OXFORD PAPERBACK REFERENCE

The Oxford Dictionary of
Word Histories

Glynnis Chantrell is Senior Editor in the English Language Teaching department at OUP. For several years she was Senior Editor in the Dictionaries department, working on many books including the *Concise Oxford Dictionary* (9th edition), and the *New Oxford Dictionary of English* (responsible for Word Histories). Glynnis taught modern languages for many years, and is multi-lingual. She has taught at every level, including adults.

Oxford Paperback Reference

The most authoritative and up-to-date reference books for both students and the general reader.

ABC of Music
Accounting
Allusions
Archaeology
Architecture
Art and Artists
Art Terms
Astronomy
Better Wordpower
Bible
Biology
British History
British Place-Names
Buddhism*
Business
Card Games
Catchphrases
Celtic Mythology
Chemistry
Christian Art
Christian Church
Chronology of English
  Literature*
Classical Literature
Classical Myth and Religion*
Computing
Contemporary World History
Dance
Dates
Dynasties of the World
Earth Sciences
Ecology
Economics
Encyclopedia
Engineering*
English Etymology
English Folklore
English Grammar
English Language
English Literature
Euphemisms
Everyday Grammar
Finance and Banking
First Names
Food and Drink
Food and Nutrition
Foreign Words and Phrases
Geography
Handbook of the World
Humorous Quotations
Idioms
Internet
Islam
Irish Literature

Jewish Religion
Kings and Queens of Britain
Language Toolkit
Law
Linguistics
Literary Quotations
Literary Terms
Local and Family History
London Place-Names
Mathematics
Medical
Medicinal Drugs
Modern Design*
Modern Slang
Music
Musical Terms
Musical Works
Nursing
Ologies and Isms
Philosophy
Phrase and Fable
Physics
Plant Sciences
Plays*
Pocket Fowler's Modern
  English Usage
Political Quotations
Politics
Popes
Proverbs
Psychology
Quotations
Quotations by Subject
Reverse Dictionary
Rhyming Slang
Saints
Science
Shakespeare
Slang
Sociology
Statistics
Synonyms and Antonyms
Twentieth-Century Art
Weather
Weights, Measures, and Units
Word Histories
World History
World Mythology
World Place-Names*
World Religions
Zoology

*forthcoming

The Oxford Dictionary of

Word Histories

Edited by GLYNNIS CHANTRELL

OXFORD
UNIVERSITY PRESS

OXFORD

UNIVERSITY PRESS

Great Clarendon Street, Oxford OX2 6DP

Oxford University Press is a department of the University of Oxford.
It furthers the University's objective of excellence in research, scholarship,
and education by publishing worldwide in

Oxford New York

Auckland Bangkok Buenos Aires Cape Town Chennai
Dar es Salaam Delhi Hong Kong Istanbul Karachi Kolkata
Kuala Lumpur Madrid Melbourne Mexico City Mumbai Nairobi
São Paulo Shanghai Taipei Tokyo Toronto

Oxford is a registered trade mark of Oxford University Press
in the UK and in certain other countries

British Library Cataloguing in Publication Data

Data available

Library of Congress Cataloging in Publication Data

Data available

ISBN 0-19-860893-4

2

Designed by Jane Stevenson
Typeset in Swift and Arial
by Selwood Systems, Midsomer Norton
Printed in Great Britain by
Clays Ltd, St Ives plc

Preface

A fascination for words and how they developed is what I hope to share with you throughout the pages of this book. The stories involve relationships: shared roots (e.g. *stare* and *starve* both from base meaning 'be rigid'); common ancestry (*mongrel* related to *mingle* and *among*); surprising commonality (*wage* and *wed*); typical formation (*blab, bleat, chatter, gibber* imitative of sounds); influence by association (*cloudscape* on the pattern of *landscape*), and shared wordbuilding elements (*hyperspace, hypersonic, hyperlink*). Colourful popular beliefs are explored about words such as *posh* and *snob*; idioms reveal how and when they came about (*happy as a sandboy, say it with flowers*). So much of what we say reveals our social history: discover the connection in a Roman soldier's mind of *salary* with *salt*, and how the notion of *public school* has changed since first instituted. Each word reveals the richness of its past and communicates afresh.

Introduction

Word Histories

The following pages detail the origins and sense development of thousands of core words of the English language with dates indicating the period in which the first example of use currently evidenced is recorded. Additional histories outside this core group are included for words with a particularly interesting story to tell; links between words are given where these enhance the picture; well-known idioms with dates of original use add their colour.

Origins of English

The words that form part of our everyday English are derived from a wide range of sources mostly within the Indo-European family of languages: the earliest are Germanic from the Anglo-Saxon Britain of the 5th century onwards (*e.g. eat, drink, house, husband, wife*), Norse from the Scandinavian invaders of the 9th and 10th centuries (*e.g. call, law, leg, root, window*), and Romantic from the period of the Norman Conquest in the 11th century (*liberty, clergy, conflict, marvel, nuptial*), Latin added its influence intermittently through various periods of advancement in art and learning, from early contact with the Roman Empire to the later mission of St Augustine in AD 597 to the Renaissance of the 15th to 17th centuries to the development of technology from the 18th century onwards. Major political and social disruptions have added fuel to language change, and in recent times through increased travel and communication, words from languages all over the world have been adopted into English.

Regional spelling variations were once great from early times to Middle English: these became more standardized with the development of printing from the 15th century. William Caxton, the first English printer (1422–91) allowed certain practical considerations to influence spelling: for example it became common to add a final -*e* to words to fill a line of print and Caxton added an -*h*- to ghost, which thereby influenced other words such as *ghastly*. Also, although the East Midland dialect was the more widespread, Caxton used the form of English common in the south-east of England which then gave the dialect a prominence; the growing influence of London as the capital reinforced this use which has persisted to the present day Printing allowed the language to be recorded in glossaries and dictionaries (the first

···

published in 1604), which also resulted in standardization.

Regional variations in pronunciation were also marked until the 14th century when major changes, especially in vowel sounds, occurred. This known as the 'great vowel shift', developed during the lifetime of the poet Chaucer, reducing the number of long vowels from seven to five. Other vowels were also affected but the spellings very often remained unaltered, which accounts for the number of 'silent' vowel sounds at the ends of words (e.g. *name*: this once rhymed with *farmer*). A gulf started to open between the written word and the spoken word. There are now many varieties of English used all over the world: the accents, words and usage vary in the same way as the regional forms and dialects of the British Isles. Rapid communication worldwide has resulted in a flourishing language that grows richer and stronger.

GLYNNIS CHANTRELL

Oxford 2001

Acknowledgements

My warm and special thanks go to Elizabeth Knowles for her semantic and historical insights and advice, to Philip Durkin for his philological expertise, to Ken Moore for his programming flair and support, and to the Oxford Dictionaries Department for the wealth of its research resources.

a [Middle English] This indefinite article used as a determiner before nouns (as in *a book*) and expanded to *an* before vowels (as in *an understanding*) is the weak form of Old English *ān* meaning 'one'. *An* was often kept before *w* (e.g. *an wood*) and *y* (e.g. *an yere*) in the 15th century, and was regularly kept before *h* (e.g. *an house*, *an hundred*) until the 17th century.

WORDBUILDING

The prefix **a-**

1 [from Greek] adds the sense

■ **not** [atheistic]

■ **without** [acephalous]

NOTE: **an-** sometimes replaces **a-** before a vowel [anaemia]

2 [Old English, unstressed form of *on*] adds the sense

■ **to, towards** [aback]

■ **in the process of** [a-hunting]

■ **in a specified state** [aflutter]

■ **on** [afoot]

■ **in** [nowadays]

WORDBUILDING

The prefix **ab-** [from Latin] adds the sense

■ **from** [abduct, abort]

---

abacus [late Middle English] This was originally a board strewn with sand on which figures and geometrical diagrams could be drawn; the word has come into English from Latin, from Greek *abax, abak-* 'slab, drawing board'. Of Semitic origin, *abacus* is probably related to Hebrew *'ābāq* 'dust'. It was not until the late 17th century that the name *abacus* was applied to a frame for making calculations by moving beads along wires.

abandon [late Middle English] The original sense of *abandon*, from Old French *abandoner*, was 'bring under control, subjugate'; this verb was based on the Old French phrase *a bandon* 'at one's disposal, under one's jurisdiction'. Later the sense became 'give in to the control of, surrender to'. From the mid 16th to the

mid 17th century, *abandon* also meant 'banish' (Shakespeare *Taming of the Shrew*: Abandon'd from your bed).
→ BAN

abase [late Middle English] *Abase* is from Old French *abaissier*, composed of *a-* (from Latin *ad* 'to, at') and *baissier* 'to lower', based on late Latin *bassus* 'short of stature'. The spelling has been influenced by *base* 'ignoble'. The common modern use is as a reflexive verb, e.g. *he would not abase himself by such behaviour* and the concept is one of 'belittlement, making base'; this has moved on from the early literal semantic strand of 'to lower' (Shakespeare *Richard III*: Will she yet abase her eyes on me).

abash [Middle English] *Abash* 'cause to feel disconcerted' is from Anglo-Norman French *abaiss-*; a comparable form is Old French *esbaiss-*, the lengthened stem of *esbair*, whose semantic elements are *es-* 'utterly' and *bair* 'astound'. The base of *bair* is thought to be *bah!*, a natural expression of astonishment; one of the early meanings in English was 'stand speechless in amazement'.
→ ABEYANCE

abate [Middle English] Early use was in legal contexts meaning 'put a stop to (a nuisance)'. The Old French verb *abatre* 'to fell' gave English *abate*; the elements at the base of the French source are Latin *ad* 'to, at' and *batt(u)ere* 'to beat'. This notion of 'beating repeatedly' developed into one of 'giving way', hence the current English sense of *abate* 'become less intense' (e.g. *the noise abated gradually*). An Anglo-Norman French word gave English **abatement**, which dates from the same period as *abate*.

abattoir [early 19th century] Adopted from French, *abattoir* is from *abattre* 'to fell'. This is the same verb involved in the history of *abate*. The English synonym *slaughterhouse* had long been in use from Middle English.
→ SLAUGHTER

abbot [Old English] Aramaic *'abbā* 'father' is the base of a group of words, of which the earliest is Old English *abbod*, which came via ecclesiastical Latin from Greek *abbas* 'father'. The combination *Abba father* is used by devotional writers when invoking the first person of the Trinity (Mark 14:36 (*Authorized Version*): And he said, Abba, father, all things are possible unto thee). Related words include, in the Middle English period, **abbey** (via Old French from medieval Latin *abbatia* 'abbacy') and **abbess** (from Old French *abbesse*, from ecclesiastical Latin *abbatissa*). Late Middle English **abbacy** is from ecclesiastical Latin *abbacia*.

abbreviate [late Middle English] The base is the Latin adjective *brevis* 'short'. The immediate source of the spelling is late Latin *abbreviat-*, the past participial stem of the verb *abbreviare* 'shorten'. Early examples of *abbreviate* are in contexts where narration is shortened or abridged by the omission of details whilst still retaining the substance of the text.
→ BRIEF

abdicate [mid 16th century] Latin *abdicat-*, from the verb *abdicare* 'renounce', is the source of English *abdicate*. The elements in the Latin formation are *ab-* 'away, from' and *dicare* 'declare'. This notion of 'declaration' is seen in early use when the verb meant 'disinherit (a child)' or 'disown'. Examples of *abdicate* 'give up sovereignty' where the throne or crown is relinquished, date from the early 18th century.

abduct [early 17th century] Latin *ab-* 'away, from' and *ducere* 'to lead' form the base of *abduct*. The English form is from the Latin past participial stem *abduct-* meaning 'led away'. The noun **abduction**, from late Latin *abductio(n-)*, dates from the same period.

aberrant [mid 16th century] This is literally 'wandering away', the meaning of Latin *aberrant-*, from the verb *aberrare*; in the formation are the elements *ab-* 'away, from' and *errare* 'to stray'. **Aberration** was first recorded a little later in the 16th century meaning 'divergence from the recognized path' and comes from Latin *aberratio(n-)*.

abet [late Middle English] It is now associated with acts of wrongdoing but in early use, *abet* focused on the act of 'urging' and this typically involved something good as well as bad; the word is from Old French *abeter*, from *a-* (from Latin *ad* 'to, at') and *beter* 'hound, urge on'. The phrase *aid and abet*, in legal contexts from the late 18th century, shows the use of two verbs reinforcing each other to convey the notion 'give active assistance'.
→ BAIT

abeyance [late 16th century] The formality of the word *abeyance* is retained from its early use as a legal term meaning 'a state of being without an owner or claimant'; the Old French source (*abeance* 'aspiration to a title') is from *abeer* 'to aspire after'. The notion of aspiration stems from Old French *beer* 'to (stand and) gape'.

abhor [late Middle English] The semantic core in *abhor* is 'shuddering'; it comes from Latin *abhorrere* 'shudder away from'. A notion of 'causing horror' existed in the English verb (Shakespeare *Othello*: I cannot say Whore, It does abhor me now I speak the word). The adjective **abhorrent**, from the present participle of the same Latin verb, dates from the late 16th century.

abide [Old English] Old English *ābīdan* 'wait' is made up of *ā-* 'onwards' and *bīdan* 'remain'. The sense 'endure' is seen in late Middle English texts when the semantics include both 'wait and persist' and 'wait and withstand'; in the late 15th century, negative phrases such as *can't abide* meaning 'can't tolerate' arose. *Abide* has occasionally been confused with the archaic verb *aby* meaning 'buy' or 'atone for' (Shakespeare *Julius Caesar*: Some will dear abide it).

abject [late Middle English] Current meanings are 'brought to a low condition' (F. Trollope: The most abject poverty is preferable to domestic service) and 'self-abasing', 'despicable'. The early recorded sense of *abject* in English was 'rejected': Latin *abjectus*, the past participle of *abicere* 'to reject', is the source and the elements in the formation are *ab-* 'away' and *jacere* 'to throw'. At first the word was pronounced on the second syllable like the Latin source.

able [late Middle English] The adjective *able* had the senses 'easy to use' and 'suitable' in early use as well as the more familiar senses 'having the qualifications or means' to do something; it comes from Old French *hable*, from Latin *habilis* 'handy'. The base verb is Latin *habere* 'to hold', the root too of **ability**, also late Middle English, which came from Old French *ablete*, from Latin *habilitas* (from *habilis*).

abled [1980s] This is taken from *disabled*.

ablution [late Middle English] The original use of *ablution* was as a term in alchemy and chemistry meaning 'purification by using liquids'. A mid 16th-century sense development was 'purification of the body by washing', which was by extension from religious use of the term. Latin *ablutio(n-)* is the source, from the verb *abluere*, made up of *ab-* 'away' and *luere* 'to wash'. The plural *ablutions*, referring to a building with washing facilities and toilets, is found in military contexts from the mid 20th century.

abnormal [mid 19th century] This spelling is an alteration, by association with Latin *abnormis* 'monstrous', of the 16th-century English word *anormal*. The latter was an adoption of a French variant of *anomal*, the variant being influenced by Latin *norma* 'rule, pattern'. The

abode [Middle English] A verbal noun from *abide, abode* 'house, home' first meant 'act of waiting'.
→ ABIDE

abolish [late Middle English] 'Put an end to' was the early English sense of *abolish* from Old French *aboliss-*, the lengthened stem of *abolir* (from Latin *abolere* 'destroy'). This is also the base of **abolition** from Latin *abolitio(n-)*, recorded from the early 16th century.

abominable [Middle English] *Abominable* was once widely believed to be from *ab-* 'away from', and Latin *homine* from *homo* 'human being', giving the sense 'inhuman, beastly'. It was frequently spelt *abhominable* until the 17th century: this is in fact the only spelling in the first folio of Shakespeare where it occurs 18 times. The word comes via Old French from Latin *abominabilis*, from *abominari* 'deprecate (as an ill omen)'. This Latin verb is the base too of Middle English **abomination** (from Latin *abominatio(n-)*) and **abominate** recorded from the mid 17th century. The base elements are *ab-* 'away, from' and *omen, omin-* 'omen'.

aborigine [mid 19th century] This is a shortening of the 16th-century plural *aborigines* 'original inhabitants', which in classical times referred to the early people of Italy and Greece. The word comes from the Latin phrase *ab origine* 'from the beginning'. Now both *Aborigines* and *Aboriginals* are standard plural forms when referring to Australian Aboriginal people: this specialized application of the term dates from the 1820s.

abortive [Middle English] The early use of *abortive* was as a noun for a stillborn child or animal, it came into English via Old French from Latin *abortivus*, from *aboriri* 'to miscarry'. It is commonly used figuratively now in phrases such as *abortive attempts*. The Latin verb *aboriri* is the source of **abort** which is recorded from the mid 16th century; the base elements are *ab-* 'from' and *oriri* 'be born'. The noun **abortion**, also mid 16th century, is from Latin *abortio(n-)*.

abound [Middle English] *Abound* 'exist in large numbers', 'proliferate' is based on *unda* 'a wave' which gives the core semantics of surging growth and movement. The early sense was 'overflow, be abundant'. From Old French *abunder*, the origin is Latin *abundare* 'to overflow', from *ab-* 'from' and *undare* 'surge'. There was a period when *abound* was erroneously connected to Latin *habere* 'to have' and was spelt with an initial *h-* in English and in French.

about [Old English] Old English *onbūtan* is formed from *on* 'in, on' and *būtan* 'outside of'.
→ BUT[2]

above [Old English] Old English *abufan* was originally an adverb; the prefix *a* meant 'on' and the remaining element, *bufan*, is made up of *bi* 'by' and *ufan* 'above'.

abracadabra [late 17th century] This was originally a mystical word engraved and used as a charm to ward off illness. It is Latin, first recorded in a 2nd-century poem by the Gnostic physician Serenus Sammonicus; the base is Greek. When the word was used as a charm, it was usually written out in the form of a triangle, with 'A' on the first line, 'AB' on the next, 'ABR' on the third, and so on; the paper was put into an amulet and worn around the neck.

abrasion [mid 17th century] *Abrasion* is from Latin *abrasio(n-)*, from the verb *abradere* 'scrape away'. The verb **abrade** is recorded from the late 17th century. *Ab-* 'away, from' and *radere* 'to scrape' are the elements of the Latin source verb, base too of **abrasive** (mid 19th century), formed from Latin *abras-* 'abraded'.

abridge [Middle English] *Abridge* was first recorded in the sense 'deprive of'; it comes from Old French *abregier*, also involved in the formation of **abridgement** (late Middle English) from Old French *abregement*. The base verb is late Latin *abbreviare* 'to cut short'. The prime current sense (dating from late Middle English) relates to cutting short texts; rare uses now include 'reduce to a small size' and 'shorten in duration' (Shakespeare *Two Gentlemen of Verona*: Thy staying will abridge thy life).
→ ABBREVIATE

abroad [Middle English] *Abroad* has a parallel in the phrase *at large*. It is made up of the prefix *a-* 'on, at' and *broad*. One of the early senses was 'out of one's home'; in late Middle English this was extended to 'in or into foreign countries'. In the early 19th century, the word developed the additional sense 'dazed, confused' (Thackeray *Vanity Fair*: At the twelfth round the … champion was all abroad).

abrupt [late 16th century] The notions of 'suddenness' and 'curtailment' come from the Latin source *abruptus* (past participle of *abrumpere*), which meant 'broken off, steep'. In literary contexts *abrupt* has been used as a noun meaning 'abyss' (Milton *Paradise Lost*: Upborn with indefatigable wings Over the vast abrupt).

abscess [mid 16th century] The noun *abscess* is from Latin *abscessus* 'a going away', from the verb *abscedere*, from *ab-* 'away from' and *cedere* 'go'. It describes the 'going away', in other words, the elimination of infected matter from a swollen area within body tissue through pus.

abscond [mid 16th century] The early sense was 'hide, conceal (oneself)', given by Latin *abscondere* 'hide', made up of *ab-* 'away, from' and *condere* 'stow'. Later, movement became associated with the meaning which became 'get away hurriedly and secretly'.

abseil [1930s] This is from the German verb *abseilen*, from *ab* 'down' and *Seil* 'rope'. A technique in mountaineering, the activity of *abseiling* involves descending a near-vertical surface by using a doubled rope coiled around the body of the abseiler and fixed at a higher point.

absent [Middle English] Latin *absens*, *absent-* 'being absent, being away', the present participle of *abesse*, is the source of English *absent*. The word is also used in North American formal language as a preposition meaning 'without': *absent a willingness to negotiate, you can't have collective bargaining*. Late Middle English **absence** is from Old French, from Latin *absentia*.

absolute [late Middle English] Latin *absolvere* 'to set free', 'acquit', formed from *ab-* 'from' and *solvere* 'loosen', is the base of *absolute*, **absolution**, and **absolve**. Early use of *absolute* in English was as a past participle meaning 'unrestricted, disengaged', adopting the sense of the Latin source *absolutus*; the adjectival use, as in *absolute truth*, *absolute nightmare* developed the meaning 'unqualified'.

absorb [late Middle English] Latin *absorbere*, from *ab-* 'from' and *sorbere* 'to suck in' has given *absorb* in English. The sense 'engross (a person's attention)' arose in the late 18th century, extended in the next century to 'assimilate mentally' in contexts of learning and taking in facts. **Absorption** (late 16th century) from Latin *absorptio(n-)*, had the early sense 'a swallowing up' and is from the Latin verb *absorbere*; so too **absorbent**, dating from the early 18th century, from the Latin present participle *absorbent-* 'swallowing up'.

abstain [late Middle English] *Abstain* is commonly used in political voting contexts, religious contexts in connection with fasting, or in phrases such as *abstain from alcohol*. It is based on the elements *ab-* 'from' and *tenere* 'to hold' in the Latin verb *abstinere*, which gave the Old French source of the English word. From the same base are **abstinence** (Middle English) via Old French from Latin *abstinentia*, and **abstinence** (late Middle English) via Old French from Latin *abstinent-* 'abstaining'. Early 16th-century **abstention** captured the action of 'keeping back' or 'restraining', and comes from late Latin *abstentio(n-)*.

abstract [Middle English] The Latin form *abstractus*, source of English *abstract*, meant literally 'drawn away' and is the past participle of *abstrahere* from the base elements *ab-* 'from' and *trahere* 'draw off'. The use in connection with art dates from the mid 19th century; in this context *abstract* means 'not representing external, recognizable reality', the artistic effect being achieved through shapes, forms, colours, and textures. Late Middle English **abstraction** is from Latin *abstractio(n-)*.

abstruse [late 16th century] *Abstruse* means 'obscure', 'difficult to understand' and gains its core meaning from a notion of pushing something to a distance (from one's understanding). It is from Latin *abstrusus* 'put away, hidden', from *abstrudere* 'conceal'. The base verb is *trudere* 'to push'.

absurd [mid 16th century] Latin *absurdus*, the source of English *absurd*, meant 'out of tune', which led to a notion of 'irrational'; Latin *surdus* 'deaf, dull' is related. The 20th-century **Theatre of the Absurd** plays on the 'irrationality' of life: major exponents of this type of drama are Samuel Beckett, Eugène Ionesco, and Harold Pinter, who abandon conventional dramatic form to portray the futility of human struggle in a senseless world.

abundance [Middle English] Latin *abundare* 'overflow' is the base of *abundance*, **abound**, and **abundant**. These English words centre around the core sense 'large quantity', which is taken up in the solo whist term *abundance* 'a call undertaking to take nine or more tricks'.
→ABOUND

abuse [late Middle English] The Latin elements *ab-* 'away' (= 'in the wrong direction', 'wrongly') and *uti* 'to use' are at the root of English *abuse*, whose spelling comes from Latin *abus-* 'misused'.
→USAGE

abut [late Middle English] *Abut* in the sense 'have a common boundary' is from Anglo-Latin *abuttare*, from *a-* (from Latin *ad* 'to, at') and Old French *but* 'end'. The late 16th-century sense 'lean upon' is from Old French *abouter* literally meaning 'strike at' and related to Old French *but* 'end': this has a Germanic origin. The noun **abutment** (mid 17th century) is comparable with French *aboutement* 'joining end to end'.

abysmal [mid 17th century] This was initially recorded as a literal use in the sense 'very deep'. It is based on the Middle English, now poetic, word *abysm* from medieval Latin *abysmus*, an alteration of late Latin *abyssus* 'bottomless pit': the ending was assimilated to the Greek ending *-ismos*. *Abysmal* in the modern sense 'appalling' dates from the early 19th century.

abyss [late Middle English] Originally an *abyss* was an 'infernal pit'; it came into English via late Latin from Greek *abussos* 'bottomless', the elements of which are *a-* 'without' and *bussos* 'depth'.

academy [late Middle English] The word *academy* was first used with reference to the garden where Plato taught; it came into English via French or Latin, from Greek *akadēmeia*; the base here is *Akadēmos*, the demigod after whom Plato's garden was named. The adjective **academic** dates from the mid 16th century and, slightly later, **academe** was recorded in the sense 'academy'. This was extended to the 'academic community' (once only used in the poetic phrase *groves of academe* translating Horace's *silvas Academi*): the source is Latin *academia*, reinforced by Greek *Akadēmos*. The modern Latin form **academia** (e.g. *he spent his working life in academia*) was adopted in the 1950s.

acceleration [late 15th century] Latin *celer* 'swift' is the root of both *acceleration* (from Latin *acceleratio(n-)*) and early 16th-century **accelerate**, which first meant 'hasten the occurrence of' (from the Latin verb *accelerare* 'hasten').

accent [late Middle English] The first recorded meaning of *accent* was 'intonation', from Latin *accentus* 'tone, signal, or intensity' translating Greek *prosōidia*. The base elements of the Latin are *ad-* 'to' and *cantus* 'song', 'a song sung to music'. The sense 'intonation' arises from the notion of a musical rise and fall being added to speech.

accept [late Middle English] This is from Latin *acceptare*, a frequentative (= verb of repeated action) of *accipere* meaning 'take something to oneself', from *ad-* 'to' and *capere* 'take'. The adjective **acceptable** dating from the same period, and mid 16th-century **acceptance** are both from Old French.

access [Middle English] The prime current meaning is 'a means to gain entry'; this was first recorded in English in the early 17th century, but an *access* in early examples was used for 'a sudden attack of illness', from Latin *accessus* 'way of approach' (from the verb *accedere* 'to approach'). The Latin elements *ad-* 'to' and *cedere* 'to give way', 'yield' form the base of other members of the same word family. The adjective **accessible** dates from late Middle English and is from late Latin *accessibilis*; **accede** is also late Middle English and was first used in the general sense 'come forward, approach', and **accession**, often used in formal contexts, started out (late 16th

century) with the general sense 'something added' from Latin *accessio(n-)*.

accident [late Middle English] 'An event' was the early meaning of *accident* which comes via Old French from Latin *accident-* 'happening'; the base elements are *ad-* 'towards, to' and *cadere* 'to fall'. Although often associated with misfortune, the notion of 'chance' is also present in phrases such as *happy accident*. **Accidental** in late Middle English meant 'incidental' and was also used as a term in philosophy (Aristotelian thought) meaning 'relating to properties not essential to a thing's nature'; the immediate source is late Latin *accidentalis*.

acclaim [early 17th century] The early sense of *acclaim* was 'express approval'; Latin *acclamare* is the source, from *ad-* 'to' and *clamare* 'to shout'. The change in the ending from *-am* to *-aim* was due to association with *claim*. Current senses involving enthusiastic praise, date from the 17th century.

accolade [early 17th century] Adopted from French, *accolade* 'award given as a recognition of merit' comes from Provençal *acolada*, which has the literal meaning of 'an embrace around the neck', a gesture made when bestowing a knighthood on someone. The elements here are Latin *ad-* 'at, to' and *collum* 'neck'.

accommodate [mid 16th century] Latin *accommodat-*, the past participial stem of *accommodare* 'make fitting', is the source of *accommodate*: the base is the Latin adjective *commodus* 'fitting'. The noun **accommodation**, recorded from the beginning of the 17th century, is from Latin *accommodatio(n-)*. The association with provision of lodging was an early sense.

accompany [late Middle English] This verb is from Old French *accompagner* but the spelling underwent a change due to association with the word *company*. The Old French form was based on *compagne* from Old French *compaignon* 'companion'. This is also at the root of **accompaniment** dating from the early 18th century, which comes from French *accompagnement*.

accomplice [mid 16th century] *Accomplice* is an alteration of Middle English *complice* 'an associate' introduced via Old French from late Latin *complex, complic-* 'allied'. Here the formative elements are *com-* meaning 'together' and the root of *plicare* 'to fold', capturing the close bond forged by an *accomplice*: the notion of secrecy implies wrongdoing, reflected in legal contexts. The prefix *ac-* is not explained by any analogous form in Latin or French: it may have arisen from the indefinite article in *a complice* or by the influence of *ac-* in *accomplish*.

accomplish [late Middle English] The core sense here is one of 'drawing to completion'; the form is from Old French *acompliss-*, the lengthened stem of *acomplir*, based on Latin *ad-* 'to' and *complere* 'to complete'.

accord [Old English] This is from Old French *acorder* 'reconcile, be of one mind', from Latin *ad-* 'to' and *cor, cord-* 'heart'. Two Middle English members of this family are **accordance** from Old French *acordance*, and **accordant** from Old French *acordant* 'bringing to an agreement'.

accordion [mid 19th century] The name of this musical instrument is from German *Akkordion*, from the Italian verb *accordare* 'to tune'.

accost [late 16th century] The meaning was originally 'lie or go alongside', from French *accoster*, from Italian *accostare*. Latin *costa* 'rib, side' is the base. In English the word was sometimes spelt *accoast* as it was for a time consciously connected with *coast* from its now obsolete meaning 'sail along the coast of'. Eventually the meaning 'go up to and speak to' became predominant, which reinforced the *accost* spelling and pronunciation.

account [Middle English] 'Counting' and 'to count' were the early senses of the noun and verb respectively. Old French *acont* and *aconter* (based on *conter* 'to count') gave the English form *account*. Middle English **accountant** is from the present participle of Old French *aconter*, a French law term; the original word was an adjective meaning 'liable to give an account', therefore coming to describe a person who must do so.

accoutrement [mid 16th century] French *accoutrer* from Old French *acoustrer* 'to clothe, equip' gave rise to *accoutrement* in English. The base noun is Old French *cousture* 'sewing'. The English word is used to refer to additional items of dress or equipment associated with a particular activity, for example *the accoutrements of religious ritual*.

accrue [late Middle English] This word, now commonly used in financial contexts, is from Old French *acreue*, the past participle of *acreistre* 'to increase', from Latin *accrescere* 'become larger'. The early meaning of the Old French noun was 'whatever grows on the earth or in a wood to the profit of the owner of that land'.

accumulate [late 15th century] Latin *cumulus* 'a heap' (the base of the verb *accumulare*) is involved in the semantics of *accumulate* which means 'gather together'.

accurate [late 16th century] Latin *accuratus* meant 'done with care', based on the noun *cura* 'care'; English *accurate*, which comes from the Latin, has the sense 'correct in all details', although in Latin this applied only to things and not people.

accuse [Middle English] *Accuse* is from Old French *acuser*, from Latin *accusare* 'to call to account', the base being *causa* 'reason, motive' or 'lawsuit'. The grammatical term **accusative** was first recorded slightly later in the Middle English period and comes from the Latin phrase (*casus*) *accusativus*, literally 'relating to an accusation or (legal) case', translating Greek (*ptōsis*) *aitiatikē* '(the case) relating to that which is caused'. The noun **accusation**, also dating from late Middle English, was introduced via Old French from Latin *accusatio(n-)*.

ace [Middle English] An *ace* denoted the 'one' on dice in Middle English; it comes via Old French from Latin *as* 'unity, a unit'. It is often ranked as the highest value in a suit of playing cards, and the associated worth and 'excellence' are transferred to many uses and contexts, e.g.: *he served an ace*, *a motorcycle ace*, *Ace! You've done it!*, *it wasn't our intention to ace Phil out of a job* (North American sense of 'outdo').

acerbic [mid 19th century] The word form is based on Latin *acerbus* 'sour-tasting'. Current use is figurative in phrases such as *acerbic wit*, *acerbic comment*.

ache [Old English] The Old English noun was *æce*; the verb *acan*; in Middle and early modern English the noun was spelt *atche* and rhymed with the letter name 'aitch' but the verb was spelt and pronounced as it is today. The pronunciation of these two parts of speech became similar in around 1700. The modern spelling is largely due to Dr Johnson, who mistakenly assumed its derivation to be from Greek *akhos* 'pain' and so spelt the verb like the noun.

achieve [Middle English] The early sense was 'complete successfully', from Old French *achever* 'come or bring to a head', from the phrase *a chief* 'to a head'. The spelling *chieve* was also common in Middle English but this is now obsolete.

acid [early 17th century] 'Sour-tasting' was the early sense of *acid*, from Latin *acidus*, from *acere* 'be sour'. It is used as a chemical term as well as referring, popularly, to a 'sour substance'; from the 1960s, it has served as a slang term, first recorded in the US, for the drug LSD. An **acid test**, commonly figurative for a test which is conclusive of the value or success of something, derives from the original use of *acid* as a test for gold using nitric acid.

acknowledge [late 15th century] This is from the obsolete Middle English verb *knowledge*, influenced by obsolete *acknow* meaning 'acknowledge, confess'.

acme [late 16th century] Greek *akmē* 'highest point' is the source of this word. Until the 18th century, it was often consciously used as a Greek word and written in Greek letters.

acne [mid 19th century] *Acne* came via modern Latin from Greek *aknas*, a misreading of *akmas*, the accusative plural of *akmē* 'highest point, peak, or facial eruption'.
→ ACME

acolyte [Middle English] English *acolyte* is from Old French *acolyt* or ecclesiastical Latin *acolytus*, from Greek *akolouthos* 'follower'. The word refers to 'an assistant', and now, in the Roman Catholic Church in particular, 'someone who attends a priest, performing duties such as assisting at the altar'; until 1 January 1973, *acolyte* was one of the four Minor Orders (formal clerical grades below the rank of deacon) of the Roman Catholic Church.

acorn [Old English] Old English *æcern* has a Germanic origin; it is related to Dutch *aker*, as well as to English *acre*. The semantic root of the word appears to have been 'fruit of the unenclosed land; natural produce of the forest'. This was extended to fruit without any specification, but later in English, Low German, and Scandinavian, the application became restricted to the most important fruit produced by the forest: the *acorn*. It became respelt by this supposed connection with the *oak* and, in the 16th century, the popular fancy was that *corn* was part of the name. During the 15th and 16th centuries, refashioned spellings included: *ake-corn*, *oke-corn*, *ake-horn*, and *oke-horn*.
→ ACRE

acoustic [mid 17th century] Greek *akoustikos*, from *akouein* 'to hear', has given English *acoustic*. The plural *acoustics* has been used, since the late 17th century, for the branch of physics dealing with the properties of sound; it has also been used, from the late 19th century, for the qualities of a building that determine how sound is transmitted within it.

acquaint [Middle English] This is from Old French *acointier* 'make known', via late Latin from Latin *accognoscere*, the elements of which are *ad-* 'to' and *cognoscere* 'come to know'. Based on the same verb is Middle English **acquaintance** which originally meant 'mutual knowledge', 'being acquainted', from Old French *acointance* (from *acointier*).

acquiesce [early 17th century] There is a notion of peacefully leaving an argument unspoken in *acquiesce* which comes from Latin *acquiescere*, from *ad-* 'at' and *quiescere* 'to rest'. **Acquiescent** which was recorded in use from the same period, is from Latin *acquiescent-* 'remaining at rest'; this Latin sense was seen in early use of the English verb.

acquire [late Middle English] The late Middle English spelling *acquere* is from Old French *aquerre*, based on Latin *acquirere* 'get in addition': the formative elements are *ad-* 'to' and *quaerere* 'seek'. The English spelling was modified around 1600 by association with the Latin word. **Acquisition**, also late Middle English, started out in the sense 'act of acquiring something' and comes from Latin *acquisitio(n-)*, from the verb *acquirere*, the base verb too of **acquisitive** which appears much later, from about the mid 19th century.

acquit [Middle English] Originally conveying the sense 'pay a debt, discharge a liability', *acquit* is from Old French *acquiter*, from medieval Latin *acquitare* 'pay a debt'; here the root verb is *quitare* 'to set free'. Up until the 16th century, the i sound in *acquit* was long (as in *require*).

acre [Old English] Old English *æcer* was the amount of land a yoke of oxen could plough in a day. The word has a Germanic origin and is related to Dutch *akker* and German *Acker* 'field', from an Indo-European root shared by Sanskrit *ajra*, Latin *ager*, and Greek *agros*: these all meant 'field', but originally specified untenanted land, open country, or forest. The development of agriculture influenced the sense, which started to focus on enclosure and then the definition of land area by size.

acrid [early 18th century] The formation of *acrid* is irregular, from Latin *acer*, *acri-* 'sharp, pungent' and the suffix *-id*; the spelling was probably influenced by *acid*.

acrobat [early 19th century] *Acrobat* was adopted from French *acrobate*, from Greek *akrobatēs*; the semantic roots are *akron* 'tip' and *bainein* 'to walk', found in the Greek adjective *akrobatos* 'walking on tiptoe'.

across [Middle English] Early use was as an adverb meaning 'in the form of a cross'; the word comes from Old French *a croix*, *en croix* 'in or on a cross', later regarded as being from *cross* prefixed by *a-*.

act [late Middle English] The noun *act* is from Latin *actus* 'event, thing done', *act-* 'done', from the verb *agere*; it was reinforced by the French noun *acte*. The verb was probably influenced by the noun, but its use was limited to Scotland at first; more than a century elapsed between its appearance in the work of the Scottish poet Robert Henryson (1430?–1506?) and its first appearance in English. As for related forms, Middle English **active** had the sense 'preferring action to contemplation': it appears to derive from Latin *activus*, from *act-* 'done', although it may come from the theological Latin phrase *vita activa* 'active life', which is the earliest application of the word in both French and English. Other related words include **action**, late Middle English, introduced via Old French from Latin *actio(n-)* and **activity** from French *activité* or late Latin *activitas*.

actor [late Middle English] An *actor* was originally an agent or an administrator; the form is Latin, meaning 'doer, actor', from *agere* 'do, act'. The theatrical sense dates from the 16th century.

actual [Middle English] Old French *actuel* 'active, practical' gave *actual* in English; the base is Latin *actus* 'thing done'. Late Middle English **actuality** had the sense 'activity'; its source is Old French *actualite* or medieval Latin *actualitas*, from *actualis* 'active, practical'. The modern French word *actualité* (usually meaning 'news') is sometimes used in English to mean 'truth', a sense not found in French (*Independent* 10 November 1992: When asked why the company had not been advised to include the potential military use, he [= Alan Clark] said it was 'our old friend economical ... with the *actualité*').

actuary [mid 16th century] An *actuary* started out as the name for a clerk or registrar of a court; the source is Latin *actuarius* 'bookkeeper', from *actus* 'event'. The current term in insurance contexts dates from the mid 19th century.

acumen [late 16th century] *Business acumen* suggests the sharpness of mind required for making good decisions; *acumen* is an adoption of a Latin word meaning 'sharpness, point', from *acuere* 'sharpen'.

acute [late Middle English] *Acute* first described a disease or its symptoms and came from Latin *acutus*, the past participle of *acuere* 'to sharpen', from *acus* 'needle'.

WORDBUILDING

The prefix **ad-** [from Latin *ad* 'to'] adds the sense

■ **motion, direction** [advance, adduce]

■ **reduction, change** [adapt; adulterate]

■ **addition** [adjunct]

In the 16th century the use of *ad-* and its variants was extended to replace *a-* from different origins such as Latin *ab-* (e.g. *advance*, from French *avancer* based on late Latin *abante* 'in front').

---

adage [mid 16th century] Adopted from French, *adage* describing a traditional maxim, is from Latin *adagium* 'saying', based on an early form of *aio* 'I say'.

adamant [Old English] A noun originally, *adamant* came from Old French *adamaunt-*, via Latin from Greek *adamas*, *adamant-*, 'untameable, invincible'. It was the name of an alleged rock or mineral, to which vague and fabulous properties were ascribed, but the essential characteristic was its hardness. It was later used to denote the hardest metal or stone of the period, which explains its extension to 'diamond', the hardest naturally occurring substance. The elements making up the form are *a-* 'not' and *daman* 'to tame'. Early medieval Latin writers explained the word as coming from *adamare* 'take a liking to' and associated *adamant* with the loadstone or magnet, and the word passed into modern languages with this confusion of meaning. The phrase *to be adamant*, suggesting firm conviction, dates from the 1930s, although adjectival use had been implied in such collocations as *an adamant heart* since the 16th century.

adapt [late Middle English] Latin *aptus* 'fit' is at the core of this word's meaning. It comes from French *adapter*, from Latin *adaptare* (from *ad-* 'to' and *aptare*). This verb is also the base of **adaptation** (early 17th century) from French, from late Latin *adaptatio(n-)*.

add [late Middle English] The specific use associated with arithmetic arose in the late 15th century, but *add* is essentially 'put (something) to'. It is from Latin *addere*, from *ad-* 'to' and the base of *dare* 'to put'; these elements are at the root of **addition**, also dating from late Middle English, from Latin *additio(n-)*.

adder [Old English] The Old English form was *nædre* 'serpent, adder', a word of Germanic origin related to Dutch *adder* and German *Natter*; the northern English dialect form *nedder* still exists. The initial *n* of the spelling was lost in Middle English by wrong division of the phrase *a naddre*; comparable words where the same process has happened are: *apron*, *auger*, and *umpire*.

addicted [mid 16th century] The obsolete adjective *addict* 'bound or devoted (to someone)' has given rise to this word; the source is Latin *addict-* 'assigned (by decree); devoted', from the verb *addicere*, from *ad-* 'to' and *dicere* 'say'. **Addiction** is first recorded slightly later in the 16th century referring to a person's inclination or proclivity for something; the immediate source is Latin *addictio(n-)*. The early 20th century saw the appearance of **addict** in the language in the context of alcohol and other drugs: this noun is from the obsolete verb *addict*, which was a back-formation (by removal of the suffix) from *addicted*.

additive [late 17th century] This was originally used as an adjective; it derives from late Latin *additivus*, from the Latin verb *addere* 'to add'. The noun dates from the 1940s.

addle [Middle English] 'Rotten' was the early meaning of *addle* which was used to describe eggs. The phrase *addle egg* often referred to an infertile egg, and the notion of abortiveness led to many wordplays on *addle* and *idle*. The word form arose from Old English *adela* 'liquid filth, stinking urine', a word of Germanic origin related to Dutch *aal* and German *Adel* 'mire, puddle'. The mid 17th century saw the introduction of **addled**, formed from the adjective *addle*; it seems to have existed before the verb. The phrase *addled Parliament* was given as a nickname to the parliament of 1614 which met on April 5 and was dissolved on June 7 without a single act being passed.

address [Middle English] This was first used as a verb in the senses 'set upright' and 'guide, direct', which developed into 'write directions for delivery on' and 'direct spoken words to'. The source is Old French, based on Latin *ad-* 'towards' and *directus* 'put straight'. The noun is mid 16th-century in origin in the sense 'act of approaching or speaking to someone'.

adept [mid 17th century] An *adept* person is 'skilled' at something: the Latin source *adeptus* 'achieved' (the past participle of *adipisci* 'attain') has given this notion of complete proficiency.

adequate [early 17th century] 'Made equal to in size or extent' is the meaning of the Latin source *adacquatus*, the past participle of the verb *adaequare*, based on *aequus* 'equal'.

adhere [late 15th century] Latin *adhaerere* is the base of *adhere* as well as **adherent** (late Middle English), **adhesion** (late 15th century), and **adhesive** (late 17th century); the literal meaning of the Latin is 'stick to'.

adieu [late Middle English] This poetic and literary word for 'goodbye' is from Old French, from *a* 'to' and *Dieu* 'God'; Spanish **adios** has the same meaning. *Adieu* was used to the person being left, in the sense 'I commend your safety to God', whereas *farewell* was the recommendation to the person setting forth.

adjacent [late Middle English] Latin *adjacent-*, from which this word comes, means 'lying near to'; it is part of *adjacere*, composed of *ad-* 'to' and *jacere* 'lie down'.

adjective [late Middle English] Old French *adjectif, -ive* is the source, from Latin *adject-* 'added', literally 'thrown towards', from the verb *adicere*. The term was originally used in the phrase *noun adjective*, translating Latin *nomen adjectivum*, a translation of Greek *onoma epitheton* 'attributive name'.

adjourn [Middle English] Now *adjourn* suggests 'break off (until a later time)', but the early sense was 'summon someone to appear on a particular day', so time is the semantic essence. It comes from Old French *ajorner*, from the phrase *a jorn* (*nome*) 'to an (appointed) day'.

adjust [early 17th century] The notion of 'bringing in close proximity' is present in *adjust* which, primarily, had the senses 'harmonize discrepancies' and 'assess (loss or damages)'. The source was the obsolete French verb *adjuster*, from Old French *ajoster* 'to approximate', based on Latin *ad-* 'to' and *juxta* 'near'.

adjutant [early 17th century] An *adjutant* was originally an 'assistant', 'a helper'; the origin is Latin *adjutant-* 'being of service to', from *adjutare*, a frequentative (= verb of repeated action) of *adjuvare* 'assist'. The term is commonly associated now with military contexts and describes an officer assisting a senior officer with administrative matters.

admiral [Middle English] An *admiral* was initially an emir or Saracen commander; Old French *amiral, amirail* is the direct source and the form came via medieval Latin from Arabic *'amīr* 'commander' (from *'amara* 'to command'). The prefix *ad-* is a Latinization. The ending *-al* was from Arabic *-al-* meaning 'of the', used in titles (e.g. *'amīr-al-'umarā* 'ruler of rulers'); this was later assimilated to the familiar Latinate suffix *-al*. The modern maritime use owes its existence to the office of 'Ameer of the Sea', created by the Arabs in Spain and Sicily. This was continued by the Christian kings of Sicily, and adopted later by the Genoese, the French, and subsequently the English under Edward III as 'Amyrel of the Se' or 'admyrall of the navy'. The original use of the title became obsolete about 1500 and *admiral* alone was used as the naval term. **Admiralty** is a late Middle English word, from Old French *admiralte*.

admiration [late Middle English] Latin *admirari* has given *admiration* (which originally meant 'marvelling, wonder'), **admirable** (also late Middle English), and **admirable** which came via Old French from Latin *admirabilis* 'to be wondered at'. **Admire** is recorded from the late 16th century. The base elements are *ad-* 'at' and *mirari* 'wonder'.

admit [late Middle English] *Admit* is from Latin *admittere*, from *ad* 'to' and *mittere* 'send'; the core notion is extended from 'sending to' to 'accepting and allowing in'. In the same family is **admission**, also a late Middle English word, from Latin *admissio(n-)*; **admissible** dates from the early 17th century and is from medieval Latin *admissibilis*.

admonish [Middle English] Middle English *amonest* meant 'urge, exhort' and came from Old French *amonester*, based on Latin *admonere* 'urge by warning'. Later, the final *-t* of *amonest* was taken to indicate the past tense, and the present tense changed following the pattern of verbs such as *abolish*; the prefix became *ad-* in the 16th century by association with the Latin form.

ado [late Middle English] *Ado* was originally 'action', 'business'; it is from northern Middle English *at do* 'to do', from Old Norse *at* (which was used to mark an infinitive) and *do*. This parallel between *at do* and *to do* can be seen in the sense 'fuss' apparent in the phrases *without more ado* and *what a to do!*.

adolescence [late Middle English] Adopted from French, from Latin *adolescentia*, *adolescence* is based on the verb *adolescere* 'grow to maturity'. The noun **adolescent** was also late Middle English, coming via French from Latin *adolescent-* 'coming to maturity'. The elements in the Latin verb are *ad-* 'to' and *alescere* 'grow, grow up', the base here being *alere* 'nourish'. The adjectival use of *adolescent* dates from the late 18th century.

adopt [late 15th century] *Adopt* includes a notion of 'choosing'; it comes via French from Latin *adoptare*, from *ad-* 'to' and *optare* 'choose'. **Adoption** is Middle English, from Latin *adoptio(n-)*; **adoptive** is late Middle English, via Old French from Latin *adoptivus*, from *adoptare* 'select for oneself'.
→ OPTION

adore [late Middle English] The semantic strands of 'worship' and 'spoken prayer' are interwoven in the word *adore*, which came into the language via Old French from Latin *adorare* 'to worship' (from *ad-* 'to' and *orare* 'speak, pray'). The adjective **adorable** came into use in the early 17th century meaning 'worthy of divine worship'; the source is French, from Latin *adorabilis*. The current meaning 'lovable, inspiring great affection' dates from the early 18th century.

adorn [late Middle English] Latin *ornare* 'to deck, add lustre' is involved in this word form, which came into English via Old French from Latin *adornare*.

adroit [mid 17th century] This is an adoption from French, from the phrase *à droit* 'according to right', 'properly'. The current sense is 'skilful in using the hands or mind'.

adulation [late Middle English] The noun *adulation* is from Latin *adulatio(n)-*, from *adulari*

'fawn on'. **Adulate** is not recorded until the mid 18th century, based on the same Latin verb.

adult [mid 16th century] *Adult* is from Latin *adultus*, the past participle of *adolescere* 'to grow to maturity'.
→ ADOLESCENCE

adulterate [early 16th century] The early use was adjectival (as in *adulterate remedies*) from Latin *adulterat-*, the past participial stem of the verb *adulterare* 'corrupt'.

adultery [late 15th century] This word comes from the obsolete noun *adulter* (as does **adulterous**), from Latin *adulter* 'adulterer'; it replaced an earlier form spelt *avoutrie*, from Old French *avouterie*. **Adulterer** is recorded from the early 16th century and comes from the obsolete verb *adulter* 'commit adultery', from Latin *adulterare* 'debauch, corrupt', replacing an earlier Middle English noun *avouterer*, from Old French *avoutrer* 'commit adultery'. The ultimate origin of this group of words is unknown.

advance [Middle English] The noun is from Old French *avance*, the verb from Old French *avancer*, based on late Latin *abante* 'in front'. The initial *a-* was mistaken for a form of the Latin prefix *ad-* in the 16th century and was assimilated to it; the error was influenced by words such as *adventure*, which was changed from *aventure*. The *d* was occasionally added artificially in French but remained mute, but in English the spelling became permanent.

advantage [Middle English] Old French *avantage* led to *advantage* in English; it is formed from *avant* 'in front', from late Latin *abante*.
→ ADVANCE

advent [Old English] *Advent* has its origin in Latin *adventus* 'arrival', from *advenire*, literally 'come to'. The earliest recorded sense in English was as the name of the period preceding the festival of the Nativity in the Christian religion; it now includes the four preceding Sundays. Something that is **adventitious** happens according to chance; this is recorded from the early 17th century and is from Latin *adventicius* 'coming to us from abroad' (from *advenire* 'arrive').

adventure [Middle English] The Latin base *adventurus* meant 'about to happen' (from *advenire* 'arrive'); this gave the noun *aventure* and the verb *aventurer* in Old French, the source of English *adventure*. In the late 15th century an **adventurer** was a gambler; the word stems from French *aventurier*, from *aventurer* 'venture upon'.

adverb [late Middle English] An *adverb* modifies the meaning of an adjective, verb, or other adverb, and it does this by 'adding' to the sense. The form is from Latin *adverbium*, the semantic elements being *ad-* 'to' (expressing addition) and *verbum* 'word, verb'.

adversary [Middle English] This word for an opponent is from Old French *adversarie*, from Latin *adversarius* 'opposed', 'opponent'; this is from *adversus* 'against, opposite', the base too of late Middle English **adverse** from Old French *advers*. The two core semantic strands are 'turning' and 'towards', found in Latin *advertere*, which also gave rise to Middle English **adversity**.
→AVERSE

advertise [late Middle English] Late Middle English is the period when *advertise*, **advert** (used formally in the verb sense 'refer to in speaking or writing'), and **advertisement** were first recorded in use. Latin *advertere* 'turn towards' is the base verb. *Advert* involved turning one's own attention to something whereas *advertise* now involves turning the attention of others. *Advertisement* was originally 'a statement calling attention to something'; its source is Old French *advertissement*, from the verb *advertir*; it started to be abbreviated to **advert** in the mid 19th century.
→ADVERSARY

advice [Middle English] *Advice* is from Old French *avis*, based on Latin *ad* and *visum*, the past participle of *videre* 'to see'. The original sense was 'a way of looking at something', 'a judgement', which led later to 'an opinion given'. The word was occasionally written *advis* by French scribes in the 14th to 16th centuries; the spelling was introduced into English by Caxton (the first English printer) and this became a permanent change. Middle English **advise** is from Old French *aviser* and is based on Latin *ad-* 'to' and *visere*, a frequentative (= verb of repeated action) of *videre* 'to see'. The original senses included 'look at' and 'consider', which led to 'consult with others'.

advocaat [1930s] This word for a liqueur made of eggs, sugar, and brandy, is an adoption of the Dutch word for 'advocate': it was originally considered 'a lawyer's drink' and this was the meaning of the full form in Dutch: *advocatenborrel*.

advocate [Middle English] An *advocate* may describe a professional who pleads for a client in a court of justice, or in Scotland a barrister, or generally refer to someone who publicly supports a cause or policy. The core notion is one of 'calling to one's assistance'; this arises from the elements *ad-* 'to' and *vocare* 'to call' in the Latin verb *advocare* 'call (to one's aid)'; the immediate source of the English is Old French

avocat. The noun **advocacy** dating from late Middle English came via Old French from medieval Latin *advocatia*.

aegis [early 17th century] An *aegis* was originally a piece of armour or a shield, especially that of a god. The word came into English via Latin from Greek *aigis* 'shield of Zeus'. It is now often used in the phrase *under the aegis of* meaning 'under the protection of'.

aeon [mid 17th century] Now this word is often seen in the plural in phrases such as *aeons ago*; it entered English via ecclesiastical Latin from Greek *aiōn* 'age'.

aerial [late 16th century] In early use *aerial* had the sense 'thin as air, imaginary'; it came via Latin *aerius* from Greek *aerios*, based on *aēr* 'air'. The word has been used since the early 20th century for a rod or wire etc. by which radio signals are transmitted.

aerobic [late 19th century] The two main elements are the prefix *aero-* (from Greek *aēr* 'air') and Greek *bios* 'life'. The word is used in biology (e.g. *simple aerobic bacteria*, where *aerobic* means 'requiring free oxygen') and in sports contexts (e.g. *aerobics*, *aerobic exercise*), where the sense relates to the efficiency of the body's cardio-vascular system in absorbing and transporting oxygen.

aeroplane [late 19th century] An *aeroplane*, semantically, is something that 'wanders through the air'. The formation is from French *aéroplane*, from *aéro-* 'air' and Greek *-planos* 'wandering'.

aesthetic [late 18th century] The early sense was 'relating to perception by the senses'; the source is Greek *aisthētikos*, from *aistheta* 'material things', from *aisthesthai* 'perceive'. This was opposed to things that were thinkable, in other words, immaterial things. The sense 'concerned with beauty' was coined in German in the mid 18th century, and adopted into English in the early 19th century, but its use was controversial until much later in the century. **Aesthete** was formed on the pattern of pairs such as *athlete*, *athletic*.

afar [Middle English] In Middle English this was *of feor* 'from far'.

affable [late Middle English] 'Talking' and therefore being communicative in a sociable way, is at the semantic core of *affable*: this came via Old French from Latin *affabilis*, from the verb *affari* (composed of *ad-* 'to' and *fari* 'speak').

affair [Middle English] This is from Old French *afaire*, from *à faire* 'to do'. English spellings in the early period were often with an *-e* ending, reflecting the French; all the examples of the spelling without a final -e are northern, a form which became generally widespread due to Caxton (the first English printer). The history of the English word *ado* is parallel to that of the French phrase *à faire*; French **affaire** was adopted in the early 19th century into English alongside *affair* but without the diversity of meaning; it is literally 'affair (of the heart)'.

→ ADO

affect¹ [late Middle English] The original sense of *affect* 'have an affect on' was 'attack as a disease'; it is from French *affecter* or Latin *affect-* 'influenced, affected', from the verb *afficere* 'work on'.

affect² [late Middle English] *Affect* 'pretend to' as in *affected to admire his music* is from French *affecter* or Latin *affectare* 'aim at', a frequentative (= verb of repeated action) of *afficere* 'work on, influence'. The base elements are *ad-* 'at, to' and *facere* 'do'. The early recorded sense was 'like, love', which led to '(like to) assume'. The noun **affectation** is recorded from the mid 16th century and comes from Latin *affectatio(n-)*, based on *afficere*: this same base verb is the source too of Middle English **affection** (via Old French from Latin *affectio(n-)*), and **affectionate** dating from the late 15th century when it meant 'disposed, inclined towards': it comes from French *affectionné* 'beloved' or medieval Latin *affectionatus* 'devoted'.

affect³ [late 19th century] This noun used in psychology contexts to denote an emotion or desire, was coined in German from Latin *affectus* 'disposition', from *afficere* 'to influence'.

affidavit [mid 16th century] A legal term from medieval Latin, *affidavit* means literally 'he has stated on oath', from the verb *affidare*.

affiliate [mid 18th century] Parent companies have *affiliates* and the 'family' associations are due to the medieval Latin verb *affiliare* 'adopt as a son' (from *ad-* 'towards' and *filius* 'son'). **Affiliation** (late 18th century) is from French, from medieval Latin *affiliatio(n-)*, from the verb *affiliare*.

affinity [Middle English] The prime semantic notion in *affinity* is 'touching', 'bordering'; this is carried through into the modern senses where similarity or a shared bond is conveyed. The first sense recorded was 'relationship by marriage'; the word came via Old French from Latin *affinitas*, from *affinis* 'related' (literally 'bordering on'), from *ad-* 'to' and *finis* 'border'.

affirm [Middle English] The early sense was 'make firm'; *affirm* comes via Old French from Latin *affirmare* 'assert', from *ad-* 'to' and *firmus* 'strong'. **Affirmative** (late Middle English) had

the sense 'assertive, positive' and came via Old French from late Latin *affirmativus*.

afflict [late Middle English] The early senses of *afflict* were 'deject' and 'humiliate'; the word comes from Latin *afflictare* 'knock about, harass', or from *afflict-* 'knocked down, weakened', both from the verb *affligere*. Middle English **affliction** was originally the 'infliction of pain or humiliation', specifically 'religious self-mortification'; the form is via Old French from Latin *afflictio(n-)*. The base is Latin *fligere* 'to strike, dash'.

affluent [late Middle English] *Affluent* 'wealthy' is a use recorded from the mid 18th century, but it was first used to describe water flowing freely. The form came via Old French from Latin *affluent-* 'flowing towards, flowing without restriction', from the verb *affluere* (from *ad-* 'to' and *fluere* 'to flow'). This Latin verb is also the base of **afflux** 'a flow (of water, air)' recorded from the early 17th century, from medieval Latin *affluxus*.

afford [late Old English] Old English *geforthian* is from *ge-* (a prefix implying completeness) and *forthian* 'to further' (from *forth*). The original sense was 'promote, perform, accomplish', later coming to mean 'manage, be in a position to do'. The association with wealth is recorded from late Middle English.

→ FORTH

affranchise [late 15th century] Old French *franc* 'free' is at the root of *affranchise* 'release from servitude'; the English spelling is from Old French *afranchiss-*, the lengthened stem of *afranchir*.

affray [Middle English] Now a dated legal term describing an instance of group fighting in a public place that disturbs the peace, *affray* first had the general sense 'disturbance, fray'. It comes from Anglo-Norman French *afrayer* 'disturb, startle', based on an element of Germanic origin related to Old English *frithu* 'peace, safety'.

affront [Middle English] First used as a verb, *affront* is from Old French *afronter* 'to slap in the face, insult', based on Latin *ad frontem* 'to the face'.

aficionado [mid 19th century] This started out as a term for a devotee of bullfighting; it is a Spanish word meaning 'amateur', the past participle of *aficioner* 'become fond of' used as a noun, based on Latin *affectio(n-)* '(favourable) disposition towards'. Now it is used to describe any ardent follower of a hobby or activity; examples of this extended usage date from the 1880s.

→ AFFECT²

afraid [Middle English] This is the past participle of the obsolete verb *affray*, from Anglo-Norman French *afrayer*.
→AFFRAY

after [Old English] Old English *æfter* is Germanic in origin and related to Dutch *achter*. The spelling of **afterwards** was influenced by *after*; in Old English the form was *æftewearde*, from *æftan* 'aft' and the suffix *-wards*.

aftermath [late 15th century] The early meaning of *aftermath* was to descibe new grass growing after the harvest or after mowing. It is made up of *after* (used as an adjective) and the dialect word *math* 'mowing': the origin is Germanic and German *Mahd* is related. The current meaning referring to a condition or situation resulting from an unpleasant event is found in texts dating from the mid 17th century (W. S. Churchill *Victory*: The life and strength of Britain … will be tested to the full, not only in the war but in the aftermath of war).

again [Old English] The Old English forms *ongēan*, *ongægn*, etc., are Germanic in origin; a relative is German *entgegen* 'opposite'. The root seems to have meant, primarily, 'direct', 'straight'; the full form became 'in a direct line with', 'opposite', leading to ideas of meeting, opposition, reversal, and recurrence. A variant in the south arose around 1130 which became corrupted before 1400 to **against**.

age [Middle English] This is from Old French, based on Latin *aetas*, *aetat-*, from *aevum* 'age, era'. The Old French word *ege* was pronounced with three syllables but the earliest recorded English equivalent was pronounced with two; the modern words in English and French (*age* and *âge*) are reduced further.

agenda [early 17th century] The early meaning was 'things to be done'; it is the Latin neuter plural of *agendum*, gerund of *agere* 'do'.

agent [late Middle English] The original meaning was 'someone or something that produces an effect'; the origin is Latin *agent-* 'doing', from the verb *agere*. **Agency** is recorded from the mid 17th century and comes from medieval Latin *agentia*.

agglomerate [late 17th century] Latin *glomus* 'ball' is at the core of *agglomerate* which comes from the Latin verb *agglomerare* 'add to'.

agglutinate [mid 16th century] Latin *gluten* 'glue' is the base of *agglutinate*. The form is from Latin *agglutinat-*, from the verb *agglutinare* 'cause to adhere'.

aggravate [mid 16th century] *Aggravate* replaced an earlier word spelt *aggrege*, and is from the Latin verb *aggravare* 'make heavy'.

The main elements here are *ad-* (expressing increase) and *gravis* 'heavy'. *Aggravate* in the sense 'annoy' dates from the 17th century and has been used with this meaning by writers ever since. The use is still regarded as incorrect by some traditionalists who think it too radical a departure from the etymological meaning 'make heavy'. This is however typical of the meaning change in many words long accepted without comment.

aggregate [late Middle English] 'Flock' is at the semantic core of *aggregate*. The source verb here is Latin *aggregare* 'herd together', from *ad-* 'towards' and *grex*, *greg-* 'a flock'. *Aggregate* involves a notion of the combination of many often disparate elements.

aggression [early 17th century] An *aggression* was originally 'an attack', from Latin *aggressio(n-)*, from *aggredi* 'to attack'; the elements in the verb are *ad-* 'towards' and *gradi* 'proceed, walk'. In the same family is **aggressive** which dates from the early 19th century, coming from Latin *aggress-* 'attacked' (from the verb *aggredi*).

aggrieved [Middle English] Middle English *aggrieved*, as the past participle of the rare verb *aggrieve*, had the sense 'distressed'; it comes from Old French *agrever* 'make heavier', 'make more severe', based on Latin *aggravare*. The French word changed its prefix from *agrever* to *aggraver* under the influence of the Latin.
→AGGRAVATE

aggro [1960s] *Aggro* is an abbreviation of *aggravation* or of *aggression*.

aghast [late Middle English] This is the past participle of the obsolete verb *agast*, *gast* 'frighten', from Old English *gæsten*. The spelling with *-gh-* was originally Scots and became general by about 1700, probably influenced by *ghost*.
→GHASTLY

agile [late Middle English] *Agile* is essentially descriptive of activity: it came via French from Latin *agilis*, from *agere* 'do'.

agitate [late Middle English] The original sense was 'drive away', from Latin *agitare* 'agitate, drive', a frequentative (= verb of repeated action) of *agere* 'do, drive'. The noun **agitation** dates from the mid 16th century when it meant 'action, being active': the source is Latin *agitatio(n-)*. The Latin form **agitator** (mid 17th century) first referred to a delegate of private soldiers in the Parliamentary army during the English Civil War; it came to describe a person urging others to rebel from about the mid 18th century, usually about political issues.

agnostic [mid 19th century] An *agnostic* believes that nothing can be known of the existence or nature of God; the word is made up of the prefix *a-* meaning 'not' and *gnostic* 'relating to knowledge', based on Greek *gnōstos* 'known'. Used more generally, *agnostic* may simply refer to a 'sceptic' or 'someone who wavers in taking a point of view', such as in political alignment.

ago [Middle English] Middle English *ago*, *agone* were past participial forms of the obsolete verb *ago* 'to pass', used to express the passage of time. The phrase *long ago* is essentially 'a long time having gone by'. The spelling *agone* was also common but dialect use shortened the word in some areas; it is still however found in certain dialects. *Ago* became the ordinary spelling in prose, from Caxton (the first English printer).

agog [mid 16th century] There is a sense of intense amazement and anticipation in *agog* and originally this was caused by amusement and merriment: it is from Old French *en gogues*, from *en* 'in' and the plural of *gogue* 'fun'. The 1960s phrase *a gogo* meaning 'galore' (as in *interactive games software a gogo*) has the same base: it is from French *à gogo*, from Old French *gogue* 'fun'.

agony [late Middle English] *Agony* referred originally to 'mental' anguish alone; the word came into English via Old French and late Latin from Greek *agōnia*, from *agōn* 'contest' (the base too of **agonize**). The Greek sense development moved from struggle for victory in the games, to any struggle, to mental struggle specifically (such as the torment of Christ in the Garden of Gethsemane). The extension in English to an idea of 'physical' suffering dates from the early 17th century.

agree [late Middle English] When we *agree* to something, there is a core notion of trying to please; the word is from Old French *agreer*, based on Latin *ad-* 'to' and *gratus* 'pleasing'. In the same family is late Middle English **agreeable** from Old French *agreable*, from *agreer* 'make agreeable to': **agreement** from Old French, dates from the same period.

agriculture [late Middle English] This is from Latin *agricultura*, from *ager*, *agr-* 'field' and *cultura* 'growing, cultivation'.

ague [Middle English] *Ague* came via Old French from medieval Latin *acuta* (*febris*) 'acute (fever)'; this was the first sense recorded in English. It came to be applied to malarial fever and at first referred to the burning feverish stage; later this changed and the word denoted the cold shivering stage. Hence the late 16th-century use for any fit of shivering.

aid [late Middle English] The noun is from Old French *aide*; the verb is from Old French *aidier*, based on Latin *adjuvare*, from *ad-* 'towards' and *juvare* 'to help'.

ail [Old English] The Old English forms *eglian* and *eglan* are from *egle* 'troublesome', which is Germanic in origin; Gothic *agls* 'disgraceful' is related. *Ail* means 'trouble in mind or body'.

aim [Middle English] *Aim* is from Old French *amer*, a variant of *esmer*. These bring with them the notion of evaluation before a direction is taken, from the Latin verb *aestimare* meaning 'assess, estimate'. The word was reinforced by Old French *aemer*, *aesmer* from late Latin *ad-aestimare*, an intensified form of *aestimare*.

aisle [late Middle English] The early spellings *ele*, *ile* are from Old French *ele*, from Latin *ala* 'wing'. The spelling change in the 17th century was due to confusion with *isle*, which may derive from the idea of a detached portion of a church; the word was also influenced by French *aile* 'wing'.

ajar [late 17th century] *A-* 'on' is prefixed to obsolete *char*, which in Old English was *cerr*, meaning 'a turn, return'.

akimbo [late Middle English] This is from *in kenebowe* in Middle English, probably from Old Norse; it has been compared with Icelandic *keng-boginn* (literally 'bent in a horseshoe curve'), but gaps remain in the evidence.

alacrity [late Middle English] Latin *alacritas* is the source, from *alacer* 'brisk'.

alarm [late Middle English] *Alarm* started out as an exclamation meaning 'to arms!'; it stems from Old French *alarme*, from the Italian phrase *all' arme!* 'to arms!'. The variant spelling *alarum* existed in English in early times because of the way the *-r-* was rolled when pronouncing the word; this form became restricted specifically to the peal of a warning bell or clock. The original exclamation as a call to arms, is seen in the phrase *alarums and excursions*, a stage direction found in Shakespeare's *Henry VI* and *Richard III*; this has resulted in playful use by more recent writers for confused fighting and skirmishing (W. Raleigh *Shakespeare*: The whole First Act of *Coriolanus* is … full of alarums and excursions and hand-to-hand fighting).

alas [Middle English] This expression of dismay is from Old French *a las*, *a lasse*, from *a* 'ah' and *las(se)* (from Latin *lassus* 'weary'). Late Middle English **alack** is a comparable exclamation, from *a* 'ah!' and *lak* 'lack'. It originally expressed dissatisfaction and the notion 'shame that it should be the case'; this came to convey regret or surprise, as in *alack-a-day*.

albatross [late 17th century] This is an alteration (influenced by Latin *albus* 'white') of 16th-century *alcatras*, applied to various seabirds including the frigate bird and pelican, from Spanish and Portuguese *alcatraz*. The source is Arabic *al-ġaṭṭās* 'the diver'. The word sometimes carries with it an idea of misfortune and burdensome guilt: this is with allusion to Coleridge's *Ancient Mariner* in which an albatross is shot by the mariner and worn symbolically as a burden of guilt for the disaster befalling the crew in their becalmed ship (1798: Instead of the Cross the Albatross About my neck was hung).

albeit [late Middle English] This form comes from the phrase *all be it* meaning 'although it be (the case that)'.

albino [early 18th century] An *albino* describes a person or animal with a congenital absence of pigment in the skin and hair. The word is from Spanish or Portuguese: the Portuguese used the term to refer to albinos among African blacks. The base is Latin *albus* 'white'.

Albion [Old English] Taken from Latin and probably of Celtic origin, *Albion* is probably related to Latin *albus* 'white' (in allusion to the white cliffs of Dover). The phrase *perfidious Albion* which dates from the mid 19th century, translates the French *la perfide Albion*, alluding to the alleged treachery of England to other nations.

album [early 17th century] This is the Latin neuter form of *albus* 'white' used as a noun meaning 'a white (= blank) tablet' on which public notices were written. Taken into English from the German use of the Latin phrase *album amicorum* 'album of friends', it was originally used consciously as a Latin word with Latin inflections (e.g. *in albo*). The adopted word referred to a book for inserting souvenirs such as autographs and drawings.

albumen [late 16th century] This is a Latin word meaning 'egg white', from *albus* 'white'.

Alcatraz This rocky island in San Francisco bay, associated with a famous penitentiary, owes its name to Spanish *alcatraz* 'pelicans', which were once common there. Robert Stroud, a convicted murderer imprisoned on Alcatraz for 73 years (54 of which were in solitary confinement), became an expert and world authority on birdlife: the film *Birdman of Alcatraz* (produced in 1962 in Stroud's lifetime) detailed his story.

alchemy [late Middle English] The word *alchemy* came via Old French and medieval Latin from Arabic *alkīmiyā'*: the elements are *al* 'the' and *kīmiyā'* which comes from Greek *khēmia*, *khēmeia* 'art of transmuting metals'. In early use

alchemy referred to the chemistry of the Middle Ages and 16th century; the search for a way of transmuting baser metals into gold, for the 'alkahest' (or universal solvent), and for the panacea (or universal remedy), were the main practical aims of this early chemistry.

alcohol [mid 16th century] This is an adoption of an earlier French form of *alcool*, or it comes from medieval Latin, from Arabic *al-kuhl* 'the kohl'. In early use the term referred to powders such as kohl used to stain the eyelids, and especially powders obtained by sublimation. Later from the mid 17th century, it came to describe any distilled or rectified spirit: *alcohol of wine* was the most familiar of these rectified spirits.

alcove [late 16th century] French *alcôve* is the source of *alcove*, from Spanish *alcoba*, from Arabic *al-kubba* 'the vault'.

alder [Old English] Old English *alor*, *aler* are Germanic in origin and related to German *Erle*; forms spelt with *-d-* are recorded from the 14th century.

alderman [Old English] Old English *aldormann* was originally used in the general sense 'a man of high rank', from *aldor*, *ealdor* 'chief, patriarch' (literally 'old one') and *man*. The *aldor* was a natural rank, the name of the chief of a clan, but the addition of the suffix *-man* added an official political dimension. Later the sense 'warden of a guild' arose; then, as the guilds became identified with the ruling municipal body, the word meant 'local magistrate, municipal officer'.

ale [Old English] The Old English word *alu*, *calu* referred especially to unhopped or the paler varieties of beer. The form is Germanic in origin; related is Old Norse *ọl*. *Ale* and *beer* were synonyms originally. Around 1524, *beer* was often hopped and now is generic for malt liquors; the late 16th-century proverb *Turkey, heresy, hops, and beer came into England all in one year* reflects the association. However, *ale* continues to be applied to paler kinds of liquors for which the malt has not been roasted. Some areas still use *beer* and *ale* interchangeably.
→ BEER; BRIDAL

alert [late 16th century] A military term originally, *alert* comes from French *alerte*, from Italian *all' erta* 'to the watchtower'.

alexandrine [late 16th century] French *alexandrin* has given *alexandrine*; it is based on the word, *Alexandre*. The person to which this refers is disputed; some refer it to Alexander the Great, who was the subject of an Old French poem in this metre (six iambic feet); others derive it from *Alexandre Paris*, a French poet who used this verse (and who in fact wrote about Alexander the Great in one of his poems).

alfresco [mid 18th century] This is from the Italian phrase *al fresco* meaning 'in the fresh (air)'.

algebra [late Middle English] *Algebra* is a word from Italian, Spanish, and medieval Latin, from Arabic *al-jabr* 'the reunion of broken parts', 'bone-setting', from *jabara* 'reunite, restore'. The original sense, which was 'the surgical treatment of fractures', probably came via Spanish, where it survives; the mathematical sense comes from the title of a book, *'ilm al-jabr wa'l-mukābala* 'the science of restoring what is missing and equating like with like', by the mathematician al-Kwārizmī
➔ ALGORITHM

algorithm [late 17th century] *Algorithm* initially denoted the Arabic or decimal notation of numbers; it is a variant, influenced by Greek *arithmos* 'number', of Middle English *algorism* which came via Old French from medieval Latin *algorismus*. The Arabic source, al-Kwārizmī 'the man of Kwārizm' (now Khiva), was the cognomen of the 9th-century mathematician Abū Ja'far Muhammad ibn Mūsa, author of widely translated works on algebra and arithmetic.

alias [late Middle English] A Latin word, *alias* means literally 'at another time, otherwise'. It is used in English as 'a false or assumed identity'. The term *aliasing* has been taken up in specialist fields such as computing (= the use of an alternative name referring to a file, command, address, etc., in order to access it) and telecommunications (= misidentification of a signal frequency, introducing distortion or error).

alibi [late 17th century] The first use was as an adverb meaning 'elsewhere', which was the sense in Latin. The noun use dates from the late 18th century.

alien [Middle English] *Alien* is now often used to refer to a foreigner or something strange and unfamiliar, and, since the 1950s in science fiction, to beings from another planet. The word came via Old French from Latin *alienus* 'belonging to another', from *alius* 'other'. From the same base is early 16th-century **alienate** (from the Latin form *alienat-* meaning 'estranged') and late Middle English **alienation** (from Latin *alienatio(n-)*). The phrase *alienation effect* dates from the 1940s and is a translation of German *Verfremdungseffekt*; this term used in the theatre refers to audience objectivity when there is no identification with the actors.

alight[1] [Old English] Old English *ālīhtan* 'descend' is from *ā-* (used for emphasis) and *līhtan* 'descend'.
➔ LIGHT[3]

alight[2] [late Middle English] This is probably from the phrase *on a light* (= lighted) *fire*. Modern use has seen a change in the position of the word in a sentence from this early attributive use; now it is only used predicatively, as in *kept the candles alight* and *all alight*; this is because of association with word forms such as *ablaze*, *afire*, etc.

align [late 17th century] The French phrase *à ligne* 'into line' is part of the verb form *aligner*, source of *align* in English. Late 18th-century **alignment** is from French *alignement*, from *aligner*.

alike [Old English] Old English *gelīc* is Germanic in origin and related to Dutch *gelijk* and German *gleich*; the word was reinforced in Middle English by Old Norse *álíkr* (adjective) and *álíka* (adverb).

aliment [late 15th century] Latin *alimentum* 'nourishment' (from *alere* 'nourish') is the source of *aliment*, late 16th-century **alimentary**, and, from the same period, **alimentation** which was originally used in the sense 'maintenance, support'.

alimony [early 17th century] The early sense of *alimony*, now mainly used in the US for maintenance payments made after a divorce settlement, was 'nourishment, means of subsistence'. It comes from Latin *alimonia* 'nutriment', from *alere* 'nourish'. The informal word *palimony* makes use of the term *alimony* and involves compensation made by one partner of an unmarried couple to the other after separation: the amicable arrangement is conveyed by the prefix *pal*.

alive [Old English] 'In life' was the literal meaning of Old English *on līfe*. The spelling *on live* was still current in the 17th century.

alkali [late Middle English] The chemistry term *alkali* used to denote a saline substance derived from the ashes of various plants, including glasswort; the formation of the word is from medieval Latin, from Arabic *al-kalī* 'calcined ashes (of the glasswort etc.)', from *kalā* 'fry, roast'. Early 19th-century **alkaloid** (a class of compounds including for example morphine, quinine, and strychnine) was coined in German from *alkali*.

all [Old English] *All* has a Germanic origin; it is related to Dutch *al* and German *all*.

allay [Old English] Old English *ālecgan* meant 'lay down or aside'. In the sense development, *allay* often overlapped with the obsolete verb *allege* (from Old French) meaning 'lighten' in a network of uses. The 'laying down or aside' of *allay* sometimes involved laws and customs, sometimes a course of action or a principle; it also involved quelling violence or strong passions: this notion of 'quell' added to the confusion with *allege* 'make lighter'.

allege [Middle English] Middle English *allege* had the early sense 'declare on oath'; the source is Old French *esligier* 'to clear at law', based on Latin *lis*, *lit-* 'lawsuit'; it was confused in sense with Latin *allegare* 'allege'. **Allegation** is late Middle English and comes from Latin *allegatio(n-)*, from *allegare* 'allege'.

allegiance [late Middle English] This is from Anglo-Norman French, a variant of Old French *ligeance*, from *lige*, *liege*, perhaps by association with Anglo-Latin *alligantia* 'alliance'.

allegory [late Middle English] An *allegory* can be interpreted to reveal a hidden meaning and the base semantics are Greek *allos* 'other' and *-agoria* 'speaking', components of the word *allegoria*. *Allegory* came into English from Old French *allegorie*.

allergy [early 20th century] There is a notion of something 'alien' present in *allergy* which comes from German *Allergie*, from Greek *allos* 'other'; it was formed on the pattern of German *Energie* 'energy'.

alleviate [late Middle English] The source of this word is late Latin *alleviare* 'lighten', from Latin *allevare*. The base is Latin *levare* 'raise', influenced by *levis* 'light'.

alley [late Middle English] Old French *alee* 'walking or passage' is the source of *alley*; the Old French base is *aler* 'to go', from Latin *ambulare* 'to walk'.

alligator [late 16th century] This is from Spanish *el lagarto* 'the lizard', probably based on Latin *lacerta*.

alliteration [early 17th century] The word *alliteration* describes the occurrence of the same letter or sound at the beginning of adjacent or closely connected words. The form is from medieval Latin *alliteratio(n-)*, from Latin *ad-* (which in this instance expresses addition) and *littera* 'letter'. The verb **alliterate** dates from the late 18th century and is a back-formation (by removal of the suffix) from *alliteration*.

allocation [late Middle English] *Allocation* is from medieval Latin *allocatio(n-)*, and mid 17th-century **allocate** is from the medieval Latin stem *allocat-*, both from the verb *allocare* 'allot'. The base verb is *locare* 'to place'.
→ LOCATE

allot [late 15th century] *Allot* is from Old French *aloter*, from *a-* (from Latin *ad* 'to') and *loter* 'divide into lots'.

allow [Middle English] This was originally used to mean 'commend, sanction' and 'assign as a right'. Both meanings were adopted from Old French *alouer* in about 1300. The source was Latin *allaudare* 'to praise', reinforced by medieval Latin *allocare* 'to place'. The semantic strands intertwined to mean 'assign with approval'. Late Middle English **allowance** is from Old French *alouance*, from *alouer*.
→ ALLOCATION

alloy [late 16th century] The noun is from Old French *aloi*, the verb from French *aloyer*, both from Old French *aloier*, *aleier* 'combine', from Latin *alligare* 'bind'. In early use the term denoted the comparative purity of gold or silver; the sense 'mixture of metals' arose in the mid 17th century.

allude [late 15th century] *Allude* 'hint at, suggest' is from Latin *alludere* 'play with', from *ad-* 'towards' and *ludere* 'to play'. **Allusion** dates from the mid 16th century and first denoted a pun, metaphor, or parable: the word comes from French, or from late Latin *allusio(n-)*, from the verb *alludere*.

allure [late Middle English] An Old French falconry term, *luere* 'a lure', is the semantic root of the notion of 'enticement' in *allure*; the first sense was 'tempt', coming from Old French *aleurier* 'attract': the prefix *a-* is from Latin *ad* 'to'.

alluvion [mid 16th century] Now a word used in legal contexts to describe the deposition by the sea or a river causing an increase in land area, *alluvion* originally meant a flood carrying suspended material which was then deposited; it comes from French, from Latin *alluvio(n-)*, from *ad-* 'towards' and *luere* 'to wash'. Recorded from the mid 17th century is **alluvium**; this is a deposit of clay, silt, and sand left by flowing flood water; the word is an adoption of the Latin neuter of *alluvius* 'washed against', from *ad-* 'towards' and *luere* 'to wash'. **Alluvial** dates from the early 19th century.

ally [Middle English] *Ally* started out as a verb; it is from Old French *alier*, from Latin *alligare* 'to bind together', based on *ligare* 'to bind'; the noun is partly via Old French *alie* 'allied'. **Alliance** is also a Middle English word, from Old French *aliance*, from *alier* 'to ally'.
→ ALLOY

alma mater [mid 17th century] This phrase is used with reference to a university or college once attended, but first had the general sense 'someone or something providing nour-

ishment'; in Latin the literal meaning is 'bounteous mother'. It was a title given by the Romans to several goddesses but in particular to Ceres and Cybele, both representing 'fostering motherfigures'.
➔ALUMNUS

almanac [late Middle English] The ultimate origin is unknown but the word came into English via medieval Latin from Greek *almenikhiaka*. At the time of Roger Bacon (1214?–1294) and Chaucer, *almanacs* were permanent tables of the apparent movements and positions of the sun and moon, from which astronomical data for any year could be calculated. In the 15th century *almanacs* started to be prepared for periods of time (10, 30 years, etc.), but within the next century they were prepared for the year. Astrological and weather predictions appeared as a feature in the 17th century. The statistics associated with almanacs are a modern addition.

almost [Old English] Old English *æl mæst* meant 'for the most part'.
➔ALL; MOST

alms [Old English] Old English *ælmysse, ælmesse* come from Christian Latin *eleemosyna*, from Greek *eleēmosunē* 'compassion'; the base is *eleos* 'mercy'. Middle English **almoner** is from Old French *aumonier*, based on medieval Latin *eleemosynarius*.

aloe [Old English] Old English *alewe, alwe* denoted the fragrant resin or heartwood of certain oriental trees; it came via Latin from Greek *aloē*; in late Middle English it was reinforced by Old French *aloes* 'aloe', causing the word to be frequently used in the plural in English. The emollient **aloe vera** is a term from the early 20th century and is modern Latin, literally 'true aloe', probably in contrast to the American agave, which closely resembles aloe vera: both plants were formerly classified together in the lily family.

aloft [Middle English] *Aloft* is from Old Norse *á lopt, á lopti*, from *á* 'in, on, to' and *lopt* 'air'.

alone [Middle English] This is made up of *all* and *one*. A rare use meaning 'unique, having no equal' is illustrated in Shakespeare's *Two Gentlemen of Verona*: All I can is nothing To her, whose worth makes other worthies nothing; She is alone.

aloof [mid 16th century] In this word, the prefix *a-* expresses direction and the second element is *luff*, a sailing term which was originally an adverb meaning 'away and to windward!', that is to say with the ship's head kept close to the wind and away from a lee shore

towards which it might drift. This led to the sense 'at a distance'.

alphabet [early 16th century] Greek *alpha* and *bēta*, the first two letters of the Greek alphabet, are the elements in *alphabet*, from late Latin *alphabetum*.

already [Middle English] The word is made up of *all* (as an adverb) and *ready*, the literal meaning therefore being 'in a completely prepared state'.

also [Old English] Old English *alswā* meant 'quite so, in that manner, similarly'.

altar [Old English] The Old English forms *altar, alter* are based on late Latin *altar, altarium*, from Latin *altus* 'high'. Early use described a raised structure on which to make offerings to a god. Reference to the *altar* in the Christian Church for celebration of the Eucharist, dates from Middle English.

alter [late Middle English] Old French *alterer* has given *alter* in English; it comes from late Latin *alterare*, from Latin *alter* 'other'. **Alteration** is also a late Middle English word from Old French, or from late Latin *alteratio(n-)*.

altercation [late Middle English] A noisy argument is sometimes described as an *altercation*; this word comes from Latin *altercatio(n-)*, from the verb *altercari* 'wrangle'. **Altercate** is recorded from the mid 16th century and comes from the Latin form *altercat-* meaning 'wrangled' (from *altercari*).

alternate [early 16th century] *Alternate* is from the Latin form *alternat-* meaning 'done by turns', from *alternare*, based on Latin *alternus* 'every other'. The word **alternative** appeared slightly later in the mid 16th century in the sense 'alternating, alternate': the source is French *alternatif, -ive* or medieval Latin *alternativus*. The base is Latin *alter* 'other'.

altitude [late Middle English] *Altitude* is from Latin *altitudo*, from *altus* 'high'.

alto [late 16th century] This musical term comes from the Italian phrase *alto (canto)* 'high (song)'.

altruism [mid 19th century] Selfless concern for others is known as *altruism*; the source of the word is French *altruisme*, from Italian *altrui* 'somebody else', from Latin *alteri huic* 'to this other'.

alumnus [mid 17th century] A Latin word originally meaning 'nursling, pupil', *alumnus* is from *alere* 'nourish'. It is mostly in US use now, describing a graduate or former student. The feminine equivalent **alumna** came into use in the late 19th century from Latin.

always [Middle English] This was the genitive case of *all way*, the inflection probably giving the sense 'at every time' as opposed to 'at one uninterrupted time'; the two are no longer distinct.

amalgam [late 15th century] *Amalgam* 'mixture', 'blend' is from French *amalgame* or medieval Latin *amalgama* (used regularly in alchemy contexts), from Greek *malagma* 'an emollient'. Two other words from this Greek root came into use in the early 17th century: **amalgamate** from medieval Latin *amalgamare* 'form into a soft mass', and **amalgamation**.

amass [late 15th century] *Amass* 'gather together in large amounts' is from French *amasser* or medieval Latin *amassare*, based on Latin *massa* 'lump'.
→ MASS

amateur [late 18th century] This is an adopted French word from Italian *amatore*, from Latin *amator* 'lover'; the base verb is *amare* 'to love'.

amaze [Old English] The origin of Old English *āmasian* is unknown. It is perhaps based on the root of two north Germanic verbs referring to pointless activity, as well as Norwegian forms meaning 'fuss' and 'start to dream', and Swedish 'walk lazily'.

Amazon [late Middle English] The word *Amazon* occurs in various uses: firstly as a name for a member of a legendary race of female warriors who were thought by the Greeks to live in Scythia. The word came via Latin from Greek *Amazōn*: it was explained by the Greeks as 'breastless', as if coming from *a-* 'without' and *mazos* 'breast'. The fable was that the Amazons cut off the right breast so as not to interfere with their use of the bow, but probably this is a folk etymology of an unknown foreign word. Another use of the name is for the river *Amazon* which was was called after legendary female warriors believed to live on its banks; it bore various names after its discovery in 1500 before the one eventually chosen. A third example of *Amazon* is as a verb from the 1990s meaning 'put out of business': the success of an Internet bookseller called *Amazon.com.Inc* led to phrases such as *businesses are being* 'Amazoned', *or reshaped by the Internet*.

ambassador [late Middle English] The origin is French *ambassadeur*, from Italian *ambasciator*, based on Latin *ambactus* 'servant'. There were many early variant spellings of the word: *embassador* was much more common than *ambassador* in the 17th to 18th century, and was in fact the common spelling in the US in the 19th century.

amber [late Middle English] Originally *amber* (a fossilized resin) was also a term for 'ambergris' (a waxlike substance from sperm whales, used in perfume manufacture) because of some confusion between the substances. It is from Old French *ambre*, from Arabic *'anbar* which at first meant 'ambergris', and then later 'amber'.

ambidextrous [mid 17th century] The sense elements here are Latin *ambi-* 'on both sides' and *dexter* 'right-handed', found in late Latin *ambidexter*, the source of *ambidextrous* 'able to use the right and left hands with equal skill'. The Latin focus on 'right'-handedness on both sides shows the tendency to consider the 'right' as the 'strong' and 'correct' hand, a perception which persisted in educational contexts for a considerable time.

ambient [late 16th century] In phrases such as *ambient temperature* or *ambient music* the sense relates to the immediate environs: the word is from French *ambiant* or Latin *ambient-* 'going round', from the verb *ambire*. In the late 19th century **ambience** came into use, composed from *ambient* and the suffix *-ence*, or from French *ambiance*, source of the English variant **ambiance**, which describes the 'atmosphere and character of a particular place'.

ambiguity [late Middle English] This comes from Old French *ambiguite* or Latin *ambiguitas*, from *ambiguus* 'doubtful'; in the same family is **ambiguous** recorded from the early 16th century meaning 'indistinct, obscure'; this is from Latin *ambiguus* 'doubtful', from *ambigere* 'waver, go around', the main two sense elements being *ambi-* 'both ways' and *agere* 'to drive'.

ambition [Middle English] *Ambition* came via Old French from Latin *ambitio(n-)*, from *ambire* 'go around (canvassing for votes)'. The related late Middle English word **ambitious** is from Old French *ambitieux* or Latin *ambitiosus*, from *ambitio(n-)*. The sense progression in Latin moved from going round generally, to going round to canvass votes, to seeking honour, to ostentation, and finally to keen desire. The sense 'desire for honour' was adopted first in the modern languages.

amble [Middle English] An *amble* in Middle English was a horse's gait: the source is Old French *ambler*, from Latin *ambulare* 'to walk'.

ambrosia [mid 16th century] This came into English via Latin from the Greek word which meant 'elixir of life', from *ambrotos* 'immortal'. *Ambrosia* in Greek and Roman mythology, was the food of the gods; it is extended to describe anything pleasing to the taste or sense of smell.

ambulance [early 19th century] This is a French word formed from the phrase *hôpital* *ambulant* which was a 'mobile field hospital' drawn in convoy by horses; Latin *ambulant-* 'walking' is the base. General use began apparently during the Crimean War (1853–6). The word was extended to the vehicle rather than the whole hospital around the mid 19th century. Later that century, the phrase **ambulance chaser** came into use as a result of the reputation gained by certain lawyers for attending accidents and encouraging victims to sue.

ambush [Middle English] At first *ambush* had the sense 'place troops in hiding in order to surprise an enemy'; the noun is from Old French *embusche*, the verb from *embuschier*, based on a late Latin word meaning 'to place in a wood'.
➔ BUSH

ameliorate [mid 18th century] This is an alteration of *meliorate*, influenced by French *améliorer*, from *meilleur* 'better'.

amen [Old English] This is taken from ecclesiastical Latin, from Greek *amēn*; the source is Hebrew *'āmēn* 'truth, certainty', used adverbially to express agreement, and adopted in the Septuagint as a solemn expression of belief or affirmation.

amenable [late 16th century] The semantic root of *amenable* is 'threat' despite the 'open, responsive' connotation of the word in modern use; the early meaning was in fact 'liable to answer (to a law or tribunal)'; it was an Anglo-Norman French legal term, from Old French *amener* 'bring to'. This is based on the verb *mener* 'bring', from Late Latin *minare* 'drive (animals)', from Latin *minari* 'threaten'.

amend [Middle English] This is from Old French *amender*, based on Latin *emendare*. An early meaning of the English plural *amends* (as in *make amends*) was 'money paid to compensate injury or offence'; it comes from Old French *amendes* 'penalties, fine', the plural of *amende* 'reparation', from *amender*. Middle English **amendment** started out with the meaning 'improvement, correction', from Old French *amendement*, from *amender*.
➔ EMEND

amenity [late Middle English] At the core of *amenity* is Latin *amoenus* 'pleasant'; Old French *amenite* or Latin *amoenitas* have given rise to the form in English.

amethyst [Middle English] This precious stone was believed to prevent intoxication; the word comes via Old French from Latin *amethystus*, from Greek *amethustos* 'not drunken'.

amiable [late Middle English] *Amiable* was originally 'kind' and 'lovely, lovable'; it comes via Old French from late Latin *amicabilis* 'amicable'. The current sense, influenced by modern French *aimable* 'trying to please', dates from the mid 18th century.

amicable [late Middle English] The early sense of *amicable* was 'pleasant, benign' and was used to describe things not people; it comes from late Latin *amicabilis*, from Latin *amicus* 'friend'.

amiss [Middle English] This is probably from Old Norse *á mis* 'so as to miss', from *á* 'on' and *mis* (related to *miss*).
➔ MISS

ammunition [late 16th century] This comes from obsolete French *amunition*, an alteration (by wrong division) of *la munition* 'the munition'. At first the word referred to stores of all kinds.

amnesty [late 16th century] This comes via Latin from Greek *amnēstia* 'forgetfulness', a meaning found in early use in English. It now usually denotes an official pardon for people who have been convicted of political offences; this is extended to contexts where authorities undertake to take no action against a specified offence: *a month-long weapon amnesty*. A special use of *oblivion* reflected the same meaning: e.g. the *Act of Oblivion* granted a general pardon and exempted those who had taken up arms against Charles II (1660 Act) and William III (1690 Act) from the consequences of earlier actions. The word *amnesty* features in the title **Amnesty International**, an independent organization in support of human rights, supporting prisoners of conscience. The organization was awarded the Nobel Peace Prize in 1977.

amok [mid 17th century] *Amok* came via Portuguese from Malay *amok* meaning 'rushing in a frenzy'. Originally this was a noun for a Malay in a homicidal frenzy after taking opium; the adverb use as in *run amok* dates from the late 17th century.

among [Old English] Old English *ongemang* is from *on* 'in' and *gemang* 'assemblage, mingling'. The *-st* of **amongst** is probably by association with words such as *against*.

amorous [Middle English] Via Old French from medieval Latin *amorosus*, *amorous* is based on Latin *amor* 'love'.

amount [Middle English] Early use was as a verb meaning 'go up, rise'; it is from Old French *amunter*, from *amont* 'upward', literally 'uphill', from Latin *ad montem*. The notion of increasing in quantity or amount arose in the late 16th century. The noun use dates from the early 18th century.

amphibian [mid 17th century] An *amphibian* originally meant 'having two modes of existence'; it is from modern Latin *amphibium* 'an amphibian', from Greek *amphibion* (a noun use of *amphibios* 'living both in water and on land'). **Amphibious** dates from the same period. The base elements are *amphi* 'both' and *bios* 'life'.

amphitheatre [late Middle English] Coming via Latin from Greek *amphitheatron*, the main elements are *amphi* 'on both sides' and *theatron* 'place for beholding'.

ample [late Middle English] This is an adoption of a French word, from Latin *amplus* 'large, capacious, abundant', the base too of late Middle English **amplify** and mid 16th-century **amplitude**.

amputate [mid 16th century] This is from the Latin verb *amputare* 'lop off', based on *putare* 'to prune'.

amtrac [Second World War] *Amtrac* is a blend of *amphibious* and *tractor*; the vehicle is used for landing assault troops on a shore.

amuse [late 15th century] From 'deception' to 'entertainment', *amuse* has undergone a change of focus. The early sense was 'delude, deceive' and came from Old French *amuser* 'entertain, deceive', from *a-* (expressing causal effect) and *muser* 'stare stupidly'. Current senses relating to entertainment date from the 17th century at the time when the noun **amusement** (from French) is recorded meaning 'musing, diversion of the attention'.

anachronism [mid 17th century] An *anachronism* refers to an event to an incorrect date. The source is Greek *anakhronismos*, from *ana-* 'backwards' and *khronos* 'time'. In the early 19th century **anachronic** was formed from *anachronism*, on the pattern of pairs such as *synchronism, synchronic*.

anagram [late 16th century] An *anagram*, a term for a word or phrase formed by rearranging the letters of another, is from French *anagramme* or modern Latin *anagramma*. The base elements are Greek *ana-* 'back anew' and *gramma* 'letter'.

analogy [late Middle English] An *analogy* is commonly a comparison between one thing and another. The early sense was 'appropriateness, correspondence'; it comes from French *analogie*, via Latin from Greek, from *analogos* 'proportionate'. This is also the base of **analogous** (mid 17th century) and **analogue** (early 19th century) from French.

analysis [late 16th century] *Analysis* has come via medieval Latin from Greek *analusis*, from *analuein* 'unloose', from *ana-* 'up' and *luein*

'loosen'. **Analyse** dates from the same period and was influenced by French *analyser*. **Analytic** (early 17th century) has come via Latin from Greek *analutikos*: the term was adopted in the late 16th century as a noun denoting the branch of logic dealing with analysis, referring specifically to Aristotle's treatises on logic, the Analytics (Greek *analutika*).

anarchy [mid 16th century] The semantic elements are *an-* 'without' and *arkhos* 'chief, ruler'; the word came into English via medieval Latin from Greek *anarkhia*, from *anarkhos*.

anathema [early 16th century] An ecclesiastical Latin word for an 'excommunicated person, excommunication', *anathema* comes from the Greek word meaning 'thing dedicated', later coming to mean 'thing devoted to evil, accursed thing', from *anatithenai* 'to set up'.

anatomy [late Middle English] This is from Old French *anatomie* or late Latin *anatomia*, from Greek, from *ana-* 'up' and *tomia* 'cutting' (from *temnein* 'to cut').

ancestor [Middle English] 'One who goes before' is the literal meaning of *ancestor*, from Old French *ancestre*, from Latin *antecessor* based on *ante* 'before' and *cedere* 'go'.

anchor [Old English] Old English *ancor* (also *ancra*) comes via Latin from Greek *ankura*; the Middle English spelling *ancre* was reinforced by Old French *ancre*. The current form is from *anchora*, an erroneous Latin spelling. The verb (from Old French *ancrer*) dates from Middle English.

ancient [late Middle English] *Ancient* comes from Old French *ancien*, based on Latin *ante* 'before'. In the mid 16th century an **ancient** was also used to mean 'a flag' or 'standard-bearer' (Shakespeare *Henry IV* part ii: Welcome ancient Pistol). The spelling is an alteration of *ensign* by association with *ancien*, an early English form of the adjective *ancient*.

ancillary [mid 17th century] Now meaning 'supporting' or 'subordinate', *ancillary* is from Latin *ancillaris*, from *ancilla* 'maidservant'. The reference to maidservants was kept occasionally as an affected use (Thackeray *Henry Esmond*: The ancillary beauty was therefore the one whom the Prince had selected).

and [Old English] Old English *and, ond* are of Germanic origin; related are Dutch *en* and German *und*.

anecdote [late 17th century] This is from French, or via modern Latin from Greek *anekdota* 'things unpublished', from *an-* 'not' and *ekdotos*, (from *ekdidōnai* 'publish'). The word came to be used for any short story. This was as a result of the use by the Byzantine historian Procopius (*c.*500–*c.*562) of the Greek to refer to the Unpublished Memoirs of the Emperor Justinian, which were tales of the private life of the court.

angel [Old English] Old English *engel* is ultimately via ecclesiastical Latin from Greek *angelos* 'messenger'; it was superseded in Middle English by forms derived from Old French *angele*. The Greek sense passed into English and was extended, through theological writers, to indicate 'a person regarded as a messenger of God', such as a pastor or minister. A transferred use of *angel* was as the name of an old English gold coin, known in full as the *angel-noble*: its device was the archangel Michael standing over and piercing the dragon. Last coined by Charles I, the coin was used to ward off scrofula (known as 'the King's evil') from a patient: hence the expression *touched by an angel*. The adjective **angelic** is late Middle English from French *angélique*, via late Latin from Greek *angelikos* (from *angelos*).

angelica [early 16th century] Medieval Latin (*herba*) *angelica* meant 'angelic (herb)'; the name derives from the belief that it was efficacious against poisoning and disease.

anger [Middle English] English *anger* is from Old Norse *angr* 'grief', *angra* 'vex'. Original use was in the Old Norse senses; current senses date from late Middle English. *Anger* is one of the seven deadly sins of the Christian tradition, the others being: pride, covetousness, lust, gluttony, envy, and sloth.

angina [mid 16th century] This Latin word for 'quinsy' came into English originally with the same meaning. It is from Greek *ankhonē* 'strangling', associated with the symptom of a feeling of suffocation of *angina pectoris*, a disease characterized by severe pain in the lower left side of the chest.

angle¹ [late Middle English] Latin *angulus* 'corner' gave *angle* in Old French which was adopted in English. Late Middle English **angular** (from Latin *angularis*) started out as an astrological term relating to any of the houses that begin at the four cardinal points of a chart.

angle² [Old English] This fishing term was originally *angul*, a noun in Old English meaning 'fish-hook'; the verb dates from late Middle English.

Anglican [early 17th century] This word comes from medieval Latin *Anglicanus*; its adoption was suggested by *Anglicana ecclesia* 'the English church' in the Magna Carta. **Angle** is from Latin *Anglus*, (plural) *Angli* 'the people of

Angul', a district of Schleswig (now in northern Germany), named because of its shape; it is Germanic in origin and related to Old English *angul*.
→ ANGLE²; ENGLISH

angst [1920s] An adoption of German *Angst* 'fear'.

anguish [Middle English] *Anguish* implies tension and comes via Old French from Latin *angustia* 'tightness', the plural of which meant 'straits, distress': the base is *angustus* 'narrow'. The word **anguished** dating from the early 17th century, is the past participle of the rare verb *anguish*, from Old French *anguissier*, from ecclesiastical Latin *angustiare* 'to distress' (from Latin *angustia*).

animal [Middle English] The noun is from Latin *animal*, based on Latin *animalis* 'having breath' from *anima* 'breath'; the adjective is via Old French from Latin *animalis*. Early use associated *animal* with sensation and will (sometimes meaning 'psychical') as functions of the brain and nervous system, as opposed to *vital* (associated with the heart and lungs) and *natural* (functions of nutrition and assimilation.

animate [late Middle English] The source of *animate* in English is Latin *animare* 'instil with life', from *anima* 'life, soul'. The noun **animation** (from Latin *animatio(n-)*, from *animare*) meant 'encouragement' in the mid 16th century; its use to mean 'liveliness' dates from the early 19th century. **Animator** (mid 16th century) is a Latin word adopted into English.

animatic [1970s] An *animatic* is a preliminary version of a film; it either comes from *animat(ed)* and *-ic*, or it is a blend of *animated* and *schematic*.

animatronics [1970s] A blend of *animated* and *electronics*.

animosity [late Middle English] *Animosity* was originally 'spirit, courage'; the source is Old French *animosite* or late Latin *animositas* based on Latin *animus* 'spirit, mind'. The current sense retains the notion of strength of spirit but this involves ill feeling directed to someone else; this use dates from the early 17th century.

ankle [Old English] Old English *ancleow* has a Germanic origin; it was superseded in Middle English by forms from Old Norse; related forms are Dutch *enkel* and German *Enkel*, from an Indo-European root shared by *angle*.
→ ANGLE¹

annals [mid 16th century] The Latin base is *annus* 'year'. The word in English is from Latin

annales (libri) 'yearly (books)', giving a historical record of the events throughout each year (Shakespeare *Coriolanus*: If you have writ your Annales true, 'tis there).
→ANNUAL

anneal [Old English] Old English *onælan* is from *on* and *ælan* 'burn, bake' (from *āl* 'fire, burning'). The original sense was 'set on fire', hence in late Middle English it came to mean 'subject to fire, alter by heating'. The sense 'heat and allow to cool slowly' for the purpose of removing internal stresses from metal or glass, dates from the mid 17th century.

annex [late Middle English] The source is Old French *annexer* or Latin *annectere* 'connect', made up of the elements *ad-* 'to' and *nectere* 'tie, fasten'. The noun *annex* refers to a building joined to the main building, or to an addition to a document. Verbal uses are commonly found in political contexts relating to appropriation of territory (*Zululand was annexed to Natal in 1897*), or in legal contexts (*the first ten amendments were annexed to the Constitution in 1791*).

annihilate [late Middle English] Originally an adjective meaning 'destroyed, annulled', *annihilate* is from late Latin *annihilatus* 'reduced to nothing', from the verb *annihilare*; the semantic elements here are *ad-* 'to' and *nihil* 'nothing'. The sense 'destroy utterly' dates from the mid 16th century, the period when **annihilation** (from late Latin *annihilatio(n-)*) was first recorded.

anniversary [Middle English] Latin *anniversarius* 'returning yearly' is the source of *anniversary*; the Latin base elements are *annus* 'year' and *versus* 'turning'.

annotation [late Middle English] This is from French, or from Latin *annotatio(n-)*, from the verb *annotare* 'to mark' which is the source too of **annotate** (late 16th century). The base is Latin *nota* 'a mark'.

announce [late 15th century] The semantic base of *announce* is Latin *nuntius* 'messenger' (also the base of *nuncio* describing a papal ambassador). The form is from French *annoncer*, from Latin *annuntiare*, from *ad-* 'to' and *nuntiare* 'declare, announce'.

annoy [Middle English] The early sense was 'be hateful to'; it comes from Old French *anoier*, based on Latin *in odio* in the phrase *mihi in odio est* 'it is hateful to me'.

annual [late Middle English] Old French *annuel* is the immediate source, from late Latin *annualis*, based on Latin *annus* 'year'. The notion

of a 'yearbook' recording events of the past year, arose in the late 17th century.
→ANNALS

annuity [late Middle English] This is from French *annuité*, from medieval Latin *annuitas*, from Latin *annuus* 'yearly', from *annus* 'year'.

annul [late Middle English] Introduced into English via Old French from late Latin *annullare*, *annul* is based on the Latin elements *ad-* 'to' and *nullum* 'nothing'.

annunciation [Middle English] The immediate source is Old French *annonciation*, from late Latin *annuntiatio(n-)*, from the verb *annuntiare*. Early use was in religious contexts before the word became generalized to an 'official declaration'. **Annunciate** is late Middle English; this was originally a past participle, from medieval Latin *annunciat-*, a variant of Latin *annuntiat-* from the verb *annuntiare* 'to announce'.

anode [mid 19th century] An *anode* is a positively charged electrode; the word form is from Greek *anodos* 'way up', from *ana* 'up' and *hodos* 'way'.

anodyne [mid 16th century] Introduced via Latin from Greek *anōdunos* 'painless', the base elements of *anodyne* are *an-* 'without' and *odunē* 'pain'.

anoint [Middle English] The immediate source is Old French *enoint* 'anointed', past participle of *enoindre*, from Latin *inungere*. The base is *ungere* 'anoint, smear with oil'.

anomaly [late 16th century] An *anomaly* is 'an irregularity'. The word has come via Latin from Greek *anōmalia*, from *anōmalos*, the source too of **anomalous** (mid 17th century) based on *an-* 'not' and *homalos* 'even'.

anon [Old English] *Anon* in Old English was *on ān* 'into one', *on āne* 'in one'. The original sense was 'in or into one state, course, etc.', which developed into the temporal sense 'at once'.

anonymous [late 16th century] This came via late Latin from Greek *anōnumos* 'nameless' based on *an-* 'without' and *onoma* 'name'.

anorak [1920s] This word for a type of garment is from Greenland Eskimo *anoraq*. The British English informal sense used disparagingly, dates from the 1980s and derives from the anoraks worn by trainspotters, regarded as typifying anyone who is socially inept, having unfashionable and solitary interests.

anorexia [late 16th century] This is based on Greek *an-* 'without' and *orexis* 'appetite'; it came into English via late Latin.

another [Middle English] *Another* was written as *an other* until the 16th century.

answer [Old English] Old English *andswaru* (noun), *andswarian* (verb), are Germanic in origin, from a base shared by *swear*.
➔ SWEAR

ant [Old English] The dialect word *emmet* for an ant is, like *ant*, from Old English *æmete*, which has a West Germanic origin; another related word is German *Ameise*. The derivative **antsy**, dating from the mid 19th century, is probably from the phrase *have ants in one's pants*; it means 'agitated', 'restless'.

antagonist [late 16th century] The core notion is 'struggle' and the direct source of the English spelling is either French *antagoniste* or late Latin *antagonista*, from Greek *antagōnistēs*. The base verb is Greek *antagōnizesthai* 'struggle against', the origin of **antagonize** which started out with this literal sense in the mid 18th century. The root is *agōn* 'contest'. **Antagonism** (early 19th century) is from French *antagonisme*.

antecedent [late Middle English] This is from Old French or from Latin *antecedent-* 'going before', from *antecedere*, from *ante* 'before' and *cedere* 'go'.

antelope [late Middle English] *Antelope* was originally the name of a fierce mythical creature with long serrated horns, said to live on the banks of the Euphrates: a similar beast is depicted in heraldry. The English word is via Old French and medieval Latin from late Greek *antholops*, of unknown origin and meaning. The modern term in zoology dates from the early 17th century.

antenna [mid 17th century] This is a Latin alteration of *antemna* 'yard' (of a ship), used in the plural to translate Greek *keraioi* 'horns (of insects)', used by Aristotle. Lateen sails had long ascending yards reminiscent of antennae.

anterior [mid 16th century] French *antérieur* or Latin *anterior* (the comparative of *ante* 'before') gave *anterior* in English.

anthem [Old English] Old English *antefn*, *antifne* was a composition sung antiphonally; the source is late Latin *antiphona*. The spelling with *th*, which began in the 16th century was on the pattern of similar words such as *Antony*, *Anthony*.
➔ ANTIPHON

anther [early 18th century] It is either French *anthère* or modern Latin *anthera* which has given the botanical word *anther* in English, which describes the part of a stamen which contains the pollen. The origin is Greek *anthēra* 'flowery', from *anthos* 'flower'.

anthology [mid 17th century] In Greek, the word originally denoted a collection of the 'flowers' of verse, that is to say small choice poems or epigrams, by various authors. The same symbolism is expressed by the French moralist and essayist Montaigne (1533–92) in his *Essais*: j'ai seulement fait ici un amas de fleurs étrangères (= I have only made up a bunch of other men's flowers). *Anthology* comes via French or medieval Latin from Greek *anthologia*, (based on *anthos* 'flower' and *legein* 'gather').

anthracite [late 16th century] Originally an *anthracite* referred to a gem described by Pliny said to resemble coals, supposedly hydrophane. The word is from Greek *anthrakitēs*, from *anthrax, anthrak-* 'coal'.

anthrax [late Middle English] This Latin word meaning 'carbuncle' passed into English with the same sense; the origin is *anthrax, anthrak-* 'coal, carbuncle', and gave its name to the disease because of the skin ulceration in humans.

antibiotic [mid 19th century] The first sense was 'doubting the possibility of life in a particular environment', but this was a rare use; it comes from *anti-* and Greek *biōtikos* 'fit for life' (based on *bios* 'life'). Early scientific use of the term was first recorded in the late 19th century, as a translation of French *antibiotique* 'destroying living matter, especially microorganisms'. The medicine known as an *antibiotic* has been described so since the mid 20th century.

anticipation [late Middle English] The Latin verb *anticipare* 'act in advance', based on *ante-* 'before' and *capere* 'take', is the base of both *anticipation* (from Latin *anticipatio(n-)*) and **anticipate**. *Anticipate* is recorded from the mid 16th century in the senses 'to take something into consideration' and 'mention something before the proper time'.

antics [early 16th century] This is the plural of *antic*, from Italian *antico* 'antique', used to mean 'grotesque', 'absurd from incongruity' (Marlowe *Edward II*: My men, like satyrs, ... Shall with their goat-feet dance the antic hay). The word now commonly describes foolish, outrageous, or amusing behaviour.

antidote [late Middle English] An *antidote* is 'something given against' the effects of a poison; it has come via Latin from Greek *antidoton*, the neuter of *antidotos* 'given against', from the elements *anti-* 'against' and *didonai* 'give'.

antiphon [late Middle English] An *antiphon*, part of traditional Western Christian liturgy, is a short sentence recited or sung before or following a canticle. The form came via ecclesiastical Latin from Greek *antiphōna* 'harmonies', the neuter plural of *antiphōnos* 'responsive' (from *anti* 'in return' and *phōnē* 'sound'). The word **antiphonary**, a book of plainsong for the Divine Office, dates from the early 17th century; it too is based on Greek *antiphōna*.

antipodes [late Middle English] This came via French or late Latin from Greek *antipodes* 'having the feet opposite', from *anti* 'against, opposite' and *pous, pod-* 'foot'. The term referred originally to the inhabitants of opposite sides of the earth; it is now used more specifically of Australia and New Zealand, by inhabitants of the northern hemisphere.

antiquity [Middle English] The base here is *ante* 'before'. *Antiquity* comes from Old French *antiquite*, from Latin *antiquitas*, from *antiquus* 'old, former'. The same base has given several related words: **antique** (late 15th century) first used just as an adjective, and **antiquated** (late 16th century) whose early sense was 'old, of long standing'; finally the two synonyms **antiquary** (mid 16th century) and **antiquarian** (early 17th century), both from Latin *antiquarius*.

antler [late Middle English] This, in early use, was limited to the lowest (forward-directed) branch of the antler; the form comes from Anglo-Norman French, a variant of Old French *antoillier*, whose origin is unknown. The current sense dates from the early 19th century.

anvil [Old English] In Old English the spelling was *anfilte*, from the Germanic base of *on* and a verbal stem meaning 'beat'.

anxiety [early 16th century] French *anxiété* or Latin *anxietas* gave *anxiety* in English; the base is Latin *anxius*, from *angere* 'to choke'; **anxious**, recorded from the early 17th century, is also based on *anxius*.

any [Old English] Old English *ænig* has a Germanic origin; it is related to Dutch *eenig* and German *einig*.
→ ONE

aorta [mid 16th century] This is from Greek *aortē* which was used in the plural by Hippocrates for the branches of the windpipe, and by Aristotle for the great artery; the source verb is *aeirein* 'raise'.
→ ARTERY

apart [late Middle English] *Apart* comes from Old French, from Latin *a parte* 'at the side'.

apartment [mid 17th century] There is a notion of separation, staying apart, in *apartment*; early use was as a suite of rooms for the use of a particular person or group. The source is French *appartement*, from Italian *appartamento*, from *appartare* 'to separate', from *a parte* 'apart'.

apathy [early 17th century] This has entered the language from French but the origin is Greek *apatheia*, from *apathēs* 'without feeling'; **apathetic** (mid 18th century) was formed on the pattern of *pathetic*.

ape [Old English] Old English *apa* is Germanic in origin; relatives include Dutch *aap* and German *Affe*. It was the generic name before the introduction of *monkey* in the 16th century. It is often in the context of mimicry of humans, a use which has arisen through the verb *to ape* which involves copying human gestures.

aperture [late Middle English] This is from Latin *apertura*, from *apert-* 'opened', from *aperire* 'to open'.

apex [early 17th century] *Apex* is Latin for 'peak, tip'.

aphrodisiac [early 18th century] The name *Aphrodite*, goddess of beauty, fertility, and sexual love, in Greek mythology, is part of *aphrodisiac*, which comes from Greek *aphrodisiakos*.

aplomb [late 18th century] 'Perpendicularity, steadiness' are the early meanings of *aplomb*; the word is from French, from *à plomb* 'according to a plummet'. The self-assurance associated with current use has developed from the steadiness conveyed by the early literal sense.

apocalypse [Old English] Coming via Old French and ecclesiastical Latin from Greek *apokalupsis*, *apocalypse* is from the base verb *apokaluptein* 'uncover, reveal'. In the early 17th century the **apocalyptic** referred to St. John with reference to the Apocalypse in the book of Revelation.

apology [mid 16th century] Used in legal contexts at first, an *apology* was a formal defence against an accusation; it is from French *apologie*, or via late Latin from Greek *apologia* 'a speech in one's own defence'. **Apologetic** was already in use from late Middle English as a noun denoting a formal justification; this was from French *apologétique* or late Latin *apologeticus*, based on Greek *apologeisthei* 'speak in one's own defence' (from *apologia*). The current sense 'expressing regret' dates from the mid 19th century. **Apologize**, late 16th century from the same base, originally meant 'make a defensive argument'; the verb has always been used in English as if it were a direct derivative of *apology*.

apoplexy [late Middle English] This is from Old French *apoplexie*, via late Latin from Greek *apoplēxia*, from *apoplēssein* 'disable by a stroke'. **Apoplectic** is not recorded until the early 17th century and comes from French *apoplectique* or late Latin *apoplecticus*, from Greek *apoplēktikos*.

apostle [Old English] Old English *apostol* comes via ecclesiastical Latin from Greek *apostolos* 'messenger', from *apostellein* 'send forth'. The bird known as an **apostlebird** is named from the supposed habit of these birds of going about in flocks of twelve, drawing on an association with the twelve chief disciples of Christ.

apostrophe [mid 16th century] Now a punctuation mark, *apostrophe* originally referred to the omission of one or more letters; it is via late Latin from Greek *apostrophos* 'accent of elision', from *apostrephein* 'turn away'.

apothecary [late Middle English] Greek *apothēkē* 'storehouse' is the base; *apothecary* came via Old French from late Latin *apothecarius*, from Latin *apotheca*. The English word is archaic and describes a person who prepared and sold medicines and drugs.

apotheosis [late 16th century] An *apotheosis* is the highest point in the development of something. The word came via ecclesiastical Latin from Greek *apotheōsis*, from *apotheoun* 'make a god of'; the elements are *apo* 'from' and *theos* 'god'.

appal [Middle English] From Old French *apalir* 'grow pale', based on *palir* 'to pale', *appal*, at first, paralleled the Old French meaning. This later became 'make pale' and developed into 'horrify' in late Middle English.

apparatus [early 17th century] This is a Latin word, from *apparare* 'make ready for', from *ad-* 'towards' and *parare* 'make ready'.

apparel [Middle English] The verb *to apparel* in early use had the sense 'make ready or fit'; as a noun it meant 'furnishings, equipment'; the source is Old French *apareillier*, based on Latin *ad-* 'to' (which expresses change) and *par* 'equal'. The core notion is one of making equal and therefore appropriate or suitable.

apparent [late Middle English] *Apparent* and **apparition** are based on Latin *apparere* 'appear'; the former is from Old French *aparant*, from Latin *apparent-* 'appearing'. *Apparition* first described 'the action of appearing', from Latin *apparitio(n-)* 'attendance'. This is reflected in its use as a term for a ghost or ghostlike image of a person.
→ APPEAR

appeal [Middle English] Recorded first in legal contexts, *appeal* is from the Old French noun *apel*, and as a verb from *apeler*, from Latin *appellare* 'to address, accost, call upon'. The base is Latin *pellere* 'to drive': the notion of 'drive towards' led to 'direct oneself to' and from there to 'approach and speak to'. Late Middle English **appellant** is from French *apelant*, literally 'appealing'; its use in English refers to someone appealing to a higher court for a jurisdiction.

appear [Middle English] *Appear* is from Old French *apareir*, from Latin *apparere*, from *ad-* 'towards' and *parere* 'come into view'. Late Middle English **appearance** is from Old French *aparance*, *aparence*, from late Latin *apparentia*, from the same base verb.

appease [Middle English] 'Bring to a peaceful state' is the literal sense of *appease* which comes from Old French *apaisier*, made up of the prefix *a-* (from Latin *ad* 'to, at') and *pais* 'peace'.

append [late Middle English] This is from Latin *appendere* 'hang on', from *ad-* 'to' and *pendere* 'hang'; so too is **appendix** recorded in the mid 16th century in the sense 'section of subsidiary matter at the end of a book or document'. The anatomy term dates from the early 17th century.

appetite [Middle English] 'Seeking' and 'desire' are involved in *appetite*, which is from Old French *apetit*: this comes from Latin *appetitus* 'desire for', from *appetere* 'seek after'.

applause [late Middle English] *Applause* and **applaud** (late 15th century) are based on Latin *ad-* 'to' and *plaudere* 'to clap', elements of the verb *applaudere*. The spelling of *applaud* was reinforced by French *applaudir*.

apple [Old English] Old English *æppel* has a Germanic root and is related to Dutch *appel* and German *Apfel*. The word features in many expressions: *a rotten apple* refers to a person in a group who is likely to have a detrimental influence, from the idea of the effect a rotten apple has on any fruit with which it is in contact. *The apple of one's eye* is someone of whom one is very proud: this originally denoted the pupil of the eye, considered to be a globular solid body, extended as a symbol of something cherished. The Australianism *she's apples* meaning everything is in good order, comes from *apples and spice* or *apples and rice*, rhyming slang for 'nice'.

applet [1990s] This computing term is a blend of *application* and *-let*.

apply [late Middle English] The Latin elements *ad-* 'to' and *plicare* 'to fold' (giving Latin *applicare* 'fold, fasten to') are the base of a family of words in English: *apply* is from Old French *aplier*; Middle English **application** came via

Old French from Latin *applicatio(n-)*; **applicable** (mid 16th century) started out in the sense 'compliant' and comes from Old French, or from medieval Latin *applicabilis*; **applicator** (mid 17th century) derives its form from Latin *applicat-* meaning 'fastened to'; **applicant** (early 19th century) is based on *application*, with the suffix *-ant*.

appointment [Middle English] The source is Old French *apointement*, from *apointer* which also gave Middle English **appoint**. The base is the French phrase *a point* 'to a point', suggesting 'bringing to a focus', whether this involves a decision in fixing a time or venue, or in choosing a suitable person for a position.

appraise [late Middle English] The original sense was 'set a price on'; it is an alteration (by association with *praise*) of the archaic verb *apprize* which had the same sense. The meaning 'assess the value or quality of' dates from the mid 19th century.

appreciate [mid 16th century] This is from the late Latin verb *appretiare* 'appraise, set at a price', from *ad-* 'to' and *pretium* 'price'. The senses 'raise in value' and 'rise in value' have been used in the US from the late 18th century.

apprehend [late Middle English] The early sense was 'grasp, get hold of (physically or mentally)'; the immediate source is either French *appréhender* or Latin *apprehendere*, from *ad-* 'towards' and *prehendere* 'lay hold of'. Late Middle English **apprehension** first meant 'learning, acquisition of knowledge' and comes from late Latin *apprehensio(n-)*. **Apprehensive**, also late Middle English in the sense 'relating to perception or understanding' is from French *appréhensif* or medieval Latin *apprehensivus*. The 'fear' aspect of the semantics in this group is first found in the 17th century.

apprentice [Middle English] This is from Old French *aprentis*, from *apprendre* 'learn', from Latin *apprehendere* 'apprehend'. The Old French spelling is on the pattern of words ending in *-tis*, *-tif* (from Latin *-tivus*).

apprise [late 17th century] *Apprise* 'inform' is from French *appris*, *apprise*, the past participle of *apprendre* 'learn, teach', from Latin *apprehendere*.
→ APPREHEND

approach [Middle English] 'Bringing near' is involved in *approach* which is from Old French *aprochier*, *aprocher*; the source is ecclesiastical Latin *appropiare* 'draw near', from *ad-* 'to' and *propius* (the comparative of *prope* 'near').

approbation [late Middle English] Via Old French from Latin *approbatio(n-)*, *approbation* is based on the verb *approbare* 'approve': the elements are *ad-* 'to' and *probare* 'try, test' (from *probus* 'good').

appropriate [late Middle English] *Appropriate* and *appropriation* are both late Middle English and are based on the Latin elements *ad-* 'to' and *proprius* 'own, proper', making up the verb *appropriare* 'make one's own'. They came into English from late Latin forms.

approve [Middle English] This is from Old French *aprover*, from Latin *approbare* 'approve'. The original sense was 'prove, demonstrate', later 'corroborate, confirm', which led to 'pronounce to be satisfactory'.
→ APPROBATION

approximate [late Middle English] Early use was in the adjectival sense 'close, similar' from late Latin *approximatus*, the past participle of *approximare*, from *ad-* 'to' and *proximus* 'very near'; the current adjectival sense 'close to the actual but not exact' dates from the early 19th century. The verb, originally meaning 'bring close', had arisen earlier in the mid 17th century.

apricot [mid 16th century] This is from Portuguese *albricoque* or Spanish *albaricoque*, from Spanish Arabic *al* 'the' and *barḳūḳ*, a word which came via late Greek from Latin *praecoquum*, a variant of *praecox* 'early-ripe'. The spelling was influenced by Latin *apricus* 'ripe' and French *abricot*.

apron [Middle English] Middle English *naperon* was from an Old French diminutive of *nape*, *nappe* 'tablecloth', from Latin *mappa* 'napkin'. The *n* was lost by wrong division of *a napron*; this also occurred in the formation of the word *adder*.
→ ADDER

apt [late Middle English] Originally *apt* meant 'suited, appropriate'; the source is Latin *aptus* 'fitted', the past participle of *apere* 'fasten'. The English word may also mean 'quick to learn' in modern use, as in *an apt pupil*. Late Middle English **aptitude** meant 'natural propensity'; this came via Old French from late Latin *aptitudo*, from *aptus*; the notion of 'natural ability in the acquisition of skills' arose in the mid 16th century.

aquarelle [mid 19th century] The technique of painting with thin transparent watercolours known as *aquarelle* owes its name to a French term, from Italian *acquarella* 'watercolour', a diminutive based on Latin *aqua* 'water'.

aquarium [mid 19th century] This is the Latin neuter of *aquarius* 'of water', used in English as a noun on the pattern of *vivarium*. In classical Latin *aquarium* meant 'watering place for cattle'.

aquatic [late 15th century] The early sense was 'watery, rainy'; *aquatic* is from Old French *aquatique* or Latin *aquaticus*. The base is Latin *aqua* 'water', a combining form in many English words: *aqualung* (1950s); *aquanaut* (based on Greek *nautēs* 'sailor'); *aquaplane* (originally US); *aquarobics* (1980s); *aquatint* (late 18th century, based on Italian *acqua tinta* 'coloured water'); *aqueduct* (mid 16th century, based on Latin *ducere* 'to lead'); *aquifer* (early 20th century, based on Latin *ferre* 'to bear').

aquiline [mid 17th century] This is from Latin *aquilinus*, from *aquila* 'eagle'. It may mean 'like an eagle' in English, but it is also used to describe a nose or profile which is curved like an eagle's beak.

arable [late Middle English] From Old French or from Latin *arabilis*, *arable* is from *arare* 'to plough'. It has the sense 'suitable for growing crops'.

arbitrary [late Middle English] 'Dependent on one's will or pleasure, discretionary' was the early meaning of *arbitrary* from Latin *arbitrarius*, based on *arbiter* 'judge, supreme ruler'. The form was perhaps influenced by French *arbitraire*. Latin *arbiter* is the base too of the English verb **arbitrate** (mid 16th century) and of **arbitration** (late Middle English from Latin *arbitratio(n-)*).

arbour [Middle English] In early use an *arbour* was also a lawn or flower bed as well as a shady garden. It is from Old French *erbier*, from *erbe* 'grass, herb', from Latin *herba*. The phonetic change to *ar-* (common in words having *er-* before a consonant) was assisted by association with Latin *arbor* 'tree'.

arc [late Middle English] An *arc* started out as a term for the path of a celestial object, especially the sun, from horizon to horizon; it came via Old French from Latin *arcus* 'bow, curve'.

arcade [late 17th century] This is an adoption from French, from Provençal *arcada* or Italian *arcata*, based on Latin *arcus* 'a bow'.

arcane [mid 16th century] Something that is *arcane* is only understood by a few; the source is Latin *arcanus*, from *arcere* 'to shut up', from *arca* 'a chest', giving a core notion of mystery.

arch [Middle English] *Arch* is from Old French *arche*, based on Latin *arcus* 'bow'.

archaeology [early 17th century] The early sense was 'ancient history', from modern Latin *archaeologia*, from Greek *arkhaiologia* 'ancient history', from *arkhaios* 'ancient'. The current sense relating to the study of history through the excavation of sites and the analysis of artefacts, dates from the mid 19th century.

archer [Middle English] This is from Old French *archier*, based on Latin *arcus* 'bow'; **archery** (late Middle English) comes from Old French *archerie*, from *archier*.

archetype [mid 16th century] This is via Latin from Greek *arkhetupon* 'something moulded first as a model', from *arkhe-* 'primitive' and *tupos* 'a model'.

archipelago [early 16th century] From Italian *arcipelago*, the base elements of *archipelago* are Greek *arkhi-* 'chief' and *pelagos* 'sea'. The word was originally used as a proper name (*the Archipelago* 'the Aegean Sea'); the general sense 'group of islands' arose because the Aegean Sea is remarkable for its large numbers of islands.

architect [mid 16th century] Greek *arkhi-* 'chief' and *tektōn* 'builder' are the key elements here. The word came into English from French *architecte*, from Italian *architetto*, via Latin from Greek. The noun **architecture** dates from the same period and comes from Latin *architectura*.

archive [early 17th century] The first recorded sense of *archive* was 'place where records are kept'; it comes from French *archives* (plural), from Latin *archiva*, *archia*, from Greek *arkheia* 'public records'. The base is *arkhē* 'government'. The verb dates from the late 19th century.

ardent [Middle English] This is from Old French *ardant* from Latin *ardens*, *ardent-*, from *ardere* 'to burn'; also based on this Latin verb is **ardour** (late Middle English) which is via Old French from Latin *ardor*. Both words convey enthusiasm and passion in English; *ardent* however is found in poetic and literary contexts with its literal sense of 'burning': *the ardent flames*.

arduous [mid 16th century] The root is Latin *arduus* 'steep, difficult'.

area [mid 16th century] Originally a 'space allocated for a specific purpose', *area* is from Latin, literally 'a vacant piece of level ground'. The historical unit of measurement, the **are**, dating from the late 18th century, came via French from Latin *area*.

arena [early 17th century] This is a Latin word meaning 'sand', 'a sand-strewn place of combat', which referred to the central part of an amphitheatre. Here spectacular displays or combats would take place: the sand was there originally to soak up the blood spilled by the combatants. The word gradually became transferred to the whole amphitheatre. Since the

1940s, the word *arena* has been used for theatre productions in-the-round (e.g. *arena theatre*, *arena stage*); the style was introduced by Glenn Hughes, director of the Washington School of Drama, in 1932, and was first known as *Penthouse* from the location of the first productions.

argue [Middle English] This is from Old French *arguer*, from Latin *argutari* 'prattle', a frequentative (= verb of repeated action) of *arguere* 'make clear, prove, accuse'. Middle English **argument** had the sense 'process of reasoning'; it comes via Old French from Latin *argumentum*. Late Middle English **argumentative** is from Old French *argumentatif, -ive* or late Latin *argumentativus*, from *argumentari* 'conduct an argument'.

argy-bargy [late 19th century] Noisy quarelling or wrangling is known as an *argy-bargy*. This was originally a Scots rhyming jingle based on *argue*.

arid [mid 17th century] The source is French *aride* or Latin *aridus*, from *arere* 'be dry or parched'.

arise [Old English] Old English *ārīsan* is from *ā-* 'away' (used for emphasis) and the verb *rise*. In ordinary language the simple verb *rise* has superseded *arise* in most senses.

aristocracy [late 15th century] The term originally denoted the government of a state by its best citizens, later by the rich and well born, which led, in the mid 17th century, to the sense 'nobility', regardless of the form of government. The origin is Old French *aristocratie*, from Greek *aristokratia*, from *aristos* 'best' and *-kratia* 'power'. **Aristocrat** (late 18th century) is from the French word *aristocrate* used during the French Revolution.

arithmetic [Middle English] Greek *arithmos* 'number' is the base of *arithmetic* from Old French *arismetique*; this is based on Latin *arithmetica*, from Greek *arithmētikē* (*tekhnē*) '(art) of counting'.

ark [Old English] Old English *ærc* is from Latin *arca* 'chest'. The **Holy Ark** is a chest housing the Torah scrolls in a synagogue. *Ark* also describes a ship, particularly Noah's Ark, from which the expression *went out with the Ark* derives.

arm¹ [Old English] Old English *arm*, *earm*, denoting a limb, shares a Germanic origin with Dutch *arm* and German *Arm*.

arm² [Middle English] The verb *arm* 'supply with weapons' is from Old French *armer*. Old French words have also given rise to the Middle English noun **arms** (based on Latin *arma*) and late Middle English **army** (based on Latin

armata, the feminine past participle of *armare* 'to arm'). The Latin verb *armare* is the base too of mid 16th-century **armada**, an adoption from Spanish, and late 16th-century **armadillo**, a Spanish diminutive of *armado* 'armed man' (because of the armour-like bony casing over the body).

armistice [early 18th century] The source is either French, or modern Latin *armistitium*, from *arma* 'arms' and *-stitium* 'stoppage'.

armour [Middle English] This is from Old French *armure*, from Latin *armatura* (which also gave **armature**), from *armare* 'to arm'. **Armoury** is also Middle English when it too meant 'armour': it is from Old French *armoirie*, *armoierie*, from *armoier* 'to blazon', from *arme* 'weapon'. The change in the second syllable in the 17th century was due to association with *armour*.

aroma [Middle English] This was usually in the plural at first denoting fragrant plants or spices; it came via Latin from Greek *arōma* 'spice'. The adjective **aromatic** arose in late Middle English via Old French and late Latin from Greek *arōmatikos*. It was connected with a spicy smell or taste from the 19th century, whereas *aroma*'s association with 'smell' alone (dissociated from spices) is much more recent. Late Middle English **aromatize** is from Old French *aromatiser*, via late Latin from Greek *arōmatizein* 'to spice'.

arouse [late 16th century] This is from *rouse*, on the pattern of the pair *rise* and *arise*.

arrange [late Middle English] This is from Old French *arangier*, from *a-* (from Latin *ad* 'to, at') and *rangier* 'put in order'.
→ RANGE

arrant [Middle English] This is a variant of *errant*, originally used in phrases such as *arrant thief* which was an 'outlawed, roving thief'. Its use in phrases such as *arrant nonsense* expresses the sense 'utter'.

array [Middle English] The early noun sense (from Old French *arei*) was 'preparedness', the early verb sense (from Old French *areer*) was 'place in readiness'. The formative elements are Latin *ad-* 'towards' and a Germanic base meaning 'prepare'. *Array* is associated with order, often martial order as in *battle array*.

arrears [Middle English] The word *arrear* was first used in the phrase *in arrear*, coming from the adverb *arrear* meaning 'behind, overdue', from Old French *arere*. Medieval Latin *adretro*, from *ad-* 'towards' and *retro* 'backwards', is the source.

arrest [late Middle English] This is from Old French *arester*, based on Latin *ad-* 'at, to' and *restare* 'remain, stop'.

arrive [Middle English] *Arrive* was first used in sailing contexts when it meant 'reach the shore after a voyage'; it comes from Old French *ariver*, based on Latin *ad-* 'to' and *ripa* 'shore'. The noun **arrival** is late Middle English from Anglo-Norman French *arrivaille*.

arrogant [late Middle English] Via Old French from Latin *arrogant-* 'claiming for oneself', English *arrogant* is from the Latin verb *arrogare*.

arrow [Old English] Old English *arewe*, *arwe*, is from Old Norse.

arrowroot [late 17th century] The tubers of the Caribbean *arrowroot* plant were used to absorb poison from arrow wounds. The word is an alteration of Arawak *aru-aru* (literally 'meal of meals') by association with *arrow* and *root*.

arsenal [early 16th century] At first this was a dock for the construction and repair of ships; the word comes from French, or from obsolete Italian *arzanale*, based on Arabic *dār-aṣ-ṣinā ʿa*, from *dār* 'house' and *al-* '(of) the' and *sinā ʿa* 'art, industry'.

arsenic [late Middle English] *Arsenic* first denoted the yellow orpiment, arsenic sulphide; it comes via Old French from Latin *arsenicum*, from Greek *arsenikon* 'yellow orpiment', identified with *arsenikos* 'male', but in fact from Arabic *al-zarnīk* 'the orpiment', based on Persian *zar* 'gold'.

arson [late 17th century] This was an Anglo-Norman French legal term, from medieval Latin *arsio(n-)*, from Latin *ardere* 'to burn'.

art [Middle English] This came via Old French from Latin *ars*, *art-*, from a base meaning 'put together, join, fit'. 'Skill' was an early meaning of *art* in English. An *art* may also be a subject area where skill is obtained or displayed, such as *the Arts* as branches of study at university. *Art* as the application of skill according to aesthetic principles (in painting, sculpture, architecture, etc.), is a term from the early 17th century. One particular aspect of this, **art deco**, was shortened from French *art décoratif* 'decorative art', from the 1925 Exhibition title *Exposition des Arts décoratifs* in Paris. The related noun **artist** came into use in the early 16th century referring to a master of the liberal arts (= the medieval trivium, including Grammar, Logic, and Rhetoric, and quadrivium, including Arithmetic, Geometry, Music, and Astronomy); it is from French *artiste*, from Italian *artista*, from *arte* 'art' (from Latin *ars*, *art-*).

artefact [early 19th century] Literally 'something made using art', *artefact* is from Latin *arte* 'by art' and *factum* 'something made' (the neuter past participle of *facere* 'to make').

artery [late Middle English] This is from Latin *arteria*, from Greek *artēria*, probably from *airein* 'raise'. *Arteries* were popularly thought by the ancients (who referred the word to Greek *aēr* 'air') to be air ducts as they do not contain blood after death. Medieval writers thought they contained an ethereal fluid distinct from that of the veins: this was referred to as *spiritual blood* or *vital spirits*.
→AORTA

artesian [mid 19th century] The term comes from French *artésien* 'from Artois', a region and former province of north-west France where wells of this type were first made in the 18th century. A perpendicular bore into a hole or basin of the strata produces a constant supply of water which rises spontaneously to the ground's surface.

article [Middle English] *Article* was first recorded as denoting a separate clause of the Apostles' Creed; it comes from Old French, from Latin *articulus* 'small connecting part', a diminutive of *artus* 'joint'. The root is Latin *ar-* 'join': an obsolete use of *article* is 'joint connecting two parts of the body'. It also meant 'juncture', in time phrases: e.g. *just in the article of time*, *just in the article of falling*. Since 'joining' and 'separating' are closely associated semantically, *article* readily applies to distinct parts, e.g. *articles of agreement*, *articles of association* as well as to distinct topics (*articles of a magazine*) and distinct items (*articles of trade* referring to commodities). As for *article* as a grammar term, Latin *articulus* was used to refer to the highly inflected *definite article* in Greek meaning 'the'; the reference to the *indefinite article* (= 'a', 'an') is part of modern grammar reference.

articulation [late Middle English] The early senses of *articulation* were 'joint' and 'joining', from Latin *articulatio(n-)*, from the verb *articulare*. **Articulate** dates from the mid 16th century and is from Latin *articulatus*, the past participle of *articulare* 'divide into joints, utter distinctly', from *articulus* 'small connecting part'.
→ARTICLE

artifice [late Middle English] Now 'cunning expedients used to trick others', *artifice* was originally 'workmanship'; the origin is Old French, from Latin *artificium*, based on *ars*, *art-* 'art' and *facere* 'make'. Late Middle English **artificial** is from Old French *artificiel* or Latin *artificialis*, from *artificium* 'handicraft'.

artillery [late Middle English] There is a notion of arrangement and order in *artillery* which comes from Old French *artillerie*. This is from *artiller*, an alteration of *atillier* 'equip, arm' which, in turn, is probably a variant of *atirier*: the elements are *a-* (from Latin *ad* 'to, at') and *tire* 'rank, order'.

artisan [mid 16th century] Originally a French word from Italian *artigiano*, *artisan* is based on Latin *artitus*, the past participle of *artire* 'instruct in the arts' (from *ars, art-* 'art'). An *artisan* currently describes someone employed or skilled in any of the industrial arts.
➜ ART

Aryan [late 15th century] This is based on Sanskrit *ārya* 'noble'. *Aryan* is used by some as an equivalent of the term Indo-European for a language family. In the 19th century, the notion of an *Aryan* race corresponding to a definite Aryan language became current and was taken up by nationalistic historical and romantic writers. One of these was De Gobineau (1816–82), an anthropologist who linked the idea to a notion of inferiority of certain races. Later the term *Aryan race* was revived and used as propaganda in Nazi Germany (1933–45).

as [Middle English] *As* is a reduced form of Old English *alswā* 'similarly'. It was commmonly written in combinations such as *forasmuch*, *inasmuch*, *whereas*.
➜ ALSO

asbestos [early 17th century] This came via Latin from Greek *asbestos* 'unquenchable' (a term applied by Dioscurides to quicklime), from *a-* 'not' and *sbestos* (from *sbennumi* 'quench').

ascend [late Middle English] This is from Latin *ascendere*, from *ad-* 'to' and *scandere* 'to climb'. The same base gave rise to the following from the same period: **ascendant** (via Old French from Latin *ascendent-* 'climbing up'); also **ascension** first used to refer to the ascent of Christ (via Old French from Latin *ascensio(n-)*). Late 16th-century **ascent** is from *ascend*, on the pattern of the pair *descend* and *descent*.

ascertain [late Middle English] In *ascertain*, the semantic core is 'make sure'. The early meaning was 'assure, convince', from Old French *acertener*, based on Latin *certus* 'settled, sure'.

ascetic [mid 17th century] Suggestive of severe self-discipline and abstention from indulgence, *ascetic* is from medieval Latin *asceticus* or Greek *askētikos*. The base is *askētēs* 'monk', from *askein* 'to exercise'.

ascribe [Middle English] The origin is Latin *ascribere*, from *ad-* 'to' and *scribere* 'write'.

ash[1] [Old English] The *ash* meaning 'powdery residue' was *æsce, æxe* in Old English, forms of Germanic origin related to Dutch *as* and German *Asche*. The festival **Ash Wednesday** derives its name from the custom of marking the foreheads of penitents with ashes on that day.

ash[2] [Old English] As a name for a tree, *ash* was *æsc* in Old English. The Germanic origin is shared by Dutch *es* and German *Esche*. The distinctive winged seeds of the tree are known as **ash-keys**.

ashamed [Old English] Old English *āscamod* was the past participle of *āscamian* 'feel shame', from *ā-* (used for emphasis) and the verb *to shame*.
➜ SHAME

aside [Middle English] This was originally *on side*.

ask [Old English] Old English *āscian, āhsian, axian* are West Germanic in origin.

aspect [late Middle English] At first an *aspect* was the action or a way of looking at something; it comes from Latin *aspectus*, from *aspicere* 'look at'.

aspic [late 18th century] This comes from the French word meaning literally 'asp' describing a small southern European viper. A proverbial phrase *froid comme un aspic* exists in French meaning 'as cold as an asp': this has been suggested as the source of the association.

aspire [late Middle English] *Aspire* is from French *aspirer* or Latin *aspirare*, from *ad-* 'to' and *spirare* 'breathe'. **Aspiration** dates from the same period when it meant 'action of pronouncing a sound with an exhalation of breath', from Latin *aspiratio(n-)*.

aspirin [late 19th century] This was coined from German, from *acetylierte Spirsäure* 'acetylated salicylic acid'; the element *Spir-* is from the plant genus name *Spiraea*.

ass [Old English] Old English *assa* describing a member of the horse family, is from a Celtic word related to Welsh *asyn* and Breton *azen*, based on Latin *asinus*. It is a word used in biblical and natural history contexts, proverbs, and fables, and is also common in Ireland. The more common term however is *donkey*.

assail [Middle English] The base elements of *assail* 'attack' are Latin *ad-* 'to' and *salire* 'to leap'. The spelling is from Old French *asaill-*, the stressed stem of *asalir*, from medieval Latin *assalire*, from Latin *assilīre*.

→ASSAULT

assassin [mid 16th century] Either from French, or from medieval Latin *assassinus*, *assassin* is in origin from Arabic *ḥašīšī* 'hashish-eater'. It used to be applied to certain Muslim fanatics at the time of the Crusades (11th, 12th, and 13th centuries) who were sent out by their sheik to murder the Christian leaders: this led to the association with murder of any public figure. The verb **assassinate** (early 17th century) is from the medieval Latin verb *assassinare* 'kill' (from *assassinus*).

assault [Middle English] The noun is from Old French *asaut*, the verb from *assauter*, based on Latin *ad-* 'to' and *saltare*, a frequentative (= verb of repeated action) of *salire* 'to leap'.

→ASSAIL

assay [Middle English] 'Trying out by testing' is the key feature of *assay*, first used in the general sense 'a test of the merit of someone or something' and now referring more specifically to metals or to measurement of immunological activity. *Assay* is from Old French *assai* (noun) and *assaier* (verb), variants of *essai* 'a trial' and *essayer* 'to try'. The base is Latin *exagium* 'weighing', which became used in the wider sense 'examination, trial'.

→ESSAY

assemble [Middle English] This word is from Old French *asembler*, based on Latin *ad-* 'to' and *simul* 'together'. Also dating from Middle English is **assembly** from Old French *asemblee*, the feminine past participle of *asembler*.

assent [Middle English] The verb is from Old French *as(s)enter*, the noun from *as(s)ente*, from the Latin base verb *assentire*, made up of *ad-* 'towards' and *sentire* 'feel, think'.

assertion [late Middle English] The Latin base elements *ad-* 'to' and *serere* 'to join' give a notion of 'coming together' to *assertion* which adds to the confidence with which such a statement is made. The word is from Latin *assertio(n-)*, from the verb *asserere* 'claim, affirm', the source too of **assert** (early 17th century).

assess [late Middle English] The source is Old French *assesser*, based on Latin *assidere* 'sit by' (from *ad-* 'to, at' and *sedere* 'sit'): this verb meant 'levy tax' in medieval Latin. From the same period, **assessor** is from Old French *assessour*, from Latin *assessor* 'assistant judge': in medieval Latin the meaning was 'assessor of taxes'.

→ASSIZE

asset [mid 16th century] This was first used in the plural in the sense 'sufficient estate to allow the discharge of a will'; it comes from an Anglo-Norman French legal term, from Old French *asez* 'enough', based on Latin *ad* 'to' and *satis* 'enough'.

assiduity [late Middle English] From Latin *assiduitas*, *assiduity* is based on *assiduus* 'occupied with'; this is also involved in the formation of the adjective **assiduous** (mid 16th century); the base verb is *assidere* 'be engaged in doing'. Current semantics involve 'care' and 'diligence', features of being occupied and attentive to the task in hand.

→ASSESS

assign [Middle English] *Assign* is from Old French *asigner*, *assiner*, from Latin *assignare* 'allot', made up of *ad-* 'to' and *signare* 'to sign'. Late Middle English **assignation** was originally 'a command', 'appointment to office', or 'allotment of revenue' and came via Old French from Latin *assignatio(n-)*, from the verb *assignare*. **Assignment**, also late Middle English, is from Old French from the same base.

assimilate [late Middle English] The source is the Latin verb *assimilare* 'absorb, incorporate', from *ad-* 'to' and *similis* 'like'.

assist [late Middle English] *Assist* is from Old French *assister*, from Latin *assistere* 'take one's stand by', from *ad-* 'to, at' and *sistere* 'take one's stand'. Dating from the same period are: **assistance** (from Old French, or from medieval Latin *assistentia*) and **assistant** (from Old French, or from medieval Latin *assistent-* 'taking one's stand beside').

assize [Middle English] 'Sitting' and 'assessment' are two core semantic elements of the legal term *assize*, from Old French *assise* (the feminine past participle of *asseeir* 'sit, settle, assess'). The base verb is Latin *assidere* 'sit by'.

→ASSESS

associate [late Middle English] *Associate* was first used as a verb in the sense 'join with in a common purpose', and as an adjective in the sense 'allied'. The source is the Latin verb *associare* 'to join', from *ad-* 'to' and *socius* 'sharing, allied'. The noun **association** is recorded from the mid 16th century in the sense 'uniting in a common purpose'; it comes from medieval Latin *associatio(n-)*, from Latin *associare* 'to unite'.

assuage [Middle English] Based on Latin *ad-* 'to' (expressing change) and *suavis* 'sweet', *assuage* is from Old French *assouagier*, *asouagier*. It is used in phrases such as *assuaged their fears* and gives a notion of 'make less intense'.

assumption [Middle English] The word *assumption* was first used with reference to the reception of the Virgin Mary into heaven; it is from Old French *asompsion* or Latin *assumptio(n-)*, from the verb *assumere*. This verb (source too of late Middle English **assume**) is based on the elements *ad-* 'towards' and *sumere* 'take'.

assure [late Middle English] This is from Old French *assurer*, based on Latin *ad-* 'to' (expressing change) and *securus* 'safe'. **Assurance** dates from the same period in the sense 'confidence in one's own abilities'; it comes from the same Old French verb. Its use as a synonym for Insurance dates from the late 16th century, and now tends to be used specifically of *Life Assurance*.
→ SECURITY

asterisk [late Middle English] This came via late Latin from Greek *asteriskos* 'small star', a diminutive of *astēr*.

asteroid [early 19th century] This is from Greek *asteroeidēs* 'starlike', from *astēr* 'star'.

astonish [early 16th century] The early form was *astonished*, in the sense 'stunned, bewildered, dismayed'; it is from obsolete *astone* 'stun, stupefy', from Old French *estoner*, based on Latin *ex-* 'out' and *tonare* 'to thunder'.

astound [Middle English] *Astound* was first used as an adjective in the sense 'stunned'; it comes from *astoned*, the past participle of obsolete *astone*.
→ STUN

astray [Middle English] The early sense was 'distant from the correct path'; it comes from an Anglo-Norman French variant of Old French *estraie*, the past participle of *estraier*, which is perhaps based on Latin *extra* 'out of bounds' and *vagari* 'wander'.

astringe [mid 16th century] This comes from French, from Latin *astringent-* 'pulling tight', from the verb *astringere*, from *ad-* 'towards' and *stringere* 'bind, pull tight'.

astronomy [Middle English] *Astronomy* at first was also a term for astrology; the origin is Old French *astronomie*, via Latin from Greek, from the adjective *astronomos* 'star-arranging'. Greek and Latin *astronomia* was a later and more scientific word than *astrologia*, and probably referred to the mapping out of constellations. In English the distinction between *astrology* and *astronomy* was more or less complete by the 17th century, a comparable process to that undergone by the terms *alchemy* and *chemistry*.

astute [early 17th century] This is from obsolete French *astut* or Latin *astutus*, from *astus* 'craft'.

asunder [Old English] Old English *on sundran* was 'in or into a separate place'.

asylum [late Middle English] At first an *asylum* was a 'place of refuge, especially for criminals'; it came via Latin from Greek *asulon* 'refuge', from *asulos* 'inviolable', from *a-* 'without' and *sulon* 'right of seizure'. Current senses referring to political refuge or to an institution for the mentally ill, date from the 18th century.

at [Old English] Old English *æt* has a Germanic origin; it is related to Old Frisian *et* and Old Norse *at*, from an Indo-European root shared by Latin *ad* 'to'.

athlete [late Middle English] This comes via Latin from Greek *athlētēs*, from *athlein* 'compete for a prize', from *athlon* 'prize'. Mid 17th-century **athletic** came into the language from French *athlétique* or Latin *athleticus*, from Greek *athlētikos* (from *athlētēs*). In ancient Greece and Rome, an *athlete* took part in public games involving running, leaping, boxing, and wrestling. Now the term is used more loosely.

atlas [late 16th century] This was originally used to refer to a person who supported a great burden; it has come via Latin from Greek *Atlas*, the name of one of the Titans who was punished for his part in their revolt against Zeus by being made to support the heavens. The word **Atlantic** (late Middle English) is also based on this name; the term originally referred to Mount Atlas in Libya, hence to the sea near the west African coast, later extended to the whole ocean.

atmosphere [mid 17th century] This word meaning literally 'ball of vapour' is from modern Latin *atmosphaera*, from Greek *atmos* 'vapour' and *sphaira* 'globe'.

atom [late 15th century] An *atom* is literally 'something which cannot be cut into parts'; it is from Old French *atome*, via Latin from Greek *atomos* 'indivisible', based on *a-* 'not' and *temnein* 'to cut'. An *atom* was also the smallest medieval measure of time; an hour was made up of 22,560 atoms (Latin *atomus* 'twinkling of an eye'). The modern scientific adoption of the term began in the 19th century; the classical writers Leucippus and Democritus, in their philosophical writings, had described ultimate particles of matter forming the universe by a *concourse of atoms*.

atone [Middle English] This meant originally 'make or become united or reconciled' and use was rare before the 16th century; it was formed from the phrase *at one*. Later it was by backformation (removal of the suffix) from **atonement** (early 16th century) when it denoted unity or reconciliation, especially between God and man. The form is made up of *at one* and the suffix *-ment*, influenced both by medieval Latin *adunamentum* 'unity' and the earlier English word *onement* (from an obsolete verb *one* 'to unite').

atrocious [mid 17th century] This is based on Latin *atrox*, *atroc-* 'cruel', as is **atrocity** which started out in the mid 16th century in the sense 'cruelty': the immediate source is French *atrocité* or Latin *atrocitas*.

attach [Middle English] The early meaning was 'seize by legal authority', 'arrest', from Old French *atachier* or *estachier* 'fasten, fix', based on an element of Germanic origin related to *stake*. The sense 'arrest' arose in English and Anglo-Norman French as an ellipsis of 'attach by some tie to the jurisdiction of the court'. The English sense 'fasten' is a recent adoption from modern French.

attack [early 17th century] The noun is from French *attaque* (from Italian *attacco* 'an attack'), the verb from *attaquer* (from Italian *attaccare* 'join battle'). The base is an element of Germanic origin shared by *attach*; 'joining' is a key semantic feature.

attain [Middle English] The early senses were 'bring to justice' and 'reach (a state)'; the origin is Old French *ateindre*, from Latin *attingere*, from *ad-* 'at, to' and *tangere* 'to touch'. The same base (and the notion of bringing to justice) gave rise to **attainder** in late Middle English, from Anglo-Norman French: this refers historically to the forfeiture of land and civil rights as a result of sentence to death for treason. The Middle English word **attaint**, now an archaic verb meaning 'affect with disease or corruption' has been influenced by *taint*; the Latin base *tangere* 'to touch' remains part of the core meaning.

attempt [late Middle English] This is from Old French *attempter*, from Latin *attemptare*, from *ad-* 'to' and *temptare* 'to tempt'. The semantic roots here are 'trying', 'testing', and 'stretching'.

attend [Middle English] The early sense was 'apply one's mind, one's energies to'; the source is Old French *atendre* 'give one's attention to', from Latin *attendere*. The base elements are *ad-* 'to' and *tendere* 'stretch', senses which were extended to the notion of making an effort to focus on and deal with a matter. Late Middle English **attendance**, **attentive**, and **attendant** (first used as an adjective) are from Old French. **Attention** is from Latin *attentio(n-)*.

attenuate [mid 16th century] *Attenuate* (from Latin *attenuare* 'make slender') is based on *tenuare* 'make thin', from *tenuis* 'thin'. Current semantics involve lessening the force or intensity of something.

attest [early 16th century] This is from French *attester*, from Latin *attestari*, from *ad-* 'to' and *testari* 'to witness' (from *testis* 'a witness').

attic [late 17th century] Early use was as an architectural term designating a small order (column and entablature) above a taller one. The word is from French *attique*, from Latin *Atticus* 'relating to Athens or Attica', indicating the cultural association with this type of architecture. The phrase *attic storey*, used from the mid 18th century, described a low space above the main tall façade, which eventually gave *attic* the sense 'highest storey of a building'.

attire [Middle English] This is from Old French *atirier*, *atirer* 'equip', from *a tire* 'in order'. The ultimate origin is not known.

attitude [late 17th century] First used as a technical term for the placing or posture of a figure in art, *attitude* is from French, from Italian *attitudine* 'fitness, posture', from late Latin *aptitudo*. The base is the Latin adjective *aptus* 'fit'. The notion 'attitude of mind' dates from the 19th century.
→APT

attorney [Middle English] This term used in legal and business contexts for someone appointed to act for another, is from Old French *atorne*, the past participle of *atorner* 'assign', from *a* 'towards' and *torner* 'turn'. By the Judicature Act of 1873, the title *attorney*, never used in Scotland, was abolished in England; the role was merged with the 'Solicitors of the Supreme Court'. *Attorney* remains in US use.

attract [late Middle English] This is from Latin *attract-* 'drawn near', from the verb *attrahere*, from *ad-* 'to' and *trahere* 'draw'. The word **attraction** used from the same period, first described the action of a poultice drawing matter from the tissues; it comes from Latin *attractio(n-)*, based on the same Latin verb as *attract*. **Attractive** (also late Middle English) had the sense 'absorbent', coming from French *attractif*, *-ive*, from late Latin *attractivus*.

attribute [late 15th century] The noun is from Old French *attribut*, the verb from Latin *attribut-* 'allotted': both from the verb *attribuere*, from *ad-* 'to' and *tribuere* 'assign'.

attrition [late Middle English] *Attrition* was first used as a term in scholastic theology meaning 'sorrow for sin falling short of contrition'; it is from late Latin *attritio(n-)*, from *atterere* 'to rub'. The terms *attrition* and *contrition* were used in a comparison of degree of sorrow for sin, the fulfilment being complete affliction and repentance.

auburn [late Middle English] This is from Old French *auborne*, *alborne*, from Latin *alburnus* 'whitish', from *albus* 'white'. The original sense was 'yellowish white', but the word became associated with *brown* because in the 16th and 17th centuries it was often written *abrune* or *abroun*. Other terms based on Latin *albus* 'white' include: *albatross*, *albino*, *album*, *albumen*, and *daub*.

auction [late 16th century] This comes from Latin *auctio*(-) 'increase', from the verb *augere* 'to increase'. The notion of prices going ever higher in bids, was already captured in Latin usage.

audacity [late Middle English] Latin *audax*, *audac-* 'bold' (from *audere* 'to dare') is the base of *audacity* and mid 16th-century **audacious**.

audience [late Middle English] The source is Old French, from Latin *audientia*, from *audire* 'hear', the base too of **audible** (late 15th century) from late Latin *audibilis*.

audit [late Middle English] This comes from Latin *auditus* 'hearing', from *audire* 'hear', in medieval Latin *auditus* (*compoti*) 'audit (of an account)'. An *audit* was originally listened to as an oral presentation.

audition [late 16th century] The early meaning of *audition* was 'power of hearing or listening', from Latin *auditio*(n-), from *audire* 'hear'. The sense 'interview for a role as a singer, actor, etc.' dates from the late 19th century.

auditorium [early 17th century] An *auditorium* was originally a general word for 'a place for hearing'; it is taken from the Latin neuter of *auditorius* 'relating to hearing'.

augment [late Middle English] This is from the Old French verb *augmenter* or late Latin *augmentare*, from Latin *augere* 'to increase'.

augur [late Middle English] This was first used as a noun; it is a Latin word meaning 'diviner'. The roots may be Latin *avis* 'bird' and *-gar* (from a base meaning 'talk'). An *augur* predicted future events by watching the flight and feeding of birds etc. **Augury**, from the same period and meaning 'divination', is from Old French *augurie* or Latin *augurium* 'interpretation of omens', from Latin *augur*.

aunt [Middle English] This is from Old French *ante*, from Latin *amita*. From the 13th to the 17th centuries, the phrase *my naunt* occurs in literature (by mistaken division of *mine aunt*). This is still found in dialect. The modern French *tante* 'aunt' may be from Old French *t'ante* 'thy aunt'.

aura [late Middle English] Originally a gentle breeze, *aura* comes via Latin from a Greek word meaning 'breeze, breath'. Current senses 'distinctive atmosphere', 'emanation', date from the 18th century.

aureole [Middle English] This comes from Old French *aureole*, from Latin *aureola* (*corona*) 'golden (crown)', the feminine of *aureolus*, based on *aurum* 'gold'.

auspice [mid 16th century] *Auspice* was originally the observation of bird-flight in divination. It is from French, or from Latin *auspicium*, from *auspex* 'observer of birds', from *avis* 'bird' and *specere* 'to look'. **Auspicious** 'favourable' (late 16th century) is formed from *auspice*.

austere [Middle English] *Austere* comes via Old French from Latin *austerus*, from Greek *austēros* 'severe'.

authentic [late Middle English] The origin is Old French from late Latin *authenticus*, from Greek *authentikos* 'principal, genuine'. In the early 17th century **authenticate** arose, from medieval Latin *authenticare* 'establish as valid', from late Latin *authenticus* 'genuine'.

author [Middle English] The early general sense 'a person who invents or causes something' existed alongside the sense 'composer of a book'; the source is Old French *autor*, from Latin *auctor*, from *augere* 'increase, originate, promote'. The spelling with *th* arose in the 15th century, and perhaps became established under the influence of *authentic*. It appears originally to have been a scribal variant. It is impossible to say when the modern pronunciation became established.

authority [Middle English] This comes from Old French *autorite*, from Latin *auctoritas*, from *auctor* 'originator, promoter'. Late Middle English **authorize** is from Old French *autoriser*, from medieval Latin *auctorizare*, from the same noun base.
→ AUTHOR

autoclave [late 19th century] This is from French, from *auto-* 'self' and Latin *clavus* 'nail' or *clavis* 'key'. This type of container, used for chemical reactions involving high temperature and pressure, is self-fastening.

autograph [early 17th century] The source is French *autographe* or late Latin *autographum*, from Greek *autographon*, neuter of *autographos* 'written with one's own hand'. The base elements are *autos* 'self' and *graphos* 'written'.

autopsy [mid 17th century] An early sense was 'personal observation'; it is from French *autopsie* or modern Latin *autopsia*, from Greek.

The base is *autoptēs* 'eyewitness', from *autos* 'self' and *optos* 'seen'.

avail [Middle English] This is from the obsolete verb *vail* 'be of use or value' and is apparently spelt on the pattern of pairs such as *amount* and *mount*. The source is Old French *valoir*, from Latin *valere* 'be strong, be of value'. Late Middle English **available** (based on *avail*) meant 'effectual, serviceable' and 'legally valid'. The common current sense 'ready and able to be used' dates from the early 19th century.

avalanche [late 18th century] *Avalanche* comes from French (influenced by the verb *avaler* 'descend'). It is an alteration of the Alpine dialect word *lavanche*; where the dialect word originates remains a mystery.

avant-garde [late Middle English] In early use this denoted the vanguard of an army; it reflects the meaning of the French source. Current senses relating to new and unusual or experimental ideas, especially in the arts, date from the early 20th century.

avarice [Middle English] This comes from Old French, from Latin *avaritia*, from *avarus* 'greedy', the base too of **avaricious** (late Middle English) from Old French *avaricieux*.

avast [early 17th century] The nautical term *avast* is from Dutch *hou'vast*, *houd vast* 'hold fast!'.

avenge [late Middle English] This is from Old French *avengier*, from *a-* (from Latin *ad* 'to') and *vengier*, from Latin *vindicare* 'vindicate'.

avenue [early 17th century] The early meaning of *avenue* was 'way of approaching a problem'; it is from the French feminine past participle of *avenir* 'arrive, approach', from Latin *advenire*, from *ad-* 'towards' and *venire* 'come'.

average [late 15th century] This is from French *avarie* 'damage to a ship or cargo', earlier 'customs duty', via Italian from Arabic *'awār* 'damage to goods'; the suffix *-age* is on the pattern of *damage*. Originally an *average* was a duty payable by the owner of goods about to be shipped; this became the financial liability from any goods lost or damaged at sea, and specifically the fair apportionment of this liability between the vessel's owners and those of the cargo (late 16th century). This led to the general sense of calculating the mean (mid 18th century).

averse [late 16th century] This is from Latin *aversus* 'turned away from', the past participle of *avertere*. From the same base and dating from the same period is **aversion** which originally described the action of turning away or averting one's eyes; it comes from Latin *aversio(n-)*.

avert [late Middle English] The early meaning was 'divert or deter someone from a place or a course of action'; it is from Latin *avertere*, from *ab-* 'from' and *vertere* 'to turn'; this was reinforced by Old French *avertir*.

aviary [late 16th century] From Latin *aviarium*, *aviary* is based on *avis* 'bird'.

aviation [mid 19th century] This is an adoption from French, formed irregularly from Latin *avis* 'bird'. **Aviate** is a back-formation (by removal of the suffix) from the noun; **aviator** (late 19th century) is from French *aviateur*.

avid [mid 18th century] The source is French *avide* or Latin *avidus*, from *avere* 'crave'.

avoid [late Middle English] This is from Old French *evuider* 'clear out, get rid of', from *vuide* 'empty'. The notion of leaving empty or alone led to 'withdraw', 'retreat', and then 'keep away from'.
→ VOID

avoirdupois [Middle English] First denoting merchandise sold by weight, this is from Old French *aveir de peis* 'goods of weight'. The *aveir* in this phrase is an infinitive (= 'to have') used as a noun.
→ POISE

avow [Middle English] The first senses were 'acknowledge, approve' and 'vouch for'; the word comes from Old French *avouer* 'acknowledge', from Latin *advocare* 'summon in defence'.

await [Middle English] This is from Anglo-Norman French *awaitier*, from *a-* (from Latin *ad* 'to, at') and *waitier* 'to wait'.

awake [Old English] Old English *āwæcnan* and *āwacian* were both used in the sense 'come out of sleep'. **Awaken** in Old English was *onwæcnan*, from *on* 'on' and *waken*.

award [late Middle English] This was originally 'issue a judicial decision' and also denoted the decision itself. The source is Anglo-Norman French *awarder*, variant of Old French *esguarder* 'consider, ordain', from *es-* (from Latin *ex* 'thoroughly') and *guarder* 'watch (over)'. The base is a word of Germanic origin related to *ward*.
→ GUARD

aware [Old English] Old English *gewær* has a West Germanic origin and is related to German *gewahr*. An early meaning was 'vigilant, cautious' as well as 'informed'.

away [Old English] Old English *onweg*, *aweg* meant 'on one's way'.

awe [Old English] Old English *ege* meant 'terror, dread'; it was replaced in Middle English by forms from the related Old Norse *agi*. Old English **awful** and late 16th-century **awesome** (the early sense of which was 'filled with awe') are based on *awe*.

awkward [late Middle English] The original meaning was 'the wrong way round, upside down'; it is based on the obsolete word *awk* 'backwards, perverse, clumsy' (from Old Norse *afugr* 'turned the wrong way').

awning [early 17th century] *Awning* was originally a nautical term describing a sheet of canvas forming a shelter against the elements on a ship's deck; the origin is unknown.

axe [Old English] Old English *æx* has a Germanic origin; it is related to Dutch *aaks* and German *Axt*. The spelling with a final *-e* became prevalent in the 19th century; *ax* was common before.

axis [late Middle English] This is a Latin word meaning 'axle, pivot'. It tends to be used for the figurative and transferred senses of the related word *axle*, such as the *axis of the earth*, at either end of which are the poles.

axle [Middle English] This was originally *axle-tree*, the 'tree' being the beam of wood carrying the opposite wheels of a carriage; it is from Old Norse *ǫxultré*.

azure [Middle English] *Azure* at first was the name of a blue dye and the precious stone 'lapis lazuli': ultramarine was made from powdered lapis lazuli. The word is from Old French *asur*, *azur*, from medieval Latin *azzurum*, *azolum*, from Arabic *al* 'the' and *lāzaward* (from Persian *lāžward* 'lapis lazuli').

Bb

babble [Middle English] Adopted from Middle Low German *babbelen* or formed independently in English as a frequentative (= verb of repeated action), *babble* is based on the repeated *ba-ba-ba*, made by a young baby or child practising speech sounds. The same process is seen in *mama*, and *papa*. Other languages share this language feature, e.g. French *babiller* 'to prattle' (based on *ba*) and French *maman* 'mummy' (based on *ma*). The word focuses on sound and the onomatopoeia lends itself readily to a description of water as in *babbling brook*.

babe/baby [late Middle English] Both of these words are probably imitative of an infant's speech which features repetition of the sound *ba*; similarly **babby** heard in dialect. *Babe* has changed its semantics and usage, from a poetical rather formal word in biblical texts (where *babe* = 'infant'), to its informal use today. In the US in the early part of the 20th century, both *babe* and *baby* started to be heard as affectionate, casual forms of address used by men when talking to women. In the later part of the century and currently, however, they have become descriptive of sexual attractiveness in both men and women: *he's a real babe*; *what a babe!*.

babel [Middle English] Genesis 11 tells the story of *Babel*, where God, angered by the arrogance of builders who thought they could reach heaven by erecting a tower, confused their language so that they could no longer understand each other. The word was originally Hebrew for 'Babylon' (based on an Akkadian (= a language of ancient Babylonia) phrase meaning 'gate of God'), but the biblical association caused its adoption into English use in the general sense of 'a confusion of sounds'. In the early 17th century a *babel* was extended to describe any scene of confusion such as a noisy assembly of people. It is also, influenced by the colourful biblical story, used metaphorically to mean 'lofty' (Dickens *Dombey and Son*: Babel towers of chimneys) or 'something visionary' (Milton *Paradise Lost*: And still with vain designe New Babels, had they wherewithall, would build).

baboon [Middle English] The first recorded sense of *baboon* known at present is 'a grotesque figure' used in architectural carving, seen in all manner of gaping poses as gargoyles on ancient buildings. Adopted from Old French *babuin* or from medieval Latin *babewynus*, the base sense was probably Old French *baboue* 'muzzle' or 'grimace'. Its use in zoology is perhaps inspired by the exaggerated facial expressions typical of an ape's behaviour.

baccalaureate [mid 17th century] The *baccalaureate* qualification started out as a 'university degree of bachelor' and comes from French *baccalauréat* or medieval Latin *baccalaureatus*. The source was the academic medieval Latin *baccalarius* 'bachelor', which became *baccalaureus* by wordplay on *bacca lauri* 'laurel berry': laurels were traditionally, by association with the ancient Greek practice of celebrating the achievement of a victor, awarded to congratulate scholars. The modern *baccalaureate*, as an examination and qualification enabling admission to a university course, dates from 1970. It has diversified into the European Baccalaureate (instituted in the EU) and the International Baccalaureate.

bacchanal [mid 16th-century] This word is used as both a noun and an adjective with reference to **Bacchus** (in Greek *Bakkhos*), the god of wine. The association with the **Bacchanalia**, the Roman festival in honour of the god, with its renowned free-flowing wine and licentious behaviour, gave the parallel sense 'drunken revelry or orgy'; so too **bacchant**, which describes both 'a priest of Bacchus' and 'a drunken reveller'.

bachelor [Middle English] The immediate source was Old French *bacheler*, of which one sense was 'a young man hoping to become a knight' by being in the service of and benefiting from the experience of an older knight. The word retained this same denotation in English as well as having the sense common in current use: 'unmarried man'. The academic sense relating to a university degree is also recorded in the Middle English period.
→ BACCALAUREATE

back [Old English] The Old English noun *bæc* has a Germanic origin; it is related to Middle Dutch and Old Norse *bak*. The adverb, seen in phrases such as *rolled back*, dates from late Middle English and is a shortening of **aback**. The adjective is either an attributive use of the noun (e.g. *back pain*) or an elliptical use of the adverb (e.g. *back rent*). The verb is based on the noun and also dates from late Middle English.

bacon [Middle English] The word *bacon* was adopted from Old French, from a Germanic word meaning 'ham, flitch'; it is related to *back*. In early use *bacon* was not merely the cured flesh of a pig, it referred to 'fresh pork' too and, until the 18th century, it was also the word for a pig's carcass. A rare use is found in Shakespeare where a *bacon* is a 'rustic' but this meaning was short-lived; here it is a short form of *chaw-bacon*, referring to the fact that pork was the meat eaten mostly by the rural population.

bacterium [mid 19th century] This modern Latin term is formed from Greek *baktērion* 'little staff', a diminutive of *baktēria* 'staff or cane'; the first bacteria to be discovered were rod-shaped. The word **bacillus**, a pathogenic bacterium, also meant 'little rod' in late Latin.

bad [Middle English]   The source of this derogatory adjective is not altogether clear but is perhaps Old English *bæddel* 'hermaphrodite' or 'womanish man', and so it probably owes its semantic core to homophobic feelings. The sense is reflected in the obsolete word *badling* (Old English) which was an 'effeminate or worthless man'.

badge [late Middle English] This word's origin remains unknown; the forms *bage* (Old French) and *hagia* (Anglo-Latin) are comparable but may derive from the English word. Early use in English was as a heraldic term for an emblem which distinguished a knight or all the retainers of a noble house.
→ BADGER

badger [early 16th century] *Badger* is probably based on *badge*, with reference to the animal's distinctive markings: the *badge* may be two black facial stripes (Eurasian *Meles meles*) or a white facial stripe (North American *Taxidea taxus*). Use as a verb arose in the late 18th century and reflects the popularity at that time of badger-baiting, a pastime where badgers were drawn from their setts by dogs and killed for sport (illegal in the UK since 1830). The name *Brock* often applied to these much-loved creatures, is a use of the Old English word *broc* for *badger*.
→ BAIT

badminton [mid 19th century] The source is *Badminton* in SW England, the name of the country seat of the Duke of Beaufort. As a word in general use, the first reference is as a summer drink: a mixture of claret, sugar, and soda water. Perhaps this refreshed the spectators of the game of *badminton* played in the grounds of the mansion

baffle [late 16th century] When first used, the verb *baffle* was 'to cheat or deceive' somebody. Maybe it is related to French *bafouer* meaning 'to ridicule' or to the obsolete French word *beffer* 'mock, deceive'. There was originally a very active sense of 'hoodwinking' seen when Defoe in his *Political History of the Devil* writes: he had not had a Mind to cheat or baffle the poor Man; later the passive became common with the sense of 'being hoodwinked' to the point of confusion.

bag [Middle English] The origin is uncertain; *bag* comes perhaps from Old Norse *baggi*. It is not found in other Germanic languages, but Old French *bague* probably shows the same word.
→ BAGGAGE

bagatelle [mid 17th century] As the name of a game, *bagatelle* is English in origin and use and dates from the early 19th century. The earlier sense reflected in phrases such as *a mere bagatelle* was an adoption from French (meaning 'something regarded as too unimportant to be worth considering') from Italian *bagatella*; the base is perhaps Italian *baga* 'baggage' or alternatively the early semantic core may be 'little berry' based on a diminutive of Latin *baca* 'berry'.

baggage [late Middle English] The semantics of *baggage* lie in the Old French source *bagage* meaning 'property packed up ready to be transported', from the verb *baguer* 'tie up' or from *bagues* 'bundles'; there is also perhaps a connection with *bag*. Its use as an insult may have been influenced in sense by French *bagasse* 'prostitute'.
→ BAG

bail¹ [Middle English] The legal term *bail* gives temporary freedom to a person in custody if someone is willing to give a surety, the base is the Latin verb *bajulare* 'bear a burden'. The adoption of *bail* into English was from Old French with the literal sense 'custody', 'jurisdiction', from *bailler* 'take charge of'. In Old French there was an additional notion of 'delivery', reflected in legal contexts. Thus there has probably been a shift in sense from the act of the magistrate 'taking charge' to the 'release' associated with the safeguard of a surety. Related words are **bailie** and **bailiff** (originally used interchangeably): they derive from Latin *bajulus* 'carrier' or 'manager', i.e. someone bearing a burden of responsibility.

bail² [Middle English] The *bail* associated with cricket is one of the crosspieces bridging the stumps; it is also a 'bar' in many applications, e.g. a bar on a printer to hold paper, or one separating horses in a stable, or even as a mountaineering term as part of a crampon. The likely base is Latin *baculum* 'rod'. In Middle English a *bail* was an outer wall of a castle (now **bailey**), made of a palisade of stakes; the source is probably Old French *baile* 'palisade', 'enclosure'.

bail³ [early 17th century] This is the *bail* of *bail out* involving, in its literal interpretation, 'scooping water'; it comes from the obsolete noun *bail* 'bucket', from French *baille*. The source is Latin *bajulus* 'carrier', which is, by extension, someone carrying a burden and therefore has a connection with the legal *bail*.
→ BAIL¹

bairn [Old English] *Bairn*, a Scots and northern English word for 'child', was originally spelt *bearn* and has Germanic roots.
→ BEAR¹

bait [Middle English] The Old Norse origin was *beit* 'pasture, food', and, as a verb, *beita* 'to hunt or chase', in essence 'cause to bite'. When the verb was first used in English it was in the context of tormenting a chained or confined animal by setting dogs on it: the notions of food and hunting have come together in the *bait* of the fisherman, while the notion of harassment is involved in the figurative use of 'baiting' someone to provoke a reaction. In slang, the noun *bait* is found meaning a 'temper' (R. Kipling, *Stalky & Co.*: 'What a bait you're in,' said Stalky).
→ ABET; BITE

baize [late 16th century] *Baize*, the felt-like covering for billiard and card tables, is now usually green, but the word comes from French *baies*, the feminine plural form of *bai* 'chestnut-coloured'. The name is presumably from the original colour of the cloth, although records indicate that a number of colours of *baize* existed.
→ BAY⁴

bake [Old English] Germanic in origin, the early word was *bacan*, related to Dutch *bakken* and German *backen*; **baker** dates from the same period. **Baxter** a 'female baker' was used as late as the 16th century in northern English, but not in the south after 1400. It came to be applied to both men and women and is still found in Scottish dialect; it remains a common family name. As for the expression **baker's dozen**, this was first recorded in the late 16th century, from the bakers' custom of adding an extra loaf to each dozen sold to give the retailer his profit. The phrase *in-bread* was also heard because the baker would throw an extra loaf or two into the oven so as not to incur a penalty for short weight. A *baker's dozen* as a colourful expression for the number 13 is matched by *a sitting of eggs* from the 19th century, referring to the number of eggs in a clutch placed under a hen for incubation.
→ BATCH

balaclava [late 19th century] A *balaclava* first denoted the type of woollen covering for the head and neck worn by soldiers on active service in the Crimean War (1854) and was named after the village of *Balaclava* in the Crimea. Originally worn for warmth, the *balaclava* now has associations with disguise in terrorist activities, etc.

balance [Middle English] The literal use of *balance* is for a weighing device. From Old French *balance*, the word is based on late Latin (*libra*) *bilanx* '(balance) with two scale-pans', composed of *bi-* 'twice', 'having two' and *lanx* 'scale-pan'.

balcony [early 17th century] The ultimate origin of *balcony* is probably Germanic; the immediate source is Italian *balcone*, based on *balco* 'a scaffold' from a Germanic root meaning 'beam'. The English word was pronounced with the stress on the second syllable until about 1825, reflecting the Italian source.

bald [Middle English] The likely semantic base of *bald* is 'white patch', leading to the archaic English sense 'marked or streaked with white'. The Welsh *ceffyl bal* provides a comparison, denoting a horse with a white mark on its face. Several Indo-European synonyms of *bald* show a connection with 'smooth', 'bright', 'shiny' rather than with 'hairless' as such.

balderdash [late 16th century] Originally a *balderdash* was a frothy liquid, and later it came to describe a rather unappetizing mixture of drinks; it keeps its negative connotation in the modern sense 'utter nonsense'; the origin is unknown.

bale¹ [Middle English] A *bale* of hay or paper describes the bundle into which these are bound or packed. The likely source is Middle Dutch from Old French; the ultimate origin is Germanic and the word is related to **ball**.
→ BALL¹

bale² [Old English] The *bale* found in **baleful** ('menacing') is Germanic in origin; it is recorded in Old English as *balu, bealu* meaning 'evil'.

ball¹ [Middle English] The *ball* which means 'sphere' is Germanic and comes from the Old Norse word *bǫllr*.

ball² [early 17th century] The *ball* which means 'a dance' is from the French word *bal*, from late Latin *ballare* 'to dance'; it is related to two Greek verbs: *ballizein* 'to dance' and *ballein* 'to throw'.

ballad [late 15th century] Originally a *ballad* was a light simple song and sprang from Old French *balade*; the pronunciation reflected this source initially. In French and English the sense was transferred from the notion of 'dancing' present in Provençal *bulada*, meaning both 'dance' and 'a song to dance to' (based on the late Latin word *ballare* 'to dance'). The early semantic core is reflected in *ballet*, which is related. The two spellings *ballad* and *ballet* were confused in the 17th century, because of the common practice of changing the suffix *-ad* to *-at(e)* or *-et*. In English, it was not until the mid 18th century that *ballad* came to denote a 'narrative poem'.
→ BALL²

ballast [mid 16th century] The origin of *ballast* is uncertain but it is probably either from Low German or has a Scandinavian source. The word exists in most of the European languages as the type of load that is carried in transport for weight only and not for commercial gain. If the word is originally Scandinavian, then the basic meaning is 'bare or mere load', as preserved in Old Swedish and Old Danish *barlast*, but if it is originally Low German, then the basic meaning is probably 'bad load' (from *bal* 'bad').

ballet [mid 17th century] A French word initially, from Italian *balletto* 'little dance' (diminutive of *ballo* 'a dance'), *ballet* is based on late Latin *ballare* 'to dance'. So too is **ballerina**, first recorded in the late 18th century, an adoption this time of the feminine of Italian *ballerino* 'dancing master'.
→ BALL²

ballistic [late 18th century] The base element of *ballistic* 'projectile' is **ballista** (from a Latin word based on Greek *ballein* 'to throw'); it describes two weapons: a type of catapult for hurling large stones at the enemy in ancient warfare, and secondly a large crossbow for firing a spear. The expression *go ballistic* dating from the 1970s meaning 'go berserk or haywire' was originally a US usage: the reference is probably to a *ballistic missile* guided during the propulsion phase but which then goes into freefall.

balloon [late 16th century] A *balloon* was originally a game played with a large inflated leather ball. It derives from French *ballon* or Italian *ballone* 'large ball'. The expression *when the balloon goes up* is probably with allusion to the release of a balloon to mark the start of an event.

ballot [mid 16th century] From Italian *ballotta*, a diminutive of *balla* 'ball', a *ballot* was originally a small coloured ball placed in a container to register a vote.
→ BALL¹

balm [Middle English] This 'fragrant resinous substance', a 'preparation for embalming', owes its original meaning to Old French *basme*, from Latin *balsamum* 'balsam'. The Greek *balsamon* is the source of both *balm* and **balsam**: it was the name of an oily resin exuded by various trees and shrubs. The figurative sense 'soothing influence' began in the mid 16th century. **Balm of Gilead** is an oleo-resin prized as an antiseptic: the name is modern and assumes that this is the substance mentioned in the Bible as found in Gilead and called *balm* in the English translation (Jeremiah 24: Is there no balm in Gilead; is there no physician there?). But the Hebrew word *tsŏri* was not identified with Greek *balsamon* by the Vulgate, which has Latin *resina* 'resin'.

balsa [early 17th century] A *balsa* was originally a kind of South American raft or fishing boat and is an adoption of this Spanish word for 'raft'. Also known as **balsa wood**, this lightweight wood from a fast-growing tropical American tree is used chiefly for making models and rafts.

baluster [early 17th century] A *baluster* is so named because part of this type of short decorative pillar resembles the curving calyx tube of a flower. The source is French *balustre*, from Italian *bulaustro*, from *balaust(r)a* 'wild pomegranate flower' (via Latin from Greek *balaustion*). A **balustrade** is supported by *balusters* and comes from the same French source.

bamboozle [early 18th century] The origin is unknown but the word first appeared around the year 1700. Mentioned in the *Tatler* No. 230 in an article about 'the continual Corruption of our English Tongue' it was one of several slang words such as *banter*, *sham*, *bubble* ('to blubber'), *bully*, and *mob* in vogue at the time. Scottish writers used *bumbaze* and *bumbaze* 'to confound' from around 1725.

ban [Old English] In *ban* the concepts of 'give an order' and 'prohibit' dominate in current usage. Old English *bannan* was 'summon by a public proclamation', from a Germanic origin, reinforced by Old Norse *banna* 'to curse', 'to prohibit'. The noun is partly from the verb and partly from the related Old French *ban* 'proclamation, summons, banishment'. A *ban* was once a formal ecclesiastical denunciation; this became, more generally 'a curse' illustrated by the following quotations in Byron's *Werner*: A prodigal son, beneath his father's ban,

and Shakespeare's *Hamlet*: With Hecate's ban thrice blasted, thrice infected.
→ BANNS

banal [mid 18th century] The original *banal* related to feudal service and meant 'compulsory': from this came a notion of 'common to everyone' and so 'quite ordinary and everyday'. The direct source is French, from *ban* 'a proclamation or call to arms' but the ultimate origin is Germanic.
→ BAN

banana [late 16th century] *Banana* is a native Niger-Congo word introduced into English via Portuguese or Spanish, the languages of the first European discoverers of the fruit. *Bananas* in its 20th-century sense 'crazy' is recorded frequently from the 1960s; much earlier (1935) in A. J. Pollock's *Underworld Speaks* the usage is defined: *He's bananas, he's sexually perverted; a degenerate*. However the origin of the sense is unclear. Interestingly, in *Jeeves in the Offing*, P. G. Wodehouse uses the expression **banana oil** to mean 'nonsense': The sort of banana oil that passes between statesmen at conferences ... before they tear their whiskers off and get down to cases.

band¹ [late Old English] The *band* used to denote 'a thin strip' was first recorded in late Old English in the sense 'something that restrains, binds, or unites'. From Old Norse, the word was reinforced in late Middle English by Old French *bande*, of Germanic origin. Its variant *bend* is retained in heraldry in **bend sinister**, a broad diagonal stripe from top right to bottom left of a shield (a supposed sign of bastardy). As for associated words: **bandage**, a long narrow strip for binding, is an adoption from French and is also based on *bande*; **bandbox**, a box for carrying hats, was originally for carrying neckbands (which were in the form of narrow strips).
→ BIND; BOND

band² [late Middle English] The *band* meaning 'group' comes from Old French *bande* and is of Germanic origin. There is a relationship with *banner*; associations with military companies wearing sashes of a certain colour or collected under a certain banner have been suggested through links between French *bande* 'troop', late Latin *bandum* 'banner', and Italian *banda* 'sash', 'ribbon'. Certainly the *band* used in musical contexts started out as a military usage (mid 17th century), which led to the idiomatic phrase *when the band begins to play* suggesting the imminence of an event of a serious nature.
→ BANNER

bandit [late 16th century] Derived from Italian *bandito*, the past participle of *bandire*, the literal meaning is 'banned (person)'.
→ BAN; BANISH

bandy¹ [late 17th century] *Bandy*, often used descriptively as in the phrase *bandy legs* means 'curving outwards'. Perhaps the obsolete word *bandy* 'a curved stick used in hockey' led to this use.

bandy² [late 16th century] Now commonly used in the phrase *bandy words with*, this verb was originally used to describe the passing to and fro of a ball; it perhaps has its origin in French *bander* 'take sides at tennis', from *bande* 'band, crowd'.
→ BAND²

bane [Old English] A *bane*, originally *bana*, a 'thing causing death', 'poison', is of Germanic origin. As well as its use in the phrase *bane of one's life*, it is commonly found in plant names, e.g.: **baneberry** (mid 18th century) is literally a 'poison berry'; **bugbane**, a tall plant of the buttercup family, is part of the species *C. foetida*, originally used to drive away bedbugs; **cowbane** (or *water hemlock*) is so named because of being poisonous to grazing cattle; **wolfbane**, a mountain plant of the genus Aconitum, is from modern Latin *lycoctonum*, translating a Greek word meaning 'wolfslayer'. Its poisonous qualities are illustrated by Keats in *Ode on Melancholy*: Go not to Lethe, neither twist Wolf's-bane tight-rooted, for its poisonous wine.

bang [mid 16th century] This word imitates the sound made; it is possibly Scandinavian in origin and may be compared with Old Norse *bang* 'hammering'.

banish [late Middle English] From Old French *baniss-*, the lengthened stem of *banir*, the verb *banish* is ultimately of Germanic origin and related to *ban*.
→ BAN

banister [mid 17th century] *Banister*, in early use also spelt *barrister*, is an alteration of *baluster*.
→ BALUSTER

banjo [mid 18th century] *Banjo* was originally a black American alteration of **bandore**: this in turn is a variant of **bandora** describing a kind of bass lute with a scallop-shaped body and metal strings, played typically by consorts of the late 16th and 17th centuries, but of uncertain derivation linguistically; compare with Dutch *bandoor* and Spanish *bandurria*; the base is probably Greek *pandoura* a 'three-stringed lute'. Also for comparison with *bandora* is **bandura**, a Ukrainian stringed instrument.

bank¹ [Middle English] From Old Norse *bakki*, the *bank* now describing a raised ridge of ground etc., is of Germanic origin; it is related to *bench*. In phrases such as *banks of speakers* and *banks of oars*, where the sense is a set of similar

things in sloping rows, French *banc* is the semantic source of the same ultimate origin.
→ BENCH

bank² [late 15th century] The financial *bank* was originally 'a money dealer's table' and comes from French *banque* or Italian *banca*, from medieval Latin *banca*, *bancus*, of Germanic origin. **Banker** is a mid 16th-century word from French *banquier*.
→ BANK¹; BENCH

bankrupt [mid 16th century] *Bankrupt* is from Italian *banca rotta*, literally 'broken bench', from *banca* and *rompere* 'to break'. The change in the ending came about by association with Latin *rupt-* 'broken'.
→ BANK²

banner [Middle English] From Old French *baniere*, the word *banner* is ultimately Germanic.
→ BAND²

banns [Middle English] This word commonly heard in the phrase *banns of marriage* is a plural of *ban* 'proclamation'; it was pronounced with a long *a* sound from the 15th to the 17th centuries.
→ BAN

banquet [late 15th century] *Banquet* is literally 'little bench', from a French diminutive of *banc* 'bench'. The meaning has been transferred to refer to the food itself in the same way that *table* and *board* are sometimes used in English (e.g. Chaucer's *Canon's Yeoman's Prologue and Tale*: Scho wolde suffre him no thing for to pay For bord ne clothing). There has been a sense reversal in that in early use a *banquet* was often a light snack between meals or merely a single course of sweetmeats, fruit, or wine; now the word describes a feast.
→ BANK¹

banshee [late 17th century] A *banshee* in Irish legend, is a female spirit who wails a warning of an imminent death in a house; the word is ultimately from Old Irish *ben side* 'woman of the fairies'.

banyan [late 16th century] The Indian fig tree known as a *banyan* comes from Portuguese, from a Gujarati word for 'a man of the trading caste', from Sanskrit. The word originally denoted a Hindu merchant, but in the mid 17th century came to be applied by Europeans to one particular tree under which traders had built a pagoda. The branches of this tree spread over a wide area often covering several hectares; they produce aerial roots which later become accessory trunks.

baptism [Middle English] The Greek verb *baptizein* 'immerse, baptize' is the source of a family of words in English, all of which date from Middle English: *baptism* is from Old French *baptesme*, via ecclesiastical Latin from ecclesiastical Greek *baptismos* 'ceremonial washing'; **baptist** is from Old French *baptiste* and was originally 'a person who baptizes someone'; **baptistery** (in early times a separate building to the church, where baptisms took place) is from Old French *baptistere* 'bathing place', and **baptize** has come via Old French from ecclesiastical Latin *baptizare*.

bar¹ [Middle English] The noun *bar* meaning 'long rigid piece of wood, metal, etc.' is from Old French *barre*, from late Latin *barra*, but earlier etymological detail is lacking. The development of sense (with the semantic strands relating to shape and obstruction) had largely taken place before the word was adopted into English. The legal use of *bar* appeared quite early but was extended to specific applications: in the late 16th century the expression *be called to the bar* is recorded, reflecting the use of *bar* as a partition in the Inns of Court separating the readers (= lecturers in law) from the rest of the hall: having gained a certain standing students were called from the body of the hall to take a principal part in the mootings of the house. **Barrister** first recorded in late Middle English is based on *bar*.

bar² [early 20th century] The technical term *bar* denoting a unit of pressure is from Greek *baros* 'weight'.

barb¹ [Middle English] A *barb* commonly denotes a sharp projection (from an arrow, fish-hook, etc.) angled away from the main point to make extraction difficult. Early use was in the broad sense 'appendage' (e.g. 'beard', 'feathers under the beak of a hawk', 'wattles of a cock', etc.); this included, in some contexts, reference to a piece of linen worn by nuns over or under the chin. The source is Old French *barbe*, from Latin *barba* 'beard', which forms the base of some fish and animal names: a *barb* is a freshwater fish with barbels around the mouth; so too is the late Middle English word **barbel** (via Old French from late Latin *barbellus* 'little barbel', diminutive of *barbus*, although it later referred specifically to the fleshy filaments themselves. There is also the word **barbet**, the name for a poodle until the early 19th century.

barb² [mid 17th century] A type of small hardy horse known as a *barb* derives its name from French *barbe*, from Italian *barbero* 'coming from Barbary'. Originally the breed came from north Africa. Barbary was a former name for the Saracen countries of north and northwest Africa, together with Moorish Spain.

barbarian [Middle English] *Barbarian* (from Old French *barbarien* or from Latin *barbarus*) was first an adjective used depreciatively of a person with different speech and customs. At the base of this word and others in the same family is Greek *barbaros* 'foreign' (usually with reference to speech). In late Middle English the following four words came into use: **barbaric** is from Old French *barbarique* or via Latin from Greek *barbarikos*; **barbarism** from Old French *barbarisme* based on Greek *barbarismos*, from *barbarizein* 'speak like a foreigner'; **barbarize** first used in the sense 'speak using barbarisms' from late Latin *barbarizare*, from Greek *barbarizein*; also **barbarous** based on Latin *barbarus*. A later addition to the group formed on the same base was **barbarity** recorded in the mid 16th century.

barbecue [mid 17th century] An early *barbecue* was 'a wooden framework for sleeping on, or for storing meat and fish to be dried'. The word comes from Spanish *barbacoa*, perhaps from Arawak (West Indies) *barbacoa* which was a 'wooden frame on posts'. In contemporary contexts *barbecue* is used in Aerospace technology in the phrases *barbecue mode* and *barbecue manoeuvre* describing the rotation of a spacecraft to allow the heat of the sun to fall on all sides.

barber [Middle English] This word comes via Anglo-Norman French from Old French *barbe* 'beard'.
→ BARB¹

bard¹ [Middle English] Of Celtic origin, *bard* was a derogatory word in Scotland in the 16th century for an itinerant musician, but was later romanticized by Sir Walter Scott (*Lay of the Last Minstrel*: The last of all the bards was he Who sung of Border chivalry). Shakespeare is sometimes referred to as the *Bard* or the *Bard of Avon*.

bard² [early 18th century] When meat is *barded* with rashers of bacon to keep it moist and basted, there is a connection with 'armour'. The noun is from French *barde*, a transferred sense of *barde* 'armour protecting the breast and flanks of a warhorse'; the base is an Arabic word meaning 'saddlecloth', 'padded saddle'.

bare [Old English] An old word of Germanic origin, *bare* is related to Dutch *baar* and the dated German word *bar* 'naked'; the original short vowel has lengthened in both these languages and in modern English. There is a link with Lithuanian *basas* 'barefoot'.

bargain [Middle English] The noun is from Old French *bargaine*; the verb from *bargaignier*. A link has been suggested with Latin *barca* 'barge' and the notion of carrying goods to and fro, but difficulties of form and sense devel-

opment make the connection unclear. The origin is probably Germanic with a link to German *borgen* 'to borrow'.

barge [Middle English] A *barge* was originally a small seagoing vessel. From Old French, the base is perhaps Greek *baris* 'Egyptian boat'.

bargeboard [mid 19th century] The first element of this word is from the mid 16th-century architectural prefix *barge-*, relating to the gable of a building, perhaps coming from medieval Latin *bargus* 'gallows'.

baritone [early 17th century] The strands of meaning in the elements that make up *baritone* are 'heaviness' and 'stretching'. The origin is Italian *baritono*, from Greek *barutonos*, from *barus* 'heavy' and *tonos* 'tone, tension'.

bark¹ [Old English] The sharp noise of a dog's *barking* (in Old English, *beorc* as a noun and *beorcan* as a verb), has a Germanic root; there is a possible relationship with *break*.
→ BREAK¹

bark² [Middle English] The *bark* of a tree is from Old Norse and is perhaps related to *birch*.
→ BIRCH

barley [Old English] One of the early words for *barley* was *bere*. The form *bærlic* first appears as an adjective or in attributive use in the name *Bærlic-croft*. Several Indo-European synonyms derive from sources which capture the 'sharp' and 'prickly' characteristics of this cereal.
→ BARN¹

barmy [late 15th century] The early sense of *barmy* was 'frothy'; it later came to mean 'excited'. The noun **barm**, the froth on fermenting malt liquor, was *beorma* in Old English and is West Germanic in origin. In the late 19th century the use of *barmy* to mean 'crazy' is recorded but, despite the spelling, this has a different source: it is an alteration of **balmy**, a slang word meaning 'soft', 'weak-minded'.

barn¹ [Old English] *Barn* as a farm building is literally a 'barley house' and in Old English was *bern*, *berern*, from *bere* 'barley' and *ern* 'house'.
→ BARLEY

barn² [1940s] *Barn* as a unit of area used especially in the field of particle physics, is apparently from the phrase *as big as a barn door*, long established as a comparative measure of height and width.

barnacle [late 16th century] The marine crustacean called a *barnacle* gets its name from medieval Latin *bernaca*; earlier details are unknown. In Middle English it denoted the barnacle goose, whose breeding grounds were long unknown and which was believed to hatch from the shell of the crustacean to which the goose gave its name.

baron [Middle English] *Baron* denoting a member of the lowest order of the British nobility comes from Old French, from medieval Latin *baro*, *baron-* meaning a 'man', a 'warrior'; the origin is probably Germanic. The word **baronet** was recorded in late Middle English and came from Anglo-Latin *baronettus*, from Latin *baro*. The word did not originally denote a nobleman, but rather a gentleman, summoned by the king to attend parliament; the current use as the lowest hereditary titled British order was instituted in the early 17th century.

baroque [mid 18th century] A *baroque*, now encapsulating a notion of ornate detail in style, was originally the name of an irregularly shaped pearl. The word came via French from Portuguese *barroco*, Spanish *barrueco*, or Italian *barocco* but the ultimate origin is unknown.

barque [Middle English] *Barque*, also spelt **bark**, is from Old French, probably via Provençal from late Latin *barca* 'ship's boat'. The verb **embark** is from French *embarquer* (the prefix *em-* supplying the sense 'in') thus expressing 'go into the boat'.

barracks [late 17th century] This military term is from French *baraque*, from Italian *baracca* or Spanish *barraca* meaning a 'soldier's tent'; earlier details are unknown. However **barrack** as a verb meaning 'jeer loudly' has been in use from the late 19th century and is probably from Northern Irish dialect.

barrel [Middle English] This word derives from from Old French *baril*, from medieval Latin *barillus* 'small cask'. Celtic words such as Welsh *baril* have sometimes been cited as the source but these are in fact from English. A **barrelhouse** as a North American word for a disreputable liquor bar gets its name from the rows of barrels stacked along the walls.
→ BAR[1]

barricade [late 16th century] An adoption from French, *barricade* is from *barrique* 'cask', from Spanish *barrica*. The 'day of the barricades' in Paris on 12 May 1588 during the Huguenot Wars was characterized by the use of barrels to build defences and obstruct access; hence the current sense of *barricade*.
→ BARREL

barrier [late Middle English] A *barrier* in early use was a palisade or fortification defending an entrance or access. Old French *barriere* is the immediate source but further details are not known with certainty.

barrow[1] [Old English] A *barrow* that carries a load as in *wheelbarrow*, *hand-barrow* was *bearwe* in Old English and Germanic in origin; it is related to the verb *bear*.
→ BEAR[1]; BIER

barrow[2] [Old English] A Germanic source gave *beorg* which meant 'mountain, hill' in Old English. There is a relationship with Dutch *berg* and German *Berg* and, over time, the word was applied to lower hills and mounds. *Barrow* disappeared from general use before 1400 but was retained in south-western dialect where it has become part of place-names such as Bull Barrow in Dorset, Cadon Barrow in Cornwall and Trentishoe Barrow in North Devon. The archaeological sense 'burial mound' present in Old English has persisted in, for example, the *barrows* of Salisbury Plain.

barter [late Middle English] 'Deception' is a likely early semantic component of *barter*; comparable is Old French *barater* 'to deceive'. The sense 'exchange goods for other goods' must often have involved inequality of perceived value and therefore disappointment, a feeling of being deceived. A recent use of *barter* in the field of broadcasting developed in the 1980s; in this context the 'exchange' is the broadcasting of a television or radio programme traded against the right to sell some of the advertising time available while the programme is being broadcast.

bascule [late 19th century] The name *bascule* for a type of bridge with a section raised and lowered by counterweights, once denoted a lever or pulley apparatus. The form *bascule* comes from a French word (earlier spelt *bacule*) for 'see-saw', from *battre* 'to bump' and *cul* 'buttocks'.

base[1] [Middle English] *Base* as the bottom or foundation of something comes from Old French, itself via Latin *basis* 'base, pedestal' from Greek. In English in the late 16th century **basis** denoted a base or pedestal, reflecting the Latin. The Greek root means, literally, 'stepping', therefore giving a notion of 'something on which one steps or stands'. *Base* is also an element of the adjective **basic** 'forming an essential foundation'.

base[2] [late Middle English] This adjective meaning 'low, ignoble' is from Old French *bas*, from medieval Latin *bassus* 'short': this was found in classical Latin as a cognomen, i.e. a type of nickname added to the personal name of an ancient Roman citizen and typically passed down from father to son. Early senses included 'low, short' and 'inferior in quality'; from this notion of poor quality arose a sense 'low in the social scale', and so in the mid 16th century, through its negative associations, 'reprehensibly cowardly', 'selfish', 'mean'.

basement [mid 18th century] It is likely that this word comes from archaic Dutch *basement* 'foundation', perhaps from Italian *basamento* 'base of a column'.

bash [mid 17th century] *Bash* was first used as a verb. It is imitative of the sound made by the action itself and in this way akin to other onomatopoeic words such as *bang*; it is perhaps a blend of *bang* and *smash*. As a slang word a *bash* is a 'party', a 20th-century usage.

basilica [mid 16th century] *Basilica* is a Latin word, literally 'royal palace', based on Greek *basileus* 'king'. This Greek root has also given rise to: the aromatic herb **basil**, literally 'royal' perhaps because it was used as royal medicine or as a royal unguent; and **basilisk** which has come via Latin from Greek *basiliskos* with the senses 'little king', 'serpent' (specifying a type distinguished by a crown-like spot), and a 'wren' (with a gold crown-like crest). In English a *basilisk* may be either a mythical reptile hatched by a serpent from a cock's egg, or alternatively a zoological term for a bright green lizard of Central America.

basin [Middle English] Medieval Latin *bacinus* 'water container' is the base of Old French *bacin*, from which *basin* in English is derived. The root is perhaps Gaulish. The Old French diminutive *bacinet* 'little basin' gave rise, because of its shape, to the military term **basinet** once worn as a close-fitting steel helmet; this was first recorded in Middle English. Comparable, though in a very different context, is **bassinet**, adopted from French in the mid 19th century; this is a diminutive of *bassin* 'basin' and captures the shape of a child's wicker cradle.

bask [late Middle English] *Bask* now suggests lying and relaxing in warmth and light, but originally it meant 'bathe' usually specifically in warm water or warm liquid: there is perhaps a relationship with Old Norse *batha* 'bathe'.

bass¹ [late Middle English] This musical term is an alteration of the adjective *base*. It has kept the pronunciation of the source word but was influenced in spelling by the Italian musical term *basso* 'bass voice'; the literal and first recorded sense is 'low'. This Italian root has given rise to other musical terms such as **bassoon**.
→ BASE²

bass² [late Middle English] *Bass*, the name of the common perch or various spiny-finned freshwater and marine fishes similar to the perch (e.g. *sea bass*, *black bass*, etc.), is an alteration of the English dialect word *barse*. Of Germanic origin, it is related to Dutch *baars* and German *Barsch*.

bastard [Middle English] Coming into English via Old French from medieval Latin *bastardus*, the word *bastard* is semantically colourful: it is perhaps from *bastum* 'packsaddle' and comparable to Old French *fils de bast*, literally 'packsaddle son' describing the offspring of an amorous itinerant mule driver, stopping to use a packsaddle for a pillow but gone again by sunrise.

bat¹ [late Old English] The Old English spelling of this 'implement used for striking' was *batt* 'club, stick, staff' and is perhaps, partly, from Old French *batte*, from *battre* 'to strike'. This same Old French verb, from Latin *battuere* 'to beat', is also the base of the English verb **batter** 'strike repeatedly' and the **batter** for making pancakes (from Old French *bateure* 'the action of beating').
→ BATTLE

bat² [late 16th century] The nocturnal mammal known as a *bat* (a spelling found from around 1575) may have got its name by association with medieval Latin *batta, blacta* 'insect that shuns the light', leading to an alteration of the earlier Middle English spelling *bakke* from a Scandinavian source: in Scots and northern English, *backie-bird* still exists. The plural **bats** is used colloquially to describe someone whose sanity is in question; this use arose in the early 20th century from the phrase *have bats in the belfry*; **batty** 'crazy' dates from the same period.

bat³ [late 19th century] The *bat* of *bat one's eyelashes* was originally a US word: the source is dialect *bat* 'to wink, blink', a variant of obsolete *bate* meaning 'to flutter'.

batch [late 15th century] The early senses of *batch* described 'the process of baking' and 'a quantity produced at one baking'. An Old English word related to *bacan* 'bake' is the source. Current senses such as 'a group' and 'a quantity produced at one time' date from the early 18th century.
→ BAKE

bathos [mid 17th century] This is a Greek word and was first recorded in English in the Greek sense 'depth'. The current application of *bathos* in literary works is to describe an anticlimax created by a ludicrous switch in mood from the sublime to the trivial: introduced by Alexander Pope in the early 18th century. He published the *Bathos* in the *Miscellanies* (third volume) in 1728, which was a lively satire giving descriptions of bad authors, identified by initials.

batman [mid 18th century] Initially a *batman* was an orderly in charge of a *bat horse* 'packhorse' which carried the officer's baggage; now he is an officer's personal assistant. Old French

bat is the source of the first element, from medieval Latin *bastum* 'packsaddle'. The parallel feminine word **batwoman** came into use during the Second World War.
→ BASTARD

battery [Middle English] The original *battery* referred to 'metal articles wrought by hammering' (a sense arising from Old French *baterie*, from *battre* 'to strike', from Latin *battuere*). Later a notion of 'set' became predominant and the word came to describe 'a number of pieces of artillery used together (for 'beating' the enemy)' and in the mid 18th century 'a number of Leyden jars' (= early electrical capacitors) connected up so as to discharge simultaneously', which gave the current use of *battery* as a source of electrical power. The general meaning 'set' dates from the late 19th century. The phrase **batterie de cuisine** which is used in culinary contexts in English is a 'set of equipment for the kitchen', a sense which derives from the earlier military use.

battle [Middle English] The noun *battle* is from Old French *bataille*, based on late Latin *battualia* describing 'military or gladiatorial exercises', from Latin *battuere* 'to beat'. **Battalion**, recorded from the late 16th century, is from French *bataillon* (from Italian *battaglione* from *battaglia* 'battle', from the Latin base).

battlement [late Middle English] The type of parapet described as a *battlement* is from Old French *bataillier* which meant 'fortify with movable defence turrets'; there is a possible relationship with *battle*.

battleship [late 18th century] This is a shortening of *line-of-battle ship*, originally the largest type of wooden warship.

bauble [Middle English] *Baubles* are associated with the decoration of Christmas trees but in former times, there was an association with jesters who used a *bauble* (a baton topped with a carved head with asses' ears) as their mock emblem of office. Cromwell referred to this mock emblem as he saw it, at the dismissal of the Rump Parliament on 20 April 1653, when he said Take away that fool's bauble, the mace. The direct source of the word is Old French *baubel* 'child's toy', hence 'something which would please a child' such as a brightly coloured ornament; further details of the origin are unknown.

baulk [late Old English] The verb *baulk* (US variant *balk*) is used with a sense of 'refusal' in phrases such as *baulk at an idea*, *baulk at doing something*. This notion developed, together with the verb senses 'hesitate' and 'hinder' in late Middle English, through a use of the noun as 'obstacle'. The early spelling of the noun was *balc*, from an Old Norse word for 'partition'. The first English usage was 'unploughed ridge', later 'land left unploughed by mistake', which was then extended to 'blunder', 'omission'. An archaic use which illustrates this strand of meaning is *baulk a chance* (i.e.'miss a chance').

bawdy [early 16th century] *Bawdy* has gained its sexual overtones, in phrases such as *bawdy jokes* and *bawdy house*, from **bawd** 'a woman in charge of a brothel', a late Middle English word shortened from the now obsolete *bawdstrot*, from Old French *baudestroyt* 'procuress' (from *baude* 'shameless').

bawl [late Middle English] Early use referred to the sound made by an animal ('howl, bark'). *Bawl* is imitative and is possibly related to medieval Latin *baulare* 'to bark' or to Icelandic *baula* 'to low'.

bay¹ [late Middle English] Often found in place names (*Bay of Biscay*, *Cardigan Bay*), this geographical term is from Old French *baie*, from Old Spanish *bahia*, but earlier details of the origin are unknown. The sense associations are 'recess' and 'projection'.

bay² [late Middle English] The *bay* of **bay tree**, **bay laurel** originally denoted the laurel berry and came via Old French *baie* from Latin *baca* 'berry'.

bay³ [late Middle English] Any recess known as a *bay* such as *bay window*, *loading bay* derives its sense from Old French *baie*, from the verb *baer* 'to gape' (from medieval Latin *batare*). The ultimate origin is not known.

bay⁴ [Middle English] A brown horse with black points, referred to as a *bay* derives its name from the Old French *bai* 'bay-coloured', from Latin *badius*, which Varro mentions in a list of colour adjectives appropriate to horses.

bay⁵ [Middle English] The word was first recorded as a noun describing the howling of hounds in pursuit of a quarry. It is imitative and comes from Old French *(a)bai* 'barking', *(a)batier* 'to bark'. The verb *bay* 'bark' was influenced in later use by the phrase *at bay* describing the position of the hunted animal when unable to flee further, and the reaction of the hounds.

bayonet [late 17th century] A *bayonet* first described a kind of short dagger. The origin is a French word based on *Bayonne*, a town in SW France where these daggers were first made.

bazaar [late 16th century] A Persian word for 'market' is the ultimate source of *bazaar* which came into English from Italian *bazarro* from

Turkish; it first described an oriental marketplace with a range of shops and stalls.

be [Old English] Old English *bēon* was an irregular and defective verb whose full conjugation derives from several originally distinct verbs from different Indo-European roots: *am* and *is* come from a root shared by Latin *sum* and *est*; *was* and *were* are from a root meaning 'remain'; but *be* and *been* are from a root shared by Latin *fui* 'I was', *fio* 'I become' and Greek *phuein* 'bring forth, cause to grow'. The origin of the form *are* is uncertain.

WORDBUILDING

The prefix **be-** [Old English, weak form of *bī* 'by'] adds the sense

■ **all over** [bespatter]
■ **thoroughly** [bewilder]
■ **covered with** [bejewelled]

The prefix **be-** makes

■ **verbs transitive** [bemoan (from moan)]
■ **verbs from adjectives and nouns** [befool, befriend]

---

beach [mid 16th century] *Beach* was first used to refer to shingle on the seashore. It is perhaps related to Old English *bece* 'brook'; this is an element that survives in place names like Wis*bech* and Sand*bach* and assumes the existence of an intermediate sense 'pebbly river valley'.

beacon [Old English] From a West Germanic root, Old English *bēacn* was 'a sign', 'a portent'. In Middle English, a *beacon* was a signal fire on a pole, a hill, or other high place. Senses showed connections with height (*Brecon Beacons*), light (such as a lighthouse), or warning (e.g. radio transmitter).
→ BECKON

bead [Old English] The spellings of *bead* in Old English were *gebed* and *bedu* 'prayer'; related Germanic forms are Dutch *bede* and German *Gebet* which have the same sense. Current meanings of *bead* derive from the use of a rosary, each bead representing a prayer; this connection is seen too in Middle English **beadsman** 'a person who prays for the souls of others'.
→ BID

beadle [Old English] Old English *bydel* was 'a person making a proclamation', a word gradually superseded in Middle English by forms from Old French *bedel*, ultimately of Germanic origin and related to German *Büttel* 'bailiff, beadle'. The spelling *bedel* survives in English as a University executive officer with processional duties as a mace-bearer; a *beadle* is now usually

a church or college officer. An obsolete English synonym of *beadle* is *bumble*, from the name of the beadle, a particularly pompous town official, in Dickens's *Oliver Twist*.
→ BID

beagle [late 15th century] This type of small hound perhaps derives its name from the Old French word *beegueule* 'open-mouthed', from *beer* 'open wide' and *gueule* 'throat'.

beak [Middle English] The *beak* of *bird's beak* is from Old French *bec*, from Latin *beccus*, with a Celtic origin. The colloquial reference to a judge as a *beak* is not recorded until the late 18th century and is probably from criminals' slang. There are also examples of the word used as part of schoolboys' slang meaning 'schoolmaster' (J. Betjeman *Summoned by Bells*: Comparing bruises, other boys could show Far worse ones that the beaks and prefects made.).

beaker [Middle English] A *beaker* was originally 'a large drinking container', from the Old Norse word *bikarr*, perhaps based on Greek *bikos* 'drinking bowl'. The *Beaker folk* is a phrase used in archaeology to refer to a people associated with the making of pottery drinking vessels without a handle, characteristic of the early Bronze Age in western Europe.

beam [Old English] An early sense of *beam* was 'tree' which is illustrated in **hornbeam**, a member of the birch family. The word is of West Germanic origin and related to Dutch *boom* and German *Baum*, both of which also mean 'tree'.

bean [Old English] The vegetable *bean* is Germanic in origin and related to Dutch *boon* and German *Bohne*. **Beanfeast**, now sometimes abbreviated to **beano** (originally printers' slang) and used in the context of a happy celebratory event, was recorded in the early 19th century; it was an annual dinner given to employees by their employers, where beans and bacon formed an indispensable part of the menu. A colloquial use of *bean* to mean 'head' started in the US in the early 20th century; this, in the 1940s, seems to have given rise to **beanie**, a type of close-fitting hat worn on the back of the head. The word *beanie* is also part of the US proprietary name **Beanie Baby**, a soft toy animal stuffed with plastic beans, popularly collected. In a different context in the 1970s the compound **bean-counter** arose in the US for an accountant; negative associations developed and it tends to be used now of anyone excessively concerned with figures, e.g. (*Chicago Tribune*, 22 December 1992): Bill Clinton ... angrily derided as 'bean counters' leaders of national women's groups who complained that he has nominated too few women to his administration.

bear¹ [Old English] This word for 'carry' was *beran* in Old English and is of Germanic origin. It shares an Indo-European root with Sanskrit *bharati*, Greek *pherein*, and Latin *ferre* 'carry'.

bear² [Old English] *Bear* as the name of an animal was *bera* in Old English and is of West Germanic origin. Close relations are Dutch *beer* and German *Bär*. The phrase **bear garden** is recorded from the late 16th century and was originally 'a place set apart for bear-baiting'; bear gardens were often used for other rough sports, hence the figurative meaning 'scene of uproar'.

beard [Old English] *Beard* is West Germanic in origin and related to Dutch *baard* and German *Bart*.
→ BARB¹

beast [Middle English] Latin *bestia* is the base of a family of words: *beast* is from Old French *beste*; **bestial** (late Middle English) has come via Old French from late Latin *bestialis*: there was an earlier noun used as a collective term for domestic animals which remained in Scots as a legal and technical term in farming contexts; **bestiality** (late Middle English) is from Old French *bestialite*. In the 1980s *beast* started to be recorded as prison slang for a sex offender.

beat [Old English] The Old English word was *bēatan*, of Germanic origin; its sense of 'striking' became extended to 'overcoming', 'conquering'. The idiom *beat about the bush* alludes to preparations made to flush out game birds; the notion of preparation gave a sense of 'tentative preliminaries'.

beatitude [late Middle English] The *Beatitudes* are the blessings listed in the Sermon on the Mount (Matthew 5: 3–11): the Latin word *beātus* 'blessed' is the root of *beatitude* and other words in the family such as **beatification** first recorded (early 16th century) in the sense 'action of making blessed', **beatify** (mid 16th century) first used in the sense 'make blessed or supremely happy', and **beatific** (mid 17th century).

beatnik [1950s] This has *beat* (from *beat generation*) as its main element with the suffix *-nik* added on the pattern of *sputnik*, perhaps influenced by the US use of the Yiddish ending *-nik*, denoting someone or something who acts in a particular way. The *beat generation* referred in the 1950s and early 1960s to young people who valued self-expression and had a musical preference for modern jazz.
→ BEAT

beauty [Middle English] *Beauty* is based on Latin *bellus* 'beautiful', 'fine' and has come into English from Old French *beaute*.

beaver [Old English] Old English *beofor*, *befor* as names for this semi-aquatic rodent are from Germanic forms, related to Dutch *bever* and German *Biber*. An Indo-European root meaning 'brown' is the semantic base. The verb *beaver away* owes its sense to the hard work associated with the animal.

because [Middle English] The origin of *because* is the phrase *by cause*, influenced by Old French *par cause de* 'by reason of'. In early use it was often followed by 'that' or 'why' and a subordinate clause, as in Chaucer's *Franklin's Tale*: By cause that he was hire Neighebour.

beck¹ [Middle English] Used as the common word for 'a brook' in northern areas of England once occupied by the Danes and Norwegians, *beck* often refers in literature to a brook with a stony bed or following a rugged course, typical of such areas. The word comes from Old Norse *bekkr* and is of Germanic origin; related forms are Dutch *beek* and German *Bach*.

beck² [Middle English] The *beck* of *beck and call* is from an archaic abbreviated form of *beckon*.

beckon [Old English] *Beckon* is West Germanic in origin. It has a connection with *beacon* through the notion of 'mute signal' which in *beckon* is a signal to approach.
→ BEACON

become [Old English] From a Germanic root, Old English *becuman* meant 'come to a place'. Dutch *bekomen* and German *bekommen* 'get, receive' are related.
→ COME

bed [Old English] Dutch *bed* and German *Bett* are related to English *bed* (of Germanic origin) for 'a place to lie down and sleep' and 'a place to nurture young plants'. A root sense of 'dig' (leading to 'dug-out place') has been suggested but this primitive notion did not remain in Germanic.

bedlam [late Middle English] *Bedlam* was an early form of *Bethlehem*, referring to the hospital of St Mary of Bethlehem in London, used as an asylum for the insane. It was later used as a general name for any similar asylum and then, in the mid 17th century, to describe any scene of confusion and chaos.

bee [Old English] Old English *bēo*, of Germanic origin, is related to Dutch *bij* and German dialect *Beie*. The industry of the *bee* has resulted in expressions such as *a sewing bee* where a group meets for communal work. **Beeline** is recorded from the early 19th century in *make a* *beeline for something*, with reference to the straight line supposedly taken instinctively by a bee when returning to the hive. The expression *the bee's knees* referred originally to something small and insignificant but US slang use reversed this sense to one of size and importance.

beech [Old English] Old English *bēce* is of Germanic origin and related to Latin *fāgus* 'beech', Greek *phagos* 'oak with edible fruit'. *Fagus* is the genus which includes the common beech.

beef [Middle English] Old French *boef*, from Latin *bōs*, *bov-* 'ox' has given *beef* in English.

beefeater [early 17th century] This popular word for a Yeoman of the Guard was originally derogatory and referred to a well-fed servant. The current sense dates from the late 17th century. The form *beaufet* has been cited as a phonetic link between *buffet* and *beefeater* but it is merely an 18th-century bad spelling.

beer [Old English] West Germanic in origin, *beer* is based on monastic Latin *biber* 'a drink', from Latin *bibere* 'to drink'. Close relations are Dutch *bier* and German *Bier*. **Beer money** as an expression dates from the early 19th century when an allowance of money was made to servants instead of an allocation of beer.

beetle[1] [Old English] *Beetle* as an insect (in Old English *bitula*, *bitela*) means, in essence, 'biter', from the base of *bītan* 'to bite'. The verb in the sense 'hurry' arises from an association with the scurrying of the insect: e.g. (in Noël Coward's *Relative Values*: There was … a terrible scene … and Freda beetled off to America.).

beetle[2] [Old English] *Beetle* as a type of hammer is Germanic in origin and related to *beat*.
→ BEAT

beetle[3] [mid 16th century] This as an adjective is a back-formation from *beetle-browed* 'having bushy eyebrows'. This was used to criticise someone's appearance. In Middle English *brow* was always an eyebrow and not the forehead; it has been suggested that the comparison is with the tufted antennae of certain beetles, which may have been called eyebrows in both English and French. The verb *beetle* which means 'overhang' (e.g. *great beetling brows*), was apparently used as a nonce-word (= coined for one occasion) by Shakespeare and was later adopted by other writers.

befall [Old English] Old English *befeallan* 'to fall' was even in early use chiefly figurative while *feallan* was literal; it is related to German *befallen*.
→ FALL

before [Old English] Old English *beforan*, literally 'by in front' is of Germanic origin and related to German *bevor*. **Beforehand** was originally two words in Middle English and was probably influenced by Old French *avant main* of which it is a direct translation.

beg [Middle English] *Beg* is probably from Old English *bedecian*, of Germanic origin; the noun **beggar**, which comes from the verb, dates from the same period.

begin [Old English] Old English *beginnan* is Germanic in origin, related to Dutch and German *beginnen*. The root sense is probably 'open up' from which the semantic transition to 'begin' is common.

beguile [Middle English] *Beguile* started out with the sense 'deceive, deprive of by fraud'; the elements which compose the word are *be-* 'thoroughly' and the obsolete verb *guile* 'to deceive'.
→ GUILE

behalf [Middle English] Occurring in the phrases *on behalf of* and *on his/her, etc. behalf*, this word is formed from a mixture of the earlier phrases *on his halve* and *bihalve him*, both meaning 'on his side'.

behave [late Middle English] *Behave* is from *be-* 'thoroughly' and *have* in the sense 'have or bear (oneself) in a particular way'; this corresponds to modern German *sich behaben*. **Behaviour**, dating from the same period, is from *behave* following the pattern of *demeanour* and influenced by the obsolete noun *haviour* 'having'.
→ HAVE

behind [Old English] Old English *bihindan* is from *bi* 'by' and *hindan* 'from behind'. **Behindhand** (mid 16th century) was formed on the pattern of *beforehand*.

behold [Old English] Old English *bihaldan* is from *bi-* 'thoroughly' and *haldan* 'to hold'. Parallel Germanic words have the sense 'maintain, retain'; the notion of 'looking' is found only in English. **Beholden** dating from late Middle English is the archaic past participle of *behold*, but the senses 'obliged to (a person)', 'duty bound' are not actually found in other parts of the verb.

beige [mid 19th century] The colour associated with *beige* is due to the word's early use to denote a woollen fabric which was usually undyed and unbleached. The immediate source is French, but earlier details are unknown.

belated [early 17th century] *Belated* started out with the meaning 'overtaken by darkness' (Milton *Paradise Lost*: Faerie Elves Whose midnight

Revels ... some belated Peasant sees); the form is the past participle of obsolete *belate* 'to delay'.

belch [Old English] *Belch*, in Old English *belcettan*, is probably imitative of the noise produced.

beleaguer [late 16th century] From Dutch *belegeren* 'camp round', from *be-* '(all) about' and *leger* 'a camp', *beleaguer* is literally 'surround with troops'. The notions of 'hostility' and 'annoyance' are reflected in transferred uses (*Guardian* 30 May 1992: It was the Tories, though initially beleaguered by the new spirit, who learnt how to master it in its macro-societal form).

belfry [Middle English] The early spelling was *berfrey*, from Old French *berfrei*, later *belfrei*, of West Germanic origin. The change in the first syllable was due to association with *bell*. Initially *belfry* had nothing to do with bells, but rather with shelter as it was a moveable tower used when besieging an emplacement. The sense shifted to 'tower for protecting watchmen', then to 'watchtower', 'beacon tower', 'bell tower' and eventually 'place where a bell is hung'.
→ BELL[1]

belie [Old English] Old English *beléogan* meant 'deceive by lying', from *be-* 'about' and *léogan* 'to lie'. The current senses 'fail to give a true impression of' and 'fail to fulfil (a claim)' date from the 17th century.

believe [late Old English] The Old English forms *belýfan*, *beléfan* are by alteration of *geléfan*, of Germanic origin: Dutch *geloven* and German *glauben* are related. Compare with Middle English **belief**, an alteration of Old English *geléafa*.

bell¹ [Old English] *Bell* has Germanic roots and is related to Dutch *bel*, and perhaps to the *bell* of a stag. Many interesting idioms are associated with *bell*: e.g. *bell the cat* ('take danger upon oneself'), an allusion to a fable in which the mice suggest hanging a bell around the cat's neck to have warning of its approach; *be saved by the bell* ('escape a situation'), with reference to the bell marking the end of a boxing round or contest; also *bells and whistles* ('attractive extras'), an allusion to the bells and whistles of old fairground organs.

bell² [Old English] *Bell* as the cry of a stag at rutting time was *bellan* in Old English, which meant 'to bellow'; German *bellen* 'to bark, bray' is related.
→ BELL[1]

belligerent [late 16th century] *Belligerent* 'showing hostility' is from Latin *belligerant-* 'waging war', from the verb *belligerare*, from *bellum* 'war', a form which had already given

rise to **bellicose** (from Latin *bellicosus*, from *bellicus* 'warlike') in late Middle English.

bellow Middle English The verb *bellow* meaning 'shout out' is of uncertain etymology but is perhaps from late Old English *bylgan*.

bellows [Middle English] *Bellows* used for blowing air into a fire, is probably from Old English *belga*, plural of *belig* 'bag' (now **belly**), a shortened form of the earlier *blæstbelig* 'blowing-bag'. The semantic base is 'swell, be inflated'.

belong [Middle English] This verb started out in the sense 'be assigned to in an appropriate way'; the form is composed of the intensifier *be-* (used to give emphasis) and the archaic verb *long* 'to belong', based on Old English *gelang* 'at hand', 'together with', thus with notions of 'proximity' and 'unity'.

beloved [late Middle English] *Beloved* is the past participle of the obsolete verb *belove* 'be pleased with', 'be pleasing', which later came to mean 'love'.

below [late Middle English] *Below* (from *be-* 'by' and the adjective *low*) was not common until the 16th century when the word developed a prepositional use and was frequent in Shakespeare (*Measure for Measure*: At the consecrated Fount, a League below the Citie).

belt [Old English] *Belt* is Germanic in origin, from Latin *balteus* 'girdle'. The phrase *belt up* is RAF slang from the 1930s, and *belt along* 'race along at great speed' is dialect and part of US usage dating from the 1890s.

belvedere [late 16th century] The name of this raised turret for viewing the surroundings encapsulates its purpose as the literal meaning of *belvedere* is 'fair sight', from Italian *bel* 'beautiful' and *vedere* 'to see'. The pronunciation is probably a result of the early adoption of the word into French.

bemoan [Old English] The spelling in Old English was *bemænan* 'complain, lament'. The change in the second syllable during the 16th century was due to association with *moan*, to which it is related.

bench [Old English] Old English *benc* is of Germanic origin, related to Dutch *bank* and German *Bank*. The early word described a long seat without a back. It entered legal contexts as the *bench* where judges sat, and was later transferred to the office of judge itself as in *be raised to the bench*.
→ BANK[1]

bend [Old English] In Old English *bendan* (of Germanic origin) was 'put in bonds' or 'make a bow taut by means of a string'. The verb was

also used in the phrase *bend up* leading to an association with the curved shape of the bow.
→ BAND¹

beneath [Old English] The Old English forms *binithan*, *bineothan* (of Germanic origin) literally meant 'by below'; compare with *before*.
→ NETHER

benefit [late Middle English] A *benefit* was originally a kind deed or something well done; the word comes from Old French *bienfet*, from Latin *benefactum* 'good deed' (from Latin *bene facere* 'do good (to)'). Other words based on these same Latin elements are: **benifice** (Middle English) which came via Old French from Latin *beneficium* 'favour, support'; **beneficial** (late Middle English) from late Latin *beneficialis*, from *beneficium*; **beneficent** (early 17th century) from Latin *beneficent-* (stem of *beneficentior*, comparative of *beneficus* 'favourable, generous'); **beneficiary** (early 17th century) from Latin *beneficiarius*, from *beneficium* 'support'.

benevolent [late Middle English] The source is Old French *benivolent*, from Latin *bene volent-* 'well wishing', whose sense comes from *bene* 'well' and *velle* 'to wish'.

benign [Middle English] *Benign* with its gentle associations is from Old French *benigne*, from Latin *benignus*, probably from *bene* 'well' and *-genus* '-born'.
→ GENTLE

benumb [late 15th century] A sense of 'taking away' is captured by Middle English *benumb* which comes from obsolete *benome*, the past participle of *benim* 'to deprive' (made up of the prefix *be-* expressing removal, and Old English *niman* 'take').

bequeath [Old English] The Old English form *becwethan* is composed of *be-* 'about' (a prefix expressing transitivity) and *cwethan* 'say'; the Middle English noun **bequest** (from *be-* 'about' and Old English *cwis* 'speech') was influenced by *bequeath*.
→ QUOTH

berate [mid 16th century] *Berate* is from *be-* 'thoroughly' and the late Middle English verb *rate* 'to scold'.

bereave [Old English] The original sense of Old English *berēafian* was 'deprive of' in general. **Bereft** ('lacking') recorded from the late 16th century is the archaic past participle of *bereave*.

beret [early 19th century] The English word has been adopted from French *béret* 'Basque cap', from Old Provençal *berret*, based on late Latin *birrus* 'hooded cape'. Also from Latin *birrus*

is *biretta*, a type of hat worn by Roman Catholic clergymen.

berry [Old English] Old English *berie* is of Germanic origin, related to Dutch *bes* and German *Beere*. The early history of the word is uncertain but conjectures have included reference to both a root meaning 'bare' (as in 'uncovered fruit') and the Sanskrit form *bhas-* 'to eat'.

berserk [early 19th century] Originally a noun denoting a wild Norse warrior who fought in a frenzied state, *berserk* is from the Old Norse noun *berserkr*, probably from *birn-*, *bjorn* 'bear' and *serkr* 'coat'; however another possible source is *berr* 'bare' (i.e. without armour).

berth [early 17th century] *Berth* started out in the sense 'adequate sea room', probably from a nautical use of the verb *bear*, thus giving 'room made by bearing off' (bear off = push away). In modern usage the common figurative expression is *give a wide berth to something* meaning 'avoid'.

beseech [Middle English] Old English *sēcan* 'seek', 'try to get' is the main element of this verb prefixed by the intensifier *be-* (used to give emphasis). Whereas in *seek* a northern form has been generalized, it is southern *seech* which has become standard in the compound *beseech*.
→ SEEK

beside [Old English] Old English *be sīdan* meant 'by the side' and was written as two words. By 1200 it was in use as an adverb and preposition. The sense 'besides, in addition' is often evidenced as in Oliver Goldsmith's *Vicar of Wakefield*: We can readily marry her to another and what is more, she may keep her lover beside.

besiege [Middle English] 'Sit down in front of' is the primary sense of *besiege*, which owes its prefix to an alteration of the earlier word *assiege* (from Old French *asegier*). Latin *sedium* 'a sitting' is the root form. The literal sense has lent itself to vivid figurative use, e.g. Pope *Epistle of Horace*: Fools with Compliments besiege ye.

besotted [late 16th century] This is the past participle of *besot* 'make foolishly affectionate', from *be-* 'cause to be' and the obsolete word *sot* 'foolish'.

best [Old English] The Old English forms *betest* (adjective), *betost*, *betst* (adverbs) are of Germanic origin, related to Dutch and German *best*. As in all the modern Germanic languages, the *t* before the *s* has been reduced.
→ BETTER

bestow [Middle English] *Bestow* as in *bestow a gift on somebody* was first used in the senses 'place' and 'apply'. It is made up of be- (used to give emphasis) and Old English *stōw* 'a place'.

bet [late 16th century] *Bet* is perhaps a shortening of the obsolete noun *abet* 'abetment', meaning encouragement to do something. The origin is not clear, nor is it known whether the noun or the verb appeared first.

betray [Middle English] *Betray* is from be- 'thoroughly' and the obsolete verb *tray* 'betray', from Old French *trair*. The Latin base verb is *tradere* meaning 'hand over'.

betroth [Middle English] *Truth* is one of the elements of *betroth* (in Middle English *betreuthe*). The change in the second syllable was due to association with *troth*, also a word for 'truth', later coming to mean 'faith'.

better [Old English] The Old English spelling was *betera*, of Germanic origin; related to Dutch *beter* and German *besser*.
→ BEST

between [Old English] The first element *be-* of Old English *betwēonum* is literally 'by'; the second is a Germanic word related to *two*. The same is true of *betwēox* (**betwixt**) which dates from the same period.

bevel [late 16th century] *Bevel* 'a slope', 'make sloping', used in carpentry and stonework contexts, is first recorded as an adjective in the sense 'oblique'. An Old French diminutive of *baif* 'open-mouthed' (from *baer* 'to gape') is the source.
→ BAY[5]

beverage [Middle English] The Latin verb *bibere* 'to drink' is the base of English *beverage*. Normally it is a general word for any drink but in Devonshire it may also mean 'small (= weak) cider'. The direct source is Old French *bevrage*. The abbreviation **bevvy** came into use in the late 19th century. Another word that has possibly been shortened from *beverage* is US **Bevo** which has the sense 'inferior' from its early proprietary name for a brand of non-alcoholic cereal-based drink produced during the Prohibition era.

beware [Middle English] This is from the phrase *be ware* literally 'be aware'; *ware* was common until 1500, especially in the warning *ware thee!* There was also in Old English the word *wǣr* meaning 'cautious' common in *to be ware* 'to be on one's guard' whose imperative amounted to *ware thee*: this resulted in the involved development of *beware*. The way the phrase was used made its treatment as a single word logical and as early as 1300 it is found written as such. Phrases before 1500 included: *beware thee, be ware to thee, beware thyself, ware to thee, to be ware, to ware oneself*.

bewilder [late 17th century] The literal sense is '(make to) go thoroughly astray'; the components are *be-* 'thoroughly' and the obsolete verb *wilder* 'lead, go astray', whose origin is unknown, although it is likely that it was extracted from *wilderness* by analogy with *wander*.

beyond [Old English] The early spelling *begeondan* is made up of *be* 'by' and *geondan*, a word of Germanic origin related to *yon* and *yonder*.

bias [mid 16th century] *Bias* is now seen in people's views and opinions but the early sense was 'oblique line' and, as an adjective, 'oblique'. It became common in technical contexts particularly in the game of bowls. *Bias* comes from French *biais* from Provençal, and is perhaps based on Greek *epikarsios* 'oblique'. The speculation that it comes from Latin *bifax* 'looking both ways' is not tenable phonetically.

bib [late 16th century] The *bib* of *baby's bib* probably comes from archaic *bib* 'to drink (something alcoholic)': the likely source is Latin *bibere* 'to drink', although it may have originated independently imitating repeated lip movements. The verbal *bib* is found in combinations such as *wine-bibber*.
→ IMBIBE

Bible [Middle English] *Bible* has come via Old French from ecclesiastical Latin *biblia*, from Greek (*ta*) *biblia* '(the) books', plural of *biblion*: this was originally a diminutive of *biblos* 'papyrus, scroll', of Semitic origin.

biceps [mid 17th century] This Latin word is literally *two-headed*, from *bi-* 'two' and *-ceps* (from *caput* 'head'). Examples of *bicep* have been found since the 1970s, which reflects an interpretation of *biceps* as a plural.

bicycle [mid 19th century] The *velocipede* (literally 'rapid foot') was the early form of *bicycle*, formed from *bi-* 'two' and Greek *kuklos* 'wheel'. The abbreviation **bike** was not long to follow, in the late 19th century. A **tricycle** as a name for a 3-wheeled coach drawn by two horses, once a form of transport in Paris, dates from the 1820s, with the abbreviation **trike** appearing in the 1880s. As for **unicycle**, this was first recorded as a US word in the 1860s in connection with gymnastic displays.

bid [Old English] The early verb was *bēodan* 'to offer, command', of Germanic origin; Dutch *bieden* and German *bieten* are related. The *bid* associated with requesting, greeting, and inviting someone to do something, was *biddan* 'ask' in Old English, of Germanic origin; a relative is German *bitten* 'ask'.

biddy [early 17th century] Old biddy is derogatory and suggests an interfering or annoying elderly woman, but a biddy was originally 'a chicken'; the origin is unknown. The word was probably influenced by the use of biddy in the US for an Irish maidservant, which arose from the pet form of Bridget; this was extended as a general derogatory word for a 'woman' in slang use: (C. P. Snow Affair: I believe she's the bloodiest awful specimen of a party biddy).

bier [Old English] Bier 'a movable frame for carrying a coffin' is Germanic in origin; the Old English form was bēr, related to German Bahre. The modern English spelling dates from 1600 and seems to be due to the influence of French bière.
→ BARROW¹; BEAR¹

big [Middle English] The early sense was 'strong', 'mighty' and was used by writers in Northumbria and north Lincolnshire at the end of the 13th century; the origin is perhaps therefore Norse but the derivation is unknown. The word soon developed a notion of 'vehement, forceful' which persisted in dialect. The association with size followed, which led to the semantic feature of 'grown tall, grown large' reflected in uses from the mid 16th century. An added sense of 'older' is seen in combinations such as big brother from the mid 19th century; however the expression Big Brother is watching you is a specific reference to the name of the head of state in Orwell's novel Nineteen Eighty-four written in 1949. The reference in this instance is to a ruthlessly powerful state authority.

bigamy [Middle English] Old French bigamie is the source of bigamy: it is based on the adjective bigame 'bigamous', from late Latin bigamus, from bi- 'twice' and Greek -gamos 'married'.

big cheese [1920s] The second element cheese has probably come via Urdu from Persian čīz 'thing': the phrase the cheese was used earlier to mean 'first-rate', i.e. the thing.

bigot [late 16th century] A bigot first denoted a superstitious religious hypocrite; the immediate source is French but further than that is not known. The noun **bigotry** arose in the late 17th century; based on bigot it was reinforced by French bigoterie.

bigwig [early 18th century] This word has come about because of the large wigs formerly worn by socially important men.
→ WIG

bikini [1940s] This swimwear owes its name to Bikini Atoll where an atom bomb was exploded in 1946. The name seemed appropriate to the supposed 'explosive' effect that the garment had when it became a fashion item. The association between the first syllable of the placename and the prefix bi- 'two' led to the coinage of **monokini** in the 1960s when the bottom half of the bikini was the 'one' item worn.

bill¹ [Middle English] The bill associated with a written list or catalogue of items comes from Anglo-Norman French bille, probably based on medieval Latin bulla 'seal, sealed document'.
→ BULL²

bill² [Old English] The Old English noun was bile 'a beak' but the origin is unknown. In the early 17th century bill and coo arose as an expression for lovers showing affectionate behaviour to each other; this came about by association with doves billing, i.e. gently stroking their bills together. The original Middle English meaning of the verb bill was 'peck'.

bill³ [Old English] German Bille 'axe' is related to this West Germanic word for a weapon in the shape of a hook. It was mentioned in Old English poetry as a kind of broadsword. The **billhook** used for pruning trees illustrates a compound of bill.

billet¹ [late Middle English] A billet (from Anglo-Norman French billette, a diminutive of bille) was once a short written document; in the mid 17th century, it came to be a 'written order requiring a householder to lodge the bearer of the billet'; this was usually a soldier, hence the current meaning 'temporary lodging for a soldier' which is part of military vocabulary. The verb use dates from the late 16th century.
→ BILL¹

billet² [late Middle English]
→ BILLIARD

billiard [late 16th century] The plural billiards was the early form but this quickly became used as a singular. French billard, a diminutive of bille 'tree trunk' is the source of this name for the cue used in the game (literally 'little tree trunk'); it was soon transferred to the game itself. This French diminutive also gave the architectural term billet in English, describing a short cylindrical insert introduced at intervals in a moulding; the immediate source is Old French billette and billot, based on medieval Latin billa, billus 'branch, trunk', probably from a Celtic root.

billow [mid 16th century] Old Norse bylgja has given billow 'great wave' in English. It was not known before 1550 but may have been part of dialect use before that. The sense is 'swelling up'.

bimbo [early 20th century] A bimbo was originally a contemptuous word for 'fellow, chap' and is derived from a masculine Italian form, whose literal meaning was 'little child'; the use was transferred to females in the late 1920s and came to describe 'an attractive woman perceived as unintelligent or frivolous'. In the 1980s **bimbette** entered the vocabulary to describe a young 'adolescent bimbo'.

bin [Old English] The original general meaning was 'receptacle'; more specifically it was also 'a manger in a stable' and 'a container for foodstuffs such as grain or bread'; **breadbin** is an example where the sense is specified. The Celtic root has also given Welsh *ben* 'cart'. The notion of 'container for rubbish' dates from the mid 19th century.

bind [Old English] Old English *bindan* has a Germanic origin; Dutch and German *binden* are related. These are from an Indo-European root shared by Sanskrit *bandh*. The vowel sound in *bind* was originally short, but this, in line with other words with *-nd*, became lengthened in midland and southern English. The word **bine** as in the plant name **woodbine** describes the flexible stem of climbing plants and is a dialect form of *bind*.
→ BOND

binnacle [late 15th century] The early spelling for this 'housing for a ship's compass' was *bittacle*, from Spanish *bitácula*, *bitácora* or Portuguese *bitacola*. Latin *habitāculum* 'dwelling place' is the base form, from *habitare* 'to inhabit'. The change in spelling to *binnacle* occurred in the mid 18th century.

birch [Old English] Old English forms were *bierce*, *birce*, from a Germanic root; German *Birke* is related. A northern spelling *birk* is found, providing a word pair comparable with *church* and *kirk*. The word is perhaps related to *bright*, the sense association being the white bark of the tree.

bird [Old English] The modern spelling is a metathesis (= transposition of letters) of Old English *brid* 'chick, fledgling'. The origin is not known and there is no corresponding form in any other Germanic language. *Fowl* was the older generic word (Chaucer *Canterbury Tales—General Prologue*: And smale foweles maken melodye That slepen al the nyght with open ye), but later this came to distinguish certain types of poultry. *Bird* was used to refer to 'a girl' as early as 1300 but the disparaging connotation did not become common until the 20th century. As for other uses, the idiom *give someone the bird* is theatre slang; at first the expression included the phrase *big bird* referring to geese and their hissing; this was the noise made to express criticism of a performance. In a completely different context, the golf term **birdie** (one stroke under par at a hole) came into use in the late 18th century as a diminutive, from a US slang use of *bird* for any first-rate thing.

biretta [late 16th century]
→ BERET

birth [Middle English] *Birth* is from Old Norse *byrth*. The early literal sense 'bringing forth offspring' lent itself readily to figurative use by Shakespeare as 'beginning', e.g. *Winter's Tale*: Not yet on summer's death, nor on the birth Of trembling winter.
→ BEAR¹

biscuit [Middle English] Originally biscuits were cooked in a twofold process: they were first baked and then dried out in a slow oven so that they would keep. Old French *bescuit* gave rise to the English word, based on Latin *bis* 'twice' and *coctus*, the past participle of *coquere* 'to cook'.

bishop [Old English] The meaning of Old English *biscop*, *bisceop* is literally 'overseer', from Greek *episkopos*, formed from *epi* 'above' and *-skopos* '-looking'. In **bishopric** (also found in Old English as *bisceoprice*), the final element *rice* means 'realm'.

bit¹ [Old English] The notion of 'small piece' has arisen from the early sense of Old English *bita* 'mouthful', of Germanic origin, related to German *Bissen*. There is a basic sense of 'biting' shared by **bit** used in equestrian contexts for part of a horse's bridle; this in Old English was *bite* related to Dutch *beet* and German *Biss*.
→ BITE

bit² [1940s] This unit of information in computing contexts is a blend of *binary* and *digit*.

bitch [Old English] Old English *bicce* has a Germanic source. There is a Scots form *bick*. Whether there is a relationship between the English word and French *biche* meaning both 'bitch' and 'fawn' is not known. The derogatory reference to a woman as a 'bitch' arose in late Middle English.

bite [Old English] Related to Dutch *bijten* and German *beissen*, Old English *bītan* is from Germanic. The semantic root is 'cleave', 'split'. The verb originally inflected like *write* and *bote* (now *bit*) is still found in Lancashire.

bitter [Old English] Dutch and German *bitter* share a Germanic origin with this word, which is probably from the root of the verb 'bite', with the original sense 'cutting, sharp'. The idiom *to the bitter end* may have a connection with this adjective, but another conjecture is that the *bitter* is a nautical reference. W. H. Smyth in his *Sailor's Word-book* of 1867 writes: When a chain or rope is paid out to the bitter-end, no more remains to be let go.
→ BITE

bivouac [early 18th century] 'A night watch by the whole army' was the original meaning of *bivouac*. The origin is French, probably from Swiss German *Bîwacht* 'additional guard at night', apparently referring to a citizens' patrol giving support to the ordinary town watch. The word is said to have been introduced into English during the Thirty Years War (1618–48). The abbreviation **bivvy** is recorded from the early 20th century.

bizarre [mid 17th century] This adjective meaning 'strange', 'odd' came into English from French, from Italian *bizzarro* which meant 'angry'. The ultimate origin remains unknown.

black [Old English] The source of Old English *blæc* is Germanic. In the same period *sweart* was in use, and related forms are common across Europe: German *schwarz*, Swedish *svart*, etc. It is however *black* which has become generalized in English while *swart* is kept in poetry (Keith Douglas *Vergissmeinnicht*, 1943: But she would weep to see today how on his skin the swart flies move). There are many compounds, e.g.:
■ **blackball** (late 18th century) derives from the practice of registering an adverse vote by placing a black ball in a ballot box.
■ **Black Death** is in fact a modern compound (earlier phrases were *the* (*great*) *pestilence*, *great death, the plague*); it is said to have been introduced into English history by Mrs Markham (the pseudonym of Mrs Penrose) in 1823, and into medical literature by a translation of German *der Schwarze Tod* (1833). The epithet *Black* is actually of uncertain origin; its equivalent was first found in Swedish and Danish chroniclers.
■ **Black Maria**, a colloquial name for a police van from the mid 19th century, was originally a US usage and is said to be named after a black woman called Maria Lee, who kept a boarding house in Boston and helped police escort drunk and disorderly customers to jail.
■ **black sheep** which arose as an expression in the late 18th century comes from the proverb *there is a black sheep in every flock*.

blackguard [early 16th century] This was originally a two word phrase for a body of attendants or servants, especially menials who were responsible for the kitchen utensils, but the exact significance of the epithet 'black' is uncertain. The sense 'scoundrel, villain' dates from the mid 18th century, and was formerly considered highly offensive.

blackmail [mid 16th century] The original *blackmail* was protection money levied by Scottish border chiefs who offered immunity from plunder to farmers in the border counties. The second element is obsolete *mail* 'tribute, rent', from Old Norse *mál* 'speech, agreement'.

bladder [Old English] A Germanic source led to Old English *blædre*; related forms are Dutch *blaar* and German *Blatter*.
→ BLOW¹

blade [Old English] The common senses of Old English *blæd* were 'leaf of a plant' and 'flat section (of an oar, sword, etc.)'; the root is Germanic and related forms are Dutch *blad* and German *Blatt*. The semantic feature 'cutting part' appears around 1330.

blame [Middle English] *Blame* as a verb is from the Old French *blamer, blasmer*, from a popular Latin variant of ecclesiastical Latin *blasphemare* 'reproach, revile, blaspheme', from Greek *blasphēmein*.
→ BLASPHEME

blanch [Middle English] *Blanch*, commonly used by cooks to describe the light boiling of vegetables, was first recorded with the meaning 'make white (by withdrawing colour)', although it was soon applied to culinary processes such as removing the skin from almonds by dipping them in boiling water. The form is from Old French *blanchir*, from *blanc* 'white'; the ultimate origin is Germanic.
→ BLANK

blancmange [late Middle English] An early spelling was *blancmanger*, from Old French *blanc mangier*, made up of *blanc* 'white' and *mangier* 'eat' (used as a noun to mean 'food'). The shortened form without -*er* arose in the 18th century. The dish started out as a mixture of chicken or other meat, minced with cream, sugar, rice, eggs, almonds, etc. Later it came to describe an opaque jelly dessert.

bland [late Middle English] In early use *bland* was 'gentle in manner', from Latin *blandus* 'soft, smooth'. This Latin adjective also forms the base of the Middle English noun **blandishment** 'a flattering statement', from Old French *blandiss-*, the lengthened stem of *blandir*, from Latin *blandīrī*.

blank [Middle English] The early sense was 'white, colourless'; the form is from Old French *blanc* 'white'; ultimately the source is Germanic. The expression *to blank somebody* meaning 'to ignore somebody deliberately'

dates from the 1970s, but *blank out* as in *blanked out the memory* has been in use since the 1950s.
→ BLANCH

blanket [Middle English] Undyed woollen cloth was called *blanket* in Middle English; the word comes via Old Northern French from Old French *blanc* 'white'. The ultimate origin is Germanic.

blare [late Middle English] Imitative *blare* was first recorded with the sense 'to roar', 'to bellow'. It comes from Middle Dutch *blaren*, *bleren*, or Low German *blaren*. Current senses date from the late 18th century.

blaspheme [Middle English] Greek *blasphēmos* 'evil-speaking' is the root of *blaspheme*, which came via Old French from ecclesiastical Latin *blasphemare* 'reproach, revile, blaspheme', from the Greek verb *blasphēmein*. The noun **blasphemy** from the same period is from Old French, via ecclesiastical Latin from Greek *blasphēmia* 'slander, blasphemy'.
→ BLAME

blatant [late 16th century] This is perhaps an alteration of Scots *blatand* 'bleating'. It was first used by Spenser as an epithet for a thousand-tongued monster produced by the mythological Cerberus (the watchdog guarding the infernal regions) and Chimaera (a creature with a lion's head, goat's body, and a serpent's tail): he saw this as a symbol of calumny, which he called the *blatant beast*. It was subsequently used to mean 'clamorous', 'offensive to the ear', first with reference to people (mid 17th century), later to describe things (late 18th century); the sense 'unashamedly conspicuous' arose in the late 19th century. Thus there has been a shift from drawing attention to the ear to drawing attention to the eye.

blaze¹ [Old English] Old English *blæse* was a 'torch', 'a bright fire', from a Germanic root. The plural *blazes* in various phrases expressing exasperation such as *what the blazes!* and *go to blazes!* is a reference to Hell and the flames associated with it.
→ BLAZE²

blaze² [mid 17th century] The *blaze* denoting a white spot or stripe on the face of an animal is ultimately of Germanic origin; related to German *Blässe* 'blaze' and *blass* 'pale'. There is probably a connection with *blemish*; the expression *blaze a trail* involves 'marking' a trail.
→ BLAZE¹

blaze³ [late Middle English] The early sense of *blaze* was 'blow out on a trumpet'. The origin is Middle Low German or Middle Dutch *blāzen* 'to blow'; English **blast** is related.
→ BLOW¹

blazer [late 19th century] Now the word for a brightly-coloured sporting jacket, *blazer* originally, in the mid 17th century, meant quite simply 'a thing that blazes or shines'.

bleach [Old English] The Old English adjective *blæc* 'pale' gave the noun *blæco*; the root form is Germanic. The verb *blæcan* is common Germanic.
→ BLEAK

bleak [Old English] Old English *blāc* was 'shining, white'; in later use it came from synonymous Old Norse *bleikr*; the ultimate origin is Germanic. Obsolete senses include 'wan', 'pale', 'sickly'. It was not until the 16th century that the modern English spelling became current. The development of sense included 'bare of vegetation' and 'cheerless'.
→ BLEACH

blear [Middle English] There is a likely connection between *blear* 'dim, misty' and Middle High German *blerre* 'blurred vision' and Low German *blarroged* 'bleary-eyed'.

bleed [Old English] Old English *blēdan* has a Germanic root. It has been transferred to many figurative uses: e.g. plants oozing sap are said to *bleed*, and in printing contexts, any cutting into the print (by over-trimming with a binder's knife) is also known as *bleeding*. The idiom *the heart bleeds* suggests 'bleeds inwardly with sorrow'. The verb's transitive use, such as *bleed someone (with leeches)*, dates from the early 15th century.
→ BLOOD

bleep [1950s] This is imitative of the sound; **bleeping** has been used euphemistically since the same decade for the informal word *bleeding*, by association with the 'bleeps' used to dub expletives in broadcast texts.

blemish [late Middle English] This was first used as a verb and comes from Old French *ble(s)miss*, the lengthened stem of *ble(s)mir* 'to make pale', 'injure'; the root is probably Germanic.

blend [Middle English] This word probably has a Scandinavian origin connected to Old Norse *blanda* 'to mix'.

bless [Old English] Old English *blēdsian*, *blētsian* are perhaps based on *blōd* 'blood', the likely original semantic core being 'mark or consecrate with blood'. The meaning was influenced by the word's use to translate Latin *benedīcere* 'to praise', 'to worship' and Greek *eulogein* meaning essentially 'speak well of'; these in turn translated Hebrew *brk* 'to bend', hence 'bend the knee (in praise)'. There is therefore a series of rich associations, pagan, Jewish, and Christian, mixed together in the English words *bless* and *blessing*; there is also a later association with *bliss*. There is no corresponding verb to *bless* in other Germanic languages.

blight [mid 16th century] A term for an inflammation of the skin when first used, *blight* now refers to a plant disease or is used figuratively with a notion of 'spoiling', 'damaging'. The word entered literature from the speech of farmers apparently but the origin is not known. Suggestions have included a connection with Icelandic *blettr* 'stain' or with *black*, *bleach*, and *bleak*, or it may be onomatopoeic. The negative association comes across in the word **blighter** used contemptuously from the early 19th century.

Blighty [early 20th century] Despite appearances, this is not based on *blight*; it was first used by soldiers serving in India to refer to Britain as home. An Anglo-Indian alteration of Urdu *bilāyatī*, *wilāyatī* meaning 'foreign, European', the word is based on Arabic *wilāyat*, *wilāya* 'dominion, district'.

blimey [late 19th century] This is a mild expletive but its original unaltered form was *blind me!* or *blame me!* **Gorblimey** is an altered form of *God blind me!*

blind [Old English] Dutch, German, and English *blind* are related and share a Germanic root. As for compounds:
■ **blindfold**, dating from the mid 16th century is an alteration, by association with *fold*, of *blindfeld*; this is the past participle of the now obsolete *blindfell* 'to strike blind', from Old English *geblindfellian*.
■ **blind man's buff** (early 17th century) as a game involving bumping into objects as an inevitable part of the blindfold search for someone, has *buff* 'a blow' as part of the phrase, from Old French *bufe*.

blink [Middle English] *Blink* is from *blenk*, a Scots variant of *blench* 'to flinch'; it was reinforced by Middle Dutch *blinken* 'to shine'. Early senses included 'to deceive', 'to flinch' as well as 'open the eyes after sleep': these led to the main current sense 'open and close the eyes rapidly' which started in the mid 16th century. **Blinking** as an adjective meant 'with half-open eyelids', 'winking' and it is this literal sense which is conveyed in the line: *The portrait of a blinking idiot*, taken from Shakespeare's *Merchant of Venice*; this is different from the 20th-century use of *blinking idiot* where *blinking* is an expletive and a euphemism for *bloody*.

blip [late 19th century] *Blip* imitates a sudden rap or tap, the initial sense of the word. In the 1940s it named the small elongated marks projected on a radar screen. The modern noun sense 'unexpected halt or change in what is happening' became common from the 1970s.

bliss [Old English] This word from a Germanic root is related to *blithe* 'happy' (*blīthe* in Old English, related to Dutch *blijde*). *Bless* and *bliss* have influenced each other from an early period, which has meant a gradual semantic distinction between *blitheness* as an earthly lightness of heart and the heavenly *bliss* of the 'blessed'.

blithe [Old English]
➔ BLISS

blizzard [early 19th century] A US word originally, a *blizzard* was 'a violent blow', but the origin is unknown. It is probably onomatopoeic; suggestive words with possible influence are *blow*, *blast*, *blister*, and *bluster*. The word was applied to a snowy squall in the American press in reports of the severe winter of 1880–81, but apparently it was used colloquially in the West considerably earlier.

bloat[1] [late 17th century] *Bloat* first meant 'cause to swell'; the source is the obsolete adjective *bloat* 'swollen, soft', perhaps from Old Norse *blautr* 'soft, flabby'. In US slang a *bloat* is a contemptible person, a usage dating from the late 19th century. The negative connotation is reflected in phrases such as *bloated capitalists*.

bloat[2] [late 16th century] This *bloat* used in the compound *bloat herring* 'a bloater' from the late 16th to mid 17th century is perhaps related to the adjective *bloat* 'soft'; its origin is obscure. Bloated herrings were steeped in brine for a time before smoking; this contrasted with red or dried herrings usually left in dry salt for 10 days and then smoked.

blob [late Middle English] Initially a *blob* was a bubble, perhaps symbolic of a drop of liquid. This use has remained in northern dialect. Some association with *blow* may be involved, from the action of the lips in forming a bubble.
➔ BLUBBER

block [Middle English] When *block* was first used it was a log or tree stump; the word came via Old French from Middle Dutch *blok* but the ultimate origin is unknown. The verb *to block* first described putting blocks in the way as an obstacle. **Blockade** dates from the late 17th century and is based on *block*, probably influenced by *ambuscade*. By the 20th century a **blockbuster** came to denote a huge aerial bomb in the 1940s but was later applied to any film or book having a huge impact when released.

blood [Old English] Old English *blōd* has a Germanic source and is related to German *Blut* and Dutch *bloed*. The origin of the adjective

bloody, in use from the mid 17th century to add emphasis to an expression, is not certain but is thought to have a connection with the 'bloods' (aristocratic rowdies) of the late 17th and early 18th centuries; hence the phrase *bloody drunk* (= as drunk as a blood) meant 'very drunk indeed'. From the mid 18th century until quite recently, *bloody* as a swear word was regarded as unprintable; the likely reason is that people believed mistakenly that it implied a blasphemous reference to the blood of Christ, or that the word was an alteration of 'by Our Lady'; hence a widespread caution in its use even in phrases such as *bloody battle* although merely a reference to bloodshed.

bloom [Middle English] The early word for 'flower' in English was *blossom*. Old Norse *blóm* 'flower, blossom', *blómi* 'prosperity', *blómar* 'flowers' are the source of *bloom* in English, which shares a base with the verb *blow* 'to burst into flower'. In late Middle English **blooming** started to be used as a euphemism for *bloody*.

bloomer [late 19th century] A *bloomer* is equivalent to *blooming error* and is thought to be Australian prison slang. In the 1930s another **bloomer** entered the vocabulary as a name for a type of loaf but it is not clear how this came about.

bloomers [mid 19th century] *Bloomers* were trousers gathered at the ankle and worn with a short skirt; they were named after Mrs Amelia J. Bloomer (1818–94), an American social reformer who advocated wearing this type of clothing. In the late 19th century, *bloomers* were considered appropriate for activities such as cycling; at the beginning of the 20th century, the name started to be applied to loose knee-length knickers and then colloquially, to any knickers.

blossom [Old English] The Old English noun *blōstm*, *blōstma*, and the verb *blōstmian* are Germanic in origin; Dutch *bloesem* is related. The two words *blossom* and *bloom* have become differentiated: *blossom* once a general word for 'flower', now is limited to the flowers associated with fruiting, whereas *bloom* is associated with the beauty of the full flower itself.
→ BLOOM; BLOW²

blouse [early 19th century] A *blouse* once described a loose garment drawn in at the waist by a belt, worn by workmen. The immediate source is French but earlier details are unknown. It was in the late 19th century that the current use of *blouse* for a woman's shirt-like garment came into use.

blow¹ [Old English] Old English *blāwan* 'send out air' and the related German word *blähen* 'blow up', 'to swell' are Germanic forms, from

an Indo-European root shared by Latin *flare* 'to blow'.

blow² [Old English] From Germanic, Old English *blōwan* 'to blossom', 'to produce flowers' is related to Dutch *bloeien* and German *blühen*.
→ BLOOM; BLOSSOM

blowsy [early 17th century] A woman described as *blowsy* would look coarse, untidy, and red-faced; the word comes from obsolete *blowze* 'a beggar's female companion', but the origin is unknown.

blubber [late Middle English] The *blubber* describing whale fat also, in early use, described both the foaming of the sea and a bubble on the surface of the water. Perhaps it is comparable with *blob* and *blotch* and symbolic of seething bubbles popping and breaking. The verb *blubber* 'to cry noisily' has a figurative association with the noun and dates from the same period, while the abbreviation **blub** appeared much later in the early 19th century.

blue [Middle English] This colour adjective comes from Old French *bleu*. Ultimately of Germanic origin, it is related to Old English *blǣwen* 'blue' and Old Norse *blár* 'dark blue'. The *blaeberry* a Scots and northern English name for 'bilberry' takes its first syllable *blue* (related to *blue*) from dialect meaning 'blackish-blue'. The **blues** to describe 'depression' arose in the mid 18th century as an elliptical form of *blue devils* describing the horrors of 'delirium tremens'. Amongst the compounds with an interesting history are:

■ **blue-chip** (early 20th century), a US word originally from the *blue chip* used in gambling games, usually bearing a high value.

■ **blue-plate** (1940s), a US word describing a restaurant meal in which a full main course is ordered as a single menu item, makes reference to the original blue plates on which fixed-price restaurant meals were once served. These were divided into compartments to hold the various portions making up the meal.

■ **blueprint** (late 19th century) as in *a blueprint for success* may now indicate any plan, template, or model, but the name comes from a process in which prints were composed of white lines on a blue ground or of blue lines on a white ground.

■ **bluestocking** (late 17th century) originally described a man wearing blue worsted stockings instead of the formal black silk ones; the word was extended to mean 'wearing informal dress'. Later a *bluestocking* came to be applied to any person attending the literary assemblies held by three London society ladies around 1750, where some of the men preferred to wear less formal dress. The women who participated became known as *blue-stocking ladies* or *blue-stockingers*.

bluff¹ [late 17th century] Nowadays *bluff* involves 'dissimulation', 'an attempt to deceive', a usage which made its appearance in the US around the middle of the 19th century when it referred to *bluffing* in the game of poker. The early meanings of *bluff* were 'to blindfold' and 'to hoodwink'; the source is Dutch *bluffen* 'brag', or *bluf* 'bragging'.

bluff² [early 17th century] *Bluff* 'steep cliff' or 'promontory' was recorded originally as a nautical adjective meaning 'broad' describing a ship's bows. The origin is not known. The Canadian sense 'grove, clump of trees' dates from the mid 18th century.

bluff³ [early 18th century] The early word meant 'surly, abrupt in manner' and was a figurative use of *bluff* 'cliff'. The current positive connotation 'direct and good-natured' dates from the early 19th century.

blunder [Middle English] *Blunder* conjures up an image of someone not quite seeing what is physically there as an obstacle, or not quite perceiving implications; the word is probably Scandinavian in origin and related to *blind*. A compound associated with *blunder* is **blunderbuss**, a mid 17th-century alteration of Dutch *donderbus*, literally 'thunder gun'.

blunt [Middle English] The origin is uncertain; it is perhaps Scandinavian in origin and related to Old Norse *blunda* 'to shut the eyes'; another possibility suggested is that *blunt* might be a form related to *blind*. The early meaning in English was 'dull, insensitive'. Obsolete senses include 'barren' and 'without refinement'.

blur [mid 16th century] 'A smear that partially obscures something' was the early meaning of *blur*. There is perhaps a connection with *blear*.
→ BLEAR

blurb [early 20th century] The American humorist Gelett Burgess who died in 1951 coined *blurb*. In *Burgess Unabridged* 7 Blurb he defined it as 1. A flamboyant advertisement; an inspired testimonial. 2. Fulsome praise; a sound like a publisher…"On the 'jacket' of the 'latest' fiction, we find the blurb; abounding in agile adjectives and adverbs, attesting that this book is the 'sensation of the year'". The jacket of a comic book by Burgess (1907) carried an image of a young lady facetiously dubbed Miss Blinda Blurb.

blush [Old English] Old English *blyscan* 'to turn red' is related to modern Dutch *blozen*. The verbal root appears to be 'burn', 'glow'. The history of the word remains very obscure.

board [Old English] A word with a complicated history, Old English *bord* (of Germanic origin) had the semantic features 'plank' and 'border, rim', which may signify two different words but the two were associated at an early date. Dutch *boord* and German *Bort* are related. *Board* was reinforced in Middle English by the influence of Old French *bort* 'edge, ship's side' and Old Norse *borth* 'board, table'.

boat [Old English] The origin of Old English *bāt* and its relationship with forms in other languages is unclear. The word appears to have been adopted in Low German as *bôt* and in Dutch as *boot* from English or Norse. There are pointers to a Germanic form *baito- preserved only in Old Norse and Old English.

bob [late Middle English] *Bob* is a mystery word. No certain origin is known for either the *bob* which describes the motion of moving up and down (although it may be onomatopoeic), or the *bob* which describes a short haircut. These both date from Middle English. It seems that the word used from the late 17th century by change-ringers of church bells (as in *bob minor* rung on 6 bells, and *bob triple* rung on 7, etc.), is based on the noun sense 'rapid up and down movement'. The coin *bob* 'shilling' has been so called since the late 18th century but again the origin is not known.

bobby [mid 19th century] Sir Robert Peel, British Home Secretary from 1828–30, established the Metropolitan Police and policemen became known as both *bobbies* and *peelers*. *Bobby* is a pet form of his first name.

bobsleigh [mid 19th century] A US word originally for two short sleighs coupled together used for hauling logs, a *bobsleigh* makes use of *bob* in the sense 'short'. This same meaning is seen in **bobcat** because of its short tail; also in **bobtail**, originally recorded as a humorous word for a kind of broad-headed arrow, probably because it looked as though it had been cut short.

bode [Old English] 'Proclaim', 'foretell' were the meanings of Old English *bodian*, from *boda* 'a messenger'. The word is Germanic in origin and related to German *Bote*.
→ BID

bodice [mid 16th century] The original spelling was *bodies*, the plural of *body*; it has retained the original pronunciation. The word probably first denoted an undergarment, then known as a *pair of bodice*, although this sense is not recorded until the early 17th century.

bodkin [Middle English] The origin is perhaps Celtic linked with Irish *bod*, Welsh *bidog*, and Scottish Gaelic *biodag* 'dagger'. This was the first sense recorded in English and is used by Shakespeare in *Hamlet*: When he himself might his quietus make With a bare bodkin?. Another early use was for a sharp instrument for piercing cloth; now, in needlework, a *bodkin* is, on the contrary, blunt with a large eye for threading tape and other thick threads through material.

body [Old English] The Old English spelling was *bodig* but the word's origin is unknown.

bog [Middle English] A *bog* describing soft, muddy ground is from Irish or Scottish Gaelic *bogach*, from *bog* 'soft'.

bogey[1] [late 19th century] This golf term for 'one stroke over par' is perhaps from *Bogey* as a name for the Devil, in this instance thought of as taking part in the game as an imaginary player.

bogey[2] [mid 19th century] This name for a mischievous spirit was first recorded as a proper name applied to the Devil, who is sometimes referred to as *Colonel Bogey*. The origin is unknown but it it is probably related to early 16th-century *bogle* 'goblin, phantom'. Related to *bogle* and *hogey* is the verb **boggle** 'look with astonishment' which arose in the late 16th century, probably from a dialect use.

bogus [late 18th century] A *bogus* was first recorded in the US as a term for a machine for making counterfeit money; it is now used as an adjective meaning 'not genuine'. The origin is unknown.

boil[1] [Middle English] From Old French *boillir*, *boil* is based on Latin *bullire* 'to bubble', from *bulla* 'a bubble'.

boil[2] [Old English] A *boil* as a pus-filled swelling was *byle*, *hyl* in Old English from a West Germanic source. Related are Dutch *buil* and German *Beule*.

boisterous [late Middle English] A variant of the earlier word *boistuous* 'rustic, coarse, boisterous', *boisterous* originally meant 'rough, stiff'. The origin is unknown.

bold [Old English] Relatives of *bold* are Dutch *boud* and German *bald* 'soon'. The Old English form was *bald*, of Germanic origin.

bollard [Middle English] The early word was the name for the short posts on a ship's deck or on a quayside. It comes perhaps from Old Norse *bolr* 'tree trunk', and is possibly related to *baulk*.

bolster [Old English] The early sense of *bolster* was 'long, thick pillow'. Of Germanic origin, it is related to Dutch *bolster* and German *Polster*.

bolt [Old English] 'Arrow' was the original meaning of *bolt* which now describes a metal bar, a flash of lightning, etc. Dutch *bout* and German *Bolzen* 'arrow, bolt for a door' are related, but the origin is unknown. In another context, a *bolt* of cloth illustrates a transferred use of the noun. As for the active verbal use, this expresses 'fly like an arrow' and conveys unleashed darting speed, dating from Middle English; later (late 18th century) the same speed is captured in the colloquial use of *bolting food*, when the semantic concept is haste in a single action.

bomb [late 17th century] French *bombe*, from Italian *bomba* has given English *bomb*; the probable base is Latin *bombus* 'booming, humming', from Greek *bombos*, of imitative origin.

bombard [late Middle English] A *bombard* was an early form of cannon, from Old French *bombarde*, probably (like *bomb*) based on Latin *bombus* 'booming, humming'. The verb became current in the late 16th century from French *bombarder*; slightly earlier that century, a **bombardier** denoted a soldier in charge of a *bombard*.

bombast [mid 16th century] Inflated language on a trivial subject, known as *bombast* has been supposed, erroneously, to have been named with reference to the Swiss physician Paracelsus (P. A. T. Bombast von Hohenheim). It in fact reflects a figurative use of an obsolete word for 'cotton wool used as padding'. The source is Old French *bombace*, from medieval Latin *bombax*, *bombac-*: this was an alteration of *bombyx* 'silk'.

bonanza [early 19th century] *Bonanza* first referred in the US to success when mining. It is a Spanish word meaning 'fair weather, prosperity', from Latin *bonus* 'good'.

bonce [mid 19th century] This slang word for 'head' was originally a large marble; the origin remains unknown.

bond [Middle English] A variant of *band* → BAND[1]

bondage [Middle English] *Bondage* is from Anglo-Latin *bondagium*, from Middle English *bond* meaning 'serf' and, earlier, 'peasant, householder' (from Old Norse *bóndi* 'tiller of the soil', based on *búa* 'dwell'). *Bond* 'physical restraint' has influenced the sense.

bone [Old English] Dutch *been* and German *Bein* are related to Old English *bān*, all of Germanic origin. The phrase **bone idle** which arose in the early 19th century expresses *idle through to the bone*.

bonfire [late Middle English] The first syllable is from *bone*. The word originally described a large open-air fire on which bones were burnt. This was sometimes as part of a celebration, sometimes for burning heretics or proscribed literature. Dr Johnson accepted the mistaken idea that the word came from French *bon* 'good'.

bonnet [late Middle English] A type of soft brimless hat for men was once known as a *bonnet*. The source is Old French *bonet*, from medieval Latin *abonnis* 'headgear'. It was in the late 15th century that it came to denote the distinctive type of hat worn by a woman or a child with a brim framing the face and ribbons tied under the chin.

bonny [late 15th century] *Bonny* as in *bonny child* is perhaps related to Old French *bon* 'good'.

bonus [late 18th century] This was probably originally Stock Exchange slang, coming from Latin *bonus* 'good'. This is a masculine adjectival form used in place of *bonum* (neuter) 'good', 'good thing'.

boo [early 19th century] *Bo* was in use from Middle English to surprise and shock somebody; *boo* was probably an alteration of this. *Boo* used in disapproval was imitative of the lowing of oxen; like *hiss* and *hoot*, the sound was considered to be derisive.

boob[1] [1950s] A US word originally for 'breast', this is an abbreviation of **booby**, a 1930s alteration of dialect *bubby*. There is perhaps a connection with German dialect *Bübbi* 'teat'.

boob[2] [early 20th century] *Boob* meaning 'mistake' is an abbreviation of *booby* 'stupid or childish person' in use two centuries earlier and probably derived from Spanish *bobo*, from Latin *balbus* 'stammering'. **Boo-boo** which arose in the 1950s in the US for 'mistake' is a reduplication of *boob*.

book [Old English] Of Germanic origin, Old English *bōc* had the meaning 'a piece of writing, a charter'; the original sense referring to a simple leaf or writing tablet became plural (i.e. written sheets, hence book) and then extended the meaning to the singular. The verb *bōcian* was 'to grant by charter'. This connection with 'charter' is seen in **bookland**, also dating from Old English, which once referred to land granted by charter into private ownership and eventually was applied to all land that was not *folcland*, i.e. land subject to traditional communal obligations. The placename *Buckland* comes from this. Related to *book* are Dutch *boek* and German *Buch*, and probably English *beech* (it has been suggested that runes were first made on beech tablets or cut in the bark of beech trees).

boom[1] [late Middle English] Ultimately imitative in that it is descriptive of the production of a deep resonant sound, this word is perhaps from Dutch *bommen* 'to hum, buzz'; its first use in English was as a verb. This probably led, in the late 19th century, to the extended sense 'burst into sudden economic activity' as in *business is booming*; this usage first appeared in the US and picks up the semantic strands of suddenness and speed.

boom[2] [mid 16th century] The nautical *boom* 'spar securing the bottom of a ship's sail' was first recorded in the general sense 'beam, pole' and comes from Dutch, 'tree, pole'; until the mid 18th century, a *boom* also referred to a pole set up to mark a channel in a waterway. Other senses include 'barrier stretched across a river to obstruct navigation' and, in North America, 'a line of floating timber to guide the path of floating logs'. In the 1930s, the word came to be applied in broadcasting contexts to a movable arm supporting a camera or microphone.
→ BEAM

boon [Middle English] A *boon* in the sense 'blessing' comes from Old Norse *bón*; it was originally 'a request for a favour'. It gradually came to refer to a 'gift' or 'gratuity', and also to any unpaid service that a landlord expected as his due from a tenant. Thus there has been a shift of emphasis from asking to receiving, with implicit expectation; current use is now focused on the value that the recipient of a gift or benefit places on it. Despite the positive connotation, the *boon* of *boon companion* is not the same word ; this particular phrase dates from the mid 16th century and has the meaning 'convivial companion' (e.g. Tennyson *Becket*: My comrade, boon companion, my co-reveller): the adjective (late Middle English) is essentially 'good', from French *bon*.

boor [mid 16th century] An ill-mannered or clumsy person is referred to as a *boor* but the early word meant 'peasant'. It comes from Low German *būr* or Dutch *boer* 'farmer'. In Dutch three words have remained distinct for the following three semantic aspects: *boer* 'peasant', *buur* 'neighbour', and *bouwer* 'builder'; however in German, under the influence of *bauen* 'to cultivate, build', *Bauer* has merged all three senses in the single word: 'farmer', 'yokel', and 'builder'.

boost [early 19th century] The origin of this word is unknown but it was first recorded in the US in the sense 'to push from below'.

boot[1] [Middle English] This word for a type of footwear is from Old Norse *bóti* or its source,

Old French *bote*. The ultimate origin is unknown but thare is perhaps a connection with archaic *bot* 'blunt, stumpy'. Johnson, in his dictionary of 1755 describes a limited use of the *boot*: ... a covering for the leg, used by horsemen. The plural *boots* started to be recorded in the sense 'person' in combinations such as *bossyboots* and *slyboots* from the early 17th century. Late in the following century a **boots** came to describe a hotel employee taking care of duties such as shoecleaning. In other contexts, the *boot* of a car appears to be derived from an earlier use of the word for compartments of a coach where attendants sat in front of or behind the body of the vehicle. In computing, the verbs *boot* and *reboot* date from the late 20th century; these are abbreviations of **bootstrap** and extend the notion 'assist in putting on (a boot)' to 'assist in loading (an operating system)'.

boot² [Old English] The *boot* in the phrase *to boot* ('to the good') was *bōt* 'advantage, remedy' in Old English and is of Germanic origin. Related words are Dutch *boete* and German *Busse* 'penance, fine', as well as English *better* and *best*.

booth [Middle English] From Old Norse *búth*, based on *búa* 'dwell', English *booth* was first used in the general sense 'a temporary dwelling or shelter'. The word **bothy** 'hut', 'labourer's one roomed lodging' may be related. Some have put forward the conjecture that *booth* was adopted from Slavonic; cognates are Czech *bouda* and Polish *buda*.

bootleg [late 19th century] The formation of this word is due to the smugglers' practice of concealing bottles inside the long leg part of their boots.

booty [late Middle English] *Booty* first referred to plunder that was acquired in common and then divided; the source is Middle Low German *būte, buite* 'exchange, distribution', but earlier details of the origin are uncertain. The notion of sharing gradually became a less prominent feature of the meaning.

booze [Middle English] The early spelling was *bouse*, from Middle Dutch *būsen* 'to drink to excess'. The current phonetic spelling *booze*, dating from the 18th century, reflects the pronunciation of Middle English. The form is perhaps dialectal.

border [late Middle English] From Old French *bordeure, border* (and its variant **bordure** retained as a heraldic term) are ultimately Germanic and related to *board*. As in certain other words in English, the *-ure* ending weakened through *-ur* to *-er*, thus masking the etymology.

bore¹ [Old English] The *bore* (*borian* in Old English) meaning 'to pierce, hollow out' is Germanic in origin; a cognate is German *bohren*.

bore² [mid 18th century] The origin of *bore* meaning 'make weary through tedium' is unknown. The noun and the verb appeared after 1750 and there may be an allusion to some anecdote, now forgotten. Its use in the phrase *French bore* alluding to someone suffering from the supposedly French malady of 'ennui', suggests a possible French origin. 'Ennui' is often likened to the English malady of 'spleen', once regarded as the seat of melancholy.

bore³ [early 17th century] A *bore* describes a steep-fronted wave caused by the meeting of two tides, or the constriction of a spring tide up a narrow estuary. The word is perhaps from Old Norse *bára* 'wave'; it was used in the general sense 'billow, wave' in Middle English.

borough [Old English] The early words *burg* and *burh* denoted 'a fortress, a citadel' and then later the sense became 'a fortified town' and eventually 'town', 'district'. Other Germanic relatives are Dutch *burg* and German *Burg*. In Middle English a huge variety of spellings of *borough* existed; **burgh** is a Scots form; the derivative **burgher** meaning 'inhabitant of a borough' was reinforced by Dutch *burger*, from *burg* 'castle'. **Bourgeois** adopted from French (from late Latin *burgus* 'castle') is related.

borrow [Old English] Germanic in origin, Old English *borgian* meaning 'to borrow against security' is related to Dutch and German *borgen*. The security assured the safe return otherwise the item would be forfeited. Current use merely emphasizes the temporary nature of the loan.

bosom [Old English] The origin of Old English *bōsm* is West Germanic; related words are Dutch *boezem* and German *Busen*.

boss¹ [early 19th century] Introduced into the US originally by settlers, *boss* is from Dutch *baas* meaning 'master'. The word soon found verbal expression in *boss about*.

boss² [Middle English] *Boss* 'round protuberance' is used in many contexts, e.g. it may refer to a swelling on a plant or on an animal's body; it describes a round ornamental metal stud or a projection in the middle of a shield; it also appears in architectural and geological contexts. The word is from Old French *boce* of which the origin is unknown.

boss-eyed [mid 19th century] There is apparently a connection here with dialect *boss* 'to miss, bungle', but the origin is unknown. The *boss* in **boss shot** 'bad aim', 'unsuccessful attempt' appears to be related.

botany [late 17th century] This comes from the earlier word *botanic* borrowed from French *botanique*, based on Greek *botanikos*. The base is Greek *botanē* 'plant'. The explorer Captain James Cook, who landed there in 1770, used the term to name *Botany Bay* because of the large variety of plants collected there by his companion, Sir Joseph Banks.

botch [late Middle English] The early sense of *botch* was 'repair'; 'clumsiness' became a feature of this over time with the semantic notion of 'patching'. The origin remains unknown. **Bodge**, an alteration of *botch*, is recorded from the mid 16th century.

both [Middle English] The origin is Old Norse *báthir*.

bother [late 17th century] First recorded as a noun in the dialect sense 'noise, chatter', *bother* is Anglo-Irish in origin; it is probably related to Irish *bodhaire* 'noise', *bodhraim* 'to deafen', 'to annoy'. The verb was originally a dialect word in the early 18th century and meant 'to confuse with noise'. Moving closer to the present day, the form **bovver** (1960s) as in *bovver boots* represents a cockney pronunciation of *bother*.

bottle [late Middle English] This word is first recorded as denoting a leather bottle and comes from Old French *boteille*, from medieval Latin *butticula* 'little cask', a diminutive of late Latin *buttis* 'wineskin'. In recent colloquial use the phrases *have lots of bottle* and *bottle out* are to do with courage; the first recorded examples are criminals' slang from the 1970s.
→ BUTT⁴

bottom [Old English] Old English *botm* has a Germanic source; related words are Dutch *bodem* 'bottom, ground' and German *Boden* 'ground, earth'. The sense 'buttocks' dates from the late 18th century.

boudoir [late 18th century] Adopted from French, this is literally a 'sulking-place', from *bouder* 'to pout, sulk'.

bough [Old English] Old English *bōg*, *bōh* 'bough' or 'shoulder' is Germanic in origin; cognates are Dutch *boeg* 'shoulders' or 'ship's bow' and German *Bug* 'ship's bow' or 'horse's hock or shoulder'. The association with 'tree' seems to be exclusively English, whereas the core meaning in related forms is 'shoulder or foreleg'.
→ BOW³

boulder [late Middle English] This is a shortening of the earlier word *boulderstone* and has a Scandinavian source. The original sense descibed a 'water-worn rounded stone' used for paving.

boulevard [mid 18th century] A French borrowing, a *boulevard* was 'a horizontal section of a rampart', and later came to describe a 'promenade on the site of a rampart'. The German word *Bollwerk* 'bulwark' gave rise to the French word.

bounce [Middle English] The 'rebound' sense was not present in the early usage of Middle English *bunsen* which was 'to beat, thump'. It is perhaps imitative, or possibly from Low German *bunsen* 'to beat' or Dutch *bons* 'a thump'. The recurrent movement associated with *bounce* featured from the early 16th century. Sense development is similar to that of *bang*.

bound¹ [early 16th century] The early use of *bound* 'leap' was as a noun (from French *bond*). The verb is from *bondir* 'resound', later 'rebound', from late Latin *bombitare*, from Latin *bombus* 'humming'. When a man is described as a **bounder**, with the accompanying disapproval because of his anti-social behaviour, there is a connection with the slang term *bounder* for a four-wheeled cab (mid 19th century) which 'bounded' over rough roads causing discomfort.

bound² [Middle English] Early senses included 'landmark' and 'borderland'; now it is common in phrases such as *out of bounds* and *beat the bounds* (when the boundaries of a parish are traced out by striking certain points with rods). The source of the word is Old French *bodne*, from medieval Latin *bodina*, earlier *butina*, but the ultimate origin is unknown. **Boundary** (early 17th century) is a variant of the dialect word *bounder* 'limit, landmark', perhaps suggested by and on the pattern of *limitary* 'subject to restriction'. Another word meaning 'boundary' (specifically of a field) is **bourn**; it too is from Old French *bodne* and dates from the early 16th century.

bound³ [Middle English] This is the *bound* of *bound for* when someone is heading for a destination. The early spelling was *boun* which meant 'ready, dressed', from Old Norse *búinn*, the past participle of *búa* 'to get ready'. The final *-d* is either euphonic or added through the influence of the word *bound* meaning 'obliged'.

bound⁴ [late 15th century] 'Under obligation' was the early sense of this *bound* as in *duty bound*. It is the past participle of *bind*.

bounty [Middle English] Initially *bounty* was 'goodness', 'generosity', from Old French *bonte* 'goodness'. The Latin base is *bonus* 'good'. The sense 'monetary reward' dates from the early 18th century. **Bountiful**, an early 16th-century word, is based on *bounty* and is common in the phrase *Lady Bountiful*, a character in Farquhar's *Beaux' Stratagem* (1707).

bouquet [early 18th century] A dialect variant of Old French *bos* 'wood' gave French *bouquet* 'clump of trees', which entered English with the meaning 'bunch of flowers'. The use referring to the aroma from wine dates from the mid 19th century.
→ BUSH

bourgeois [mid 16th century]
→ BOROUGH

bout [mid 16th century] A *bout* is used for any period during which an activity takes place or when something occurs, as in *boxing bout*, *bout of flu*. The original meaning of the word was 'curve', 'circuit': dialect *bought* 'bend, loop' gave rise to this; the origin is probably Low German.

boutique [mid 18th century] Adopted from the French word meaning 'small shop', *boutique* comes via Latin from Greek *apothēkē* 'storehouse'. The Spanish word *bodega*, a shop selling wine, is related.

bow¹ [Old English] The *bow* of an archer or musician was *boga* 'bend, bow, arch' in Old English, from a Germanic source. It is related to Dutch *boog* and German *Bogen*, and also to the verb *bow* 'stoop', 'bend over'. In Old English *bow* formed part of compounds such as *rainbow* and *elbow*.

bow² [Old English] Old English *būgan* 'to bend, stoop' is Germanic and related to German *biegen*, also to the noun *bow* 'arc'.

bow³ [early 17th century] The *bow* of a ship (a sense recorded only since 1600) is from Low German *boog*, Dutch *boeg*, 'shoulder', 'ship's bow'.
→ BOUGH

bowel [Middle English] Old French *bouel* has given *bowel* in English, from Latin *botellus* 'little sausage', a diminutive of *botulus*: this last word is the base of **botulism**, a form of food poisoning, adopted from German *Botulismus*, originally 'sausage poisoning'.

bower [Old English] The *bower* often associated in poetry with a lady's private retreat has a connection with German *Bauer* 'birdcage'. Old English *būr* meant 'dwelling, inner room', from a Germanic root; possibly related to this is Old English *bȳre* 'byre', 'cowshed'. The outdoor *bower* keeps a notion of 'cover' and 'retreat' because of overarching branches forming a canopy.

bowl¹ [Old English] Historically a *bowl* was distinguished from a *basin* by its pronounced hemispherical shape, a basin being wider and shallower, but these distinctions have become confused regionally. Old English *bolle*, *bolla*, from Germanic, are related to Dutch *bol* 'round object', and English **boll**, a 'bubble' (now a word for 'a rounded seed capsule' of plants such as cotton or flax).

bowl² [late Middle English] The *bowl* used in sports contexts had the early general sense 'ball'. From Old French *boule* (a word still common in modern French, for example the game of *boules*), the base is Latin *bulla* 'a bubble'.

bowser [1920s] This type of tanker used in the fuelling of vehicles such as aircraft or for water, owes its name to a company of oil storage engineers.

box¹ [late Old English] The *box* describing a type of container is probably from late Latin *buxis*, from Latin *pyxis* 'boxwood box', from Greek *puxis*, the name of the tree yielding hard timber for making boxes. This Greek word has also given **pyx**, a term used in the Christian Church for a box storing the consecrated bread of the Eucharist. As for *box* in compounds:
■ **Christmas box**, a gift or gratuity given to tradesman in Britain, has given rise to **Boxing Day**, the day associated with the tradition since the early 19th century; it has nothing to do with the sport of boxing, an origin sometimes popularly believed.
→ BOX³

box² [late Middle English] Pugilistic *box* was first recorded as a noun (as in *a box on the ear*) and had the general sense 'a blow'; the origin is not known.

box³ [Old English] This name for a slow-growing evergreen shrub often used for hedging, came via Latin from Greek *puxos*.
→ BOX¹

boy [Middle English] A *boy* was originally 'a male servant'; the origin is obscure; it is apparently identical with East Frisian *boy* 'young gentleman' and, thought by many to be identical with Dutch *boef* 'knave'. Although *boy* is used positively and indulgently in phrases such as *that's the boy* and *one of the boys*, the connotation of lower status persisted alongside this in its use as a form of address for summoning and giving orders to slaves or servants. This negative association has connections with the phrase *good ole boy* used to refer to a white male of the southern US portrayed as believing in simple pleasures, but with deep social and racial prejudices (1982 S. B. Flexner *Listening to America* 286: A loyal southerner, with all the charm and prejudice the term conveys, has been widely called a *good ole boy* since the mid-1960s).

boycott [late 19th century] This is from the name of Captain Charles C. Boycott (1832–97), an Irish land agent, who, in 1880, was one of the first to be ostracized by the Irish Land League who were campaigning to reduce rents and gain agrarian reforms.

brace [Middle English] 'Clasp, fasten tightly' were the meanings of the early verb; the direct source is Old French *bracier* 'to embrace', from *brace* 'two arms', from Latin *bracchia*, 'arms', based on Greek *brakhiōn*. The semantic strands which have developed from this core sense of 'two arms' are 'a pair', as in *a brace of pheasant*; 'something which clasps' such as a brace for teeth; 'something which gives support' such as a brace to support flats used in theatrical scenery; and 'something which serves as a measure' (originally the distance between the fingertips with arms outstretched).

bracelet [late Middle English] Adopted from Old French, from *bras* 'arm', the base is Latin *bracchium*. The word has been used to denote a piece of armour for covering the arm, and is also a slang term for handcuffs.

bracket [late 16th century] This support, made of stone, wood, or metal, is apparently from or via French *braguette* 'codpiece', 'corbel' from Spanish. The base is Latin *brāca*, singular of *brācae* 'breeches'; it has been suggested that the architectural *bracket* may have derived its name from a resemblance to the codpiece of a pair of breeches. An erroneous connection with Latin *bracchium* 'arm', because of the notion of 'support', seems to have affected the sense development.

brae [Middle English] Old Norse *brá* 'eyelash' has given both the form and visual colour to this Scots and northern English word for a steep bank along a river valley or a hill slope. A similar sense development occurred in *brow*.
→ BROW

brag [Middle English] *Brag* was first recorded as an adjective 'boastful', and noun 'a boast'. The source is not known; the related French word *braguer* 'to flaunt' is recorded only later, and late 16th-century **braggart** 'boaster' may be referred to this verb; however in the case of *brag*, some of the English forms go back to 1300. The origin has been sought in Norse and Celtic, and various conjectures have been made: possibly that the French might be from Old Norse *brak* 'creaking noise', or perhaps that Old Norse *bragr* 'the best' may be involved in the word's history. An early sense of the verb described the noise made by a trumpet: 'sound loudly'.

braid [Old English] The twisting and intricacy associated with braiding have arisen from the senses of the Old English verb *bregdan*, from a Germanic source. The three early meanings were: 'make a sudden movement', 'change

sudddenly', and 'interweave'; the Dutch verb *breien* is related. The early noun adds to the semantic picture: it meant 'a subtlety'.

brain [Old English] Old English *brægen* has a West Germanic origin; a related form is Dutch *brein*.

braise [mid 18th century] A culinary method involving stewing in a tightly-closed pan, *braise* is from the French verb *braiser*, which is based on *braise* 'live coals': formerly the cooking container was placed in the midst of these.
→ BRAZIER[1]

brake[1] [late 18th century] The origin of this word for 'cause to slow down' or for a device which slows or stops forward movement, is not known. There may be a connection with late Middle English *brake* 'winch of a crossbow', 'pump handle' (perhaps related to French *braquer* 'point a cannon'), or with late Middle English *brake* 'a bridle' (possibly from Old Dutch).

brake[2] [Old English] *Bracu*, an early word for 'a thicket' was first recorded in the plural in *fearnbraca* 'thickets of fern'; it is related to Middle Low German *brake* 'branch, stump'. This is a different word from Middle English **brake** 'a fern', which is perhaps an abbreviation of *bracken*, the final -*n* being interpreted as a plural ending.

branch [Middle English] Late Latin *branca* 'paw' gave Old French *branche*, source of the English word.

brand [Old English] There is a Germanic root in *brand*, originally 'a burning' and 'a piece of smouldering wood'; German *Brand* is related. The verb sense 'mark permanently with a hot iron' dates from late Middle English, giving rise to the mid 17th-century noun sense 'mark of ownership made by branding'; almost two centuries later the current prime sense in commercial contexts developed, denoting a type of product manufactured under a particular name. A special early use of *brand* in poetry for 'a sword' illustrates a link with *brandish*.
→ BURN[1]

brandish [Middle English] Ultimately of Germanic origin, *brandish* is from Old French *brandiss-*, the lengthened stem of *brandir* 'wave about'; and related to *brand*.

brandy [mid 17th century] *Brandwine* and *brandewine* were earlier forms of *brandy*. These came from Dutch *brandewijn*, from *branden* 'to burn, distil' and *wijn* 'wine'. The abbreviated form was used familiarly as early as 1657 and the fuller form was kept in official use (such as in customs' tariffs and parliamentary acts) until the end of the 17th century, when it gradually became regarded as a compound made up of *brandy* and *wine*.

brash [early 19th century] This adjective meaning *self-assertive in a rude way*, 'ostentatious' was originally dialect; it is perhaps a form of *rash*.
→ RASH¹

brass [Old English] The origin of Old English *bræs* is unknown. Related words in Old Frisian and Middle Low German simply meant 'metal'. The sense 'cheek', 'effrontery' appeared in late Middle English from a notion of hardness associated with metal, thus insensitivity. The derivative golf term **brassie** for a number two wood, dates from the late 19th century, because the wood was originally shod with brass. Interesting compounds of *brass* include:
■ **brass hat**, which is a late 19th-century phrase for a high-ranking officer in the armed forces, so named because of the gilt insignia on their caps. The slang phrase **top brass** (originally US) is associated.
■ **brass monkey**, also dating from the late 19th century, derives from a type of brass rack or 'monkey' in which cannon balls were stored and which contracted in very cold weather, ejecting the balls: hence the expression *cold enough to freeze the balls off a brass monkey*.

brassiere [early 20th century] This was originally a French word dating from the 17th century, meaning 'bodice, child's vest'. The English abbreviation **bra** for *brassiere* 'woman's undergarment for supporting the breasts' (first abbreviated as *bras*) arose in the 1930s.

brat [mid 16th century] A derogatory word for 'a child', this is perhaps associated with the synonymous Scots word *bratchet*, from Old French *brachet* 'hound, bitch'. Alternatively it may be from the dialect form *brat* for 'a rough garment', 'a rag', based on Old Irish *bratt* 'cloak'.

brave [late 15th century] *Brave* was adopted from French, from Italian *bravo* 'bold' or Spanish *bravo* 'courageous, untamed, savage', based on Latin *barbarus*. The Scots **braw** 'fine' (late 16th century) is a variant. Related to these is the noun **bravado**, also late 16th century: it is from Spanish *bravada*, from *bravo* 'bold'. **Bravery**, recorded slightly earlier in the mid 16th century, had the sense 'bravado' and came from French *braverie* or Italian *braveria* 'boldness', based on Latin *barbarus*.
→ BARBARIAN

bravo [mid 18th century] This exclamation used to express appreciation is from French, from the Italian word whose literal meaning is 'bold'. This same Italian adjective gave the

noun **bravura** 'great technical skill', which came into English at the same time.
→ BRAVE

brawn [Middle English] *Brawn* is descriptive of muscular strength and is also a term for a type of pressed potted meat. Its source is Old French *braon* 'fleshy part of the leg', from a Germanic root; a related word is German *Braten* 'roast meat'.

bray [Middle English] The loud harsh *bray* of a donkey stems from Old French *brait* 'a shriek', the verb being from *braire* 'to cry'; these senses passed directly into English. The ultimate origin is perhaps Celtic.

brazen [Old English] Old English *bræsen* meant 'made of brass', a usage which has persisted in poetry and literary language, from *bræs* 'brass' (Tennyson *Lady of Shalott*: The sun came dazzling through the leaves, And flamed upon the brazen greaves Of bold Sir Lancelot). The ultimate origin of the word is unknown. As with *brass* the semantic transference to 'audacity' is present in phrases such as *brazen hussy*.

brazier¹ [late 17th century] From French *brasier*, from *braise* 'hot coals', a *brazier* has a connection with the culinary term *braise*.

brazier² [Middle English] This word for a 'worker in brass' is probably based on *brass*, on the pattern of *glass* and *glazier*.
→ BRASS

breach [Middle English] The central notion of *breach* is 'breaking' whether this be to form 'a gap' or to 'sever' a bond such as a promise or a set of rules (*breach of the peace*). From Old French *breche*, the origin is ultimately Germanic.
→ BREAK¹

bread [Old English] A Germanic source relates Dutch *brood*, German *Brot*, and Old English *brēad* 'morsel of food'; there are pointers to a root meaning 'break'. Its importance as the staple part of the diet is shown in the compound **breadwinner** for a person obliged to work to provide essential food for the family; also in the phrase *take the bread out of someone's mouth*, where *bread* is 'means of subsistence'. With the relative affluence of recent times, the focus sometimes shifts to the 'basic' nature of this food, as in, for example, the phrase *on the breadline*, which was recorded as being used in the US to refer to any group of poor people at subsistence level needing help.
→ LOAF

breadth [early 16th century] Formed on the pattern of *length*, this measure is from obsolete *brede* which had the same sense; it is related to *broad*.

break¹ [Old English] The Old English form of *break* was *brecan*, which has a Germanic source and is related to Dutch *breken* and German *brechen*. It has an Indo-European root shared by Latin *frangere* 'to break', which gave English words such as *fracture*.

break² [mid 19th century] *Break*, and its variant *brake* as in *shooting brake*, a dated word for an estate car, is perhaps from 16th-century *brake* 'cage', later 'a framework'; its origin is unknown.

breakfast [late Middle English]
➔ BREAK¹; FAST²

breast [Old English] A Germanic source has given Old English *brēost*, Dutch *borst*, and German *Brust*, all related. The early word also meant 'chest' in general, and was considered the seat of the affections and the emotions. *Breast* is confined to Germanic; there is no Indo-European name for the breast; there may be a connection with Old Saxon *brustian* 'to bud', but not as has been suggested, English *berstan* 'to burst'.

breath [Old English] Dutch *adem* and German *Athem* 'breath' are in current use but their English relative *ethem* from a shared West Germanic root, gave way to Old English *bræth*, originally 'a smell, scent'; also from a Germanic source, it is related to *brood*. An early progression in the sense development was to 'vapour given off by a heated object' in Middle English, and in this same period the word was applied to exhalation by a person or animal. The verb **breathe** (also Middle English) based on *breath*, had the senses 'exhale' and 'steam'.
➔ BROOD

breathalyser [1960s] This is a noun based on a blend of *breath* and *analyse*.

breech [Old English] This word, common in the phrase *breech birth*, owes this particular sense of 'buttocks' to association with the meaning originally recorded for Old English *brēc*, which was a 'garment covering the loins and thighs'. This is in fact the plural of *brōc* of Germanic origin; Dutch *broek* is related. This English plural was interpreted as a singular form. Later the sense developed to mean 'the hind part' of anything, such as the back part of a rifle. Middle English **breeches** 'short trousers' is a repluralization.

breed [Old English] From a Germanic source, Old English *brēdan*, related to German *brüten*, meant 'to produce (offspring), bear (a child)'. The semantic root meant 'warmth', 'fostering', 'hatching'. The pair *brood/breed* are analogous to *food/feed* and *blood/bleed*.
➔ BROOD

breeze¹ [mid 16th century] This is probably from Old Spanish and Portuguese *briza* 'north-east wind', which was the original sense in English applied by English navigators of the 16th century to trade-winds on the Atlantic seaboard of the West Indies and Spanish Main. The extension to the sense 'gentle fresh wind' is predominant in English.

breeze² [late 16th century] *Breeze* as in *breeze blocks* is from French *braise* 'live coals'. Small cinders mixed with sand and cement make up this type of brick.

breve [Middle English] This is a variant of *brief* and is first recorded as referring to an authoritative letter from a monarch or pope. In the musical sense dating from 1460, the term was originally used in a series where a *long* was of greater time value than a *breve*. In printing contexts from the late 19th century, a *breve* has indicated a mark over a short or unstressed vowel.

brevity [late 15th century]
➔ BRIEF

brew [Old English] The Old English verb *brēowan*, Dutch *brouwen*, and German *brauen* are from a Germanic source and are related. The Germanic root (shared by *broth*) meant 'make a decoction', 'infuse' and thus had a wider sense than the English word; the same root is perhaps to be found in Latin *dēfrutum* describing new wine which has been boiled down. **Brewery**, which is recorded from the mid 17th century is based on *brew* and is probably formed on the pattern of Dutch *brouwerij*.
➔ BROTH

bribe [late Middle English] Both the noun and verb forms of *bribe* appear in Chaucer (c. 1342–1400) and the works of some of his contemporaries, but their history prior to then is obscure. There may possibly have been a sense development as follows (if the sense of Old French *bribe* is the original): 'piece of bread', 'alms', 'living from alms', 'professional begging'. The original sense of the English verb *bribe* (from Old French *briber*, *brimber* 'beg') was 'rob, extort', which led to the noun meanings 'theft, stolen goods', and 'money extorted or demanded for favours'. In the early 16th century, the verb came to mean 'offer money as an inducement'.

bric-a-brac [mid 19th century] This comes from French, from the obsolete phrase *à bric et à brac* 'at random'.

brick [late Middle English] English *brick* is found only from the middle of the 15th century. It was probably introduced by Flemish workmen; Old French *brique* 'a form of loaf' probably reinforced the adoption from Low German. Burgundian and Hainault dialect still have the phrase *brique de pain* 'piece of bread'. The ultimate origin is unknown; in English the word denoted the substance before coming to describe the shaped object.

bridal [late Middle English] The elements *brȳd* 'bride' (of Germanic origin) and *ealu* 'ale-drinking' made up Old English *brȳd-ealu* which meant 'wedding-feast'. Since the late 16th century, the word has been associated with adjectives ending in *-al*. The root sense of noun **bride** is uncertain but it may possibly be 'cook, brew, make broth', the duties of a daughter-in-law in the primitive family; the sense 'daughter-in-law' is the only one occurring in certain developments, e.g. medieval Latin *bruta*, Old French *bru*. Of the compounds based on *bride*, Old English had *brȳdguma*, from *brȳd* 'bride' and *guma* 'man'. The change in the second syllable forming **bridegroom** was due to association with *groom*. Another compound, **bridesmaid** was an alteration in the late 18th century of the earlier word *bridemaid*, by the insertion of the letter *s*.

bridge [Old English] The Old English form of the noun for a structure over a river or road was *brycg*; of Germanic origin, it is related to Dutch *brug* and German *Brücke*. The game of *bridge* dates from the late 19th century, but in this case the origin is unknown.

bridle [Old English] The early form of this word was *brīdel* in the case of the noun, and *brīdlian* as a verb. The origin is a Germanic root meaning 'pull, twitch' and the Dutch noun *breidel* is related. The sense 'show displeasure and unwillingness to cooperate' as in *she bridled at his remarks* arises by association with the action of a horse when reined in.

brief [Middle English] The Old French, from which this word comes, had the same spelling, the source is Latin *brevis* 'short'. The noun is via late Latin *breve* 'a note, dispatch', hence 'an official letter'. The late 15th-century noun **brevity** is from Old French *brievete*, from Latin *brevitas* (from *brevis* 'brief').

brigade [mid 17th century] Adopted from French, the word *brigade* comes from Italian *brigata* 'company', from *brigare* 'to contend'. The base noun is *briga* 'strife', the source too of late Middle English **brigand**, which denoted 'an irregular foot soldier' as well as 'bandit', 'member of a marauding gang': the core meaning is that of Italian *brigante*, literally 'a person contending'. In the late 17th century **brigadier** was also adopted from French.

bright [Old English] Old English *beorht* has a Germanic origin but it is now lost in all the languages except English. Dating from the same period is *(ge)beorhtnian*, now **brighten**.

brilliant [late 17th century] This adjective is from French *brillant* 'shining', the present participle of *briller*, from Italian *brillare*, probably from Latin *beryllus* 'beryl'. The abbreviation **brill** meaning 'great, wonderful' came into use in the 1980s.

brim [Middle English] *Brim* was originally the edge of the sea or any stretch of water; it may be related to German *Bräme* 'trimming'.

brimstone [late Old English] This is probably from Old English *bryne* 'burning' and *stān* 'stone'.

brine [Old English] The origin of Old English *brīne* remains unknown; a comparable form is Dutch *brijn*.

bring [Old English] Old English *bringan* 'cause to come along' is from Germanic; related are Dutch *brengen* and German *bringen*. The stem is not known outside Germanic.

brink [Middle English] *Brink* has a Scandinavian origin.

brisk [late 16th century] The probable source of *brisk* is French *brusque*.
➔ BRUSQUE

brisket [Middle English] This cut of meat is perhaps from Old Norse *brjósk* 'cartilage, gristle'.

bristle [Middle English] This is from the same base as Old English *byrst*, of Germanic origin, related to German *Borste*. Scots *birse* has persisted for 'bristle'.

brittle [late Middle English] Related to Old English *brēotan* 'to break up', *brittle* is ultimately of Germanic origin.

broach [Middle English] The verb *broach* 'raise, introduce' (as in *broach a subject*) is from Old French *brochier*, based on Latin *brocchus, broccus* 'projecting'. The earliest recorded sense was 'prick with spurs', generally 'pierce with something sharp', which gave rise in late Middle English to the sense 'pierce (a cask) to draw off liquor' and 'open and start using the contents of (a bottle)'. The figurative use 'raise and start a discussion about', dates from the late 16th century. A ship is sometimes said to *broach*, i.e. veer, but this is a different word of unknown origin, dating from the early 18th century.

broad [Old English] Old English *brād*, Dutch *breed* and German *breit* share a Germanic origin. The informal North American noun usage referring to a woman as a *broad* is an early 20th-century development. The late Middle English term **broadcloth** originally denoted cloth made 72 inches wide, as opposed to 'strait' cloth which was 36 inches wide. The word now implies quality rather than width.

broadcast [mid 18th century] *Broadcast* was first recorded in the sense 'sown by scattering', from *broad* and the past participle of *to cast*. The word's use in the contexts of radio and television dates from the early 20th century.

brocade [late 16th century] Italian *brocco* 'twisted thread' is at the base of this word introduced into English from Spanish and Portuguese *brocado* and influenced by French *brocart*.

brochure [mid 18th century] The French source word meant literally 'something stitched', from *brocher* 'to stitch'.
→ BROACH

brock [Old English] Old English *brocc, broc* 'badger' is Celtic in origin; related are Welsh and Cornish *broch*, Irish and Scottish Gaelic *broc*, and Breton *broc'h*.
→ BADGER

brogue [late 16th century] This word for a type of strong outdoor shoe is from Scottish Gaelic and Irish *bróg*, from Old Norse *brók*. It was originally a rough shoe of untanned hide worn in the wilder parts of Ireland and the Highlands of Scotland. The **brogue** referring to a marked accent when speaking English (recorded in use from the early 18th century), is perhaps by allusion to this type of rough footwear.
→ BREECH

broil [late Middle English] *Broil*, used commonly in North America as a culinary term, also had the sense 'burn, char' initially. It comes from Old French *bruler* 'to burn', but earlier details remain uncertain.

broker [Middle English] Initially a *broker* was a retailer or pedlar; the source is Anglo-Norman French *brocour*, but the ultimate origin remains unknown.

bronze [mid 17th century] *Bronze* was first recorded in use as a verb and derives from French, from Italian *bronzo*, probably based on Persian *birinj* 'brass'. A bronze currency was introduced in Great Britain in 1860 instead of copper; however, from traditional habit, 'a copper' is still the familiar name for a bronze coin.

brooch [Middle English] This is a variant of *broach*, a noun originally meaning 'skewer, bodkin', from Old French *broche* 'a spit for roast-ing'. The Latin base is *brocchus, broccus* 'projecting'.
→ BROACH

brood [Old English] Old English *brōd* 'family', 'hatching' is Germanic in origin; related forms are Dutch *broed* and German *Brut*. The sense 'think deeply about something sad' was originally (late 16th century), used with an object, i.e. 'nurse (feelings) in the mind', a figurative use of the notion of a hen nursing chicks under her wings.
→ BREED

brook[1] [Old English] The origin of Old English *brōc* is unknown; it is related to Dutch *broek* and German *Bruch* 'marsh'.

brook[2] [Old English] Old English *brūcan* meant 'to use', 'possess'. Germanic in origin, it is related to Dutch *bruiken* and German *brauchen*. The current sense 'tolerate' (as in *brook no dissent*) dates from the mid 16th century, a figurative use of an earlier sense 'to digest' (= make use of food), 'to stomach'.

broom [Old English] Old English *brōm* was the name of the shrub. Of Germanic origin, it is related to Dutch *braam* and English *bramble*. The name was applied to an implement for sweeping in Middle English when it was made of broom, heather, or similar twigs.

broth [Old English]
→ BREW

brothel [mid 16th century] The original word was *brothel-house*; the first element is from late Middle English *brothel* 'worthless man, prostitute', related to Old English *brēothan* 'to degenerate, deteriorate'.

brother [Old English] A Germanic source relates Old English *brōthor*, Dutch *broeder*, and German *Bruder*, from an Indo-European root shared by Latin *frāter*. Middle English **brotherhood** is probably from obsolete *brotherred* (based on Old English *-rǣden* 'condition, state'); a comparable form is *kindred*. The change of suffix was due to association with words ending in *-hood* and *-head*.

brow [Old English] In Old English *brū*, of Germanic origin, was 'eyelash, eyebrow'. Current senses such as *brow of a hill*, arose in Middle English.
→ BRAE

brown [Old English] 'Dark', 'dusky' was the meaning of Old English *brūn*. The association with 'gloom' gave rise to the phrase *in a brown study* meaning 'absorbed in one's thoughts'. The Germanic source of *brown* also gave Dutch *bruin* and German *braun*. In Middle English it gained a sense of 'burnished', referring to steel, as well as that of colour. The mid 16th-century word **brunette**, is from the French feminine of *brunet*, a diminutive of *brun* 'brown'.

browse [late Middle English] The early sense of *browse* was 'feed on leaves'; the source is Old French *broster*, from *brost* 'young shoot', probably of Germanic origin. The use 'look through (books) in a casual way' is not recorded before the late 19th century.

bruise [Old English] Old English *brȳsan* 'crush', 'injure or damage with a blow by something blunt' was reinforced in Middle English by Old French *bruisier* 'to break'.

brunch [late 19th century] A word blend from *breakfast* and *lunch*.

brunt [late Middle English] The origin of *brunt* is unknown but the early meaning was 'a blow', 'an attack', also denoting the force or shock of something. Possibly formed as an onomatopoeia, it was first recorded in the 14th century.

brush[1] [Middle English] A *brush* for sweeping is from Old French *broisse*; most French etymologists identify it with *brush* 'undergrowth, brushwood', a bunch of twigs such as broom being used for the implement. The verb is partly from Old French *brosser* 'to sweep'.

brush[2] [Middle English] *Brush* meaning 'undergrowth' is from Old French *broce*, perhaps based on Latin *bruscum*, a word for an excrescence on a maple.

brusque [mid 17th century] This has been adopted from the French word meaning 'lively, fierce', from Italian *brusco* 'sour'.
→ BRISK

brute [late Middle English] The noun use of *brute* dates from the early 17th century; initially *brute* was an adjective, from Old French *brut(e)*, from Latin *brutus* 'dull, stupid'. This same Latin base gave **brutal** from the late 15th century, which was first recorded with the sense 'relating to the lower animals', coming into English from Old French, or from medieval Latin *brutalis*.

bubble [Middle English] *Bubble* is partly imitative, partly an alteration of *burble*. The late 18th-century phrase **bubble and squeak** for a mixture of fried cooked cabbage and potatoes, is from the sounds of the mixture cooking.

buccaneer [mid 17th century] *Buccaneers* were originally European hunters in the Caribbean. The word is from French *boucanier*, from *boucan* 'a frame for cooking or curing meat', from Tupi (from the Amazon Valley) *mukem*.

buck[1] [Old English] Partly from *buc* 'male deer' (of Germanic origin, related to Dutch *bok* and German *Bock*), *buck* is reinforced by Old English *bucca* 'male goat', of the same ultimate origin. The phrases *buck someone up* and *buck up one's ideas* have a connection with the sharp jerk of the *buck*'s butting movements. *Buck* has been used meaning 'man' and in the 18th century described 'a dashing fellow, a dandy'; it had associations with lively spirit rather than elegance: this latter aspect arose in the 19th century.

buck[2] [mid 19th century] This informal word for 'a dollar' is of unknown origin.

buck[3] [mid 19th century] The *buck* which denotes an article placed in front of a card-player as a reminder of whose turn it is to deal at poker, is the word which has given the phrase *the buck stops here*. Its origin is unknown.

bucket [Middle English] *Bucket* is from Anglo-Norman French *buquet* 'tub, pail', perhaps from Old English *būc* 'belly, pitcher'.

buckle [Middle English] This word for a fastener is from Old French *bocle*, from Latin *buccula* 'cheek strap of a helmet'; the base is Latin *bucca* 'cheek'. The verb *to buckle* under a weight or strain is from French *boucler* 'to bulge'. A **buckler**, a Middle English word for a small round shield, is from Old French (*escu*) *bocler*, literally '(shield) with a boss', from *bocle* 'buckle, boss'.

bud [late Middle English] The origin of *bud* for a new shoot of a plant, is unknown.

buddy [mid 19th century] This was originally a US word and is perhaps an alteration of *brother*. The informal form of address **bud** dates from the same period and is an abbreviation of *buddy*.

budge [late 16th century] This movement verb is from French *bouger* 'to stir', based on Latin *bullīre* 'to boil'.

budgerigar [mid 19th century] Of Aboriginal origin, *budgerigar* is perhaps an alteration of Kamilaroi *gijirrigaa*, which is also found in related languages.

budget [late Middle English] Old French *bougette*, a diminutive of *bouge* 'leather bag', has given English *bulge*. Latin *bulga* 'leather bag, knapsack' is the source, of Gaulish origin. The word originally denoted a pouch or wallet, and later its contents. In the mid 18th century, the Chancellor of the Exchequer, in presenting his annual statement, was said 'to open the budget'. In the late 19th century, the use of

the term was extended from governmental to private or commercial finances.
➜ BULGE

buff [mid 16th century] The yellowish beige colour *buff* is probably from French *buffle*, from Italian *bufalo*, from late Latin *bufalus* 'buffalo'. The original sense in English was 'buffalo', later 'oxhide' or 'the colour of oxhide'. In the early 20th century the word *buff* was applied to enthusiastic fire-watchers, because of the buff uniforms formerly worn by New York volunteer firemen; this led to the usage 'enthusiast' as in *a computer buff*.

buffer¹ [mid 19th century] A *buffer* as a shock-absorbing piston and, figuratively, as something which serves to lessen the impact of something, is probably from the obsolete verb *buff*, imitative of the sound of a blow to a soft body.

buffer² [mid 18th century] The *buffer* in *old buffer* referring to an elderly man who is perceived as being old-fashioned and out-of-touch is probably from obsolete *buff*, or from the dialect verb *buff* 'stutter, splutter' (which may be the same word). In late Middle English *buffer* had the sense 'stammerer'.

buffet¹ [early 18th century] A *buffet* originally referred to a piece of dining-room furniture. It was adopted from French, from Old French *bufet* 'stool', but earlier details of the origin are unknown.

buffet² [Middle English] This verb describing the action of repeated and violent blows, is from Old French *buffeter*, and the noun comes from *buffet*, a diminutive of *bufe* 'a blow'.

buffoon [mid 16th century] This is from French *bouffon*, from Italian *buffone* (from medieval Latin *buffo* 'a clown'). It is connected with Italian *buffare* 'to puff' and some refer the word to the notion of puffing out the cheeks as a comic gesture. It was originally recorded as a rare Scots word for a kind of pantomime dance; in the late 16th century a *buffoon* was a professional jester.

bug [early 17th century] The origin of *bug* 'insect' is unknown. Current verb senses such as 'annoy' and 'fit with an eavesdropping device' date from the early 20th century.

bugbear [late 16th century] This is probably made up of obsolete *bug* 'bogey, ghost' (whose origin is unknown) and *bear*. It once referred to a sort of hobgoblin perhaps in the shape of a bear which was said to devour naughty children; later it became an object of needless dread (needless because imaginary).

bugger [Middle English] A *bugger* was originally a heretic, specifically an Albigensian (belonging to a heretic sect of southern France in the 12th and 13th centuries). The direct source is Middle Dutch, from Old French *bougre* 'heretic'; this came from medieval Latin *Bulgarus* 'a Bulgarian', particularly one belonging to the Orthodox Church and therefore regarded as a heretic by the Roman Church. The sense 'sodomite' appeared in the 16th century from an association of heresy with forbidden sexual practices; its use as a general insult dates from the early 18th century.

bugle [Middle English] The early English sense was 'wild ox', hence the compound *buglehorn* for the horn of an ox used to give signals, originally during hunting. The word comes via Old French from Latin *būculus*, a diminutive of *bōs* 'ox'.

build [Old English] Old English *byldan* is from *bold*, *botl* 'dwelling'; the origin is Germanic.
➜ BOWER

bulb [late Middle English] *Bulb* comes via Latin from Greek *bolbos* 'onion, bulbous root'. Directly based on *bulb* is the adjective **bulbous** which dates from the late 16th century.

bulge [Middle English] This is from Old French *boulge*, from Latin *bulga* 'leather bag'. The original meaning was 'wallet'; other senses to do with 'swelling' presumably derived from association with the shape of a full bag. In the early 17th century, a *bulge* referred to 'a ship's bilge', but gradually the word **bilge**, already in use from the late 15th century and probably a variant form, became predominant.
➜ BUDGET

bulk [Middle English] The earliest recorded senses ('cargo as a whole' and 'heap, large quantity') are probably from Old Norse *búlki* 'cargo'; other senses arose perhaps by alteration of obsolete *bouk* 'belly, body'. The compound **bulkhead**, dating from the late 15th century is not from the same source: it is based on Old Norse *bálkr* 'partition'.

bull¹ [late Old English] In Old English this was *bula* but it was only recorded in place names; it derives from Old Norse *boli*. The related English word **bullock** (late Old English *bulluc*) is a diminutive of *bula*. Later in the Old English period it denoted a male ox. The Stock Exchange usage, which originally referred to stock bought at a low price for selling at a profit later, arose in the early 18th century.

bull² [Middle English] The *bull* of *papal bull* is from Old French *bulle*, from Latin *bulla* 'a bubble, rounded object' which, in medieval Latin, became 'seal or sealed document'.

bull³ [early 17th century] The *bull* meaning 'nonsense' is usually associated with **bullshit**, a usage which dates from the early 20th century. The earlier meaning was 'an expression containing a ludicrous inconsistency' and was sometimes known as *Irish bull*; its origin is unknown.

bulldoze [late 19th century] This verb was originally US in the sense 'intimidate' and is made up of *bull* (suggesting size, by association with the animal) and *-doze* (an alteration perhaps of the noun *dose* 'quantity'). The early context was the whipping of black slaves as a punishment for non-compliance with orders; later this was extended to more general contexts of coercion and force. A **bulldozer** in the US of the 1870s was someone who took part in the practice of *bulldozing* slaves, as well as being a term for a type of pistol. The word's application to a type of heavy tractor dates from the 1930s.

bullet [early 16th century] Originally a *bullet* was 'a cannon ball'. The word is from French *boulet, boulette* 'small ball', a diminutive of *boule*, from Latin *bulla* 'a bubble'. The plural *bullets* is also slang in English for 'peas' and 'beans'.

bulletin [mid 17th century] First recorded as denoting an official warrant in some European countries, *bulletin* is from French, from Italian *bullettino*, a diminutive of *bulletta* 'passport', itself a diminutive of *bulla* 'seal'.

bullion [Middle English] Introduced into English from Anglo-Norman French in the sense 'a mint', *bullion* is a variant of Old French *bouillon*, based on Latin *bullire* 'to boil'. The sense progression from boiling to melting to molten metal, is purely an English development.

bully¹ [mid 16th century] This *bully* 'intimidating person' is probably from Middle Dutch *boele* 'lover', having undergone a reversal from its positive connotation to a negative one. Original use was as a term of endearment applied to either sex, later becoming a familiar form of address to a male friend. An attributive use meaning 'admirable, gallant, jolly' is seen in Shakespeare's *Midsummer Night's Dream*: What sayest thou, bully Bottom. The current noun use with its notion of aggression dates from the late 17th century. The phrase **bully pulpit** used from the early 20th century for a position of authority affording an opportunity to speak on any subject, was apparently originally used by President Theodore Roosevelt when explaining his personal view of the presidency (*Outlook* (New York) 27 February 1909: I have got such a bully pulpit!).

bully² [late 19th century] The hockey term *bully* originally denoted a scrum in Eton football; its origin is unknown.

bully³ [mid 18th century] The *bully* of *bully beef* is an alteration of French *bouilli* 'boiled'.

bulrush [late Middle English] This word for a type of waterplant is probably from *bull* (= the animal) conveying the sense 'large or coarse', as is the case in words such as *bullfrog*.

bum¹ [late Middle English] *Bum* 'buttocks' is of unknown origin. Interesting compounds based on this word are:
■ **bum bailiff**, a word from the early 17th century for a bailiff empowered to collect debts or arrest debtors. The association is with the approach made from behind as an element of surprise.
■ **bumboat**, apparently from *bum*, is a late 17th-century word for a small boat offering provisions for sale to moored vessels. The term originally denoted a scavenger's boat removing refuse etc. from ships and often also bringing produce for sale.

bum² [mid 19th century] *Bum* 'vagrant' is probably from *bummer* dating from the same period, which is perhaps from German *Bummler*, from *bummeln* 'to stroll, loaf about'. The US compound:
■ **bum steer** meaning 'a useless piece of advice', arose in the 1920s; the *steer* element carries the sense 'advice, guidance'.
→ STEER

bumble [late Middle English] The early sense was 'hum, drone' (as in **bumble bee**); the word is a frequentative of the sound word *boom*; it developed the additional meaning 'move around in a confused manner'.
→ BOOM¹

bumf [late 19th century] This word for what is perceived as useless printed information is an abbreviation of the slang phrase *bum-fodder*, which has the same sense.

bump [mid 16th century] This imitative word was first recorded in use as a verb; it is perhaps of Scandinavian origin. Based on this in a humorous formation, is the adjective **bumptious**, an early 19th-century word on the pattern of *fractious*.

bumpkin [late 16th century] English *bumpkin*, which describes a socially inept or unsophisticated person, is perhaps from Dutch *boomken* 'little tree' or Middle Dutch *bommekijn* 'little barrel', used to denote a dumpy person.

bun [late Middle English] The origin of *bun* is not known. It was originally a small soft round sweet bread or cake with currants; in Scotland

and Jamaica it is a rich fruit cake or currant bread.

bunch [late Middle English] The origin is a mystery, but the first meaning recorded was 'hump', 'goitre'.

bundle [Middle English] Perhaps Old English *byndelle* 'a binding' is the source of *bundle*, reinforced by Low German and Dutch *bundel*, to which *byndelle* is related.

bungalow [late 17th century] The Hindi word *baṅglā* 'belonging to Bengal' has given English *bungalow*.

bungee [1930s] The *bungee* of *bungee-jumping* is first recorded as denoting an elasticated cord for launching a glider; its origin is not known.

bunion [early 18th century] This is ultimately from Old French *buignon*, from *buigne* 'swelling (on the head) caused by a blow'.

bunker [mid 16th century] Originally Scots, a *bunker* was a seat or bench: it is perhaps related to mid 18th-century *bunk* describing a narrow bed.

bunkum [mid 19th century] A word for 'nonsense', 'twaddle', *bunkum* was originally spelt *buncombe*, referring to *Buncombe* County in North Carolina, a place mentioned in an inconsequential speech made in around 1820 by its congressman, solely with the aim of pleasing his constituents. The abbreviation **bunk** came into use in the early 20th century.

bunny [early 17th century] This was originally used as a term of endearment to a person, later as a pet name for a rabbit; it is based on dialect *bun* 'squirrel, rabbit', of unknown origin, also used as a term of endearment. The Australian use of the word in the sense 'victim' dates from the early 20th century.

buoy [Middle English] English *buoy* is probably from Middle Dutch *boye*, *boeie*, from a Germanic base meaning 'signal'. The verb is from Spanish *boyar* 'to float', from *boya* 'buoy'. The adjective **buoyant** (late 16th century) is from French *bouyant* or Spanish *boyante* 'floating', the present participle of *boyar* 'to float'.

burden [Old English] A West Germanic source gave Old English *byrthen*, which is related to the verb *bear* 'to carry'. English forms with the -*d*- spelling appeared early in the 12th century; comparable pairs are *murder* for *murther* and dialect *furder* for *further*.
→ BEAR¹

bureau [late 17th century] Adopted from French, the original meaning was 'baize', which was used to cover writing desks. There is a colour connection in that the word is from

Old French *burel*, probably from *bure* 'dark brown', based on Greek *purros* 'red'. The 19th-century derivatives **bureaucracy** and **bureaucrat** are also from French words.

burgeon [Middle English] Late Latin *burra* 'wool' gave Old French *borjon* 'bud', on which *bourgeonner* 'put out buds' is based; English *burgeon* comes from this.

burglary [early 16th century] *Burglary* is from legal French *burglarie*, from *burgler*; this or Anglo-Latin *burglator* are the source of English *burglar* which is related to Old French *burgier* 'to pillage'. The verb **burgle** was originally a humorous and colloquial back-formation from **burglar**, first recorded in the late 19th century.

burlesque [mid 17th century] The ultimate origin of *burlesque* is unknown, but it was adopted from French, which is from Italian *burlesco*, from *burla* 'mockery'.

burly [Middle English] The early meaning of *burly* was 'dignified, imposing', which is probably accounted for by an unrecorded Old English word meaning 'stately, fit for the bower'. The current sense conveys notions of strength and size.
→ BOWER

burn¹ [Old English] Old English *birnan* 'be on fire' and *bærnan* 'consume by fire' are both from the same Germanic base; they are related to German *brennen*.

burn² [Old English] The Old English forms *burna* and *burn(e)* 'small stream' are Germanic in origin and related to Dutch *bron* and German *Brunnen* 'well'. The Middle English word **bourn** is a southern English variant.

burnish [Middle English] When a metal is highly polished through rubbing, it has gone through the process of *burnishing*; the verb comes from Old French *burniss-*, the lengthened stem of *burnir*, variant of *brunir* 'to make brown', from *brun* 'brown'.

burr [Middle English] The early meaning of *burr* was 'prickly seed case'; it is probably Scandinavian in origin and related to Danish *burre* 'bur, burdock' and Swedish *kard-borre* 'burdock'. The notion of roughness may have a link with the *burr* referring to the rough pronunciation of the letter *r* such as the uvular trill of a Northumberland accent; *burr* may also refer to a rough buzzing noise.

burrow [Middle English] This word for a tunnel made by a small animal as a shelter, is a variant of *borough*.
→ BOROUGH

bursar [late Middle English] When *bursar* denotes a person in charge of the finance in a

college, or alternatively, a student holding a bursary, the source is medieval Latin *bursarius*, from *bursa* 'bag, purse'; in Greek *bursa* meant 'leather'. The word **bursary** was first recorded in the late 17th century as a room in a college used by a bursar; this form is from medieval Latin *bursaria*, from *bursa*.
→ PURSE

burst [Old English] A Germanic source is the basis of Old English *berstan*; Dutch *bersten* is related.

burton [Second World War] The phrase *gone for a burton* means 'lost', 'gone irretrievably' and was originally RAF slang: perhaps it was a euphemism based on going off for a *Burton* ale, from Burton-upon-Trent.

bury [Old English] The Old English verb *byrgan* is West Germanic in origin; and is related to the verb *borrow* and the noun *borough*. From the same period and related to *bury* is *byrgels* (**burial**) 'a place of burial, grave'; this was interpreted as plural in Middle English, hence the loss of the final -*s*.
→ BOROUGH; BORROW

busby [mid 18th century] A *busby* was originally a large bushy wig; the word's origin is unknown.

bush [Middle English] The source is Old French *bos, bosc*, variants of *bois* 'wood', reinforced by Old Norse *buski*. Of Germanic origin, *bush* is related to Dutch *bos* and German *Busch*. The sense 'uncultivated country' such as the *bush* of Australia, New Zealand, and Africa, is probably directly from Dutch *bos*. The phrase *go bush* is used in Australia for leaving one's usual surroundings, and arose by association with convicts escaping into wild country.

business [Old English] Old English *bisignis* meant 'anxiety'; the sense 'state of being busy' was used from Middle English down to the 18th century, but is now differentiated as *busyness*. The use 'appointed task' dates from late Middle English, and all the other current senses have developed from this. The abbreviation **biz** (mid 19th century) was originally US.

busk [mid 17th century] When musicians *busk* in the streets for money, the verb is from obsolete French *busquer* 'to seek', from Italian *buscare* or Spanish *buscar*; the origin is Germanic. Originally in nautical use meaning 'to cruise about, tack', the word later gained the extended sense of 'go about selling things', hence 'go about performing' (mid 19th century).

bust[1] [mid 17th century] A *bust* is first recorded as describing the upper part or torso of a large sculpture. The source is French *buste*, from Italian *busto*, but the origin of the Romanic word has not been ascertained.

bust[2] [mid 18th century] A variant of *burst*, the word *bust* was originally a US usage as a noun meaning 'an act of bursting or splitting'.

bustard [late 15th century] This word is perhaps an Anglo-Norman French blend of Old French *histarde* and *oustarde*, both from Latin *avis tarda* 'slow bird': the name is a mystery, as bustards are fast runners. The largest European bird, the great bustard *Otis tarda* was formerly found in England but is now extinct.

bustle [late Middle English] The hurry and busy activity associated with *bustle* are notions brought perhaps by a variant of obsolete *buskle*, a frequentative of *busk* 'to prepare', from Old Norse. Late 18th-century **bustle** as a fashion item for holding out the back of a skirt, is a term of unknown origin.

busy [Old English] The verb form in Old English was *bisgian*, and the adjective was *bisig*; Dutch *bezig* is related but the origin is unknown. The slang use of the noun *busy* for 'policeman' arose in the early 20th century.

but[1] [Old English] In Old English this conjunction was *be-ūtan, butan, būta* 'outside, without, except'.

but[2] [early 18th century] Scots *but* (as in *but and ben*) describing an outer room in a two-roomed cottage, is from the conjunction *but* in its early sense 'outside', specifically 'into the outer part of a house'.

butch [1940s] Used as an informal word for 'masculine in manner and appearance', *butch* is perhaps an abbreviation of *butcher*.

butcher [Middle English] This is from an Anglo-Norman French variant of Old French *bochier*, from *boc* 'he-goat', probably sharing the same ultimate origin as *buck* 'male goat'. The early word emphasized the act of slaughter rather than the selling of meat. Middle English **butchery** was a slaughterhouse or meat market, coming from Old French *boucherie*, from *bouchier* 'butcher'.

butler [Middle English] English *butler* is from Old French *bouteillier* 'cup-bearer', from *bouteille* 'bottle'. The verb **buttle** came into use in the mid 19th century, as as back-formation from *butler*.

butt[1] [Middle English] This verb meaning 'to strike against' something is from Old French *boter*; the origin is Germanic.

butt[2] [Middle English] This is the *butt* of phrases such as *the butt of her jokes*. The earliest use of the word was as an archery term for 'a mound on which a target could be set up'; it comes from *but*, an Old French word of unknown origin, and it was perhaps influenced by French *butte* 'rising ground'. Its figurative use as 'target' is seen in Shakespeare's *Henry V*: To which is fixed as an aim or butt Obedience.

butt³ [late Middle English] The *butt* of *cigarette butt* is apparently related to Dutch *bot* 'stumpy'; a dialect use of *butt* arose in the late Middle English period and meant 'buttock' in phrases such as *butte of porke*; this was later extended in US use to 'buttocks' more generally. As for the verb in the sense ' lie flat against' as in *the gutter butted against the wall*, this is partly from *butt* 'target', reinforced by *abut*.
➔ BUTT²; BUTTOCK

butt⁴ [late Middle English] A *butt* in the sense 'cask' is from Old French *bot*, from late Latin *buttis*.

butter [Old English] Old English *butere* is West Germanic in origin; Dutch *boter* and German *Butter* are relatives, based on Latin *butyrum*, from Greek *bouturon*. Compounds include:
■ **butterfly**, an Old English formation whose elements are perhaps due to the cream or yellow colour of common species, or to an old belief that the insects stole butter.
■ **butterfly effect**, part of chaos theory in the 1980s describing the fact that minute localized change in a complex system may have a large effect elsewhere; the phrasal elements are from the notion that a butterfly fluttering in Rio de Janeiro could change the weather in Chicago.
■ **butterwort** which is named from the plant's supposed ability to keep cows in milk, and so maintain the supply of butter.

buttery [Middle English] The common British English use of *buttery* is to refer to a room in a college where provisions are sold to students. This word is from Anglo-Norman French *boterie* 'butt-store', from Old French *bot* 'cask'.
➔ BUTT⁴

buttock [Old English] This was formerly identical with Old English *buttuc* which originally meant 'short ridge of land', probably from the base of *butt* 'stub', 'hind end'.
➔ BUTT³

button [Middle English] Related to English *butt* 'strike against', the word *button* is from Old French *bouton* 'bud', 'knob', 'button'; the origin is Germanic. The word started out with a connotation of shape, but the purpose of the object became the main focus as the word became extended to various applications.
➔ BUTT¹

buttress [Middle English] Old French *boter* 'to strike or thrust' gave (*ars*) *bouterez* 'thrusting (arch)', whence English *buttress* describing a structure built against a wall to support it.
➔ BUTT¹

buxom [Middle English] The original sense was 'compliant, obliging', later developing to 'lively and good-tempered', influenced by the traditional association of plumpness and good health with an easy-going nature. The formation of the word is from the stem of Old English *būgan* 'to bend' and the common suffix *-some* 'apt to'.
➔ BOW²

buy [Old English] A Germanic source gave Old English *bycgan* 'obtain by paying a price'. The sense progression to a notion of influencing someone by bribery, arose in the mid 17th century. Slang uses are seen in phrases such as *he bought it* meaning 'he was killed', evidenced from the early 19th century; the same phrase from the early 20th century could also mean 'he believed it'.

buzzard [late Middle English] Old French *busard* is the source, based on Latin *būteō* 'falcon'. The buzzard was considered an inferior kind of hawk which was useless for falconry; this led, apparently, to its use as a derogatory description of an ignorant or stupid person; the force weakened over time and the phrase *old buzzard* may convey nothing more than 'old chap'. In dialect a *buzzard* is sometimes 'a moth' or 'cockchafer' but this word is based on the sound verb *buzz*.

by [Old English] Old English *bī, bi, be* are Germanic in origin; related forms are Dutch *bij* and German *bei*.

bye-bye [early 18th century] This child's word to express *goodbye* is also found from the mid 19th century as the plural **bye-byes**, from the sound *bye-bye*, long used as a refrain in lullabies.

by-law [Middle English] This is probably from obsolete *byrlaw* which meant 'local law or custom', from Old Norse *bȳjar* 'of a town'. The first syllable eventually became associated with *by*. The first recorded reference to the local custom is in Kent in the 13th century, and involved settlement of boundary disputes between neighbours by specially appointed arbitrators out of court.

byre [Old English]
➔ BOWER

byte [1960s] The computer term *byte* for 'a group of bits' is an arbitrary formation based on the words *bit* and *bite*.
➔ BIT²

Cc

cab [early 19th century] A *cab*, in current use, is a *taxi cab* or the driver's compartment of a vehicle such as a lorry, bus, or train. In North American English, when this compartment is directly above the engine of a truck, it is known as a **cabover**, a late 20th-century truncation of *cab over engine*. The derivation of *cab* is by shortening *cabriolet*, a French word which, in the mid 18th century, described a light two-wheeled carriage with a hood, drawn by one horse. The motion of the carriage led to the name, from French *cabriole* 'a goat's leap', from *cabrioler* 'to leap in the air'. *Cab* continued to be used to describe the *cabriolet*'s improved successor, the *hansom*, and also became generalized to any public carriage with two or four wheels, drawn by one horse and seating two or four people. The word **cabbie** for a cab's driver, dates from the mid 19th century.

→ CABRIOLE; CAPER

cabal [late 16th century] Historically, *cabal* was a committee of five ministers under Charles II, whose surnames began with C, A, B, A, and L (they were Clifford, Arlington, Buckingham, Ashley (Earl of Shaftesbury), and Lauderdale). However the first recorded use of *cabal* (from French *cabale*) was in reference to the Cabbala, the ancient Jewish tradition of mystical interpretation of the Bible, first transmitted orally using esoteric methods such as ciphers. It reached the height of its influence in the later Middle Ages and remains significant in Hasidism (a movement founded in reaction to the rigid academicism of rabbinical Judaism). Medieval Latin *cabala* is the source of several variants of Cabbala, including *Kabbalah* (the preferred modern spelling), *Kabbala*, *Cabala*, and *Qabalah*, based on a rabbinical Hebrew word for 'tradition'.

cabaret [mid 17th century] A *cabaret* in early use, described a French inn (S. Pepys *Diary* 23 Sept.: In most cabaretts in France they have writ upon the walls 'Dieu te regarde'.). The source is Old French, meaning literally 'wooden structure', which comes via Middle Dutch from Old Picard *camberet* 'little room'. Current senses referring to entertainment in a nightclub, or to the nightclub itself, date from the early 20th century.

cabbage [late Middle English] The word *cabbage* has led to the compound **Cabbagetown** in Canadian English to describe a run-down urban area; it springs from the nickname of a depressed area of Toronto, where the inhabitants were said to exist on a diet of cabbage. *Cabbage* is from Old French (Picard dialect) *caboche* 'head', a variant of Old French *caboce*, whose origin is unknown. In the Channel Islands French *caboche* is used to mean 'cabbage'. The word **cabochon** is from the same Old French source: it dates from the mid 16th century, and means literally 'little head', describing a gem that has been polished but not faceted.

caber [early 16th century] A *caber* is a roughly trimmed tree trunk used in the Scottish Highland sport of *tossing the caber*, which involves heaving the trunk into the air so that it lands on its opposite end. The word is from Scottish Gaelic *cabar* 'pole'.

cabin [Middle English] *Cabin* is from Old French *cabane*, from Provençal *cabana*, from Latin *capanna*, *cavanna*. The word **cabinet** (mid 16th century) is formed on *cabin* by addition of the suffix *-et*; obsolete senses include 'little cabin'. However, French *cabinet* has influenced other uses such as the archaic meaning 'boudoir' and the current 'ornamental piece of furniture fitted with compartments'. A connection with *gabinetto* 'closet, chest of drawers', an Italian dialectal word related to *cabin*, has been suggested in the derivation. In political contexts, *the Cabinet* commonly refers to the small select body of chief ministers who meet to discuss government policy: this was originally known as the *Cabinet Council*, distinguished from the *Privy* (= *private*) *Council*.

cable [Middle English] This is from an Anglo-Norman French variant of Old French *chable*, from late Latin *capulum* 'halter (for catching cattle)'. In early use, a *cable* was a strong thick rope made of fibre such as hemp; now *rope* is commonly used when the material is fibre, whereas *cable* is used when made of wire. The word has been adopted by some writers instead of *camel* in the biblical quotation it is easier for a camel to go through the eye of a needle than for a rich man to enter the kingdom of God: this is a variant interpretation of Greek *kamēlon* in Matthew 19:24 (J. Cheke *Gospel St. Matthew*: It is easier for a cable to passe thorough a nedels eie).

caboodle [mid 19th century] The phrases *the whole caboodle* and *the whole kit and caboodle* mean 'the whole lot, the whole number'. *Caboodle* was originally a US usage, perhaps from the phrase *kit and boodle* which had the same meaning: *kit* often refers to 'equipment' and *boodle* (from a Dutch word for 'possessions') is an informal word for money.

cabriole [late 18th century] This is a French word adopted into English. Its literal meaning is, 'light leap', from *cabrioler* (earlier *caprioler*), from Italian *capriolare* 'to leap in the air'. In the late 18th century, a curved **cabriole leg** characteristic of Chippendale and Queen Anne furniture, derived its name from the resemblance to the front legs of a leaping animal.
➔ CAB

cachet [early 17th century] A *cachet* suggests 'respect' and 'prestige': e.g. *no other shipping company had quite the cachet of Cunard*. It basically describes 'a distinguishing mark or seal'. Adopted from French, from the sense 'to press' of *cacher*, the word is based on Latin *coactare* 'constrain'. This notion of constraint has led to the word's additional use for 'a flat capsule containing a dose of unpleasant-tasting medicine' (tightly sealed).

cack [Old English] In Old English, the prefix *cac-* was part of *cachūs* 'privy'. The verb, meaning 'defecate', dates from late Middle English and is related to Middle Dutch *cacken*, based on Latin *cacare* 'defecate'. In the mid 19th century, **cack-handed** was recorded meaning 'left-handed' or 'clumsy'. The use of *cack* in this informal phrase, was with derogatory reference to left-handedness.

cackle [Middle English] This is probably from Middle Low German *kākelen*; it is partly imitative of the sound made, reinforced by *kāke* 'jaw, cheek'. The evidence is not clear as to whether the word has been adopted from one language to another (cf. Dutch *kakelen*, Swedish *kackla*, Danish *kagle*) or whether it has arisen separately in imitation of animal sounds.

cacophony [mid 17th century] 'A harsh discordant mixture of sounds', *cacophony* has come into English from French *cacophonie*, from Greek *kakophōnia*: the base elements are *kakos* 'bad' and *phōnē* 'sound'.

cad [late 18th century] This is a dated term sometimes used humorously to describe a man who behaves dishonourably towards a woman, and appears to have arisen at the universities as a colloquial insult for a 'man of low, vulgar manners': it may have originated at Oxford in a contemptuous application to townsmen in the 'town and gown' rivalry. *Cad* however once referred to any passenger picked up by the driver of a horse-drawn coach for his personal profit. It is an abbreviation of *caddie* or *cadet*.
➔ CADDIE

cadaver [late Middle English] A medical term for a 'corpse', *cadaver* is also used in literary contexts. It is Latin, from the verb *cadere* 'to fall'.

caddie [mid 17th century] This was originally Scots and comes from French *cadet* 'younger'. Many French terms were adopted in Scots as a result of the close relationship of the 'Auld Alliance', the political alliance between Scotland and France which began with the treaty of 1295 between John Balliol and Philip IV of France. Early use of *caddie* was in reference to a gentleman joining the army without a commission with the intention of learning the profession and following a military career. Later it came to mean 'odd-job man'. The current golfing sense 'person who assists by carrying a golfer's clubs' dates from the late 18th century.

cadence [late Middle English] Early use was recorded as 'rhythm or metrical beat'. The word has come via Old French from Italian *cadenza*, based on Latin *cadere* 'to fall'. **Cadenza** (mid 18th century) is used as a musical term for a virtuoso solo passage usually inserted near the end of a movement in a concerto or other work. The phrase *have a cadenza* is used informally in South African English to mean 'be extremely agitated': this is said to be from Danny Kaye's *The Little Fiddle*, a humorous recording made in the 1940s.

cadet [early 17th century] The first recorded use was in the sense 'younger son or daughter': it was adopted from French, from Gascon dialect *capdet*, a diminutive based on Latin *caput* 'head'. The notion 'little head' or 'inferior head' gave rise to that of 'younger, junior'. A *cadet* is now common in military contexts and means 'trainee'.

cadge [early 17th century] The dialect sense 'carry about' was the early recorded use of *cadge*, which now means 'ask for something to which one is not strictly entitled'. It is a backformation (by removal of the suffix) from the noun *cadger* (late 15th century), which in northern English and Scots was 'an itinerant dealer'. This led to the verb sense 'hawk, peddle', from which the modern sense has been extended.

cahoots [early 19th century] Originally a US word and part of the phrase *in cahoots with* 'colluding with', *cahoot* may be from French *cahute* 'poor hut, cabin', suggesting complicity in an intimate closed environment.

cairn [late Middle English] A *cairn* is a mound of rough stones; it is from Scottish Gaelic *carn*. This word is found in all the Celtic languages, e.g. Old Irish *carn*, Welsh *carn* 'heap'. In Welsh there is also *carn* 'hoof, knife haft', indicating an earlier sense 'horn': it is possible that the primary sense is 'cairn on a mountain top' (– the horn on its head). The word enters into the names of several mountains in Wales and Scotland, e.g. *Cairngorms* (northern Scotland), from Scottish Gaelic *carn gorm* 'blue cairn'. A **Cairn terrier** (the smallest breed of terrier in Great Britain) is said to be so named because it was once used to hunt amongst cairns.

cake [Middle English] The word has a Scandinavian origin and is related to Swedish *kaka* and Danish *kage*. The ulterior history is unknown but the stem cannot be related, as formerly supposed, to Latin *coquere* 'to cook'. A *cake* first denoted a small flat bread roll baked hard on both sides by being turned in the process. This use of *cake* for a rounded flattened shape has influenced phrases such as *fish cake*, *potato cake*. In Scotland, parts of Wales, and the north of England, a *cake* sometimes describes a thin hard-baked brittle kind of oaten bread. This has given rise to the phrase *Land of Cakes* applied in banter to Scotland or the Scottish Lowlands (R. Burns *On Captain Grose's Peregrinage*: Hear, land o' Cakes, and brither Scots).

calamity [late Middle English] This is from Old French *calamite*, from Latin *calamitas* 'damage', 'disaster', 'adversity'. Latin writers associated this with *calamus* 'straw, corn stalk' referring it to damage to crops by hail, mildew, etc., but this is doubtful. Some refer it to a lost form (*calamis*) meaning 'injured'. **Calamity Jane** (1930s), used to describe someone expecting adversity, was the nickname of Martha Jane Burke (*c*.1852–1903), an American frontierswoman and markswoman.

calculate [late Middle English] This verb is from late Latin *calculare* 'to count'. The base is Latin *calculus* 'a small pebble (as used on an abacus)' source too of the term **calculus**, a branch of mathematics.

calendar [Middle English] From Old French *calendier*, from Latin *kalendarium* 'account book', *calendar* is based on Latin *kalendae* referring to the 'first day of each month (of the Roman calendar)'. Old English **calends** indicated an appointed time: its Latin source, *kalendae*, referred to the time when accounts were due and when the order of days was proclaimed: related words are Latin *calare* and Greek *kalein* 'call, proclaim'. The *Julian calendar* was introduced by Julius Caesar in 46 BC: the year consisted of 365 days, every fourth year having 366 days. It was superseded by the Gregorian calendar, though it is still used by some Orthodox churches. The Gregorian calendar was a modification of the Julian, introduced in 1582 by Pope Gregory XIII. To bring the calendar back into line with the solar year, 10 days were suppressed and centenary years were made leap years, only if divisible by 400. Scotland adopted this 'New Style' in 1600, but England and Wales did not follow until 1752, by which time 11 days had to be suppressed.

calf¹ [Old English] Old English *cælf* 'young bovine animal' has a Germanic origin and is related to Dutch *kalf* and German *Kalb*. In transferred use the word sometimes refers to something that appears to be born of something larger, for example an iceberg detached from a coast glacier, or (from Old Norse *kálfr*) a small island lying close to a larger one, as in *the Calf of Man* near the Isle of Man.

calf² [Middle English] The *calf* which describes the fleshy lower back part of the leg, is from Old Norse *kálfi*, but earlier details of the origin are unknown.

calibre [mid 16th century] The first recorded sense was 'social standing or importance'. It comes via French from Italian *calibro*, perhaps from Arabic *kalib* 'a mould (for casting metal)', based on Greek *kalapous* 'shoemaker's last'. Weight is a feature of *calibre*: e.g. the *calibre* of a mounted gun determines the weight of the projectile it can throw. This leads to a notion of 'weight' with regard to a person's character and personal ability.

calliper [late 16th century] This is apparently an alteration of *calibre*. It is an instrument for measuring external or internal dimensions and *culliper compasses* measure the calibre of a bullet. Several 16th-century writers assign the same origin to both *calliper* and *calibre*. The origin cited is *caliver*, the name of a type of harquebus (a portable gun fired from a forked rest), a word often used in the sense of *calibre* in the 16th and 17th centuries.

call [late Old English] Old English *ceallian* is from Old Norse *kalla* 'summon loudly' Middle English *callen* was originally northern.

calligraphy [early 17th century] The origin is Greek *kalligraphia*, from *kalligraphos* 'person who writes beautifully'. The base elements are *kallos* 'beauty' and *graphein* 'write'.

callous [late Middle English] The early English sense reflected the Latin source *callosus* 'hard-skinned'. The transference to 'insensitive to others' feelings' has a parallel in the phrase *thick-skinned*.

callow [Old English] Old English *calu* 'bald' is West Germanic in origin, probably from Latin *calvus* 'bald'. This was later extended to mean 'unfledged'; it was also applied to the down of unfledged birds which led to an association with the 'down' on a youth's cheek and chin and, figuratively, to the present sense 'immature, inexperienced' (C. Brontë *Shirley*: In all the voluptuous ease of a yet callow pacha).

calm [late Middle English] English *calm* with its notion of 'peace' and 'undisturbed serenity' came via one of the Romance languages from Greek *kauma* 'heat (of the day)'. Portuguese and Old Spanish *calma* also mean 'heat of the day', but Italian *calma* has no sense of heat, just of calm and quiet weather.

calque [1930s] A French adoption, meaning literally 'copy, trace', *calque* is from French *calquer* 'to trace', via Italian from Latin *calcare* 'to tread'.

cam [late 18th century] A *cam* is a projection on a rotating part in machinery. It is from Dutch *kam* 'comb', as in *kamrad* 'cog wheel'.

camber [late Middle English] *Camber* 'a slightly convex shape of a horizontal surface such as a road', is from Old French *cambre*, a dialect variant of *chambre* 'arched'. The base is Latin *camurus* 'curved inwards'.

camera [late 17th century] *Camera* was first recorded as a 'council or legislative chamber' in reference to Italy or Spain; it is a Latin word meaning 'vault, chamber', from Greek *kamara* 'object with an arched cover'. The *Radcliffe Camera* in Oxford owes its name to its rounded design: the Radcliffe building was described as a *camera* in the Latin statute of 1856. It is now used as a Reading Room in connection with the Bodleian Library under the name 'Camera Bodleiana'. The Latin phrase *in camera* is used in legal contexts to mean 'in the judge's private chamber' instead of in open court. In the 19th century, the Latin *camera* 'chamber' was applied in English to a device recording visual images in the form of photographs; **camera obscura**, literally 'dark chamber', had existed earlier (early 18th century), so too **camera lucida**, literally 'bright chamber' (mid 18th century). A *camera obscura* is a darkened box with a convex lens for projecting the image of an external object on to the screen inside; a *camera lucida* is an instrument in which rays of light are reflected by a prism to produce an image on a sheet of paper.

camouflage [First World War] This was adopted from French, from *camoufler* 'to disguise', which was originally thieves' slang. It comes from Italian *camuffare* 'to disguise, deceive', perhaps by association with French *camouflet* 'a whiff of smoke in the face'.

camp[1] [early 16th century] A *camp* describing a place with temporary accommodation, is from French *camp*, *champ*, from Italian *campo*. The base is Latin *campus* 'level ground', which was specifically applied to the *Campus Martius* in Rome, used for games, athletic practice, and military drill. The late 20th-century word **camporee** used mainly in North American English to describe a local camping event for scouts, is a blend of *camp* and *jamboree*.

camp[2] [early 20th century] The adjective *camp* meaning 'ostentatiously effeminate' is of unknown origin.

campaign [early 17th century] A *campaign* was first recorded as a tract of open land. It is from French *campagne* 'open country', via Italian from late Latin *campania*, from *campus* 'level ground'. The change in sense to 'a series of military operations' arose from an army's practice of 'taking the field' (i.e. moving from a fortress or town to open country) at the start of summer.

can[1] [Old English] Old English *cunnan* 'know' (in Middle English 'know how to') is related to Dutch *kunnen* and German *können*. It is from an Indo-European root shared by Latin *gnoscere* 'know' and Greek *gignōskein* 'know'. The current sense 'be able' comes through the notion of assimilated knowledge.
→ CUNNING

can[2] [Old English] Old English *canne* was a container for liquids; this could be of any material, shape, or size, and sometimes described a drinking cup. It is related to Dutch *kan* and German *Kanne*. It is either of Germanic origin or from late Latin *canna*. The word is now more specifically used of a cylindrical container made of metal. The phrase *in the can* is a slang expression meaning 'in prison' (originally a US usage); the same phrase may mean 'completed' in cinematography contexts when a film or film sequence has just been shot to a satisfactory standard. The idiom *carry the can* is said to be services' slang referring to the beercan which one soldier carries for all his companions, thus extended to mean 'bear responsibility': this origin however is unverified.

canal [late Middle English] This term for an artificial waterway or tubular duct is from an Old French alteration of *chanel* 'channel', from Latin *canalis* 'pipe, groove, channel'. The base is Latin *canna* 'cane'.

cancel [late Middle English] The early sense was 'obliterate or delete writing by drawing or stamping lines across it', which, in legal contexts, rendered documents void. It is from Old French *canceller*, from Latin *cancellare*, from *cancelli* 'crossbars'. This Latin base and the notion of 'crossbars' gave rise to the anatomy term **cancellous** in the mid 19th century, referring to bone tissue with a meshlike structure. The notion of 'obliteration' is captured in computing contexts, where the term **cancelbot**, coined in the 1990s, denotes a program that searches for and deletes specified mailings from Internet newsgroups: it is formed from the verb *cancel* and the *bot* syllable of *robot*.

cancer [Old English] This is a Latin word for 'crab', 'creeping ulcer', translating Greek *karkinos*: this is said to have been applied to such tumours because the swollen veins around them resembled the limbs of a crab. The spelling *canker* was usual until the 17th century but *cancer* gradually superseded this as a more technical term. The Latin word was reintroduced in Middle English in astronomy as the zodiac sign *Cancer*.
→ CANKER

candid [mid 17th century] The early sense in English reflected that of Latin *candidus* 'white'. Subsequent early senses were 'pure, innocent', 'unbiased', and 'free from malice'; these led to 'frank' in the late 17th century. This notion of 'frankness' led to the phrase **candid camera**, which involves informal photography frequently without the knowledge of the subject, giving unposed true-to-life results.
→ CANDOUR

candidate [early 17th century] *Candidate* is based on Latin *candidus* 'white'. It is from Latin *candidatus* 'white-robed', an adjective also used as a noun to denote a candidate for office whose traditional attire was a white toga.

candle [Old English] Old English *candel* is from Latin *candela*, from *candere* 'to be white or glisten'. Old English *Candelmæsse* derives its name from the tradition of blessing candles at this Christian festival held on 2 February. It commemorates the purification of the Virgin Mary and the presentation of Christ in the Temple. Another name associated with candle-burning is the zoological term **candlefish** (late 19th century) which arose because the Chinook Indians formerly burnt the oily bodies of these fish as candles.

candour [late Middle English] The early English sense was that of the Latin source *candor* 'whiteness'. The current meaning, 'openness and honesty in expression', dates from the mid 18th century. The development of the senses paralleled that of *candid*.

candy [mid 17th century] Early use was as a verb ('preserve by coating and impregnating with sugar'); the noun use is from late Middle English *sugar-candy*, from French *sucre candi*

'crystallized sugar'. The source is Arabic *sukkar* 'sugar' and *ḳandı* 'candied', based on Sanskrit *khaṇḍa* 'fragment'. Compounds include:

■ **candyman** now meaning somebody who sells illegal drugs. In earlier use (mid 19th century) the word described a ragman who gave toffee in exchange for goods.

■ **candy-striper**, an informal term in North American usage for a female voluntary nurse in a hospital: the name derives from the candy-striped uniforms of such nurses.

canine [late Middle English] Latin *canis* 'dog' is the base of *canine*, which means 'characteristic of a dog' as in *canine teeth*. It is also used in astronomy contexts for constellations: **Canis Major** (the Great Dog), and **Canis Minor** (the Little Dog): these constellations are said to represent hounds following Orion, the hunter of Greek mythology.

canister [late 15th century] In early use, a *canister* denoted a basket. It is from Latin *canistrum* 'basket for bread, fruit, or flowers', from Greek *kanastron* 'wicker basket', from *kanna* 'cane, reed'. Now, typically, a *canister* is made of metal; the shape tends to be round or cylindrical.

canker [Middle English] The early word described a tumour. It is from Old French *chancre*, from Latin *cancer* 'crab'. In current use, *canker* describes fungal disease, an ulcerous condition, or inflammation. In literary use, however, it is extended to 'a malign and corrupting influence' (Bacon *Of Honour and Reputation*: Enuie which is the canker of Honour).
→ CANCER

cannibal [mid 16th century] This word is from the Spanish plural *Caníbales*, a variant (recorded by Columbus) of *Caribes*, the name of a West Indian people reputed to eat humans.

cannon [late Middle English] This large heavy piece of artillery derives its name from French *canon*, from Italian *cannone* 'large tube', from *canna* 'cane, reed'. The spellings *cannon* and *canon* occurred alongside each other until about 1800, but the current spelling became more frequent after about 1660.

canny [late 16th century] The original word was Scots. It is a comparatively modern word, based on *can* in the obsolete sense 'know'. The current meaning is 'showing shrewdness' and 'careful and cautious' (R. Burns *Auld Farmers New-year Salutation*): Hamely, tawie, quiet and cannie). In the north of England, the word is used to express approbation as in *Canny New-castle*.

canon[1] [Old English] *Canon* 'general rule' is from Latin, from Greek *kanōn* 'rule', reinforced in Middle English by Old French *canon*. The sense development is uncertain: a *canon* is also a musical term for a piece in which the same melody is begun in different parts successively so that the imitations overlap. The musical association is also found in **canon cancrizans** (late 19th century) which includes the medieval Latin word *cancrizans* 'walking backwards' (from *cancer* 'crab'). Here the theme of the *canon* is repeated backwards in the second part.

canon² [Middle English] This had the early sense 'canon regular', a member of certain orders of clergy living communally according to an ecclesiastical rule in the same way as monks. It is from Old French *canonie*, from Latin *canonicus* 'according to rule'. The sense referring to a member of the clergy on the staff of a cathedral, dates from the mid 16th century.

canopy [late Middle English] *Canopy* is from medieval Latin *canopeum* 'ceremonial canopy', which is an alteration of Latin *conopeum* 'mosquito net over a bed'. The source is Greek *kōnōpeion* which described a 'couch with mosquito curtains', from *kōnōps* 'mosquito'.

cant [early 16th century] *Cant* describing either 'hypocritical and sanctimonious talk on a moral or religious issue' or alternatively 'a catchword temporarily in fashion', is probably from Latin *cantare* 'to sing'. The early meaning was 'musical sound, singing'; in the mid 17th century this gave rise to the senses 'whining manner of speaking' and 'form of words repeated mechanically' (such as the pleas made by beggars, referred to as *the canting crew*): this led to the sense 'jargon' specific to certain groups (Dickens *Nicholas Nickleby*: All love—bah! That I should use the cant of boys and girls—is fleeting enough).

cantankerous [mid 18th century] The origin is unknown. It is perhaps a blend of Anglo-Irish *cant* 'auction' and *rancorous* 'bitter and resentful'.
→ RANCOUR

canteen [mid 18th century] This was originally a type of shop in a barracks or garrison town, selling provisions and liquor to soldiers. The form comes from French *cantine*, from Italian *cantina* 'cellar'. A French use of *cantine* for a small compartmented case for carrying bottles of wine, may have given rise to the sense 'case containing cutlery'. The notion, from early usage, of 'organized provision for a group' has been extended to one of 'fostered group spirit and beliefs' in the expression **canteen culture**: this arose in the 1980s for the type of conservative resistance to more modern codes of practice, said to exist within

the police force and fostered by discussions in the informality of canteen meetings.

canter [early 18th century] Early use was as a verb; it is short for *Canterbury pace* or *Canterbury gallop*, which suggested the supposed easy pace of medieval pilgrims to Canterbury. The shrine of Thomas à Becket (St Thomas of Canterbury) was in pre-Reformation times a favourite place of pilgrimage; this was the shrine to which Chaucer's narrators of his *Canterbury Tales* were heading as a company of pilgrims.

canticle [Middle English] A *canticle* is a hymn or chant, typically with a biblical text. It comes from Latin *canticulum* 'little song', a diminutive of *canticum*, from *canere* 'sing'.

canton [early 16th century] This word denotes a subdivision of a country, such as a state of the Swiss Federation, or it refers, in heraldry, to a square charge in the upper corner of a shield. It comes from Old French, literally 'corner', from Provençal, based on a Romance word related to medieval Latin *cantus* 'side, corner'. The verb was reinforced by French *cantonner* 'to quarter'.

canvas [late Middle English] This is from Old Northern French *canevas*, based on Latin *cannabis* 'hemp', from Greek.

canvass [early 16th century] The first recorded sense was 'toss in a canvas sheet': this was a punishment or as part of a sport. The word is from *canvas*. Later extended senses include 'criticize, discuss' (as if 'tossing about' an issue: mid 16th century) and 'propose for discussion'; this came to be 'seek support' as in the phrase *canvass for votes*.

canyon [mid 19th century] This word for 'a deep gorge' is from Spanish *cañón* 'tube', based on Latin *canna* 'reed, cane'. Other words based on Latin *canna* are *can*, *canal*, *cannon*, *cannula*, *canvas*, and *channel*.

cap [Old English] Old English *cæppe* 'hood' is from late Latin *cappa*, perhaps from Latin *caput* 'head'.

capable [mid 16th century] The first recorded sense was 'able to take in', physically or mentally. The spelling is from French, from late Latin *capabilis*, from Latin *capere* 'take or hold'.

capacity [late Middle English] From French *capacité*, from Latin *capacitas*, *capacity* is based on Latin *capax*, *capac-* 'that can contain', from *capere* 'take or hold'. This 'holding' may refer physically to containers, or mentally to a person's ability to take in information.

cape¹ [mid 16th century] *Cape* 'a sleeveless cloak' is from French, from Provençal *capa*, from late Latin *cappa* 'covering for the head'.
→ CAP

cape² [late Middle English] *Cape* 'promontory' (as in *Cape of Good Hope*) is from Old French *cap*, from Provençal, based on Latin *caput* 'head'.

caper [late 16th century] To *caper* is 'to skip about in a playful way'; a *caper* is 'an amusing escapade'. The word is an abbreviation of **capriole**, which came via French from Italian *capriola* 'leap', from *capriolo* 'roebuck'. The semantic association, therefore, is 'frolicking', the base being Latin *capreolus*, a diminutive of *caper*, *capr-* 'goat'.
→ CABRIOLE

capillary [mid 17th century] Defining a tube with a hairlike thinness, *capillary* is from Latin *capillaris*, from *capillus* 'hair', influenced by Old French *capillaire*.

capital¹ [Middle English] Early use of *capital* ('most important, chief, largest' and 'wealth') was as an adjective in the sense 'relating to the head or top', later 'standing at the head or beginning'. The spelling is via Old French from Latin *capitalis*, from *caput* 'head'.

capital² [Middle English] This term used in architecture for the distinct broader part at the head of a column, is from Old French *capitel*, from late Latin *capitellum* 'little head', diminutive of Latin *caput*.

capitulate [mid 16th century] *Capitulate* was first recorded as meaning 'parley, draw up terms'. It is from French *capituler*, from medieval Latin *capitulare* 'draw up under headings': this is from Latin *capitulum*, a diminutive of *caput* 'head'. It now means 'cease to resist an opponent or an unwelcome demand'.

caprice [mid 17th century] A *caprice* is a 'sudden unaccountable change of mood'. It comes from French, from Italian *capriccio*, which is literally 'head with the hair standing on end', hence 'horror'. This eventually became 'a sudden start, a sudden change', under the influence of Italian *capra* 'goat' which is associated with frisky movement: the base elements are *capo* 'head' and *riccio* 'hedgehog'. **Capricious** 'unpredictable' (early 17th century) is from French *capricieux*, from the same Italian base.

capsize [late 18th century] This is perhaps based on Spanish *capuzar* 'sink (a ship) by the head', from *cabo* 'head' and *chapuzar* 'to dive or duck'.

capstan [late Middle English] A *capstan*, used to wind rope or cable on board ship, is probably from Provençal *cabestan*, from *cabestre* 'halter'. The Latin source is *capistrum*, from *capere* 'seize'. The word occurred in English in the 14th century and may have been learnt from the shipmen of Marseilles or Barcelona at the time of the Crusades.

captain [late Middle English] Early use was as a general term for 'a chief or leader'. The derivation is Old French *capitain* (superseding earlier *chevetaigne* 'chieftain'), from late Latin *capitaneus* 'chief'. The base is Latin *caput*, *capit-* 'head'.

caption [late Middle English] Early use was in the sense 'seizing, capture'. *Caption* is from Latin *captio(n-)*, from *capere* 'take, seize'. The early senses 'arrest' and 'a warrant for arrest' gave rise in the late 17th century to *caption* as a 'statement of where, when, and by whose authority a warrant was issued'. Such a statement was usually appended to a legal document, hence the sense 'heading or appended wording' from the late 18th century.

captive [late Middle English] The word *captive* is from Latin *captivus*, from *capere* 'seize, take', the base too of the mid 16th-century noun **capture** which came via French. The related verb **captivate** dates from the early 16th century and is from the late Latin verb *captivare* 'take captive' (from *captivus*).

Capuchin [late 16th century] 'A friar belonging to a branch of the Franciscan order that observes a strict rule drawn up in 1529', *Capuchin* is from obsolete French, an earlier form of *capucin*, from Italian *cappuccino*. This is based on *cappuccio* 'hood, cowl', from *cappa* 'cape': the Capuchin friars wear sharp-pointed hoods. The name has also been applied to a South American monkey with a cap of hair on its head which has the appearance of a cowl, as well as to a breed of pigeon with neck and head feathers resembling a cowl.

car [late Middle English] The early recorded use of *car* was in the general sense 'wheeled vehicle', which might describe a carriage, chariot, cart, wagon, etc. It comes from Old Northern French *carre*, based on Latin *carrum*, *carrus* 'wheeled vehicle'. The origin is Celtic. From the 16th to the 19th centuries, the word was mainly poetic and conveyed splendour and solemnity: Tennyson *Ode to Wellington*: And a reverent people behold The towering car, the sable steeds. In the US a *car* nearly always refers to a railway vehicle, e.g. *passenger-car*, *freight-car*.

carafe [late 18th century] Adopted from French, from Italian *caraffa*, *carafe* is probably based on Arabic *garafa* 'draw water'. The association now is with the serving of wine. The word has long been in use in Scotland, but appeared later in England where it is often treated as if still a French word.

carat [late Middle English] This is a measure of the purity of gold (the early use of the English word) as well as a unit of weight for precious stones and pearls. It comes via French from Italian *carato*, from Arabic *ḳīrāṭ*, a unit of weight. The base is Greek *keration* 'fruit of the carob' (also denoting a unit of weight), a diminutive of *keras* 'horn', which visually captured the shape of the carob's elongated seed pod.

caravan [late 15th century] The early use of *caravan* was to describe a group of people such as traders or pilgrims travelling together across a desert in Asia or North Africa. The word comes from French *caravane*, from Persian *kārwān*. The sense 'covered horse-drawn wagon' dates from the early 19th century; during this period it also described a third class 'covered carriage' on a railway. A **caravanserai** (late 16th century) is from Persian *kārwānsarāy*, literally a 'caravan palace': the word is either synonymous with the early sense of *caravan* or it describes an inn with a central courtyard for travellers.

carbine [early 17th century] A *carbine* in more recent use is a light automatic rifle. It comes from French *carabine*, from *carabin* 'mounted musketeer', a word of unknown origin. A **carabineer** was a cavalry soldier whose principal weapon was a *carbine*; the word dates from the mid 17th century, from French *carabinier* (from *carabine*).

carboy [mid 18th century] A large globular glass bottle with a narrow neck, used for holding acids or other corrosive liquids, is known as a *carboy*. The term is from Persian *ḳarāba* 'large glass flagon (for wine, rose-water, etc.)'.

carbuncle [Middle English] A *carbuncle* is a bright red gem and usually refers to a garnet; it is also used to denote a severe abscess. It comes from Old French *charbuncle*, from Latin *carbunculus* 'small coal', from *carbo* 'coal, charcoal'. The red colour is by association with a lighted coal.

carcass [Middle English] Carcass is from Anglo-Norman French *carcois*, a variant of Old French *charcois*. In later use, the word is from French *carcasse*; the ultimate origin remains unknown. From around 1750 *carcass* ceased to be used for the dead body of a person in ordinary language except in contempt; it was restricted to the dead body of an animal although originally it referred to both.

carcinoma [early 18th century] This medical term has come via Latin from Greek *karkinōma*, from *karkinos* 'crab'.
→ CANCER

card¹ [late Middle English] The first recorded sense of *card* was 'playing card'; it is from Old French *carte*, from Latin *carta*, *charta*, from Greek *khartēs* 'papyrus leaf'.

card² [late Middle English] The *card* used as a verb to mean 'comb and clean (raw wool)' is from Old French *carde*, from Provençal *carda*, from *cardar* 'tease, comb'. This is based on Latin *carere* 'to card'.

cardigan [mid 19th century] This term arose during the Crimean War. The name is due to James Thomas Brudenel, the 7th Earl of *Cardigan* (1797–1868), leader of the Charge of the Light Brigade, whose troops are thought to have first worn this type of garment.

cardinal [Old English] This ecclesiastical term is from Latin *cardinalis*, from *cardo*, *cardin-* 'hinge'. The sense has arisen through the notion of the important function of such priests as 'pivots' of church life. *Cardinal red* is by association with the deep scarlet colour of a cardinal's cassock.

care [Old English] Old English *caru* (noun) and *carian* (verb) are Germanic in origin; they are related to Old High German *chara* 'grief, lament', *charon* 'grieve', and Old Norse *kǫr* 'sickbed'. **Careless** (in Old English *carlēas*) meant 'free from care'.

career [mid 16th century] The first recorded sense was 'racecourse'; a *career* was also 'a charge' of a horse, often in the expression *to pass a career* at a tournament or in battle (Milton *Paradise Lost*: Mortal combat or career with Lance). The word is from French *carrière*, from Italian *carriera*, based on Latin *carrus* 'wheeled vehicle'. The sense 'stages in professional employment' is extended from a notion of progressing along a course.

caress [mid 17th century] Based on Latin *carus* meaning 'dear', *caress* is from French *caresser* (verb) and *caresse* (noun), the source of which was Italian *carezza*.

cargo [mid 17th century] *Cargo* is from Spanish *cargo*, *carga*, from late Latin *carricare*, *carcare* 'to load', from Latin *carrus* 'wheeled vehicle'.
→ CHARGE

caricature [mid 18th century] Adopted from French, from Italian *caricatura*, *caricature*, with its sense of exaggeration to dramatic or amusing effect, is based on Italian *caricare* 'load, exaggerate', from Latin *carricare* 'to load'.

carnage [early 17th century] Latin *caro, carn-* 'flesh' is the base of *carnage* describing 'the killing of large numbers of people'. The English spelling came from French, from Italian *carnaggio*, from medieval Latin *carnaticum*.

carnival [mid 16th century] *Carnival* is from Italian *carnevale*, from medieval Latin *carnelevamen* 'Shrovetide', The Latin elements here are *caro, carn-* 'flesh' and *levare* 'put away', associated with feasting before fasting at Lent.

carol [Middle English] From Old French *carole*, English *carol* 'religious folk song or popular hymn associated with Christmas', has been recorded as 'a ring dance', 'merrymaking' (where dancing is the main feature), and 'band of singers'. It has also been used to mean 'ring of standing stones', with reference to Stonehenge. The ulterior etymology of Old French *carole* is unclear; there are many indications that the first syllable was originally *co-*, which could point to a base in Greek *chorus*. Another conjecture is that 'ring' is the original sense of the noun, perhaps with Latin *corolla* 'little crown' as the source.

carouse [mid 16th century] *Carouse* (which formerly rhymed with *house*) was originally an adverb meaning 'right out, completely' in the phrase *drink carouse*, from German *gar aus trinken*. This resulted in the current meaning 'drink heavily, have a drinking bout'.

carp [Middle English] The verb *carp* 'complain', 'find fault with' was first recorded in the sense 'talk, chatter'. It comes from Old Norse *karpa* 'brag', and was later influenced by Latin *carpere* 'pluck at, slander'.

carpenter [Middle English] *Carpenter* is from Anglo-Norman French, from Old French *carpentier, charpentier*, from late Latin *carpentarius* (*artifex*) 'carriage(-maker)'. The base is late Latin *carpentum* 'wagon', of Gaulish origin.
→ CAR

carpet [Middle English] A *carpet* originally denoted a thick fabric used as a cover for a table or bed. This is where the expression *on the carpet* originates: this was the covering of the council table, where official documents for discussion were placed. The word is from Old French *carpite* or medieval Latin *carpita*, from obsolete Italian *carpita* 'woollen counterpane'. Latin *carpere* 'pluck, pull to pieces' is the base. The Latin *carpita* may have been originally given to a fabric formed of unravelled cloth or shreds of cloth patched together. Compounds of interest are:
■ **carpet-bagger**, used in North American English for a political candidate who seeks election where (s)he has no local connections; this was applied after the American Civil War (1861–

5) to any immigrant from the northern to the southern States, whose property qualification was simply the contents of the carpet-bag carried.
■ **carpet knight** arose in the late 16th century: it is now archaic but described a man who avoided hard work, preferring leisure activities or philandering: it refers to a knight's exploits being restricted to a carpeted boudoir rather than the field of battle.

carriage [late Middle English]
→ CARRY

carrion [Middle English] From Anglo-Norman French and Old Northern French *caroine*, Old French *charoigne, carrion*, which describes 'the decaying flesh of dead animals', is based on Latin *caro* 'flesh'.

carry [late Middle English] The root of the verb *carry* had two semantic strands: 'remove, transport' and 'support'. It is from Anglo-Norman French and Old Northern French *carier*, based on Latin *carrus* 'wheeled vehicle'. This is also the base of **carriage** first recorded in the same period; the compound:
■ **carriage dog** is recorded from the early 19th century, because Dalmatians were formerly trained to run behind a carriage as guard dogs.

cart [Middle English] *Cart* (in early use meaning a 'carriage' of any kind) is from Old Norse *kartr*, probably influenced by Anglo-Norman French and Old Northern French *carete*, a diminutive of *carre*.
→ CAR

cartel [late 19th century] This word comes from from German *Kartell* 'challenge, cartel', via French from Italian *cartello*, a diminutive of *carta*, from Latin *carta* 'paper'. It was originally used to refer to the coalition of the Conservatives and National Liberal parties in Germany (1887), and hence to any political combination; later the reference was extended to a trade agreement (early 20th century). This involves the maintenance of prices at a high level and the restriction of competition.
→ CARD[1]

cartoon [late 16th century] A *cartoon* first described a full-size drawing made as a preliminary design for a painting or other work of art. It comes from Italian *cartone*, from *carta*, from Latin *carta, charta* 'papyrus leaf'. The sense referring to a simple drawing showing the features of its subject in a humorous and exaggerated way, dates from the mid 19th century.
→ CARD[1]

cartridge [late 16th century] A *cartridge* is basically a 'casing', whether for a spool of film or an explosive charge of some kind. This is from French *cartouche*, from Italian *cartoccio*, based on Latin *carta* 'papyrus leaf'. **Cartridge paper**, a mid-17th century term, was originally used to make cartridge cases.

carve [Old English] Old English *ceorfan* 'cut, carve', is West Germanic in origin and related to Dutch *kerven*. The verbs *cut* and *carve* were once equivalent; the alliterative phrase *cut and carve* goes back to the 14th century, and reflects this equivalence.

cascade [mid 17th century] Adopted from French, from Italian *cascata* (from *cascare* 'to fall'), *cascade* is based on Latin *casus* 'falling'.
➔ CASE¹

case¹ [Middle English] The *case* which means 'an instance', 'a legal action', etc. is from Old French *cas*, from Latin *casus* 'a fall', related to *cadere* 'to fall'. The grammatical use of *case* referring to inflected forms in languages such as German is taken directly from Latin, in which it translates Greek *ptōsis*, literally 'fall'.

case² [late Middle English] The *case* meaning 'container' is from Old French *casse*, *chasse*, the modern forms of which are *caisse* 'trunk, chest', *châsse* 'reliquary, frame'. These are based on Latin *capsa*, related to *capere* 'to hold'. Latin *capsa* is also the base of late Middle English **capsule**, a general term at first for 'a small container'. The same base gave rise to late Middle English **casement** (from Anglo-Latin *cassimentum*) which was first recorded as an architectural term for a hollow moulding, and now refers to a type of window.

cash [late 16th century] In early use a *cash* was a box for money. It is from Old French *casse* or Italian *cassa* 'box', from Latin *capsa*. It is now the 'money' itself in coins or notes. The word **cashier** (late 16th century) is from Dutch *cassier* or French *caissier*, from *caisse* 'cash'. The verb however has a different source. It started out in the sense 'dismiss or disband troops': Flemish *kasseren* 'disband (troops)' or 'revoke (a will)' is the direct source, from French *casser* 'revoke, dismiss', from Latin *quassare* 'quash'.
➔ CASE²

casino [mid 18th century] This type of public room or building where gambling games are played derives its name from Italian. The literal meaning is 'little house', from *casa* 'house', from Latin *casa* 'cottage'.

cask [early 16th century] The source is either French *casque* or Spanish *casco* 'helmet'. The current senses 'barrel-like container' and 'the quantity contained in such a container' appear only in English; from the late 16th to the late 18th centuries the word also meant 'helmet'.

casket [late Middle English] This word for a small ornamental box, is perhaps an Anglo-Norman French form of Old French *cassette* 'small case' (hence also English **cassette**), a diminutive of *casse*. In the US, a *casket* is used to mean 'coffin'.
➔ CASE²

casserole [early 18th century] This originally French word for a stew, or the pot in which a stew is cooked, is a diminutive of *casse* 'spoon-like container', from Old Provençal *casa*, from late Latin *cattia* 'ladle, pan'. The base is Greek *kuathion* 'little cup', a diminutive of *kuathos*.

cassock [mid 16th century] A *cassock* is a full-length garment worn by certain Christian clergy members. The word comes from French *casaque* 'long coat', from Italian *casacca* 'riding coat'. It is probably based on Turkic *kazak* 'vagabond'. A *cassock* once referred to a long coat worn by some soldiers in the 16th and 17th centuries; the ecclesiastical use appears to have arisen in English in the 17th century.

cast [Middle English] *Cast* 'throw' is from Old Norse *kasta* 'to cast or throw'. *Throw* has largely taken over in ordinary language to express this simple sense, whereas *cast* now appears archaic or literary except in specialized uses such as *cast a line* in fishing. It is also used figuratively: the type of *cast* (mid 17th century) involved in a play, film, or similar production, derives its name from a special use of the verb in the sense 'arrange in a specified form or style'.

castanets [early 17th century] This word for musical instruments (made usually of small concave pieces of wood) joined in pairs clicked as a rhythmic accompaniment to Spanish dancing, is from Spanish *castañeta*, a diminutive of *castaña*, from Latin *castanea* 'chestnut'.

caste [mid 16th century] The general sense in early use was 'race, breed'. It is from Spanish and Portuguese *casta* 'lineage, race, breed', feminine of *casto* 'pure, unmixed', from Latin *castus* 'chaste'. The common current use is to refer to the hereditary classes of Hindu society. There are four basic classes: Brahman (priest), Kshatriya (warrior), Vaisya (merchant or farmer), and Sudra (labourer). The spelling *caste* is hardly found before 1800; it was previously written *cast* and assumed, apparently, to be a particular application of *cast*.

castigate [early 17th century] Latin *castigare* 'reprove', from *castus* 'pure, chaste' is the source of English *castigate*.

castle [late Old English] *Castle* is from Anglo-Norman French and Old Northern French *castel*, from Latin *castellum* 'little fort', a diminutive of *castrum*. The Latin plural *castra* gave *Chester* in English present in the names of fortified places in Britain which had originally been Roman encampments; the ending -*caster* as in *Lancaster* is a variant. The phrase *build castles in Spain* 'daydream, create an idle fancy', is a Gallicism used by modern writers: the French phrase varies as to the location (sometimes *Asia*, sometimes *Albania*) which suggests the expression refers basically to building castles in a foreign country where one has no real base. The phrase *build castles in the air* is equivalent.

castor¹ [late 17th century] The first recorded sense was 'container with holes in the top' for sprinkling sugar or pepper. It was originally a variant of *caster*, in the general sense 'something that casts'. **Caster sugar** (mid 19th century) is so named because it was suitable for use in a *castor*.

castor² [late Middle English] The early sense was recorded as 'beaver'. It is from Old French or Latin, from Greek *kastōr*. It now refers more commonly to a reddish-brown oily substance secreted by beavers, used in perfumes and medicines. **Castor oil**, a pale yellow oil obtained from castor beans used as a purgative, owes its name perhaps to the fact that it succeeded *castor* in this medicinal use.

casual [late Middle English] The early senses were 'not regular or permanent' and 'happening by chance'; the form is from Old French *casuel* and Latin *casualis*, from *casus* 'fall'.
→ CASE¹

casualty [late Middle English] The early recorded sense was 'chance, a chance occurrence'. It comes from medieval Latin *casualitas*, from *casualis*, on the pattern of words such as *penalty*.

cat [Old English] Old English *catt(e)* is Germanic in origin and related to Dutch *kat* and German *Katze*. The spelling was reinforced in Middle English by forms from late Latin *cattus*. The original source is not known; history points to Egypt as the earliest home of the domestic cat and the name is generally sought in that area. Amongst the compounds are:

■ **catcall** (mid 17th century) which originally denoted a kind of whistle or squeaking instrument used to express disapproval at a theatre.

■ **catgut** (late 16th century) involves the word *cat* but the reason remains unexplained. Used for the strings of musical instruments and for surgical sutures, it is made of the dried twisted intestines of sheep or horses but not cats.

■ **caterwaul** (late Middle English) is formed from *cat* and the imitative word *waul*.

cataclysm [early 17th century] This word for a large-scale, violent event in the natural world, originally denoted the biblical Flood described in Genesis. French *cataclysme* is the source of *cataclysm* which came via Latin from Greek *kataklusmos* 'deluge', from *kata*- 'down' and *kluzein* 'to wash'.

catacomb [Old English] This is from late Latin *catacumbas*, the name of the subterranean cemetery of St Sebastian on the Appian Way near Rome. This is the area where the bodies of the apostles Peter and Paul were said to have been placed. The evidence is unclear as to whether the name originally belonged to the cemetery itself or the locality. The word was not generalized to other subterranean cemeteries until the 17th century: first to those around Rome which had been covered over and long forgotten until they were discovered by chance in 1578; then to others as at Naples, Egypt, Syracuse, etc. Gradually the application widened to such places as the *catacombs* of Paris which were worked-out stone quarries. The spelling *catacomb* was reinforced in late Middle English by French *catacombes*.

catalogue [late Middle English] *Catalogue* came via Old French and late Latin from Greek *katalogos*, from *katalegein* 'pick out or enrol'.

catamaran [early 17th century] This word describes a yacht or other boat with twin hulls in parallel; it is from Tamil *kaṭṭumaram*, which means literally 'tied wood'.

catapult [late 16th century] This is from French *catapulte* or Latin *catapulta*, from Greek *katapeltēs*. The base elements are *kata*- 'down' and *pallein* 'hurl'.

cataract [late Middle English] Latin *cataracta* 'waterfall, floodgate' is the source. This also meant 'portcullis', which probably gave rise to the medical sense describing blurring of the eye lens due to increasing opacity. The origin is Greek *kataraktēs* 'down-rushing', based on the elements *kata*- 'down' and *arassein* 'strike, smash'.

catastrophe [mid 16th century] The first recorded sense was 'denouement'. The word came via Latin from Greek *katastrophē* 'overturning, sudden turn', from *kata*- 'down' and *strophē* 'turning'.

catch [Middle English] This verb also meant 'chase' in early use, but eventually the result of the action became semantically dominant. It is from Anglo-Norman French and Old Northern French *cachier*, a variant of Old French *chacier*, based on Latin *captare* 'try to catch', from *capere* 'take'. In the 1970s the expression **catch-22** 'a dilemma from which there is no escape' became current; it is from the title of a novel by Joseph Heller (1961), in which the main character feigns madness to avoid dangerous combat missions, but this very desire is taken to prove his sanity.

→ CHASE[1]

category [late Middle English] The word was first used in philosophy. The source is French or late Latin, from Greek *katēgoria* 'statement, accusation', from *katēgoros* 'accuser'.

cater [late 16th century] This verb is from obsolete *cater* 'caterer', from Old French *acateor* 'buyer', from *acater* 'buy'.

caterpillar [late Middle English] This is perhaps from a variant of Old French *chatepelose*, meaning literally 'hairy cat', influenced by obsolete *piller* 'ravager' because of the association with the damage done to plants by caterpillars. The connection with *cat* is found in other languages, e.g. Swiss German *Teufelskatz* (literally 'devil's cat'), Lombard *gatta* (literally 'cat'). Also the French word *chaton* means 'catkin', because of the resemblance to a hairy caterpillar.

catharsis [early 19th century] The medical sense 'purgation' was the early usage. It is from Greek *katharsis*, from *kathairein* 'cleanse': the base is *katharos* 'pure'. The notion of 'release' from strong or repressed emotions through drama derives from Aristotle's *Poetics*.

catholic [late Middle English] The early sense related to the 'catholic church' or the 'church universal' applied to the whole body of believers as distinguished from an individual congregation. It is from Old French *catholique* or late Latin *catholicus*, from Greek *katholikos* 'universal': the base elements are *kata* 'in respect of' and *holos* 'whole'. The general sense is 'all-embracing'.

catkin [late 16th century] This is from obsolete Dutch *katteken* 'kitten'.

→ CATERPILLAR

cattle [Middle English] In early use *cattle* also denoted personal property or wealth; under the feudal system 'movable' property constituted personal property. The direct source is Anglo-Norman French *catel*, a variant of Old French *chatel*. The spelling *cattle* has existed chiefly from around 1700.

→ CHATTEL

cauldron [Middle English] This word comes from Anglo-Norman French *caudron*, based on Latin *cal(i)darium* 'cooking-pot', from *calidus* 'hot' (Shakespeare *Macbeth*: Double, double, toil and trouble, Fire burn, and Cauldron bubble). An alternative spelling is *caldron* which was favoured in dictionaries from Johnson onwards; the *l* is an insertion of the Renaissance in imitation of Latin; the *l* has been rec-

ognized gradually in pronunciation. Scots still has *caudron*.

cauliflower [late 16th century] This is from obsolete French *chou fleuri* 'flowered cabbage' (the flower being the white head), probably from Italian *cavolfiore* or modern Latin *cauliflora*. The original English form *colieflorie* or *cole-flory*, had its first element influenced by *cole*; the second element was influenced by *flower* during the 17th century.

cause [Middle English] This is from Old French, from Latin *causa* (noun) and *causare* (verb). In the early period, Latin *causa* came down as French *chose* 'matter', 'thing', also as Spanish and Italian *cosa* (with the same meaning). At a later period medieval Latin *causa*, used in philosophy and legal contexts, influenced English *cause*.

causeway [late Middle English] The first element of *causeway* is from the synonym *causey*, now an archaic or dialect term, from Anglo-Norman French *causee*, based on Latin *calx* 'lime, limestone': this material was used for paving roads. The first recorded sense of *causey* was 'mound, embankment, dam'. A *causeyway* was a way across a mound or, a raised footpath by the side of a carriage road which might be submerged in wet weather: this was contracted to *causeway*.

caustic [late Middle English] English *caustic* came via Latin from Greek *kaustikos*, from *kaustos* 'combustible', from *kaiein* 'to burn'. This Greek verb is the base too of late Middle English **cauterize** which came into the language via Old French.

caution [Middle English] At first a *caution* denoted bail or a guarantee, senses which are now chiefly Scots and US. The word is from Latin *cautio(n-)*, from *cavere* 'take heed'.

cavalry [mid 16th century] This is from French *cavallerie*, from Italian *cavalleria*, from *cavallo* 'horse'. The base is Latin *caballus*, source too of **cavalier** (which came via French from Italian and dates from the same period) and **cavalcade** (late 16th century) which at first meant 'a ride, raid on horseback': this is from French, from Italian *cavalcata*, from *cavalcare* 'to ride'.

cave [Middle English] *Cave* is from Old French, from Latin *cava*, from *cavus* 'hollow'. The usage *cave in* may be from the synonymous dialect expression *calve in* 'yield to pressure', influenced by obsolete *cave* 'excavate, hollow out'. All the earliest instances of *cave in* in print are from the US: the phrase is thought to be East Anglian originally however.

cavern [late Middle English] *Cavern* is from Old French *caverne* or from Latin *caverna*, from *cavus* 'hollow'. English *cavern*, with notions of vastness and indefinite extent, is vaguer and more rhetorical than *cave*: the latter is the exact equivalent, however, of French *caverne*.

cavity [mid 16th century] *Cavity* is from French *cavité* or late Latin *cavitas*, from Latin *cavus* 'hollow'.

cease [Middle English] *Cease* is from Old French *cesser*, from Latin *cessare* 'stop', from *cedere* 'to yield'.

cede [early 16th century] *Cede* is from French *céder* or Latin *cedere* 'to yield'.

ceiling [Middle English] At first *ceiling* was the action associated with the late Middle English verb *ceil* meaning 'line (the interior of a room) with plaster or panelling'. It is perhaps related to Latin *celare*, French *céler* 'conceal'. The sense describing the upper interior surface of a room, dates from the mid 16th century.

celebrate [late Middle English] The first recorded sense was 'perform (a religious ceremony) publicly'; it is from Latin *celebrat-*, a form of the verb *celebrare* 'celebrate', from *celeber, celebr-* 'frequented or honoured'.

celebrity [late Middle English] The early recorded sense was 'solemn ceremony'. The source is Old French *celebrite* or Latin *celebritas*, from *celeber, celebr-* 'frequented or honoured'.

celestial [late Middle English] *Celestial* came via Old French from medieval Latin *caelestialis*, from Latin *caelestis*, from *caelum* 'heaven'.

cell [Old English] *Cell* comes from Old French *celle* or Latin *cella* 'storeroom, chamber'; in late Latin *cella* also denoted 'a monk's or hermit's cell'. Some of the Latin senses (e.g. the Latin word was also used for the cell of a honeycomb) appeared in English comparatively late. The earliest English sense appears to have been 'monastery, nunnery', which was frequent in medieval Latin.

cellar [Middle English] The early general sense was 'storeroom', from Old French *celier*, from late Latin *cellarium* 'storehouse', from *cella* 'storeroom, chamber'. It is impossible to be sure when the notion of 'storeroom' started to give way to that of 'underground chamber'.

cement [Middle English] As a noun, *cement* is from Old French *ciment*, as a verb, from *cimenter*, from Latin *caementum* 'quarry stone'. The base is Latin *caedere* 'to hew'. In English, the name appears to have been given to broken or pounded stone or tiles mixed with lime to form a setting mortar; eventually the term was applied to the mortar itself, and then to the modern sense of strong setting mortar in general, however made.

cemetery [late Middle English] *Cemetery* came via late Latin from Greek *koimētērion* 'dormitory', from *koiman* 'put to sleep'. The transference of sense to 'burial ground' is found in the work of Christian writers.

cenotaph [early 17th century] This is from French *cénotaphe*, from late Latin *cenotaphium*. The base elements are Greek *kenos* 'empty' and *taphos* 'tomb'.

censor [mid 16th century] The first sense recorded was in reference to 'either of two magistrates who held censuses and supervised public morals'. It is from Latin, from *censere* 'assess'. The word is used in universities and colleges as a title for various officials, e.g. at Oxford and Cambridge it is the title of the official Head of the Non-collegiate (= unattached) Students. The use to describe someone with the official duty of inspecting books and dramatic pieces before publication, dates from the mid 17th century.

censure [late Middle English] A *censure* (now 'formal disapproval') was first recorded as a 'judicial sentence'. The spelling is from Old French *censurer* (verb), *censure* (noun), from Latin *censura* 'judgement, assessment'. The base verb in Latin is *censere* 'assess'.

census [early 17th century] The early word denoted a poll tax. It is from Latin, applied to the registration of citizens and property in ancient Rome, usually for taxation, from *censere* 'assess'. The current sense 'official count of a population', dates from the mid 18th century.

cent [late Middle English] The first recorded sense was 'a hundred'. *Cent* is from French *cent*, Italian *cento*, or Latin *centum* 'hundred'. The use of *cent* as a monetary unit was apparently first mentioned in 1782 in a letter from Robert Morris to the US Congress; his particular proposal was not taken up but may have suggested the name. Prior to the coining of the US cent, accounts were kept in dollars and ninetieths (from the time when the Spanish piastre, known as a 'dollar' to colonists, was worth 90 pence of the money of account of Maryland and Pennsylvania).

centigrade [early 19th century] This is from French, from Latin *centum* 'a hundred' and *gradus* 'step'.

centre [late Middle English] This word is from Old French or from Latin *centrum*, from Greek *kentron* 'sharp point, stationary point of a pair of compasses'. It is related to *kentein* 'to prick'. The spelling which prevailed from the 16th to the 18th century was *center* in Shakespeare, Milton, Pope, etc. This is now the prevalent spelling in the US. It was the entry of the spelling *centre* (from technical contexts) in Johnson's dictionary which led to the general adoption of this in British English.

century [late Middle English] A *century* first described a company in the ancient Roman army, made up of one hundred men. It comes from Latin *centuria*, from *centum* 'hundred'. The time sense 'one hundred years' dates from the early 17th century.

cereal [early 19th century] Early use was as an adjective, as in *cereal seeds*, *cereal grounds*, *cereal grasses*. It is from Latin *cerealis*, from *Ceres*, the name of the Roman goddess of agriculture.

ceremony [late Middle English] *Ceremony* is from Old French *ceremonie* or Latin *caerimonia* meaning 'religious worship', or in the plural, 'ritual observances'.

certain [Middle English] This is from Old French, based on Latin *certus* 'settled, sure'. The words *certainer* and *certainest* were common up to the middle of the 18th century, but are rare now. Other words based on Latin *certus* 'sure' are *ascertain*, *certificate*, *certify*, and *certitude*.

cesspool [late 17th century] A *cesspool*, in early use, denoted a trap under a drain to catch solids. It is perhaps an alteration, influenced by *pool*, of archaic *suspiral* 'vent, water pipe, settling tank', from Old French *souspirail* 'air hole'. This is based on Latin *sub-* 'from below' and *spirare* 'breathe'. Mid 19th-century **cesspit** is prefixed by *cess* as the supposed base of *cesspool*.

chafe [late Middle English] The first recorded sense was 'make warm'. It comes from Old French *chaufer* 'make hot', based on Latin *calefacere*, from *calere* 'be hot' and *facere* 'make'. The sense 'rub' developed from a notion of using friction to restore heat; this became associated with abrasion and thus irritation (Dickens *Old Curiosity Shop*: To chafe and vex me is part of her nature).

chaff [Old English] Old English *ceaf* 'seed husks' is probably from a Germanic base meaning 'gnaw', related to Dutch *kaf*, and **chafer** 'a large flying beetle', destructive to plant roots. The word **chaffinch** (in Old English *ceaffinc* 'chaff finch') is so named because it forages around barns, picking seeds out of the chaff.

chagrin [mid 17th century] *Chagrin* was also, in early use, *shagreen*, a kind of leather with a rough surface; the early figurative sense was 'melancholy'. In around 1700 the word was often referred to as an affected and Frenchified term. The noun comes from French *chagrin*, the

verb from *chagriner*, but earlier details of the origin are unknown. The current sense is 'annoyance at being humiliated, or having failed'.

chain [Middle English] *Chain* is from Old French *chaine*, *chaeine*, from Latin *catena* 'a chain'.

chair [Middle English] *Chair* is from Old French *chaiere*, via Latin from Greek *kathedra* 'seat'. Modern French now has *chaire* 'bishop's throne, professorial cathedra' and the variant *chaise* 'chair'. The Middle English word *cathedral* is related (= the place containing the bishop's throne).

chalet [late 18th century] This has been adopted from Swiss French and is a diminutive of Old French *chasel* 'farmstead', based on Latin *casa* 'hut, cottage'.

chalice [Middle English] 'A large cup or goblet', *chalice* came via Old French from Latin *calix*, *calic-* 'cup'.

chalk [Old English] Old English *cealc* also meant 'lime'; it is related to Dutch *kalk* and German *Kalk*, from Latin *calx* 'lime'. The shift in English to the sense 'limestone' is associated with the fact that *chalk* is the chief 'limestone' of the SE of England. The expression *by a long chalk* meaning 'to a great degree' refers to the use of chalk lines drawn in various games for scoring points.

challenge [Middle English] *Challenge* was first recorded in the noun sense 'accusation' (from Old French *chalenge*) and the verb sense 'accuse' (from Old French *chalenger*). The Latin base is *calumnia* 'false accusation' which also gave **calumny** 'a false statement damaging someone's reputation' in late Middle English.

chamber [Middle English] The early recorded use of *chamber* was in the sense 'private room'. It is from Old French *chambre*, from Latin *camera* 'vault, arched chamber', from Greek *kamara* 'object with an arched cover'.

chamberlain [Middle English] A *chamberlain* used to denote a servant in a bedchamber. The origin is Old French based on Old Saxon *kamera*, from Latin *camera* 'vault'; the suffix *-lain*, forming the noun, is equivalent to *-ling* (as in *hireling*, *sapling*) and means 'person belonging to'. Now the term may refer, historically, to an officer who managed the household of a monarch, or an officer who received revenue on behalf of a public body.

chameleon [Middle English] This word comes via Latin from Greek *khamaileōn*, from *khamai* 'on the ground' and *leōn* 'lion'. Already in ancient Greek, the word was also used as the name of various plants, because of their ability to change colour.

champion [Middle English] A *champion* was first recorded as meaning 'a fighting man'. It is from Old French, from medieval Latin *campio(n-)* 'fighter', from Latin *campus* (an arena where such a fighter fought). The flower known as a **campion** is perhaps related. The name was originally used for the rose campion, whose name in Latin (*Lychnis coronaria*) and Greek (*lukhnis stephanōmatikē*) means 'campion fit for a crown', and which was said in classical times to have been used for victors' garlands.

chance [Middle English] From Old French *cheance*, from *cheoir* 'fall, befall', English *chance* is based on Latin *cadere*.

chancellor [late Old English] *Chancellor* is from Old French *cancelier*, from late Latin *cancellarius* meaning 'porter, secretary', but originally denoting a court official stationed at the grating which separated the public from the judges. The base is Latin *cancelli* 'crossbars', which also gave rise, via Old French, to Middle English **chancel**: this is the part of a church near the altar reserved for the clergy and choir.

chandelier [mid 18th century] This term for a large decorative hanging light, is based on Latin *candere* 'be white, glisten'. It comes from Old French *chandelier* which also gave Middle English **chandler**, a 'candlemaker or candle seller'.

change [Middle English] The noun is from Old French *change*, the verb from *changer*, from late Latin *cambiare*, from Latin *cambire* 'to barter'. The origin is probably Celtic.

channel [Middle English] *Channel* is from Old French *chanel*, from Latin *canalis* 'pipe, groove, channel', from *canna* 'reed'.
→ CANAL

chant [late Middle English] The early recorded sense of *chant* was 'sing'. The source is Old French *chanter* 'sing', from Latin *cantare*, a frequentative (= verb of repeated action) of *canere* 'sing'. *Chant* is part of the name **Chanticleer** given to a domestic cock especially in fairy tales: it is from Old French *Chantecler* (from *chanter* 'sing, crow' and *cler* 'clear') in the fable *Reynard the Fox*.

chaos [late 15th century] A *chaos*, in early use, was 'a gaping void or chasm', but later it came to mean 'formless primordial matter'; the prime current sense is 'disorder'. It came into English via French and Latin from Greek *khaos* 'vast chasm, void'.

chap [late 16th century] This informal word for 'man' used to denote a buyer or customer. It is an abbreviation of *chapman* (in Old English *cēapman*), from *cēap* 'bargaining, trade' and *man*. The current sense dates from the early 18th century. The origins of the verb *chap* meaning 'become rough and sore' (late Middle English) and the noun *chap* meaning 'lower jaw' (mid 16th century) are unknown: the plural of this noun is commonly replaced by the synonym *chops* as in *chubby chops*.

chapel [Middle English] The word comes via Old French from medieval Latin *cappella*, a diminutive of *cappa* 'cap or cape'. The first *chapel* was a sanctuary in which St Martin's cloak (preserved by the Frankish kings as a sacred relic) was kept. Borne in battle and used to give sanctity to oaths, it was preserved under the care of its *cappellani* 'chaplains'. Later the word *chapel* was applied generally to any sanctuary containing holy relics attached to a palace, then to any holy place, and finally to a place for worship.
→ CHAPLAIN

chaperone [late Middle English] In early use a *chaperone* was recorded as a 'hood or cap', regarded as giving protection. It is from the French feminine of *chaperon* 'hood'. The current use referring to a person providing protection by accompanying another, dates from the early 18th century.

chaplain [Middle English] *Chaplain* is from Old French *chapelain*, from medieval Latin *cappellanus*, which was originally a custodian of the cloak of St Martin. The base is medieval Latin *cappella*, which originally meant 'little cloak'.
→ CHAPEL

chapter [Middle English] Latin *capitulum* 'little head', 'head of a plant', 'capital of a column', later meaning 'chapter of a book', 'section of a law' is the base of English *chapter*. The direct source is Old French *chapitre*. The spelling *chapiter* existed beside *chapter* until the middle of the 17th century: it is still found occasionally meaning 'capital of a column'.

char[1] [late 17th century] The verb *char* 'partially burn' is apparently a back-formation (by removal of the suffix) from **charcoal**, a late Middle English word. *Charcoal* is an amorphous form of carbon obtained as a residue when organic matter such as wood or bone is heated in the absence of air.

char[2] [late 16th century] The early spelling of this informal word for 'tea' was *cha*, but use was rare before the early 20th century. It is from Chinese (Mandarin dialect) *chá*.

character [Middle English] This is from Old French *caractere*, via Latin from Greek *kharaktēr* 'a stamping tool'. The early sense 'distinctive mark' led, in the early 16th century, to 'token, feature, or trait', and later 'a description, especially of a person's qualities', giving rise to 'distinguishing qualities'.

charade [late 18th century] Perhaps imitative in origin, *charade* has come via French from modern Provençal *charrado* 'conversation', from *charra* 'chatter'.

charge [Middle English] The general early senses were 'to load' as a verb (from Old French *charger*), and 'a load' (from Old French *charge*), as a noun. The word has come via late Latin *carricare*, *carcare* 'to load', from Latin *carrus* 'wheeled vehicle'.
→ CAR; CARGO

charger [Middle English] The type of *charger* which describes a large flat dish, is from Anglo-Norman French *chargeour*, from *chargier* 'to load'. This is from late Latin *car(ri)care* 'to load'.

chariot [late Middle English] *Chariot* is from Old French, based on Latin *carrus* 'wheeled vehicle'.

charisma [mid 17th century] The first recorded sense of *charisma* was 'a divinely conferred talent'. The word came via ecclesiastical Latin from Greek *kharisma*, from *kharis* 'favour, grace'. The word now expresses 'compelling charm'. **Charismatic** has been used in religious contexts in the phrase *charismatic movement* since the 1930s; within certain Western Churches, worshippers have favoured the restoration of the *charismata* or spiritual gifts (such as speaking in tongues) to a central place in the life of the Church.

charity [late Old English] Latin *carus* 'dear' is the base; the direct source of the word in English is Old French *charite*. The early sense of *charity* was 'Christian love of one's fellows'. In translations of the Bible, *charity* and *love* were often used interchangeably for the source word; however in the Revised Version of 1881, the word *love* was substituted in all instances. A notion of 'generosity' and 'spontaneous goodness' became associated with *charity*.

charlatan [early 17th century] 'An itinerant seller of supposed remedies' was once described as a *charlatan*, which is from French, from Italian *ciarlatano*. The base is the Italian verb *ciarlare* 'to babble', fast talking being an essential skill for this type of salesman.

charm [Middle English] A *charm*, in early use, meant 'incantation, magic spell' and, as a verb, 'to use spells' (Shakespeare *Midsummer Night's Dream*: Never harm, nor spell, nor charm, Come our lovely lady nigh. So good night, with lullaby). It is from Old French *charme* (noun), *charmer* (verb), from Latin *carmen* 'song, verse, incantation'. The 17th century saw the figurative extension of the word to 'a trait or quality, such as female beauty, which exerts a fascinating influence'.

chart [late 16th century] This comes from French *charte*, from Latin *charta* 'paper, papyrus leaf'.

charter [Middle English] *Charter* is related to *chart* and *card*. The direct source is Old French *chartre*, from Latin *chartula*, a diminutive of *charta* 'paper'. The *Magna Charta* or *Magna Carta* was the *Great Charter* signed by King John in 1215 guaranteeing the fundamental liberties of the English people. A **charter party** (dating from late Middle English) is from French *charte partie*. It was a deed between a shipowner and a merchant for the hire of a ship and the delivery of cargo. The medieval Latin phrase *charta partita* 'divided charter' was one written in duplicate on a single sheet, then divided in such a way that the two parts could be fitted together again as proof of authenticity.

charwoman [late 16th century] The first element of this word is from obsolete *char* or *chare* meaning 'a turn of work, an odd job, chore': it is obscurely related to *chore* (Shakespeare *Antony and Cleopatra*: The Maid that Milkes, And doe's the meanest chares).
→ CHORE

chary [Old English] Old English *cearig* 'sorrowful, anxious' is West Germanic in origin and related to *care*. The current sense 'suspiciously reluctant' arose in the mid 16th century.

chase¹ [Middle English] Old French *chacier* (verb) and *chace* (noun) have given *chase* 'pursue' in English. The base is Latin *captare* 'continue to take', from *capere* 'take'.

chase² [late Middle English] *Chase* 'engrave' is apparently from the earlier word *enchase* which came from Old French *enchasser*.

chasm [late 16th century] A *chasm* originally denoted an opening up of the sea or land, as in an earthquake. It is from Latin *chasma*, from Greek *khasma* 'gaping hollow'.

chasten [early 16th century] Latin *castus* 'morally pure, chaste' is the base of *chasten*, formed from the now obsolete English verb *chaste*, from Old French *chastier*, from Latin *castigare* 'castigate', 'make chaste'.

chastise [Middle English] This word was apparently formed irregularly from the obsolete verb *chaste* 'correct or amend by discipline', involved in the formation of *chasten*.

chastity [Middle English] This is from Old French *chastete*, from Latin *castitas*, from *castus* 'morally pure', the base too of Middle English **chaste**.

chat [Middle English] This is a shortening of **chatter**, which is imitative of quick repeated sounds.

chattel [Middle English] A *chattel*, now often used in legal contexts as in *goods and chattels*, is 'a personal possession'. The source of the word is Old French *chatel*, from medieval Latin *capitale*, from Latin *capitalis* 'of the head', from *caput* 'head'.
→ CAPITAL¹; CATTLE

chauffeur [late 19th century] This was originally used in the general sense 'motorist'. It was adopted from French and its literal meaning is 'stoker' (by association with steam engines), from *chauffer* 'to heat'.

chauvinism [late 19th century] This term for 'exaggerated patriotism' or 'prejudiced support for one's own cause' owes its coinage to Nicolas Chauvin, a Napoleonic veteran noted for his extreme patriotism. He was popularized as a character by the Cogniard brothers in *Cocarde Tricolore* (1831). After the fall of Napoleon, the term *chauvin* was used to ridicule any old soldier of the Empire who maintained admiration for the emperor and his acts.

cheap [late 15th century] This word relates now to low value, but it comes originally from the obsolete phrase *good cheap* meaning 'a good bargain'; the opposite phrase *dear cheap* 'high prices', 'scarcity' existed alongside. In Old English, *cēap* was a noun with the sense 'bargaining, trade', based on Latin *caupo* 'small trader, innkeeper'. It is found in placenames such as *Cheapside* and *Eastcheap* where the element *cheap* means 'market'. Compounds involving *cheap* include:
■ **cheapjack** (mid 19th century) which has the same notion of trading: it means a seller of cheap inferior goods. In North American usage this may also be used as an adjective meaning 'of inferior quality'.
■ **cheapskate** (late 19th century), which was originally US: *skate* means 'a worn-out horse' or 'a mean, contemptible, or dishonest person', but its origin is unknown.

cheat [late Middle English] This is a shortening of *escheat* 'reversion of property to the State', which was the original sense.

check¹ [Middle English] The word *check* was originally used in the game of chess. The noun and exclamation are from Old French *eschec*, from medieval Latin *scaccus*, via Arabic from Persian *šāh* 'king'. The verb is from Old French *eschequier* 'play chess, put in check'. The sense 'stop, restrain, or control' arose from the use in chess, and led in the late 17th century to 'examine the accuracy of, verify'. Middle English **checkmate** is from Old French *eschec mat*, from Arabic *šāh māta*, from Persian *šāh māt* 'the king is dead'.

check² [late Middle English] Check 'pattern of small squares' is probably from *chequer*.

cheek [Old English] Old English *cē(a)ce, cēoce* 'cheek, jaw' is West Germanic in origin and related to Dutch *kaak*. The phrase *cheek by jowl* is a use of two synonymous terms: the wording was originally *cheek by cheek*. The use of the word to mean 'effrontery' suggests open confidence in facing someone; *have the cheek* has a parallel in the expression *have the face* to do something (Dickens *Bleak House*: On account of his having so much cheek).

cheer [Middle English] Cheer is from Old French *chiere* 'face', from late Latin *cara*, from Greek *kara* 'head'. The original sense was 'face', hence 'expression, mood', later specifically 'a good mood'.

chemist [late Middle English] In early use a *chemist* denoted an alchemist. The word comes via French from modern Latin *chimista*, from *alchimista* 'alchemist', from *alchimia* 'alchemy'.
→ ALCHEMY

chenille [mid 18th century] This term for a tufty velvety yarn is a use of a French word meaning 'hairy caterpillar', from Latin *canicula* 'small dog', a diminutive of *canis*.

cheque [early 18th century] This originally denoted a counterfoil, or a form with a counterfoil; it is a variant of *check* in the sense 'device for checking the amount of an item'.

chequer [Middle English] Chequer is from *exchequer*, which originally meant 'chessboard', a sense which was transferred to *chequer*. This gave rise to *chequered* meaning 'marked like a chessboard'; hence the sense 'pattern of squares' which dates from the early 16th century.

cherish [Middle English] The early sense was 'hold dear, make much of', the source being Old French *cheriss-*, the lengthened stem of *cherir* 'hold dear'. The base is Latin *carus* 'dear'.

cherub [Old English] Old English *cherubin* is ultimately (via Latin and Greek) from Hebrew *kĕrūb*, plural *kĕrubim*. A rabbinic folk etymology, which explains the Hebrew singular form as representing Aramaic *kĕ-rabyā* 'like a child', led to the representation of the cherub as a child.

chess [Middle English] *Chess* is from Old French *esches*, the plural of *eschec* 'a check'.
→CHECK[1]

chest [Old English] Old English *cest*, *cyst* is related to Dutch *kist* and German *Kiste*, based on Greek *kistē* 'box'. The anatomical *chest* as a 'container' for the heart and lungs dates from the early 16th century.

chic [mid 19th century] Adopted from French, *chic* 'elegantly fashionable' is probably from German *Schick* 'skill'.

chicane [late 17th century] A *chicane* describes a sharp double bend forming an obstacle on a motor racing track; it is also an old word for *chicanery* 'trickery'. The origin is the French noun *chicane*, and verb *chicaner* 'quibble', but earlier details of the origin are unknown.

chief [Middle English] From Old French *chief*, *chef*, English *chief* is based on Latin *caput* 'head'.

chieftain [Middle English] The original spelling was that of Old French *chevetaine*, from late Latin *capitaneus* 'chief'. The spelling was altered by association with *chief*.
→CAPTAIN

chiffon [mid 18th century] This word was originally used in the plural, denoting trimmings or ornaments on a woman's dress. It is from French, from *chiffe* 'rag' and now refers to a light transparent fabric usually made of silk or nylon.

child [Old English] Old English *cild* has a Germanic origin. The Middle English plural *childer* or *childre* became *childeren* or *children* by association with plurals such as *brethren* ending in *-en*. *Child* is sometimes used in ballads as a kind of title meaning 'youth of gentle birth' (Shakespeare *King Lear*: Child Rowland, to the dark town come). It is also sometimes used affectionately as a form of address (*come, child!*) **Childhood** in Old English was *cildhād*, the suffix of which was originally an independent noun meaning 'person, condition, or quality'.

chill [Old English] Old English *c(i)ele* 'cold, coldness' has a Germanic origin and is related to *cold*.

chime [Middle English] *Chime* 'bell, bell sound' was first recorded as meaning 'cymbal' as a noun, and 'ring out' as a verb. It is probably from Old English *cimbal*, later interpreted as *chime bell*.
→CYMBAL

chimney [Middle English] A *chimney* was first recorded as 'a fireplace or furnace' and comes from Old French *cheminee* 'chimney, fireplace'. The origin is late Latin *caminata*, perhaps from *camera caminata* 'room with a fireplace', from Latin *caminus* 'forge, furnace', from Greek *kaminos* 'oven'.

chin [Old English] Old English *cin(n)* is Germanic in origin and related to Dutch *kin*, from an Indo-European root shared by Latin *gena* 'cheek' and Greek *genus* 'jaw'.

chine [Middle English] *Chine* used in butchery contexts to refer to the backbone of an animal, is from Old French *eschine*, based on a blend of Latin *spina* 'spine' and a Germanic word meaning 'narrow piece'.
→SHIN

chink [mid 16th century] A *chink* meaning 'a narrow opening or crack' is related to **chine** (in Old English *cinu* 'cleft, chink', of Germanic origin) meaning 'narrow ravine' in placenames such as *Blackgang Chine* on the Isle of Wight.

chintz [early 17th century] The early spelling was *chints*, the plural of *chint*, a stained or painted calico cloth imported from India. It is from Hindi *chīṃṭ* meaning 'spattering, stain'.

chip [Middle English] *Chip* is related to Old English *forcippian* 'to cut off'.

chipper [mid 19th century] This informal word meaning 'lively' corresponds perhaps to northern English dialect *kipper* which also means 'lively'.

chirrup [late 16th century] The word *chirp* (imitative of a short sharp high-pitched sound) has been altered by trilling the *-r-* to form *chirrup*.

chisel [late Middle English] *Chisel* is from Old Northern French, based on Latin *cis-* (found in late Latin *cisorium* 'cutting instrument'): this is a variant of *caes-*, the stem of *caedere* 'to cut'.
→SCISSORS

chit[1] [late Middle English] The *chit* used in expressions such as *chit of a girl* was originally recorded with the meaning 'whelp, cub, kitten'; the sense carries the derogatory implication of 'immaturity' and 'lack of respect'. It is perhaps related to the dialect word *chit* 'sprout', which is also the source of early 17th-century *chit* meaning 'induce (a potato) to sprout by placing it in a cool light place'.

chit[2] [late 18th century] The *chit* meaning 'note, voucher' and usually indicating an amount of money owed, is an Anglo-Indian word from Hindi *ciṭṭhī* 'note, pass'. **Chitty** is an informal word for *chit*.

chivalry [Middle English] *Chivalry* describes 'courteous behaviour' originally associated with an ideal knight, educated in the medieval knightly system with its religious, moral, and social code. It also referred historically to knights, noblemen, and horsemen collectively. Old French *chevalerie* is the source, from medieval Latin *caballerius*; the base is Latin *caballus* 'horse'. Late Middle English **chivalrous** had the sense 'characteristic of a medieval knight': the direct source is Old French *chevalerous*, from *chevalier*.

chivvy [late 18th century] *Chivvy* means 'tell someone to do something repeatedly'. It is probably from the ballad title *Chevy Chase*, celebrating a skirmish (probably the battle of Otterburn in 1388) on the Scottish border. Originally use was as a noun for a hunting cry; the term later meant 'a pursuit', hence the verb sense 'to chase, worry' which arose in the mid 19th century.

chock [Middle English] This is a 'wedge' or 'block' used to prevent movement or keep something steady (*chocks away!*). It is probably from an Old Northern French variant of Old French *couche*, *çoche* 'block, log'; the ultimate origin is unknown. The phrase **chock-a-block** arose in nautical use in the mid 19th century with reference to tackle having the two blocks run close together: the *chock* element is from **chock-full** 'filled to overflowing'. **Chocker**, a naval slang term, was used as an abbreviation of *chock-a-block* during the Second World War, with the special meaning 'tired of something, disgusted with something', although it is also used to mean 'full'. The phrase **chock-full** dates from late Middle English but the origin is unknown; it was later associated with *chock*.

chocolate [early 17th century] The term was first recorded as 'a drink made with chocolate'. It comes from French *chocolat* or Spanish *chocolate*, from Nahuatl *chocolatl* 'food made from cacao seeds'; it was influenced by the unrelated word *cacaua-atl* 'a drink made from cacao'.

choir [Middle English] The early spellings *quer*, *quere* are from Old French *quer*, from Latin *chorus*. The spelling change in the 17th century was due to association with Latin *chorus* and modern French *chœur*. The spelling variant *quire* has never been altered in the English Prayer book (In Quires and Places where they sing, here followeth the Anthem).

choke [Middle English] *Choke* 'have difficulty in breathing' is from the Old English verb *ācēocian*, from *cēoce* 'jaw'. The **choke** (late 17th century) which refers to the mass of inedible silky fibres at the centre of a globe artichoke has probably arisen because of a confusion of the last syllable of *artichoke* with *choke* 'breathe with difficulty'. **Artichoke** came instead from a north Italian word, via Spanish from Arabic.

➔ CHEEK

chokey [early 17th century] The Hindi sense 'customs or toll house, police station' was the early sense in English. The word is Anglo-Indian, from Hindi *caukī*, influenced by *choke*. The use is now informal, meaning 'prison'.

choose [Old English] Old English *cēosan* is Germanic in origin and related to Dutch *kiezen*. A relative of *choose* is Middle English **choice** from Old French *chois*, from *choisir* 'choose' (ultimately from the base of *choose*).

chop[1] [late Middle English] *Chop* 'cut something into small pieces' is a variant of *chap* 'become cracked and sore'. The adjective **choppy**, now often describing the sea as 'having many small waves', meant 'full of chaps or clefts' in the early 17th century.

chop[2] [late Middle English] The *chop* commonly heard in the phrase *chop and change* was first recorded in the sense 'barter, exchange'. It is perhaps related to Old English *cēap* 'bargaining, trade'; the *chap-* of *chapman* is comparable.

chop-chop [mid 19th century] Pidgin English *chop-chop* is based on Chinese dialect *kuai-kuai*. Also pidgin English and comparable is **chopstick** dating from the late 17th century: the first element is from *chop* 'quick' and the word translates Chinese dialect *kuaizi*, meaning literally 'nimble ones'.

chops [late Middle English]
➔ CHAP

chord[1] [Middle English] The early spelling of this musical term for a group of notes sounded together as a basis of harmony, was *cord*, from *accord*. The spelling change in the 18th century was due to confusion with *chord* 'string (of a harp, etc.)'. The original sense was 'agreement, reconciliation', later 'a musical concord or harmonious sound'; the current sense dates from the mid 18th century.

chord[2] [mid 16th century] Early use was in the anatomical sense, as in *spinal chord*. Later it was applied in other contexts such as mathematics, where it refers to a straight line joining the ends of an arc. It was a later spelling (influenced by Latin *chorda* 'rope') of *cord*. The idiom *strike a chord* is a figurative reference to the 'strings' of the mind visualized as a musical instrument.

chore [mid 18th century] Originally a dialect word and a US usage, *chore* is a variant of obsolete *char* or *chare* found in *charwoman*.

chortle [1872] This was coined by Lewis Carroll in *Through the Looking Glass*; it is probably a blend of *chuckle* and *snort*.

chorus [mid 16th century] The word comes via Latin from Greek *khoros*. A *chorus* in English first denoted a character speaking the prologue and epilogue in a play, whose role was to comment on events.

Christ [Old English] Old English *Crīst* is via Latin from Greek *Khristos*, 'anointed (one)', from *khriein* 'anoint', translating Hebrew *māšīah* 'Messiah'. Also from Latin *Christus* 'Christ' are: **Christmas** which in Old English was *Crīstes mæsse* = Christ's Mass; **christen** which in Old English was *crīstnian* 'make Christian', from *crīsten* 'Christian'; **Christendom** which in Old English was *crīstendōm*; late Middle English **Christian** (from Latin *Christianus*), and Middle English **Christianity** from Old French *crestiente*, from *crestien* 'Christian', influenced by late Latin *christianitas*.

chrome [early 19th century] As well as naming a decorative or protective chromium plate finish, *chrome* denotes compounds or alloys of chromium. The word comes from French, from Greek *khrōma* 'colour', this because of the brilliant colours of chromium compounds.

chronic [late Middle English] *Chronic* is from French *chronique*, via Latin from Greek *khronikos* 'of time', from *khronos* 'time'. This gives the sense 'persisting for a long time' in relation to illness, which stems from the word's use in ancient medical texts. In British English it is also used informally to mean 'of very poor quality'; this dates from the early 20th century (e.g. *the film was chronic*) and is connected with 'constant, unending' tedium.

chronicle [Middle English] This word comes from Anglo-Norman French *cronicle*, a variant of Old French *cronique*, via Latin from Greek *khronika* 'annals'. The base is Greek *khronos* 'time'; a *chronicle* gives a factual account of historical events, or records a series of events.

chubby [early 17th century] The early recorded meaning was 'short and thickset, like a chub', a chub being a thick-bodied European river fish. The term *chub* dates from late Middle English, but its origin is unknown.

chuck [late 17th century] This informal word meaning 'throw' is from early 17th-century *chuck* 'touch (someone) playfully under the chin': this is probably from Old French *chuquer*, later *choquer* 'to knock, bump' (of unknown ultimate origin). The phrase *the chuck* expressing rejection (*give somebody the chuck*) dates from the late 19th century.

chuck [late 17th century] *Chuck* as a term for a device for gripping a workpiece in a tool such as a drill, is a variant of *chock* 'wedge'. The same word is applied to a cut of beef.
→ CHUNK

chuckle [late 16th century] The early sense was 'laugh convulsively'; it comes from *chuck* meaning 'to cluck' in late Middle English. Mid 18th-century **chucklehead** 'stupid person' was formed from early 18th-century *chuckle* 'big and clumsy', which is probably related to the butchery term *chuck* 'a cut of beef (typically used for stewing)'.

chuffed [1950s] This is from the dialect word *chuff* meaning 'plump or pleased'.

chum [late 17th century] This was originally Oxford University slang for 'a room-mate'. It is probably short for *chamber-fellow*.
→ COMRADE; CRONY

chump [early 18th century] The first recorded sense of *chump* was 'thick lump of wood'. It is probably a blend of *chunk* and either *lump* or *stump*. Now a *chump* may refer to 'a stupid person' or to a cut (= thick end) of lamb.

chunder [1950s] *Chunder* means 'vomit': it is probably from the rhyming slang *Chunder Loo* 'spew', from the name of a cartoon character *Chunder Loo of Akim Foo*. The character was devised by Norman Lindsay (1879–1969) and used in advertisements for Cobra boot polish in the Sydney *Bulletin* in the early 20th century.

chunk [late 17th century] This word for 'a thick solid piece of something' is apparently an alteration of *chuck* 'cut of beef', 'device for gripping'.

church [Old English] Old English *cir(i)ce* is related to Dutch *kerk* and German *Kirche*. Scots and northern English *kirk* is from the same Old English word. The base is medieval Greek *kurikon*, from Greek *kuriakon* (*dōma*) 'Lord's (house)', from *kurios* 'master or lord'.

churl [Old English] Old English *ceorl* is West Germanic in origin and related to Dutch *kerel* and German *Kerl* 'fellow'. It is also related to *carl* (from Old Norse *karl* '(free)man') used in Scots to mean 'fellow', but archaic in English use: it had the meaning 'man of low birth' and denoted a peasant originally.

chute [early 19th century] *Chute* 'sloping channel' was originally a North American usage; it is a French word originally meaning 'fall' (referring to water or rocks), from Old French *cheoite*, the feminine past participle of *cheoir* 'to fall'. The base is Latin *cadere* 'to fall'. The word in English has been influenced by *shoot*.

cigar [early 18th century] *Cigar* is from French *cigare*, or from Spanish *cigarro*, probably from Mayan *sik'ar* 'smoking'. Mid 19th-century

cigarette was adopted from French: it is a diminutive of *cigare*. The abbreviation **ciggy** dates from the 1960s.

cinch [mid 19th century] *It's a cinch* expresses 'it's an easy (= sure) thing'; the early recorded sense however was 'a girth for a saddle' (used mainly in Mexico and the western US), from Spanish *cincha* 'girth'.

cinder [Old English] Old English *sinder* was first recorded with the sense 'slag' and is Germanic in origin; it is related to German *Sinter*. The similar but unconnected French *cendre* (from Latin *cinis* 'ashes') has influenced both the sense development and the spelling. *Cinder* still has the sense 'slag' in technical use as in *forge-cinder* 'iron slag from a forge' and *mill-cinder* 'slag from a rolling-mill'. The name of the fairy tale character **Cinderella** was formed by adding the diminutive suffix *-ella* to *cinder* on the pattern of the French equivalent of the name: *Cendrillon*.

cipher [late Middle English] A *cipher* in early use was either a 'symbol for zero' or an 'arabic numeral'. The word is from Old French *cifre*, based on Arabic *ṣifr* 'zero'. This notion of 'nothing' is captured in the figurative use referring to a person as 'somebody of no importance' (Thackeray *Henry Esmond*: To the lady and lord rather—his lordship being little more than a cypher in the house). *Cipher* in the context of codes, dates from the early 16th century.

circle [Old English] *Circle* is from Old French *cercle*, from Latin *circulus* 'small ring', a diminutive of *circus* 'ring'. The spelling *cercle* was common in Middle English reflecting the French spelling, but the Latin form influenced the change to *circle* from the 16th century. The term used as an area or gallery of a theatre (*dress circle*, *upper circle*), is an extension of the *circle* referring to a 'circus ring'.

circuit [late Middle English] The base elements of *circuit* are Latin *circum* 'around' and *ire* 'go'. The word came via Old French from Latin *circuitus*, from *circuire*, a variant of *circumire* 'go round'. **Circuitous** dates from the mid 17th century and is from medieval Latin *circuitosus* (from *circuitus* 'a way around').

circulate [late 15th century] Early use was as an alchemical term meaning 'distil something in a closed container, allowing condensed vapour to return to the original liquid'. It comes from the Latin verb *circulare* 'move in a circular path' (from *circulus* 'small ring'). The prime current sense 'move or cause to move continuously', dates from the mid 17th century.

circumcise [Middle English] The source is either Old French *circonciser* or Latin *circumcis-* 'cut around', from the verb *circumcidere* (from the elements *circum* 'around, about' and *caedere* 'to cut'). Examples of other words prefixed by *circum* 'around' are: **circumnavigate** (early 17th century); **circumscribe** 'draw round' (late Middle English) whose final syllable is from Latin *scribere* 'write'; **circumspect** 'wary' (also late Middle English), whose final syllable is based on Latin *specere* 'to look'.

circumstance [Middle English] This is from Old French *circonstance* or Latin *circumstantia*, from *circumstare* 'encircle, encompass'; the base elements are Latin *circum* 'around' and *stare* 'stand'. Like *assistance*, this was originally a noun that could not be made plural: it merely described an action (= the act of standing around) or a state (= standing around). However it is now frequently determinate (B. Disraeli *Vivian Grey*: Man is not the creature of circumstances. Circumstances are the creatures of men); the singular is sometimes poetical or rhetorical (Shakespeare *Hamlet*: You speak like a green girl Unsifted in such perilous circumstance).

circus [late Middle English] The early use of *circus* was to refer to the arena of Roman antiquity. It is a use of the Latin word meaning 'ring or circus'. The sense 'travelling company of performers' dates from the late 18th century. The phrase *bread and circuses* translating a line from one of Juvenal's satires, is used allusively for 'food and entertainment' especially when provided by a government to maintain goodwill.

cistern [Middle English] This word for a 'tank for storing water' is from Old French *cisterne*, from Latin *cisterna*, from *cista* 'box'.

citadel [mid 16th century] This is from French *citadelle*, or from Italian *cittadella*, based on Latin *civitas* 'city': this referred to the inner small fortified city, round which the larger city of later times grew.

city [Middle English] This is from Old French *cite*, from Latin *civitas*, from *civis* 'citizen'. Originally denoting a town, and often used as a Latin equivalent to Old English *burh* 'borough', the term was later applied to foreign and ancient cities and to the more important English boroughs. The connection between city and cathedral grew up under the Norman kings, as the episcopal sees (many had been established in villages) were removed to the chief borough of the diocese. The noun **citizen** dates from the same period as *city* and is from Anglo-Norman French *citezein*, an alteration (probably influenced by *deinzein* 'denizen') of Old French *citeain* based on Latin *civitas* 'city'.

civic [mid 16th century] Civic comes from French *civique* or Latin *civicus*, from *civis* 'citizen'. The original use was in *civic garland*, *civic crown*, etc., translating Latin *corona civica*, which was a garland of oak leaves and acorns given in ancient Rome to a person who saved a fellow citizen's life.

civilian [late Middle English] A *civilian* first denoted a practitioner of civil law: it is from Old French *civilien* used in the phrase *droit civilien* 'civil law'. The current sense describing a person not in the armed services, arose in the early 19th century; *civvy* is a late 19th-century abbreviation of *civilian*. The phrase **civil service** (late 18th century) originally applied to the part of the service of the British East India Company conducted by staff who did not belong to the Army or Navy. Late Middle English **civil** came via Old French from Latin *civilis* 'relating to citizens', from *civis* 'citizen'; from the same period is **civility** from Old French *civilite*, from Latin *civilitas* (from *civilis*). In early use the term denoted the state of being a citizen and hence 'good citizenship' or orderly behaviour. The sense 'politeness' arose in the mid 16th century.

claim [Middle English] Latin *clamare* 'to call out' is the base of English *claim*. The immediate source of the noun is Old French *claime*, and the verb is from Old French *clamer*.

clairvoyant [late 17th century] This was first recorded as meaning 'clear-sighted, perceptive'. It was adopted from French, from *clair* 'clear' and *voyant* 'seeing' (from *voir* 'to see'). The current term for someone with the supernatural ability to perceive events in the future, dates from the mid 19th century.

clam [early 16th century] This term for a type of mollusc is apparently from the earlier word *clam* meaning 'a clamp', from Old English *clam(m)* 'a bond or bondage'. The origin is Germanic; related terms are Dutch *klemme*, German *Klemme* and English *clamp*.

clamber [Middle English] *Clamber* is probably from *clamb*, the obsolete past tense of *climb*; an equivalent verb *climber* was in use in the 16th and 17th centuries.

clammy [late Middle English] This is from dialect *clam* 'to be sticky or adhere', which is of Germanic origin and related to *clay*; it was first found spelt as *claymy*.

clamour [late Middle English] *Clamour* came via Old French from Latin *clamor*, from *clamare* 'to cry out'.

clamp [Middle English] The *clamp* meaning 'a brace for holding something together' is probably of Dutch or Low German origin and related to *clam*.

clan [late Middle English] *Clan* is from Scottish Gaelic *clann* 'offspring, family', from Old Irish *cland*, from Latin *planta* 'sprout'.

clandestine [mid 16th century] This word meaning 'kept secretive, done secretly' is from French *clandestin* or Latin *clandestinus*, from *clam* 'secretly'.

clap [Old English] Old English *clappan* 'throb, beat' is imitative in origin. The sense 'strike the palms of the hands together' dates from late Middle English. The expression **claptrap** (mid 18th century) is based on *clap* and started out denoting something designed to elicit applause: it now means 'absurd talk'.

claret [late Middle English] *Claret* originally denoted a light red or yellowish wine, as distinct from a red or white: this contrast ceased around 1600 after which it was used for red wines generally. It is now applied to the red wines imported from Bordeaux. It is from Old French *(vin) claret* and medieval Latin *claratum (vinum)* 'clarified (wine)', from Latin *clarus* 'clear'.

clarify [Middle English] *Clarify* started out with the senses 'set forth clearly' and 'make pure and clean'. The source is Old French *clarifier*, from late Latin *clarificare*, from Latin *clarus* 'clear'.

clarinet [mid 18th century] This musical term is from French *clarinette*, a diminutive of *clarine* denoting a kind of bell; it is related to Middle English **clarion** 'a shrill narrow tubed war trumpet', from medieval Latin *clario(n-)*, from Latin *clarus* 'clear'.

clarity [Middle English] In early use, *clarity* had the sense 'glory, divine splendour'; it comes from Latin *claritas*, from *clarus* 'clear'. The current sense 'quality of being clear', dates from the early 17th century.

class [mid 16th century] The early sense of *class* was 'a group taught together'; it comes from Latin *classis* 'a division of the Roman people, a grade, or a class of pupils'.

classic [early 17th century] *Classic* is from French *classique* or Latin *classicus* 'belonging to a class or division', later 'of the highest class', from Latin *classis* 'division, grade, etc.'. The association with 'classes' in school or college probably influenced the connection with ancient authors (*the classics*) studied by students; this in turn probably led to its transference to the languages Greek and Latin. **Classical** was first recorded in the late 16th century in the sense 'outstanding of its kind', and is based on Latin *classicus* 'belonging to a class'.

clause [Middle English] This word came into English via Old French *clause* from Latin, based on Latin *claus-* from the verb *claudere* 'to close'. The Latin source included the senses 'conclusion of a legal formula' and 'a section of law'. Early use of *clause* in English was to denote both 'a distinct part of a sentence' and 'a separate article or proviso in a legal document'

clay [Old English] Old English *clǣg* is West Germanic in origin; it is related to Dutch *klei*, as well as to English *cleave* and *climb*.

clean [Old English] Old English *clǣne* 'clear, pure' is West Germanic in origin and related to Dutch and German *klein* 'small'. Old High German had the senses: clear, pure, clean, neat, delicate, fine, small. The verb **cleanse** was *clǣnsian* in Old English, from *clǣne*; since in Middle English the form was usually *clense*, the modern spelling seems to be an artificial assimilation to *clean*. At first *cleanse* was in ordinary use, but later it became more elevated than *clean* and retained in figurative use (Dryden—translating Ovid *Cinyra & Myrrha* in *Fables*: Not all her od'rous tears can cleanse her crime). In the 1990s, *cleanse* started to be used in the transferred sense 'ethnically cleanse' with reference to the purging of areas of ethnic or religious minority groups.

clear [Middle English] *Clear* is from Old French *cler*, from Latin *clarus* 'clear, bright'. Some of the senses are partly due to association with the native English word *clean*: e.g. 'unsullied' as in Shakespeare's *Macbeth*: Duncan ... has been So clear in his great Office; another adverbial sense is '(escaped) completely' (= clean away) as in Swift's *Ode to Sir W. Temple*: She soars clear out of sight. In modern use, *clear* has the predominant notion of 'unencumbered, free, rid' not found in *clean*.

cleave[1] [Old English] Old English *clēofan* 'split, sever' is Germanic in origin and related to Dutch *klieven* and German *klieben*.

cleave[2] [Old English] The origin of Old English *clifian*, *clifian*, *clifan* 'cling' is West Germanic; related forms are Dutch *kleven*, German *kleben*, and English *clay* and *climb*.

clef [late 16th century] This term for a musical symbol placed at the left hand end of a stave is from French, from Latin *clavis* 'key'.

cleft [Middle English] The early spelling of this word describing a 'fissure' was *clift*. Of Germanic origin, it is related to Dutch *kluft*, German *Kluft*, and to English *cleave*. The form of the word was altered in the 16th century by association with *cleft* 'split, divided', the past

participle of *cleave*. In the 16th to 18th centuries, the word seems to have been almost completely confused with *cliff* (in Old English *clif*).

clench [Old English] *Clench*, in early use, had the sense of *clinch* 'fix securely'. Of Germanic origin, it is related to *cling*.

cleric [early 17th century] *Cleric* is from ecclesiastical Latin *clericus* 'clergyman', (the base too of Middle English **clergy**). This is from Greek *klērikos* 'belonging to the Christian clergy', from *klēros* 'lot, heritage' (Acts 1:26).

clerk [Old English] Old English *cleric, clerc* had the senses 'ordained minister, man in a religious order'. The source is ecclesiastical Latin *clericus* 'clergyman' and the spelling was reinforced by Old French *clerc*, from the same source. The scholarship of the Middle Ages was limited to a great degree to the clergy who undertook all the writing and secretarial work of the time: this led to a notion of 'scholar' which became associated with the work of a notary, recorder, accountant, and finally 'penman' in general. The use describing an 'office employee maintaining records and undertaking administrative tasks' dates from the early 16th century. As for the pronunciation, the rhyme with *bark* is evidenced in the south of England from the 15th century.

clever [Middle English] The early sense was 'quick to catch hold', only recorded in this period. It is perhaps of Dutch or Low German origin, and related to *cleave*. In the late 16th century, probably through regional and colloquial use, the term came to mean 'manually skilful'. The notion of 'possessing mental agility' dates from the early 18th century. The sense development has similarities with that of *nimble*, *adroit*, *handy*, and *neat*.

client [late Middle English] This is from Latin *cliens, client*, a variant of *cluens* 'heeding', from *cluere* 'hear', 'obey', giving a notion of someone 'at the call of another' such as a patron. The term originally denoted a person under somebody's protection and patronage, which led to its application to a person 'protected' by a legal or other adviser. Mid 16th-century **clientele** had the sense 'clientship, patronage': it came via French from Latin *clientela* 'clientship' (from *cliens, client-*).

climate [late Middle English] This is from Old French *climat* or late Latin *clima, climat-*, from Greek *klīma* 'slope, zone'; the base is Greek *klinein* 'to slope'. The term originally denoted a zone of the earth between two lines of latitude, then any region of the earth, and later, a region considered with reference to its atmospheric conditions. **Clime** is from late Latin *clima* 'zone' and also dates from late Middle English.

climax [mid 16th century] The word *climax* was first used in rhetoric in which a number of propositions are set forth in a series, one rising above the other in force or effectiveness of expression. It is from late Latin, from Greek *klimax* 'ladder, climax'. The sense 'culmination' arose in the late 18th century from popular misuse of the learned word.

climb [Old English] Old English *climban* is West Germanic in origin and related to Dutch and German *klimmen*, also to *clay* and *cleave*. The root sense 'adhere' led to 'get up by clinging'. The *i* in the spelling was mostly pronounced as a short sound in the dialects; clear evidence of the long *i* (rhyming with *eye*) is not found before the 16th century. In other modern languages the comparable forms have mostly lost the *b* from the spelling: it was lost in pronunciation from all of them.

clinch [late 16th century] The early senses were 'something that grips' and, as a verb, 'fix securely': *clinch* is a variant of *clench*.

cling [Old English] Old English *clingan* 'stick together' is of Germanic origin; it is related to Middle Dutch *klingen* 'adhere', Middle High German *klingen* 'climb', and also to English *clench*.

clinic [mid 19th century] *Clinic* is first recorded as the 'teaching of medicine at the bedside'. It is from French *clinique*, from Greek *klinikē (tekhnē)* 'bedside (art)', from *klinē* 'bed'.

clique [early 18th century] This is an adoption of a French word, which refers to a group sharing common interests but not readily allowing others to join in. The source is Old French *cliquer* 'make a noise'. The modern sense is related to **claque**, a group hired to applaud or heckle a performer: this practice first occurred at the Paris opera in the early 19th century. *Claque* is from French *claquer* 'to clap'.

cloak [Middle English] The word *cloak* is from Old French *cloke*, a dialect variant of *cloche* 'bell' or, because of its bell shape, 'cloak'. The source is medieval Latin *clocca* 'bell'. The expression *cloak and dagger* associated with intrigue and subterfuge, is a translation of the French phrase *de cape et d'épée*. The notion of 'concealment' is a natural extension from the voluminous cover-all characteristics of the garment.

clock [late Middle English] *Clock* is from Middle Low German and Middle Dutch *klocke*, based on medieval Latin *clocca* 'bell'. The early sense was 'bell' in English, which then became 'the gong of a striking watch'. The slang phrase *clock something* meaning 'notice, observe something' dates from the mid 20th century; *clock*

had already come to mean 'face' in the earlier part of the century (leading to a notion of 'facing' and 'observing').

clod [late Middle English]
→ CLOT

clog [Middle English] A *clog* was first recorded as 'a block of wood to impede an animal's movement'; the term for a type of wooden shoe arose in late Middle English. The origin is unknown. The verb meaning 'block' derived this notion from the early use 'impede an animal by fitting with a clog encumbrance'.

cloister [Middle English] The early sense was 'place of religious seclusion'; it comes from Old French *cloistre*, from Latin *claustrum, clostrum* 'lock, enclosed place', from *claudere*, 'to close'.

clone [early 20th century] From Greek *klōn* 'twig', English *clone* is commonly used to refer to a person or thing regarded as identical to another. This meaning is an extension of the biological term for a group of cells produced asexually from one stock, to which they are genetically identical.

close[1] [Middle English] *Close* meaning 'only a short distance away' or 'enclosed place' is from Old French *clos*, from the Latin noun *clausum* 'enclosure' and adjective *clausus* 'closed' (the past participle of *claudere*). A diminutive of Old French *clos* 'closed' gave late Middle English **closet** which first denoted a private or small room.

close[2] [Middle English] The verb *close* 'move or cause to move so as to cover up (an opening)', 'come or bring to an end', etc. is from Old French *clos-*, the stem of *clore*, from Latin *claudere* 'to shut'. The same Latin verb is the base of late Middle English **closure** which came into English from Old French, from late Latin *clausura*.

clot [Old English] Old English *clot(t)* is Germanic in origin and related to German *Klotz*. With reference to a person, a *clot* was originally (mid 17th century) 'a clumsy person' but it came to be associated with stupidity.

cloth [Old English] The ultimate origin of Old English *clāth* 'fabric for covering or wrapping', related to Dutch *kleed* and German *Kleid*, is unknown. The verb **clothe** was only recorded in the past participle *geclāded* in Old English: this is from the noun *clāth*. The plural **clothes** was *clāthas* (= cloths) in this same early period. Later (in Middle English) came **clothier**, at first spelt *clother*: the change in the ending was due to association with the common suffix *-ier* used to denote occupations.

cloud [Old English] Old English *clūd* meant 'mass of rock or earth'; it is probably related to *clot*. The term for a 'visible mass of condensed watery vapour' dates from Middle English. The phrase **cloud cuckoo land** 'a state of over-optimistic fantasy' (late 19th century) is a translation of Greek *Nephelokokkugia* (the form elements of which are *nephelē* 'cloud' and *kokkux* 'cuckoo'). This was the name of the city built by the birds in Aristophanes' comedy *The Birds*.
→ CLOT

clout [Old English] Old English *clūt* had the sense 'a patch or metal plate'. It is related to Dutch *kluit* 'lump, clod', as well as to Old English *clot*. The shift of sense to 'heavy blow', which dates from late Middle English, is difficult to explain; possibly the change occurred first in the verb (with a progression from 'put a patch on' to 'hit hard').
→ CLOT

clown [mid 16th century] The origin is perhaps Low German. The early sense was 'an unsophisticated country person': this became extended to mean 'ill-bred' (Tennyson *In Memoriam*: The churl in spirit … By blood a king, at heart a clown). The use to describe a fool or jester, such as in a circus, developed within a short period; in Shakespeare, a *clown* often refers to a jester retained as court (*As You Like It*: The roynish Clown, at whom so oft Your Grace was wont to laugh).

cloy [late Middle English] 'Disgust or sicken' is the current sense of *cloy* which is a shortening of the obsolete verb *accloy* 'choke'. Another sense was 'stop up' from Old French *encloyer* 'drive a nail into', from medieval Latin *inclavare*; the base is *clavus* 'a nail'.

club [Middle English] This term for a heavy stick with a thick end, is from Old Norse *clubba*, a variant of *klumba*; it is related to *clump*. The use of *club* for a society or association dedicated to a particular interest dates from the early 17th century; it was formed obscurely from *club* 'beat with a club' and first used as a verb meaning 'combine into a mass'.

clue [late Middle English] *Clue* is a variant of the archaic word *clew*. The original sense was 'a ball of thread'; hence one used to guide a person out of a labyrinth either literally or figuratively. This was used in the story of the Greek legendary hero, Theseus, who slew the Cretan Minotaur, escaping from the Labyrinth with Ariadne's ball of thread which unravelled along the path of his escape. The sense relating to 'a piece of information used in the detection of something' dates from the early 17th century.

clump [Middle English] *Clump* first denoted a heap or lump; it was reinforced by Middle Low German *klumpe* and Middle Dutch *klompe*; related is English *club*.

clumsy [late 16th century] *Clumsy* is from obsolete *clumse* 'make numb, be numb'. The origin is probably Scandinavian, related to Swedish *klumsig*.

cluster [Old English] Old English *clyster* is probably related to *clot* 'thick mass', a word of the same period of Germanic origin.
→ CLOT

clutch[1] [Middle English] *Clutch* 'grasp' meant, in early use, 'bend, crook'. It is a variant of the obsolete verb *clitch* 'close the hand', from Old English *clyccan* 'crook, clench'. The origin is Germanic.

clutch[2] [early 18th century] This term for a 'group of eggs' is probably a southern variant of the northern English dialect word *cletch*. This is related to Middle English *cleck* 'to hatch' (from Old Norse *klekja*).

clutter [late Middle English] *Clutter* started out as a verb. It is a variant of dialect *clotter* 'to clot', influenced by *cluster* and the imitative Old English word *clatter*.
→ CLOT

coach[1] [mid 16th century] The noun *coach* was first used to describe a horse-drawn carriage, which in the 16th and 17th centuries was usually a royal state vehicle. It comes from French *coche*, from Hungarian *kocsi* (*szekér*) '(wagon) from *Kocs*', the name of a town in Hungary. The notion of 'transportation' influenced its extension and application to 'railway carriage' and 'single-decker bus'. The *coach* meaning 'to train' (early 18th century) or 'trainer' is a figurative use of *coach*, from the idea of 'move forward, move along, progress'.

coagulate [late Middle English] This is from Latin *coagulat-*, from the verb *coagulare* 'curdle', from *coagulum* 'rennet'.

coal [Old English] Old English *col* meant 'glowing ember' and 'charred remnant'. It is Germanic in origin and related to Dutch *kool* and German *Kohle*. The sense 'combustible mineral used as fuel' dates from Middle English. The dog known as a **collie** (mid 17th century) is thought to derive its name from the word *coal*: the breed was originally black. **Collier**, based on *coal* had the original sense 'maker of charcoal', which survives in US use: such a person usually brought it to market, hence 'person selling charcoal', later 'person selling coal', from which the current senses arose.

coalition [early 17th century] The early sense was 'fusion', from medieval Latin *coalitio(n)*, from the verb *coalescere* 'grow together'. Its use in political contexts where an alliance for combined action is agreed upon between different parties for a temporary period, dates from the early 18th century.

coarse [late Middle English] The first recorded senses were 'ordinary' (describing cloth) and 'inferior'. The origin is uncertain; until the 17th century it was identical in spelling with *course*, and possibly derived from this, in the sense 'habitual or ordinary manner'. Both words were originally pronounced /kurs/; the spelling *coarse* seems to have appeared at the same time that the pronunciation of *course* changed to /kors/. It is difficult to say when the notion of 'inferior quality' developed into 'lacking delicacy of texture'. This lack of delicacy became associated figuratively with vulgar language and behaviour.

coast [Middle English] Early usage was as a word for the 'side of the body', from Old French *coste*, from Latin *costa* 'rib, flank, side'. The connection with the sea arose from the phrase *coast of the sea* meaning 'side of the sea'. The verb was used to mean 'move along the edge of' and 'sail along the coast'. The notion of 'move easily without effort' has arisen through an early 19th-century US usage 'slide down a snow-covered slope in a sled', 'freewheel down a hill on a bicycle': this derives from French *côte* 'hillside'. The word **coaster** for a small round mat (late 19th century), started out as a term for a low round tray for a decanter: the notion comes from 'coasting' (= making the circuit of) the table after dinner.

coax [late 16th century] *Coax* is from obsolete *cokes* meaning 'simpleton', the origin of which is unknown. The original sense was 'pet, fondle', hence 'persuade by caresses or flattery': the underlying sense is 'make a simpleton of'. The parallel notions 'make a fool of', 'make a pet of' are also seen in the word *fond* (meaning both 'befooled' and 'affectionate').
→ FOND

cob [late Middle English] A *cob* is used to describe many things where the underlying general sense appears to be 'stout, rounded, sturdy'. Amongst the uses are: 'loaf of bread', 'a hazel bush', 'a male swan', 'a roundish lump of coal', 'a powerfully built short-legged horse', 'the central woody part of a maize ear'. In early use a *cob* referred to a strong man or leader. The origin remains unknown.

cobalt [late 17th century] This is from German *Kobalt* 'imp, demon (of the mines)', from the belief that cobalt was harmful to the ores with which it occurred. It was also associated with ill health by the miners of the Harz or Erzgebirge (mountain ranges in Germany). The word passed from German into all the European languages.

cobweb [Middle English] The early spelling was *cop(pe)web*: the first element is from obsolete *coppe* 'spider'.

coccyx [late 16th century] The name for this small triangular bone at the base of the spinal column came via Latin from Greek *kokkux* 'cuckoo': the shape of the bone resembles a cuckoo's bill.

cock[1] [Old English] Old English *cocc* is from medieval Latin *coccus*; it was reinforced in Middle English by Old French *coq*. Wherever the name arose originally, it is probably echoic, representing the cock's cry by imitation. The crowing of the cock in the early morning led to time expressions such as *first, second, third cock, etc.* (Chaucer *Miller's Tale*: When that the firste cok hath crowe; and *Bible* Mark 14:30: Before the cock crow twice, thou shalt deny me thrice). A *cock* is used in other senses and sometimes refers to a type of tap for stopping the flow of liquid, or to a spout. The phrase **cock-a-hoop** 'extremely pleased' (mid 17th century) comes from the expression *set cock a hoop*, which apparently denotes the action of turning on the tap and allowing liquor to flow before a drinking session. 'Shape' may be a core feature of the word: some stopcocks resemble a cock's head with a comb. The use of the word *cock* in firearms for a lever in a matchlock, flintlock, percussion lock, is due to the original shape of these mechanisms.

cock[2] [late Middle English] This *cock* meaning 'small pile' of a material such as hay or straw (e.g. *haycock*), is perhaps of Scandinavian origin and related to Norwegian *kok* 'heap', 'lump', Danish *kok* 'haycock', and Swedish *koka* 'clod'.

cockney [late Middle English] A *cockney* was originally 'a pampered child'. Its origin is not at all certain; one theory, now not given credence, was a possible connection with *cokeney* meaning 'cock's egg' already in use in this period and describing a small misshapen egg (probably from *cock* and *ey*, an obsolete word for 'egg'). The notion of 'smallness' and the connotation of disparagement were found in a later use of *cockney* describing 'a town-dweller regarded as puny or affected'. This usage led to the current sense 'native of the east end of London', which was initially applied in a derogatory way.

cockpit [late 16th century] A *cockpit* first described a place hollowed out for cock-fighting. The association with injury and bloodshed led, in the early 18th century, to the term being used in a nautical context for an area in the aft lower deck of a man-of-war: wounded sailors were treated there in the heat of battle. The use was then extended to apply to the well in a sailing yacht where the vessel was steered, which accounts for the current general sense of a *cockpit* housing the controls of other vehicles such as an aircraft or racing car.

cockroach [early 17th century] The early written form was *cacaroch* which is fairly close to its source: Spanish *cucaracha*. The spelling changed by association with words more familiar to the English ear: *cock* and *roach*.

cocksure [early 16th century] The meaning 'absolutely sure' owes more to the word *cock* 'cockerel' with its strutting, confident image, than it does to the real source of the word which is the obsolete *cock* used euphemistically for 'God'.

cocktail [early 17th century] Early use was an adjective describing a creature with a tail like that of a cock, specifically a horse with a docked tail. Because hunters and coach-horses were generally docked, the term developed a sense of 'non-thoroughbred' when applied to racehorses in the early 19th century: the suggestion was that there had been a cock-tailed horse in the pedigree. This notion of 'adulteration, lack of purety' probably led to the current *cocktail* as a term for a drink, first recorded as a US usage, from the idea of an 'adulterated' spirit.

coco [mid 16th century] Used in combinations such as *coco palm*, *coco matting*, this was originally a term for 'coconut' and came from a Spanish and Portuguese word meaning 'grinning face', inspired by the three holes on the base of the nut. The **coconut** was only referred to as the *nut of India* or *Indian nut* when first introduced to the English markets, after its discovery in India by the Portuguese. Because of the confusion with *cocoa*, the spelling *coker* was commonly used at the Port of London.

cocoa [early 18th century] Cocoa is an alteration of Spanish *cacao*. The Spanish spelling itself was used in English almost two centuries earlier to mean 'cocoa bean'.
→ CHOCOLATE

cocoon [late 17th century] A French word *cocon* is the source of *coccoon*, which in turn came from medieval Provençal *coucoun* 'eggshell', a diminutive of *coca* 'shell'. The verb dates from the mid 19th century.

coddle [late 16th century] Coddle was used originally to mean 'boil gently' in connection with the cooking of fruit, but where the word

comes from is not absolutely clear. The modern sense 'look after somebody in an indulgent way' is probably a dialect variant of the obsolete *caudle* 'give gruel to an invalid', based on the Latin *caldum* 'hot drink'.

code [Middle English] From Latin *codex*, this word came into English via Old French. It was originally a systematic collection of statutes made by one of the later Roman emperors, used particularly with reference to Justinian. The earliest modern sense sprang up in the mid 18th century in relation to the penal code. The Latin word **codex** has passed into English as 'a list of statutes', having moved in Latin from the early simple meaning of a 'a block of wood', to 'a block split into leaves or tablets' thus 'a book'. The related term **codicil** is from Latin *codicillus*, a diminutive of *codex*, and thus applies to a 'small' part of a legal document.

codger [mid 18th century] A colloquial and depreciatory term for an elderly man, it is probably a variant of *cadger*.

codpiece This male fashion accessory in the shape of a pouch worn over other clothing and over the genitals, is based on Old English *codd* first meaning 'bag', later written *cod* and meaning 'scrotum'. The fish we call **cod** may have got its name from the same word, thus 'bag fish' because of its shape, but this origin is not certain; **cuttlefish** (first only referred to as *cuttle*) is related to Old English *codd* being so named because of its inkbag.

codswallop [1960s] A *load of codswallop* is an informal way of saying 'lot of nonsense'; the origin of the first element of the word is sometimes said to be the name of Hiram Codd who, in 1878, invented a bottle for fizzy drinks; this theory has not been confirmed. The element *wallop* may be from a colloquial use of the word from the 1930s for 'beer' or any alcoholic drink.
→ WALLOP

coerce [late Middle English] The current sense of *coerce* is 'persuade by threats or by using force'; early use involved constraint to force obedience or compliance. The word is based on the Latin elements *co-* 'jointly' and *arcere* 'hold back', giving the verb *coercere* 'restrain'. The noun **coercion** dates from the same period and has the same Latin source. The adjective **coercive** is not recorded until the late 16th century; the suffix *-ive* was added to the English verb.

coffee [late 16th century] Probably introduced via the Dutch word *koffie*, English *coffee* has its source in Turkish *kahveh*, from Arabic. Arab lexicographers believe the original meaning to have been 'wine'.

coffer [Middle English] This is from Old French *coffre* 'chest', via Latin from Greek *kophinos* 'basket'. The association with 'stored valuables' has led to *coffers* having the sense 'financial reserves' rather than 'containers'. The word **coffret** is a diminutive, thus 'small chest'.

coffin [Middle English] *Coffin* shares the same source as *coffer*, and in Middle English also meant 'chest, casket'. Its immediate source was Old French *cofin* 'little basket'. The shape led to the term's use in cookery for a 'mould for a pie' but this is now obsolete.

cog [Middle English] This word meaning 'wheel transferring motion to another', is probably of Scandinavian origin and related to Swedish *kugge* and Norwegian *kug*.

cogent [mid 17th century] *Cogent* 'logical and convincing' is from Latin *cogent-* 'compelling', from the verb *cogere*, from *co-* 'together' and *agere* 'drive'.

cogitate [late 16th century] This formal word meaning 'think deeply' is from the Latin verb *cogitare* 'consider', from *co-* 'together' and *agitare* 'turn over, consider'. The first person singular of this Latin verb is seen in the philosophical term **cogito** meaning literally 'I think', in Descartes's formula (1641) *cogito, ergo sum* 'I think therefore I am'.

coherent [mid 16th century] The first recorded sense was 'logically related to'; it comes from Latin *cohaerent-* 'sticking together', from the verb *cohaerere*. The past participle of this is *cohaes-* 'cleaved together', which gave mid 17th-century **cohesion** on the pattern of *adhesion*.

cohort [late Middle English] *Cohort* 'band of people' is from Old French *cohorte*, or from Latin *cohors*, *cohort-* 'yard, retinue'. The syllable *hort-* (found in Latin *hortus* 'garden') is related to English *garden*, which comes from a root meaning 'to enclose'.
→ COURT

coil [early 16th century] Early use was as a verb. *Coil* is from Old French *coillir*, from Latin *colligere* 'gather together'. *Coil* meaning 'confusion, turmoil' is used in the phrase shuffle off this mortal coil in Shakespeare's *Hamlet*. The origin of the word remains unknown but it was probably in spoken use in nautical contexts before the datings of the written evidence.
→ COLLECT

coin [Middle English] *Coin* is from Old French *coin* 'wedge, corner, die', *coigner* 'to mint', from Latin *cuneus* 'wedge'. The original sense was 'cornerstone', later 'angle or wedge' (senses now spelt *quoin*); in late Middle English, the term denoted a die for stamping money, or a piece of money produced by such a die. Early 17th-century **coign** is a variant of *coin* in the late Middle English sense 'projecting corner or cornerstone'. The phrase *coign of vantage* meaning 'a favourable position for observation or action' was first used by Shakespeare (*Macbeth* i. iv. 7), and later popularized by Sir Walter Scott.

coincide [early 18th century] The early sense was 'occupy the same space': it comes from medieval Latin *coincidere*, from *co-* 'together with' and *incidere* 'fall upon or into'.

colander [Middle English] This is based on Latin *colare* 'to strain'.

collaboration [mid 19th century] This is from Latin *collaboratio(n-)*, from *collaborare* 'work together', from *col-* 'together' and *laborare* 'to work'.

collapse [early 17th century] The early form was *collapsed*, from medical Latin *collapsus*, the past participle of *collabi*, from *col-* 'together' and *labi* 'to slip'.

collar [Middle English] *Collar* is from Old French *colier*, from Latin *collare* 'band for the neck, collar', from *collum* 'neck'. The Middle English spelling was *coler*.

collateral [late Middle English] Early use was as an adjective; it is from medieval Latin *collateralis*, from *col-* 'together with' and *lateralis* (from *latus*, *later-* 'side'). The sense 'something pledged as security for repayment of a loan', originally a US usage, is from the phrase *collateral security* which is something pledged in addition to the main contractual obligation. More recently from the 1970s, the phrase *collateral damage* has arisen in military contexts, describing damage inflicted over and beyond what is intended or expected by an aggressor, usually 'alongside' a military target.

collation [Middle English] *Collation* 'light meal', 'action of collating' came via Old French from Latin *collatio(n-)*, from *conferre* 'bring together'. Used in the plural originally in English, the term referred to John Cassian's *Collationes Patrum in Scetica Eremo Commorantium* 'Conferences of, or with, the Egyptian Hermits' (AD 415–20), from which a reading would be given in Benedictine communities before a light meal.

colleague [early 16th century] *Colleague* is from French *collègue*, from Latin *collega* 'partner in office', from *col-* 'together with' and *legare* 'depute'.

collect [late Middle English] *Collect* 'gather together' is from Old French *collecter* or medieval Latin *collectare*, from Latin *collect-* 'gathered together'. The Latin base verb *colligere* is from *col-* 'together' and *legere* 'choose or collect'. The *collect* meaning 'prayer' (Middle English) is from Old French *collecte*, from Latin *collecta* 'a gathering together'; an obsolete use of *collect* was as a term for 'a gathering' for an act of worship.

college [late Middle English] This is from Old French, from Latin *collegium* 'partnership, association', from *collega* 'partner in office'. Early use included the general senses 'gathering', 'reunion of companions'.
➜ COLLEAGUE

collision [late Middle English] *Collision* is from late Latin *collisio(n-)*, from Latin *collidere* 'strike together', the base too of **collide** (early 17th century). This verb had the early sense 'cause to collide', the base elements being *col-* 'together' and *laedere* 'to strike or damage'. The intransitive use 'come into collision' was much objected to as an Americanism when first used in the context of trains or ships in collision, around 1860–70.

collusion [late Middle English] *Collusion* is from Latin *collusio(n-)*, from *colludere* 'have a secret agreement', a base shared by **collude** (early 16th century), the elements of which are *col* 'together' and *ludere* 'to play'.

colonel [mid 16th century] This word for a military rank is from obsolete French *coronel*, an earlier form of *colonel*. The source is Italian *colonnello* 'column of soldiers', from *colonna* 'column', from Latin *columna*. The form *coronel*, source of the modern pronunciation, was usual until the mid 17th century.

colony [late Middle English] The first sense of *colony* documented in English was 'a settlement formed mainly of retired soldiers', acting as a garrison in newly conquered territory in the Roman Empire (such as London, Bath, and Chester in Britain). The word is from Latin *colonia* 'settlement, farm', from *colonus* 'settler, farmer', from *colere* 'cultivate'. The modern application of *colony* to a new community of settlers subject to the parent state, dates from the 16th century.

colossus [late Middle English] A *colossus* is a statue that is much bigger than life-size. The word comes via Latin from Greek *kolossos*, which was applied by Herodotus to the statues of Egyptian temples. This Greek form is the base of the word **Colosseum** used as a name since medieval times for a vast amphitheatre in Rome (started in *c*. AD 75): it is the neuter of Latin *colosseus* 'gigantic'. **Colossal** 'huge' (early 18th century) is from French, from *colosse*, from Latin *colossus*.

colour [Middle English] The noun is from Old French *colour* (from Latin *color*), the verb from Old French *colourer* (from Latin *colorare*). *Colour* has been the normal spelling in English from the 14th century, with *color* being used occasionally from the 15th century under Latin influence: this is now the prevalent spelling in the US. The military rank **colour sergeant** has arisen with reference to the sergeant's responsibility for carrying one of the regiment's colours in an honour guard.

colt [Old English] This is perhaps related to Swedish *kult*, applied to boys or half-grown animals.

column [late Middle English] This is partly from Old French *columpne*, reinforced by its source, Latin *columna* 'pillar'.

WORDBUILDING

The prefix **com-** [from Latin *cum* 'with'] adds the sense

■ **with** [combine]

■ **together** [compact]

■ **altogether** [commemorate]

Variants of the prefix *com-* are: *co-* (especially before vowels), *col-* (before *l*), *cor-* (before *r*), and *con-* (mostly before consonants other than *b*, *m*, and *p*).

---

coma [mid 17th century] This medical term is modern Latin, from Greek *kōma* 'deep sleep'; related to *koitē* 'bed' and *keisthai* 'lie down'.

comb [Old English] Old English *camb* is Germanic in origin and related to Dutch *kam* and German *Kamm*. The semantic root may be 'tooth'.

combat [mid 16th century] The verb is from French *combattre*, from late Latin *combattere*, from *com-* 'together with' and *battere* (a variant of Latin *batuere* 'to fight'). The adjective **combatant** was used from late Middle English in heraldry meaning literally 'in fighting stance', to describe two lions facing one another with raised forepaws: it is a use of the present participle of Old French *combatre* 'to fight'.

combe [Old English] Old English *cumb* 'small valley, hollow' was found in charters as part of some placenames in southern England, many of which survive. It is Celtic in origin, related to *cwm*, a term for a rounded hollow in the mountains of Wales. The current general application of the word to a short valley or hollow on a hillside or coastline (especially in southern England) dates from the late 16th century.

combine [late Middle English] *Combine* is from Old French *combiner* or late Latin *combinare* 'join two by two', from com- 'together' and Latin *bini* 'two (yoked) together'. From the same period is **combination** from late Latin *combinatio(n-)*, from the verb *combinare*.

combustion [late Middle English] This word is from late Latin *combustio(n-)*, from Latin *comburere* 'burn up'. Late 15th-century **combust** is from obsolete *combust* 'burnt, calcined', from Latin *combustus* (the past participle of *comburere*).

come [Old English] Old English *cuman* is Germanic in origin and related to Dutch *komen* and German *kommen*.

comedy [late Middle English] The early *comedy* was a word for a genre of drama as well as for a narrative poem with a happy ending (as in Dante's *Divine Comedy*). It comes from Old French *comedie*, via Latin from Greek *kōmōidia*: this is from *kōmōidos* 'comic poet', composed of *kōmos* 'revel' and *aoidos* 'singer'. A **comedian**, in the late 16th century, was a comic playwright: it comes from French *comédien*, from Old French *comedie*. The reference to an entertainer whose act centres on making people laugh, dates from the late 19th century.

comely [Middle English] This was probably shortened from *becomely* 'fitting, becoming', from *become*.
→ BECOME

comet [late Old English] *Comet* is from Latin *cometa*, from Greek *kometēs* 'long-haired (star)', from *komē* 'hair'. It was reinforced by Old French *comete*.

comfort [Middle English] In early use the noun (from Old French *confort*) meant 'strengthening, support, consolation'; as a verb (from Old French *conforter*) the senses were 'strengthen, give support, console'. The source is late Latin *confortare* 'strengthen', from com- (giving emphasis) and Latin *fortis* 'strong'. The sense 'something producing physical ease' arose in the mid 17th century. Middle English **comfortable** meant 'pleasing' as well as 'strengthening, encouraging'; it is from Anglo-Norman French *confortable*, from *conforter* 'to comfort'.

comic [late 16th century] This word comes via Latin from Greek *kōmikos*, from *kōmos* 'a revel'. Pre-dating this from late Middle English in the sense 'relating to or in the style of comedy' is **comical**, based on Latin *comicus*.

command [Middle English] *Command* is from Old French *comander* 'to command', from late Latin *commandare*, from com- (giving emphasis) and *mandare* 'commit, command'. Middle English was also the period when **commandment** (from Old French *comandement*) and

commander (from Old French *comandeor*) were recorded. The word *commandment* was originally spelt with an *e* before the final *-ment* and the four syllables were still found in the works of 16th- and 17th-century writers as well as in 19th-century dialect speech from Scotland to West Somerset. The trisyllabic spelling was already in evidence however in the 13th century and became prevalent in literary language in the 17th–18th centuries: in the early period, the first syllable was often stressed.

commandeer [early 19th century] *Commandeer* 'take possession of officially' is from Afrikaans *kommandeer*, from Dutch *commanderen*, from French *commander* 'to command'.

commando [late 18th century] This was first recorded as a word for a militia, originally consisting of Boers in South Africa. It is from Portuguese (an earlier form of *comando*), from *commandar* 'to command', from late Latin *commandare*.
→ COMMAND

commemoration [late Middle English] This is from Latin *commemoratio(n-)*, from the verb *commemorare* 'bring to remembrance'. **Commemorate** dates from the late 16th century and is from Latin *commemorat-* from *commemorare*. The base elements are Latin com- 'altogether' and *memorare* 'relate', from *memor* 'mindful'.

commence [Middle English] *Commence* is from Old French *commencier*, *comencier*, based on Latin com- (giving emphasis) and *initiare* 'begin'.

commend [Middle English] *Commend* is from Latin *commendare*, from com- (giving emphasis) and *mandare* 'commit, entrust'. From the same period is **commendation** from Old French, from Latin *commendatio(n-)*, from *commendare* 'commit to the care of'. Originally in the plural, the word once referred to a liturgical office ending with a prayer commending the souls of the dead to God.
→ COMMAND

commensurate [mid 17th century] *Commensurate* 'corresponding in size or degree', is from Latin *commensuratus*, from com- 'together' and *mensuratus*, the past participle of *mensurare* 'to measure'.

comment [late Middle English] A *comment* was first recorded as meaning 'expository treatise' and 'explanatory note'. It comes from Latin *commentum* 'contrivance' (a form of the verb *comminisci* 'to devise'), which in late Latin came also to mean 'interpretation'. **Commentary** dates from this same period and is from Latin *commentarius*, *commentarium* (an adjective, used as a noun), based on *comminisci*. Mid 19th-century **commentate** is a back-formation (by removal of the suffix) from **commentator**.

commerce [mid 16th century] The first recorded sense referred to social dealings between people. The source is French, from Latin *commercium* 'trade, trading', from the base elements *com-* 'together' and *merx, merc-* 'merchandise'.

commiserate [late 16th century] Latin *miser* 'wretched' is the base of *commiserate*, whose direct source is Latin *commiserat-*, past participial stem of the verb *commiserari* 'lament with'.

commission [Middle English] A *commission* is commonly an instruction or command; it came into English via Old French from Latin *commissio(n-)*, from *committere* 'entrust'. Late Middle English **commissioner** 'a person appointed by a commission', is from medieval Latin *commissionarius*, from Latin *commissio*.
➔ COMMIT

commissionaire [mid 17th century] This word for a uniformed door attendant at a building such as a hotel or theatre is from French, from medieval Latin *commissarius* 'person in charge', from Latin *committere* 'entrust'.

commit [late Middle English] This is from Latin *committere* 'join, entrust', which in medieval Latin meant 'put into custody': it is from *com-* 'with' and *mittere* 'put or send'.

committee [late 15th century] A *committee* was first recorded as meaning 'a person to whom something has been entrusted': it is based on the verb *commit*.

commode [mid 18th century] A *commode* first referred to a chest of drawers of a type popular in the 18th century. From French and meaning in its literal sense 'convenient, suitable', it is based on Latin *commodus*. Its use as a word for a piece of furniture containing a concealed chamber pot, dates from the early 19th century.

commodity [late Middle English] From Old French *commodite* or Latin *commoditas, commodity* 'useful thing', 'raw material that can be bought and sold', is based on Latin *commodus* 'convenient'.

common [Middle English] Old French *comun* is the direct source of English *common*. The related noun **commonality** was rarely used before the 1950s, but from the mid 16th century meant 'a sharing of features'. It was first recorded in late Middle English in the sense 'people without special rank or position' and was a variant of **commonalty**, dating from the

same period. The source is Old French *comunalte*, from medieval Latin *communalitas*, from Latin *communis* 'common, general'. Latin *communis* is the base of these words including Middle English **commoner** first recorded as a word for a citizen or burgess.

commonplace [mid 16th century] This was originally written *common place*, a translation of Latin *locus communis*, rendering Greek *koinos topos* 'general theme'.

commonwealth [late Middle English] First denoting public welfare, this was originally written as two words and is equivalent to the archaic phrase *the commonweal* 'the welfare of the public'.

commotion [late Middle English] The Latin elements *com-* 'altogether' and *motio* 'motion' form the Latin noun *commotio(n-)*, which has given *commotion* in English.
➔ MOTION

commune[1] [late 17th century] Early use was as a term for the smallest French territorial division from an administrative point of view. It is French, from medieval Latin *communia*, the neuter plural of Latin *communis* 'common, general'. The adjective **communal** (early 19th century) was first recorded in contexts relating to a *commune*, especially the Paris Commune, the group which seized the municipal government in the French Revolution and played a leading part in the Reign of Terror until suppressed in 1794. It comes from French, from late Latin *communalis*, from *communis* 'common, general'.

commune[2] [Middle English] The verb *commune* 'share one's intimate thoughts with someone', is from Old French *comuner* 'to share', from *comun* 'common'.

communication [late Middle English] *Communication* is from Old French *comunicacion*, from Latin *communicatio(n)*, from the verb *communicare* 'to share': this is a base shared by the verb **communicate** which dates from the early 16th century.
➔ COMMON

communion [late Middle English] This is from Latin *communio(n)*, from *communis* 'common'.

communism [mid 19th century] *Communism* is from French *communisme*, from *commun* 'common'.

community [late Middle English] This is from Old French *comunete*, reinforced by its source, Latin *communitas*, from *communis* 'common'.

commute [late Middle English] The early recorded sense of *commute* was 'interchange (two things)'. The source of the word is Latin *commutare*, from *com-* 'altogether' and *mutare* 'to change'. *Commute* meaning 'travel between home and one's place of work', originally meant to buy and use a *commutation ticket*, the US term for a season ticket: this is because the daily fare was 'commuted' to a single payment.

compact [late Middle English] *Compact* 'packed together closely and neatly' is from Latin *compact-*, from the verb *compingere* 'to join', from *com-* 'together' and *pangere* 'fasten'.

companion [Middle English] This word is from Old French *compaignon*, literally 'one who breaks bread with another', based on Latin *com-* 'together with' and *panis* 'bread'.

company [Middle English] *Company* is from Old French *compainie* which is related to *compaignon* 'companion'.

comparison [Middle English] *Comparison* is from Old French *comparesoun*, from Latin *comparatio(n-)*, from *comparare* 'to pair, match'. This Latin verb is also the base of **compare** recorded from late Middle English (from Old French *comparer*): the base elements are *com-* 'with' and *par* 'equal'.

compartment [mid 16th century] Late Latin *compartiri* 'divide' is the base of Italian *compartimento* which gave French *compartiment*, source of the English word *compartment*.

compass [Middle English] The noun is from Old French *compas*, the verb from Old French *compasser*, based on Latin *com-* 'together' and *passus* 'a step or pace'. Several senses ('measure', 'artifice', 'circumscribed area', and 'pair of compasses') which appeared in Middle English are also found in Old French, but their development and origin are uncertain. The transference of sense to the magnetic compass is held to have occurred in the related Italian word *compasso*, inspired by the circular shape of the compass box.

compassion [Middle English] The word *compassion* came into English via Old French from ecclesiastical Latin *compassio(n-)*, from *compati* 'suffer with'. **Compassionate**, dating from the late 16th century and based on *compassion* was influenced by archaic French *compassioné* 'feeling pity'.

compatible [late Middle English] This was adopted from French, from medieval Latin *compatibilis*, from *compati* 'suffer with'.

compatriot [late 16th century] This word for a fellow citizen or national of a country, is from French *compatriote*, from late Latin *compatriota*

(translating Greek *sumpatriōtēs*), from *com-* 'together with' and *patriota* 'patriot'.
→ PATRIOT

compel [late Middle English] The base elements of Latin *compellere*, from which *compel* derives, are *com-* 'together' and *pellere* 'drive'.

compendium [late 16th century] This was originally a Latin word meaning 'profit, saving' (literally 'that which is weighed together'). In English it refers to 'a collection' of information in a publication, for example, or of things systematically gathered. The base elements are Latin *com-* 'together' and *pendere* 'weigh'.

compensation [late Middle English] *Compensation* came via Old French from Latin *compensatio(n-)*. The Latin base verb is *compensare* 'weigh against', which is also the source of **compensate** (mid 17th century): this was first recorded in the sense 'counterbalance'. The Latin formative elements are *com-* 'together' and *pendere* 'weigh'.

compete [early 17th century] This word is from Latin *competere* in its late sense 'strive or contend for (something)': the elements here are *com-* 'together' and *petere* 'aim at, seek'. The noun **competition** from late Latin *competitio(n-)* 'rivalry' dates from the same period. **Competitor** (early 16th century) is from French *compétiteur* or Latin *competitor*.

competent [late Middle English] *Competent* was first recorded in the sense 'suitable, adequate'. It comes from Latin *competent-*, from the verb *competere* in its earlier sense 'be fit or proper'.

compile [Middle English] This is from Old French *compiler* or its apparent source, Latin *compilare* 'plunder', 'plagiarize'. Late Middle English **compilation** came via Old French from Latin *compilatio(n-)*, from *compilare*.

complacent [mid 17th century] The early sense recorded was 'pleasant'; it comes from Latin *complacent-* 'pleasing', from the verb *complacere*. **Complacency** dates from the same period and is from medieval Latin *complacentia*, from Latin *complacere* 'to please'.

complain [late Middle English] *Complain* is from Old French *complaindre*, from medieval Latin *complangere* 'bewail', made up of *com-* (giving emphasis) and *plangere* 'to lament'. **Complaint**, dating from the same period, is from Old French *complainte*, the feminine past participle of *complaindre* 'to lament'.

complement [late Middle English] A *complement* is something which contributes additional or contrasting features to something else so as to emphasize its quality. The early

recorded sense was 'completion', the source being Latin *complementum*, from *complere* 'fill up'.
→COMPLETE; COMPLIMENT

complete [late Middle English] *Complete* is from Old French *complet* or Latin *complētus*, the past participle of *complere* 'fill up, finish, fulfil'. Here *com-* reinforces *plere* 'to fill'.

complex [mid 17th century] When first recorded, *complex* was used to refer to 'a group of related elements'. The source is Latin *complexus*, the past participle (used as a noun) of *complectere* 'embrace, comprise'; it was later associated with *complexus* 'plaited', which adds to the notion of intricacy. The adjective is partly via French *complexe*.

complexion [Middle English] This came via Old French from Latin *complexio(n-)* 'combination' from *complectere* 'embrace, comprise'. The term originally referred to a person's physical constitution (a late Latin sense) or to temperament once believed to be determined by a combination of the four bodily humours: blood, phlegm, yellow bile, and black bile. This gave rise, in the late 16th century, to the meaning 'natural colour and texture of a person's skin' as a visible sign of this temperament.
→HUMOUR

complication [late Middle English] *Complication* is from late Latin *complicatio(n-)*, from Latin *complicare* 'fold together'. **Complicate** dates from the early 17th century when it meant 'combine, entangle, intertwine': this is from the Latin form *complicat-*, from *com-* 'together' and *plicare* 'to fold'.

complicity [mid 17th century] This is based on Middle English *complice* 'an associate', from Old French, from late Latin *complex, complic-* 'allied', from Latin *complicare* 'fold together'. It was not until the 1940s that the word **complicit** was recorded in use: this is a back-formation (by removal of the suffix) from *complicity*.
→ACCOMPLICE

compliment [mid 17th century] As a noun, *compliment* is from French *compliment*, as a verb from French *complimenter*. Both stem from Italian *complimento* 'fulfilment of the requirements of courtesy'. The base is Latin *complementum* 'completion, fulfilment', reflected in the earlier English spelling *complement*: this was gradually replaced by the French form between 1655 and 1715.

comply [late 16th century] *Comply* is from Italian *complire*, Catalan *complir*, Spanish *cumplir*, from Latin *complere* 'fill up, fulfil'. The

original sense was 'fulfil, accomplish', later 'fulfil the requirements of courtesy', which led to the meanings 'be agreeable', 'oblige', and 'obey'.
→COMPLETE

component [mid 17th century] Latin *component-*, the source of English *component*, meant 'putting together'. The Latin elements are *com-* 'together' and *ponere* 'to put'.
→COMPOUND[1]

compose [late Middle English] The early recorded use was in the general sense 'put together, construct'. The word is from Old French *composer* (from Latin *componere* 'put together') influenced by Latin *compositus* 'composed' and Old French *poser* 'to place'. Dating from the same period is **composition** which came via Old French from Latin *compositio(n-)* (from *componere*); also **compositor**, now a printing term but originally Scots for an umpire or arbiter (from Anglo-Norman French *compositour*). The noun **composure** arose later and, in the late 16th century, had the meaning 'composing, composition': this is based on *compose* by the addition of the suffix *-ure*.

compost [late Middle English] This word for decayed organic material is from Old French *composte*, from Latin *composita, compositum* 'something put together' (forms of the verb *componere* 'put together').

compound[1] [late Middle English] The verb *compound* 'make up a (composite) whole' was *compoune* in late Middle English, from Old French *compoun-*, the present tense stem of *compondre* (from Latin *componere* 'put together'). The final *-d* was added in the 16th century on the pattern of words such as *expound* and *propound*. The use of *compound* in the sense 'make (something bad) worse' (e.g. *this compounded their problem*) arose through a misinterpretation of the phrase *compound a felony* which strictly speaking means 'forbear from prosecuting a felony in exchange for a consideration such as money'. The misinterpretation led to a change in legal use and in general use, gradually accepted as standard English.

compound[2] [late 17th century] A *compound* describes an area enclosed by a fence, which originally arose with reference to a specific type of enclosure in SE Asia in which a house or factory stood. It comes from Portuguese *campon* or Dutch *kampoeng*, from Malay *kampong* 'enclosure, hamlet'.

comprehend [Middle English] This is from Old French *comprehender*, or Latin *comprehendere*, from *com-* 'together' and *prehendere* 'grasp'. Late Middle English **comprehension** is from French *compréhension* or Latin comprehensio(n-), from the verb *comprehendere* 'seize, comprise'. The related word **comprehensive** dates from the early 17th century and is from French *compréhensif, -ive*, from late Latin *comprehensivus* (from the verb *comprehendere*).

compress [late Middle English] *Compress* is either from Old French *compresser* or late Latin *compressare*, based on the elements *com-* 'together' and *premere* 'to press'; or it is directly from *compress-* 'pressed together', from the verb *comprimere*. **Compression** also dates from late Middle English and comes via Old French from Latin *compressio(n-)*, from *comprimere* 'press together'.

comprise [late Middle English] *Comprise* was originally a French word meaning 'comprised'; it is the feminine past participle of *comprendre*, from Old French *comprehender*.
→ COMPREHEND

compromise [late Middle English] At first *compromise* was recorded as denoting mutual consent to arbitration. It comes from Old French *compromis*, from late Latin *compromissum* 'a consent to arbitration' (a form of the verb *compromittere*). The formative elements are *com-* 'together' and *promittere* 'to promise'.
→ PROMISE

compulsion [late Middle English] Latin *compellere* 'to drive, force' is the base of several words in English: *compulsion* came via Old French from late Latin *compulsio(n-)*; **compulsory** dates from the early 16th century as a noun for a legal mandate which had to be obeyed: it derives from medieval Latin *compulsorius*, from *compuls-* 'driven, forced'; **compulsive**, which dates from the late 16th century in the sense 'compulsory', is from medieval Latin *compulsivus*. The use of *compulsive* and *compulsion* as terms in psychology relating to an irresistible impulse to behave in a certain way, date from the early 20th century.

compunction [Middle English] 'A feeling of guilt or moral scruple' is expressed by the word *compunction* (as in *without compunction*). The source of the word is Old French *componction*, from ecclesiastical Latin *compunctio(n-)*, from Latin *compungere* 'prick sharply'.

compute [early 17th century] From French *computer* or Latin *computare*, *compute* is based on *com-* 'together' and *putare* 'to settle (an account)'. **Computation** is recorded from late Middle English. The early meanings centred on 'calculation' and 'estimation': often these were to do with astronomy and the calendar.

comrade [mid 16th century] The spelling *comrade* existed alongside *camerade* in early

recorded examples: this comes from French *camerade, camarade*, from Spanish *camarada* 'room-mate', from Latin *camera* 'chamber'. A *comrade* was originally someone who shared the same room or tent, and was often specifically a fellow soldier.
→ CHUM

con[1] [late 19th century] Originally a US usage, *con* 'persuade someone to do or believe something by deception', is an abbreviation of *confidence*, as in *confidence trick*.

con[2] [late 16th century] This *con* meaning 'disadvantage', commonly found in the phrase *pros and cons*, is from Latin *contra* 'against'.

con[3] [early 17th century] The *con* found in the first syllable of the phrase *conning tower* is apparently a weakened form of obsolete *cond* 'conduct, guide', from Old French *conduire*, from Latin *conducere* 'to lead'. *Con* is used in nautical contexts for 'direct the steering of (a ship)'.

concave [late Middle English] This is from Latin *concavus*, from *con-* 'together' and *cavus* 'hollow'.

conceal [Middle English] The direct source of *conceal* is Old French *conceler*, from Latin *concelare*, of which the formative elements are *con-* 'completely' and *celare* 'to hide'.

conceive [Middle English] This is from Old French *concevoir*, from Latin *concipere*, from *com-* 'together' and *capere* 'take'. Late Middle English **conceit** meant 'idea or notion', and also referred to an 'article considered quaint and decorative'; it continues to refer to a fanciful or clever verbal expression (e.g. *the idea of the wind's singing is a prime romantic conceit*). The formation of the word is from *conceive*, on the pattern of pairs such as *deceive, deceit*. The Latin verb *concipere* 'conceive' is also the base of several other related words in this group: Middle English **conception** (which came via Old French from Latin *conceptio(n-)*); **concept** (mid 16th century from Latin *conceptum* 'something conceived') whose early meanings were 'thought', 'frame of mind', and 'imagination'; also **conceptual** (mid 17th century from medieval Latin *conceptualis*).

concentrate [mid 17th century] Early recorded use was in the sense 'bring towards a centre'; it is a Latinized form of **concentre** 'concentrate (something) into a small area' (from Latin *con-* 'together' and *centrum* 'centre'), or from French *concentrer* 'to concentrate'. The meaning 'focus one's attention' dates from the early 20th century.

concern [late Middle English] *Concern* is from French *concerner* or late Latin *concernere* (in medieval Latin 'be relevant to'). The base elements are con- (the prefix here giving emphasis) and cernere 'sift, discern', conveying a notion of 'going over and through something in a detailed manner'.

concert [late 16th century] The verb concert (earliest in the sense 'unite, cause to agree') is from French concerter, from Italian concertare 'harmonize'. The noun use, dating from the early 17th century (in the sense 'a combination of voices or sounds'), is from French concert, from Italian concerto, from concertare.

concession [late Middle English] This is from Latin concessio(n-), from the verb concedere, base of **concede** (late 15th century): the source is French concéder or Latin concedere, from con- 'completely' and cedere 'yield'.

conciliate [mid 16th century] The first recorded meaning of conciliate was 'gain (goodwill)'; it comes from Latin conciliat-, from the verb conciliare 'combine, gain', from con-cilium 'council'.
→ COUNCIL

concise [late 16th century] The basic meaning of concise is 'cut to small size': it comes from French concis or Latin concisus, the past participle of concidere 'cut up, cut down' (from con- 'completely' and caedere 'to cut').

conclude [Middle English] 'Convince' was the early sense of conclude: it is from Latin concludere, from con- 'completely' and claudere 'to shut'. **Conclusion** dates from late Middle English and is from Latin conclusio(n-), from the verb concludere, the base too of **conclusive** (late 16th century in the sense 'summing up, concluding'), from late Latin conclusivus.

concoct [mid 16th century] Latin concoct-, the source of English concoct, means literally 'cooked together', from the verb concoquere. The original sense was 'refine or purify metals or minerals by heating', which later became 'cook (up)'.

concourse [late Middle English] The first recorded meaning was 'crowd of people'; it is from Old French concours, from Latin concursus, from the verb concurrere 'run together'. The meaning 'large open central area inside or at the front of a public building' was originally a US usage and dates from the mid 19th century.
→ CONCUR

concrete [late Middle English] Early senses were 'formed by cohesion', 'solidified'. The word comes from French concret or Latin concretus, the past participle of concrescere 'grow together'. Early use was also as a grammatical term describing a quality belonging to a substance (usually expressed by an adjective such as white, e.g. white paper) as opposed to the quality itself (expressed by an abstract noun such as whiteness); later concrete came to be used to refer to nouns embodying attributes (e.g. fool, hero), as opposed to the attributes themselves (e.g. foolishness, heroism). This is the basis of the modern use as the opposite of 'abstract'. The noun sense 'building material' dates from the mid 19th century.

concubine [Middle English] This word for a 'woman living with a man who has lower status than his wife or wives', is from Old French, from Latin concubina, from con- 'with' and cubare 'to lie'.

concur [late Middle English] Early senses included 'collide' and 'act in combination'. The source is Latin concurrere 'run together, assemble in crowds'. Now the common meaning is 'be in agreement'. Late Middle English **concurrent** 'happening at the same time' is from Latin concurrent- 'running together, meeting', from the verb concurrere.

concussion [late Middle English] This word describing a condition resulting from a violent blow, is from Latin concussio(n-), from the verb concutere 'dash together, shake'.

condemn [Middle English] The first recorded meaning of condemn was 'sentence (someone) to a particular punishment'. The source of the word in English is Old French condemner, from Latin condemnare, based on damnare 'inflict loss on'. The prefix con- adds emphasis to the verb.
→ DAMN

condense [late Middle English] This is from Old French condenser or Latin condensare, from condensus 'very thick', from con- 'completely' and densus 'dense'. **Condensation** was not recorded until the early 17th century and comes from late Latin condensatio(n-), from condensare 'press close together'.

condescend [Middle English] 'Give way' and 'defer' were the first recorded meanings of condescend, which is via Old French from ecclesiastical Latin condescendere. The semantic components are con- 'together' and descendere 'descend'.

condiment [late Middle English] This word for a substance that adds flavour to food, is from Latin condimentum, from condire 'to pickle'.

condition [Middle English] The noun is from Old French condicion, the verb from Old French condicionner, from Latin condicio(n-) 'agreement'. The source verb is Latin condicere 'agree upon', from con- 'with' and dicere 'say'.

condom [early 18th century] This is often said to be named after a physician who invented it, but no such person has been traced.

condone [mid 19th century] *Condone* 'accept and allow (behaviour) to continue' is from Latin *condonare* 'refrain from punishing' (from *con-* 'altogether' and *donare* 'give').

conducive [mid 17th century] *Conducive* 'making a certain situation likely or possible' is from *conduce*, a late Middle English verb (from Latin *conducere* 'bring together') used to mean 'lead or bring'. It is formed on the pattern of words such as *conductive*.

conduct [Middle English] *Conduct* is from Old French, from Latin *conduct-* 'brought together', from the verb *conducere*. The term originally referred to some provision for safe passage, such as an escort or pass, surviving in the phrase *safe conduct*; later the verb sense 'lead, guide' arose, which led to 'manage' and 'management' in late Middle English, later 'management of oneself, behaviour' (mid 16th century). The original form of the word was *conduit*, which was preserved only in the sense 'channel'; in all other uses the spelling was influenced by Latin. The Latin verb *conducere* 'bring together' is also the base of late Middle English **conductor** which was a term initially for a military leader: this comes via Old French from Latin *conductor*.
→ CONDUIT

conduit [Middle English] *Conduit* meaning 'channel' is from Old French, from medieval Latin *conductus*, from Latin *conducere* 'bring together'.

cone [late Middle English] A *cone* in early use referred to an apex or vertex. It comes from French *cône*, via Latin from Greek *kōnos*.

confection [Middle English] *Confection* had the early general sense 'something made by mixing', especially a medicinal preparation. It comes via Old French from Latin *confectio(n-)*, from *conficere* 'put together'.

confederacy [late Middle English] *Confederacy* (from Old French *confederacie*), **confederate** (from ecclesiastical Latin *confoederatus*), and **confederation** (from Old French *confederacion* or late Latin *confederatio(n-)*) are all recorded from late Middle English. The source is Latin *confoederare* 'join together in league' based on *foedus* 'league, treaty'.

confer [late Middle English] The early recorded general sense was 'bring together', as well as 'have discussions'. It is from Latin *conferre*, from *con-* 'together' and *ferre* 'bring'. The notions of 'bringing' and 'sharing' led to its use in phrases such as *confer a degree, title or*

favour *on* a worthy person. The noun **conference** dates from the early 16th century in the general sense 'conversation, talk' and is from French *conférence* or medieval Latin *conferentia*.

confessor [Old English] The early use of *confessor* was in reference to 'a person who avows religious faith in the face of opposition'; it comes from Old French *confessour*, from ecclesiastical Latin *confessor*. Latin *confess-* 'acknowledged' is the base, which is shared by late Middle English **confess**. Dating from the same period is the noun **confession** which came into English via Old French from Latin *confessio(n-)*, based on the verb *confiteri* 'acknowledge'. The formative elements are *con-* (a prefix giving emphasis) and *fateri* 'declare, avow'.

confetti [early 19th century] *Confetti* originally referred to the real or imitation sweets thrown during Italian carnivals. It is from an Italian word for 'sweets', from Latin *confectum* 'something prepared', the neuter past participle of *conficere* 'put together'.
→ CONFECTION

confidant [mid 17th century] 'A person with whom one shares a confidence' is called a *confidant* or, feminine, *confidante*. The word is an alteration of *confident*, which, as a noun in the early 17th century, was used in the same sense. The change in spelling was probably to represent the pronunciation of French *confidente* 'having full trust'.

confide [late Middle English] The early recorded meaning was 'place trust (in)'. It is from Latin *confidere* 'have full trust'. The sense 'impart as a secret' dates from the mid 18th century.

confidence [late Middle English] Latin *confidentia* is the source of English *confidence*. The Latin base verb is *confidere* 'have full trust'. **Confident** arose in the late 16th century and is from French *confident(e)*, from Italian *confidente*, from Latin *confident-* 'having full trust'. The elements are *con-* (giving emphasis) and *fidere* 'to trust'.

confine [late Middle English] This was first recorded as a noun and is from French *confins* (plural), from Latin *confinia*, from *confinis* 'bordering': this is made up of *con-* 'together' and *finis* 'end, limit' (or in the plural *fines* 'territory'). The verb senses are from French *confiner*, based on Latin *confinis*.

confirm [Middle English] *Confirm* is from Old French *confermer*, from Latin *confirmare* 'make firm, establish', which is also the base of the word **confirmation** dating from the same period. The latter is via Old French from Latin *confirmatio(n-)*. The Latin elements *con-* 'together' and *firmus* 'firm' are involved in both derivations.

confiscate [mid 16th century] Latin *confiscat-* (from the verb *confiscare* 'store in a chest, consign to the public treasury') is the source of English *confiscate*. The Latin base forms are *con-* 'together' and *fiscus* 'chest, treasury'.

conflagration [late 15th century] 'Consumption by fire' was the early meaning of this word, from Latin *conflagratio(n-)*, based on *con-* (giving emphasis) and *flagrare* 'to blaze'.

conflate [late Middle English] The early meanings were 'fuse or melt down metal'; it is from Latin *conflat-*, from the verb *conflare* 'kindle, fuse', from *con-* 'together' and *flare* 'to blow'.

conflict [late Middle English] *Conflict* is from Latin *conflict-* 'struck together, fought', from the verb *confligere*, from *con-* 'together' and *fligere* 'to strike'; the noun is via Latin *conflictus* 'a contest'.

conform [Middle English] Early records show *conform* in the sense 'make (something) like another thing'. It is from Old French *conformer*, from Latin *conformare*, from *con-* 'together' and *formare* 'to form'. **Conformity** (late Middle English) is from Old French *conformite* or late Latin *conformitas*, and **conformation** dates from the early 16th century in the sense 'conforming, adaptation': the source is Latin *conformatio(n-)*, from *conformare* 'to shape, fashion'.

confound [Middle English] *Confound* is from Old French *confondre*, from Latin *confundere* 'pour together, mix up'.
→ CONFUSE

confront [mid 16th century] French *confronter*, from medieval Latin *confrontare*, has given *confront* in English. The Latin base elements are *con-* 'with' and *frons, front-* 'face'.

confuse [Middle English] The early meanings recorded for *confuse* were 'rout' and 'bring to ruin'. The word is from Old French *confus*, from Latin *confusus*, the past participle of *confundere* 'mingle together'. Originally all senses of the verb were passive, and therefore appeared only as the past participle *confused*; the active voice occurred rarely until the 19th century when it began to replace *confound*. **Confusion** dates from Middle English and is from Latin *confusio(n-)*, from the verb *confundere*.
→ CONFOUND

congeal [late Middle English] 'Become semi-solid' is the meaning of *congeal* which is based on the Latin word *gelu* 'frost'. *Congeal* is from Old French *congeler*, from Latin *congelare*, from *con-* 'together' and *gelare* 'freeze'.

congested [mid 19th century] This is the past participle of *congest* which was used in late Middle English in the sense 'heap up, accumulate'. It comes from Latin *congest-* 'heaped up' based on the elements *con-* 'together' and *gerere* 'bring'. **Congestion**, via Old French from Latin *congestio(n-)*, also dates from late Middle English.

conglomerate [late Middle English] Early recorded use was as an adjective describing something gathered up into a rounded mass. The word is from Latin *conglomeratus*, the past participle of *conglomerare*, from *con-* 'together' and *glomus, glomer-* 'ball'. The geological use of the term for a 'coarse-grained sedimentary rock' dates from the early 19th century; other noun senses ('large corporation' and 'number of different things grouped together') are later.

congratulate [mid 16th century] *Congratulate* is from Latin *congratulat-*, based on the elements *con-* 'with' and *gratulari* 'show joy' (from *gratus* 'pleasing'). **Congratulation** was already recorded in late Middle English and is from Latin *congratulatio(n-)*, from the verb *congratulari*.

congregate [late Middle English] Latin *grex, greg-* 'a flock' is the base of both *congregate* and **congregation**, which were first recorded in the same period. *Congregate* is from Latin *congregat-*, from the verb *congregare* 'collect (into a flock, unite'; *congregation* was first used in the senses 'gathering', 'deliberative body', and 'group abiding by a common religious rule': it comes from Latin *congregatio(n-)*, from *congregare*.

congress [late Middle English] A *congress* once denoted an encounter during battle: it is from Latin *congressus*, from *congredi* 'meet', literally 'walk together'. The word in English refers to any 'coming together' reflected in obsolete or archaic uses such as *social congress*, *sexual congress*; now it commonly refers to a 'formal meeting'.

conifer [mid 19th century] This is from Latin; the literal meaning is 'cone-bearing'.

conjecture [late Middle English] The early recorded senses were 'to divine' and 'divination'. The word comes from Old French, or from Latin *conjectura*, from *conicere* 'put together in thought'. The base forms are *con-* 'together' and *jacere* 'to throw'. Now the meanings involve the formation of an opinion on the basis of incomplete information.

conjugal [early 16th century] *Conjugal* relates to marriage and is based on the Latin word *jugum* 'yoke'. The word comes from Latin *conjugalis*, from *conjux*, *conjug-* 'spouse'; the prefix *con-* means 'together'.

conjure [Middle English] *Conjure* 'make to appear unexpectedly', used also to mean 'oblige by oath'. The origin is Old French *conjurer* 'to plot', 'exorcize', from Latin *conjurare* 'band together by making an oath'; this became 'invoke' in medieval Latin. The elements are *con-* 'together' and *jurare* 'swear'. **Conjuror** also dates from Middle English and is partly from *conjure* and partly from Old French *conjureor*, *conjurere*, from medieval Latin *conjurator* (from Latin *conjurare* 'conspire').

conk [early 19th century] *Conk* is an informal word. When used to mean 'nose' it is perhaps an alteration of **conch** 'shell' and influenced by shape. The origin of the verb *conk* in the phrase *conk out* 'fail', is not known but it arose during the First World War.

conker [mid 19th century] This was originally a dialect word for a snail shell, with which the game of *conkers* (or a similar form of it) was originally played. The origin may be English *conch* 'shell', but the word was associated with and was frequently spelt *conquer* in the 19th and early 20th centuries: an alternative name for the game was *conquerors*.

connect [late Middle English] Although recorded in late Middle English in the sense 'be united physically', use of *connect* was rare before the 18th century. It is from Latin *connectere*, from *con-* 'together' and *nectere* 'to bind'. Late Middle English **connection** is from Latin *connexio(n-)*, from *connectere*; the spelling *-ct* (18th century) is from *connect*, formed on the pattern of word pairs such as *collect*, *collection*.

connivance [late 16th century] When first recorded, *connivance* 'willing complicity' also had the Latin sense 'winking'. It comes from French *connivence* or Latin *conniventia*, from *connivere* 'shut the eyes (to)'. The verb **connive** dates from the early 17th century and is from French *conniver* or Latin *connivere* 'shut the eyes (to)', from *con-* 'together' and an unrecorded word related to *nictare* 'to wink'.

connotation [mid 16th century] This term for an idea or feeling invoked in addition to the primary meaning of a word, is from medieval Latin *connotatio(n-)*, from *connotare* 'mark in addition'; the base elements are Latin *con-* 'together with' and *notare* 'to note' (from *nota* 'a mark').

conquer [Middle English] Initially *conquer* also had the general sense 'acquire, attain'; it is from Old French *conquerre*, based on Latin *conquirere* 'gain, win'. The elements here are

con- (expressing completion) and *quaerere* 'seek'.

conquest [Middle English] *Conquest* is from Old French *conquest(e)*, based on Latin *conquirere* 'gain'.

conscience [Middle English] In early use, *conscience* also meant 'inner thoughts or knowledge'. It comes via Old French from Latin *conscientia*, from *conscient-* 'being privy to'; the base verb is *conscire*, from *con-* 'with' and *scire* 'know'. The adjective **conscientious** dates from the early 17th century and is from French *consciencieux*, from medieval Latin *conscientiosus* (from Latin *conscientia*). The abbreviation **conchie** arose in the First World War in reference to a conscientious objector to military service for reasons of pacifism.

conscious [late 16th century] *Conscious* always had the meaning 'being aware' but once had the additional meaning 'being aware of wrongdoing'. It is based on Latin *conscius* 'knowing with others' or 'having knowledge oneself' (from *conscire* 'be privy to').

conscript [late 18th century] Early use was recorded as a noun; it is from French *conscrit*, from Latin *conscriptus*, the past participle of *conscribere* 'enrol'. The verb is a back-formation (by removal of the suffix) from **conscription** in the early 19th century which came into English via French: conscription was introduced in France in 1798. This is from late Latin *conscriptio(n-)* 'levying of troops', from Latin *conscribere* 'write down together, enrol'.

consecrate [late Middle English] This is based on Latin *sacer* 'sacred' and is from the Latin verb *consecrare* 'dedicate, devote as sacred'.

consecutive [early 17th century] This is from French *consécutif*, *-ive*, from medieval Latin *consecutivus*. Latin *consecut-* 'followed closely' is the base, from the verb *consequi*.

consensus [mid 17th century] This is a Latin word meaning 'agreement'; it comes from Latin *consens-* 'agreed', from the verb *consentire*.

consent [Middle English] The noun *consent* is from Old French *consente*, the verb from Old French *consentir*, from Latin *consentire*, formed from *con-* 'together' and *sentire* 'feel'.

consequence [late Middle English] This came via Old French from Latin *consequentia*, from *consequent-* 'following closely', the source too of **consequent**, dating from the same period.

conservative [late Middle English] The early recorded sense was 'aiming to preserve'; it is from late Latin *conservativus*, from the verb *conservare* 'to conserve'. Current senses such as 'averse to change' and 'conventional' date from the mid 19th century. One of the most common current uses of the word is as *Conservative*, designating one of the main English political parties; the word was first used in this sense by J. Wilson Croker in an article published on 1 January 1830 (Attached to what is called the Tory, and which might with more propriety be called the Conservative, party). The word 'Tory' had been in use for almost 150 years but was soon taken over by the new term.

conservatory [mid 16th century] Early use was in the sense 'something that preserves': it is from late Latin *conservatorium*, from *conservare* 'to preserve'. The reference to 'a greenhouse or ornamental house for plants' dates from the mid 17th century. The word may also apply to a public institution for special instruction in music, a common application in the US, whereas the French term *conservatoire* is more common in British English in this equivalent specialized use; in this case it translates the Italian *conservatorio*, a hospital originally for the rearing of foundlings, to whom a musical education was given.

conserve [late Middle English] The noun is from Old French *conserve*, the verb from Old French *conserver*, from Latin *conservare* 'to preserve', the elements of which are *con-* 'together' and *servare* 'to keep'. *Conserve* was a more common word than *preserve* in Middle English and early modern English; this changed in the early 18th century. The 19th century saw the word regain its currency under the influence of *conservative* and *conservation*, etc. **Conservation** dates from late Middle English when it had the general sense 'conserving, preservation'. It comes from Latin *conservatio(n-)*, from the verb *conservare*.

consider [late Middle English] This word is from Old French *considerer*, from Latin *considerare* 'examine'. It is perhaps based on *sidus*, *sider-* 'star' and may have been originally a term in astrology or augury contexts. **Consideration** dates from the same period and is via Old French from Latin *consideratio(n-)*.

considerable [late Middle English] *Considerable*, in early texts, has the meaning 'capable of being considered'. It is from medieval Latin *considerabilis* 'worthy of consideration', from Latin *considerare* 'examine'. The modern sense 'of notable size or merit' dates from the mid 17th century.

considerate [late 16th century] In early use, this word is recorded as meaning 'showing careful thought'; it is from Latin *consideratus*, the past participle of *considerare* 'examine'.
→ CONSIDER

consign [late Middle English] 'Mark with the sign of the cross' at a baptism or confirmation, as a sign of dedication to God, was the meaning of *consign* in early examples. It is from French *consigner* or Latin *consignare* 'mark with a seal'. It now means 'give into a person's custody'.

consist [late Middle English] Latin *consistere* 'stand firm or still, exist' (from *con* 'together' and *sistere* 'stand (still)') is the source of a family of words: *consist* was first recorded in the sense 'be located or inherent in'; **consistency** (late 16th century) first denoted permanence of form and is from Latin *consistentia*; and **consistent**, also late 16th century in the sense 'consisting or composed of', is from Latin *consistent-* 'standing firm or still, existing'.

consolation [late Middle English] *Consolation* is via Old French from Latin *consolatio(n-)*, from the verb *consolari*. The verb **console** (from French *consoler*) is recorded from the mid 17th century and replaced the earlier Latinate word *consolate* which had been in use from the late 15th century. The Latin base elements are *con-* 'with' and *solari* 'soothe'.

console [mid 17th century] The *console* which describes a panel or set of controls, or an ornamental bracket supporting a surface, is from French, perhaps from *consolider*, from Latin *consolidare* 'make firm'.

consolidate [early 16th century] The early recorded meaning was 'combine into a single whole'; it is from Latin *consolidare*, from *con-* 'together' and *solidare* 'make firm' (from *solidus* 'solid').

consort [late Middle English] Early recorded meanings were 'companion' and 'colleague'. *Consort* is via French from Latin *consors* 'sharing, partner', from *con-* 'together with' and *sors*, *sort-* 'lot, destiny'. Now indicating 'a partner in marriage', the word is used in combinations such as *prince consort* which was a title conferred on Prince Albert, the husband of Queen Victoria. The verb senses of *consort* are probably influenced by similar senses (now obsolete) of the verb *sort*.

consortium [early 19th century] The early sense of *consortium* was 'partnership': it is a Latin word, from *consors* 'sharing, partner'.

conspicuous [mid 16th century] This word is based on Latin *conspicuus*, from *conspicere* 'look at attentively'.

conspire [late Middle English] *Conspire* is from Old French *conspirer*, from Latin *conspirare* 'agree, plot', from *con-* 'together with' and *spirare* 'breathe'. **Conspirator** (late Middle English) is from Old French *conspirateur*, from Latin *conspirator*, based on the verb *conspirare* 'agree, plotted'. **Conspiracy**, also late Middle English, is from Anglo-Norman French *conspiracie*, an alteration of Old French *conspiration*, based on Latin *conspirare*.

constable [Middle English] The governors of certain royal castles in England are known as *constables*: this was a title recorded early in the history of the word. It is from Old French *conestable*, from Latin *comes stabuli* 'count (head officer) of the stable'. The use as a term for 'a police officer' dates from the mid 19th century. The word **constabulary** is recorded from the late 15th century when it denoted the district under the charge of a constable: it is from medieval Latin *constabularia* (*dignitas*) '(rank) of constable', from *constabulus*, based on Latin *comes stabuli*.

constant [late Middle English] In early use the meaning was 'staying resolute or faithful': it comes from Old French, from Latin *constant-* 'standing firm', from the elements *con-* 'with' and *stare* 'stand'. The noun senses ('situation' and 'a quantity that does not change') date from the mid 19th century. **Constancy** (late 15th century) is from Latin *constantia*.

constellation [Middle English] This word is based on Latin *stella* 'star'; it was an astrological term when first recorded, referring to the relative positions of the 'stars' (= planets) which were thought to influence events. The phrase *my constellation* meant *my stars* and could refer to one's character as determined by these stars (Shakespeare *Twelfth Night*: I know thy constellation is right apt For this affayre). The spelling came into English via Old French from late Latin *constellatio(n-)*.

consternation [early 17th century] This is from Latin *consternatio(n-)*, from the verb *consternare* 'lay prostrate, terrify'.

constipation [late Middle English] The early recorded meaning was 'contraction of body tissues'. It is from late Latin *constipatio(n-)*, based on the elements *con-* 'together' and *stipare* 'to press, cram'.

constitution [Middle English] A *constitution* once referred to a law, as well as to a body of laws or customs. It comes from Latin *constitutio(n-)*, from *constituere* 'establish, appoint'. The base elements are *con-* 'together' and *statuere* 'set up'; the notion of the 'way in which something is made up' led (mid 16th century) to an association with the 'physical character of the body in regard to health'.

constrain [Middle English] *Constrain* is from Old French *constraindre*, from Latin *constringere* 'bind tightly together'. The noun **constraint** recorded from late Middle English in the sense

'coercion', is from Old French *constreinte*, the feminine past participle of *constraindre*.

constriction [early 18th century] This is based on Latin *constrict-* 'bound tightly together', from the verb *constringere*, which gave rise also to **constrict** in the mid 18th century.
→ CONSTRAIN

construct [late Middle English] This is from Latin *construct-* 'heaped together, built', from the verb *construere*, from *con-* 'together' and *struere* 'to pile, build'. The noun **construction** is also late Middle English: it came via Old French from Latin *constructio(n-)*. **Constructive** is recorded from the mid 17th century when it meant 'derived by inference' (e.g. *constructive liability*): it is from late Latin *constructivus*.

construe [late Middle English] *Construe* is from Latin *construere* 'heap together', 'connect grammatically'; in late Latin the meanings included 'analyse the construction of a sentence'. From an early date *construe* was pronounced with the stress on the first syllable, the final syllable being reduced to *-stre* and *-ster*: *conster* continued to be the pronunciation to the 19th century even after it had disappeared as a written form.

consult [early 16th century] The early recorded meaning of *consult* was 'deliberate together, confer'. It is from French *consulter*, from Latin *consultare*, a frequentative (= verb of repeated action) of *consulere* 'take counsel'. The noun **consultation** was recorded earlier and dates from late Middle English : it is from Latin *consultatio(n-)*, from *consultare*.

consume [late Middle English] Latin *consumere* (from *con-* 'altogether' and *sumere* 'take up') gave *consume* in English: it was reinforced by French *consumer*. Dating from the same period and based on the same Latin verb is **consumption** from Latin *consumptio(n-)*. It was used as a medical term for tuberculosis, because of the wasting nature of the disease. The related word **consumptive** dates from the mid 17th century and is from medieval Latin *consumptivus*, from Latin *consumpt-* 'consumed'.

consummate [late Middle English] Early recorded use was as an adjective (*with consummate elegance, with consummate ease*) meaning 'completed, accomplished'. It comes from the Latin form *consummat-*, from the verb *consummare* 'bring to completion'. This is based on the elements *con-* 'altogether' and *summa* 'sum total' (the feminine of *summus* 'highest, supreme').

contact [early 17th century] *Contact* is from Latin *contactus*, from *contact-* 'touched, grasped, bordered on', from the verb *contingere*. The formative elements are *con-* 'together with' and *tangere* 'to touch'.

contagion [late Middle English] This is from Latin *contagio(n-)*, from *con-* 'together with' and the base of *tangere* 'to touch'. **Contagious**, recorded in this same early period, is from late Latin *contagiosus*, from *contagio*.

contain [Middle English] Contain is from Old French *contenir*, from Latin *continere*, from *con-* 'altogether' and *tenere* 'to hold'.

contaminate [late Middle English] This is from Latin *contaminat-*, from the verb *contaminare* 'make impure', from *contamen* 'contact, pollution'. The base is Latin *tangere* 'to touch'.

contemplation [Middle English] Via Old French from Latin *contemplatio(n-)*, *contemplation* is based on the Latin verb *contemplari*. This is also involved in the formation of late 16th-century **contemplate**, from the Latin verb *contemplari* 'survey, observe': the base is Latin *templum* 'place for observation'. Middle English **contemplative** is from Old French *contemplatif*, *-ive*, or Latin *contemplativus*; it is used as a noun in English to refer to a person devoted to religious meditation, such as a member of a *contemplative order*.

contemporary [mid 17th century] Contemporary is from medieval Latin *contemporarius*, from *con-* 'together with' and *tempus*, *tempor-* 'time'.

contempt [late Middle English] Contempt is from Latin *contemptus*, from *contemnere* 'view with contempt' (which gave **contemn** used in the same sense in English). **Contemptible** is also late Middle English and comes from Old French, or from late Latin *contemptibilis*. **Contemptuous** is recorded from the mid 16th century when it had the early meaning 'despising law and order'. It comes from medieval Latin *contemptuosus*, from Latin *contemptus* 'contempt'.

contend [late Middle English] Contend had the sense 'compete for (something)' in early examples. It is from Old French *contendre* or Latin *contendere*, from *con-* 'with' and *tendere* 'to stretch, strive'. **Contention**, from the same period, is from Latin *contentio(n-)*, from *con-tendere* 'strive with', the base too of **contentious** from Old French *contentieux*, from Latin *contentiosus*.

content¹ [late Middle English] Content 'peacefully happy' is via Old French from Latin *contentus* 'satisfied', the past participle of *continere* 'hold'. The word **contentment** dates from late Middle English when it referred to the payment of a claim (which 'satisfied' the obligation): it comes from French *contentement*, from Latin *contentus*.

content² [late Middle English] This word meaning 'things that are held or included', is from medieval Latin *contentum* (in the plural *contenta* 'things contained'), neuter past participle of *continere*.
→ CONTAIN

contest [late 16th century] Early use was recorded as a verb in the sense 'swear to, attest'. The word comes from Latin *contestari* 'call upon to witness, initiate an action (by calling witnesses)'. The senses 'wrangle, strive, struggle for' arose in the early 17th century, whence the current noun and verb meanings.

context [late Middle English] The early use of *context* referred to the construction of a text. It is from Latin *contextus*, from *con-* 'together' and *texere* 'to weave'.

continent¹ [mid 16th century] The geographical term *continent* is from the Latin phrase *terra continens* 'continuous land'.
→ CONTAIN

continent² [late Middle English] The adjective *continent* meaning 'able to exercise self-restraint', 'able to control bladder and bowel functions', is from Latin *continent-* 'holding together, restraining oneself', from the verb *continere*. The word first passed into the modern languages with the meaning 'restraining one's passions'.

contingent [late Middle English] In early examples, *contingent* meant 'of uncertain occurrence'. It comes from Latin *contingere* 'befall', from *con-* 'together with' and *tangere* 'to touch'. The noun sense was originally 'something happening by chance', then 'a person's share resulting from a division, a quota'; the current meaning dates from the early 18th century. **Contingency** (mid 16th century) in early use was as a philosophical term meaning 'the fact of being so without having to be so'. It is from late Latin *contingentia* (in its medieval Latin sense 'circumstance'), from *contingere* 'befall'.

continue [Middle English] Continue is from Old French *continuer*, from Latin *continuare* 'make continuous', from *continuus*. In Middle English there was frequent confusion between *continue* and *contain*, spelt *contene*. The adjective **continuous** arose in the mid 17th century, based on Latin *continuus* 'uninterrupted', from *continere* 'hang together'.

contort [late Middle English] This is from Latin *contort-* 'twisted round, brandished', from the verb *contorquere* 'twist together'.

contour [mid 17th century] *Contour* is a word adopted from French, from Italian *contorno*: this is from *contornare* 'draw in outline', from *con-* 'together' and *tornare* 'to turn'.

contraband [late 16th century] This is from Spanish *contrabanda* 'smuggling', from Italian *contrabando* 'unlawful dealing', from *contra-* 'against' and *bando* 'proclamation, ban'. The word *contraband* was used for a captured slave during the American Civil War, because of the decision by General Butler in 1861 that it was forbidden to take and make use of any such slave.

contract [Middle English] *Contract* is via Old French from Latin *contractus*, from *contract-* 'tightened', from the verb *contrahere*. The elements are *con-* 'together' and *trahere* 'to draw'. This may convey a notion of 'get smaller' (= draw together tightly) or, as a noun, 'binding' (= drawing together tightly under legal constraint). Late Middle English **contraction** is via Old French from Latin *contractio(n-)*, from *contrahere* 'draw together'.

contradiction [late Middle English] This came via Old French from Latin *contradictio(n-)*, from the verb *contradicere*, base too of **contradictory** used in late Middle English as a term in logic for a proposition or principle which contradicts another. This is from late Latin *contradictorius*, from Latin *contradict-* 'spoken against'. The verb **contradict** dates from the late 16th century and is based on Latin *contradicere*, which was originally *contra dicere* 'speak against'.

contraption [early 19th century] Association with the word *trap* may have influenced the formation of *contraption*, which is perhaps from *contrive* on the pattern of pairs such as *conceive*, *conception*.

contrary [Middle English] This is from Anglo-Norman French *contrarie*, from Latin *contrarius*, from *contra* 'against'. The original stress in the pronunciation was on the second syllable, following French and Latin, but the poets from Chaucer to Spenser and Shakespeare use both *'contrary* and *con'trary*. The latter pronunciation is common in dialect speech and often conveys the sense 'perverse, self-willed' as in the nursery rhyme: Mary, Mary, quite contrary.

contrast [late 17th century] *Contrast* was first recorded as a term in fine art in the sense 'juxtapose so as to bring out differences in form and colour'. It is from French *contraste* (noun), *contraster* (verb), via Italian from medieval Latin *contrastare*. The Latin base elements are *contra-* 'against' and *stare* 'stand'.

contravention [mid 16th century] The Latin elements *contra-* 'against' and *venire* 'come' are at the base of *contravention*, which is via French from medieval Latin *contraventio(n-)*. **Contravene** dates from the same period and is from late Latin *contravenire*.

contribution [late Middle English] A *contribution* used to refer specifically to a tax or levy. It is from late Latin *contributio(n-)*, from Latin *contribuere* 'bring together, add', the source too of the English verb **contribute**, also late Middle English. The base is Latin *tribuere* 'bestow'.

contrite [Middle English] This word meaning 'feeling remorse' is from Old French *contrit*, from Latin *contritus*, based on the elements *con-* 'together' and *terere* 'rub, grind'. These are also at the root of Middle English **contrition** which came via Old French from late Latin *contritio(n-)*, from *contrit-* 'ground down', from the verb *conterere*.

contrive [Middle English] This is from Old French *contreuve-*, the stressed stem of *controver* 'imagine, invent', from medieval Latin *contropare* 'compare'. Early use was with both negative and positive connotations: invention was done with skill or malice.

control [late Middle English] The early sense of the verb was 'check or verify accounts': this was usually by making reference to a duplicate register. It is from Anglo-Norman French *controller* 'keep a copy of a roll of accounts', from medieval Latin *contrarotulare*, from *contrarotulus* 'copy of a roll'. The noun is perhaps via French *contrôle*. A **controller**, recorded in Middle English, was a person who kept a duplicate accounts register: this is from Anglo-Norman *contrerollour*.

controversy [late Middle English] This is from Latin *controversia*, from *controversus* 'turned against, disputed': the prefix *contro-* is a variant of *contra-* 'against', and *versus* is from the verb *vertere* 'to turn'.

conundrum [late 16th century] The origin is unknown, but the word was first recorded in a work by the English pamphleteer Thomas Nashe (1567–1601), as a term of abuse for a crank or pedant, later coming to denote a whim, fancy, or pun. Current senses date from the late 17th century.

conurbation [early 20th century] A *conurbation* is an extended urban area; it is based on the Latin noun *urbs*, *urb-* 'city' (the *con-* prefix adds the notion of 'together').

convalesce [late 15th century] *Convalesce* is from Latin *convalescere*, from *con-* 'altogether' and *valescere* 'grow strong' (from *valere* 'be well').

convene [late Middle English] *Convene* is from Latin *convenire* 'assemble, agree, fit', from *con-* 'together' and *venire* 'come'.
→ CONVENTION

convenience [late Middle English] *Convenience* is from Latin *convenientia*, from *convenient-* 'assembling, agreeing', from the verb *convenire*. **Convenient**, also late Middle English, had the early recorded senses 'becoming' and 'befitting, suitable' and is from Latin *convenient-* 'assembling, agreeing, fitting'. The prime current meaning is 'fitting in well with a person's needs'; it also has a notion of 'involving little effort'. In colloquial and dialect use, *convenient* was also 'handy' as seen in Thackeray's *Vanity Fair*: Heretics used to be brought thither convenient for burning hard by.

convent [Middle English] *Convent* is from Old French, from Latin *conventus* 'assembly, company', from the verb *convenire*. The original spelling was *covent* (surviving in the place name *Covent Garden*); the modern form dates from the 16th century.
→ CONVENE

convention [late Middle English] The first recorded meaning was 'large meeting or conference'; it came via Old French from Latin *conventio(n-)* 'meeting, covenant', from the verb *convenire*. The sense 'the way in which something is usually done', dates from the late 18th century.

converge [late 17th century] This is from late Latin *convergere*, from *con-* 'together' and Latin *vergere* 'incline'.

conversant [Middle English] This is from the Old French present participle of *converser*. The original sense was 'habitually spending time in a particular place or with a particular person'; it now expresses the notion of 'being familiar with or knowledgeable about something'.
→ CONVERSE[1]

conversation [Middle English] *Conversation* once had the meanings 'living among' and 'familiarity, intimacy'. It comes via Old French from Latin *conversatio(n-)*, from the verb *conversārī* 'keep company (with)'.

converse[1] [late Middle English] *Converse* has meant 'engage in conversation' since the early 17th century (Shakespeare *Comedy of Errors*: Did you converse sir with this gentlewoman?...I never spake with her in all my life); however, it used to mean 'live among, be familiar with' in early use (Chaucer translating Boethius In whos houses I hadde conuersed and haunted). It is from Old French *converser*, from Latin *conversārī* 'keep company (with)', from *con-* 'with' and the Latin verb base *vertere* 'to turn'.

converse[2] [late Middle English] *Converse* '(something) having characteristics which are the reverse of something else already mentioned', is from Latin *conversus* 'turned about', the past participle of *convertere*.

convert [Middle English] 'Turn round', 'send in a different direction' were the early recorded meanings of *convert*. The source of the word is Old French *convertir*, based on Latin *convertere* 'turn about', from *con-* 'altogether' and *vertere* 'turn'. **Conversion** is also Middle English, when it meant 'turning of sinners to God': this came via Old French from Latin *conversio(n-)*, from *convers-* 'turned about' (from the verb *convertere*). **Convertible** is recorded slightly later in the sense 'interchangeable', from Old French, from Latin *convertibilis*. Its use to refer to a car with a collapsible hood started out as a US usage in the early 20th century.

convex [late 16th century] This is from Latin *convexus* 'vaulted, arched'.

convey [Middle English] The early sense was 'escort'. The word comes via Old French from medieval Latin *conviare*, from *con-* 'together' and Latin *via* 'way'. The Renaissance spellings *conveigh* and *convehith* imply a mistaken derivation from Latin *convehere* 'carry with', to which *convey* is not related.
→ CONVOY

convict [Middle English] This verb, like English *convince*, comes from Latin *convict-* 'demonstrated, refuted, convicted', from *convincere* There is a basic notion of 'conquering'. The noun is from obsolete *convict* 'convicted'. **Conviction** dates from late Middle English and is from Latin *convictio(n-)*, from the verb *convincere*.

convince [mid 16th century] *Convince* was first recorded in the sense 'overcome, defeat in argument': it is from Latin *convincere*, from *con-* 'with' and *vincere* 'conquer'.

convivial [mid 17th century] The early recorded sense was 'fit for a feast, festive'. The word is from Latin *convivialis*, from *convivium* 'a feast', from *con-* 'with' and *vivere* 'to live'.

convocation [late Middle English] The origin is Latin *convocatio(n-)*, from the verb *convocare*, from *con-* 'together' and *vocare* 'call'. This Latin verb also gave **convoke**, recorded from the late 16th century.

convoluted [late 18th century] This is the past participle of *convolute*, from Latin *convolutus* 'rolled together, intertwined', from the verb *convolvere*.

convoy [late Middle English] Originally Scots and used as a verb meaning 'convey', 'conduct', and 'act as escort', *convoy* is from French *convoyer*, from medieval Latin *conviare*.
→ CONVEY

convulsion [mid 16th century] Originally in the sense 'cramp, spasm', *convulsion* is from Latin *convulsio(n-)*, from the verb *convellere*. The medical use describing an agitated condition marked by involuntary spasms alternating with periods of relaxation, was already a sense in Latin, reflected in Pliny's writings and those of the medical writers. **Convulse**, which is recorded almost a century later, is from Latin *convuls-* 'pulled violently, wrenched', based on the elements *con-* 'together' and *vellere* 'to pull'.

cooee [late 18th century] This exclamation used to attract attention is imitative of a signal used by Australian Aboriginals, which was copied by settlers.

cook [Old English] Originally a *cōc* was always masculine and was applied either to the domestic officer in charge of the preparation of food in a large household, monastery, college, ship, etc., or to a tradesman preparing and selling food. It is from popular Latin *cocus*, from Latin *coquus*.

cookie [early 18th century] The US word *cookie* is from Dutch *koekje* 'little cake'. The term has been applied in computing, since the 1980s, to a packet of data passed between computers or programs to allow access to or to activate certain features; it is also a packet of data sent by an Internet server to a browser.

cool [Old English] Of Germanic origin, Old English *cōl* was a noun, *cōlian* the verb; they are related to Dutch *koel*, also to *cold*. The word **coolant**, based on *cool*, is recorded from the 1930s, formed on the pattern of *lubricant*.

coop [Middle English] The Middle English *cowpe* is apparently identical with Middle English *cupe* 'basket'; it is related to Dutch *kuip* 'vat' and German *Kufe* 'cask', based on Latin *cupa*. It used to refer to a kind of basket placed over fowls when sitting or being fattened, and now forms part of the phrase *hen coop*. As a slang term it sometimes means 'prison' (P. G. Wodehouse *Stiff Upper Lip*: I accompanied Constable Oates to the village coop).

cooper [Middle English] In Middle English this was often spelt *cowper*, which is found as a surname pronounced *Cooper*. It is from Middle Dutch, Middle Low German *kūper*, from *kūpe* 'tub, vat', based on Latin *cupa*. A *cooper* makes and repairs wooden containers such as casks and tubs; the term also refers to someone in the trade of bottling and retailing wine. The

word is not a derivative of *coop* which seems never to have had the sense 'cask' in English.

cooperation [late Middle English] This is from Latin *cooperatio(n-)*, from the verb *cooperari* 'work together'; it was later reinforced by French *coopération*. The verb **cooperate** arose in the late 16th century and is from ecclesiastical Latin *cooperat-*: the formative elements are *co-* 'together' and *operari* 'to work'. **Cooperative** (early 17th century) is from late Latin *cooperativus*.

co-opt [mid 17th century] A word used to mean 'appoint to membership of a committee', *co-opt* is from Latin *cooptare*, from *co-* 'together' and *optare* 'choose'.

coordinate [mid 17th century] This was first recorded with the senses 'of the same rank' and 'place in the same rank'. It is formed (on the pattern of *subordinate*) from the prefix *co-* 'together' and the Latin base *ordo* 'order'. Dating from the same period is **coordination** (from French or from late Latin *coordinatio(n-)*) which had the sense 'placing in the same rank'.

cop¹ [early 18th century] The verb *cop* 'catch' is perhaps from the obsolete *cap* 'arrest', from Old French *caper* 'seize' (from Latin *capere*). It is found recorded in nearly all northern English glossaries, but is now a slang term in general use. The noun used informally to mean 'police officer' is a shortened form of *copper*, probably from the verb *cop* and therefore literally 'catcher'. The phrase *not much cop* meaning 'not much good', is in essence 'not much of an acquisition' (H. Pinter *The Caretaker*: At least they're comfortable. Not much cop, but I mean they don't hurt).

cop² [late 18th century] *Cop* is found in many names of hills, e.g. *Mowl Cop* (in Cheshire), *Fin Cop* (in Derbyshire). It is possibly from Old English *cop* 'summit, top'.

cope [Middle English] *Cope*, now meaning 'contend with, deal effectively with something difficult', was first recorded in the sense 'meet in battle, come to blows'. The source is Old French *coper*, *colper*, from *cop*, *colp* 'a blow': this is via Latin from Greek *kolaphos* 'blow with the fist'.

coping [mid 16th century] This term used in building contexts for the top course of a brick or stone wall is from the verb *cope* 'cover with a coping', originally meaning 'dress in a cope (= cape)': this *cope* is from medieval Latin *capa*, a variant of the earlier *cappa*.
→ CAPE¹

copious [late Middle English] *Copious* is from Old French *copieux* or Latin *copiosus*, from *copia* 'plenty'.

copper¹ [Old English] Old English *copor*, *coper* (related to Dutch *koper* and German *Kupfer*), is based on late Latin *cuprum*, from Latin *cyprium aes* 'Cyprus metal': Cyprus was the chief source.

copper² [mid 19th century]
→ COP¹

coppice [late Middle English] Describing an area of woodland in which the trees or shrubs have been periodically cut back to ground level, *coppice* is from Old French *copeiz*, based on medieval Latin *colpus* 'a blow'. The word *copse*, dating from the late 16th century, is shortened from *coppice*. Both *coppice* and *copse* have sometimes been treated dialectally as plurals.
→ COPE

copulate [late Middle English] The early meaning was 'join': it is from the Latin form *copulat-* from the verb *copulare* 'fasten together', from *copula* 'connection, linking'. The base elements are *co-* 'together' and *apere* 'fasten'.

copy [Middle English] 'A transcript or reproduction of a document' was an early sense of *copy*, from Old French *copie*, from Latin *copia* 'abundance'. Latin phrases such as *copiam describendi facere* 'give permission to transcribe' led to medieval Latin *copia* 'transcript' and the sense development in English.

corbel [late Middle English] A *corbel* is an architectural term for a piece of stone jutting out from a wall, or a short piece of timber under a beam: both support weight. It comes from an Old French diminutive of *corp* 'crow', from Latin *corvus* 'raven'. This is perhaps because of the shape of a corbel originally cut slantwise so that the profile resembled a crow's beak. The term developed a notion of ornamentation, not present in early use, from Sir Walter Scott's The corbels were carved grotesque and grim (*Lay of the Last Minstrel*), a line which captured the popular imagination.

cord [Middle English] This is from Old French *corde* 'string of a musical instrument', 'rope', from Latin *chorda*, from Greek *khordē* 'gut, string of a musical instrument'. The word *chord* is a refashioning of *cord*.
→ CHORD²

cordial [Middle English] An early meaning of this word was 'belonging to the heart'; it comes from medieval Latin *cordialis*, from Latin *cor*, *cord* 'heart'. The adjective was applied to drinks meaning 'comforting', 'invigorating the heart' (Spenser *Faerie Queene*: Costly Cordialles she did apply).

cordon [late Middle English] A *cordon* once referred to an ornamental braid worn on clothing. It comes from Italian *cordone* and French *cordon*, both from Latin *chorda* 'string, rope'.

The earliest modern noun usage is as the architectural term for a projecting band of stone on the face of a wall: this dates from the early 18th century. The notions of 'thin ribbon' or 'encircling band' predominate in the use of *cordon* which describes, for example, a 'fruit tree trained to grow as a single stem' or 'circle of troops or police positioned to prevent free passage'. A **cordon bleu** was the sky-blue ribbon worn by knights of the highest order of chivalry under the Bourbon Kings; the phrase was extended to other first-class distinctions.
→ CORD

core [Middle English] The origin is uncertain: it has been suggested that it comes from Latin *cor* 'heart', but the original meaning, 'hard central part of a fruit', does not agree with any sense of the Latin. Others have proposed French *corps* 'body' or *cor* 'horn' as the origin. The primary sense of *core* was formerly expressed by *colk* which remains in dialect and refers to the 'core of an apple or of a horn', 'a heart of wood', etc. Its origin is also uncertain but it may be the same word as *coke* (which is essentially a 'solid remaining part after reduction of the main substance').

cork [Middle English] This is from Dutch and Low German *kork*, from Spanish *alcorque* 'cork-soled sandal'. The source elements are Arabic *al-* 'the' and (probably) Spanish Arabic *ḳurk*, *ḳork*, based on Latin *quercus* 'oak, cork oak'.

corn¹ [Old English] Of Germanic origin, *corn* is related to Dutch *koren* and German *Korn*. The adjective **corny**, which dates from the 1930s meaning 'unsophisticated' is from an earlier sense which expressed 'rustic, appealing to country folk'. Of the compounds of *corn*:

■ **corn dolly** is a popular corruption of *kirn dolly*; *kirn* was a feast held on completion of the harvest. A *corn dolly* is made with the last handful of corn.

■ **corn snake** derives its name through its association with cornfields where it is often found.

■ **corn snow**, snow with a rough granular surface formed from alternate thawing and freezing, is based on a use of *corn* in the dialect sense 'granule'.

corn² [late Middle English] *Corn* 'a small area of thickened skin on the foot caused by pressure', is via Anglo-Norman French from Latin *cornu* 'horn'.

corner [Middle English] This is from an Anglo-Norman French word based on Latin *cornu* meaning 'horn, tip, corner'.

cornet¹ [late Middle English] In music this was originally a wind instrument made of a horn. It is from an Old French diminutive of a variant of Latin *cornu* 'horn'. The shape of the instrument gave the association for the word's use as a 'conical wafer' for ice-cream, recorded from the early 20th century. The Italian word *cornetto*, literally 'little horn', was used in early music of the 16th and 17th centuries for a wooden wind instrument with finger-holes and a cup-shaped mouthpiece.

coronary [mid 17th century] The first recorded sense was 'resembling a crown'. The word is from Latin *coronarius*, from *corona* 'wreath, crown'. In medical contexts, the term refers to blood vessels, nerves, or ligaments which encircle a part of the body, and often specifically the arteries which surround and supply the heart.

coronation [late Middle English] *Coronation* came via Old French from medieval Latin *coronatio(n-)*, from *coronare* 'to crown, adorn with a garland', from *corona* 'crown'. The word is used in the culinary term **coronation chicken**: this dish of cold cooked chicken served in a sauce flavoured with apricots and curry powder, was created for the coronation of Queen Elizabeth II in 1953.

coroner [Middle English] A *coroner* was once an official responsible for safeguarding the private property of the Crown. The word comes from Anglo-Norman French *coruner*, from *corune* 'a crown' and reflects the Latin title *custos placitorum coronae* 'guardian of the pleas of the crown'. Now the word refers to an official who holds enquiries into suspicious or sudden deaths, and, in Britain, into cases of treasure trove.

coronet [late Middle English] This comes from Old French *coronete* 'small crown or garland', a diminutive of *corone*.
➔ CROWN

corporation [late Middle English] This is from Latin *corporatio(n-)*, from Latin *corporare* 'combine in one body'. **Corporate** is recorded from the late 15th century and is from Latin *corporatus* 'formed into a body', based on *corpus*, *corpor-* 'body'.

corpse [Middle English] In early contexts, a *corpse* referred to the living body of a person or animal. It is an alteration of the archaic word *corse* 'body' by association with Latin *corpus*: this change also took place in French (Old French *cors* becoming *corps*). The *p* was originally silent, as in French; the final *e* was rare before the 19th century, but now distinguishes *corpse* from the word *corps* used commonly in military contexts.

correct [Middle English] Early examples are of *correct* as a verb. It is from Latin *correct-*, the past participial stem of the verb *corrigere* 'make straight, amend': the base elements are *cor-* 'together' and *regere* 'to guide'. The adjective is via French. **Correction** is also Middle English and is via Old French from Latin *correctio(n-)*, from *corrigere* 'make straight, bring into order'. Based on the same Latin verb is **corrigible**, which in late Middle English had the sense 'deserving punishment': it comes via French from medieval Latin *corrigibilis*.

correspond [late Middle English] This word is from Old French *correspondre*, from medieval Latin *correspondere*, from *cor-* 'together' and Latin *respondere* 'respond'. Related and dating from the same period are: **correspondence** (via Old French from medieval Latin *correspondentia*), and **correspondent** (from Old French *correspondant* or medieval Latin *correspondent-* 'corresponding'). This was first used as an adjective but has been used to describe a person employed to report on a particular subject for publication, from the early 18th century; initially this was a contributor of letters to a periodical.
➔ RESPONSE

corridor [late 16th century] A *corridor* was first used as a military term for a strip of land along the outer edge of a ditch, protected by a parapet. It is from French, from Italian *corridore*, an alteration (by association with *corridore* 'runner') of *corridoio* 'running-place', from *correre* 'to run'. The base is Latin *currere* 'to run'. The current sense ('long passage in a building') dates from the early 19th century.

corroborate [mid 16th century] If someone *corroborates* an account or story, the facts are strengthened. *Corroborate* was first recorded in the sense 'make physically stronger': it is from the Latin verb *corroborare* 'strengthen'. The base elements are Latin *cor-* 'together' and *roborare*, from *robur* 'strength'.

corrode [late Middle English] *Corrode* is from Latin *corrodere*, from *cor-* (giving emphasis) and *rodere* 'gnaw'. Dating from the same period is **corrosion** from Old French, or from late Latin *corrosio(n-)*, from Latin *corrodere* 'gnaw through'. **Corrosive**, also late Middle English, is from Old French *corosif*, *-ive*, from medieval Latin *corrosivus*, from Latin *corros-* 'gnawed through'.

corrugate [late Middle English] This is from Latin *corrugat-*, from the verb *corrugare* 'to wrinkle', based on *ruga* 'a wrinkle', prefixed by *cor-* giving emphasis.

corrupt [Middle English] *Corrupt* is from Latin *corruptus*, the past participle of *corrumpere* 'mar, bribe, destroy', from *cor-* 'altogether' and *rumpere* 'to break'. Middle English **corruption**

is via Old French from Latin *corruptio(n-)*, from *corrumpere*.

corset [Middle English] This is from a diminutive of Old French *cors* 'body', from Latin *corpus*. The sense 'close-fitting undergarment' dates from the late 18th century, by which time the sense '(outer) bodice' had mainly historical reference.

cortex [late Middle English] This is a Latin word meaning literally 'bark (of a tree)'.

cosmetic [early 17th century] In early contexts this was a noun referring to the art of beautifying the body. *Cosmetic* is via French from Greek *kosmētikos*, from *kosmein* 'arrange or adorn', from *kosmos* 'order or adornment'. The use of the word for a preparation used in beautifying the skin, dates from the mid 17th century.

cosmonaut [1950s] This is based on *cosmos*, on the pattern of *astronaut* and Russian *kosmonavt*.
➔ COSMOS

cosmopolitan [mid 17th century] This is based on **cosmopolite** ('a cosmopolitan person'), a word recorded from the early 17th century. **Cosmopolis** (a city inhabited by people from many different countries) dates from the mid 19th century, and is from Greek *kosmos* 'world' and *polis* 'city'.

cosmos [Middle English] The universe seen as a well-ordered whole is termed the *cosmos*. It comes from Greek *kosmos* 'order or world'.

cosset [mid 16th century] A *cosset* was a noun for a lamb brought up by hand; later it came to refer to a spoiled child: the verb use developed from the noun. It is probably from Anglo-Norman French *coscet* 'cottager', from Old English *cotsæta* 'cottar', 'dweller in a cot'.

cost [Middle English] The noun is from Old French *coust*, the verb from Old French *couster*, based on Latin *constare* 'stand firm, stand at a price'.

costermonger [early 16th century] The first element, *Costard*, was a kind of large apple (oval in shape and ribbed) often mentioned from the 14th to the 17th centuries after which the word faded from common use. The second element *-monger* means 'dealer'. This was an apple-seller originally but now refers in London to a person selling fruit, fish, vegetables, etc. from a barrow.

costume [early 18th century] This is from French, from Italian *costume* 'custom, fashion, habit', from Latin *consuetudo* 'custom'. The word is used in historical art to refer to the fashion of the time to which a scene belongs, or to the features proper to the time and locality. This was transferred to a manner of dressing, and then later to the dress itself.

cot[1] [mid 17th century] This word commonly used for an infant's bed, was originally an Anglo-Indian word for a light bedstead. The origin is Hindi *khāṭ* 'bedstead, hammock'.

cot[2] [Old English] Once a small, simple cottage, and now used as a term for a small shelter for livestock, this *cot* is Germanic in origin; it is comparable with Old Norse *kytja* 'hovel'. It is related to *cote*.

cote [Old English] Early examples reflected the sense 'cottage'; it now refers to a shelter for mammals or birds such as pigeons. Germanic in origin, it is related to *cot* which has the same meanings.

cottage [late Middle English] This is from Anglo-Norman French *cotage* and Anglo-Latin *cotagium*, from English *cot* or *cote*, both once used to describe a simple cottage.

couch [Middle English] Early recorded examples were as a noun denoting something to sleep on, and as a verb in the sense 'lay something down'. *Couch* is from Old French *couche* (noun), *coucher* (verb), from Latin *collocare* 'place together'.

cough [Middle English] *Cough* has an imitative origin; it is related to Dutch *kuchen* 'to cough' and German *keuchen* 'to pant'.

council [Old English] A *council* first referred to an 'ecclesiastical assembly'. It comes from Anglo-Norman French *cuncile*, from Latin *concilium* 'convocation, assembly', from *con* 'together' and *calare* 'summon'. Late Middle English **councillor** is an alteration of *counsellor*, by association with *council*.

counsel [Middle English] The noun is via Old French *counseil*, the verb via Old French *conseiller*, from Latin *consilium* 'consultation, advice', related to *consulere* 'take counsel'. Dating from the same period is **counsellor** which had the general sense 'adviser': this is from Old French *conseiller* (from Latin *consiliarius*) and Old French *conseillour*, both based on Latin *consilium* 'consultation or advice'.

count[1] [Middle English] This word used in mathematical calculation, in numbering, and in determining significance (*it counts for nothing*), is from the Old French noun *counte*, and the Old French verb *counter*, from Latin *computare* 'calculate'. The verb *tell* used to be the word for 'to enumerate', 'to number'.
➔ COMPUTE

count² [late Middle English] This title for a foreign nobleman is from Old French *conte*, from Latin *comes*, *comit-* 'companion, overseer, attendant': in late Latin this referred to a 'person holding a state office'. The base elements are *com-* 'together with' and *it-* 'gone' (from the verb *ire* 'go'). Middle English **countess** is from Old French *contesse*, from late Latin *comitissa*, the feminine of *comes* 'companion'.

countenance [Middle English] This is from Old French *contenance* 'bearing, behaviour', from *contenir* 'contain'. The early sense was 'bearing, demeanour', as well as 'facial expression', hence 'the face'.
→ CONTAIN

counter¹ [Middle English] The first recorded sense was 'a small disc used as a placemarker or to record points in a game'. *Counters* began to be used for keeping a tally in accounting and were of various shapes and sizes. It was in the late 17th century that the word came to be used for a surface across which goods were exchanged for money. It is from Old French *conteor*, from medieval Latin *computatorium*, from Latin *computare* 'count'.
→ COMPUTE

counter² [late Middle English] 'Speak in opposition' is the sense of *counter* in examples such as *the second argument is difficult to counter*. The word is from Old French *contre* (from Latin *contra* 'against') or directly from the prefix *counter-* (from Anglo-Norman French *countre-*, Old French *contre*) used in phrases such as *counter-attack* and *counter-espionage*.

counterfeit [Middle English] The Latin base elements of *counterfeit* are *contra-* 'in opposition' and *facere* 'make'. The direct source is Anglo-Norman French *countrefeter*, from Old French *contrefait*, the past participle of *contrefaire*.

counterpane [early 17th century] This is an alteration of *counterpoint*, from Old French *contrepointe*, based on medieval Latin *culcitra puncta* 'quilted mattress' (*puncta*, literally meaning 'pricked', from the verb *pungere*). The change in the ending was due to association with the word *pane* in an obsolete sense 'cloth'.

country [Middle English] *Country* came via Old French *cuntree*, from medieval Latin *contrata* (*terra*) '(land) lying opposite'. The base is Latin *contra* 'against, opposite'.

county [Middle English] The source of *county* is Old French *conte*, from Latin *comitatus*, from *comes*, *comit-* 'companion, overseer'. The word seems earliest to have referred to a meeting held periodically to transact the business of a shire.
→ COUNT²

couple [Middle English] The noun is from Old French *cople* (from Latin *copula*), the verb from Old French *copler* (from Latin *copulare*). The base elements are *co-* 'together' and *apere* 'fasten'. The term **couplet** (late 16th century) used in poetry for a pair of successive (usually rhyming) lines, means literally 'little pair', a diminutive of French *couple*, from Old French *cople*.
→ COPULATE

coupon [early 19th century] An early *coupon* was a detachable portion of a stock certificate handed over in return for payment of interest. The word is from French, meaning literally 'a piece cut off', from *couper* 'cut', from Old French *colper*.
→ COPE

courage [Middle English] The word *courage* once referred to the heart as the seat of feelings (Shakespeare *Henry VI* part iii: This soft courage makes your Followers faint). It is from Old French *corage*, from Latin *cor* 'heart'. Middle English **courageous** is from Old French *corageus*, from *corage*.

courier [late Middle English] The base is Latin *currere* 'to run'; in English a *courier* first referred to a person sent to run with a message. The early source was Old French *coreor*; later it came from French *courier* (now *courrier*), from Italian *corriere*.

course [Middle English] *Course* is from Old French *cours*, from Latin *cursus*, from the verb *currere* 'to run'. The same Latin base (via Old French *corsier*) gave Middle English **courser** referring, in literary and poetic contexts, to a swift horse.

court [Middle English] This is from Old French *cort*, from Latin *cohors*, *cohort-* 'yard or retinue'. The verb is influenced by Old Italian *corteare*, Old French *courtoyer*. **Courtier** (Middle English) is via Anglo-Norman French from Old French *cortoyer* 'be present at court', from *cort*. **Courteous** in Middle English meant 'having manners fit for a royal court'; the origin is Old French *corteis* (based on Latin *cohors*). The change in the ending in the 16th century was due to association with words ending in *-eous*. Dating from the same period is **courtesy** from Old French *cortesie*.
→ COHORT

cousin [Middle English] This is from Old French *cosin*, from Latin *consobrinus* 'mother's sister's child', from *con-* 'with' and *sobrinus* 'second cousin' (from *soror* 'sister').

cove [Old English] This word's use for a small sheltered bay dates from the late 16th century. It was *cofa* 'chamber, cave' in Old English. Of

Germanic origin, it is related to German *Koben* 'pigsty, pen'.

covenant [Middle English] *Covenant* is from Old French; it is the present participle of *covenir* 'agree', from Latin *convenire*.
→ CONVENE

cover [Middle English] *Cover* is from Old French *covrir*, from Latin *cooperire*, from *co-* (giving emphasis) and *operire* 'to cover'. The noun is partly a variant of *covert*. Middle English **coverlet** is from Anglo-Norman French *covrelet*, from Old French *covrir* 'to cover' and *lit* 'bed'.

covert [Middle English] First recorded with the general senses 'covered' and 'a cover', *covert* is from Old French, 'covered', the past participle of *covrir*.

covet [Middle English] *Covet* is from Old French *cuveitier*, based on Latin *cupiditas* 'desire'. **Covetous** (also Middle English) is from Old French *coveitous*, based on Latin *cupiditas*.

cow¹ [Old English] Referring to the fully grown female animal of a domesticated breed of ox, *cow* (in Old English *cū*) is Germanic in origin. It is related to Dutch *koe* and German *Kuh*, from an Indo-European root shared by Latin *bos* and Greek *bous* 'ox'.

cow² [late 16th century] The verb *cow* 'cause to submit', is probably from Old Norse *kúga* 'oppress'

coward [Middle English] This is from Old French *couard*, based on Latin *cauda* 'tail', possibly with reference to a frightened animal with its tail between its legs, depicted in heraldry from the early 16th century. **Cowardice** (Middle English) is from Old French *couardise*.

cower [Middle English] This is from Middle Low German *kūren* 'lie in wait'; the ultimate origin remains unknown.

cowl [Old English] Old English *cugele*, *cūle* is from ecclesiastical Latin *cuculla*, from Latin *cucullus* 'hood of a cloak'.

cox [mid 19th century] This is an abbreviation of **coxswain** made up of obsolete *cock* 'small boat' and *swain* 'youth'.

coy [Middle English] This is from Old French *coi*, *quei*, from Latin *quietus*. The original sense was 'quiet, still' (especially in behaviour), later 'modestly retiring', and hence (of a woman) 'affecting to be unresponsive to advances'.
→ QUIET

crabbed [Middle English] *Crabbed* and *crabby* are synonyms; early examples of *crabbed* showed the sense 'perverse, wayward'. It is from the zoological word *crab*, because of the crab's sideways gait and habit of snapping,

thought to suggest a perverse or irritable nature. *Crabbed* may also describe writing that is ill-formed and hard to decipher. The *crab* in *crab apple* (characterized by its sourness) may have been influenced by *crabbed* but, originally, it is probably unrelated.

cradle [Old English] Old English *cradol* is of uncertain origin; it is perhaps related to German *Kratte* 'basket'.

craft [Old English] Old English *cræft* meant 'strength, skill'. Germanic in origin, it is related to Dutch *kracht*, German *Kraft*, and Swedish *kraft* 'strength'. The change of sense to 'skill' occurred only in English. Its use with reference to a 'boat' originally in the expression *small craft* indicating 'small trading vessels', may be elliptical, referring to vessels requiring a small amount of 'craft' or skill to handle, as opposed to large ocean-going ships.

crafty [Old English] Old English *cræftig* occasionally meant 'strong, powerful'; 'skilful' became the common usage and this became associated with the negative connotation 'artful', 'wily' (Chaucer *Canon's Yeoman's Prologue and Tale*: Sin that he is so crafty and so sly).

cram [Old English] Old English *crammian* is Germanic in origin; it is related to Dutch *krammen* 'to cramp or clamp'. The primary meaning was 'to press, squeeze'.

crane [Middle English] This term for a tall machine used for lifting heavy objects is a figurative use of *crane* for a type of long-legged long-necked bird. It is of Germanic origin (from an Indo-European root shared by Latin *grus* and Greek *geranos*). The same sense development occurred in the related German *Kran* and Dutch *kraan*, and in French *grue*. The verb 'stretch one's neck upwards', dates from the late 16th century.

crank¹ [Old English] Old English *cranc* was recorded in *crancstæf*, a weaver's implement. The primary notion is 'something bent together' and it is related to *crincan* 'to bend'. In current use it refers to part of an axle or shaft, and as a verb it includes the meaning 'turn (a handle) in order to start an engine'.
→ CRINGE

crank² [early 17th century] The *crank* which means 'eccentric person' is perhaps from the dialect word *crank* meaning 'weak, shaky'.

cranky [late 18th century] In early examples this informal word had the sense 'sickly, in poor health'. It is perhaps from the obsolete (*counterfeit*) *crank* referring to 'a rogue feigning sickness', from Dutch or German *krank* 'sick'. It now means 'eccentric' or 'ill-tempered'.

cranny [late Middle English] Referring to a 'small narrow space', *cranny* is apparently from Old French *crane* 'notched', from *cran*, from popular Latin *crena* 'notch'. The etymology is uncertain.

crap [Middle English] *Crap* is related to Dutch *krappe*, from *krappen* 'pluck or cut off', and perhaps also to Old French *crappe* 'siftings', Anglo-Latin *crappa* 'chaff'. The original sense was 'chaff', later coming to mean 'residue from rendering fat' as well as 'dregs of beer'. Current senses denoting 'something of poor quality', 'rubbish', 'nonsense', 'excrement', date from the late 19th century: the common notion is one of 'rejected matter'.

craps [early 19th century] A term for a gambling game, *craps* is perhaps from *crab* or *crab's eyes*, denoting the lowest throw (two ones) at dice.

crash [late Middle English] *Crash* is imitative, perhaps partly suggested by *craze* and *dash*.

crass [late 15th century] *Crass* (as in *crass stupidity*) is used with relation to a grossly insensitive lack of intelligence. It was first recorded as meaning 'dense or coarse (in constitution or texture)'. It comes from Latin *crassus* 'solid, thick'.

crate [late Middle English] English *crate* 'a slatted wooden case for transporting goods' may be related to Dutch *krat* 'tailboard of a wagon', used earlier to mean 'box of a coach'. The origin remains unknown.

crater [early 17th century] This is via Latin from Greek *kratēr* 'large bowl for mixing wine with water', from *krasis* 'mixture'.

cravat [mid 17th century] This is from French *cravate*, from *Cravate* 'Croat' (the source is German *Krabat*, from Serbo-Croat *Hrvat*). The association is the linen scarf worn by Croatian mercenaries in France. The cravat came into fashion in France in the 17th century; when first introduced it was made of lace or linen, or muslin edged with lace. It was tied in a bow which had long flowing ends. It was also worn by women. More recently the name was given to a linen or silk handkerchief passed once (or twice) round the neck outside the shirt collar and tied in a bow in front; also to a long woollen comforter wrapped around the neck to protect the wearer from the cold.

crave [Old English] Old English *crafian* meant 'demand, claim as a right'. Germanic in origin, it is related to Swedish *kräva*, Danish *kræve* 'demand'. The current sense 'feel a strong desire for', dates from late Middle English.

craven [Middle English] Middle English *cravant* meant 'defeated' and is perhaps via Anglo-Norman French from Old French *cravante*, the past participle of *cravanter* 'crush, overwhelm' (based on Latin *crepare* 'burst'). The change in the ending in the 17th century was due to association with past participles ending in *-en*. The current notion is 'showing contemptible cowardice'.

craw [late Middle English] *Craw* is a term for the crop of birds and insects; it is also transferred to mean 'stomach' (Byron *Don Juan*: As tigers combat with an empty craw). It is from or related to Middle Dutch *crāghe* or Middle Low German *krage* 'neck, throat'.

crawl [Middle English] The origin is unknown; it is possibly related to Swedish *krafla* 'to grope' and Danish *kravle* 'crawl, climb up'. The word was rare in Middle English and apparently only found in northern use.

crayon [mid 17th century] *crayon* is an adopted word from French, from *craie* 'chalk', from Latin *creta*.

craze [late Middle English] The early recorded sense was 'break, shatter, produce cracks'. It is perhaps of Scandinavian origin and related to Swedish *krasa* 'crunch'. A fuller form *acrase* is recorded in the 16th century; if this existed earlier, *crase* may have been a shortened form of this (from Old French *acraser*, a variant of *écraser* 'to crush'). The word's use to mean 'insane or irrational fancy' dates from the early 19th century; this developed from the earlier sense 'flaw' in health.

crease [late 16th century] This is probably a variant of *crest*.
→ CREST

create [late Middle English] *Create*, **creation**, **creator**, and **creature** all date from the Middle English period. The early recorded sense of *create* is 'form out of nothing', used with reference to a divine or supernatural being. It comes from Latin *creat-*, from the verb *creare* 'produce', the base of the other related English words. *Creation* is via Old French from Latin *creatio(n-)*; *creator* is from Old French *creatour*, *creatur*, from Latin *creator*. *Creature* had the early meaning 'something created' and is via Old French from late Latin *creatura*.

credential [late Middle English] This is from medieval Latin *credentialis*, from *credentia* (which gave English **credence**, from Latin *credent-* 'believing'). The original use was as an adjective in the sense 'giving credence to, recommending', frequently in *credential letters* or *papers*, hence *credentials* (mid 17th century).

credible [late Middle English] This is from Latin *credibilis*, from *credere* 'believe'. **Credibility**, which dates from the mid 16th century, is from medieval Latin *credibilitas* (from Latin *credibilis*).

credit [mid 16th century] The original senses recorded were 'belief' and 'credibility'. The word is from French *crédit*, probably via Italian *credito* from Latin *creditum* (from *credere* 'believe, trust'). This notion of 'belief' and 'trust' passed into contexts where trust was placed in the ability of a customer to pay for goods. The word **creditor** was recorded already from late Middle English, and is from Old French *crediteur*, from Latin *creditor*.

creed [Old English] This is from Latin *credo* 'I believe'.

creep [Old English] Old English *crēopan* 'move with the body close to the ground' is Germanic in origin and related to Dutch *kruipen*. The verb sense 'move slowly in order to to avoid being noticed' dates from Middle English.

crescent [late Middle English] An early spelling was *cressant*, from Old French *creissant*, from Latin *crescere* 'grow'. The spelling change in the 17th century was due to the influence of the Latin.

crest [Middle English] *Crest* comes from Old French *creste*, from Latin *crista* 'tuft, plume'. The word **crestfallen** dates from the late 16th century and is figurative, from the original use referring to a mammal or bird having a fallen or drooping crest.

cretin [late 18th century] *Cretin* used abusively now, was formerly a medical term referring to a person deformed physically and mentally handicapped as a result of congenital thyroid deficiency. The word is from French *crétin*, from Swiss French *crestin* 'Christian' (from Latin *Christianus*), used to mean 'human creature' apparently in these early contexts, countering the notion of 'bestial creature' suggested by the severe deformities.

crevice [Middle English] This is from Old French *crevace*, from *crever* 'to burst', from Latin *crepare* 'to rattle, crack'. Also from Old French *crevace* is **crevasse**, dating from the early 19th century. This word has been adopted by Alpine climbers in Switzerland, and in the US from the French of Louisiana, and refers to a deep open crack as opposed to a narrow fissure defined by *crevice*.

crew [late Middle English] English *crew* is from Old French *creue* 'augmentation, increase', the feminine past participle of *croistre* 'to grow', from Latin *crescere*. Originally the word referred to a 'band of soldiers serving as reinforcements'; hence it came to denote any organized armed band or, more generally, a company of people (late 16th century). The phrase:

■ **crew cut** dates from the 1940s and was apparently first adopted as a hairstyle by boat crews of Harvard and Yale universities.

crib [Old English] The early sense of *crib* was 'manger'. The word is Germanic in origin and is related to Dutch *krib*, *kribbe* and German *Krippe*.

cricket[1] [late 16th century] The sporting term *cricket* has an uncertain origin. The word is found in a document dated 1598 and the evidence then given takes the game back to the end of the reign of Henry VIII. The word appears to be the same as French *criquet* which was described as a game of skill or as a type of bat in a bowling game. It is doubtful that the game was a development of stoolball referred to frequently from 1567 to 1725 although some have surmised there to be a connection. Many changes have been made to the game since the 17th century when the bats were hockey sticks, the wicket was two stumps with one long bail, and the ball trundled ('bowled') along the ground.

cricket[2] [Middle English] *Cricket*, referring to a type of insect with a characteristic chirping sound, is from Old French *criquet*, from *criquer* 'to crackle', of imitative origin.

crime [Middle English] Early senses were 'wickedness' and 'sin'. It comes via Old French from Latin *crimen* 'judgement, offence', based on *cernere* 'to judge'. **Criminal** is late Middle English as an adjective and comes from late Latin *criminalis*, from Latin *crimen*, *crimin-* ; noun use dates from the early 17th century.

cringe [Middle English] Middle English spellings included *crenge* and *crenche*. It is related to Old English *cringan*, *crincan* 'bend, yield, fall in battle' and is Germanic in origin, related to Dutch *krengen* 'heel over' and German *krank* 'sick'.
→ CRANK[1]

cripple [Old English] This is from two Old English words *crypel* and *crēopel*, both of Germanic origin and related to *creep*. The sense is either 'one who can only creep' or 'someone contracted in body and limbs'.
→ CREEP

crisis [late Middle English] A *crisis* once referred to the turning point of a disease. It is medical Latin, from Greek *krisis* 'decision', from *krinein* 'decide'. The general sense 'decisive point' dates from the early 17th century.

crisp [Old English] Originally *crisp* was used to describe hair in the sense 'curly'. It is from

Latin *crispus* 'curled'. Other senses may result from symbolic interpretation of the sound of the word.

criterion [early 17th century] This is from Greek *kritērion* 'a means of judging', from *kritēs* 'a judge'.

critic [late 16th century] This is via Latin *criticus* from Greek *kritikos*, from *kritēs* 'a judge', from *krinein* 'judge, decide'. When first used the adjective **critical** related to the crisis of a disease; it comes from late Latin *criticus*.

crock [late Middle English] The word *crock* used commonly in the phrase *old crock*, is perhaps from Flemish, and probably related to *crack*. Originally a Scots term for an old ewe, it came in the late 19th century to denote an old or broken-down horse.

crockery [early 18th century] *Crockery* is from obsolete *crocker* 'potter', from **crock**, spelt in Old English *croc*, *crocca* 'earthenware pot'. This is Germanic in origin and related to Old Norse *krukka* and probably to Dutch *kruik* and German *Krug*.

crocodile [Middle English] Spellings in Middle English included *cocodrille* and *cokadrill* from Old French *cocodrille*, via medieval Latin from Latin *crocodilus*. The base is Greek *krokodilos* 'worm of the stones', from *krokē* 'pebble' and *drilos* 'worm'. In the 16th century, the spelling was changed to conform with the Latin and Greek forms. The compound:
■ **crocodile tears** dates from the mid 16th century and is said to derive from a belief that crocodiles wept while devouring or luring their prey.

crone [late Middle English] This came via Middle Dutch *croonje, caroonje* 'carcass, old ewe' from Old Northern French *caroigne* meaning both 'carrion' and 'cantankerous woman'.
→ CARRION

crony [mid 17th century] Originally Cambridge university slang, *crony* is from Greek *khronios* 'long-lasting' (here used to mean 'contemporary'), from *khronos* 'time'.
→ CHUM

crook [Middle English] The early term meant 'hooked tool or weapon'. It is from Old Norse *krókr* 'hook'. A noun sense 'deceit, guile, trickery' was recorded in Middle English but was obsolete by the 17th century. Middle English **crooked** is based on *crook*, probably modelled on Old Norse *krókóttr* 'crooked, cunning'.

croon [late 15th century] Originally Scots and northern English, *croon* is from Middle Low German and Middle Dutch *krōnen* 'groan,

lament'. The use of *croon* in standard English was probably popularized by Robert Burns.

crop [Old English] *Crop* is Germanic and related to German *Kropf*. From Old English to the late 18th century there existed a sense 'flower head, ear of corn', which became extended to 'cultivated plant grown on a large scale commercially'. There were also senses referring to the top of something such as the top of a whip, whence the extension to *hunting crop, riding crop*.

cross [late Old English] Early use was to refer to a 'monument in the form of a cross'. It comes from Old Norse *kross*, from Old Irish *cros*, from Latin *crux*. The adjective *cross* meant 'transverse, lying across', then 'adverse', which led to 'angry' (mid 17th century). Compounds include:
■ **crosspatch** (early 18th century) based on the obsolete word *patch* meaning 'fool, clown', perhaps from Italian *pazzo* 'madman'.
■ **crossword**, said to have been invented by the journalist Arthur Wynne, whose puzzle (called a 'word-cross') appeared in a Sunday newspaper, the *New York World*, on 21 December 1913.

crotchety [early 19th century] This word meaning 'irritable' is based on **crotchet** in the sense 'perverse or unfounded belief' and which in Middle English meant 'hook'. *Crotchet* is from Old French *crochet*, a diminutive of *croc* 'hook', from Old Norse *krókr*. The sense 'hook' is the association which has given the musical term, due to the way it is represented.

crouch [late Middle English] This is perhaps from Old French *crochir* 'be bent', from *croche* 'crozier, shepherd's crook', perhaps related to English **crotch** (mid 16th century), based on Old Norse *krókr* 'hook'.

croupier [early 18th century] In early use, this was a term for a person standing behind a gambler to give advice. It has been adopted from French, from Old French *cropier* 'pillion rider, rider on the croup', related to Old French *croupe* 'rump'.

crowd [Old English] Old English *crūdan* 'press, hasten' is Germanic in origin and related to Dutch *kruien* 'push in a wheelbarrow'. In Middle English the senses 'move by pushing' and 'push one's way' arose, leading to the sense 'congregate', and hence (mid 16th century) to the noun.

crown [Middle English] The noun is from Anglo-Norman French *corune* (Old French *corone*), the verb from Anglo-Norman French *coruner* (Old French *coroner*), from Latin *corona* 'wreath, chaplet'.

crucial [early 18th century] *Crucial* in early texts had the sense 'cross-shaped'. It is from French, from Latin *crux, cruc-* 'cross'. The sense 'decisive', 'very important' (*at a crucial stage*) has developed from Francis Bacon's Latin phrase *instantia crucis* 'crucial instance', which he explained as a metaphor from a *crux* or finger-post marking a fork at a crossroad. The physicists Newton (1642-1727) and Boyle (1627-91) took up the metaphor in *experimentum crucis* 'crucial experiment', a decisive test showing which of several hypotheses is correct.

crucible [late Middle English] This is from medieval Latin *crucibulum* 'night lamp, crucible' which may originally have been a lamp hanging in front of a crucifix. It is from Latin *crux, cruc-* 'cross'.

crucify [Middle English] This is from Old French *crucifier*, from late Latin *crucifigere*, from Latin *crux, cruc-* 'cross' and *figere* 'fix'. The figurative sense arose in the early 17th century. Also Middle English is **crucifix** (via Old French and ecclesiastical Latin from Latin *cruci fixus* 'fixed to a cross'). **Crucifixion** dates from late Middle English and is from ecclesiastical Latin *crucifixio(n-)*, from the verb *crucifigere*.

crud [late Middle English] *Crud* is a variant of *curd*, which was its original sense. The earliest modern meanings, 'filth' and 'nonsense' (originally US), date from the 1940s.

crude [late Middle English] This is from Latin *crudus* 'raw, rough'.

cruel [Middle English] *Cruel* is via Old French from Latin *crudelis*, related to *crudus* 'rough'. **Cruelty**, also Middle English, is from Old French *crualte*, based on Latin *crudelitas*, from *crudelis*.

cruise [mid 17th century] This is probably from Dutch *kruisen* 'to cross', from *kruis* 'cross', from Latin *crux*. Late 17th-century **cruiser** is from Dutch *kruiser*, from *kruisen*.

crumb [Old English] Old English *cruma* is Germanic and related to Dutch *kruim* and German *Krume*. The final *-b* was added in the 16th century, perhaps from *crumble* but also influenced by words such as *dumb*, where the original final *-b* is kept but no longer pronounced. The exclamation **crumbs** has been in recorded use from the late 19th century: it is a euphemism for *Christ*.

crumble [late Middle English] This is probably from an Old English word related to *crumb*.

crummy [mid 19th century] Also spelt **crumby**, this word was used earlier in the literal senses 'crumbly' and 'like or covered with crumbs'. It now expresses the notions 'unpleasant', 'in poor condition'.

crumple [Middle English] This is from obsolete *crump* 'make or become curved', from Old English *crump* 'bent, crooked', of West Germanic origin; it is related to German *krumm*.

crusade [late 16th century] Originally spelt *croisade, crusade* is from French *croisade*, an alteration (influenced by Spanish *cruzado*) of earlier *croisée*. This meant literally 'the state of being marked with the cross', based on Latin *crux, cruc-* 'cross'. In the 17th century the form *crusado*, from Spanish *cruzado*, was introduced; the blending of these two forms led to the current spelling, first recorded in the early 18th century.

crush [Middle English] *Crush* is from Old French *cruissir*, 'gnash (teeth)' or 'crack'; the origin is unknown.

crust [Middle English] This is from Old French *crouste*, from Latin *crusta* 'rind, shell, crust'.

cry [Middle English] *Cry* is first recorded with the meanings 'ask for earnestly', 'ask for loudly'. The verb is from Old French *crier*, the noun from Old French *cri*, the source for both being Latin *quiritare* 'raise a public outcry', literally 'call on the *Quirites* (= Roman citizens) for help'. Early examples of *cry* centre around 'sound': this was sometimes in sorrow or distress. The association with tears with or without sound is recorded from around the mid 16th century.

crypt [late Middle English] *Crypt*, first recorded as meaning 'cavern', is from Latin *crypta*, from Greek *kruptē* 'a vault', from *kruptos* 'hidden'. This is the base too of the adjective **cryptic** (early 17th century), from late Latin *crypticus*, from Greek *kruptikos*.

crystal [late Old English] Early examples showed *crystal* as a term for ice or a mineral resembling it. It is from Old French *cristal*, via Latin from Greek *krustallos* 'ice, crystal'. The chemistry sense dates from the early 17th century.

cubicle [late Middle English] The first recorded sense was 'bedroom'; it comes from Latin *cubiculum*, from *cubare* 'lie down'.

cucking-stool [Middle English] Once used as a chair to which disorderly women were tied and then ducked under water, a *cucking-stool* is from obsolete *cuck* 'defecate'. It is Scandinavian in origin and derives its name from the type of stool containing a chamber pot, which was often used for this form of punishment.

cuckold [late Old English] This word for the husband of an unfaithful wife is from Old

French *cucuault*, from *cucu* 'cuckoo', by association with the cuckoo's habit of laying its egg in another bird's nest. The equivalent words in French and other languages are applied to both the bird and the person; *cuckold* has never been applied to the bird in English.

cud [Old English] Old English *cwidu*, *cudu* is Germanic in origin and is related to German *Kitt* 'cement, putty' and Swedish *kåda* 'resin'.

cue [mid 16th century] The *cue* that serves as a signal for action is of unknown origin, but the **cue** referring to a long wooden rod used in games such as snooker, arose in the mid 18th century to denote a long plait or pigtail: this word is a variant of *queue*.

culinary [mid 17th century] *Culinary* is from Latin *culinarius*, from *culina* 'kitchen'.

culminate [mid 17th century] A term used in astronomy and astrology originally, this is from the late Latin form *culminat-* (meaning 'exalted'), based on Latin *culmen* 'summit'.

culpable [Middle English] The first recorded sense was 'deserving punishment'. *Culpable* is from Old French *coupable*, *culpable*, from Latin *culpabilis*, from *culpare* 'to blame', from *culpa* 'fault, blame'.

culprit [late 17th century] This was once part of the formula *Culprit, how will you be tried?*, said by the Clerk of the Crown to a prisoner pleading not guilty. This is perhaps as a result of a misinterpretation of the written abbreviation *cul. prist*, standing for Anglo-Norman French *Culpable: prest d'averrer notre bille* '(You are) guilty: (We are) ready to prove our indictment'. In later use this may have been influenced by Latin *culpa* 'fault, blame'.

cult [early 17th century] *Cult* was originally homage paid to a divine being. It is from French *culte* or Latin *cultus* 'worship', from *cult-* 'cultivated, worshipped', from the verb *colere*. The sense of the word in phrases such as *religious cults* has often focused on external rites and ceremonies, with suspicion of any difference from the mainstream. From the 1960s, the word in English has come to refer to cultural phenomena appealing to a relatively small (often young) audience (e.g. *cult figures*, *cult status*).

cultivate [mid 17th century] This word comes from medieval Latin *cultivat-*, from the verb *cultivare* 'prepare for crops', from *cultiva (terra)* 'arable (land)'. The base verb is *colere* 'cultivate, inhabit'.

culture [Middle English] The base for the noun and the verb is Latin *colere* 'tend, cultivate'. In early examples, a *culture* was 'a cultivated piece of land': this is from French *culture* or directly from Latin *cultura* 'growing, cultivation'. In late Middle English the meaning was 'cultivation of the soil' and this developed during the early 16th century into 'cultivation (of the mind, faculties, or manners)'. Reference to the arts and other examples of human achievement, dates from the early 19th century.
→ CULTIVATE

cumbersome [late Middle English] In early examples, the meaning was 'difficult to get through'. The first element is *cumber* a Middle English verb in the sense 'overthrow, destroy', which probably came from *encumber*.

cummerbund [early 17th century] This word for a sash worn round the waist, is from Urdu and Persian *kamar-band*, from *kamar* 'waist, loins' and *-bandi* 'band'. The sash was formerly worn in the Indian subcontinent by domestic workers and office workers of low status.

cumulate [mid 16th century] The early verb meant 'gather in a heap'. It comes from the Latin verb *cumulare* 'to heap', from *cumulus* 'a heap'. Current senses such as 'gather and combine' and 'be gathered together' date from the early 20th century

cunning [Middle English] This comes perhaps from Old Norse *kunnandi* 'knowledge', from *kunna* 'know' (which is related to the verb *can*), or perhaps from Middle English *cunne*, an obsolete variant of *can*. The original sense was '(possessing) erudition or skill' and had no implication of deceit; the sense 'deceitfulness' dates from late Middle English.
→ CAN[1]

cup [Old English] This is from popular Latin *cuppa*, probably from Latin *cupa* 'tub'. *Cup* is the first element of **cupboard** which in late Middle English referred to a table or sideboard on which cups, plates, etc. were displayed.

cur [Middle English] A *cur* is now depreciative in that it focuses on the aggressive nature of a dog or its poor condition; it also expresses contempt when used as an insult of a person. However it was first used generally in the sense 'dog'. It probably comes from the phrase *cur-dog*, perhaps from Old Norse *kurr* 'grumbling'.

curate [Middle English] *Curate* is from medieval Latin *curatus*, from Latin *cura* 'care'. The phrase **curate's egg** arose in the early 20th century from a cartoon in *Punch* (1895) depicting a meek curate who, given a stale egg at the bishop's table, assures his host that 'parts of it are excellent'. The verb **curate** (late 19th century) is a back-formation (by removal of the suffix) from *curator* which in late Middle English was an ecclesiastical pastor. It was also (and still is in Scottish Law) the guardian of a minor; the origin is Old French *curateur* or, in later use, directly from Latin *curator*, from *curare*. The current sense ('custodian of a museum') dates from the mid 17th century. The primary notion in all these words is 'care and attention'.

→ CURE

curb [late 15th century] A *curb* is a check or restraint; early use was to denote a strap fastened to a horse's bit. It comes from Old French *courber* 'bend, bow', from Latin *curvare*. The semantic core is therefore shape-related (the device forming part of the bit caused the horse to bend its neck). The meaning came to include a notion of 'holding back'.

→ CURVE

curdle [late 16th century] This is a frequentative (= verb of repeated action) of the obsolete word *curd* 'congeal'.

cure [Middle English] The verb is from Old French *curer*, the noun from Old French *cure*, both from Latin *curare* 'take care of', from *cura* 'care'. The original noun senses were 'care, concern, responsibility', in particular spiritual care, hence its use to mean 'a Christian minister's pastoral charge'. In late Middle English the senses 'medical care' and 'successful medical treatment' arose, and hence 'remedy'.

curfew [Middle English] A *curfew* was initially a regulation requiring people to extinguish fires at a fixed hour in the evening, or it referred to a bell rung at that fixed time. The origin is Old French *cuevrefeu*, from *cuvrir* 'to cover' and *feu* 'fire'. The current usage referring to a regulation requiring people to stay indoors, dates from the late 19th century.

curious [Middle English] *Curious* is from Old French *curios*, from Latin *curiosus* 'careful', from *cura* 'care', with emphasis on 'detailed, focused attention'. The meaning 'strange, unusual' arose in the early 18th century. **Curiosity** is late Middle English and comes from Old French *curiousete*, from Latin *curiositas*, from *curiosus* 'careful'. The word **curio** for 'a rare and intriguing object' dates from the mid 19th century and is an abbreviation of *curiosity*.

curl [late Middle English] *Curl* is from obsolete *crulle* meaning 'curly', from Middle Dutch *krul* (Chaucer *Prologue*: A yong Squier ... With lokkes crulle as they were leyd in presse).

currant [Middle English] This comes from the phrase *raisons of Corauntz*, translating Anglo-Norman French *raisins de Corauntz* 'grapes of Corinth', which was their original source.

current [Middle English] The early adjective meant 'running, flowing' and is from Old French *corant* 'running', from *courre* 'to run', from Latin *currere* 'to run'.

cursor [Middle English] Early use of this word was to refer to a runner or running messenger. It is Latin for 'runner', from Latin *curs-* '(having) run', from the verb *currere*. From the late 16th century, a *cursor* was used as a term for a 'sliding part of a rule, marked with a hairline for pinpointing a position', and, in computing contexts it has come to refer to a 'movable indicator on a computer screen'. The word **cursory** captures the early notion of 'speed' present in the Latin base and means 'hasty and lacking detail'. This dates from the early 17th century and is from Latin *cursorius* 'relating to a runner', from *cursor*.

curt [late Middle English] Early examples of *curt* reflected the sense 'short, shortened'. The origin is Latin *curtus* 'cut short, abridged'. Now there is an additional notion of 'rudeness' in the brevity.

curtail [late 15th century] *Curtail* comes from the obsolete term *curtal* for a 'horse with a docked tail', from French *courtault*. This is from French *court* 'short', from Latin *curtus*. The change in the ending was due to the association of ideas with *tail* and perhaps also with French *tailler* 'to cut'.

curtain [Middle English] This is from Old French *cortine*, from late Latin *cortina*, a translation of Greek *aulaia*, from *aulē* 'court'. The late Latin word in the derivation is found in the Vulgate in Exodus, in the phrase *decem cortinas* referring to 'ten curtains' with which to make a tabernacle. This was for use as a sanctuary for the Ark of the Covenant by the Israelites during the Exodus and until the building of the Temple. A compound using *curtain* is:
■ **curtain-raiser** (late 19th century) was originally used in the theatre to denote a short opening piece performed before a play.

curtsey [early 16th century] *Curtsey* is a variant of *courtesy*. Both forms were used to denote the expression of respect or courtesy by a gesture, especially in phrases such as *do courtesy*, *make courtesy*. This led to the current use, which arose in the late 16th century.

curve [late Middle English] The verb is from Latin *curvare* 'to bend', from *curvus* 'bent'. The noun dates from the late 17th century

cushion [Middle English] This word reflects the original purpose of a *cushion*: it is from Old French *cuissin*, based on a Latin word meaning 'cushion for the hip', from *coxa* 'hip, thigh'.

The Romans also had a word *cubital* 'elbow-cushion', from *cubitus* 'elbow'.

cushy [First World War] This was originally an Anglo-Indian word from Urdu k͟ushī 'pleasure', from Persian k͟uš.

custard [late Middle English] Early spellings included *crustarde* and *custarde*; the word described an open pie containing meat or fruit in a spiced or sweetened sauce thickened with eggs. It comes from Old French *crouste* 'crust'. The composition of the dish changed apparently around 1600. It is now commonly made with beaten eggs and milk, and sometimes, as a similar preparation, served in the form of a thick sauce.
→ CRUST

custody [late Middle English] *Custody* is from Latin *custodia*, from *custos* 'guardian'. The noun **custodian**, based on *custody*, is recorded much later, in the late 18th century: its spelling is on the pattern of *guardian*.

custom [Middle English] This is from Old French *coustume*, based on Latin *consuetudo*: the core elements are *con-* (giving emphasis) and *suescere* 'become accustomed'. **Customary** (late Middle English) is from medieval Latin *custumarius*, from *custuma*, from Anglo-Norman French *custume*.

customs [late Middle English] Original examples were in the singular when a *custom* was a customary due paid to a ruler, later coming to refer to a duty levied on goods on their way to market.

cut [Middle English] It is likely that this word existed in Old English but no recorded examples have been found. The origin is probably Germanic linked to Norwegian *kutte* and Icelandic *kuta* 'cut with a small knife', *kuti* 'small blunt knife'.

cute [early 18th century] Early examples showed *cute* as meaning 'clever, shrewd'. It is a shortening of *acute*. *Cute* in the sense 'attractive, pretty' was originally a US colloquial usage (A. Huxley *Grey Eminence*: The tiny boy … looking almost 'cute' in his claret-coloured doublet and starched ruff).
→ ACUTE

cutlass [late 16th century] The origin of *cutlass* describing a short sword with a slightly curved blade, is French *coutelas*, based on Latin *cultellus* 'small knife'.

cutler [Middle English] A *cutler* (from Old French *coutelier*, from *coutel* 'knife') describes a person who makes or sells cutlery. The source is Latin *cultellus*, a diminutive of *culter* 'knife, ploughshare'. This also gave the English word **coulter**, which is a vertical cutting blade fixed at the front of a ploughshare. **Cutlery**, also Middle English, is from Old French *coutellerie* (from *coutelier*).

cutlet [early 18th century] *Cutlet* is literally 'little rib'. It comes from French *côtelette*, an earlier spelling of which was *costelette*, a diminutive of *coste* 'rib' (from Latin *costa*).

cwm [mid 19th century] This is a Welsh word related to *combe*.
→ COMBE

cycle [late Middle English] This is from Old French via late Latin from Greek *kuklos* 'circle'. The adjective **cyclic** is not recorded before the late 18th century: it is from French *cyclique* or Latin *cyclicus*, from Greek *kuklikos* (from *kuklos* 'circle').

cyclone [mid 19th century] This term in meteorology for a system of winds rotating inwards to an area of low barometric pressure, probably has its origin in Greek *kuklōma* 'wheel, coil of a snake', from *kuklos* 'circle'. The change of spelling from *-m* to *-n* is unexplained.

cylinder [late 16th century] The shape and movement of a *cylinder* are captured in the word's origin. *Cylinder* comes via Latin from Greek *kulindros* 'roller', from *kulindein* 'to roll'.

cymbal [Old English] The shape of a cymbal is central to its name: it comes via Latin *cymbalum* from Greek *kumbalon*, from *kumbē* 'cup'. The word was readopted in Middle English from Old French *cymbale*.

cynic [mid 16th century] The word started out with reference to a member of a school of ancient Greek philosophers who displayed a contempt for ease and pleasure; this movement, founded by Antisthenes, flourished in the 3rd century BC and was revived in the 1st century AD. From Latin *cynicus*, from Greek *kunikos*, *cynic* is probably originally from *Kunosarges*, the name of a gymnasium where Antisthenes taught, but it was popularly taken to mean 'doglike, churlish': *kuōn*, *kun-*, 'dog' became a nickname for a Cynic.

cyst [early 18th century] *Cyst* is from late Latin *cystis*, from Greek *kustis* 'bladder'. The word in English describes a bladderlike sac containing fluid, or a protective vesicle.

Dd

dab [Middle English] *Dab* is symbolic of a light striking movement. Sometimes this lightness of touch is translated as expertise. The verb **dabble** (mid 16th century) is either a frequentative (= verb of repeated action) of *dab* or comes from obsolete Dutch *dabbelen*. The phrase:

■ **dab hand** is recorded from the 1820s; the element *dab* in this expression was in use before 1700 for 'expert', 'skilful person'. It may be a derivative of *dab* 'touch lightly', or possibly a corruption of *adept* and *dapper*, but this is merely conjecture.

dad [mid 16th century] This is probably imitative of an infant's speech when early syllables include the repetition of *da*. **Daddy**, recorded slightly earlier, is based on *dad*.

dado [mid 17th century] The architectural term *dado* first denoted the main part of a pedestal above the base. It is an Italian word whose original literal meaning was 'dice or cube', from Latin *datum* 'something given', 'starting point'.

daft [Old English] Old English *gedæfte* meant 'mild, meek' and is Germanic in origin; it is related to Gothic *gabadan* 'become or be fitting'. The sense 'lacking intelligence, silly' arose in Middle English; a comparable development is seen in the synonym *silly* which moved from a notion of 'defenceless, innocent' to 'foolish'. *Daft* often has a notion of indulgence associated with the word, from an early semantic core of 'inoffensive'. An idea of 'playfulness' is also involved (R. Burns *Twa Dogs*: In a frolic daft). Possibly related to *daft* is informal **daffy** 'mildly eccentric' (late 19th century), from northern English dialect *daff* 'simpleton'.
→ DEFT

dagger [late Middle English] This is perhaps from the obsolete verb *dag* 'to pierce, stab', influenced by Old French *dague* 'long dagger'.

dainty [Middle English] *Dainty* in early examples meant 'titbit, (something) pleasing to the palate'. The source is Old French *daintie*, *deintie* 'choice morsel, pleasure', from Latin *dignitas* 'worthiness or beauty'. Latin *dignus* 'worthy' is the base.

dairy [Middle English] The Middle English spelling *deierie* was from *deie* 'dairymaid', which in Old English was *dæge* 'female servant'. The origin is Germanic; it is related to Old Norse *deigja* as well as to English *dough* and the second element of Old English *hlæfdige* 'woman to whom homage is due'.
→ DOUGH; LADY

dais [Middle English] This was originally a table for distinguished guests. The source is Old French *deis*, from Latin *discus* which first meant 'disc or dish' and later came to mean 'table'. The sense development in English moved from 'table' to 'high table on a platform' to 'raised end of the hall occupied by the high table' to 'canopy covering this raised area'. Little used after the Middle English period, the word was revived by antiquarians in the early 19th century with the disyllabic pronunciation.
→ DISH

daisy [Old English] Old English *dæges ēage* meant 'day's eye' because the flower opens in the morning and closes at night concealing its yellow disk. *Push up daisies* is an evocative idiom used to mean 'be in one's grave' (W. Owen *Poems*: 'Pushing up daisies' is their creed, you know).

dale [Old English] Old English *dæl* is Germanic in origin, related to Old Norse *dalr*, Dutch *dal*, and German *Tal*. The semantic root appears to be 'deep or low place'. The word is a living geographical name in the north, probably from the native word being reinforced by Norse: *Clydesdale*, *Borrowdale*, *Dovedale*.
→ DELL

dally [Middle English] *Dally* 'linger', 'have a casual romantic liaison', is from Old French *dalier* 'to chat' (commonly used in Anglo-Norman French). The origin is unknown. **Dalliance** started out with the meaning 'conversation' in Middle English and is based on *dally*. **Dilly-dally** arose in the early 17th century and is a reduplication (= repetition of an element with a small change) of *dally*.

dam¹ [Middle English] *Dam* 'a barrier' is from Middle Low German or Middle Dutch. Related are Dutch *dam* and German *Damm*, as well as the Old English verb *fordemman* 'to close up'.

dam² [late Middle English] The female parent of an animal, especially a domestic mammal, is known as a *dam*; currently the word is commonly used in connection with horses. Early examples however show the term as meaning 'a human mother'. The word is an alteration of *dame*.

damage [Middle English] An Old French word is the source, from *dam*, *damne* 'loss or damage', from Latin *damnum* 'loss or hurt'. Slang use meaning 'cost' as in *what's the damage?* dates from the mid 18th century.
➜ DAMN

dame [Middle English] In early use *dame* was recorded as meaning a 'female ruler'; it comes via Old French from Latin *domina* 'mistress'. The role of *pantomime dame* dates from the early 20th century. Latin *domina* also gave rise to **damsel** in Middle English, from Old French *dameisele*, *damisele*.

damn [Middle English] This is from Old French *dam(p)ner*, from Latin *dam(p)nare* 'inflict loss on', from *damnum* 'loss, damage'. In expressions such as *darn it!*, **darn** is a euphemism of the expletive *damn*; it was originally a US usage dating from the late 18th century. Middle English **damnation** is via Old French from Latin *dam(p)natio(n-)*.

damp [Middle English] 'Noxious inhalation' was the early noun sense. It is West Germanic in origin and related to a Middle Low German word meaning 'vapour, steam, smoke'.
➜ DANK

dance [Middle English] The verb is from Old French *dancer*, the noun from Old French *dance*; the origin is obscure. The Romanic form is generally thought to be an adoption of an Old High German word meaning 'to draw (towards oneself)', 'to stretch'.

dandelion [late Middle English] This name is from French *dent-de-lion*, a translation of medieval Latin *dens leonis* 'lion's tooth' because of the jagged shape of the plant's leaves.

dandruff [mid 16th century] The first element is unknown; the second (-*ruff*) is perhaps related to Middle English *rove* 'scurfiness'.

dandy [late 18th century] This is perhaps a shortened form of 17th-century *Jack-a-dandy* 'conceited fellow', in which the last element represents *Dandy*, a pet form of the given name *Andrew*. In English *dandy* was in vogue in London around 1813–1819 for the 'swell' (= fashionable man) of the period. One meaning is 'splendid', reflected in the phrase *fine and dandy* which originated in the US.

danger [Middle English] This is from Old French *dangier*, based on Latin *dominus* 'lord'. The original sense was 'jurisdiction or power of a lord or master', specifically the 'power to harm' (Shakespeare *Merchant of Venice*: You stand within his danger, doe you not). From this arose the current meaning 'potential for causing harm'. Middle English **dangerous** meant 'arrogant', 'fastidious', and 'difficult to please' at first: it is from Old French *dangereus*, from *dangier*.

dank [Middle English] *Dank* is probably of Scandinavian origin and related to Swedish *dank* 'marshy spot'. There is no original connection between *dank* and *damp* but recently the latter has acquired the sense of *dank* and has largely taken its place.

dapper [late Middle English] This is probably from a Middle Low German or Middle Dutch word meaning 'strong, stout'. In early use it was appreciative but now it is sometimes used humorously.

Darby and Joan [late 18th century] This phrase for 'a devoted old married couple' is from a poem written in 1735 in the *Gentleman's Magazine*, which contained the lines: 'Old Darby, with Joan by his side … They're never happy asunder.'

dare [Old English] Old English *durran* is of Germanic origin; related to Gothic *gadaursan*, from an Indo-European root shared by Greek *tharsein* and Sanskrit *dhṛṣ-* 'be bold'. The original 3rd person singular *he dare* and, in the past tense, *he durst*, remain undisturbed to the present day: northern dialects retain them and they are often preferred in literary English (Tennyson *In Memoriam*: Nor dare she trust a larger lay). The compound:
■ **dare-devil** is a contraction of *someone ready to dare the devil* and is one of several phrases where this type of formation occurs (*cutthroat*, *scarecrow*).

dark [Old English] Old English *deorc* is probably of Germanic origin and distantly related to German *tarnen* 'conceal'. There is no corresponding adjective in other Germanic languages, but the Old High German verb *tarchanjan* which would correspond to a West German form *darknjan* (unattested), appears to contain the same stem.

darling [Old English] Old English *dēorling* became *dereling* in Middle English and is related to *dear*. The letters *er* followed by a consonant regularly undergo change to *ar*, which resulted in the modern spelling.

darn [early 17th century] *Darn* 'mend' may be from dialect *dern* 'to hide', from Old English *diernan*, which is West Germanic in origin; a comparable form is Middle Dutch *dernen* 'stop holes in (a dyke)'. The English verb appears about 1600 from which time many examples start to be recorded; it may be that this way of repairing a tear or hole was introduced during this period.

dart [Middle English] This is from the accusative of Old French *darz*, *dars*, from a West Germanic word meaning 'spear, lance'.

dash [Middle English] The early recorded sense of *dash* was 'strike forcibly against'. It is probably symbolic of forceful movement and related to Swedish and Danish *daska* 'to slap with an open hand'. Onomatopoeic words such as *bash*, *clash*, and *crash* are comparable. In the 16th century *dash* was commonly used in the sense 'destroy, confound, bring to nothing' in connection with the rejection of a bill in parliament: this sense survives in the phrase *dash someone's hopes*. The compound:
■ **dashboard** (mid 19th century) was originally a board or leather apron on the front of a vehicle to stop mud from being splashed by the horses' heels into the interior; it also referred to movable side pieces of a cart which served the same protective purpose. This was transferred to the control panel in motor vehicles at the beginning of the 20th century.

dastard [late Middle English] A *dastard* now refers to a 'despicable coward' (Scott *Lochinvar*: A laggard in love and a dastard in war) but originally it meant 'stupid person'. It is probably from *dazed*, influenced by *dotard* and *bastard*. **Dastardly** is recorded from the mid 16th century in the sense 'dull or stupid': the form is based on *dastard*.

data [mid 17th century] This was originally recorded as a term in philosophy referring to 'things assumed to be facts'. It is the Latin plural of **datum** 'a piece of information', literally 'something given', the neuter past participle of *dare* 'give'. Although plural, *data* is often treated as a singular as a mass noun meaning 'information'. The common current application of the word is in computing contexts.
→ DADO

date[1] [Middle English] This word specifying time is via Old French from medieval Latin *data*, the feminine past participle of *dare* 'give'. It comes from the Latin formula used in dating letters, *data* (*epistola*) ... '(letter) given or delivered ...' when recording a particular time or location (e.g. *Data Romae prid. Kal. Apr.* 'given at Rome on the 31st March').

date[2] [Middle English] The source of the word *date* referring to a fruit and the plant bearing it, is Old French, via Latin from Greek *daktulos* 'finger', because of the fingerlike shape of the plant's leaves.

daub [late Middle English] This is from Old French *dauber* 'clothe in white', 'clothe', 'white-

wash', 'plaster', from Latin *dealbare* 'whiten, whitewash'. The Latin base is *albus* 'white'. All the English uses have developed from that of 'plaster'.

daughter [Old English] Old English *dohtor* is Germanic in origin. Related to Dutch *dochter* and German *Tochter*, it is from an Indo-European root shared by Greek *thugatēr*. The spelling *daughter* appeared in the 16th century when it was substituted in Cranmer's edition of the Bible for Coverdale's and Tindale's *doughter*: it was used by Shakespeare and later writers. This seems to have a southern origin.

daunt [Middle English] This is from Old French *danter*, from Latin *domitare*, a frequentative (= verb of repeated action) of *domare* 'to tame'. With 'taming' there has arisen a notion of 'intimidation'.

dawdle [mid 17th century] This is related to dialect *daddle*, *doddle* 'dally'.

dawn [late 15th century] *Dawn*, first recorded as a verb, is a back-formation (by removal of the suffix) from Middle English *dawning*, a verbal form expressing the 'beginning of daylight; appearance of light'. **Dawning** remains a literary word for 'dawn'; it is an alteration of earlier *dawing*, from Old English *dagian* 'to dawn', of Germanic origin.
→ DAY

day [Old English] Old English *dæg* is Germanic in origin and related to Dutch *dag* and German *Tag*. Late Middle English **daily** is based on *day*. There is no relationship with Latin *dies*; the semantic root is thought to be 'burn' associated with the heat of summer.

daze [Middle English] *Daze* is a back-formation (by removal of the suffix) from *dazed*, from Old Norse *dasathr* 'weary'; a comparable form is Swedish *dasa* 'lie idle'. In English the sense 'benumb with cold' may have been the earliest; in Icelandic the verb *dasa-sk* is 'become weary and exhausted from an effect such as cold'.

dazzle [late 15th century] The early sense was 'be dazzled'. It is a frequentative (= verb of repeated action) of the verb *daze*.
→ DAZE

WORDBUILDING

The prefix **de-** [from Latin *de* 'off, from'] adds the sense
■ **down, away** [descend]
■ **completely** [denude]
■ **formation from** [deverbal]

The prefix **de-** [via Old French *des-* from Latin *dis-*] also denotes removal or reversal [deaerate; de-ice]

deacon [Old English] Old English *diacon* came via ecclesiastical Latin from Greek *diakonos* 'servant, messenger, waiting man', which in ecclesiastical Greek meant 'Christian minister'. The feminine **deaconess** dates from late Middle English.

dead [Old English] Old English *dēad* is Germanic in origin and related to Dutch *dood* and German *tot*. An early spelling of **deadly** was *dēadlīc* (Old English) which meant 'mortal, in danger of death'.
→ DIE¹

deaf [Old English] Old English *dēaf* has a Germanic origin; it is related to Dutch *doof* and German *taub*, from an Indo-European root shared by Greek *tuphlos* 'blind'. The semantic root is probably 'dull in perception'.

deal¹ [Old English] Old English *dǣlan* meant 'divide', 'participate', and is Germanic in origin; it is related to Dutch *deel* and German *Teil* 'a part'. The sense 'divide' gave rise to 'distribute', hence 'give out cards' and 'inflict (a blow) on'; the sense 'participate' gave rise to 'have dealings with', hence 'take part in commercial trading' (e.g. *they were prohibited from dealing in the company's shares*) and 'take measures concerning something' (e.g. *deal with the economic crisis*).
→ DOLE

deal² [Middle English] The wood known as *deal* is from Middle Low German and Middle Dutch *dele* 'plank'.

dean [Middle English] This comes from Old French *deien*, from late Latin *decanus* 'chief of a group of ten', from Latin *decem* 'ten'. Modern senses of *dean* in English come from monastic and civil uses of the late Latin term, such as 'head or president of ten monks in a monastery', 'head of a body of canons of a cathedral church'.

dear [Old English] Old English *dēore* is Germanic in origin and related to Dutch *dier* 'beloved', also to Dutch *duur* and German *teuer* 'expensive'.

dearth [Middle English] The Middle English spelling was *derthe* (*dear* with the suffix *-th*) which had the early sense 'shortage and dearness of food' (F. Bacon *Of Seditions and Troubles*: The Causes and Motives of Seditions are … Dearths: Disbanded Souldiers). No example of the word has been found in Old English, but there is a correspondence with an Old Norse form meaning 'glory, splendour': this meaning was also found in English but it was a rare occurrence. English examples of the sense 'costliness' are also found but not frequently.

'Scarcity' in a general context, is a figurative and transferred sense.
→ DEAR

death [Old English] Old English *dēath* has a Germanic origin and is related to Dutch *dood* and German *Tod*.

debase [mid 16th century] The early senses recorded were 'humiliate' and 'belittle'; the form comes from *abase*, prefixed by *de-*. The word has been used in the context of lowering the value of a coin, by reducing the content of precious metal, since the early 17th century.
→ ABASE

debate [Middle English] *Debate* came via Old French, from the Latin prefix *dis-* (expressing reversal) and *battere* 'to fight'. **Debatable** (late Middle English) is from Old French, from *debatre* 'contend over', or from Anglo-Latin *debatabilis*, from the same source as *debate*.

debauch [late 16th century] This is from French *débaucher* meaning 'turn away from one's duty', 'entice away from the service of one's master', from Old French *desbaucher*. The ultimate origin is uncertain. French etymologists have suggested a derivation in French from *bauche* meaning 'place of work' (giving *desbaucher* 'draw away from the workshop'); also *bauche* 'a course of stones in building' has been suggested as a base (giving *desbaucher* 'bring order into disarray'). However, the meaning 'draw away from service', as in English, is the earliest recorded in French.

debenture [late Middle English] A *debenture* in early use was a voucher issued by a royal household, giving the right to claim payment for goods or services. It is probably from Latin *debentur* 'are owing' (from *debere* 'owe'), used as the first word of a certificate recording a debt. In the 17th century, vouchers known as *debentures* were given to soldiers and sailors certifying the audited amount of pay owing: the Parliamentary Army received these during the Civil War apparently from November 1641 onwards. In some cases such certificates were secured upon and redeemed in forfeited land, which was especially the case in Ireland. The current term for a 'long-term security, secured against assets', dates from the mid 19th century.

debilitate [mid 16th century] This is from Latin *debilitat-*, from the verb *debilitare*, 'to weaken', from *debilitas*, the source of Middle English **debility**. The base is Latin *debilis* 'weak'.

debit [late Middle English] 'Debt' was the early recorded sense of *debit*. The origin is French *débit*, from Latin *debitum* 'something

owed'. The verb sense 'remove from a customer's account' dates from the 17th century; the current noun sense 'a sum of money due', dates from the late 18th century.
→ DEBT

debonair [Middle English] Early examples showed *debonair* with the meanings 'meek' or 'courteous'. The word, very common in Middle English, comes from Old French *debonaire*, from the phrase *de bon aire* 'of good disposition'. Modern examples add a notion of 'lightness of heart'.

debris [early 18th century] This is an adoption of French *débris*, from obsolete *débriser* 'to break down'.

debt [Middle English] An early spelling was *dette*; it comes from Old French, based on Latin *debitum* 'something owed', the past participle of *debere* 'owe'. The related word **debtor**, also Middle English is from Old French *det(t)or*, from Latin *debitor*. The spelling change in both English words was in imitation of the Latin.

decade [late Middle English] A *decade* in early recorded examples referred to each of ten parts of a literary work. The word is via Old French and late Latin from Greek *deka* 'ten'. The reference to a period of ten years dates from the early 17th century.

decadence [mid 16th century] This is from French *décadence*, from medieval Latin *decadentia* 'a declining, a decaying'. In English the word is often applied to a particular period of decline in art such as the period following Raphael and Michelangelo.
→ DECAY

decant [mid 17th century] This verb is from medieval Latin *decanthare*, from the Latin prefix *de-* 'away from' and *canthus* 'edge, rim', a word used by the alchemists to denote the angular lip of a beaker. Greek *kanthos* 'corner of the eye' is the base.

decapitate [early 17th century] Latin *caput*, *capit-* 'head' is the base element of the word, which comes from late Latin *decapitare* 'decapitate'. The *de-* prefix expresses removal.

decay [late Middle English] *Decay* is from Old French *decair*, based on Latin *decidere* 'fall down or off'. The elements are *de-* 'away from' and *cadere* 'to fall'.

decease [Middle English] This is from Old French *deces*, from Latin *decessus*, the past participle (used as a noun meaning 'death') of *decedere* 'to die'. The Latin word was a euphemism for *mors* 'death'; in English *decease* is still euphemistic. It is the common legal and technical term used where the incidence of death is in question.

deceit [Middle English] *Deceit* is from the Old French past participle of *deceveir* 'deceive' used as a noun. Middle English **deceive** is from Old French *deceivre*, from Latin *decipere* 'catch, ensnare, cheat'. 'Ensnare, take unawares' was an early sense in English (Milton *Paradise Lost*: He it was whose guile ... deceived Tho mother of mankind). Related words are **deception** (late Middle English) from late Latin *deceptio(n-)*, and **deceptive** (early 17th century) from Old French *deceptif*, *-ive* or late Latin *deceptivus*.

decency [mid 16th century] In early examples *decency* had the sense 'appropriateness, fitness'. Latin *decentia* is the source, from *decent-* 'being fitting': this latter form gave rise to English **decent** meaning 'suitable, appropriate', recorded from the same period.

decide [late Middle English] *Decide* was 'bring to a settlement' in early contexts. It comes from French *décider*, from Latin *decidere* 'determine': the elements are *de-* meaning 'off' and *caedere* 'to cut'. **Decision**, also late Middle English, is from Latin *decisio(n-)*. The adjective **decisive** dates from the early 17th century and is from French *décisif*, *-ive*, from medieval Latin *decisivus*.

deciduous [late 17th century] *Deciduous* is based on Latin *deciduus*, from *decidere* 'fall down or off'.

decimal [early 17th century] This is from the medieval Latin adjective *decimalis*, from Latin *decimus* 'tenth'. The word in English and French, like the Latin source, once referred to tithes. It now commonly refers to numerical notation as in the *decimal classification system* or *Dewey system* (S. C. Bradford *Documentation*: In 1883, a decimal classification was introduced in the Bodleian Library ... and ... is still in use). In the phrase *decimal coinage*, the reference is to a monetary system where each successive division is ten times the value of that below it.

decimate [late Middle English] This is from Latin *decimat-*, from the verb *decimare* 'take as a tenth', from *decimus* 'tenth'. English *decimate* originally alluded to the Roman punishment of executing one man in ten of a mutinous legion. In Middle English the term *decimation* denoted the levying of a tithe, and later the tax imposed by Cromwell on the Royalists (1655).

decipher [early 16th century]
→ CIPHER

deck [late Middle English] This is probably from Middle Dutch *dec* 'covering, roof, cloak', *dekken* 'to cover'. Originally it referred to a canvas material used to make a covering on a ship; the term then came to mean the covering itself, and later a solid surface serving as either a roof or a floor. In nautical contexts, 16th-century writers sometimes use *deck* to mean 'poop', as in early seagoing craft there was only a deck at the stern. Nautical *deck* seems to be known in English 160 years earlier than in Dutch. The compound **double-decker**, originally a US usage, referred in the mid 19th century to a 'double-decked ship' and to a 'double-decked streetcar'. The use of the noun *deck* in English to refer to a pack of cards, dates from the late 16th century. The verb use also arose in the 16th century and primarily expresses the action of 'covering' or 'clothing' (Shakespeare *Hamlet*: I thought thy bride-bed to have deck sweet maide, And not have strew'd thy grave).

declare [Middle English] *Declare* is from Latin *declarare*, from *de-* 'thoroughly' and *clarare* 'make clear' (from *clarus* 'clear'). Related words dating from late Middle English are; **declaration** from Latin *declaratio(n-)*, from *declarare* 'make quite clear'; also **declarative** from Old French *déclaratif, -ive* or Latin *declarativus*.

decline [late Middle English] This is from Old French *decliner*, from Latin *declinare* 'bend down, turn aside': the elements here are *de-* 'down' and *clinare* 'to bend'. An early use of the word was with the meaning 'turn away from the straight course'; this developed into 'turn aside from, refuse'. **Declension** from the same period is from Old French *declinaison*, from *decliner* 'to decline'. The change in the ending was probably due to association with words such as *ascension*.

decompose [mid 18th century] Early use was with the meaning 'separate into simpler constituents'. It comes from French *décomposer*, from *de-* (a prefix expressing reversal) and *composer*.

decoration [late Middle English] Latin *decus, decor-* 'beauty, honour, or embellishment' is the base of both *decoration* (from late Latin *decoratio(n-)*) and **decorate** dating from the mid 16th century. The English verb originally meant 'to grace or honour' and comes from Latin *decoratus* 'embellished', the past participle of *decorare*.

decorum [mid 16th century] First used as a literary term denoting suitability of style, *decorum* comes from the neuter form of the Latin adjective *decorus* 'seemly'. The latter is also the base of the adjective **decorous** recorded from the mid 17th century in the sense 'appropriate, seemly'.

decoy [mid 16th century] At first the English word was simply *coy* (a place constructed for entrapping ducks). The source is Dutch *de kooi*

'the decoy', from Middle Dutch *de kouw* 'the cage': Latin *cavea* 'cage' is the base. This notion of confinement reflects the practice of using tamed ducks as *decoys* to lead wild ones along channels into captivity.

decrease [late Middle English] The noun is from Old French *decreis*, the verb from Old French *decreistre*, based on Latin *decrescere*, from *de-* 'down' and *crescere* 'grow'.

decree [Middle English] Early *decrees* were edicts issued by an ecclesiastical council to settle a point of doctrine or discipline. The word is from Old French *decre, decret*, from Latin *decretum* 'something decided', from *decernere* 'decide'. The *nisi* in the term **decree nisi** (late 19th century) is the Latin word for 'unless'; the phrase represents a court order stating when a marriage will end 'unless' a good reason to prevent divorce is produced.

decrepit [late Middle English] This word describing someone who is elderly and infirm owes its extended sense to the noise of creaking. The source is Latin *decrepitus*, from *de-* 'down' and *crepitus*, the past participle of *crepare* 'to rattle, creak'. **Decrepitude** dates from the early 17th century.

decry [early 17th century] *Decry*, now 'publicly denounce', formerly had the sense 'decrease the value of coins by royal proclamation'. The base is the verb *cry*.
→ CRY

dedicate [late Middle English] The early sense of *dedicate* was 'devote to sacred use by solemn rites'. The source is Latin *dedicat-* from the verb *dedicare* 'devote, consecrate'. The notion of introducing an artistic work such as a book or piece of music, with words addressed to a friend or patron, dates from the early 16th century. The adjective **dedicated** used to describe a person who is single-mindedly loyal and conscientious, arose in the mid 20th century. It is often extended and applied now in transport contexts in the sense 'allocated to a particular purpose', e.g. *dedicated route, dedicated service*. Late Middle English **dedication** is from Latin *dedicatio(n-)*.

deduce [late Middle English] Early examples of *deduce* included the sense 'lead or convey' as well as 'draw as a logical conclusion'. It is from Latin *deducere*, from *de-* 'down' and *ducere* 'lead'. A related late Middle English word is **deduct** from the Latin verb *deducere* 'take away'. *Deduct* and *deduce* were not distinguished in sense until around the middle of the 17th century. The noun **deduction** from Latin *deductio(n-)* is also a late Middle English word.

deed [Old English] Old English *dēd*, *dæd* is Germanic in origin and related to Dutch *daad* and German *Tat*, from an Indo-European root shared by the English word *do*. The early sense referred to an 'act'. Later, in Middle English, it became a legal term for a document that is signed and delivered usually concerning ownership of property.
→ DO

deem [Old English] Old English *dēman* also had the sense 'act as judge'. The word is Germanic in origin and is related to Dutch *doeman*.
→ DOOM

deep [Old English] The Old English adjective was *dēop*, and adverbial spellings were *dīope*, *dēope*. The origin is Germanic; Dutch *diep* and German *tief* are related. **Depth** is late Middle English, a word form based on *deep*.
→ DIP

deer [Old English] The Old English word *dēor* was also originally a term for any quadruped: the now archaic phrase *small deer* meaning 'small creatures collectively' reflects this early use (Shakespeare *King Lear*: But mice and rats, and such small deer, Hath been Tom's food for seven long year). The origin is Germanic and related words are Dutch *dier* and German *Tier*, also simply meaning 'animal'.

defame [Middle English] *Defame* is from Old French *diffamer*, from Latin *diffamare* 'spread an evil report', from *dis-* (expressing removal) and *fama* 'report'.

default [Middle English] This is from Old French *defaut*, from *defaillir* 'to fail', based on Latin *fallere* 'disappoint, deceive'. Early senses of the noun included 'lack' and 'defect'; a current legal use of the verb is 'failure to fulfil an obligation'.

defeat [late Middle English] Early recorded senses were 'undo, destroy, annul'; *defeat* comes from Old French *desfait* 'undone', the past participle of *desfaire*, from medieval Latin *disfacere* 'undo'. The word **defeatist** dates from the First World War and is from French *défaitiste*, from *défaite* 'defeat'.

defecate [late Middle English] Early use was in the sense 'clear of dregs, purify'. Latin *defaecat-* is the source of the form, from the verb *defaecare*, the elements of which are *de-* (expressing removal) and *faex*, *faec-* 'dregs'. The current sense dates from the mid 19th century.

defect [late Middle English] *Defect* meaning 'imperfection' was influenced by Old French *defect* 'deficiency'. It is from Latin *defectus*, the past participle of *deficere* 'desert or fail', from *de-* (expressing reversal) and *facere* 'do'. The verb *defect* (late 16th century) meaning 'abandon

one's country or a cause in favour of an opposing one' is also from the Latin verb *deficere*. The noun **defection** expressed the same early notion of 'falling short' and meant 'imperfection' and 'failure' (C. Brontë *Villette*: I underwent ... miserable defections of hope, intolerable encroachments of despair), as well as 'desertion'.

defend [Middle English] Latin *defendere* 'ward off', 'guard' (from *de-* 'off' and *-fendere* 'to strike') is the base of several words in English dating from the Middle English period. *Defend* is from Old French *defendre*; **defence** is from Old French *defens*, from late Latin past participles of *defendere*; **defender** is from Old French *defendeor*. The adjective **defensible** was first recorded as meaning 'capable of giving protective defence' when referring to such things as a weapon or fortified place: the direct source is late Latin *defensibilis*. The shortened form *fencible* is sometimes used to refer to a type of military corps used for defensive service in the home country. **Defensive** is from Old French *défensif*, *-ive*, from medieval Latin *defensivus*.
→ OFFENCE

defer¹ [late Middle English] One of the early meanings of *defer* 'put off to a later time' was 'put on one side'. The word comes from Old French *differer* which meant both 'defer' and 'differ', from Latin *differre*: the elements are *dis-* 'apart' and *ferre* 'carry'. In the 17th century, the English spelling was often *differ*.
→ DIFFER

defer² [late Middle English] *Defer* 'submit humbly' (e.g. *he deferred to Tim's superior knowledge*) is from Old French *deferer*, from Latin *deferre* 'carry away, refer (a matter)'. The base elements here are *de-* 'away from' and *ferre* 'carry'.

defiance [Middle English] In early contexts a *defiance* was a renunciation of an allegiance or friendship. It comes from Old French, from *defier* 'defy'. The word's use as a description of an act of open resistance to authority, dates from the early 18th century. The adjective **defiant** (late 16th century) is from French *défiant* or directly from the English noun *defiance*.

deficient [late 16th century] The origin of the word is Latin *deficient-* 'failing', from the verb *deficere*. *Deficient* was originally used in the theological phrase *deficient cause* denoting a failure or deficiency with a particular consequence. This concept first appeared in St Augustine in his discussion on the origin of evil: his doctrine was that evil lacked anything positive and therefore could have no *efficient* merely a *deficient* cause or result. This came

into vogue in English during the Calvinistic-Arminian controversy in the 16th-17th centuries. *Deficient* in general current use focuses on the notion of 'lack' and 'falling short'.
→DEFECT

deficit [late 18th century] This has come via French from Latin *deficit* 'it is lacking', from the verb *deficere*. The Latin word was used formerly in inventories to record what was missing.
→DEFECT

defile [late Middle English] *Defile* 'sully, spoil' is an alteration of the obsolete word *defoul*, from Old French *defouler* 'trample down'. The spelling was influenced by the obsolete verb *befile* 'befoul, defile'.

define [late Middle English] An early sense was 'bring to an end'. The source is Old French *definer* 'terminate, determine', from a variant of Latin *definire*, from *de-* (expressing completion) and *finire* 'finish' (from *finis* 'end'). **Definition**, dating from the same period, is from Latin *definitio(n-)*, from the verb *definire* 'set bounds to'.

definite [mid 16th century] This is from the Latin form *definitus* meaning 'defined, set within limits', the past participle of *definire*. **Definitive** was recorded from late Middle English and is from Old French *definitif, -ive*, from Latin *definitivus*, from the verb *definire*. *Definitive* is sometimes confused in use with *definite* but it has the additional notion of 'having an authoritative basis' (e.g. *the definitive biography*); *definite* simply means 'clearly decided' (e.g. *he is definite about his choice*).
→DEFINE

deflation [late 19th century] The early recorded sense was 'a release of air from something inflated'. The word is based on the English verb **deflate** from the same period, composed of the prefix *de-* (expressing reversal) and the element *-flate* as in *inflate*.
→INFLATE

deflect [mid 16th century] This is from Latin *deflectere*, from *de-* 'away from' and *flectere* 'to bend'. **Deflection** (early 17th century) is from late Latin *deflexio(n-)*, from *deflectere* 'bend away'.

deform [late Middle English] *Deform* is from Old French *desformer* via medieval Latin from Latin *deformare*, from *de-* (expressing reversal) and *forma* 'a shape'. Dating from the same period and based on the same verb is **deformation** (from Latin *deformatio(n-)*); **deformity** came via Old French from Latin *deformitas*, from *deformis* 'misshapen'.

defraud [late Middle English] This is from Old French *defrauder* or Latin *defraudare*, from *de-* 'from' and *fraudare* 'to cheat' (from *fraus*, *fraud-* 'fraud').

defray [late Middle English] This is from French *défrayer*, from *dé-* (expressing removal) and obsolete *frai* 'cost, expenses'. The noun base is medieval Latin *fredum* meaning 'a fine for breach of the peace'. The early general sense of *defray* was 'spend money'.

deft [Middle English] In early use meaning 'gentle, meek', *deft* is a variant of *daft*. It also had a notion of 'skilful' in early contexts and gradually acquired the sense 'neat in action', which also became transferred to 'neat in person': 'neat and pretty' is a use still found regionally in dialect.
→DAFT

defunct [mid 16th century] 'Deceased' was the first recorded sense. *Defunct* comes from Latin *defunctus* meaning 'dead', the past participle of *defungi* 'carry out, finish', from *de-* (expressing reversal) and *fungi* 'perform'. The current meaning, 'no longer in use or in fashion', dates from the mid 18th century.

defy [Middle English] The sense development of *defy* seems to have been: 'renounce an allegiance', 'declare hostility against' and 'issue a challenge to fight' (Milton *Paradise Lost*: Th'infernal Serpent ... Who durst defie th'Omnipotent to Arms). The source is Old French *desfier*, based on Latin *dis-* (expressing reversal) and *fidus* 'faithful'.

degenerate [late 15th century] This adjective comes from Latin *degeneratus* 'no longer of its kind', from the verb *degenerare*. The base is the Latin adjective *degener* 'debased', from *de-* 'away from' and *genus*, *gener-* 'race, kind'. In early examples, the 'change in kind' did not always imply debasement; it sometimes simply described a change in nature or character. The noun **degeneration** from the same period is from late Latin *degeneratio(n-)*, from the verb *degenerare* (source too of the English verb *degenerate*: mid 16th century).

degrade [late Middle English] *Degrade* is from Old French *degrader*, from ecclesiastical Latin *degradare*, from *de-* 'down, away from' and Latin *gradus* 'step'. The notion of moving to a lower rank was associated with dishonour. **Degradation** (mid 16th century) was first recorded in the sense 'deposition from an office or rank as a punishment': this is from Old French, or from ecclesiastical Latin *degradatio(n-)*, from the verb *degradare*.

degree [Middle English] Early senses of *degree* were 'step', 'tier', 'rank', or 'relative state'. The source of the form is Old French, based on Latin *de-* 'down' and *gradus* 'step or grade'. In heraldry, *degree* still refers to a 'step': this use, referring sometimes to the rung of a ladder is seen in early general contexts: (Shakespeare *Julius Caesar*: He then unto the Ladder turnes his Backe ... scorning the base degrees By which he did ascend). The academic use of *degree* arose from the preliminary steps (Bachelorship and License) at the Mastership or Doctorate, attained in stages; it dates from the 13th century and has been associated with the progress of an apprentice who, after serving his time, would gain a testimonial of skill and a licence to practise his particular trade.

deify [Middle English] The first recorded sense was 'make godlike in character'. The origin is Old French *deifier*, from ecclesiastical Latin *deificare*, from *deus* 'god'.

deign [Middle English] *Deign* is from Old French *degnier*, from Latin *dignare*, *dignari* 'deem worthy', from *dignus* 'worthy'. A now obsolete use expressed the idea 'accept graciously' (Shakespeare *Antony and Cleopatra*: Thy pallat then did daine The roughest Berry, on the rudest Hedge).

deject [late Middle English] Early use included the sense 'overthrow, abase, degrade' as well as the still current sense 'dishearten'. It is from the Latin verb *deicere*, from *de-* 'down' and *jacere* 'to throw'. **Dejection** dating from the same period is from Latin *dejectio(n-)*, from *deicere*.

delectable [late Middle English] *Delectable* 'giving delight' (Bunyan *Pilgrim's Progress*: The Shepherds there, who welcomed them ... unto the delectable Mountains) came via Old French from Latin *delectabilis*, from *delectare* 'to charm'. This word is rare now in ordinary speech, except when used ironically or humorously. Its pronunciation in Shakespeare put stress on the first syllable rather than the second, now currently widespread. The noun **delectation** came via Old French from Latin *delectatio(n-)*, from *delectare*.
→ DELIGHT

delegate [late Middle English] Both the noun and the verb are from the Latin verb *delegare* 'send on a commission', from *de-* 'down' and *legare* 'depute'. The noun **delegation** dates from the early 17th century: it meant both 'act or process of delegating' and 'delegated power'. The origin is Latin *delegatio(n-)*, from *delegare*.

delete [late Middle English] 'Destroy' was the early recorded sense of *delete*, from Latin *delet-*, the past participial form of the verb *delere* 'blot out, efface'.

deliberate [late Middle English] *Deliberate*, both as an adjective and verb, comes from Latin *deliberare* 'consider carefully', from *de-* 'down' and *librare* 'weigh'. The base is *libra* 'scales'. The saying *he who hesitates is lost* was first found in J. Addison's *Cato* [1713] in the form: In spite of all the virtue we can boast The woman that deliberates is lost. **Deliberation** is via Old French from Latin *deliberatio(n-)*, from the same verb. The direct source of **deliberative** (late 15th century) is either French *délibératif*, *-ive* or Latin *deliberativus*.

delicacy [late Middle English] Currently the word conveys a notion of 'fineness and sensitivity' but 'voluptuousness' and 'luxuriousness' were the senses first recorded for *delicacy*: the form is based on the adjective **delicate** whose early meanings included 'delightful' and 'charming'. Senses also expressed in Middle English, but which are now obsolete, included 'voluptuous', 'self-indulgent', 'fastidious', and 'effeminate'. The word is from French *délicat* or Latin *delicatus*, but the ultimate origin remains unknown. French *délicat* describes the quality 'of exquisite fineness' and is the source of both German *Delikatessen* and Dutch *delicatessen*, whence English **delicatessen** in the late 19th century. It was originally a US usage referring to prepared foods for sale.

delicious [Middle English] Early contexts include the sense 'characterized by sensuous indulgence'. The word came via Old French from late Latin *deliciosus*, from Latin *deliciae* (plural) 'delight, pleasure'.

delight [Middle English] The verb is from Old French *delitier*, the noun from Old French *delit*, from Latin *delectare* 'to charm, allure, please'. The *-gh-* was added in the 16th century by association with *light*; *delite* and *delyte* were common early spellings.

delineate [mid 16th century] 'Trace the outline of something' was the meaning found in early examples of *delineate*. It is from the Latin verb *delineare* 'to outline', which is based on *linea* 'line'. The Latin prefix *de-* means 'out, completely'. Current senses involve 'precision' either in indicating a boundary or in a description or portrayal of something.

delinquent [late 15th century] Latin *delinquent-* (from the verb *delinquere* 'to offend') is the source of the English form. The elements in the formation are *de-* 'away' and *linquere* 'to leave'. It is now typically used with regard to a young person involved in minor crime. The noun **delinquency** dates from the mid 17th century and is from ecclesiastical Latin *delinquentia*, from *delinquent-*.

delirium [mid 16th century] This is a Latin word adopted into English, from the verb *delirare* 'deviate, be deranged'. The literal meaning is 'deviate from the furrow', from *de-* 'away' and *lira* 'a ridge between furrows'.

deliver [Middle English] *Deliver* is from Old French *delivrer*, based on Latin *de-* 'away' and *liberare* 'set free'. The word's use to mean 'launch (a blow, an attack), throw (a ball)' arose towards the end of the 16th century. Middle English **deliverance** is from Old French *delivrance*, from the verb *delivrer*. **Delivery** (late Middle English) is from Anglo-Norman French *delivree*, the feminine past participle of *delivrer*.

dell [Old English] Germanic in origin, *dell*, used in poetic and literary language to mean 'small valley', is related to Dutch *del* and German dialect *Telle*.
→ DALE

delta [mid 16th century] This word for a triangular tract of sediment deposited at the mouth of a river owes its name to the the shape of the Greek letter *delta*. In geographical contexts, it was originally used specifically in the phrase *the Delta* referring to the River Nile.

delude [late Middle English] This is from Latin *deludere* 'to mock', from *de-* (here with pejorative force) and *ludere* 'to play'. The noun **delusion** at this same period, had the meaning 'act of deluding or of being deluded': it comes from late Latin *delusio(n-)*, from *deludere*. Late 15th-century **delusory** is from late Latin *delusorius*, from the same source verb.

deluge [late Middle English] This is from an Old French variant of *diluve* 'flood', from Latin *diluvium*, from *diluere* 'wash away'. The English word *antediluvian* meaning literally 'before the (biblical) Flood' (= very antiquated) is also based on Latin *diluvium*.

delve [Old English] Old English *delfan* 'to dig' is West Germanic in origin and is related to Dutch *delven*. Early use was literal but in late Middle English the verb came to mean 'dig into' in an investigative way.

demagogue [mid 17th century] In ancient Greece and Rome, a *demagogue* was often an orator who took on the cause and spoke in support of the common people. It is from Greek *dēmagōgos*, from *dēmos* 'the people' and *agōgos* 'leading' (from the verb *agein* 'to lead'). Now the word commonly refers to a political leader who seeks support by appealing to popular prejudices.

demand [Middle English] The noun is from Old French *demande*, the verb from Old French *demander*. Latin *demandare* meant 'hand over, entrust' but the sense 'demand' developed in

medieval Latin. The base elements are *de-* 'formally' and *mandare* 'to order'.

demean [early 17th century] In *demean* ('cause a severe loss in the dignity of and respect for somebody or something') *de-* 'away, down' is prefixed to the adjective *mean*, on the pattern of *debase*.

demeanour [late 15th century] This comes from the archaic Middle English verb *demean*, which in early use meant 'manage, control' and later was used reflexively to mean 'conduct oneself', e.g. *no man demeaned himself so honourably*. The source was Old French *demener* 'to lead', based on Latin *de-* 'away' and *minare* 'drive (animals), drive on with threats'. *Demeanour* refers to 'behaviour'; the word was probably influenced by the obsolete noun *havour* 'behaviour'.

demented [mid 17th century] This is the past participle of the earlier verb *dement* meaning 'drive mad' which came from Old French *dementer* or late Latin *dementare*. The Latin adjective *demens* 'out of one's mind', is the base of this and of **dementia** (early 19th century).

demise [late Middle English] Early use was as a legal term; it is still used with reference to the conveyance of an estate by will or lease. The source is an Anglo-Norman French word, from Old French *desmettre* 'to dismiss', which in the reflexive meant 'abdicate'; it is based on Latin *dimittere* 'to dismiss'. *Demise* now is essentially 'end', whether this be a person's death (*her tragic demise*), or failure (*demise of industry*), or transfer of property.
→ DISMISS

democracy [late 16th century] This comes from French *démocratie*, via late Latin from Greek *dēmokratia*, from *dēmos* 'the people' and *-kratia* 'power, rule'. **Democratic** is recorded from the early 17th century and is from French *démocratique*, via medieval Latin from Greek *dēmokratikos*, from *dēmokratia*. A **democrat** (late 18th century) first signified an opponent of the aristocrats in the French Revolution of 1790; French *démocrate* is the source, formed on the pattern of *aristocrate* 'aristocrat'.

demolish [mid 16th century] This comes from French *démoliss-*, the lengthened stem of *démolir*, from Latin *demoliri*. The formative elements are *de-* (expressing reversal) and *moliri* 'construct' (from *moles* 'mass'). **Demolition** dating from the same period, is via French from Latin *demolitio(n-)*.

demon [Middle English] This is from medieval Latin, from Latin *daemon*, from Greek *daimōn* 'deity, genius'; the English sense 'evil spirit' is from Latin *daemonium* 'lesser spirit', from Greek *daemonion*. The spelling **daemon** was common from the mid 16th century until the 19th century. From the 1980s, this term has been in use in computing for a background process handling requests for services such as print spooling and file transfer: it is perhaps from *d(isk) a(nd) e(xecution) mon(itor)* or from *de(vice) mon(itor)*, but it could be merely a transferred use of *demon*. The device stays dormant when not required.

demonstrate [mid 16th century] Latin *demonstrare* 'to point out' gave rise to English *demonstrate* which had the same meaning in early contexts. Essentially there is a notion of 'making aware in a clear and public way' which led in the mid 19th century to a connection with public protest. The same Latin verb is the source of several words recorded from late Middle English: **demonstrable** (from Latin *demonstrabilis*); **demonstration** (from Latin *demonstratio(n-)*) whose meanings included 'proof provided by logic' and 'sign, indication'; also **demonstrative** (from Old French *demonstratif, -ive*, from Latin *demonstrativus*) which meant 'serving as conclusive evidence of' and 'making manifest'.

demur [Middle English] *Demur* 'raise doubts or objections', was first recorded as meaning 'linger, delay'. The source of the verb is Old French *demourer*, based on Latin *de-* 'away, completely' and *morari* 'delay'.

demure [late Middle English] Early meanings of *demure* were 'sober, serious, reserved'. The origin is perhaps Old French *demoure*, the past participle of *demourer* 'remain, stay', influenced by Old French *mur* 'grave' (from Latin *maturus* 'ripe or mature'). The sense 'reserved, shy' dates from the late 17th century.
→ DEMUR

den [Old English] Old English *denn* 'wild animal's lair' has a Germanic origin and is related to German *Tenne* 'threshing floor' and English *dene* 'vale'. The word came to be used for a private room set aside for work, in the late 18th century; a century later examples of the word are recorded referring to a child's hideaway 'home'.

denigrate [late Middle English] Early use was recorded as 'blacken, make dark'. Latin *denigrare* 'to blacken' is the source, from *de-* 'away, completely' and *nigrare* (from *niger* 'black'). The sense has developed into the figurative 'disparage'.

denim [late 17th century] The original phrase was *serge denim*, from French *serge de Nîmes* which was a kind of serge from the manufacturing town of *Nîmes* in France.

denote [late 16th century] *Denote* 'be a sign of', 'stand as a name for' is from French *dénoter* or Latin *denotare*, from *de-* 'thoroughly' and *notare* 'observe, note'. The root is Latin *nota* 'a mark'.

denounce [Middle English] The original senses recorded were 'proclaim, announce' and 'proclaim someone wicked, cursed, a rebel, etc.'. The source is Old French *denoncier*, from Latin *denuntiare* 'give official information', based on *nuntius* 'messenger'.

dent [Middle English] *Dent* was first recorded as a noun designating a blow with a weapon; the word is a variant of *dint*.
→ DINT

dentist [mid 18th century] *Dentist* and **denture** (late 19th century) are both based on French *dent* 'tooth', from Latin *dens, dent-*. **Dentition** recorded earlier (late 16th century) first denoted the development of teeth as a process: it comes from Latin *dentitio(n-)*, from *dentire* 'teethe'.

denude [late Middle English] This is from Latin *denudare*, from *de-* 'completely' and *nudare* 'to bare' (from *nudus* 'naked').

deny [Middle English] The Latin elements *de-* 'formally' and *negare* 'say no' form the base of *deny*. The direct source of the word is Old French *deni-*, the stressed stem of *deneier*, from Latin *denegare*.

depart [Middle English] *Depart* is from Old French *departir*, based on Latin *dispertire* 'to divide'. The original sense was 'separate', also 'take leave of each other', which gave rise to 'go away'. **Departure** was recorded in late Middle English and is from Old French *departeure*, from the verb *departir*.

department [late Middle English] This is from Old French *departement*, from *departir* 'depart'. The original sense was 'division or distribution', later 'separation', hence the notion of 'a separate part' (mid 18th century) whether referring to a division of a company or an administrative district of a country.
→ DEPART

depend [late Middle English] Early senses included 'hang down' and 'wait or be in suspense'. The source of the word is Old French *dependre*, from Latin *dependere*, from *de-* 'down' and *pendere* 'hang'. The noun **dependent** or **dependant**, now 'a person who depends on another', referred to a dependency in late Middle English: from Old French, the literal meaning is 'hanging down from'. Up to the 16th century, both the noun and the adjective ended in *-ant* reflecting the French participial form. Now the adjective is consistently spelt *dependent*; the spelling change was due to association with the Latin participial stem *dependent-*. The noun *dependant* however has shown variations in modern British and US English spelling, with the variant *-ent* ending becoming standard. Another related form is **dependency** (late 16th century) which is commonly used to denote a country or province subject to the control of another. The phrase *dependency culture* dates from the 1980s; it describes a social or political climate in which people rely on the State to provide for them.

depict [late Middle English] This is from Latin *depict-*, from the verb *depingere* 'portray', from *de-* 'completely' and *pingere* 'to paint'.

depilatory [early 17th century] The Latin adjective *depilatorius* is the source of *depilatory*. The base verb is Latin *depilare* 'strip of hair', from *de-* (expressing removal) and *pilare* (from *pilus* 'hair').

deplete [early 19th century] This comes from the from the Latin verb *deplere*, from *de-* (expressing reversal) and *plere* 'fill' (from *plenus* 'full'). Early use was in medical contexts describing the emptying of the bodily system by bleeding or purgatives.

deplore [mid 16th century] The early senses of *deplore* were 'weep for' and 'regret deeply'. The word is from French *déplorer* or Italian *deplorare*: their source is Latin *deplorare*, from *de-* 'away, thoroughly' and *plorare* 'bewail'. **Deplorable** (early 17th century) is from French *déplorable* or late Latin *deplorabilis*, from the verb *deplorare*.

deploy [late 18th century] *Deploy* 'move into position' often used in military contexts, is from French *déployer*, from Latin *displicare* and late Latin *deplicare* 'unfold'. The formative elements are *dis-*, *de-* 'un-' and *plicare* 'to fold'.
→ DISPLAY

deport [late 16th century] This was first recorded meaning 'conduct oneself in a certain manner'; it is from French *déporter*, from Latin *deportare*, from *de-* 'away' and *portare* 'carry'. The word's use to mean 'expel from a country' dates from the mid 17th century. **Deportment** (early 17th century) denoted behaviour in general and is from French *déportement*, from the verb *déporter*.

depose [Middle English] This is from Old French *deposer*, from Latin *deponere* 'lay aside'. The early sense was 'remove from office'. A now obsolete sense was 'put aside for safekeeping' which is associated with **deposit** recorded from the late 16th century, found especially in the phrases *in deposit* or *on deposit*. The noun comes from Latin *depositum*, the verb from

medieval Latin *depositare*, both from Latin *deponere*.

depot [late 18th century] A *depot*, now 'a place for storage', was initially an 'act of depositing'. It comes from French *dépôt*, from Latin *depositum* 'something deposited'.
→ DEPOSE

deprave [late Middle English] The first recorded sense of *deprave* was 'pervert the meaning or intention of something': it comes from Old French *depraver* or Latin *depravare*, from *de-* 'down, thoroughly' and *pravus* 'crooked, perverse'. 'Corrupt in moral character or habits' was a sense that arose early in English. **Depravity** dating from the mid 17th century is an alteration (influenced by *deprave*) of obsolete *pravity*, from Latin *pravitas* based on *pravus*.

deprecate [early 17th century] *Deprecate* 'express disapproval of' meant 'pray against' in early examples. It is from Latin *deprecari* 'pray against (as being evil)', from *de-* (expressing reversal) and *precari* 'pray'.

depreciate [late Middle English] The first sense recorded for *depreciate* was 'disparage'. The source of the word is late Latin *depreciare*, from Latin *de-* 'down' and *pretium* 'price'. The transitive 'lower the market price of' is a sense which arose in the mid 17th century.

depress [late Middle English] The notion of 'weight' is at the core of *depress* which comes from Old French *depresser*, from late Latin *depressare*; this is a frequentative (= verb of repeated action) of *deprimere* 'press down'. The noun **depression**, also late Middle English, is from Latin *depressio(n-)*, from *deprimere*. **Depressive** recorded from the early 17th century, is from French *dépressif*, *-ive* or medieval Latin *depressivus*, from *deprimere*.

deprive [Middle English] 'Depose from office' was the early sense of *deprive*: it comes via Old French from medieval Latin *deprivare*, from *de-* 'away, completely' and *privare* 'bereave, deprive'. **Deprivation** (late Middle English in the sense 'removal from office') is from medieval Latin *deprivatio(n-)*, from the verb *deprivare*.
→ PRIVATE

deputy [late Middle English] *Deputy* is from Old French *depute*, from late Latin *deputatus*; the source verb is Latin *deputare* 'consider to be, assign', from *de-* 'away' and *putare* 'think over, consider'. This Latin verb is the base too of **depute** and **deputation** (both late Middle English): a *deputation* was originally an 'appointment to an office or function'.

derange [late 18th century] This is from French *déranger*, from Old French *desrengier*, literally 'move from orderly rows'. The senses 'make insane' and 'throw into confusion, disarrange' were both found in early contexts in English.

derelict [mid 17th century] This is from Latin *derelictus*, the past participle of *derelinquere* 'abandon', from *de-* 'completely' and *relinquere* 'forsake'.

deride [mid 16th century] Latin *deridere* 'scoff at' has given *deride* in English as well as the earlier noun **derision** (recorded in late Middle English): this came via Old French from late Latin *derisio(n-)*. **Derisory** meant 'derisive' in the early 17th century and is from late Latin *derisorius*; **derisive** was formed in the mid 17th century by adding the suffix *-ive* to *derision*.

derive [late Middle English] *Derive* was 'draw a fluid through or into a channel' in early contexts. It is from Old French *deriver* or Latin *derivare*, from *de-* 'down, away' and *rivus* 'brook, stream'. **Derivation**, a word from the same period, often referred specifically to the drawing of pus or blood, but also had the sense 'formation of a word from another word'. The source is Latin *derivatio(n-)*, from the verb *derivare*. **Derivative** was first recorded as an adjective meaning 'having the power to draw off', and as a noun meaning 'a word derived from another'. It comes from French *dérivatif*, *-ive*, from Latin *derivativus*.

derogatory [early 16th century] The early sense recorded was 'impairing in force or effect'. Late Latin *derogatorius*, based on the verb *derogare* 'abrogate', is the source of the form in English. The Latin base elements are *de-* 'aside, away' and *rogare* 'ask'.

derrick [early 17th century] A *derrick*, now a type of crane, first denoted a hangman as well as the gallows structure. The word comes from the surname of a London hangman.

descend [Middle English] This comes from Old French *descendre*, from Latin *descendere*, from *de-* 'down' and *scandere* 'to climb'. The noun **descent** dating from the same period is from Old French *descente*, from *descendre*.

describe [late Middle English] Latin *describere*, from *de-* 'down' and *scribere* 'write', has given rise to *describe*; it is the base too of **description** (via Old French from Latin *descriptio(n-)*) and **descriptive** (mid 18th century from late Latin *descriptivus*).

desert[1] [late Middle English] *Desert* 'abandon' is from Old French *deserter*, from late Latin *desertare*, from Latin *desertus* 'left waste'.

desert[2] [Middle English] This word for a dry barren area of land came via Old French from late Latin *desertum* 'something left waste', the neuter past participle of *deserere* 'leave, forsake'.

desert[3] [Middle English] *Desert* as in the phrase *just deserts* came via Old French from *deservir* 'serve well'.
→ DESERVE

deserve [Middle English] The origin is Old French *deservir*, from Latin *deservire* 'serve well or zealously'.

design [late Middle English] The early verb meant 'to designate'. Latin *designare* 'to designate', reinforced by French *désigner*, is the source of the English form. The noun, first recorded as meaning 'a plan, a scheme' is via French from Italian. The word's use in the sense 'a drawing to show the look or function of something' dates from the mid 17th century.

designate [mid 17th century] This is from Latin *designare*, based on *signum* 'a mark'. Verb use dates from the late 18th century. The noun **designation** was found from late Middle English in the sense 'action of marking': this is from Latin *designatio(n-)*, from *designare*.

desire [Middle English] The noun is from Old French *desir*, the verb from Old French *desirer*, from Latin *desiderare* 'to desire'. Late Middle English **desirable** is from Old French, suggested by Latin *desiderabilis*, from *desiderare*.

desist [late Middle English] *Desist* is via Old French from Latin *desistere*, from *de-* 'down from' and *sistere* 'to stop'.

desk [late Middle English] The source of *desk* is medieval Latin *desca*, probably based on Provençal *desca* 'basket' or Italian *desco* 'table, butcher's block', both based on Latin *discus*. A *desk* referring to a reception point or counter, dates from the mid 20th century.
→ DISC

desolate [late Middle English] This is from Latin *desolatus*, the past participle of *desolare* 'abandon', from *de-* 'thoroughly' and *solus* 'alone'. **Desolation**, also late Middle English, is from late Latin *desolatio(n-)*, from *desolare*.

despair [Middle English] 'Loss of hope' is the core notion of *despair*. The noun is via Anglo-Norman French from Old French *desespeir*; the verb from Old French *desperer*, from Latin *desperare*, from *de-* 'down from' and *sperare* 'to hope'. **Desperation** (late Middle English) came via Old French from Latin *desperatio(n-)*. **Desperate** originally meant 'in despair' in late Middle English and is from Latin *desperatus* 'deprived of hope'. The noun **desperado**

dating from the early 17th century, is a pseudo-Spanish alteration of the obsolete noun *desperate*. Both *desperate* and *desperado* originally denoted a person in despair or in a desperate situation, hence someone made reckless by despair.

despise [Middle English] *Despise* is from Old French *despire*, from Latin *despicere*, from *de-* 'down' and *specere* 'look at'. **Despicable** 'deserving to be despised' (mid 16th century) comes from late Latin *despicabilis*, from *despicari* 'look down on'.

despite [Middle English] Originally used as a noun meaning 'contempt, scorn' in the phrase *in despite of*, *despite* is from Old French *despit*, from Latin *despectus* 'looking down on' (from *despicere*).
→ DESPISE

despond [mid 17th century] The source of *despond* is Latin *despondere* 'give up, abandon', from *de-* 'away' and *spondere* 'to promise'. The word was originally used as a noun in *Slough of Despond*, a deep boggy place in John Bunyan's *The Pilgrim's Progress*, between the City of Destruction and the gate at the beginning of the hero Christian's journey.

despot [mid 16th century] This is from French *despote*, via medieval Latin from Greek *despotēs* 'master, lord, absolute ruler' (in modern Greek the common appellation of a bishop). Originally, after the Turkish conquest of Constantinople, the term denoted a petty Christian ruler under the Turkish empire. The current sense dates from the late 18th century.

dessert [mid 16th century] This comes from the French past participle of *desservir* 'clear the table', from *des-* (expressing removal) and *servir* 'to serve'.

destiny [Middle English] *Destiny* is via Old French from Latin *destinata*, the feminine past participle of *destinare* 'make firm, establish'. Middle English **destined** is the past participle of *destine* 'predetermine, decree', from Old French *destiner* (from Latin *destinare*). **Destination**, late Middle English from Latin *destinatio(n-)* had the original sense 'directing someone or something towards a particular purpose'; later the meaning 'being destined for a particular place' arose, hence (from the early 19th century) the place itself.

destitute [late Middle English] The early sense was 'deserted, abandoned, empty'. It is from Latin *destitutus*, the past participle of *destituere* 'forsake', from *de-* 'away from' and *statuere* 'to place'.

destroy [Middle English] *Destroy* is from Old French *destruire*, based on Latin *destruere*, from

de- (expressing reversal) and *struere* 'build'. The word's use to mean 'ruin financially or professionally' dates from the late 18th century. **Destruction**, also Middle English, is from Latin *destructio(n-)*, from the verb *destruere*. **Destructive** dating from the late 15th century, came via Old French from late Latin *destructivus*, from the verb *destruere*.

desultory [late 16th century] *Desultory* 'lacking purpose or enthusiasm' also had the literal sense 'skipping about' in early use. The source is Latin *desultorius* 'superficial' (literally 'relating to a vaulter'), from *desultor* 'vaulter', from *desilire* 'to leap'.

detach [late 16th century] The early sense recorded for *detach* was 'discharge a gun'. The word is from French *détacher*, earlier *destacher*, from *des-* (expressing reversal) and *attacher* 'attach'. **Detachment** (mid 17th century) is from French *détachement*, from *détacher*. The word's application to a part of a military unit, is recorded early.

detail [early 17th century] *Detail* in early contexts, referred to 'minor items or events regarded collectively'. The origin of the noun is French *détail*; the verb comes from French *détailler*, from *dé-* (expressing separation) and *tailler* 'to cut'. Latin *talea* 'twig, cutting' is the base. The verb use in English meaning 'assign to a specific duty' (e.g. *the ships were detailed to keep watch*) dates from the early 18th century.

detain [late Middle English] *Detain* had the sense 'be afflicted with sickness or infirmity'. It comes from Old French *detenir*, from a variant of Latin *detinere*, from *de-* 'away, aside' and *tenere* 'to hold'. **Detention** in late Middle English meant 'the withholding of what is claimed or due'; the source of the word is late Latin *detentio(n-)*, from Latin *detinere* 'hold back'. In school contexts, the sense relating to a pupil being kept back as a punishment, dates from the late 19th century.

detect [late Middle English] This comes from Latin *detect-*, from the verb *detegere* 'uncover', from *de-* (expressing reversal) and *tegere* 'to cover'. The original senses were 'uncover, expose' and 'give someone away', and later 'expose the real or hidden nature of something or someone'. The current senses have been partly influenced by **detective**, a mid 19th-century word based on the form *detect*. **Detection** dates from the late 15th century when it meant 'revelation of what is concealed' from late Latin *detectio(n-)*, from Latin *detegere*.

deter [mid 16th century] The origin is Latin *deterrere*, from *de-* 'away from' and *terrere* 'frighten'. The word **deterrent** is recorded from the early 19th century and is from Latin *deterrent-*, from the verb *deterrere* 'deter'. Later in the century, the word came to denote a weapon owned by a State to ward off threat of attack.

detergent [early 17th century] Early use was as an adjective; the source of the word is Latin *detergent-* 'wiping away', from the verb *detergere*, from *de-* 'away from' and *tergere* 'to wipe'. The noun use arose towards the end of the 17th century.

deteriorate [late 16th century] At first the verb *deteriorate* was used transitively in the sense 'make worse'. It comes from late Latin *deteriorare* 'make worse', from Latin *deterior* 'worse'.

determine [late Middle English] This comes from Old French *determiner*, from Latin *determinare* 'limit, fix', from *de-* 'completely' and *terminare* 'terminate'. **Determination** in late Middle English meant both 'settlement of a controversy by a judge or by reasoning' and 'authoritative opinion'; the source is Old French from Latin *determinatio(n-)*. Also from the same period is **determinable** which came into English via Old French from late Latin *determinabilis* 'finite'.

detest [late 15th century] This is from Latin *detestari*, from *de-* 'down' and *testari* 'witness, call upon to witness' (from *testis* 'a witness'). The core semantic elements focus on the public and obvious nature of the dislike.

detonation [late 17th century] *Detonation* is from French *détonation*, from the verb *détoner*, from Latin *detonare* 'thunder down'. **Detonate** (early 18th century) is from the same Latin verb: the formative elements are *de-* 'down' and *tonare* 'to thunder'.

detriment [late Middle English] The sense first recorded was 'loss sustained by damage'. *Detriment* comes via Old French from Latin *detrimentum*. The first element *detri-* is the stem of *deterere* 'to wear away'.

deuce[1] [late 15th century] The *deuce* meaning 'the two on dice', 'a throw of two', 'a tennis score of equality where two clear points are required to win', is from Old French *deus* 'two', from Latin *duos*.

deuce[2] [mid 17th century] *Deuce* used as a euphemism for the devil as in *what the deuce!*, is from Low German *duus*, probably having the same origin as the *deuce* used in gaming: two aces at dice is the worst throw.

devastate [mid 17th century] This is from the Latin verb *devastare* 'lay waste', from *de-* 'thoroughly' and *vastare* 'lay waste'.

develop [mid 17th century] The first recorded sense was 'unfold, unfurl'. The word is from French *développer*, based on Latin *dis-* 'un-' and a second element of unknown origin found also in *envelop*. The verb's use in photographic contexts dates from the mid 19th century.

deviation [late Middle English] *Deviation* came via French from medieval Latin *deviatio(n-)*, from Latin *deviare* 'turn out of the way': the base elements are *de-* 'away from' and *via* 'way'. **Deviate** dates from the mid 16th century as an adjective in the sense 'remote': this form also comes from late Latin *deviare*. The verb dates from the mid 17th century.

device [Middle English] The original sense of *device* was 'desire or intention', found now only in *leave a person to his or her own devices*. This has come to be associated with the sense 'plan, scheme, trick' (as in *cunning device*). The source of the word form is Old French *devis*, based on Latin *divis-* 'divided', from the verb *dividere*.

devil [Old English] Old English *dēofol* (related to Dutch *duivel* and German *Teufel*) came via late Latin from Greek *diabolos* 'accuser, slanderer', a word used in the Septuagint to translate Hebrew *śatan* 'Satan'. The source is the Greek verb *diaballein* 'to slander', from *dia* 'across' and *ballein* 'to throw'.

devious [late 16th century] This is based on Latin *devius* (from *de* 'away from' and *via* 'way'). The original sense was 'remote or sequestered'; the later sense 'departing from the direct route' gave rise to the figurative sense 'deviating from the straight way' and hence 'skilled in underhand tactics'.

devise [Middle English] The verb is from Old French *deviser*, from the Latin verb *dividere* 'divide', a sense reflected in the original English sense of the verb. Another early use was to mean 'look at attentively, meditate on' which led to the notion of underhand plotting. The noun is a variant of *device*.

devoid [late Middle English] This is the past participle of obsolete *devoid* 'cast out', from Old French *devoidier*.

devolve [late Middle English] The sense in early contexts was 'roll down': it is from Latin *devolvere*, from *de-* 'down' and *volvere* 'to roll'. **Devolution** dates from the late 15th century in the sense 'transference by default': the source is late Latin *devolutio(n-)*, from Latin *devolvere*. Political use as 'transference of power to a local administration' dates from the mid 18th century.

devotion [Middle English] *Devotion* is from Latin *devotio(n-)*, from *devovere* 'consecrate'.

Divine worship and personal worship were both early senses in English. **Devote**, from the same verb, arose in the late 16th century in the sense 'dedicate formally, consecrate': the Latin elements are de- 'formally' and *vovere* 'to vow'.

devour [Middle English] *Devour* is from Old French *devorer*, from Latin *devorare*, from *de-* 'down' and *vorare* 'to swallow'.

devout [Middle English] Old French *devot*, from Latin *devotus* 'devoted' (the past participle of *devovere*), gave *devout* in English.
→ DEVOTION

dew [Old English] Old English *dēaw* is Germanic in origin; it is related to Dutch *dauw* and German *Tau*.

dexterity [early 16th century] At first *dexterity* referred to 'mental adroitness'. It is from French *dextérité*, from Latin *dexteritas*, from *dexter* 'on the right'. This adjective is also the base of **dexterous** which started out in the early 17th century with the meaning 'mentally adroit, clever'.

WORDBUILDING

The prefix **di-** [from Greek *dis* 'twice'] adds the sense

■ twice; two; double [dichromatic]

■ containing two atoms [dioxide]

The prefix **di-** [from Latin] is a variant spelling of **dis-**

WORDBUILDING

The prefix **dia-** [from Greek *dia* 'through'] adds the sense

■ through [diaphanous]

■ across [diameter]

■ apart [dialysis]

---

diabolic [late Middle English] This comes from Old French *diabolique* or ecclesiastical Latin *diabolicus*, from *diabolus* 'devil'.

diadem [Middle English] The Greek word *diadema* (from *diadein* 'to bind round') from which English *diadem* derives, meant 'band, fillet of cloth' and this was especially with reference to the regal fillet of Persian kings adopted by Alexander of Macedon and his successors. The band was either plain or decorated with jewels and was worn as a symbol of honour.

diagnose [mid 19th century] *Diagnose* is a back-formation (by removal of the suffix) from modern Latin **diagnosis** recorded in the late

17th century; the source is Greek, from *diagignōskein* 'distinguish, discern', from *dia* 'apart' and *gignōskein* 'recognize, know'.

diagonal [mid 16th century] *Diagonal* comes from Latin *diagonalis*, from Greek *diagōnios* 'from angle to angle', from *dia* 'through' and *gōnia* 'angle'.

diagram [early 17th century] Greek *dia* 'through' and *graphein* 'write' are the elements of the verb *diagraphein* 'mark out by lines', the source of the Latin and Greek noun *diagramma*: English *diagram* derives from this. The Greek word sometimes referred to a geometrical figure and sometimes to a written list or register: this sense of 'enumeration' was reflected in English in the 17th century but is now obsolete.

dial [Middle English] In early use a *dial* was a mariner's compass as well as an instrument telling the time by the length of the sun's shadow. The word comes from medieval Latin *diale* 'clock-dial', based on Latin *dies* 'day'. In English, the word has also become a slang term for 'face' since the early 19th century (*Punch* 5 April 1933: The major hesitated, and then a grin lamped up his dial).

dialect [mid 16th century] *Dialect* is from French *dialecte*, or via Latin from Greek *dialektos* 'discourse, way of speaking', from *dialegesthai* 'converse with'. Old French *dialectique* or its Latin source from Greek *dialektikē (tekhnē)* '(art) of debate' gave rise to the English form **dialectic** in philosophy: it was recorded in late Middle English as the art of investigating the truth of opinions. In early English use it was a synonym of 'logic' applied to formal rhetorical reasoning.
→ DIALOGUE

dialogue [Middle English] This comes from Old French *dialoge*, via Latin from Greek *dialogos*, from *dialegesthai* 'converse with, speak alternately': the formative elements are *dia* 'through' and *legein* 'speak'. The tendency in English is to confine the sense to a conversation between two people, perhaps by associating the prefix *dia-* with *di-*. The phrase *dialogue of the deaf* arose in the 1970s as a translation of the French phrase *dialogue de sourds*, describing a discussion in which neither party attempts to understand the other's point of view (H. Kissinger *The White House Years* 1977: The Nixon-Gandhi conversation that turned into a classic dialogue of the deaf).

diameter [late Middle English] This comes from Old French *diametre*, via Latin from Greek *diametros (grammē)* '(line) measuring across', from *dia* 'across' and *metron* 'measure'. **Diametric** is recorded from the mid 16th century in the sense 'of or along a diameter': it derives from Greek *diametrikos* (from *diametros* 'measuring across').

diamond [Middle English] *Diamond* is from Old French *diamant*, from medieval Latin *diamas*, *diamant-*, a variant of Latin *adamans*. The spelling was influenced by many technical words beginning with the prefix *dia-*. **Diamantine** (mid 16th century) originally meant 'hard as diamond' whereas the current sense is 'made from or reminiscent of diamonds'; the origin of the form is French *diamantin*, from *diamant* 'diamond'.
→ADAMANT

diaper [Middle English] Originally, *diaper* seems to have denoted a costly silk fabric, but the word has been applied since the 15th century to a linen fabric woven with a small simple pattern. It is from Old French *diapre*, from medieval Latin *diasprum*, based on Greek *dia* 'across' and *aspros* 'white' (the composite sense being either 'white at intervals' or 'pure white'). Babies' nappies were originally made from pieces of *diaper*, which gave rise to the US application of the word.

diaphanous [early 17th century] The word derives from medieval Latin *diaphanus*, from Greek *diaphanēs*, from *dia* 'through' and *phainein* 'to show'.

diaphragm [late Middle English] This comes from late Latin *diaphragma*, from Greek, from *dia* 'through, apart' and *phragma* 'a fence'. The Greek noun meant 'barrier, midriff'.

diary [late 16th century] Latin *diarium* is the source of English *diary*, a recording of daily events: the base is Latin *dies* 'day'.

diaspora [late 19th century] This is a Greek word used to refer to Jews living outside Israel or any large group of people living away from their homeland, from *diaspeirein* 'disperse': the semantic elements here are *dia* 'across' and *speirein* 'scatter'. The term originated in the Septuagint (Deuteronomy 28:25) in the phrase *esē diaspora en pasais basileias tēs gēs* 'thou shalt be a dispersion in all kingdoms of the earth'.

diatribe [late 16th century] In modern use a *diatribe* is a violent criticism of a person or work. The source is French, via Latin from Greek *diatribē* 'spending of time, discourse', from *dia* 'through' and *tribein* 'to rub'. An archaic use of the word in English was as a term for a critical dissertation.

dice
→DIE²

dicky [late 18th century] The colloquial word *dicky* meaning 'unhealthy, not functioning properly', was originally used to mean 'almost over'. It is perhaps from the given name *Dick*, in the old saying *as queer as Dick's hatband*.

dictate [late 16th century] The Latin verb *dictare* 'to dictate' gave rise to *dictate*, **dictator** (late Middle English adopted from Latin), **dictation** (mid 17th century from late Latin *dictatio(n-)*), and **dictatorial** (early 18th century based on Latin *dictatorius*).

diction [mid 16th century] This was first recorded as meaning 'phrase, word'. It comes from Latin *dictio(n-)*, from the verb *dicere* 'to say'. It currently refers to 'a style of enunciation' and 'the choice of words in writing or speech'. Apparently the word was not found in English dictionaries before Johnson.

dictionary [early 16th century] The medieval Latin phrase *dictionarium* (*manuale*) or *dictionarius* (*liber*) 'manual or book of words', is the source of *dictionary* in English.
→DICTION

didactic [mid 17th century] The origin is Greek *didaktikos*, from *didaskein* 'teach'.

diddle [early 19th century] A slang term for 'cheat', *diddle* is probably from the name of Jeremy *Diddler*, a character in Kenney's farce *Raising the Wind* (1803), who constantly borrowed small sums of money which he failed to repay. The name may have been based on an earlier verb *diddle* 'walk unsteadily, swerve', related to *dither*.

diddy [late 18th century] The informal word *diddy* meaning 'small' is probably a child's corruption of *little*.

didicoi [mid 19th century] This dialect word for a 'gypsy' is perhaps an alteration of Romany *dik akei* 'look here'.

die¹ [Middle English] The verb *die* is of Germanic origin, it is related to *dead*. No example of the word has been found in Old English literature; the sense was expressed by *steorfan* and *sweltan* or by a periphrase equivalent to *be dead*. It is generally believed that the word was lost early in Old English and re-adopted in late Old English or early Middle English from Old Norse *deyja*. The colloquial phrase *to die for* meaning 'highly desirable' is recorded as early as 1898 but most examples occur from the 1980s onwards. Of the compounds:
■ **diehard**, dating from the mid 19th century, for 'a person who strongly resists change', derives from the verbal expression *to die hard* meaning 'disappear or change slowly'.

die² [Middle English] This word for a small cube of which the faces are marked with spots numbering from one to six used in games of chance, is from Old French *de*, from Latin *datum* 'something given' (the neuter past participle of *dare* 'to give'). The inference in late popular Latin was that *datum* meant 'something given by lot or fortune' and was therefore applied to the dice that determined this. The singular *die* is uncommon in modern standard English; *dice* tends to be used for both the singular and the plural. The term *die* is also applied to various devices including an engraved stamp for impressing a design on a softer material, such as when coining money. Often used in pairs, these stamps are usually dissimilar (as the faces of a gaming die) for impressing unlike designs on the opposite sides of the thing stamped.

diet¹ [Middle English] The noun *diet* in the context of food, is from Old French *diete*, the verb from Old French *dieter*, via Latin from Greek *diaita* 'a way of life'. **Dietary** (late Middle English) is from medieval Latin *dietarium*, from Latin *diaeta*.

diet² [late Middle English] The *diet* that means 'legislative assembly' is from medieval Latin *dieta* which was both 'a day's work, wages, etc.', and 'meeting of councillors'. A famous example is the *Diet of Worms* in 1521, which was a meeting of the imperial *diet* of Charles V, the Holy Roman Emperor. Martin Luther was summoned to Worms (a town on the Rhine in western Germany), where he committed himself to the cause of Protestant reform. His teaching was later formally condemned in the Edict of Worms.

differ [late Middle English] Early senses included 'put off, defer'. The source of the word is Old French *differer* 'differ, defer', from Latin *differre* 'differ, defer' (from *dis-* 'from, away' and *ferre* 'carry'). The two meanings in French have continued from the 14th century to the present day, whereas in English, the two forms *differ* and *defer* have become distinct. Late Middle English **different** is via Old French from Latin *different-* 'carrying away, differing'; the verb **differentiate** (early 19th century) is from medieval Latin *differentiare* 'carry away from', from Latin *differentia* 'difference'.
➔ DEFER¹

difficult [late Middle English] This is a back-formation (by removal of the suffix) from **difficulty** dating from the same period in the senses 'requiring effort or skill' and 'something difficult'. This word was probably formed directly from Latin *difficultas*, from *dis-* (expressing reversal) and *facultas* 'ability, opportunity'.

diffident [late Middle English] The current meanings 'shy' and 'modest' derive from the early sense 'lacking confidence or trust in someone or something'. The source of the form is Latin *diffident-*, from the verb *diffidere* 'fail in trust', from *dis-* (expressing reversal) and *fidere* 'to trust'.

diffract [early 19th century] This is from Latin *diffringere* 'break into pieces', from *dis-* 'away, from' and *frangere* 'to break'.

diffuse [late Middle English] The verb is from Latin *diffundere* 'pour out', from *dis-* 'away' and *fundere* 'pour'; the adjective is via French *diffus* or Latin *diffusus* 'extensive', from *diffundere*. Late Middle English **diffusion** meant 'pouring out, effusion' and is from Latin *diffusio(n-)*, from *diffundere*.

dig [Middle English] This is perhaps from Old English *dic* 'ditch'.

digest [late Middle English] *Digest* is from Latin *digerere* 'distribute, dissolve, digest', from *di-* 'apart' and *gerere* 'carry'. This same verb is the base of the noun *digest* used for a compilation of information, from Latin *digesta* 'matters methodically arranged', from *digestus* 'divided'. Dating from the same period are: **digestible** (via Old French from Latin *digestibilis*) and **digestion** (via Old French from Latin *digestio(n-)*).

digit [late Middle English] This comes from Latin *digitus* 'finger, toe'; the use of the word to mean 'numeral (from 0 to 9)' is due to the practice of counting on the fingers. **Digital** dates from the late 15th century and is from Latin *digitalis*, from *digitus* 'finger, toe'; the technical use of the word in communications, arose in the mid 20th century.

dignity [Middle English] *Dignity* is from Old French *dignete*, from Latin *dignitas*, from *dignus* 'worthy'. This Latin adjective is also the base of the verb **dignify** (late Middle English) from Old French *dignefier*, from late Latin *dignificare*.

dilapidate [early 16th century] The early sense recorded for *dilapidate* is 'waste, squander'. The Latin verb *dilapidare* is the source, meaning literally 'scatter as if throwing stones', from *di-* 'apart, abroad' and *lapis, lapid-* 'stone'. Examples of the noun **dilapidation** 'squandering' are found from late Middle English: this is from late Latin *dilapidatio(n-)*, from Latin *dilapidare*.

dilate [late Middle English] *Dilate* is from Old French *dilater*, from Latin *dilatare* 'spread out', from *di-* 'apart' and *latus* 'wide'.

dilatory [late Middle English] This is from late Latin *dilatorius* 'delaying', from Latin *dilator* 'delayer', from *dilat-*, the past participial stem of *differre* 'defer'.

dilemma [early 16th century] The first recorded sense of *dilemma* was 'a form of argument involving a choice between equally unfavourable alternatives', in logic. This notion of double difficulty is captured by the expression *on the horns of a dilemma*. The word came into English via Latin from Greek *dilēmma*, from *di-* 'twice' and *lēmma* 'premise'.

diligent [Middle English] *Diligent* came via Old French from Latin *diligens, diligent-* 'assiduous', from *diligere* 'love, take delight in'. Middle English **diligence** had the sense 'close attention, caution' and is via Old French from Latin *diligentia*, from *diligent-*; the same word form was used to denote a public stagecoach in the late 17th century. This is the adoption of the French word from the phrase *carrosse de diligence* 'coach of speed' ('speed' is a special use of *diligence* found also in English at one time but now obsolete).

dilute [mid 16th century] Latin *diluere* 'wash away, dissolve' is the source of English *dilute*. It is also the base of mid 17th-century **diluvial** 'relating to a flood' (from late Latin *diluvialis*, from *diluvium* 'deluge').
→ DELUGE

dimension [late Middle English] The first recorded sense of *dimension* was 'a measurable extent such as length or breadth'. It comes via Old French from Latin *dimensio(n-)*, from *dimetiri* 'measure out'. The word's use to describe 'an aspect or feature of a situation' (e.g. *a water feature can add a new dimension to your garden*) dates from the 1920s.

diminish [late Middle English] This is a blend of archaic *minish* 'diminish' (based on Latin *minutia* 'smallness') and obsolete *diminue* 'speak disparagingly' (based on Latin *deminuere* 'lessen' which in late Latin became *diminuere*); the base is *minuere* 'make small'. **Diminution** (Middle English) came via Old French from Latin *deminutio(n-)*, from the verb *deminuere*. **Diminutive** (late Middle English) from Old French *diminutif, -ive*) was first used as a grammatical term.

din [Old English] Old English *dyne, dynn* (noun), *dynian* (verb), are Germanic in origin. Old High German *tuni* (noun) and Old Norse *dynr* (noun), *dynja* 'come rumbling down', are related.

dine [Middle English] This is from Old French *disner*, probably from *desjëuner* 'to break fast', from *des-* (expressing reversal) and *jëun* 'fasting' (from Latin *jejunus*). Middle English **dinner** is also from Old French *disner*: here it is an infinitive used as a noun.

dingy [mid 18th century] This is perhaps based on Old English *dynge* 'dung'. Early dialect use was in the sense 'soiled, dirty'.
→ DUNG

dinky [late 18th century] This is from Scots and northern English dialect *dink* 'neat, trim'. The ultimate origin is unknown. The word has been used from the 1980s for either partner of a well-off working couple with no children: in this use it is an acronym from *double income, no kids*, on the pattern of *yuppy*.

dinosaur [mid 19th century] This is from modern Latin *dinosaurus*, from Greek *deinos* 'terrible' and *sauros* 'lizard'. The word was coined in 1841. Figurative use referring to somebody or something that has not adapted to changing circumstances, dates from the 1950s.

dint [Old English] Old English *dynt* meant 'a stroke with a weapon'; it was reinforced in Middle English by the related Old Norse word *dyntr*. The ultimate origin is unknown. The phrase *by dint of* is literally 'by force of'. The meaning associated with *dent* describing an impression left in a surface, dates from the late 16th century: it is used figuratively to mean 'effect produced'.
→ DENT

diocese [Middle English] *Diocese* is from Old French *diocise*, from late Latin *diocesis*, from Latin *dioecesis* 'governor's jurisdiction, diocese'. The Greek form *dioíkēsis* meant 'administration, diocese', from *dioikein* 'keep house, administer'.

dip [Old English] Old English *dyppan*, of Germanic origin, is related to *deep*. The phrase *dip into* (a book or subject of study) meaning 'read short passages, touch lightly upon' dates from the late 17th century. The slang term *dip* meaning 'pick pockets' is found from the early 19th century.
→ DEEP

diploma [mid 17th century] A *diploma* was originally a general word for a 'state paper'. It came via Latin from Greek *diplōma* 'folded paper', from *diploun* 'to fold', from *diplous* 'double'.

diplomatic [early 18th century] This word is connected with *diploma*. The early sense was 'relating to original or official documents'; it comes from modern Latin *diplomaticus* and French *diplomatique*, from Latin *diploma*. **Diplomacy** arose towards the end of the 18th century and is from French *diplomatie*, from *diplomatique* 'diplomatic', on the pattern of French *aristocratie* 'aristocracy'. **Diplomat** dating from the early 19th century, is from French *diplomate*, a back-formation (by removal of the suffix) from *diplomatique*.

direct [late Middle English] Latin *dirigere* 'to guide' (from *di-* 'distinctly' or *de-* 'down' and *regere* 'put straight') is the source of a group of contemporaneous words in English. *Direct* is from Latin *directus*, the past participle of *dirigere*; **direction** from Latin *directio(n-)*, was first recorded as meaning 'management of someone or something'; **directive** is from medieval Latin *directivus* and was first used as an adjective; **director** is from Anglo-Norman French *directour*, from late Latin *director* 'governor'; **directory**, now 'a book listing details or directions' had the general sense 'something that directs' and is from late Latin *directorium*, from *director* 'governor'.

dirt [Middle English] This comes from Old Norse *drit* 'excrement', an early sense in English.

WORDBUILDING

The prefix dis- [from Latin or via French des-]

expresses **negation** [disadvantage]

denotes **reversal or absence** [disaffirm]

denotes **removal** [disafforest]

denotes **separation** [discarnate]

denotes **expulsion** [disbar]

denotes **intensification** [disgruntled]

---

disadvantage [late Middle English] *Disadvantage* comes from Old French *desavantage*, from *des-* (expressing reversal) and *avantage* 'advantage'.

disagree [late 15th century] Early senses included 'be inconsistent, fail to correspond' and 'refuse to agree to'. The source of the word is Old French *desagreer*. **Disagreeable** dating from late Middle English in the sense 'discordant, incongruous', is from Old French *desagreable*, based on *agreer* 'agree'.

disappoint [late Middle English] *Disappoint* was formerly 'deprive of an office or position'. Old French *desappointer* is the source. The sense developed to focus on the sense of failure to fulfil expectation.

disaster [late 16th century] This is from Italian *disastro* 'ill-starred event', from *dis-* (expressing negation) and *astro* 'star' from Latin *astrum*. **Disastrous** from the same period, had the sense 'ill-fated' and is from French *désastreux*, from Italian *disastroso* (from *disastro* 'disaster').

disc [mid 17th century] *Disc* originally referred to the seemingly flat round form of the sun or moon. It comes from French *disque* or Latin *discus*.

discard [late 16th century] The original sense recorded was 'reject (a playing card)'; the

word is formed from the prefix *dis-* 'away' and *card*.
→ CARD[1]

discern [late Middle English] This came via Old French from Latin *discernere*, from *dis-* 'apart' and *cernere* 'to separate'. In early contexts the word was recorded as meaning 'mark as separate or distinct'.

discharge [Middle English] 'Relieve of (an obligation)' was the early sense of *discharge* which comes from Old French *descharger*, from late Latin *discarricare* 'unload'. The elements are *dis-* (expressing reversal) and *carricare* 'to load'. 'Release from custody' is a sense dating from the mid 16th century.
→ CHARGE

disciple [Old English] This is from Latin *discipulus* 'learner', from *discere* 'learn'; it was reinforced by Old French *deciple*. The Latin verb *discere* is also the source of Middle English **discipline** which meant 'mortification by scourging oneself': this came via Old French from Latin *disciplina* 'instruction, knowledge'. The adjective **disciplinary** (late 15th century) was originally used with reference to ecclesiastical order: the source is medieval Latin *disciplinarius*, from Latin *disciplina*.

discomfit [Middle English] *Discomfit* usually found in the verb phrase *be discomfited* had the early sense 'defeat in battle'. It comes from Old French *desconfit*, the past participle of *desconfire*, based on Latin *dis-* (expressing reversal) and *conficere* 'put together'.
→ CONFECTION

discomfort [Middle English] Early examples are as a verb in the sense 'dishearten, distress', from Old French *desconforter*; the noun is from Old French *desconfort*, from *des-* (expressing reversal) and *conforter* 'to comfort'.
→ COMFORT

disconcert [late 17th century] 'Upset the progress of' was the meaning of *disconcert* in early contexts. It comes from obsolete French *desconcerter*, from *des-* (expressing reversal) and *concerter* 'bring together'. In English the meaning developed into 'ruffle' and 'fluster' and, in the form *disconcerting*, came to mean 'upsetting' in the early 19th century.

discord [Middle English] The noun is from Old French *descord*, the verb from Old French *descorder*, from Latin *discordare*. The base is Latin *discors* 'discordant', from *dis-* (expressing negation, reversal) and *cor*, *cord-* 'heart'. 'Being at variance' is the core notion whether in opinions, harmony of sound, or in consistency.

discotheque [1950s] This is from French *discothèque*, which was originally 'a record library', on the pattern of *bibliothèque* 'library'. The abbreviation **disco** dates from the 1960s and was originally a US usage.

discount [early 17th century] The early word denoted a reduction in the amount or value of something. The noun comes from obsolete French or (in commercial contexts) from Italian (*di*)*scontare*. Medieval Latin *discomputare* is the source, from Latin *dis-* (expressing reversal) and *computare* 'count'.
→ COMPUTE

discourse [late Middle English] A *discourse* was formerly 'the process of reasoning' as used in the phrase *discourse of reason*. It is from Old French *discours*, from Latin *discursus* 'running to and fro' (which became, in medieval Latin, 'argument'). The Latin verb *discurrere* is the base, from *dis-* 'away' and *currere* 'to run'. The English verb was influenced by French *discourir*. **Discursive** (late 16th century) is from medieval Latin *discursivus*, from Latin *discurrere*.

discover [Middle English] The early sense was 'make known': it comes from Old French *descovrir*, from late Latin *discooperire*, from Latin *dis-* (expressing reversal) and *cooperire* 'cover completely'.
→ COVER

discreet [Middle English] *Discreet* 'careful and circumspect in speech or action' is from Old French *discret*, from Latin *discretus*, the past participle of *discernere* 'discern'. The sense arose from late Latin *discretio* 'discernment', the source of the English word **discretion** in Middle English. Classical Latin *discretio* meant 'separation' which led to the notion of 'fine judgement'.

discrete [late Middle English] *Discrete* 'individually separate and distinct' is from Latin *discretus* 'separate'.
→ DISCREET; DISCERN

discriminate [early 17th century] This is from Latin *discriminare* 'distinguish between', from *discrimen* 'distinction', from the verb *discernere*. The notion of making prejudicial distinctions in the treatment of different groups of people on grounds of race, sex, etc., arose in the late 19th century.
→ DISCERN

discuss [late Middle English] The semantic core in *discuss* is one of 'shaking and separating': Latin *quatere* 'shake' is the base verb. Early senses of *discuss* included 'dispel, disperse' and 'examine by argument'. The source is the Latin form *discuss-* from *discutere* meaning 'dash to pieces' and later 'investigate'. **Discussion** dates from Middle English when it referred to

a judicial examination: it comes via Old French from late Latin *discussio(n*), from *discutere*.

disdain [Middle English] The noun is from Old French *desdeign*, the verb from Old French *desdeignier*, from Latin *dedignari*. The prefix *de-* in this verb expresses reversal and *dignari* means 'consider worthy'.

disease [Middle English] The early sense was 'lack of ease; trouble, inconvenience'. Old French *desaise* 'lack of ease' is the source of the word in English, from *des-* (expressing reversal) and *aise* 'ease'. The 'lack of ease' soon became associated with illness. **Diseased** is recorded from late Middle English and is the past participle of *disease* 'deprive of ease' (from Old French *desaisier*, from *desaise*).

disembark [late 16th century] This is from French *désembarquer*, Spanish *desembarcar*, or Italian *disimbarcare*, based on Latin *barca* 'ship's boat'.

disfigure [late Middle English] Old French *desfigurer*, based on Latin *figura* 'figure', is the source of *disfigure*.

disgorge [late 15th century] This is from Old French *desgorger*, from *des-* (expressing removal) and *gorge* 'throat'.

disgrace [mid 16th century] Early use was as a verb. It comes via French from Italian *disgrazia* (noun), *disgraziare* (verb), from *dis-* (expressing reversal) and Latin *gratia* 'grace'. 'Spoil the grace of something' was an early sense in English, now obsolete; 'shame' and 'dishonour' became the main notions in *disgrace*.

disgruntle [mid 17th century] This is from *dis-* (used as an intensifier) and the dialect verb *gruntle* 'utter little grunts'. Vocal displeasure is therefore associated with being *disgruntled*.
→ GRUNT

disguise [Middle English] An early meaning recorded was 'change one's usual style of dress', with no implication of concealing one's identity. It is from Old French *desguisier*. The word soon developed a notion of concealment; it was also used for 'disfigure, alter in appearance from the natural condition', a meaning now obsolete (Shakespeare *The Rape of Lucrece*: Her cheeks with chaps and wrinkles were disguised; Of what she was no semblance did remain.)

disgust [late 16th century] *Disgust* expresses 'strong distaste' and is from early modern French *desgoust* or Italian *disgusto*, from Latin *dis-* (expressing reversal) and *gustus* 'taste'. This word and its cognates appear after 1600 and are not found in Shakespeare.

dish [Old English] Old English *disc* 'plate, bowl' (related to Dutch *dis*, German *Tisch* 'table')

is based on Latin *discus*. The word's slang use to refer to an attractive person (*what a dish!*), dates from the beginning of the 20th century; it is comparable with *delicious* used informally to describe someone's sexual appeal.
→ DISC

dishevel [late Middle English] This is perhaps from the Old French verb *descheveler*, based on *chevel* 'hair' from Latin *capillus*. The original sense was 'having the hair uncovered'; later it meant 'hanging loose' referring to the hair itself, from which the sense 'disordered, untidy' developed.
→ UNKEMPT

dishonest [late Middle English] Early senses included 'dishonourable, unchaste'. *Dishonest* is from Old French *deshoneste*, Latin *dehonestus*. **Dishonesty** from the same period meant 'dishonour, sexual misconduct': this form is from Old French *deshoneste* 'indecency'.

disinherit [late Middle English] This spelling superseded the earlier verb *disherit*. It is composed of *dis-* (expressing removal) and *inherit* in the obsolete sense 'make someone an heir'.

disinter [early 17th century] This is from French *désenterrer*, from *dis-* (expressing reversal) and *enterrer* 'to bury'.

dislocate [late 16th century] This is probably a back-formation from **dislocation** (from Old French, or from medieval Latin *dislocatio(n-)*), but perhaps from medieval Latin *dislocatus* 'moved from a former position', from the verb *dislocare*. The base is Latin *locare* 'to place'.

dislodge [late Middle English] *Dislodge* is from Old French *deslogier*, from *des-* (expressing reversal) and *logier* 'encamp', from *loge* 'lodge'. One of the early uses was in military contexts.
→ LODGE

dismal [late Middle English] This is from the earlier noun *dismal*, from Anglo-Norman French *dis mal*, from medieval Latin *dies mali* 'evil days': these referred to the two days in each month believed in medieval times to be unlucky. Also known as Egyptian days, they are said to have been discovered or computed by Egyptian astrologers. They were January 1, 25; February 4, 26; March 1,28; April 10, 20; May 3, 25; June 10, 16; July 13, 22; August 1, 30; September 3, 21; October 3, 22; November 5, 28; December 7, 22. Some medieval writers connected them with the plagues of ancient Egypt.

dismantle [late 16th century] *Dismantle* in early examples included the meaning 'destroy the defensive capability of (a fortification)'. Old French *desmanteler* (literally 'take a man's cloak from his back') is the source of the word, from

des- expressing reversal and *manteler* 'fortify'. Latin *mantellum* 'cloak' is the base.
→ MANTLE

dismay [Middle English] *Dismay* is from Old French, based on Latin *dis-* (expressing negation) and the Germanic base of *may*. The core sense is apparently 'deprive of power or ability'.

dismiss [late Middle English] This word appears to have occurred first in the form *dismissed* used by Caxton to translate the French word *desmis*; this is probably how *dismiss* came to be the accepted English representation of Latin *dimittere* 'send away'. The English synonym *dismit* was in use earlier which may have influenced the prefix. In the 16th and 17th centuries, various spellings were in use including *dimit*, *dimiss*, and *demit*.

disobey [late Middle English] This comes from Old French *desobeir*, based on Latin *oboedire* 'obey'. Late Middle English **disobedient** is from Old French *desobedient*, based on Latin *oboedient-* 'obeying'. **Disobedience** from the same period, is from Old French *desobedience*, from an alteration of ecclesiastical Latin *inoboedientia*.
→ OBEY

disoblige [late 16th century] *Disoblige* 'offend someone by going against their wishes' was first recorded with the sense 'release from an obligation'. It comes from French *désobliger*, based on Latin *obligare* 'oblige'.

disorder [late 15th century] Early use was as a verb in the sense 'upset the order of'. The form is an alteration after *order*, of the earlier verb *disordain*, from Old French *desordener*. It is ultimately based on Latin *ordinare* 'ordain'. The notion of public disturbance and commotion dates from the early 16th century.

disorganize [late 18th century] The word *disorganize* is a word dating from the French Revolution; French *désorganiser* is the source.

disorient [mid 17th century] *Disorient*, another term, chiefly in US use, for *disorientate* is from French *désorienter* 'turn from the east'.

disparage [late Middle English] The early word meant both 'marry someone of unequal rank' and 'bring discredit on' (Chaucer *Reeve's Tale*: Who dorste be so boold to disparge my doghter that is come of swich lynage). The source is Old French *desparagier* 'marry someone of unequal rank', based on Latin *par* 'equal'. The sense 'vilify, speak of slightingly' dates from the mid 16th century.

disparate [late Middle English] *Disparate* 'essentially different in kind' comes from Latin *disparatus* 'separated', from the verb *disparare*, from *dis-* 'apart' and *parare* 'to prepare'. The word was influenced in sense by Latin *dispar* 'unequal'.

disparity [mid 16th century] *Disparity* 'great difference' is from French *disparité*, from late Latin *disparitas*, based on Latin *paritas* 'parity'.

dispatch [early 16th century] *Dispatch* comes from Italian *dispacciare* 'hasten' or Spanish *despachar* 'expedite', from *dis-, des-* (expressing reversal) and the base of Italian *impacciare* 'entangle, hinder', Spanish *empachar* 'hinder'. 'Speed' is at the core of the word, seen also in transferred use such as *dispatch* for an official communication (e.g *mentioned in dispatches*): such communications are often conveyed at speed by special messenger. The English spelling was uniformly *dispatch* until the early part of the 19th century; somehow, however, the word was entered under *des-* in Johnson's Dictionary even though Johnson himself always wrote *dispatch*. Since about 1820, there has therefore been the diversity of *despatch* as a variant.

dispel [late Middle English] The Latin elements *dis-* 'apart' and *pellere* 'to drive', which make up the verb *dispellere*, are the base forms of *dispel* in English.

dispense [late Middle English] *Dispense* came via Old French from Latin *dispensare* 'continue to weigh out or disburse', from the verb *dispendere*, based on *pendere* 'weigh'. The phrase *dispense with* 'do without', has developed from administrative contexts where there was a relaxation of a penalty, giving exemption. The use of *dispense* in pharmacy for making up medicine to a prescribed formula, dates from the early 16th century; there is a sense connection with **dispensary** (late 17th century from medieval Latin *dispensarium*), both the name of a book containing formulae for making up medicines, and a place for dispensing medicines. Related words in this group are late Middle English **dispensation** (from Latin *dispensatio(n-)*) and the adjective **dispensable**. The latter dates from the early 16th century with the meaning 'permissible in special circumstances': it comes from medieval Latin *dispensabilis*. It came to mean 'unimportant, not necessary' from the mid 17th century.

disperse [late Middle English] This comes from Latin *dispers-*, a form of the verb *dispergere* 'to scatter', from *dis-* 'widely' and *spargere* 'strew'. **Dispersion**, dating from the same period, is from late Latin *dispersio(n-)*, from Latin *dispergere*.

display [Middle English] The early meaning was 'unfurl (a banner or sail), unfold'. The word comes from Old French *despleier*, from Latin *displicare* 'scatter, disperse', which came to mean 'unfold' in medieval Latin. In English the notion of 'unfurling' led to 'causing to notice'; this sometimes included an ostentatious show (Shakespeare *King Lear*: The very fellow that … Display'd so saucily against your Highness).
→ DEPLOY

dispose [late Middle English] The source of *dispose* is Old French *disposer*, from Latin *disponere* 'arrange'; the spelling was influenced by Latin *dispositus* 'arranged' and Old French *poser* 'to place'. The sense may involve 'placing at appropriate points' (e.g. *disposed in a circle*) or 'making fit or ready' (e.g. *prolactin disposes you towards sleep*); the proverb *Man proposes, but God disposes* uses *dispose* to mean 'determine the course of events'. The notion 'get rid of' in *dispose of*, arose in the early 17th century. Late Middle English **disposition** came via Old French from Latin *dispositio(n-)*, from *disponere*. It involves a notion of placement and order as in *disposition of troops in the field*, or one of constitution, humour, or inclination (Swift *Gulliver*: I rose up with as melancholy a Disposition as ever I had in my Life). This latter use is possibly of astrological origin: *dispositions* were described as saturnine, jovial, martial, mercurial, and venereal.

dispute [Middle English] *Dispute* came via Old French from Latin *disputare* 'to estimate', which came, in late Latin, to mean 'to dispute'. The base elements are *dis-* 'apart' and *putare* 'reckon'. **Disputable** dates from the late 15th century and is from Latin *disputabilis*, from the verb *disputare*.

disrupt [late Middle English] This comes from Latin *disrupt-*, the past participial stem of *disrumpere* 'break apart'.

dissect [late 16th century] The Latin base elements of *dissect* are *dis-* 'apart' and *secare* 'to cut'.

disseminate [late Middle English] This is from Latin *disseminare* 'scatter', from *dis-* 'abroad' and *semen, semin-* 'seed'.

dissent [late Middle English] The origin is Latin *dissentire* 'differ in sentiment'.

dissertation [early 17th century] Early use was in the sense 'discussion, debate'. The origin is Latin *dissertatio(n-)*, from *dissertare* 'continue to discuss', from *disserere* 'examine, discuss'. The use of the word to refer to a scholarly essay submitted for a degree, dates from the late 19th century.

dissident [mid 16th century] *Dissident*, now 'in opposition to official policy', was first recorded with the general meaning 'differing in opinion or character'. It comes from Latin *dissident-* 'sitting apart, disagreeing', from *dis-* 'apart' and *sedere* 'sit'. **Dissidence** (mid 17th century) is from Latin *dissidentia*.

dissipate [late Middle English] The Latin verb *dissipare* 'scatter', from *dis-* 'apart, widely' and *supare* (unattested) 'to throw', gave rise to *dissipate* and **dissipation** in English. The latter meant 'complete disintegration' in early use.

dissolute [late Middle English] This comes from Latin *dissolutus* 'disconnected, loose', from the verb *dissolvere* 'loosen'. The common current sense is 'overindulging in sensual pleasures'.
➔ DISSOLVE

dissolve [late Middle English] Early use included the sense 'break down into component parts'. Latin *dissolvere* is the source, from *dis-* 'apart' and *solvere* 'loosen or solve'. **Dissolution** is recorded from the same period from Latin *dissolutio(n-)*, from the verb *dissolvere*. It became associated with the dismissal of a political assembly or constituted body, in the mid 16th century.

dissonant [late Middle English] The early sense was 'clashing'. It derives from Old French, or from Latin *dissonant-*, from the verb *dissonare* 'be inharmonious', from *dis-* 'apart' and *sonare* 'to sound'. **Dissonance**, also late Middle English, is from Old French, from late Latin *dissonantia*.

dissuade [late 15th century] This is from Latin *dissuadere*, from *dis-* (expressing reversal) and *suadere* 'advise, persuade'.

distaff [Old English] Old English *distæf* was a 'spindle on which to wind wool ready for spinning': the first element is apparently related to Middle Low German *dise*, *disene* 'distaff, bunch of flax'; the second is English *staff* 'stick'. The extended sense 'concerning women', as in *marriage is still the passport to distaff power*, arose because spinning was traditionally done by women. The phrase *distaff side* dates from the late 19th century and refers to the female side of a family: while women did the spinning, the men did the weaving. *St Distaff's Day*, the day after the Feast of the Epiphany (January 7), was the day women resumed their spinning and other daily work after the holidays.

distance [Middle English] 'Discord, debate' was an early sense of *distance* which is either from Old French or from Latin *distantia* 'standing apart', 'remoteness', from the verb *distare* 'stand apart'. This base verb also gave **distant**, recorded from late Middle English; the formative elements are *dis-* 'apart' and *stare* 'stand', which led to the notion of 'extent or interval of space between objects or people'.

distend [late Middle English] This comes from Latin *distendere*, from *dis-* 'apart' and *tendere* 'to stretch'.

distil [late Middle English] *Distil* is from Latin *distillare* 'fall in drops', a variant of *destillare* 'trickle or drip down', from *de-* 'down, away' and *stillare* (from *stilla* 'a drop'). This verb is the base too of **distillation** dating from the mid 19th century.

distinction [Middle English] A *distinction* was first recorded as meaning a 'subdivision', a 'category'. It came via Old French from Latin *distinctio(n-)*, from the verb *distinguere* 'put apart': the elements are *dis-* 'apart' and *stinguere* 'put out' (from a base meaning 'to prick'). Related forms are late Middle English **distinct** (from Latin *distinctus* 'separated, distinguished') which had the early sense 'differentiated', and **distinctive** from the same period (from Latin *distinctivus*) meaning 'serving to differentiate'. The verb **distinguish** (late 16th century) was formed irregularly from French *distinguer* or from Latin *distinguere*.

distort [late 15th century] 'Twist to one side' was the sense first recorded for *distort*. It is from the Latin verb *distorquere* 'twist apart'.

distract [late Middle English] Early meanings included 'pull in different directions' as well as the current 'stop from attending or concentrating fully'. The word is from Latin *distract-*, from the verb *distrahere* 'draw apart'. This is the base too of late Middle English **distraction** from Latin *distractio(n-)*.

distraught [late Middle English] This is an alteration of the obsolete adjective *distract* (from Latin *distractus* 'pulled apart'); it was influenced by *straught*, the archaic past participle of *stretch*.

distress [Middle English] The noun is from Old French *destresce*, the verb from Old French *destrecier*, based on Latin *distringere* 'stretch apart'.
➔ DISTRICT

distribute [late Middle English] The Latin verb *distribuere* 'divide up' is the source of *distribute* and the base of **distribution** (from Latin *distributio(n-)*); the base elements are *dis-* 'apart' and *tribuere* 'assign'.

district [early 17th century] A *district* was originally the territory under the jurisdiction of a feudal lord. The word is from French, from medieval Latin *districtus* which meant 'the constraining and restraining of offenders (i.e the exercise of justice)' and '(territory of) jurisdiction'. The classical Latin verb was *distringere* 'draw apart'.

disturb [Middle English] *Disturb* is from Old French *destourber*, from Latin *disturbare* 'throw into turmoil', from *dis-* 'utterly' and *turbare* 'disturb' (from *turba* 'tumult'). Middle English **disturbance** is from Old French *destourbance*, from *destourber*; early use included the notion 'breach of the public peace'.

ditch [Old English] Old English *dīc* is Germanic in origin and related to Dutch *dijk* 'ditch, dyke' and German *Teich* 'pond, pool'. The verb *ditch* meaning 'leave in the lurch' is a colloquial use dating from the early 20th century. In aviation contexts, the verb *ditch* 'bring (an aircraft) down in the sea in an emergency', dates from the middle of the 20th century.
→ DYKE

ditto [early 17th century] Original use was in the sense 'in the aforesaid month'. It comes from a Tuscan dialect variant of Italian *detto* 'said', from Latin *dictus* 'said'.

divan [late 16th century] A *divan* was first used to denote a legislative body in the Middle East. The word came via French or Italian from Turkish *dīvān*, from Persian *dīwān* 'anthology, register, court, or bench'. As a piece of furniture, a *divan* was originally, in the early 18th century, a low bench or raised section of floor used as a long seat against the wall of a room, common in Middle Eastern countries; European imitation of this led to the sense 'low flat sofa or bed' in the late 19th century.

dive [Old English] Old English *dūfan* 'dive, sink' and *dȳfan* 'immerse' are Germanic in origin. The noun *dive* meaning 'disreputable place' is a US usage originally and was often used in connection with an illegal drinking den.
→ DEEP; DIP

divers [Middle English] *Divers* used in literary language to mean 'of varying types', has come via Old French from Latin *diversus* 'diverse', from *divertere* 'turn in separate ways'. **Diverse** 'showing much variety' is a Middle English variant of *divers*. **Diversity**, also Middle English, is via Old French from Latin *diversitas*, from *diversus* 'diverse' (the past participle of *divertere*).
→ DIVERT

divert [late Middle English] *Divert* came via French from Latin *divertere*, from *di-* 'aside' and *vertere* 'to turn'. It acquired a notion of 'entertainment and recreation' in the mid 16th century (Daniel Defoe *Robinson Crusoe*: I used

frequently to visit my Boat ... sometimes I went out in her to divert my self). **Diversion** dating from the same period, is from late Latin *diversio(n-)*, from Latin *divertere* 'turn aside'. From the 1950s, the word has also been applied to an alternative route by-passing a temporarily-closed road.

divest [early 17th century] *Divest* 'deprive of power or rights' is an alteration of *devest*, from Old French *desvestir*, from *des-* (expressing removal) and Latin *vestire* (from *vestis* 'garment').

divide [Middle English] *Divide* is from Latin *dividere* 'force apart, remove'. The noun dates from the mid 17th century. **Division** dates from late Middle English and is from Old French *devisiun*, from Latin *divisio(n-)*, from the verb *dividere*.

dividend [late 15th century] *Dividend* started out with the general sense 'portion, share'. It comes from Anglo-Norman French *dividende*, from Latin *dividendum* 'something to be divided', from the verb *dividere*. The spelling was often *dividente* or *dividend* in error in early use as the ending *-end* was unusual; it conformed to the Latin type in the 17th century.
→ DIVIDE

divine[1] [late Middle English] *Divine* 'godlike' and, informally, 'delightful', came via Old French from Latin *divinus*, from *deus* 'godlike' (related to *deus* 'god'). The phrase *the divine right of kings* stating that legitimate kings derive their power from God alone, came into specific use in the 17th century; it was a claim made prominently by the Stuart kings. **Divinity**, recorded slightly earlier, is from Old French *divinite*, from Latin *divinitas*, from *divinus* 'belonging to a deity'.

divine[2] [late Middle English] *Divine* 'discover by intuition' is from Old French *deviner* 'predict', from Latin *divinare*, from *divinus* 'belonging to a deity'. **Divination** (late Middle English) is from Latin *divinatio(n-)*, from *divinare* 'predict'.
→ DIVINE[1]

divorce [late Middle English] The noun is from Old French *divorce*, from Latin *divortium*, based on *divertere* 'turn in separate ways'; the verb from Old French *divorcer*, from late Latin *divortiare*, from *divortium*. **Divorcee** dates from the early 19th century and is from French *divorcé(e)* 'divorced man (or woman)'.
→ DIVERT

divulge [late Middle English] 'Announce publicly' was the first recorded meaning of *divulge* which derives from Latin *divulgare*. The formative elements are *di-* 'widely' and *vulgare* 'publish' (from *vulgus* 'common people').

dizzy [Old English] Old English *dysig* meant 'foolish' and is West Germanic in origin; it is related to Low German *dusig*, *dösig* 'giddy' and Old High German *tusic* 'foolish, weak'.

do [Old English] Old English *dōn* is Germanic in origin; it is related to Dutch *doen* and German *tun*, from an Indo-European root shared by Greek *tithēmi* 'I place' and Latin *facere* 'make, do'.

dock¹ [late Middle English] *Dock* 'an enclosed area of water in a port' is from Middle Dutch, Middle Low German *docke*. The ultimate origin is unknown.

dock² [late 16th century] *Dock* describing the enclosure in a criminal court where a defendant stands, is probably originally slang and related to Flemish *dok* 'chicken coop, rabbit hutch'. The ultimate origin is unknown.

dock³ [late Middle English] The original noun sense was 'the solid part of an animal's tail', whence the verb sense 'cut short (an animal's tail)', later generalized to 'reduce, deduct'. The word is perhaps related to Frisian *dok* 'bunch, ball (of string etc.)' and German *Docke* 'doll'. The word **docket** (late 15th century) is perhaps from *dock*. The word originally denoted a summary or abstract; hence, in the early 18th century, 'a document giving particulars of a consignment'.

doctor [Middle English] Early senses of *doctor* included 'learned person' and 'Doctor of the Church'. It comes via Old French from Latin *doctor* 'teacher' (from *docere* 'teach'). **Doctorate** (mid 17th century) is from medieval Latin *doctoratus* meaning 'made a doctor'.

doctrine [late Middle English] *Doctrine* is from Old French, from Latin *doctrina* 'teaching, learning', from *doctor* 'teacher', from *docere* 'teach'.

document [late Middle English] This is from an Old French word, from Latin *documentum* 'lesson, proof', which became in medieval Latin 'written instruction, official paper'. The base is the Latin verb *docere* 'teach'. **Documentary** (early 19th century) is based on *document*: this is a truncated element in the formation of the word **docudrama** dating from the 1960s; similarly **docutainment** (1970s) is a blend of *documentary* and *entertainment*: the word is a North American usage referring to films including documentary materials intended to inform and entertain.

doff [late Middle English] *Doff* 'remove' is a contraction of *do off*.
→ DON²

dogma [mid 16th century] *Dogma* is via late Latin from Greek *dogma* 'opinion', from *dokein* 'seem good, think'. This word is the base of **dogmatic** dating from the early 17th century when it was a noun for a philosopher or physician (of a school based on a priori assumptions): the direct source is late Latin from Greek *dogmatikos*. *Dogma* is also the base of **dogmatism** from French *dogmatisme*, from medieval Latin *dogmatismus*.

doily [late 17th century] This word for a small ornamental mat made either of lace or of paper with a lace pattern, is from *Doiley* or *Doyley*, the name of a 17th-century London draper. It was originally a term for a woollen material used for summer wear, said to have been introduced by this draper. The current word was originally part of the phrase *doily napkin* and dates from the early 18th century.

doldrums [late 18th century] The early form was singular *doldrum* meaning 'a dull, sluggish person': the source is perhaps the adjective *dull*. The word is now used in the plural in the phrase *the doldrums* ('a state of depression or stagnation'), on the pattern of *tantrums*.

dole [Old English] Old English *dāl*, of Germanic origin, meant 'division, portion, or share'. It is now used as a term for 'a benefit paid by the state', 'a charitable gift', or even, in poetry, 'a person's lot or destiny'.
→ DEAL¹

doll [mid 16th century] This first denoted a mistress; it is the pet form of the given name *Dorothy*. The sense 'small model of a human figure' dates from the late 17th century; *poppet* and *puppet* were in use earlier in this sense.

■ **dolly tub** meaning 'washtub for clothes' (late 19th century) is based on dialect *dolly* which is used as a term for various contrivances thought to resemble a doll in some way. Here the *dolly* in *dolly tub* is a type of short wooden pole for stirring the washing.

dollar [mid 16th century] This is from early Flemish or Low German *daler*, from German *T(h)aler*, short for *Joachimsthaler*, a coin from the silver-mine of Joachimsthal ('Joachim's valley'), now called *Jáchymov*, in the Czech Republic. The term was later applied to a coin used in the Spanish-American colonies, which was also widely used in the British North American colonies at the time of the American War of Independence, hence adopted as the name of the US monetary unit in the late 18th century.

dollop [late 16th century] A *dollop* was first used as a word for a clump of grass or weeds in a field. It is perhaps Scandinavian in origin and related to Norwegian dialect *dolp* 'lump'.

dolphin [late Middle English] This is from Old French *dauphin*, from Provençal *dalfin*, via Latin from Greek *delphin*. The French word *dauphin* was also used as a title for the eldest son of the King of France. It was a nickname meaning 'dolphin' but was first used as this specific regal title in the 14th century from the family name of the lords of the Dauphiné (a region and former province of SE France)

domain [late Middle English] A *domain* was formerly 'heritable or landed property'. The word is from French *domaine*, an alteration by association with Latin *dominus* 'lord' of Old French *demeine* 'belonging to a lord'.

dome [early 16th century] A *dome* in early use denoted a stately building; this particular sense comes directly from Latin *domus* 'house'. The source of the word in other senses is French *dôme*, from Italian *duomo* 'cathedral, dome', from Latin *domus* 'house'. The distinctive shape associated with the word has given the name *The Dome*, built as part of millennium celebrations and now a landmark in London.

Domesday [Middle English] *Domesday* was apparently a popular name applied to the *Domesday Book* (a record of the extent and ownership etc. of land in England in 1086 made by order of William I) during the 12th century because the book was regarded as a final authority. The allusion is to *doomsday* 'the Day of Judgement'.

domestic [late Middle English] This is from French *domestique*, from Latin *domesticus*, from *domus* 'house'. The form **domesticate** is recorded from the mid 17th century and derives from medieval Latin *domesticare* 'domesticate', from Latin *domesticus* 'belonging to the house'.

domicile [late Middle English] This word comes via Old French from Latin *domicilium* 'dwelling', from *domus* 'home'.

dominant [late Middle English] *Dominant* is via Old French from Latin *dominant-* 'ruling, governing', from the verb *dominari*, the base too of **domination** (also late Middle English) which is via Old French from Latin *dominatio(n-)*. The verb **dominate** dates from the early 17th century and is also from Latin *dominari*. The base is Latin *dominus* 'lord, master', which gave rise to **dominion** via Old French from medieval Latin *dominio(n-)*, already recorded from Middle English.

domineer [late 16th century] *Domineer* is from Dutch *domineren*, from French *dominer*, from Latin *dominari*.
→ DOMINANT

don[1] [early 16th century] This is commonly now a term for a university teacher. In early use, it referred to the Spanish title prefixed to a male forename. It comes from Spanish, from Latin *dominus* 'lord, master'.

don[2] [late Middle English] This verb meaning 'put on' is a contraction of *do on*.
→ DOFF

donor [Middle English] *Donor* is from Old French *doneur*, from Latin *donator*, from *donare* 'give'. **Donation** (late Middle English) is via Old French from Latin *donatio(n-)*, from the verb *donare*, based on *donum* 'gift'. **Donate**, recorded from the late 18th century as a back-formation (by removal of the suffix) from *donation*.

doodle [early 17th century] *Doodle* was originally a noun denoting a fool, but later use as a verb developed in the sense 'make a fool of, cheat'. The origin of the form is Low German *dudeltopf, dudeldopp* 'simpleton'. Current senses relating to 'scribbling in an absent-minded way' date from the 1930s.

doom [Old English] Old English *dōm* meant 'statute, judgement'. The word is Germanic in origin, from a base meaning 'to put in place'. *Doom* 'terrible fate' dates from late Middle English. **Doomsday** was, in Old English, *dōmes dæg*.
→ DO

door [Old English] Old English *duru, dor* is Germanic in origin and related to Dutch *deur* 'door' and German *Tür* 'door', *Tor* 'gate'. They are from an Indo-European root shared by Latin *foris* 'gate, leaf of a door' and Greek *thura* 'door'.

dormant [late Middle English] 'Fixed in position' and 'latent' were the meanings of *dormant* in early examples. It comes from an Old French word meaning 'sleeping', from the verb *dormir*, from Latin *dormire* 'to sleep'. This Latin verb gave rise to **dormitory** in late Middle English, from Latin *dormitorium*, neuter (used as a noun) of *dormitorius*.

dose [late Middle English] *Dose* as in 'a quantity (of medicine, of radiation, etc.)' is from French, via late Latin from Greek *dosis* 'giving, gift', from *didonai* 'give'. The phrase *like a dose of salts* meaning 'very fast and efficiently' comes from the use of Epsom salts as an aperient.

do-si-do [1920s] This term used in country dancing where two dancers move round each other back to back was originally a US usage. It is an alteration of French *dos-à-dos* 'back-to-back'.

dossier [late 19th century] *Dossier* is from a French word for a bundle of papers with a label on the back, from *dos* 'back', based on Latin *dorsum*.

dot [Old English] Old English *dott* was the 'head of a boil'. The word is recorded only once in Old English, and after that not until the late 16th century, when it is found in the sense 'a small lump or clot', perhaps influenced by Dutch *dot* 'a knot'. The sense 'small mark or spot' dates from the mid 17th century.

dote [Middle English] *Dote*, now 'be extremely fond of', once had the sense 'act or talk foolishly'. The origin is uncertain; it is related to Middle Dutch *doten* 'be silly'. **Dotage**, the 'period of life when a person is old and weak', was recorded from late Middle English, and is based on *dote*.

double [Middle English] *Double* is via Old French from Latin *duplus* 'duple'. The verb is from Old French *dobler*, from late Latin *duplare*, from *duplus*.

doublet [Middle English] A *doublet* as a word for either of a pair of similar things, is from an Old French word meaning 'something folded'; it also denoted a fur-lined (= double) coat, from *double* 'double'. This type of coat was worn by men from the 14th to 18th centuries; it was close-fitting, sometimes with sleeves and sometimes without. The word was rarely applied to a similar garment worn by women.

doubt [Middle English] The noun *doubt* is from Old French *doute*, the verb from Old French *douter*, from Latin *dubitare* 'hesitate', from *dubius* 'doubtful'. The compound ▪ **doubting Thomas** dating from the early 17th century as a name for someone who is sceptical and refuses to believe something without proof, is with biblical allusion to the apostle Thomas (John 20: 24–9). He earned his nickname by saying that he would not believe that Christ had risen again until he could see and touch his wounds.
→ DUBIOUS

dough [Old English] Old English *dāg* is Germanic in origin and related to Dutch *deeg* and German *Teig*, from an Indo-European root meaning 'smear, knead'. **Duff** (mid 19th century) as in *plum duff* is a northern English form of *dough*.

dour [late Middle English] This word meaning 'relentlessly severe' was originally Scots. It is probably from Scottish Gaelic *dúr* 'dull, obstinate, stupid', perhaps from Latin *durus* 'hard'.

down[1] [Old English] Old English *dūn*, *dūne* 'towards a lower place' were shortened from *adūne* 'downward', from the phrase *of dūne* 'off the hill'. **Downward** is Middle English and is a shortening of Old English *adūnweard*.

down[2] [Middle English] The *down* describing 'soft fine fluffy feathers' is from Old Norse *dúnn*.

down[3] [Old English] *Down* referring to a gently sloping hill and commonly used in the phrase *the Downs* in southern England, was *dūn* 'hill' in Old English (related to Dutch *duin* 'dune'). It is perhaps ultimately of Celtic origin and related to Old Irish *dún* and obsolete Welsh *din* 'fort', which are from an Indo-European root shared by *town*.
→ TOWN

dowry [Middle English] A *dowry* was a term for a widow's life interest in her husband's estate. It comes from Anglo-Norman French *dowarie*, from medieval Latin *dotarium*; the base verb is Latin *dotare* 'endow', from *dos*, *dot-* 'dowry'. Latin *dare* 'give' is related.

doze [mid 17th century] *Doze* 'sleep lightly' had the sense 'stupefy, bewilder, make drowsy' in early use. It is perhaps related to Danish *døse* 'make drowsy'.

dozen [Middle English] This is from Old French *dozeine*, based on Latin *duodecim* 'twelve'.

drab [mid 16th century] This adjective meaning 'lacking brightness' was first used as a noun for undyed cloth. It is probably from Old French *drap* 'cloth'.
→ DRAPERY

draconian [late 19th century] This word meaning 'excessively harsh' is from the Greek name *Drakōn*. Draco was an Athenian legislator whose codification of Athenian Law was notorious for its severity: the death penalty was imposed for trivial crimes.

drag [Middle English] This is from Old English *dragan* or Old Norse *draga* 'to draw'; the noun is partly from Middle Low German *dragge* 'grapnel'. The meaning 'boring event' (*what a drag!*) is recorded from the early 19th century; slang use of the noun in the phrase *main drag* meaning 'main street' is found from the mid 19th century; *in drag* in the sense 'in women's clothes' dates from the end of that century.

dragon [Middle English] This is from Old French, via Latin from Greek *drakōn* 'serpent', which was an early meaning of the English word.

drama [early 16th century] This came via late Latin from Greek *drama*, from *dran* 'do, act'. **Dramatis personae** (mid 18th century) and meaning literally 'persons of the drama', is a Latin phrase used to list the characters in a play.

drapery [Middle English] At first *drapery* meant 'cloth, fabrics'. It is from Old French *draperie*, from *drap* 'cloth'. A back-formation of this is **drape** which is recorded from the mid

19th century. The noun **draper** dates from late Middle English when it referred to a maker of woollen cloth: the source of the word is Old French *drapier*, from *drap* 'cloth', from late Latin *drappus*.

drastic [late 17th century] This adjective was originally applied to the effect of medicine: it comes from Greek *drastikos*, from *dran* 'do'.

drat [early 19th century] This is a shortening of the phrase *od rat*, a euphemism for *God rot*.

draught [Middle English] *Draught* was first recorded as meaning both 'drawing, pulling' and 'something drawn, a load'. Old Norse *dráttr* is the source and the origin is Germanic; it is related to German *Tracht*. *Draft* is a phonetic spelling of *draught*.
→ DRAW

draw [Old English] Old English *dragan* is from a Germanic source and is related to Dutch *dragan* and German *tragen* as well as to English *draught*. The main semantic branches include: 'cause to move by the application of force' (*drawn by horses*), 'come, go' (*drew near*), 'take in, attract' (*felt drawn to her*), 'take out' (*drew the cork*), 'extend' (*drew out the meeting*), and 'depict' (*drew a picture*).

drawl [late 16th century] This is probably slang originally, from Low German or Dutch *dralen* 'to delay, linger'.

dray [late Middle English] A *dray* used to denote a sledge. It comes perhaps from Old English *dræge* 'dragnet', related to *dragan* 'to pull'. It now commonly refers to a cart.
→ DRAW

dread [Old English] Old English *ádrædan*, *ondrædan* 'regard with awe', 'fear greatly' is West Germanic in origin and related to Old High German *intratan* (the prefix of which is from a base meaning 'against').

dream [Middle English] Of Germanic origin, *dream* is related to Dutch *droom* and German *Traum*, and probably also to Old English *dréam* 'joy, music'.

dreary [Old English] Old English *dréorig* meant 'gory, cruel' as well as 'melancholy', from *dréor* 'gore'. Of Germanic origin, it is related to German *traurig* 'sorrowful'.
→ DROWSY; DRIZZLE

dredge[1] [late 15th century] *Dredge* 'clean out the bed of a harbour', was first recorded as a noun and was originally in the phrase *dredge-boat*. It is perhaps related to Middle Dutch *dregghe* 'grappling hook'.

dredge[2] [late 16th century] This *dredge* meaning 'sprinkle with a powdered substance',

is from obsolete *dredge* 'sweetmeat, mixture of spices', from Old French *dragie*, perhaps via Latin from Greek *tragēmata* 'spices'.

drench [Old English] Old English *drencan* 'force to drink', *drenc* 'a drink or draught' are Germanic in origin and related to the German verb *tränken*, and the noun *Trank*.
→ DRINK

dress [Middle English] *Dress* had the early sense 'put straight'. It comes from Old French *dresser* 'arrange, prepare', based on Latin *directus* 'direct, straight'.

dresser [late Middle English] The piece of furniture known as a *dresser* is now either a sideboard with shelves above for displaying or storing plates and utensils, or in North American usage a chest of drawers with a mirror. Originally it described a kitchen sideboard or table on which food was prepared. The word is from Old French *dresseur*, from *dresser* 'prepare'.
→ DRESS

dribble [mid 16th century] This is a frequentative (= verb of repeated action) of obsolete *drib*, a variant of *drip*. The original sense was 'shoot an arrow short or wide of its target', which was also a sense of *drib*. The word used to mean 'fall slowly in drops' and may also have been influenced by *drivel*. A **driblet** meaning 'a small drop or stream of liquid' dates from the late 16th century when it denoted a 'small sum of money': this too is based on obsolete *drib*. The phrase *dribs and drabs* is formed by reduplication (= repetition of an element with a small change).

drift [Middle English] In early contexts a *drift* was a 'mass of snow, leaves, etc.'. It is originally from Old Norse *drift* 'snowdrift'; in later use it derives from Middle Dutch *drift* 'course, current'. The verb 'move in an aimless manner' is a mid 19th-century development.
→ DRIVE

drill [early 17th century] The *drill* meaning 'make a hole in' is from Middle Dutch *drillen* 'bore, turn in a circle'. The *drill* meaning 'furrow' or 'machine for making small furrows' (early 18th century) is perhaps from the same source.

drink [Old English] Old English *drincan*, *drinc* is Germanic in origin and related to Dutch *drinken* and German *trinken*. The colloquial phrase *the drink* referring to the sea, dates from the mid 19th century.

drip [Old English] From a Germanic source, Old English *dryppan*, *drýpen* is related to Danish *dryppe*. The slang use of the word to refer to a

'feeble or dull person', dates from the middle of the 20th century.
→DROP

drive [Old English] Old English *drīfan* is of Germanic origin; Dutch *drijven* and German *treiben* are related. The noun *drive*, which comes from the verb, was applied to a road for vehicles or a private access to a house, from the early 19th century.

drizzle [mid 16th century] This is probably based on Old English *drēosan* 'to fall', of Germanic origin; *dreary* may be related.
→DREARY

droll [early 17th century] *Droll* 'curious and unusual in a way that provokes dry amusement', is from French *drôle*, perhaps from Middle Dutch *drolle* 'imp, goblin'.

drone [Old English] Old English *drān*, *drǣn* 'male bee' is from a West Germanic verb meaning 'to resound, boom'; it is related to Dutch *dreunen* 'to drone', German *dröhnen* 'to roar', and Swedish *dröna* 'to drowse'.

drool [early 19th century] *Drool* is a contraction of **drivel**, of which the early sense was 'let saliva flow from the mouth or let mucus flow from the nose'. The origin of *drivel* is uncertain.

droop [Middle English] *Droop* is from Old Norse *drúpa* 'hang the head'; it is related to *drip* and *drop*.
→DRIP

drop [Old English] Old English *dropa* (noun), *droppian* (verb) are Germanic in origin and related to German *Tropfen* 'a drop', *tropfen* 'to drip'. The primary sense is 'a small globule of liquid that falls': the semantic components of this are highlighted in various ways. The notion of 'tiny size' is illustrated in the phrase *a drop in the ocean* referring to an infinitesimally small or insignificant part: it has the variant *a drop in the bucket* which seems to have been the earlier of the two expressions. Dickens's *Christmas Carol* is where the first recorded example with *ocean* is found (The dealings of my trade were but a drop of water in the … ocean of my business). Another semantic component is 'falling' and this is seen in the word's use in slang, for example *the drop* referring to hanging by the gallows. The shape of a *drop* is captured in references to pendants of precious stone or glass, for example as part of a chandelier.
→DRIP; DROOP

drought [late Old English] The early word *drūgath* meant 'dryness'. It is Germanic in origin and related to *dry*; of similar development is Dutch *droogte* from *droog* 'dry'. In meteorological use, an *absolute drought* is a

period of 15 consecutive days or more when no more than 0.2 mm of rain falls on any day; a *partial drought* is a period of at least 29 consecutive days when the average daily rainfall is no more than 0.2 mm.

drown [Middle English] This was originally a northern English word; it may be related to Old Norse *drukkna* 'to be drowned' but the origin is obscure.
→DRINK

drowsy [late 15th century This is probably from the stem of Old English *drūsian* 'be languid or slow', a verb of Germanic origin. It is related to *dreary*. The verb **drowse** is a back-formation (by removal of the suffix) from *drowsy*.

drudge [Middle English] The noun is known from about 1500, the verb about 50 years later. The origin is unknown, but there is perhaps a connection with *drag* (Johnson *Dictionary of the English Language*: *Lexicographer*, a writer of dictionaries; a harmless drudge, that busies himself in tracing the original, and detailing the significance of words).
→DRAG

drum [Middle English] *Drum* is probably from Middle Dutch or Low German *tromme*, of imitative origin. The word was not common before 1575 and may be a shortening of the earlier word *drumslade* (an alteration of Low German *trommelslag* 'drum beat') common in the 16th century. All the continental languages have the initial letters *tr-* in their corresponding forms, but English had *dr-* apparently from the beginning.

drunken [Old English] This adjective is the archaic past participle of *drink*.
→DRINK

dry [Old English] Old English *drȳge* (adjective), *drȳgan* (verb), are Germanic in origin; Middle Low German *dröge*, Dutch *droog*, and German *trocken* are related. The word's application to lack of emotion or cordiality is figurative and arose in Middle English; the notion of *dry humour* dates from the mid 16th century. The first sense of the noun **dryer** (formed from *dry*) in Middle English was literal: 'a person who dries'.

dual [late Middle English] *Dual* 'consisting of two parts' was first recorded as a noun denoting (until the late 16th century) either of the two middle incisor teeth in each jaw. Latin *dualis* is the source of the word, from *duo* 'two'.

dub[1] [late Old English] The early sense was 'make a knight'. The source is suppposed to be Old French *adober* 'equip with armour', but the ultimate origin is unknown. Some have suggested a Germanic origin but there is no such

Germanic verb as *dubban* 'to strike'. *Dub* as a fishing term for dressing an artificial fly, is from the obsolete meaning 'dress or adorn'.

dub² [1920s] *Dub* 'provide (a film) with a soundtrack' is an abbreviation of *double*.

dubious [mid 16th century] The early sense recorded was 'morally suspect'. The source of the English is Latin *dubiosus*, from *dubium* 'a doubt', a neuter form of *dubius* 'doubtful'.

duck¹ [Old English] Old English *duce* describing this swimming bird, is from the Germanic base of the verb *duck* 'to dip under'. It is sometimes used as a term of endearment (Shakespeare *Midsummer Night's Dream*: O dainty duck, o deare!; Dickens *Old Curiosity Shop*: How is he now, my duck of diamonds). The use of the word in cricket to signify no score, is short for a *duck's egg*, because of the similarity in shape between the egg's outline and the figure zero. Of compounds with *duck*:

■ **ducks and drakes** dates from the late 16th century and is a game where flat stones are thrown so that they skim across the surface of the water: this is by association with the movement of these water birds.

duck² [Middle English] This verb meaning 'plunge, dive' is of Germanic origin and related to Dutch *duiken* and German *tauchen* 'dive, dip, plunge'. The colloquial sense 'avoid, dodge' was originally a US usage.

duct [mid 17th century] Early *duct* meant 'course' or 'direction'. It comes from Latin *ductus* 'leading, aqueduct' from the verb *ducere* 'to lead'. The Latin spelling *ductus* was current in English in early contexts. The adjective **ductile** is recorded from Middle English in the sense 'malleable': Latin *ductilis* (from *ducere*) is the source.

dud [Middle English] The origin of *dud* meaning 'something that fails to work properly', 'something unsatisfactory' is unknown. The early use of this word was to denote an 'item of clothing'.

dude [late 19th century] This slang term (probably from German dialect *Dude* 'fool') appeared in New York at the beginning of 1883 for a man affecting fastidiousness in his dress and bearing to show 'good form'; it was extended to describe a 'dandy'. At the same time the word was applied to a non-westerner or city-dweller spending his holidays on a ranch in the western US. Through black English in the 20th century, the word is used approvingly in reference to a person of one's own circle (e.g. *cool dude*), meaning simply 'guy', 'fellow'.

due [Middle English] The early sense of *due* was 'payable'; it comes from Old French *deu* 'owed', based on Latin *debitus* 'owed', from *debere* 'owe'.

duel [late 15th century] This is from Latin *duellum*, an archaic and literary form of *bellum* 'war' used in medieval Latin with the meaning 'combat between two persons'; it was partly influenced by *dualis* 'of two'. The original sense was 'single combat used to decide a judicial dispute'; the word's use for a 'contest to decide a point of honour' dates from the early 17th century.

duet [mid 18th century] *Duet* is from Italian *duetto*, a diminutive of *duo* 'duet', from Latin *duo* 'two'.

duffer [mid 19th century] This derogatory word is from Scots *dowfart* 'stupid person', from *douf* 'spiritless'.

duke [Middle English] A *duke* was originally the ruler of a duchy: it is from French *duc*, from Latin *dux*, *duc-* 'leader', related to *ducere* 'to lead'. The sense 'leader', for example of an army, was found in English but is now obsolete. It has been used in the plural as a slang term for 'fist, hand' since the late 19th century: this is from the rhyming slang *Duke of Yorks* (= forks, i.e. fingers). **Duchy** dates from Middle English and is via Old French from medieval Latin *ducatus*, from Latin *dux*, which is also the base of late Middle English **duchess** (via Old French from medieval Latin *ducissa*). In English the spelling *dutchess* was common until about 1810.

dulcet [late Middle English] *Dulcet* as in *dulcet tones* was spelt *doucet* earlier, from an Old French diminutive of *doux*, from Latin *dulcis* 'sweet'. The Latin form influenced the modern spelling.

dull [Old English] Old English *dol* meant 'stupid': the word is Germanic in origin, related to Dutch *dol* 'crazy' and German *toll* 'mad, fantastic, wonderful'. The sense 'causing depressed spirits', 'tedious', dates from the 17th century: this notion is transferred to descriptions of the weather, suggesting 'gloomy', 'cheerless'. **Dolt** recorded since the mid 16th century and now a dated term for a 'stupid person' is perhaps a variant of *dulled*, the past participle of *dull*. The noun **dullard** is Middle English and is from Middle Dutch *dullaert*, from *dul* 'dull'.

dumb [Old English] Of Germanic origin, *dumb* is related to Old Norse *dumbr* and Gothic *dumbs* 'mute', also to Dutch *dom* 'stupid' and German *dumm* 'stupid'. The original sense may have been 'not understanding'. The slang word **dumbo** was originally a US usage; it dates from the 1960s. The compound:

■ **dumb-bell** dates from the early 18th century and originally referred to an apparatus similar to that used to ring a church bell but without the bell making it therefore noiseless or 'dumb'.

■ **dumbfound** (mid 17th century) is a blend of *dumb* and *confound*.

■ **dumbsize** used commercially to describe the reducing of staff in a company to a size where work can no longer be carried out productively, dates from the 1990s and is used humorously, on the pattern of *downsize*.

dummy [late 16th century] This word is based on *dumb*. The original sense was 'a person who cannot speak', then (mid 18th century) 'an imaginary fourth player in whist'. This gave rise to 'a substitute for the real thing' (e.g. a rubber teat, a blank round of ammunition) and 'a model of a human being' (mid 19th century).

dump [Middle English] This comes perhaps from an Old Norse word related to Danish *dumpe* and Norwegian *dumpa* 'fall suddenly': the latter was the original sense in English. In later use the word, like *thump* is partly imitative.

dumps [early 16th century] This was originally singular in the sense 'a dazed or puzzled state'. It is probably a figurative use of Middle Dutch *domp* 'haze, mist'. The phrase *the dumps* was in early use for 'depression'.

dumpy [mid 18th century] *Dumpy* 'short and stout' is from **dumpling** (early 17th century): this is apparently from the rare adjective *dump* 'of the consistency of dough', although *dumpling* is recorded much earlier.

dun [Old English] Old English *dun*, *dunn* describing a dull greyish-brown colour, is Germanic in origin and probably related to *dusk*.

dunce [early 16th century] The surviving sense of *dunce* is 'a person who shows no capacity for learning'. Originally it was an epithet for a follower of John Duns Scotus, a scholastic theologian whose works on theology, philosophy, and logic were used as university textbooks. His followers, called Scotists, were a sect who predominated in scholastic circles until the 16th century when the humanists, and later the reformers, attacked and ridiculed them for making what they saw as useless distinctions. The *Dunsmen* or *Dunses* spoke out in their turn against the 'new learning' and the name *Duns* became synonymous with 'hair-splitter'. A notion of 'obstinacy' developed, from where the idea of 'person impervious to learning' sprang.

dunderhead [early 17th century] The origin of *dunderhead* is obscure, but it may be connected with the obsolete Scots word *dunder*, *dunner* meaning 'resounding noise'. The change in Dutch *donderbus* to *blunderbuss* may indicate an association in English between *dunder* and *blunder*: the word suggests doltish stupidity.

→ DIN

dung [Old English] *Dung*, of Germanic origin, is related to German *Dung*, Swedish *dynga*, Icelandic *dyngja* 'dung, dunghill, heap', and Danish *dynge* 'heap'. The original sense is uncertain. For a period during the 18th century, the word passed into tailors' slang to denote a journeyman working by the piece: a *Dung* worked to the detriment of a *Flint* who worked by the day not submitting to pressure from the master to work more quickly. A word probably based on *dung* is **dunny** 'toilet' recorded from the early 19th century in the sense 'dung': it is from dialect *dunnekin* 'privy', probably from *dung* and archaic slang *ken* 'house'. The Scots *dunny* for an underground passage or cellar, is probably a different word.

dungeon [Middle English] A *dungeon* was once a 'castle keep' as well as a dark vault for confinement. It comes from Old French, perhaps originally with the sense 'lord's tower' or 'mistress tower'; it is based on Latin *dominus* 'lord, master'. The word is essentially a doublet (= of the same derivation but having a different meaning) of *dominion*.

→ DOMINANT

dunk [early 20th century] This colloquial word is from Pennsylvanian German *dunke* 'dip', from German *tunken* 'to dip or plunge'.

dupe [late 17th century] *Dupe* 'a victim of deception', is from dialect French *dupe* 'hoopoe', from the bird's supposedly stupid appearance.

duplex [mid 16th century] The adjective is recorded first and is from Latin *duplex, duplic-*, from *duo* 'two' and *plicare* 'to fold'. The noun dates from the 1920s; in North American usage, it is a residential building divided into two apartments, but it may also refer to a semi-detached house or a flat on two floors.

duplicate [late Middle English] The early sense was 'having two corresponding parts'. The source of the form is Latin *duplicat-*, from the verb *duplicare* 'to double', from *duplic-* 'twofold'. **Duplication** from the same period, was used in the mathematical sense 'multiplication by two': it is from Old French, or from Latin *duplicatio(n-)*, from *duplicare*.

duplicity [late Middle English] *Duplicity* is from Old French *duplicite* or late Latin *duplicitas*, from Latin *duplic-* 'twofold'.

→ DUPLEX

durable [Middle English] The early sense recorded for *durable* was 'steadfast'. It came via Old French from Latin *durabilis*, from *durare* 'to last'. This Latin verb also gave rise to the noun **duration** in late Middle English: it came via Old French from medieval Latin *duratio(n-)*. The base is Latin *durus* 'hard'. In the 1914–1918 war, the phrase *for four years or the duration of the war* was used as a term of enlistment: this led to the expression *for the duration* referring initially to 'for the time a war lasts' but becoming extended to 'for the indeterminate period that a process continues'.

duress [Middle English] The early senses were 'harshness', 'severity', 'cruel treatment'. English *duress* is via Old French from Latin *duritia*, from *durus* 'hard'.

dusk [Old English] Old English *dox* 'dark, swarthy' and *doxian* 'darken in colour' are of Germanic origin. Old High German *tusin* 'darkish' is related. The relation of modern English *dusk* to Old English *dox* is unclear: few English words ending in *-sk* are Old English in origin. Middle English spellings included *deosc* and *dosc*: the final consonant group *-sc* normally develops later into *-sh* as in *ash*, *dish*, *fish*.
→ DUN

dust [Old English] Of Germanic origin, Old English *dūst* is related to Dutch *duist* 'chaff, meal-dust, bran'. The primary semantic notion is 'that which rises in a cloud like smoke'; an earlier form *dunst* gave rise to many Germanic forms including German *Dunst* 'vapour'. The expression *shake the dust off one's feet* is with biblical allusion to Matthew 10:14.

duty [late Middle English] This is from Anglo Norman French *duete*, from Old French *deu*. *Duty* is associated with 'what is owed' to a higher or respected party. This is sometimes an expression of polite respect (Shakespeare *Hamlet*: Our duties to your honor) or moral obligation (Wordsworth *Ode to Duty*: Stern Daughter of the Voice of God! O Duty!) or what is owed financially to a higher authority (*customs duty*).
→ DUE

dwarf [Old English] Old English *dweorg*, *dweorh* is Germanic in origin and related to Dutch *dwerg* and German *Zwerg*. The word often refers to a member of a race of diminutive people in Germanic, especially Scandinavian, folklore and mythology; *dwarves* in this context are supposed, like elves, to have special skill in working metals. The slang term **dweeb** which arose in the 1980s is probably a blend of *dwarf* and *feeble*.

dwell [Old English] Old English *dwellan* meant 'lead astray' and 'hinder, delay': these latter two meanings did not survive this period. Later, in Middle English, the meaning was 'tarry', 'remain in a place'. Germanic in origin, English *dwell* is related to Middle Dutch *dwellen* 'stun, perplex' and Old Norse *dvelja* 'delay, tarry, stay'.

dwindle [late 16th century] This is a frequentative (= verb of repeated action) of the Scots and dialect verb *dwine* 'fade away, pine away', from Old English *dwīnan*, a Germanic word in origin. Related are Middle Dutch *dwīnen* and Old Norse *dvína*. *Dwindle* was used in Shakespeare but found rarely before 1650 (Shakespeare *Henry IV part 1*: Bardoll, am I not falne away vilely … do I not bate? Do I not dwindle?).

dye [Old English] The Old English noun spelling was *dēag*, the verb *dēagian*. There is no record of the noun from Old English to the late 16th century when it was re-formed from the verb. The distinction of spelling between *die* and *dye* is fairly recent; both words were spelt *die* in Johnson's Dictionary. The expression *dyed in the wool* refers to the colouring process being more thorough in the raw state of the material, rather than at a later stage.

dyke [Middle English] A general word for 'a trench or ditch' at first, *dyke* is from Old Norse *dík*. The term used for a long wall or embankment built against flooding, has been influenced by Middle Low German *dīk* 'dam' and Middle Dutch *dijc* 'ditch, dam'.
→ DITCH.

dynamic [early 19th century] Originally a term in physics, *dynamic* is from French *dynamique*, from Greek *dunamikos*. The Greek adjective *dunamis* meaning 'power' is the root of this form and of **dynamism**, first recorded slightly later.

dynasty [late Middle English] *Dynasty* is either from French *dynastie* or via late Latin from Greek *dunasteia* 'lordship, power'. The base is Greek *dunastēs*, from the verb *dunasthai* 'be able'.

WORDBUILDING

The prefix **dys-** [from Greek *dus-*; related to German *zer-*, also to Old English *tō-*] adds the sense

- bad [dysentery]
- difficult [dyspepsia]

---

dysentery [late Middle English] This is from Old French *dissenterie*, or via Latin from Greek *dusenteria*, from *dusenteros* 'afflicted in the bowels', from *dus-* 'bad' and *entera* 'bowels'.

dyspepsia [early 18th century] This came via Latin from Greek *duspepsia*, from *duspeptos* 'difficult to digest'.

Ee

each [Old English] Old English *ælc* is related to Dutch *elk* and German *jeglich*, based on a West Germanic phrase meaning 'ever alike'. The early use of *each* corresponded to the current use of *every* (literally a compound word meaning 'ever each'). However unlike *every*, *each* could always be used from the earliest times in the context of just two items as opposed to several.

eager [Middle English] Early senses included 'sharp to the senses, pungent, sour'. The word is from Old French *aigre* 'keen', from Latin *acer*, *acr-* 'sharp, pungent'. The meaning 'full of keen desire' when describing somebody's attitude, seems to be an English development, unlike other now obsolete senses which came from their Old French source; these were: 'biting' (e.g. Shakespeare *Henry VI* part iii: Vex him with eager Words); also 'brittle, imperfectly tempered' in descriptions of metals (*eager gold*); and 'fierce' (Malory *Morte d'Arthur*: With an egyr countenaunce).

ear[1] [Old English] Old English *ēare*, the organ of hearing, is a Germanic word in origin and related to Dutch *oor* and German *Ohr*. These forms come from an Indo-European root shared by Latin *auris* and Greek *ous*. Senses in English relate to various aspects: the function (= hearing) of the ear, as in the proverb walls have ears; a person as a type of listener (*a sympathetic ear*); and musical discrimination (as in the phrase *ear candy*, a US expression from the 1970s for music that is pleasant but with no deeper merit). The phrase *within earshot* dating from the early 17th century, was influenced by the imagery of the word *bowshot*.

ear[2] [Old English] Of Germanic origin, Old English *ēar* referring to the seed-bearing head of a cereal plant such as a spike of corn, is related to Dutch *aar* and German *Ähre*.

earl [Old English] The word *earl* (*eorl* in Old English and Germanic in origin) originally denoted a man of noble rank, as opposed to a churl (= peasant) or ordinary freeman. It was also specifically a hereditary nobleman directly above the rank of thane (= a man who held land granted by the King). It was later an equivalent of *jarl* (a Norse or Danish chief) and, under Canute and his successors, applied to the governor of divisions of England such as Wessex and Mercia. In the late Old English period, as the Saxon court came increasingly under Norman influence, the word was applied to any nobleman bearing the continental title of count.
→ COUNT[2]

early [Old English] The Old English adverb was *ǣrlīce*, based on *ǣr* 'ere' (= before) from a Germanic source related to Dutch *eer* and German *eher*. *Early* was influenced by Old Norse *árliga*. Adjective use dates from Middle English; it often indicates the first part of a period of time and in the 19th century was used in the phrase *small and early* to indicate an early evening party (Dickens *Our Mutual Friend*: Mrs Podsnap added a small and early evening to the dinner). It may also have the sense 'premature' as in *early retirement* and *take an early bath* (a phrase from the 1960s in sporting contexts).

earn [Old English] Old English *earnian* is West Germanic in origin, from a base shared by Old English *esne* 'labourer'. The primary sense is 'obtain in reward for labour'. The notion of gaining a reputation (Spenser *Faerie Queene*: The which shall nought to you but foul dishonour earn) or a particular name (e.g. *earned him a nickname*) dates from the late 16th century.

earnest [Old English] Old English *eornoste* 'serious' and *eornost* 'seriousness' (e.g. *in earnest*) are Germanic in origin and related to the German noun *Ernst*. The adjective seems to have died out in Old English and developed afresh later; no clear examples are found in Middle English. Early contexts showed the word to involve intense or violent feeling, which is often excluded in modern usage.

earth [Old English] The origin of Old English *eorthe* is Germanic; related words are Dutch *aarde* and German *Erde*. Early uses included 'ground', 'soil' as well as the 'world' as a dwelling place. Its use as the burrow of an animal dates from the late 16th century. In figurative extension, one of the most recent phrases is *to feel the earth move* to express a sensation of ecstasy: the first recorded occurrence is in Ernest Hemingway's *For Whom the Bell Tolls*: 'Did thee feel the earth move?' 'Yes. As I died. Put thy arm around me, please'. The word **earthling**, although now associated with science fiction, dates from the late 16th century with the meaning 'inhabitant of the earth'.

earwig [Old English] The *earwig* is so named because it was once thought to crawl into the human ear. This same idea is found in synonyms in other languages such as French *perce-oreilles*, literally 'ear-piercer', and German *Ohrwurm*, literally 'ear worm'. The spelling in Old English was *ēarwicga*, the elements of which are *ēare* 'ear' and *wicga* 'earwig' which is probably related to English *wiggle*.

ease [Middle English] *Ease* is from Old French *aise*, based on Latin *adjacens* which means 'lying close by' (the present participle of *adjacere*). The earliest senses of the French were 'elbow room' and 'opportunity': the latter sense passed into English but is now obsolete. 'Absence of pain or trouble' was found early as a meaning of *ease* in English contexts: the phrase *little ease* was sometimes used as the name of a prison cell too small to allow any comfortable position for the prisoner. The notion of 'facility' as opposed to 'difficulty' is not recorded before the early 17th century (Tennyson *Lucretius*: Seeing with how great ease Nature can smile). The notion of an 'unconstrained position or attitude' arose in the early 19th century, and is illustrated in the military phrase *stand at ease*. The verb is originally from Old French *aisier*, from the phrase *a aise* 'at ease'.

easel [late 16th century] The core semantic notion in *easel* is one of 'bearing a load'; it comes from Dutch *ezel* 'ass'. The word *horse* is used in English in a similar way to denote a supporting frame (e.g. *clothes horse*).

east [Old English] Old English *ēast-*, Germanic in origin, is related to Dutch *oost* and German *ost*, from an Indo-European root shared by Latin *aurora* and Greek *auōs* meaning 'dawn'. **Eastern** in Old English was *ēasterne* and is based on *east*.

Easter [Old English] Old English *ēastre* is Germanic in origin and related to German *Ostern* and English *east*. According to Bede the word is derived from *Ēastre*, the name of a goddess associated with the Spring.

easy [Middle English] Early senses included 'comfortable' and 'quiet, tranquil'. The source of the word is Old French *aisie*, the past participle of *aisier* 'put at ease, facilitate'. Sense development in English has been affected by *ease*. The notion of *easy listening* for a category of music which is popular but not loud or otherwise intrusive and demanding, dates from the 1960s. The colloquial word:

■ **easy-peasy** from the 1970s is a reduplication of *easy*; it means 'childishly easy' and the childish word intensifies the sense.
→ EASE

eat [Old English] Old English *etan* is Germanic in origin and related to Dutch *eten* and German *essen*, from an Indo-European root shared by Latin *edere* and Greek *edein*. The two main semantic strands involve 'consume in order to nourish, take into the mouth' and 'destroy by devouring, corrode, gnaw away at'. **Edible** (late 16th century) is from late Latin *edibilis*, from Latin *edere* 'eat'. The word **eatery** is a relatively recent word for a restaurant; it arose in the US in the early 20th century.

eaves [Old English] Old English *efes* was a singular form meaning 'overhanging edge of a roof'. Germanic in origin, it is related to German dialect *Obsen*, and also probably to *over*. The final *-s*, mistaken as a plural, has led to occasional use of the word *eave* as a singular. The verb **eavesdrop** is an early 17th-century back-formation (by removal of the suffix) from late Middle English *eavesdropper* meaning 'a person who listens in to conversations, from under the eaves'. This in turn is from the obsolete noun *eavesdrop* 'the ground on to which water drips from the eaves', probably from Old Norse *upsardropi*, from *ups* 'eaves' and *dropi* 'a drop'.
→ OVER

ebb [Old English] The Old English noun *ebba* and verb *ebbian* 'flow back' are West Germanic in origin and related to Dutch *ebbe* (noun) and *ebben* (verb). Ultimately they are also related to the preposition *of* which had the primary sense 'away from'.
→ OF

ebullient [late 16th century] The first recorded sense was the literal 'boiling' from Latin *ebullient-*, present participial stem of the verb *ebullire* 'to boil up'. The elements are *e-* (a variant of *ex-*) 'out' and *bullire* 'to boil'. The sense 'bubbling over with enthusiasm' dates from the mid 17th century.

eccentric [late Middle English] Early use of *eccentric* was as a noun referring to a circle or orbit which did not have the earth precisely at its centre. It comes via late Latin from Greek *ekkentros*, from *ek* 'out of' and *kentron* 'centre'. The word's use in describing people as 'odd and whimsical' arose in texts in the late 17th century.

ecclesiastic [late Middle English] *Ecclesiastic*, often a synonym of *ecclesiastical*, relates to the Christian Church (an early sense contrasted with *secular*) or its clergy (a sense which arose later towards the end of the 16th century). The word is from French *ecclésiastique*, or via late Latin from Greek *ekklēsiastikos*, from *ekklēsiastēs* 'member of an assembly'. The source is Greek *ekklēsia* 'assembly, church', based on *ekkalein* 'summon out'.

echelon [late 18th century] 'A formation of troops' is an early sense of *echelon*. It comes from French *échelon*, from *échelle* 'ladder', from Latin *scala*. The notion of 'steps of a ladder' is reflected in modern figurative use in the context of company hierarchy or strata of society.

echo [Middle English] This is from Old French or Latin, from Greek *ēkhō*, related to *ēkhē* 'a sound'. In Greek mythology, the character *Echo* was regarded as a mountain nymph: an Oread. The myth recounts that Echo was deprived of speech by Hera, wife of Zeus, to stop her chattering: she was left only able to repeat what others said.

eclipse [Middle English] *Eclipse* comes from Old French via Latin from Greek *ekleipsis*: the verb base is *ekleipein* 'fail to appear, forsake its accustomed place', from *ek* 'out' and *leipein* 'to leave'.

ecology [late 19th century] The original spelling was *oecology*. The word is based on Greek *oikos* 'house', asociated with one's environment or habitat.

economic [late Middle English] This came via Old French and Latin from Greek *oikonomikos*, from *oikonomia* 'economy'. Originally a noun, the word referred to household management or to a person who had this particular skill, hence the early use of the adjective (late 16th century) meaning 'relating to household management'. Modern senses involving profitability and saving money date from the mid 19th century. **Economy** (late 15th century) was first recorded as the 'management of material resources': from French *économie* or via Latin from Greek *oikonomia* 'household management', it is based on *oikos* 'house' and *nemein* 'manage'. Current senses date from the 17th century. The phrase *economy size* (1950s) does not refer to a limited size, but quite the opposite; it has more to do with a purchaser's economic choice of buying a large quantity of an item for a discounted price. **Economics** in the late 16th century denoted the science of household management; the plural suffix -s was originally on the pattern of Greek *ta oikonomika* (plural), the name of a treatise by Aristotle. Current use dates from the late 18th century.

ecstasy [late Middle English] The first recorded sense of *ecstasy* was 'emotional or religious frenzy'. Old French *extasie* is the direct source, which came via late Latin from Greek *ekstasis* 'standing outside oneself'. The base elements are *ek-* 'out' and *histanai* 'to place'. Classical senses included 'insanity' and 'bewilderment'; this developed to mean 'withdrawal of the soul from the body'; in later medical writers, the sense 'trance' was used. These senses blended in the modern languages. **Ecstatic** is a late 16th-century word from French *extatique*, from Greek *ekstatikos*.

ecumenical [late 16th century] This adjective relating to a number of different Christian Churches was originally used in the sense 'belonging to the universal Church'. It comes via late Latin from Greek *oikoumenikos* from *oikoumenē* 'the (inhabited) earth'.

eddy [late Middle English] This word for a small whirlpool is probably from the Germanic base of the Old English prefix *ed-* meaning 'again, back'.

edge [Old English] Old English *ecg* 'the sharpened side of a blade' is a Germanic word in origin and related to Dutch *egge*, German *Ecke* 'corner', and Old Norse *eggja* (from an Indo-European root shared by Latin *acies* 'edge' and Greek *akis* 'point'). The sense 'corner', present in Dutch and German, is not found in the sense development of English *edge*. The compound:
■ **edge city** dates from 1991; it is a US phrase for an urban area on the outskirts of a city usually beside a major road. It was originally coined by J. Garreau in a book of the same name.
→ EAR²; EGG²

edict [Middle English] The Latin source *edictum* meant 'something proclaimed'; it is the neuter past participle of *edicere*, from *e-* (a variant of *ex-*) 'out' and *dicere* 'say, tell'. *Edict*, an 'official proclamation' in English, is particularly famous historically in the phrase *Edict of Nantes*, signed in 1598 by Henry IV of France granting toleration to Protestants and ending the French Wars of Religion. It was revoked by Louis XIV in 1685 which resulted in the emigration of the Huguenots to England.

edifice [late Middle English] *Edifice* is via Old French from Latin *aedificium*, from *aedis* 'dwelling' and *facere* 'make'. It is now a formal word in English for 'building'.

edify [Middle English] The word *edify* is from Old French *edifier*, from Latin *aedificare* 'to build', from *aedis* 'dwelling' and *facere* 'make'. The word originally meant 'construct a building', and 'strengthen', which led to 'build up' morally or spiritually. **Edification** (late Middle English), a formal word for instruction, is from Latin *aedificatio(n-)*, from *aedificare*.
→ EDIFICE

edition [late Middle English] This is from French *édition*, from Latin *editio(n-)*, from *edere* 'to put out, produce'. The individual elements in the formation here are *e-* (a variant of *ex-*) 'out' and *dare* 'give'. An early, now obsolete sense, was 'making public'. The verb **edit** dates from the late 18th century: partly a back-formation (by removal of the suffix) from mid 17th-century **editor**, it was reinforced by French *éditer* 'to edit'. *Editor* is a Latin word meaning 'producer (of games), publisher', from the verb *edere*.

educate [late Middle English] This is from the Latin verb *educare* 'rear, bring up (children)', related to *educere* 'lead out' (which has given the formal English word **educe** 'develop something latent'). The noun **education** is found from the mid 16th century: the source is Latin *educatio(n-)*.

eerie [Middle English] *Eerie* 'strange and frightening' was originally northern English and Scots in the sense 'fearful'. The focus therefore moved from feelings of fear to the cause of the fear. It comes probably from Old English *earg* 'cowardly', which has a Germanic source and is related to German *arg*.

efface [late 15th century] The early recorded sense was 'pardon or be absolved from (an offence)'; current senses include 'rub out (writing or a mark)' and the figurative use 'wipe out (a memory)'. The source verb is French *effacer*, from *e-* (from Latin *ex-* 'away from') and *face* 'face'. The notion of 'effacing oneself' to the point of being unobserved or overlooked, dates from the late 19th century.

effect [late Middle English] *Effect* 'result, consequence' is from Old French, or from Latin *effectus*, from *efficere* 'accomplish, work out', of which the formative elements are *ex-* 'out', thoroughly' and *facere* 'do'. *Effects* 'personal belongings' arose from the obsolete sense 'something acquired on completion of an action'. **Effective** 'having a result' also dates from the late Middle English period and is from Latin *effectivus*, from *efficere*.

effeminate [late Middle English] This is from Latin *effeminatus*, the past participle of *effeminare* 'make feminine', from *ex-* (expressing a change of state) and *femina* 'woman'.

effervesce [early 18th century] Latin *effervescere* (made up of *ex-* 'out, up' and *fervescere* 'begin to boil') is the origin of *effervesce* and **effervescent** which was recorded slightly earlier. Latin *fervere* 'be hot, boil' is the base verb. In English the notion of 'heat' was conveyed at first but the focus transferred to that of 'bubbling'.

effete [early 17th century] *Effete* 'affected, over-refined' was originally, in early texts, 'no longer fertile, past bearing young'. It comes from Latin *effetus* 'worn out by bearing young', from *ex-* 'out' and *fetus* 'breeding'. The current sense in English suggests 'having exhausted one's vigour', which is sometimes extended to 'ineffectual', 'effeminate'.

efficacy [early 16th century] Latin *efficacia*, from *efficax*, *efficac-* 'effective' is the source of the English word. **Efficacious** from this same period is also from Latin *efficax*, from *efficere* 'accomplish'.
→ EFFECT

efficient [late Middle English] Early senses included 'making' and 'causing', usually in the phrase *efficient cause*, a term in philosophy for 'an agent that brings something into being': Latin *efficere* 'accomplish' is the source. The current sense 'working in a competent way' dates from the late 18th century. **Efficiency**, late 16th century in the sense 'the fact of being an efficient cause', is from Latin *efficientia*, from *efficere*.
→ EFFECT

effigy [mid 16th century] Latin *effigies* is the source of English *effigy*. This is from the Latin verb *effingere* 'to fashion (artistically)', from *ex-* 'out' and *fingere* 'to shape'. Early examples in English include the senses 'portrait' and 'image'.

effloresce [late 18th century] Latin *flos*, *flor-* 'flower' is the base of *effloresce* 'turn to a fine powder on exposure to air'. The direct source of the spelling is Latin *efflorescere*, from *e-* (a variant of *ex-*) 'out' and *florescere* 'begin to bloom' (from *florere* 'to bloom'). Early use in English included 'burst forth into something resembling a flower'.

effluent [late Middle English] The adjectival sense 'flowing out' was the first recorded. It is from Latin *effluent-*, the present participial stem of *effluere* 'flow out' (from *ex-* 'out' and *fluere* 'to flow'). The noun dates from the mid 19th century. **Effluence**, also late Middle English, is from medieval Latin *effluentia*, from Latin *effluere*. This group of English words is primarily found in scientific contexts involving water or fluid motion.

effort [late 15th century] This is a French adoption, from Old French *esforcier*, based on Latin *ex-* 'out' and *fortis* 'strong'. In English, the meaning involves 'a visibly strenuous attempt to achieve something' and sometimes it describes the achievement itself.

effrontery [late 17th century] From French *effronterie*, English *effrontery* is based on late

Latin *effrons*, *effront-* 'shameless, barefaced, unblushing'. The base elements are *ex-* 'out' and the noun *frons* which meant both 'forehead' and 'the ability to blush'.

effusion [late Middle English] Latin *effundere* 'pour out' (from *ex-* 'out' and *fundere* 'pour') is the source of *effusion* (from Latin *effusio(n-)*) and the verb **effuse** dating from the same period.

egalitarian [late 19th century] This is from French *égalitaire*, based on *égal* 'equal', from Latin *aequalis*.
→ EQUAL

egg¹ [Middle English] *Egg* from Old Norse superseded the earlier spelling *ey* from Old English *æg*. In 1490 Caxton wrote: What sholde a man in thyse dayes now wryte, egges or eyren, certaynly it is harde to playse every man. The word **egghead** for a 'a knowledgeable or academic person' is by analogy with a bald head and the association of age and wisdom. The compound: ■ **egg plant**, an alternative term for aubergine was first used to describe a variety of the plant bearing white fruit whose shape and colour led to the association with *egg*.

egg² [Middle English] The verb *egg* 'urge' as in *egg on* is from Old Norse *eggja* 'incite'. The colloquial word **eggy** 'irritated' dates from the 1930s, and is from the notion of being 'urged on, incited to anger'.

egoism [late 18th century] This is from French *égoïsme* and modern Latin *egoismus*, from Latin *ego* 'I': **ego** was adopted into English in the early 19th century meaning 'a person's sense of self-esteem'. **Egotism**, dating from the early 18th century is sometimes used as a variant of *egoism* and comes from French *égoïste*; the *-t-* is euphonic (= for ease of pronunciation). The term **egocentric** arose in the early 20th century, on the pattern of words such as *geocentric*.

egregious [mid 16th century] The word *egregious* started out meaning 'remarkably good': it comes from Latin *egregius* 'illustrious', literally 'standing out from the flock' (from *ex-* 'out' and *grex*, *greg-* 'flock'). The derogatory sense 'outstandingly bad' (late 16th century) probably arose as an ironical use.

either [Old English] Old English *ægther* 'each of two' is a contracted form of *æg(e)hwæther* which is of Germanic origin.
→ WHETHER

ejaculate [late 16th century] This is from the Latin verb *ejaculari* 'dart out', from *e-* (a variant of *ex-*) 'out' and *jaculari* 'to dart'. The base is Latin *jaculum* 'dart, javelin', from *jacere* 'to throw'.

eject [late Middle English] The Latin verb *eicere* 'throw out' is the source of English *eject*, from *e-* (a variant of *ex-*) 'out' and *jacere* 'to throw'.

eke [Old English] Old English *ēacian*, *ēcan* had the sense 'increase'; it is Germanic originally and related to Old Norse *auka*. The current meaning is 'make last longer by being frugal' (as in *eke out the stew to provide an extra portion*).

elaborate [late 16th century] In early contexts, the adjective *elaborate* meant 'produced by effort of labour'. The verb was a term in biology for 'produce (a substance) from its elements or simpler constituents': this may have been the earliest sense in English due to the use of the Latin word in writings on alchemy or medicine. The Latin verb *elaborare* 'work out' is the source of the form, from *e-* (a variant of *ex-*) 'out' and *labor* 'work'. The verb's use to mean 'explain something in more detail' dates from the 1930s.

elapse [late 16th century] 'Slip away' was the early sense; the word comes from Latin *elaps-*, the past participial stem of the verb *elabi* 'slip away', from *e-* (a variant of *ex-*) 'out, away' and *labi* 'to glide, slip'. The association with passing time developed early in the word's history.
→ LAPSE

elastic [mid 17th century] The adjective *elastic* originally described a gas in the sense 'expanding spontaneously to fill the available space' (some supposed air particles to act like a coiled spring). It is from modern Latin *elasticus*, from Greek *elastikos* 'propulsive', from *elaunein* 'to drive'. The noun *elastic* for a piece of cord woven with india rubber, dates from the mid 19th century.

elate [late Middle English] Early use was as an adjective. It comes from Latin *elat-*, the past participial stem of the verb *efferre* 'raise', from *ex-* 'out, from' and *ferre* 'to bear'. The verb dates from the late 16th century; late Middle English **elation** (from Old French *elacion*) had the verbal sense 'lifting' in early contexts and came to mean 'high spirits' in the mid 18th century.

elbow [Old English] Old English *elboga*, *elnboga*, literally 'arm-bend', has a Germanic origin and is related to Dutch *elleboog* and German *Ellenbogen*. The first element **ell** (*eln* in Old English) is a former measure of length equivalent to six hand breadths (used for textiles).
→ BOW¹

elder [Old English] Old English *ieldra*, *eldra* 'greater in age' is a Germanic word related to German *älter*. The comparative of *old*, it was originally equivalent to the modern form *older*

(Shakespeare *The Merchant of Venice*: How much more elder art thou then thy looks) but is now in more resticted use.
➔ OLD

elect [late Middle English] This is from Latin *elect-*, the past participial stem of the verb *eligere* 'pick out', from *e-* (a variant of *ex-*) 'out' and *legere* 'to pick'. In early use *elect* was often found following the noun, a use still found in phrases such as *president elect*. The phrase *the elect* meaning 'those chosen by God' is first found in religious writings in the early 16th century. **Election** (Middle English) came via Old French from Latin *electio(n-)*. Its use in political contexts where choices are made by popular vote, dates from the mid 17th century. Late Middle English **elective** is from Old French *electif*, *-ive*, from late Latin *electivus*, and **eligible** dating from the same period is via French from late Latin *eligibilis*.

electric [mid 17th century] *Electric* is from modern Latin *electricus*, from Latin *electrum* 'amber', from Greek *ēlektron*. This association arose because rubbing amber causes electrostatic phenomena. The figurative 'causing a thrill' dates from the late 18th century.

elegant [late 15th century] Early use was in connection with tasteful attire and sometimes even had the unfavourable sense 'foppish'. It comes from French, or from Latin *elegans*, *elegant-*, related to *eligere* 'choose, select'.
➔ ELECT

elegy [early 16th century] This word for a 'lament' is from French *élégie*, or via Latin from Greek *elegeia*, from *elegos* 'mournful poem'.

element [Middle English] The early use of the word referred to a fundamental constituent. It comes via Old French from Latin *elementum* 'principle, rudiment', translating Greek *stoikheion* 'step, component part'. In ancient and medieval philosophy, the *elements* earth, water, air, and fire were thought to compose all material bodies. The word is used in modern chemistry for more than 100 substances which are provisionally supposed to be simple bodies and primary constituents of matter. Late Middle English **elementary** (from Latin *elementarius*) had the sense 'composed of the four elements, earth, air, fire, and water'. Current senses such as 'easy, rudimentary' date from the mid 16th century; the misquotation 'elementary my dear Watson' attributed to Sherlock Holmes in Arthur Conan Doyle's detective fiction is taken from the interchange: ... 'Excellent', I cried. 'Elementary', said he.

elevate [late Middle English] *Elevate* is from Latin *elevare* 'to raise', based on *levis* 'light', as is the noun **elevation** from the same period

(from Latin *elevatio(n-)*). **Elevator** dating from the mid 17th century as a term for a type of muscle is modern Latin, from Latin *elevare*; later, such as in the late 19th-century US usage for a 'lift' in a building, the word is directly from *elevate*.

elf [Old English] *Elf* is Germanic in origin and related to German *Alp* 'nightmare'; the early belief was that these dwarfish supernatural beings possessed great magical powers, that they caused nightmares, substituted changelings for stolen children, produced diseases, etc. The Germanic belief in elves is probably the principal source of the medieval superstition regarding fairies. Originally *elf* was masculine and *elven* was feminine, but in the 13th and 14th centuries, the two forms seem to have been used interchangeably for both sexes. **Elfin** first used by Spenser in the *Faerie Queene* in the late 16th century is based on *elf* and was probably suggested by Middle English *elvene land* meaning 'land of elves' and by *Elphin*, the name of a character in Arthurian romance.

elicit [mid 17th century] *Elicit* is from the Latin verb *elicere* 'draw out by trickery or magic', from *e-* (a variant of *ex-*) 'out' and *lacere* 'entice, deceive'.

elide [mid 16th century] The early sense recorded for *elide* was 'annul, do away with, destroy (the force of evidence)', chiefly as a Scots legal term. It comes from Latin *elidere* 'crush out', from *e-* (a variant of *ex-*) 'out' and *laedere* 'to dash'. Based on the same Latin verb is the noun **elision** which dates from the late 16th century: the direct source is late Latin *elisio(n-)*.

eliminate [mid 16th century] 'Drive out, expel' was the early sense of *eliminate* from Latin *eliminare* 'turn or thrust out of doors', based on *limen*, *limin-* 'threshold'. The sense 'kill, murder' dates from the early 18th century.

elite [late 18th century] This comes from French *élite* 'selection, choice', from *élire* 'to elect', from a variant of Latin *eligere* 'pick out'.
➔ ELECT

elixir [late Middle English] This word came into English via medieval Latin from Arabic *al-'iksīr*, from *al* 'the' and *'iksīr* from Greek *xērion* 'powder for drying wounds' (from *xēros* 'dry'). Early use of the word was in alchemy: it was a term for a preparation thought to be able to change metals into gold, and in the phrase *elixir of life* it was a preparation thought to be able to prolong life indefinitely. It came later to be used for a sovereign remedy for disease and was applied to quack medicines from the early 17th century; it sometimes denoted a type of compound tincture and is found used figuratively for the quintessence of something, its secret principle.

elk [late 15th century] The name of this type of large deer is probably from Old English *elh*, *eolh*, with the substitution of *k* for *h*. Other words which have undergone this change are dialect *selk* (Old English *seolh* 'seal') and *fark* (Old English *færh* 'farrow, litter of pigs').

elocution [late Middle English] Oratorical or literary style was known as *elocution*; it is from Latin *elocutio(n-)* (from *eloqui* 'speak out') which Roman rhetoricians used in this same sense. The word has been used to mean 'a way of speaking, manner of oral delivery' and 'the art of public speaking' since the early 17th century.
→ ELOQUENCE

elongate [late Middle English] 'Move away, set at a distance' were found as early meanings of *elongate* from late Latin *elongare* 'place at a distance': the Latin elements are *e-* (a variant of *ex-*) 'away' and *longe* 'far off', *longus* 'long'. The noun **elongation** from late Latin *elongatio(n-)* also dates from the late Middle English period.

elope [late 16th century] In early contexts *elope* had the general sense 'abscond, run away'; this was usually in the context of a wife running away from her husband in the company of a paramour. The source is Anglo-Norman French *aloper*, perhaps related to *leap*. The notion of running away to be married soon became associated with the verb.
→ LEAP

eloquence [late Middle English] An Old French word from Latin *eloquentia* (from *eloqui* 'speak out') is the source of *eloquence*. **Eloquent** is also a late Middle English word via Old French.
→ ELOCUTION

else [Old English] Old English *elles* is Germanic in origin and related to Middle Dutch *els* and Swedish *eljest*. It is a synonym of *other* and may be interpreted as 'something in addition' or 'something different' as seen in the phrase *something else*. The colloquial expression *or else* added as a threat or warning has the meaning 'or else you may imagine the terrible alternative or retribution': it dates from Middle English.

elucidate [mid 16th century] *Elucidate* is from late Latin *elucidare* 'make clear', from *e-* (a variant of *ex-*) 'out' and *lucidus* 'lucid'.

elude [mid 16th century] Early senses included 'delude' (partly because of confusion with *illude*) and 'baffle, disappoint'. The source is Latin *eludere*, from *e-* (a variant of *ex-*) 'out, away from' and *ludere* 'to play'. The adjective

elusive based on the same Latin verb dates from the early 18th century.

elver [mid 17th century] This word for a 'young eel' is a variant of dialect *eel-fare* meaning both 'the passage of young eels up a river' and 'a brood of young eels': *fare* has its original sense 'a journey'.

emaciate [early 17th century] This comes from Latin *emaciare* 'make thin', from *e-* (a variant of *ex-* expressing a change of state) and *macies* 'leanness'.

emanate [mid 18th century] The Latin verb *emanare* 'flow out' made up of *e-* (a variant of *ex-*) 'out' and *manare* 'to flow', is the source of *emanate* in English. Early use was in the context of ideas, principles, courses of action originating from a person or something as a source. When it later came to be used in a physical sense, the meaning remained associated with intangible things such as light and gases.

emancipate [early 17th century] *Emancipate* is from Latin *emancipare* 'transfer as property', from *e-* (a variant of *ex-*) 'out' and *mancipium* 'slave'. In Roman Law it was the setting free of a child or wife from the power of the *pater familias*, the head of the household; in modern use, the association has been with the liberation of slaves which has affected figurative extensions.

emasculate [early 17th century] This is from Latin *emasculare* 'castrate', from *e-* (a variant of *ex-*, expressing a change of state) and *masculus* 'male'. Figurative use focuses on loss of strength and vigour.

embargo [early 17th century] This term for 'an official ban' is an adoption of a Spanish word, from *embargar* 'arrest', based on Latin *in-* 'in, within' and *barra* 'a bar'.

embark [mid 16th century] This comes from French *embarquer*, from *em-* 'in' and *barque* 'bark, ship'.

embarrass [early 17th century] 'Hamper, impede' was the sense found in early texts. The word is from French *embarrasser* 'obstruct', from Spanish *embarazar*, probably from Portuguese *embaraçar* (from *baraço* 'halter'). The notion of 'difficulty' led to the verb being used in the passive as *be embarrassed* very often in the context of debt, and from the early 19th century with an extra dimension of 'awkwardness and shame'.

embassy [late 16th century] Originally this had the spelling variant *ambassy* and as well as being an official residence, it denoted the position of ambassador or the sending out of ambassadors. The source is Old French *ambasse*, based on Latin *ambactus* 'servant'.

→AMBASSADOR

embellish [late Middle English] The English spelling is from Old French *embelliss-*, the lengthened stem of *embellir*, based on *bel* 'handsome', from Latin *bellus*. The early word meant 'make beautiful' but gradually it has acquired more of a sense of 'heighten the effect of something with additions'.

ember [Old English] Old English *æmyrge* is originally Germanic and related to Old High German *eimuria* 'pyre', Danish *emmer*, Swedish *mörja* 'embers'. The *-b-* was added in English for ease of pronunciation.

embezzle [late Middle English] The ultimate origin of *embezzle* is unknown. The first sense recorded was 'steal' and the direct source is Anglo-Norman French *embesiler*, from the synonymous verb *besiler*; in Old French *besillier* meant 'maltreat, ravage'. The current sense 'misappropriate (money placed in one's trust)' dates from the late 16th century.

emblem [late Middle English] This is from Latin *emblema* 'inlaid work, raised ornament', from Greek *emblēma* 'insertion', from *emballein* 'throw in, insert'. In English an *emblem* was used as a term for an ornament of inlaid work (Milton *Paradise Lost*: The ground more colour'd then with stone Of costliest Emblem); later (early 17th century) it became a symbolical representation.

emboss [late Middle English] This is from the Old French base of obsolete French *embosser*, from *em-* 'into' and *boce* 'protuberance'.

embrace [Middle English] 'Encircle, surround, enclose' are among the early senses of *embrace* which was formerly also spelt *imbrace*. Old French *embracer* is the source, based on Latin *in-* 'in' and *bracchium* 'arm'. The notion of *embracing a faith or political belief* dates from the mid 16th century.

embrocation [late Middle English] This is from medieval Latin *embrocatio(n-)*, from the verb *embrocare*, based on Greek *embrokhē* 'lotion'. An *embrocation* is rubbed on the body to relieve pain from sprains and strains.

embroider [late Middle English] Anglo-Norman French *enbrouder* (from *en-* 'in, on' and Old French *brouder*, *broisder* 'decorate with embroidery') has given rise to *embroider* and the contemporaneous **embroidery**.

embroil [early 17th century] *Embroil* is from French *embrouiller* 'to muddle'. It is now commonly used in contexts where someone

becomes involved in a difficult situation: e.g. *she became embroiled in a dispute*.

embryo [late Middle English] This comes via late Latin from Greek *embruon* 'fetus', from *em-* 'into' and *bruein* 'swell, grow'. **Embryonic** arose much later in the mid 19th century and is based on late Latin *embryo*, *embryon-* 'embryo'; figurative use in the sense 'at a rudimentary stage' is found recorded from the same period.

emend [late Middle English] *Emend*, originally 'free (a person) from faults', is from Latin *emendare*, from *e-* (a variant of *ex-*) 'out of' and *menda* 'a fault'. The word's use in the context of text correction dates from the late 18th century.

→AMEND

emerge [late 16th century] Early senses included 'become known' and 'come to light'. Latin *emergere* is the source verb, from *e-* (a variant of *ex-*) 'out, forth' and *mergere* 'to dip'. The noun **emergency** (from medieval Latin *emergentia*, from Latin *emergere*) in the mid 17th century had the senses 'unforeseen occurrence' and 'issuing from concealment'; the political phrase *state of emergency*, often synonymous with 'war', arose at the end of the 19th century.

emery [late 15th century] *Emery* as in *emery board*, *emery paper* is from French *émeri*, from Old French *esmeri*, from Italian *smeriglio*. This is based on Greek *smuris*, *smiris* 'polishing powder'.

emetic [mid 17th century] *Emetic* 'causing vomiting' is from Greek *emetikos*, from *emein* 'to vomit'.

emigrant [mid 18th century] This is from Latin *emigrant-*, the present participial stem of the verb *emigrare* 'migrate from': this is the source too of late 18th-century **emigrate**. The base elements are *e-* (a variant of *ex-*) 'out of' and *migrare* 'migrate'.

eminence [Middle English] *Eminence* 'recognised superiority in a field' is from Latin *eminentia*, from *eminere* 'jut, project'. The word has been used as a title since the mid 17th century but it is now only used with reference to Cardinals. **Eminent** is late Middle English from the same Latin source verb.

emissary [early 17th century] This word for a person sent as a diplomatic representative is from Latin *emissarius* 'scout, spy', from *emittere* 'send out'.

→EMISSION

emission [late Middle English] The first recorded sense of *emission* was 'emanation'; it comes from Latin *emissio(n-)*, from *emittere* 'send out'. **Emit** is also from Latin *emittere* and dates from the early 17th century.

emollient [mid 17th century] This word meaning 'softening', 'calming' comes directly from the Latin verb form *emollient-*, the present participial stem of *emollire* 'make soft': the base here is the adjective *mollis* 'soft'. It is commonly used to convey soothing properties in phrases such as *emollient cream* or *emollient words*.

emolument [late Middle English] *Emolument* comes from Latin *emolumentum* which was probably, in its original use, a payment made to a miller for grinding corn. The verb *emolere*, source of the noun, meant 'to grind up' (the prefix *e-* here adding the notion of 'thoroughly'). The near-synonym *salary* started out as a 'payment for salt'.
→ MEAL²; MILL; SALARY

emotion [mid 16th century] *Emotion* was first used to denote a public disturbance or commotion, and comes from French *émotion*. The basic notion is one of 'movement' provided by the Latin source words *movere* 'move' and *e-* 'out'. The sense developed to convey 'excitement' and, from the mid 17th century, 'mental agitation'. The current meaning (now more generalized) which describes instinctive feelings such as pity, hate, and love, arose in the early 1800s. A century on, **emote**, a back-formation (by removal of the suffix) from *emotion*, started to be used in the US as an evocative way of describing how an actor portrays feelings in a theatrical manner.

emoticon [1990s] A blend of *emotion* and *icon*, this coinage has emerged as part of the explosion of new words in technology; it describes any of the keyboard-generated facial expressions (such as a smile or a frown) seen at the end of e-mail communications.

empathy [early 20th century] The Greek word *empatheia* (from *em-* 'in' and *pathos* 'feeling') is the source of this word first used in psychology in the early part of the century; it was coined to translate German *Einfühlung* used by the psychologists Lipps, Groos, and others. Terms which are also based on *pathos* are: *sympathy*; *antipathy*; and scientific terms such as *protopathic* (describing sensory nerve fibres); as well as those prefixed by *patho-*.

emphasis [late 16th century] This comes via Latin from Greek; the word originally meant 'appearance' or 'show' and later denoted a figure of speech where more is implied than is actually said. It is this later usage which was first picked up in English. The Greek verb *emphainein* 'to exhibit' is the source, which is made up of *em-* 'in, within' and *phainein* 'to show'. Other words which contain the notion of 'showing' based on Greek *phainein* are: *diaphanous* (showing through); *fantastic* (revealed to the imagination); *hierophant* (revealer of the esoteric); *phantasm* (figment of the imagination); *phase* (appearance of something); it has also provided the prefix *pheno-*.

empire [Middle English] *Empire* has come via Old French from Latin *imperium*, related to *imperare* 'to command'; this verb originally contained a sense of 'making preparations for' an event, as seen in its base elements *in-* 'towards' and *parare* 'prepare, contrive'. The initial letters *imp-* of the Latin are kept in English in the related words: *imperial*; *imperative*; *imperious*. The word **emperor** (from Latin *imperator* 'military commander') dates from Middle English too and was used to represent the title given to the head of the Roman Empire. It later gained a more general sense of sovereignty and was applied to rulers of wide territories extending beyond those of a kingdom. Queen Victoria assumed the title of **Empress** of India in 1876.

employ [late Middle English] *Employ* comes from Old French *employer* and was first used to describe the action of applying or making use of something for a specific purpose. Another early spelling of this word was *imploy*, reflecting the spelling of the Latin base verb *implicari* 'be involved in, be attached to'. In the 16th and 17th centuries the meanings 'enfold, entangle' and 'imply', which mirrored the classical Latin meanings, gained currency. Shakespeare's use of *employ* and *employment* reflects various nuances of sense, for example in *The Merchant of Venice* the following advice is given: Employ your chiefest thoughts to courtship, and in *King John* there is the offer: At your employment, at your service, sir!, already giving a glimpse of current use.
→ IMPLICATE; IMPLY

emporium [late 16th century] An *emporium* was originally a centre of commerce, and is now sometimes the name given to a large retail outlet where variety is the key feature. It comes via Latin from Greek *emporion*, from *emporos* 'merchant'. The semantic stem is 'journey', which evokes all the colourful associations of trade routes of the past.

empty [Old English] Old English *æmtig, æmetig* meant 'at leisure, unoccupied' as well as 'empty'; it comes from *æmetta* 'leisure', perhaps from *ā* 'no, not' and *mōt* 'meeting'. The word is used colloquially to mean 'hungry' (Daniel Defoe *Robinson Crusoe*: I found my self empty).
→ MOOT

emulate [late 16th century] The Latin verb *aemulari* 'to rival, equal', from *aemulus* 'rival' is the source of English *emulate* 'match, surpass'. In computing contexts, the term has been adopted to mean 'reproduce the function or action of (a different computer or software system)'.

emulsion [early 17th century] *Emulsion* was originally a term for a milky liquid made by crushing almonds in water. It is from modern Latin *emulsio(n-)*, from the verb *emulgere* 'milk out', from *e-* (a variant of *ex-*) 'out' and *mulgere* 'to milk'. The phrase *emulsion paint* dates from the 1940s.

WORDBUILDING

The prefix **en-** [from French, from Latin *in-*] adds the sense

- **put into** [embed]
- **brought into the condition of** [encrust]
- **in; into** [ensnare]

It also **intensifies** [entangle] and **forms verbs** together with the suffix **-en** [enliven]

[Note: **in-** is a commonly found by-form of **en-**]

The prefix **en-** [from Greek] adds the sense

- **within** [empathy; enthusiasm]

The prefix **-em** is a variant spelling of **-en** assimilated before *-b-* [emblazon] assimilated before *-p-* [emplacement]

---

enable [late Middle English] This was formerly also written as *inable*. The core sense of the verb is 'give power to'; in early contexts this was by investing somebody with legal status, by empowering someone legally; later the verb acquired a more general notion of 'make possible'. From the 1960s, it has been used in computing contexts simply to mean 'turn on, make operational'.
→ABLE

enact [late Middle English] This was formerly also written as *inact*. It is based on *act*, suggested by medieval Latin *inactare, inactitare*.
→ACT

enamel [late Middle English] Original use was as a verb; the spelling was sometimes formerly *inamel*. The source of the word is the Anglo-Norman French verb *enamailler*, from *en-* 'in, on' and *amail* 'enamel'. The ultimate origin is Germanic. *Enamel* is a semi-transparent glassy substance applied to hard surfaces for ornament or as a protective coating: in the 19th century it was used as a lining for cooking pots. The dentistry term for the hard glossy coating of teeth is from French *émail* and dates from the early 18th century.

enamour [Middle English] This is from Old French *enamourer*, from *en-* 'in' and *amour* 'love'. In English the word was also spelt *inamour* in early contexts. It is commonly used in the passive *be enamoured* (Shakespeare *Midsummer*

Night's Dream: Me thought I was enamoured of an Ass).

enchant [late Middle English] 'Put under a spell' and 'delude' were among the early senses of *enchant* which was also written *inchant* formerly. The source is French *enchanter*, from Latin *incantare*, from *in-* 'in' and *cantare* 'sing'. The current meaning 'delight' is found from the late 16th century and reflects the modern French use of *enchanter*. **Enchantress** dates from late Middle English and is from Old French *enchanteresse*. The woodland plant:

■ **enchanter's nightshade** (late 16th century) was believed by early botanists to be the herb used in potions by the enchantress Circe of Greek mythology, who charmed Odysseus' companions and turned them into pigs. Odysseus protected himself with the mythological herb *moly*.

enclave [mid 19th century] This is a French adoption, from Old French *enclaver* 'enclose, dovetail', based on Latin *clavis* 'key'. Its current use in English is to refer to a piece of territory surrounded by peoples who are culturally or ethnically distinct; it sometimes refers to a group of people who are socially distinct.

enclose [Middle English] The early sense recorded was 'shut in, imprison'. The word comes from Old French *enclos*, the past participle of *enclore*, based on Latin *includere* 'to shut in'. **Enclosure** is late Middle English from legal Anglo-Norman French and Old French, from *enclos* 'closed in'. The word's use to refer to a document enclosed with another in an envelope dates from the late 16th century.

encounter [Middle English] 'Meet as an adversary' was an early sense of *encounter* which was also spelt *incounter* formerly. The verb is from Old French *encontrer*, the noun from Old French *encontre*, based on Latin *in-* 'in' and *contra* 'against'. The core sense of 'meeting' came gradually to include the notion of 'by chance, casually' in some contexts; however the initial notion of 'facing problems in a conflict' is seen in combinations such as *encountered hostilities, encountered fierce opposition in the House*. The phrase *encounter therapy* has been used since the 1960s, originating in the US, for a type of group therapy through body contact and emotional expression.

encourage [Middle English] *Incourage* was an early variant spelling of *encourage* from French *encourager*, from *en-* 'in' and *corage* 'courage'. The early meaning was 'inspire with courage'; it was towards the end of the 17th century that the verb acquired a notion of 'stimulate someone to action by reward or approval'.

encroach [late Middle English] 'Obtain unlawfully, seize' was the early sense of *encroach* also occasionally spelt *incroach* formerly. It is from Old French *encrochier* 'seize, fasten upon', from *en-* 'in, on' and *crochier*. The base is *croc* 'hook', from Old Norse *krókr*. The meaning acquired a notion of 'making insidious advances to obtain something' usually involving somebody else's territory.

encrypt [1950s] This was originally a US word made up of the prefix *en-* 'in' and Greek *kruptos* 'hidden'; it refers to the conversion of data into cipher or code to prevent unauthorized access. Common now in computing contexts, it is found in phrases such as *public-key encryption* where a key code is obtained to encrypt messages, which may only be deciphered by a second 'private' key known only to the recipient: this is sometimes used for safe transmission of payments, signatures, and data sent via the Internet.

encumber [Middle English] Early use included the meanings 'cause trouble to' and 'entangle'; formerly the spelling variant *incumber* was also found. It is from Old French *encombrer* 'block up', from *en-* 'in' and *combre* 'river obstruction'. Use in English often includes a notion of 'burden' as well as 'obstruction'. Middle English **encumbrance** was 'an encumbered state': the origin is Old French *encombrance*.

encyclopedia [mid 16th century] A modern Latin word, *encyclopedia* is from pseudo-Greek *enkuklopaideia* for *enkuklios paideia* 'all-round education' (a 'circle' of arts and sciences thought by the Greeks to be essential to a liberal education). The English spelling with *-ae-* as in *encyclopaedia* is still found, influenced by the retention of the Latin word in titles such as *Encyclopaedia Britannica*. In early use the word referred to a general course of education; it was in the 17th century that it became a term for a literary work.

end [Old English] Old English *ende* (noun) and *endian* (verb) are Germanic in origin and related to Dutch *einde*, German *Ende* (nouns), Dutch *einden*, German *enden* (verbs). The first recorded meaning of **ending**, which in Old English was spelt *endung*, was 'termination, completion'.

endeavour [late Middle English] 'Exert oneself' was the early sense of *endeavour* from the phrase *put oneself in devoir* 'do one's utmost; make it one's duty (to do something)': *devoir*, from Old French, is an archaic English word for 'duty'.

endemic [mid 17th century] This word meaning 'regularly found among particular people or in a certain area' is from French *endémique* or modern Latin *endemicus*: the source is Greek *endēmios* 'native' (based on *dēmos* 'people'). When referring to plants and animals the opposite term is *exotic*.

endorse [late 15th century] The early literal sense was 'write on the back of'; the word was sometimes formerly written as *indorse* especially in law books and it continues to be found in legal and statutory use. American dictionaries approve the *indorse* spelling, but *endorse* prevails in English commercial use. It comes from medieval Latin *indorsare*, from Latin *in-* 'in, on' and *dorsum* 'back'.

endow [late Middle English] Formerly the alternative spelling *indow* existed: early senses included 'provide a dower or dowry', the source being legal Anglo-Norman French *endouer*, from *en-* 'in, towards' and Old French *douer* 'give as a gift'. Latin *dotare* 'endow' is the source of the second element. The vow *With all my worldly goods I thee endow* taken from the Book of Common Prayer (1569), traditionally part of the marriage service, illustrates early use. **Endowment** also dates from late Middle English; its use in insurance contexts is found from the mid 19th century.
→ DOWRY

endure [Middle English] *Endure* is from Old French *endurer*, from Latin *indurare* 'harden', from *in-* 'in' and *durus* 'hard'. An obsolete English sense is 'harden' as in Spenser's *Faerie Queene*: *And manly limbs endur'd with little care Against all hard mishaps and fortuneless misfare.* **Endurance** (late 15th century in the sense 'continued existence, ability to last') is from Old French, from *endurer* 'make hard'; it was also formerly written as *indurance*.

enema [late Middle English] This is via late Latin from Greek *enienai* 'send or put in', from *en-* 'in' and *hienai* 'send'.

enemy [Middle English] This is from Old French *enemi*, from Latin *inimicus*, from *in-* 'not' and *amicus* 'friend'. *The great enemy* is sometimes used to mean 'death': this is a biblical allusion to 1 Corinthians 15:26. The phrase *enemy of the people* is commonly found in political contexts as a form of indictment by popular leaders against their oppponents (Joseph Conrad *Nostromo*: Comrade Fidanza … you have refused all aid from that doctor. Is he really a dangerous enemy of the people?). The noun **enmity** is also Middle English and is from Old French *enemi(s)tie*, based on Latin *inimicus*.

energy [mid 16th century] The early use of the word *energy* was with the meaning 'force or vigour of expression': this sense derives from an imperfect understanding of Aristotle's use of *energeia* for the kind of metaphor which calls up a mental picture of something 'in action'. French *énergie* or late Latin is the direct source of the English word, from Greek *energeia*, from *en-* 'in, within' and *ergon* 'work'. **Energetic** dating from the mid 17th century meant 'powerfully effective' initially: the origin is Greek *energētikos*, from *energein* 'operate, work in or upon' (based on *ergon*).

enervate [early 17th century] The Latin verb *enervare* 'weaken (by extraction of the sinews)', gave rise to *enervate* 'cause to feel drained of energy' in English; the base elements are *e-* (a variant of *ex-*) 'out of' and *nervus* 'sinew'.

enforce [Middle English] 'Strive' and 'impel by force' were senses found for *enforce* in early examples of its use. It was formerly also spelt *inforce*. It also expressed a notion of 'reinforcing' a military body or 'strengthening' a fortress. The notion of law enforcement dates from the early 17th century. The origin is Old French *enforcir*, *enforcier*, based on Latin *in-* 'in' and *fortis* 'strong'.

enfranchise [late Middle English] *Infranchise* was once a variant spelling of *enfranchise* from Old French *enfranchiss-*, the lengthened stem of *enfranchir*. The base elements here are *en-* (expressing a change of state) and *franc*, *franche* 'free'. Basically, the word means 'make free' but it is now often associated with the right to vote: this political link dates from the late 17th century.

engage [late Middle English] Formerly also written as *ingage*, *engage* is from French *enguger*, ultimately from the base of English *gage*. The word originally meant 'to pawn or pledge something, mortgage (land)'; later it expressed the idea 'pledge oneself (to do something)', which led in the mid 16th century to 'enter into a contract'. A century later, the senses 'involve oneself in an activity', 'enter into combat' arose: this development gave rise to the notion 'involve someone or something else'. The connection with betrothal dates from the early 18th century. **Engagement**, a French adoption, from *engager*, is found from the early 17th century in the general sense 'a legal or moral obligation'. Its use for an 'appointment' made with another person for a business or social meeting, is found from the early 19th century.
→ WAGE

engender [Middle English] A former variant spelling was *ingender*. The word in English is from Old French *engendrer*, from Latin *ingenerare*, from *in-* 'in' and *generare* 'beget'. The base is Latin *genus* 'breed, race'. The figurative use

'give rise to' occurred early in the word's sense development.
→ GENERATION

engine [Middle English] Old French *engin* is the source of the word, from Latin *ingenium* 'talent, device', from *in-* 'in' and *gignere* 'beget'. The original meaning was 'ingenuity, cunning', which survives in Scots in the word *ingine*; this was an early alternative English spelling of *engine*. The sense developed into 'the product of ingenuity; a plot or snare'; it also came to denote a 'tool, weapon' (Milton *Paradise Lost*: That two-handed engine … Stands ready to smite); later it referred specifically to a large mechanical weapon. This gave rise to 'machine' in the mid 17th century, used commonly later in combinations such as *steam engine*, *internal-combustion engine*. **Engineer** dates from Middle English as a term for a designer and constructor of fortifications and weapons; in early use it came via Old French from medieval Latin *ingeniator*, from *ingeniare* 'contrive, devise' (from Latin *ingenium*). In later use it is from French *ingénieur* or Italian *ingegnere*, also based on Latin *ingenium*, its ending influenced by words ending in *-eer*.
→ INGENIOUS

English [Old English] Even in Old English the adjective *Englisc* had lost its etymological sense of 'belonging to the Angles' and denoted the early Germanic settlers of 5th-century Britain (the Angles, Saxons, and Jutes) or their language which is now called *Old English*. In the 11th century, *English* came to be applied to all natives of England including the Celtic and Scandinavian elements of the population. However after the Norman Conquest, descendants of the invaders were regarded as French, *English* being restricted to people who were settled in England prior to the Conquest.
→ ANGLICAN

engorge [late 15th century] The early sense recorded was 'gorge; eat or fill to excess'. This was probably first used in English with reference to hawks. Old French *engorgier* 'feed to excess' is the source, from *en-* 'into' and *gorge* 'throat'. The current sense 'fill or be congested with blood' dates from the early 19th century.

engross [late Middle English] This was formerly also written as *ingross*. It is based on late Latin *grossus* 'large'. The chief current sense is 'absorb all the attention of somebody': this dates from the early 18th century. A current legal usage is 'produce (a legal document) in its final form'; this is from Anglo-Norman French *engrosser*, based on medieval Latin *grossa* 'large writing'. Obsolete senses include 'buy up wholesale' which usually involved buying up the whole stock of a commodity in order to retail it at a monopoly price: this comes via Old French from medieval Latin *in grosso* 'wholesale'.

enhance [Middle English] This is from Anglo-Norman French *enhauncer*, probably based on Latin *in-* (expressing intensive force) and *altus* 'high'; a former alternative spelling was *inhance*. The word originally meant 'elevate' both literally and figuratively; later it came to mean 'exaggerate, make to appear greater' as well as 'raise the value or price of something'. Current senses such as 'improve the quality of' date from the early 16th century.

enigma [mid 16th century] This comes via Latin from Greek *ainigma* 'riddle', from *ainissesthai* 'speak allusively or obscurely', from *ainos* 'fable'. In English an *enigma* may be a short piece of prose or verse in which something is described intentionally in obscure metaphors or it may simply refer to something puzzling. One of the codes broken by the codebreakers at Bletchley during the Second World War was known as *Enigma*: this was done using Colossus, the world's first electronic programmable computer. **Enigmatic** (early 17th century) is from French *énigmatique* or late Latin *aenigmaticus*, based on Greek *ainigma*. This conveys mystery and is often used descriptively in association with Leonardo da Vinci's *Mona Lisa*: the sitter was the wife of Francesco del Giocondo and her *enigmatic smile* has become one of the most famous images in Western art.

enjoy [late Middle English] *Enjoy* is from Old French *enjoier* 'give joy to' or *enjoïr* 'enjoy', both based on Latin *gaudere* 'rejoice'. Although usually expressing 'have the benefit of', *enjoy* is sometimes used in phrases such as *enjoy poor health* where the noun has a favourable sense and the adjective qualifies this adversely.

enlarge [Middle English] Formerly also written as *inlarge*, *enlarge* is from Old French *enlarger*, from *en-* (expressing a change of state) and *large* 'large'.

enlighten [Middle English] The early sense was 'make luminous'. In early use the word is from Old English *inlīhtan* 'to shine'; later it is from the prefix *en-*, or *in-* (used as an intensifier) and either *lighten* or the noun *light*. The sense 'give intellectual understanding to' dates from the late 17th century (Milton *Paradise Lost*: Reveal to Adam what shall come ... As I shall thee enlighten).

enliven [mid 17th century] 'Restore to life' and 'give life to' were the early senses of *enliven* which was also formerly written as *inliven*. The word comes from the 16th-century verb *enlive*, *inlive* which was used in the same sense. Here the prefix *en-* or *in-* is an intensifier: the base noun is *life*.
➔ LIFE

enormity [late Middle English] *Enormity* is via Old French from Latin *enormitas*, from *enormis*: the formative elements are *e-* (a variant of *ex-*) 'out of' and *norma* 'pattern, standard'. The word originally meant 'deviation from a standard (such as legal or moral rectitude)' and 'transgression, crime'. Current senses have been influenced by **enormous** 'abnormal, strikingly irregular (for example in size)': this word is recorded from the mid 16th century and is based on Latin *enormis* 'unusual, huge'.

enough [Old English] Old English *genōg* is originally Germanic and related to Dutch *genoeg* and German *genug*. In modern English *enough* normally follows an adjective (*happy enough*) or adverb (*soon enough*) but in Old and Middle English it often preceded them.

enquire [Middle English] The spelling in Middle English was *enquere*, from Old French *enquerre*, based on Latin *inquirere* (*quaerere* 'to seek' being the base verb). It is an alternative form of *inquire* which is often given by dictionaries as standard. *Enquire* is frequently used for 'ask a question'.
➔ INQUIRE

enrage [late 15th century] Formerly also written as *inrage*, this word is from French *enrager*, from *en-* 'into' and *rage* 'rage, anger'. The word sometimes meant 'be distracted (by hunger or thirst)', sometimes 'become angry'; the sense 'make furious' dates from the late 16th century.

enrich [late Middle English] Old French *enrichir* from *en-* 'in' and *riche* 'rich' is the source of *enrich* in English. The early sense was the literal one: 'make wealthy'.

enrol [late Middle English] *Enrol* is from Old French *enroller*, from *en-* 'in' and *rolle* 'a roll': names were originally written on a roll of parchment. Formerly the spelling *inroll* was sometimes found. The connection with enlisting and joining an army arose in the late 16th century.

ensconce [late 16th century] 'Fortify' and 'shelter within or behind a fortification' were early senses of *ensconce* formerly also spelt *insconce*. The prefix *en-*, *in-* 'in' was added to the now archaic noun *sconce* meaning 'small fort': this is from Dutch *schans* 'brushwood'. The meaning developed into 'settle into a comfortable and secure position' in the early 19th century (Dickens *The Old Curiosity Shop*: Ensconcing themselves ... in the warm chimney-corner).

ensign [late Middle English] *Ensign*, both 'flag' and a term for a military rank, is from Old French *enseigne*, from Latin *insignia* 'signs of office'. The now archaic word *ancient* for a 'standard' or 'flag' is an alteration of *ensign*.
→ INSIGNIA

ensue [late Middle English] *Ensue* is from Old French *ensivre*, from Latin *insequi*, based on *sequi* 'to follow'. It was also formerly spelt *insue*. The notion of 'follow' is at the core of the word: sometimes in early contexts this was 'follow in (the steps of)', 'follow the guidance of', 'pursue'; the focus then fell on 'sequence and result' (Tennyson *In Memoriam*: That out of distance might ensue Desire of nearness doubly sweet).

ensure [late Middle English] Early senses included 'convince' and 'make safe'. It is from Anglo-Norman French *enseurer*, an alteration of Old French *aseurer*, which later became *assurer*. It was once used in commercial contexts in the same way as *insure*: this latter has now become the specialized term in this field.
→ ASSURE; INSURANCE

entail [late Middle English] The early term *entail* referred to settlement of property; it was also sometimes spelt *intail*. The base noun is Old French *taille* 'notch, tax'. The simple general use of *entail* to mean 'bring on as a necessary consequence', dates from the early 19th century.

entangle [mid 16th century] This word is based on *tangle*; the primary reference may have been to oars being caught in 'tangle' which was seaweed.
→ TANGLE

enter [Middle English] *Enter* is from Old French *entrer*, from Latin *intrare*, from *intra* 'within'. It has been used as a stage direction from this early period, reflecting corresponding Latin stage directions. The word's use to mean 'put oneself forward as a competitor in (an event)' dates from the late 17th century, from the notion of inserting one's name on a list. **Entry** is also Middle English and is from Old French *entree*, based on Latin *intrata*, the feminine past participle of *intrare*. Early use was both for the action of gaining access, or physical access such as a door, passage, or gate. **Entrance** dates from the late 15th century as the 'right or opportunity of admission': the source is Old French, from *entrer* 'enter'.

enterprise [late Middle English] This is from an Old French word meaning 'something undertaken', the feminine past participle of *entreprendre* used as a noun, based on Latin *pre(he)ndere* 'to take'. The word gradually acquired an additional sense of an undertaking that is bold or momentous. The phrase *enterprise culture* grew up in the 1980s for a model of a capitalist society which specifically encourages entrepreneurial activity and financial self-reliance.

entertain [late Middle English] From French *entretenir*, *entertain* is based on Latin *inter* 'among' and *tenere* 'to hold'. The word originally meant 'maintain, continue' (seen in archaic phrases such as *entertain a correspondence with someone*); this later (late 15th century) developed into 'maintain in a certain condition, treat in a certain way' (Shakespeare *Henry VI* part i: I am sorry, that with reverence I did not entertain thee as thou art). The meaning 'show hospitality' existed from the same period. It was the early 17th century when the verb started to be used in the context of *entertaining an idea*. The noun **entertainment** dates from the early 16th century; its use for a public performance intended to amuse an audience is recorded from the early 18th century.

enthrall [late Middle English] Initially *enthrall* had the sense 'enslave' but it now usually means 'captivate'. The prefix *en-*, *in-* is an intensifier added to *thrall* which may be interpreted as 'slave' or 'slavery'. The spelling in early examples was sometimes formerly *inthrall*.
→ THRALL

enthrone [early 16th century] This word based on *throne* gradually replaced late Middle English *enthronize*.
→ THRONE

enthusiasm [early 17th century] 'Religious fervour' was once referred to as *enthusiasm* which comes from French *enthousiasme*, or via late Latin from Greek *enthousiasmos*. Greek *enthous* 'possessed by a god, inspired' (the second element of which is from *theos* 'god') is the base. The related words **enthusiast** and **enthusiastic** are contemporaneous. *Enthusiast* denoted a person believing himself or herself to be divinely inspired, which reflects the Greek *enthousiastēs* 'person inspired by a god': the direct source of the English word is either French *enthousiaste* or ecclesiastical Latin *enthusiastes* 'member of a heretical sect'. *Enthusiastic* is from Greek *enthousiastikos*, from *enthous*. The verb **enthuse** dates from the early 19th century as a US colloquial usage often used humorously: it is a back-formation (by removal of the suffix) from *enthusiasm*.

entice [Middle English] Early senses included 'incite' and 'provoke (to anger)' from Old French *enticier*: this is probably from a root meaning 'set on fire', based on an alteration of

Latin *titio* 'firebrand'. *Intice* was an alternative spelling in English formerly.

entire [late Middle English] Formerly also spelt *intire*, *entire* is from Old French *entier*, based on Latin *integer* 'untouched, whole', from *in-* 'not' and the root of *tangere* 'to touch'. The literal meanings of Latin *integer* ('whole, unbroken') survived in early French and Middle English, but the figurative senses ('untainted, upright') tended to disappear. Middle English **entirety** is from Old French *entierete*, from Latin *integritas*, from *integer*.
→ INTEGER

entitle [late Middle English] *Entitle* is via Old French from late Latin *intitulare*, from *in-* 'in' and Latin *titulus* 'title'. *Intitle* once existed as an alternative spelling in English.

entity [late 15th century] Initially this word denoted a thing's existence. It comes from French *entité* or medieval Latin *entitas*, from late Latin *ens*, *ent-* 'being' (from *esse* 'to be').

entomb [late Middle English] Sometimes written *intomb* in early examples, *entomb* is from Old French *entomber*, from *en-* 'in' and *tombe* 'tomb'.

entrails [Middle English] This word is from Old French *entrailles*, from medieval Latin *intralia*, an alteration of Latin *interanea* 'internal things', based on *inter* 'among'.

entrap [mid 16th century] The source is Old French *entraper*, from *en-* 'in' and *trappe* 'a trap'.

entreat [late Middle English] The early sense recorded was 'treat, act towards (someone) in a certain manner'; the source is Old French *entraitier*, based on *traitier* 'to treat', from Latin *tractare* 'to handle'. An alternative early spelling was *intreat*. Late Middle English **entreaty** had the senses 'treatment (of a subject)', 'treatment (of people)', 'management (of cattle)'; it is based on *entreat*, on the pattern of *treaty*. The current sense 'earnest request, supplication' dates from the late 16th century.

entrench [mid 16th century] Based on *trench*, this word initially had the literal sense 'place within a trench'. In the late 16th century it came to be used in political contexts for 'safeguard the position of (somebody or a group)'.
→ TRENCH

entrepreneur [early 19th century] *Entrepreneur* was once also a job title for the director of a musical institution as well as denoting a person who sets up a business. It comes from French, from *entreprendre* 'undertake'.
→ ENTERPRISE

enumerate [early 17th century] *Enumerate* is from Latin *enumerare* 'count out', from *e-* (a variant of *ex-*) 'out' and *numerus* 'number'.

enunciate [mid 16th century] This is from Latin *enuntiare* 'announce clearly', from *e-* (a variant of *ex-*) 'out' and *nuntiare* 'announce'. The base noun is Latin *nuntius* 'messenger'.

envelop [late Middle English] *Envelop* is from Old French *envoluper*, from *en-* 'in' and a second element (also found in *develop*) of unknown origin. The word **envelope** dates from the mid 16th century in the sense 'wrapper, enveloping layer': it comes from French *enveloppe*, from *envelopper* 'envelop'. The sense 'covering of a letter' dates from the early 18th century.

environs [mid 17th century] This word for the surrounding area of a district is an adoption of the French plural of *environ* 'surroundings': the base elements are Old French *en* 'in' and *viron* 'circuit' (from *virer* 'to turn, veer'). The verb **environ** dating from Middle English is current in formal use; it is from Old French *environer* 'to surround', a meaning which has passed into English.

envisage [early 19th century] *Envisage* is from French *envisager*, from *en-* 'in' and *visage* 'face'.

envoy [mid 17th century] Literally meaning 'sent (person)', *envoy* is from French *envoyé*, the past participle of *envoyer* 'send'. The phrase *en voie* 'on the way' is the source, based on Latin *via* 'way'.

envy [Middle English] *Envy* is one of the traditional seven deadly sins said to lead to damnation in Christian theology. Early senses included 'hostility, enmity'. The noun *envy* is from Old French *envie*, the verb from Old French *envier*, from Latin *invidere* 'regard maliciously, grudge'. Latin *in-* 'into' and *videre* 'to see' are the base elements. Middle English **envious** is from Old French *envieus*, from *envie* 'envy', on the pattern of Latin *invidiosus* 'invidious'.

ephemera [late 16th cent.] *Ephemera* 'things that exist or are used for a short time', sometimes describe collectable memorabilia. It is the plural of *ephemeron*, the Greek neuter of *ephēmeros* 'lasting only a day'. As a singular noun the word originally denoted a plant said by ancient writers to last only one day, or an insect with a short lifespan, and therefore was applied (in the late 18th century) to a person or thing of short-lived interest. Current use has been influenced by plurals such as *trivia* and *memorabilia*. The adjective **ephemeral** also dates from the late 16th century and is based on Greek *ephēmeros*.

epic [late 16th century] First recorded as an adjective, *epic* came via Latin from Greek *epikos*, from *epos* 'word, song', related to *eipein* 'say'. Typical epics are the Homeric poems (the *Iliad* and the *Odyssey*); these are often regarded as embodying the nation's history most worthy of remembrance. Some writers refer to a *national epic*, a phrase which has been extended to any imaginative work such as a film (e.g. *a Hollywood biblical epic*).

epicentre [late 19th century] This is from Greek *epikentros* 'situated on a centre', from *epi* 'upon' and *kentron* 'centre'.

epicure [late Middle English] An *epicure* first denoted a disciple of the Greek philosopher *Epicurus* (341–270 BC) who founded a school which advocated hedonism. The word came via medieval Latin from Greek *Epikouros* 'Epicurus'. In current use an *epicure* takes particular pleasure in fine food and drink.

epidemic [early 17th century] This was first recorded as an adjective. The source of the word is French *épidémique*, from *épidémie* which is via late Latin from Greek *epidēmia* 'the prevalence of disease'. The Greek base *epidēmios* 'prevalent' is made up of *epi* 'upon' and *dēmos* 'the people'.

epilation [late 19th century] This comes from French *épiler*, from *é-* (expressing removal) and Latin *pilus* 'strand of hair', on the pattern of *depilation*.

epilepsy [mid 16th century] *Epilepsy* is from French *épilepsie*, or via late Latin from Greek *epilēpsia*, from *epilambanein* 'seize, attack', from *epi* 'upon' and *lambanein* 'take hold of'. **Epileptic** (early 17th century) is from French *épileptique*, via late Latin from Greek *epilēptikos*, from *epilēpsia*.

epilogue [late Middle English] *Epilogue*, a comment or conclusion at the end of a book or play, is from French *épilogue*, via Latin from Greek *epilogos*, from *epi* 'in addition' and *logos* 'speech'.

epiphany [Middle English] *Epiphany*, the festival commemorating the manifestation of Christ to the Gentiles as represented by the Magi, is from Greek *epiphainein* 'reveal'. The sense relating to the Christian festival is via Old French *epiphanie* and ecclesiastical Latin *epiphania*.

episcopal [late Middle English] This is from French *épiscopal* or ecclesiastical Latin *episcopalis*, from *episcopus* 'bishop', from Greek *episkopos* 'overseer'. The word in English means 'of a bishop, governed by bishops' and is found in combinations such as *Methodist Episcopal* and *Reformed Episcopal*, religious denominations constituted on the principle of episcopacy.
→ BISHOP

episode [late 17th century] An *episode* initially denoted a section between two choric songs in Greek tragedy. The word is from Greek *epeisodion*, the neuter of *epeisodios* 'coming in besides'. The elements here are: *epi* 'in addition' and *eisodos* 'entry' (from *eis* 'into' and *hodos* 'way'). The use of the word for an instalment in a radio and, eventually, television drama dates from the early 20th century.

epistle [Old English] This came via Latin from Greek *epistolē*, from *epistellein* 'send news', from *epi* 'in addition' and *stellein* 'send'. The word was reintroduced in Middle English from Old French. Now, when referring to an ordinary modern letter, it is only applied humorously; the usual use is with reference to a letter written in ancient times or as a term for a poetical work composed in the form of a letter. The *epistles* of the New Testament are letters from the apostles, forming part of the canon of Scripture.

epitaph [late Middle English] Old French *epitaphe* is the source; this came via Latin from Greek *epitaphion* 'funeral oration', the neuter of *ephitaphios* 'over or at a tomb', from *epi* 'upon' and *taphos* 'tomb'.

epithet [late 16th century] This word for an adjective or descriptive phrase came from French *épithète*, or via Latin from Greek *epitheton*, the neuter of *epithetos* 'attributed', from *epitithenai* 'add'. The formative elements here are *epi* 'upon' and *tithenai* 'to place'.

epitome [early 16th century] *Epitome* 'a perfect example of a particular quality or type' is via Latin from Greek *epitomē*, from *epitemnein* 'abridge', from *epi* 'in addition' and *temnein* 'to cut'.

epoch [early 17th century] The Latin form *epocha* is found in early examples: it was originally in the general sense of a date from which succeeding years were numbered (for example the date of the birth of Christ). Modern Latin *epocha* is the source, from Greek *epokhē* 'stoppage, fixed point of time', from *epe-khein* 'stop, take up a position'. The base elements are *epi* 'upon, near to' and *ekhein* 'stay, be in a certain state'.

equable [mid 17th century] 'Fair, equitable' was the sense of *equable* in early examples. The origin is Latin *aequabilis*, from *aequare* 'make equal'. The common current sense is 'not easily disturbed; calm'.

→ EQUATE

equal [late Middle English] *Equal* is from Latin *aequalis*, from *aequus* 'even, level, equal'. The noun use to denote a person of the same standing, socially or in ability, etc., dates from the late 16th century. Late Middle English **equality** is via Old French from Latin *aequalitas*, from *aequalis*.

equanimity [early 17th century] Early senses included 'fairness, impartiality'. The word is from Latin *aequanimitas*, from *aequus* 'equal' and *animus* 'mind'.

equate [Middle English] 'Make equal, balance' was the early sense recorded. It is from Latin *aequare* 'make level or equal', from *aequus*. Current senses date from the mid 19th century. **Equation** dates from late Middle English and is from Latin *aequatio(n-)*, from *aequare*; use in mathematics arose in the late 16th century. The same Latin verb is the base of **equator**, also late Middle English, from medieval Latin *aequator*, found in the phrase *circulus aequator diei et noctis* 'circle equalizing day and night'.

→ EQUAL

equerry [early 16th century] Formerly also spelt *esquiry*, the word *equerry* is from Old French *esquierie* 'company of squires, prince's stables', from Old French *esquier* 'esquire'; it is perhaps associated with Latin *equus* 'horse'. The historical sense referring to an officer of the household of a prince or noble, in charge of the stables, is apparently based on Old French *esquier d'esquierie* 'squire of stables'.

equestrian [mid 17th century] This is based on Latin *equester* 'belonging to a horseman', from *eques* 'horseman, knight', from *equus* 'horse'.

equilibrium [early 17th century] The early sense was 'well-balanced state of mind'. Latin *aequilibrium* is the source, from *aequi-* 'equal' and *libra* 'balance'.

equine [late 18th century] This is from Latin *equinus*, from *equus* 'horse'.

equinox [late Middle English] The *equinox* occurs twice a year when the sun crosses the celestial equator and day and night are of equal length. The word is from Old French *equinoxe*

or Latin *aequinoctium*, from *aequi-* 'equal' and *nox*, *noct-* 'night'.

equip [early 16th century] *Equip* is from French *équiper* 'equip', probably from Old Norse *skipa* 'to man (a ship)', from *skip* 'ship'. **Equipment** dates from the early 18th century and is from French *équipement*, from *équiper*.

equity [Middle English] This word is from Old French *équité*, from Latin *aequitas*, from *aequus* 'equal'. It was adopted as the name of an actors' trade union from the early 20th century in the UK, US, and several other countries, to which all professional actors must belong. **Equitable** dating from the mid 16th century is from French *équitable*, from *équité*.

equivalent [late Middle English] The word *equivalent* once described people who were equal in power or rank. The source is Old French from late Latin *aequivalere* 'be of equal worth', from *aequi-* 'equally' and *valere* 'be worth'. **Equivalence** recorded from the same period came via Old French from medieval Latin *aequivalentia*, from *aequivalere*.

equivocate [late Middle English] *Equivocate* 'use ambiguous language to conceal the truth' was first recorded in the sense 'use a word in more than one sense'. It is from late Latin *aequivocare* 'call by the same name', from *aequivocus*. The adjective **equivocal** meaning 'open to more than one interpretation' dates from the mid 16th century: it is from late Latin *aequivocus*, from Latin *aequus* 'equally' and *vocare* 'to call'.

era [mid 17th century] This is from late Latin *aera* which was a number used as a basis for reckoning, an epoch from which time was reckoned: this is the plural of *aes*, *aer-* 'money, counter'.

eradicate [late Middle English] The early sense was 'pull up by the roots'. It comes from Latin *eradicare* 'tear up by the roots', from *e-* (a variant of *ex-*) 'out' and *radix*, *radic-* 'root'. The modern sense 'remove entirely' dates from the mid 17th century.

erase [late 16th century] This was originally a heraldic term meaning 'represent the head or limb of an animal with a jagged edge'. It comes from Latin *eras-*, the past participial stem of *eradere* 'scrape away', from *e-* (a variant of *ex-*) 'out' and *radere* 'scrape'.

erect [late Middle English] *Erect* and **erection** date from the same period; their source is Latin *erigere* 'to set up', from *e-* (a variant of *ex-*) 'out' and *regere* 'to direct'. **Erectile** dates from the mid 19th century and is from French *érectile*, from Latin *erigere*.

ergonomic [1950s] This term for the study of people's efficiency in their working environment is based on Greek *ergon* 'work', on the pattern of the term *economics*.

ermine [Middle English] This is from Old French *hermine*, probably from medieval Latin (*mus*) *Armenius* 'Armenian (mouse)'. The belief that the ermine derived its name from Armenia (in the Caucasus of SE Europe) was common in the 14th century.

erosion [mid 16th century] This word came via French from Latin *erosio(n-)*, from *erodere* 'wear or gnaw away', the source of the English verb **erode** which dates from the early 17th century. The base elements are *e-* (a variant of *ex-*) 'out, away' and *rodere* 'gnaw'. These words are used in geological contexts from the late 18th century.

erotic [mid 17th century] This is from French *érotique*, from Greek *erōtikos*, from *erōs*, *erōt-* 'sexual love'. This Greek word gave the name *Eros* (the god of love in Greek mythology) on which the adjective **erogenous** is based: this dates from the late 19th century.

err [Middle English] The early sense of *err* was 'wander, go astray'. The source is Old French *errer*, from Latin *errare* 'to stray'.

errand [Old English] Old English *ærende* was a 'message, mission'; it is a Germanic word related to Old High German *ārunti*, and obscurely to Swedish *ärende* and Danish *ærinde*. The modern colloquial use of the word to mean a short journey made to deliver a message or make a purchase for the sender, dates from the mid 17th century.

errant [Middle English] This word was used first of all in the sense 'travelling in search of adventure' as in *knight errant*: this is from Old French *errant* 'travelling', the present participle of *errer*, from late Latin *iterare* 'go on a journey'. The base is Latin *iter* 'journey'. The word's use to mean 'straying from accepted standards' is from Latin *errant-*, the present participial stem of the verb *errare* 'to wander'. **Arrant** is a Middle English variant of *errant* which was originally found in phrases such as *arrant thief* (=roving thief). It is now commonly heard in the phrase *arrant nonsense*.

erratic [late Middle English] This is from Old French *erratique*, from Latin *erraticus*, from *errare* 'to stray, err'. It was first used in connection with planets described as *erratic stars*; it had the sense 'prone to wander'. The sense 'unpredictable in movement' dates from the mid 19th century.

error [Middle English] *Error* has come via Old French from Latin *error*, from *errare* 'to stray, err'. Until the end of the 18th century, the spelling was often *errour*, a form given by Johnson. The word was spelt *error* in Bailey's Dictionary of 1753 and this is the one that has prevailed. However, in the sense 'wandering', the spelling *error* was used in conscious imitation of the Latin. This sense is now only in poetic use (Tennyson *Gareth and Lynette*: The damsel's headlong error thro' the wood). Latin *errare* 'to wander' has also given rise to late Middle English **erroneous** based on Latin *erroneus*, from *erro(n-)* 'vagabond'. The English word meant 'wandering, roving' in certain early examples.

erudite [late Middle English] *Erudite* 'showing great knowledge' is from Latin *eruditus*, the past participle of *erudire* 'instruct, train (= bring out of an untrained state)': the base is *rudis* 'rude, untrained'.

eruption [late Middle English] This word comes from Old French, or from Latin *eruptio(n-)*, from the verb *erumpere* 'break out', from *e-* (a variant of *ex-*) 'out' and *rumpere* 'burst out, break'. As a geological term, the word is found from the mid 18th century. **Erupt** dates from the mid 17th century and is from Latin *erupt-*, the past participial stem of *erumpere*.

escalator [early 20th century] This was originally a US trade name; the word is formed from the verb *escalade* 'climb a wall by ladder', on the pattern of *elevator*. The verb **escalate** arose in the 1920s in the sense 'travel on an escalator': it is a back-formation (by removal of the suffix) from *escalator*. Current senses include 'increase rapidly' usually with reference to prices, and 'become or make more serious' (e.g. *it was feared it could escalate the war*): the latter use became popular around the time of the Vietnam War during the late 1960s and early '70s.

escape [Middle English] This is from Old French *eschaper*, based on medieval Latin *ex-* 'out' and *cappa* 'cloak'. The use of *escape* for a 'mental distraction' in connection with an activity such as reading dates from the mid 19th century. The medieval Latin element *cappa* 'cloak' is the base too of **escapade** first recorded in the mid 17th century also meaning 'an escape'; it is now 'an incident which involves adventure and daring'. It comes from French, from Provençal or Spanish, from *escapar* 'to escape'.

escarpment [early 19th century] This geographical term for a long steep slope is from French *escarpement*, *escarpe* 'scarp', from Italian *scarpa* 'slope'.

eschew [late Middle English] *Eschew* 'deliberately avoid' is from Old French *eschiver*; it is

ultimately Germanic in origin and related to German *scheuen* 'shun, dread'.
→ SHY

escort [late 16th century] An *escort* was originally a body of armed men escorting travellers. It comes via French from Italian *scorta*, the feminine past participle of *scorgere* 'to conduct, guide', based on Latin *ex-* 'out of' and *corrigere* 'set right'. The notion of 'accompanying, keeping company with' a woman is a US usage dating from the end of the 19th century.
→ CORRECT

escutcheon [late 15th century] The word *escutcheon* 'a shield or emblem bearing a coat of arms' is in current idiomatic use in the phrase *a blot on one's escutcheon* which expresses the notion of 'a stain on one's reputation'. It comes from Anglo-Norman French *escuchon*, based on Latin *scutum* 'shield'.

esoteric [mid 17th century] *Esoteric* 'likely to be understood only by a small group of people' is from Greek *esōterikos*: this is from *esōterō*, the comparative of *esō* 'within', from *es*, *eis* 'into'. The Greek word was first used by Lucian with regard to Aristotle's work which he classified into *esoteric* and *exoteric*. Later writers used the word for the secret doctrines said to have been taught by Pythagoras to a few specially chosen disciples.

especial [late Middle English] This comes via Old French from Latin *specialis* 'belonging to a particular species, special as opposed to general', from *species*. In Old French the word had developed a secondary meaning: 'pre-eminent'. In English the word *especial* was used as a synonym of *special* but later the two words came to exist side by side but with distinct meanings in use, *especial* coming to be restricted to the sense 'important'.
→ SPECIAL

esplanade [late 16th century] An *esplanade* once denoted an area of flat ground on top of a rampart. The word is a French adoption, from Italian *spianata*, from Latin *explanatus* 'flattened, levelled'. The base verb is *explanare* 'make plain'.
→ EXPLAIN

espouse [late Middle English] The early sense recorded was 'take as a spouse'. The source is Old French *espouser*, from Latin *sponsare* 'espouse, betroth', from *sponsus* 'betrothed'. The transferred use of the verb to mean 'make one's own, adopt, embrace' when talking about a cause, a doctrine, a way of life, etc., dates from the early 17th century (Wordsworth *White Doe*: Espouse thy doom at once, and cleave To fortitude without reprieve).

Espousal, also late Middle English, is from Old French *espousaille*, from Latin *sponsalia* 'betrothal', from *sponsare*.

espy [Middle English] This is from Old French *espier*, which is ultimately Germanic in origin and related to Dutch *spieden* and German *spähan*. Early meanings included 'act as a spy upon' and 'keep a look out'; the emphasis then moved to a notion of 'perception and discovery' (S. T. Coleridge *Sibylline Leaves*: Can she the bodiless dead espy).
→ SPY

esquire [late Middle English] *Esquire* is from Old French *esquier*, from Latin *scutarius* 'shield-bearer', from *scutum* 'shield'. The word first referred to a young nobleman in training for knighthood. It continued to denote a man belonging to the higher order of the English gentry ranking immediately below a knight: classes of *esquires* within this group have been defined by some but the boundaries between them are disputed as confusing *esquire* and *gentleman*. Its use as a polite title appended to a man's name arose from the word's application as a courtesy title given to a young nobleman. In the US the title belongs officially to lawyers and public officers; in British English it is now reserved for ceremonious occasions or letter addresses.
→ SQUIRE

essay [late 15th century] The early sense of the verb was 'test the quality of': it is an alteration of *assay*, by association with Old French *essayer*: this is based on late Latin *exagium* 'weighing', from the base of *exigere* 'ascertain, weigh'. The noun *essay* dates from the late 16th century and is from Old French *essai* 'trial'; it was used to mean 'an attempt or endeavour' (C. Brontë *Villette*: Is this your first essay at teaching?). In writing contexts, it referred inintially to 'a first draft' but came to mean 'a composition' (Dickens *Our Mutual Friend*: She could write a little essay on any subject). This particular use is apparently taken from the French philosopher and essayist Montaigne (1533–92) whose *Essais* were first published in 1580.
→ ASSAY

essence [late Middle English] *Essence* is via Old French from Latin *essentia*, from *esse* 'to be'. An early meaning was 'being, existence'. In alchemy it was used in the phrase *fifth essence* which was a supposed substance distinct from the recognized four elements of fire, air, earth, and water. The alchemists believed this substance to be latent in all bodies and thus to be extractable by distillation: this probably led to the word's use for 'an extract obtained from a plant with therapeutic qualities', reinforced by the sense 'indispensable quality or constituent'. Middle English **essential** had the sense 'in the highest degree': it is from late Latin *essentialis*, from Latin *essentia*.

→ QUINTESSENCE

establish [late Middle English] This word was recorded earlier as *stablish*. It comes from Old French *establiss-*, the lengthened stem of *establir*, from Latin *stabilire* 'make firm'. The Latin adjective *stabilis* meaning 'stable' is the base.

estate [Middle English] 'State or condition' was the early meaning of *estate*; this remains in the phrase *the (holy) estate of matrimony*. Sometimes the notion of 'condition' means with respect to worldly property and possessions seen in examples such as *country estate* and *wind up an estate*. The source is Old French *estat*, from Latin *status* 'state, condition'. The base verb is Latin *stare* 'to stand'. In English the word is sometimes used to define three basic divisions in politics, originally defined as the Clergy, the Barons and Knights, and the Commons; this evolved into the Lords Spiritual, the Lords Temporal, and the Commons. The latter was often referred to as the *third estate*, but the other two are not usually enumerated in this way. These earlier divisions led to the less precise use of *estate* in the phrase *the estates of the realm* referring to The Crown, the House of Lords, and the House of Commons. The *fourth estate* has become a humorous way of referring to the Press.

esteem [Middle English] The word was first recorded as a noun in the senses 'worth, reputation' and 'valuation'. It comes via Old French from Latin *aestimare* 'to estimate'. The verb was originally in the Latin sense as well as meaning 'appraise', used figuratively to mean 'assess the merit of'. Current senses date from the 16th century. The adjective **estimable** arose in the late 15th century in the sense 'able to be estimated or appraised'; it has come via Old French from Latin *aestimabilis*, from *aestimare*. The English word was found earlier in *inestimable*.

→ ESTIMATE

estimate [late Middle English] *Estimate* is from Latin *aestimare* 'determine, appraise'. The noun originally meant 'intellectual ability, comprehension' but this did not survive beyond late Middle English; later it developed the sense '(making) a valuation'. The verb originally meant 'to think well or badly of someone or something' (late 15th century), later becoming more generalized as 'regard as being, consider to be'. **Estimation** dates from late Middle English in the senses 'comprehension, intuition' and 'valuing, a valu-

ation': it comes from Latin *aestimatio(n-)*, from *aestimare*.

→ ESTEEM

estrange [late 15th century] Found in phrases such as *estranged wife*, *estrange* is from Old French *estranger*, from Latin *extraneare* 'treat as a stranger'. The Latin word is based on *extraneus* 'not belonging to the family', used as a noun to mean 'stranger'.

→ STRANGE

estuary [mid 16th century] This was originally a tidal inlet of any size. Latin *aestuarium* 'tidal part of a shore' is the source, from *aestus* 'tide'.

etch [mid 17th century] This is from Dutch *etsen*, from German *ätzen*, from a base meaning 'cause to eat'. This type of engraving is done by 'eating away' the surface of metals, glass, and stone, by the application of acid.

→ EAT

eternity [late Middle English] Old French *eternite* is the source, from Latin *aeternitas*, from *aeternus* 'without beginning or end', from *aevum* 'age'. **Eternal** is also late Middle English and comes via Old French from late Latin *aeternalis*, from Latin *aeternus*. The word is common in religious contexts, and as a noun phrase *the Eternal* is sometimes found meaning 'God' (Milton *Paradise Lost*: His trust was with th'Eternal to be deem'd Equal in strength).

ether [late Middle English] This is from Old French, or via Latin from Greek *aithēr* 'upper air', from the base of *aithein* 'burn, shine'. Originally the word denoted a substance believed to occupy space beyond the sphere of the moon. The use of *ether* as a name for the rarefied substance formerly believed to permeate all space arose in the mid 17th century; its application as a term for a volatile liquid used as an anaesthetic is found in medical contexts from the mid 18th century. The adjective **ethereal** (early 16th century) is based on Greek *aitherios* (from *aithēr*).

Ethernet [1970s] This is a blend of *ether* and *network*.

ethic [late Middle English] At first this term referred to ethics or moral philosophy. It comes from Old French *éthique*, from Latin *ethice*, from Greek *(hē) ēthikē (tekhnē)* '(the science of) morals'. The base is Greek *ēthos* 'nature, disposition'.

→ ETHOS

ethnic [late Middle English] This, like *gentile*, was first used with reference to a person not belonging to the Christian or Jewish faith. It comes via ecclesiastical Latin from Greek *ethnikos* 'heathen', from *ethnos* 'nation'. Current senses date from the mid 19th century. The phrase *ethnic minority* arose in the 1940s; references to *ethnic cleansing* are found in texts from the 1990s.

ethos [mid 19th century] *Ethos* 'the characteristic spirit of a culture' is modern Latin from Greek *ēthos* 'nature, disposition', which in the plural means 'customs'.

etiquette [mid 18th century] This is from French *étiquette* 'list of ceremonial observances of a court'. The French word also meant 'label', from Old French *estiquette*; it is this primary sense that is represented by English *ticket*. In English, the word referred to the ceremonial of a court and similar observances in polite society.
→ TICKET

Eucharist [late Middle English] This is from Old French *eucariste*, based on ecclesiastical Greek *eukharistia* 'thanksgiving', from Greek *eukharistos* 'grateful', from *eu* 'well' and *kharizesthai* 'offer graciously'. Greek *kharis* 'grace' is the base.

eulogy [late Middle English] 'High praise' was the first sense recorded for *eulogy*. The source is medieval Latin *eulogium*, *eulogia* (from Greek *eulogia* 'praise'), apparently influenced by Latin *elogium* 'inscription on a tomb' (from Greek *elegia* 'elegy'). The current sense 'a speech given in praise' dates from the late 16th century.

eunuch [Old English] This word came via Latin from Greek *eunoukhos*, literally 'bedroom guard', from *eunē* 'bed' and a second element related to *ekhein* 'to hold'.

euphemism [late 16th century] The word *euphemism* for 'a mild word or expression substituted for one considered blunt and embarrassing' is from Greek *euphēmismos*, from *euphēmizein* 'use auspicious words'. The formative elements are *eu* 'well' and *phēmē* 'speaking'.

euphoria [late 17th century] This originally described the well-being produced in a sick person by the use of drugs. It is modern Latin, from Greek, from *euphoros* 'borne well, healthy', from *eu* 'well' and *pherein* 'to bear'.

eureka [early 17th century] This is from Greek *heurēka* 'I have found it' (from *heuriskein* 'to find'), said to have been uttered by Archimedes when he hit upon a method of determining the purity of gold. The noun (a term for an alloy of copper and nickel used for electrical filament and resistance wire) dates from the early 20th century.

euthanasia [early 17th century] This was first used in the literal sense 'easy death'. It is from Greek, from *eu* 'well' and *thanatos* 'death'.

evacuate [late Middle English] The early sense was 'clear the contents of'. It comes from the Latin verb *evacuare* 'empty (the bowels)', from *e-* (a variant of *ex-*) 'out of' and *vacuus* 'empty'. The noun **evacuation** is also late Middle English and is from late Latin *evacuatio(n-)*, from *evacuare*. **Evacuee** dates from the early 20th century; it was originally in the French form *évacué*, the past participle of *évacuer* (from Latin *evacuare*).

evade [late 15th century] This is from French *évader*, from Latin *evadere* from *e-* (a variant of *ex-*) 'out of' and *vadere* 'go'. **Evasion** is late Middle English when it meant 'prevaricating excuse': this came via Old French from Latin *evasio(n-)*, from *evadere*. **Evasive**, from the same source verb, dates from the early 18th century.

evaluate [mid 19th century] This is a back-formation (by removal of the suffix) from *evaluation*, from French *évaluer*, from *es-* (from Latin *ex-*) 'out, from' and Old French *value* 'value'.

evangelist [Middle English] The first recorded use of *evangelist* was as a term for each writer of the four gospels, Matthew, Mark, Luke, or John; the word comes from Old French *évangéliste*, via ecclesiastical Latin from ecclesiastical Greek *euangelistēs*, from *euangelizesthai* 'evangelize'. **Evangelical** dates from the mid 16th century; it comes via ecclesiastical Latin from ecclesiastical Greek *euangelikos*, from *euangelos* 'bringing good news'. The formative elements are *eu-* 'well' and *angelein* 'announce'.

evaporate [late Middle English] Latin *evaporare* 'change into vapour' (based on *vapor* 'steam, vapour') is the source of *evaporate* in English.

even [Old English] Old English *efen* 'smooth' and *efne* (adverb) are Germanic in origin and related to Dutch *even*, *effen* and German *eben*.
■ **even-steven** (mid 19th century) is a rhyming phrase meaning 'equal(ly)', used as an intensive.

evening [Old English] Old English *ǣfnung* 'dusk falling, the time around sunset' is from *ǣfnian* 'to approach evening', from *ǣfen*: this is Germanic in origin and related to Dutch *avont* and German *Abend*. A short form of *even* is **eve** which dates from late Middle English in the sense 'close of day':
■ **evensong** was *ǣfensang* in Old English and was originally applied to the pre-Reformation service of vespers.

event [late 16th century] This is from Latin *eventus*, from *evenire* 'result, happen', from *e-* (a variant of *ex-*) 'out of' and *venire* 'come'. **Eventual** dates from the early 17th century in the sense 'relating to an event or events': this is also from Latin *eventus*, on the pattern of *actual*. The word **eventing** has been used in equestrian contexts since the 1960s: it was suggested by *three-day event*, horse trials held on three consecutive days.

ever [Old English] Old English *æfre* is of unknown origin.

every [Old English] Old English *æfre ælc* is literally 'ever each'; the compound **everywhere** is Middle English and was formerly written as two words:
■ **Everyman** used to denote any ordinary and typical human being has been recorded in this sense since the early 20th century: it was the name of the principal character in a 15th-century morality play.
➔ EACH

evict [late Middle English] In early contexts *evict* was 'recover property, or the title to property, by legal process'. It comes from Latin *evincere* 'overcome, defeat' (which also gave the formal English word **evince** 'reveal the presence of'). The base elements are *e-* (a variant of *ex-*) 'out' and *vincere* 'conquer'.

evidence [Middle English] This came via Old French from Latin *evidentia*, from *evident-* meaning 'obvious to the eye or mind'. This also gave rise to **evident** (late Middle English): the formative elements are *e-* (a variant of *ex-*) 'out' and *videre* 'to see'.

evil [Old English] Old English *yfel* is Germanic in origin and related to Dutch *euvel* and German *Übel*.

evoke [early 17th century] The first sense of *evoke* recorded was 'invoke (a spirit or deity)': it is from Latin *evocare*, from *e-* (a variant of *ex-*) 'out of, from' and *vocare* 'to call'. The sense 'activate in the mind' dates from the mid 19th century. **Evocative** 'bringing strong feelings to mind' comes from Latin *evocativus*, from the verb *evocare*.

evolve [early 17th century] *Evolve* was first used in the general sense 'make more complex, develop'. It comes from Latin *evolvere*, from *e-* (a variant of *ex-*) 'out of' and *volvere* 'to roll'. **Evolution** dating from the same period is from Latin *evolutio(n-)* 'unrolling', from the verb *evolvere*. Early senses related to physical movement, first recorded in describing a tactical 'wheeling' manoeuvre in the realignment of troops or ships. Current senses stem from a notion of 'opening out' and 'unfolding', giving rise to a general sense of 'development'.

ewer [late Middle English] This is from Anglo-Norman French *ewer*, a variant of Old French *aiguiere*, based on Latin *aquarius* 'of water', from *aqua* 'water'.

WORDBUILDING

The prefix **ex-** [from Latin *ex* 'out of'] adds the sense
■ **out** [exclude]
■ **upward** [extol]
■ **thoroughly** [excruciate]
■ **removal or release** [excommunicate]
■ **inducement of a state** [exasperate]
■ **a former state** [ex-husband]
The prefix **ex-** [from Greek *ex* 'out of'] adds the sense
■ **out** [exodus]

exacerbate [mid 17th century] This is from Latin *exacerbare* 'make harsh', from *ex-* (expressing the inducement of a state) and *acerbus* 'harsh, bitter'. The noun **exacerbation** was already recorded in late Middle English; it originally meant 'provocation to anger'.

exact [late Middle English] Early use was as a verb. It comes from Latin *exact-*, the past participial stem of the verb *exigere* 'complete, ascertain, enforce', from *ex-* 'thoroughly' and *agere* 'perform'. The adjective dates from the mid 16th century and reflects the Latin *exactus* 'precise'.

exaggerate [mid 16th century] This is from Latin *exaggerare* 'heap up', from *ex-* 'thoroughly' and *aggerare* 'heap up' (from *agger* 'heap'). The word originally meant 'pile up, accumulate', later 'intensify praise or blame', 'dwell on a virtue or fault', which gave rise to the current 'represent (something as being) larger or more important than it actually is'.

exalt [late Middle English] *Exalt* is from Latin *exaltare* 'raise aloft', from *ex-* 'out, upward' and *altus* 'high'. **Exaltation** meant 'the action of raising high' in late Middle English: the source is late Latin *exaltatio(n-)*, from Latin *exaltare*.

examine [Middle English] This comes from Old French *examiner*, from Latin *examinare* 'weigh, test', from *examen* literally 'tongue of a balance'. **Examination** is late Middle English in the sense 'testing (one's conscience) by a standard': it comes via Old French from Latin *examinatio(n-)*, from *examinare*. The word's use for 'a test of knowledge' is recorded early in its history.

example [late Middle English] *Example* is from Old French, from Latin *exemplum* 'sample, imitation', from *eximere* 'take out', from *ex-* 'out' and *emere* 'take'. The related word **exemplary** dates from the late 16th century and is from late Latin *exemplaris*, from Latin *exemplum*.
➔ SAMPLE

exasperate [mid 16th century] *Exasperate* is from Latin *exasperare* 'irritate to anger', based on *asper* 'rough'.

excavate [late 16th century] *Excavate* is from Latin *excavare* 'hollow out', from *ex-* 'out' and *cavare* 'make or become hollow' (from *cavus* 'hollow'). This verb is the base too of **excavation** (early 17th century) from French, or from Latin *excavatio(n-)*.

exceed [late Middle English] The early sense was 'go over (a boundary or specified point)'. It is from Old French *exceder*, from Latin *excedere* 'go out, surpass', from *ex-* 'out' and *cedere* 'go'. Dating from the same period is **excess** which comes via Old French from Latin *excessus*, from *excedere*; also **excessive** which comes from Old French *excessif, -ive*, from medieval Latin *excessivus*, from Latin *excedere*.

excel [late Middle English] The origin of this word is Latin *excellere* 'surpass', from *ex-* 'out, beyond' and *celsus* 'lofty'. From the same base is the contemporaneous word **excellence** from Latin *excellentia*. **Excellency** (from Latin *excellentia*) was recorded slightly earlier in the sense 'excellence'; the use of the word as a title dates from the mid 16th century. The adjective **excellent** is late Middle English in the general sense 'excelling, outstanding', referring to either a good or bad quality: it is from Old French, from Latin *excellent-* 'being pre-eminent', from *excellere*. The current appreciatory sense dates from the early 17th century.

except [late Middle English] This is from Latin *except-*, the past participial stem of the verb *excipere* 'taken out', from *ex-* 'out of' and *capere* 'take'. These elements are also at the base of late Middle English **exception** (which came via Old French from Latin *exceptio(n-)*).

excerpt [mid 16th century] Early use was as a verb; it comes from Latin *excerpt-*, the past participial stem of *excerpere* 'pluck out', from *ex-* 'out of' and *carpere* 'to pluck'.

exchange [late Middle English] The noun is from Old French *eschange*, the verb from Old French *eschangier*, based on *changer* 'to change'. The spelling was influenced by Latin *ex-* 'out, utterly'.
➔ CHANGE

exchequer [Middle English] This is from Old French *eschequier*, from medieval Latin *scaccarium* 'chessboard', from *scaccus* . The original sense in English was 'chessboard'. Current senses derive from the department of State established by the Norman kings to deal with the royal revenues, named *Exchequer* from the chequered tablecloth on which accounts were kept by means of counters. The spelling was influenced (mistakenly) by Latin *ex-* 'out', after words such as *exchange*.
➔ CHECK[1]; CHEQUER

excise[1] [late 15th century] The general sense 'a tax or toll' was the first recorded. It is from Middle Dutch *excijs, accijs*, perhaps based on Latin *accensare* 'to tax', from *ad-* 'to' and *census* 'tax'.
➔ CENSUS

excise[2] [late 16th century] The verb *excise* meaning 'cut out surgically' was used originally meaning 'notch or hollow out'. The source is Latin *excis-*, the past participial stem of *excidere* 'cut out', from *ex-* 'out of' and *caedere* 'to cut'.

excite [Middle English] The first sense recorded was 'stir someone up, incite someone to do something'. It is from Old French *exciter* or Latin *excitare*, a frequentative (= verb of repeated action) of *exciere* 'call out or forth'. The sense 'cause strong feelings of enthusiasm in' dates from the mid 19th century.

exclaim [late 16th century] *Exclaim* is from French *exclamer* or Latin *exclamare* 'shout out', from *ex-* 'out' and *clamare* 'to shout'. **Exclamation** (late Middle English) is from Latin *exclamatio(n-)*, from *exclamare*.

exclude [late Middle English] *Exclude* is from Latin *excludere* 'shut out', from *ex-* 'out' and *claudere* 'to shut'. This verb has given rise too to late Middle English **exclusion** from Latin *exclusio(n-)*. **Exclusive** dates from the late 15th century as a noun denoting something that excludes or causes exclusion: it is from medieval Latin *exclusivus*, from Latin *excludere*.

excommunicate [late Middle English] This is from ecclesiastical Latin *excommunicare* 'exclude from communication with the faithful', from *ex-* 'out' and Latin *communis* 'common to all', on the pattern of Latin *communicare*.
➔ COMMUNICATION

excrement [mid 16th century] The word *excrement* is from French *excrément* or Latin *excrementum*, from *excernere* 'to sift out': the formative elements are *ex-* 'out' and *cernere* 'sift'. This base verb also gave rise to **excrete** in the early 17th century in the sense 'cause to excrete'.

excruciate [late 16th century] Based on Latin *crux, cruc-* 'a cross', English *excruciate* is from Latin *excruciat-*, the past participial stem of the verb *excruciare* 'torment'.

excursion [late 16th century] The first recorded senses of *excursion* were 'act of running out' and 'sortie' as in the phrase *alarums and excursions*. It comes from Latin

excursio(n-), from the verb *excurrere* 'run out', from *ex-* 'out' and *currere* 'to run'.
→ ALARM

excuse [Middle English] This is from Old French *escuser* (verb), from Latin *excusare* 'to free from blame', from *ex-* 'out' and *causa* 'accusation, cause'.

execrate [mid 16th century] *Execrate* is from the Latin verb *exsecrari* 'to curse', based on *sacrare* 'to dedicate' (from *sacer* 'sacred'). The adjective **execrable** was already found in late Middle English in the sense 'expressing or involving a curse': it is via Old French from Latin *execrabilis*, from *exsecrari*.

execute [late Middle English] This is from Old French *executer*, from medieval Latin *executare*, from Latin *exsequi* 'follow up, carry out, punish'. The formative elements are *ex-* 'out' and *sequi* 'follow'. Also late Middle English and from the same Latin verb is **execution** which has come via Old French from Latin *executio(n-)*. Another related form from the same period is **executive** from medieval Latin *executivus*. The use of the word in business contexts as a role in the management hierarchy dates from the early 20th century. The noun **executor**, commonly found as a legal term, was recorded the earliest in this group and is via Anglo-Norman French.

exempt [late Middle English] *Exempt* is from Latin *exemptus*, the past participle of *eximere* 'take out, free'. Dating from the same period is **exemption** which is from Old French, or from Latin *exemptio(n-)*, from *eximere*.

exercise [Middle English] The early sense was 'application of a faculty, right, or process'. However, the notion of 'activity practised to stay healthy or improve health' was present in early examples of the word in use. It has come via Old French from Latin *exercitium*, from *exercere* 'keep busy, practise', from *ex-* 'thoroughly' and *arcere* 'keep in or away'.

exert [mid 17th century] 'Perform, practise' was the first sense recorded. *Exert* is from Latin *exserere* 'put forth', from *ex-* 'out' and *serere* 'bind'.

exhale [late Middle English] The word meant 'be given off as vapour' in early examples. It is from Old French *exhaler*, from Latin *exhalare* 'breathe out', from *ex-* 'out' and *halare* 'breathe'. **Exhalation**, also late Middle English, is from Latin *exhalatio(n-)*, from *exhalare*.

exhaust [mid 16th century] First used in the general sense 'draw off or out', *exhaust* is from Latin *exhaust-*, the past participial stem of *exhaurire* 'drain out', from *ex-* 'out' and *haurire* 'draw (water), drain'. The noun **exhaustion** was first

recorded slightly later and is from late Latin *exhaustio(n-)*, from Latin *exhaurire*. Although first used literally, these words were soon applied to people with the notion of being drained of energy.

exhibit [late Middle English] Early senses included 'submit for consideration', and specifically 'present a document as evidence in court'. It is from Latin *exhibit-*, the past participial stem of *exhibere* 'hold out', from *ex-* 'out' and *habere* 'hold'. **Exhibition** also dates from late Middle English in the sense 'maintenance, support'; this led, in the mid 17th century, to the word's application to 'a scholarship awarded to a student in the form of financial support'. It has come via Old French from late Latin *exhibitio(n-)*, from Latin *exhibere*.

exhilarate [mid 16th century] This is based on Latin *hilaris* 'cheerful'. The direct source is Latin *exhilarare* 'make cheerful'. The prefix *ex-* here expresses inducement of a state.

exhort [late Middle English] *Exhort* is from Old French *exhorter* or Latin *exhortari* 'encourage', from *ex-* 'thoroughly' and *hortari* 'encourage'. The noun **exhortation** from Latin *exhortatio(n-)* is recorded slightly earlier.

exhume [late Middle English] This is from medieval Latin *exhumare*, from *ex-* 'out of' and *humus* 'ground'.

exile [Middle English] The noun is partly from Old French *exil* 'banishment' and partly from Old French *exile* 'banished person'; the verb is from Old French *exiler*. The common base is Latin *exilium* 'banishment', from *exul* 'banished person'.

existence [late Middle English] This is from Old French, or from late Latin *existentia*, from Latin *exsistere* 'come into being', from *ex-* 'out' and *sistere* 'take a stand'. The verb **exist** dates from the early 17th century and is probably a back-formation (by removal of the suffix) from *existence*.

exit [mid 16th century] This was first used as a stage direction alongside *exeat*. It is an adoption of Latin *exit* 'he or she goes out', the third person singular present tense of *exire*, from *ex-* 'out' and *ire* 'go'. The noun use (late 16th century) is from Latin *exitus* 'going out', from the verb *exire*; *exit* meaning 'door' is found from the late 17th century. A recent phrase associated with this sense is *exit poll* in political contexts dating from the 1980s in the US: this involves asking voters on their way out of a polling station how they have voted, as a way of predicting the eventual outcome.

exonerate [late Middle English] *Exonerate* 'absolve from blame' is from Latin *exonerare* 'free from a burden', from ex- 'from' and onus, oner- 'a burden'.

exorbitant [late Middle English] This was originally a legal term describing a case that is outside the scope of a law. The word comes from late Latin exorbitant-, the present participial stem of exorbitare 'go off the track', from ex- 'out from' and orbita 'course, track'. The common current sense is 'unreasonably high' when describing prices; this meaning was present early in the word's history.

exorcize [late Middle English] This word is from French exorciser or ecclesiastical Latin exorcizare, from Greek exorkizein 'exorcise', from ex- 'out' and horkos 'oath'. The word originally meant 'conjure up or command (an evil spirit)'; the specific sense of driving out an evil spirit dates from the mid 16th century. The noun **exorcism**, also late Middle English came via ecclesiastical Latin from ecclesiastical Greek exorkismos, from exorkizein.

exotic [late 16th century] English exotic is via Latin from Greek exōtikos 'foreign', from exō 'outside'. It was once used generally with the meaning 'belonging to another country' but the tendency now is to use the adjective with plants meaning 'introduced from abroad, not indigenous' (as opposed to endemic). The notion of 'foreign origin' has also given the word a dimension of glamour from the attraction of something unfamiliar and mysterious. This same notion is part of the association with strip-tease in the phrase exotic dancer, first introduced in US use.

expand [late Middle English] Expand comes from Latin expandere 'to spread out', from ex- 'out' and pandere 'to spread'. The same verb is the base of **expansion** (early 17th century) from late Latin expansio(n-). The noun **expanse** is found from the mid 17th century and is from modern Latin expansum 'something expanded', the neuter past participle of expandere.

expatiate [mid 16th century] Expatiate now means 'speak or write at length' but the first sense recorded was 'roam freely'. It comes from Latin exspatiari 'move beyond one's usual bounds', from ex- 'out, from' and spatiari 'to walk' (from spatium 'space').

expatriate [mid 18th century] This word was first found as a verb. It comes from medieval Latin expatriare 'gone out from one's country', from ex- 'out' and patria 'native country'.

expect [mid 16th century] The early sense was 'defer action, wait'. It is from Latin exspectare 'look out for', from ex- 'out' and spectare 'to look', a frequentative (= verb of repeated action) of specere 'see'. A common current sense

'look for something as rightfully due or owing' is well illustrated by Nelson's famous phrase at Trafalgar: England expects that every man will do his duty. With reference to pregnancy, the verb meaning 'anticipate the birth of' is found from the early 20th century. The notion of 'anticipation' however is lost in the phrase I expect used colloquially for 'I suppose': this is often said to be an Americanism but it is very common in British English. **Expectation** is a word recorded from the mid 16th century, from Latin expectatio(n-), from the verb expectare.

expectorant [mid 18th century] The medicine known as an expectorant owes its origin to Latin expectorant-, the present participial stem of expectorare 'expel from the chest', from ex- 'out' and pectus, pector- 'breast'.

expedient [late Middle English] This is from Latin expedire 'extricate, put in order'. The original sense was neutral; the depreciatory sense, implying disregard of moral considerations, dates from the late 18th century (e.g. either side could break the agreement if it were expedient to do so).
➔ EXPEDITE

expedite [late 15th century] The early sense was 'perform quickly'. It comes from Latin expedire 'extricate (originally by freeing the feet)', 'put in order by freeing from difficulties', from ex- 'out' and pes, ped- 'foot'.

expedition [late Middle English] Expedition came via Old French from Latin expeditio(n-), from expedire 'extricate'. Early senses included 'prompt supply of something' and 'setting out with aggressive intent'. The notions of 'speed' and 'purpose' are retained in current senses. Expedition meaning 'a journey undertaken with the purpose of exploration' dates from the late 16th century.
➔ EXPEDITE

expel [late Middle English] The early general sense was 'eject, force to leave'. It comes from Latin expellere, from ex- 'out' and pellere 'to drive'. **Expulsion** is also a late Middle English word from Latin expulsio(n-), from expellere 'drive out'.

expend [late Middle English] Latin expendere 'pay out' (from ex- 'out' and pendere 'weigh, pay') is the source of a group of related words in English: firstly expend 'use up'; also late Middle English **expense** from an Anglo-Norman French alteration of Old French espense, from late Latin expensa (pecunia) '(money) spent'; **expensive** 'costly', which was also in the early 17th century descriptive of a person as 'lavish or extravagant'; finally **expenditure**, a mid 18th-century word based on the verb expend and suggested by the obsolete (medieval Latin) noun *expenditor* 'an officer in charge of expenditure'.

→ SPEND

experience [late Middle English] *Experience* is via Old French from Latin *experientia*, from *experiri* 'to try'. In early use it had the meaning 'experiment'; this led to a notion of 'gaining knowledge from observation' and therefore 'knowledge' itself.

→ EXPERIMENT; EXPERT

experiment [Middle English] This is from Old French, or from Latin *experimentum*, from *experiri* 'to try'. **Experimental** dates from the late 15th century when it meant 'having personal experience' as well as 'experienced, observed': it is from medieval Latin *experimentalis*, from Latin *experimentum*.

→ EXPERIENCE; EXPERT

expert [Middle English] *Expert*, first used as an adjective, is from French, from Latin *expertus*, the past participle of *experiri* 'to try'. Noun use dates from the early 17th century. The word **expertise** is a mid 19th-century adoption from French, from *expert*.

→ EXPERIENCE; EXPERIMENT

expiate [late 16th century] The early sense was 'end (rage, sorrow, etc.) by suffering it to the full'. It comes from Latin *expiare* 'appease by sacrifice', from *ex-* 'out' and *piare* (from *pius* 'pious'). The word is common in religious contexts.

expire [late Middle English] Old French *expirer* is the source of *expire* from Latin *exspirare* 'breathe out', from *ex-* 'out' and *spirare* 'breathe'. The word has two main semantic strands in English: 'breathe out, exhale' and 'breathe one's last, come to an end'. **Expiration**, also late Middle English, at first denoted a vapour or exhalation: it is from Latin *exspiratio(n-)*, from the verb *exspirare*.

explain [late Middle English] *Explain* and **explanation** (from Latin *explanatio(n-)*) both date from late Middle English: their source is Latin *explanare*, based on *planus* 'plain'. Early senses included 'smooth out' and 'spread out flat'; in the early 16th century, it came to mean 'give details of (a matter)', and later 'make intelligible by clarification'.

expletive [late Middle English] This word was used first as an adjective. It is from late Latin *expletivus*, from *explere* 'fill out', from *ex-* 'out' and *plere* 'to fill'. The general noun sense 'word used merely to fill out a sentence' (early 17th century) was applied specifically to an oath or swear word in the early 19th century. The phrase *expletive deleted* gained a high profile in the 1970s in the submission of recorded conversations involving President Nixon to the Committee on the Judiciary of the House of Representatives (30 April 1974).

explicate [mid 16th century] *Explicate* 'analyse and develop (an idea) in detail' is from Latin *explicat-*, the past participial stem of *explicare* 'to fold' (from *ex-* 'out' and *plicare* 'to fold'). The adjective **explicable**, also mid 16th century, is from French, or from Latin *explicabilis*, from *explicare*.

explicit [early 17th century] *Explicit* is from French *explicite* or Latin *explicitus*, the past participle of *explicare* 'to unfold'. An early sense was 'free from intricacies' (Milton *Samson Agonistes*: That commonly called the plot, whether intricate or explicit). The meaning 'leaving nothing merely implied' dates from the early 17th century, but the word's application to material in magazines and films, etc. that is 'sexually explicit' dates from the 1970s.

→ EXPLICATE

explode [mid 16th century] In early contexts *explode* meant 'reject scornfully, discard'. The source of the word is Latin *explodere* 'drive out by clapping, hiss off the stage', from *ex-* 'out' and *plaudere* 'to clap'. The sense 'expose as unfounded' as in *the new findings exploded his theory* is derived from the original sense of the word; the sense 'blow up' arose in the late 18th century and evolved via an old sense 'expel with violence and sudden noise': it was perhaps influenced by the obsolete verb *displode* 'burst with a noise'. The noun **explosion** arose in the early 17th century from Latin *explosio(n-)* 'scornful rejection', from the verb *explodere*.

exploit [Middle English] The noun is from Old French *esploit*, based on Latin *explicare* 'unfold'. The early notion of 'success, progress' gave rise to the sense 'attempt to capture', 'military expedition', hence the current sense of the noun. Current verb senses date from the mid 19th century and are taken from modern French *exploiter*.

→ EXPLICATE

explore [mid 16th century] The first recorded sense was 'investigate (why)'. It is from French *explorer*, from Latin *explorare* 'search out', from *ex-* 'out' and *plorare* 'utter a cry'. The noun **exploration** first denoted an investigation and arose at the same time as *explore*: this is from French, or from Latin *exploratio(n-)*, from the verb *explorare*. The current sense dates from the early 19th century.

exponent [late 16th century] The early word was an adjective in the sense 'expounding'. It comes from the Latin verb *exponere* 'put out'. Examples such as *an early exponent of the teachings of Thomas Aquinas* illustrate the word in the

sense 'a person who believes in and tries to make public the benefits of a theory or practice': this usage is recorded from the early 19th century.
→ EXPOUND

export [late 15th century] The early sense was 'take away'. It comes from Latin *exportare*, from *ex-* 'out' and *portare* 'carry'. Current senses date from the 17th century.

expose [late Middle English] This is from Old French *exposer*, from Latin *exponere* 'publish, explain', but influenced by Latin *expositus* 'put or set out' and Old French *poser* 'to place'. **Exposition** was recorded slightly earlier and comes from Latin *expositio(n-)*, from the verb *exponere*. However **exposure** is not found until the early 17th century: it is based on the verb *expose*, on the pattern of words such as *enclosure*. The word **exposé** is an early 19th-century adoption of the French past participle of *exposer*: the literal meaning is 'shown, set out'.

expound [Middle English] The early spelling *expoune* existed alongside *expound(e)* which had the sense 'explain (what is difficult)' in early contexts. It comes from Old French *espon-*, the present tense stem of *espondre*, from Latin *exponere* 'expose, publish, explain' (from *ex-* 'out' and *ponere* 'put'). The origin of the final *-d* recorded from the Middle English period is uncertain but may have been because of the frequent occurrence of the past participle *expound*.
→ COMPOUND¹

express¹ [late Middle English] *Express* included both 'convey in words' and 'press out, obtain by squeezing or wringing' in its early use; the latter was used figuratively to mean 'extort'. The origin is Old French *expresser*, based on Latin *ex-* 'out' and *pressare* 'to press'. **Expression** is also late Middle English and is from Latin *expressio(n-)*, from *exprimere* meaning 'press out, form (an image) by pressure' and 'express': this is the base verb too of **expressive** which is recorded from the same period in the sense 'tending to press out': the direct source is French *expressif, -ive* or medieval Latin *expressivus*.

express² [early 18th century] This *express* is an extension of *express* discussed in the next entry. The early use was in delivery contexts as a verb meaning 'send by express messenger'. The sense 'operating at high speed' (as in *express airmail service*) is from *express train*: this got its name because it served a particular destination without intermediate stops, reflecting an earlier sense of *express*: 'done or made for a special purpose'. The word *express* was later interpreted in the sense 'rapid' because of the

train association. Senses relating to *express delivery* date from the institution of this postal service in 1891.
→ EXPRESS³

express³ [late Middle English] Old French *expres* is the source of the English word *express* used in phrases such as *it was his express wish*. It comes from Latin *expressus* 'distinctly presented', the past participle of *exprimere* 'to press out, express', from *ex-* 'out' and *primere* 'press'.

expropriate [late 16th century] This word comes from medieval Latin *expropriare* 'take from the owner', from *ex-* 'out, from' and *proprium* 'property', the neuter singular of *proprius* 'own'.

expunge [early 17th century] Latin *expungere* 'mark for deletion by means of points' is the source of English *expunge*. The formative elements are *ex-* 'out' and *pungere* 'to prick'.

expurgate [early 17th century] *Expurgate* 'remove objectionable material from (a text)' was originally used meaning 'purge of excrement'. It is from the Latin verb *expurgare* 'cleanse thoroughly', from *ex-* 'out' and *purgare* 'cleanse'.

exquisite [late Middle English] *Exquisite* once meant 'carefully ascertained, precise'. It at times had the negative connotation 'over-laboured'. The spelling is from the Latin past participial stem *exquisit-* from the verb *exquirere* 'seek out' (from *ex-* 'out' and *quaerere* 'seek'). The meaning association with workmanship of a high standard dates from the mid 16th century.

extant [mid 16th century] The early recorded sense was 'accessible, able to be publicly seen or reached'. It is from Latin *exstant-* 'being visible or prominent, existing', from the verb *exstare*, from *ex-* 'out' and *stare* 'to stand'. It is now often used in connection with documents meaning 'surviving, still in existence'.

extempore [mid 16th century] Used in examples such as *extempore public speaking* and *he recited the poem extempore*, this word is from Latin *ex tempore* 'on the spur of the moment' (literally 'out of the time').

extend [late Middle English] Latin *extendere* 'stretch out' (from *ex-* 'out' and *tendere* 'stretch') gave rise to *extend*, as well as **extension** (from late Latin *extensio(n-)*) and **extensive** (from French *extensif, -ive* or late Latin *extensivus*). Middle English **extent** used first in the sense 'valuation of property (usually for taxation purposes)' is from Anglo-Norman French *extente*, from medieval Latin *extenta*, the feminine past participle of Latin *extendere*. The *extent* relating to the space or degree to which something is extended, dates from the early 17th century.

extenuate [late Middle English] The sense 'make thin, emaciate' was found in early texts. The Latin verb *extenuare* 'make thin' is the source, based on *tenuis* 'thin'. The sense 'lessen the seriousness of' as in the legal phrase *extenuating circumstances* dates from the late 16th century.

exterior [early 16th century] This is the use of a Latin word in English: it is the comparative of Latin *exter* 'outer'.

exterminate [late Middle English] 'Drive out, banish' was the sense found in early contexts. It is from Latin *exterminat-*, the past participial stem of *exterminare* 'drive out, banish': the base elements are *ex-* 'out' and *terminus* 'boundary'. The sense 'destroy' (mid 16th century) comes from the Latin of the Vulgate.

extern [mid 16th century] Early use was as an adjective in the sense 'external'. The source is French *externe* or Latin *externus*, from *exter* 'outer'. The word was used by Shakespeare to mean 'outward appearance'; current senses such as 'non-resident' date from the early 17th century.

external [late Middle English] *External* is from medieval Latin, based on Latin *exter* 'outer'.

extinct [late Middle English] The early recorded sense was 'no longer alight'. The spelling is from the Latin past participial stem *exstinct-*, from the verb *exstinguere* 'to extinguish'. *Extinct* is used in connection with species of animals that have died out, from the late 17th century. The noun **extinction** is also late Middle English: this is from Latin *exstinctio(n-)*, from *exstinguere*.

extinguish [mid 16th century] This is from Latin *exstinguere*, from *ex-* 'out' and *stinguere* 'quench'. In early medical use it meant 'reduce (an inflammation)', but generally it is 'put out (a fire, a light, or anything bright)'; this led to contexts of 'putting out hope, passion, etc.' which are associated figuratively with light or burning.
➔ DISTINCTION

extol [late Middle English] *Extol* is from Latin *extollere*, from *ex-* meaning 'out, upward' and *tollere* 'to raise'. An early sense in English was 'raise' which came to be 'raise high by praise' (the current sense) in the early 16th century.

extortion [Middle English] *Exacting money by force* is the meaning of *extortion*; legal contexts record the word from the early 17th century. It is from late Latin *extortio(n-)*, from Latin *extor-*

quere 'to wrest': this is the source too of **extort** which dates from the early 16th century. Latin *ex-* 'out' and *torquere* 'to twist' are the base elements.

extra [mid 17th century] *Extra* 'additional' is probably a shortening of *extraordinary*, suggested by similar forms in French and German.

extraction [late Middle English] *Extraction* came via Old French from late Latin *extractio(n-)*, from Latin *extrahere* 'draw out', which is also the source of late Middle English **extract**. The formative base elements are Latin *ex-* 'out' and *trahere* 'to draw'. The notion of 'get out by force or effort' (early 17th century) was influenced by the word's use in surgical operations such as in dentistry.

extradition [mid 19th century] This is an adoption from French, from the prefix *ex-* meaning 'out, from' and *tradition* meaning 'delivery'. In an *extradition* procedure, a person accused or convicted of a crime is taken out of a foreign country and delivered to the home country authorities. The verb **extradite** dating from the same period is a back-formation (by removal of the suffix) from *extradition*.

extramural [mid 19th century] The first recorded sense of *extramural* was 'outside the walls of a town or city'. Latin *extra muros* 'outside the walls' is part of the formation of the word. The meaning has become extended to mean 'outside the bounds of a community' referring to study that is undertaken by people not registered as full-time students within a particular educational establishment.

extraordinary [late Middle English] The Latin phrase *extra ordinem* 'outside the normal course of events' is the base of the Latin adjective *extraordinarius* which gave *extraordinary* in English. An *envoy extraordinary* was once a minister sent on special diplomatic business, but it now designates a second class of diplomatic minister ranked next to ambassador. The notion of 'astonishing' dates from the late 16th century and this may be accompanied by admiration (*such extraordinary talent!*) or, if something is considered strange, quite the opposite (*what extraordinary behaviour!*).

extrapolate [late 19th century] *Extrapolate*, meaning 'extend the application of (a method) to an unknown situation assuming that the same patterns will continue', is composed of *extra-* meaning 'outside' and a shortened form of *interpolate*.

extravagant [late Middle English] Early senses included 'unusual, abnormal' and 'unsuitable'. The word comes from the medieval Latin form *extravagant-*, the present participial stem of *extravagari* 'diverge greatly'. The base elements are Latin *extra-* 'outside' and *vagari* 'to wander'. Shakespeare uses the word to mean 'wandering, roaming' (*Othello*: An extravagant, and wheeling stranger, Of here, and every where). The sense 'wasteful' dates from the early 18th century. The noun **extravagance** is recorded much later from the mid 17th century, adopted from French. The source is also medieval Latin *extravagant-*.

extravaganza [mid 18th century] An *extravaganza* is now 'an elaborate and spectacular entertainment or production', but in early use it meant 'extravagance in language or behaviour'. Italian *estravaganza* 'extravagance' is the source of the word: the change in spelling in English was due to association with words beginning with *extra-*.

extreme [late Middle English] This comes via Old French from Latin *extremus*, literally 'outermost', the superlative of *exterus* 'outer'. The common meanings of *extremus* were 'utmost', 'endmost', 'farthest', 'last'. The word **extremity** is also late Middle English and is from Old French *extremite* or Latin *extremitas*, from *extremus*.

extricate [early 17th century] Latin *ex-* 'out' and *tricae* 'perplexities' are the base elements of the word form *extricate*, of which the early sense was 'unravel, untangle'. The source verb is Latin *extricare* 'unravel'.

extrinsic [mid 16th century] The early sense recorded was 'outward'. The source is late Latin *extrinsecus* 'outward', from Latin *extrinsecus* 'outwardly', based on *exter* 'outer'.

extrovert [early 20th century] This is from *extro-* (a variant of *extra-*, on the pattern of *intro-*) and Latin *vertere* 'to turn'.

extrude [mid 16th century] This is from Latin *extrudere*, from *ex-* 'out' and *trudere* 'to thrust'. The notion of 'force out' was also applied to people in early contexts (B. Jonson *Poetaster*: Say he should extrude me his house today).

exuberant [late Middle English] 'Overflowing, abounding' were the early senses recorded for *exuberant* from French *exubérant*, from the Latin present participial stem of the verb *exuberare* 'be abundantly fruitful'. The base is Latin *uber* 'fertile'. The usual sense now is 'overflowing with delight', first recorded in the early 16th century.

exude [late 16th century] *Exude* 'discharge' is from Latin *exsudare*, from *ex-* 'out' and *sudare* 'to sweat'.

exult [late 16th century] *Exult* is from Latin *exsultare*, a frequentative (= verb of repeated action) of *exsilire* 'leap up', from *ex-* 'out, upward' and *salire* 'to leap'.

eye [Old English] The origin of Old English *ēage* is Germanic; related forms are Dutch *oog* and German *Auge*. In poetry *eye* is sometimes used in references such as the *eye of heaven* meaning the sun (Spenser *Faerie Queene*: Her angels face, As the great eye of heaven, shyned bright) or *eyes of heaven* referring to the stars. The expression *to turn a blind eye* is with allusion to Nelson at the Battle of Trafalgar (1805) who is said to have put a telescope to his blind eye saying 'I really do not see the signal'. The word **eyelet** dates from late Middle English as *oilet*, from Old French *oillet*, a diminutive of *oil* 'eye', from Latin *oculus*. The change in the first syllable in the 17th century was due to association with *eye*.

eyrie [late 15th century] This is from medieval Latin *aeria, aerea, eyria*, probably from Old French *aire*. The source is thought to be Latin *area* 'level piece of ground', which in late Latin became 'nest of a bird of prey'.

Ff

fable [Middle English] *Fable* is from Old French *fable*, from Latin *fabula* 'story', from *fari* 'to speak'. In early use, as well as referring to any general fictitious narrative, the word was also found with the current meaning: 'a short story conveying a lesson, usually though the portrayal of animals as the main characters'. The semi-legendary Greek storyteller Aesop (6th century BC) is associated with this type of moral animal fable.

fabric [late 15th century] This comes from French *fabrique*, from Latin *fabrica* 'something skilfully produced', from *faber* 'a worker in a material such as metal or stone'. A *fabric* was originally 'a building', then later 'a machine or appliance'. The core sense, as is the case with Latin *fabrica*, is 'something made', which led to the prime current meaning 'cloth, textile': in the mid 18th century this was any manufactured material. *Fabric* may also refer to the roof, floors, and walls of a building: this usage dates from the mid 17th century. The related verb **fabricate** arose in late Middle English: Latin *fabricare* 'manufacture' is the source, from *fabrica*. It has come to be used in a negative sense: 'make up, invent (a lie)'; this started towards the end of the 18th century.

fabulous [late Middle English] 'Known through fable' and 'unhistorical' were the early senses of *fabulous*. The source of the word is French *fabuleux* or Latin *fabulosus* which meant 'celebrated in fable', from *fabula* 'discourse, narrative, story'. The notion of 'astonishing' led to associations with 'incredible' interpreted as both 'beyond belief' (mid 16th century) and 'wonderful, marvellous' (mid 20th century). The colloquial abbreviation **fab** for 'marvellous' dates from the 1960s: it was popularized in the phrase *the fab four* referring to the pop group *the Beatles* at the height of their popularity at that time.
→ FABLE

facade [mid 17th century] This is an adoption of French *façade*, from *face* 'face', on the pattern of Italian *facciata*. Primarily used of buildings, it started to be used in a figurative way (*her flawless public façade masked private despair*), from around the middle of the 19th century.

face [Middle English] *Face* is from Old French, based on Latin *facies* 'form, appearance, face'. The word **facial**, now commonly a noun for a beauty treatment to the face, was recorded early in the 17th century in adjectival use as a theological term meaning 'face to face, open'. It is from medieval Latin *facialis*, from *facies*. The current senses of the adjective ('affecting the face', 'of the face') date from the early 19th century. The idiom *fly in the face of* is taken literally from the notion of a dog attacking someone; figuratively it means 'act in opposition to'. The recent colloquialism 'in your face' arose in the US in the 1970s: it is both a way of expressing scorn and a phrase meaning 'blatant'.

facet [early 17th century] This is from French *facette*, literally 'little face', a diminutive of *face* 'face, side'. The figurative use 'particular aspect of something' is found in examples from the early 19th century.

facetious [late 16th century] The general sense 'witty, amusing' was the first recorded for *facetious*, which comes from French *facétieux*, from *facétie*. Latin *facetia* 'jest' is the base noun, from *facetus* 'witty'. The common current sense is 'flippant'.

facile [late 15th century] *Facile* meant 'easily accomplished' in early examples. This is now often used with a connotation of disparagement. It comes from French, or from Latin *facilis* 'easy', from *facere* 'to do, make'.

facilitate [early 17th century] This is from French *faciliter*, from Italian *facilitare*, which is based on *facile* 'easy' (from Latin *facilis*). The sense combines both 'make easier' and 'help to move forward'.

facility [early 16th century] *Facility* primarily meant 'the means or unimpeded opportunity for doing something'. The source here is either French *facilité* or Latin *facilitas*, from *facilis* 'easy'. The plural *facilities* meaning 'amenities' or 'resources' which enable something to be done, dates from the early 19th century.

facsimile [late 16th century] This was originally written *fac simile*, denoting the making of an exact copy, usually a copy of a piece of writing. It is modern Latin, from Latin *fac!* (the imperative of *facere* 'make') and *simile* (the neuter of *similis* 'like'). The abbreviation **fax** dates from the 1940s.

fact [late 15th century] *Fact* is from Latin *factum*, the neuter past participle of *facere* 'do'. The original sense was 'an act or feat'; this developed later into 'a bad deed, a crime', surviving in the legal phrase *before* (or *after*) *the fact*. The earliest of the current senses ('truth, reality') dates from the late 16th century. **Factual** is recorded from the mid 19th century: the formation is based on *fact*, on the pattern of *actual*.
→ FEAT

faction [late 15th century] This originally expressed the action of doing or making something; now it is applied to a small dissentient group within a larger one, often in the sphere of politics. It came via French from Latin *factio(n-)*, from *facere* 'do, make'. The adjective **factious** 'inclined towards dissension' dates from the mid 16th century and is from French *factieux* or Latin *factiosus* (from *factio*).

factor [late Middle English] In early use a *factor* was a 'doer, perpetrator' and in Scots, 'agent': the word is is still used in Scots for 'a land agent'. It is from French *facteur* or Latin *factor* (from the verb *facere* 'to do'). It is a term used in maths (*the two factors z and y*) and in physiology (*factor VIII*) and may generally be something that acts and contributes to a result, or an element of something which contributes to a process.

factory [late 16th century] The original use of the word was to denote an establishment for traders carrying on business in another country. It comes via Portuguese *feitoria*. The current word describing 'a place where goods are manufactured or assembled, usually by machine' is based on late Latin *factorium* which was literally 'an oil press'. The notion of *factory farm* originated in the US in the late 19th century.

factotum [mid 16th century] This word for an employee undertaking all kinds of tasks was originally in the phrases *dominum* (or *magister*) *factotum* translated roughly as 'master of everything', and *Johannes factotem* meaning 'John do-it-all' or 'Jack of all trades'. It is from medieval Latin, from Latin *fac!* 'do!' (the imperative of *facere*) and *totum* 'the whole thing' (the neuter of *totus* 'all').

faculty [late Middle English] This comes from Old French *faculte*, from Latin *facultas*, from *facilis* 'easy'. It basically means 'the power of doing something' and the Latin source verb is *facere* 'make, do'. *Faculty* may also be 'a kind of ability' which has led to the word's use for a department of knowledge in a university. In psychology the word has been applied to various 'powers' of the mind such as the will,

memory, or reason; phrenologists associated these with cranial bumps and congenital aptitudes. These applications have affected popular language.

fad [mid 19th century] *Fad* 'short-lived enthusiasm' was originally dialect: it is probably the second element of *fidfad*, a contraction of *fiddle-faddle* 'trifling talk'. **Faddy** dates from the early 19th century and is probably from the same source as *fad*.

fade [Middle English] The early sense of *fade* was 'grow weak, waste away'. The word comes from Old French *fader*, from *fade* 'dull, insipid', probably based on a blend of Latin *fatuus* 'silly, insipid' and *vapidus* 'vapid'. The sense 'lose freshness' (*faded colours*) developed alongside the early English meaning 'lose strength'.

faff [late 18th century] *Faff* was originally a dialect word in the sense 'blow in puffs or small gusts', describing the wind. It is imitative of the sound. The current sense may have been influenced by dialect *faffle* initially meaning 'stammer, stutter', later 'flap in the wind', which came to mean 'fuss or dither' at about the same time as *faff*, in the late 19th century.

faggot [Middle English] *Faggot* was first recorded in the sense 'bundle of sticks for fuel'. It comes from Old French *fagot*, from Italian *fagotto*, based on Greek *phakelos* 'bundle'. Towards the end of the 16th century, the word came to be used from dialect as an abusive term for a woman; later, in the early 20th century this was applied as offensive slang in US English to a male homosexual. The abbreviation **fag** in this latter context dates from the 1920s.

fail [Middle English] The verb is from Old French *faillir*, the noun from Old French *faille*, based on Latin *fallere* 'to deceive'. An earlier sense of the noun was 'failure to do or perform a duty', surviving in the phrase *without fail*. The main semantic strands are: 'be absent, wanting, or inadequate', 'have a deficiency', and 'fall short in performance'. **Failure** was first spelt *failer* in the mid 17th century, meaning both 'non-occurrence' and 'cessation of supply'. It is from Anglo-Norman French *failer* for Old French *faillir*.

faint [Middle English] The senses of *faint* in early examples were 'sickly, oppressive' and 'cowardly': the latter survives in *faint heart*. The verb sense 'swoon' is recorded early in the word's history. The source of the spelling is Old French *faint*, the past participle of *faindre* 'to feign' ('simulated' is an obsolete English meaning of *faint*). The adjectival sense 'hardly perceptible' dates from the mid 17th century.
→ FEIGN; FEINT¹

fair¹ [Old English] Old English *fæger* meant 'pleasing, attractive'. The origin is Germanic; it is related to Old High German *fagar*. In all the older senses, *fair* was formerly used in contrast with *foul* still seen in the phrase *by fair means or foul*. In connection with complexion and hair, examples are not found until the middle of the 16th century. The notion of 'equitable' 'unbiased' dates from Middle English.

fair² [Middle English] A *fair* in Middle English described a 'periodic gathering for the sale of goods'. It comes from Old French *feire*, from late Latin *feria*, the singular of Latin *feriae* 'holy days', times when this type of fair was often held.

fairy [Middle English] *Fairy* was a collective term for fairies or it meant fairyland, in early use. It is from Old French *faerie*, from *fae*, 'a fairy', from Latin *fata* 'the Fates' (plural of *fatum*). The archaic spelling variant **faerie** was first attested in the late 16th century by Spenser in his title *Faerie Queene*: it probably existed in Middle English. Late Middle English **fay** from Old French *fae, faie* (from Latin *fata*) is a poetic or literary word for *fairy*.
→ FATE

faith [Middle English] *Faith* is from Old French *feid*, from Latin *fides*. The Latin had the following meanings: 'belief and trust', 'a pledge or evidence inspiring belief', and 'fidelity'. In English the strands are : 'belief and trust' (such as *belief in God*), 'inducement to belief' (such as *make faith*, an obsolete phrase meaning 'affirm, give surety'), and 'obligation resulting from trust' (e.g. Milton *Samson Agonistes*: Who to save Her country from a fierce destroyer, chose Above the faith of wedlock-bands). **Faithfully** is late Middle English and its use in the polite formula *Yours faithfully* (= with firm allegiance to you) at the end of letters was an early usage.

fake [late 18th century] *Fake* 'not genuine' was originally slang; the origin is uncertain. It is perhaps ultimately related to German *fegen* 'sweep, thrash'. The verb was part of thieves' cant from the early 19th century meaning 'tamper with (something) for the purpose of deception'. The sense 'counterfeit' arose in the early 20th century.

fall [Old English] Old English *f(e)allan* is Germanic in origin, related to Dutch *vallen* and German *fallen*. The noun is partly from the verb, partly from Old Norse *fall* 'downfall, sin'. The verb has many figurative uses including idiomatic expressions such as *his face fell*, which is a Hebraism from the biblical reference in *Genesis* 4:5: And Cain was very wroth, and his countenance fell. Moral overtones are by association with the biblical *Fall* of Man caused by Adam giving way

to temptation: this is carried over into senses such as *fall* 'lose one's chastity' (Shakespeare *Othello*: It is their Husbands faults if Wives do fall) and 'become pregnant'. Some slang uses are relatively recent such as *fall about* meaning 'to laugh': this is first recorded in the 1960s. The use of the noun *Fall* in North American English to mean 'Autumn' is from the early phrase *fall of the leaf* recorded from the mid 16th century.

fallacy [late 15th century] *Fallacy* gradually superseded Middle English *fallace* and in early examples meant 'deception, guile'. It comes from Latin *fallacia*, from *fallax, fallac-* 'deceiving', from *fallere* 'to deceive'. The word was a term in logic in the late 16th century for a deceptive or misleading argument; it came to be generalized as a 'delusive notion based on false reasoning' at the beginning of the 17th century.

fallible [late Middle English] This is from medieval Latin *fallibilis*, from Latin *fallere* 'to deceive'. The Latin adjective had the sense 'deceitful' but in late medieval Latin it became reversed to 'deceivable'.

fallow¹ [Old English] In Old English the verb *fealgian* meant 'to break up land for sowing'. Of Germanic origin, the word is related to Low German *falgen*. The sense now is 'leave unsown' referring to land which has been ploughed and harrowed.

fallow² [Old English] Germanic in origin, Old English *falu, fealu* is related to Dutch *vaal* and German *fahl, falb*. Describing the colour pale brown or reddish yellow, it is now most commonly found in the word *fallow deer*, a Eurasian deer which has a reddish-brown coat in the summer.

false [Old English] Old English *fals* 'fraud, deceit' is from Latin *falsum* 'fraud, falsehood', the neuter past participle of *fallere* 'to deceive'. It was reinforced or reborrowed in Middle English from Old French *fals, faus* meaning 'false'. As well as the notion 'erroneous, contrary to fact', the word also implies 'deceitful, sham' in certain contexts. The verb **falsify** in late Middle English meant 'prove (a statement) to be false': this is from French *falsifier* or medieval Latin *falsificare*, from Latin *falsificus* 'making false' (from *falsus* 'false').

falter [late Middle English] The early senses were 'stammer' and 'stagger'. The word's etymology is obscure but it is perhaps from the verb *fold* which was occasionally used to describe the faltering of the legs or tongue; the *-ter* suffix is on the pattern of *totter*. It is possible that association with the word *fault* has influenced recent use of the word.

fame [Middle English] *Fame* also meant 'reputation' in early contexts, which survives in the phrase *house of ill fame*. The word comes via Old French from Latin *fama* 'report, fame'. The adjective **famed** 'renowned' is also Middle English, the past participle of the archaic verb *fame*, from Old French *famer*, from Latin *fama*. **Famous** dates from late Middle English and is from Old French *fameus*, from Latin *famosus* 'famed', from *fama*. Andy Warhol (*c.* 1928–87), an American painter, graphic artist, and film-maker, is quoted as saying In the future everybody will be world famous for fifteen minutes: this led to the phrase *fifteen minutes of fame* meaning a 'period of brief notoriety'.

familiar [Middle English] The first senses recorded for *familiar* were 'intimate' and 'on a family footing'. It comes from Old French *familier*, from Latin *familiaris* 'intimate', from *familia* 'household servants, household, family'. It sometimes means 'too intimate, taking liberties with (somebody)'. The notion of intimate association is illustrated in the phrase *familiar spirit* in contexts of witchcraft or spiritualism, where a demon is supposed to act in conjunction with a particular person or under their influence. The related noun **familiarity**, also recorded in use from Middle English, meant 'close relationship' and 'sexual intimacy': this is via Old French from Latin *familiaritas*, from *familiaris*.
→FAMILY

family [late Middle English] The early sense recorded referred to 'all the descendants of a common ancestor' as well as 'the servants of a household or the retinue of a nobleman'. The word comes from Latin *familia* 'household servants, household, family', from *famulus* 'servant'. It is now used in contexts where there is an idea of 'grouping' of related people or things: one example is in modern scientific classification where a *family* is a group of allied genera. The word is also used, chiefly in the US, as a slang term for the members of a local unit of the Mafia; it was popularized in the 1972 film *The Godfather* by Francis Ford Coppola. The phrase *in the family way* meaning 'pregnant' dating from the late 18th century was in use earlier meaning 'in a domestic way, in a domestic setting'.

famine [late Middle English] This is from Old French, from *faim* 'hunger', from Latin *fames*.

famish [late Middle English] *Famish* is from obsolete *fame* 'to starve, famish', from Old French *afamer*, based (like *famine*) on Latin *fames* 'hunger'.

fan [Old English] Old English *fann* was a noun denoting a device for winnowing grain. The Old English verb spelling was *fannian*. Latin *vannus* 'winnowing fan' is the origin of the word in English. Use of the word for a device to cool the face dates from the mid 16th century.
→VANE

fanatic [mid 16th century] Early use of the word was as an adjective, from French *fanatique* or Latin *fanaticus* meaning 'of a temple, inspired by a god' (from *fanum* 'temple'). It originally described behaviour or speech that possession by a god or demon might cause, which led to the earliest sense of the noun: 'a religious maniac' (mid 17th century). The word **fan**, an abbreviation of *fanatic*, dates from the late 19th century in the US. A **fanzine** is also originally a US word which was coined in the 1940s for a magazine produced by amateurs for enthusiasts of a particular entertainment: this is a blend of *fan* and *magazine*.

fancy [late Middle English] *Fancy* is a contraction of *fantasy*. In early use it was a synonym of *imagination*. The word developed various semantic nuances including: 'mental image', 'inventive design', and 'caprice' (F. Nightingale *Notes on Nursing*: Such cravings are usually called the 'fancies' of patients). It is also used as a term in breeding animals in order to develop points of beauty and excellence (e.g. *pigeon-fancying*). The term:
■ **fancy man** dates from the early 19th century and is primarily 'a man that is fancied', in other words 'a sweetheart'; it is also used pejoratively, influenced by its use in slang for a man living from a prostitute's earnings.
→FANTASY

fanfare [mid 18th century] This comes from French and is probably of imitative origin. The word describes a flourish played on brass instruments. It is also used as a specialized term for a style of bookbinding decoration developed in Paris in the 16th century: in this technique, a continuous interlaced ribbon divides the whole surface of both covers of the book into symmetrical compartments varying in shape and size.

fang [late Old English] *Fang* first denoted booty or spoils. It comes from Old Norse *fang* 'to capture, grasp'. A sense 'trap, snare' is recorded from the mid 16th century; both this and the original sense survive in Scots. The current sense 'large sharp tooth' (also mid 16th century) reflects the same notion of 'something that catches and holds'.

fantastic [late Middle English] The early sense recorded was 'existing only in the imagination, unreal'; the word comes from Old French *fantastique*, via medieval Latin from Greek *phantastikos*. The Greek source verbs were *phantazein* 'make visible' and *phantazesthai* 'have visions, imagine', from *phantos* 'visible' (related to *phainein* 'to show'). From the 16th to the 19th centuries the Latinized spelling *phantastic* was also used. The modern use of the word to mean 'wonderful, excellent' dates from the 1930s.

fantasy [late Middle English] This is from Old French *fantasie*, from Latin *phantasia*, from the Greek word meaning 'imagination, appearance' and later 'phantom', from *phantazein* 'make visible'. From the 16th to the 19th centuries the Latinized spelling *phantasy* was also used. The recent phrase *fantasy football* arose in the 1980s and was originally a US usage: it denotes a competition in which participants select imaginary teams from players in the existing league, scoring points according to actual performances.
→ FANTASTIC

far [Old English] Old English *feorr* is Germanic in origin and related to Dutch *ver*, from an Indo-European root shared by Sanskrit *para* and Greek *pera* 'further'.
→ FURTHER

farce [early 16th century] This is an adoption of a French word meaning literally 'stuffing', from *farcir* 'to stuff' (from Latin *farcire*). An earlier sense of 'forcemeat stuffing' became used metaphorically for comic interludes 'stuffed' into the texts of religious plays: this led to the current usage 'a comic drama featuring buffoonery'.

fare [Old English] Old English *fær*, *faru* meant 'travelling, a journey or expedition'; the verb *faran* meant both 'to travel' and 'get on (well or badly)'. The origin is Germanic and related forms are Dutch *varen* and German *fahren* 'to travel', as well as Old Norse *ferja* 'ferry boat'. *Fare* as 'an amount paid for a journey' stems from an earlier meaning: 'a journey' for which a price is paid. The word as a term for 'food' was originally used with reference to the quality or quantity of food provided, probably from the idea of *faring* well or badly (Milton *Paradise Lost*: After such delicious Fare). The expression **farewell** is late Middle English from the imperative of *fare* and the adverb *well*, wishing a 'safe journey'.
→ FORD

farm [Middle English] This comes from Old French *ferme*, from medieval Latin *firma* 'a fixed payment (in money or kind)', from Latin *firmare* 'to fix, settle'. It is based on Latin *firmus* 'constant, firm'. The noun originally referred to a fixed annual amount payable as rent or tax; this is reflected in the historical verb sense 'allow (someone) to keep the revenues from a tax, on payment of a fee' (Shakespeare *Richard II*: We are enforced to farm out our royal Realm). It later gave rise to the sense 'to subcontract'. The noun came to be a term for a lease, and, in the early 16th century, land leased specifically for farming. The verb sense 'grow crops or keep livestock' dates from the early 19th century. A **farmer** in late Middle English was somebody who collected taxes: the word is from Old French *fermier*, from medieval Latin *firmarius*, *firmator*, from *firma*. The modern sense of *farmer* has arisen from the word's earlier use to denote a bailiff or steward who farmed land on the owner's behalf, a tenant farmer.
→ FIRM²

farrier [mid 16th century] *Farrier* 'a smith who shoes horses' is from Old French *ferrier*, from Latin *ferrarius*, from *ferrum* 'iron, horseshoe'.

farrow [Old English] Old English *fearh*, *færh* was a 'young pig'; now the noun use is 'a litter of pigs'. Of West Germanic origin, it is from an Indo-European root shared by Greek *porkos* and Latin *porcus* 'pig'.

fascinate [late 16th century] 'Bewitch, put under a spell' was the first sense recorded for *fascinate*. It comes from Latin *fascinare* 'bewitch', from *fascinum* 'spell, witchcraft'. The figurative use meaning 'attract and hold spellbound' developed early in the word's history.

fascism [early 20th century] This word comes from Italian *fascismo*, from *fascio* 'bundle, political group', from Latin *fascis* 'bundle'. The term *fascism* was first used of the totalitarian right-wing nationalist regime of Mussolini in Italy (1922–43); the regimes of the Nazis in Germany and of Franco in Spain were also *fascist*. Views held tend to include a belief in the supremacy of one national or ethnic group and a contempt for democracy. In ancient Rome a bundle of rods with a projecting axe blade known as *fasces* were carried by a lictor as a symbol of a magistrate's power. These items were carried in Fascist Italy as emblems of authority.

fashion [Middle English] The word *fashion* originally meant 'make, shape, or appearance' as well as 'a particular make, style'. Old French *façon* is the source, from Latin *factio(n-)*, from *facere* 'do, make'. The phrase *out of fashion* once meant 'out of shape'. It was in the mid 16th century that the word came to denote a mode of dress currently adopted by society. *In fashion* and *out of fashion* were both used by Shakespeare to mean 'in vogue' or 'out of vogue' (*Julius Caesar*: Slaying is the word. It is a deed in fashion).

fast¹ [Old English] Old English *fæst* meant 'firmly fixed in place, steadfast' (as in *fast friend*) and the adverb *fæste* meant 'firmly, securely'.

Of Germanic origin, the word is related to Dutch *vast* and German *fest* 'firm, solid' and *fast* 'almost'. In Middle English the adverb developed the senses 'strongly, vigorously' (which is comparable with *hard* in *run hard*), and 'close, immediate' (just surviving in the archaic and poetic *fast by*, comparable with *hard by*). This led to 'closely, immediately' and 'quickly'; the idea of rapid movement was later reflected in adjectival use. The compound:

■ **fast food** dates from the 1950s for food served in catering outlets where it is kept hot or semi-prepared ready to serve quickly.

fast² [Old English] Old English *fæstan* 'abstain from or go without food' has a Germanic origin; it is related to Dutch *vasten* and German *fasten*, as well as to Old Norse *fasta*, the source of the noun.

fasten [Old English] Old English *fæstnian* meant 'make sure, confirm' and 'immobilize'. Of West Germanic origin, it is related to *fast* 'fixed in place'.
→ FAST¹

fastidious [late Middle English] This comes from Latin *fastidiosus*, from *fastidium* 'loathing'. The word originally meant 'disagreeable, distasteful', later 'disgusted'. Current senses ('attentive to accuracy', 'concerned about personal cleanliness') date from the 17th century.

fat [Old English] The meaning of Old English *fætt* was 'well fed, plump' and 'fatty, oily', both with favourable and unfavourable connotations. The word is West Germanic in origin and related to Dutch *vet* and German *feist*.

fatal [late Middle English] The early use of *fatal* is recorded as 'destined by fate' and 'ominous'. It comes from Old French, or from Latin *fatalis* 'decreed by fate', from *fatum* 'that which has been spoken'. The noun **fatality** (from French *fatalité* or late Latin *fatalitas*) is recorded from the late 15th century when it denoted the quality of causing death or disaster. The prime current sense 'an occurrence of death by accident, in war, or by disease' dates from the mid 19th century.
→ FATE

fate [late Middle English] *Fate* is from Italian *fato* or (later) from its source, Latin *fatum* 'that which has been spoken', from *fari* 'to speak'. The primary sense of the Latin *fatum* was 'doom or sentence of the gods'; this changed to 'one's lot'. In the plural *the Fates* refer to the three goddesses of Greek and Roman mythology, supposed to determine the course of human life.

father [Old English] Old English *fæder* is Germanic in origin and related to Dutch *vader* and German *Vater*, from an Indo-European root shared by Latin *pater* and Greek *patēr*. The name:

■ **Father Christmas** is of obscure origin. His conventionalized image is comparatively recent: in late medieval Europe he became identified with St Nicholas (Santa Claus); in England Father Christmas was a personification of Christmas, a genial red-robed old man who appeared in many 16th-century masques and in mummers' plays. There was a great revival of the celebration of Christmas in the 19th century and Father Christmas acquired (from St Nicholas) the association of present-bringing.

fathom [Old English] Old English *fæthm* is a Germanic word in origin and related to Dutch *vadem*, *vaam* and German *Faden* 'six feet'. The original sense in the singular was 'something which embraces', in the plural meaning 'the outstretched arms'; this gave rise to the word's use as a unit of measurement based on the span of the outstretched arms, later standardized to six feet. The sense 'understand' found in the verb is from the notion 'embrace'.

fatigue [mid 17th century] The early use of the word was to mean 'a task or duty causing weariness'; this is seen in the military use of the plural *fatigues*, duties sometimes allocated as a punishment. It comes via French from Latin *fatigare* 'tire out', from *ad fatim*, *affatim* 'to satiety or surfeit; to bursting'.

fatuous [early 17th century] This is based on Latin *fatuus* 'foolish'.

faucet [late Middle English] An early *faucet* was a bung for the vent-hole of a cask, or a tap for drawing liquor from a container. It comes from Old French *fausset*, from Provençal *falset*, from *falsar* 'to bore'. The current sense 'tap' in North American usage dates from the mid 19th century.

fault [Middle English] The spelling in Middle English was *faut(e)* 'lack, failing', from Old French, based on Latin *fallere* 'to deceive'. The -*l*- was added (in French and English) in the 15th century to conform with the Latin word, but this did not become standard in English until the 17th century, remaining silent in pronunciation until well into the 18th. The word expresses 'error' sometimes accompanied by blame and sometimes not; this is seen in its use in sporting contexts with loss of points following an erroneous shot or move (late 16th century).

fauna [late 18th century] Commonly found in the phrase *flora and fauna*, this word for 'the animals of a particular habitat or geological period' is a modern Latin application of *Fauna*, the name of a rural goddess. She was the sister of *Faunus*, an ancient Italian pastoral god, grandson of Saturn, associated with wooded places.

favour [Middle English] The early noun sense was 'liking, preference'. It comes via Old French from Latin *favor*, from *favere* 'show kindness to' (related to *fovere* 'cherish'). In the late 16th century, a *favour* was something given as a sign of preference, a gift as a token of affection. An example of this is the *favour* worn conspicuously by medieval knights. Sometimes a ribbon or cockade worn at a ceremony such as at a wedding or coronation was known as a *favour* too. The adjective **favourable** is Middle English and is via Old French from Latin *favorabilis*, from *favor*.

favourite [late 16th century] Early examples show *favourite* as a noun. It comes from obsolete French *favorit*, from Italian *favorito*, the past participle of *favorire* 'to favour'. Latin *favor* 'kindness; kindly regard' is the base. The phrase *favourite son* is part of US English and refers to 'a man who has endeared himself to a particular country or state'. It is also specifically used as a commendatory title given to George Washington.
→ FAVOUR

fawn¹ [late Middle English] The zoological word *fawn* from Old French *faon*, based on Latin *fetus* 'offspring'. The association with colour dates from the beginning of the 19th century.

fawn² [Old English] Old English *fagnian* meant 'make or be glad'; this was often used of an animal such as a dog showing delight by wagging its tail. Of Germanic origin, *fawn* is related to *fain*. The current sense is 'make a servile display of affection'. The archaic word **fain** as in *the traveller was fain to proceed* is related: in Old English this was *fægen* 'happy, well pleased' from a base meaning 'rejoice'.

faze [mid 19th century] This informal word meaning 'disturb, disconcert' (as in *she was not fazed by his show of anger*) was originally US, a variant of dialect *feeze* 'drive or frighten off', from Old English *fēsian*, whose origin is unknown.

fear [Old English] Old English *fær* meant 'calamity, danger' and the verb *færan* meant both 'to frighten' and 'to revere'. The origin is Germanic and related forms are Dutch *gevaar* and German *Gefahr* 'danger'. The noun *fear* sometimes mixes the notions 'dread' and 'reverence' as in *fear of God*.

feasible [late Middle English] *Feasible* 'possible to do' is from Old French *faisible*, from *fais-*, the stem of *faire* 'do, make', from Latin

facere. An informal use of the word reflects the meaning 'likely, probable'.

feast [Middle English] The noun is from Old French *feste*, the verb from Old French *fester*, from Latin *festa*, the neuter plural of *festus* 'joyous'. The main semantic strands are 'festival' and 'banquet'. As a festival, a *feast* is sometimes a religious anniversary accompanied by rejoicing (as opposed to a *fast*); sometimes it is a village festival held annually, originally on the feastday of the saint to whom the parish church was dedicated. *Movable feasts* refer to dates such as Easter which vary from year to year, whereas *immovable feasts* are the fixed celebrations such as Christmas Day.

feat [late Middle English] The general sense 'action or deed' was found in early examples of *feat*, which is from Old French *fait*, from Latin *factum*. The current sense is 'achievement, noteworthy act'.
→ FACT

feather [Old English] Old English *fether* is Germanic in origin, related to Dutch *veer* and German *Feder*, from an Indo-European root shared by Sanskrit *patra* 'wing', Latin *penna* 'feather', and Greek *pteron*, *pterux* 'wing'. The idiom *a feather in one's cap* denoting 'a sign of honour' is associated with the word *favour*, once worn as a sign of special preference for example by knights jousting in honour of a particular lady.
→ FAVOUR

feature [late Middle English] This was originally 'a physical feature' or 'the form or proportions of the body'. It comes from Old French *faiture* 'form', from Latin *factura*. The word's tranferred use as a 'distinctive part of something' dates from the late 17th century. A *feature* in a newspaper is a mid 19th-century development; in connection with films, examples are found from the early 20th century.

feckless [late 16th century] *Feckless* 'lacking in efficiency or vitality' is based on Scots and northern English dialect *feck*, a shortening of *effeck*: this is a variant of *effect*.

federal [mid 17th century] *Federal* is based on Latin *foedus*, *foeder-* 'league, covenant'. It was used to mean 'relating to a treaty or covenant', and from combinations such as *federal union* (= union sealed by a covenant) came to be 'relating to a political union of two or more states'. The abbreviation **fed** was used in the late 18th century to denote a member of the Federalist party who advocated a union of American colonies after the War of Independence; from the early 20th century the abbreviation has been used to mean 'federal agent' (usually of the FBI). **Federation** (early 18th century) comes from

French *fédération*, from late Latin *foederatio(n-)*, from the verb *foederare* 'to ally' (from *foedus*).

fee [Middle English] *Fee* is from an Anglo-Norman French variant of Old French *feu*, *fief*, from medieval Latin *feodum*, *feudum*. The ultimate origin is Germanic. Historically a *fee* was an estate of land usually held in return for feudal service (but still in the ownership of the lord). In legal contexts this notion has remained in phrases such as *in fee* referring to an estate of inheritance in land; theoretically in English Law all landed property is held feudally of the Crown. *Hold in fee* is also used figuratively meaning 'hold as one's absolute possession' (Tennyson *In Memoriam*: I know thee of what force thou art, To hold the costliest love in fee). Currently a *fee* is a 'payment' in various contexts.

feeble [Middle English] This word is from Old French *fieble*, which was spelt *fleible* earlier. Latin *flebilis* 'lamentable' is the source, from *flere* 'to weep'. As well as 'lacking physical strength', *feeble* meant 'lacking intellectual or moral strength' from the earliest times.

feed [Old English] The Old English verb *fēdan* is Germanic in origin and related to Dutch *voeden*. The semantic core is 'supply' rather than the nourishment itself: this is seen in extended use such as *feed a slot-machine with coins*, *feed chords to a jazz soloist*, *feed a pond with water from a stream*, *feed a spindle with thread*.
→ FOOD

feel [Old English] Old English *fēlan* has a West Germanic origin; it is related to Dutch *voelen* and German *fühlen*. The semantic strands are 'explore by touch', 'perceive', and 'experience as a sensation'. The notion of having a personal conviction of something is recorded from the early 17th century; this is seen especially in the common modern construction *feel that* … (Trollope *Barchester Towers*: She felt that she might yet recover her lost ground).

feign [Middle English] *Feign* is from Old French *feign-*, the stem of *feindre*, from Latin *fingere* 'to mould, contrive'. Old French *feindre* meant 'avoid one's duty by false pretences, shirk': this was sometimes found in English (Chaucer *Boke of the Duchesse*: Noon of hem … feyned To singe). Senses taken from Latin in Middle English included 'make something' and 'invent a story, excuse, or allegation', hence 'make a pretence of a feeling or response' (e.g. *she feigned nervousness*).
→ FICTION; FIGMENT

feint[1] [late 17th century] This fencing term for a deceptive or pretended blow is from French *feinte*, the past participle (used as a noun) of *feindre* 'to feign'.

feint[2] [mid 19th century] This word used in phrases such as *feint paper* describing paper printed with faint lines as a handwriting guide, is a variant of *faint*.
→ FAINT

feisty [late 19th century] Meaning 'excitable and assertive', this US slang word originated in dialect from the earlier noun *feist*, *fist* 'a small dog'. This in its turn came from *fisting cur*, a derogatory term for a lapdog, from Middle English *fist* meaning 'to break wind' (of West Germanic origin).
→ FIZZLE

feline [late 17th century] This is from Latin *felinus*, from *feles* 'cat'.

fell[1] [Old English] Old English *fellan* 'cut down' is Germanic in origin and related to Dutch *vellen* and German *fällen*.
→ FALL

fell[2] [Middle English] This word for a 'hill' is from Old Norse *fjall*, *fell* 'hill'; it is probably related to German *Fels* 'rock'.

fell[3] [Middle English] This *fell* means 'deadly or ferocious'; it is from Old French *fel*, the nominative of *felon* 'wicked (person)'. The phrase *in one fell swoop* originally referred to the sudden descent of a bird of prey in deadly pursuit of its quarry; this led to the extended sense 'with a single blow, all in one go'.
→ FELON

fell[4] [Old English] A *fell* sometimes describes a 'an animal's hide'. Of Germanic origin, it is related to Dutch *vel* and German *Fell*, from an Indo-European root shared by Latin *pellis* and Greek *pella* 'skin'. A derivative from the same root is *film*.
→ FILM

fellow [late Old English] Late Old English *fēolaga* meant 'a partner or colleague', literally 'one who lays down money in a joint enterprise'. It comes from Old Norse *félagi*, from *fé* 'cattle, property, money' and the Germanic base of *lay* 'place down'. As well as being used generally now for 'person, man', it is also a specific term in universities for an incorporated senior member of a college, an elected graduate receiving a stipend for research, or (in certain universities) a member of the governing body.
→ LAY[1]

felon [Middle English] This comes from an Old French word meaning literally 'wicked, a wicked person', from medieval Latin *fello*, *fellon-*, whose origin is unknown. The most probable of the conjectures about the history of the Latin is that it derives from *fel* 'gall', which would give an original sense of 'somebody or something full of bitterness'. The English word was used as an adjective meaning 'cruel, fierce' as well as a noun. The legal term **felony** also dates from Middle English and is from Old French *felonie*, from *felon*.

felt [Old English] This word for a kind of cloth made by rolling or pressing wool to form a smooth surface is West Germanic in origin. It is related to Dutch *vilt* and *filter*.
→ FILTER

female [Middle English] This is from Old French *femelle*, from Latin *femella*, a diminutive of *femina* 'a woman'. The change in the ending was due to association with *male*, but the words *male* and *female* are not linked etymologically.

feminine [late Middle English] This is from Latin *femininus*, from *femina* 'woman'. This is also the base of **feminism** and **feminist**, both late 19th century from French *féminisme* and *féministe* respectively.

fen [Old English] Old English *fen(n)* 'marshy land; low land covered in shallow water' is Germanic in origin and related to Dutch *veen* and German *Fenn*. *The Fens* are low-lying areas of eastern England mainly in Lincolnshire, Cambridgeshire, and Norfolk which were formerly marshland but since the 17th century largely drained for agriculture.

fence [Middle English] The early sense recorded for *fence* was 'defending, defence' and it is in fact a shortening of *defence*. The use of the word for 'railing' developed early. Association with the art of fencing arose in the late 16th century.
→ FEND

fend [Middle English] The early use of *fend* was to mean 'defend': it is a shortening of the verb *defend*.
→ FENCE

feral [early 17th century] *Feral* 'in a wild state' is based on Latin *fera* 'wild animal', from *ferus* 'wild'.

ferment [late Middle English] The noun is from Old French *ferment*, the verb from Old French *fermenter*, based on Latin *fermentum* 'yeast', from *fervere* 'to boil'. **Fermentation** (from late Latin *fermentatio(n-)* 'fermenting') is also late Middle English.

ferocity [mid 16th century] This comes either from French, or from Latin *ferocitas*, from *ferox*, *feroc-* 'fierce'. This is also the base of **ferocious** which is recorded from the mid 17th century.

ferret [late Middle English] This word is from Old French *fuiret*, an alteration of *fuiron*, based on late Latin *furo* 'thief, ferret', from Latin *fur* 'thief'. Verb use was also early; the figurative

use of *ferret about* 'hunt about' arose in the late 16th century.

ferry [Middle English] *Ferry* is from Old Norse *ferja* 'a ferry boat'. Germanic in origin, it is related to *fare*.
→ FARE

fertile [late Middle English] *Fertile* 'bearing or producing in abundance' came via French from Latin *fertilis*, from *ferre* 'to bear'. In early use the English word was usually applied to the soil and the land, rarely animals.

fervour [Middle English] *Fervour* 'intense feeling' came via Old French from Latin *fervor*, from *fervere* 'to boil'. Middle English **fervent** came via Old French from Latin *fervent-*, the present participial stem of *fervere*.

fester [late Middle English] This comes from the rare word *fester* 'a fistula', later 'a festering sore', or from the Old French verb *festrir*, from Latin *fistula* 'pipe, reed, fistula'. The transferred sense 'allow (malice) to rankle' dates from the early 17th century.

festival [Middle English] Early use was as an adjective. It comes via Old French from medieval Latin *festivalis*, from Latin *festivus*, from *festum* (in the plural *festa* 'feast'). **Festivity** from Old French *festivite* or Latin *festivitas*, from *festivus*, is late Middle English. **Festive** dates from the mid 17th century, also from Latin *festivus*.

festoon [mid 17th century] *Festoon* is from French *feston*, from Italian *festone* 'festal ornament', believed to be from *festa* 'feast'. The core meaning would therefore be 'decoration for a feast'.

fetch [Old English] Old English *fecc(e)an* is a variant of *fetian*, probably related to *fatian* 'to grasp'. The origin is Germanic and German *fassen* is related. The colloquial *fetching* meaning 'alluring, attractive' dates from the late 19th century.

fetid [late Middle English] This is from Latin *fetidus* (often erroneously spelled *foetidus*), from *fetere* 'to stink'.

fetish [early 17th century] This was originally a word for any object used by the peoples of West Africa as an amulet or charm. It comes from French *fétiche*, from Portuguese *feitiço* 'charm, sorcery' (originally an adjective meaning 'made by art'). Latin *factitius* 'made by art' is the base. In psychology *fetish* is a term for sexual desire produced by a stimulus which in itself is non-sexual: this dates from the early 20th century.

fetlock [Middle English] This word is of Germanic origin, probably related to German *Fessel* 'fetlock' and to English *foot*. The word was

easily interpreted as 'foot lock' (= lock of hair at the foot) and this notion influenced some early spellings.
→ FOOT

fetter [Old English] Old English *feter* is from a Germanic source; it is related to Dutch *veter* 'a lace', from an Indo-European root shared by *foot*.
→ FOOT

fettle [late Middle English] The general sense 'get ready, prepare', specifically 'prepare oneself for battle, gird up' was found in early use. It comes from dialect *fettle* 'strip of material, girdle', from Old English *fetel* which is Germanic in origin. A related word is German *Fessel* 'chain, band'. English *fettle* is commonly found in the phrase *in fine fettle* meaning 'in fine condition'.

feud [Middle English] The Middle English spelling was *fede* 'hostility, ill will'; it comes from Old French *feide*, from Middle Dutch, Middle Low German *vēde*, of Germanic origin.
→ FOE

feudal [early 17th century] *Feudal* is from medieval Latin *feudalis*, from *feudum*.
→ FEE

fever [Old English] Old English *fēfor* is from Latin *febris*; the spelling was reinforced in Middle English by Old French *fievre* (also from *febris*). Some refer the word to a root meaning 'be restless'. The plant:
■ **feverfew** used in herbal medicine was *feferfuge* in Old English, from Latin *febrifuga*, from *febris* 'fever' and *fugare* 'drive away'.

few [Old English] Old English *fēawe, fēawa* is Germanic in origin; it is related to Old High German *fao*, from an Indo-European root shared by Latin *paucus* and Greek *pauros* 'small'. The phrase *the Few* referring with respect to the RAF pilots who took part in the Battle of Britain, is an allusion to a speech of Sir Winston Churchill (1940: Never in the field of human conflict was so much owed by so many to so few).

fiasco [mid 19th century] This is an adoption of an Italian word meaning literally 'bottle, flask', in the phrase *far fiasco*, literally 'make a bottle'. Figuratively this means 'fail in a performance' but the reason for the figurative sense remains unexplained.

fib [mid 16th century] This informal word for 'a lie' is perhaps a shortening of the obsolete compound *fible-fable* 'nonsense', a reduplication of *fable*.

fibre [late Middle English] Coming via French from Latin *fibra* 'fibre, filament, entrails', *fibre* was originally used as a term for the 'lobe of

the liver' following Latin usage. The word's use to mean 'filament' dates from the early 17th century; it is not until the beginning of the 20th century that the word refers to dietary material resistant to the action of digestive enzymes.

fickle [Old English] Old English *ficol* meant 'deceitful': the origin is Germanic. The sense 'changeable in disposition' dates from Middle English.

fiction [late Middle English] The early sense of *fiction* was 'invented statement'. The word came via Old French from Latin *fictio(n-)*, from *fingere* 'to form, contrive'. The application to literature dates from the late 16th century. **Fictitious** is recorded from the early 17th century and is based on Latin *ficticius* (from *fingere*).
→ FEIGN; FIGMENT

fiddle [Old English] Old English *fithele* was a violin or similar instrument and originally this was not an informal or depreciatory term. It is related to Dutch *vedel* and German *Fiedel*, based on Latin *vitulari* 'celebrate a festival, be joyful', perhaps from *Vitula*, the name of a Roman goddess of joy and victory. The verb *fiddle* 'toy with idly' dates from the mid 16th century and the sense 'cheat' is a slang use from the early 17th century.

fidelity [late Middle English] This comes from Old French *fidelite* or Latin *fidelitas*, from *fidelis* 'faithful', from *fides* 'faith'.

fidget [late 17th century] *Fidget* is from obsolete or dialect *fidge* 'to twitch'; it is perhaps related to Old Norse *fikja* 'move briskly, be restless or eager'.

field [Old English] Old English *feld* also denoted a large tract of open country (comparable with *veld*). It is West Germanic in origin and related to Dutch *veld* and German *Feld*.

fiend [Old English] Old English *fēond* was 'an enemy, the devil, a demon'. Of Germanic origin it is related to Dutch *vijand* and German *Feind* 'enemy'.

fierce [Middle English] *Fierce* is from Old French *fiers* 'fierce, brave, proud', from Latin *ferus* 'untamed'.

fight [Old English] The Old English verb form *feohtan* and noun forms *feoht(e), gefeoht* are West Germanic in origin; they are related to Dutch *vechten, gevecht* and German *fechten, Gefecht* (verbs and nouns respectively). The *good fight* is a biblical phrase (1 Timothy 6:12: Fight the good fight of faith, lay hold on eternal life) quoted in the Irish-born clergyman J. S. B. Monsell's hymn

The Fight for Faith of 1863 (Fight the good fight with all thy might).

figment [late Middle English] Initially *figment* was an invented statement or story. It is from Latin *figmentum*, related to *fingere* 'to form, contrive'. The current sense, often used in the phrase *figment of the imagination* dates from the early 17th century.
→ FEIGN; FICTION

figure [Middle English] Early senses included 'distinctive shape of a person or thing', 'representation of something material or immaterial', and 'numerical symbol', among others. The word is from Old French *figure* (noun), *figurer* (verb), from Latin *figura* 'shape, figure, form' (related to *fingere* 'form, contrive'). Mid 19th-century **figurine** came via French, from Italian *figurina*, a diminutive of *figura*.

filament [late 16th century] This was adopted from French, or it is from modern Latin *filamentum*, from Late Latin *filare* 'to spin', from Latin *filum* 'thread'. *Filament* is also used as a term for a conducting wire (originally some form of carbon and now commonly tungsten) forming part of an electric bulb or thermionic valve: this application dates from the late 19th century.

file¹ [late Middle English] The *file* which means 'place in a folder in an organized way for easy reference' was first used meaning 'string documents on a thread or wire to keep them in order'. The source is French *filer* 'to string', *fil* 'a thread', both from Latin *filum* 'a thread'.
→ FILE²

file² [late 16th century] This *file* which refers to a line of people or things one behind the other (as in *in single file*) is from French *file*, from *filer* 'to string'.

file³ [Old English] Old English *fíl* 'tool for smoothing a hard or rough material' is of West Germanic origin; related words are Dutch *vijl* and German *Feile*.

filibuster [late 18th century] This word from French *flibustier*, first applied to pirates who pillaged the Spanish colonies in the West Indies. In the mid 19th century (via Spanish *filibustero*), the term referred to American adventurers who incited revolution in several Latin American states: this gave rise to the historical sense 'person engaging in unauthorized warfare against a foreign state'. When the verb was used initially it described tactics for sabotaging US congressional proceedings: this led to the word's use (especially as *filibustering*) for an action such as prolonged speaking, a deliberate obstruction to progress in a legislative assembly.

filigree [late 17th century] The earlier spellings for this word describing fine ornamental work usually in gold or silver were *filigreen* and *filigrane*. The word comes from French *filigrane*, from Italian *filigrana*. The formative elements are Latin *filum* 'thread' and *granum* 'seed'.

fill [Old English] Old English *fyllan* (verb) and *fyllu* (noun) have a Germanic source; they are related to the Dutch verbs *vullen* and German *füllen*, and the noun *Fülle*. The semantic strands include 'make full', 'occupy completely', and 'satisfy'. The phrase variations *drink, eat one's fill* were already in use in Old English.
→ FULL¹

fillet [Middle English] Early use of the word was to denote a band worn round the head. Old French *filet* 'thread' based on Latin *filum* 'thread' is the source of the word in English. Current senses all involve the notion 'thin strip' (e.g. *fillet of beef, fillet impressed on a book cover*, etc.).

fillip [late Middle English] 'Something which acts as a stimulus' is a *fillip*. An archaic sense is a 'flick of the finger', which arises from the first recorded use of the word as a verb meaning 'make a fillip with the fingers'. It is a word symbolic of the action.
→ FLICK; FLIP

filly [late Middle English] *Filly* 'a young female horse' is from Old Norse *fylja*, Germanic in origin; it is related to *foal*.
→ FOAL

film [Old English] Old English *filmen* meant 'membrane'. The origin is West Germanic. The word has been used in photography since the mid 19th century. The verb dates from the early 17th century in the sense 'cover as if with a film', with more specific application to photographs and films becoming common in the 19th and 20th centuries.
→ FELL⁴

Filofax [1930s] This represents a colloquial pronunciation of *file of facts*.

filter [late Middle English] A *filter* in early examples was 'a piece of felt'. It comes from French *filtre*, from medieval Latin *filtrum* 'felt used as a filter', of West Germanic origin. Figurative use of the noun dates from the early 17th century; **filtrate** dates from this period too and is from modern Latin *filtrare* 'to filter', from medieval Latin *filtrum*.
→ FELT

filth [Old English] Of Germanic origin, Old English *fylth* meant both 'rotting matter, rottenness' and 'corruption, obscenity'; it is related to Dutch *vuilte*. The compound:

■ **filthy lucre** (early 16th century) is with biblical allusion to Titus 1:11 (For there are many unruly and vain talkers … teaching things which they ought not, for filthy lucre's sake).
→ FOUL

fin [Old English] Old English *finn*, *fin* is Germanic in origin and related to Dutch *vin* and probably ultimately to Latin *pinna* 'feather, wing'.

final [Middle English] The adjectival sense 'conclusive' was the first recorded. It comes from Old French, or from Latin *finalis*, from *finis* 'end'. It is recorded as a noun meaning 'deciding game' from the late 19th century, when it was also used for 'last of a series of examinations' (from colloquial use at Oxford). In the mid 18th century the word **finale** was adopted from Italian mainly in musical and entertainment contexts: this is also from Latin *finalis*.
→ FINISH

finance [late Middle English] *Finance* is from Old French, from *finer* 'make an end; settle a debt', from *fin* 'end'. The original sense was 'payment of a debt, compensation, or ransom'; this later developed into 'taxation, revenue'. Current senses date from the 18th century, and reflect sense development in French. **Financier**, early 17th century, is from French, from *finance*.
→ FINE²

find [Old English] Old English *findan* is Germanic in origin, related to Dutch *vinden* and German *finden*. The main nuances of meaning in English are 'come upon by chance', 'discover by searching', and 'provide for': the latter is illustrated by the phrase *all found*, sometimes reduced to *found* (Dickens *Nicholas Nickleby*: An annual salary of five pounds … and 'found' in food and lodging).

fine¹ [Middle English] *Fine* 'of very high quality' is from Old French *fin*, based on Latin *finire* 'to finish'. **Finery**, late 17th century, is based on *fine*, on the pattern of nouns such as *bravery*. Related to *fine* is the late Middle English word **finesse** which meant 'purity, delicacy' in early examples: this is the adoption of a French word.
→ FINISH

fine² [Middle English] *Fine* 'payment' is from Old French *fin* 'end, payment', from Latin *finis* 'end': this word in medieval Latin denoted a sum paid on settling a lawsuit. The original sense in English was 'conclusion' (surviving in the phrase *in fine*). Also used in the medieval Latin sense, the word came to denote a penalty of any kind, later specifically a monetary penalty.

finger [Old English] *Finger* is Germanic in origin and related to Dutch *vinger* and German *Finger*. The word is used in many idiomatic expressions including: *point the finger (of scorn)* (early 19th century), *lay a finger on somebody* (mid 19th century), *fingers crossed* (1920s), *pull one's finger(s) out* (1940s).

finish [Middle English] This comes from Old French *feniss-*, the lengthened stem of *fenir*, from Latin *finire*, from *finis* 'end'. The use of the word to describe 'the completed and perfected state of something' dates from the late 18th century; in sporting contexts the meaning 'end point of a race' dates from the late 19th century. Latin *finitus* meaning 'finished' (the past participle of *finire*) gave rise to late Middle English **finite**.

fire [Old English] The Old English noun *fyr* and the verb *fyrian* 'supply with material for a fire' are West Germanic in origin; they are related to Dutch *vuur* and German *Feuer*. The association with passion and emotion was made early in the word's development.

firm¹ [Middle English] *Firm* meaning 'having a solid surface or structure' comes from Old French *ferme*, from Latin *firmus*. 'Not yielding to pressure' is the core of the word.

firm² [late 16th century] The *firm* referring to 'a company or business' is from Spanish and Italian *firma*, via medieval Latin from Latin *firmare* 'fix, settle' which came to mean 'confirm by signature'. The base is the adjective *firmus* 'firm'. The word in English originally referred to an autograph or signature; later, in the mid 18th century, it became the name under which the business of a firm was transacted, hence the firm itself (late 18th century).
→ FARM

firmament [Middle English] This poetical word for the heavens came via Old French from Latin *firmamentum*, from *firmare* 'fix, settle'. It was a word adopted in the Vulgate translating the Hebrew word which probably meant 'expanse', used for 'vault of the sky' as a fixed structure.

first [Old English] Old English *fyr(e)st* is Germanic in origin and related to Old Norse *fyrstr* and German *Fürst* 'prince', from an Indo-European root shared by Sanskrit *prathama*, Latin *primus*, and Greek *prōtos*.

fiscal [mid 16th century] This financial term is either from French, or from Latin *fiscalis*, from *fiscus* 'purse, treasury, rush basket'.

fish [Old English] Old English *fisc* was a noun denoting any animal living exclusively in water; the verb spelling was *fiscian*. Of Germanic origin, *fish* is related to Dutch *vis* and

German *Fisch*. The expression *queer fish* for an 'odd person' dates from the mid 18th century. Old English *fiscere* 'fisherman' is related to Dutch *visser* and German *Fischer*.

fissure [late Middle English] This is from Old French, or from Latin *fissura*, from *findere* 'to split': this Latin verb is also the base of **fission** 'splitting' (early 17th century) from Latin *fissio(n-)*.

fist [Old English] Old English *fȳst* is originally West Germanic, related to Dutch *vuist* and German *Faust*. The informal word **fisticuffs** dates from the early 17th century and is probably from obsolete *fisty* meaning 'relating to the fists or to fist fighting' and the verb *cuff* 'strike with the open hand'.

fit¹ [Old English] Old English *fitt* meant 'conflict' and, in Middle English, 'a position of danger or excitement' as well as 'a short period'. The current sense 'sudden attack of illness' dates from the mid 16th century.

fit² [late Middle English] The origin of *fit* meaning 'be the right shape or size for' and 'in good health', etc., is unknown. The word may be from the same ultimate root as the Dutch and Flemish form *vitten* 'to suit, adapt' of the 16th–17th centuries. The phrase *survival of the fittest* dates from the mid 19th century. 'Sexually attractive' became a slang use in British English during the 1980s.

fix [late Middle English] This is partly from Old French *fix* meaning 'fixed' and partly from medieval Latin *fixare* meaning 'to fix'. They are both from Latin *fixus*, the past participle of *figere* 'to fix or fasten'. The noun dates from the early 19th century. **Fixation** is a late Middle English word and was originally an alchemical term for the process of reducing a volatile spirit to a permanent form. The origin is medieval Latin *fixatio(n-)*, from *fixare*. Use of *fixation* 'obsessive attachment' as a term in psychology dates from the early 20th century. The word **fixture** (late 16th century in the sense 'fixing, becoming fixed') is an alteration first found in Shakespeare of obsolete *fixure* (from late Latin *fixura*, from Latin *figere* 'to fix'). The *t* was inserted in the spelling on the pattern of *mixture*.

fizzle [late Middle English] The early sense of *fizzle* was 'break wind quietly': it is probably imitative of the sound (as is mid 17th-century **fizz**) but may be related to Middle English *fist*. Current senses date from the 19th century.
→ FEISTY

flab [1950s] *Flab* is a back-formation (by removal of the suffix) from late 17th-century **flabby**, an alteration of the earlier adjective

flappy. *Flabby* (together with *aghast*) may also have suggested **flabbergast**, first mentioned in 1772 as a new piece of fashionable slang and probably an arbitrary invention.

flaccid [early 17th century] *Flaccid* 'drooping, lacking force' comes from French *flaccide* or Latin *flaccidus*, from *flaccus* 'flabby'.

flag¹ [mid 16th century] The *flag* which is used as the emblem of a country (as in *the American flag*) is perhaps onomatopoeic expressing the idea of something flapping in the wind, or from obsolete *flag* 'drooping'. The ultimate origin is unknown. It is found however in all the modern Germanic languages and was apparently recorded first in English.

flag² [late Middle English] This *flag* meaning 'a flat stone slab' included the sense 'turf, sod' in early examples. It is probably of Scandinavian origin and related to Icelandic *flag* 'a spot from which a sod has been cut' and Old Norse *flaga* 'slab of stone'.

flag³ [mid 16th century] The *flag* meaning 'become tired' had the early sense 'flap about loosely, hang down'; it is related to obsolete *flag* 'hanging down'. The formation may be partly onomatopoeic with a notion of 'flap' but implying less energetic movement.
→ FLAG¹

flagon [late Middle English] This comes from Old French *flacon*, based on late Latin *flasco*, *flascon-*, of unknown origin.
→ FLASK

flagrant [late 15th century] The early sense recorded was 'blazing, resplendent'. It comes from French, or from Latin *flagrant-*, the present participial stem of the verb *flagrare* 'to blaze'. The word's use meaning 'glaring, scandalous' with reference to an offence or a crime (e.g. *flagrant violation of the law*), dates from the early 18th century.

flail [Old English] Of West Germanic origin, *flail* is based on Latin *flagellum* 'whip'; it was probably influenced in Middle English by Old French *flaiel* or Dutch *vlegel*. The word has been used historically as a term for a military weapon and during the 'Popish Plot' (1678–81) a *Protestant flail* is said to have been carried by people fearing attack by Papists: this weapon was a short staff loaded with lead and secured to the wrist by a strap. The Popish Plot was a fictitious plot concocted by Titus Oates and attributed to the Jesuits involving a supposed plan to kill Charles II and massacre Protestants. The 'discovery' of the plot led to widespread panic and a number of trials and executions.

flair [late 19th century] This word for 'instinctive aptitude' comes from French, from *flairer*

'to smell', based on Latin *fragrare* 'smell sweet'. The notion is one of having the ability to detect the 'scent, essence' of something and the know-how to react accordingly.
→ FRAGRANT

flake [Middle English] The immediate source of *flake* as in *snow flake* is unknown; the senses derive perhaps from different words. It is probably of Germanic origin. **Flaky**, based on *flake*, is recorded from the late 16th century; in the 1960s it started to be used as a slang term in the US meaning 'odd, eccentric' (perhaps from a notion of 'not holding together' psychologically).
→ FLAG²; FLAW

flake [late 15th century] The informal word *flake* as in *flake out through exhaustion* dates, in this sense, from the 1940s. The word however existed much earlier meaning 'become languid' and sometimes referred to a garment meaning 'fall in folds'. The word is a variant of obsolete *flack*.
→ FLAG³

flamboyant [mid 19th century] This word is an adoption from the French present participle of *flamboyer*; its literal meaning is 'flaming, blazing' but it is used figuratively to mean 'ostentatious and lively'. The base is French *flambe* 'a flame'.

flame [Middle English] This comes from Old French *flame* (noun), *flamer* (verb), from Latin *flamma* 'a flame'. The word is sometimes used to mean 'the object of one's love' (as in *old flame*); its association with passion is found in very early examples of the word. A recent use is in computing contexts in the phrase *flame mail* for communications that are liable to be 'hot', i.e. troublesome. **Flammable** is recorded from the early 19th century and is from Latin *flammare*, from *flamma*.

flan [mid 19th century] This is the adoption of a French word which originally denoted a round cake. It is from Old French *flaon*, from medieval Latin *flado, fladon-*, of West Germanic origin. Dutch *vlade* 'custard' is related.

flank [late Old English] This is from Old French *flanc*, of Germanic origin. The ulterior etymology is disputed; it is likely that it was adopted from the Germanic word that appears in Old High German *hlancha*, Middle Dutch *lanke* and early Middle English *lonke* (related to English *lank*).

flannel [Middle English] *Flannel* is probably from Welsh *gwlanen* 'woollen article', from *gwlân* 'wool'. The word's use for a piece of soft cloth for washing the face and hands dates from the early 19th century. As for the slang

use of *flannel* meaning 'nonsense, flattery', this dates from the 1920s.

flap [Middle English] This is probably imitative; equivalent words in form and meaning are Dutch *flappen* 'to strike, clap' and German *flappen* 'to clap, applaud'. The slang use *flap about something* meaning 'become agitated or panic about something' dates from the early 20th century.

flare [mid 16th century] The early sense recorded for *flare* was 'spread out (one's hair)'. The origin is unknown. Current senses date from the 17th century associated with flames and light suddenly spreading. The notion of anger *flaring up* dates from the mid 19th century.

flash [Middle English] 'Splash water about' is the first meaning found in examples of *flash*. It is probably imitative. The use of the word in connection with fire or light is now the most common application: this is not found before the second half of the 16th century. This may have arisen because of the coincidence of the initial similar sounds of *flame*. The origin of *flash in the pan* is with allusion to the priming of a firearm, the flash arising from an explosion of gunpowder within the lock.
→ FLUSH¹

flask [Middle English] The early sense was 'cask or skin for holding liquor'. It comes from medieval Latin *flasca*. From the mid 16th century the word denoted a case of horn, leather, or metal for carrying gunpowder. The sense 'glass container' (late 17th century) was influenced by Italian *fiasco*, from medieval Latin *flasco*.
→ FLAGON

flat¹ [Middle English] *Flat* 'smooth and even' is from Old Norse *flatr*. The compound
■ **flatline** arose in the 1980s meaning 'to die'; its origin is with reference to the continuous straight line displayed on a heart monitor, indicating death.

flat² [early 19th century] *Flat* 'apartment' was originally a floor or storey. It is an alteration of obsolete *flet* 'floor, dwelling', of Germanic origin and related to *flat* meaning 'smooth and even'.

flattery [Middle English] This comes from Old French *flaterie*, from *flater* 'stroke, flatter' The origin is probably Germanic; the adjective *flat* 'smooth and even' may be related. Middle English **flatter** is perhaps a back-formation (by removal of the suffix) from *flattery*.

flatulent [late 16th century] This word came via French from modern Latin *flatulentus*, from Latin *flatus* 'blowing', from *flare* 'to blow'.

flavour [late Middle English] The early sense recorded was 'fragrance, aroma'. Old French *flaor* is the source, perhaps based on a blend of Latin *flatus* 'blowing' and *foetor* 'stench'. The -*v*- appears to have been introduced in Middle English by association with *savour*. The meaning associated with 'taste' dates from the late 17th century.

flaw [Middle English] This is perhaps from Old Norse *flaga* 'slab'. The original sense was 'a flake of snow' and later it came to mean 'a fragment or splinter'. This gave rise in the late 15th century to the sense 'defect or imperfection'.

flax [Old English] Old English *flæx* is West Germanic in origin; it is related to Dutch *vlas* and German *Flachs*, from an Indo-European root shared by Latin *plectere* and Greek *plekein* 'to plait, twist'.

flay [Old English] Old English *flēan* is originally Germanic; it is related to Middle Dutch *vlaen*.

flea [Old English] Old English *flēa*, *flēah* is of Germanic origin; related words are Dutch *vlo* and German *Floh*.

fleck [late Middle English] Early use was as a verb. It is perhaps from Old Norse *flekkr* (noun), *flekka* (verb), or from Middle Low German, Middle Dutch *vlecke* 'blow, mark of a blow'. The noun is not found before the 16th century.

fledge [mid 16th century] This word comes from the obsolete adjective *fledge* 'ready to fly', from Old English. The origin is Germanic; Dutch *vlug* 'quick, agile' is related. **Fledgling** is found from the mid 19th century, on the pattern of *nestling*.
→ FLY¹

flee [Old English] Old English *flēon* is Germanic in origin; it is related to Dutch *vlieden* and German *fliehen*. The two verbs *flee* and *fly* are often confused together in their history; this was already true in Old English. *Flee* has become archaic and is usually confined to poetry and rhetoric.

fleece [Old English] Old English *flēos*, *flēs* has a West Germanic origin; related words are Dutch *vlies* and German *Vlies*. The word has been used as a fashion term from the 1990s for a jacket made of fleece-like material. The verb meaning 'to obtain a lot of money from someone by deception' dates from the late 16th century.

fleet¹ [Old English] This nautical word (*flēot* in Old English) was first recorded with the meaning 'ship, shipping'. It is from *flēotan* 'to float, swim'.
→ FLEET³

fleet² [early 16th century] *Fleet* 'fast and nimble' (as in *fleet of foot*) is probably from Old

Norse *fljótr*, of Germanic origin. Although the word is not found in examples before the 16th century, it is probably much older.
→ FLEET³

fleet³ [Old English] Old English *flēotan* meant 'float, swim'; the current use of this *fleet* is in phrases such as *a look of horror fleeted across his face*. The word is Germanic in origin, related to Dutch *vlieten* and German *fliessen*. **Fleeting** (as in *for a fleeting moment*) is also Old English when it meant 'floating, swimming'.
→ FLIT; FLOAT

flesh [Old English] Old English *flæsc* is Germanic in origin and related to Dutch *vlees* and German *Fleisch*. *Flesh* meaning 'descendants' as in *flesh and blood* is chiefly of biblical origin. The compound:
■ **fleshpots** (early 16th century) is with biblical allusion to the *fleshpots of Egypt* (Exodus 16:3: Would to God that we had died by the hand of the Lord in the land of Egypt, when we sat by the flesh pots, and when we did eat bread to the full).

flex [early 16th century] *Flex* 'bend' is from Latin *flex-*, the past participial stem of *flectere* 'to bend'. The word *flex* meaning 'cable' is an abbreviation of *flexible* and dates from the early 20th century. **Flexible** is late Middle English from Old French, or from Latin *flexibilis*, from *flectere*: this is the base of the compound **flexitime** used since the 1970s in business contexts where employees have the flexibility to vary their daily starting and finishing times.

flick [late Middle English] This is a symbolic word: *fl-* is frequently found at the start of words denoting sudden movement.

flicker [Old English] Old English *flicorian, flycerian* meant 'to flutter'. The word is probably Germanic, related to Low German *flickern* and Dutch *flikkeren*.

flight [Old English] Old English *flyht* described the 'action or manner of flying'. The word's origin is Germanic, related to Dutch *vlucht*. This was probably merged in Middle English with an unrecorded Old English word related to German *Flucht* and to *flee* reflected in the use of *flight* to mean 'an escape'. **Flighty** 'fickle and irresponsible' is found from the mid 16th century, based on *flight*.
→ FLY¹

flimsy [early 18th century] This is probably from **flimflam** 'nonsensical talk' which dates from the mid 16th century and is a reduplication symbolic of the sound of this type of chatter.

flinch [mid 16th century] The early sense recorded was 'slink or sneak off'. It comes from Old French *flenchir* 'turn aside'. Of West Germanic origin it is related to German *lenken* 'to guide, steer'.

fling [Middle English] 'Go violently' was the sense found in early examples. The word is perhaps related to Old Norse *flengja* 'to flog'. The prime current sense 'throw or hurl forcefully' is based on an earlier sense 'reckless movement of the body' and dates from the early 19th century. During this same period the sense 'period of self-indulgence or enjoyment' arose.

flip [mid 16th century] The sense 'make a fillip (= flicking movement) with the fingers' is the first recorded for *flip*. It is probably a contraction of *fillip*. The phrase *egg flip* (late 17th century) used for a type of drink is perhaps from *flip* in the sense 'whip up'. The informal word **flipping** used to express mild annoyance is an early 20th-century usage based on *flip*.
→ FILLIP

flippant [early 17th century] The word *flippant* is based on *flip* perhaps on the pattern of heraldic terms such as *couchant* and *rampant*. Early senses included 'nimble' and 'talkative', hence 'playful', giving rise to the current use 'lacking seriousness'.

flirt [mid 16th century] This word is apparently symbolic, the elements *fl-* and *-irt* both suggesting sudden movement; *flick* and *spurt* are comparable. The original verb senses were 'give someone a sharp blow' and 'sneer at'; the earliest noun senses were 'joke, gibe' and 'flighty girl' (defined by Dr Johnson as 'a pert young hussey'), with a notion originally of cheeky behaviour, later playfully amorous behaviour.

flit [Middle English] Early use was in the Scots and northern English sense 'move house'. It comes from Old Norse *flytja*.

flitch [Old English] Old English *flicce* originally denoted the salted and cured side of any meat whereas now, in butchery contexts, it is 'a side of bacon'. Of Germanic origin, it is related to Middle Low German *vlicke*.

float [Old English] The Old English verb *flotian* has a Germanic origin; it is related to *fleet* 'pass quickly', reinforced in Middle English by Old French *floter*, also from Germanic. The relatively recent word **floatel** (1950s) is a blend of *float* and *hotel*.
→ FLEET[3]

flock[1] [Old English] Old English *flocc* is of unknown origin. The original sense was 'a band or body of people': this became obsolete, but has been reintroduced as a transferred use of the sense 'a number of animals kept together'.

flock[2] [Middle English] This word for a soft material for stuffing cushions or quilts is from Old French *floc*, from Latin *floccus* 'lock or tuft of wool'.

floe [early 19th century] This word for a sheet of floating ice superseded *flake* in the sense 'fragment, flat piece'. It is probably from Norwegian *flo*, from Old Norse *fló* 'layer'.

flog [late 17th century] This was originally a slang word and may be imitative or alternatively from Latin *flagellare* 'to whip', from *flagellum* 'a whip'.

flood [Old English] Old English *flōd* is a Germanic word; it is related to Dutch *vloed* and German *Flut*. The word is sometimes used poetically to refer to 'water' and is contrasted with words such as *fire* or *field* (= land) as in Shakespeare's *Othello*: I spake ... Of moving accidents of flood and field.
→ FLOW

floor [Old English] Old English *flōr* is Germanic in origin and related to Dutch *vloer* and German *Flur*. Its use with reference to legislative assemblies where the members sit dates from the late 18th century; this notion of 'area or focus of activity' is also reflected in the context of film and television shots in the phrase *on the floor* (= in production). The verb *floor* is often associated with sporting contests such as boxing or horse-racing (from the mid 17th century) and is found in figurative use ('flabbergast') from the early 19th century.

floozie [early 20th century] This informal word for a girl or woman with a reputation for promiscuity, is perhaps related to *flossy* or to dialect *floosy* meaning 'fluffy'.

flop [early 17th century] This is a variant of *flap*.
→ FLAP

floral [mid 18th century] This word is based on Latin *flos, flor-* 'flower': this is also the base of **floret** (late 17th century), **florid** (mid 17th century from Latin *floridus*), **florescence** (late 18th century from modern Latin *florescentia*), as well as **florist** (early 17th century) on the pattern of French *fleuriste* or Italian *florista*.

floss [mid 18th century] This is from French (*soie*) *floche* 'floss (silk)', from Old French *flosche* 'down, nap of velvet', of unknown origin.

flotsam [early 17th century] *Flotsam* is from Anglo-Norman French *floteson*, from *floter* 'to float'.

flounce[1] [mid 16th century] *Flounce* meaning 'move in an angry manner' is perhaps of Scandinavian origin and related to Norwegian *flunsa* 'hurry', or it may be symbolic like *bounce* or *pounce*.

flounce² [early 18th century] This word for a 'wide ornamental strip of material gathered into a frill' is from an alteration of obsolete *frounce* 'a fold or pleat', from Old French *fronce*. The origin is Germanic.
→ RUCK²

flounder [late 16th century] This word meaning 'struggle helplessly' is perhaps a blend of *founder* and *blunder*, or it is perhaps symbolic: *fl-* is often found at the beginning of words connected with swift or sudden movement.

flour [Middle English] *Flour* is a specific use of *flower* in the sense 'the best part', used originally to mean 'the finest quality of ground wheat'. The two spellings remained in use alongside each other until the early 19th century.

flourish [Middle English] *Flourish* is from Old French *floriss-*, the lengthened stem of *florir*, based on Latin *florere*, from *flos, flor-* 'a flower'. The noun senses 'ornamental curve' and 'florid expression' come from an obsolete sense of the verb, 'adorn': this was originally effected with flowers.

flout [mid 16th century] This is perhaps from Dutch *fluiten* 'whistle, play the flute, hiss (in derision)'; German dialect *pfeifen auf*, literally 'pipe at', has a similar extended meaning.

flow [Old English] Old English *flōwan* has a Germanic origin; it is related to Dutch *vloeien*. The phrase *go with the flow* meaning 'relax and let things progress naturally' is found from the 1970s.
→ FLOOD

flower [Middle English] The Middle English form was *flour*, from Old French *flour, flor*, from Latin *flos, flor-*. The original spelling was no longer in use by the late 17th century except in its specialized sense 'ground grain'.
→ FLOUR

flu [mid 19th century]
→ INFLUENZA

fluctuate [mid 17th century] Latin *fluctuare* 'to undulate' (from *fluctus* 'flow, current, wave', from *fluere* 'to flow') gave rise to *fluctuate* in English. The figurative use 'waver, move indecisively (from one opinion to another)' dates from the early 17th century.

flue [late 16th century] The origin is unknown. The primary reference may be to the *fluing* (= splaying) of the sides of chimneys in houses of the 16th century.

fluent [late 16th century] Early examples include the literal sense 'flowing freely or abundantly'. The word is from the Latin form *fluent-* from the verb *fluere* 'to flow'. **Fluency** (early 17th century) is from Latin *fluentia*, from *fluere*.

fluff [late 18th century] This is probably a dialect alteration of 16th-century *flue* 'down, nap, fluff', apparently from Flemish *vluwe*. The English word may involve an onomatopoeic modification in imitation of the puffing away of some light substance. The association with the theatre and *fluffing lines* dates from the end of the 19th century. The colloquial expression *bit of fluff* for 'a young woman' arose at the beginning of the 20th century.

fluid [late Middle English] Early use was as an adjective. It comes from French *fluide* or Latin *fluidus*, from *fluere* 'to flow'. Noun use dates from the mid 17th century in physics contexts; medical use is recorded from the early 18th century.

fluke [mid 19th century] This was originally a term in games such as billiards denoting a lucky stroke. It is perhaps a dialect word.

flume [Middle English] The early word denoted a river or stream. It comes from Old French *flum*, from Latin *flumen* 'river', from *fluere* 'to flow'. The sense 'artificial channel' dates from the mid 18th century; 'water chute for amusement' is a late 20th-century usage.

flummox [mid 19th century] This is probably of dialect origin; *flummock* 'to make untidy, confuse' is recorded in western counties and the north Midlands.

flunk [early 19th century] The early general sense was 'back down, fail utterly': this originated in the US. It is perhaps related to *funk* 'state of great fear' or to US *flink* 'be a coward' (a variant perhaps of *flinch*).

flunkey [mid 18th century] This was originally Scots: it is perhaps from *flank* in the sense 'a person who stands at one's flank'.

flurry [late 17th century] *Flurry* is from obsolete *flurr* 'fly up, flutter, whirr' (an imitative word), probably influenced by *hurry*.

flush¹ [Middle English] *Flush* as in *flushed cheeks, flushed out the catheter* was first recorded in the sense 'move rapidly, spring up', especially in the context of a bird which might 'fly up suddenly'. It is symbolic, *fl-* frequently beginning words connected with sudden movement; perhaps influenced by *flash* with regard to the movement, and *blush* with regard to colour.
→ FLASH

flush² [mid 16th century] *Flush* currently has the prime meanings 'completely level' and

'having plenty (of money)'. It is probably related to the verb *flush*. Early uses included 'abundantly full, overflowing'; the development of the word to mean 'level, in the same plane' is probably from the image of a river running full and level with its banks.
→ FLUSH¹

flush³ [early 16th century] This term for a hand of cards all of the same suit is perhaps from French *flux* (formerly *flus*), from Latin *fluxus* 'a flow'. This specialized use may be compared with English *run* also used in cards contexts.

fluster [early 17th century] The early sense was 'make slightly drunk'. It is perhaps of Scandinavian origin and related to Icelandic *flaustra* 'hurry, bustle'.

flute [Middle English] This is from Old French *flahute*, probably from Provençal *flaüt*, perhaps a blend of *flaujol* 'flageolet' and *laüt* 'lute'. The early *flute* was blown through a mouthpiece at the end; in about the middle of the 18th century, this was superseded by the *German flute* or *transverse flute* which is blown through a mouthpiece at the side. The word sometimes refers to a type of glass for sparkling wines: this arose in the mid 17th century. Its use to describe a 'channel' or 'groove' dates from the early 18th century.

flutter [Old English] Old English *floterian, flotorian* is a frequentative form (= verb of repeated action) meaning in essence 'float to and fro'. The use of the word to convey 'tremulous excitement' dates from the mid 18th century (*all of a flutter*). In medical contexts, *flutter* is found from the early 20th century describing heart fibrillation.

flux [late Middle English] *Flux* 'the process of flowing' is from Latin *fluxus*, from *fluere* 'to flow'. The meaning 'continuous succession of changes' as in the phrase *in a state of flux* dates from the early 17th century.

fly¹ [Old English] Old English *flēogan* 'move through the air, flee' has a Germanic origin; it is related to Dutch *vliegen* and German *fliegen*.
→ FLEE; FLY²

fly² [Old English] Old English *flȳge, flēoge* denoted any winged insect. Of West Germanic origin, it is related to Dutch *vlieg* and German *Fliege*.
→ FLY¹

foal [Old English] *Foal* and *filly* are related. The word in Old English was *fola*; Germanic in origin, it is related to Dutch *veulen* and German *Fohlen*.
→ FILLY

foam [Old English] The origin of *foam* is West Germanic and the spellings in Old English were *fām* in the case of the noun, and *fǣman* for the verb; Old High German *feim* (noun), *feimen* (verb) are related. *The foam* is sometimes used poetically to refer to 'the sea'. The use of the word as a term for rubber or plastic in a cellular mass (e.g. *foam rubber*) dates from the 1930s.

fob¹ [mid 17th century] Early use of this term for a chain attached to a watch, was to refer to a fob pocket in the waistband of breeches. This was a small pocket for carrying a watch or other valuables. The origin is uncertain; it is probably related to German dialect *Fuppe* 'pocket': this may, if the word originally referred to a secret pocket, be connected with the verb *fob* 'deceive'.

fob² [late 16th century] The first sense recorded was 'cheat out of', a colloquial usage. The origin is uncertain but it is perhaps related to German *foppen* 'deceive, cheat, banter', or to English *fop*.
→ FOP

focus [mid 17th century] The term started out as in geometry and physics; the astronomer Kepler was the first to use the word in a geometrical sense in a work written in 1604. From Latin, the literal meaning is 'domestic hearth'; the conjecture is that the optical sense 'burning point of a lens' (= the point at which rays meet after reflection or refraction) already existed. Kepler's use was as the 'burning point' of a parabolic mirror, the geometrical focus of its curvature. The figurative use of *focus* as the centre of activity dates from the early 19th century; the phrase *focus group* in marketing and political contexts for a group of people chosen as representative of the population, questioned about opinions as part of consumer research, dates from the 1980s. The adjective **focal** is recorded from the late 17th century and is either from modern Latin *focalis* (from Latin *focus*) or directly from *focus*.

fodder [Old English] Related to Dutch *voeder* and German *Futter*, English *fōdor* is Germanic in origin. Originally *fodder* was a general word for 'food'; its use became more specific and is now restricted to dried food such as hay or straw for stall-feeding of cattle. The phrase *cannon fodder* referring to young infantry soldiers dates from the First World War.
→ FOOD

foe [Old English] Old English *fāh* meant 'hostile' and *gefā* meant 'enemy'. The origin is West Germanic. The phrase *the arch foe* sometimes refers to the Devil (Milton *Paradise Lost*: The arch foe subdu'd Or Captive drag'd in Chains).
→ FEUD

fogey [late 18th century] This word for a person considered to be old-fashioned or narrow-minded is related to earlier slang *fogram*; its origin is unknown but it was first found in Scots use. It may be connected with *foggy* meaning 'flabby, bloated' or 'moss-grown'.

foggy [late 15th century] *Foggy* was used to mean 'covered with fog (= a type of coarse grass)', 'mossy', 'boggy', 'flabby and puffy' (referring to 'people or animals') and 'thick, murky'. The derivation is perhaps from *fog* meaning 'coarse grass'. The weather term **fog** (mid 16th century) is perhaps a back-formation (by removal of the suffix) from *foggy*. At the turn of the 20th century, *fog* became associated with London (J. Ashby-Sterry *Lazy Minstrel*: 'Tis sometimes yellow, sometimes brown, A London Fog!).

foible [late 16th century] Early use was as an adjective meaning 'feeble'. It is from an obsolete French word (in Old French *fieble*). Both current noun senses ('minor eccentricity' and, as a fencing term, 'the blade from the middle to the point') also formerly occurred as senses of the word *feeble* and all date from the 17th century.
→ FEEBLE

foil[1] [Middle English] The verb *foil* currently means 'prevent'; in early contexts the sense was 'trample down'. It is perhaps from Old French *fouler* 'to full cloth; to trample', based on Latin *fullo* 'fuller'.
→ FULL[2]

foil [Middle English] The *foil* used in phrases such as *silver foil, a perfect foil for his activities*, comes via Old French from Latin *folium* 'leaf'.

foil[3] [late 16th century] The *foil* used as a fencing term for a light blunt-edged fencing sword is of unknown origin.

foist [mid 16th century] The early sense of *foist* was 'to palm a false die, so as to produce it at the right moment'. It comes from Dutch dialect *vuisten* 'take in the hand', from *vuist* 'fist'. The Dutch word is now used for a game in which one player holds a number of coins in one hand and others have to guess how many.
→ FIST

fold[1] [Old English] Old English *falden, fealden* 'double or bend over' is Germanic in origin and related to Dutch *vouwen* and German *falten*. The term's use in cookery as *fold in* dates from the early 20th century. The word has long meant 'fail, falter'; examples from the 1920s onwards show *fold up* in contexts of shows and plays being closed due to lack of support; this has

gradually transferred to contexts such as companies folding through financial failure.

fold[2] [Old English] Old English *fald* 'pen, enclosure' has a Germanic origin; it is related to Dutch *vaalt*.

foliage [late Middle English] The early spelling was *foilage* used to describe 'a design resembling leaves'. It is from Old French *feuillage*, from *feuille* 'leaf', from Latin *folium*. The change in the first syllable was due to association with Latin *folium*.
→ FOIL

folio [late Middle English] This is an English use of a Latin word, the ablative case of *folium* 'leaf'; in medieval Latin it was used in references to mean 'on leaf so-and-so'. The original sense of *in folio* (from Italian *in foglio*) was 'in the form of a full-sized sheet or leaf folded once': this designated the largest size of book.

folk [Old English] Old English *folc* is Germanic originally; it is related to Dutch *volk* and German *Volk*. Archaic uses of *folk* include 'a people, a nation' and 'the common people (often in relation to a superior)'. References to *folk music* are found from the late 19th century, specifying music of popular origin.

follicle [late Middle English] This comes from Latin *folliculus* 'little bag', a diminutive of *follis* 'bellows'.

follow [Old English] Old English *folgian* is originally a Germanic word related to Dutch *volgen* and German *folgen*. The sense 'go after somebody as an attendant' is probably the closest to the original meaning of the verb. The notion *follow an argument or reasoning* dates from the mid 19th century (Lewis Carroll *Alice in Wonderland*: I think I should understand that better … if I had it written down: but can't quite follow it as you say it).

folly [Middle English] This comes from Old French *folie* 'madness' from *fol* 'fool, foolish'; in modern French the word also means 'delight, favourite dwelling' which is comparable with the English use of the word for a costly ornamental building serving no practical purpose.

foment [late Middle English] *Foment* is from French *fomenter*, from late Latin *fomentare*, from Latin *fomentum* 'poultice, lotion': the base is Latin *fovere* 'to heat, cherish'. The early use referred to bathing a part of the body with warm or medicated lotions. The common current sense is 'stir up (violent sentiment or action)'.

fond [late Middle English] 'Infatuated, foolish' was the early sense recorded. The word comes from obsolete *fon* 'a fool, be foolish', of

unknown origin. The phrase *be fond of* 'have a liking for' was formerly *be fond on* (Shakespeare *A Midsummer Night's Dream*: He may prove More fond on her, than she upon her love).
→ FUN

fondle [late 17th century] The early sense was 'pamper'. The word is a back-formation (by removal of the suffix) from the obsolete noun *fondling* meaning 'a much-loved or petted person', based on *fond*.

font¹ [late Old English] This word for a receptacle in a church for baptismal water is from Latin *fons*, *font-* 'spring, fountain', occurring in the ecclesiastical Latin phrase *fons* or *fontes baptismi* 'baptismal water(s)'.

font² [late 16th century] This printing term was originally used for the action or process of casting or founding. It now refers to a set of type for one particular face and size. It comes from French *fonte*, from *fondre* 'to melt'. A variant spelling is *fount* which was the usual form in British English until the introduction of computer typesetting.

fontanelle [mid 16th century] This was formerly a term for a hollow of the skin between muscles. It is the adoption of a French word from modern Latin *fontanella*, from an Old French diminutive of *fontaine* 'fountain'. The semantic connection with *fountain* may have to do with the fact that the hollow between muscles was regarded as a suitable place to insert a seton (= absorbent material introduced below and protruding above the skin to facilitate drainage), since *fontanelle* also formerly denoted an outlet for bodily secretions. It may however be analogous to Italian *fontanella*, denoting both a small fountain and the hollow of the neck. The current sense referrring to a specific part of a baby's skull dates from the mid 18th century.

food [late Old English] Old English *fōda* is Germanic in origin. The phrase *food for thought* was first recorded in the early 19th century. Combinations which grew up in the 1990s are *food miles* referring to the distance food has to travel from its point of origin to the consumer, and *food desert* as an inner city area abandoned by retailers who have moved to an out-of-town site.
→ FODDER

fool [Middle English] This comes from Old French *fol* 'fool, foolish', from Latin *follis* 'bellows, windbag': this, by extension, came to mean 'an empty-headed person'. *Fool* in modern English is used with a much stronger sense than it had in earlier times. The word:

■ **foolhardy** (Middle English) is from Old French *folhardi*, from *fol* 'foolish' and *hardi* 'bold'.

foolscap [late 17th century] The term *foolscap* for a paper size is said to be named from a former watermark representing a fool's cap.

foot [Old English] Old English *fōt* is Germanic originally and related to Dutch *voet* and German *Fuss*, from an Indo-European root shared by Sanskrit *pad*, *pāda*, Greek *pous*, *pod-*, and Latin *pes*, *ped-* 'foot'. The colloquial exclamation *my foot* is first found in the early part of the 20th century. The metrical unit *foot* used as a division in verse is a translation from Latin and Greek and is commonly thought to refer to the movement of the foot in beating time. The lineal measure equal to 12 inches was originally based on the length of a man's foot.
→ FETTER

footle [late 19th century] This word for engaging in fruitless activity is perhaps from dialect *footer* 'to idle, potter about', from 16th-century *foutre* 'worthless thing': this comes from Old French, whose literal meaning is 'have sexual intercourse with'.

fop [late Middle English] Now meaning 'a man overly concerned with his appearance', *fop* originally meant 'fool'. It may be related to *fob* 'deceive'.
→ FOB²

for [Old English] This is probably a reduction of a Germanic preposition meaning 'before' (in place or time); it is related to German *für*. In Old English *for* and *fore* were used indiscriminately as prepositions; they were gradually differentiated in Middle English. The archaic conjunction **forasmuch** was written, in Middle English, as *for as much*, translating Old French *por tant que* 'for so much as'.
→ FORE

WORDBUILDING

The prefix **for-** [Old English] adds the sense

■ **prohibition** [forbid]
■ **abstention** [forgive]
■ **neglect** [forget]
■ **renunciation** [forgo]
■ **intensification** [forlorn]

---

forage [Middle English] *Forage* is from Old French *fourrage* (noun), *fourrager* (verb), from *fuerre* 'straw'. The origin is Germanic.
→ FODDER

foray [Middle English] *Foray* 'sudden incursion into enemy territory' is a back-formation (by removal of the suffix) from *forayer* 'raider'.

The source is Old French *forrier* 'forager', from *fuerre* 'straw'.
→ FORAGE

forbear [Old English] In Old English the spelling was *forberan*. The original senses were 'endure' and 'bear with' which led to 'endure the absence of something, do without' as well as 'bear up against, control oneself'. These gave rise to the meaning 'refrain from' in Middle English.
→ BEAR¹

forbid [Old English] The spelling *forbēodan* was the Old English form; corresponding words are Dutch *verbieden* and German *verbieten*. The core sense is 'bid someone not to'. The phrase *God forbid ...!* is recorded early in the word's history.

force [Middle English] This word comes from Old French *force* (noun), *forcer* (verb), based on Latin *fortis* 'strong'. Specialized use of the word in physics dates from the mid 17th century. *Force* as a word for an army is found early in its history; the phrase *the force* referring to the police as a body is found in examples from the mid 19th century.

ford [Old English] This word for a shallow place in a stream or river, of West Germanic origin, is related to Dutch *voorde*.
→ FARE

fore [Old English] Early use was as a preposition. It is related to Dutch *voor* and German *vor*. The adjective (e.g. *fore wings*) and noun (e.g. *to the fore*, *the fore of the ship*) represent the prefix *fore-* used independently from the late 15th century. The nautical phrase *fore and aft* (early 17th century) perhaps translates a phrase of Low German origin; a comparable phrase in modern Dutch is *van voren en van achteren*.

WORDBUILDING

The prefix **fore-** [Old English] adds the sense

- In front [foreshorten]
- beforehand [forebode]
- situated in front [forecourt]
- front part of [forebrain]
- near the bow [forecastle]
- preceding [forefathers]

---

forebear [late 15th century] *Bear*, the second element of this word for 'ancestor', is a variant of obsolete *beer* 'someone who exists' (from the verb *be* and the suffix *-er*). A *forebear* is thus literally 'a person existing before'.

foreclose [Middle English] This is from Old French *forclos*, the past participle of *forclore*: the elements are *for-* 'out' (from Latin *foras*

'outside') and *clore* 'to close'. The original sense was 'bar from escaping', which in late Middle English became 'shut out' and 'bar from doing something': this led specifically to 'bar someone from redeeming a mortgage' (early 18th century).

foreign [Middle English] The Middle English spelling was *foren*, *forein*, from Old French *forein*, *forain*: this is based on Latin *foras*, *foris* 'outside', from *fores* 'door'. The current spelling arose in the 16th century, by association with words such as *sovereign*. The use of *foreign* in the medical phrase *foreign body* dates from the mid 18th century.

foremost [Old English] Old English *formest*, *fyrmest* are based on *forma* 'first', which is ultimately a superlative formed from the Germanic base of *fore*. The current spelling arose by association with the two elements *fore* and *most*.
→ FIRST; FORMER

forensic [mid 17th century] This word is based on Latin *forensis* 'in open court, public', from *forum*. *Forensic medicine* is thus the application of medical knowledge in the domain of Law, in the investigation of crime.
→ FORUM

forest [Middle English] Early use was to describe 'a wooded area kept for hunting'; it was also any uncultivated land. The word comes via Old French from late Latin *forestis* (*silva*) , literally '(wood) outside' from Latin *foris* 'outside'. As a legal delimitation it once referred to a woodland district usually belonging to the King, designated for hunting: special laws applied and officers were appointed to uphold these. The *New Forest* in southern Hampshire was reserved as Crown property in 1079 by William I as a royal hunting area. Middle English **forester** is from Old French *forestier*, from *forest*.
→ FOREIGN

forestall [Old English] Old English *foresteall* was 'an ambush'; as a verb the earliest sense (in Middle English) was 'intercept and buy up (goods) before they reach the market, so as to raise the price': this was formerly an offence.
→ STALL

forfeit [Middle English] A *forfeit* was originally a crime or transgression, which led to the notion of a fine or penalty for this. The word is from Old French *forfet*, *forfait*, the past participle of *forfaire* 'to transgress'. The formative elements here are *for-* 'out' (from Latin *foris* 'outside') and *faire* 'do' (from Latin *facere*). The word's use in a trivial way in games and minor breaches of rules dates from the early 17th century (Shakespeare *Measure for Measure*: The strong

Statutes Stand like the forfeites in a Barbers shop, As much in mock, as mark).

forge¹ [Middle English] Early use of *forge* 'smithy', 'shape (a metal object)' was also in the general sense 'make, construct'. The word derives from Old French *forger*, from Latin *fabricare* 'to fabricate': this is from *fabrica* 'manufactured object, workshop'. The use of the word in connection with fraudulent imitation arose early in the word's history. The noun is via Old French from Latin *fabrica*.
→ FABRIC

forge² [mid 18th century] This word used in phrases such as *forge ahead* was originally used in connection with ships. It is perhaps an aberrant pronunciation of *force*.
→ FORCE

forget [Old English] Old English *forgietan* is West Germanic in origin and related to Dutch *vergeten* and German *vergessen*. The etymological sense is 'miss one's hold' but this physical application is not recorded in any Germanic language. The compound:
■ **forget-me-not** dates from the mid 16th century and translates the Old French name *ne m'oubliez mye*, the flower is said to have the virtue of ensuring that anyone wearing it would never be forgotten by a lover.

forgive [Old English] Old English *forgiefan* is Germanic in origin and related to Dutch *vergeven* and German *vergeben*. Early use included association with the remittance of debt or with pardoning an offence.
→ GIVE

fork [Old English] Old English *forca*, *force* was an agricultural implement; it is based on Latin *furca* 'pitchfork, forked stick', reinforced in Middle English by Anglo-Norman French *furke* (also from Latin *furca*). The *fork* used for holding food dates from late Middle English. Figuratively it is sometimes associated with a dilemma. *Morton's Fork* is an example of a dilemma in which either choice brings discredit: John Morton (c.1420–1500) was the Archbishop of Canterbury and minister of Henry VII who tried to levy forced loans by arguing that the rich could afford to pay and so could those who lived frugally since they must have amassed savings. It was towards the mid 19th century that *fork* came to be used in phrases such as *fork in the road*.

forlorn [Old English] Old English *forloren* meant 'depraved, morally abandoned'; it is the past participle of *forlēosan* 'to lose'. Of Germanic origin it is related to Dutch *verliezen* and German *verlieren*. The prime current sense 'pitifully sad' dates from the 16th century.

form [Middle English] The noun is from Old French *forme*, the verb from Old French *fo(u)rmer*, from Latin *formare* 'to form', both based on Latin *forma* 'a mould or form'. The same source led to late Middle English **formation** (from Latin *formatio(n-)*) and **formative** (late 15th century from Old French *formatif*, *-ive* or medieval Latin *formativus*): the use of *formative* to mean 'relating to development' as in *formative period* is found in examples from the mid 19th century.

formal [late Middle English] *Formal* is from Latin *formalis*, from *forma* 'shape, mould'. The use of the word to mean 'prim, stiff' is recorded from the early 16th century; slightly later examples show *formal* in the sense 'officially sanctioned'. **Formality** recorded from the mid 16th century meaning 'accordance with legal rules or conventions', is from French *formalité* or medieval Latin *formalitas*, from *formalis*.
→ FORM

format [mid 19th century] This word came via French and German from Latin *formatus* (*liber*) 'shaped (book)', the past participle of *formare* 'to form'.

former [Middle English] This comes from Old English *forma* and the suffix *-er* forming a comparative meaning 'earlier'.

formidable [late Middle English] This comes either from French, or from Latin *formidabilis*, from *formidare* 'to fear'. In modern use the word has developed a notion of 'difficult to overcome' (*formidable adversary*), as well as simply one of impressive size commanding respect (*formidable talent*).

formula [early 17th century] In early examples the sense was 'a fixed form of words (for use on ceremonial or social occasions)'. It comes from a diminutive of Latin *forma* 'shape, mould'. The use of the word in chemistry dates from the mid 19th century.

fornicate [mid 16th century] *Fornicate* is from ecclesiastical Latin *fornicari* 'to arch', from Latin *fornix*, *fornic-* 'vaulted chamber'; later this Latin word was used to mean 'brothel'.

forsake [Old English] Old English *forsacan* 'to renounce, refuse' is West Germanic in origin and related to Dutch *verzaken*. It is formal in modern use but familiar as part of the traditional Christian wedding service (Book of Common Prayer: And forsaking all other keep thee only unto her).

fort [late Middle English] This is from Old French *fort* or Italian *forte*, from Latin *fortis* 'strong'. Middle English **fortress** is from Old French *forteresse* 'strong place', based on Latin *fortis*.

forth [Old English] *Forth* is Germanic in origin and related to Dutch *voort* and German *fort*, from an Indo-European root shared by *fore-*. **Forthright** was spelt *forthriht* in Old English and meant 'straight forward, directly'.

fortify [late Middle English] Late Latin *fortificare*, from Latin *fortis* 'strong' has given *fortify* and **fortification** (both via French).

fortnight [Old English] *Fortnight* is a contraction of Old English *fēowertīene niht* meaning 'fourteen nights', reflecting an ancient Germanic method of reckoning by nights.

fortuitous [mid 17th century] This is based on Latin *fortuitus*, from *forte* 'by chance', from *fors* 'chance, luck'.

fortune [Middle English] *Fortune* came via Old French from Latin *Fortuna*, the name of a goddess personifying luck or chance. Late Middle English **fortunate** is from Latin *fortunatus*, from *fortuna*.

forum [late Middle English] This is originally a Latin word meaning literally 'what is out of doors'. In English it originally described an enclosure around a house; it is related to *fores* '(outside) door'. The use of the word to mean 'a place where ideas can be exchanged' dates from the mid 18th century.

forward [Old English] Old English *forward* meant 'towards the future', as in the phrase *from this day forward*; it was a variant of Old English *forthweard*.
→ FORTH

fossil [mid 16th century] This word was first used for a fossilized fish found and believed to have lived in water underground. It comes from French *fossile*, from Latin *fossilis* 'dug up', from *fodere* 'dig'. *Fossil* was first used as a contemptuous term for a person around the middle of the 19th century.

foster [Old English] Old English *fōstrian* 'feed, nourish' is from *fōster* 'food, nourishment', of Germanic origin. The sense 'bring up another's child' dates from Middle English. The word was also once used to mean 'bring up one's own child'. The compounds **foster-father**, **foster-mother**, **foster-child**, and **foster-brother** all date from Old English. *Foster-mother* has also been used to mean a wet nurse, her husband being *foster-father* to the child she fed, with *foster-brother* and *foster-sister* referring to children reared at the same breast.
→ FOOD

foul [Old English] Old English *fūl* is originally Germanic and related to Old Norse *fūll* 'foul', Dutch *vuil* 'dirty', and German *faul* 'rotten, lazy'. These are from an Indo-European root shared by Latin *pus*, Greek *puos* 'pus', and Latin *putere* 'to stink'.

found¹ [Middle English] *Found* 'establish' is from Old French *fonder*, from Latin *fundare* 'to lay a base for', from *fundus* 'bottom, base'. **Foundation** is late Middle English from Old French *fondation*, from Latin *fundatio(n-)*, from *fundare*.

found² [early 16th century] *Found* 'melt and mould' is from French *fondre*, from Latin *fundere* 'melt, pour'. **Foundry** dates from the early 17th century: the earlier spelling was *foundery*; it was perhaps suggested by French *fonderie*.

founder [Middle English] *Founder* 'fill with water and sink' was originally recorded as meaning 'knock to the ground'. It comes from Old French *fondrer*, *esfondrer* 'submerge, collapse', based on Latin *fundus* 'bottom, base'.

fountain [Middle English] 'Natural spring of water' was the early sense recorded. The origin is Old French *fontaine*, from late Latin *fontana*, the feminine of Latin *fontanus* (an adjective from *fons*, *font-* 'a spring'). **Fount** 'source' is recorded from the late 16th century and is a back-formation (by removal of the suffix) from *fountain*, on the pattern of the pair *mountain*, *mount*.

fowl [Old English] Old English *fugol* was originally the general term for a bird. Of Germanic origin the word is related to Dutch *vogel* and German *Vogel*.
→ FLY¹

fox [Old English] This is of Germanic origin, related to Dutch *vos* and German *Fuchs*. An association soon arose with the characteristics of artfulness and cunning. The adjective **foxy** is found in examples from the early 16th century meaning 'foxlike' but has been used from the early 20th century as slang in the US meaning 'attractive, sexy' (*foxy lady*).

foyer [late 18th century] At first the word *foyer* meant the 'centre of attention or activity'. It is from a French word meaning 'hearth, home', based on Latin *focus* 'domestic hearth'.
→ FOCUS

fraction [late Middle English] This came via Old French from ecclesiastical Latin *fractio(n-)* 'breaking (bread)', from Latin *frangere* 'to break', the base too of **fracture** from the same period (from French, or from Latin *fractura*). The adjective **fractious** is based on *fraction*, probably on the pattern of the pair *faction*, *factious*; the common current senses of the word are 'unruly' and 'easily irritated' (both early 18th century).

fragile [late 15th century] The initial sense was 'morally weak'. The word is from Latin *fragilis*, from *frangere* 'to break'. The sense 'liable to break' dates from the mid 16th century.

fragment [late Middle English] This is either an adoption of the French word or it is from Latin *fragmentum*, from *frangere* 'to break'.

fragrant [late Middle English] *Fragrant* is from French, or from Latin *fragrant-*, present participial stem of the verb *fragrare* 'smell sweet'. **Fragrance** is recorded from the mid 17th century and is either from French, or from Latin *fragrantia*, from *fragrare*.

frail [Middle English] Old French *fraile*, from Latin *fragilis* gave rise to *frail* in Middle English. **Frailty** (from Old French *frailete*) dates from the same period in the sense 'weakness in morals'.
➔ FRAGILE

frame [Old English] Of Germanic origin, the Old English verb *framian* meant 'be useful, be of service'. The general sense in Middle English was 'make ready for use', which probably led to the verb sense 'create (a plan or concept)' (e.g. *the management group framed the proposals*); it also gave rise to the specific meaning 'prepare timber for use in building', and later 'make the wooden parts of a building', essentially the framework giving the noun sense 'structure' in late Middle English. The slang use 'concoct a false accusation against someone' was originally US and dates from the 1920s.
➔ FROM

franchise [Middle English] An early *franchise* denoted a grant of legal immunity. It is from Old French, based on *franc, franche* 'free'. The sense 'the right to vote in public elections' dates from the late 18th century and its use for 'an authorization to carry out commercial activities' arose in the 20th century.
➔ FRANK¹

frank¹ [Middle English] *Frank* 'open, honest, and direct' started out in English in the sense 'free'. It comes from Old French *franc*, from medieval Latin *francus* 'free', from *Francus* 'a Frank': only Franks had full freedom in Frankish Gaul which they conquered in the 6th century. Another Middle English sense was 'generous' which led to the current sense.

frank² [early 18th century] *Frank* 'to stamp (in order to indicate postage)' is from the adjective *frank* 'open, honest': an early sense of the verb was 'to free of obligation'.

frankincense [late Middle English] This is from Old French *franc encens*, literally 'high-quality incense', from *franc* in an obsolete sense

'superior, of high quality' (which also existed in English) and *encens* 'incense'.
➔ FRANK¹

frantic [late Middle English] The early spelling was *frentik* which meant 'insane, violently mad', from Old French *frenetique* 'frenetic'.
➔ FRENETIC

fraternity [Middle English] This is from Old French *fraternite*, from Latin *fraternitas*: this in turn is from *fraternus* from *frater* 'brother'. **Fraternal** is late Middle English from medieval Latin *fraternalis*, from Latin *fraternus*.

fraud [Middle English] *Fraud* is from Old French *fraude*, from Latin *fraus, fraud-* 'deceit, injury'. **Fraudulent** is late Middle English from Old French, or from Latin *fraudulentus*, from *fraus, fraud-*.

fraught [late Middle English] The early meanings were 'laden' and 'provided, equipped'. It is the past participle of obsolete *fraught* 'load with cargo', from Middle Dutch *vrachten*, from *vracht* 'ship's cargo'. The current sense is 'filled with' (e.g. *fraught with danger*).
➔ FREIGHT

fray¹ [late Middle English] *fray* 'unravel' is from Old French *freiier*, from Latin *fricare* 'to rub'.

fray² [late Middle English] *Fray* 'disturbance' is from the archaic verb *fray* 'to quarrel', from *affray* 'startle': this comes from Anglo-Norman French *afrayer*.
➔ AFFRAY

frazzle [early 19th century] This is perhaps a blend of *fray* 'unravel' and the obsolete *fazle* 'ravel out', of Germanic origin. The word was originally East Anglian dialect; it came into standard British English via US usage.

freckle [late Middle English] This is an alteration of dialect *frecken*, from Old Norse *freknur* (plural).

free [Old English] The Old English adjective *frēo* and verb *frēon* are Germanic in origin; related words are Dutch *vrij* and German *frei*, from an Indo-European root meaning 'to love', shared by *friend*. **Freedom** is also an Old English word. The word **freebie** 'something given free of charge' arose in the 1940s in the US: it is an arbitrary formation from *free*.
➔ FRIEND

freebooter [late 16th century] This word for a lawless adventurer is from Dutch *vrijbuiter*, from *vrij* 'free' and *buit* 'booty', and the noun suffix *-er*.
➔ FILIBUSTER

freelance [early 19th century] It is now used in business contexts for someone who works for different companies not under permanent contract, but *freelance* once denoted a mercenary. It was originally written as two words.

freeze [Old English] Old English *frēosan* was first recorded in the phrase *hit frēoseth* 'it is freezing, it is so cold that water turns to ice'. Of Germanic origin, it is related to Dutch *vriezen* and German *frieren*, from an Indo-European root shared by Latin *pruina* 'hoar frost' and *frost*.

freight [late Middle English] The sense found in early examples was 'the hire of a ship for transporting goods'. It comes from Middle Dutch, Middle Low German *vrecht*, a variant of *vracht* 'ship's cargo'. The current noun sense is 'goods transported in bulk'.
→ FRAUGHT

French [Old English] Old English *Frencisc* is Germanic in origin, from the base of *Frank*, a word for a member of a Germanic people that conquered Gaul in the 6th century. *Frank* was *Franca* in Old English: it is perhaps from the name of a weapon and related to Old English *franca* 'javelin'. The idiomatic expression:
■ **French leave** (mid 18th century) is said to derive from the French custom of leaving a dinner or ball without saying goodbye to the host or hostess. The phrase was first recorded shortly after the Seven Years War (1756–63) when France and Britain were struggling for supremacy overseas; the equivalent French expression is *filer à l'Anglaise*, literally 'to escape in the style of the English'.

frenetic [late Middle English] The early meaning recorded was 'insane'. The source is Old French *frenetique*, via Latin from Greek *phrenitikos*, from *phrenitis* 'delirium'. Greek *phrēn* 'mind' is the base.
→ FRANTIC

frenzy [Middle English] This is from Old French *frenesie*, from medieval Latin *phrenesia*, from Latin *phrenesis*, from Greek *phrēn* 'mind'.

frequent [late Middle English] 'Profuse, ample' was the meaning of *frequent* in early examples. It comes from French, or from Latin *frequens, frequent-* 'crowded, frequent'. The ultimate origin is unknown. The word **frequency** is found from the mid 16th century: it gradually superseded late Middle English *frequence* and originally denoted a gathering of people. Latin *frequentia* is the source, from *frequens*.

fresco [late 16th century] A painting done rapidly in watercolour on wet plaster on a wall or ceiling is described by the Italian word *fresco*, literally 'cool, fresh'. The word was first recorded in the phrase *in fresco*, representing Italian *affresco, al fresco* 'on the fresh (plaster)'.

fresh [Old English] Old English *fersc* meant 'not salt, fit for drinking'. It was superseded in Middle English by forms from Old French *freis, fresche*; both are ultimately of Germanic origin and related to Dutch *vers* and German *frisch*. The use of *fresh* to mean 'cheeky, forward' is perhaps influenced by German *frech* 'impudent, saucy': it is found in English from the mid 19th century.

fret[1] [Old English] The current sense is 'worry' but Old English *fretan* meant 'devour, consume'. The origin is Germanic and related words are Dutch *vreten* and German *fressen*.
→ EAT

fret[2] [late Middle English] *Fret* describing a repeated ornamental design is from Old French *frete* 'trelliswork', the origin of which is unknown. The *fret* associated with music dates from the early 16th century, but again the origin remains unknown.

friar [Middle English] This is from Old French *frere*, from Latin *frater* 'brother'.

friction [mid 16th century] *Friction* denotes chafing or rubbing of the body or limbs, formerly frequently used in medical treatment. It comes via French from Latin *frictio(n-)*, from *fricare* 'to rub'.

fridge [1920s] This is an abbreviation, probably influenced by the proprietary name *Frigidaire*.

friend [Old English] Old English *frēond* is originally Germanic and related to Dutch *vriend* and German *Freund*, from an Indo-European root meaning 'to love', shared by *free*.
→ FREE

frieze [mid 16th century] This comes from French *frise*, from medieval Latin *frisium*, a variant of *frigium*, from Latin *Phrygium (opus)* '(work) of Phrygia'. Phrygia is an ancient region of west central Asia Minor which reached the peak of its power in Asia Minor in the 8th century.

frigate [late 16th century] An early *frigate* was a light, fast boat which was rowed or sailed. It comes from French *frégate*, from Italian *fregata*, of unknown origin. Current use is as the name of a type of warship with a mixed armament, originally introduced for convoy escort work.

fright [Old English] Old English *fryhto, fyrhto* is Germanic in origin and related to Dutch *furcht* and German *furcht*.

frigid [late Middle English] This comes from Latin *frigidus*, from *frigere* 'be cold', from the noun *frigus* meaning 'cold'.

fringe [Middle English] *Fringe* is from Old French *frenge*, based on late Latin *fimbria*, which earlier was a plural noun meaning 'fibres, shreds'.

frippery [mid 16th century] Early use of the word was as a collective for old or second-hand clothes. It comes from French *friperie*, from Old French *freperie*, from *frepe* 'rag'. The ultimate origin is unknown.

frisk [early 16th century] Early use was in the sense 'a playful skip or leap'. It comes from obsolete *frisk* 'lively, frisky', from Old French *frisque* 'alert, lively, merry'. The origin is perhaps Germanic. The word in contexts such as *frisk someone for offensive weapons* was originally slang; it dates from the late 18th century.

fritter[1] [early 18th century] *Fritter* 'waste' is based on the obsolete verb *fitter* 'break into fragments, shred'; it is perhaps related to German *Fetzen* 'rag, scrap'.

fritter[2] [late Middle English] The *fritter* of culinary contexts is from Old French *friture*, based on Latin *frigere* 'to fry'.
→ FRY[1]

frivolous [late Middle English] This is based on Latin *frivolus* 'silly, trifling'.

frizz [late Middle English] Early use was in the sense 'dress (a wash leather) with pumice'. It comes from French *friser*. The meaning 'form into a mass of curls' dates from the late 16th century. **Frizzle** 'form into tight curls' is based on *frizz* and is found in examples from the mid 16th century.

frizzle [mid 18th century] The *frizzle* which means 'fry with a sizzling noise' is from the verb *fry* probably influenced by *sizzle*.
→ FRY[1]

frock [late Middle English] This comes from Old French *froc*, of Germanic origin. The sense 'priest's or monk's gown' is preserved in *defrock*.

frog [Old English] Old English *frogga* is Germanic in origin and related to Dutch *vors* and German *Frosch*. Used as a general term of abuse in Middle English, the term was applied specifically to the Dutch in the 17th century; its application to the French (late 18th century) is probably partly alliterative, partly from the reputation of the French for eating frogs' legs.

frolic [early 16th century] This is from Dutch *vrolijk* 'merry, cheerful'.

from [Old English] Old English *fram*, *from* has a Germanic origin; it is related to Old Norse *frá*, from which Middle English **fro** derives.

frond [late 18th century] This is from Latin *frons*, *frond-* 'leaf'.

front [Middle English] The early word referred to the forehead. It is from Old French *front*, from Latin *frons*, *front-* 'forehead, front'. **Frontal** in the mid 17th century meant 'relating to the forehead': it is from modern Latin *frontalis*, from Latin *frons*.

frontier [late Middle English] *Frontier* is from Old French *frontiere*, based on Latin *frons*, *front-* 'front'.

frontispiece [late 16th century] The early sense recorded was in architectural contexts as 'the principal face of a building'. It comes from French *frontispice* or late Latin *frontispicium* 'facade', from Latin *frons*, *front-* 'front' and *specere* 'to look'. The change in the ending (early in the word's history) was by association with *piece*.

frost [Old English] Old English *frost*, *forst* is Germanic in origin and related to Dutch *vorst* and German *Frost*.
→ FREEZE.

froth [late Middle English] *Froth* is from Old Norse *frotha*, *frauth*.

frown [late Middle English] Old French *froignier*, from *froigne* 'surly look' has given *frown* in English; it is of Celtic origin.

frugal [mid 16th century] This comes from Latin *frugalis*, from *frugi* 'economical, thrifty', from *frux*, *frug-* 'fruit'.

fruit [Middle English] *Fruit* is from Old French, from Latin *fructus* 'enjoyment of produce, harvest', from *frui* 'enjoy'; this is related to *fruges* 'fruits of the earth', the plural (and most common form) of *frux*, *frug-* 'fruit'. **Fruition** in late Middle English meant 'enjoyment': it comes via Old French from late Latin *fruitio(n-)*, from *frui*; the current senses 'producing fruit', 'realization of a plan' (dating from the late 19th century) arose by association with *fruit*.

frump [mid 16th century] This is probably a contraction of late Middle English *frumple* 'wrinkle', from Middle Dutch *verrompelen*. The word originally referred to a mocking speech or action; later as *frumps* it meant 'the sulks'; this led to the word's use for a bad-tempered, and eventually a dowdy woman (early 19th century).

frustrate [late Middle English] This is from Latin *frustrare* 'to disappoint' from *frustra* 'in vain'. **Frustration** (mid 16th century) is from Latin *frustratio(n-)*, from *frustrare*.

fry¹ [Middle English] *Fry* 'cook (food) in hot fat' is from Old French *frire*, from Latin *frigere*.

fry² [Middle English] *Fry* 'young fish' is from Old Norse *frjó*.

fudge [early 17th century] This is probably an alteration of obsolete *fadge* 'to fit'. Early usage was as a verb in the sense 'turn out as expected', also 'merge together': this probably gave rise to its use in confectionery. In the late 17th century the verb came to mean 'fit together in a clumsy or underhand manner', which included facts or figures being cobbled together in a superficially convincing way: this led to the exclamation *fudge!* meaning 'nonsense!' and to use of the word for 'a piece of late news inserted in a newspaper page'.

fuel [Middle English] This comes from Old French *fouaille*, based on Latin *focus* 'hearth' which in late Latin came to mean 'fire'. In the medieval Latin of England and France the plural *focalia* (singular *focale* or *focalium*) are often found in charters concerning the obligation to furnish fuel and the right to demand supplies of fuel. *Fuel poverty* is a phrase found from the 1970s referring to the inability to afford the cost of adequate domestic heating, lighting, and power.

fugitive [late Middle English] *Fugitive* is from Old French *fugitif*, *-ive*, from Latin *fugitivus*, from *fugere* 'to flee'.

fulcrum [late 17th century] This word was originally used in the general sense 'a prop or support'. It is taken from Latin in which the literal meaning is 'post of a couch', from *fulcire* 'to prop up'.

fulfil [late Old English] Late Old English *fullfyllan* meant 'fill up, make full'. The notion of *fulfilling a prophecy* is a Hebraism. Reflexive use as in *fulfil oneself* (by developing one's gifts to the full) is a development of a use by Tennyson in 1842 (*Gardener's Daughter*: My desire ... By its own energy fulfill'd itself).
→ FILL; FULL¹

full¹ [Old English] *Full* 'having no empty space' is Germanic in origin and related to Dutch *vol* and German *voll*. The nautical use of *full* describing sails as 'filled with wind' dates from the early 17th century.

full² [Middle English] This verb used in textile contexts for cleaning, shrinking, and felting cloth by heat, pressure, and moisture is probably a back-formation (by removal of the suffix) from **fuller**, influenced by Old French *fouler*

'press hard upon' or medieval Latin *fullare*, based on Latin *fullo* 'fuller'.

fulsome [Middle English] The early sense was 'abundant'. It is based on *full*. The main current sense is 'excessively flattering'.
→ FULL¹

fumble [late Middle English] *Fumble* is from Low German *fommeln* or Dutch *fommelen*.

fume [late Middle English] This comes from the Old French verb *fumer*, from Latin *fumare* 'to smoke'. The sense 'show seething anger' dates from the early 16th century.

fumigate [mid 16th century] The early sense recorded was 'to perfume'. It comes from Latin *fumigare* 'to fumigate', from *fumus* 'smoke'. The notion of disinfection is associated with the verb from the late 18th century.

fun [late 17th century] 'A trick or hoax' was the early meaning of *fun*, from the obsolete verb *fun* 'to cheat or hoax': this was a dialect variant of late Middle English *fon* 'make a fool of, be a fool', related to *fon* 'a fool'. The ultimate origin is unknown. **Funny** dates from the mid 18th century. The compounds:

■ **funny ha-ha** and **funny peculiar** were coined by Ian Hay in his novel *Housemaster* (1936).

■ **funny money** dates from the 1930s in US English; it describes money that is forged or otherwise useless
→ FOND

function [mid 16th century] This comes from French *fonction*, from Latin *functio(n-)*, from *fungi* 'to perform'.

fund [mid 17th century] *Fund* is from Latin *fundus* 'bottom, piece of landed property'. The earliest sense was 'the bottom or lowest part', later 'foundation, basis'; the association with money has perhaps arisen from the idea of landed property being a source of wealth.

fundamental [late Middle English] The source of *fundamental* is French *fondamental*, or late Latin *fundamentalis*: these are based on Latin *fundamentum*, from *fundare* 'to found'. The noun, often used in the plural as *fundamentals*, dates from the mid 17th century.

funeral [late Middle English] This comes from Old French *funeraille*, from medieval Latin *funeralia*, the neuter plural of late Latin *funeralis*, from Latin *funus*, *funer-* 'funeral, death, corpse'.

fungus [late Middle English] This is the use of a Latin word in English; it is perhaps from Greek *spongos*. The word has sometimes been used to mean 'a beard' since the early 20th century (P.G. Wodehouse *Sam the Sudden*: Where

did you get the fungus?): this is probably a shortening of *face fungus*.
→ SPONGE

funk¹ [mid 18th century] This *funk* used in the phrase *in a blue funk* was first recorded as Oxford University slang: it is perhaps from *funk* in the slang sense 'tobacco-smoke', or from obsolete Flemish *fonck* 'disturbance, agitation'.
→ FUNK²

funk² [early 17th century] This *funk* used since the 1950s in musical contexts (for a style of popular dance music of US black origin) was in use earlier with the sense 'musty smell'; this is still current in North American English. It is perhaps from French dialect *funkier* 'blow smoke on', based on Latin *fumus* 'smoke'.

funnel [late Middle English] This is apparently via Old French from Provençal *fonilh*, from late Latin *fundibulum*, from Latin *infundibulum*, from *infundere*, from *in-* 'into' and *fundere* 'to pour'.

fur [Middle English] Use as a verb was recorded first. It is from Old French *forrer* 'to line, sheathe', from *forre* 'sheath', of Germanic origin. Middle English **furrier** is from Old French *forreor*, from *forrer*. The change in the ending in the 16th century was due to association with words ending in *-ier* such as *clothier*.

furbish [late Middle English] This is from Old French *forbiss-*, the lengthened stem of *forbir*, of Germanic origin.

furious [late Middle English] The source of *furious* is Old French *furieus*, from Latin *furiosus*, from *furia* 'fury'.

furl [late 16th century] *Furl* is from French *ferler*, from Old French *fer, ferm* 'firm' and *lier* 'bind' (from Latin *ligare*).

furlong [Old English] Old English *furlang* is from *furh* 'furrow' and *lang* 'long'. The word originally denoted the length of a furrow in a common field (formally regarded as a square of ten acres). It was also used as the equivalent of the Roman *stadium*, one eighth of a Roman mile, which gave rise to the current sense.
→ STADIUM

furnace [Middle English] This comes from Old French *fornais(e)*, from Latin *fornax, fornac-*, from *fornus* 'oven'.

furnish [late Middle English] The early general sense was 'provide or equip with what is necessary or desirable'. The source is Old French *furniss-*, the lengthened stem of *furnir*: the word is ultimately of West Germanic origin.

furniture [early 16th century] *Furniture* in early examples denoted the action of furnishing. It is from French *fourniture*, from

fournir, from Old French *furnir* 'to furnish'. The common modern sense 'large movable items such as tables and chairs' dates from the late 16th century; specialist application to fittings such as 'door handles, door knockers' arose in the early 18th century.

furrow [Old English] Old English *furh* is Germanic in origin and related to Dutch *voor* and German *Furche*. They share an Indo-European root with Latin *porca* 'ridge between furrows'.

further [Old English] Old English *furthor* (adverb), *furthra* (adjective), *fyrthrian* (verb) are of Germanic origin and related to *forth*. The primary sense is 'more forward, more onward'. In standard English, the word *farther* is usually used if the intended meaning is 'more far', i.e. the comparative use of *far*, whereas *further* tends to be chosen when the notion of *far* is absent (as in *nothing further to say*). **Furthest** is late Middle English, formed as a superlative of *further*.
→ FORTH

furtive [early 17th century] This comes from French *furtif, -ive* or Latin *furtivus*, from *furtum* 'theft'.

fury [late Middle English] *Fury* came into English via Old French, from Latin *furia*, from *furiosos* 'furious'. The base verb is Latin *furere* 'be mad, rage'.

fuse¹ [late 16th century] *Fuse* 'blend together' is from Latin *fundere* 'to pour, melt'. **Fusion**, recorded slightly earlier, is from Latin *fusio(n-)*, from *fundere*.

fuse² [mid 17th century] *Fuse* as in the *fuse of a bomb* is from Italian *fuso*, from Latin *fusus* 'spindle'.

fuselage [early 20th century] This is the adoption of a French word, from *fuseler* 'shape into a spindle', from *fuseau* 'spindle'.

fuss [early 18th century] This is perhaps an Anglo-Irish word. It may echo the sound of something bubbling or express the action of 'puffing and blowing'. **Fussy** is found from the early 19th century; it was applied to clothing as 'having excessive detail' in the middle of the 19th century.

fusty [late 15th century] *Fusty* is from Old French *fuste* 'smelling of the cask', from *fust* 'cask, tree trunk', from Latin *fustis* 'cudgel'.

futile [mid 16th century] *Futile* is from Latin *futilis* 'leaky, futile', apparently from *fundere* 'to pour'.

future [late Middle English] This word comes via Old French from Latin *futurus*, the future participle of *esse* 'to be': the source is the stem *fu-*, ultimately from a base meaning 'to grow, become'.

fuzz [late 16th century] This word for a fluffy mass of hair or fibre is probably of Low German or Dutch origin; comparable words are Dutch *voos*, Low German *fussig* 'spongy'. The slang word **fuzz** referring to the 'police' dates from the 1920s; it is originally US but the origin remains unknown.

Gg

gab [early 18th century] This informal word meaning 'to chat' is a variant of *gob*. **Gabby**, based on *gab* is recorded from the same period and was originally Scots.
→ GOB¹

gabble [late 16th century] This word is from Dutch *gabbelen*. The origin is imitative, reflecting rapid unintelligible talk. The word has sometimes been used to describe the sound made by geese (Byron *Marino Faliero*: The geese in the Capitol … gabbled Till Rome awoke).

gaberdine [early 16th century] *Gaberdine* is from Old French *gauvardine*, an earlier spelling of which was *gallevardine*, perhaps from Middle High German *wallevart* 'pilgrimage'. The original meaning was 'a garment worn by a pilgrim'; it was a type of smock made of coarse material (Shakespeare *Merchant of Venice*: You call me misbeliever … And spit upon my Jewish gaberdine). The textile sense referring to cloth of fine worsted is first recorded in the early 20th century.

gable [Middle English] Coming via Old French from Old Norse *gafl*, *gable* is of Germanic origin. Related words are Dutch *gaffel* and German *Gabel* 'fork': the point of the gable was originally the fork of two crossed timbers supporting the end of the roof-tree.

gad [late Middle English] *Gad* as in *gad about* is probably a back-formation (by removal of the suffix) from obsolete *gadling* which first meant 'companion' but later had the meaning 'wanderer, vagabond'. The origin is Germanic. Another view as to the origin is that it is from obsolete *gad* meaning 'rush about like an animal stung by gad-flies' which is a possibility but many quotations do not favour this theory.

gadget [late 19th century] This word was originally in nautical use: it is probably from French *gâchette* 'a lock mechanism' or from the French dialect word *gagée* 'tool'.

gag¹ [Middle English] *Gag* 'something placed over the mouth to prevent the person from crying out' is perhaps related to Old Norse *gagháls* 'with the neck thrown back', or it may be imitative of a person choking.

gag² [mid 19th century] This *gag* meaning 'joke' was originally theatrical slang but its origin is unknown. It may be connected with the notion of thrusting something down the throat of a credulous listener who would 'swallow' the story. It may alternatively be onomatopoeic in origin with the original sense 'meaningless chatter'.

gaga [early 20th century] *Gaga* 'slightly mad' is from French, 'senile, a senile person'. It is a reduplication based on *gâteux*, a variant of the hospital slang word *gâteur* 'bed-wetter'.

gaggle [Middle English] (as a verb): *Gaggle* as in *gaggle of geese*, *gaggle of reporters* is originally imitative of the noise that a goose makes. Dutch *gaggelen* and German *gackern* are comparable. Many artificial terms were invented in the 15th century as collectives referring to groups of people or animals; unlike most of the others, *gaggle* was actually adopted in use.

gain [late 15th century] Early use was as a noun (from Old French *gaigne*) when it meant 'booty'. The verb is from Old French *gaignier*. The origin is Germanic. The phrase *gain ground* was originally in military use when terrain was taken from an adversary. From the 1990s the expression *no gain without pain* became frequent expressing the notion that success in something requires effort.

gainsay [Middle English] This is from the obsolete prefix *gain-* 'against' and the verb *say*. In current use it is a literary word.

gait [late Middle English] Originally Scots, *gait* 'a manner of walking' is a variant of *gate* which meant 'way' in Middle English: Old Norse *gata* is the source, related to German *Gasse* 'alley, lane'. The spelling *gait* was rare until the 17th century.

gaiter [early 18th century] This word for a protective covering for the ankle and lower leg is from French *guêtre*, which probably has a Germanic source and is related to *wrist*.

gala [early 17th century] The early use of *gala* reflects the sense 'showy or festive dress'. It has come via Italian and Spanish from Old French *gale* 'rejoicing'. Now it describes a social occasion with entertainment, or it refers to a swimming competition or similar sports meeting.

galaxy [late Middle English] Originally this word referred specifically to the Milky Way. It has come via Old French from medieval Latin *galaxia*, from Greek *galaxias* (*kuklos*) 'milky (vault)' (from *gala*, *galakt-* 'milk'). Figurative use dates from the late 16th century. **Galactic** is recorded from the mid 19th century and is based on Greek *galaktias*, a variant of *galaxias* 'galaxy'.

gale [mid 16th century] This word for a very strong wind is perhaps related to Old Norse *galinn* 'mad, frantic', but the origin remains obscure.

gall[1] [Old English] Old English *gealla* was a word for 'bile'. It is Germanic in origin and related to Dutch *gal* and German *Galle* 'gall', from an Indo-European root shared by Greek *kholē* and Latin *fel* 'bile'. The current figurative sense is 'impudent behaviour' (e.g. *he had the gall to demand a huge fee*).

gall[2] [Old English] This *gall* describes a sore on the skin caused by chafing; the figurative use is 'anger'. In Old English *gealle* was a 'sore on a horse'; it is perhaps related to *gall* 'bile'. The spelling was superseded in Middle English by forms from Middle Low German or Middle Dutch.

gallant [Middle English] The early sense recorded for *gallant* is 'finely dressed'. The source is Old French *galant*, from *galer* 'have fun, make a show', from *gale* 'pleasure, rejoicing'. The sense 'politely attentive to women' was adopted from French into English in the 17th century; the accentuation *ga'llant* differentiates this use. **Gallantry** arose in the late 16th century meaning 'splendour, ornamentation': this is from French *galanterie*, from *galant*.

gallery [late Middle English] This was originally a term for a long passage partly open at the side to form a colonnade. It came via Old French from Italian *galleria* 'gallery', which earlier also meant 'a church porch', from medieval Latin *galeria*: this is perhaps an alteration of *galilea* 'Galilee' (= a porch or chapel at the church entrance, perhaps referring to Galilee as an outlying portion of the Holy Land). The use of *gallery* in the theatre for the highest part of the auditorium containing the cheapest seats, dates from the late 17th century.

gallivant [early 19th century] This is perhaps a humorous alteration of *gallant*.

gallon [Middle English] This unit of volume for liquids is from Anglo-Norman French *galon*, from the base of medieval Latin *galleta*, *galletum* 'pail, liquid measure'. The origin may be Celtic.

gallop [early 16th century] The verb *gallop* is from Old French *galoper*, a variant of Old Northern French *waloper*. No satisfactory origin

has been found for these words; it may be that the word is a compound of Germanic *hlaupen* (unattested) 'to leap, run'.
→WALLOP

gallows [Old English] Old English *galga*, *gealga* is Germanic in origin and related to Dutch *galg* and German *Galgen*; it was reinforced in Middle English by Old Norse *gálgi*. Both a singular and a plural form were used in English, the plural presumably designating the two posts of the frame. The plural has been predominant since the 13th century.

galore [early 17th century] This word is from Irish *go leor* whose literal sense is 'to sufficiency'.

galosh [Middle English] A *galosh* originally denoted a type of clog. It comes via Old French from late Latin *gallicula*, a diminutive of Latin *gallica* (*solea*) 'Gallic (shoe)'. The current use of the word for a waterproof overshoe dates from the mid 19th century.

galumph [1872] Now meaning 'move in a clumsy and ponderous way', *galumph* started out in the sense 'prance in triumph'. It was coined by Lewis Carroll in *Through the Looking Glass* and may be a blend of *gallop* and *triumph*.

galvanize [early 19th century] The early sense was 'stimulate by electricity'. It comes from French *galvaniser* based on *Galvani* the name of an Italian anatomist (1737–98) best known for his discovery of the twitching reaction of frogs' legs in an electric field. The figurative use of the word ('shock into activity') dates from the mid 19th century (Charlotte Brontë *Villette*: *Her approach always galvanized him to new and spasmodic life*).

gambit [mid 17th century] The word has an involved history; its application to chess seems to have first occurred in Spain as *gambito* which was adopted into Italian as *gambitto*. The native spelling *gambetto* meaning literally 'tripping up' (from *gamba* 'leg') was taken up later. The early English spelling was *gambett* from Italian *gambetto*; the later English spelling *gambit* is from Spanish. The word describes a method of opening the game of chess, the original one being the offer of a bishop's pawn (= King or Queen's gambit).

gamble [early 18th century] *Gamble* is from obsolete *gamel* 'play games', or from the verb *game*.

gambol [early 16th century] *Gambol* 'a playful jump' is an alteration of obsolete *gambade*, via French from Italian *gambata* 'trip up', from *gamba* 'leg'. The *-ade* ending of the early spelling was soon confused with the then common endings *-aud* and *-auld*: the *-d* was then dropped.

game[1] [Old English] Old English *gamen* 'amusement, fun' and *gamenian* 'play, amuse oneself' are Germanic in origin. The expression *to be game* (early 18th century) meaning 'to be brave and ready to do something adventurous' is from the use of *game* as a term for 'game-cock'.

game[2] [late 18th century] *Game* meaning 'injured, lame' as in *game leg* was apparently originally north Midland dialect (as *gam*) but its origin is unknown. A variant dialect form of *game* is **gammy** which in the mid 19th century meant 'bad, false'.

gammon [late 15th century] In early use this culinary word referred to the haunch of a pig. It comes from Old Northern French *gambon*, from *gambe* 'leg'.

gamut [late Middle English] This word is from medieval Latin *gamma ut*, originally the name of the lowest note in the medieval scale (bass G an octave and a half below middle C), then applied to the whole range of notes used in medieval music. The Greek letter Γ (gamma) was used for bass G, with *ut* indicating that it was the first note in the lowest of the hexachords or six-note scales. Notes in each hexachord were named using syllables of a Latin hymn for St John the Baptist's Day in which each line began on the next note of the scale: *Ut* queant laxis *re*sonare fibris *Mi*ra gestorum *fa*muli tuorum, *Sol*ve polluti *la*bii reatum, Sancte Iohannes. A seventh note, *si*, was added later, from the initial letters of Sancte Iohannes. The scheme was adapted in the 19th century to form solmization systems such as the Tonic Sol-fa.

gang [Old English] *Gang* is from Old Norse *gangr*, *ganga* 'gait, course, going', of Germanic origin. It is related to Scots *gang* 'go'. The original meaning was 'going, a journey'; later in Middle English the sense 'way, passage' is exemplified. At the same time the word was used for 'a set of things which go together'; it led in the early 17th century to its application in nautical use to 'a crew', in other areas 'a group of workmen', and generally to any group often in a depreciatory sense. **Gangster**, based on *gang*, dates from the late 19th century; this was altered in US black English slang to **gangsta** in the 1980s and is used literally as well as specifying a type of rap music.

gannet [Old English] Old English *ganot* is Germanic in origin and related to Dutch *gent* 'gander'. The word is used sometimes to describe a greedy person: this was applied first of all to a greedy sailor as slang in the 1920s.

gantry [late Middle English] In Middle English this was a four-footed wooden stand for barrels. It is probably from dialect *gawn* (a contraction of *gallon*) and *tree*.

gaol
→ JAIL

gap [Middle English] *Gap* is from an Old Norse word meaning 'chasm', 'wide-mouthed outcry' which formed part of the mythological name *Ginnunga-gap*. In geographical contexts *gap* is commonly used in the US for a mountain pass. The notion of 'break' or 'hiatus' is at the core of the word; this is reflected in the compound *gap year* common since the 1980 for an academic year taken as a break from formal education between leaving school and starting further education.
→ GAPE

gape [Middle English] This is from Old Norse *gapa* 'open one's mouth'. An early English sense was 'open the mouth wide in order to bite or swallow something'. **Gawp** recorded from the late 17th century is perhaps an alteration of *gape*.
→ GAP

garage [early 20th century] This is an adoption of a French word, from *garer* 'to shelter'.

garb [late 16th century] *Garb* is via French from Italian *garbo* 'elegance'. The origin is Germanic. Obsolete senses in English include 'grace, elegance' and 'a person's outward bearing or carriage'. The connection with 'fashion' soon arose in the early 17th century.
→ GEAR

garbage [late Middle English] In early examples, *garbage* meant 'offal': it comes from Anglo-Norman French but the ultimate origin is unknown. Its use to mean 'refuse' is recorded from the late 16th century. The word has been used in computing since the 1960s in the phrase *garbage in, garbage out* abbreviated to *GIGO*: this expresses the idea that if the input of the program is wrong then the output will naturally be wrong as well.

garble [late Middle English] 'Sift out, cleanse' was the early meaning of *garble*, from Anglo-Latin and Italian *garbellare*, from Arabic *garbala* 'sift'. The source is perhaps late Latin *cribellare* 'to sieve', from Latin *cribrum* 'sieve'.

garden [Middle English] This word comes from Old Northern French *gardin*, a variant of Old French *jardin*, of Germanic origin. The idiomatic phrase *to cultivate one's garden* meaning 'to tend to one's own affairs' is a translation from Voltaire's *Candide* (1759): All that is very well, answered Candide, but let us take care of our garden. Middle English **gardener** is from Old French *gardinier*, from *gardin*.
→ YARD[2]

gargantuan [late 16th century] *Gargantuan* 'enormous' is from *Gargantua*, the name of a voracious giant in the French satirist Rabelais' book of the same name (1534).

gargle [early 16th century] This comes from French *gargouiller* 'to gurgle, bubble', from *gargouille* 'throat'.
→ GARGOYLE

gargoyle [Middle English] Old French *gargouille*, the source of the English word, meant 'throat' and 'gargoyle'; the association is with water passing through the throat and mouth of the figure. It is related to Greek *gargarizein* 'to gargle', imitating the sounds made in the throat.

garment [Middle English] The origin is Old French *garnement* 'equipment', from *garnir* 'to equip'.
→ GARNISH

garner [Middle English] This was originally a noun meaning 'granary, storehouse for corn': it comes from Old French *gernier*, from Latin *granarium* 'granary', from *granum* 'grain'.

garnish [Middle English] The early sense recorded was 'equip, arm': the source is Old French *garnir* meaning both 'fortify, defend' and 'provide, prepare': this is probably of Germanic origin and related to *warn*. The prime current sense 'decorate, embellish' dates from the late 17th century.

garret [Middle English] 'Watchtower' was the first meaning recorded for *garret* from Old French *garite*: this word (like *garrison*) is from *garir* 'to defend, provide'. The word's use for a room on the top floor of a house or within the roof space arose early in its history (late 15th century).

garrison [Middle English] The Middle English sense was 'safety, means of protection'. Old French *garison* is the source, from *garir* 'defend, provide', of Germanic origin. Confusion with French *garnison* (from *garnir* 'to garnish') which meant both 'supplies' and 'garrison' apparently led *garrison* to take on the meaning 'fortress'.

garrulous [early 17th century] *Garrulous* is based on Latin *garrulus* from *garrire* 'to chatter, prattle'.

garter [Middle English] This is from Old French *gartier*, from *garet* 'bend of the knee, calf of the leg', probably of Celtic origin. The highest order of English knighthood has as its badge *the Garter*, a dark-blue velvet ribbon worn below the left knee and edged and buckled with gold bearing the words *Honi soit qui mal y pense*. These words were thought originally to

have been said by Edward III when he tied a garter belonging to the Countess of Salisbury to his leg after the garter fell to the floor as she danced with him.

gas [mid 17th century] This word was invented by the Belgian chemist J. B. van Helmont (1577–1644), to denote an occult principle which he believed to exist in all matter. It was suggested by Greek *khuos* 'chaos', with Dutch g representing Greek *kh*. The word in Portuguese and French is *gaz*, a spelling which was used by English writers for a while. *Gas* of a sort suitable for lighting or heating purposes dates from the late 18th century. The first experiments using coal-gas for lighting are said to have been made by the rector of Crofton, Dr Clayton, in about 1688; gas-lighting in its practical application was due to Murdoch (1792–1808).

gash [Middle English] The early spelling was *garse*, from Old French *garcer* 'to chap, crack', perhaps based on Greek *kharassein* 'sharpen, scratch, engrave'. The current spelling is recorded from the mid 16th century.

gasket [early 17th century] A *gasket* at first was a cord securing a furled sail to the yard of a sailing ship. It comes perhaps from French *garcette* 'thin rope'. The term for a flat ring used as a seal against the pressure of gas or liquids such as in an internal combustion engine, dates from the early 20th century.

gasp [late Middle English] This word comes from Old Norse *geispa* 'to yawn'.

gastronomy [early 19th century] French *gastronomie* is the direct source, from Greek *gastronomia*, an alteration of *gastrologia*, based on Greek *gastēr*, *gastr-* 'stomach'.

gate [Old English] Old English *gæt*, *geat* (plural *gatu*) is Germanic in origin; a related form is Dutch *gat* 'gap, hole, breach'.

gather [Old English] Old English *gaderian* has a West Germanic origin; it is related to Dutch *gaderen*. The sense 'understand, deduce' is recorded from the early 16th century. The word's use in sewing contexts dates from the late 16th century.
→ TOGETHER

gaudy [late 15th century] This word meaning 'extravagantly showy' is probably from Middle English *gaud* denoting a trick or pretence. This came perhaps via Anglo-Norman French from Old French *gaudir* 'to rejoice', from Latin *gaudere*. *Gaud* is still in current use in English for 'something showy', which may have been influenced by the obsolete word *gaud* for 'a large ornamental bead in a rosary'.

gauge [Middle English] This was originally a standard measure; it comes from Old French *gauge* (noun), *gauger* (verb), variants of Old Northern French forms whose source is unknown. The spelling *gage* has been adopted in recent American dictionaries, whereas *gauge* prevails in British English.

gaunt [late Middle English] The origin is unknown. Norwegian *gand* 'thin pointed stick' and Swedish dialect *gank* 'a lean horse' have been compared. It may be from Old French *gent* 'elegant': an obsolete English sense is 'slender, not fat'.

gauntlet[1] [late Middle English] This comes from Old French *gantelet*, a diminutive of *gant* 'glove'. It is apparently of Germanic origin but is only found in Scandinavian cognates. The phrases *throw down the gauntlet* and *take up the gauntlet* are translations of French phrases and come from the medieval custom of throwing down a glove to challenge an oppponent who would show acceptance by picking it up.

gauntlet[2] [mid 17th century] *Gauntlet* as in *run the gauntlet* is an alteration of *gantlope* (from Swedish *gatlopp*, from *gata* 'lane' and *lopp* 'course') by association with *gauntlet* 'glove'.

gauze [mid 16th century] The thin transparent fabric known as *gauze* is from French *gaze*, perhaps from *Gaza*, the name of a town in Palestine.

gawk [late 17th century] Early examples show the word *gawk* in noun use. It is perhaps related to obsolete *gaw* 'to gaze', from Old Norse *gá* 'heed'.

gay [Middle English] Early use of *gay* is recorded in the sense 'light-hearted and carefree'; it comes from Old French *gai* whose origin is unknown. The word developed the notion 'addicted to social pleasures' often with an association of loose morality as in *gay dog* or *gay Lothario* (a character in Rowe's *Fair Penitent* 1703); it was extended in slang use to refer to a woman living by prostitution. The use of the word to mean 'homosexual' is found in examples from the 1930s (as an adjective); the first citation found to date illustrating this sense is prison slang. Noun use is found from the 1970s. The noun **gaiety** dates from the mid 17th century and is from French *gaieté*, from *gai*.

gaze [late Middle English] *Gaze* like the later (late 17th century) **gawk** 'stare openly and stupidly' is perhaps related to obsolete *gaw* 'to gaze', from Old Norse *gá* 'heed'. There may be a connection between *gaze* and mid 18th-century **gazebo**, a small type of summer house from which one may 'gaze' at the garden. The *-ebo* ending is in imitation of Latin future tenses, creating a pseudo form meaning 'I will gaze'.

gazette [early 17th century] *Gazette* came via French from Italian *gazzetta*, which originally in Venetian Italian was *gazeta de la novità* 'a halfpennyworth of news': the news-sheet sold for a *gazeta*, a Venetian coin of very little value. The verb phrase *to be gazetted* was used to mean 'be the subject of an announcement in a gazette' and 'be named in a gazette as being appointed to a military command'. **Gazetteer** is also early 17th century when it meant 'journalist': this is via French from Italian *gazzettiere* (from *gazzetta*). The current use of the word for a geographical index comes from a late 17th-century gazetteer called *The Gazetteer's: or, Newsman's Interpreter: Being a Geographical Index*.

gazump [1920s] Early use was in the sense 'swindle'; it derives from Yiddish *gezumph* 'to overcharge'. Current use in connection with bids in house purchase dates from the 1970s. In the late 1980s the opposite term **gazunder** was coined by a humorous blend of *gazump* and *under*, when the property market stagnated and lower and lower bids were offered as prices fell.

gear [Middle English] Of Scandinavian origin, English *gear* is associated with Old Norse *gervi*. Early senses expressed the general meaning 'equipment or apparatus'; later it came to mean 'mechanism': which led (early 19th century) to its main current use in automotive contexts. Recently *gear* has been used as slang for 'drugs'.

geek [late 19th century] This informal word for either an unfashionable person or an obsessive enthusiast (e.g. *computer geek*) is US slang from the related English dialect word *geck* 'fool', from a Germanic source. It is related to Dutch *gek* 'mad, silly'. In Webster's *New International Dictionary of the English Language* of 1954, the definition read: *Geek*, a carnival 'wild man' whose act usually includes biting off the head off a live chicken or snake.

geezer [late 19th century] An informal word for a 'man', *geezer* represents a dialect pronunciation of the earlier form *guiser* meaning 'mummer'. In recent use it sometimes has a connotation of shady dealing.

geld [Middle English] This verb meaning 'castrate' is from Old Norse *gelda*, from *geldr* 'barren'. In early use the word was used generally with reference to men as well as animals but current use is restricted to the latter. Examples of figurative use meaning 'weaken, enfeeble' are found from the 16th century. The noun **gelding** once meaning 'a eunuch' and now usually applied to a castrated male horse, is late Middle English from Old Norse *geldingr*, from *geldr*.

gem [Old English] Old English *gim* is from Latin *gemma* 'bud, jewel', influenced in spelling in Middle English by Old French *gemme*.

gen [Second World War] This was a term first used in the armed services: it may be from the first syllable of the phrase *general information* (as in the official formula *for the general information of all ranks*). Other possibilities are that it is a truncation of *genuine* or extracted from *intelligence*.

gender [late Middle English] *Gender* is from Old French *gendre* (now *genre*), based on Latin *genus* 'birth, family, nation'. Use of the word as a grammatical term meaning 'a type or class of noun' reflected a sense of Latin *genus*. Another early meaning was 'kind, sort, genus' as in the now obsolete phrase *the general gender* 'the common sort (of people)'. (Shakespeare *Hamlet*: The great love the general gender bear him). The words *gender* and *sex* both define 'the state of being male or female' but they are used in slightly different ways: whereas *sex* tends to refer to biological differences, *gender* refers to social or cultural differences.

gene [early 20th century] *Gene* is from German *Gen*, from *Pangen* (from Greek *pan-* 'all' and *genos* 'race, kind, offspring'), a supposed ultimate unit of heredity. The rapid advances in research in genetics in the later part of the 20th century has led to many new phrases: *gene therapy*, *gene family*, *gene superfamily*, *gene mapping*, etc. The adjective **genetic** (mid 19th century) started out meaning 'arising from a common origin': this is from **genesis**, on the pattern of pairs such as *antithesis* and *antithetic*.

genealogy [Middle English] This came via Old French and late Latin from Greek *genealogia*, from *genea* 'race, generation' and *-logia* 'speaking, discourse'.

general [Middle English] This came via Old French from Latin *generalis* 'relating to the (whole) kind', from *genus*, *gener-* 'class, race, kind'. The Latin word came to be used in contrast to *specialis*: this antithetical use remains in all the European languages. The noun primarily denotes a person having overall authority: in military use it started out meaning a 'commander of the whole army' as an abbreviation of *captain general*, from French *capitaine général* 'commander-in-chief', but it came to be a specific military rank used as a title. The word **generality** (late Middle English) is from Old French *generalite*, from late Latin *generalitas*, from *generalis*.

generation [Middle English] *Generation* came via Old French from Latin *generatio(n-)*, from the verb *generare* 'create', from *genus*, *gener-* 'stock, race' (the base too of **generic** dating from the late 17th century). **Generate** is found in examples from the early 16th century in the sense 'beget, procreate': it comes from the Latin verb *generare*.

generosity [late Middle English] This initially denoted nobility of birth: it comes from Latin *generositas*, from *generosus* 'magnanimous', from *genus*, *gener-* 'stock, race'. Current senses involving kindness and magnanimity date from the 17th century. The adjective **generous** is found from the late 16th century and is via Old French from Latin *generosus*. The original sense was 'of noble birth', hence 'characteristic of noble birth, courageous, magnanimous, not mean' (a sense already present in Latin).

genial [mid 16th century] *Genial* is from Latin *genialis* 'nuptial, productive', from *genius*. The Latin sense was adopted into English; hence the English sense 'mild and conducive to growth' which dates from the mid 17th century (*genial climate*), which later developed into 'cheerful, kindly, jovial' (mid 18th century).
→ GENIUS

genie [mid 17th century] The early use referred to a guardian or protective spirit: it comes from French *génie*, from Latin *genius*. *Génie* was adopted in the current sense by the 18th-century French translators of *The Arabian Nights' Entertainments*, because of its resemblance in form and sense to Arabic *jinnī* 'jinnee'.
→ GENIUS

genius [late Middle English] This is a use of a Latin word meaning 'attendant spirit present from one's birth' and by extension 'innate ability or inclination', from the root of *gignere* 'beget'. The original English sense 'tutelary spirit attendant on someone' gave rise in the late 16th century to the notion of 'a person's characteristic disposition', which led to the sense 'a person's natural ability'. Finally the word acquired the meaning 'exceptional natural ability', recorded from the mid 17th century.

genteel [late 16th century] 'Fashionable, stylish' was the early sense of *genteel*, a re-adoption of French *gentil* 'well-born' (previously adopted in the 13th century and later developing into *gentle*). From the 17th century to the 19th century the word was used in such senses as 'of good social position', 'having the manners of a well-born person', and 'well bred'. In the middle of the 19th century the word started to be ridiculed and used in an ironic or derogatory

way because of its association with people who dreaded being taken for 'common people' or those who set too much store by marks of social superiority.
→GENTLE

gentile [late Middle English] This word comes from Latin *gentilis* 'of a family or nation; of the same clan', used in the Vulgate to refer to non-Jews. The source is Latin *gens, gent-* 'family, race', from the root of *gignere* 'beget'.

gentle [Middle English] *Gentle* 'mild' is from Old French *gentil* 'high-born, noble', from Latin *gentilis* 'of the same clan' The original sense was 'nobly born' which led to 'courteous, chivalrous' and later (mid 16th century) 'mild, moderate in action or disposition'. Middle English **gentility** (from Old French *gentilite*, from *gentil*) meant initially 'honourable birth'. The compound:
■ **gentleman** (Middle English and based on *gentle*) started out with the meaning 'man of noble birth', translating Old French *gentilz hom*. In later use it denoted a man of a good family (especially one entitled to a coat of arms) but not of the nobility. The phrase *gentlemen's agreement* was originally a US usage and is binding by honour but not enforceable at law. **Gent** was originally (from the mid 16th century) a standard written abbreviation of *gentleman*; it has been a colloquial usage since the early 19th century.
→GENTEEL; GENTILE

gentry [late Middle English] The first sense recorded was 'superiority of birth or rank'. It is apparently an altered form of obsolete *gentrice* 'noble birth': the final sound may have been taken to be plural. This form was from Old French *genterise*, based on *gentil*. In modern English use it specifies the class immediately below the nobility.
→GENTLE

genuine [late 16th century] 'Natural' and 'proper' were the early meanings. *Genuine* is from Latin *genuinus*, from *genu* 'knee', with reference to the Roman custom of a father acknowledging paternity of a newborn child by placing it on his knee. Later it was associated with 'birth, race, stock'. The sense 'not counterfeit' dates from the mid 17th century; its use to describe people as 'free from affectation' is recorded from the late 19th century. From the 1970s it has been applied in the specialized context of horse- or greyhound-racing to describe an animal as 'able to be relied on to do its best'.

geography [late 15th century] The source of the word *geography* in English is French *géographie* or Latin *geographia*, from Greek *geo-*

graphia. The base elements are *gē* 'earth' and *-graphia* 'writing'.

geology [late 18th century] This is from modern Latin *geologia*, from Greek *gē* 'earth' and *-logia* 'discourse'. As a term for a distinct branch of physical science, the word occurs first in English. In early use it denoted the science of the Earth in general.

geometry [Middle English] *Geometry* is via Old French from Latin *geometria*, from Greek, from *gē* 'earth' and *metria* 'measuring'. **Geometric** dates from the mid 17th century and is via French from Latin *geometricus*, from Greek *geōmetrikos*, from *geōmetrēs*.

geriatric [1920s] This word is made up of Greek *gēras* 'old age' and *iatros* 'doctor', on the pattern of *paediatric*.

germ [late Middle English] The early term referred to a portion of an organism capable of developing into a new one or part of one. It came via Old French from Latin *germen* 'seed, sprout'. The sense 'micro-organism' dates from the late 19th century when it originally was used vaguely to mean the 'seed' of a disease. Also based on Latin *germen* are **germinate** (late 16th century from Latin *germinare* 'to sprout, bud') and **germinal** (early 19th century).

German [mid 16th century] This is from Latin *Germanus*, a word used to designate related peoples of central and northern Europe and perhaps a name given by Celts to their neighbours. It may be a derivative of Old Irish *gair* 'neighbour'. The name does not appear to have been applied to these people by themselves.

germane [early 17th century] This is a variant of Middle English *german* (with which it was once synonymous) from Old French *germain*, from Latin *germanus* 'genuine, of the same parents'. The current sense 'pertinent' has arisen from a usage in Shakespeare's *Hamlet* (The word had been more cousin german to the phrase, if he could have carried the canon by his side). The phrase *cousin german* remains an old-fashioned term for *cousin*.

gerrymander [early 19th century] This is a use of the name of Governor Elbridge *Gerry* of Massachusetts combined with *salamander*: this arose through the supposed similarity between a salamander and the shape of a new voting district on a map drawn when Governor Gerry was in office (1812). It was felt that this creation favoured his party: the map (with claws, wings, and fangs added), was published in the Boston *Weekly Messenger*, with the title *The Gerry-Mander*. The verb is now used generally for political manipulation of electoral boundaries.

gestation [mid 16th century] The word *gestation* has the notion of 'carrying' at its core. It was first used for an excursion on horseback or in a carriage, considered to be a form of exercise: it comes from Latin *gestatio(n-)*, from *gestare* 'carry, carry in the womb'.

gesticulate [early 17th century] This comes from Latin *gesticulari* 'to gesticulate', from *gesticulus*, a diminutive of *gestus* 'action'.

gesture [late Middle English] This is from medieval Latin *gestura*, from Latin *gerere* 'to bear, wield, perform'. The original sense was 'bearing, deportment' (as in *gesture of the body*) which led to 'the use of posture and bodily movements for effect in oratory' (James Boswell *Life of Johnson*: His unqualified ridicule of rhetorical gesture, or action). The figurative use of *gesture* to mean 'a friendly action made to elicit a favourable response' arose in the early part of the 20th century.

get [Middle English] *Get* is from Old Norse *geta* 'obtain, beget, guess', related to Old English *gietan* (found in *begietan* 'beget', *forgietan* 'forget'). It is from an Indo-European root shared by Latin *praeda* 'booty, prey', *praehendere* 'get hold of, seize', and Greek *khandanein* 'hold, contain, be able'. The phrase **giddy-up** dating from the 1920s used as an encouragement to a horse was originally *giddap* in US English: this reproduces a pronunciation of *get up*.

geyser [late 18th century] Icelandic *Geysir*, literally 'gusher' and the name of a particular spring in Iceland, has given *geyser* in English; it is related to Icelandic *geysa* 'to gush'. Non-Icelanders used the word for any of the springs of this type in Iceland and it was then extended to others throughout the world.

ghastly [Middle English] This word is from obsolete *gast* 'to terrify', from Old English *gæstan*, which is Germanic origin and related to *ghost*. The *gh* spelling is by association with *ghost*. The sense 'objectionable' dates from the mid 19th century.
→ GHOST

ghetto [early 17th century] Two possible origins include Italian *getto* 'foundry' (because the first ghetto was established in 1516 on the site of a foundry in Venice), or Italian *borghetto*, a diminutive of *borgo* 'borough'. In Italy the word referred to the quarter of a city to which Jews were restricted, a use which became more widespread elsewhere, e.g. *the Warsaw Ghetto*.

ghost [Old English] Old English *gāst* meant 'spirit, soul'. The word is known only in the West Germanic languages; related forms are Dutch *geest* and German *Geist*. It appears however to be pre-Germanic in origin with a base meaning 'fury, anger'; outside Germanic, derivatives seem to point to the primary sense 'to wound, tear, pull to pieces'. The *gh-* spelling occurs first in Caxton, probably influenced by Flemish *gheest*. **Ghostly** had the spelling *gāstlic* in Old English from *gāst* 'ghost'.

ghoul [late 18th century] *Ghoul* is from Arabic *ġūl*, a desert demon believed to rob graves and devour corpses.

GI [1930s] This abbreviation of *government* (or *general*) *issue* originally denoted equipment supplied to US forces. It is now applied to a private soldier in the US.

giant [Middle English] The early spelling was *geant*; the first syllable was later influenced by Latin *gigant-*. It comes from Old French, via Latin from Greek *gigas, gigant-*. The Greek word and its Latin transliteration denoted, in classical use, a mythical race of beings of great size and strength, sons of Gaea (= Earth) and Uranus (= Heaven) or Tartarus (= Hell), who were destroyed after warring with the gods. The Vulgate used the word to refer to men of huge stature and strength: this led to the wider sense current in the Romance languages and in English. The adjective **gigantic** which arose in the early 17th century meaning 'like or suited to a giant' is based on Latin *gigas*.

gibberish [early 16th century] This is perhaps from **gibber** 'speak rapidly and unintelligibly', the *-ish* suffix denoting a language as in *Spanish, Swedish*, etc. *Gibberish* is found earlier however in written examples.

gibbet [Middle English] *Gibbet* 'a gallows' is from Old French *gibet* 'staff, cudgel, gallows', a diminutive of *gibe* 'club, staff'. The origin is probably Germanic. In later use the word came to designate an upright post with a projecting arm from which the bodies of criminals were hung in irons or chains after execution.

giddy [Old English] Old English *gidig* meant 'insane' from the literal meaning 'possessed by a god'; it is from the same base as *God*. Current senses date from late Middle English.

gift [Middle English] This is from Old Norse *gipt*.
→ GIVE

gig¹ [late 18th century] This *gig* as a term for a light two-wheeled carriage or a fast narrow boat adapted for rowing or sailing is apparently a transferred sense of obsolete *gig*: this meant originally 'a flighty girl' but it was also applied to various objects or devices that whirled.

gig² [1920s] The origin of the musical term *gig* is unknown.

giggle [early 16th century] This word, like *cackle*, is imitative of the sound. Dutch *giggelen* and German *gichern* are synonymous.

gigolo [1920s] The original sense was 'dancing partner': it comes from French, formed as the masculine of *gigole* 'dance hall woman; tall thin woman', from colloquial *gigue* 'leg'.

gild [Old English] Old English *gyldan* (found in the past particple *gegyld* 'gilded') is Germanic in origin and related to *gold*. The figurative use 'give false brilliance to' dates from the late 16th century. Middle English **gilt** is the archaic past participle of *gild*. The expression *gild the lily* meaning 'improve what is already beautiful' is a misquotation from Shakespeare's *King John*: To gild refined gold, to paint the lily; to throw perfume on the violet,... is wasteful, and ridiculous excess.

gimmick [1920s] The origin of *gimmick* first recorded in American English is unknown but it is possibly an approximate anagram of *magic*, the original sense of the word being 'a piece of magicians' apparatus'.

gingerly [early 16th century] The early sense of *gingerly* was 'daintily' in descriptions of dancing or walking. At first it meant 'with small elegant steps' but it became depreciative and conveyed 'mincingly'. From the 17th century the word was recorded with reference to bodily movements generally and involved caution or distaste. It comes perhaps from Old French *gensor* 'delicate', the comparative of *gent* 'graceful', from Latin *genitus* '(well-) born'.

gird [Old English] Old English *gyrdan* is Germanic in origin; it is related to Dutch *gorden* and German *gürten*. The idiom *gird (up) one's loins* is a use of a biblical phrase. The noun **girder** (early 17th century) is based on *gird* in the archaic sense 'brace, strengthen'.
→ GIRDLE; GIRTH

girdle [Old English] Old English *gyrdel* is Germanic in origin and related to Dutch *gordel* and German *Gürtel*.
→ GIRD; GIRTH

girl [Middle English] In early use, this word referred to a child or young person of either sex. It is perhaps related to Low German *gör* 'child'. In the late 18th century **gal** started to be used occasionally, representing a particular pronunciation. The phrase *the girl next door* to describe an ordinary and likeable young woman arose in film contexts in the 1950s. The compound:

■ **girl Friday** (1940s) was coined on the pattern of *man Friday*, the name of a character in Daniel Defoe's *Robinson Crusoe* (1719), who helped the shipwrecked Crusoe.

giro [late 19th century] This word for a system of electronic file transfer used in Europe and Japan came via German from an Italian word meaning 'circulation (of money)'.

girth [Middle English] *Girth* was initially used in the sense 'a band attached to a saddle': it is from Old Norse *gjorth*. The sense referring to measurement around the circumference of something dates from the mid 17th century.

gist [early 18th century] *Gist* is from Old French; it was the third person singular present tense of *gesir* 'to lie', from Latin *jacere*. The Anglo-French legal phrase *cest action gist* 'this action lies' stated that there were sufficient grounds to proceed; *gist* was adopted into legal English denoting the grounds themselves (i.e. the real point of an action). More general use of the word began in the early 19th century.

give [Old English] Old English *giefan*, *gefan* is Germanic in origin; it is related to Dutch *geven* and German *geben*. The idiomatic phrase *give and take* is found in contexts from the early 16th century.

gizzard [late Middle English] The early spelling was *giser* which is from Old French, based on Latin *gigeria* 'cooked entrails of fowl'. The final *-d* was added in the 16th century.

glacial [mid 17th century] This is either from French, or from Latin *glacialis* 'icy', from *glacies* 'ice', the base too of **glacier** (mid 18th century), apparently a French Savoyard word from *glace* 'ice'.

glad [Old English] Old English *glæd* was originally in the sense 'bright, shining'; it is Germanic in origin and related to Old Norse *glathr* 'bright, joyous' and German *glatt* 'smooth', as well as to Latin *glaber* 'smooth, hairless'. In modern English the sense has weakened from 'delighted and rejoicing' to 'pleased'. The expression *glad rags* was first used in US English at the beginning of the 20th century meaning 'smart clothes'. The *glad eye* (= a look intending to attract the opposite sex) dates from around the same period in British English.

glade [late Middle English] The origin of *glade* is unknown. It is perhaps related to *glad* or *gleam*, with reference to the comparative brightness of a clearing: obsolete senses of *glade* include 'a gleam of light' and 'a bright space between clouds'. By the end of the 17th century when the word had perhaps become merely literary, many writers associated the word not with sunshine but with shade.

glamour [early 18th century] *Glamour* was originally Scots in the sense 'enchantment, magic': it is an alteration of *grammar*. Although *grammar* itself was not used in this sense, the

Latin word *grammatica* (from which it derives) was often used in the Middle Ages to mean 'scholarship, learning', including the occult practices popularly associated with learning. The notion of 'magical beauty' became associated with *glamour* in the mid 19th century; in US English in the 1930s, the word came to mean 'attractiveness, feminine beauty'.

glance [late Middle English] *Glance* is first recorded as meaning 'rebound obliquely' with reference to a blow by a weapon. It is probably a nasalized form of obsolete *glace* in the same sense, from Old French *glacier* 'to slip', from *glace* 'ice', based on Latin *glacies*. The use of the word to mean 'give a momentary look' is recorded from the late 16th century.

glare [Middle English] The sense found in early examples is 'shine brilliantly or dazzlingly'. The word comes from Middle Dutch and Middle Low German *glaren* 'to gleam, glare' and is perhaps related to *glass*. The sense 'stare' occurred first in the adjective *glaring* in late Middle English. The notion of 'look fiercely and fixedly' dates from the early 17th century.
→ GLASS

glass [Old English] Old English *glæs* is Germanic in origin; related words are Dutch *glas* and German *Glas*. The word is often used as a truncated form of various names for instruments and objects such as *hour-glass*, *looking-glass*, *magnifying-glass*, *weather-glass*, *field-glass*, etc.
→ GLARE

glaze [late Middle English] The early spelling was *glase* and the source of the word is *glass*. The figurative use in connection with eyes is first found in Shakespeare's *Richard II*: For Sorrowes eyes glazed with blinding tears, Divides one thing entire to many objects.

gleam [Old English] Of Germanic origin, Old English *glæm* meant 'brilliant light' but the sense changed to describe rather a subdued or transient appearance of light.

glean [late Middle English] This is from Old French *glener*, from late Latin *glennare*, probably of Celtic origin. The literal sense is 'gather ears of corn left by the reapers'; this was soon extended to gathering small quantities generally and particularly snippets of information.

glee [Old English] Old English *glēo*, of Germanic origin, meant 'entertainment, music, fun'; it was and remained in Middle English chiefly poetic. It was rarely used after the 15th century and was almost completely absent from literature in the 17th century. Johnson considered it merely a comic word. It became common again around the end of the 18th

century but the reason for its revival remains a mystery. The use of the word as a musical term to denote 'a song for men's voices in three or more parts usually sung unaccompanied' dates from the mid 17th century.

glib [late 16th century] Early use included the sense 'smooth, unimpeded': it is ultimately of Germanic origin and related to Dutch 'slippery' and German *glibberig* 'slimy'. The use of the word used contemptuously in connection with speech or writing developed early in the word's history.

glide [Old English] Old English *glīdan* has a Germanic source; it is related to Dutch *glijden* and German *gleiten*. No cognates are known outside Germanic.

glimpse [Middle English] Early use of the word reflected the sense 'shine faintly': it is probably of Germanic origin and related to Middle High German *glimsen* and late Middle English **glimmer** which is probably Scandinavian in origin and related to Swedish *glimra* and Danish *glimre*. *Glimpse* developed the sense 'come into view' and then came to mean (during the late 18th century) 'catch sight of something coming into view'.

glint [Middle English] In early examples the meaning of *glint* was 'move quickly or obliquely'. It is a variant of dialect *glent*, probably of Scandinavian origin and related to Swedish dialect *glänta, glinta* 'to slip, slide, gleam'. Use was rare in the 15th century; its reappearance was first in Scottish writers of the 18th century (Robert Burns *How Long and Dreary is Night*: How slow ye move, ye heavy hours! ... It was na sae ye glinted by, When I was wi' my dearie).

glisten [Old English] Old English *glisnian* is Germanic in origin; it is related to Middle Low German *glisen*. The noun dates from the mid 19th century. Late Middle English **glister** is probably from Middle Low German *glistern* or Middle Dutch *glisteren*.

glitch [1960s] *Glitch* was originally a US usage but the origin is unknown. The original sense was 'a sudden surge of current', hence 'malfunction, hitch' in astronautical slang.

glitter [late Middle English] This comes from Old Norse *glitra*. The word **glitterati** for the fashionable set of people engaged in a glamorous activity such as show business dates from the 1950s in the US and is a blend of *glitter* and *literati* (from Latin meaning 'those acquainted with letters'). **Glitzy** was originally a North American usage of the 1960s and is based on *glitter*, suggested by *ritzy*, and perhaps also by German *glitzerig* 'glittering'.

gloaming [Old English] Old English *glōmung*, from *glōm* 'twilight', is Germanic in origin. The core sense seems to be 'the glow' of sunset.
→ GLOW

gloat [late 16th century] Of unknown origin, *gloat* is perhaps related to Old Norse *glotta* 'to grin' and Middle High German *glotzen* 'to stare'. The original sense was 'give a sideways or furtive look', hence 'cast amorous or admiring glances'; the current sense ('feel smug about') dates from the mid 18th century.

globe [late Middle English] This was initially a general term for a 'spherical object': it is either from Old French, or from Latin *globus*. The phrase *the globe* meaning 'the Earth' dates from the mid 16th century: in this period *the globes* began to be used to refer to spherical structures on which were depicted the *terrestrial globe* as the configuration of the Earth and the *celestial globe* as the arrangement of the constellations (Mrs Gaskell *Wives and Daughters*: I suppose you've been taught music, and the use of the globes, and French, and all the usual accomplishments).

gloom [late Middle English] Early use was as a verb. It may be a back-formation (by removal of the suffix) from **gloomy**, a word of unknown origin. In Scots use the noun first meant 'a sullen look'; the sense 'darkness, deep shadow' may have been a new formation from Milton: it occurs nine times in his poems (Milton *On Christ's Nativity*: Though the shady gloom Had given day her room, The Sun himself with-held his wonted speed). Later examples of *gloom* are associated with depressing darkness influenced by the figurative use 'state of melancholy' which is found in examples from the mid 18th century. The phrase *doom and gloom* dates from the 1940s and originated in the US.
→ GLUM

glory [Middle English] This comes from Old French *glorie*, from Latin *gloria* 'glory', the base too of Middle English **glorious** (from Old French *glorieus*, from Latin *gloriosus*) and **glorify** (from Old French *glorifier*, from ecclesiastical Latin *glorificare*, from late Latin *glorificus*).

glossary [late Middle English] This word for an alphabetical list of terms is from Latin *glossarium*, from *glossa* 'explanation of a difficult word', from Greek *glōssa* 'word needing explanation, language, tongue'. This is the base too of the word **gloss** 'an explanation', mid 16th century and an alteration of the noun *gloze*, (from Old French *glose* 'comment') influenced by Latin spelling.

glove [Old English] Old English *glōf* is Germanic in origin. Common idiomatic expressions including the word *glove* are: *fit like a glove*

and *hand in glove* which both date from the late 18th century although the latter was in existence earlier as *hand and glove*. The expression *to take the gloves off* meaning 'to use no mercy' dates from the 1920s.

glow [Old English] Of Germanic origin, Old English *glōwan* is related to Dutch *gloeien* and German *glühen*. The association with passion or emotion dates from the early 17th century.

glower [late 15th century] This is perhaps a Scots variant of the synonymous dialect word *glore*, or it may be from obsolete *glow* 'to stare', both possibly of Scandinavian origin.

glue [Middle English] The noun is from Old French *glu*, the verb from Old French *gluer*, from late Latin *glus*, *glut-*, from Latin *gluten*. This Latin word is also the base of late Middle English **glutinous** which comes either from Old French *glutineux* or from Latin *glutinosus*.

glum [mid 16th century] *Glum* is related to dialect *glum* 'to frown', a variant of *gloom*.
→ GLOOM

glut [Middle English] This is probably via Old French from Latin *gluttire* 'to swallow'.
→ GLUTTON

glutton [Middle English] This word is from Old French *gluton* 'glutton', from Latin *glutto(n-)* related to *gluttire* 'to swallow, gulp down', *gluttus* 'greedy', and *gula* 'throat'. Middle English **gluttony** is from Old French *glutonie*, from *gluton*.

gnarled [early 17th century] *Gnarled* is a variant of *knarled*, from *knar* 'knot in wood'. **Gnarl** is recorded from the early 19th century: it is a back-formation (by removal of the suffix) from *gnarled*.

gnash [late Middle English] This may be related to Old Norse *gnastan* 'a gnashing'. It was first recorded at the end of the 15th century; it is apparently a modification of an older verb spelt *gnast*.

gnaw [Old English] Old English *gnagen* has a Germanic origin; it is related to German *nagen* and is ultimately imitative.

gnome [mid 17th century] This comes from French, from modern Latin *gnomus*, a word used by the Swiss physician Paracelsus (c.1493–1541) as a synonym of *Pygmaeus*, denoting a mythical race of very small people said to inhabit parts of Ethiopia and India.
→ PYGMY

go [Old English] Old English *gān* is a Germanic word in origin; it is related to Dutch *gaan* and German *gehen*. The form *went* was originally the past tense of *wend*. The compound:

■ **go-cart** was first recorded in the late 17th century when it denoted a baby walker: the first element *go* is from the obsolete sense 'walk'. The variant **go-kart** for a small racing car arose in the 1950s with *kart* as a deliberate alteration of *cart*.

goad [Old English] Old English *gād* is Germanic in origin.

goal [Middle English] The early sense recorded was 'limit, boundary': the origin is unknown. It was used for the end point of a race from the early 16th century; soon afterward it became figurative for the focus of one's ambition and striving.

gob[1] [mid 16th century] This *gob* used informally for 'mouth' is perhaps from Scottish Gaelic *gob* 'beak, mouth'. The compound: ■ **gobsmack** dates from the 1980s and means 'astound' either with reference to the shock of a blow to the mouth, or to the action of clapping a hand to one's mouth in astonishment.

gob[2] [late Middle English] This *gob* meaning 'lump' is from Old French *gobe* 'mouthful, lump', from *gober* 'to swallow, gulp'. The origin is perhaps Celtic. The verb **gobble** 'eat rapidly' (early 17th century) is probably based on *gob*; it may have influenced the *gobble* which is imitative of the sound made by a turkey (late 17th century).

goblet [late Middle English] This comes from Old French *gobelet*, a diminutive of *gobel* 'cup', of which the origin is unknown.

goblin [Middle English] *Goblin* is from Old French *gobelin*; it is possibly related to German *Kobold* describing a spirit of Germanic mythology who haunts houses or who lives underground in caves and mines, or it may be related to Greek *kobalos* 'mischievous goblin'. In medieval Latin *Gobelinus* occurs as the name of a mischievous spirit, said to haunt Évreux in northern France in the 12th century. The word **gremlin** in use since the 1940s was perhaps suggested by *goblin*.

God [Old English] Of Germanic origin, the word *God* is related to Dutch *god* and German *Gott*. The exclamation **gosh** (mid 18th century) is a euphemism for *God* as is late 18th-century **golly**.
■ **God's Acre**, is a phrase for the 'churchyard' dating from the early 17th century, from German *Gottesacker*, Dutch *Godsakker*.
■ **God Save the Queen** seems to have a 17th-century origin for the complete words and tune of this British national anthem. The ultimate origin is obscure: the phrase 'God save the King' occurs in various passages in the Old Testament, while as early as 1545 it was a watch-word in the navy, with 'long to reign over us' as a countersign.
■ **godsend** (early 19th century) is from *God's send*, that is 'what God has sent'.

gofer [1960s] This informal word for someone who runs errands is from *go for* (= go and fetch).

goggle [Middle English] The early sense was 'look to one side, squint': it is probably from a base symbolic of oscillating movement.

goitre [early 17th century] This comes from French. It is either a back-formation (by removal of the suffix) from *goitreux* 'having a goitre', or it comes from Old French *goitron* 'gullet': both are based on Latin *guttur* 'throat'.

gold [Old English] *Gold* is Germanic in origin and related to Dutch *goud* and German *Gold*, from an Indo-European root shared by *yellow*. **Golden** is Middle English and superseded the earlier *gilden*. The phrase *golden age* dates from the mid 16th century and refers to an idyllic period in the past: this translates the Greek and Roman poets' name for the first period of history, when the human race was believed to live in an ideal state.
➜ YELLOW

golf [late Middle English] This term was originally Scots: it is perhaps related to Dutch *kolf* 'club, bat', used as a term in several Dutch games; *golf*, however, is recorded before these games.

goo [early 20th century] This word for 'a sticky substance' was originally US and is perhaps from *burgoo*, a nautical slang term for porridge, based on Persian *bulgūr* 'bruised grain' (a word found in *bulgar wheat*).

good [Old English] Old English *gōd* has a Germanic source; it is related to Dutch *goed* and German *gut*. The phrase *the great and the good* 'all the distinguished and worthy people' often used ironically, dates from the mid 19th century. The noun **goodness**, spelt *gōdnes* in Old English, is sometimes used in exclamatory phrases where it refers to the goodness of God (e.g. *for goodness' sake*, *surely to goodness*). The compound:
■ **Good Friday** illustrates *good* in the sense 'holy, observed as a holy day'.

goodbye [late 16th century] *Goodbye* is a contraction of *God be with you!*; *good* was substituted into the phrase on the pattern of phrases such as *good morning*.

goon [mid 19th century] This may be from dialect *gooney* 'booby'; it was influenced by the subhuman cartoon character 'Alice the Goon', created by the American cartoonist E. C. Segar (1894–1938).

gopher [late 18th century] This zoological term is perhaps from Canadian French *gaufre* 'honeycomb': the gopher 'honeycombs' the ground with its burrows.

gore¹ [Old English] The current sense 'blood that has been shed' dates from the mid 16th century. Old English *gor* meant 'dung, dirt' and is Germanic in origin; it is related to Dutch *goor* and Swedish *gorr* 'muck, filth'.

gore² [late Middle English] The verb *gore* had the early sense 'stab, pierce': its origin is unknown.

gore³ [Old English] *Gore* 'a triangular piece of material' (as in *gored skirt*) was *gāra* in Old English and designated 'a triangular piece of land'. It is Germanic in origin and related to Dutch *geer* and German *Gehre*, also probably to Old English *gār* 'spear': a spearhead was triangular.

gorge [Middle English] (as a verb): The main noun use of *gorge* now is to describe a narrow valley between hills; this arose in the mid 18th century. An archaic use of the word however is as a word for 'throat' (from Old French *gorge* 'throat'). The verb comes from Old French *gorger*, from *gorge*, based on Latin *gurges* 'whirlpool'. In heraldry **gorged** (also based on French *gorge*) describes the neck encircled by a coronet or collar.

gorgeous [late 15th century] *Gorgeous* initially described sumptuous clothing. The word derives from Old French *gorgias* 'fine, elegant'; the origin remains unknown.

gorilla [mid 19th century] This is from an alleged African word for a wild or hairy person, found in the Greek account of the voyage of the Carthaginian explorer Hanno in the 5th or 6th century BC. It was adopted in 1847 as the specific name of the ape.

gormless [mid 18th century] The original spelling was *gaumless* made up of dialect *gaum* 'understanding' (from Old Norse *gaumr* 'care, heed') and the suffix *-less*.

gospel [Old English] Old English *gōdspel* is from *gōd* 'good' and *spel* 'news, a story', translating ecclesiastical Latin *bona annuntiatio* or *bonus nuntius*: these were used to gloss ecclesiastical Latin *evangelium*, from Greek *euangelion* 'good news'. After the vowel was shortened in Old English, the first syllable was mistaken for *god*.
→ SPELL²

gossamer [Middle English] This is apparently from *goose* and *summer*, perhaps from the time of year around St Martin's summer, that is early November, when geese were eaten: gossamer was common then.

gossip [late Old English] Late Old English *godsibb* meaning 'godfather, godmother, baptismal sponsor' was literally 'a person related to one in God', from *god* 'God' and *sibb* 'a relative'. In Middle English the sense was 'a close friend, a person with whom one gossips', hence 'a person who gossips', coming later, in the early 19th century, to mean 'idle talk' (from the verb which dates from the early 17th century).

gouge [late Middle English] This comes from Old French, from late Latin *gubia*, *gulbia*, perhaps of Celtic origin; comparable words are Old Irish *gulba* 'beak' and Welsh *gylf* 'beak, pointed instrument'.

gout [Middle English] This comes from Old French *goute*, from medieval Latin *gutta* whose literal meaning is 'a drop': gout was believed to be caused by the dropping of diseased matter from the blood into the joints.

govern [Middle English] *Govern* is from Old French *governer* (the base too of Middle English **government**), from Latin *gubernare* 'to steer, rule': the base verb is Greek *kubernan* 'to steer'. Middle English **governess** was originally spelt *governeress* meaning 'a female ruler': it is from Old French *governeresse*, the feminine of *governeour* 'governor' (which gave English **governor** in this same period), from Latin *gubernator*, from *gubernare*.

gown [Middle English] Old French *goune* is the source, from late Latin *gunna* 'fur garment'; it is probably related to Byzantine Greek *gouna* 'fur, fur-lined garment'.

grab [late 16th century] This verb corresponds to Middle Low German and Middle Dutch *grabben*; it is perhaps related to *grip*, *gripe*, and *grope*. The verb has been used since the 1970s in computing contexts to express the idea of capturing a frame of video or television footage to be stored in digitized form in computer memory.

grace [Middle English] *Grace* came via Old French from Latin *gratia* 'pleasing quality, favour, gratitude', from *gratus* 'pleasing, thankful'. The word once conveyed the sense 'attitude', 'way of proceeding' which is still reflected in the phrase *airs and graces* (Thackeray *Vanity Fair*: Old Sir Pitt ... chuckled at her airs and graces, and would laugh by the hour together at her assumptions of dignity and imitations of genteel life). Other semantic strands include 'gracefulness', 'favour' (as in *divine grace*), and 'thanks': this latter is illustrated in the phrase *say grace* which was originally, and until the 16th century, almost exclusively *say graces*.

Middle English **gracious** came via Old French from Latin *gratiosus* 'attracting favour, pleasing', from *gratia*. The word, since the mid 18th century, has been used as a substitute for the word *God* in exclamations such as *oh gracious!*, *gracious sake!*, *good gracious!* The phrase *gracious living* referring to an elegant way of life, arose in the 1930s.

grade [early 16th century] Latin *gradus* 'step' is the base of several words in English: *grade* (the direct source of which is French) was originally used as a unit of measurement of angles (a degree of arc); the term later (early 19th century) referred to degrees of merit or quality; the phrase *make the grade* arose in US English at the beginning of the 20th century. **Gradual** was already found from late Middle English and is from medieval Latin *gradualis*: the original sense of the adjective was 'arranged in degrees' developing from the late 17th century into 'taking place by degrees'. The noun refers to the altar steps in a church, from which the antiphons were sung. **Graduate** is also late Middle English from medieval Latin *graduare* 'take a degree'. **Gradation** dates from the mid 16th century and is from Latin *gradatio(n-)*; the noun **gradient** is recorded from the mid 19th century and is based on *grade*.

graffiti [mid 19th century] This is the adoption of an Italian word in the plural form (singular *graffito*), from *graffio* 'a scratch'.

graft[1] [late Middle English] The early spelling of this horticultural term was *graff*, from Old French *grafe*, via Latin from Greek *graphion* 'stylus, writing implement' (with reference to the tapered tip of the scion), from *graphein* 'write'. The final *-t* is typical of phonetic confusion between *-f* and *-ft* at the end of words; *tuft* is comparable. The use of the word in surgical contexts (e.g. *skin graft*) is recorded from the late 19th century.

graft[2] [mid 19th century] The *graft* which means 'work' is perhaps related to the phrase *spade's graft* 'the amount of earth that one stroke of a spade will move', based on Old Norse *groftr* 'digging'.

grain [Middle English] This word was used originally in the sense 'seed, grain of corn': it comes from Old French *grain*, from Latin *granum*. As well as meaning 'seed' or referring to particles resembling a seed (e.g. *grain of sand*), the word has been used to describe granular texture (as in photography or engraving). This extended into describing the arrangement of particles or fibres as in *grain of the wood*, giving idiomatic phrases such as *go against the grain* (mid 17th century).

gram [late 18th century] This metric unit of mass is from French *gramme*, from late Latin *gramma* 'a small weight', from Greek.

grammar [late Middle English] The source of this word is Old French *gramaire*, via Latin from Greek *grammatikē (tekhnē)* '(art) of letters', from *gramma, grammat-* 'letter of the alphabet, something written'. In early English *grammar* meant specifically Latin grammar as Latin was the only language taught grammatically. It was in the 17th century that it became a generic term where the language had to be specified (*Latin grammar, French grammar*). The adjective **grammatical** is not found before the early 16th century and is from late Latin *grammaticalis*, via Latin from Greek *grammatikos*, from *gramma*.
→ GLAMOUR

granary [late 16th century] *Granary* is from Latin *granarium*, from *granum* 'grain'.

grand [Middle English] *Grand* is from Old French *grant, grand*, from Latin *grandis* 'full-grown, big, great'. The original uses were to denote family relationships (e.g. *grand-niece* following Old French usage) and as a title (*the Grand*, translating Old French *le Grand*); this led to the senses 'of the highest rank' and 'of great importance'. The noun **grandeur** (from French, from *grand*) is recorded in use from the late 16th century denoting tall stature.

grandiose [mid 19th century] This is an adoption from French, from Italian *grandioso*, from *grande* 'grand'.

grange [Middle English] The early sense recorded was 'granary barn': it comes from Old French, from medieval Latin *granica (villa)* 'grain house or farm', based on Latin *granum* 'grain'.

granite [mid 17th century] *Granite* is from Italian *granito* whose literal meaning is 'grained', from *grano* 'a grain', from Latin *granum*.

granny [mid 17th century] This is based on *grannam*, representing a colloquial pronunciation of *grandam* (an archaic word for 'grandmother').

grant [Middle English] *Grant* is from Old French *granter* 'to consent to support', a variant of *creanter* 'to guarantee', based on Latin *credere* 'entrust'.

granule [mid 17th century] *Granule* is from late Latin *granulum*, a diminutive of Latin *granum* 'grain'. **Granular** dates from the late 18th century, based on late Latin *granulum*.

grape [Middle English] This is from an Old French word meaning 'bunch of grapes', a sense which was adopted into English. It is probably from *graper* 'gather (grapes)', from *grap* 'hook' (used in harvesting grapes). The origin is Germanic.

graphic [mid 17th century] *Graphic* came via Latin from Greek *graphikos*, from *graphē* 'writing, drawing'. The noun is often in the plural as *graphics*; it referred to *diagrams* as an aid to mathematical calculation in the late 19th century but became part of computing terminology from the 1960s. **Graph**, dating from the late 19th century and a common term in mathematics, is an abbreviation of *graphic formula*.

grapple [Middle English] *Grapple* was first used as a noun for a grappling hook: it is from Old French *grapil*, from Provençal, a diminutive of *grapa* 'hook'. It is Germanic in origin and related to *grape*. The verb dates from the mid 16th century.
→ GRAPE

grasp [late Middle English] *Grasp* may be related to *grope*. Examples from the late 17th century reflect the transferred sense 'understand, take in mentally'. The phrase *grasp the nettle* is recorded in the late 19th century.
→ GROPE

grass [Old English] Old English *græs* has a Germanic source; it is related to Dutch *gras*, German *Gras* and also ultimately to *green* and *grow*. The compound:
■ **grass widow** arose in the early 16th century as a phrase for an unmarried woman with a child. It derives perhaps from the idea of the couple having lain on the grass together instead of in bed. The current use referring to a wife whose husband is often away for long periods dates from the mid 19th century; Dutch *grasweduwe* and German *Strohwitwe* (literally 'straw widow') are comparable.

grate¹ [late Middle English] *Grate* 'to shred' is from Old French *grater*, of Germanic origin; it is related to German *kratzen* 'to scratch'. The verbal phrase *grate upon* 'irritate' is found from the early 17th century.

grate² [Middle English] This *grate* denoting a metal frame for holding fuel in a fireplace was originally a general word for 'a grating': it comes from Old French, based on Latin *cratis* 'hurdle'.

gratis [late Middle English] *Gratis* 'free' is a Latin word originally, a contraction of *gratiis* 'as a kindness', from *gratia* 'grace, kindness'.

gratitude [late Middle English] This has come into English from Old French, or from medieval Latin *gratitudo*, from Latin *gratus* 'pleasing, thankful'. This Latin adjective is also the base of late Middle English **gratify** which

at first meant 'make pleasing' (from French *gratifier* or Latin *gratificari* 'give or do as a favour') and mid 16th-century **grateful** (from obsolete *grate* 'pleasing, agreeable, thankful').

gratuitous [mid 17th century] This is from Latin *gratuitus* 'given freely, spontaneous' and the suffix *-ous*.

gratuity [late 15th century] In early examples the word denoted graciousness or favour: the source is Old French *gratuité* or medieval Latin *gratuitas* 'gift', from Latin *gratus* 'pleasing, thankful'.

grave¹ [Old English] Germanic in origin, Old English *græf* 'place of burial' is related to Dutch *graf* and German *Grab*.

grave² [late 15th century] *Grave* was originally used to describe a wound as 'severe, serious': the source is Old French *grave* or Latin *gravis* 'heavy, serious'.

gravel [Middle English] This is from an Old French diminutive of *grave*, a variant of Old French *greve* 'shore'.

gravity [late 15th century] *Gravity* was first used in the sense 'seriousness': it comes from Old French, or from Latin *gravitas* 'weight, seriousness', from *gravis* 'heavy'. The term in physics dates from the 17th century. Latin *gravitas* is also the base of **gravitate** (mid 17th century) from modern Latin *gravitare*.

gravy [Middle English] *Gravy* initially described a spicy sauce: it may be from a misreading (*gravé*) of Old French *grané*, probably from *grain* 'spice', from Latin *granum* 'grain'.

graze [Old English] Old English *grasian* 'eat grass' is from *græs* 'grass'. It may have led to the word **graze** meaning 'scrape and damage the skin' (from a notion of skimming the surface) dating from the late 16th century, as a specific use. Modern sense development of *graze* includes the notion of eating little and often at irregular intervals rather than at mealtimes (1970s) and sampling television programmes by switching from channel to channel (1980s).

grease [Middle English] *Grease* is from Old French *graisse*, based on Latin *crassus* 'thick, fat'. The phrase *grease somebody's palms* suggesting bribery dates from the early 16th century; *grease the wheels* meaning 'help something to go more smoothly' is found from the early 19th century.

great [Old English] Old English *grēat* 'big, coarse, thick, stout' has a West Germanic origin; it is related to Dutch *groot* and German *gross*. Colloquial use of *great* as an adverb meaning 'wonderfully, really well' (e.g. *doing* *great*) is originally part of US English from the 1940s.

greedy [Old English] Old English *grædig* is Germanic in origin. The noun **greed** is recorded from the late 16th century; it is a back-formation (by removal of the suffix) from *greedy*.

Greek [Old English] Old English *Grēcas* 'the Greeks' is from Latin *Graeci*, the name given by the Romans to the people who called themselves the Hellenes. The source is Greek *Graikoi*, which according to Aristotle was the prehistoric name of the Hellenes.

green [Old English] Old English *grēne* was the adjective spelling, *grēnian* the verb. Of Germanic origin, *green* is related to Dutch *groen*, German *grün*, as well as to *grass* and *grow*. It was often used to describe a sickly complexion in phrases such as *green and wan*, *green and pale*: this was indicative of fear, jealousy, a bad mood, or sickness. The compound:
■ **green-eyed monster** meaning 'jealousy' is from Shakespeare's *Othello* (O beware jealousy. It is the green eyed monster).

greet [Old English] Old English *grētan* 'approach, attack, or salute' is West Germanic origin; it is related to Dutch *groeten* and German *grüssen* 'to greet'. *Send greeting* is a phrase dating from Old English; the compound *greetings card* dates from the late 19th century.

gregarious [mid 17th century] This is based on Latin *gregarius* from *grex*, *greg-* 'a flock'.

gremlin [1940s]
→ GOBLIN

grenade [mid 16th century] The word *grenade* first described a 'pomegranate': it comes from a French alteration of Old French (*pome*) *grenate*, on the pattern of Spanish *granada*. The bomb was so named because of its shape, supposedly resembling a pomegranate. The term **grenadier** (from French) dates from the late 17th century, based on French *grenade*.

grey [Old English] Of Germanic origin, Old English *græg* is related to Dutch *grauw* and German *grau*. Its figurative use to mean 'dismal, sad' is found in examples from the early 18th century; it also has a connotation of 'faceless, anonymous' dating from the 1960s, first mentioned in connection with politicians.

grid [mid 19th century] This is a back-formation (by removal of the suffix) from Middle English **gridiron**, originally spelt *gredire* (an alteration of *gredile* 'griddle' by association with *iron*).

griddle [Middle English] This word was first used to denote a gridiron: it comes from Old

French *gredil*, from Latin *craticula*, a diminutive of *cratis* 'hurdle'.
→ CRATE; GRATE²; GRILL

grieve [Middle English] Early senses included 'harm, oppress'; *grieve* is from Old French *grever* 'to burden, encumber', based on Latin *gravare*, from *gravis* 'heavy, grave'. The Middle English noun **grief** 'hardship, hurt, sorrow' is from Old French *grief*, from *grever*. The phrase *come to grief* 'end in disaster' dates from the mid 19th century. **Grievance** (also Middle English when it included the sense 'injury') is from Old French *grevance*, from *grever*.
→ GRAVE²

grievous [Middle English] This formal word meaning 'very severe' (as in the legal phrase *grievous bodily harm*) comes from Old French *greveus*, from *grever* 'to burden, encumber'.
→ GRIEVE

grill [mid 17th century] The noun is from French *gril*, the verb form French *griller*, from Old French *graille* 'grille'.

grille [mid 17th century] This word meaning 'grating' is from French, from medieval Latin *craticula*, a diminutive of *cratis* 'hurdle'.
→ CRATE; GRATE²; GRIDDLE

grim [Old English] The origin of this word is Germanic; it is related to Dutch *grim* and German *grimm*. The word is used to mean 'uninviting' when describing scenes from the early 19th century. The idiomatic phrase 'hang or cling on like grim death' dates from the mid 19th century.

grimace [mid 17th century] This is the adoption of a French word, from Spanish *grimazo* 'caricature', from *grima* 'fright'.

grime [Middle English] This is from Middle Low German and Middle Dutch.

grin [Old English] Old English *grennian* of Germanic origin meant 'bare the teeth in pain or anger'; it is probably related to *groan*. The word **gurn** 'pull a grotesque face' which arose in the early 20th century, is a dialect variant of *grin*.

grind [Old English] Old English *grindan* is probably Germanic in origin. Although no cognates are known, it may be distantly related to Latin *frendere* 'rub away, gnash'.

grip [Old English] Old English forms included *grippa* (verb), *gripe* 'grasp, clutch' (noun), *gripa* 'handful, sheath'. The phrase *come to grips with* is from the image of hand-to-hand combat and dates from the mid 17th century. Figurative use of *lose one's grip* is found from the late 19th century.
→ GRIPE

gripe [Old English] Old English *grīpan* meant 'grasp, clutch'; the origin is Germanic and Dutch *grijpen*, German *greifen* 'seize' are related. The sense 'affect with intestinal pain' dates from the 17th century; the sense 'grumble' is of US origin and dates from the 1930s.
➔ GRIP; GROPE

grisly [Old English] Of Germanic origin, Old English *grislic* meant 'terrifying'; it is related to Dutch *griezelig*.

grit [Old English] Old English *grēot* 'sand, gravel' has a Germanic source; related words include German *Griess* and English *groats* 'hulled or crushed grain' (late Old English *grotan*). With reference to toughness of character, the word is originally US slang found from the early 19th century.

grizzle [mid 18th century] The verb *grizzle* meaning 'cry fitfully' had the early sense 'show the teeth, grin'; the origin remains unknown.

grizzled [late Middle English] This adjective meaning 'streaked with grey hair' is based on the Middle English adjective *grizzle* as in *grizzle-haired*, which derives from Old French *grisel*, from *gris* 'grey'. **Grizzly** (early 19th century) is also based on *grizzle*.

groan [Old English] Old English *grānian* has a Germanic origin; it is related to German *greinen* 'grizzle, whine', *grinsen* 'grin', and also probably to *grin*.

grocer [Middle English] Originally this word denoted 'a person who sold things in the gross' (= in large quantities). It comes from Old French *grossier*, from medieval Latin *grossarius*, from late Latin *grossus* 'gross'.

grog [mid 18th century] This word for alcoholic drink is said to be from *Old Grog*, the reputed nickname (given to him because of his grogram cloak) of Admiral Vernon (1684–1757): in 1740 he first ordered diluted rum to be served out to sailors instead of the traditional neat rum.

groin [late Middle English] The early spelling was *grynde*, perhaps from Old English *grynde* 'depression, abyss'.

grommet [early 17th century] First recorded in nautical use in the sense 'a circle of rope used as a fastening', *grommet* is from obsolete French *grommette*, from *gourmer* 'to curb'. The ultimate origin is unknown. Current senses ('eyelet', 'surgical tube') date from the mid 20th century.

groom [Middle English] The first sense recorded was 'boy', becoming later 'man, male servant'; the origin is unknown. It was in the early 17th century that examples of *groom* for *bridegroom* were first recorded.

groove [Middle English] An early *groove* was a mine or shaft. It comes from Dutch *groeve* 'furrow, pit'. The *groove* cut into a gramophone record (early 20th century) led to the phrase *in the groove* expressing the enjoyment of music played well, particularly jazz in early contexts.
➔ GRAVE[1]

grope [Old English] Old English *grāpian* has a West Germanic origin; it is related to *gripe*.
➔ GRIPE

gross [Middle English] The early sense was 'thick, massive, bulky'. The origin is Old French *gros, grosse* 'large, thick, coarse', from late Latin *grossus*. A recent colloquial use of *gross* is to mean 'disgusting': this arose in the US in the 1950s.

grotesque [mid 16th century] (as noun): This word comes from French *crotesque* which was the earliest spelling in English, from Italian *grottesca*. This formed part of the phrases *opera grottesca* 'work resembling that found in a grotto' and *pittura grottesca* 'painting resembling one found in a grotto'. 'Grotto' here probably denoted a room in an ancient Roman building revealed by excavations and containing murals in the grotesque style (interweaving human and animal forms with flowers and foliage). The informal 1960s word **grotty** is based on *grotesque*.

grotto [early 17th century] This is from Italian *grotta*, via Latin from Greek *kruptē*.
➔ CRYPT

grouch [late 19th century] *Grouch* is a variant of obsolete *grutch*, from Old French *grouchier* 'to grumble, murmur', of unknown origin. Early 19th-century **grouse** may be related.
➔ GRUDGE

ground [Old English] Old English *grund* has a Germanic source and is related to Dutch *grond* and German *Grund*. The main semantic nuances are: 'bottom' (*break ground*), 'foundation' (*grounds for divorce*), 'surface of the earth' (*above ground*), and 'soil' (*till the ground*).

group [late 17th century] French *groupe* is the source, from Italian *gruppo*, of Germanic origin; it is related to *crop*. The basic sense would appear to be 'lump' or 'mass'. In English specific senses associated with art came first (e.g. a group depicted in a design, a group of musical notes, a group of columns in architecture); wider use was transferred from these.
➔ CROP

grout [mid 17th century] This word for 'a mortar for filling crevices' is perhaps from obsolete *grout* 'sediment', (plural) 'dregs', or it may be related to French dialect *grouter* 'grout a wall'.

grove [Old English] Old English *grāf* is Germanic on origin. The phrase *groves of Academe* used to refer to the academic world translates Horace's *silvas Academi*.

grovel [Middle English] This is a back-formation (by removal of the suffix) from the obsolete adverb *grovelling* based on obsolete *groof*, *grufe* 'the face or front'. This element was found in the phrase *on grufe*, from Old Norse *á grúfu* 'face downwards'.

grow [Old English] Old English *grōwan* originally referred chiefly to plants. The origin of the word is Germanic; Dutch *groeien* is related.
→ GRASS; GREEN

grub [Middle English] *Grub* 'dig, poke' is perhaps related to Dutch *grobbelen* and to English *grave*. The compound:
■ **Grub Street** referring to a class of impoverished journalists and writers was the name of a street (which later changed to Milton Street) in Moorgate, London, where such authors lived in the 17th century.

grudge [late Middle English] This is a variant of obsolete *grutch* 'complain, murmur, grumble', from Old French *grouchier*, of unknown origin. The phrase *bear a grudge* is found in examples from the mid 17th century.
→ GROUCH

gruel [Middle English] This word describing a thin liquid food of oatmeal comes from Old French and is Germanic in origin. The adjective **gruelling** 'extremely tiring and demanding' dates from the mid 19th century and is from the verb *gruel* 'to exhaust, punish', from an old phrase *get one's gruel* 'receive one's punishment'.

gruesome [late 16th century] This is based on Scots *grue* 'to feel horror, shudder' (of Scandinavian origin). Rare before the late 18th century, the word was popularized by Sir Walter Scott (*Tales of my Landlord*: He's as grave and grewsome an auld Dutchman as e'er I saw).

gruff [late 15th century] 'Coarse-grained' was the meaning of *gruff* in early examples: it is from Flemish and Dutch *grof* 'coarse, rude', of West Germanic origin. The sense 'rough, surly' dates from the early 18th century.

grumble [late 16th century] This is based on obsolete *grumme*, which is probably of Germanic origin and related to Dutch *grommen*. The near-synonym **grump** dating from the early 18th century is imitative of inarticulate sounds expressing displeasure.

grunge [1960s] This word for grime is a back-formation (by removal of the suffix) from *grungy*, perhaps suggested by *grubby* and *dingy*. Its association with music dates from the 1970s but it was only popularized as a generic term from the 1990s due to the international success of several American groups particularly from Seattle.

grunt [Old English] Old English *grunnettan* is of Germanic origin and related to German *grunzen*; it was probably originally an imitative formation.

guarantee [late 17th century] The early sense recorded referred to a person as a 'guarantor'. The use of the word for 'something given or acting as security' dates from the early 19th century. The source is perhaps Spanish *garante*, corresponding to French *garant*, later influenced by French *garantie* 'guaranty'.
→ WARRANT

guard [late Middle English] 'Care, custody' was the early sense of *guard* from Old French *garde*, of West Germanic origin. The phrase *guard against* is found in examples from the early 18th century. Late Middle English **guardian** is from Old French *garden*, of Germanic origin.
→ WARD; WARDEN

gubbins [mid 16th century] This was initially a word for 'fragments'; it is from obsolete *gobbun* 'piece, slice, gob', from Old French. Current senses include 'miscellaneous items' and 'gadget': these date from the early 20th century.

guerrilla [early 19th century] This word for a member of an independent group taking part in irregular fighting is from a Spanish diminutive of *guerra* 'war'. It was introduced during the Peninsular War, a campaign waged on the Iberian peninsula between the French and the British assisted by Spanish and Portuguese forces from 1808 to 1814 during the Napoleonic Wars.

guess [Middle English] The origin of *guess* is uncertain; it is perhaps from Dutch *gissen* and is probably related to *get*. In the 14th century *guess* was the usual translation of Latin *aestimare*, which probably affected some of the senses. The phrase 'I guess' meaning 'I am pretty sure' originated in the northern US in the late 17th century.

guest [Old English] *Guest* is from Old Norse *gestr*, of Germanic origin; it is related to Dutch *gast* and German *Gast*, from an Indo-European root shared by Latin *hostis* 'enemy' (which originally meant 'stranger'). The notion of a *guest appearance* on stage as an occasional performer rather than as a member of the regular cast is found from the beginning of the 20th century. The phrase *be my guest* 'do as you wish' dates from the 1950s. The compound:

■ **guest house** was first used for an inn as well as a house or apartment for the reception of strangers. The modern sense describing a lodging house run commercially for paying guests dates from the 1920s.

guide [late Middle English] The noun is from Old French *guide*, the verb from Old French *guider*, of Germanic origin. The capitalized spelling *Guide* (originally as *Girl Guide*) has denoted a member of the Girl Guides Association (corresponding to the Scout Association) since the early 20th century. The movement was established in 1910 by Lord Baden-Powell with his wife and sister.

guild [late Old English] This is probably from Middle Low German and Middle Dutch *gilde*, of Germanic origin. The guilds mentioned pre-Conquest served much the same purpose as modern burial and benefit societies, but they also provided masses for the souls of the dead. They always had a strong religious element in their constitution; their meetings were apparently convivial. As they developed over time some became purely religious confraternities and some developed into municipal corporations. Post-Conquest the *guild of merchants* became an incorporated society giving exclusive trading rights to its members within the town (a practice already common on the Continent). The *trade guilds* came into prominence in the 14th century for people practising the same craft for the promotion of their common interests.
→ YIELD

guile [Middle English] This word for 'cunning intelligence' is from Old French, probably from Old Norse.
→ WILE

guillotine [late 18th century] This is from a French word for a device named after Joseph-Ignace *Guillotin* (1738–1814), the French physician who recommended its use for executions in 1789 at the time of the French Revolution. In the mid 19th century in the US, *guillotine* came to be used in political contexts, especially for a method of shortening the discussion of a bill in parliament by fixing a day when the Committee stage must close.

guilt [Old English] The origin of Old English *gylt* 'failure of duty', 'fault (of someone)' is unknown. No equivalent forms are known in other Germanic languages. Legal use of the term is recorded early; the phrase *guilt by association* is an example of a modern usage dating

from the 1940s. **Guilty** was spelt *gyltig* in Old English; its association with the conscience and feelings of guilt dates from the late 16th century (Shakespeare *Henry VI* part iii: Suspicion always haunts a guilty mind).

guise [Middle English] *Guise* is from Old French, of Germanic origin. Early senses included 'manner, way' and 'characteristic manner, custom': the latter became very common in the 16th century and first half of the 17th century (Pope translating Homer's *Odyssey*: It never was our guise To slight the poor, or ought humane despise).

gulf [late Middle English] This comes from Old French *golfe*, from Italian *golfo*, based on Greek *kolpos* 'bosom, gulf'. The current figurative meaning of a great division or difference between two groups is by association with the biblical reference in Luke 16:26 (Between you and us there is a great gulf set). Literally a *gulf* often describes a long landlocked portion of sea opening through a strait and it often takes its name from the adjoining land, e.g. *Persian Gulf*, the site of the *Gulf War* of 1991 following Iraq's invasion of Kuwait. The phrase *Gulf War Syndrome* was coined at this time, describing a range of symptoms affecting veterans of this conflict.

gullet [late Middle English] *Gullet* is from Old French *goulet*, a diminutive of *goule* 'throat', from Latin *gula*.

gullible [early 19th century] *Gullible* is based on the late 16th-century verb **gull** 'fool, deceive', of which the origin is unknown.

gully [mid 16th century] The early sense recorded was 'gullet': the source is French *goulet*.
→ GULLET

gulp [Middle English] This is probably from Middle Dutch *gulpen*, of imitative origin.

gum[1] [Middle English] *Gum* 'sticky secretion' is from Old French *gomme*, based on Latin *gummi* via Greek from Egyptian *kemai*. In confectionery *gum* was applied to a type of sweet pastille in the early 19th century; the use of the word for *chewing gum* is recorded from the mid 19th century in the US. The compound:

■ **gumshoe**, an informal North American English usage for a detective arose in the early 20th century and is taken from *gumshoes* referring to 'sneakers' and suggesting stealth.

gum[2] [Old English] Old English *gōma* referred to the 'inside of the mouth or throat'. It is Germanic in origin and related to German *Gaumen* 'roof of the mouth'.

gun [Middle English] Early spellings included *gunne* and *gonne*, perhaps from a pet form of the Scandinavian name *Gunnhildr*, from *gunnr* and *hildr*, both meaning 'war'. Female personal names were sometimes given to engines of war.

gunge [1960s] This word was perhaps suggested by *goo* and *gunk*.

gung-ho [Second World War] This expression meaning 'enthusiastic to take part' (usually in fighting) is from Chinese *gōnghé*, taken to mean 'work together' and adopted as a slogan by US Marines under General E. Carlson (1896–1947). He organised 'kung-hoi' meetings to discuss general problems and explain orders to promote cooperation.

gunk [1930s] This was originally a US usage and came from the proprietary name of a detergent.

gurgle [late Middle English] *Gurgle* is either imitative, or it comes directly from Dutch *gorgelen*, German *gurgeln*, or medieval Latin *gurgulare*: the common base is Latin *gurgulio* 'gullet'.

guru [early 17th century] This is from Hindi and Punjabi, from Sanskrit *guru* 'weighty, grave, dignified' (comparable with Latin *gravis*): this led to 'elder, teacher'.

gust [late 16th century] This is from Old Norse *gustr*, related to *gjósa* 'to gush'. The late appearance of the word in English may mean that it was preserved in nautical use or through dialect. The verb is found from the early 19th century (S. T. Coleridge *Letters*: The Pride, like the bottom-swell of our lake, gusts up again).

gusto [early 17th century] This is the adoption of an Italian word, from Latin *gustus* 'taste'. From the beginning it meant both 'particular liking (for something)' and 'keen enjoyment': the latter intensified sense became very common from the beginning of the 19th century.

gut [Old English] *Gut* is probably related to Old English *gēotan* 'to pour'. The word *guts* was used commonly for 'stomach, bowels'; it became more informal and came to mean 'force of character, courage' from the late 19th century. The notion of 'basic' as in *gut reaction* arose in the 1960s.

gutter [Middle English] The noun was a name for a 'watercourse' in early examples whether natural or artificial; in later use it became a 'brook, channel'. The figurative use associated with low birth (e.g. *only moneyed privilege had kept him out of the gutter*) dates from the mid 19th century. *Gutter* is from Old French *gotiere*, from Latin *gutta* 'a drop'. The verb dates from late Middle English, originally meaning 'cut grooves in' and later, in the early 18th century, it started to describe the action of a candle melting rapidly when becoming channelled on one side.

guttural [late 16th century] This is from French, or from medieval Latin *gutturalis*, from Latin *guttur* 'throat'.

guy¹ [early 19th century] This informal word for a 'man, person' was originally recorded to describe a figure representing *Guy* Fawkes, one of the conspirators in the Gunpowder Plot on 5 November 1605 when Catholic extremists intended to blow up James I and his parliament. A *guy* effigy is burnt traditionally each year on the same day in commemoration of the plot.

guy² [late Middle English] This *guy* as a term for a 'rope for steadying and guiding' is probably of Low German origin, related to Dutch *gei* 'brail' and German *Geitaue* 'brails': these are small ropes for temporarily furling a fore-and-aft sail.

guzzle [late 16th century] This comes perhaps from Old French *gosillier* 'chatter, vomit', from *gosier* 'throat', from late Latin *geusiae* 'cheeks'. It is recorded in dialect in English for 'throat' (mid 17th century) and as a verb 'throttle, strangle' (late 19th century).

gymkhana [mid 19th century] Urdu *gendkānah* 'racket court' (from Hindi *gemd* 'ball' and Persian *kānah* 'house') is the source of English *gymkhana*. The spelling was altered by association with *gymnastic*.

gymnasium [late 16th century] This word came via Latin from Greek *gumnasion*, from *gumnazein* 'exercise naked', from *gumnos* 'naked'. The abbreviation **gym** arose in the late 19th century. Other words dating from the same period as *gymnasium* are **gymnast** (from French *gymnaste* or Greek *gumnastēs* 'trainer of athletes', from *gumnazein*) and **gymnastic** (via Latin from Greek *gumnastikos*, from *gumnazein*).

gypsy [mid 16th century] This was originally *gipcyan*, short for *Egyptian*: gypsies were popularly supposed to have come from Egypt. The spelling *gipsy* has become common in recent years. The name given to the people by themselves is Romany: this is also the language of the gypsies, a greatly corrupted dialect of Hindi with a large number of words from various European languages. The plant **gypsywort** (late 18th century), a member of the mint family, derives its name from the reputation of having been used by gypsies to stain the skin brown.

gyrate [early 19th century] The Greek word *guros* meaning 'a ring' is the base of English *gyrate*. The direct source is Latin *gyrat-*, the past participial stem of *gyrare* 'to revolve'.

Hh

haberdasher [Middle English] This word is probably based on Anglo-Norman French *hapertas*, which may have been the name of a fabric: further details of the origin are unknown. In early use it was a term for a dealer in a variety of household goods, but in the course of the 16th century it also became applied specifically to a hatter. Current senses as a term for a dealer in dressmaking goods and, in North American usage, a dealer in men's clothing, date from the early 17th century.

habit [Middle English] *Habit* is from Old French *(h)abit*, from Latin *habitus* 'condition, appearance', from *habere* 'to have, consist of'. The word originally referred to 'dress or attire' characteristic of a particular profession or function, e.g. *a monk's habit*; later it came to mean 'physical or mental constitution'. It was in the late 16th century that *habit* referred to an habitual practice. The adjective **habitual** is recorded from late Middle English meaning 'part of one's character': this is from medieval Latin *habitualis*, from *habitus*.

habitation [late Middle English] This word came via Old French from Latin *habitatio(n-)*, from *habitare* 'to inhabit', the source too of **habitable** in the same period (via Old French from Latin *habitabilis*). The now common environmental term **habitat** was adopted from Latin in the late 18th century from its use in books written in Latin on flora and fauna: the literal meaning is 'it dwells', from *habitare*.

hack¹ [Old English] Old English *haccian* meant 'cut in pieces'. It is West Germanic in origin and related to Dutch *hakken* and German *hacken*. Slang use includes phrases such as *I can't hack it* meaning ' I can't cope with it'; this arose in US English in the 1950s. From the 1980s this word and the noun **hacker** have been adopted in computing contexts of gaining unauthorized access to data by 'cutting in' to program code.

hack² [Middle English] This *hack* may refer in a depreciative way to a journalist or serve as a term in horse-riding contexts. The first sense recorded was 'a horse for ordinary riding'; the application to journalism dates from the early 19th century. The word is an abbreviation of Middle English **hackney** which probably derives from *Hackney* in East London, where horses were pastured. Originally an ordinary riding horse (as opposed to a war horse or draught horse), a *hackney* was especially one available for hire: this gave *hackney carriage*. It also led to the verb *hackney* meaning 'use (a horse) for general purposes'; later this was extended to 'make commonplace by overuse' (e.g. *hackneyed old sayings*).

hackle [late Middle English] The early use of *hackle* was as a term for a long narrow feather on the neck or saddle of a domestic cock: it is a variant of the synonym *hatchel* (Middle English *hechele*) which is West Germanic in origin. The root is probably Germanic *hak-* 'prick, stab'. The idiomatic expression *his/her hackles rose* referring to a person's reaction of anger (an extension of the image of a cock's hackles rising aggressively) dates from the late 19th century.
→ HOOK

haemorrhage [late 17th century] This word is an alteration of obsolete *haemorrhagy*, via Latin from Greek *haimorrhagia*, from *haima* 'blood' and the stem of *rhēgnunai* 'to burst'.

haft [Old English] Old English *hæft* 'knife or dagger handle' is Germanic in origin and related to Dutch *heft*, *hecht* and German *Heft*. The semantic root would appear to be 'anything that is grasped or taken hold of'.
→ HEAVE

hag [Middle English] This word used disparagingly (*old hag*) is literally 'an evil spirit in female form, a witch': it derives perhaps from Old English *hægtesse*, *hegtes*, related to Dutch *heks* and German *Hexe* 'witch'. The ultimate origin remains unknown.

haggard [mid 16th century] First used in falconry to mean 'wild, untamed, having adult plumage', *haggard* is from French *hagard* and may be related to English *hedge*. Later it was influenced by *hag*. During the 17th century the word became applied to people, initially to the 'wild' expression of the eyes.

haggis [late Middle English] This word for a Scottish dish of chopped offal mixed with suet and oatmeal is probably from the earlier word *hag* meaning 'to hack, hew', from Old Norse *hǫggva*.

haggle [late 16th century] *Haggle* 'to dispute, bargain' included the sense 'hack, mangle, mutilate' in early examples: it comes from Old Norse *hǫggva* 'hew'.

hail¹ [Old English] The noun was *hagol* or *hægl* 'pellets of frozen rain' in Old English; the verb was *hagalian*: these forms are Germanic in origin and are related to Dutch *hagel* and German *Hagel*. Figurative use describing something falling like hail dates from the late 16th century (Shakespeare *A Lover's Complaint*: That not a heart which in his level came Could 'scape the hail of his all-hurting aim).

hail² [Middle English] This *hail* used in contexts of attracting attention is from the obsolete adjective *hail* 'healthy'. This occurred in greetings and toasts, such as Middle English *wæs hæil* (now *wassail*) 'be in (good) health!', from Old Norse *ves heill*. This formula and the reply *drinkhail* 'drink good health' were probably introduced by Danish-speaking inhabitants of England: the popular spread of the custom meant that by the 12th century the usage was considered by the Normans to be characteristic of Englishmen.
→ HALE; WHOLE

hair [Old English] Old English *hær* has a Germanic source; related forms are Dutch *haar* and German *Haar*. The plural *hairs* was used in early times similar to French usage of the plural *cheveux*. Of the idiomatic expressions, *not to turn a hair* was first applied (early 19th century) to horses who did not show any signs of sweating, i.e. the heat did not curl and roughen their coat (Jane Austen *Northanger Abbey*: Hot! he [*sc* a horse] had not turned a hair till we came to Walcot Church). The phrase *let one's hair down* started out as *let down the back hair* (mid 19th century) with the notion of relaxing and becoming less formal. From the 1990s *bad hair day* became popular in the context of any day when everything seems to go wrong from a personal point of view; it was originally a US usage.

halcyon [late Middle English] The first use of the word was as a name for a mythological bird said by ancient writers to breed in a nest floating on the sea at the winter solstice charming the wind and waves into calm for a fourteen-day period. It came via Latin from Greek *alkuōn* 'kingfisher' (sometimes spelt *halkuōn*) by association with *hals* 'sea' and *kuōn* 'conceiving'.

hale [Old English] *Hale* is a northern variant of *hāl* 'whole'. Early senses included 'free fom injury' and 'free from disease'. The word's use in the expression *hale and hearty* dates from the mid 19th century.
→ WHOLE

half [Old English] Old English *h(e)alf* is originally Germanic; related forms are Dutch *half* and German *halb* (adjectives). The earliest meaning of the Germanic base was 'side', which was a noun sense in Old English. Middle English **halve** is based on *half*.

hall [Old English] Old English *h(e)all* was originally a roofed space located in the centre of a community for the communal use of a tribal chief and his people. Of Germanic origin it is related to German *Halle*, Dutch *hall*, and to Norwegian and Swedish *hall*, from a root meaning 'conceal'. The word is evocative of space, illustrated by the now obsolete cry *a hall! a hall!* asking people to clear the way, for example to make way for dancing (Shakespeare *Romeo and Juliet*: A hall, a hall, give room, and foot it girls). *Hall* as a word for a lobby or vestibule in a house, dates from the mid 17th century.

hallmark [early 18th century] The word *hallmark* certifying a standard of purity of articles of gold, silver, or platinum comes from *Goldsmiths' Hall* in London, where articles were tested and stamped with a mark.

hallow [Old English] The Old English verb *hālgian* and noun *hālga* are Germanic originally, related to Dutch and German *heiligen* 'to hallow'. The word for the festival of **Halloween** dates from the late 18th century; it is a contraction of *All Hallow Even* 'the eve of All Saints' Day'. The noun *hallow* meant 'saint' until around 1500 after which it was rarely used.
→ HOLY

hallucination [early 17th century] The word *hallucination* is from Latin *hallucinatio(n-)*: this is from the verb *hallucinari* 'go astray in thought', from Greek *alussein* 'be uneasy or distraught'. The early sense of **hallucinate** recorded from the mid 17th century was 'be deceived, have illusions': the source is Latin *hallucinat-*, the past participial stem of *hallucinari*.

halo [mid 16th century] This was originally a circle of light such as that around the sun; it came via medieval Latin from Latin *halos*, from Greek *halōs* which referred to the 'disc of the sun or moon'. From around the middle of the 17th century, the word came to be applied to the circle of light depicted around Christ's head or those of the saints. Its use for an effect in photography is found from the 1940s.

halt [late 16th century] This word was originally found in the phrase *make halt*, from German *haltmachen*, from *halten* 'to hold'. This was military vocabulary (as in the command *company, halt!*) which then passed into hunting contexts, travelling, and gradually into general use. The archaic adjective *halt* meaning 'lame' (Tennyson *Guinevere*: If a man were halt or hunch'd) is from a different source and was first recorded in Old English as *halt* and *healt*, it is Germanic in origin.

halter [Old English] The Old English form was *hælftre* from a Germanic source meaning 'something by which to hold things'. It is related to German *Halfter*. The *f* was lost in Middle English, a process that also occurred in Middle Dutch and Middle High German.

ham¹ [Old English] Old English *ham*, *hom* was originally a word for the back of the knee, from a Germanic base meaning 'be crooked'. In the late 15th century the term came to refer to the back of the thigh, hence the thigh or hock of an animal. The compound:

■ **hamstring** used from the mid 16th century for any of the five tendons at the back of the knee or, in animals, the great tendon at the back of the hock, is recorded as a verb from the mid 17th century in the sense 'cut the hamstrings of' in order to lame. Figurative use expresses 'destroy the efficiency of (somebody or something)'.

ham² [late 19th century] This term used to describe an excessively theatrical actor was originally a US usage perhaps by using the first syllable of *amateur*; the US slang term *hamfatter* 'inexpert performer' may also be a corruption of this. The sense 'amateur radio operator' dates from the early 20th century.

hamlet [Middle English] *Hamlet* is from Old French *hamelet*, a diminutive of *hamel* 'little village'; it is related to *home* which was *hám* in Old English.

hammer [Old English] Old English *hamor*, *hamer* has a Germanic origin; related forms are Dutch *hamer*, German *Hammer*, and Old Norse *hamarr* 'rock, crag'. The original sense was probably 'stone tool, stone weapon'. The expression *hammer and tongs* meaning 'with energy and speed' (early 18th century) is by association with the blacksmith showering blows on the iron taken by the help of tongs from the fire.

hammock [mid 16th century] The Spanish form *hamaca* was in use as the early spelling; the word came via Spanish from Taino (= an extinct Caribbean language) *hamaka*; the last syllable was altered in the 16th century conforming to English words ending in *-ock*.

hamper¹ [Middle English] This word, now used for a large carrier of food and picnic utensils, at first defined any large case or casket but from 1500 was usually of wickerwork. The origin is Anglo-Norman French *hanaper* 'case for a goblet', from Old French *hanap* 'goblet', Germanic originally.

hamper² [late Middle English] This word now used to mean 'impede progress' originally meant 'shackle, entangle, catch'. It was first found in northern writers and is perhaps related to German *hemmen* 'restrain'.

hand [Old English] Old English *hand*, *hond* is Germanic in origin, related forms are Dutch *hand* and German *Hand*. This is one of the elements of Middle English **handicraft**, an alteration of *handcraft* formed on the pattern of **handiwork**. In Old English the latter was spelt *handgeweorc*, the element *geweorc* meaning 'something made': this was interpreted in the 16th century as *handy* and *work* meaning literally 'a thing made manually'. **Handy** came to mean 'convenient' in the late 17th century. Also based on *hand* is Old English **handle**: this gained the colloquial sense 'title' in the early 19th century (e.g. *a handle to one's name*) and included 'nickname' as one of its senses by the late 19th century.

handicap [mid 17th century] This apparently comes from the phrase *hand in cap*, originally a pastime in which one person claimed an article belonging to another and offered something in exchange, any difference in value being decided by an umpire. All three deposited forfeit money in a cap; the two opponents showed their agreement or disagreement with the valuation by bringing out their hands either full or empty. If both were the same, the umpire took the forfeit money; if not it went to the person who accepted the valuation. The term *handicap race* was applied from the late 18th century to a horse race in which an umpire decided the weight to be carried by each horse, the owners showing acceptance or dissent in a similar way. By the late 19th century *handicap* came to mean the extra weight given to the superior horse.

handle [Old English]
➔ HAND

handsome [Middle English] *Handsome* is based on *hand*. The original sense was 'easy to handle or use', which led to the word being used in some contexts to mean 'suitable' and 'apt, clever' in the mid 16th century. The current appreciatory uses ('good-looking', 'striking, of fine quality') followed soon after.

hang [Old English] Old English *hangian* was an intransitive verb of West Germanic origin, related to Dutch and German *hangen*: it was reinforced by the Old Norse transitive verb *hanga*. The past tense is sometimes found now as *hung* and sometimes as *hanged*. This is due partly to development of weak and strong verb inflections: the northern strong past participle inflection *hung* penetrated into general English in the 16th century which led to the new past tense *hung*. *Hanged* persisted probably through its retention and use, despite being generally archaic, in the law courts: it remains a specialized use in the context of capital punishment.

hangar [late 17th century] This was originally 'a shelter'. The word comes from French; it is probably from Germanic bases meaning 'hamlet' and 'enclosure'.

hank [Middle English] *Hank* was found in the 14th century apparently from Old Norse *hǫnk*. Swedish *hank* 'string' and Danish *hank* 'handle (of a basket), ear (of a pot)' are associated forms.

hanker [early 17th century] This is probably related to *hang*; Dutch *hunkeren* is associated. The notion is one of 'hanging' on the periphery of something, longing to participate.

hanky-panky [mid 19th century] This may be an alteration of *hokey-pokey*. It started out referring to 'jugglery' or 'underhand dealing'. Its association with sexual activity dates from the 1930s.

haphazard [late 16th century] This word expressing the unpredictable nature of an outcome is composed of Middle English *hap* 'luck, fortune' (from Old Norse *happ*) and *hazard*.

hapless [late Middle English] This is based on Middle English *hap* in the early sense 'good fortune'.
→ HAPHAZARD

happen [late Middle English] This spelling superseded the verb *hap*: it is based on the now archaic noun *hap* 'luck'. The early sense was 'occur by chance'. The phrase *it's all happening* dates from the 1960s.
→ HAPHAZARD

happy [Middle English] The early sense of *happy* was 'lucky'. It derives from the noun *hap* 'luck'.
→ HAPHAZARD

harangue [late Middle English] This word, first found in Scottish writers, is from Old French *arenge*, from medieval Latin *harenga*. The origin is perhaps Germanic. Its spelling was later altered to conform with the modern French form *harangue*.

harass [early 17th century] The source of *harass* is French *harasser*, perhaps from *harer* 'set a dog on'. This is from Germanic *hare* used as a cry of encouragement to a dog to attack. Early senses included 'to weary, tire out' but the notion of intimidation of people arose during the 19th century, illustrated commonly from the 1970s in the phrase *sexual harassment*

describing unwanted and persistent offensive sexual advances or bullying.

harbinger [Middle English] This comes from Old French *herbergere*, from *herbergier* 'provide lodging for', from *herberge* 'lodging': the origin here is Old Saxon *heriberga* 'shelter for an army, lodging' (from *heri* 'army' and a Germanic base meaning 'fortified place'). The term was originally applied to a person who provided lodging, later to somebody who went ahead to find lodgings for a group such as an army or a nobleman and his retinue: this gave rise to the sense 'herald' recorded from the mid 16th century.
→ HARBOUR

harbour [late Old English] Of Germanic origin, Old English *hereborg* was 'a shelter, refuge'; the verb was *herebeorgian* 'occupy shelter': these forms are related to Dutch *herberge* and German *Herberge*, as well as to French *auberge* 'inn'. The figurative verb use 'cherish privately' arose early and was used of both kind and evil thoughts; it gradually became associated most commonly with grievance and resentment.
→ HARBINGER

hard [Old English] Old English *h(e)ard* is Germanic in origin and related to Dutch *hard* and German *hart*. The main semantic strands are 'resisting force or pressure' (*hard substance*), 'severe; difficult to bear or deal with' (*hard life, hard case*), 'harsh' (*hard view, hard line*), and 'intense, strenuous' (*hard labour*).

hardy [Middle English] The early sense was 'bold, daring'; the form is from Old French *hardi*, the past participle of *hardir* 'become bold', of Germanic origin. The word has been used in horticultural contexts from the mid 17th century.
→ HARD

harem [mid 17th century] This is from Arabic *ḥaram*, *ḥarīm* which is literally 'prohibited' or 'a prohibited place', thus 'sanctuary, women's quarters' and, by extension, 'women'. The base verb is Arabic *ḥarama* 'be prohibited'.

harlequin [late 16th century] *Harlequin* is sometimes used as an adjective meaning 'in varied colours'. When capitalized the word is the name of a mute character, masked and dressed in a diamond-patterned costume, who played a leading role in the **harlequinade**, a section of a traditional pantomime; as pantomime developed from being a prologue into a dramatized story, the denouement included a transformation scene in which Harlequin and his mistress Columbine performed a dance. *Harlequin* comes from obsolete French, from the earlier word *Herlequin* (or *Hellequin*), the leader of a legendary troop of demon horsemen. It may ultimately be related to Old English *Herla cyning* 'King Herla', a mythical figure sometimes identified with Woden.

harlot [Middle English] 'Vagabond or beggar' was the early meaning of *harlot*; later it came to denote 'a lecherous man or woman', eventually specifying a 'promiscuous female'. It derives from Old French *harlot, herlot* 'young man, knave, vagabond'. Earlier details of the word's history are uncertain.

harm [Old English] Old English *hearm* (noun), *hearmian* (verb) are Germanic in origin; related words are German *Harm* and Old Norse *harmr* 'grief, sorrow'.

harmony [late Middle English] *Harmony* is via Old French from Latin *harmonia* 'joining, concord', from Greek, from *harmos* 'joint'. The adjective **harmonic** is recorded from the late 16th century in the senses 'relating to music' and 'musical': the form came via Latin from Greek *harmonikos*, from *harmonia*.

harness [Middle English] *Harness* is from Old French *harneis* 'military equipment', from Old Norse, composed of the elements *herr* 'army' and *nest* 'provisions'. In English the word was also used at first to describe the portable equipment of an army but this was only during the Middle English period. It also referred to the equipment of a horse for riding or driving but it gradually came to specify straps and fastenings.

harpoon [early 17th century] Originally this was a barbed dart or spear. It comes from French *harpon*, from *harpe* 'dog's claw, clamp', via Latin from Greek *harpē* 'sickle'.

harpy [late Middle English] A *harpy* is used to refer to a grasping unscrupulous woman; this is by association with the rapacious monster of Greek and Roman mythology depicted as a bird of prey with a woman's face. The word is from Latin *harpyia*, from the Greek plural *harpuiai* meaning 'snatchers'.

harridan [late 17th century] This word for a belligerent old woman was originally slang: it is perhaps from French *haridelle* 'old horse'.

harrow [Middle English] This term for an agricultural tool is from Old Norse *herfi*; it is obscurely related to Dutch *hark* 'rake'. The verb use 'to distress' dates from the early 16th century.

harsh [Middle English] *Harsh* is from Middle Low German *harsch* 'rough', the literal meaning of which was 'hairy', from *haer* 'hair'.

harum-scarum [late 17th century] This reduplication based on *hare* and *scare* was first used as an adverb in early examples recorded.

harvest [Old English] Old English *hærfest* 'autumn' is Germanic in origin; related forms include Dutch *herfst* and German *Herbst*, from an Indo-European root shared by Latin *carpere* 'pluck' and Greek *karpos* 'fruit'.

hassle [late 19th century] This was originally a dialect word in the sense 'hack or saw at'. The origin is unknown but it may be a blend of *haggle* and *tussle*.

hassock [Old English] The early use of Old English *hassuc* as a term for a firm clump of grass in marshy ground. The origin is unknown. It was at the beginning of the 16th century that *hassock* came to describe a thick firm cushion on which to rest the feet or kneel.

haste [Middle English] The noun *haste* is from Old French *haste*, the verb from Old French *haster*, of Germanic origin. Based on the noun is the contemporaneous word **hasty** from Old French *hasti, hastif*. The related verb **hasten** is found in examples from the mid 16th century as an extended form of *haste*, formed on the pattern of other verbs ending in *-en*.

hat [Old English] Old English *hætt* is Germanic in origin, related to Old Norse *hǫttr* 'hood'. The compound:
■ **hat-trick** originally referred in the late 19th century to the club presentation of a new hat (or some equivalent) to a bowler taking three wickets successively.
→ HOOD

hatch[1] [Old English] The word now describes an opening allowing through-passage, but in Old English *hæcc* was the lower half of a divided door. Of Germanic origin, it is related to Dutch *hek* 'paling, screen'.

hatch[2] [Middle English] This word used in the context of producing young from an egg was spelt *hacche* in Middle English; it is related to Swedish *häcka* and Danish *hække*.

hatch[3] [late 15th century] *Hatch* 'shade with parallel lines' was first used in the sense 'inlay with strips of metal': it comes from Old French *hacher* 'chop up', from *hache*.
→ HATCHET

hatchet [Middle English] This is from Old French *hachette*, a diminutive of *hache* 'axe', from medieval Latin *hapia*. The origin is Germanic.
■ **hatchet man** dates from the late 19th century in the US, derived figuratively from an early use of the phrase for 'a hired Chinese assassin' who carried a hatchet with the handle cut off. The usual extended sense (from the 1940s) is 'a journalist employed to attack a person's reputation'.

hate [Old English] Old English *hatian* (verb) and *hete* (noun) are Germanic in origin and related to Dutch *haten* (verb), German *hassen* (verb) and *Hass* 'hatred'. Middle English **hatred** is based on *hate*: the suffix *-red* is from Old English *ræden* 'condition'.

haughty [mid 16th century] This is an extended form of obsolete *haught* (which was formerly spelt *haut*): it comes from Old French, from Latin *altus* 'high'.

haul [mid 16th century] Originally used in the nautical sense 'trim sails for sailing closer to the wind', *haul* is a variant of the archaic verb *hale* 'drag forcibly' (from Old French *haler*).

haunch [Middle English] This comes from Old French *hanche* of Germanic origin. The early spelling in English was *hanch*; it was not displaced by *haunch* until the 18th century.

haunt [Middle English] The early sense was 'to frequent (a place)'. The source is Old French *hanter*, of Germanic origin; it is distantly related to *home*. The figurative use meaning 'constantly occupy one's thoughts' arose early in the word's history.
→ HOME

have [Old English] Old English *habban* is Germanic in origin, related to Dutch *hebben* and German *haben*. There is also probably a connection with English *heave*.
→ HEAVE

haven [late Old English] Old English *hæfen* is from Old Norse *hǫfn*; related to Dutch *haven* and German *Hafen* 'harbour'. The literal meaning in English is 'harbour' but the figurative generalization 'safe place' arose early.

haversack [mid 18th century] This is from French *havresac*, from obsolete German *Habersack* which described a bag used by soldiers to carry oats as horse feed. Dialect *Haber* 'oats' and *Sack* 'sack, bag' are the elements making up the German noun.

havoc [late Middle English] *Havoc* is from Anglo-Norman French *havok*, an alteration of Old French *havot* of unknown origin. The word was originally used in the phrase *cry havoc* (reflecting Old French *crier havot*): this meant 'to give an army the order *havoc*', the signal to start plundering.

hawk [late 15th century] The verb *hawk* meaning 'peddle' is a back-formation (by removal of the suffix) from **hawker**: this is first found in written examples in the early 16th century and is probably from Low German or Dutch and related to **huckster** (also of Low German origin and found in Middle English as a term for for a retailer at a stall).

hay [Old English] Old English *hēg*, *hīeg*, *hīg* is Germanic in origin; Dutch *hooi* and German *Heu* are related. The word:
■ **haywire** dates from the early 20th century in the US: its idiomatic application to mean 'erratic, out of control' is by association with hay-baling wire in makeshift repairs.
→ HEW

hazard [Middle English] This was initially a gambling game with two dice: it comes via Old French and Spanish from Arabic *az-zahr* 'chance, luck', either from Persian *zār* or Turkish *zar* 'dice'. **Hazardous** is recorded from the mid 16th century: this adjective is from French *hasardeux*, from *hasard* 'chance'.

haze [early 18th century] This was originally a word for fog or hoar frost: it is probably a back-formation (by removal of the suffix) from **hazy** which in the early 17th century was in nautical use meaning 'foggy'. The origin is unknown.

he [Old English] Old English *he*, *hē* has a Germanic source; a related form is Dutch *hij*. Old English **his** is the genitive singular form of *he*, *hē* 'he' and *hit* 'it'. Old English **him** is the dative singular form of these same forms. In the 10th century *him* started to be used for the accusative as well, in north-midland dialect; this continued to spread and before 1400 became the general literary form.

head [Old English] Of Germanic origin, Old English *hēafod* is related to Dutch *hoofd* and German *Haupt*. The semantic strands include: the literal meaning, an extension of this referring to anything resembling a head (e.g. *flower heads*, *nail head*), and figurative use (e.g. *head of the corporation*). Of the phrases *head to head* and *head over heels* date from the 18th century. The word **headlong** was *headling* in Middle English: the adverbial suffix *-ling* was altered in late Middle English by association with words ending in *-long*.

heal [Old English] Old English *hǣlan* meant 'restore to sound health'. Of Germanic origin, it is related to Dutch *heelen* and German *heilen*. **Health** (in Old English *hǣlth*) is related.
→ WHOLE

heap [Old English] The Old English noun *hēap* and verb *hēapian* are Germanic in origin; they are related to Dutch *hoop* and German *Haufen*, both nouns. The word is sometimes used to indicate a large number or amount (*heaps of time*); this is found from the mid 17th century. Colloquially a *heap* occasionally means 'a battered old car': this started out in US usage in the 1920s.

hear [Old English] Old English *hīeran*, *hēran* is Germanic in origin; it is related to Dutch *hooren* and German *hören*. The expression *Hear! Hear!* now used to express approval was originally (late 17th century) *Hear him! Hear him!* shouted out to draw attention to the speaker for example in the House of Commons.

hearken [Old English] Old English *heorcnian* is probably related to Middle English *hark* of Germanic origin and related to German *horchen*. The spelling with *ea* dating from the 16th century is due to association with *hear*.

hearse [Middle English] This comes from Anglo-Norman French *herce* 'harrow, frame', from Latin *hirpex* 'a kind of large rake', from Oscan *hirpus* 'wolf' (with reference to the animal's teeth). The earliest recorded use in English was as a term for a 'latticework canopy placed over the coffin (whilst in church) of a distinguished person': this probably arose from the late Middle English sense 'triangular frame (shaped like the ancient harrow) for carrying candles at certain services'. The current sense dates from the mid 17th century.

heart [Old English] Old English *heorte* is Germanic in origin, related to Dutch *hart* and German *Herz*, from an Indo-European root shared by Latin *cor*, *cord-* and Greek *kēr*, *kardia*.

hearth [Old English] Of West Germanic origin, Old English *heorth* is related to Dutch *haard* and German *Herd* 'floor, ground, fireplace'. The expression *hearth and home* is found from the mid 19th century.

heat [Old English] Old English *hætu* (noun), *hætan* (verb) are Germanic in origin; they are related to Dutch *hitte* (noun) and German *heizen* (verb). The popular quotation *If you can't stand the heat, get out of the kitchen* is associated with the Democratic statesman Harry S. Truman, the 33rd American President, but attributed by him to Harry Vaughan in 1952.
→ HOT

heath [Old English] Old English *hæth* is from a Germanic source; related forms are Dutch *heide* and German *Heide*. In Middle English *heath* was often contrasted as an area with *holt* or *wood*.

heathen [Old English] Old English *hæthen* is Germanic originally; it is related to Dutch *heiden* and German *Heide*. *Heathen* is generally regarded as a specifically Christian use of a Germanic adjective meaning 'inhabiting open country', from the base of *heath*.
→ HEATH

heave [Old English] Old English *hebban* is Germanic; it is related to Dutch *heffen* and German *heben* 'lift up'. The phrase:

■ **heave-ho** (late Middle English) is a combination of the imperative *heave!* and the natural exclamation *ho*. It was originally in a nautical phrase said when hauling a rope.

heaven [Old English] Related to Dutch *hemel* and German *Himmel*, Old English *heofon* is from a Germanic source. The word's use in exclamations such as *Heavens!* and *Heavens Above!* dates from the late 16th century.

heavy [Old English] Spelt *hefig* in Old English, *heavy* is of Germanic origin; it is related to Dutch *hevig*. Its use as a noun meaning 'a tough well built person' dates from the 1930s; the plural phrase *the heavies* has referred to the more serious newspapers from the 1950s.
→ HEAVE

heckle [Middle English] The early sense recorded for *heckle* was 'dress (flax) by splitting and straightening the fibres ready for spinning': it comes from *heckle* 'flax comb', a northern and eastern form of *hackle*. The sense 'interrupt (a public speaker) with aggressive questions to bring out weaknesses in the argument' arose in the mid 17th century; the word *tease* is comparable in its sense development.
→ HACKLE

hectic [late Middle English] The early spelling was *etik* which came via Old French from late Latin *hecticus*, from Greek *hektikos* 'habitual': the base is Greek *hexis* 'habit, state of mind or body'. The original sense was 'symptomatic of one's physical condition' associated specifically with the symptoms of tuberculosis (*hectic fever*); this led in the early 20th century to the sense 'characterized by feverish activity'.

hedge [Old English] Old English *hegg* is Germanic in origin and related to Dutch *heg* and German *Hecke*. Based on *hedge* is **hedgerow**, the second element here being obsolete *rew* 'hedgerow' which was assimilated to *row* 'line'.

heed [Old English] Old English *hedan* was originally intransitive; it is West Germanic in origin and related to Dutch *hoeden* and German *hüten*.

heel¹ [Old English] Old English *hēla*, *hæla* 'back part of the foot' is Germanic in origin; it is related to Dutch *hiel*. The word *heel* meaning 'despicable person' may be associated but its origin is uncertain: it is found in examples from the early 20th century.

heel² [Old English] The gardening term *heel* (as in *heel in new plants to prevent moisture loss from the roots*) was *helian* 'cover, hide' in Old English. Of Germanic origin, it is from an Indo-European root shared by Latin *celare* 'hide'.

hefty [mid 19th century] This was originally a US dialect word formed from late Middle English *heft* 'the weight of someone', a late derivative of *heave*, perhaps following the pattern of pairs such as *weave* and *weft*, *thieve* and *theft*.

height [Old English] Old English *hēhthu* meant 'top of something'. Of Germanic origin, it is related to Dutch *hoogte*.
→ HIGH

heinous [late Middle English] This comes from Old French *haineus*, from *hair* 'to hate', of Germanic origin.

heir [Middle English] *Heir* is via Old French from Latin *heres*. Based on *heir* is the compound:
■ **heirloom** (late Middle English); the second element *loom* formerly had the senses 'tool, heirloom'.

heist [mid 19th century] This word for 'a robbery' represented a local pronunciation of *hoist*; it was first used as slang in the US.
→ HOIST

helicopter [late 19th century] This word is from French *hélicoptère*, from Greek *helix* 'spiral' and *pteron* 'wing'.

hell [Old English] Old English *hel(l)* is Germanic in origin, related to Dutch *hel* and German *Hölle*, from an Indo-European root meaning 'to cover or hide'. Old Norse *Hel* was the proper name of the goddess of the infernal regions. The word **heck** (a euphemistic alteration of *hell*) arose in the late 19th century, originally part of northern English dialect.

hello [late 19th century] This is a variant (like *hallo*) of the earlier word *hollo*, related to *holla*.

helm [Old English] This nautical word in Old English was *helma* which is probably related to **helve** 'weapon handle' (in Old English *helfe*), related to *halter*.
→ HALTER

helmet [late Middle English] *Helmet* is from an Old French diminutive of *helme*, of Germanic origin; it is related to the Old English archaic synonym **helm** as well as Dutch *helm* and German *Helm*. They share an Indo-European root meaning 'to cover or hide'.

help [Old English] Old English *helpan* (verb), *help* (noun) are of Germanic origin; related to Dutch *helpen* and German *helfen*. The compound:
■ **helpmate** (spelt in the late 17th century *helpmeet*) is from an erroneous reading of Genesis 2:18, 20, where Adam's future wife is described as 'an help meet for him' (i.e. a suitable helper for him). The variant *helpmate* came into use in the early 18th century.

helter-skelter [late 16th century] This rhyming jingle of unknown origin was initially used as an adverb. It is perhaps symbolic of running feet or based on Middle English *skelte* 'hasten'.

hem [Old English] The sense 'border of a piece of cloth' was the first recorded. It is West Germanic in origin. Verb senses date from the mid 16th century.

henchman [Middle English] This is composed of Old English *hengest* 'male horse' and *man*, the original sense being probably 'groom'. In the mid 18th century the sense 'principal attendant of a Highland chief' was popularized by Sir Walter Scott: this gave rise to the current (originally US) usage meaning 'a follower ready to show fidelity by engaging in crime'.

her [Old English] Old English *hire* was the genitive and dative form of *hio*, *heo* 'she'.

herald [Middle English] The noun is from Old French *herault*, the verb from Old French *herauder*, of Germanic origin.

herb [Middle English] *Herb* came via Old French from Latin *herba* 'grass, green crops, herb'. Although *herb* has always been spelled with an *h*, pronunciation without it was usual until the 19th century and is still standard in the US. The word **herbal** was first recorded as a noun in the early 16th century: it comes from medieval Latin.

herd [Old English] Old English *heord* has a Germanic origin; it is related to German *Herde*. From the early 17th century *the herd* has sometimes referred to 'the common people', the rabble' (Shakespeare *Julius Caesar*: When he perceiv'd the common Herd was glad he refus'd the Crown).

here [Old English] Old English *hēr* is Germanic in origin and related to Dutch and German *hier*; it is apparently from the Germanic stem *hi-* 'this' but the nature of the formation is unclear. There are many idiomatic phrases incorporating the word *here*: for example, *here's to …* in toasts to somebody's health is recorded from the late 16th century (Shakespeare: *Romeo and Juliet*: Here's to my love). *Here, there, and everywhere* dates from the same period (Marlowe *Doctor Faustus*: That I may be here and there and everywhere). *Here today and gone tomorrow* dates from the late 17th century. The word **hither** (in Old English *hider*) is related to *here*.
→ HE

hereditary [late Middle English] *Hereditary* is from Latin *hereditarius*, from *hereditas* 'heirship, inheritance', from *heres*, *hered-* 'heir'. The form **heredity** is recorded from the late 18th century meaning 'hereditary character'; its use in biological contexts is found from the late 19th century: it comes via French from Latin *hereditas*.

heresy [Middle English] This comes from Old French *heresie*, based on Latin *haeresis* 'school of thought', from Greek *hairesis* 'choice': this same word in ecclesiastical Greek meant 'heretical sect'. The base verb is *haireomai* 'to choose, take for oneself'. **Heretic** is Middle English from Old French *heretique*, via ecclesiastical Latin from Greek *haeretikos* 'able to choose' (in ecclesiastical Greek 'heretical').

heritage [Middle English] This is from Old French *heritage*, from *heriter* 'inherit', from Latin *heres*, *hered-* 'heir'. *Heritage*, since the 1970s, has been popular in combinations such as *heritage centre*, *heritage coast*, *heritage trail* where there is focus on cultural heritage as worthy of preservation.

hermetic [mid 17th century] *Hermetic* commonly refers to a seal as 'complete and airtight'. As *Hermetic* it relates to an ancient occult tradition encompassing alchemy, astrology, and theosophy. It comes from modern Latin *hermeticus*, an irregular formation from *Hermes Trismegistus*, a legendary figure regarded by Neoplatonists and others as the author of certain works on astrology, magic, and alchemy.

hermit [Middle English] This is from Old French *hermite*, from late Latin *eremita*, from Greek *erēmitēs*, from *erēmos* 'solitary'.

hero [Middle English] Early use of *hero* was with mythological reference to men of superhuman strength or ability who were favoured by the Gods, described, for example, in Homer. The word came via Latin from Greek *hērōs*. It became applied to literary characters as the principle subject of a story or drama at the end of the 17th century. **Heroine** is recorded slightly earlier than this and is via French or Latin from Greek *hērōinē*, the feminine of *hērōs*. **Heroic** is late Middle English from Old French *heroique* or Latin *heroicus*, from Greek *hērōikos* 'relating to heroes' (from *hērōs* 'hero').

hesitate [early 17th century] This word comes from Latin *haesitare* 'to stick fast, leave undecided', from *haerere* 'to stick, stay'.

het up [mid 19th century] This comes from dialect *het* 'heated, hot' surviving in Scots and northern English.

heuristic [early 19th century] This word which means 'enabling somebody to learn something for themselves' is formed irregularly from Greek *heuriskein* 'to find'.

hew [Old English] Old English *hēawan* is Germanic in origin and related to Dutch *houwen* and German *hauen*.

heyday [late 16th century] In early use *heyday* referred to 'good spirits' or 'passion': it derives from archaic *heyday!*, an exclamation of joy or surprise.

hiatus [mid 16th century] This was originally 'a physical gap or opening': it comes from a Latin word meaning literally 'gaping', from *hiare* 'to gape'.

hibernate [early 19th century] This comes from Latin *hibernare*, from *hiberna* 'winter quarters', from *hibernus* 'wintry'.

hide[1] [Old English] The Old English verb *hȳdan* 'keep out of sight' has a West Germanic source. The children's game *hide-and-seek* (mid 17th century) was originally set in motion by the cry *all hid!* and this served as a name for the game for a while. (Shakespeare *Love's Labour's Lost*: All hid, all hid, an olde infant play).

hide[2] [Old English] Old English *hȳd* 'skin of an animal' has a Germanic source; related forms are Dutch *huid* and German *Haut*. The idiomatic phrase *neither hide nor hair* dates from the mid 19th century.

hideous [Middle English] This is from Old French *hidos*, *hideus*, from *hi(s)de* 'fear', the origin of which is unknown. The Middle English spelling was *hidous*, but the ending changed to *-eous* during the 16th century.

hierarchy [late Middle English] This came via Old French and medieval Latin from Greek *hierarkhia*, from *hierarkhēs* 'sacred ruler'. The earliest sense denoted a system of orders of angels and heavenly beings; other senses relating to organization according to status or similar classification date from the 17th century.

higgledy-piggledy [late 16th century] This is a rhyming jingle probably with reference to the herding together of pigs in a disorderly and confused way.

high [Old English] Old English *hēah* is Germanic in origin, related to Dutch *hoog* and German *hoch*. The sense describing an elated emotional state dates from the early 18th century; the association with a drug-enhanced state of euphoria is found from the 1930s. Amongst the idiomatic expressions are: *high and mighty* which in Middle English was first used with reference to dignity; it was later (19th century) that the sense 'arrogant' became a depreciative connotation. The phrase *high and dry* is from nautical contexts of the early 19th century.

hilarity [late Middle English] 'Cheerfulness' was the first sense recorded for *hilarity*. It comes from French *hilarité*, from Latin *hilaritas* 'cheerfulness, merriment', from *hilaris* 'cheerful'. **Hilarious** is recorded form the early 19th century meaning 'cheerful': it is based on Latin *hilaris*, from Greek *hilaros*. The sense 'exceedingly amusing' dates from the 1920s.

hill [Old English] Old English *hyll* is Germanic in origin; it comes from an Indo-European root shared by Latin *collis* and Greek *kolōnos* 'hill'. The expression *over the hill* was originally a US usage from the 1950s.

hind¹ [Middle English] *Hind* as in *hind leg* is perhaps a shortened form of Old English *behindan* 'behind'.
→ BEHIND

hind² [Old English] This zoological term for a female deer is Germanic in origin; it comes from an Indo-European root meaning 'hornless', shared by Greek *kemas* 'young deer'.

hinder [Old English] Germanic in origin, Old English *hindrian* meant 'injure, damage'; it is related to German *hindern*. The senses 'keep back, delay, impede, obstruct' are found in examples from late Middle English.
→ BEHIND

hinge [Middle English] This was spelt *henge* in Middle English; it is related to *hang*.
→ HANG

hint [early 17th century] The early sense was 'occasion, opportunity': it is apparently from obsolete *hent* 'grasp, get hold of', from Old English *hentan*, of Germanic origin; The basic notion is 'something that may be taken advantage of'.
→ HUNT

hippy [1950s] This is based on the originally US term *hip* meaning 'following the latest fashion'.

hire [Old English] Old English *hȳrian* 'employ (someone) for wages' and *hȳr* 'payment under contract for the use of something' are West Germanic in origin; they are related to Dutch *huren* (verb) and *huur* (noun).

hiss [late Middle English] This was first recorded as a verb. It is imitative of the sound made but was not recorded until the end of the 14th century. It was not known in the earlier stage of any Germanic language.

history [late Middle English] This word came via Latin from Greek *historia* 'finding out, narrative, history', from *histōr* 'learned, wise man', from an Indo-European root shared by *wit*. Also based on Greek *historia* are: late Middle English **historian** (from Old French *historien*, from Latin *historia*) and **historic** dating from the early 17th century in the sense 'relating to or in accordance with history' (via Latin from Greek *historikos*, from *historia*).

histrionic [mid 17th century] This word meaning 'over-theatrical' had the early sense 'dramatically exaggerated, hypocritical'. It derives from Late Latin *histrionicus*, from Latin *histrio(n-)* 'actor'.

hit [late Old English] The Old English spelling *hittan* had the sense 'come upon, find': it is from Old Norse *hitta* 'come upon, meet with', of unknown origin. The main strands of meaning in English are 'strike, reach with a blow' (Shakespeare *Twelfth Night*: O for a stone-bow to hit him in the eye), 'come upon' as in *hit the trail* (reflecting the Old Norse sense and mostly found from the early 16th century) and 'aim, direct one's course' (Thomas Hardy *Jude the Obscure*: I've seen her hit in and steer down the long slide on yonder pond).

hitch [Middle English] The early sense was 'lift up with a jerk'. The origin is unknown. The sense 'hitch-hike' dates from the 1930s.

hive [Old English] Old English *hȳf* as a receptacle for a swarm of bees is Germanic in origin. It is probably related to Old Norse *húfr* 'hull of a ship' and Latin *cupa* 'tub, cask'. Early *hives* were conical and made of straw.

hoard [Old English] This word has a Germanic source and is related to German *Hort* (noun), *horten* (verb). The words *hoard* and *horde* have some similarities in meaning and are pronounced the same, so they are therefore sometimes confused. A *hoard* is 'a secret stock or store of something', as in *a hoard of treasure*, while a *horde* is a disparaging word for 'a large group of people', as in *hordes of fans descended on the stage*. Instances of *hoard* being used instead of *horde* are not uncommon: around 10 per cent of citations for *hoard* in the British National Corpus are for the incorrect use.

hoarding [early 19th century] This word for a large board for displaying advertisements is based on obsolete *hoard* used in the same sense (which is probably based on Old French *hourd*).

hoarse [Old English] Old English *hās* is of Germanic origin, related to Dutch *hees*. The spelling with *r* was influenced in Middle English by an Old Norse cognate.

hoax [late 18th century] This was first used as a verb: it is probably a contraction of *hocus* although there is no direct evidence.

hob [late 16th century] This word commonly used for a cooking appliance, is an alteration of *hub*. In the late 17th century *hob* was 'a metal shelf by a fireplace' but earlier versions were in the form of a mass of clay behind the fire.

hobble [Middle English] Hobble is probably of Dutch or Low German origin and related to Dutch *hobbelen* 'rock from side to side'; this is taken to be a diminutive of *hobben* 'rock in the manner of a boat on the waves'. The word's specialized application to the tying together of a horse's legs to prevent it from straying dates from the early 19th century (the earlier spelling in this sense was *hopple*).

hobby [late Middle English] Early spellings included *hobyn* and *hoby*, from pet forms of the given name *Robin*. Originally (like *dobbin*) a word for 'pony', it came to denote a toy horse or hobby horse: this led in the early 19th century to the notion of 'a pastime, something done for pleasure'.

hobnob [early 19th century] The early meaning was 'drink together'. It is from the archaic phrase used by two people drinking each other's health: *hob or nob*, *hob and nob* which probably meant 'give and take' (from dialect *hab nab* 'have or not have').

hock [mid 19th century] This *hock* meaning 'deposit (something) with a pawnbroker' is from Dutch *hok* 'hutch, prison, debt'.

hocus [late 17th century] This is from an obsolete noun meaning 'trickery', from **hocus-pocus** (early 17th century): this is a representation of a pseudo-Latin phrase *hax pax max Deus adimax* used by conjurors as a magic formula.

hod [late 16th century] Hod is a variant of northern English dialect *hot* 'a basket for carrying earth': it comes from Old French *hotte* 'pannier' and is probably Germanic in origin.

hoe [Middle English] This comes from Old French *houe* of Germanic origin; it is related to German *Haue*.
→HEW

hoist [late 15th century] This is an alteration of dialect *hoise* which is probably from Dutch *hijsen* or Low German *hiesen*, but in fact recorded earlier. The association of lifting by means of a mechanical appliance is found from the late 16th century.

hoity-toity [mid 17th century] This was a noun in early use; the first sense recorded was 'boisterous or silly behaviour'. It comes from obsolete *hoit* 'indulge in riotous mirth'. The origin is unknown. An early example of the word's use to mean 'haughty' is found in Keats's *Cap and Bells* (1820): See what hoity-toity airs she took.

hold¹ [Old English] Old English *haldan*, *healdan* 'grasp, keep fast, keep in charge' is Germanic in origin and related to Dutch *houden* and German *halten*; the noun is partly from Old Norse *hald* 'hold, support, custody'. The original Germanic sense is accepted as being 'watch over' but the verb already had a diverse sense development in Old English.

hold² [late 16th century] This word for a large compartment in a ship is from obsolete *holl*, from Old English *hol* 'hole'. The addition of -d was due to association with the verb *hold* meaning 'grasp, keep'.

hole [Old English] Old English *hol* and *holian* (verb) are Germanic in origin, related to Dutch *hol* 'cave' or (as an adjective) 'hollow', and German *hohl* 'hollow', from an Indo-European root meaning 'cover, conceal'. Transferred uses of *hole* from the late 15th century added a notion of 'secrecy': it once referred to any place where unlawful activity took place such as unlicensed printing (late 17th century). There was also a notion of 'dinginess' with the sense 'dungeon' (early 16th century); this was also seen in the generalized sense 'dingy lodging place, dismal place' (early 17th century).

holiday [Old English] In Old English the spelling was *hāligdæg*, literally 'holy day'.
→HOLY

hollow [Old English] Old English *holh* 'cave' is obscurely related to *hole*. The adjective dates from Middle English when it was used literally as the opposite of *solid*; figurative use applied to people in the sense 'vain, lacking substance, insincere' (e.g. *hollow promises*) is found from the early 16th century.
→HOLE

holster [mid 17th century] This word corresponds to and is contemporary with Dutch *holster*, of unknown origin.

holt [late Middle English] This word for the den of an otter was used originally in dialect to mean 'a grip or hold'; it is a variant of *hold*.
→HOLD¹

holy [Old English] Old English *hālig* is Germanic in origin, related to Dutch and German *heilig*.
→WHOLE

homage [Middle English] This is from Old French, from medieval Latin *hominaticum* from *homo, homin-* 'man'. The original use of the word was for the ceremony in which a vassal declared himself to be his lord's 'man'.

home [Old English] Old English *hām* is Germanic in origin and related to Dutch *heem* and German *Heim*. Early use included reference to a collection of dwellings as a *home*, synonymous with the compound:

■ **homestead**, *hāmstede* in Old English meaning 'a settlement'.

homily [late Middle English] This word for a religious discourse intended to educate came via Old French from ecclesiastical Latin *homilia*, from the Greek word meaning 'discourse, conversation' (in ecclesiastical use 'sermon') from *homilos* 'crowd'.

honcho [1940s] This informal word is from Japanese *hanchō* 'group leader', a term brought back to the US by servicemen stationed in Japan during the occupation following the Second World War.

hone [Middle English] *Hone* is from Old English *hān* 'stone' (frequently applied originally to a stone serving as a landmark). It is recorded as meaning 'whetstone' for giving a fine edge to cutting tools during the 1300s. Of Germanic origin, it is related to Old Norse *hein*. The verb sense 'sharpen' is found from the early 19th century.

honesty [Middle English] This is from Old French *honeste*, from Latin *honestas*, from *honestus*, from *honos*. The original sense was 'honour, respectability', later 'decorum, virtue, chastity'. The plant *honesty* is so named from its diaphanous seed pods, translucency symbolizing lack of deceit. The adjective **honest** dates from the same period and was originally used in the sense 'held in or deserving of honour'. It comes via Old French from Latin *honestus*. The compound:
■ **honest broker** denoting an impartial mediator dates from the late 19th century as a translation of German *ehrlicher Makler* with reference to the Prussian minister and German statesman Bismarck: he was the driving force behind the unification of Germany, orchestrating wars with Denmark (1864), Austria (1866), and France (1870–1) to achieve this.
➔ HONOUR

honey [Old English] Old English *hunig* is Germanic in origin, related to Dutch *honig* and German *Honig*. Of the compounds:
■ **honeycomb** was *hunigcamb* in Old English.
■ **honeymoon** was originally, in the mid 16th century, the period of time following a wedding. The original reference was to 'sweet' affection changing like the moon which, no sooner full, begins to wane; later the sense came to specify 'the first month after marriage'.

honour [Middle English] This is from Old French *onor* (noun), *onorer* (verb), from Latin *honor*, the base too of Middle English **honourable** (via Old French from Latin *honorabilis*) and **honorific** (first recorded in the mid 17th century from Latin *honorificus*).

hood [Old English] Old English *hōd* has a West Germanic source; related forms are Dutch *hoed* and German *Hut* 'hat'. Based on *hood* is the verb:
■ **hoodwink** (mid 16th century) originally used in the sense 'to blindfold'; the second element is from an obsolete sense of *wink* 'close the eyes'.
➔ HAT

hoof [Old English] Old English *hōf* is Germanic in origin and related to Dutch *hoef* and German *Huf*. The phrase *hoof it* meaning 'walk' (as opposed to 'ride'), dates from the mid 17th century; its use to mean 'dance' is found from the 1920s.

hook [Old English] Of Germanic origin, Old English *hōc* is related to Dutch *hoek* 'corner, angle, projecting piece of land' and German *Haken* 'hook'. The phrase *by hook or by crook* suggests difficulty and intricate manoeuvring; it is recorded early in the word's development.

hoop [late Old English] Late Old English *hōp* is of West Germanic origin, related to Dutch *hoep*. Its association with women's fashion in holding skirts out to display their fullness dates from the mid 16th century, first in farthingales (16th to 17th centuries), then in hoop-skirts (18th century) and later in crinolines (19th century). The connection with bands of colour such as the *hooped caps* of horse-racing is found from the late 19th century.

hoot [Middle English] The early sense of *hoot* was 'make sounds of derision'; it may be imitative in origin.

hop [Old English] Of Germanic origin, Old English *hoppian* 'to spring' is related to German dialect *hopfen* and German *hopsen*. The expression *on the hop* dates from the mid 19th century.

horde [mid 16th century] This word originally referred to a tribe or troop of Tartar or other nomads who lived in tents or wagons migrating from place to place in search of new pasture or to plunder and wage war. The form comes from Polish *horda*, from Turkish *ordu* '(royal) camp'. *Golden Horde* was the name of a Tartar and Mongol army who took over Kiptchak maintaining an empire in eastern Russia and western and central Asia from the 13th century until 1480: the richness of the leader's camp gave the attribute *Golden*.

horizon [late Middle English] *Horizon* came via Old French from late Latin *horizon*, from Greek *horizōn (kuklos)* 'limiting (circle)'. **Horizontal**, recorded from the mid 16th century is from French, or from modern Latin *horizontalis*, from late Latin *horizon*.

horn [Old English] Germanic in origin, *horn* is related to Dutch *hoorn* and German *Horn*, from an Indo-European root shared by Latin *cornu* and Greek *keras*. In Scottish Law the *horn* was used from the late Middle English period in forms of legal process for the proclamation of outlawry; the verb *horn* is found recorded from the late 16th century in this same legal context and with proclaiming someone a rebel.

horoscope [Old English] This word came via Latin from Greek *hōroskopos*, from *hōra* 'time' and *skopos* 'observer'.

horror [Middle English] *Horror* came via Old French from Latin *horror*, from *horrere* 'tremble, shudder' and '(of hair) stand on end'. This Latin verb is the base of several words in English: Middle English **horrible** is via Old French from Latin *horribilis*; **horrid** in the late 16th century had the sense 'rough, bristling' and is from Latin *horridus*; **horrendous** (mid 17th century) is based on Latin *horrendus*, the gerundive of *horrere*; **horrific** (mid 17th century) is from Latin *horrificus* which also gave rise to **horrify** in the late 18th century (via Latin *horrificare*).

hose [Old English] Old English *hosa* is of Germanic origin, related to Dutch *hoos* 'stocking, water hose' and German *Hosen* 'trousers'. Originally singular, the word denoted a covering for the leg sometimes including the foot but sometimes only reaching as far as the ankle.

hospice [early 19th century] This is from French, from Latin *hospitium*, from *hospes, hospit-* 'host'.
→ HOST[1]

hospital [Middle English] *Hospital* came via Old French from medieval Latin *hospitale*, the neuter of Latin *hospitalis* 'hospitable', from *hospes, hospit-* 'host'. At first the word named a hospice or a hostel for the reception of pilgrims and travellers. It also came to describe a charitable institution for the housing of the needy: *Greenwich Hospital* for example was originally a home for superannuated seamen. From the early 16th century a *hospital* was also a charitable institution for the education of children, a term remaining in Scottish Law and the names of ancient institutions such as *Heriot's Hospital*, Edinburgh. Use of the word to denote an institution providing medical treatment dates from the mid 16th century.
→ HOST[1]

hospitality [late Middle English] *Hospitality* is from Old French *hospitalite*, from Latin *hospitalitas*, from *hospitalis* 'hospitable'.
→ HOSPITAL

host[1] [Middle English] This word for a person who receives and entertains guests is from Old French *hoste*, from Latin *hospes, hospit-* 'host, guest'.

host[2] [Middle English] This word for a 'crowd' is from Old French *ost, hoost*, from Latin *hostis* 'stranger, enemy' which later, in medieval Latin, came to mean 'army'.

hot [Old English] Old English *hāt* has a Germanic source and is related to Dutch *heet* and German *heiss*.

hotchpotch [late Middle English] This is a variant of the contemporaneous word **hotchpot** from Anglo-Norman French and Old French *hochepot*, from a combination of *hocher* 'to shake' (probably of Low German origin) and *pot* 'pot'.

hotel [mid 18th century] *Hotel* is from French *hôtel*, from Old French *hostel* (which also gave Middle English **hostel** 'lodging place'); the noun **hotelier** dates from the early 20th century from French *hôtelier*, from Old French *hostelier* 'innkeeper'.

hour [Middle English] *Hour* is from Anglo-Norman French *ure*, via Latin from Greek *hōra* 'season, hour'.

house [Old English] Old English *hūs* (noun), *hūsian* (verb) are Germanic in origin, related to Dutch *huis*, German *Haus* (nouns), and Dutch *huizen*, German *hausen* (verbs). The semantic root may be 'hide'. The word's use in theatre contexts meaning 'playhouse' or an 'audience' (e.g. *full house, well-received by the house*) dates from the mid 17th century.

how [Old English] Old English *hū* is of West Germanic origin; related to Dutch *hoe*.
→ WHO, WHAT

hub [early 16th century] Early use was as a term for 'a shelf at the side of a fireplace used for heating pans; a hob'. Its origin is unknown. It appears to have been a dialect word; it was not recorded in dictionaries until the 19th century when it appeared first in the American Webster of 1828.
→ HOB

huddle [late 16th century] The early sense was 'conceal'; it may be of Low German origin, ultimately perhaps from the root *hud-* 'to cover'.

hue [Old English] Old English *hīw, hēow* included the sense 'form, appearance'. Of Germanic origin, it is related to Swedish *hy* 'skin, complexion'. The sense 'colour, shade' dates from the mid 19th century. The phrase:
■ **hue and cry** is late Middle English from the Anglo-Norman French legal phrase *hu et cri*, literally 'outcry and cry', from Old French *hu* 'outcry' (from *huer* 'to shout').

hug [mid 16th century] This is probably of Scandinavian origin and related to Norwegian *hugga* 'comfort, console'.

huge [Middle English] This is a shortening of the synonymous Old French word *ahuge*, of unknown origin.

hulk [Old English] Old English *hulc* meant 'fast ship'; it was probably reinforced in Middle English by Middle Low German and Middle Dutch *hulk*. It is probably of Mediterranean origin and related to Greek *holkas* 'cargo ship'. The generalized use 'large unwieldy mass, large person' dates from late Middle English.

hull[1] [Middle English] This word for the main body of a ship is perhaps the same word as *hull* 'outer covering of a fruit' or it may be related to *hold*.
→ HOLD[2]

hull[2] [Old English] This word for the outer covering of a fruit was *hulu* in Old English, related to Dutch *huls*, German *Hülse* 'husk, pod' and German *Hülle* 'covering'.

human [late Middle English] The early spelling was *humaine*, from Old French *humain(e)*, from Latin *humanus*, from *homo* 'man, human being'. The present spelling became usual in the 18th century. The noun **humanity** is recorded from Middle English via Old French from Latin *humanitas*, from *humanus*.
→ HUMANE

humane [late Middle English] This was the earlier form of *human*; it became restricted to the senses 'showing compassion', 'without inflicting pain', and 'civilizing' in the 18th century.
→ HUMAN

humble [Middle English] *Humble* is from Old French, from Latin *humilis* 'low, lowly', from *humus* 'ground'. Middle English **humility** (via Old French) is also based on Latin *humilis*; so too **humiliate** (from late Latin *humiliare* 'make humble').

humid [late Middle English] *Humid* is from French *humide* or Latin *humidus*, from *humere* 'be moist'. **Humidity** (from Old French) dates from the same period.

humour [Middle English] This came via Old French from Latin *humor* 'moisture', from *humere* 'be moist'. The original sense was 'bodily fluid' surviving in *aqueous humour* and *vitreous humour*, fluids in the eyeball. It was used specifically for any of the cardinal humours which were thought to be the four chief fluids of the body (blood, phlegm, choler, and melancholy). This gave rise to the notion of 'mental disposition' (thought to be caused by the relative proportions of the humours). In the 16th century, sense development continued giving 'state of mind, mood' and 'whim, fancy', hence *to humour someone* 'to indulge a person's whim'. The association with amusement arose in the late 17th century.

hump [early 18th century] This is probably related to Low German *humpe* 'hump', also to Dutch *homp*, Low German *humpe* 'lump, hunk (of bread)'.

hundred [late Old English] This is composed of *hund* 'hundred' (from an Indo-European root shared with Latin *centum* and Greek *hekaton*) and a second element meaning 'number'. The word is Germanic in origin and related to Dutch *honderd* and German *hundert*. The noun sense 'subdivision of a county' (as in *Chiltern Hundreds*) is of uncertain origin: it may originally have been equivalent to a hundred hides of land. A hide is an ancient measure of land typically equal to between 60 and 100 acres, being the growing area which would support a family and its dependants. The manorial rights of *the Chiltern Hundreds* belonged to the Crown: the whole area contained the Chiltern Hills and included five hundreds (or strictly four and a half) in Oxfordshire and three in Buckinghamshire.

hunger [Old English] Old English *hungor* (noun), *hyngran* (verb) are originallly Germanic and related to Dutch *honger* and German *Hunger*. **Hungry** (in Old English *hungrig*) is of West Germanic origin, related to Dutch *hongerig* and German *hungrig*.

hunk [early 19th century] This is probably of Dutch or Low German origin.

hunky-dory [mid 19th century] This word meaning 'just fine' was originally US: *hunky* is from Dutch *honk* 'home, base', a term used in games; the origin of *dory* is unknown.

hunt [Old English] Old English *huntian* is Germanic in origin. The sense in change-ringing referring to changing the position of bells in a simple progression dates from the late 17th century is probably based on the idea of the bells pursuing one another.

hutch [Middle English] *Hutch* comes from Old French *huche*, from medieval Latin *hutica*, of unknown origin. The original sense was 'storage chest', surviving in North American usage.

hybrid [early 17th century] This was first used as a noun; it is from Latin *hybrida* 'offspring of a tame sow and wild boar, child of a freeman and slave, etc.'. Figurative use dates from the mid 19th century (Charles Darwin *Life and Letters*: I will tell you what you are, a hybrid, a complex cross of lawyer, poet, naturalist, and theologian!).

hydrant [early 19th century] This word was coined in French from Greek *hudōr* 'water'. The word **hydrate** is from the same Greek base and dates from the same period.

hydraulic [early 17th century] This is via Latin from Greek *hudraulikos* from *hudro-* 'water' and *aulos* 'pipe'. The Greek adjective was used as a noun for a type of musical instrument played by means of water; the extension to other kinds of water-driven engines is first found in Latin authors.

hygiene [late 16th century] *Hygiene* came via French from modern Latin *hygieina*, from Greek *hugieinē (tekhnē)* meaning '(art) of health', from *hugiēs* 'healthy'.

hymn [Old English] This came via Latin from Greek *humnos* 'ode or song in praise of a god or hero', used in the Septuagint (a Greek version of the Old Testament) to translate various Hebrew words, and hence in the New Testament and other Christian writings. It appears to have been in the early 16th century that the final *-n* was dropped in pronunciation.

WORDBUILDING

The prefix **hyper-** [from Greek *huper* 'over, beyond'] adds the sense

- **over; beyond** [hyperspace]
- **exceeding** [hypersonic]
- **relating to hypertext** [hyperlink]

---

hyphen [early 17th century] This word came into English via late Latin from Greek *huphen* 'together', from *hupo* 'under' and *hen* 'one'.

hypnotic [early 17th century] *Hypnotic* is from French *hypnotique*, via late Latin from Greek *hupnōtikos* 'narcotic, causing sleep', from *hupnoun* 'put to sleep'. The base is Greek *hupnos* 'sleep' which is also at the base of late 19th-century **hypnosis**.

hysteric [mid 17th century] The word *hysteric* came into English via Latin from Greek *husterikos* 'of the womb', from *hustera* 'womb': hysteria was thought to be specific to women and associated with the womb. The noun **hysteria** dates from the early 19th century, from Latin *hystericus*.

I i

I [Old English] Of Germanic origin, the personal pronoun *I* is related to Dutch *ik* and German *ich*, from an Indo-European root shared by Latin *ego* and Greek *egō*.
→ EGOISM

ice [Old English] Old English *īs* is related to Dutch *ijs* and German *Eis*. There are no certain cognates outside Germanic. The expression *break the ice* dates from the late 16th century; at first this referred to making a passage for boats, then it began to be used figuratively for making a start in some undertaking, eventually extending to its modern sense 'break through cold reserve'. The use of the word *ice* in confectionery, arose during the 18th century (Thackeray *Vanity Fair*: He went out and ate ices at a pastry-cook's shop). Based on *ice* is Middle English **icicle**. The second element is from the dialect word meaning *ickle* 'icicle' from Old English *gicel*. Spellings in Middle English included *ysse-íkkle* and *yse-yckel*; the word was apparently pronounced as if a compound of two words in the 17th century. Other combinations include:
■ **iceberg** (late 18th century) which is from Dutch *ijsberg*, from *ijs* 'ice' and *berg* 'hill'.
■ **ice cream** (mid 18th century) which is an alteration of *iced cream* 'cream cooled by means of ice'.
■ **ice house** (late 17th century) which was a structure partly or wholly underground, built with non-conducting walls for the storage of ice kept from the winter for use during the rest of the year.

icon [mid 16th century] An *icon* was originally a 'simile'. It came via Latin from Greek *eikōn* 'likeness, image'. In the early 17th century the Greek spelling was used in the title *Eikon Basilike* of a book purported to be meditations by Charles I, published at about the date when he was executed: the title is literally 'royal image'. It had such strong popular appeal that 47 editions were published; Parliament found it necessary to make reply with Milton's *Eikonoklastes* (literally 'image breaker') which refuted the earlier book paragraph by paragraph. Current senses of *icon* referring to representational symbols date from the mid 19th century onwards; use as a word to describe a person seen as representing a movement or culture is found from the 1950s.

idea [late Middle English] Early use of this word was as a term in philosophy adopted from Platonic thought: in this thinking an *idea* is an eternally existing pattern from which individual things derive their existence but are only imperfect copies. It comes via Latin from Greek *idea* 'form, pattern', from the base of *idein* 'to see'. The word **ideal** dates from the same period as a term in Platonic philosophy meaning 'existing as an archetype': it is from late Latin *idealis*, from Latin *idea*. **Idealism** is recorded from the late 18th century again as a philosophical term often contrasted with *realism*: this is from French *idéalisme* or German *Idealismus*, from late Latin *idealis*.

identical [late 16th century] The early sense recorded for *identical* was 'expressing an identity' in logic and maths. It comes from medieval Latin *identicus*, from late Latin *identitas*.
→ IDENTITY

identity [late 16th century] In early examples *identity* meant 'the quality of being identical': it comes from late Latin *identitas*, from Latin *idem* 'same'. The phrase *identity crisis* arose in the 1950s and, in the US during the 1980s *identity theft* was coined: this is the stealing of personal information as a means of perpetrating fraud. The verb **identify** is found from the mid 17th century in the sense 'treat as being identical with': this form is from medieval Latin *identificare*, from a combination of late Latin *identitas* and Latin -*ficare* (from *facere* 'make').

idiom [late 16th century] This comes from French *idiome*, or via late Latin from Greek *idiōma* 'private or peculiar phraseology', from *idiousthai* 'make one's own': the base is Greek *idios* 'own, private'. **Idiomatic** (early 18th century) is from Greek *idiōmatikos* 'peculiar, characteristic', from *idiōma*.

idiosyncracy [early 17th century] This was originally in the sense 'physical constitution peculiar to an individual'. The source is Greek *idiosunkrasia*, from *idios* 'own, private', *sun* 'with', and *krasis* 'mixture'.

idiot [Middle English] This was a word in Middle English for a person of low intelligence: it came via Old French from Latin *idiota* 'ignorant person', from Greek *idiōtēs* 'private person, layman, ignorant person': this is based on *idios* 'own, private'.

idle [Old English] Old English *īdel* included the sense 'empty, useless': it was often found in the combination *idle yelp* 'boasting'. Of West Germanic origin, it is related to Dutch *ijdel* 'vain, frivolous, useless' and German *eitel* 'bare, worthless'.

idol [Middle English] *Idol* is from Old French *idole*, from Latin *idolum* 'image, form' (used in ecclesiastical Latin in the sense 'idol'), from Greek *eidōlon*, from *eidos* 'form, shape'. Figurative use for a thing or person revered as an object of excessive devotion dates from the mid 16th century. **Idolater** is late Middle English from Old French *idolatre*, based on Greek *eidololatrēs*, from *eidōlon* and *latrēs* 'worshipper'.

idyll [late 16th century] This comes from Latin *idyllium* (which was the accepted spelling in English at first), from Greek *eidullion* 'a short descriptive poem', a diminutive of *eidos* 'form, picture'.

if [Old English] Old English *gif* is of Germanic origin; related to Dutch *of* and German *ob*. The informal word **iffy** meaning 'doubtful' is found in US usage from the 1930s.

ignition [early 17th century] *Ignition* initially denoted the heating of a substance to the point of combustion or chemical change. The word is from medieval Latin *ignitio(n-)*, from the verb *ignire* 'set on fire'. This Latin verb is the source of **ignite** which, in the mid 17th century, had the sense 'make intensely hot'. The base is Latin *ignis* 'fire'.

ignoble [late Middle English] The early sense of *ignoble* was 'of humble origin'. from French, or from Latin *ignobilis*, from *in-* 'not' and *gnobilis*, an older form of *nobilis* meaning 'noble'. Depreciative use dates from the late 16th century.

ignominious [late Middle English] This word comes from French *ignominieux* or Latin *ignominiosus*, from *ignominia*, made up of *in-* 'not' and a variant of *nomen* 'name'. **Ignominy** dates from the mid 16th century, from French *ignominie* or Latin *ignominia*.

ignoramus [late 16th century] This was first used as the endorsement formerly made by a Grand Jury on an indictment brought before them that they considered to be backed by insufficient evidence to bring before a petty jury. A Latin word, it means literally 'we do not know', which in legal use is 'we take no notice of it', from *ignorare* 'not to know'. The current phrase used by the Grand Jury is 'not a true bill' or 'not found' or 'no bill'. The modern sense may derive from the name of a character in George Ruggle's *Ignoramus*, a satirical comedy written in 1615 exposing lawyers' ignorance.

ignorance [Middle English] This came via Old French from Latin *ignorantia*, from *ignorant-*, the present participial stem of *ignorare* 'not to know', from *in-* 'not' and *gno-*, a base meaning 'know'. **Ignorant** (late Middle English) is via Old French from Latin *ignorant-*. The verb **ignore** dates from the late 15th century in the sense 'be ignorant of', from French *ignorer* or Latin *ignorare*; current senses conveying the notion 'refuse to acknowledge' date from the early 19th century.

ilk [Old English] Old English *ilca* meant 'same'. Of Germanic origin, it is related to *alike*. The phrase *of that ilk* meaning 'of the same place' is a Scots use often found in the name of landed families such as *Wemyss of that ilk* = Wemyss of Wemyss. The phrase *that ilk* meaning 'that set, that sort' is a popularized interpretation based on this use.
→ ALIKE

ill [Middle English] The early senses included 'wicked', 'malevolent', 'harmful', and 'difficult'. *Ill* comes from Old Norse *illr* 'evil, difficult' but the ultimate origin is unknown. Although *ill* has been synonymous with *evil* in some contexts since the 12th century, the two words are not related.

illegitimate [mid 16th century] This is from late Latin *illegitimus* (from *in-* 'not' and *legitimus* 'lawful'), suggested by *legitimate*. The use of the word to mean 'not born in wedlock' was the earliest sense in English.

illicit [early 16th century] *Illicit* is from French, or from Latin *illicitus* 'not allowed', from *in-* 'not' and *licitus*, the past participle of *licere* 'allow'.

illuminate [late Middle English] This comes from Latin *illuminat-*, the past participial stem of the verb *illuminare* 'to throw light on, brighten': the elements here are *in-* 'upon' and *lumen*, *lumin-* 'light'. The sense 'enlighten intellectually' dates from the mid 16th century. The Latin verb is the source too of Middle English **illumination** (via Old French from late Latin *illuminatio(n-)*) and **illumine** from the same period (from Old French *illuminer*). Reference to the decoration of an initial letter or word in a manuscript with brilliant colours is recorded towards the end of the 17th century; in this same period the plural *illuminations* is found as a term for decorative lights in a town as a symbol of festivity.

illusion [Middle English] The first sense recorded for *illusion* was 'deception, attempt to fool'. It came via Old French from Latin *illusio(n-)*, from *illudere* 'to mock, ridicule, make sport of', from *in-* 'against' and *ludere* 'play'. The prime current sense is 'a false idea or belief' (dating from the late 18th century) which is extended from 'deceptive appearance' (Shakespeare *Hamlet*: Stay illusion, If there be any good thing to be done ... Speak to me). The Latin verb *illudere* is also the source of the poetic **illude** (late Middle English), **illusory** (late 16th century from ecclesiastical Latin *illusorius*), and **illusive** (early 17th century from medieval Latin *illusivus*).

illustration [late Middle English] The core notion in *illustration* is one of 'light'; the early sense was 'illumination; spiritual or intellectual enlightenment', the sense history paralleling that of *illumination*. It came via Old French from Latin *illustratio(n-)*, from the verb *illustrare* 'light up' (from *in-* 'upon' and *lustrare* 'illuminate'). **Illustrate** (early 16th century) is from Latin *illustrare*: the early sense was 'shed light on' but the figurative 'elucidate and explain' soon developed. It was in the mid 17th century that the notion of elucidation became linked to drawings.

illustrious [mid 16th century] This word is based on Latin *illustris* 'clear, bright'. Its use to mean 'renowned, noble' is found from the late 16th century, and is sometimes found as a courtesy title.

image [Middle English] *Image* is from Old French, from Latin *imago* 'imitation, likeness, idea'. **Imagery** is also Middle English when it referred to 'statuary, carved images collectively': this is from Old French *imagerie*, from *imager* 'make an image', from *image*.
→ IMITATION

imagine [Middle English] Latin *imago, imagin-* 'image, idea' is the base of several words in English: *imagine* via Old French from a combination of Latin *imaginare* 'form an image of, represent' and *imaginari* 'picture to oneself'; **imagination** from the same period via Old French from Latin *imaginatio(n-)*, from the verb *imaginari*; **imaginative** (late Middle English) via Old French from medieval Latin *imaginativus* and **imaginary** (late Middle English) from Latin *imaginarius*.

imbecile [mid 16th century] Early use as an adjective was in the description 'physically weak'. The word came via French from Latin *imbecillus* 'weak, feeble', perhaps literally 'without a supporting staff' based on Latin *baculum* 'stick, staff'. The current sense conveying stupidity dates from the early 19th century.

imbibe [late Middle English] The senses 'absorb moisture', 'cause to absorb moisture' and 'take into solution' were the first recorded for *imbibe* which is from Latin *imbibere*. The elements in the formation are *in-* 'in' and *bibere* 'to drink'.

imbue [late Middle English] 'Saturate' was the early sense. The word is from French *imbu* 'moistened', from Latin *imbutus*, the past participle of *imbuere* 'to moisten'. The modern sense 'inspire (with a feeling or quality)' is found in examples from the mid 16th century (Milton *Paradise Lost*: Thy words with Grace Divine Imbu'd).

imitation [late Middle English] The source of this word is Latin *imitatio(n-)*, from the verb *imitari* 'to copy'. **Imitate** dates from the mid 16th century from the same Latin verb; it is related to Latin *imago* 'image, copy'.

immaculate [late Middle English] 'Free from moral stain' was the meaning in early examples. The source is Latin *immaculatus*, from *in-* 'not' and *maculatus* 'stained' (from *macula* 'spot'). The phrase *Immaculate Conception* referring to the conception of the Virgin Mary as free from the taint of original sin, is found from the late 17th century; it was declared an article of faith of the Roman Catholic Church in 1854. *Immaculate* 'spotlessly clean' dates from the early 18th century.

immature [mid 16th century] Early senses included 'premature' which almost always referred to death. It is from Latin *immaturus* 'untimely, unripe', from *in-* 'not' and *maturus* 'ripe'.

immediate [late Middle English] The first use recorded was 'nearest in space or order'. *Immediate* is from Old French *immediat*, or from late Latin *immediatus*, from *in-* 'not' and *mediatus* 'intervening' (the past participle of *mediare*). The use of *immediate* in time contexts meaning 'instant' dates from the mid 16th century.

immense [late Middle English] This word came via French from Latin *immensus* 'immeasurable', from *in-* 'not' and *mensus* 'measured' (the past participle of *metiri*). The word conveyed the meaning 'immeasurably large' at first. The slang use 'superlatively good' arose in the mid 18th century.

immersion [late 15th century] This comes from late Latin *immersio(n-)*, from *immergere* 'dip into', the source too of **immerse** in the early 17th century. The elements in the formation are *in-* 'in' and *mergere* 'to dip'. The word's use in education contexts (e.g. *immersion course*) began as a North American usage in the 1960s.

immigrate [early 17th century] This is from Latin *immigrare*, from *in-* 'into' and *migrare* 'migrate'. The word **immigrant** from the same Latin verb is recorded from the late 18th century, formed on the pattern of *emigrant*.

imminent [late Middle English] This is from Latin *imminent-*, the present participial stem of the verb *imminere* 'overhang, impend', from *in-* 'upon, towards' and *minere* 'to project'. This last element belongs to a group of cognate classical Latin words referring to 'jutting' and 'threatening': *mentum* 'chin', *minae* 'threats', and *mons* 'mount'.

immune [late Middle English] Latin *immunis* 'exempt from public service' (from *in-* 'not' and *munis* 'ready for service') is the source of *immune* and **immunity** (from Latin *immunitas*). The early sense of *immune* was 'free from (a liability)' and this general meaning was common from the 15th to 17th centuries. Senses relating to physiological resistance date from the late 19th century when the word was reintroduced (perhaps from French or German use) in connection with investigation into the nature of infectious diseases and their prevention by inoculation.

imp [Old English] Old English *impa*, *impe* meant 'young shoot, scion', the verb *impian* meant 'to graft', based on Greek *emphuein* 'to implant'. In late Middle English, the noun was used to mean 'a descendant', especially of a noble family, and later a child of the devil or a person regarded as such (Scott *Kenilworth*: Either Flibbertigibbet … or else an imp of the devil in good earnest). This led in the early 17th century to the sense 'a little devil' or 'mischievous child'.

impact [early 17th century] Verb use is recorded first in the sense 'press closely, fix firmly'. It comes from Latin *impact-*, the past participial stem of *impingere* 'drive in'. Figurative use of the noun *impact* for 'the effect of something on someone' dates from the early 19th century.
→ IMPINGE

impair [Middle English] In Middle English the spelling was *enpeire*; it comes from Old French *empeirier* 'make worse', based on late Latin *pejorare*, from Latin *pejor* 'worse'. The current spelling is due to association with words derived from Latin beginning with *im-*.

impale [mid 16th century] The early sense was 'enclose with stakes or pales'. The source is French *empaler* or medieval Latin *impalare*, from Latin *in-* 'in' and *palus* 'a stake'. The meaning 'thrust a stake through the body' is recorded from the late 17th century.

impart [late Middle English] 'Give a share of' was the sense in early examples; it is from Old French *impartir*, from Latin *impartire*. The elements here are *in-* 'in' and *pars*, *part-* 'part'. The use of the word in phrases such as *impart knowledge* date from the mid 16th century. The adjective **impartial** dates from the late 16th century meaning 'not taking one side or the

other' (Shakespeare *Richard II*: Impartial are our eyes and ears).

impatient [late Middle English] Early senses included 'lacking patience' and 'unbearable'. The word comes via Old French from Latin *impatient-* meaning 'not bearing, impatient', from *in-* 'not' and *pati* 'suffer, bear'. The notion of 'eagerness' is found in contexts from the late 16th century.

impeach [late Middle English] 'Hinder, prevent' was an early sense of *impeach*, which was formerly spelt *empeche*. It comes from Old French *empecher* 'impede', from late Latin *impedicare* 'catch, entangle' (based on *pedica* 'a fetter', from *pes*, *ped-* 'foot'). The sense 'accuse of treason against the state' is recorded from the late 16th century.
→ IMPEDE

impeccable [mid 16th century] The theological sense 'not liable to sin' was the first recorded for *impeccable* from Latin *impeccabilis*: the base elements are *in-* 'not' and *peccare* 'to sin'. The notion of 'faultless' is found in examples from the early 17th century.

impede [late 16th century] *Impede* comes from Latin *impedire* 'shackle the feet of', based on *pes*, *ped-* 'foot'. **Impediment** dates from late Middle English and is from Latin *impedimentum*, from *impedire*. Meaning 'hindrance', it is well-known from the Book of Common Prayer as part of the marriage service: If either of you do know of any impediment.
→ IMPEACH

impel [late Middle English] The early sense was 'propel'. The source is Latin *impellere*, from *in-* 'towards' and *pellere* 'to drive'.

impend [late 16th century] *Impend* is from Latin *impendere*, from *in-* 'towards, upon' and *pendere* 'to hang'. Figurative use ('be about to happen') has been much more common than the literal.

imperative [late Middle English] This was first used as a grammatical term to describe a mood of the verb used for ordering or suggesting: it is from late Latin *imperativus* literally 'specially ordered': this translated Greek *prostatikē enklisis* 'imperative mood', from *imperare* 'to command'. The base elements are *in-* 'towards' and *parare* 'make ready'.

imperfect [Middle English] Early spellings included *imparfit* and *imperfet* via Old French from Latin *imperfectus*: the elements in the formation are *in-* 'not' and *perfectus* 'completed'. The spelling change in the 16th century was due to association with the Latin form. Late Middle English **imperfection** came via Old

French from late Latin *imperfectio(n-)*, from *imperfectus*.

imperial [late Middle English] This came via Old French from Latin *imperialis*, from *imperium* 'command, authority, empire'. *Imperial* (like mid 16th-century **imperious** 'having a commanding demeanour' from Latin *imperiosus*) is related to *imperare* 'to command'.
→ EMPIRE

impersonal [late Middle English] *Impersonal* was first found as a term in grammar: it comes from late Latin *impersonalis*, from Latin *in-* 'not' and *personalis* 'relating to a person'.

impersonate [early 17th century] The early sense was 'personify'. The word is composed of the prefix *in-* 'into' and Latin *persona* 'person', on the pattern of *incorporate*.

impertinent [late Middle English] The first sense recorded was 'not pertinent to a particular matter'. The source is either Old French, or late Latin *impertinent-* meaning 'not having reference to', from Latin *in-* 'not' and *pertinere* 'pertain'. The early notion of 'not belonging' is illustrated in Coleridge's *Friend*: The more distant, disjointed and impertinent to each other and to any common purpose, will they appear. The current meaning 'insolent' is recorded from the late 17th century.
→ PERTAIN

impervious [mid 17th century] This is based on Latin *impervius*, from *in-* 'not' and *pervius* 'pervious'. Figurative and literal use have run in parallel.

impetuous [late Middle English] *Impetuous* is from Old French *impetueux*, from late Latin *impetuosus*, from *impetere* 'to assail, attack'. Early use was also in the sense 'having much impetus' found in descriptions of water or wind.

impetus [mid 17th century] This is an adoption of a Latin word meaning 'assault, force', from *impetere* 'assail', from *in-* 'towards' and *petere* 'seek'.

impinge [mid 16th century] *Impinge* is from Latin *impingere* 'drive something in or at', from *in-* 'into' and *pangere* 'fix, drive'. The word originally meant 'thrust at forcibly' which became 'come into forcible contact'; this led in the mid 18th century to 'encroach on' (Scott *Waverley*: Heaven forbid that I should do aught that might … impinge upon the right of my kinsman').

implacable [late Middle English] The source of English *implacable* is Latin *implacabilis* literally 'not appeasable' based on Latin *placare* 'appease'.

implant [late Middle English] The source is late Latin *implantare* 'engraft', from Latin *in-* 'into' and *plantare* 'to plant'. Use in surgical contexts dates from the late 19th century.

implement [late Middle English] The early use of *implement* was to refer to an 'article of furniture, equipment, or dress'. It is partly from the medieval Latin plural *implementa* and partly from late Latin *implementum* 'filling up, fulfilment': these both derive from Latin *implere* 'fill up', which later developed the sense 'employ'. The verb dates from the early 18th century.

implicate [late Middle English] *Implicate* is from Latin *implicatus*, the past participle of *implicare* 'fold in'. The original sense was 'entwine, entangle'; the earliest modern sense 'convey (a meaning) indirectly by what one says' dates from the early 17th century but appears earlier in **implication**. The early sense of this noun (from Latin *implicatio(n-)*, from *implicare*) was 'entwining, being entwined'.
→ EMPLOY; IMPLY.

implicit [late 16th century] The source of *implicit* is either French *implicite* or Latin *implicitus*, a later form of *implicatus* 'entwined' (the past participle of *implicare*). The early sense in English was 'entangled' (Milton *Paradise Lost*: The humble Shrub, And bush with frizl'd hair implicit). The current sense 'implied' is recorded from the late 17th century.
→ IMPLY

implode [late 19th century] Formed on the pattern of *explode*, *implode* is from the prefix *in-* 'within' and Latin *plodere* or *plaudere* 'to clap'.

implore [early 17th century] *Implore* is from French *implorer* or Latin *implorare* 'invoke with tears'. Sometimes the sense is 'beseech' (Shakespeare *Measure for Measure*: Implore her … that she make friends To the strict deputie).

imply [late Middle English] This word is from Old French *emplier*, from Latin *implicare*, from *in-* 'in' and *plicare* 'to fold'. The original sense was 'entwine, entangle'; in the 16th and 17th centuries the word also meant 'employ'.
→ EMPLOY; IMPLICATE

impolite [early 17th century] 'Unpolished' was the sense recorded in early examples. It comes from Latin *impolitus*, from *in-* 'not' and *politus* 'polished'. The notion of 'not polished in manners' (i.e. rude, uncivil) dates from the early 18th century.
→ POLITE

import [late Middle English] The first sense recorded was 'signify'. Latin *importare* 'bring in' is the source, which became in medieval Latin 'imply, mean, be of consequence' (from *in-* 'in' and *portare* 'carry'). The application of the word in international commerce dates from the mid 16th century.

important [late Middle English] This comes from medieval Latin *important-*, from the verb *importare* 'be of consequence', the source too of **importance** dating from the early 16th century (via French from medieval Latin *importantia*).

importune [mid 16th century] *Portunus*, the name of the god who protected harbours (from *portus* 'harbour') is at the base of *importune*. The safety and calm associated with this protection is negated in *inopportune* 'troublesome, bringing problems'. The word comes from French *importuner* or medieval Latin *importunari*, from Latin *importunus* 'inconvenient, unseasonable'.
→ OPPORTUNE

impose [late 15th century] The early meaning was 'impute'. The origin of the word is French *imposer*, from Latin *imponere* 'inflict, deceive' (from *in-* 'in, upon' and *ponere* 'put'); it was influenced by *impositus* 'inflicted' and Old French *poser* 'to place'. **Imposition** is late Middle English from Latin *impositio(n-)*, from the verb *imponere*.

impossible [Middle English] This is either from Old French, or from Latin *impossibilis*, from *in-* 'not' and *possibilis*. The word is often modified by an adverb specifying the context in which something is possible, e.g. *physically impossible, mathematically impossible*. Late Middle English **impossibility** is from Old French *impossibilite* or Latin *impossibilitas*, from *impossibilis*.
→ POSSIBLE

impostor [late 16th century] In early use this was spelt *imposture*. The source of the word is French *imposteur*, from late Latin *impostor*, a contraction of *impositor*: the base is Latin *imponere* 'deceive'.
→ IMPOSE

impotent [late Middle English] *Impotent* is via Old French from Latin *impotent-* 'powerless', from *in-* 'not' and *potent-* 'having power'. The word's use to refer to lack of sexual power dates from the early 17th century.
→ POTENT

impoverish [late Middle English] An early spelling included *empoverish*: the source is Old French *empoveriss-*, the lengthened stem of *empoverir* 'make poor', based on *povre* 'poor'.

impregnable [late Middle English] This comes from Old French *imprenable*, from *in-* 'not' and *prendre* 'take' (from Latin *prehendere*). The current spelling arose in the 16th century, perhaps influenced by Old French variants.

impregnate [early 17th century] 'Fill' was the first sense recorded for *impregnate* which comes from late Latin *impregnat-*, the past participial stem of *impregnare* 'make pregnant'.

impress [late Middle English] The early sense was 'apply with pressure'. *Impress* is from Old French *empresser*, from *em-* 'in' and *presser* 'to press', influenced by Latin *imprimere* 'press in'. The sense 'make (someone) feel admiration and respect' dates from the mid 18th century. Late Middle English **impression** is via Old French from Latin *impressio(n-)*, from *imprimere*. It was used as a word for a 'printed copy' from the mid 16th century. The phrase *under the impression that ...* is found from the mid 19th century. The term **Impressionism** applied to a style in painting is from French *impressionnisme*, from *impressionniste*: this was originally applied unfavourably to Monet's painting entitled *Impression: Soleil levant* (1872).
→ IMPRINT

imprint [late Middle English] This was originally spelt *emprint*, from Old French *empreinter*, based on Latin *imprimere*; this verb means literally 'press in' based on Latin *premere* 'to press'.

impromptu [mid 17th century] This word was first used as an adverb. It is from French, from Latin *in promptu* 'in readiness', from *promptus* 'prepared, ready'.
→ PROMPT

improper [late Middle English] This is from French *impropre* or Latin *improprius*, from *in-* 'not' and *proprius* 'one's own, proper'. The sense 'not in accordance with good manners' is found in examples from the mid 18th century.

improvement [late Middle English] The early spelling was *emprowement* used to mean 'profitable management or use, profit'. It derives from Anglo-Norman French, from *emprower* (based on Old French *prou* 'profit', ultimately from Latin *prodest* 'is of advantage'). **Improve** is recorded from the early 16th century when early spellings included *emprowe* and *improwe*, from Anglo-Norman French *emprower*. The ending *-owe* was changed to *-ove* under the influence of *prove*. The original sense was 'make a profit, increase the value of', subsequently 'make greater in amount or degree': this led to 'make or become better' from the early 17th century.

improvise [early 19th century] This comes from French *improviser* (or its source, Italian *improvvisare* from *improvviso* 'extempore') from Latin *improvisus* 'unforeseen'. The base is Latin *provisus*, the past participle of *providere* 'make preparation for'.

impudent [late Middle English] 'Immodest' and 'indelicate' were the senses reflected in early examples. The source is Latin *impudent-*, from *in-* 'not' and *pudent-* 'ashamed, modest' (from *pudere* 'be ashamed'). The notion 'disrespectful' is associated with the word from the mid 16th century.

impulsive [late Middle English] 'Tending to impel' was the first sense recorded: it comes from French *impulsif, -ive* or late Latin *impulsivus*, from Latin *impuls-* 'driven onwards'. The prime current sense 'acting without forethought' dates from the mid 18th century. **Impulse** (from Latin *impuls-* 'driven on') dates from the early 17th century; it was first used as a verb in the sense 'give an impulse to'; the noun is from *impulsus* 'impulsion, outward pressure', both from the verb *impellere*.

impunity [mid 16th century] This comes from Latin *impunitas*, from *impunis* 'unpunished'. The prefix *in-* 'not' is combined here with either *poena* 'penalty' or *punire* 'punish'.

impure [late Middle English] *Impure* meant 'dirty, containing offensive matter' in early examples. It is from Latin *impurus*, from *in-* 'not' and *purus* 'pure'. The same Latin base gave rise to late Middle English **impurity** from French *impurite* or Latin *impuritas*.

in [Old English] Old English *in* (preposition), *inn(e)* (adverb) are of Germanic origin; related forms are Dutch *in* (preposition) and German *ein* (adverb). These are from an Indo-European root shared by Latin *in* and Greek *en*. Old English **inner** (the early spellings of which included *innerra* and *innra*) is a comparative of *in*, and based on *in* is the Old English word **inning** (originally *innung* 'a putting or getting in'): the current cricketing sense dates from the mid 19th century. Compounds based on *in* include:

■ **indeed** recorded from Middle English when it was written in two words as *in deed*.

■ **indoor** found from the early 18th century was initially spelt *within-door*; this is also the base of **indoors** (late 18th century) which was written *within doors* in early examples. *See box opposite*

WORDBUILDING

The prefix **in-¹** [representing English *in* or the Latin preposition *in*] adds the sense

■ **in** [inborn]

■ **towards** [influx]

---

inadvertent [mid 17th century] This is from the prefix *in-* 'not' and Latin *advertent-*, the present participial stem of *advertere* 'turn the mind to'. The noun *inadvertence* was already long in use from late Middle English.

inane [mid 16th century] This is from Latin *inanis* 'empty, vain'. The sense 'silly, senseless' dates from the beginning of the 19th century (Shelley *Cenci*: Some inane and vacant smile).

inarticulate [early 17th century] The word is composed of the prefix *in-* 'not' and the adjective *articulate*; the sense 'not clearly pronounced' corresponds to that of late Latin *inarticulatus*.
→ ARTICULATION

inaugural [late 17th century] This is the adoption of a French word, based on *inaugurer* 'inaugurate', from Latin *inaugurare* 'take omens from the flight of birds'. This Latin verb also gave rise to **inaugurate** in the late 16th century: the base is Latin *augurare* 'to augur'.

incandescent [late 18th century] This comes from French, from Latin *incandescent-*, the present participial stem of *incandescere* 'glow', based on *candescere* 'become white' (from *candidus* 'white'). The prefix *in-* here intensifies the meaning.

incantation [late Middle English] This came via Old French from late Latin *incantatio(n-)*, from *incantare* 'chant, bewitch' based on *cantare* 'to sing'. The prefix *in-* (as in *incandescent*) intensifies the meaning.

incapacity [early 17th century] This word comes from French *incapacité* or late Latin *incapacitas*, from *in-* (expressing negation) and *capacitas*, based on Latin *capere* 'to hold'.
→ CAPACITY

incarcerate [mid 16th century] Latin *carcer* 'prison' is the base of this word from medieval Latin *incarcerare* 'imprison'.

incarnation [Middle English] This was first used as a term in Christian theology. It came via Old French from ecclesiastical Latin *incarnatio(n-)*, from the verb *incarnare* 'make flesh', the source of late Middle English **incarnate**. The formative elements are *in-* 'into' and *caro, carn-* 'flesh'.

incendiary [late Middle English] *Incendiary* is from Latin *incendiarius* 'causing conflagration', from *incendium* 'conflagration', from *incendere* 'set fire to'.

incense¹ [Middle English] This word for a substance burnt for its sweet smell was originally spelt *encense* and comes from Old French *encens*, from ecclesiastical Latin *incensum* 'something burnt, incense': this is the neuter past participle of *incendere* 'set fire to'. The base elements in the formation are *in-* 'in' and the base of *candere* 'to glow'.

WORDBUILDING

The prefix **in-²** [from Latin] adds the sense

■ **not** [infertile] *see table below*

■ **without** [inappreciation]

Common words prefixed by or incorporating *in-* = not

From Latin

Middle English	innumerable
late Middle English	illiterate
late Middle English	immortal
late Middle English	immutable
late Middle English	imprudent
late Middle English	incomplete
late Middle English	incredible
late Middle English	inexcusable
late Middle English	infinite
late Middle English	inflexible
late Middle English	inseparable
late Middle English	insoluble
late Middle English	intolerable
late Middle English	inviolable
late Middle English	irrational
late Middle English	irreligious
late Middle English	irreverent
late Middle English	irrevocable
late 15th century	indeterminable
late 15th century	indigestible
late 15th century	inimitable
late 15th century	intractable
mid 16th century	indistinct
late 16th century	immodest
late 16th century	improbable
late 16th century	inconsolable
early 17th century	inaudible
early 17th century	inclement
mid 17th century	insalubrious
mid 17th century	insincere
mid 18th century	intolerant

From Old French

Middle English	incorrigible
Middle English	incorruptible
Middle English	incurable
late Middle English	inaccessible
late Middle English	inequality
late Middle English	invariable

From French

late 16th century	infertile
late 16th century	inhospitable
mid 17th century	irreproachable
late 17th century	incontestable
mid 18th century	indecision

From Old French or Latin

late Middle English	indubitable
late Middle English	insatiable
late Middle English	interminable

From Old French, from Latin

Middle English	invisible
late Middle English	impenetrable
late Middle English	inconstant
late Middle English	inestimable
late Middle English	inexpert
late Middle English	irreparable

From French or Latin

late 16th century	indecent

From French, from Latin

early 16th century	inelegant

From French, from medieval Latin

late Middle English	imperceptible

From French or medieval Latin

early 16th century	impalpable
early 17th century	illegal

From French or late Latin

mid 17th century	inconvertible
late 17th century	impermeable

From late Latin

late Middle English	imperturbable
late Middle English	inanimate
late Middle English	indivisible
early 16th century	inopportune
mid 16th century	indisputable
early 17th century	insubstantial
early 17th century	irrefutable

From medieval Latin

late Middle English	incompatible
late Middle English	indirect
late 15th century	incombustible
late 16th century	incapable
late 16th century	irresistible
early 17th century	intangible

incense² [late Middle English] The verb *incense* meaning 'make very angry' started out in the general sense 'inflame or excite someone with a strong feeling'. It comes from Old French *incenser*, from Latin *incendere* 'set fire to'.

incentive [late Middle English] *Incentive* is from Latin *incentivum* 'something that sets the tune or incites', from *incantare* 'to chant or charm'. In the context of a payment made to encourage harder work, the word is found from the 1940s.

incessant [late Middle English] *Incessant* came via Old French from late Latin *incessant-*, from *in-* 'not' and Latin *cessant-* 'ceasing' (from the verb *cessare*).

incest [Middle English] The word *incest* is from Latin *incestus, incestum* 'unchastity, incest', from *in-* 'not' and *castus* 'chaste'. **Incestuous** dates from the early 16th century and is from late Latin *incestuosus*, from Latin *incestus*.

inch [late Old English] Old English *ynce* is from Latin *uncia* 'twelfth part', from *unus* 'one' The word is not found in other Germanic languages.
➔ OUNCE

incident [late Middle English] This came via Old French from Latin *incident-*, the present participial stem of *incidere* 'fall upon, happen to' (based on *cadere* 'to fall'). Dating from the same period and based on the same verb is **incidence** (from Old French, or medieval Latin *incidentia*): this was first recorded meaning 'casual event or circumstance' but later, from the early 19th century, came to denote an 'occurrence of a disease, crime, or similar undesirable event'. **Incidental** (from medieval Latin *incidentalis*) is found from the early 17th century.

incinerate [late 15th century] Latin *cinis, ciner-* 'ashes' is the base of *incinerate*, which is from medieval Latin *incinerare* 'burn to ashes'.

incision [late Middle English] Latin *incidere* 'cut into' is the source of several words: *incision* (from late Latin *incisio(n-)*); **incisive** first used in late Middle English in the sense 'cutting, penetrating' (from medieval Latin *incisivus*); **incise** in the mid 16th century (from French *inciser*) and, in the late 17th century, **incisor** from the medieval Latin word meaning literally 'cutter'.

incite [late 15th century] *Incite* is from French *inciter*, from Latin *incitare*, from *in-* 'towards' and *citare* 'rouse, set in rapid motion'.

incline [Middle English] The sense first recorded for *incline* was 'bend (the head, the body, or oneself) towards something'. The notion of mentally leaning towards something

was also found in early examples. The word was formerly also written as *encline*, from Old French *encliner*, from Latin *inclinare*. The base elements are *in-* 'towards' and *clinare* 'to bend'. Late Middle English **inclination** is from Latin *inclinatio(n-)*, from *inclinare*.

include [late Middle English] 'Shut in' was an early meaning of *include*, from Latin *includere*, from *in-* 'into' and *claudere* 'to shut'. Latin *includere* is also the base of **inclusive** (late 16th century from medieval Latin *inclusivus*) and **inclusion** (early 17th century from Latin *inclusio(n-)*).

incognito [mid 17th century] This is the adoption of an Italian word meaning literally 'unknown'. The source is Latin *incognitus* used in the same sense and based on *cognoscere* 'to know'.

income [Middle English] *Income* meant 'entrance, arrival' in early texts; this use is now only Scots. The early word was from Old Norse *innkoma*, but later use is from *in* and *come*. The current sense 'money received regularly for work or through investments' dates from the late 16th century.

incommunicado [mid 19th century] This is from Spanish *incomunicado*, the past participle of *incomunicar* 'deprive of communication'.

incompetent [late 16th century] 'Not legally competent' was the early sense of *incompetent*. It is either from French, or from late Latin *incompetent-*, from *in-* 'not' and Latin *competent-* 'being fit or proper'.
➔ COMPETENT

incomprehensible [late Middle English] This word was found in examples before its opposite *comprehensible*. The source is Latin *incomprehensibilis*, from *in-* 'not' and *comprehensibilis* 'able to be understood'.
➔ COMPREHEND

incongruous [early 17th century] The base of this word is Latin *incongruus*, from *in-* 'not' and *congruus* 'agreeing, suitable' (from the verb *congruere*). There is often stress on a notion of absurdity from a mismatch (Daniel Defoe *Robinson Crusoe*: I have since often observed, how incongruous and irrational the common Temper of Mankind is).

inconsequent [late 16th century] This word meaning 'not following logically' is from Latin *inconsequent-*, from *in-* 'not' and *consequent-* 'overtaking, following closely'. The sense 'unimportant' is recorded from the mid 18th century.
➔ CONSEQUENCE

inconsiderable [late 16th century] 'Impossible to imagine' was the sense reflected in early use of the word. The origin is either French, or late Latin *inconsiderabilis*, from *in-* 'not' and *considerabilis* 'worthy of consideration'.
→ CONSIDERABLE

inconsiderate [late Middle English] The early sense recorded was 'not properly considered'. It comes from Latin *inconsideratus*, from *in-* 'not' and *consideratus* 'examined, considered'. Later, in the early 17th century, the word conveyed the meaning 'thoughtless' (Shakespeare *King John*: Rash, inconsiderate, fiery voluntaries).
→ CONSIDERATE

inconspicuous [early 17th century] Latin *inconspicuus* (from *in-* 'not' and *conspicuus* 'clearly visible') is the base of *inconspicuous*. The early sense was 'invisible, indiscernible'.

incontinent [late Middle English] 'Lacking self-restraint' was the first sense recorded. The form is either from Old French, or from Latin *incontinent-*, from *in-* 'not' and *continent-* 'holding together'. The medical sense dates from the early 19th century.

inconvenience [late Middle English] Senses recorded in early use were 'incongruity, inconsistency' and 'unsuitability'. The word came via Old French from late Latin *inconvenientia* 'incongruity, inconsistency': the formative elements are *in-* 'not' and Latin *convenient-* 'agreeing, fitting'. **Inconvenient** dates from the same period and originally meant 'incongruous' or 'unsuitable'. It came via Old French from Latin *inconvenient-*. Current senses such as 'awkward, not opportune' date from the mid 17th century.
→ CONVENIENCE

incorporate [late Middle English] This comes from late Latin *incorporat-*, the past participial stem of *incorporare* 'embody'. This verb is based on the prefix *in-* 'into' and Latin *corporare* 'form into a body' (from *corpus*, *corpor-* 'body'). The sense 'become constituted as a legal corporation' dates from the 1950s.

incorrect [late Middle English] Latin *incorrectus* (from *in-* 'not' and *correctus* 'made straight, amended') is the base of *incorrect*. Originally used in the general sense 'uncorrected', the word was later applied specifically to a book containing errors because it had not been corrected for the press. This led to 'not in accordance with a set of standards', e.g. *grammatically incorrect* (late 17th century).
→ CORRECT

increase [Middle English] Written formerly also as *encrease*, this word is from Old French *encreistre*, from Latin *increscere*, from *in-* 'into' and *crescere* 'grow'.

incredulous [16th century] This is based on Latin *incredulus* (from *in-* 'not' and *credulus* 'believing, trusting', from *credere* 'to believe').

increment [late Middle English] *Increment* is from Latin *incrementum*, from the stem of *increscere* 'grow'.
→ INCREASE

incriminate [mid 18th century] The word *incriminate* is from late Latin *incriminare* 'accuse', from *in-* 'into, towards' and Latin *crimen* 'crime'.

incubation [early 17th century] The verb *incubare* 'lay on' (from *in-* 'upon' and *cubare* 'to lie') is the source of both *incubation* (from Latin *incubatio(n-)*) and **incubate** (mid 17th century).

inculcate [mid 16th century] This verb meaning 'instil (an attitude) by persistent instruction' is from Latin *inculcat-*, the past participial stem of *inculcare* 'press in', from *in-* 'into' and *calcare* 'to tread' (from *calx*, *calc-* 'heel').

incumbent [late Middle English] This comes from Anglo-Latin *incumbens*, *incumbent-*, from Latin *incumbere* 'lie or lean on', from *in-* 'upon' and a verb related to *cubare* 'lie'. The noun sense meaning 'holder of an office' is peculiar to English.

incur [late Middle English] *Incur* meaning 'bring upon oneself, be subject to' is from Latin *incurrere*, from *in-* 'towards' and *currere* 'run'.

incursion [late Middle English] This was formerly also written as *encursion*. It is from Latin *incursio(n-)*, from the verb *incurrere*, literally 'run towards'.
→ INCUR

indebted [Middle English] The Middle English spelling was *endetted*, from Old French *endette* 'involved in debt', the past participle of *endetter*. The spelling change in the 16th century was due to association with medieval Latin *indebitare* (based on Latin *debitum* 'debt').

indefatigable [early 17th century] This is either from French, or from Latin *indefatigabilis*, from *in-* 'not' and *de-* 'away, completely' and *fatigare* 'wear out'.

indefinite [mid 16th century] From Latin *indefinitus*, the word *indefinite* is based on the elements *in-* 'not' and *definitus* 'defined, set within limits'.
→ DEFINITE

indelible [late 15th century] The early spelling was *indeleble*. It comes from French, or from Latin *indelebilis*, from *in-* 'not' and *delebilis* 'able to be defaced' (from *delere* 'efface, delete'). The ending was altered under the influence of the common suffix *-ible*.

indemnity [late Middle English] *Indemnity* is from French *indemnite*, from late Latin *indemnitas*, from *indemnis* 'unhurt, free from loss'. This Latin adjective is the base too of **indemnify** recorded from the early 17th century: the base is Latin *damnum* 'loss, damage'.

indent [late Middle English] This was first used as a verb meaning 'give a zigzag outline to, divide by a zigzag line'. It comes from Anglo-Norman French *endenter* or medieval Latin *indentare*, from *en-*, *in-* 'into' and Latin *dens*, *dent-* 'tooth'. **Indenture** dating from the same period is related: it came via Anglo-Norman French from medieval Latin *indentura*, based on *indentare* 'give a zigzag outline to'. Now a word for a formal legal agreement, this was historically in the form of a deed of contract of which copies were made for each contracting party with the edges indented for identification. The early spelling was *endenture*.

independent [early 17th century] This was formed partly on the pattern of French *independant*. **Independence** is recorded slightly later in the mid 17th century and is based on *independent*, partly on the pattern of French *indépendance*.

indeterminate [early 17th century] This comes from late Latin *indeterminatus*, from *in-* 'not' and Latin *determinatus* 'limited, determined'.
→ DETERMINE

index [late Middle English] This is from Latin *index* 'forefinger, informer, sign', from *in-* 'towards' and a second element related to *dicere* 'say' or *dicare* 'make known'. The original sense 'index finger' (with which one points) was extended to mean 'pointer' in the late 16th century; figuratively it became something that serves to point to a fact or conclusion. This led to a list of topics in a book ('pointing' to their location).
→ INDICATION

indication [late Middle English] This is from Latin *indicatio(n-)*, from the verb *indicare* 'point out' (from *in-* 'towards' and *dicare* 'make known'). This same Latin verb gave rise to late Middle English **indicative** (from French *indicatif*, *-ive*, from late Latin *indicativus*) and **indicate** in the early 17th century.

indict [Middle English] Early spellings included *endite* and *indite*, from Anglo-Norman French *enditer*. The word is based on Latin *indicere* 'proclaim, appoint', from *in-* 'towards' and *dicere* 'pronounce, utter'. The Middle English

noun **indictment** was initially spelt *enditement* or *inditement*, from Anglo-Norman French *enditement*, from *enditer*.

indifferent [late Middle English] The early sense was 'having no partiality for or against'. It came via Old French from Latin *indifferent-* 'not making any difference', from *in-* 'not' and *different-* 'differing'. The phrase *be indifferent to* dates from the early 16th century; the notion 'not particularly good' is found associated with the word from the mid 17th century. **Indifference** (from Latin *indifferentia*) dates from late Middle English in the sense 'being neither good nor bad'.
→ DIFFER

indigenous [mid 17th century] *Indigenous* is based on Latin *indigena* 'a native' whose root is an element related to *gignere* 'to beget'.

indigestion [late Middle English] This is from late Latin *indigestio(n-)*, from *in-* (expressing negation) and *digestio*.
→ DIGEST

indignation [late Middle English] 'Disdain, contempt' was the early meaning of *indignation* from Latin *indignatio(n-)*. The base verb is *indignari* 'regard as unworthy', which also gave rise (late 16th century) to **indignant** and **indignity** (from French *indignité* or Latin *indignitas*). The formative elements are *in-* 'not' and *dignus* 'worthy'.

indigo [mid 16th century] This comes from Portuguese *índigo*, via Latin from Greek *indikon*, from *indikos* 'Indian (dye)'.

indiscreet [late Middle English] This was originally spelt *indiscrete* in the sense 'lacking discernment or judgement'. It comes from late Latin *indiscretus* (from *in-* 'not' and *discretus* 'separate, distinguishable') which in medieval Latin came to mean 'careless, indiscreet'. Latin *discernere* 'separate out, discern' is the base. Middle English **indiscretion** is from late Latin *indiscretio(n-)*, literally 'lack of discernment'.
→ DISCREET

indiscriminate [late 16th century] 'Haphazard, not selective' was the sense of *indiscriminate* in early examples. The form is from *in-* 'not' and Latin *discriminatus* (the past participle of *discriminare* 'distinguish between'). The current sense 'making no distinctions' dates from the late 18th century.

indispensable [mid 16th century] In early use *indispensable* meant 'not to be allowed or provided for by ecclesiastical dispensation'. Medieval Latin *indispensabilis* is the source, from *in-* 'not' and *dispensabilis* 'able to be disbursed'. The meaning 'absolutely necessary' is found from the late 17th century.

indisposed [late Middle English] This is either a compound of *in-* 'not' and *disposed*, or it is the past participle of *indispose* 'make unwell or unwilling'. Early examples reflected the meaning as 'not properly arranged, not well organized'; the meaning 'not well' is recorded from the late 16th century.

individual [late Middle English] 'Indivisible' was the early meaning of *individual* from medieval Latin *individualis*, from Latin *individuus* 'not divisible'. The base is Latin *dividere* 'to divide'. The noun use 'single human being' dates from the early 17th century.

indolent [mid 17th century] This is from late Latin *indolent-*, from *in-* 'not' and *dolere* 'suffer or give pain'. The Latin senses are reflected in the English use of *indolent* in medical contexts. The senses 'idleness' and 'idle' arose in the early 18th century.

indomitable [mid 17th century] 'Untameable' was the early sense. The origin is late Latin *indomitabilis* 'not able to be tamed', from *in-* 'not' and Latin *domitare* 'to tame'.

induce [late Middle English] *Induce* is from Latin *inducere* 'lead in', from *in-* 'into' and *ducere* 'to lead', or from French *enduire*. **Induction** dates from the same period and is from Latin *inductio(n-)*, from the verb *inducere*. The word's use to denote 'a process of being initiated' is recorded from the early 16th century.

indulgence [late Middle English] *Indulgence* came via Old French from Latin *indulgentia*, from the verb *indulgere* 'give free rein to': this is also the source of **indulgent** (early 16th century) and **indulge** (early 17th century) when it meant 'treat with excessive kindness'.

industry [late Middle English] The first sense recorded for *industry* was 'hard work'. It derives from either French *industrie* or Latin *industria* 'diligence'. The meaning 'trade, manufacture' is found from the mid 16th century. The adjective **industrious** recorded from the late 15th century in the sense 'skilful, clever, ingenious' is from French *industrieux* or late Latin *industriosus*, from Latin *industria*.

inebriate [late Middle English] Early use was as an adjective. It is from Latin *inebriatus*, the past participle of *inebriare* 'intoxicate' (based on *ebrius* 'drunk').

inept [mid 16th century] 'Not apt, unsuitable' was the early sense of *inept*, from Latin *ineptus*. The formative elements are *in-* 'not' and *aptus* 'fitting'.

inert [mid 17th century] *Inert* is from Latin *iners, inert-* 'unskilled, inactive', from *in-* (expressing negation) and *ars, art-* 'skill, art'.

The noun **inertia** dates from the early 18th century as a term in physics: it is from Latin, from *iners, inert-*.

inevitable [late Middle English] *Inevitable* is from Latin *inevitabilis*, from *in-* 'not' and *evitabilis* 'avoidable' (from *evitare* 'to avoid').

infallible [late 15th century] French *infaillible* or late Latin *infallibilis* (from *in-* 'not' and Latin *fallere* 'deceive') gave rise to *infallible* in English. **Infallibility** (early 17th century) is from obsolete French *infallibilité* or medieval Latin *infallibilitas*.

infamous [late Middle English] This comes from medieval Latin *infamosus*, from Latin *infamis* (based on *fama* 'fame').

infant [late Middle English] *Infant* is from Old French *enfant*, from Latin *infant-* 'unable to speak', from *in-* 'not' and *fant-* from the verb *fari* 'to speak'. The same source also gave rise to **infancy** (from Latin *infantia* 'childhood, inability to speak') and **infantile** (from French, or from Latin *infantilis*) in the same period.

infantry [late 16th century] The word *infantry* is from French *infanterie*, from Italian *infanteria*, from *infante* 'youth, infantryman', from *infant-* 'not speaking'.
→ INFANT

infatuate [mid 16th century] This is from Latin *infatuat-*, the past participial stem of the verb *infatuare* 'make foolish', from *in-* 'into' and *fatuus* 'foolish'.

infect [late Middle English] *Infect* and **infection** (via Latin *infectio(n-)*) are both from Latin *inficere* 'to taint, dip in', from *in-* 'into' and *facere* 'put, do'. They are recorded from the same period.

infer [late 15th century] The early sense recorded for *infer* is 'bring about, inflict'. The source of the form is Latin *inferre* 'bring in, bring about', which in medieval Latin came to mean 'deduce'. The base elements are *in-* 'into' and *ferre* 'bring'. *Infer* expresses the idea that something in the speaker's words enables the listener to 'deduce' what is meant; this is distinct from the use of *imply* which expresses the notion that something in the speaker's words 'suggests' a certain meaning. The word **inference** dates from the late 16th century and is from medieval Latin *inferentia*, based on the same Latin verb as *infer*.

inferior [late Middle English] This is a use of the Latin comparative of *inferus* 'low' and was first used to mean 'lower in position'. **Inferiority** dating from the late 16th century is probably from medieval Latin *inferioritas*, from Latin *inferior*.

infernal [late Middle English] *Infernal* is from Old French, from Christian Latin *infernalis*, from Latin *infernus* 'below, underground': this was used by Christians to mean 'hell', on the pattern of *inferni* (masculine plural) 'the shades' and *inferna* (neuter plural) 'the lower regions'. The word **inferno** dates from the mid 19th century and is via Italian from Christian Latin *infernus*.

infest [late Middle English] This was found in the sense 'torment, harass' in early examples. It comes from French *infester* or Latin *infestare* 'assail', from *infestus* 'hostile'. The current sense 'trouble in large numbers' dates from the mid 16th century.

infidel [late 15th century] *Infidel* is from French *infidèle* or Latin *infidelis*, literally 'not faithful' (the source too of late Middle English **infidelity**): the base is Latin *fides* 'faith', related to *fidere* 'to trust'. The word originally referred to a person of a religion other than one's own, specifically a Muslim (to a Christian), a Christian (to a Muslim), or a Gentile (to a Jew).

infinity [late Middle English] The word *infinity* is from Old French *infinite* or Latin *infinitas*, from *infinitus* meaning literally 'not finished'.

infirm [late Middle English] This was first used in the general sense 'weak, frail'. It is from Latin *infirmus*, from *in-* 'not' and *firmus* 'firm'. The word **infirmary** (late Middle English) is based on the same Latin adjective: it derives from medieval Latin *infirmaria*.

inflammation [late Middle English] Latin *flamma* 'flame' is the base of *inflammation* (from Latin *inflammatio(n-)*) and Middle English **inflame** (from Latin *inflammare*). The related word **inflammable** dates from the early 17th century and came into English via French.

inflate [late Middle English] The Latin verb *flare* 'to blow' is the base of *inflate* which literally means 'blow into'. Middle English **inflation** referred to 'the condition of being inflated with a gas': it is from Latin *inflatio(n-)*, from *inflare* 'blow into'. The economics sense dates from the mid 19th century.

inflect [late Middle English] The early sense of 'inflect' was 'bend or deflect something inwards'. The source is Latin *inflectere*, from *in-* 'into' and *flectere* 'to bend'. **Inflection** dates from the same period describing 'the action of bending inwards': it is from Latin *inflexio(n-)*, from the verb *inflectere*. The word's use in grammar contexts focuses on a notion of modification and dates from the mid 17th century.

inflict [mid 16th century] 'Afflict, trouble' was the first sense recorded for *inflict* from Latin *inflict-*, the past participial stem of *infligere* 'strike against'. **Infliction** (mid 16th century) is from late Latin *inflictio(n-)*, from the verb *infligere*.

influence [late Middle English] *Influence* is from Old French, or from medieval Latin *influentia* 'inflow', from Latin *influere* 'flow into'. The word originally had the general senses 'an influx' and 'flowing matter' and was also used specifically in astrology to denote 'the flowing in of ethereal fluid (affecting human destiny)'. The sense 'an imperceptible or indirect action exerted to cause changes' was established in Scholastic Latin by the 13th century but not recorded in English until the late 16th century.

influenza [mid 18th century] This is a use of an Italian word meaning literally 'influence', from medieval Latin *influentia* The Italian word also has the sense 'an outbreak of an epidemic'. It was applied specifically to an influenza epidemic which began in Italy in 1743 and was later adopted in English as the name of the disease.
→ INFLUENCE

influx [late 16th century] Initially this denoted an inflow of liquid, gas, or light: it comes from late Latin *influxus*, from *influere* 'flow in'.
→ INFLUENCE

inform [Middle English] Early spellings included *enforme* and *informe* which meant both 'give form or shape to' and 'form the mind of, teach'. The source is Old French *enfourmer*, from Latin *informare* 'shape, fashion, describe' (from *in-* 'into' and *forma* 'a form'). The noun **information** arose in late Middle English when it was also used in the sense 'formation of the mind, teaching': it is via Old French from Latin *informatio(n-)*.

infrequent [mid 16th century] The early senses were 'little used', 'seldom done', and 'uncommon'. The form is from Latin *infrequent-* from *in-* 'not' and *frequent-* 'frequent'.

infringe [mid 16th century] *Infringe* is from Latin *infringere*, from *in-* 'into' and *frangere* 'to break'. **Infraction** (from Latin *infractio(n-)*, from the verb *infringere*) was already found in examples in late Middle English.

infuriate [mid 17th century] *Infuriate* is from medieval Latin *infuriare* 'make angry', from *in-* 'into' and Latin *furia* 'fury'.

infuse [late Middle English] This word is from Latin *infus-*, the past participial stem of *infundere* 'pour in'. The noun **infusion** from the same period initially denoted the pouring in of a liquid: it comes from Latin *infusio(n-)*, from the verb *infundere*. As a term for 'a dilute liquid extract' such as a herbal drink, *infusion* dates from the mid 16th century.

ingenious [late Middle English] *Ingenious* is from French *ingénieux* or Latin *ingeniosus*, from *ingenium* 'mind, intellect'. **Ingenuity** dates from the late 16th century when it also had the senses 'nobility' and 'ingenuousness'. It comes from Latin *ingenuitas* 'ingenuousness', from *ingenuus* 'inborn'. The current meaning arose by confusion of *ingenuous* with *ingenious*.
→ ENGINE

ingenuous [late 16th century] This word meaning 'innocent and unsuspecting' is from Latin *ingenuus* literally 'native, inborn' (from *in-* 'into' and an element related to *gignere* 'beget'). The original sense was 'noble, generous', giving rise to 'honourably straightforward, frank', hence 'innocently frank' (late 17th century).

ingest [early 17th century] *Ingest* is from Latin *ingest-*, the past participial stem of *ingerere* 'bring in', from *in-* 'into' and *gerere* 'to carry'.

inglenook [late 18th century] The second element of *inglenook* is from Scots *ingle* first recorded in the early 16th century: this is perhaps from Scottish Gaelic *aingeal* 'light, fire' or Irish *aingeal* 'live ember'.

ingot [late Middle English] An *ingot* was originally a mould in which metal is cast. It is perhaps from *in* and Old English *goten*, the past participle of *geotan* 'to pour, cast'.

ingrain [late Middle English] This was originally written as *engrain* in the sense 'dye with cochineal or in fast colours'. It is composed of *en-* or *in* used as an intensifier and the verb *grain*. The adjective is from *in grain* 'fast-dyed', from the old use of *grain* meaning 'kermes, cochineal'.

ingratiate [early 17th century] This is based on Latin *in gratiam* 'into favour', on the pattern of the obsolete Italian verb *ingratiare*, an earlier form of *ingraziare*.

ingratitude [Middle English] This word is from Old French, or from late Latin *ingratitudo*, from Latin *ingratus* 'ungrateful', the source too of the formal or literary word **ingrate** for 'an ungrateful person'.

ingredient [late Middle English] *Ingredient*, essentially something which 'goes into' a mixture, is from Latin *ingredient-*, the present participial stem of *ingredi* 'enter', from *in-* 'into' and *gradi* 'to walk'.

inhabit [late Middle English] Early spellings included *inhabite* and *enhabite*, from Old French *enhabiter* or Latin *inhabitare* 'dwell in' (based on *habere* 'to have'). **Inhabitant** is also late Middle English via Old French from Latin *inhabitare*.

inhalation [early 17th century] Latin *halare* 'to breathe' is the base of the word *inhalation* (the direct source of which is medieval Latin *inhalatio(n-)*) and of early 18th-century **inhale** (from Latin *inhalare* 'breathe in'). The current use of *inhale* has arisen by influence of its opposite: *exhale*. The word **inhaler** dates from the late 18th century.

inherent [late 16th century] *Inherent* is from Latin *inhaerent-*, the present participial stem of *inhaerere* 'stick to': this verb is formed from the prefix *in-* 'in, towards' and the verb *haerere* 'to stick'. First examples of use of the English word were with the meaning 'contained in, sticking or fixed in', but the figurative sense was also recorded early.

inherit [Middle English] The Middle English spelling was *enherite* which meant 'receive as a right', from Old French *enheriter*. Late Latin *inhereditare* 'appoint as heir' is the source, from Latin *in-* 'in' and *heres, hered-* 'heir'. The noun **inheritance** is recorded later in the Middle English period: this was formerly also written as *enheritance* and is from Anglo-Norman French *enheritaunce* 'being admitted as heir', from Old French *enheriter*.

inhibit [late Middle English] The early sense recorded was 'forbid (a person) to do something'. It comes from Latin *inhibere* 'to hinder', literally 'hold in' (from *in-* 'in' and *habere* 'hold'). This Latin verb also gave rise to late Middle English **inhibition** (from Latin *inhibitio(n-)*) which at first conveyed the sense 'forbidding, a prohibition'. Use in psychology contexts dates from the late 19th century.

inhuman [late Middle English] This was originally written *inhumane*; both spellings were stressed on the final syllable. The source is Latin *inhumanus*, from *in-* 'not' and *humanus* 'relating to a human being'. Latin *inhumanus* is also the base of **inhumanity** (from Old French *inhumanite* or Latin *inhumanitas*) recorded from the late 15th century.
→ HUMAN

inhumane [late Middle English] 'Inhuman, brutal' was the early sense recorded for *inhumane*. It was originally a variant of *inhuman* but became rare in this use after 1700. The modern word is a combination of the prefix *in-* 'not' and *humane*: the current sense dates from the early 19th century.

iniquity [Middle English] This comes from Old French *iniquite*, from Latin *iniquitas*. The Latin adjective *iniquus* is the base from a combination of *in-* 'not' and *aequus* 'equal, just'. *Iniquity* (sometimes called *the Vice*) was used as the name of a comic character in the old morality plays who represented a particular vice depicted in the drama (Shakespeare *Richard III*: Thus like the formal vice iniquity, I moralize two meanings in one word).

initial [early 16th century] *Initial* is from Latin *initialis*, from *initium* 'beginning', from *inire* 'go in(to)' It was used as a noun for 'an initial letter' from the early 17th century and as *initials* representing a signature from the early 18th century. Latin *inire* is also the base of **initiate** recorded from the mid 16th century in the context of admitting someone to a secret society: this is from Latin *initiare* 'begin'; an *initiate* as a name for a novice is found from the early 19th century. **Initiation** dates from the late 18th century and is via French from Latin *initiare*.

injection [early 16th century] This word is from Latin *injectio(n-)*, from the verb *inicere* 'throw in' (from *in-* 'into' and *jacere* 'throw'). The verb **inject** dates from the late 16th century when it meant 'throw in': this comes from Latin *inject-*, the past participial stem of *inicere*.

injunction [late Middle English] This word for an authoritative warning is from late Latin *injunctio(n-)*, from Latin *injungere* 'enjoin, impose'.

injury [late Middle English] *Injury* is from Anglo-Norman French *injurie*, from Latin *injuria* 'a wrong', from *in-* (expressing negation) and *jus, jur-* 'right'. **Injure** and **injurious** date from the same period: *injure* is a back-formation (by removal of the suffix) from *injury* which was an earlier spelling of the verb (displaced between 1580 and 1640); *injurious* is from French *injurieux* or Latin *injuriosus*.

injustice [late Middle English] *Injustice* is from Old French, from Latin *injustitia*, from *in-* 'not' and *justus* 'just, right'.

ink [Middle English] Early spellings included *enke* and *inke*. Old French *enque* is the source, via late Latin from Greek *enkauston* (from *enkaiein* 'burn in'), which was a term for the purple ink used by Roman emperors for signatures.

inkling [late Middle English] An *inkling* in early contexts was 'a mention in an undertone, a hint'; it was often part of the phrase *hear an inkling of*. The source is the rare verb *inkle* 'utter in an undertone', of which the origin is unknown. The name *The Inklings* was a name given to friends of C. S. Lewis, including novelists such as Tolkien and Charles Williams, who, from the 1930s to the 1960s, met in Lewis's Oxford rooms to read their works aloud and discuss them.

inmate [late 16th century] The first element is probably originally from *inn* but later became

associated with *in*. This was initially a person who shared a house, specifically a lodger or subtenant. In the 16th and 17th centuries there were strict by-laws about harbouring poor people as *inmates*: this was a practice that caused the number of local paupers to increase.

inn [Old English] An early *inn* was a 'dwelling place, lodging'. Of Germanic origin it is related to *in*. In Middle English the word was used to translate Latin *hospitium* which was a residence for students: this sense is preserved in the names of some buildings formerly used for this purpose, notably *Gray's Inn* and *Lincoln's Inn*, two of the *Inns of Court*. The current sense dates from late Middle English.
→ HOSPICE

innards [early 19th century] This represents a dialect pronunciation of *inwards*, used as a noun.

innate [late Middle English] *Innate* is from Latin *innatus*, the past participle of *innasci*, from *in-* 'into' and *nasci* 'be born'. It was often a word opposed to *acquired*.

innocent [Middle English] Literally meaning 'not harming', *innocent* is either from Old French, or from Latin *innocent-*, from *in-* 'not' and *nocere* 'to hurt, injure'. **Innocence**, a word dating from the same period, is from Old French, from Latin *innocentia*, from *innocent-* 'not harming'.

innocuous [late 16th century] This word is from Latin *innocuus*, from *in-* 'not' and *nocuus* 'injurious' (from *nocere* 'to hurt, injure').
→ INNOCENT

innovation [late Middle English] This is from Latin *innovatio(n-)*, from the verb *innovare* 'renew, alter', from *in-* 'into' and *novare* 'make new' (from *novus* 'new'). **Innovate** (from Latin *innovare*) is recorded from the mid 16th century and in early use was 'change to something new', a sense which is now obsolete (Scott *Rob Roy*: The dictates of my father were ... not to be altered, innovated, or even discussed). The adjective **innovative** is found from the early 17th century; since the 1970s it has focused on the notion 'novel and creative'.

innuendo [mid 16th century] *Innuendo* was initially used as an adverb meaning 'that is to say, to wit' in legal documents when introducing an explanation. It is a use of a Latin word meaning 'by nodding at, by pointing to', the ablative gerund of *innuere*, from *in-* 'towards' and *nuere* 'to nod'. The noun meaning 'allusive remark' dates from the late 17th century.

inoculate [late Middle English] In early use the word *inoculate* meant 'graft a bud or shoot into a plant of a different type'. It has a Latin source: *inoculare* 'engraft', from *in-* 'into' and *oculus* 'eye, bud'. The sense 'vaccinate' dates from the early 18th century.

inordinate [late Middle English] This word meaning 'disproportionately large' is from Latin *inordinatus*, from *in-* 'not' and *ordinatus* 'arranged, set in order'. An early meaning in English was 'not ordered, intemperate'.

inquest [Middle English] *Inquest* is from Old French *enqueste*, based on Latin *inquirere* 'seek into'. The spelling with *in-*, although found frequently in the 17th century, was not finally established until the 18th century. Early *inquests* were held for all formal or official enquiries into matters of state or public interest, for example the fixing of prices, property valuations, etc.
→ ENQUIRE

inquire [Middle English] The early spelling was *enquere* which later became *inquere*. Old French *enquerre* is the source: this came from a variant of Latin *inquirere*, based on *quaerere* 'to seek'. The spelling with *in-*, influenced by Latin, dates from the 15th century. The related words **inquisitive** (from Old French *inquisitif*, *-ive*) and **inquisitor** (from French *inquisiteur*, from Latin *inquisitor*) date from late Middle English, as does **inquisition** from the same Latin source verb *quaerere*. This originally referred to any searching examination and came via Old French from Latin *inquisitio(n-)* 'examination'. The *Spanish Inquisition* became notorious in the 16th century for its severe methods in the suppression of heresy: such ecclesiastical tribunals were originally organized by the Roman Catholic Church in the 13th century under Innocent III, under a central governing body in Rome called the Congregation of the Holy Office.
→ ENQUIRE

insane [mid 16th century] *Insane* is from Latin *insanus*, from *in-* 'not' and *sanus* 'healthy'. A now obsolete sense 'causing insanity' is illustrated in Shakespeare's *Macbeth*: Have we eaten on the insane Root, That takes the Reason prisoner? The word in its current sense was used to describe actions as well as people from the middle of the 19th century. **Insanity** (late 16th century) is from Latin *insanitas*, from *insanus*.

inscribe [late Middle English] *Inscribe* is from Latin *inscribere*, from *in-* 'into' and *scribere* 'write'. **Inscription** in this early period referred to a short descriptive or dedicatory passage at the beginning of a book: it is from Latin *inscriptio(n-)*, from the verb *inscribere*.

inscrutable [late Middle English] *Inscrutable* is from ecclesiastical Latin *inscrutabilis*, from *in-* 'not' and *scrutari* 'to search'.
→ SCRUTINY

insect [early 17th century] This was originally a term for any small cold-blooded creature with a segmented body; it comes from Latin (*animal*) *insectum* 'segmented (animal)' translating Greek *zōion entomon*. The base elements are *in-* 'into' and *secare* 'to cut'.

insecure [mid 17th century] *Insecure* is from medieval Latin *insecurus* 'unsafe', from *in-* 'not' and Latin *securus* 'free from care'; in certain senses it is from the prefix *in-* 'not' and *secure*. Use in psychology contexts dates from the 1930s.

inseminate [early 17th century] Latin *semen*, *semin-* 'seed, semen' is the base of *inseminate* from Latin *inseminare* 'to sow' (literally 'plant into'). Its use in human biology contexts dates from the mid 19th century and in connection with *artificial insemination* from the 1920s.

insensible [late Middle English] Early use included the senses 'unable to be perceived' and 'incapable of physical sensation'. The word in some senses is from Old French *insensible* (from Latin *insensibilis*, from *in-* 'not' and *sensibilis*, from *sensus* 'sense'); in others it is from the prefix *in-* 'not' and *sensible*.

insert [late 15th century] In early examples *insert* meant 'include (text) in a piece of writing'. It is from Latin *insert-*, the past participial stem of *inserere* 'put in', from *in-* 'into' and *serere* 'to join'. **Insertion** dates from the mid 16th century and is from late Latin *insertio(n-)*, from Latin *inserere*.

insidious [mid 16th century] This is based on Latin *insidiosus* 'cunning', from *insidiae* 'an ambush or trick', from *insidere* 'lie in wait for'. The base elements here are *in-* 'on' and *sedere* 'sit'.

insight [Middle English] 'Inner sight, mental vision, wisdom' was the sense reflected in early contexts. It is probably Scandinavian and Low German in origin, related to Swedish *insikt*, Danish *indsigt*, Dutch *inzicht*, and German *Einsicht*.

insignia [mid 17th century] Based on Latin *signum* 'sign', *insignia* is a use of the Latin plural of *insigne* 'sign, badge of office', the neuter of *insignis* 'distinguished (as if by a mark)', from *in-* 'towards'.

insinuate [early 16th century] This word was first used in legal contexts in the sense 'enter (a document) on the official register'. Latin *insinuare* 'introduce tortuously' is the source, from *in-* 'in' and *sinuare* 'to curve'. Nearly all the English senses were already in Latin, the figurative uses being adopted first. The noun **insinuation** (from Latin *insinuatio(n-)*) dates from the mid 16th century.

insipid [early 17th century] *Insipid* is from French *insipide* or late Latin *insipidus*, from *in-* 'not' and *sapidus* (from *sapere* 'to taste').

insist [late 16th century] 'Persist, persevere' was the first sense recorded for *persist* from Latin *insistere* 'persist', from *in-* 'upon' and *sistere* 'stand'.

insolent [late Middle English] Early use included the sense 'extravagant, going beyond acceptable limits': it comes from Latin *insolent-* meaning 'immoderate, unaccustomed, arrogant'. The Latin verb *solere* 'be accustomed' is the base.

insomnia [early 17th century] This is a use of a Latin word, from *insomnis* 'sleepless', from *in-* (expressing negation) and *somnus* 'sleep'.

inspect [early 17th century] *Inspect* is either from Latin *inspect-*, the past participial stem of *inspicere* 'look into, examine' (from *in-* 'in' and *specere* 'look at'), or from the frequentative (= verb of repeated action) *inspectare* 'keep looking at'. **Inspector** from the same period is the adoption of a Latin word.

inspire [Middle English] *Inspire* (originally spelt *enspire*) is from Old French *inspirer*, from Latin *inspirare* 'breathe or blow into' from *in-* 'into' and *spirare* 'breathe'. The word was originally used in connection with a divine or supernatural being who would *inspire* i.e. 'impart a truth or idea to someone'. Middle English **inspiration** which was originally 'divine guidance' came via Old French from late Latin *inspiratio(n-)*, from the verb *inspirare*.

instability [late Middle English] French *instabilité* (from Latin *instabilitas*) is the source of *instability* in English. The base adjective is *instabilis*, literally 'not able to stand'.
→ STABILITY

install [late Middle English] The early sense of *install* was 'place (someone) in a new position of authority'. The source of this word (and **installation** from the same period) is medieval Latin *installare*, from *in-* 'into' and *stallum* 'place, stall'. The prime current sense 'place (equipment) in position ready for use' dates from the mid 19th century.

instalment [mid 18th century] Early use of this word was to describe an arrangement to pay by instalments. It is an alteration of the obsolete *estalment* (probably by association with *installation*), from Anglo-Norman French *esta-* *lement*: this came from Old French *estaler* 'to fix'.

instance [Middle English] *Instance* came via Old French from Latin *instantia* 'urgency', from *instare* 'be present, press upon, be at hand' (from *in-* 'upon' and *stare* 'to stand'). The original senses were 'urgency' or 'urgent entreaty': this survives in the formal phrase *at the instance of* (e.g. *prosecution at the instance of the police*). In the late 16th century the word was used to refer to a specific case cited to disprove a general assertion: this was derived from medieval Latin *instantia* 'an example to the contrary' (translating Greek *enstasis* 'objection'). This gave rise to the common current meaning 'single occurrence of something' (e.g. *a serious instance of corruption*). Related words based on Latin *instare* are late Middle English **instant** which came into the language via Old French and **instantaneous** (mid 17th century) from medieval Latin *instantaneus* (formed on the pattern of ecclesiastical Latin *momentaneus*).

instead [Middle English] This was originally written as two words. The literal meaning is 'in place'; it was rarely written as one word before 1620 but seldom written separately after 1640.
→ STEAD

instep [late Middle English] This word is of unknown origin. The West Frisian *ynstap* means 'opening in a shoe for insertion of the foot' and may be associated.

instigation [late Middle English] *Instigation* meant 'incitement' initially. It comes from Old French, or from Latin *instigatio(n-)*, from the verb *instigare* 'urge, incite'. **Instigate** dates from the mid 16th century in the sense 'urge on': Latin *in-* 'towards' and *stigare* 'prick, incite' are the base elements.

instil [late Middle English] The sense 'insert drops' was among the first recorded. The word is from Latin *instillare*, from *in-* 'into' and *stillare* 'to drop' (from *stilla* 'a drop').

instinct [late Middle English] In early examples there were the additional senses 'instigation' and 'impulse'. *Instinct* is from Latin *instinctus* 'impulse', from the verb *instinguere*: the base is Latin *stinguere* 'to prick' which gives a core notion of 'urge'.

institute [Middle English] The early sense was 'a summary of principles (usually law-related)'. It comes from Latin *instituere* 'establish', from *in-* 'in, towards' and *statuere* 'set up'. The noun is from Latin *institutum* 'something designed, precept', the neuter past participle of *instituere*. The use of the word to mean 'an organization' dates from the early 19th century. The word **institution** is found in late

Middle English meaning 'established law': it came via Old French from Latin *institutio(n-)*, from the verb *instituere*. When used referring to 'an organization' the word is found from the early 18th century.

instruct [late Middle English] *Instruct* is from Latin *instruere* 'construct, equip, teach', from *in-* 'upon, towards' and *struere* 'pile up'. Late Middle English **instruction** came via Old French from late Latin *instructio(n-)*, from the verb *instruere*.

instrument [Middle English] This word is either from Old French, or from Latin *instrumentum* 'equipment, implement', from the verb *instruere* 'construct, equip'. Its use as a word for a musical instrument was among the earliest. **Instrumental** arose in late Middle English and came via French from medieval Latin *instrumentalis*, from Latin *instrumentum*.

insufferable [late Middle English] *Insufferable* is perhaps from the now dialect French word *insouffrable*, based on Latin *sufferre* 'to endure'.
→ SUFFER

insufficient [late Middle English] 'Incapable, incompetent' was the early meaning recorded for *insufficient* which came via Old French from late Latin *insufficient-*. The literal sense is 'not sufficing' (from *in-* 'not' and Latin *sufficere* 'be enough').
→ SUFFICE

insular [mid 16th century] This was first used as a noun for 'an islander'. The source is late Latin *insularis*, from *insula* 'island' which is also the base of the verb **insulate** dating from the same period.

insult [mid 16th century] The early meaning was 'exult, act arrogantly'. Latin *insultare* 'jump or trample on' (based on Latin *saltare*, from *salire* 'to leap') is the source. The noun in the early 17th century meant 'an attack' and is from French *insulte* or ecclesiastical Latin *insultus*. The main senses in current use date from the 17th century apart from the medical *insult* meaning 'an occurrence of damage' which has been in use since the early 20th century.

insuperable [Middle English] The general sense 'invincible' was the early one recorded for *invincible* which is either from Old French, or from Latin *insuperabilis*. The formative elements are *in-* 'not' and *superabilis* (from *superare* 'overcome').

insupportable [mid 16th century] This is an adoption of a French word composed of *in-* 'not' and the adjective *supportable* 'bearable' (from *supporter* 'to support, endure').

insurance [late Middle English] The original spelling was *ensurance* used in the sense 'ensuring, assurance, a guarantee', from Old French *enseurance*, from *enseurer*. The commercial application where a company arranges to provide a guarantee of compensation for loss or illness etc. dates from the mid 17th century. The verb **insure** which is also late Middle English is first recorded with the sense 'assure someone of something': this is an alteration of *ensure*. In both British English and American English *insure* figures mostly in the commercial sense of providing financial compensation, whereas *ensure* is not used at all in this sense; however in more general contexts the two forms overlap considerably particularly in US English.
→ ENSURE

insurrection [late Middle English] *Insurrection* came via Old French from late Latin *insurrectio(n-)*, from *insurgere* 'rise up' (from *in-* 'into, towards' and *surgere* 'to rise'). From the same Latin source is **insurgent** (via French, mid 18th century) meaning 'rising in active revolt'.

intact [late Middle English] *Intact* is from Latin *intactus*, from *in-* 'not' and *tactus* (the past participle of *tangere* 'to touch').

integer [early 16th century] The early meaning of this mathematical term was 'entire, whole'. It is originally a Latin word with the core sense 'standing alone' formed from *in-* (expressing negation) and the root of *tangere* 'to touch'. Mid 16th-century **integral** (from late Latin *integralis*) is based on *integer*; so too 17th-century **integrate** and **integration** (from Latin *integrare* 'make whole') and late Middle English **integrity** (from French *intégrité* or Latin *integritas*). *Integrity* as a word for 'soundness of moral principle' dates from the mid 16th century.
→ ENTIRE

intellect [late Middle English] This is from Latin *intellectus* 'understanding', from *intellegere* 'to understand' (literally 'choose between'); although found in late Middle English, it was little used before the 16th century. **Intellectual** (from Latin *intellectualis*, from *intellectus*) dates from the same period; use in the legal phrase *intellectual property* (intangible property that is the result of creativity such as patents) is found from the mid 19th century and has become frequent recently in areas involving data transmitted electronically over the Internet. The noun use *an intellectual* for 'an intellectual person' is recorded from the mid 17th century. Words also based on Latin *intellegere* and therefore with a core notion of 'choosing' and 'discriminating' include: late Middle English **intelligence** (via Old French from Latin *intelligentia*) and **intelligible** (from Latin *intelligibilis*); so too early 16th-century **intelligent**.

intend [Middle English] The early spelling was *entend* which meant 'direct the attention to', from Old French *entendre*. The source here is Latin *intendere* 'intend, extend, direct', literally 'stretch towards'. The Middle English noun **intent** is from Old French *entent(e)*, based on Latin *intendere*; adjectival use (as in *intent upon*) is from Latin *intentus*, the past participle of *intendere*. This Latin verb also gave rise to late Middle English **intention** (via Old French *entencion*, from Latin *intentio(n-)* 'stretching, purpose') and mid 16th-century **intentional** 'existing only in intention' (from French *intentionnel* or medieval Latin *intentionalis*).

intense [late Middle English] *Intense* is either from Old French, or it comes from Latin *intensus* 'stretched tightly; strained', the past participle of *intendere* 'extend'. **Intensive** dating from the same period was first recorded meaning 'vehement, intense': this comes from French *intensif*, *-ive* or medieval Latin *intensivus*, from *intendere*. → INTEND

inter [Middle English] This verb meaning 'bury' is from Old French *enterrer*, based on Latin *in-* 'into' and *terra* 'earth'.

intercede [late 16th century] *Intercede* is from French *intercéder* or Latin *intercedere* 'intervene', from *inter-* 'between' and *cedere* 'go'.

intercept [late Middle English] Early senses included 'contain between limits' and 'halt (an effect)'. The source is Latin *intercept-*, the past participial stem of *intercipere* 'catch between', from *inter-* 'between' and *capere* 'to take'.

intercourse [late Middle English] Initially this word referred to 'communication or dealings'. Old French *entrecours* 'exchange, commerce' is the source of the form, from Latin *intercursus*, from *intercurrere* 'intervene' (literally 'run between'). The specifically sexual use arose in the late 18th century.

interest [late Middle English] The early spelling was *interess*, from Anglo-Norman French *interesse*, from Latin *interesse* 'differ, be important' (literally 'be between'). The *-t* was added partly by association with Old French *interest* 'damage, loss', apparently from Latin *interest* 'it is important'. The original sense was 'the possession of a share in or a right to something'; hence the sense 'stake, share'. The use 'wanting to know about something' arose in the 18th century. In financial contexts the word was influenced by medieval Latin *interesse* 'compensation for a debtor's defaulting'.

interfere [late Middle English] *Interfere* is from Old French *s'entreferir* 'strike each other', from *entre-* 'between' and *ferir* (from Latin *ferire* 'to strike'). **Interference** (mid 18th century) is based on *interfere*, influenced by the pattern of words such as *difference*.

interim [mid 16th century] This was first used for 'a temporary or provisional arrangement', originally for the adjustment of religious differences between the German Protestants and the Roman Catholic Church. It is a use of a Latin word meaning 'meanwhile'.

interior [late 15th century] This is a use of a Latin word which meant 'inner'; it is a comparative adjective from *inter* 'within'.

interjection [late Middle English] *Interjection* came via Old French from Latin *interjectio(n-)*, from the verb *interjicere* literally 'throw between', which also gave **interject** in the late 16th century.

interlocutor [early 16th century] This is modern Latin, from Latin *interlocut-*, the past participial stem of *interloqui* meaning 'interrupt (by speech)' (literally 'speak between').

interloper [late 16th century] An early *interloper* was an unauthorized trader trespassing on the rights of a trade monopoly. The second element *-loper* is the same found in archaic *landloper* 'vagabond' (from Middle Dutch *landlooper*).

interlude [Middle English] This was originally a light dramatic entertainment: it comes from medieval Latin *interludium*, from *inter-* 'between' and *ludus* 'play'.

intermediate [late Middle English] *Intermediate* is from medieval Latin *intermediatus*, from Latin *intermedius*, from *inter-* 'between' and *medius* 'middle'. Also from Latin *intermedius* is **intermediary** (late 18th century) from French *intermédiaire*, from Italian *intermediario*.

intermittent [mid 16th century] *Intermittent* is from Latin *intermittent-*, the present participial stem of *intermittere* 'cease', from *inter-* 'between' and *mittere* 'let go'. This Latin verb was also the source (via Latin *intermissio(n-)*) of **intermission** in late Middle English. This word's use for a break between sections of a play, concert, or film was first found from the 1920s in the USA.

intern [early 16th century] This was first used as an adjective in the sense 'internal'. It is from French *interne*, from Latin *internus* 'inward, internal'. Current senses date from the 19th century. From the same base is **internal** which in the early 16th century had the sense 'intrinsic', from modern Latin *internalis*.

interpose [late 16th century] *Interpose* is from French *interposer*, from Latin *interponere* 'put in' (literally 'put between') but influenced by both Latin *interpositus* 'inserted' and Old French *poser* 'to place'.

interpret [late Middle English] Latin *interpretari* 'explain, translate' (from *interpres*, *interpret-* 'agent, translator, interpreter') has given rise to *interpret* and both **interpreter** and **interpretation**, all three via Old French and in the same period.

interrogation [late Middle English] This is from Latin *interrogatio(n-)*, from the verb *interrogare* 'to question', from *inter-* 'between' and *rogare* 'ask'. Use in grammar and rhetoric dates from the late 16th century. Late 15th-century **interrogate** is from the same Latin verb.

interrupt [late Middle English] *Interrupt* is from Latin *interrupt-*, the past participial stem of *interrumpere* 'break, interrupt', from *inter-* 'between' and *rumpere* 'to break'.

intersect [early 17th century] This comes from Latin *intersecare* 'cut, intersect', from *inter-* 'between' and *secare* 'to cut'. The noun **intersection** is recorded from the mid 16th century, from Latin *intersectio(n-)*, from *intersecare*. As a term for a road junction, the word is found from the mid 19th century in North American usage.

intersperse [mid 16th century] This verb originally meant 'diversify (something) by introducing other things at intervals'. The source is Latin *interspers-*, the past participial stem of *interspergere* 'scatter between', from *inter-* 'between' and *spargere* 'to scatter'.

interval [Middle English] *Interval* is from Old French *entrevalle*, based on Latin *intervallum* 'space between ramparts, interval', from *inter-* 'between' and *vallum* 'rampart'.

intervention [late Middle English] This is from Latin *interventio(n-)*, from the verb *intervenire*, literally 'come between'. This Latin verb is also the source of **intervene** (late 16th century in the sense 'come in as an extraneous factor or thing'): from Latin *intervenire*.

interview [early 16th century] Formerly also written as *enterview*, *interview* is from French *entrevue*, from *s'entrevoir* 'see each other'. The association with the press trying to obtain a statement for publication by questioning someone is found from the mid 19th century; in contexts of the job application process examples are found from the early 20th century.

intestate [late Middle English] The legal term *intestate* is from Latin *intestatus*, from *in-* 'not' and *testatus* 'testified'.

intestine [late 16th century] This is from Latin *intestinum*, the neuter of *intestinus* 'internal', from *intus* 'within'.

intimate[1] [early 17th century] *Intimate* 'closely acquainted, familiar' is from late Latin *intimatus*, the past participle of Latin *intimare* 'impress, make familiar', from *intimus* 'inmost, deepest, profound'.

intimate[2] [early 16th century] The verb *intimate* 'make known' is from late Latin *intimare* 'to make known' The noun **intimation** was already recorded in late Middle English.
→ INTIMATE[1]

intimidate [mid 17th century] Based on Latin *timidus* 'timid', *intimidate* is from medieval Latin *intimidare* meaning 'to make timid'.

intone [late 15th century] This was originally written as *entone*. It comes from Old French *entoner* or medieval Latin *intonare*, from *in-* 'into' and Latin *tonus* 'tone'. **Intonation** dates from the early 17th century with reference to the opening phrase of a plainsong melody: it is from medieval Latin *intonatio(n-)*, from *intonare*.

intoxicate [late Middle English] 'To poison' was the early sense of *intoxicate*, from medieval Latin *intoxicare*, from *in-* 'into' and *toxicare* 'to poison'. The base is Latin *toxicum* 'a poison'. The association with alcohol is found from the late 16th century.
→ TOXIC

intransigent [late 19th century] This comes from French *intransigeant*, from Spanish *los intransigentes* (a name adopted by the extreme republicans in Spain in 1873–4 and to the Party of the Extreme Left in the Spanish Cortes = legislative assembly). It is based on Latin *in-* 'not' and *transigere* 'come to an understanding'.

intrepid [late 17th century] This comes from French *intrépide* or Latin *intrepidus* whose literal meaning is 'not alarmed'.

intricate [late Middle English] Latin *intricat-*, the past participial stem of the verb *intricare* 'entangle', is the source of *intricate* in English. It is from *in-* 'into' and *tricae* 'tricks, perplexities'.

intrigue [early 17th century] 'Deceive, cheat' was the sense of the verb reflected in early contexts. The spelling is from French *intrigue* 'plot' and *intriguer* 'to tangle, to plot', via Italian from Latin *intricare*. The verb sense 'arouse the curiosity of' was influenced by a later French sense 'to puzzle, make curious' which arose in the late 19th century.
→ INTRICATE

intrinsic [late 15th century] *Intrinsic* had the early general sense 'interior, inner'. French *intrinsèque* is the source, from late Latin *intrinsecus*, from the earlier adverb *intrinsecus* 'inwardly, inwards'.

introduce [late Middle English] The early sense was 'bring (a person) into a place or group'. It is from Latin *introducere*, from *intro-* 'to the inside' and *ducere* 'to lead'. Late Middle English **introduction** is from Latin *introductio(n-)*, from the verb *introducere*.

introspection [late 17th century] This is based on Latin *introspicere* 'look into' or *introspectare* 'keep looking into'.

introvert [mid 17th century] Early use was as a verb in the general sense 'turn one's thoughts inwards (in spiritual contemplation)'. It comes from modern Latin *introvertere*, from *intro-* 'to the inside' and *vertere* 'to turn'. Its use as a term in psychology dates from the early 20th century.

intrusion [late Middle English] The early sense was 'invasion, usurpation'. The source is medieval Latin *intrusio(n-)*, from Latin *intrudere* 'thrust in' (from *in-* 'into' and *trudere* 'to thrust'). **Intrude** dates from the mid 16th century when it was spelt *entrude*: the early meaning was 'usurp an office, usurp a right'. It comes from Latin *intrudere*.

intuition [late Middle English] *Intuition* at first referred to 'spiritual insight or immediate spiritual communication'. It is from late Latin *intuitio(n-)*, from Latin *intueri* 'consider or contemplate'; the formative elements are *in-* 'upon' and *tueri* 'to look'. In modern philosophy *intuition* as immediate mental apprehension of something without any reasoning involved is found from the late 16th century. **Intuitive** dates from the late 15th century when it was used to describe sight as 'accurate, unerring': the source is medieval Latin *intuitivus*, from Latin *intueri*.

inundate [late 16th century] *Inundate* is from Latin *inundat-*, the past participial stem of *inundare* 'to flood', from *in-* 'into, upon' and *undare* 'to flow'. The base is Latin *unda* 'a wave'.

inure [late Middle English] Early spellings included *enure*; it comes from an Anglo-Norman French phrase meaning 'in use or practice', from *en* 'in' and Old French *euvre* 'work' (from Latin *opera*). The modern use is usually the passive *be inured to something* conveying the sense 'be accustomed to something' (by habitual occurrence).

invade [late Middle English] The early sense was 'attack or assault (a person)'. The source is Latin *invadere*, from *in-* 'into' and *vadere* 'go'.

Also based on this is late Middle English **invasion** from late Latin *invasio(n-)* and, from the same period, **invasive** from obsolete French *invasif, -ive* or medieval Latin *invasivus*.

invalid [mid 16th century] This word meaning 'not valid' appeared earlier than its opposite *valid*: it comes from Latin *invalidus*, from *in-* 'not' and *validus* 'strong'. A special sense of *invalid* ('infirm or disabled') gave, with a change of pronunciation, the noun use 'a person disabled by illness or injury'.
→VALID

invalidate [mid 17th century] *Invalidate* is from medieval Latin *invalidat-*, the past participial stem of *invalidare* 'annul'. The base is Latin *validus* 'strong'.

invective [late Middle English] This is currently a mass noun for 'insulting or abusive language' (e.g. *he let out a stream of invective*), but original use was as an adjective meaning 'reviling, abusive'. *Invective* is from Old French *invectif, -ive*, from late Latin *invectivus* 'attacking', from the verb *invehere* (literally 'carry in'). The noun is from late Latin *invectiva (oratio)* 'abusive or censorious (language)'. **Inveigh**, formerly also written as *enveigh*, is found from the late 15th century; it now means 'speak about something with great hostility' but was first used in the sense 'carry in, introduce'; The source here too is Latin *invehere* 'carry in' and *invehi* 'be carried into, assail'.

inveigle [late 15th century] This was first recorded in the sense 'beguile, deceive' and was formerly also written as *enveigle*. It comes from Anglo-Norman French *envegler*, an alteration of Old French *aveugler* 'to blind', from *aveugle* 'blind'.

invention [Middle English] 'Finding out, discovery' was the early sense of *invention*, from Latin *inventio(n-)*, from *invenire* 'discover' (from *in-*, upon' and *venire* 'come'). This Latin verb is the source of several words: **invent** recorded from the late 15th century in the sense 'find out, discover'; **inventive** (late Middle English from French *inventif, -ive* or medieval Latin *inventivus*), and from the same period **inventory**: this is from medieval Latin *inventorium*, an alteration of late Latin *inventarium*, literally 'a list of what is found'.

inverse [late Middle English] *Inverse* is from Latin *inversus*, the past participle of *invertere* literally 'turn inside out', the source too of **invert** (mid 16th century in the sense 'turn back to front'). The word **inversion** (also mid 16th century) was first used as a term in rhetoric for the turning of an argument against the person who put it forward: this is from Latin *inversio(n-)*, from the verb *invertere*.

invest [mid 16th century] Early senses included 'clothe', 'clothe with the insignia of a rank', and 'endow with authority'. It is from French *investir* or Latin *investire*, from *in-* 'into, upon' and *vestire* 'clothe' (from *vestis* 'clothing'). The use of the word in financial contexts dates from the early 17th century and was influenced by the Italian verb *investire*.

investigation [late Middle English] This is from Latin *investigatio(n-)*, from the verb *investigare* 'trace out', the source too of **investigate** in the early 16th century.

investiture [late Middle English] This comes from medieval Latin *investitura*, from *investire* 'clothe with'.
→ INVEST

inveterate [late Middle English] When first used *inveterate* referred to disease, in the sense 'of long standing, chronic'. The source is Latin *inveteratus* 'made old', the past participle of *inveterare* (based on *vetus*, *veter-* 'old').

invidious [early 17th century] *Invidious* is from Latin *invidiosus*, from *invidia* 'ill will, envy', from *invidere* 'regard maliciously'.
→ ENVY

invigilate [mid 16th century] This word initially had the general sense 'watch over, keep watch'. It is from Latin *invigilat-*, the past participial stem of *invigilare* 'watch over', from *in-* 'upon, towards' and *vigilare* 'watch'. The base is Latin *vigil* 'watchful'.

invigorate [mid 17th century] This is from medieval Latin *invigorat-*, the past participial stem of *invigorare* 'make strong', from *in-* 'towards' and Latin *vigorare* 'make strong'. The base is Latin *vigor* 'vigour'.

invincible [late Middle English] This word appeared earlier than its opposite *vincible*. It is via Old French from Latin *invincibilis*, from *in-* 'not' and *vincibilis* 'able to be overcome' (from *vincere* 'to overcome').

invitation [late Middle English] This comes from French, or from Latin *invitatio(n-)*, from *invitare* which is also the source of mid 16th-century **invite** from Old French *inviter*.

invoice [mid 16th century] This was originally the plural (spelt *invoyes*) of obsolete *invoy* meaning literally 'a despatch of goods': it comes from obsolete French *envoy* from *envoyer* 'to send'.
→ ENVOY

invoke [late 15th century] This comes from French *invoquer*, from Latin *invocare* 'call upon as a witness, call upon for aid', from *in-* 'upon' and *vocare* 'to call'. Late Middle English **invo-**cation is via Old French from Latin *invocatio(n-)*, from the verb *invocare*.

involve [late Middle English] Early senses included 'enfold, enwrap' and 'entangle'; it was formerly also written as *envolve*. The source of the word is Latin *involvere*, from *in-* 'into' and *volvere* 'to roll'.

invulnerable [late 16th century] *Invulnerable* appeared earlier than its opposite *vulnerable*. It comes from Latin *invulnerabilis*, from *in-* 'not' and *vulnerabilis* 'capable of being wounded'.
→ VULNERABLE

ire [Middle English] This formal word for 'anger' is via Old French from Latin *ira* 'anger', the base too of late Middle English **irascible** which came via French from late Latin *irascibilis*, from *irasci* 'grow angry'. The adjective **irate** dates from the mid 19th century, from Latin *iratus*, from *ira*.

iridescent [late 18th century] This word meaning 'displaying luminous colours that appear to change' is based on Latin *iris*, *irid-* 'rainbow'.

irk [Middle English] In early examples the sense was 'be annoyed or disgusted': it is perhaps from Old Norse *yrkja* 'to work, take effect upon'.

iron [Old English] Old English *iren*, *isen*, *isern* is Germanic in origin and related to Dutch *ijzer* and German *Eisen*, and probably ultimately from Celtic. Many uses of *iron* as a defining word have arisen from the fact that the item was originally made of iron, for example *irons* for 'fetters' and *iron* for smoothing clothes: the latter dates from the early 17th century. The use of the word in medicinal preparations is found from the mid 18th century.

irony [early 16th century] This came via Latin from Greek *eirōneia* 'simulated ignorance', from *eirōn* 'dissembler'. **Ironic** dating from the mid 17th century is from French *ironique* or late Latin *ironicus*, from Greek *eirōnikos* 'dissembling, feigning ignorance', from *eirōneia*.

irradiate [late 16th century] This was first used in the sense 'emit rays, shine upon'. It is from Latin *irradiare*, from *in-* 'upon' and *radiare* 'to shine' (from *radius* 'ray').

irregular [late Middle English] 'Not conforming to rule' (for example that of the Church) was the sense of *irregular* in early examples. It comes via Old French from medieval Latin *irregularis*, from *in-* 'not' and *regularis*. Middle English **irregularity** is from Old French *irregularite*, from late Latin *irregularitas*, from *irregularis*.

irrigate [early 17th century] This comes from Latin *irrigat-*, the past participial stem of *irrigare* 'moisten', from *in-* 'into' and *rigare* 'moisten, wet'.

irritation [late Middle English] *Irritation* is from Latin *irritatio(n-)*, from the verb *irritare*, the base too of **irritate** recorded from the mid 16th century in the sense 'excite, provoke'. **Irritable** (mid 17th century) is from Latin *irritabilis*, from the verb *irritare*.

island [Old English] Old English *īegland* is from *īeg* 'island' (from a base meaning 'watery, watered') and *land*. The change in the spelling of the first syllable in the 16th century was due to association with the unrelated word **isle**: this, in Middle English, was spelt *ile*, from Old French, from Latin *insula*. The spelling with *s* (also in 15th-century French) was influenced by Latin.

isolate [early 19th century] *Isolate* is a back-formation (by removal of the suffix) from mid 18th-century *isolated*, the source of which is French *isolé*: this derives from Italian *isolato*, from late Latin *insulatus* 'made into an island'. Latin *insula* 'island' is the base. **Isolation** (mid 19th century) is based on *isolate*, partly influenced by French *isolation*. The medical context of *isolation wards* in hospitals appears at the end of the 19th century.

isometric [mid 19th century] This is based on Greek *isometria* 'equality of measure', from *isos* 'equal' and *-metria* 'measuring'.

isotonic [early 19th century] This word was first used as a musical term designating a system of tuning, characterized by equal intervals; it is commonly used in physiology contexts currently. From Greek *isotonos*, the base elements are *isos* 'equal' and *tonos* 'tone'.

issue [Middle English] 'Outflowing' was the early sense of *issue* from Old French, based on Latin *exitus*, the past participle of *exire* 'go out'. Other semantic branches of the word are 'way out' (Thackeray *The Virginians*: my Lord Castlewood departed by another issue), 'offspring' (e.g. *without male issue*), 'outcome of an action, result of a discussion' (Daniel Defoe *Robinson Crusoe*: They ... said they would much rather venture to stay there than to be carried to England to be hanged: so I left it on that issue), the legal use 'point in question' (e.g. ... *directed an issue to be tried*), and 'a giving out' (e.g. *issue of bank notes*).

it [Old English] Old English *hit* was the neuter of *he*. Of Germanic origin, it is related to Dutch *het*.
➔ HE

italic [late Middle English] This was first used in the general sense 'Italian'. It comes via Latin from Greek *Italikos*, from *Italia* 'Italy'. Senses relating to writing date from the early 17th century.

itch [Old English] Old English *gycce* (noun), *gyccan* (verb) are West Germanic in origin; they are related to Dutch *jeuk* (noun) and Dutch *jeuken*, German *jucken* (verbs). The figurative notion of hankering appears in examples from the early 16th century (Robert Browning *Filippo Baldinucci*: We fret and fume and have an itch To strangle folk).

item [late Middle English] Early use of this Latin word was as an adverb meaning 'in like manner, also'. The noun sense arose in the late 16th century from the use of the adverb to introduce each statement in a list.

itinerary [late Middle English] This word for 'a planned route' comes from late Latin *itinerarium*, the neuter of *itinerarius* 'of a journey or roads', from Latin *iter, itiner-* 'journey, road'. **Itinerant** is found from the late 16th century describing a judge travelling on a circuit: this is from late Latin *itinerant-*, the present participial stem of *itinerari* 'to travel', from Latin *iter*.

Jj

jab [early 19th century] This was originally a Scots word and is a variant of late Middle English *job* 'stab, prod', a word symbolic of a brief forceful action. Its use meaning 'inoculate' dates from the 1920s.

jabber [late 15th century] This word is imitative of rapid and excited talk. The word **jabberwocky** meaning 'meaningless language' is from the title of a nonsense poem in Lewis Carroll's *Through the Looking Glass* (1871).

jack [late Middle English] This word is from *Jack*, a pet form of the given name *John*. The term was used originally to refer to an ordinary man; from the mid 16th century it also denoted a youth which was extended to the 'knave' in cards (Dickens *Great Expectations*: He calls the knaves, Jacks, this boy!) and to 'male animal' (as in *jackass*). The word was also a term for various devices saving human labour as though one had a helper (e.g. *car jack*), and in compounds such as *jackhammer* and *jackknife*. The general sense 'labourer' arose in the early 18th century and survives in *lumberjack*, *steeplejack*, etc. Since the mid 16th century a notion of 'smallness' has arisen, as in the *jack* in bowls. The compound ■ **jackpot** (late 19th century) is based on *jack*. The term was originally used in a form of poker in which the pool accumulated until a player could open the bidding with two jacks or better.

jacket [late Middle English] *Jacket* is from Old French *jaquet*, a diminutive of *jaque*. The origin of the French word is uncertain but it may have been identical with the given name *Jacques* and be associated with a garment worn by people in country areas or rural jobs. The use of *jacket* as a protective cover for a book dates from the late 19th century.

jade[1] [late 16th century] This word for a hard usually green stone used for ornaments is from French *le jade* (earlier *l'ejade*), from Spanish *piedra de ijada* 'stone of the flank': in other words a stone for colic, which it was believed to cure.

jade[2] [late Middle English] The *jade* meaning 'worn-out horse' is of unknown origin. It forms the base of late 16th-century **jaded** which was first recorded in the sense 'disreputable'.

jagged [late Middle English] This is based on late Middle English **jag** meaning 'stab, pierce' and is perhaps symbolic of sudden movement or unevenness.

jail [Middle English] Based on Latin *cavea*, this word came into English in two forms, *jaiole* (from Old French) and *gayole* (from Anglo-Norman French *gaole*) surviving in the spelling *gaol*. The latter was originally pronounced with a hard g, as in *goat*. *Jail* is the official spelling in the US.

jam [early 18th century] This word meaning 'squeeze, pack' is probably symbolic of the action; *cram* is comparable. The **jam** used to describe a thick fruit conserve (recorded from the mid 18th century) is perhaps based on the verb. Use as a jazz term dates from the 1920s.

jamb [Middle English] *Jamb* as a term for a post of a doorway or window is from Old French *jambe* 'leg, vertical support', based on Greek *kampe* 'joint'.

jangle [Middle English] The early word meant 'talk excessively or noisily, squabble'. It comes from Old French *jangler* but earlier details of the origin are unknown. In some senses it has been influenced by *jingle*.

janitor [mid 16th century] This is an English use of a Latin word, from *janua* 'door'. It is chiefly a North American word for a doorkeeper or caretaker. *Janus* was the name of an ancient Italian deity regarded as the doorkeeper of heaven and as the guardian of doors and gates. **January** is the 'month of Janus', presiding over the entrance to the year.

jape [Middle English] This word for a practical joke is apparently combining the form of Old French *japer* 'to yelp, yap' with the sense of Old French *gaber* 'to mock'.

jar[1] [late 16th century] The *jar* that describes a container is from French *jarre*, from Arabic *jarra* 'earthen water vessel'. It has been used colloquially to refer to a 'drink of beer' from the 1920s.

jar[2] [late 15th century] This *jar* associated with a shock or a jolt was first used as a noun in the sense 'disagreement, dispute'. It is probably imitative of a harsh vibratory sound.

jargon [late Middle English] The original sense was 'twittering, chattering', which later came to describe 'gibberish'. It is from Old French *jargoun* 'warbling of birds', a word of unknown origin. The main modern sense (illustrated now in phrases such as *legal jargon*, *computer jargon*) dates from the mid 17th century.

jaundice [Middle English] The Middle English spelling was *jaunes*, from Old French *jaunice* 'yellowness', from *jaune* 'yellow'. The word *jaundiced* in figurative use for 'coloured by envy' dates from the mid 17th century, the source apparently of the verb **jaundice** (late 18th century) 'affect with envy'.

jaunt [late 16th century] *Jaunt* is of unknown origin. Originally depreciatory, early senses included 'tire a horse out by riding it up and down', 'traipse about', and (as a noun) 'troublesome journey'. The current positive sense 'excursion for pleasure' dates from the mid 17th century.

jaunty [mid 17th century] An early sense of *jaunty* was 'well-bred, genteel'. The source is French *gentil*. The word now conveys the sense 'lively, cheerful, and self-confident'.
→ GENTLE; GENTEEL

jaw [late Middle English] *Jaw* is from Old French *joe* 'cheek, jaw'; further details of the origin are unclear. The form *jowe* existed in early use in English; this spelling was soon superseded by *jaw(e)*.

jaywalk [early 20th century] This verb is formed in part on *jay* which is usually the name of a bird of the crow family but is used colloquially sometimes to mean 'silly person'.

jazz [early 20th century] The origin is unknown. Various suggestions have been made: one is that it took its name from *Jasbo* Brown, a black itinerant musician who played along the course of the Mississippi and later in Chicago cabarets; one is that it is a term from an African patois, sometimes said to mean 'excite' and sometimes 'hurry up'.

jealous [Middle English] This comes from Old French *gelos*, from medieval Latin *zelosus*. Middle English **jealousy** is from Old French *gelosie*, from *gelos*.
→ ZEAL

jean [late 15th century] Early use was as an adjective. It comes from Old French *Janne* (now *Gênes*), from medieval Latin *Janua* 'Genoa', the place of original production. The noun sense comes from *jean fustian*, literally 'fustian from Genoa', used in the 16th century as a term for a heavy twilled cotton cloth. The word **jeans**

dates from the mid 19th century as the plural of *jean*.

jeep [Second World War] This was originally US from the initials *GP*, standing for *general purpose*. This choice was influenced by 'Eugene the Jeep', a creature of great resourcefulness and power represented in the *Popeye* comic strip first introduced on 16 March 1936.

jelly [late Middle English] *Jelly* is from Old French *gelee* 'frost, jelly', from Latin *gelata* 'frozen', from *gelare* 'to freeze'. The base is Latin *gelu* 'frost'. The word referred to savoury aspic moulds of meat or fish at first; reference to fruit-flavoured jellies is found from the late 18th century.

jemmy [early 19th century] This word for a short crowbar is from the pet form of the given name *James*; the word *jack* is comparable.
→ JACK

jeopardy [Middle English] The early spelling was *iuparti*, from Old French *ieu parti* 'an (evenly) divided game'. The term was originally used in chess and other games to refer to a problem or a position in which the chances of winning or losing were evenly balanced: this led to the sense 'a dangerous situation'.

jerk [mid 16th century] *Jerk* was first recorded meaning 'a stroke with a whip'; it is probably imitative of the action. The slang use meaning 'fool, stupid person' is originally a US usage dating from the 1930s.

jerry-built [mid 19th century] The origin of this compound is unknown; it is sometimes said to be from the name of a firm of builders in Liverpool, or to allude to the walls of Jericho, which fell down at the sound of Joshua's trumpets (Joshua 6:20: … and it came to pass, when the people heard the sound of the trumpet, and the people shouted with a great shout, that the wall fell down flat).

jerrycan [Second World War] The word *jerrycan* for a metal container for liquids is based on the informal word *Jerry* for 'German', because such containers were first used in Germany.

jest [late Middle English] This comes from the earlier word *gest*, from Old French *geste*, from Latin *gesta* 'actions, exploits'. The base is Latin *gerere* 'do'. The original *jest* was 'an exploit, heroic deed' which led to the word being used for 'a narrative of such deeds' (originally in verse); later the term denoted 'an idle tale', and then by extension in the mid 16th century 'a joke'.

jet [late 16th century] This word was first used as a verb meaning 'jut out'. The source is French *jeter* 'to throw', based on Latin *jactare*, a frequentative (= verb of repeated action) of *jacere* 'to throw'. A *jet* as a type of plane (using jet propulsion for forward thrust) dates from the 1940s.

jetsam [late 16th century] Initially spelt *jetson*, this word is a contraction of *jettison*. The core notion is one of 'thrown material'.

jettison [late Middle English] *Jettison* was originally a noun denoting the throwing of goods overboard to lighten a ship in distress. It comes from Old French *getaison*, from Latin *jactatio(n-)*, from *jactare* 'to throw' The verb dates from the mid 19th century.
→ JET

jetty [late Middle English] *Jetty* (literally 'a thrown-out part') is from Old French *jetee*, the feminine past participle of *jeter* 'to throw'.
→ JET

jewel [Middle English] *Jewel* is from Old French *joel*, from *jeu* 'game, play', perhaps from Latin *jocus* 'jest'. It referred to a decorative piece worn for personal adornment at first (Shakespeare *Twelfth Night*: Here, wear this Jewel for me, tis my picture); later it specified an ornament containing a precious stone or the gem itself. The word **jeweller** (from Old French *juelier*, from *joel*) dates from the same period. **Jewellery** is recorded slightly later and comes from Old French *juelerie*, from *juelier* 'jeweller'.

jib [early 19th century] *Jib* is perhaps related to French *regimber* (earlier *regiber*) 'to buck, rear'. It may be an abbreviation of *gibbet* referring to its suspension from the mast-head. The expression *the cut of one's jib* 'one's personal appearance' was originally a sailor's figure of speech suggested by the prominence and characteristic form of the jib of a ship.
→ JIBE

jibe [mid 16th century] First used as a verb, this word meaning 'make a mocking remark' is perhaps from Old French *giber* 'handle roughly' (in modern dialect 'to kick')

jiggery-pokery [late 19th century] This is probably a variant of Scots *joukery-pawkery*, from *jouk* 'dodge, skulk', of unknown origin.

jilt [mid 17th century] This was described as 'a new cant word' in 1674 when it had the sense 'deceive, trick'. The origin is unknown.

jingo [late 17th century] This was originally a conjuror's word; its use to denote a 'vociferous supporter of policy favouring war' derives from the use of *by jingo* in a popular music-hall song adopted by those supporting Lord Beaconsfield's policy of sending of a British fleet into Turkish waters to resist Russia in 1878. The

chorus ran: 'We don't want to fight, yet by Jingo! if we do, We've got the ships, we've got the men, and got the money too'. The noun **jingoism** is recorded from the late 19th century.

jink [late 17th century] This was originally Scots in the phrase *high jinks* referring to antics at drinking parties. These usually consisted of throwing dice to decide who should perform a silly task to amuse the others in the company, or who should drink a large draught of alcohol; a forfeit was involved. The word is probably symbolic of nimble motion. Current senses associated with a sudden change in direction date from the 18th century.

jive [1920s] This word was originally part of US usage denoting meaningless or misleading speech. Its origin is unknown; the later musical sense 'jazz' gave rise to the meaning 'a dance performed to jazz' in the 1940s.

job [mid 16th century] The original sense was 'a task or piece of work'. The origin is unknown.

jockey [late 16th century] This is a diminutive of *Jock* and was originally the name for an ordinary man, lad, or underling. The word came to mean 'mounted courier', which gave rise to the current sense in the late 17th century. Another early use was 'horse-dealer' which had long been a byword for dishonesty; it probably gave rise to the verb sense 'manipulate', whereas the main verb sense may relate to the behaviour of jockeys manoeuvring for an advantageous position during a race.

jocund [late Middle English] *Jocund* came via Old French from Latin *jocundus*, a variant (influenced by *jocus* 'joke') of *jucundus* 'pleasant, agreeable', from *juvare* 'to delight'.
→ JOKE

jodhpurs [late 19th century] This name for trousers worn for horse-riding derives from *Jodhpur*, a city in western India where similar garments are worn by Indian men as part of everyday dress.

jog [early 16th century] The origin is uncertain. It appears to be an onomatopoeic word. More recent use, extended from contexts of horse-riding at a jolting pace, is in connection with keep-fit exercise: this dates from the 1960s.
→ JAGGED

join [Middle English] *Join* is from Old French *joindre*, from Latin *jungere* 'to join'. This Latin verb is also the source of several words in English. Middle English **joint** (from the Old French past participle of *joindre* 'to join') was used in butchery contexts from the late 16th century. Late Middle English **juncture** originally meant 'joining' (from Latin *junctura* 'joint'); **junction** (early 18th century from Latin *junctio(n-)*) also started out in the sense 'joining'; its use in transport contexts is found from the late 18th century.

joist [late Middle English] The early spelling was *giste*, from an Old French word for a 'beam supporting a bridge'; it is based on Latin *jacere* 'lie down'.

joke [late 17th century] Originally slang, *joke* is perhaps from Latin *jocus* 'jest, wordplay'. **Jocular** was recorded slightly earlier; this is from Latin *jocularis*, from *joculus* (a diminutive of *jocus*).

jolly [Middle English] *Jolly* is from Old French *jolif* 'merry, amorous, handsome, lively, festive', an earlier form of *joli* 'pretty', perhaps from Old Norse *jól*. Middle English **jollity** is from Old French *jolite*, from *joli*.
→ YULE

jostle [late Middle English] The early spelling was *justle*, from *just*, an earlier form of *joust*. The original sense was 'have sexual intercourse with'; current senses date from the mid 16th century.
→ JOUST

jot [late 15th century] *Jot* came via Latin from Greek *iōta*, the smallest letter of the Greek alphabet. In the noun, the notion of 'smallness' predominates (Shakespeare *Merchant of Venice*: This bond doth give thee here no jot of blood); the verb which is first found recorded in the early 18th century focuses on the short sharp action (e.g. *jotted notes down in the meeting*).

journal [late Middle English] Originally a *journal* was a book listing the times of daily prayers. It comes from Old French *jurnal*, from late Latin *diurnalis* 'belonging to a day'. The use of the word to mean 'diary' is recorded from the early 17th century; its use as a term for a daily newpaper or publication dates from the mid 18th century.

journey [Middle English] *Journey* is from Old French *jornee* 'day, a day's travel, a day's work': these were the earliest senses in English. Latin *diurnum* 'daily portion' is the base, from *diurnus* 'daily', from *dies* 'day'. The compound:
■ **journeyman** (late Middle English) is based on *journey* in the obsolete sense 'a day's work'; this is because the journeyman, once no longer bound by indentures, came to be paid by the day.

joust [Middle English] 'Join battle, engage' were the early senses recorded for *joust* from Old French *jouster* 'bring together', based on Latin *juxta* 'near'. The historical spelling from the 13th century was *just*; French influenced

the later spelling which was sometimes used by writers such as Spenser and Milton, became preferred by Johnson, and used by Scott: the pronunciation did not reflect the later (now current) spelling until relatively recently.

jovial [late 16th century] *Jovial* is from French, from late Latin *jovialis* 'of Jupiter', with reference to the supposed influence of the planet Jupiter on those born under it. *Jove* was a poetical equivalent of Jupiter, the name of the highest deity of the ancient Romans.

jowl [Old English] Old English *ceole* 'jawbone' (related to German *Kehle* 'throat, gullet') merged partly with Old English *ceafl* 'jaw' (related to Dutch *kevels* 'cheekbones').

joy [Middle English] *Joy* is from Old French *joie*, based on Latin *gaudium*, from *gaudere* 'rejoice'. The compound:
■ **joypad** used in computing contexts from the late 20th century is a blend of *joystick* and *keypad*.

jubilee [late Middle English] This word is from Old French *jubile*, from late Latin *jubilaeus* (*annus*) '(year) of jubilee', based on Hebrew *yōbēl* (which in Jewish history referred to a year of emancipation and restoration kept every fifty years). The sense of the Hebrew word was originally 'ram's-horn trumpet' with which the jubilee year was proclaimed.

jubilant [mid 17th century] This was originally used in the sense 'making a joyful noise'. It comes from Latin *jubilant-*, the present participial stem of *jubilare* 'call out, halloo'. This Latin verb was used by Christian writers to mean 'shout for joy'.

judge [Middle English] *Judge* is from Old French *juge*, from Latin *judex*, a combination of *jus* 'law' and *dicere* 'to say'. The expression *as grave (or sober) as a judge* is found from the mid 17th century. Middle English **judgement** is from Old French *jugement*, from *juger* 'to judge'. Also based on *judex* is late Middle English **judicial** from Latin *judicialis*, from *judicium* 'judgement'. Latin *judicium* also gave rise to late 16th-century **judicious** and early 19th-century **judiciary**.

jug [mid 16th century] This word is perhaps an extended use of *Jug*, a pet form of the given names *Joan*, *Joanna*, and *Jenny*. Probably because of the narrow entrance of this type of container the word (in full *stone jug*) has been used as a slang term for 'prison': this originated in the US in the early 19th century.

juggernaut [mid 19th century] This word for a large heavy vehicle is an extension of *Juggernaut*, the name (derived via Hindi from Sanskrit *Jagannātha* 'Lord of the world') for the form of Krishna worshipped in Puri, Orissa in eastern India: here in the annual festival Krishna'a image is dragged through the streets in a heavy chariot.

juggle [late Middle English] In early examples *juggle* meant 'entertain with jesting, tricks, etc.'. It is from Old French *jogler*, from Latin *joculari* 'to jest', from *joculus* (a diminutive of *jocus* 'jest'). Current senses date from the late 19th century. The word **juggler** is recorded earlier (in late Old English as *iugelere* 'magician, conjuror'); it derives from Old French *jouglere*, from Latin *joculator*, from the verb *joculari*. The current sense dates from the early 19th century.
→ JOKE

juice [Middle English] *Juice* came via Old French from Latin *jus* 'broth, vegetable juice'. Extended uses to mean power in the form of 'electricity' or 'petrol' date from the late 19th century.

jukebox [1930s] This is based on a word in Creole (Gullah *juke*) meaning 'disorderly'.

jumble [early 16th century] This is probably symbolic of disorder. Words like *bumble, fumble, mumble, tumble* convey the same notion. In the context of second-hand articles sold for charity, the word is found from the late 19th century.

jumbo [early 19th century] This word was originally applied to a large and clumsy person and is probably the second element of *mumbojumbo*. The term was popularized as the name of an elephant at London Zoo, sold in 1882 to the Barnum and Bailey circus.

jump [early 16th century] The early sense recorded was 'be moved or thrown with a sudden jerk'. It is probably imitative of the sound of feet coming into contact with the ground. The word:
■ **jumpsuit** was originally a US usage of the 1940s: it was first used for a parachutist's garment.

jumper [mid 19th century] This word was originally used for a loose outer jacket worn by sailors. It is probably from dialect *jump* 'a short coat', perhaps from Scots *jupe* which was a man's (later also a woman's) 'loose jacket or tunic', via Old French from Arabic *jubba*.

jungle [late 18th century] *Jungle* came via Hindi from Sanskrit *jāngala* 'rough and arid (terrain)'.

junior [Middle English] This word was first used as an adjective following a family name. It is a use of a Latin word, the comparative of *juvenis* 'young'.

junk [late Middle English] A *junk* was initially an old or inferior rope. The origin is unknown. The sense 'old and discarded articles' dates from the mid 19th century. The word **junkie** dating from the 1920s in the US in drug contexts is based on *junk*. The *junk* used to denote a type of sailing vessel is not related. Dating from the mid 16th century, it is from obsolete French *juncque* or Portuguese *junco*, from Malay *jong*. It was reinforced by Dutch *jonk*. Some have thought this to be of Chinese origin but the Portuguese and Dutch were established in the Malay archipelago before they visited China; they found the Javanese and Malay word applied to all large native vessels as well as to Chinese ships.

junket [late Middle English] The culinary word *junket* is from Old French *jonquette* 'rush basket', from *jonc* 'rush', from Latin *juncus*. Originally a term for a rush basket (usually used for fish and still in dialect use), it also denoted a cream cheese made at one time in a rush basket or served on a rush mat.

jury [late Middle English] *Jury* is from Old French *juree* 'oath, inquiry', from Latin *jurata*, the feminine past participle of *jurare* 'to swear'. Early juries were only composed of men and questions were asked of them which related to their own personal knowledge of an event they had witnessed or experienced. From the same Latin source is late Middle English **juror** from Old French *jureor*, from Latin *jurator*. The base is Latin *jus, jur-* 'law'.

just [late Middle English] *Just* came via Old French from Latin *justus*, from *jus* 'law, right', the base of late Old English **justice** (first recorded meaning 'administration of the law'): this came via Old French from Latin *justitia*. Adverbial use as in *that is just what I need* is from the semantic notion 'by right, rightly'.

justify [Middle English] Early senses included 'administer justice to' and 'inflict a judicial penalty on'. The source is Old French *justifier*, from Christian Latin *justificare* 'do justice to', from Latin *justus*. The sense 'give a justification of' dates from the early 17th century.
→ JUST

jut [mid 16th century] *Jut* is a variant of *jet* which was first used to mean 'jut out'.
→ JET

juvenile [early 17th century] *Juvenile* is from Latin *juvenilis*, from *juvenis* 'young, a young person'.

juxtapose [mid 19th century] The source is French *juxtaposer*, from Latin *juxta* 'next' and French *poser* 'to place'.

Kk

kaleidoscope [early 19th century] This word, coined by its inventor Sir David Brewster in 1817, is made up of Greek *kalos* 'beautiful', *eidos* 'form', and the suffix *-scope* (from Greek *skopein* 'look at'). The instrument is in the form of a tube in which mirrors reflect ever-changing patterns of coloured glass shapes on rotation. Figurative use is first recorded in Byron's *Don Juan*: This rainbow look'd like hope—Quite a celestial kaleidoscope.

kangaroo [late 18th century] This is apparently the name of a specific kind of kangaroo from an extinct Aboriginal language of North Queensland. The recent common assertion that the word means 'I don't understand', said to be the supposed reply of a native inhabitant to an immigrant to Australia, lacks foundation. The first species of kangaroo known in Europe was the great kangaroo (*Macropus giganteus*) discovered by Captain Cook in 1770.

kaput [late 19th century] This word meaning 'no longer working' comes from German *kaputt*, from French (*être*) *capot* '(be) without tricks in the card game of piquet'.

karaoke [1970s] This is a word taken from Japanese meaning literally 'empty orchestra'.

kayak [mid 18th century] This comes from Inuit *qayaq*; it is a term common to all the dialects from Greenland to Alaska.

kecks [1960s] This informal British English word for 'trousers', 'knickers', or 'underpants', is a phonetic respelling of the obsolete *kicks* meaning 'trousers'.

keel [Middle English] Of Germanic origin, this *keel* describing the structure along the base of a ship is from Old Norse *kjǫlr*. The word is not related to Middle Dutch *kiel* meaning 'boat': these are related to the British English word *keel* used to describe a flat-bottomed boat once used in the rivers Tyne and Wear for loading colliers.

keen [Old English] The prominent sense of Old English *cēne* was 'brave, daring'. Of Germanic origin, it is related to Dutch *koen* and German *kühn* 'bold, brave'. The Old English word also meant 'wise, clever'. Current senses date from Middle English; the sense 'sharp' is specifically English but its development is obscure.

keep [late Old English] Old English *cēpan* meant 'seize, take in' and 'care for, attend to'. The origin is unknown. It probably belonged to non-literary vulgar language primarily but it is recorded in literary use from c.1000 and seems to have undergone considerable sense development before that. The prime sense may have been 'lay hold on' with the hands, extended to 'watch (= lay hold on visually)'. 'Retention' is the main notion in later development.

keg [early 17th century] This word for a small barrel is a variant of Scots and US dialect *cag*, from Old Norse *kaggi*.

ken [Old English] Old English *cennan* 'tell, make known' is Germanic in origin, related to Dutch and German *kennen* 'know, be acquainted with', from an Indo-European root shared by *can* and *know*. Current senses of the verb ('know', 'recognize') date from Middle English, the noun ('range of knowledge' as in *beyond our ken*) from the mid 16th century.
→ CAN¹; KNOW

kennel [Middle English] This is from an Old Northern French variant of Old French *chenil*, from Latin *canis* 'dog'.

kerb [mid 17th century] This was initially a term for a raised border or frame. It is a variant of *curb* but is usually kept to specific use describing a stone edging to a pavement.
→ CURB

kerchief [Middle English] The early spelling was *kerchef*, from Old French *cuevrechief*, from *couvrir* 'to cover' and *chief* 'head'. It was formerly used to describe a woman's head-dress, a type of cloth covering over the hair. The word was used meaning 'cloth' as the second element of **handkerchief** from the mid 16th century.

kerfuffle [early 19th century] This is perhaps from Scots *curfuffle* (probably from Scottish Gaelic *car* 'twist, bend' and Scots *fuffle* 'to disorder'), or it may be related to Irish *cior thual* 'confusion, disorder'.

kernel [Old English] Old English *cyrnel* is a diminutive of *corn* 'seed, grain'.
→ CORN¹

kerosene [mid 19th century] The word *kerosene* is based on Greek *kēros* 'wax': this is because the solid form of paraffin is wax-like.

ketchup [late 17th century] This is perhaps from Chinese (Cantonese dialect) *k'ē chap* 'tomato juice'.

kettle [Old English] Germanic in origin, Old English *cetel*, *cietel* 'pot, cauldron' is based on Latin *catillus*, a diminutive of *catinus* 'a deep container for cooking or serving food'. In Middle English the word's form was influenced by Old Norse *ketill*.

key [Old English] Old English *cǽg*, *cǽge* is of unknown origin. It is not found in other Germanic languages. The modern pronunciation appears to be of northern origin and it is difficult to know how this became generalized. The word was often used in poetry to rhyme with *day*, *way*, *say*, *play* etc. and this particular pronunciation seems to have been standard through to the end of the 17th century.

kick [late Middle English] The origin is unknown. Middle English spellings included *kike* and *kyke*. The expression *kick over the traces* meaning 'throw off the usual restraints' is recorded from the late 18th century; this is from the image of a horse succeeding in straddling the side ropes attaching it to a cart and thereby having more freedom.

kid¹ [Middle English] The word originally denoted a young goat. It is from Old Norse *kith*, of Germanic origin; related to German *Kitze*. *Kid* was originally applied to a young child in the late 17th century and was low slang but by the 19th century it was heard frequently in familiar speech. Based on *kid* is the verb **kidnap** dating from the late 17th century: the second element is slang *nap* 'nab, seize'. It originally referred to the practice of stealing children to provide servants or labourers for the American plantations.

kid² [early 19th century] The verb *kid* 'deceive in a playful way' is perhaps from the noun *kid*, expressing the notion 'make a child or goat of' someone.

kill [Middle English] Early senses included both 'strike, beat' and 'put to death'. The origin is probably Germanic; it may be related to *quell*. The noun originally denoted a stroke or blow.

kiln [Old English] Old English *cylene* is from Latin *culina* 'kitchen, cooking stove'.

Kilroy [Second World War] Kilroy was a mythical person popularized by American servicemen. Of the many unverifiable accounts of the source of the term, one claims that James J. *Kilroy* of Halifax, Massachusetts, a shipyard employee, wrote 'Kilroy was here' on sections of warships after inspection; the phrase is said to have been reproduced by shipyard workers who entered the armed services.

kilt [Middle English] Early use was as a verb in the sense 'tuck up around the body'. Apparently Scandinavian in origin, the word is comparable with Danish *kilte (op)* 'tuck (up)' and Old Norse *kilting* 'a skirt'. The noun dates from the mid 18th century.

kin [Old English] Old English *cynn* has a Germanic origin; it is related to Dutch *kunne*, from an Indo-European root meaning 'give birth to', shared by Greek *genos* and Latin *genus* 'race'. *Kin* is the first element of Middle English **kindred**; the suffix *-red* is from Old English *rǽden* 'condition'. The insertion of *-d-* in the modern spelling is through phonetic development (as in *thunder*). The word **kinship** is more modern, dating from the early 19th century.

kind¹ [Old English] Old English *cynd(e)*, *gecynd(e)* is Germanic in origin and related to *kin*. The original sense was 'nature, the natural order' as well as 'innate character, form, or condition'; this led to the use of the word for 'a class or race distinguished by innate characteristics'.
→ KIN

kind² [Old English] Old English *gecynde* meant 'natural, native'; in Middle English the earliest sense was 'well-born or well-bred', which gave rise to 'well-disposed by nature, courteous, gentle, benevolent'. The adverb **kindly** was *gecyndelīce* in Old English meaning 'naturally, characteristically'.

kindle [Middle English] This word meaning 'light, set on fire' is based on Old Norse *kynda*, influenced by Old Norse *kindill* 'candle, torch'.

kinetic [mid 19th century] This comes from Greek *kinētikos*, from *kinein* 'to move'.

king [Old English] Old English *cyning*, *cyng* is Germanic in origin and related to Dutch *koning* and German *König*. The title first appeared in Old English as the name of the chiefs of the various Saxon and Anglian 'kins', tribes, or clans who invaded Britain and of the petty states founded by them; it was also the title of the native British chiefs with whom they fought. With the conquests of Wessex in the 9th and 10th centuries, the king of the West Saxons became the king of the English and the tribal kings came to an end. Old English **kingdom** had the early spelling *cyningdōm* and meant 'kingship'.
→ KIN

kink [late 17th century] *Kink*, originally a nautical term referring to a twist in a rope, is from Middle Low German *kinke*, probably from Dutch *kinken* 'to kink'. The adjective **kinky**, based on *kink* arose in the mid 19th century meaning 'having twists'; the sense 'perverted' dates from the 1950s.

kiosk [early 17th century] The term was first used to refer to a 'pavilion'. It comes from French *kiosque*, from Turkish *köşk* 'pavilion', from Persian *kuš*.

kip [mid 18th century] This word meaning 'a nap' was first used as a term for a 'brothel'. It may be related to Danish *kippe* 'hovel, tavern'.

kipper [Old English] Old English *cypera* was first used as a term for a male salmon in the spawning season. It is of Germanic origin and related to Old Saxon *kupiro*. It may also be related to *copper*.

kiss [Old English] The Old English verb *cyssan* is from a Germanic source; related forms are Dutch *kussen* and German *küssen*.

kit [Middle English] *Kit* 'set of items' is from Middle Dutch *kitte* 'wooden vessel', the origin of which is unknown. The original sense 'wooden tub' was later applied to other containers; the word's use for a soldier's equipment (late 18th century) probably arose from the idea of a set of articles packed in a container.

kitchen [Old English] Old English *cycene* is from West Germanic and is related to Dutch *keuken* and German *Küche*, based on Latin *coquere* 'to cook'.

kite [Old English] Old English *cȳta* was first used as a term for a bird of prey; it is probably of imitative origin and related to German *Kauz* 'screech owl'. The toy was so named because it hovers in the air like the bird.

kith [Old English] Old English *cȳthth*, of Germanic origin, is related to *couth*. The original senses were 'knowledge', 'one's native land', and 'friends and neighbours'. The phrase *kith and kin* originally referred to a person's country and relatives, later coming to specify one's friends and relatives.

kitten [late Middle English] Middle English spellings included *kitoun* and *ketoun*, from an Anglo-Norman French variant of Old French *chitoun*, a diminutive of *chat* 'cat'.

kitty [early 19th century] This word was originally used to mean 'jail'. The origin is unknown. Its use as a term for a fund of money dates from the late 19th century.

knack [late Middle English] This was originally a clever or deceitful trick. It is probably related to obsolete *knack* 'sharp blow or sound', of imitative origin. Dutch *knak* 'crack, snap' is comparable.

knacker [late 16th century] A *knacker* was originally a harness-maker and later a slaughterer of horses. The word is possibly from obsolete *knack* 'trinket' associated with the small articles belonging to a harness. It is unclear whether the verb meaning 'exhaust' represents a figurative use of 'slaughter' or of 'castrate': the latter is by association with the vulgar slang use of *knackers* for 'testicles' (perhaps derived from dialect *knacker* 'castanet', from the word *knack* imitative of a sharp abrupt noise).

knapsack [early 17th century] This is from Middle Low German, from Dutch *knapzack*, probably from German *knappen* ' to bite (food)' and *zak* 'sack'. It was first used by soldiers for carrying necessities such as food supplies.

knave [Old English] In Old English a *cnafa* was a 'boy' or 'servant'. Of West Germanic origin, it is related to German *Knabe* 'boy'. The sense 'rogue' arose early and probably developed from a use to describe a 'person of ignoble character'.

knead [Old English] Old English *cnedan* is from a Germanic source; it is related to Dutch *kneden* and German *kneten*.

knee [Old English] Old English *cnēow*, *cnēo* is Germanic in origin, related to Dutch *knie* and German *Knie*, from an Indo-European root shared by Latin *genu* and Greek *gonu*. Old English *cnēowlian* **kneel** is based on *cnēow*.

knell [Old English] Old English *cnyll* (noun), *cnyllan* (verb) are West Germanic in origin and related to Dutch *knal* (noun), *knallen* (verb) 'bang, pop, crack'. The current spelling dating from the 16th century was perhaps influenced by *bell*.

knickerbockers [mid 19th century] *Knickerbocker* was originally a word for a New Yorker (a descendant of the original Dutch settlers of the New Netherlands in America); it was named after Diedrich *Knickerbocker*, the pretended author of W. Irving's *History of New York* (1809). Plural use for loose-fitting breeches is said to have arisen from the resemblance of *knickerbockers* to the knee breeches worn by Dutch men in Cruikshank's illustrations in Irving's book. The word **knickers** (late 19th century) referred at first to 'short trousers': it is an abbreviation of *knickerbockers*.

knife [late Old English] Old English *cnif* is from Old Norse *knífr*, of Germanic origin.

knight [Old English] Old English *cniht* meant 'boy, youth, or servant'. Of West Germanic origin, it is related to Dutch *knecht* and German *Knecht*. The use of the word for a man awarded a non-hereditary title, dates from the mid 16th century.

knit [Old English] Old English *cnyttan* is West Germanic in origin; it is related to German dialect *knütten*. The original sense was 'tie in or with a knot', hence 'join, unite' (as in *a closely-knit family*); an obsolete Middle English sense 'knot string to make a net' gave rise to the handicraft sense.
→ KNOT

knob [late Middle English] This comes from Middle Low German *knobbe* 'knot, knob, bud'. Late Middle English **knobble** is a diminutive of *knob*; the adjective **knobbly** dates from the mid 19th century.

knock [Old English] The origin of Old English *cnocian* is apparently imitative of the sound. The colloquial sense 'speak disparagingly about' is recorded from the late 19th century in US usage.

knoll [Old English] Old English *cnoll* meant 'hilltop'. Of Germanic origin, it is related to German *Knolle* 'clod, lump, tuber' and Dutch *knol* 'tuber, turnip'.

knot [Old English] Old English *cnotta* is of West Germanic origin; Dutch *knot* is related. The expression *tie the knot* referring to marriage dates from the early 18th century.

know [Old English] Old English *cnāwan* (earlier *gecnāwan*) 'recognize, identify' is of Germanic origin, from an Indo-European root shared by Latin (*g*)*noscere* and Greek *gignōskein* 'know (by the senses)'. The English verb also comprises the meaning 'know (by the mind), know as a fact'. These two strands of 'apprehend' and 'comprehend' are often translated by different verbs in other European languages: e.g. French *savoir* and *connaître*, German *kennen* and *wissen*, etc.
→ CAN[1]; KEN

knowledge [Middle English] This was originally a verb in the sense 'acknowledge, recognize'. The source is an Old English compound based on *cnāwan*.
→ KNOW

knuckle [Middle English] Middle English *knokel* originally denoted the rounded shape of a joint such as the elbow or knee when bent. It comes from Middle Low German, Middle Dutch *knökel*, a diminutive of *knoke* 'bone'. In the mid 18th century the verb *knuckle* (*down*) expressed setting the knuckles down to shoot the taw in a game of marbles: this led to the notion of applying oneself with concentration.

kook [1960s] This informal word for an eccentric person is probably from *cuckoo*.

kowtow [early 19th century] This word for kneeling down and touching the forehead on the ground in worship or submission is from Chinese *kētóu*, from *kē* 'knock' and *tóu* 'head'.

L1

label [Middle English] The first sense recorded for *label* was 'a narrow strip or band'. It came from an Old French word meaning 'ribbon', the origin of which is thought to be Germanic by some scholars. In the late 15th century, a *label* was a narrow strip of material attached to a document to carry the seal; the current sense referring to a slip of paper, metal, material, etc. bearing a name or description, is recorded from the late 17th century. Association with a company as a brand-name has been found since the beginning of the 20th century.
→ LAP¹

laboratory [early 17th century] *Laboratory* is essentially a place where work is undertaken; it comes from medieval Latin *laboratorium*, from Latin *laborare* 'to labour'.

labour [Middle English] This word used as a noun is from Old French *labour*; as a verb it is from Old French *labourer*, both having as their source Latin *labor* 'toil, trouble'. As a term in childbirth it dates from the late 16th century from the core sense of 'exertion'. Association with efforts to produce commercial goods for the community arose in the late 18th century; the word was then transferred to the work-force. This had its influence on the use of *Labour* to refer to the *Labour Party* formed in 1906 by a federation of trade unions and political bodies seeking to represent the workforce as opposed to management. Related words include Middle English **labourer** for an unskilled manual worker (Luke 10:7: *the labourer is worthy of his hire*) and the adjective **laborious** found from late Middle English in the positive sense 'industrious, hard-working' as well as expressing the negative notion 'toilsome'. This is from Old French *laborieux*, from Latin *laboriosus*, from *labor*.

labyrinth [late Middle English] The word was first used to refer to the mythological maze constructed by the Greek craftsman Daedalus for King Minos of Crete to house the Minotaur, a creature half-man half-bull. The story recounted how Daedalus and his son Icarus were imprisoned by the king but escaped, helped by wings fabricated through Daedalus' skill and attached to their bodies by wax. The source of the word-form is French *labyrinthe* or Latin *labyrinthus*, from Greek *laburinthos*.

lace [Middle English] The Old French noun *laz* or *las* and the verb *lacier* gave rise to *lace*; the base is Latin *laqueus* 'noose' which was also found as an early sense in English. The fine openwork fabric made by looping or twisting fine threads, known as *lace*, was so named from the middle of the 16th century. The verb *lace* is often used figuratively: *lace with*, a late 16th-century usage, meant 'streak with colour'; the extended senses 'fortify' and 'flavour' (as in *laced with gin*, *laced with honey*) are recorded a century later.
→ LASSO

lacerate [late Middle English] *Lacerate*, often used in contexts describing the skin as damaged or scored, is from Latin *lacerat-*, the past participial stem of *lacerare* 'to mangle', from *lacer* 'mangled, torn'.

lack [Middle English] This word corresponds to and is perhaps partly from Middle Dutch and Middle Low German *lak* 'deficiency' and Middle Dutch *laken* 'lack, blame'. Early use in English reflected the meaning 'defect, failing, offence'. The verb meaning 'be deficient in' gave rise to the compound:
■ **lackland** recorded from the late 16th century and used as a sobriquet (*John Lackland*) of King John (1165–1216): he lost most of his French possessions including Normandy to Phillip II of France.

lackadaisical [mid 18th century] 'Feebly sentimental' was among the early meanings of *lackadaisical* which comes from the archaic interjection *lackaday* and its extended form *lackadaisy*. These were said in an affectedly languishing manner (Fielding *Tom Jones*: Good lack-a-day! Why there now, who … would have thought it!).

lackey [early 16th century] *Lackey* is from French *laquais*, perhaps from Catalan *alacay*, from Arabic *al-kā'id* 'the chief'. The word initially described a 'footman', particularly one used to take messages. Towards the end of the 16th century, the word was associated with servile obsequious behaviour. As a term of abuse, *lackey* has been applied specifically to a servile follower in political contexts from the 1930s.

lacquer [late 16th century] This is from obsolete French *lacre* 'sealing wax', from Portuguese *laca*. Early use of the word, until the early 18th century, was synonymous with *lac*, a dark red resinous secretion from certain homopteran insects, used to make varnish. The word as a name for a hairspray styling product dates from the 1940s.

lad [Middle English] A *lad* in early use described a 'man of low birth', a 'varlet', an 'attendant'. In the 15th century it was used to mean 'a youth' and sometimes, in pastoral poetry, 'a young shepherd'. The origin is obscure. In the 1990s, the word **ladette** came into use for a young woman behaving in a 'laddish' (= brash and crude) manner.

ladder [Old English] Old English *hlæd(d)er* is West Germanic in origin and related to Dutch *leer* and German *Leiter*. The word's use to describe an unravelled section in stockings or knitted garments was first applied by sempstresses in the early part of the 19th century.

lade [Old English] Old English *hladan* is West Germanic in origin, related to Dutch and German *laden* 'to load' and perhaps to English *lathe*. In English the word has had two semantic strands, 'load' and 'draw water': the second strand is peculiar to English.
→ LADLE

ladle [Old English] Old English *hlædel* is from *hladan* 'to lade' (= scoop up liquid).
→ LADE

lady [Old English] Old English *hlæfdige* was a woman to whom homage or obedience was due, such as the wife of a lord or the mistress of a household; the word also referred specifically to the Virgin Mary. In this word, Old English *hlāf* 'loaf' is combined with a Germanic base meaning 'knead' (related to *dough*). In *Lady Day* and other compounds where *lady* conveys a notion of possession, it represents the Old English genitive *hlæfdigan* meaning '(Our) Lady's'.
→ LORD

lag¹ [early 16th century] Early use was as a noun for the 'hindmost person (in a game, race, etc.)'; it was also a term for 'dregs'. One possible theory as to the origin is that it may be related to the dialect adjective *lag* meaning 'last'; this may be the result of a fanciful distortion of *last* from such phrases as *fog, seg, lag* said by children in games deciding the order 'first, second, last'. Another possibility is that the word is of Scandinavian origin (Norwegian dialect *lagga* 'go slowly' is comparable). *Lag* is also the base of **laggard** which dates from the early 18th century as an adjective.

lag² [late 19th century] This *lag* which conveys the meaning 'cover with strips of felt or other insulating material' is from the earlier word *lag* for a 'piece of insulating cover'.

lager [mid 19th century] This word is taken from German *Lagerbier* 'beer brewed for keeping': the first element is *Lager* 'storehouse'.

lagoon [early 17th century] *Lagoon* is from Italian and Spanish *laguna*, from Latin *lacuna* 'pool'.

lair [Old English] The Old English word spelt *leger* meant 'resting-place' or 'bed'. The word has remained in Scots as a term for a grave. Of Germanic origin, the English form is related to Dutch *leger* 'bed, camp' and German *Lager* 'storehouse'. English examples of *lair* as a place for animals to lie and rest date from Middle English.
→ LIE¹

lake [late Old English] A *lake* once denoted a pond or pool: it is from Old French *lac*, from Latin *lacus* 'basin, pool, lake'. It is usually however a large area of water forming a geographical feature, such as one of the *Great Lakes* forming the boundary between Canada and the US, or one of the expanses of water found in the *Lake District* of north west England: the *Lake Poets* refer to Coleridge, Southey, and Wordsworth who lived in this area.

lama [mid 17th century] This honorific title applied to a spiritual leader in Tibetan Buddhism is from Tibetan *bla-ma* (the initial *b* remaining silent); the literal meaning is 'superior one'.

lamb [Old English] *Lamb* is of Germanic origin; related words are Dutch *lam* and German *Lamm*. The associations in figurative use include meekness and innocence, which has led to its application as a term of affection (Shelley *Fiordispina*: And say, sweet lamb, would you not learn …?). Use of the word in religious contexts is common especially in the phrase *Lamb of God* from John 1:29: Behold the Lamb of God, which taketh away the sin of the world.

lambaste [mid 17th century] The early sense recorded for *lambaste* was 'beat, thrash': it comes from late 16th-century *lam* meaning 'beat soundly' and mid 16th-century *baste* meaning 'thrash'. The current sense 'criticize harshly' dates from the late 19th century.

lame [Old English] Old English *lama* is Germanic in origin; it is related to Dutch *lam* and German *lahm*. Figurative use in the sense 'feeble' (e.g. *lame excuse*) arose early.

lament [late Middle English] First found used as a verb, *lament* is from French *lamenter* or

Latin *lamentari* 'to wail', from *lamenta* (plural) 'weeping'. The adjective **lamentable** is recorded from late Middle English with the meaning 'mournful' and 'pitiable, regrettable': it is from Old French, or from Latin *lamentabilis*, from the verb *lamentari*.

lamp [Middle English] *Lamp* came via Old French from late Latin *lampada*, from Latin *lampas*, *lampad-* 'torch', from Greek. In the plural the word was used by Shakespeare to refer poetically to the eyes (*Comedy of Errors*: My wasting lampes some fading glimmer left); this usage is slang in current language.

lampoon [mid 17th century] The source of English *lampoon* meaning 'publicly criticize by using ridicule or irony' is French *lampon*. This is said to be from the refrain *lampons* 'let us drink!', from *lamper* 'gulp down', a nasalized form of *laper* 'to lap (liquid)'.

land [Old English] *Land* has a Germanic origin; it is related to Dutch *land* and German *Land*. The idiom *to see how the land lies* was primarily nautical dating from the early 18th century. The notion of 'securing' as in *land a job* is found in examples from the mid 19th century; this may be an extension of *land* with the connotation of success in fishing contexts (e.g. *land a large fish*).

landscape [late 16th century] This was first used as a term for a picture of natural scenery: it comes from Middle Dutch *lantscap*, from *land* 'land' and *-scap* (the equivalent of the English suffix *-ship*).

lane [Old English] This word is related to Dutch *laan*; the ultimate origin is unknown. It expresses the notion 'narrow passage' and has been used in transport contexts as a division of a highway or motorway from the 1920s.

language [Middle English] *Language* is from Old French *langage*, based on Latin *lingua* 'tongue'.

languish [Middle English] Early senses included 'become faint, feeble, or ill'; in the early 18th century it came to mean 'assume a languid or sentimentally tender expression' and was aptly applied to Sheridan's character Lydia Languish in *The Rivals* performed for the first time on 17 January 1775. Old French *lan-guiss-* gave rise to the English form: it is the lengthened stem of *languir* 'languish', from a variant of the Latin verb *languere* related to *laxus* 'loose, lax'. From the same base and dating from the same period is **languor** which came via Old French. The original senses were 'illness, disease' and 'distress' later extended to 'faintness, lassitude'; current senses date from the 18th century, when such lassitude became

associated with a romantic sometimes rather self-indulgent yearning. Late 16th-century **languid**, also based on Latin *languere*, was first recorded as 'be forced to remain in an unpleasant situation' (e.g. *languishing in a Mexican jail*): the form is from French *languide* or Latin *languidus*.

lank [Old English] Old English *hlanc* meant 'thin, not filled out'. The word is not found in other Germanic languages but is related to High German *lenken* 'to bend, turn aside'.
→ FLANK; LINK

lantern [Middle English] *Lantern* is from Old French *lanterne*, via Latin from Greek *lamptēr* 'torch, lamp', from *lampein* 'to shine'.

lap¹ [Old English] Old English *læppa* is Germanic in origin; it is related to Dutch *lap* and German *Lappen* 'piece of cloth'. The word originally referred to a fold or flap of a garment (mid 17th-century *lapel* is a diminutive of *lap*), but later more specifically to a flap that could be used as a pocket or pouch. It was also used in Middle English to refer to the front of a skirt when held up to catch or carry something, and from that it came to specify the area between the waist and knees as a place where a child could be nursed or an object held.
→ LAPEL

lap² [Middle English] This *lap* denoting 'coiling' such as 'a circuit of a racing track', 'a turn of a cable' was first found recorded as a verb meaning 'coil, fold, or wrap'. It comes from *lap* 'flap, fold'. The verb and the noun sense 'circuit' date from the mid 19th century.
→ LAP¹

lap³ [Old English] Old English *lapian* 'take up liquid by the tongue' is from a Germanic source; it is related to Middle Low German and Middle Dutch *lapen*.

lapel [mid 17th century]
→ LAP¹

lapse [late Middle English] *Lapse* is from Latin *lapsus*, from *labi* 'to glide, slip, or fall'; the verb was reinforced by Latin *lapsare* 'to slip or stumble'. Association with time as in *lapse of a hundred years* dates from the mid 18th century.

larceny [late 15th century] This legal term comes from Old French *larcin*, from Latin *latrocinium*. The base is Latin *latro(n-)* 'robber' which had the earlier meaning 'mercenary soldier', from Greek *latreus*. In legal contexts a distinction was once made between *grand larceny* and *petty larceny*: *grand larceny* was the theft of property having a value of more than 12 pence; *petty larceny* related to values of less than 12 pence.

larder [Middle English] An early *larder* was a 'store of meat'. The word derives from Old French *lardier*, from medieval Latin *lardarium*: this is from *lar(i)dum* 'bacon, lard' which gave rise (via Old French) to Middle English **lard**. Greek *larinos* 'fat' is related.

large [Middle English] *Large* was found in early examples with the meaning 'liberal in giving, lavish, ample in quantity'. The spelling came via Old French from Latin *larga*, the feminine of *largus* 'copious': the latter is the base of **largesse** 'liberality, munificence', a Middle English word from Old French.

lark [early 19th century] The word *lark* meaning 'play, have fun' is perhaps from dialect *lake* 'play', from Old Norse *leika*. It is worth noting however that the verb *skylark* had the same notion of playing and frolicking as English *lark* and was recorded earlier.

larva [mid 17th century] 'A disembodied spirit or ghost' was once described by using this Latin word which means literally 'ghost, mask'. The common modern use is as a term for the active immature form of an insect; this technical restricted use is due to the Swedish botanist Linnaeus (1707–78).

lash [Middle English] *Lash* 'strike with or as if with a whip; bind with or as if with a whip' was first recorded meaning 'make a sudden movement': the formation is probably imitative of a short sharp action. The expression *lashings of* is originally Anglo-Irish and means 'great quantities of'; it is found from the early 19th century.

lass [Middle English] *Lass* is based on the Old Norse feminine adjective *laskura* 'unmarried'. It is common in northern and north midland dialects. The word has sometimes been used with the sense 'lady love' (Spenser *Faerie Queene*: And eke that I adry, his faire lovely lasse).

lasso [mid 18th century] This word represents an American Spanish pronunciation of Spanish *lazo*, based on Latin *laqueus* 'noose'.
➔ LACE

last¹ [Old English] The Old English adverb *latost* meant 'after all others in a series'. Germanic originally, it is related to Dutch *laatst*, *lest* and German *letzt*.
➔ LATE

last² [Old English] The verb *last* conveys a notion of 'duration'. In Old English *læstan* meant 'to follow', 'endure, go on for a period of time'; from a Germanic source, it is related to German *leisten* 'afford, yield'.
➔ LAST³

last³ [Old English] Old English *læste* 'shoemaker's model of a foot on which to place and repair a shoe', 'footstep' is Germanic in origin, from a base meaning 'follow'. Related forms are Dutch *leest* and German *Leisten*.

latch [Old English] Old English *læccan* meant 'take hold of, grasp (physically or mentally)'. The origin is Germanic. The word's use as a noun for a type of door fastening dates from Middle English. The expression *latch on to* meaning 'grasp (both physically or conceptually)' dates from the 1930s.

late [Old English] Old English *læt* as an adjective included the sense 'slow, tardy'. Of Germanic origin, it is related to German *lass*, from an Indo-European root shared by Latin *lassus* 'weary'. The sense 'recently deceased', in examples such as *his late wife*, arose in Middle English. **Lately** (in Old English *lætlice*) initially meant 'slowly, tardily'. Old English **latter** was originally *lætra* 'slower', the comparative of *læt*.
➔ LET

latent [late Middle English] *Latent* is from Latin *latent-*, the present participial stem of *latere* 'be hidden'.

lateral [late Middle English] This word meaning 'at or to the side' is from Latin *lateralis*, from *latus, later-* 'side'.

lathe [Middle English] This term for a machine for shaping wood is probably from Old Danish *lad* 'structure, frame', perhaps from Old Norse *hlath* 'pile, heap'.
➔ LADE

lather [Old English] Old English *læthor* was 'washing soda' or its froth; the verb spelling was *lēthran*. Of Germanic origin, *lather* is related to the Old Norse noun *lauthr*, from an Indo-European root shared by Greek *loutron* 'bath'. The figurative use meaning 'agitation' (e.g. *got into a lather over his mistake*) dates from the early 19th century.

latitude [late Middle English] This geographical term is from Latin *latitudo* 'breadth', from *latus* 'broad'. The general notion of 'freedom from any restriction' (e.g. *too much latitude was given to them in their choice of reading matter*) is found associated with the word from the early 17th century.

latrine [Middle English] Although the word was found in Middle English, it was rare before the mid 19th century. It came via French from Latin *latrina* 'privy', a contraction of *lavatrina*, from *lavare* 'to wash'.

lattice [Middle English] *Lattice* 'a structure made of laths' is from Old French *lattis*, from *latte* 'lath', of Germanic origin. The ordered criss-cross pattern associated with the word has led to its application in many contexts, particularly in botany, zoology, and physics.

laud [late Middle English] The noun is from Old French *laude*, the verb from Latin *laudare*, both from Latin *laus*, *laud-* 'praise'. The plural *lauds* referring to a service of morning prayer in the Divine Office of the Western Christian Church, is Middle English. It derives from the frequent use of the Latin imperative *laudate!* 'praise ye!' in Psalms 148–50. Although traditionally said or chanted at daybreak, *lauds* were historically often held with matins on the previous night.

laugh [Old English] Old English *hlæhhan*, *hliehhan* is from a Germanic source; it is related to Dutch and German *lachen*, as well as to **laughter** (in Old English *hleahtor*, related to German *Gelächter*). The idiomatic phrase *to be laughing* meaning 'to be in a very fortunate position' (as in *you'll be laughing if you land that job*) arose in the 1930s.

launch[1] [Middle English] 'Hurl a missile' and 'discharge with force' were the first meanings found for *launch* in early examples; it is from Anglo-Norman French *launcher*, a variant of Old French *lancier*.

launch[2] [late 17th century] Nautical *launch* 'a large motor boat' was first used as a term for the longboat of a man-of-war: it is from Spanish *lancha* 'pinnace' (= a small boat forming part of the equipment of a warship), perhaps from Malay *lancharan*, from *lanchar* 'swift, nimble'.

launder [Middle English] *Launder* was first used as a noun for 'a person who washes linen'. It is a contraction of *lavender*, from Old French *lavandier*, based on Latin *lavanda* 'things to be washed' (from *lavare* 'to wash'). The figurative use (as in *launder money*) relating to the transferral of illegally acquired funds subsequently returned from an apparently legitimate source, was first found in the 1970s: this usage arose out of the Watergate inquiry in the US in 1973–4. The word **laundry** dates from the early 16th century as a contraction of Middle English *lavendry* from Old French *lavanderie*, from *lavandier*.

laureate [late Middle English] *Laureate* is from Latin *laureatus*, from *laurea* 'laurel wreath', from *laurus* 'laurel'. The word is sometimes short for **Poet Laureate**, an eminent poet appointed as a member of the royal household. The first person to have this title in the modern sense was the English dramatist and poet Ben Jonson (1572–1637), but the title became established with the appointment of John Dryden in 1668. The person appointed was expected to write poems for state occasions, but since Victorian times the post has carried no specific duties.

lava [mid 18th century] This is an adoption of an Italian word from Neapolitan dialect which described the lava stream from Vesuvius (a still active volcano near Naples), but which was originally a word for a stream caused by sudden rain. *Lava* derives from *lavare* 'to wash', from Latin.

lavatory [late Middle English] *Lavatory* is from late Latin *lavatorium* 'a place for washing', from Latin *lavare* 'to wash'. The word originally denoted a place in which to wash such as a bath or ancient Roman piscina, but later, in the mid 17th century, it was a room with washing facilities; the current sense 'toilet' dates from the 19th century.

lavish [late Middle English] Early use of *lavish* was as a noun denoting 'profusion': it is from Old French *lavasse* 'deluge of rain', from *laver* 'to wash', from Latin *lavare*. The verb sense, now current, meaning 'bestow in great quantities' dates from the mid 16th century.

law [Old English] Old English *lagu* is from Old Norse *lag* 'something laid down or fixed', a word of Germanic origin. The phrase combination *law and order* is found from the late 16th century.
→ LAY[1]

lawn[1] [mid 16th century] This is an alteration of dialect *laund* 'glade, pasture', from Old French *launde* 'wooded district, heath', of Celtic origin. The current use as a name for short mown grass dates from the mid 18th century.

lawn[2] [Middle English] The *lawn* associated with fine linen or cotton fabric is probably from *Laon*, the name of a city in France important for linen manufacture.

laxative [late Middle English] This word came via Old French *laxatif*, *-ive* or late Latin *laxativus*, from Latin *laxare* 'loosen'. The base is Latin *laxus* 'loose'.

lay[1] [Old English] Old English *lecgan* 'put down flat' is Germanic in origin, related to Dutch *leggen* and German *legen*. The semantic strands are: 'prostrate, cause to lie' (e.g. *lay low*), 'deposit' (e.g. *lay a wager*), 'place, set' (e.g. *laid traps in the undergrowth*), 'put forward' (e.g. *lay before the court*), and 'place in a layer, spread' (e.g. *lay the table*).
→ LIE[1]

lay[2] [Middle English] The *lay* meaning 'non-clerical' and 'not having expert knowledge' is from Old French *lai*, via late Latin from Greek *laïkos*, from *laos* 'people'.

layer [Middle English] In Middle English there was a word *layer* based on *lay* 'put down' and was a name for a mason who 'put down stones'. The word in the sense 'stratum of material covering a surface' is not found before the early 17th century; it may represent a respelling of an obsolete agricultural use of *lair* referring to soil quality.
➔ LAIR; LAY[1]

lazy [mid 16th century] This is perhaps related to Low German *lasich* 'languid, idle'. The verb **laze** is found from the late 16th century as a back-formation (by removal of the suffix) from *lazy*.

lead[1] [Old English] Old English *lǣdan* 'show the way, be ahead of' is Germanic in origin, related to Dutch *leiden* and German *leiten*. The word was commonly used to translate the Latin word *ducere* and this has influenced to a certain extent the sense development. The word **lead-erene** was coined in the 1980s as a humorous or ironic name for the first female British Prime Minister Margaret Thatcher: the formation was suggested by the pattern of female given names such as *Marlene*.
➔ LOAD

lead[2] [Old English] Old English *lēad* denoting a soft ductile bluish-grey metal is West Germanic in origin, related to Dutch *lood* 'lead' and German *Lot* 'plummet, solder'.

leaf [Old English] Old English *lēaf* is Germanic in origin, related to Dutch *loof* and German *Laub*. Some scholars believe the word to have a core notion of 'peeling away'. The essential 'thin' quality conveyed by the word was transferred early to paper (*leaf of a book*) which then provided many idioms such as *turn over a new leaf* (late 16th century) and *take a leaf out of someone's book* (early 19th century).

league [late Middle English] An early *league* was 'a binding compact for mutual protection or advantage'; it came into English via French from Italian *lega*, from *legare* 'to bind', from Latin *ligare*.

leak [late Middle English] *Leak* is probably of Low German or Dutch origin and related to *lack*. The phrase *leak out* referring to reports or facts is found from the early 19th century.

lean[1] [Old English] Old English *hleonian, hlinian* 'incline, move to a sloping position' is of Germanic origin; it is related to Dutch *leunen* and German *lehnen*, from an Indo-European root shared by Latin *inclinare* and Greek *klinein*. The verbal noun **leaning** is found in figurative use for a 'tendency, inclination' from the late 16th century.

lean[2] [Old English] Old English *hlǣne* 'not fat' is from a Germanic source. Application of the word as a noun is an elliptical use, e.g. *lean* instead of *lean meat*: a well-known illustration of this is the nursery rhyme:
Jack Sprat would eat no fat,
His wife would eat no lean.
And so betwixt them both, you see,
They licked the platter clean.

leap [Old English] Old English *hlēapan* (verb) and *hlȳp* (noun), are Germanic in origin; related forms are Dutch *lopen*, German *laufen* (verb), and Dutch *loop*, German *Lauf* (noun), all meaning 'run'. No certain connections have been established outside Germanic. The compound:
■ **leap year** (late Middle English) is probably from the fact that feast days after February in such a year fell two days later than in the previous year, rather than one day later as in other years, and so could be said to have 'leapt' a day.
➔ LOPE

learn [Old English] This word is West Germanic origin, related to German *lernen*. Old English *leornian* 'learn' gained the additional meaning 'teach' in Middle English: this is illustrated by the adjective **learned** in use from this period: a *learned person* is literally 'a person who has been taught'. In current English *learn* is found meaning both 'gain knowledge' and 'teach' but the latter is now considered not only incorrect but an 'unlearned' use.
➔ LORE

lease [late Middle English] *Lease* is from Old French *lais, leis* 'a letting', from *lesser, laissier* 'let, leave'; the source is Latin *laxare* 'make loose', from *laxus* 'loose, lax'. The word is mostly associated with property contracts but figurative use is found from the late 16th century (Shakespeare *Macbeth*: Our high plac'd Macbeth Shall live the Lease of Nature); this extension of meaning continued in such phrases as (*new*) *lease of life*, suggesting freedom to enjoy a period of life.

leash [Middle English] This is from Old French *lesse, laisse*, from *laissier* in the specific sense 'let run on a slack lead'. The word has been commonly used in sporting contexts such as coursing or hawking.
➔ LEASE

least [Old English]
➔ LESS

leather [Old English] Of Germanic origin, Old English *lether* is related to Dutch *leer* and German *Leder*, from an Indo-European root shared by Irish *leathar* and Welsh *lledr*. The plural *leathers* now associated with leather clothing worn by motorcyclists, was once used more generally and was even extended to the people wearing such clothes (Dickens *Pickwick Papers*: Out of the way, young leathers.)

leave¹ [Old English] Old English *lǣfan* meant both 'bequeath' and 'allow to remain, leave in place'. It is Germanic in origin and related to German *bleiben* 'remain'. The Germanic root has the sense 'remain, continue' found in English *life* and *live*; it is thought that this sense developed from a primary sense 'adhere, be sticky'.

leave² [Old English] Old English *lēaf* 'permission' is from a West Germanic source; related words are *love* and the archaic word **lief** found in the phrase *as lief* meaning 'as happily' (e.g. *he would just as lief eat a pincushion as eat bran*). Old English *lēof* meant 'dear, pleasant'.
→ LOVE

leaven [Middle English] *Leaven*, a substance such as yeast used to produce fermentation, is from Old French *levain*, based on Latin *levamen* 'relief': this meaning was extended from the literal sense 'means of raising', from *levare* 'to lift'.

lecher [Middle English] This is from Old French *lichiere*, *lecheor*, from *lechier* 'live in debauchery or gluttony'. Ultimately it is from West Germanic and related to *lick*. **Lecherous** and **lechery** are also Middle English via Old French from *lecheor*. The word **lech**, a back-formation (by removal of the suffix) from *lecher* appeared in the late 18th century in contexts of strong desire, particularly sexual.
→ LICK

lectern [Middle English] This word for a tall stand with a sloping top for holding a book or notes for a speaker is from Old French *letrun*, from medieval Latin *lectrum*, from Latin *legere* 'to read'. This verb is also the base of late Middle English **lecture** which, in early use, meant 'reading' or 'a text to read'. It comes from Old French, or from medieval Latin *lectura*, from the past participial stem of *legere*.

ledge [Middle English] An early *ledge* was a strip of wood or other material fixed across a door, gate, etc. It is perhaps from an early form of *lay* 'place'. The main current sense describing a 'narrow horizontal surface projecting from a wall' dates from the mid 16th century.
→ LAY¹

ledger [late Middle English] Early spellings included *legger* and *ligger* which were large bibles or breviaries, probably from variants of *lay* 'set down' and *lie* 'be set down' influenced by Dutch *legger* and *ligger*. Current senses date from the 16th century.
→ LAY¹; LIE¹

lee [Old English] Old English *hlēo*, *hlēow* meant 'shelter'. Of Germanic origin, it is probably related to *luke-* in *lukewarm*. The word is common in nautical contexts for the sheltered side of a ship, land, etc.; it is not clear whether the nautical use of Dutch *lij* shares its history with the English word.

leer [mid 16th century] Initially *leer* had the general sense 'look sideways or askance'; it is perhaps from obsolete *leer* 'cheek', from Old English *hlēor*, as though the sense were 'to glance over one's cheek'.

left [Old English] 'Weak' was the early sense of Old English *lyft*, *left* (of West Germanic origin): the left-hand side was regarded as the weaker side of the body. This negative connotation is also seen in the word *sinister* from Latin *sinister* 'left-hand'. *Left* is commonly used in political contexts; in continental systems this was traditionally applied to the section of members in the seats to the left side of the Assembly Chamber (viewed from the president's chair): this was customarily an area for those holding liberal or democratic views.

leg [Middle English] *Leg* took over from the earlier word *shank*. It is from Old Norse *leggr*; the Danish word *læg* 'calf (of the leg)' is associated, of Germanic origin. The use of *leg* for a short section (e.g. *leg of a journey*, *leg of a competition*) found from the 1920s, has developed from the nautical application of the term in the early 17th century when it described 'a short rope branching out into two or more parts'.
→ SHANK

legacy [late Middle English] When first used, the word *legacy* was also 'the function or office of a deputy' especially a papal legate: it comes via Old French from medieval Latin *legatia* 'legateship'. The base is Latin *legatus* 'a person delegated' (from *legare* 'depute, delegate, bequeath') which also gave late Old English **legate** via Old French *legat*.

legal [late Middle English] The early application of the word was in the sense 'in connection with Mosaic law': it is from French, or from Latin *legalis*, from *lex*, *leg-* 'law'. A special use of the adjective *legal* used as a noun is found in taxi-drivers' slang from the 1920s meaning 'the exact fare without any tip included'.
→ LOYAL

legend [Middle English] The first sense recorded for *legend* was 'the story of a saint's life': it is from Old French *legende*, from medieval Latin *legere* 'to read'. The prime current sense 'a traditional story popularly regarded as historical' dates from the early 17th century; this was the period when the word is first found meaning 'motto, inscription' in certain contexts. **Legendary** is recorded from the early 16th century, initially used as a noun for a collection of legends, especially detailing saints' lives: it comes from medieval Latin *legendarius*, from *legenda*.

legible [late Middle English] *Legible* is from late Latin *legibilis*, from *legere* 'to read'.

legion [Middle English] *Legion* came via Old French from Latin *legio(n-)*, from *legere* 'to choose, levy'. Although first associated with the Roman army, it has been used in more modern military contexts such as *the Foreign Legion*, a body of foreign volunteers first formed in the French army in the 19th century. Adjectival use of *legion* 'innumerable' dates from the late 17th century; in early use it was often found in the phrase *their name is legion* meaning 'they are many'. This is taken from a biblical reference: Mark 5:9: My name is Legion; for we are many, said by a man possessed by devils and miraculously cured by Jesus.

legislator [late 15th century] *Legislator* is from Latin *legis lator* (from *lex* 'law' and *lator* 'mover'), literally 'the proposer of a law'. The noun **legislation** is recorded from the mid 17th century and was first used for 'the enactment of laws': it comes from late Latin *legis latio(n-)* translated literally as 'the proposing of a law'. **Legislature** found in examples towards the end of the 17th century, is based on *legislation* and formed on the pattern of *judicature*. The verb **legislate**, a back-formation (by removal of the suffix) from *legislation* dates from the early 18th century.

legitimate [late Middle English] This was first used meaning 'born of parents lawfully married to each other': it comes from medieval Latin *legitimatus* 'made legal', from the verb *legitimare*. The source is Latin *legitimus* 'lawful', from *lex*, *leg-* 'law'. In the early 20th century the abbreviation **legit** came into colloquial use.

leisure [Middle English] *Leisure* is from Old French *leisir*, based on Latin *licere* 'be allowed'. The phrase *a lady of leisure* defining a woman who has lots of free time, dates from the 1940s. There is a notion of 'freedom of personal choice' throughout the senses: e.g. *at leisure*, *at one's leisure*.

lend [Old English] Old English *lænan* is Germanic in origin, related to Dutch *lenen*. The addition of the final *-d* in late Middle English was due to association with verbs such as *bend* and *send*. The 'temporary' flavour of *lend* gave

life to expressions such as *lend an ear* 'listen for a while'; there is also a notion of 'flexibility' inherent in this temporary aspect (e.g. *this approach lends itself to many different applications*).
→ LOAN

length [Old English] This Old English word is from Germanic and related to Dutch *lengte*. The word is commonly used in various sports contexts as a measure of distance, such as racing (mid 17th century) and swimming (early 20th century).
→ LONG¹

lenient [mid 17th century] The first use of *lenient* was to mean 'emollient': it comes from Latin *lenient-*, the present participial stem of *lenire* 'to soothe', from *lenis* 'mild, gentle'. The word was associated with an attenuated degree of severity in legal judgements from the late 18th century.

lens [late 17th century] This word for a piece of transparent substance for concentrating or dispersing light rays is an adoption of a Latin word, the literal meaning of which is 'lentil'. Shape association influenced the choice. Its connection with photography contexts arose in the mid 19th century.

Lent [Middle English] *Lent* is an abbreviation of Old English **Lenten**, originally spelt *lencten* meaning 'spring, Lent'. Of Germanic origin, it is related to *long*, perhaps because of the association with the lengthening of the day in spring. *Lent Lily* is another term for *daffodil* cultivated as an early spring flower.
→ LONG¹

leotard [early 20th century] This word is taken from the name of Jules Léotard (1839–70), a French trapeze artist.

leper [late Middle English] This is probably from an attributive use of *leper* 'leprosy', from Old French *lepre*. *Leper* came via Latin from Greek *lepra*, the feminine of *lepros* 'scaly', from *lepos*, *lepis* 'scale'. **Leprosy** (mid 16th century) superseded Middle English *lepry*: this form is based on **leprous**.

leprechaun [early 17th century] *Leprechaun* is from Irish *leipreachán*, based on Old Irish *luchorpán*, from *lu* 'small' and *corp* 'body'.

lesbian [late 19th century] The word *lesbian* came via Latin from Greek *Lesbios*, from *Lesbos*, the island home (in the eastern Aegean) of Sappho, who expressed love for women in her poetry.

less [Old English] Old English *læssa* has a Germanic source; it is related to Old Frisian *lessa*, from an Indo-European root shared by Greek *loisthos* 'last'. Related to *less* is the word **least**

(læst, læsest in Old English) from a Germanic source. Middle English **lesser** is a double comparative based on *less*.

lesson [Middle English] *Lesson* is from Old French *leçon*, from Latin *lectio* 'a reading'. In early use it was 'a public reading' or 'a portion of a book to be studied by a pupil for repetition to the teacher'. The notion 'instructive example' is found associated with the word from the late 16th century.

let [Old English] Old English *lætan* 'leave behind, leave out' is Germanic in origin, related to Dutch *laten* and German *lassen*. There is a basic notion of 'not take action to prevent' in the verb.
→ LATE

lethal [late 16th century] 'Causing spiritual death' was the early meaning of *lethal* from Latin *lethalis*. The base is Latin *lethum*, a variant (influenced by Greek *lēthē* 'forgetfulness'), of *letum* 'death'. The river *Lethe* in Greek mythology produced forgetfulness of the past in anyone who took a drink from its waters (Shakespeare *Richard III*: In the Lethe of thy angry soul, Thou drown the sad remembrance).

lethargy [late Middle English] *Lethargy* came via Old French and late Latin from Greek *lēthargia*, from *lēthargos* 'forgetful'. From the same period, **lethargic** came via Latin from Greek *lēthargikos*, from *lēthargos*: this is from the base of *lanthanesthai* 'forget'.

letter [Middle English] *Letter* is from Old French *lettre*, from Latin *lit(t)era* meaning, in the singular, 'letter of the alphabet', and in the plural, 'epistle, literature, culture'. The use of the plural *letters* to denote a qualification such as a degree (as in *letters after one's name*) dates from the late 19th century.

lettuce [Middle English] The word *lettuce* is from Old French *letues, laitues*, the plural of *laitue*, from Latin *lactuca*. The base is Latin *lac, lact-* 'milk' because of the milky juice of the *lettuce* plant.

level [Middle English] The early use of *level* was as a term for an instrument to determine whether or not a surface was horizontal. It comes from Old French *livel*, based on Latin *libella*, diminutive of *libra* 'scales, balance'. *Levellers* in the English Civil War (1642–9) strove to create a 'balance' of position or rank and called for the abolition of the monarchy, for agrarian and social reform, and for religious freedom. In idiomatic use, the expression *one's level best* dates from the mid 19th century; the synonymous phrase *one's levelest* and its opposite *one's level worst* exist in US English.

lever [Middle English] *Lever* is from Old French *levier, leveor*, from *lever* 'to lift'. The English verb dates from the mid 19th century.

levity [mid 16th century] *Levity* is from Latin *levitas*, from *levis* 'light'. It was originally descriptive of the physical quality 'lightness' but gained the figurative notion 'frivolity' in the mid 16th century (Shakespeare *Antony and Cleopatra*: Our graver business, Frowns at this levity).

levy [Middle English] First used as a noun, *levy* is from Old French *levee*, the feminine past participle of *lever* 'to raise': this comes from Latin *levare*, from *levis* 'light'. It is commonly associated with the collection of taxes or duties.

lewd [Old English] Old English *lǣwede* is of unknown origin. The original sense was 'belonging to the laity'; in Middle English the sense became 'belonging to the common people, vulgar', and later 'worthless, vile, evil' which led to the current sense 'crude and offensive'.

lexicon [early 17th century] This is a modern Latin word, from Greek *lexikon (biblion)* '(book) of words', from *lexis* 'word', from *legein* 'speak'. The adjective **lexical** is found from the mid 19th century: it is based on Greek *lexikos* 'of words'.

liable [late Middle English] This is perhaps from Anglo-Norman French, from French *lier* 'to bind', from Latin *ligare*. The literal sense would then be 'able to be bound': this is plausible but it remains odd that the word is not found in Anglo-French or the Latin of legal documents.

liaison [mid 17th century] Originally a cookery term, *liaison* is from French, from *lier* 'to bind'. The more general use of the word to mean 'intimate connection' or more specifically 'sexual relationship' dates from the early 19th century. The verb **liaise** 'communicate and cooperate' was used from the 1920s as military slang: it is a back-formation (by removal of the suffix) from *liaison*.

libel [Middle English] When first used a *libel* was 'a document, a written statement': it came via Old French from Latin *libellus*, a diminutive of *liber* 'book'. Use as a legal term referring to a published false statement damaging to someone's reputation, dates from the early 17th century.

liberal [Middle English] *Liberal* came via Old French from Latin *liberalis*, from *liber* 'free (man)'. The original sense was 'suitable for a free man', which developed into 'suitable for a gentleman' (that is, one not tied to a trade): this survives in *liberal arts* which were a mixture of arts and sciences considered 'worthy of study by a free man' (as opposed to *mechanical arts* involving manual labour). Another early sense 'generous' (used in phrases such as *liberal amounts of wine*) gave rise to an obsolete meaning 'free from restraint', leading in the late 18th century to the prime current sense 'open to new ideas'. *Liberal* has been a term in politics since the early 19th century; *the Liberal Party* emerged in the 1860s from the old Whig Party and until the First World War was one of the two major parties in Britain.

liberty [late Middle English] Latin *liber* 'free' is the base of both *liberty* (from Old French *liberte*, from Latin *libertas*) and late 16th-century **liberate** (from Latin *liberare* 'to free'). The expression *take liberties* conveying 'behave in an improperly familiar manner', dates from the mid 19th century.

library [late Middle English] *Library* came via Old French from Latin *libraria* 'bookshop', the feminine (used as a noun) of *librarius* 'relating to books', from *liber* 'book'. This Latin base is thought to be a use of Latin *liber* 'bark', which according to Roman tradition was a material used in early times as a medium for writing. In the late 17th century, a **librarian** was a term for 'a scribe or copyist'. The base of the word is Latin *librarius* meaning, when used as a noun, 'bookseller, scribe'.

licence [late Middle English] Latin *licere* 'be lawful or permitted' is the base of *licence* which came into English via Old French from Latin *licentia* 'freedom, licentiousness': this, in medieval Latin, came to mean 'authority, permission'. The phrase *poetic licence* meaning deviation from a recognized rule for artistic effect is found from the early 16th century. The verb **license** (late Middle English) gained its *-se* spelling by analogy with noun/verb pairs such as *practice* and *practise*.

lick [Old English] Old English *liccian* is West Germanic in origin and related to Dutch *likken* and German *lecken*, from an Indo-European root shared by Greek *leikhein* and Latin *lingere*. The phrase *lick someone into shape* arose in late Middle English from the image of a bear grooming its young: early bestiaries described cubs being born without shape and being moulded by the licking of their parents. The slang meaning 'thrash, beat' is found from the early 16th century.

lid [Old English] Old English *hlid* has a Germanic origin, from a base meaning 'cover'; it is related to Dutch *lid*. The notion of 'cover' is illustrated in the compound *eyelid*. The word *lid* has also been used in slang to mean 'hat' (Wodehouse *Jeeves in the Offing*: It is almost as foul as Uncle Tom's Sherlock Holmes deerstalker, which

has frightened more crows than any other lid in Worcestershire).

lido [late 17th century] This word for a public open-air swimming pool or bathing beach comes from Italian *Lido*, the name of a famous bathing beach near Venice. It comes from Italian *lido* 'shore', from Latin *litus*.

lie¹ [Old English] This *lie* meaning 'remain, stretch beneath, be in a resting position' was spelt *licgan* in Old English. Of Germanic origin, it is related to Dutch *liggen* and German *liegen*, from an Indo-European root shared by Greek *lektron*, *lekhos* and Latin *lectus* 'bed'.

lie² [Old English] Old English *lyge* (noun), *lēogan* (verb) in contexts of deceit and untruth are of Germanic origin, related to Dutch *liegen* and German *lügen*. The word **liar** is also an Old English word: *lēogere*.

life [Old English] Old English *līf* is Germanic origin, related to Dutch *lijf* and German *Leib* 'body'. The root has the meaning 'continue, last, endure'. In Old English the word referred both to the condition characterizing animals and plants from inanimate matter, as well as to the duration of this condition: *life* as a sentence of imprisonment imposed for a serious crime is a slang usage dating from the early 20th century.
→ LIVE¹

lift [Middle English] *Lift* is from Old Norse *lypta*, of Germanic origin. The use of the word to describe a compartment for lifting goods or people between levels in a building dates from the mid 19th century. This same period saw the first examples of the word used figuratively to mean 'an elevating effect or influence' as in *it gave me quite a lift to receive such good news*.
→ LOFT

light¹ [Old English] Old English *lēoht*, *līht* 'shining, bright' (noun and adjective), *līhtan* (verb) are Germanic in origin; they are related to the Dutch nouns *licht* and German *Licht*, from an Indo-European root shared by Greek *leukos* 'white' and Latin *lux* 'light'. The expression *out like a light* dates from the 1930s.

light² [Old English] Old English *lēoht*, *līht* 'of little weight', *lēohte* (adverb) are Germanic in origin; related to Dutch *licht* and German *leicht*, from an Indo-European root shared by Latin *lung*. The word *lights* for 'lungs' is a noun use of the adjective because of the relative lightness of the lungs to other internal parts.
→ LUNG

light³ [Old English] Old English *līhtan* meant 'descend' (as in *from the horse he lit down*); it also had the sense 'lessen the weight of'. It comes from the adjective *light*. Common use now is in

the phrase *light upon* in examples such as *he lit upon a possible solution*.
→ ALIGHT¹; LIGHT²

lightning [Middle English] This is a special use of *lightning*, the verbal noun from Middle English **lighten** 'shed light upon'.

like¹ [Middle English] *Like* in the sense 'similar to' is from Old Norse *líkr*, the base too of Middle English **likely** (from Old Norse *líkligr*). The verb **liken**, based on *like* dates from the same period.
→ ALIKE

like² [Old English] Old English *lícian* 'please, be pleasing' is Germanic in origin and related to Dutch *lijken*. In reference to people, the verb *like* is weaker in sentiment than *love*. The expression *I like it but it doesn't like me* applied usually in food contexts, dates from the late 19th century.

lilo [1930s] The word *lilo* describing a mattress-like inflatable for use on water is an alteration of *lie low*.

lilt [late Middle English] The early word, spelt *lulte*, had the senses 'sound (an alarm)' or 'lift up (the voice)': the origin is unknown. There may be a connection with Norwegian *lilla* 'to sing'.

limb [Old English] Old English *lim* included the senses 'organ' and 'part of the body'. It is from a Germanic source. The transferred sense referring to the main branch of a tree is recorded from the late 16th century.

limber [mid 16th century] Early use was as an adjective meaning 'easily bent'; it is commonly used now as a verb phrase *limber up* 'loosen up in preparation for exercise'. The word is perhaps from *limber* in the dialect sense 'cart shaft', with allusion to the to-and-fro motion: in Middle English this was spelt *lymour* meaning 'the detachable front part of a gun carriage', apparently related to medieval Latin *limonarius* from *limo*, *limon-* 'shaft'.

limbo¹ [late Middle English] This word is usually found in the expression *in limbo*, a medieval Latin phrase from *limbus* 'hem, border, limbo'. It either refers to the supposed abode (in some Christian beliefs) of the souls of unbaptized infants, or more generally to an undetermined period of waiting.

limbo² [1950s] This *limbo* referring to a type of West Indian dance in which the dancer bends backwards and dances under a horizontal bar which is held ever lower is from the verb *limber*
→ LIMBER

limerick [late 19th century] This is said to be from the chorus 'will you come up to Limerick?' sung between extemporized verses at a social gathering. The word now describes a humorous five-line poem with an *aabba* rhyme-scheme.

limit [late Middle English] *Limit* is from Latin *limes*, *limit-* 'boundary, frontier'. The expression *over the limit* with reference to drinking and driving dates from the 1960s. The verb *limit* is from Latin *limitare*, from *limes*, the base too of late Middle English **limitation** from Latin *limitatio(n-)*.

limousine [early 20th century] This is an adoption of a French feminine adjective meaning 'of Limousin', originally applied to a caped cloak worn in the region of *Limousin* (a former province of central France). The early version of this car had a roof that protected the outside driving seat.

limp¹ [late Middle English] This *limp* meaning 'walk unevenly or with difficulty' was originally used with the sense 'fall short of': it is related to obsolete *limphalt* 'lame', and is probably of Germanic origin. Use of the word in nautical, aviation, and other transport contexts such as *limp into port*, *limped over the airfield* is found from the 1920s.

limp² [early 18th century] This *limp* meaning 'lacking firmness' is of unknown origin; it may be related to the verb *limp*, having the basic sense 'hanging loose'.
→ LIMP¹

limpid [late Middle English] *Limpid* 'clear' is from Latin *limpidus* and may be related to *lymph*.

linchpin [late Middle English] *Linchpin*, a term for a pin passed through the end of an axle to keep a wheel in position is composed of Old English *lynis* which by itself meant 'linchpin' and the word *pin*.

linctus [late 17th century] This word for a cough mixture is an adoption of a Latin word which comes from *lingere* 'to lick'. It is literally a mixture meant to be lapped up by the tongue.

line¹ [Old English] This *line* for a straight mark or a row was *líne* in Old English when it meant 'rope' or 'series'. It is probably of Germanic origin, from Latin *linea* (*fibra*) 'flax (fibre)', from Latin *linum* 'flax'; it was reinforced in Middle English by Old French *ligne*, based on Latin *linea*. Middle English **lineage** (from Old French *lignage*) is also from Latin *linea* 'a line', so too mid 17th-century **linear** from Latin *linearis*.

line² [late Middle English] This *line* used to mean 'cover the inside of (curtains, a container, etc.)' is from obsolete *line* 'flax', with reference to the common use of linen for linings.

linen [Old English] Old English *línen* was an adjective meaning 'made of flax'. Of West Ger-

manic origin, it is related to Dutch *linnen*, German *Leinen*, also to the obsolete English word *line* 'flax'.
➔ LINE²

linger [Middle English] 'Dwell, abide' were early meanings of *linger*, a frequentative (= verb of repeated action) of obsolete *leng* 'prolong'. A Germanic word in origin, it is related to German *längen* 'make long(er)'.
➔ LONG¹

lingo [mid 17th century] *Lingo* is probably via Portuguese *lingoa* from Latin *lingua* 'tongue'.

linguist [late 16th century] Latin *lingua* 'language' is the base of *linguist* and early 19th-century **linguistic**.

liniment [late Middle English] This word for 'an embrocation for rubbing on the body' is from late Latin *linimentum*, from Latin *linire* 'to smear'.

link [late Middle English] A *link* was originally 'a loop'; as a verb it meant 'connect physically': it comes from Old Norse *hlekkr*, of Germanic origin. German *Gelenk* 'joint' is related.

links [Old English] This word used commonly in golf contexts was first found as *hlinc* meaning 'rising ground'; it is perhaps related to *lean*. *Links* in Scots use describes gently undulating sandy ground near the sea-shore covered with turf or coarse grass, which is connected to the golfing sense.
➔ LEAN¹

lint [late Middle English] The early spelling was *lynnet* 'flax prepared for spinning': this sense survives in Scots. The word is perhaps from Old French *linette* 'linseed', from *lin* 'flax'.

lintel [Middle English] *Lintel*, a horizontal support across the top of a door or window, is from Old French, based on late Latin *liminare*, from Latin *limen* 'threshold'.

lion [Middle English] *Lion* is from Anglo-Norman French *liun*, from Latin *leo, leon-*, from Greek *leōn, leont-*: the latter may have been adopted from some foreign language. Before the adoption of the Anglo-Norman French word into English, representations of Latin forms were used; the Latin word was adopted into all the Germanic languages.

lip [Old English] Old English *lippa* from a Germanic source is related to Dutch *lip* and German *Lippe*, from an Indo-European root shared by Latin *labia, labra* 'lips'. The word is used in several phrases expressing an attitude or reaction: *bite one's lip* (Middle English), *keep a stiff upper lip* (early 19th century), and *smack one's lips* (early 19th century).

liquid [late Middle English] *Liquid* is from Latin *liquidus*, from *liquere* 'be liquid', the base too of **liquefy** from the same period. The latter is from French *liquéfier* from Latin *liquefacere* 'make liquid'. The verb **liquidate** used in financial contexts arose in the mid 16th century in the sense 'set out (accounts) clearly': this is from medieval Latin *liquidare* 'make clear', from Latin 'liquidus'. The meaning 'wind up the affairs of a company' was influenced by Italian *liquidare* and French *liquider*; the sense 'kill by violent means' was influenced by Russian *likvidirovat'*.

liquor [Middle English] Early use of *liquor* was with reference to a liquid or something to drink: the form comes from Old French *lic(o)ur*, from Latin *liquor*; related to *liquare* 'liquefy', *liquere* 'be fluid'.

liquorice [Middle English] This chewy aromatic black substance used as a sweet and in medicine comes from Old French *licoresse*, from late Latin *liquiritia*, from Greek *glukurrhiza*. The base elements are *glukus* 'sweet' and *rhiza* 'root'.

lisp [Old English] Old English *wlispian* (recorded in *āwlyspian*) from the adjective *wlisp* 'lisping', is an imitative word in origin. Dutch *lispen* and German *lispeln* are associated.

lissom [late 18th century] *Lissom* expresses the notion 'thin, supple, and graceful'; it is a contraction of *lithesome*.

list¹ [early 17th century] The origin of *list* enumerating a series of items is uncertain but the word is probably identical with Old English *list* 'strip (of paper)', a word of Germanic origin. Early use was associated with catalogues of names especially of soldiers in an army.

list² [early 17th century] The origin of this *list* used in nautical contexts to mean 'lean over to one side', usually when describing a ship carrying an uneven cargo or one taking in water, is obscure. It may be a transferred use of Old English *list* meaning 'longing, inclination', a Germanic word from a base meaning 'pleasure'. The English spelling in early examples was sometimes *lust*.

listen [Old English] Old English *hlysnan* meant 'pay attention to'. The origin is Germanic. The association of the noun **listener** with radio broadcasts dates from the 1920s but general use of the word is recorded from the early 17th century.

listless [Middle English] *Listless* is based on obsolete *list* 'appetite, desire', thus the literal sense is 'without desire'.

litany [Middle English] *Litany*, a series of petitions for use in church services, is from Old

French *letanie*, via ecclesiastical Latin from Greek *litaneia* 'prayer'. The base is Greek *litē* 'supplication'. From the early 19th century, examples of the word meaning 'a tedious list or enumeration' (as in *a litany of complaints*) are found.

literal [late Middle English] *Literal* is from Old French, or from late Latin *litteralis*, from Latin *littera* 'letter'. Early use in English related to the letters of the alphabet (e.g. *literal characters*); the meanings 'verbally exact' and 'relating to the etymological sense of a word' date from the late 16th century.
→LETTER

literate [late Middle English] Latin *littera* 'letter' is the base of several English words: *literate* is from Latin *litteratus*; **literature** dating from late Middle English in the sense 'knowledge of books' came via French from Latin *litteratura*; **literary**, mid 17th century in the sense 'relating to the letters of the alphabet', is from Latin *litterarius*; **literacy** arose in the late 19th century and is based on *literate*, following the formation pattern of *illiteracy*: apart from defining 'the knowledge of reading and writing' it has come to encompass the sense 'know-how' as in *computer literacy*.

lithe [Old English] Old English *līthe* had the meanings 'gentle, meek' and 'mellow' (often referring to the weather). Of Germanic origin, it is related to German *lind* 'soft, gentle'. The current sense 'thin, supple, and graceful' was the only one recorded by Johnson.

litigious [late Middle English] This word meaning 'prone to go to law, relating to lawsuits' is from Old French *litigieux* or Latin *litigiosus* from *litigium* 'litigation'. The base, Latin *lis*, *lit-* 'lawsuit', also gave rise to the verb **litigate** recorded from the early 17th century (from Latin *litigare* 'dispute in a lawsuit').

litter [Middle English] *Litter* was first used to describe a vehicle containing a bed or seat, enclosed by curtains and carried either on men's shoulders or supported by animals. The source of the form is Old French *litiere*, from medieval Latin *lectaria*, from Latin *lectus* 'bed'. The main current meaning 'rubbish left in a public place' dates from the mid 18th century. This probably arises from the early sense and the notion of straw and rushes serving as bedding.

little [Old English] Old English *lȳtel*, of Germanic origin; related to Dutch *luttel*, German dialect *lützel*. The main uses of the word are in semantic opposition to *great* and *much*. The phrase *little by little* dates from late Middle English. Use of *little* as an adverb in such idiomatic phrases as *little did he know it, but …* arose

early in the word's history; this is restricted to the verbs *know*, *think*, *care* and their synonyms.

liturgy [mid 16th century] *Liturgy* came via French or late Latin from Greek *leitourgia* 'public service, worship of the gods', from *leitourgos* 'minister'. The semantic components here are Greek *lēitos* 'public' and *-ergos* 'working'.

live¹ [Old English] The Old English verb *libban*, *lifian* 'be alive' is Germanic in origin; related forms are Dutch *leven* and German *leben*. Of the idiomatic phrases: *live with* (as in *he had to learn to live with his decision*) dates from the 1930s; *live it up* meaning 'have an enjoyable time' is found from the 1950s; *to live with oneself* (as in *will he ever be able to live with himself?*) arose in the 1960s.
→LIFE; LEAVE¹

live² [mid 16th century] This *live* (rhyming with *hive*) is a shortening of *alive*.
→ALIVE

livelihood [Old English] Old English *līflād* meant 'way of life', made up of the elements *līf* 'life' and *lād* 'course'. The change in the word's form in the 16th century was due to association with *lively* and the suffix *-hood* used in noun formation.

livelong [late Middle English] This poetical word, found in the phrases (*all*) *the livelong day*, *the livelong night*, was originally *leve longe* meaning 'dear long'; a corresponding phrase exists in German: *die liebe lange Nacht* 'the dear long night'. The change in spelling of the first word was due to association with the verb *live* in the latter part of the 16th century.
→LIVE¹

lively [Old English] Old English *līflic* meant 'living, animate'. The sense 'vigorous, energetic' arose early; association with feelings as in *lively fear*, *lively impression*, expressing 'vivid, intense' came about in the early 16th century; *lively* meaning 'full of action or incident' (Dickens *Barnaby Rudge*: It was the liveliest room in the building) was first recorded from the late 17th century.
→LIFE

livery [Middle English] *Livery* is from Old French *livree* meaning 'delivered', the feminine past participle of *livrer*: this is from Latin *liberare* which in early use meant 'to liberate', but which in medieval Latin came to mean 'hand over'. The original sense of *livery* was 'the dispensing of food, provisions, or clothing to servants'; it was also 'an allowance of provender for horses', surviving in the phrase *at livery* and in *livery stable*. Use of the word to mean 'a special uniform worn by a servant' arose because medieval nobles provided matching clothes to distinguish their servants from those of others.

livid [late Middle English] The early sense recorded was 'of a bluish leaden colour': *livid* comes from French *livide* or Latin *lividus*, from *livere* 'be bluish'. The sense 'furiously angry' dates from the early 20th century.

load [Old English] Old English *lād* had the meaning 'way, journey, conveyance'. Of Germanic origin, it is related to German *Leite*. The verb dates from the late 15th century. Meaning development has been influenced by association with *lade* and in certain northern dialects these words are indistinguishable.
→LADE; LEAD[1]

loaf [Old English] Old English *hlāf* is Germanic in origin and related to German *Laib*. In early use the word was sometimes used to mean 'bread' but it is not clear whether this general sense or the more specific 'loaf, portion of baked bread' is the earlier. The slang term *loaf* 'head' (used from the 1930s) is probably from the rhyming slang *loaf of bread*.

loafer [mid 19th century] This word for a person who idles time away is perhaps from German *Landläufer* 'tramp', from *Land* 'land' and *laufen* (spelt in dialect *lofen*) 'to run'. The mid 19th-century verb *loaf* is probably a back-formation (by removal of the suffix) from *loafer*.

loan [Middle English] Early use of the word was to denote 'a gift from a superior'. It comes from Old Norse *lán*, of Germanic origin; related forms are Dutch *leen* and German *Lehn*.
→LEND

loath [Old English] Old English *lāth* meant 'hostile, spiteful'. Of Germanic origin, it is related to Dutch *leed* and German *Leid* 'sorrow'. The word is commonly used in the phrase *loath to …* 'disinclined to …', a use which arose early in the word's history.

loathe [Old English] Old English *lāthian* is Germanic in origin. Early use was in the structure *it loathes me* in the sense 'it is offensive or displeasing to me'; the sense has strengthened in modern use which is probably partly due to the contexts where the loathing of a particular food is involved and an association with nausea.
→LOATH

loathsome [Middle English] This word is from archaic *loath* 'disgust, loathing' suffixed with *-some*.

lob [late 16th century] Early senses included 'cause or allow to hang heavily' and 'behave like a lout'; the word comes from the archaic noun *lob* meaning 'lout' and 'pendulous object', probably from Low German or Dutch; in modern Dutch *lubbe* exists meaning 'hanging lip'. Several Germanic words of a similar sound express the notions of 'heaviness' and 'clumsiness' and the English word is perhaps onomatopoeic. The current sense 'throw (a ball or other object) in a high slow arc' dates from the mid 19th century.

lobby [mid 16th century] An early *lobby* was a 'monastic cloister'. The word comes from medieval Latin *lobia, lobium* 'covered walk, portico'; it soon came to denote a passage area between rooms in a building (Shakespeare *Henry VI* part ii: How in our voiding Lobby has thou stood, and duly waited for my coming forth?). The verb sense of political contexts (originally US) derives from the practice of frequenting the lobby of a house of legislature to influence its members into supporting a cause.
→LODGE

lobe [mid 16th century] *Lobe* came via late Latin from Greek *lobos* 'lobe, pod'. Its use in *lobe of the brain* dates from the late 17th century.

lobster [Old English] Old English *lopustre* is an alteration of Latin *locusta* 'crustacean, locust'. The application of the Latin word to a locust was from the perceived similarity in shape. *Lobster* was used as a contemptuous name for a British soldier from the mid 17th century; it was originally applied to a regiment of Roundhead cuirassiers who wore complete suits of armour; later the term was associated with the characteristic red military coats. In US slang, *lobster* has been used to describe 'a slow-witted or gullible person' from the late 19th century.

local [late Middle English] *Local* is from late Latin *localis*, from Latin *locus* 'place'. General use of the word in English was initially 'concerned with place or position'. It came to be applied more specifically to a small area with respect to its inhabitants from the late 17th century (e.g. *local laws, local government*); *locals* described the inhabitants themselves from the mid 19th century. The noun **locality** (early 17th century) is from French *localité* or late Latin *localitas*, from *localis* 'relating to a place'.

locale [late 18th century] This word for a place where something happens or where events are scheduled is from the French noun *local*, respelt to indicate stress on the final syllable. The word *morale* underwent a similar process.

locate [early 16th century] *Locate* is from Latin *locare* 'to place', from *locus* 'a place'. The original sense was as a legal term meaning 'let out on hire'; in the late 16th century it came to mean 'assign to a particular place', then (particularly in North American usage) 'establish in a place'. The prime modern sense 'discover the exact position of' dates from the late 19th century. Late 16th-century **location** is from Latin *locatio(n-)*, from the verb *locare*.

lock¹ [Old English] Old English *loc* 'a device for fastening' (such as a bar, bolt, or latch) is from a Germanic source; German *Loch* 'hole' is related. The common combination *under lock and key* was frequent from early times. The application of the word as 'a barrier' on a river is found from Middle English and, more specifically on a canal or similar waterway with sluice gates for raising and lowering the level of the water, from the late 16th century.

lock² [Old English] Old English *locc* as in *lock of hair* is Germanic in origin, related to Dutch *lok*, German *Locke*, and possibly also *lock* 'device for fastening'. The pre-Germanic root perhaps meant 'to bend'.
→LOCK¹

locket [late Middle English] The first recorded use of *locket* was to denote 'a metal plate on a scabbard'. It comes from Old French *locquet*, a diminutive of *loc* 'latch, lock'. Of Germanic origin, it is related to *lock* 'fastener'. Use of *locket* as an item of jewellery dates from the late 17th century.
→LOCK¹

locomotive [early 17th century] Early use was adjectival; the word comes from modern Latin *locomotivus*, from Latin *loco* (the ablative of *locus* 'place') and late Latin *motivus* 'motive': this was suggested by medieval Latin *in loco moveri* 'move by change of position'. **Locomotion**, dating from the mid 17th century, is from Latin *loco* 'from a place' and *motio* 'motion'.

lodge [Middle English] The early spelling was *loge*, which came via Old French *loge* 'arbour, hut' from medieval Latin *laubia*, *lobia* 'covered walk'. The origin is Germanic; German *Laube* 'arbour' is related. Early verb use was in the sense 'place (soldiers) in tents or other temporary shelter'; it was used in legal contexts from the early 18th century for 'deposit (a formal statement) in court' which led to popular use in phrases such as *lodge a complaint*.
→LOBBY

loft [late Old English] Of Germanic origin, Old English *loft* 'air, sky' is from Old Norse *lopt* 'air, sky, upper room', related to Dutch *lucht* 'light' and German *Luft* 'air'. The word is recorded as an 'attic' early in its history; it was applied more specifically to a *hay loft* from the early 16th century. The adjective **lofty** dating from Middle English is based on *loft*, but was influenced by *aloft*.

log [Middle English] At first a *log* was 'a bulky mass of wood'. The origin is unknown but it is perhaps symbolic of the notion of heaviness. The nautical term for an apparatus for determining the speed of a ship originally denoted a thin quadrant of wood loaded to float upright in the water: this came to be 'ship's journal' in which information from the log board was recorded.

loggerheads [late 16th century] A *loggerhead* was originally a 'foolish person'; it is based on dialect *logger* 'block of wood for hobbling a horse'. The phrase *at loggerheads* arose in the late 17th century; this may possibly have a connection with the word *loggerhead* as a term for an iron instrument with a long handle and a ball at the end, used for melting pitch and heating liquids; something similar may have been used as a weapon.

logic [late Middle English] *Logic* came via Old French *logique* and late Latin *logica* from Greek *logikē* (*tekhnē*) '(art) of reason'; the base is Greek *logos* 'word, reason'. **Logical**, from medieval Latin *logicalis* from late Latin *logica*, dates from the same period.

logistics [late 19th century] Early use of the word *logistics* was in the sense 'movement and supplying of troops and equipment'. The form in English is from French *logistique*, from *loger* 'to lodge'.

loin [Middle English] *Loin* is from Old French *loigne*, based on Latin *lumbus* 'loin'. From the early 16th century, it was used as a biblical and poetical word especially in the phrase *gird up one's loins*; it was extended to mean 'the seat of physical power' and so came to represent 'offspring, descendants' in phrases such as *the fruit of one's loins*.

loiter [late Middle English] *Loiter* is perhaps from Middle Dutch *loteren* 'wag about (like a loose tooth)' and 'dawdle over one's work'. It may have been introduced into England by foreign 'loiterers' or vagrants.

loll [late Middle English] This word meaning 'droop' is probably symbolic of dangling. Mid 18th-century **lollop** 'move in a lazy clumsy way' is probably based on *loll* as an onomatopoeic extension.

lollipop [late 18th century] This may be from dialect *lolly* 'tongue' and the verb *pop* 'put quickly'. The abbreviation **lolly** is found from the mid 19th century; its informal use to mean 'money' arose in the 1940s.
→POP¹

lone [late Middle English] This adjective is a shortening of *alone*.
→ALONE

long[1] [Old English] The Old English adjective *lang, long* and adverb *lange, longe* are Germanic in origin; related forms are Dutch and German *lang*. The expression *the long and the short of it* was initially *the short and the long of it* and examples date from the early 16th century. The phrase *before long (ere long)* is found from the mid 18th century.

long[2] [Old English] The Old English verb *langian* meant both 'grow long, prolong', and 'dwell in thought, yearn'. Of Germanic origin, it is related to Dutch *langen* 'present, offer' and German *langen* 'reach, extend'. The phrase *long for* was sometimes expressed as *long after* in Middle English.

longevity [early 17th century] This word meaning 'long life' is from late Latin *longaevitas*, a combination of Latin *longus* 'long' and *aevum* 'age'.

longitude [late Middle English] In early use *longitude* was both length and tallness: it comes from Latin *longitudo*, from *longus* 'long'.

loo [1940s] Many theories have been put forward about the origin of this informal word for 'a toilet': one suggests the source is *Waterloo*, a trade name for iron cisterns in the early part of the century; the evidence remains inconclusive.

look [Old English] The Old English verb *lōcian* is West Germanic in origin, related to German dialect *lugen*. *Looks* meaning 'appearance' is recorded from the mid 16th century. Association with fashion (as in *the new look*) arose in the 1930s.

loom[1] [Old English] Now an apparatus for making fabric, a *loom* was *gelōma* 'a tool' in Old English; the word was shortened to *lome* in Middle English.

loom[2] [mid 16th century] This word meaning 'apppear as a shadowy form' is probably from Low German or Dutch; East Frisian *lōmen* 'move slowly' and Middle High German *lüemen* 'be weary' are comparable forms. Early use in English was in the description of ships or of the sea, expressing the sense 'move slowly up and down'.

loon [late 19th century] This word for 'a silly person' is from the mid 17th-century North American term **loon** for a 'diver' (a large diving water bird). This is with reference to the bird's actions when escaping from danger, perhaps influenced by **loony**, a mid 19th-century abbreviation of *lunatic*.

loop [late Middle English] The origin of *loop* is unknown; Scottish Gaelic *lùb* 'loop, bend' may be associated. The modern phrase *in the loop* originated in the US in the 1970s and expresses the notion 'kept informed'. The compound:

■ **loophole** dating from the late 16th century denoting an arrow slit in a castle ramparts, is based on obsolete *loop* 'embrasure'. Its figurative use meaning 'means of escape, get-out' in phrases such as *loophole in the law*, dates from the early 17th century.

loose [Middle English] Middle English *loos* 'free from bonds' is from Old Norse *lauss*, of Germanic origin; Dutch and German *los* is related. The notion 'free from moral restraint' (e.g *loose women*) was associated with the word from late Middle English. The association with money as in *loose change* arose in the early 19th century (Jane Austen *Sense and Sensibility*: My loose cash would … be employed in improving my collection of music and books). The slang phrase *hang loose* expressing 'stay calm' arose in US English in the 1960s.

loot [early 19th century] The first examples found were of *loot* as a verb. It comes from Hindi *lūṭ*, from Sanskrit *luṇṭh-* 'rob'. The noun sense 'money' dates from the 1940s.

lop[1] [late Middle English] This *lop* commonly used to mean 'cut off (branches)' was first recorded as a noun for 'the branches and twigs of trees'. The etymology is obscure; it is not found in other Germanic languages. Norwegian dialect *lopa* exists meaning '(of bark) be loosened by moisture'.

lop[2] [late 16th century] This *lop* meaning 'hang loosely' (as in *lop-eared*) is probably a symbolic formation suggestive of limpness; the word *lob* is comparable. Early 18th-century **lopsided** is based on *lop*.

lope [Middle English] This verb meaning 'run with a long bounding stride' is a variant of Scots *loup*, from Old Norse *hlaupa* 'leap'.

loquacious [mid 17th century] This formal word meaning 'talkative' is based on Latin *loquax, loquac-*, from *loqui* 'talk'.

lord [Old English] Old English *hlāford*, from *hlāfweard* 'bread-keeper' is from a Germanic base; **laird** dating from late Middle English is a Scots form of *lord*. In its primary sense the word (not found in other Germanic languages) denoted a head of a household (= in charge of those who eat his bread); it already had a wider application before the literary period of Old English. Sense development has been much influenced by the adoption of the word as the ususal translation of Latin *dominus*. The idiomatic verb phrase *lord it (over)* is found from the late 16th century. Use of the phrase *the Lords* for the peers, temporal and spiritual, constituting the higher of the two bodies of English, Scot-

tish, and Irish legislature (originally separate) is found from the mid 1400s. This branch of the legislature now consists of English noblemen of baronial rank, the English bishops (with a few exceptions), and elected representatives of the peers of Scotland and Ireland.
→ LADY; LOAF

lore [Old English] Old English *lār* 'instruction, piece of instruction' is Germanic in origin and related to Dutch *leer* and German *Lehre*. This early sense is illustrated in Milton's *Paradise Lost*: She finish'd, and the subtle Fiend his lore Soon learn'd. The word soon came to encompass 'a body of facts or beliefs': e.g. T. Hughes *Tom Brown's School Days*: Arthur was initiated into the lore of bird's eggs. This same sense is found in phrases such as *folk lore*.
→ LEARN

lorry [mid 19th century] The origin of *lorry* is obscure; dialect *lurry* meaning 'pull, drag' exists but it is not clear if there is a connection.

lose [Old English] Old English *losian* meant 'perish, destroy' as well as 'become unable to find'. Modern uses of the verb in idiomatic expressions include: *lose it* 'become angry, lose one's self-control' from the 1970s, and *lose the plot* 'cease to understand', a phrase of the 1990s. *Lose* is based on Old English *los* 'destruction', in current English **loss**. Of Germanic origin, *loss* is related to Old Norse *los* 'breaking up of the ranks of an army'; in later use it is probably a back-formation (by removal of the suffix) from *lost*. The phrase:
■ **lost generation** was applied by the American writer Gertrude Stein (1874–1946) to disillusioned young American authors such as Ernest Hemingway, Scott Fitzgerald, and Ezra Pound, who went to live in Paris in the 1920s; Stein's home there became a focus for the avant-garde during the 1920s and 30s.
→ LOOSE

lot [Old English] Old English *hlot* has a Germanic origin; it is related to Dutch *lot* and German *Los*. The original meanings were 'the making of a decision by random selection' (as in *officers were selected by lot*) and, by extension, 'a portion assigned to someone'; the latter gave rise to the other noun senses such as *purchase a lot of land*. The notion of 'great quantity' as in 'a lot of' is found from the late 16th century; *the lot* meaning 'the whole quantity' arose as a usage in the late 19th century.

lotion [late Middle English] *Lotion* is from Old French, or from Latin *lotio(n)-*, from *lot-* 'washed', from the verb *lavare*. Early use in English included the sense 'washing, ablution', but the pharmaceutical sense was also recorded early.

lottery [mid 16th century] This is probably from Dutch *loterij*, from *lot* 'lot'.

lotus [late 15th century] This was initially a term for a type of clover or trefoil, described by Homer as food for horses. It came via Latin from Greek *lōtos*, of Semitic origin. The term was used by classical writers to denote various trees and plants; the legendary plant whose fruit induced a dreamy forgetfulness mentioned by Homer, was thought by later Greek writers to be *Ziziphus lotus*, a relative of the jujube. The word *lotus-eater* for someone indulging in pleasure and luxury rather than dealing with practical concerns, dates from the early 19th century.

loud [Old English] Of West Germanic origin, Old English *hlūd* is related to Dutch *luid* and German *laut*, from an Indo-European root meaning 'hear'. This root is shared by Greek *kluein* 'hear', *klutos* 'famous' and Latin *cluere* 'be famous'. The transferred use to colours and styles of dress is found from the mid 19th century.

lounge [early 16th century] This reflected the sense 'move indolently' in early contexts and may be a word-formation symbolic of slow movement. Use of the word to describe a type of sitting-room dates from the late 19th century. The phrase *lounge lizard* is slang from US English of the early 20th century describing a man spending his time idly in fashionable society (usually seeking out a wealthy patroness); *lounge music* to describe a type of music that is easy on the ear, dates from the 1980s in US English.

lousy [Middle English] *Lousy* is based on **louse** (an Old English word of Germanic origin). It meant both 'full of lice' and 'dirty, contemptible' from early times. The sense 'swarming, full, abundantly supplied' as in *lousy with tourists*, *lousy with money* arose in US English in the mid 19th century.

lout [mid 16th century] This may be dialectal in origin from archaic *lout* 'to bow down', of Germanic origin: this verb included the senses 'lurk', 'deceive', and 'be small', all with negative connotations.

louvre [Middle English] The first sense recorded was to describe a domed structure on a roof with side openings for ventilation: *louvre* comes from Old French *lover*, *lovier* 'skylight', probably of Germanic origin and related to *lodge*.
→ LODGE

love [Old English] Old English *lufu* is from a Germanic source; it has an Indo-European root shared by Sanskrit *lubhyati* 'desires', Latin *libet*

'it is pleasing', and *libido* 'desire'. The word was applied as a term of endearment from Middle English. The expression *love's young dream* is first recorded in Galsworthy's *Skin Game* (1920): I don't mean any tosh about love's young dream; but I do like being friends. The compound:
■ **love-in** originated in the 1960s and was originally with reference to Californian hippy gatherings.

lovely [Old English] The Old English spelling was *luflic* which meant both 'loving' and 'lovable'. The word was used as a term of approval expressing 'excellent' from the early 17th century.
→ LOVE

low¹ [Middle English] This *low* meaning 'not high, at an inferior level' is from Old Norse *lágr*. Germanic in origin, it is related to Dutch *laag*. The transferred sense 'emotionally depressed' dates from the mid 18th century. The compound:
■ **lower case** in printing contexts referred originally to the lower of two cases of type positioned on an angled stand for use by a compositor.
→ LIE¹

low² [Old English] This *low* which describes the gentle noise made by cattle (in Old English *hlōwan*) is Germanic in origin and related to Dutch *loeien*, from an Indo-European root shared by Latin *clamare* 'to shout'.

loyal [early 16th century] *Loyal* is from French, via Old French *loial* from Latin *legalis*, from *lex*, *leg-* 'law'. Early use was in contexts of faithful allegiance to the sovereign or constituted government, which in a more generalized way became 'true to obligations of duty' (Shakespeare *Othello*: Your wife my Lord, your true and loyal wife). The connection with the Latin base meaning 'law' is now obsolete; an illustration of its use is in Shakespeare's *King Lear*: Loyal and natural boy, where the sense is 'legitimate'.
→ LEGAL

lozenge [Middle English] *Lozenge*, which primarily conveys a diamond shape, is from Old French *losenge*, probably derived from the base of Spanish *losa*, Portuguese *lousa* 'slab', and late Latin *lausiae* (*lapides*) meaning 'stone slabs'. The word's use to mean 'tablet' arose in the early 16th century from the original diamond shape of these tablets.

lubricate [early 17th century] Latin *lubricare* 'make slippery', from *lubricus* 'slippery' is the source of *lubricate* in English. **Lubricant** from the same source verb is found from the early 19th century.

lucid [late 16th century] This was first found meaning 'bright, luminous', a use found in poetical and literary work (Milton *Paradise Lost*: Over his lucid Arms A Military Vest of purple flowed). The source is Latin *lucidus* (perhaps via French *lucide* or Italian *lucido*) from *lucere* 'to shine'. The base is *lux*, *luc-* 'light'. The phrase *lucid interval* was common from the early 17th century referring first to a period of apparent health between attacks of a disease and later to a period of temporary sanity between attacks of lunacy; the Latin phrase *non est compos mentis, sed gaudet lucidis intervallis* 'he is not sane but has periods of sanity' was common in English legal documents from the 13th to the 15th centuries. This influenced later sense development.

Lucifer [Old English] This is a Latin word originally, meaning 'light-bringing, morning star', from *lux*, *luc-* 'light' and *-fer* 'bearing'. It was sometimes used to refer to the planet Venus appearing in the sky before sunrise, a reference found in poetry. It was also used as a name for the rebel archangel (Satan) by association with the biblical quotation How art thou fallen from heaven, O Lucifer, son of the morning (Isaiah 14:12).

luck [late Middle English] This may be from Middle Low German or Middle Dutch *lucken*; verb use was the first recorded in English. The noun (late 15th century) is from Middle Low German *lucke*, related to Dutch *geluk*, German *Glück*, of West Germanic origin and possibly related to *lock*. The word may have come into English as a gambling term.
→ LOCK¹

lucre [late Middle English] This word for 'money' was adopted from French *lucre* or Latin *lucrum*; the phrase *filthy lucre* is with biblical allusion to Titus 1:11 in which the basic sense is 'dishonourable gain' (Teaching things which they ought not, because of filthy lucre). **Lucrative** dating from the same period is from Latin *lucrativus*, from the verb *lucrari* 'to gain', from *lucrum*.

ludicrous [early 17th century] The early sense of *ludicrous* was 'sportive, intended as a jest': it is based on Latin *ludicrus*, probably from *ludicrum* 'stage play'.

lug [late Middle English] *Lug* 'heave about' is probably of Scandinavian origin; compare with Swedish *lugga* 'pull a person's hair' (from *lugg* 'forelock'). The use of the word *lug* as a colloquial noun for 'ear' appeared in the early 16th century; there may be a connection with a general sense 'something that can be pulled'.

luggage [late 16th century] There was a connotation of inconvenience when *luggage* was first used; it was usually large and cumbersome. The base verb is *lug*.

→ LUG

lukewarm [late Middle English] The first element is from dialect *luke* which is probably from dialect *lew* 'lukewarm' and related to *lee*. The definition is found in the biblical reference: So then because thou art lukewarm, and neither cold nor hot, I will spew thee out of my mouth (Revelation 3:16). The word was applied to feelings and attitudes from the early 16th century.

→ LEE

lull [Middle English] This is imitative of sounds used to quieten a child; compare with Latin *lallare* 'sing to sleep', Swedish *lulla* 'hum a lullaby', and Dutch *lullen* 'talk nonsense'. The noun first recorded in the sense 'a soothing drink' dates from the mid 17th century.

lullaby [mid 16th century] *Lullaby* has the first element *lull* 'soothe' and the second element formed on *bye-bye*, a sound used as a refrain in lullabies; the child's word *bye-byes* for 'sleep' is influential here. The word was first used to describe the actual refrain; the noun use for a type of soothing song is found from the late 16th century.

lumber [late Middle English] The early spelling was *lomere* and it may have been symbolic of clumsy movement. In the mid 16th century the word *lumber* was found recorded meaning 'articles of furniture taking up storage space'; this may have been from the earlier verb of movement but it later became associated with the obsolete term *lumber* 'pawnbroker's shop'. The sense 'leave (someone) with unwanted items or an unwelcome task' is found from the mid 19th century.

luminous [late Middle English] *Luminous* is from Old French *lumineux* or Latin *luminosus*, from *lumen, lumin-* 'light'.

lump [Middle English] This is not found in the early stages of the Germanic languages but may be from a Germanic base meaning 'shapeless piece'; Danish *lump* 'lump', Norwegian and Swedish dialect *lump* 'block, log', and Dutch *lomp* 'rag' are comparable forms. The word was applied in disparagement meaning 'heavy, dull person' from the end of the 16th century. The idiomatic phrase *lump in one's throat* associated with emotion is recorded from the early 19th century.

lunar [late Middle English] This is from Latin *lunaris*, from *luna* 'moon'.

lunatic [Middle English] *Lunatic* is from Old French *lunatique*, from late Latin *lunaticus*, from Latin *luna* 'moon': the belief was that changes of the moon caused intermittent insanity. The

word **lunacy**, in the mid 16th century, originally referred to this type of madness and was based on the word *lunatic*.

lunch [early 19th century] This is an abbreviation of **luncheon** which was in use from the late 16th century meaning 'thick piece, hunk': this was possibly an extension of the obsolete word *lunch* 'thick piece, hunk', from Spanish *lonja* 'slice'. When it first appeared *lunch* was considered a vulgarism or a fashionable affectation. A *luncheon* was originally a light meal taken between two of the ordinary mealtimes, especially between breakfast and the midday meal.

lung [Old English] Old English *lungen* is from a Germanic source and is related to Dutch *long* and German *Lunge*, from an Indo-European root shared by *light*.

→ LIGHT²

lunge¹ [mid 18th century] This *lunge* denoting a forward thrust with the body as in fencing is from earlier *allonge*, from French *allonger* 'to lengthen'.

lunge² [early 18th century] The *lunge* denoting a long rein on which a horse is held is from French *longe*, from *allonge* 'a lengthening out'.

lurch [late 17th century] This word was first used as a noun denoting the sudden leaning of a ship to one side. The origin remains unknown. It is not the same word that forms part of the expression *leave in the lurch*; this is connected with a type of backgammon played in the 16th century known as *lurch*, a term extended to mean 'discomfiture' (because of association with a large gap in the game score).

lure [Middle English] This comes from Old French *luere*, of Germanic origin; it is probably related to German *Luder* 'bait'. Early use was in contexts of training hawks.

lurgy [mid 20th century] The origin of *lurgy* remains unknown but it was frequently used in the British radio series *The Goon Show* of the 1950s and 1960s. It is usually part of the phrase *the dreaded lurgy*, a fictitious highly-infectious disease.

lurid [mid 17th century] The early sense was 'pale and dismal in colour': it comes from Latin *luridus*, related to *luror* 'a wan or yellow colour'.

lurk [Middle English] The formation of this word may involve Middle English **lour** 'look angry or sullen' (the origin of which is unknown) and the frequentative suffix *-k* (as in *talk*): this adds a notion of repeated or frequent on-going activity. In the 1990s *lurk* became part of computing slang meaning 'read communications on a network without making one's presence known'.

luscious [late Middle English] This is perhaps an alteration of obsolete *licious*, a shortened form of *delicious*; early use was in descriptions of food or perfumes. The abbreviated form *lush* arose as a colloquial usage in the 1990s.

lush [late Middle English] This may be an alteration of obsolete *lash* meaning 'soft, lax', from Old French *lasche* 'lax', by association with *luscious*. In the late 18th century a *lush* came to mean 'a drunk': this may have been a humorous use of the earlier word.

lust [Old English] 'Pleasure' and 'delight' were among the early meanings of *lust* which is from Germanic and related to Dutch *lust* and German *Lust*. 'Sexual appetite' was also an early sense. Middle English **lusty** 'cheerful' and later (Middle English) 'healthy, strong' is based on *lust* in the early sense 'vigour'.

lustre [early 16th century] Lustre is from French, from Italian *lustro*, from the verb *lustrare*, from Latin *lustrare* 'illuminate'. The connection with ceramics arose in the early 19th century. The phrase *lack-lustre* was used by Shakespeare to mean 'lacking brightness', primarily when describing eyes; this was soon generalized (e.g. *lacklustre performance in goal*).

luxury [Middle English] Luxury was once a word for 'lechery'. It comes from Old French *luxurie, luxure*, from Latin *luxuria*, from *luxus* 'excess'. The sense 'comfort and extravagance' dates from the mid 17th century. In the plural as *luxuries* the word means 'things that are desirable but not indispensable', a use dating from the late 18th century. The adjective **luxurious** from the same Latin base is also Middle English when it meant 'lascivious': it came into the language via Old French *luxurios*, from Latin *luxuriosus*.

lychgate [late 15th century] This word for a type of covered gateway at the entrance to a churchyard has as its first element the Old English word *līc* 'body'. The gateway was used formerly at burials for sheltering a coffin until the clergyman arrived.

lynch [mid 19th century] This verb used to mean 'hang' in contexts of a mob taking it into their own hands to make a summary execution outside the law, is from the phrase *Lynch's law*, an early form of **lynch law**. The latter dates from the early 19th century and is believed to derive its name from Captain William Lynch, the head of a self-constituted judicial tribunal in Virginia in c.1780: he was said to have illegally fined and imprisoned certain Tories but no evidence of his involvement in any such act has been found.

lyre [Middle English] Greek *lura* 'lyre' is the source of *lyre* (via Old French *lire* and Latin *lyra*) and the base of late 16th-century **lyric** from French *lyrique* or Latin *lyricus*. **Lyrical**, synonymous with *lyric* when first used, came to mean 'highly enthusiastic' (as in *wax lyrical*) from the end of the 19th century.

Mm

macabre [late 19th century] This word meaning 'grim, repulsive, gruesome' is an adoption of French *macabre*, from *Danse Macabre* 'dance of death', from Old French. The source is perhaps *Macabé* 'a Maccabee'. The reference would then be to a miracle play depicting the slaughter of the Maccabees, followers of the family of Judas Maccabeus, the Jewish leader who led a revolt in Judaea against Antiochus IV Epiphanes in around 167. He is the hero of the two books of the Maccabees in the Apocrypha.

mace [Middle English] Old French *masse* 'large hammer' is the source of *mace*. There is probably a connection with the rare classical Latin word *mateola* which was an agricultural implement. The use of the word to describe a staff of office in the form of an ornamental club also dates from Middle English. The *mace*, in several legislatures, is viewed as a symbol of authority; in the House of Commons it lies on the table before the Speaker.

macerate [mid 16th century] *Macerate* is from Latin *macerare* 'make soft, soak'. As well as meaning 'soften (food) by soaking in a liquid (such as wine)', the word, in early use, meant 'cause to grow thinner or waste away (usually by fasting)': this latter sense is now archaic.

machete [late 16th century] This is an adoption of a Spanish word, probably from *macho* 'hammer'. From the mid 19th century, the word was also used as a term for a small type of guitar usually with four strings played in Portugal and Madeira; the forerunner of the ukulele, it was a plucked instrument, and is said to have been introduced into the Hawaiian islands by Portuguese sailors.
→ MACE

machine [mid 16th century] A *machine* was originally a structure of any kind. It comes from French via Latin from Doric Greek *makhana*: in Attic Greek the parallel form was *mēkhanē*, from *mēkhos* 'contrivance'. The chief semantic strands include: 'a non-mechanical structure functioning independently' (e.g. *human machine* (= body); *the machine of society*); 'structure designed for a specific purpose' (e.g. *war machine*); 'a mechanical structure for transportation' (e.g. *bathing machine*, *pedal-powered machines*); and 'a device designed to perform a specific task' (*vending machine*). **Machinate** is recorded slightly earlier than *machine* when it was used transitively in the sense 'to plot (a malicious act)' in phrases such as *machinate treason*, *machinate destruction*: it comes from Latin *machinat-*, the past participial stem of *machinari* 'contrive', from Latin *machina*.

macho [1920s] In Mexican Spanish this word means 'masculine or vigorous'. It was adopted into US English and the pejorative sense 'displaying aggressive pride in one's masculinity' may have begun in Anglophone usage. **Machismo**, also from Mexican Spanish and based on *macho*, dates from the 1940s.

mackintosh [mid 19th century] This word for a waterproof garment was named after Charles *Macintosh* (1766–1843), the Scottish inventor who originally patented the cloth (made of two layers of cloth bonded together by India rubber dissolved in naphtha). The abbreviation **mac** is found from the early 20th century.

mad [Old English] This is from Old English *gemǣd(e)d* 'maddened', a participial form related to *gemād* 'mad', of Germanic origin. 'Insane' was probably the earliest sense; Old English *wōd* (= wood) was common in this sense but became rare by the 16th century except in northern regional use. *Mad* took over as the popular term, as it did to express the sense 'feeling anger' previously expressed by *wroth* and other synonyms in Middle English. The phrase *like mad* is found from the mid 17th century, meaning *like a mad person* originally and gradually weakening in sense to mean 'very much'. The adjective **madding** is first recorded in a poetic use by Spenser in the late 16th century, meaning 'becoming mad'. In *Gray's Elegy* (1751), the phrase Far from the madding Crowd's ignoble Strife shows *madding* in the sense 'frenzied, acting madly'; Thomas Hardy uses *Far from the Madding Crowd* as the title of one of his novels (1874). Compounds involving *mad* which have become common are:

■ **mad scientist** dating from the 1940s and popularized by melodramatic horror stories and films.

■ **mad cow disease** dating from the late 1980s, a popular phrase for bovine spongiform encephalopathy, characterized in cattle by abnormal behaviour and unsteady gait.

madrigal This word for a part-song for several voices, especially from the Renaissance period, is from Italian *madrigale* (from medieval Latin *carmen matricale* 'simple song'), from late Latin *matricalis* 'maternal or primitive'. The base is Latin *matrix* 'womb'.

maelstrom [late 17th century] This is from an early modern Dutch proper name for a mythical whirlpool supposed to exist in the Arctic Ocean, west of Norway. The name was used on Dutch maps. The elements are from *maalen* 'grind, whirl' and *stroom* 'stream'. The figurative use 'state of turbulence and confusion' is found from the early 19th century.

magazine [late 16th century] *Magazine* comes from French *magasin* via Italian from Arabic *makzin, makzan* 'storehouse', from *kazana* 'store up'. The term originally meant 'store' and was often used from the mid 17th century in the title of books providing a 'store' of information useful to particular groups of people: this gave rise to the prime current sense 'periodical publication' (mid 18th century). *Magazine* 'a store for arms', a contemporary specialization of the original meaning, gave rise to the sense 'chamber for holding a supply of cartridges' in the mid 18th century.

magenta [mid 19th century] This colour owes its name to *Magenta* in northern Italy, the site of a battle in 1859 fought shortly before the dye (of bloodlike colour) was discovered.

magic [late Middle English] *Magic* in early use was also 'a magical procedure'. The source is Old French *magique*, from Latin *magicus* (adjective), late Latin *magica* (noun), from Greek *magikē (tekhnē)* '(art of) a magus': magi were regarded as magicians. The word sometimes means 'surprising and remarkable' as in *magic touch* (mid 19th century). From the 1950s it has been in use as a colloquial way of saying 'excellent'; humorous use of the compound *magic sponge*, an apparent 'cure-all' (of a sponge and cold water) for football injuries, dates from the 1960s. The word **magician** is late Middle English from Old French *magicien*, from late Latin *magica*.

magistrate [late Middle English] *Magistrate* is from Latin *magistratus* 'administrator', from *magister* 'master'. This may refer to a civil officer charged with the administration of a law (such as a coroner); however the term came to be applied increasingly to local justices in the English boroughs (such as justices of the peace) and eventually in country areas as well.

magnanimous [mid 16th century] This word meaning 'very generous' is based on Latin *magnanimus*, composed of *magnus* 'great' and *animus* 'soul'.

magnate [late Middle English] *Magnate* 'a wealthy and influential person' is from late Latin *magnas, magnat-* 'great man', from Latin *magnus* 'great'. It is often used in business contexts defined by a preceding word (e.g. *sugar magnate, oil magnate*).

magnet [late Middle English] This word was originally a name for lodestone. It comes from Latin *magnes, magnet-*, from Greek *magnēs lithos* 'lodestone': it was probably influenced by Anglo-Norman French *magnete*. The adjective **magnetic** is recorded from the early 17th century and is from late Latin *magneticus*, from Latin *magneta*, the base too of **magnetism** from modern Latin *magnetismus*.

magnificent [late Middle English] *Magnificent* came via Old French from Latin *magnificent-* 'making great, serving to magnify', based on *magnus* 'great'. The word has been attached to names (such as *Suleiman the Magnificent*) from the early 18th century.

magnify [late Middle English] Early senses included 'show honour to (God)' (illustrated in Luke 1:46: My soul doth magnify the Lord: part of the *Magnificat*, a canticle used in Christian liturgy) and 'make greater in size or importance' (Job 20:6: Though he be magnified up to the heaven). It comes from Old French *magnifier* or Latin *magnificare*, based on Latin *magnus* 'great'. 'Make larger by means of a lens' is a sense dating from the mid 17th century.

magnitude [late Middle English] The word derives from Latin *magnitudo*, from *magnus* 'great'. 'Greatness of character' was an early meaning of *magnitude*, now a rare usage (Thomas Hardy *Far from the Madding Crowd*: 'What fun it would be to send it to the stupid old Boldwood ...!' said the irrepressible Liddy ... indulging in an awful mirth ... as she thought of the moral and social magnitude of the man contemplated). In astronomy contexts, *magnitude* was a class into which bodies such as stars were placed according to their brillancy. This led in the late 16th century to phrases such as *of the first magnitude* (= the most brilliant): these distinctions were subjective originally but are now a matter of photometric measurement. Figurative use of the phrase is found from the mid 17th century (e.g. *a commercial city of the first magnitude*).

maiden [Old English] Old English *mægden* is from a Germanic diminutive meaning 'maid, virgin': this is related to German *Mädchen*, a diminutive of *Magd* 'maid', from an Indo-European root shared by Old Irish *mug* 'boy, servant'. Middle English **maid** came to exist as a doublet alongside *maiden* of which it is an abbreviation. From the earliest times, *maid* and *maiden* appear to have shared the senses 'young female' and 'virgin (of any age)'; because of this ambiguity, words such as *girl* and phrases such as *young lady* have tended to replace *maiden* in the 'young female' sense thereby limiting its application to 'virgin'. Compounds such as *housemaid*, *nursemaid*, *chambermaid* probably led to the common sense 'servant' becoming more associated with *maid* than with *maiden*.

mail[1] [Middle English] An early *mail* was a 'travelling bag': it comes from Old French *male* 'wallet', of West Germanic origin. In later use the plural *mails* for 'luggage' is seen in US use (R. L. Stevenson *Catriona*: He … emptied out his mails upon the floor that I might have a change of clothes). The notion 'by post' dates from the mid 17th century in phrases such as *mail of letters*: the sense 'letters and packages' is first found in US usage. In recent times distinctions in speed of delivery have been made in compounds such as *snail mail* and *e-mail* (1990s).

mail[2] [Middle English] This *mail* as in *coat of mail*, in early use also referred to each individual metal element in the composition of mail armour. Old French *maille* is the source, from Latin *macula* 'spot or mesh'.

maim [Middle English] *Maim* is from Old French *mahaignier*, the origin of which is unknown.

main [Middle English] *Main* is from Old English *mægen* 'physical force' (as in *with might and main*), reinforced by Old Norse *meginn*, *megn* 'strong, powerful', both from a Germanic base meaning 'have power'. The noun use referring to a principal power supply such as electricity or water dates from the early 17th century; *turn on the main* has sometimes been used humorously for 'begin to weep copiously' (Dickens *Pickwick Papers*: Blessed if I don't think he's got a main in his head as is always turned on). The adjective *main* expresses senses related to the notion of physical power (e.g. *by main force*) and to preeminence (e.g. *main points of an argument*).

maintain [Middle English] An early sense of *maintain* was 'practise (a good or bad action) habitually'. The source of the word in English is Old French *maintenir* 'protect, conserve in the same state', from Latin *manu tenere* 'hold in the hand'. The semantic strands of *maintain* are: 'support, assist' (Malory *Morte d'Arthur*: To maintain his nephew against the mighty earl), 'cause to continue' (e.g. *maintain military discipline*). Middle English **maintenance** conveyed a notion of support and in law contexts meant 'aiding a party in a legal action taken without lawful cause': this is from Old French, from *maintenir*. It also referred to support of a family by providing the means of subsistence: from

the late 17th century this was extended to use as a legal term for an allowance made to a spouse after divorce.

majesty [Middle English] *Majesty* referred to the 'greatness of God' in early examples as well as the greatness of a monarch. Old French *majeste* is the source, from Latin *majestas*, from a variant of *majus*, *major-*. The use of the word as an honorific title in phrases such as *Your Majesty* is attested as an early usage: other forms of address included *Your Grace* and *Your Highness*, commonly used when addressing Henry VIII and Elizabeth I, but these were superseded by *Your Majesty* in the 17th century.
→ MAJOR

major [Middle English] *Major* is a use of the Latin comparative of *magnus* 'great'; it was perhaps influenced by French *majeur*. The use appended to nouns indicating the more senior of two people (e.g. *Brown major*) is found from the mid 16th century. Colloquial use meaning 'serious, excessive' (as in *major sucking-up*) is found first in US examples from the 1950s. The verb usage *major in* in US English for 'study a subject as a principal course at University' dates from the early 20th century. Latin *major* is the base of **majority**, recorded from the mid 16th century when it denoted superiority: it comes from French *majorité*, from medieval Latin *majoritas*. Its use in political contexts dates from the mid 18th century.

make [Old English] Old English *macian* is of West Germanic origin; it may be from a Germanic base meaning 'fitting' or from an Indo-European base meaning 'knead, work with the hands' from which the more general meaning 'make' may have developed. The semantic branches include: 'produce' (e.g. *make a sketch*); 'cause to be or become' (e.g. *make someone a scapegoat*); 'cause (to do or occur)' (e.g. *make someone laugh*); 'perform, accomplish' (e.g. *make one's getaway*); 'behave, act' (e.g. *if I may make so bold*); 'put in order' (e.g. *make the bed*). *Make* features commonly in idiomatic phrases: of the more recent popular expressions *make my day* dates from the 1980s and was popularized as a remark made by the character Dirty Harry in the film *Sudden Impact* (1983).
→ MATCH[1]

malady [Middle English] *Malady* comes from Old French *maladie*, from *malade* 'sick', based on Latin *male* 'ill' and *habitus* 'having (as a condition)'.

malaria [mid 18th century] This is the adoption of an Italian word, from *mal'aria*, a contracted form of *mala aria* 'bad air'. The term originally referred to the unwholesome atmosphere created by exhalations from marshes, once thought to cause the disease.

male [late Middle English] Male is from Old French masle, from Latin masculus, from mas 'a male'.

malevolent [early 16th century] Latin malevolent- is the source of English malevolent meaning literally 'wishing ill'. The formative elements are male 'ill' and volent- from the verb velle 'to wish'.

malice [Middle English] Malice came via Old French from Latin malitia the source too of Middle English **malicious** (from Old French malicios). The base is Latin malus 'bad'. The phrase malice aforethought is common in modern legal language, but originally this was referred to as malice prepense (= premeditated malice), an Anglo-Norman phrase.

malign [Middle English] Malign came via Old French maligne and is based on Latin malignus 'tending to evil', from malus 'bad'. An obsolete use is in the sense 'malignant' (as in malign tumours). **Malignant** is recorded from the mid 16th century when it also meant 'likely to rebel against God or authority': this is from late Latin malignare 'contrive maliciously'. The term was used in its early sense to describe those sympathetic to the royalist cause during the English Civil War (Charles I (1642): How I have been dealt with by a Powerful malignant Party in this Kingdom, whose Designs are no less than to destroy my Person and Crown).

malinger [early 19th century] This is a back-formation (by removal of the suffix) from late 18th-century malingerer, apparently from French malingre: this was perhaps formed as mal- 'wrongly, improperly' and haingre 'weak'. The likely origin is Germanic.

mall [mid 17th century] In early use this was a name for the game of pall mall, of which it is probably a shortening. This game was popular in the 16th and 17th centuries and involved a boxwood ball being driven through an iron ring suspended at the end of a large alley (Pall Mall in London was on the site of a pall-mall alley). Use of the word mall to mean 'a sheltered walk' derives from The Mall, a tree-bordered walk in St James's Park in London, also the site of a pall-mall alley. The prime current sense 'shopping precinct' dates from the 1960s.

malleable [late Middle English] 'Able to be hammered' was the first sense recorded for malleable. The general sense 'pliable, liable to adapt' dates from the early 17th century. It came via Old French from medieval Latin malleabilis, from Latin malleus 'a hammer', the base too of late Middle English **mallet** (from Old

French maillet, from mail 'hammer'). The surname Mallet has been referred, by some, to the bearer's fearsome behaviour in battle.

malt [Old English] Old English m(e)alt is Germanic in origin; it is probably related to melt. Use of the word to mean 'malt whisky' dates from the early 18th century.
→ MELT

mammal [early 19th century] This is an Anglicized form, first used in the plural, of modern Latin mammalia, the neuter plural of Latin mammalis, an adjective from mamma 'breast'.

mammoth [early 18th century] This comes from Russian mamo(n)t and is probably of Siberian origin from a base meaning 'earth horn'. The spelling with th was always reflected apparently in the pronunciation and seems to have come into English via Dutch and German sources. Adjectival use in the sense 'gigantic' began in US English in the early 19th century.

man [Old English] Old English man(n), (plural) menn (noun), mannian (verb) are Germanic in origin; related forms include Dutch man, German Mann, and Sanskrit manu 'mankind'. In all the Germanic languages, the word had the two senses 'adult male' and 'human being', but the latter has been generally replaced by derivatives (e.g. German Mann 'man', Mensch 'human being') except in the case of English.

manacle [Middle English] Manacle is from Old French manicle 'handcuff', from Latin manicula, a diminutive of manus 'hand'. Figurative use as a 'bond or restraint' dates from the early 17th century (Shakespeare Cymbeline: For my sake, wear this, It is a Manacle of Love).

manage [mid 16th century] The early sense recorded for manage was 'put (a horse) through the paces of the manège' (= training in an enclosed area). The word is from Italian maneggiare, based on Latin manus 'hand'. The notions of supervising and controlling were soon reflected in other uses such as manage financial affairs; the idea of coping and staying in control despite difficulties (as in I don't know how I'll ever manage) dates from the mid 18th century. In medical contexts manage has had the sense 'carefully control (a disease or patient care)' from the mid 19th century.

mandate [early 16th century] Mandate is from Latin mandatum 'something commanded' (the source too of **mandatory** recorded slightly earlier from late Latin mandatorius). The base elements here are manus 'hand' and dare 'to give'. The noun sense 'authority to carry out a policy' has been influenced by French mandat and is found in examples from the late 18th century.

mandible [late Middle English] The anatomical term *mandible* for 'jaw' is from Old French, or from late Latin *mandibula*, from *mandere* 'to chew'.

mane [Old English] Old English *manu* is Germanic in origin and related to Dutch *manen*. Ultimately the word is from an Indo-European base meaning '(nape of the) neck'.

manger [Middle English] *Manger* is from Old French *mangeure*, based on Latin *manducare* 'to chew'.

mangle¹ [late 17th century] This *mangle* as a term for a machine for squeezing moisture from wet laundry, is from Dutch *mangel*, from *mangelen* 'to mangle'. This is from medieval Latin *mango, manga*, from Greek *manganon* 'axis, engine'. The early *mangle* was an oblong rectangular wooden chest filled with stones, worked backwards and forwards by a wheel mechanism: the fabric was spread on a polished surface underneath it.

mangle² [late Middle English] This *mangle* meaning 'mutilate' is from Anglo-Norman French *mahangler*, which is apparently a frequentative (= verb of repeated action) of *mahaignier* 'to maim'.

mangy [early 16th century] This is based on late Middle English **mange** (a skin disease caused by parasitic mites) from Old French *mangeue*, from *mangier* 'to eat'. Latin *manducare* 'to chew' is the base. The figurative sense 'contemptible' is found from the mid 16th century.

mania [late Middle English] *Mania* came via late Latin from a Greek word meaning literally 'madness' (characterized by excited or aggressive behaviour), from *mainesthai* 'be mad'. It was often contrasted with *melancholia*. The sense 'personal obsession' (as in *a mania for buying antiques*) dates from the late 17th century. Compounds suffixed by *-mania* are attested in English from the early 17th century onwards; noun compounds with *mania* as the second element (such as *persecution mania*) became common from the late 18th century. The related word **maniac** dates as an adjective from the early 16th century: it came via late Latin from late Greek *maniakos*, from *mania* which is also the base of early 19th-century **manic** 'characterized by mania'. The sense 'excessively enthusiastic, wild, hyperactive' (e.g. *completely manic about collecting memorabilia*) dates from the 1950s.

manicure [late 19th century] This is an adoption of a French word, from Latin *manus* 'hand' and *cura* 'care'.

manifest [late Middle English] *Manifest* 'clear, obvious' came via Old French from Latin *mani-*

festus. Verb use in spiritualist contexts such as *the ghost manifested during the trance* dates from the mid 19th century. **Manifestation**, also late Middle English, is from late Latin *manifestatio(n-)*, from the verb *manifestare* 'make public'.

manifesto [mid 17th century] This is an adoption of an Italian word from the verb *manifestare*, from Latin, 'make public'. Latin *manifestus* 'obvious' is the base.
→ MANIFEST

manikin [mid 16th century] This is from Dutch *manneken* 'little man', a diminutive of *man*. It shares the sense 'jointed model' with **mannequin** dating from the mid 18th century; this word comes from French and once denoted a young woman or man employed to show clothes to customers.

manipulate [early 19th century] This is a back-formation (by removal of the suffix) from the earlier noun *manipulation*, from Latin *manipulus* 'handful'. The transferred sense 'control and influence in an underhand and devious manner' is seen in examples from the mid 19th century.

manky [1950s] This word meaning 'inferior, worthless' is probably from obsolete *mank* 'mutilated, defective', from Old French *manque*, from Latin *mancus* 'maimed'.

manner [Middle English] *Manner* is from Old French *maniere*, based on Latin *manuarius* 'of the hand', from *manus* 'hand'. The semantic branches include: 'kind, sort' (e.g. *what manner of man is he?*); 'mode of behaviour' (e.g. *after the manner of young animals*); 'the way in which something is performed' (e.g. *in a forthright manner*). The word **mannerism** as an 'idiosyncratic habit' dates from the early 19th century; capitalized as *Mannerism* it describes a style of Italian art in the 16th century characterized by stylistic exaggeration, distorted scale and perspective, as well as unusual effects of colour and lighting

manoeuvre [mid 18th century] 'Tactical movement' (in military and nautical contexts) was the early sense of the noun *manoeuvre* which came via French from medieval Latin *manuoperare*. The base elements here are Latin *manus* 'hand' and *operari* 'to work'. The phrase *room for manoeuvre* dates from the 1950s.

manor [Middle English] Anglo-Norman French *maner* 'dwelling', from Latin *manere* 'remain' has given rise to the word *manor* in English. The phrase *to the manor born* (= naturally suited to upper-class life) is an error for or pun of *to the manner born* (= familiar with a way of living from birth). The colloquial use in police contexts of *manor* to mean 'patch, territory' (as in *the snouts on my manor*) is found from the 1920s.

mansion [late Middle English] A *mansion* was initially a word for the chief residence of a lord: it came via Old French from Latin *mansio(n-)* 'place where someone stays', from *manere* 'remain'. The same Latin verb is the base of **manse** (late 15th century) which was the principal house of an estate: this is from medieval Latin *mansus* 'house, dwelling'.

mantle [Old English] Old English *mentel* is from Latin *mantellum* 'cloak', reinforced in Middle English by Old French *mantel*. The word initially described any outer garments of men, women, and children, but it came to be restricted to long cloaks worn by women and robes worn by certain dignitaries. The word was used figuratively from early times. **Mantel** (mid 16th century) as in *mantelpiece* was originally a variant of *mantle*.

manual [late Middle English] The adjective is from Old French *manuel*, from Latin *manualis* 'held in the hand' (a word which later influenced the English spelling), from *manus* 'hand'. The noun is from Anglo-Norman French *manuel, manual* 'handle, handbook'.

manufacture [mid 16th century] Originally this word referred to something made by hand: it comes from French (re-formed by association with Latin *manu factum* 'made by hand'), from Italian *manifattura*. Reference to 'the making of articles on a large scale using machinery' dates from the early 17th century.

manure [late Middle English] The first recorded use was as a verb in the sense 'cultivate (land)': the source is Anglo-Norman French *mainoverer*, Old French *manouvrer*. The noun sense dates from the mid 16th century
➡ MANOEUVRE

manuscript [late 16th century] *Manuscript*, literally 'something written by hand' is from medieval Latin *manuscriptus*, from *manu* 'by hand' and *scriptus* the past participle of *scribere* 'to write'.

many [Old English] Old English *manig* is of Germanic origin, related to Dutch *menig* and German *manch*.

map [early 16th century] *Map* is either from late Latin *mappa* or from medieval Latin *mappa mundi* which is translated literally as 'sheet of the world'.

mar [Old English] Shakespeare's line in his *King Lear*: Mend your speech …, lest it may mar your fortunes illustrates the sense already found in Old English when *merran* meant 'hinder,

damage'. The word is from a Germanic source and is probably related to Dutch *marren* 'to loiter'. Scots use includes the sense 'perplex, trouble, annoy'.

marathon [late 19th century] The place name *Marathōn* in Greece is the source of this word: it was the scene of a victory over the Persians in 490 BC; the modern race (usually over 42.195 kilometers) is based on the tradition that a messenger ran from Marathon to Athens, a distance of 22 miles, with the news. The original account by Herodotus told of the messenger Pheidippides running 150 miles from Athens to Sparta before the battle in search of help.

maraud [late 17th century] This is from French *marauder*, from *maraud* 'rogue'. Further details in the etymology are uncertain and disputed. The French words were adopted in German in the 17th century when they were punningly associated with an imperialist general called Count Mérode whose troops had the reputation, in the Thirty Years' War, of being undisciplined.

marble [Middle English] *Marble* came via an Old French variant of *marbre* from Latin *marmor*, from Greek *marmaros* 'shining stone' (associated with *marmairein* 'to shine'). Use of the word as a term for a little glass or baked clay ball used in the children's game of *marbles* dates from the late 17th century: these were originally made of marble. The colloquial use of *marbles* referring to sanity (as in *lose one's marbles*) was first recorded in North American English examples at the beginning of the 20th century.

march [late Middle English] *March* 'walk in a military manner' is from French *marcher* 'to walk', which earlier meant 'to trample': the origin is uncertain. The phrase *get a march on* (early 18th century) meaning 'get ahead of' is from a use of *march* meaning 'the distance covered by troops in a specified period of time', usually a single day.

mardy [early 20th century] This northern English word meaning 'sulky' is from dialect *mard* 'spoilt' used to describe a child, an alteration of *marred*.
➡ MAR

mare [Old English] Old English *mearh* 'horse', *mere* 'mare' are from a Germanic base with cognates in Celtic languages meaning 'stallion'. The sense 'male horse' died out at the end of the Middle English period.

margarine [late 19th century] This comes from French, based on Greek *margaron* 'pearl', by association with the lustre of the crystals of margaric acid: this application arose from a misconception of *margarine*'s chemical nature. The abbreviation **marge** has been in use since the 1920s.

margin [late Middle English] *Margin* is from Latin *margo*, *margin-* 'edge', 'retaining wall', 'margin of a book'. The phrase *margin of* or *for error* dates from the mid 19th century. **Marginal** from the same Latin base (late 16th century) is from medieval Latin *marginalis*.

marina [early 19th century] This is from the Italian *marina* 'coastal region', from late Latin *marina*. The word originally described a coastal resort or a port area; the current modern sense 'harbour for the mooring of yachts' or 'leisure complex' based around sailing activities, is found from the 1930s, originally in US English.

marinate [mid 17th century] The word *marinate* is from Italian *marinare* 'pickle in brine', or from French *mariner* (from *marine* 'brine'). **Marinade**, dating from the late 17th century, is an English use of a French word from Spanish *marinada*, via *marinar* 'to pickle in brine' from *marino* 'briny'.

marine [Middle English] Early use was as a noun meaning 'seashore': it is from Old French *marin* 'sea', 'sailor', *marine* 'sea(shore)'. Latin *marinus* is the source of the noun and the adjective, from *mare* 'sea' (the base too of **maritime** dating from the mid 16th century). **Mariner** is also a Middle English word, from Old French *marinier*, from medieval Latin *marinarius*, from Latin *marinus*. It is attested as a surname from the late 12th century.

marital [early 16th century] *Marital* is from Latin *maritalis* 'conjugal, nuptial', from *maritus* 'husband'.

mark [Old English] The Old English noun *mearc*, *gemerce* and verb *mearcian* are Germanic in origin; they are from an Indo-European root shared by Latin *margo* 'margin'. The noun's semantic branches include: 'boundary, limit', a use which is now archaic; 'object marking a boundary' (R. L. Stevenson *Treasure Island*: A tall tree was thus the principal mark); 'omen, indicator' (R. Graves *I Claudius*: the broad-headed halberd and the long sword are marks of high rank); 'sign, badge' (e.g. *the Devil's mark*, *Mark of Cain*); 'visible marking' (e.g. *zebra-like marks*); 'target' (e.g. *hit the mark*); 'indicator of a limit' (e.g. *up to the 300 mark*); also 'attention, notice' (e.g. *a statement worthy of mark*). The phrase *God bless the mark* now used mainly in writing to apologize for a preceding or following word, was originally probably a formula to avert an evil omen and was formerly used apparently by midwives at the birth of a child bearing a birthmark.

market [Middle English] The immediate origin of *market* is uncertain; it may be a borrowing of a late Latin word in another Germanic language, or it may be from an Old French regional form, based on Latin *mercari* 'to buy'. The word refers to 'a place of trade' or the 'trade' itself.
→ MERCHANT

marmalade [late 15th century] *Marmalade* is from Portuguese *marmelada* 'quince jam', from *marmelo* 'quince', based on Greek *melimēlon*. The base elements are *meli* 'honey' and *mēlon* 'apple'. Close medieval trading relations between England and Portugal may account for the very early borrowing of the Portuguese word into English. Use of the word in connection with colour dates from the early 1920s.

maroon[1] [late 17th century] This *maroon* used in colour contexts was first found in the sense 'chestnut'. It is from French *marron* 'chestnut', via Italian from medieval Greek *maraon*. The sense relating to colour dates from the late 18th century.

maroon[2] [early 18th century] This word used to mean 'leave in a position from which there is no escape' is from *Maroon*, the name (from French *marron* 'feral') of a member of a group of black people living in the forests and mountains of Suriname and the West Indies, descended from runaway slaves. It was originally in the form *marooned* 'lost in the wilds'.

marriage [Middle English] *Marriage* is from Old French *mariage*, from *marier* 'marry' (from Latin *maritare*, from *maritus* 'married') the source too of the Middle English verb **marry**. *Marry* was a relatively rare word in comparison to *wed* in Chaucer's writings, but by the end of the 16th century it was the more usual. Extended use in the sense 'blend, link together' (e.g. *marry two flavours*) is already found in early examples.

marrow [Old English] Old English *mearg* was a word for 'bone marrow'; of Germanic origin it is related to Dutch *merg* and German *Mark* cognate with several Indo-European words meaning 'pith'. The development of the term for a type of gourd eaten as a vegetable is unclear; the compound *marrowfat* is the earliest application, followed by *vegetable marrow* (originally referring to an avocado and later to the squash); it may have developed from a notion of 'inner pulp' or from that of 'rich substance'.

marsh [Old English] Old English *mer(i)sc* was perhaps influenced by late Latin *mariscus* 'marsh'. The origin of the word is West Germanic from a base shared by *mere* now used poetically for a lake or pond.

marshal [Middle English] In early examples, a *marshall* was simply 'a person in charge of looking after horses': this developed gradually until it came to denote a high-ranking officer of state. The horse (and therefore the responsibility for its care) was important in medieval warfare. The word comes from Old French *mareschal* 'farrier, commander', from late Latin *mariscalcus*, from Germanic elements meaning 'horse' and 'servant'. Use of the word in US English to denote a legal officer with duties similar to those of a sheriff, dates from the late 18th century.
→ MARE

marsupial [late 17th century] A rare use of *marsupial* meaning 'resembling a pouch' in the phrase *marsupial muscle* was the first recorded. It comes from modern Latin *marsupialis*, via Latin from Greek *marsupion* 'pouch'.

martial [late Middle English] *Martial* meaning 'warlike, relating to war' comes from Old French, or is from Latin *martialis*, based on *Mars*, the name of the god of war in Roman mythology.

martyr [Old English] Old English *martir* came via ecclesiastical Latin from Greek *martur* which generally meant 'witness' but which in Christian use meant 'martyr'. The general sense 'person who suffers or who appears to suffer', often used humorously (e.g. *a martyr to dyspepsia*) dates from the late 16th century.

marvel [Middle English] Early use was as a noun meaning 'miracle', 'wonderful thing' from Old French *merveille*, from late Latin *mirabilia*, the neuter plural of Latin *mirabilis* 'wonderful', from *mirari* 'wonder at'. Middle English **marvellous** is from Old French *merveillus*, from *merveille*.

mascara [late 19th century] This is an adoption of an Italian word with the literal meaning 'mask', from Arabic *maskara* 'buffoon'.

mascot [late 19th century] *Mascot* is from French *mascotte*, from modern Provençal *mascotto*, the feminine diminutive of *masco* 'witch'. The French word was popularized by the operetta *La Mascotte* written by Edmond Audran; it had its premiere on 29 December 1880.

masculine [late Middle English] This came via Old French from Latin *masculinus*, from *masculus* 'male'.

mash [Old English] Old English *māsc* was first used as a brewing term. It is West Germanic origin and perhaps ultimately related to *mix*.
→ MIX

mask [mid 16th century] This is from French *masque*, from Italian *maschera*, *mascara*, probably from medieval Latin *masca* 'witch, spectre', but influenced by Arabic *maskara* 'buffoon'.

masochism [late 19th century] This is based on the name of Leopold von Sacher-*Masoch* (1835–95), the Austrian novelist who described the tendency.

mason [Middle English] *Mason*, from Old French, is probably of Germanic origin; it is perhaps related to *make*. The word is also used to denote a *Freemason*, a member of the *Free and Accepted Masons*. Early in the 17th century, the societies of freemasons (skilled workers in stone who travelled to find employment and had a system of secret signs and passwords giving admittance to important buildings being erected) began to admit honorary members. These were called *accepted masons* and were supposed to be eminent for architectural or antiquarian learning; they were initiated in the knowledge of secret signs. This status became sought after and fashionable and before the end of the 17th century, the object of these societies (lodges) became chiefly social. The constitution of the society came to embrace mutual help and brotherly feeling with a powerful network of lodges (the 'grand lodge' is situated in London) all over the world.
→ MAKE

masquerade [late 16th century] This comes from French *mascarade*, from Italian *mascherata*, from *maschera* 'mask'. Use of the word to mean 'pretence' dates from the late 17th century.

Mass [Old English] Old English *mæsse* is from ecclesiastical Latin *missa*, from Latin *miss-*, the past participial stem of *mittere* 'dismiss', perhaps from the last words of the service, *Ite, missa est* 'Go, it is the dismissal'.

mass [late Middle English] *Mass* 'large body of matter' is via Old French from Latin *massa*, from Greek *maza* 'barley cake' (perhaps related to *massein* 'to knead'). **Massive** dating from the same period is from French *massif*, *-ive*, from Old French *massis*, based on Latin *massa*.

massacre [late 16th century] This is from French, from Old French *macecre* 'slaughterhouse, butcher's shop'; the ultimate origin is uncertain.

massage [late 19th century] *Massage* is from French, from *masser* 'knead, treat with massage': this is probably from Portuguese *amassar* 'knead', from *massa* 'dough'.

mast [Old English] Old English *mæst* 'upright post' is West Germanic in origin and related to Dutch *mast* and German *Mast*.

master [Old English] Old English *mæg(i)ster* is from Latin *magister*; it was later reinforced by

Old French *maistre* 'master'. It is probably related to Latin *magis* 'more' (i.e. 'more important'). Middle English **mastery** is from Old French *maistrie*.

masticate [mid 17th century] This is from late Latin *masticare* 'to chew', from Greek *mastikhan* 'gnash the teeth' (related to *masasthai* 'to chew').

mastiff [Middle English] This word obscurely represents Old French *mastin*, based on Latin *mansuetus* 'tame'.

mat [Old English] Old English *m(e)att(e)* is West Germanic in origin, related to Dutch *mat* and German *Matte*, from late Latin *matta* 'rush mat, bedcover', from Phoenician. Use of the word in sports contexts for a piece of padded material for gymnastic displays or combat sports is found from the early 20th century. The phrase *on the mat* (early 20th century) 'being reprimanded by a superior' is with reference to the orderly room mat where an accused would stand before the commanding officer. The verb *mat* meaning 'become entangled' (e.g. *the cat's fur was matted through neglect*) dates from the mid 18th century.

match¹ [Old English] Old English *gemæcca* meant 'mate, companion'. Of West Germanic origin, it is related to the base of *make*. Use of the word to mean 'contest, competitive trial' dates from the early 16th century.
➔ MAKE

match² [late Middle English] 'Wick of a candle' was the first sense recorded. It is from Old French *meche*, perhaps from Latin *myxa* meaning 'spout of a lamp', and then later 'lamp wick'. As a word for a short thin piece of wood tipped with a combustible substance, *match* is found from the early 19th century.

mate¹ [late Middle English] This informal word is from Middle Low German *māt(e)* 'comrade', of West Germanic origin. It is related to *meat*, the underlying association being that of eating together. It has been used as a form of address (e.g. *good day, mate*) from around the beginning of the 16th century, the period when the verb *mate* is first recorded. This originally meant 'to equal, rival' (Pope, translating Homer's *Iliad*: In standing Fight he mates Achilles' Force): examples where the meaning is 'join as a couple or in alliance, take in marriage' are found from the end of the 16th century.
➔ MEAT

mate² [Middle English] The noun *mate* used in the game of chess is from Anglo-Norman French *mat*, from the phrase *eschec mat* 'check-

mate'; the verb is from Anglo-Norman French *mater* 'to checkmate'.
➔ CHECK¹

material [late Middle English] The sense in early examples was 'relating to matter': the source of the form is late Latin *materialis* 'formed of matter', an adjective from Latin *materia* 'matter'. In law (in phrases such as *material witness*) the word gained the meaning 'having a significant factual connection' towards the end of the 16th century. Use of the word to mean 'cloth' dates from the mid 19th century.

maternal [late 15th century] *Maternal* is from French *maternel*, from Latin *maternus*, from *mater* 'mother', the base too of early 17th-century **maternity** which came into English via French.

mathematical [late Middle English] *Mathematical* (from Latin *mathematicalis*) and **mathematian** (via Old French from Latin *mathematicus* 'mathematical') are from Greek *mathēmatikos*, from *mathēma* 'science', from the base of *manthanein* 'learn'. **Mathematics**, formerly used in the singular as *mathematic*, dates from the late 16th century and is from Old French *mathematique*, from Latin (*ars*) *mathematica* 'mathematical (art)', from Greek *mathēmatikē* (*tekhnē*). **Maths** is an early 20th-century abbreviation.

matinee [mid 19th century] This comes from French *matinée*, literally 'morning (as a period occupied by activity)', from *matin* 'morning': performances at one time also took place in the morning.

matriarch [early 17th century] *Matriarch* is from Latin *mater* 'mother', on the false analogy of *patriarch*.

matriculate [late 16th century] This word meaning 'be registered as a student at a college' is from medieval Latin *matriculare* 'enroll', from late Latin *matricula* 'register', a diminutive of Latin *matrix*.

matrimony [late Middle English] This came via Old French from Latin *matrimonium*, based on *mater*, *matr-* 'mother'. **Matrimonial** is also late Middle English and is via Old French from Latin *matrimonialis*, from *matrimonium*.

matrix [late Middle English] The early sense was 'womb'. It is primarily a Latin word which first meant 'breeding female' and then later 'womb', from *mater*, *matr-* 'mother'.

matron [late Middle English] The first recorded sense of *matron* was 'married woman'; it comes from Old French *matrone*, from Latin *matrona*, from *mater*, *matr-* 'mother'. The use of the word in hospital contexts, originally for someone in charge of the domestic arrangements of a charitable institution, dates from the mid 16th century.

matt [early 17th century] This word, sometimes spelt *mat* and often in combination with colours (e.g. *matt blue*) was first used as a verb; the source is French *mat*.

matter [Middle English] *Matter* came via Old French from Latin *materia* which meant both 'timber, substance' and 'subject of discourse', from *mater* 'mother'. The semantic strands in English are: 'thing, affair' (e.g. *that's another matter*); 'the basis of thought' (e.g. *subject matter*); and 'content', as opposed to *form* (in philosophy contexts and logic).

mattress [Middle English] The word *mattress* came via Old French and Italian from Arabic *maṭraḥ* 'carpet or cushion', from *ṭaraḥa* 'to throw'.

mature [late Middle English] Latin *maturus* 'timely, ripe' is the source of *mature* and, dating from the same period, **maturity** (from Latin *maturitas*). Latin *maturus* also gave rise to late Middle English **maturation** (from medieval Latin *maturatio(n-)*, from Latin *maturare*) which, when first recorded, referred to the formation of pus, and **maturate** dating from the mid 16th century from Latin *maturare* 'ripen, hasten'.

maudlin [late Middle English] Early use was as a noun referring to Mary Magdalen. It comes from Old French *Madeleine*, from ecclesiastical Latin *Magdalena*. The sense of the adjective 'self-pityingly sentimental' derives from allusion to pictures of Mary Magdalen weeping.

maul [Middle English] In early use the noun sense was 'hammer or wooden club', the verb sense was 'strike with a heavy weapon'. The source is Old French *mail*, from Latin *malleus* 'hammer'. Use of the word as a rugby term (originally for a prolonged tackle attempting to get the ball from another player and, in Rugby Union, a type of loose scrum) dates from the mid 19th century. The verb *maul* to mean 'mutilate by clawing' when describing an attack by an animal dates from the mid 19th century.

mausoleum [late 15th century] This word came via Latin from Greek *Mausōleion*, from *Mausōlos*, the name of a king of Caria in the 4th century BC. It was originally applied to his tomb in Halicarnassus.

maverick [mid 19th century] Applied to an unorthodox or independent-minded person, this word is from the name of Samuel A. *Maverick* (1803–70), a Texas engineer and rancher who did not brand his cattle.

maxim [late Middle English] In early use a *maxim* was an axiom: it comes from French *maxime*, from medieval Latin *(propositio) maxima* 'largest or most important (proposition)'.

maximum [mid 17th century] *Maximum*, first used as a noun, is from a modern Latin neuter noun use of the Latin adjective *maximus* (the superlative of *magnus* 'great'). Adjectival use dates from the early 19th century, when **maximize** was also first recorded, based on Latin *maximus*.

may [Old English] Old English *mæg* is Germanic in origin from a base meaning 'have power'; it is related to Dutch *mogen* and German *mögen*. Late Middle English **maybe** is from the phrase *it may be (that)*.
→ MAIN; MIGHT

Mayday [1920s] This international radio distress signal represents a pronunciation of French *m'aider*, from *venez m'aider* 'come and help me'.

mayhem [early 16th century] *Mayhem* comes from Old French *mayhem*. The sense 'disorder, chaos' which was originally recorded in US English dates from the late 19th century.
→ MAIM

mayor [Middle English] The source of *mayor* in English is Old French *maire*, from the Latin adjective *major* 'greater', used as a noun in late Latin.
→ MAJOR

maze [Middle English] *Maze* referred originally to delirium or delusion: it is probably from the base of *amaze*, of which the verb (used in dialect such as *she was still mazed with the drug she had taken*) is a shortening. The word's use to denote a 'labyrinth' dates from late Middle English; large-scale recreational *mazes* are traditionally made from hedges; from the early 20th century, *mazes* have been used in psychology experiments to study human and animal learning and intelligence.

me [Old English] Old English *mē* is the accusative and dative form of the personal pronoun *I*. Of Germanic origin, it is related to Dutch *mij* and German *mir* (dative), from an Indo-European root shared by Latin *me*, Greek *(e)me*, and Sanskrit *mā*. The word **myself** was *me self* in Old English; the change of *me* to *my* occurred in Middle English. A related English form is the possessive **mine** (in Old English *mīn*) also from a Germanic source.

mead [Old English] Old English *me(o)du* is Germanic in origin, related to Dutch *mee* and German *Met*, from an Indo-European root shared by Sanskrit *madhu* 'sweet drink, honey' and Greek *methu* 'wine'.

meadow [Old English] Old English *mædwe* is the oblique case of *mæd* 'meadow' (now *mead* in poetry and literary use), from the Germanic base of *mow*.
→ MOW

meagre [Middle English] The early sense of *meagre* was 'lean', from Old French *maigre*, from Latin *macer*. It was recorded early in surnames in England but it is not clear whether these are Middle English or Anglo-Norman French. The sense 'deficient in quantity' is found from the mid 17th century (e.g. *meagre rations*); in money contexts (e.g. *meagre profits*) the sense 'very small' is found in examples from the early 19th century.

meal[1] [Old English] Of Germanic origin, Old English *mæl* included the sense 'measure' surviving in words such as *piecemeal* 'measure taken at one time'. The early sense of *meal* involved a notion of 'fixed time' comparable with words such as Dutch *maal* 'meal, (portion of) time' and German *Mal* 'time', *Mahl* 'meal', from an Indo-European root meaning 'to measure'. The expression *make a meal of* dates from the early 17th century in the sense 'take advantage of', but the notion 'make unduly laborious' is relatively recent dating from the 1960s.

meal[2] [Old English] This *meal* referring to the edible part of any grain or pulse ground to powder was *melu*, *meolo* in Old English. Of Germanic origin, the word is related to Dutch *meel* and German *Mehl*, from an Indo-European root shared by Latin *molere* 'to grind'.

mean[1] [Old English] Old English *mænan* 'intend to convey' is from a West Germanic source and is related to Dutch *meenen* and German *meinen*, from an Indo-European root shared by *mind*. The noun **meaning** is late Middle English.
→ MIND

mean[2] [Middle English] This word meaning 'ungenerous' is a shortening of Old English *gemæne*, of Germanic origin, from an Indo-European root shared by Latin *communis* 'common'. The original sense was 'common to two or more persons', later 'inferior in rank', leading to the notion 'poor in quality' (e.g. *her home was mean and small*) as well as 'ignoble, small-minded': the latter gave rise to the senses 'unwilling to share' and 'unkind, spiteful' (which became common in the 19th century). The early 20th-century colloquial word **mingy** is perhaps a blend of *mean* and *stingy*.

mean[3] [Middle English] This *mean* meaning 'average' is from Old French *meien*, from Latin *medianus* 'middle'. The plural **means** (late Middle English) used in phrases such as *resolving disputes by peaceful means* arose from the early

sense 'intermediary', the source too of Middle English **meantime** and late Middle English **meanwhile**.
→ MEDIAN

meander [late 16th century] Early use of *meander* was as a noun from Latin *maeander*, from Greek *Maiandros*, the name of a river noted for its winding course: this is now known as the Menderes flowing through SW Turkey and joining the Aegean Sea south of the Greek island of Samos.

measles [Middle English] The spelling in Middle English was *maseles*, probably from Middle Dutch *masel* 'pustule'; in modern Dutch *mazelen* is the word for 'measles'. The spelling change was due to association with Middle English *mesel* 'leprous, leprosy'. **Measly** dates from the late 16th century when it described a pig or pork infected with measles; the current sense 'contemptibly small, mean' dates from the mid 19th century.

measure [Middle English] Noun use was the first recorded in the senses 'moderation', 'instrument for measuring', 'unit of capacity'. *Measure* is from Old French *mesure*, from Latin *mensura* 'process of measuring, system or instrument of measurement', from the verb *metiri* 'to measure'. The semantic branches include: 'limited extent' (e.g. *to know no measure*), 'means or result of measuring' (e.g. *a measure two yards long*), 'metrical sound or movement' (e.g. *pastoral measure*), and 'plan or course of action' (e.g. *took measures to stop the protest*).

meat [Old English] Germanic in origin, Old English *mete* meant 'food' or 'article of food' (as in *sweetmeat*). The Indo-European base may have meant 'be wet, succulent, fat'.

mechanic [late Middle English] Early use was as an adjective in the sense 'relating to manual labour': the word came via Old French or Latin from Greek *mēkhanikos*, from *mēkhanē*. The same base (via Latin) gave rise in the same period to **mechanical**. **Mechanism** is found from the mid 17th century and is from modern Latin *mechanismus*, from Greek *mēkhanē*.
→ MACHINE

medal [late 16th century] *Medal* is from French *médaille*, from Italian *medaglia*, from medieval Latin *medalia* 'half a denarius', from Latin *medialis* 'medial'. The word **medallion** dates from the mid 17th century and is from French *médaillon*, from Italian *medaglione*, an augmentative (= having the sense 'large (of its kind)') of *medaglia*.

meddle [Middle English] The early sense recorded was 'mingle, mix'. Old French *medler* is the source, a variant of *mesler*, based on Latin *miscere* 'to mix'.

median [late Middle English] This word meaning '(at the) midpoint' was originally used to denote a median vein or nerve: it comes from medieval Latin *medianus*. The base is Latin *medius* 'mid', which also gave rise to late Midde English **mediate** first used as an adjective in the sense 'interposed': this is from late Latin *mediatus*, the past participle of the verb *mediare* 'to place in the middle'.

medicine [Middle English] *Medicine* came via Old French from Latin *medicina*, from *medicus* 'physician'. Latin *medicus* is the base of several other words in English: late Middle English **medicinal** (from Latin *medicinalis*, from *medicina*); early 17th-century **medicate** (from Latin *medicari* 'administer remedies to'); also mid 17th-century **medical** (via French from medieval Latin *medicalis*) and the informal word for a doctor, **medic**.

medieval [early 19th century] This is based on modern Latin *medium aevum* 'middle age'.

mediocre [late 16th century] *Mediocre* is from French *médiocre*, from Latin *mediocris* meaning 'of middle height or degree' (literally 'somewhat rugged or mountainous', from *medius* 'middle' and *ocris* 'rugged mountain').

meditation [Middle English] The Latin verb *meditari* 'contemplate' is the base of *meditation* in English, which comes from Old French, from Latin *meditatio(n-)*. The same Latin verb is the source of mid 16th-century **meditate** from a base meaning 'measure'.

medium [late 16th century] This originally denoted something intermediate in nature or degree: it is a use of a Latin word meaning literally 'middle', the neuter of *medius*.

medley [Middle English] *Medley* conveys a notion of something intermixed and entwined: it is found in early examples referring both to hand-to-hand combat and cloth made of variegated wool. Old French *medlee*, a variant of *meslee* 'melee', is the source of the English word. The base is medieval Latin *misculare* 'to mix'.
→ MEDDLE

meek [Middle English] The early spelling was *me(o)c* which also had the sense 'courteous or indulgent'. It comes from Old Norse *mjúkr* 'soft, gentle'.

meet[1] [Old English] Old English *mētan* meant 'come upon, come across'. Of Germanic origin, it is related to Dutch *moeten*.
→ MOOT

meet[2] [Middle English] This archaic word used in phrases such as *it was not meet for us to see*

the king's dishonour was first recorded meaning 'made to fit'. It is a shortening of Old English *gemæte*, of Germanic origin.

melancholy [Middle English] *Melancholy* is from Old French *melancolie*, via late Latin from Greek *melankholia*, from *melas, melan-* 'black' and *kholē* 'bile', an excess of which was formerly believed to cause depression. Another name for *black bile* was *black humour*, one of the four chief fluids (*cardinal humours*) thought to determine a person's physical and mental qualities and disposition.

mellifluous [late 15th century] Latin *mel, mell(i)-* 'honey' and the verb *fluere* 'to flow' are the base elements of *mellifluous* (from late Latin *mellifluus*) and early 17th-century **mellifluent**.

mellow [late Middle English] The early sense of *mellow* was 'ripe, soft, sweet, and juicy' describing fruit. It is perhaps from an attributive use of Old English *melu, melw-* 'meal'. The verb dates from the late 16th century.
→ MEAL[2]

melodrama [early 19th century] This word is from French *mélodrame*, from Greek *melos* 'music' and French *drame* 'drama'.

melody [Middle English] 'Sweet music' was an early sense of *melody* from Old French *melodie*, via late Latin from Greek *melōidia* 'melody', from *melos* 'song'. The same base gave rise to late Middle English **melodious** (from Old French *melodieus*, from *melodie*) and **melodic** (dating from the early 19th century from French *mélodique*, via late Latin from Greek *melōidikos* from *melōidia*).

melt [Old English] Old English *meltan, mieltan* is Germanic in origin, related to Old Norse *melta* 'to melt, digest', from an Indo-European root shared by Greek *meldein* 'to melt' and Latin *mollis* 'soft'.
→ MALT

member [Middle English] This came via Old French from Latin *membrum* 'limb', 'part of the body', 'constituent part of something', 'member of a body of people'.

membrane [late Middle English] *Membrane* is from Latin *membrana*, from *membrum* 'limb'.

memento [late Middle English] The early use of *memento* was to denote a prayer of commemoration. It is a use of the Latin imperative (meaning literally 'remember!') of *meminisse*.

memoir [late 15th century] This is from French *mémoire* (masculine), a special use of *mémoire* (feminine) 'memory'. The early sense recorded was 'memorandum', 'record'.

memorable [late 15th century] *Memorable* is from Latin *memorabilis*, from *memorare* 'bring to mind', from *memor* 'mindful'.

memorandum [late Middle English] This Latin word means literally 'something to be brought to mind'; it is the gerundive of *memorare* 'bring to mind'. The original use was as an adjective, placed at the head of a note of something to be remembered or of a record made for future reference. The abbreviation **memo** dates from the early 18th century.

memory [Middle English] *Memory* is from Old French *memorie* (modern French *mémoire*), from Latin *memoria*, from *memor* 'mindful, remembering'. The same Latin base gave rise to late Middle English **memorial** from late Latin *memoriale* 'record, memory, monument', from Latin *memorialis* 'serving as a reminder'.

menace [Middle English] This comes via Old French from late Latin *minacia*, from Latin *minax*, *minac-* 'threatening', from *minae* 'threats'. In law contexts, the Larceny Act of 1861 made it a criminal offence to demand *money with menaces* and the phrase has been used in subsequent Acts dealing with similar offences.

menagerie [late 17th century] This word meaning 'a collection of wild animals' is from French *ménagerie*, from *ménage*. The source is Old French *mainer* 'to stay', influenced by Old French *mesnie* 'household', both ultimately based on Latin *manere* 'remain'.

mend [Middle English] *Mend* is apparently a shortening of *amend*, but the origin is uncertain.
→ AMEND

mendicant [late Middle English] Latin *mendicant-*, the present participial stem of *mendicare* 'to beg', is the source of *mendicant* in English. The origin is Latin *mendicus* 'beggar', from *mendum* 'fault'.

menial [late Middle English] 'Domestic' was the early sense of *menial* from Old French, from *mesnee* 'household'.

mental [late Middle English] *Mental* is from late Latin *mentalis*, from Latin *mens*, *ment-* 'mind'. Senses relating to the mind in an unhealthy or abnormal state date from the late 18th century. The use of *mental* in compounds such as *mental hospital* and *mental patient* is first recorded at the end of the 19th century and was the accepted term in the first half of the 20th century; it has now been largely replaced by *psychiatric*. The noun **mentality** dates from the late 17th century when it meant 'mental process': it is based on *mental*. Current senses date from the mid 19th century.

mention [Middle English] This word was originally part of the phrase *make mention of*: it came via Old French from Latin *mentio(n-)* and is related to *mind*.
→ MIND

mentor [mid 18th century] *Mentor* came via French and Latin from Greek *Mentōr*, the name of the adviser of the young Telemachus in Homer's *Odyssey* and Fénelon's *Télémaque*.

menu [mid 19th century] This is a use of a French word meaning literally 'detailed list' from the adjective *menu* meaning 'small, detailed'. The base is Latin *minutus* 'very small'.

mercenary [late Middle English] Early use was as a noun; it comes from Latin *mercenarius* 'hireling', from *merces*, *merced-* 'reward'.

merchant [Middle English] *Merchant* is from Old French *marchant*, based on Latin *mercari* 'to trade', from *merx*, *merc-* 'merchandise'. Related words include late Middle English **merchandise** (from Old French *marchandise*, from *marchand* 'merchant') and mid 17th-century **mercantile** (via French from Italian, from *mercante* 'merchant').

mercurial [late Middle English] *Mercurial* was first recorded in the sense 'relating to the planet Mercury' which is the sense of Latin *mercurialis*, the word's source. Use of the adjective to mean 'subject to unpredictable mood swings' dates from the mid 17th century.

mercy [Middle English] *Mercy* is from Old French *merci* 'pity' or 'thanks', from Latin *merces*, *merced-* 'reward', which came in Christian Latin to mean 'pity, favour, heavenly reward'.

mere [late Middle English] The early senses recorded for *mere* are 'pure' and 'sheer, downright'. Latin *merus* 'undiluted' is the source of the word.

merge [mid 17th century] 'Immerse (oneself)' was the first sense recorded for *merge* which is from Latin *mergere* 'to dip, plunge'. Use in legal contexts is from Anglo-Norman French *merger*. **Merger** dates from the early 18th century in law contexts, from Anglo-Norman French *merger* (a verb used as a noun); its use in business contexts dates from the middle of the 19th century.

meridian [late Middle English] This word comes from Old French *meridien*, from Latin *meridianum* 'noon', from *medius* 'middle' and *dies* 'day'. The use in astronomy is due to the fact that the sun crosses a meridian at noon.

meridional [late Middle English] This word meaning 'southern' came via Old French from late Latin *meridionalis*, formed irregularly from Latin *meridies* 'midday, south'.

merit [Middle English] The original sense recorded is 'deserved reward or punishment'. *Merit* came via Old French from Latin *meritum* 'due reward', from *mereri* 'earn, deserve'. **Meritorious** dates from late Middle English in the sense 'entitling a person to reward': this is based on late Latin *meritorius* (from *mereri*).

mermaid [Middle English] The first element of *mermaid* is from *mere* in the obsolete sense 'sea': this is the same word found in place names such as *Hornsea Mere*.

merry [Old English] Old English *myrige* meant 'pleasing, delightful'. In Middle English it gained the sense 'happy through intoxication'. Of Germanic origin, the word is related to *mirth*. The base must have meant 'short' in view of the Germanic and Indo-European cognates which had this same sense (e.g. Old High German *murg* 'short'). There may have been an Old English verb meaning 'to shorten' in the context of 'whiling away time'.
➙ MIRTH

mesh [late Middle English] This is probably from an unrecorded Old English word related to (and perhaps reinforced in Middle English by) Middle Dutch *maesche*, of Germanic origin. Dutch influenced the currency of many fishing terms; there were many borrowings into English in this context in Middle English.

mess [Middle English] *Mess* is from Old French *mes* 'portion of food', from late Latin *missum* 'something put on the table' (from *mittere* 'send, put'). Early senses included 'a serving of food' and 'a serving of liquid or pulpy food'; later it came to mean 'liquid food for an animal', which gave rise in the early 19th century to the senses 'unappetizing concoction' and 'predicament', on which *mess* as an 'untidy state of things' is based. In late Middle English the term also denoted any of the small groups into which the company at a banquet was divided (served from the same dishes); hence, 'a group who regularly eat together' such as in military contexts, a use recorded from the mid 16th century.

message [Middle English] This word is from Old French, based on Latin *missus*, the past participle of *mittere* 'to send'. **Messenger**, also Middle English, is from Old Northern French *messanger*, a variant of Old French *messager*, from Latin *missus*.

metal [Middle English] This is from Old French *metal* or Latin *metallum*, from Greek *metallon* 'mine, quarry, or metal'. Late Middle

English **metallic** came via Latin from Greek *metallikos*, from *metallon*.

metamorphosis [late Middle English] *Metamorphosis* came into English via Latin from Greek *metamorphōsis*, from *metamorphoun* 'transform, change shape'. The Latin source was with reference to *Metamorphoses*, a poem by Ovid in the classical tradition of tales about transformations of gods into the shapes of objects, plants, or animals. **Metamorphose** dates from the late 16th century and is from French *métamorphoser*. The word **metamorphic** is an early 19th-century formation based on the prefix *meta-* (denoting a change of condition) and Greek *morphē* 'form', influenced by the earlier words.
➙ MORPH

metaphor [late 15th century] *Metaphor* is from French *métaphore*, via Latin from Greek *metaphora*, from *metapherein* 'to transfer'. In a metaphor a word or phrase is transferred from one context to another creatong a vivid association, e.g. *he fell through a trapdoor of depression*.

mete [Old English] The *mete* of *mete out* was *metan* in Old English meaning 'to measure, determine the quantity of'. Of Germanic origin, it is related to Dutch *meten* and German *messen* 'to measure', from an Indo-European root shared by Latin *meditari* 'meditate' and Greek *medesthai* 'care for'.

meteor [mid 16th century] In early use the term denoted any atmospheric phenomenon: it comes from modern Latin *meteorum*, from Greek *meteōron* 'of the atmosphere', the neuter form (used as a noun) of *meteōros* 'lofty'. The same base gave rise to **meteorology** (early 17th century) from Greek *meteōrologia*.

meter [Middle English] A *meter* in Middle English was a 'person who measures'; it is based on *mete* 'to measure'. The current word 'a device that measures and records' dates from the 19th century.
➙ METE

methinks [Old English] Old English *mē thyncth* is from *mē* 'to me' and *thyncth* 'it seems' (from *thyncan* 'seem') This second element is related to, but distinct from, *think*.

method [late Middle English] Originally a *method* referred to a 'prescribed medical treatment for a disease'. The word came via Latin from Greek *methodos* 'pursuit of knowledge', based on *hodos* 'way'. From the late 16th century, examples of **methodical** (via late Latin from Greek *methodikos*) are found; the word **Methodist** (a denomination originating in the 18th-century evangelistic movement of Charles and John Wesley and George

Whitefield) is probably from the notion of following a specified 'method' of Bible study. The noun **methodology** is recorded from the early 19th century from modern Latin *methodologia* or French *méthodologie*.

meticulous [mid 16th century] 'Fearful, timid' was the early sense of *meticulous* which came from Latin *meticulosus*, from *metus* 'fear'. The word came to mean 'overcareful about detail', which eventually lost its negative connotation giving the current sense 'showing great attention to detail' in the early 19th century.

metre [Old English] *Metre* denoting the rhythm of a piece of poetry was reinforced in Middle English by Old French *metre*, from Latin *metrum*, from Greek *metron* 'measure'. The word *metre* used as a unit of length (late 18th century) is from French *mètre*, from the same Greek base. **Metric** dates from the mid 19th century as an adjective relating to length: it comes from French *métrique*, from *mètre*.

metronome [early 19th century] This word for a device used by musicians for marking time is from Greek *metron* 'measure' and *nomos* 'law'. The modern *metronome* dates from 1815; originally a graduated inverted pendulum was used with an adjustable sliding weight.

metropolis [late Middle English] *Metropolis* and, from the same period, **metropolitan** were both used originally in ecclesiastical contexts in connection with the authority of a bishop over others in a province. Both words came via late Latin from Greek *mētropolis* 'mother state'. The base elements are *mētēr*, *mētr-* 'mother' and *polis* 'city'.

mettle [mid 16th century] This is a specialized spelling of *metal*. It is used for figurative senses; during the 17th century it became particularly associated with 'vigour, spiritedness' initially when referring to horses and eventually to people. Although used prior to that as a variant interchangeable in all senses with *metal*, it became a separate word by the mid 18th century (Scott *Fair Maid of Perth*: Thou ken'st not the mettle that women are made of).
→ METAL

mews [late Middle English] This is the plural of *mew* 'a cage or housing for trained hawks', originally referring to the royal stables on the site of the hawk mews at Charing Cross, London. The sense 'converted dwellings' dates from the early 19th century. The source of the word is Old French *mue* 'the shedding of feathers', 'cage for birds while moulting', 'cage for keeping poultry being fattened', from *muer* 'to moult', from Latin *mutare* 'to change'.

mezzanine [early 18th century] This is an adoption of a French word, from Italian *mezzanino*, a diminutive of *mezzano* 'middle, intermediate', from Latin *medianus* 'median'. In north American English, a *mezzanine* is the lowest gallery in a theatre's auditorium, the equivalent of the dress circle.

microbe [late 19th century] *Microbe* is from French based on the Greek elements *mikros* 'small' and *bios* 'life'. The word was coined by C. Sédillot in March 1878 expressly as an alternative to many other terms used synonymously at that time.

microcosm [Middle English] Old French *microcosme* or medieval Latin *microcosmus* have given rise to *microcosm* in English. Greek *mikros kosmos* 'little world' is the base. In ecology a *microcosm* has been a term for a tiny enclosed self-sufficient ecosystem since the 1930s.

middle [Old English] Old English *middel* has a West Germanic origin; it is related to Dutch *middel* and German *Mittel*, as well as to Old English **mid**, a shortening of *amid*. Late Middle English **midst** is from the phrase *in middes* 'in the middle'.

midge [Old English] Old English *mycg(e)* is Germanic in origin; related forms are Dutch *mug* and German *Mücke*, from an Indo-European root shared by Latin *musca* and Greek *muia* 'fly'. Mid 19th-century **midget** is based on *midge*; it came to be applied as a term for a vehicle built to a smaller size specification from the 1930s.

midriff [Old English] Old English *midhrif* is from *mid* and *hrif* 'belly'; the second element shares the same Indo-European base as Latin *corpus* 'body'.

midwife [Middle English] This is probably from the obsolete preposition *mid* 'with' and the word *wife* in the archaic sense 'woman'. *Midwife* thus expresses the sense 'a woman who is with (the mother)'.

miff [early 17th century] *Miff* may be an imitative word expressing the feeling of being annoyed; a comparable form is early modern German *muff*, an exclamation of disgust.

might [Old English] Old English *miht*, *mieht* 'great and impressive power' is Germanic in origin. The adjective **mighty** was spelt *mihtig* in Old English.
→ MAY

migraine [late Middle English] This type of headache characteristically affects one side of the head. It is from French, via late Latin from Greek *hēmikrania*, from *hēmi-* 'half' and *kranion* 'skull'.

migrate [early 17th century] *Migrate* was initially a general word for 'move from one place to another'. It comes from Latin *migrare* 'to move, shift'. Use in computing contexts in the sense 'transfer (data) from one environment to another' dates from the 1980s.

milch [Middle English] *Milch* is from Old English *-milce* found only in *thrimilce* 'May' (the time of the year when cows could be milked three times a day); it comes from the Germanic base of *milk*.
→ MILK

mild [Old English] Old English *milde* was originally in the sense 'gracious, not severe, merciful'. Germanic in origin, it is related to Dutch and German *mild*, from an Indo-European root shared by Latin *mollis* and Greek *malthakos* 'soft'. The adjective was connected with food flavour from Middle English and with beer from the mid 16th century: the latter usage meant 'free from acidity' but came to have the specific meaning 'not strongly flavoured with hops'.

mildew [Old English] Old English *mildēaw*, of Germanic origin, meant 'honeydew'. The first element is related to Latin *mel* and Greek *meli* 'honey'. The word initially referred to a sweet sticky substance deposited on plants by greenfly; later it was applied to other plant diseases, then extended to a similar growth on substances such as paper and cloth exposed to damp.

mile [Old English] Old English *mil* is based on Latin *mil(l)ia*, the plural of *mille* 'thousand': the original Roman unit of distance was *mille passus* 'a thousand paces'. The expression *to be miles away* meaning 'to be lost in thought' dates from the early 20th century; *to go the extra mile* meaning 'to make more effort than is necessary as an act of goodwill' is with allusion to Matthew 5:41: And whosoever shall compel thee to go a mile, go with him twain.

militant [late Middle English] 'Engaged in warfare' was the early sense of *militant* which is from Old French or Latin, from Latin *militare* 'serve as a soldier'. The current sense 'aggressive in support of a political or social cause' dates from the early 20th century. Latin *miles, milit-* 'soldier' is the base of this and late Middle English **military** (via French *militaire* from Latin *militaris*), as well as late 16th-century **militate** 'to campaign, strive' (from Latin *militare*) and **militia** (from the Latin word meaning literally 'military service').

milk [Old English] Old English *milc* and *milcian* are Germanic in origin, related to Dutch *melk* and German *Milch*, from an Indo-European root shared by Latin *mulgere* and Greek *amelgein* 'to milk'. The proverb *it's no use crying over spilt milk*

dates from the mid 17th century; the *milk of human kindness* meaning 'compassion' is often used with allusion to Shakespeare's *Macbeth*: Yet do I fear thy nature, It is too full o' th' Milk of human kindness.

mill [Old English] Old English *mylen* is based on a variant of late Latin *molinum*, from Latin *mola* 'grindstone, mill', from *molere* 'to grind'. The idiomatic expression *to put through the mill* meaning 'cause to feel hardship' dates from the early 19th century.

milliner [late Middle English] This word, based on the place name *Milan* originally meant 'a native of Milan'; later it became 'a vendor of fancy goods from Milan'.

mimic [late 16th century] *Mimic* came via Latin from Greek *mimikos*, from *mimos* 'mime'. The word **mime** (via Latin from Greek *mimos*) is found from the early 17th century: early senses included 'mimic' and 'jester'.

minaret [late 17th century] This word for a slender tower (for example as part of a mosque) is from French, or from Spanish *minarete*, Italian *minaretto*, via Turkish from Arabic *manār(a)* 'lighthouse, minaret', based on *nār* 'fire or light'.

mince [late Middle English] *Mince* is from Old French *mincier*, based on Latin *minutia* 'smallness'. The sense 'walk with short steps and an affected daintiness' dates from the mid 16th century; later that century the first examples of the expression *mince one's words* are found. The noun meaning 'minced meat' is found from the early 19th century.

mind [Old English] Old English *gemynd* meant 'memory, thought'. The origin of the word is Germanic from an Indo-European root meaning 'revolve in the mind, think', shared by Sanskrit *manas* and Latin *mens* 'mind'.

mine [late Middle English] *Mine* is from Old French and perhaps has Celtic origins (Welsh *mwyn* means 'ore' and earlier meant 'mine'). **Miner** is Middle English from Old French *minour*, from *miner* 'to mine'.

mineral [late Middle English] The source of this word is medieval Latin *minerale*, a neuter form (used as a noun) of *mineralis*, from *minera* 'ore'.

mingle [late Middle English] *Mingle* is a frequentative (= verb of repeated action) of obsolete *meng* 'mix or blend' (related to *among*), perhaps influenced by Middle Dutch *mengelen*.
→ AMONG

miniature [early 18th century] *Miniature* is from Italian *miniatura*, via medieval Latin from Latin *miniare* 'rubricate, illuminate', from *minium* 'red lead, vermilion': this was used to mark particular words in manuscripts. It has no etymological connection with words such as *mini*, *minimum* despite the resemblance in word form and the notion of small size.

minimum [mid 17th century] This is an English use of the Latin neuter of *minimus* 'least, smallest'. **Minimal** dating from the same period is from the same Latin base. The word **minimalist** (early 20th century) was first used with reference to the Russian Mensheviks: usage in art and music dates from the 1960s.

minion [late 15th century] This word describing an underling is from French *mignon*, *mignonne*.

minister [Middle English] A *minister* in early use referred to a *minister of religion* or generally to a means of conveying something (e.g. *angels as ministers of the divine will*). The noun is from Old French *ministre*, the verb from Old French *ministrer*; the base is from Latin *minister* 'servant', from *minus* 'less'. The compound ■ **ministering angel** (early 17th century) meaning 'a kind-hearted person' is with biblical allusion to Mark 1:13 (And he was there in the wilderness forty days, tempted of Satan; and was with the wild beasts; and the angels ministered unto him). Shakespeare uses the phrase in *Hamlet*: A ministering Angel shall my sister be.

minor [Middle English] This is a use of a Latin word meaning 'smaller, less', related to *minuere* 'to lessen'. The term originally referred to a Franciscan friar, suggested by the Latin name *Fratres Minores* ('Lesser Brethren'), chosen by St Francis for the order. Based on Latin *minor* is the noun **minority**, which in the late 15th century referred to the state of being a minor. It comes from French *minorité* or medieval Latin *minoritas*.

minster [Old English] Old English *mynster* came via ecclesiastical Latin from Greek *monastērion*.
→ MONASTERY

minstrel [Middle English] *Minstrel* is from Old French *menestral* 'entertainer, servant'; this came via Provençal from late Latin *ministerialis* 'servant', from Latin *ministerium* 'ministry'.
→ MINISTER

mint¹ [Old English] Old English *minte*, a name for an aromatic plant, is from a West Germanic source. It is related to German *Minze*, and is ultimately (via Latin) from the Greek base *minthē*.

mint² [Old English] Old English *mynet* meant 'coin'. Of West Germanic origin, it is related to Dutch *munt* and German *Münze*, from Latin *moneta* 'money'.

minuet [late 17th century] This word for a slow stately ballroom dance or the music in the style of this type of dance is from French *menuet* meaning literally 'fine, delicate': this is a diminutive (used as a noun) of *menu* 'small'.

minus [late 15th century] The word *minus* comes from the Latin neuter of *minor* 'less'.

minuscule [early 18th century] *Minuscule* is from French, from Latin *minuscula* (*littera*) 'somewhat smaller (letter)'. It is a common spelling error in English to write *miniscule* which has arisen by analogy with other words beginning with *mini-* where the meaning is similarly 'very small'.

minute¹ [late Middle English] The *minute* in clock time came via Old French from late Latin *minuta*, a feminine form (used as a noun) of *minutus* meaning 'made small'. The senses 'period of sixty seconds' and 'sixtieth of a degree' derive from medieval Latin *pars minuta prima* 'first minute part'.

minute² [late Middle English] The word *minute* meaning 'extremely small' was first found with the meaning 'lesser' when referring to a tithe or tax. It comes from Latin *minutus*, the past participle of *minuere* 'to lessen'.

minute³ [late Middle English] Now usually found as *minutes* referring to recorded notes from a meeting, the word *minute* was first used in the singular in the sense 'note or memorandum'. It comes from French *minute*, from the notion of a rough copy in 'small writing' (Latin *scriptura minuta*) as distinct from the fair copy in book hand. The verb dates from the mid 16th century.

miracle [Middle English] *Miracle* came via Old French from Latin *miraculum* 'object of wonder', from *mirari* 'to wonder', from *mirus* 'wonderful'. Late Middle English **miraculous** is from French *miraculeux* or medieval Latin *miraculosus*, from Latin *miraculum*.

mirage [early 19th century] This is an adoption of a French word, from *se mirer* 'be reflected', from Latin *mirare* 'look at'.

mire [Middle English] *Mire* is from Old Norse *mýrr*, of Germanic origin.
→ MOSS

mirror [Middle English] *Mirror* is from Old French *mirour*, based on Latin *mirare* 'look at'. Early senses also included 'a crystal used in magic' and 'a person deserving imitation'.

mirth [Old English] Old English *myrgth* is from a Germanic source and is related to *merry*.
→ MERRY

misadventure [Middle English] The first recorded sense of *misadventure* was 'unfortunate incident'; use in law is found later. It comes from Old French *mesaventure*, from *mesa-venir* 'turn out badly'.

misanthropy [mid 17th century] This word comes from Greek *misanthrōpia*, from *miso-* 'hating' and *anthropos* 'man'.

miscellany [late 16th century] Miscellany is from French *miscellanées* (feminine plural), from Latin *miscellanea* (a word adopted into English meaning 'miscellaneous items'). **Miscellaneous** dates from the early 17th century and is based on Latin *miscellaneus* (from *miscellus* 'mixed', from *miscere* 'to mix'). In earlier use the word also described a person as 'having various qualities'.

mischief [late Middle English] In early examples, *mischief* denoted 'misfortune' or 'distress'. Old French *meschief* is the source, from the verb *meschever* 'come to an unfortunate end' (based on *chef* 'head'). **Mischievous** (Middle English) is from Anglo-Norman French *meschevous*, from Old French *meschever*. The early sense was 'unfortunate or calamitous', later 'having harmful effects'; the sense 'playfully troublesome' dates from the late 17th century.

miser [late 15th century] Early use of *miser* was as an adjective in the sense 'miserly': it comes from a Latin word meaning literally 'wretched'.

misery [late Middle English] Misery is from Old French *miserie*, from Latin *miseria*, from *miser* 'wretched'. This Latin base also gave rise in the same period to **miserable**, via French from Latin *miserabilis* 'pitiable', from *miserari* 'to pity'.

misnomer [late Middle English] This word meaning 'inaccurate name' is from Anglo-Norman French, from the Old French verb *mesnommer*: the formative elements are *mes-* 'wrongly' and *nommer* 'to name' (based on Latin *nomen* 'name').

misogyny [mid 17th century] Misogyny is from Greek *misos* 'hatred' and *gunē* 'woman'.

miss [Old English] The word *missan* 'fail to hit' is Germanic in origin, related to Dutch and German *missen*. The main semantic strands include: 'fail to hit or meet' (e.g. *missed the target*); 'fail' (e.g. *the engine keeps missing*); 'be without, feel the loss of' (e.g. *she's missing her mother*); and 'omit' (e.g. *he's missed the rehearsal*).

missile [early 17th century] Early use was as an adjective in the sense 'suitable for throwing (at a target)': the source is Latin *missile*, a neuter form (used as a noun) of *missilis*, from *miss-*, the past participial stem of *mittere* 'to send'.

mission [mid 16th century] The word *mission* was first used to denote the sending of the Holy Spirit into the world; it comes from Latin *missio(n-)*, from *mittere* 'send'. Mid 17th-century **missionary** is from modern Latin *missionarius*, from Latin *missio*.

missive [late Middle English] This was originally an adjective used in the phrase *letter missive*, a letter from a monarch to a dean and chapter nominating someone as bishop. The word comes from medieval Latin *missivus*, from Latin *mittere* 'send'. The current sense 'letter' dates from the early 16th century.

mist [Old English] Old English *mist* is of Germanic origin, from an Indo-European root shared by Greek *omikhlē* 'mist, fog'. Old English **misty** had the early spelling *mistig*.

mistake [late Middle English] Mistake, first used as a verb, is from Old Norse *mistaka* 'take in error', probably influenced in sense by Old French *mesprendre*.

mister [mid 16th century] This form of address is a weakened form of *master* in unstressed use before a name.
➡ MASTER

mistletoe [Old English] Old English *misteltān* is from *mistel* 'mistletoe' (of Germanic origin, related to Dutch *mistel* and German *Mistel*) and *tān* 'twig'. The first word of the compound **mistle thrush** (early 17th century) is also from Old English *mistel* 'mistletoe': this bird has a fondness for mistletoe berries.

mistress [Middle English] Mistress is from Old French *maistresse*, from *maistre* 'master'. The word **miss**, recorded from the mid 17th century is an abbreviation of *mistress*.

mite [Old English] Old English *mite* describing a tiny arachnid related to the ticks is a word of Germanic origin. Late Middle English *mite* now used in phrases such as *poor little mite* is probably from the same Germanic word but it described, during this period, a small Flemish copper coin (from Middle Dutch *mīte*). The 'small size' is reflected in the phrase *the widow's mite*, with biblical allusion to Mark 12:42 (And there came a certain poor widow, and she threw in two mites, which made a farthing): this is a small amount of money given as a donation to charity but which is as much as the giver can afford.

mither [late 17th century] Welsh *moedrodd* 'to worry, bother' may have a connection with English *mither*, the origin of which is unknown.

mitigate [late Middle English] Mitigate and the contemporaneous noun **mitigation** (from

Old French, or from Latin *mitigatio(n-)*) have the same source: Latin *mitigare* 'soften, alleviate', from *mitis* 'mild'.

mitre [late Middle English] *Mitre* 'a tall hat worn by a bishop' is from Old French, via Latin from Greek *mitra* 'turban', 'belt'.

mitten [Middle English] *Mitten* is from Old French *mitaine*, perhaps from *mite*, a pet name for a cat: mittens were often made of fur. Mid 18th-century **mitt** is an abbreviation of *mitten*.

mix [late Middle English] This word is a back-formation (by removal of the suffix) from late Middle English *mixt* (= **mixed**) taken to be a past participle. This is from Old French *mixte*, from Latin *mixtus*, the past participle of *miscere* 'to mix'. The noun **mixture**, also late Middle English, is from French *mixture* or Latin *mixtura*.

moan [Middle English] The first sense recorded for *moan* was 'complaint or lamentation'; the origin is unknown.

moat [late Middle English] *Moat* is from Old French *mote* 'mound'.

mob [late 17th century] This is an abbreviation of archaic *mobile*, short for Latin *mobile vulgus* 'excitable crowd'.

mob cap [mid 18th century] The first word of this compound is a variant of obsolete *mab* meaning 'slut'. The word *mob* was first used in the sense 'prostitute' (mid to late 17th century), later it came to denote a négligé (mid 17th century to mid 18th century). The common reference now is to a large soft hat with a decorative frill; it is associated with casual dress, first associated with the type of indoor morning wear of ladies in the 18th and early 19th centuries.

mobile [late 15th century] *Mobile* came via French from Latin *mobilis*, from *movere* 'to move'. The noun dates from the 1940s. The verb **mobilize** dates from the mid 19th century and is from French *mobiliser*, from *mobile*.

mock [late Middle English] Old French *mocquer* 'deride' is the source of *mock* and late Middle English **mockery** from Old French *moquerie*.

mode [late Middle English] Early use of *mode* was in musical contexts (as a scale of notes) and as a variant for the grammatical term *mood*. The word originates from Latin *modus* 'measure', from an Indo-European root shared by *mete*. **Modal** (from medieval Latin *modalis*, from Latin *modus*) dates from the mid 16th century as a term in logic.
→ MOOD[2]

model [late 16th century] A *model* was initially 'a set of plans of a building'. The word comes from French *modelle*, from Italian *modello*, from an alteration of Latin *modulus* 'measure'. Use of the word to describe someone employed to display clothes in a fashion show is found from the early 20th century.

modem [mid 20th century] The term *modem* is a blend of *modulator* and *demodulator*.

moderate [late Middle English] Latin *moderare* 'to control, reduce' is the source of both *moderate* and, dating from the same period, **moderation** which came via Old French from Latin *moderatio(n)*.
→ MODEST

modern [late Middle English] *Modern* is from late Latin *modernus*, from *modo* 'just now'. The word **mod** is an abbreviation of *modern* or *modernist*; in the early 1960s *mods* formed a subculture which was characterized by a liking for smart stylish clothes and motor scooters.

modest [mid 16th century] The word *modest* is from French *modeste*, from Latin *modestus* 'keeping due measure', related to *modus* 'measure'.

modicum [late 15th century] This is an English use of the Latin neuter form of *modicus* 'moderate', from *modus* 'measure'.

modify [late Middle English] *Modify* is from Old French *modifier*, from Latin *modificare*, from *modus* 'measure'. The noun **modification** in Scots law in the late 15th century was 'the assessment of a payment'. It comes from French, or from Latin *modificatio(n-)*, from *modificare*.
→ MODE

modulate [mid 16th century] 'Intone (a song)' was the early sense of *modulate*, from Latin *modulari* 'measure, make melody', from *modulus* 'measure'.

module [late 16th century] 'Allotted scale' and 'plan, model' were early senses of *module* which comes either from French, or from Latin *modulus* 'measure'. The notion of 'distinct unit' dates from the 1950s. **Modular** dates from the late 18th century and is from modern Latin *modularis*, from Latin *modulus*.

moggie [late 17th century] This informal word for a cat is a variant of *Maggie*, a pet form of the given name *Margaret*.

mohair [late 16th century] The word *mohair* is from Arabic *mukayyar* 'cloth made of goat's hair', its literal use as an adjective being 'choice, select'. The change in ending was due to association with *hair*.

moist [late Middle English] *Moist* is from Old French *moiste*, based on Latin *mucidus* 'mouldy' (influenced by *musteus* 'fresh', from *mustum*). Late Middle English **moisture** meant 'moistness'; the source is Old French *moistour*, from *moiste*.

molar [late Middle English] This word in dentistry contexts is from Latin *molaris*, from *mola* 'millstone'. A *molar* is a grinding tooth.

mole[1] [late Middle English] This word for a small burrowing mammal is from the Germanic base of Middle Dutch and Middle Low German *mol*. Use of the word to mean a 'penetration agent' working within an organization over a period to achieve a position of trust before disclosing confidential information, became prominent in the 1970s in writings on Cold War espionage.

mole[2] [Old English] Of Germanic origin, Old English *māl* meant 'discoloured spot'.

molest [late Middle English] 'Cause trouble to, vex' was the first sense recorded for *molest*: the source of the form is Old French *molester* or Latin *molestare* 'annoy', from *molestus* 'troublesome'.

moll [early 17th century] *Moll* as in *a gangster's moll* is a pet form of the given name *Mary*.

mollify [late Middle English] Early senses included 'make soft or supple'; it comes from French *mollifier* or Latin *mollificare*, from *mollis* 'soft'.

mollusc [late 18th century] This word comes from modern Latin *mollusca*, the neuter plural of Latin *molluscus*, from *mollis* 'soft'.

mollycoddle [mid 19th century] This is from *molly* 'girl or prostitute' (another word for *moll* used in the same sense) and *coddle*.
→ MOLL

molten [Middle English] This is a use of the archaic past participle of *melt*.
→ MELT

moment [late Middle English] Latin *momentum* is the source of *moment* and the base of late Middle English **momentary** (from Latin *momentarius*). The Latin word was adopted into English in the late 17th century as a term in physics (e.g. *angular momentum*): it comes from *movimentum*, from *movere* 'to move'.

monarch [late Middle English] *Monarch* is from late Latin *monarcha*, from Greek *monarkhēs*, from *monos* 'alone' and *arkhein* 'to rule'. The noun **monarchy** dates from the same period and is from Old French *monarchie*, via late Latin from Greek *monarkhia* 'the rule of one person'.

monastery [late Middle English] Greek *monos* 'alone' is the base of *monastery* (which came via ecclesiastical Latin from ecclesiastical Greek *monastērion*, from *monazein* 'live alone') and late Middle English **monastic** (via late Latin from Greek *monastikos*, from *monazein*).

money [Middle English] *Money* is from Old French *moneie*, from Latin *moneta* 'mint, money', originally given as a title to the goddess Juno in whose temple in Rome money was minted. Also based on Latin *moneta* are early 19th-century **monetary** (from French *monétaire* or late Latin *monetarius*) and late 19th-century **monetize** from French *monétiser*.
→ MINT[2]

mongrel [late Middle English] Of Germanic origin, *mongrel* is apparently from a base meaning 'mix'.
→ AMONG; MINGLE

monitor [early 16th century] This was first used to describe a school pupil with special duties. It comes from Latin, from the verb *monere* 'to warn'. The sense 'instrument for observing' (e.g. *heart monitor*) dates from the 1930s.

monk [Old English] Old English *munuc* is based on Greek *monakhos* 'solitary', from *monos* 'alone'.
→ MONASTERY

monochrome [mid 17th century] This word is based on Greek *monokhrōmatos* 'of a single colour'.

monocle [mid 19th century] Adopted from a French word, a *monocle* is a single eye-glass but the French term once meant 'one-eyed', from late Latin *monoculus* 'one-eyed'.

monogamy [early 17th century] *Monogamy* is from French *monogamie*, via ecclesiastical Latin from Greek *monogamia*, from *monos* 'single' and *gamos* 'marriage'.

monolith [mid 19th century] This came from French *monolithe*, from Greek *monolithos*, from *monos* 'single' and *lithos* 'stone'.

monologue [mid 17th century] *Monologue* is from French, from Greek *monologos* 'speaking alone'.

monopoly [mid 16th century] *Monopoly* came via Latin from Greek *monopōlion*, from *monos* 'single' and *pōlein* 'sell'.

monotone [mid 17th century] *Monotone* derives from modern Latin *monotonus*, from late Greek *monotonos*.

monsoon [late 16th century] This word for a seasonal prevailing wind is from Portuguese *monção*, from Arabic *mawsim* 'season', from *wasama* 'to mark, brand'. In specialized use the word refers to a summer wind usually accompanied by heavy and continuous rainfall.

monster [late Middle English] *Monster* is from Old French *monstre*, from Latin *monstrum* 'portent or monster', the base too of **monstrous** which in late Middle English meant 'strange or unnatural' (from Old French *monstreux* or Latin *monstrosus*). Current senses date from the 16th century. **Monstrosity** dates from the mid 16th century when it denoted an abnormality of growth: this is from late Latin *monstrositas*, from Latin *monstrosus*. The base verb is Latin *monere* 'to warn'.

month [Old English] Old English *mōnath* is Germanic in origin, related to Dutch *maand* and German *Monat*.
→ MOON

monty [late 20th century] This word in the phrase *the full monty*, only recorded towards the end of the 20th century, is of unknown origin. Among various (unsubstantiated) theories, one cites the phrase *the full Montague Burton*, apparently meaning 'Sunday-best three-piece suit' (from the name of a tailor of made-to-measure clothing in the early 20th century); another recounts the possibility of a military usage, *the full monty* being 'the full cooked English breakfast' insisted upon by Field Marshal Montgomery.

monument [Middle English] A *monument* once referred to a 'burial place': it comes via French from Latin *monumentum*, from *monere* 'remind'.

mooch [late Middle English] The early recorded sense of *mooch* was 'to hoard'. The origin is probably Anglo-Norman French *muscher* 'hide, skulk'. A dialect sense 'play truant' dates from the early 16th century; current senses date from the mid 19th century.

mood¹ [Old English] Old Englsih *mōd* included the senses 'mind' and 'fierce courage'. Of Germanic origin, it is related to Dutch *moed* and German *Mut*. **Moody** in Old English was *mōdig* in the sense 'brave or wilful'.

mood² [mid 16th century] This word used in grammar contexts (e.g. *subjunctive mood*) and logic is a variant of *mode*.
→ MODE

moon [Old English] Old English *mōna* is Germanic in origin, related to Dutch *maan* and German *Mond*, from an Indo-European root shared by Latin *mensis* and Greek *mēn* 'month', as well as Latin *metiri* 'to measure': the moon was used to measure time.
→ MONTH

moor¹ [Old English] Old English *mōr* describing a tract of uncultivated upland is from a Germanic source.

moor² [late 15th century] This word meaning 'make fast' in nautical contexts is probably from the Germanic base of Dutch *meren*.

moot [Old English] Old English *mōt* was an 'assembly or meeting' and *mōtian* meant 'to converse'. Of Germanic origin, the word is related to *meet*. The adjective (originally an attributive noun use as in *moot court*) dates from the mid 16th century; the current verb sense 'raise (a topic) for discussion' dates from the mid 17th century.
→ MEET¹

mop [late 15th century] *Mop* is perhaps ultimately related to Latin *mappa* 'napkin'. The use of *mop* in the late 17th century as the name for 'an autumn fair' is probably from the practice at the fair whereby a mop was carried by a maidservant in search of employment.

mope [mid 16th century] The early noun sense of *mope* was 'fool or simpleton'. The word may be of Scandinavian origin, associated with Swedish dialect *mopa* 'to sulk'.

moped [1950s] This is made up of syllables from the Swedish phrase (*trampcykel med*) *mo*(*tor och*) *ped*(*aler*) 'pedal cycle with motor and pedals'.

moppet [early 17th century] *Moppet* is from the obsolete word *moppe* 'baby or rag doll' suffixed by the diminutive *-et*, giving 'little doll'.

moral [late Middle English] *Moral* is from Latin *moralis*, from *mos, mor-* 'custom', (plural) *mores* 'morals'. As a noun the word was first used to translate Latin *Moralia*, the title of St Gregory the Great's moral exposition of the Book of Job, and was subsequently applied to the works of various classical writers. Late Middle English **morality** is from Old French *moralite* or late Latin *moralitas*, from Latin *moralis*. Early senses included 'ethical wisdom', 'moral qualities', 'moral allegory', and 'ethics'. Also dating from the same period is the verb **moralize** which was first used in the sense 'explain the moral meaning of': this is from French *moraliser* or medieval Latin *moralizare*, from late Latin *moralis*.

morale [mid 18th century] This word meaning 'confidence and enthusiasm' is from French *moral*. It was respelt in English to reproduce the final stress of French pronunciation.

morass [late 15th century] *Morass* is from Dutch *moeras*, an alteration (by assimilation to *moer* 'moor') of Middle Dutch *marasch*, from

Old French *marais* 'marsh', from medieval Latin *mariscus*.

moratorium [late 19th century] This is modern Latin, a neuter form (used as a noun) of late Latin *moratorius* 'delaying', from Latin *morari* 'to delay', from *mora* 'delay'.

morbid [mid 17th century] The medical sense 'indicative of disease' was the first recorded. It is from Latin *morbidus*, from *morbus* 'disease'. The extended sense 'unwholesome', 'gloomy' (as in *morbid fear*, *morbid visions*) dates from the late 18th century.

more [Old English] Old English *mara* is Germanic in origin, related to Dutch *meer* and German *mehr*.

morgue [early 19th century] This is an adoption of a French word originally used as the name of a building in Paris where bodies were kept until they could be identified.

morning [Middle English] This word was formed from Old English *morn*, on the pattern of *evening*. **Morn** was *morgen* in Old English, of Germanic origin. Middle English **morrow** (spelt *morwe* in early examples), is also from Old English *morgen*; it remains now in poetic and literary use.

moron [early 20th century] Early use was as a medical term for an adult with a mental age of about 8–12. It comes from Greek *mōron*, the neuter of *mōros* 'foolish'.

morose [mid 16th century] *Morose* is from Latin *morosus* 'peevish', from *mos*, *mor-* 'manner'.

morph [1990s] This verb meaning 'change smoothly from one image to another by computer animation techniques' is an element from *metamorphosis*.
→ METAMORPHOSIS

morsel [Middle English] *Morsel* is from an Old French diminutive of *mors* 'a bite', from Latin *mors-*, the past participial stem of *mordere* 'to bite'.

mortal [late Middle English] The word *mortal* is from Old French, or from Latin *mortalis*, from *mors*, *mort-* 'death'. **Mortality** dates from the same period and is via Old French from Latin *mortalitas*, from *mortalis*.

mortar[1] [late Old English] This *mortar* was first used in the sense 'bowl for grinding ingredients for cooking or of a medicinal compound'. It comes from Old French *mortier*, from Latin *mortarium* (to which the English spelling was later assimilated).

mortar[2] [Middle English] This *mortar* describing a bonding compound used in building con-

texts is from Old French *mortier*, from Latin *mortarium*. It is probably a transferred sense of the word *mortar* describing a bowl for pulverizing compounds.
→ MORTAR[1]

mortgage [late Middle English] This is from an Old French word meaning literally 'dead pledge', from *mort* (from Latin *mortuus* 'dead') and *gage* 'pledge'.

mortify [late Middle English] Early senses included 'put to death', 'deaden', and 'subdue by self-denial'. The word is from Old French *mortifier*, from ecclesiastical Latin *mortificare* 'kill, subdue', from *mors*, *mort-* 'death'.

mortuary [late Middle English] A *mortuary* was originally a gift claimed by a parish priest from a deceased person's estate; it comes from Latin *mortuarius*, from *mortuus* 'dead'. The current meaning 'place where dead bodies are kept prior to burial' dates from the mid 19th century.

mosaic [late Middle English] From French *mosaïque*, English *mosaic* is based on Latin *musi(v)um* 'decoration with small square stones', perhaps ultimately from Greek *mousa* 'a muse'.

moss [Old English] Old English *mos* 'bog or moss' is Germanic in origin, related to Dutch *mos* and German *Moos*.

most [Old English] Old English *māst* is Germanic in origin, related to Dutch *meest* and German *meist*.

mother [Old English] Of Germanic origin, Old English *mōdor* is related to Dutch *moeder* and German *Mutter*, from an Indo-European root shared by Latin *mater* and Greek *mētēr*. **Motherly** is also an Old English word: *mōdorlic*.

motion [late Middle English] This came via Old French from Latin *motio(n-)*, from *movere* 'to move'.
→ MOVE

motive [late Middle English] *Motive* is from Old French *motif* (an adjective used as a noun), from late Latin *motivus*, from *movere* 'to move'. The noun **motivation** is found in examples from the late 19th century: based on *motive*, it was reinforced by **motivate**.

motley [late Middle English] This word is of unknown origin but is perhaps ultimately related to Old English *mote* 'tiny piece' (related to Dutch *mot* 'sawdust').

motor [late Middle English] In early use a *motor* was a person who imparted motion. It derives from a Latin word meaning 'mover', based on *movere* 'to move'. The current sense of the noun dates from the mid 19th century.

mottle [late 18th century] *Mottle* is probably a back-formation (by removal of the suffix) from *motley*.
→ MOTLEY

motto [late 16th century] This word is an adoption of Italian *motto* 'word'.

mould¹ [Middle English] This *mould* used for creating shapes is apparently from Old French *modle*, from Latin *modulus* 'measure'.

mould² [late Middle English] This *mould* is probably from obsolete *mould*, the past participle of *moul* 'grow mouldy', of Scandinavian origin. Old Norse *mygla* 'grow mouldy' is probably associated.

mould³ [Old English] Old English *molde* (as in *leaf mould*) is from a Germanic base meaning 'pulverize or grind'.
→ MEAL²

moult [Middle English] An early spelling was *moute*, from an Old English verb based on Latin *mutare* 'to change'. The intrusive -l- is seen in other words such as *fault*.

mound [early 16th century] Early use was as a verb meaning 'enclose with a fence or hedge'. The origin is obscure. An early sense of the noun was 'boundary hedge or fence'.

mount¹ [Middle English] This word meaning 'climb up' is from Old French *munter*, based on Latin *mons, mont-* 'mountain'. The noun comes from the verb but may have been influenced by French *monte*; it sometimes refers since the mid 18th century to 'a support' on which something is placed, and in photography to 'a border and backing'.

mount² [Old English] Old English *munt* 'hill' is from Latin *mons, mont-* 'mountain', reinforced in Middle English by Old French *mont*. Middle English **mountain** is from Old French *montaigne*, based on Latin *mons*.

mourn [Old English] Old English *murnan* is from a Germanic source. The base is commonly referred to the Indo-European base of *memory*; however some scholars take the Old Norse sense of *morna* 'pine away' as primary and suggest the Indo-European base to be 'to die, wither'.

mouse [Old English] Old English *mūs*, (plural) *mȳs* is Germanic in origin, related to Dutch *muis* and German *Maus*, from an Indo-European root shared by Latin and Greek *mus*. The compound:
■ **mouse potato** used in computing contexts from the 1990s was formed on the pattern of *couch potato*.

moustache [late 16th century] This is from French, from Italian *mostaccio*, from Greek *mustax, mustak-*. Earlier British English dictionaries and some American English dictionaries used to give *mustache* (a semi-Anglicized spelling) as the main form.

mouth [Old English] Old English *mūth* is Germanic in origin, related to Dutch *mond* and German *Mund*, from an Indo-European root shared by Latin *mentum* 'chin'.

move [Middle English] *Move* is from Old French *moveir*, from Latin *movere*. The main semantic strands are: 'proceed' (e.g. *he moved awkwardly along the narrow passageway*), 'cause to feel emotion' (e.g. *moved me to tears*), and 'cause to act' (e.g. W. Golding *Rites of Passage*: What would move Captain Anderson to do as I wished). Late Middle English **movement** came via Old French from medieval Latin *movimentum*, from Latin *movere*.

mow [Old English] Old English *māwan*, of Germanic origin, is related to Dutch *maaien* and German *mähen* 'mow'.

much [Middle English] This is a shortened form of *muchel*, from Old English *micel* 'great, numerous'. *Mickle* has often been misinterpreted as meaning 'a small amount': this is because the original proverb *many a little makes a mickle* was misquoted and first recorded in the writing of George Washington in 1793 as *many a mickle makes a muckle*. *Mickle* and *muckle* are in fact variants of the same word, which still exists in dialect.

muck [Middle English] This word, initially spelt *muk*, is probably of Scandinavian origin: Old Norse *myki* 'dung' may be related, from a Germanic base meaning 'soft' and shared by English *meek*. The expression *where there's muck, there's brass* dates from the mid 19th century. The phrases *Lady Muck* and *Lord Muck*, used to refer to self-important people, date from the 1930s.

mucus [mid 17th century] This is a use of a Latin word; the adjective **mucous**, also mid 17th century, is from Latin *mucosus*.

mud [late Middle English] *Mud* is probably from Middle Low German *mudde*. Of the idioms containing the word *mud*, *as clear as mud* is found from the early 19th century; *drag through the mud* arose in the mid 19th century, and *mud sticks* is recorded from the late 19th century. *Here's mud in your eye* said in a convivial way before drinking dates from the 1920s.

muddle [late Middle English] 'Wallow in mud' was the early sense of *muddle* which comes perhaps from Middle Dutch *moddelen*, a frequentative (= verb of repeated action) of

modden 'dabble in mud'. The sense 'confuse' was initially associated with alcoholic drink (= 'intoxicate, blur the speech' in the late 17th century), giving rise to 'busy oneself in a confused way' and 'jumble up' around the middle of the 19th century.
→ MUD

muff [mid 16th century] This word describing a tube of fur for warming the hands is from Dutch *mof*, Middle Dutch *muffel*, from medieval Latin *muff(u)la*; the ultimate origin is unknown. An associated word may be the verb **muff** found from the early 19th century meaning 'handle clumsily'.

muffle [late Middle English] The verb *muffle* 'cover, conceal' is perhaps a shortening of Old French *enmoufler*.

mug [early 16th century] This *mug* for containing a drink was originally a Scots and northern English word for an earthenware bowl. The origin is probably Scandinavian; Norwegian *mugge* and Swedish *mugg* 'pitcher with a handle' may be associated. The use of *mug* to mean 'face' dates from the early 18th century: drinking mugs representing grotesque human faces were common during that century. The verb **mug** (as in *mug up on Greek mythology*) dates from the mid 19th century but its origin is unknown; it may be from mid 17th-century slang *mug* 'to drink liquor, get drunk'. The derogatory word **muggins** (mid 19th century) is perhaps a use of the surname *Muggins*, alluding to *mug* in the sense 'gullible person'.

muggy [mid 18th century] This is from regional use of *mug* 'mist, drizzle' (found in Scots, East Anglian, and Shropshire dialects), from Old Norse *mugga* 'drizzle'.

mulch [mid 17th century] This word used in gardening contexts is probably from the dialect adjective *mulch* 'soft' used as a noun, from Old English *melsc*, *mylsc*. It describes a mixture of wet straw, and leaves spread on the ground to enrich the soil or to protect the roots of newly planted trees.

mule¹ [Old English] Old English *mūl* describing the offspring of a donkey and a horse is probably of Germanic origin, from Latin *mulus*, *mula*; reinforced in Middle English by Old French *mule*. The use of *mule* to denote 'a courier for illicit drugs' dates from the 1920s in US slang.

mule² [mid 16th century] This is an adoption of a French word meaning 'slipper'. It is from late Latin *mulla*, Lat.n *mulleus* (*calceus*) which were reddish shoes worn by Roman magistrates.

mull¹ [mid 19th century] This *mull* as in *mull over* is of uncertain origin. It may be from *mull* 'mulled wine'.
→ MULL²

mull² [early 17th century] The *mull* of *mulled wine* is of unknown origin. Several theories have been put forward; one unlikely suggestion is that *mulled ale* is a corruption of *moldale* 'funeral banquet'; another is that *mull* refers to the powdered spices used in mulling; a third is that the original sense may have been 'to soften, make mild'. However the earliest examples seem to imply that the primary sense is 'to heat'

mull³ [Middle English] This *mull* is common in place names meaning 'promontory, headland' (e.g. *Mull of Kintyre*). Scottish Gaelic *maol* and Icelandic *múli* are comparable.

multiple [mid 17th century] *Multiple* is from French, from late Latin *multiplus*, an alteration of Latin *multiplex*. Early use was as a mathematical quantity.

multiply [Middle English] *Multiply* is from Old French *multiplier*, from Latin *multiplicare*, which is also the base of late Middle English **multiplication** (from Old French, or from Latin *multiplicatio(n-)*). **Multiplicity**, also late Middle English, is from late Latin *multiplicitas*, from Latin *multiplex*.
→ MULTIPLE

multitude [Middle English] This came via Old French from Latin *multitudo*, from *multus* 'many'.

mum¹ [late Middle English] *Mum* as in *mum's the word* (early 16th century) is imitative of a sound made with closed lips as an indication of an unwillingness to speak.

mum² [late Middle English] This is perhaps associated with Middle Low German *mummen* 'to mutter, disguise oneself'. Words associated with *mumming* appear to be attested earliest in Old French and to have spread to other European languages. The original sense is probably imitative of the muffled and distorted voices of the performers of traditional masked mime: they were known as *mummers*. The word **mummer** is also late Middle English from Old French *momeur*, from *momer* 'act in a mime'.

mumble [Middle English] *Mumble* is a frequentative (= verb of repeated action) based on *mum!* 'hush!'.

mummy¹ [late 18th century] This child's term for 'mother' is perhaps an alteration of the earlier word *mammy*.

mummy² [late Middle English] This word, often used in the context of ancient Egypt, initially denoted a substance taken from embalmed bodies and used in medicines. It comes from French *momie*, from medieval Latin *mumia* and Arabic *mūmiyā* 'embalmed body', perhaps from Persian *mūm* 'wax'. The word describing a dead body preserved by embalming dates from the early 17th century.

munch [late Middle English] *Munch* is a word imitative of the sound made when eating audibly; *crunch* is a similar formation.

mundane [late Middle English] The early sense recorded for mundane is 'of this earthly world'. The source is Old French *mondain*, from late Latin *mundanus*, from Latin *mundus* 'world'. The common current sense 'dull, lacking interest' dates from the late 19th century.

municipal [mid 16th century] The word *municipal* originally related to the internal affairs of a state as distinct from its foreign relations. It comes from Latin *municipalis* (from *municipium* 'free city', from *municeps*, *municip-* 'citizen with privileges', from *munia* 'civic offices') and *capere* 'take'. **Municipality** dates from the late 18th century and is from French *municipalité*, from *municipal*.

mural [late Middle English] This word comes from French, from Latin *muralis*, from *murus* 'wall'. The adjective was first used in heraldry in the phrase *mural crown* which depicts a city wall in the form of a crown; later, in the mid 16th century, the sense 'placed or executed on a wall' arose, reflected in the current noun use 'work of art depicted on a wall' (dating from the early 20th century). The phrase *extra-mural*, literally 'outside the walls', has been used in educational contexts from the late 19th century referring to courses given to people from outside the establishment.

murder [Old English] Old English *morthor* is from a Germanic source; it is related to Dutch *moord* and German *Mord*, from an Indo-European root shared by Sanskrit *mará* 'death' and Latin *mors*; reinforced in Middle English by Old French *murdre*.

murk [Old English] Old English *mirce*, from a Germanic source, was reinforced in Middle English by Old Norse *myrkr*.

murmur [late Middle English] *Murmur* is from Old French *murmure*, from *murmurer* 'to murmur', from Latin *murmurare*, from *murmur* 'a murmur'.

muscle [late Middle English] This is from French, from Latin *musculus*, a diminutive of *mus* 'mouse': some muscles were thought to be mouse-like in form. The adjective **muscular** dates from the late 17th century and is an alter-

ation of earlier *musculous* which had the same sense.

muse [Middle English] The verb *muse* 'be absorbed in thought' is from Old French *muser* 'meditate, waste time', perhaps from medieval Latin *musum* 'muzzle'.

museum [early 17th century] A *museum* once referred to a university building, specifically one erected at Alexandria by Ptolemy Soter (*c.*280 BC). The word came via Latin from Greek *mouseion* 'seat of the Muses', based on *mousa* 'muse'.

mush¹ [late 17th century] This was first recorded as a word for 'thick maize porridge': it is apparently a variant of *mash*.
→ MASH

mush² [mid 19th century] This word used to encourage dogs to pull a sled across snow is probably an alteration of French *marchez!* or *marchons!*, imperatives of *marcher* 'to advance'.

mushroom [late Middle English] This was originally a word for any fungus with a fleshy fruiting body. It is from Old French *mousseron*, from late Latin *mussirio(n-)*.

music [Middle English] *Music* is from Old French *musique*, via Latin from Greek *mousikē* (*tekhnē*) '(art) of the Muses', from *mousa* 'muse'. The word **muzak** dating from the 1930s is an alteration of *music*. Latin *musica* 'music' is the base of late Middle English **musical** (from Old French, from medieval Latin *musicalis*) and **musician** (from Old French *musicien*).

musket [late 16th century] *Musket* is from French *mousquet*, from Italian *moschetto* 'crossbow bolt', from *mosca* 'a fly'.

muslin [early 17th century] 'Mosul', the name of the place of manufacture in Iraq, is the base of *muslin*: the place was called *Mussolo* in Italian and the cloth was called *mussolina*. This was adopted into French as *mousseline* which in turn gave the English form.

must¹ [Old English] Old English *mōste* was the past tense of *mōt* 'may'. Of Germanic origin, it is related to Dutch *moeten* and German *müssen*.

must² [Old English] This *must* meaning 'grape juice' before or during fermentation is from Latin *mustum*, a neuter form (used as a noun) of *mustus* 'new'.

muster [late Middle English] *Muster* as a verb is from Old French *moustrer*; as a noun it is from Old French *moustre*. The base is Latin *monstrare* 'to show'.

musty [early 16th century] *Musty* is perhaps an alteration of *moisty* 'moist'.

mutation [late Middle English] This word comes from Latin *mutatio(n-)*, from *mutare* 'to change'; the verb **mutate** is an early 19th-century back-formation (by removal of the suffix) from this. **Mutant** arose in the early 20th century from Latin *mutare*.

mute [Middle English] *Mute* is from Old French *muet*, a diminutive of *mu*, from Latin *mutus*.

mutilate [early 16th century] Latin *mutilus* 'maimed' (from Latin *mutilare* 'maim, mutilate, lop off') is the base of *mutilate* in English.

mutiny [mid 16th century] The word *mutiny* is from obsolete *mutine* meaning 'rebellion', from French *mutin* 'mutineer'; the base is Latin *movere* 'to move'. **Mutinous**, dating from the late 16th century, also has obsolete *mutine* at its base. The noun **mutineer** is found in examples from the early 17th century and is from French *mutinier*, from *mutin* 'rebellious', from *muete* 'movement' (based on Latin *movere*).

mutt [late 19th century] This word for a 'dog' or a person regarded as stupid, is an abbreviation of *muttonhead*.

mutter [late Middle English] This is a word imitative of the sound; German dialect *muttern* is a comparable form.

mutton [Middle English] This comes from Old French *moton*, from medieval Latin *multo(n-)*, probably of Celtic origin; Scottish Gaelic *mult*, Welsh *mollt*, and Breton *maout* are comparable.

mutual [late 15th century] *Mutual* is from Old French *mutuel*, from Latin *mutuus* 'mutual, borrowed'; related to *mutare* 'to change'.

muzz [mid 18th century] This word meaning 'muddle' was first used as a verb in the sense 'study intently'. It is of unknown origin, but is based partly perhaps on an alteration of *muse*.
→ MUSE

muzzle [late Middle English] *Muzzle* is from Old French *musel*, a diminutive of medieval Latin *musum*. The ultimate origin is unknown.

muzzy [early 18th century] of unknown origin.

my [Middle English] The early spelling was *mi* used originally before words beginning with any consonant except *h-*. It is a reduced form of *min*, from Old English *mīn* 'mine'.
→ ME

myriad [mid 16th century] This was originally found as a unit meaning ten thousand. The word came via late Latin from Greek *murias*, *muriad-*, from *murioi* '10,000'.

mystery [Middle English] The early sense recorded was 'mystic presence, hidden religious symbolism'. The word comes from Old French *mistere* or Latin *mysterium*, from Greek *mustērion*. The religious element is reflected in the *mystery plays*, popular medieval dramas based on biblical stories or the lives of the saints: they were performed by members of trade guilds in Europe from the 13th century. **Mysterious** is a late 16th-century word from French *mystérieux*, from *mystère* 'mystery'. The verb **mystify** dates from the early 19th century and is from French *mystifier* (formed irregularly from *mystique* 'mystic' or from *mystère* 'mystery').
→ MYSTIC

mystic [Middle English] 'Mystical meaning' was the early sense of *mystic* which comes either from Old French *mystique*, or via Latin from Greek *mustikos*, from *mustēs* 'initiated person'. The base verb is Greek *muein* meaning both 'close the eyes or lips' and 'initiate'. The current sense of the noun ('a person believing in the spiritual apprehension of truths beyond the intellect') dates from the late 17th century.

mythology [late Middle English] Greek *muthos* 'myth' is the source of the first element of the word *mythology* (which is either from French *mythologie*, or via late Latin from Greek *muthologia*) and mid 19th-century **myth** (from modern Latin *mythus*).

Nn

nab [late 17th century] *Nab* 'catch, grab' is of unknown origin; it was also written formerly as *napp*; the final element of *kidnap* may be associated.

nag¹ [early 19th century] This *nag* meaning 'find fault, come at persistently' (e.g. *nagging pain*) was originally dialect in the sense 'gnaw'; it may be Scandinavian or Low German in origin associated with Norwegian and Swedish *nagga* 'gnaw, irritate' and Low German *(g)naggen* 'provoke'.

nag² [Middle English] The informal *nag* used as a derogatory description of an old or ailing horse is of obscure origin; it may be related to Dutch *negge* used to describe 'a small horse'.

nail [Old English] The Old English noun *nægel* is Germanic in origin. The two principal meanings 'small metal spike' and 'horny covering on the upper side of a fingertip' were already present in this early period. The word is related to Dutch *nagel* and German *Nagel*, from an Indo-European root shared by Latin *unguis* 'nail, claw' and Greek *onux* 'nail'. The verb gained the extended sense 'capture, pin down' (as in *it was her evidence that nailed him*) in the early 18th century.

naive [mid 17th century] This word originally meant 'natural and unaffected'; it comes from French *naïve*, the feminine of *naïf*, from Latin *nativus* 'native, natural'. Since the 1950s *naive* has been applied in art contexts to paintings produced in a straightforward style characterized by bold directness typical of a child.

naked [Old English] Of Germanic origin, Old English *nacod* is related to Dutch *naakt* and German *nackt*, from an Indo-European root shared by Latin *nudus* and Sanskrit *nagna*. The phrase *the naked truth* illustrates early figurative use in late Middle English.

namby-pamby [mid 18th century] This phrase meaning 'lacking energy, feeble, effeminate' is a fanciful formation based on the name of *Ambrose* Philips, an English writer of the early 18th century whose pastorals were ridiculed by the poets Carey and Pope.

name [Old English] Shakespeare questioned the accuracy of *name* in capturing the true nature of something (*Romeo and Juliet*: What's in a name? That which we call a Rose, by any other name would smell as sweet) but generally a *name* is a 'designation'. Germanic in origin, Old English *nama*, *noma* (noun), and *(ge)namian* (verb) are related to Dutch *naam* and German *Name*, from a root shared by Latin *nomen* and Greek *onoma*. Of the phrases incorporating *name*: *you name it* is found from the 1960s; *name and shame* meaning 'publicly denounce' is recorded from the 1990s. The compound:
■ **namesake** (mid 17th century) comes from the phrase *for the name's sake*.

nanny [early 18th century] This word for a person taking care of young children or used as an epithet in the phrase *nanny-goat* is a pet form of the given name *Ann*. The notion of *nanny state* is found from the 1960s with reference to a form of government perceived as overprotective and interfering. The verb dates from the 1950s. The noun *nan* (1940s) is either an abbreviation of *nanny* or a child's pronunciation of *gran*.

nap¹ [Old English] *Nap* 'sleep briefly' was *hnappian* in Old English; the source is probably Germanic. In the early 19th century, the word *catnap* came into use from *a cat's nap*, a short sleep while sitting.

nap² [late Middle English] The *nap* referring to the raised threads on the surface of fabric had the spelling *noppe* in late Middle English. It comes from Middle Dutch, Middle Low German *noppe* 'nap', *noppen* 'trim the nap from'.

nap³ [1950s] A horse who *naps* refuses to go on; the word is a back-formation (by removal of the suffix) from *nappy*, an adjective first used to describe heady beer in late Middle English. In the early 18th century, *nappy* was used in the sense 'intoxicated by drink'; it is since the 1920s that it has been applied in contexts of a disobedient horse.

nape [Middle English] The word *nape* (e.g. *nape of the neck*) is of unknown origin.

napkin [late Middle English] *Napkin* is from Old French *nap(p)e* 'tablecloth' (from Latin *mappa*) and the diminutive suffix *-kin*, thus giving 'little cloth'. The archaic word **napery** (Middle English) for 'household linen' shares the same Old French source.
➔ MAP

nappy [early 20th century] This word (as in *baby's nappy*) is an abbreviation of *napkin*.
➜ NAPKIN

narcotic [late Middle English] *Narcotic* is from Old French *narcotique*, via medieval Latin from Greek *narkōtikos*, from *narkoun* 'make numb'. The word **narcoterrorism** was coined in the 1980s: here the prefix *narco-* means 'relating to illegal narcotics'.

nark [mid 19th century] This word as in *copper's nark* meaning 'a police informer' is from Romany *nāk* 'nose'.

narrative [late Middle English] Early use was as an adjective; it comes from French *narratif*, *-ive*, from late Latin *narrativus* 'telling a story', from the verb *narrare*. This same Latin verb (meaning 'relate, tell', from *gnarus* 'knowing') is the source too of **narrate** which is recorded in use from the mid 17th century.

narrow [Old English] Old English *nearu* is Germanic in origin, related to Dutch *naar* 'dismal, unpleasant' and German *Narbe* 'scar'. Early senses in English included 'constricted' and 'mean'. This notion of 'limiting to a reduced scope' is found in the compound verb **narrowcast** 'transmit to a small audience' which is recorded from the 1930s; it is a back-formation (by removal of the suffix) from *narrowcasting*, influenced by the pattern of *broadcasting*. The phrase *the straight and narrow* meaning a course of conventionally moral, law-abiding behaviour dates from the mid 19th century: it is a misinterpretation of Matthew 7:14: Because strait is the gate, and narrow is the way which leadeth unto life, and few there be that find it.

nasal [Middle English] *Nasal* 'of the nose' is from medieval Latin *nasalis*, from Latin *nasus* 'nose'. Its use to describe a type of speech sound dates from the mid 17th century.

nasty [late Middle English] The origin of the word *nasty* is unknown. Early use was with the meaning 'offensive through being filthy'. Its application to people in the sense 'spiteful' arose in the early 19th century. The term *video nasty* for 'a horror video film' came into use in the late 20th century.

nation [Middle English] *Nation* came via Old French from Latin *natio(n-)* 'birth, race of people', from *nat-*, the past participial stem of *nasci* 'be born'. The Latin verb *nasci* is also the source of Middle English **nativity** (from Old French *nativite*, from late Latin *nativitas*) and late Middle English **native** (from Latin *nativus* 'arisen by birth'). The phrase *the natives are restless*, a stock expression in Hollywood films from the 1950s, came to refer to any trouble brewing

or any unrest. **National** dating from the late 16th century is from French, from Latin *natio(n-)*.

natter [early 19th century] The dialect sense 'grumble, fret' was the first recorded for *natter*; the word is imitative of fast chatter.

natty [late 18th century] Originally slang, *natty* 'smart and fashionable' (e.g. *natty dresser*) may be related to *neat*.
➜ NEAT

nature [Middle English] In Middle English, the *nature* of a person referred to 'physical power'; it comes from Old French, from Latin *natura* 'birth, nature, quality', from *nasci* 'be born'. Middle English **natural** in early use meant 'having a certain status by birth'; an Old French word is the direct source, from Latin *naturalis*, from *natura*.

naught [Old English] Old English *nāwiht*, *nāwuht* is from *nā* 'no' and *wiht* 'thing'.

naughty [late Middle English] This word is based on *naught*. The earliest recorded sense was 'possessing nothing'; the sense 'wicked' also dates from late Middle English and gave rise to the current senses. The expression *naughty but nice* referring to something slightly improper but enjoyable dates from the late 19th century. It was given new life in advertising slogans during the late 20th century.
➜ NAUGHT

nausea [late Middle English] Greek *nausia* (from *naus* 'ship') gave rise to Latin *nausea* 'seasickness', the source of *nausea*, **nauseous** (early 17th century from Latin *nauseosus*) and **nauseate** (mid 17th century from Latin *nauseare* 'cause to feel sick').

nautical [mid 16th century] This word is from French *nautique*, or via Latin from Greek *nautikos*, from *nautēs* 'sailor', from *naus* 'ship'.

nave [late 17th century] The *nave* of a church owes its name to its shape: it comes from Latin *navis* 'ship'.

navel [Old English] Old English *nafela* is Germanic in origin, related to Dutch *navel* and German *Nabel*, from an Indo-European root shared by Latin *umbo* 'boss of a shield', *umbilicus* 'navel', and Greek *omphalos* 'boss, navel'.

navigation [early 16th century] *Navigation* was initially a word describing the 'action of travelling on water'; it comes from French, or from Latin *navigatio(n-)*. The base is Latin *navigare* 'to sail', the source too of **navigate** (late 16th century). The early use of this verb was in the sense 'travel in a ship'; the Latin elements are *navis* 'ship' and *agere* 'drive'.

navvy [early 19th century] This word for a labourer employed in the building of roads, railways, or canals is an abbreviation of **navigator** which was used in the same sense in the late 18th century.
→ NAVIGATION

navy [late Middle English] *Navy* is from Old French *navie* 'ship, fleet', from popular Latin *navia* 'ship', from Latin *navis* 'ship'. When first recorded *navy* referred to 'ships collectively'. The adjective **naval** is also late Middle English, from Latin *navalis*, from *navis*.

near [Middle English] This comes from Old Norse *nær* 'nearer', the comparative of *ná*, corresponding to Old English *nēah* 'nigh'.

neat [late 15th century] 'Clean, free from impurities' was the first sense recorded for *neat*; the source is French *net*, from Latin *nitidus* 'shining', from *nitere* 'to shine'. The sense 'bright' (now obsolete) was recorded in English in the late 16th century, as was 'not mixed with water' (e.g. *neat gin*).

neb [Old English] Old English *nebb* 'nose, beak, peak' is Germanic in origin; it is related to Dutch *neb(be)*.
→ NIB; NIPPLE

nebulous [late Middle English] The first sense recorded was 'cloudy'; *nebulous* is from French *nébuleux*, from Latin *nebulosus*, from *nebula* 'mist'. The sense 'cloud-like, vague' dates from the early 19th century. The term **nebulizer** for a device producing a fine spray of mist came into use towards the end of the 19th century and is based on Latin *nebula*.

necessary [late Middle English] *Necessary* is from Latin *necessarius*, from *necesse* 'needful', the base too of the contemporaneous word **necessity** (from Old French *necessite*, from Latin *necessitas*) and early 17th-century **necessitate** (from medieval Latin *necessitare* 'to compel').

neck [Old English] Old English *hnecca* meant 'back of the neck'. Of Germanic origin, it is related to Dutch *nek* 'neck' and German *Nacken* 'nape'. Use of the word colloquially to mean 'impudence' (e.g. *barefaced neck*) dates from the late 19th century.

nectar [mid 16th century] *Nectar* in early use designated a 'drink of the gods' in Greek and Roman mythology. The word came via Latin from Greek *nektar*. Based on *nectar* is early 17th-century **nectarine** which included the meaning 'nectar-like' as well as serving as the name for a smooth-skinned variety of peach.

need [Old English] The Old English verb *nēodian* and noun *nēod*, *nēd* are from a Germanic source. Dutch *nood* and German *Not* 'danger' are related.

needle [Old English] Old English *nædl*, of Germanic origin, is related to Dutch *naald* and German *Nadel*, from an Indo-European root shared by Latin *nere* 'to spin' and Greek *nēma* 'thread'. The colloquial use of the verb in the sense 'irritate, annoy' dates from the late 19th century.

nefarious [early 17th century] This word meaning 'wicked, criminal' is from Latin *nefarius*, based on *nefas*, *nefar-* 'wrong' (from *ne-* 'not' and *fas* 'divine law').

negation [late Middle English] The word *negation* is from Latin *negatio(n-)*, from *negare* 'deny'. **Negative** is recorded from the same period and is from late Latin *negativus*, from *negare*; its use in photography contexts is found from the mid 19th century. **Negate**, from the same Latin verb, is first found in early 17th-century examples meaning 'nullify' and 'deny the existence of something'.

negligee [mid 18th century] A *negligee* described a kind of loose gown worn by women in the 18th century; it is from a French word meaning literally 'given little thought or attention' (the feminine past participle of *négliger* 'to neglect').

negligence [Middle English] *Negligence* came via Old French from Latin *negligentia*, from the verb *negligere* (a variant of *neglegere* 'to disregard, slight', from *neg-* 'not' and *legere* 'choose'). The adjective **negligent** is recorded from late Middle English and is from Old French, or from Latin *negligent-*, the present participial stem of *negligere*. From the early 16th century, examples of the verb **neglect** (from Latin *neglegere*) started to be found. **Negligible** (from obsolete French, from *négliger* 'to neglect') dates from the early 19th century.

negotiation [late 15th century] A *negotiation* was initially an act of dealing with another person; it is from Latin *negotiatio(n-)*, from the verb *negotiari* 'do in the course of business'. **Negotiate**, early 17th century, is from the same Latin verb based on *negotium* 'business', from *neg-* 'not' and *otium* 'leisure'. Its extended use in phrases such as *negotiate a bend safely* dates from the mid 19th century.

neigh [Old English] The Old English verb *hnægan* is imitative in origin; Dutch dialect *neijen* is a related form.

neighbour [Old English] Old English *nēahgebūr* is from *nēah* 'nigh, near' and *gebūr* 'inhabitant, peasant, farmer'.
→ BOOR

neither [Middle English] *Neither* is an alteration (by association with *either*) of Old English *nawther*: this is a contraction of *nāhwæther*, from *nā* 'no' and *hwæther* 'whether'.

nelly [mid 20th century] This informal word for 'a silly or effeminate person' is from a familiar form of the given names *Helen* or *Eleanor*. The phrase *not on your nelly* is from the rhyming slang *Nelly Duff* for *puff* (= breath of life), giving 'not on your life'.

nemesis [late 16th century] This word for someone's or something's 'downfall' is Greek; the literal meaning is 'retribution', from *nemein* 'give what is due'.

neon [late 19th century] *Neon* (as in *neon light*) comes from a Greek word with the literal meaning 'something new': it is the neuter form of the adjective *neos*.

nephew [Middle English] *Nephew* is from Old French *neveu*, from Latin *nepos* 'grandson, nephew', from an Indo-European root shared by Dutch *neef* and German *Neffe*. The euphemistic use of *nephew* to mean 'illegitimate son' dates from the late 16th century.

nepotism [mid 17th century] This word comes from French *népotisme*, from Italian *nepotismo*, from *nepote* 'nephew': the reference is to privileges bestowed on the 'nephews' of popes, who were in many cases their illegitimate sons. The general use of *nepotism* to mean 'unfair preferment of friends or family' dates from the 1950s.

nerve [late Middle English] Early use of the word included the sense 'tendon, sinew'; it comes from Latin *nervus* 'sinew'; related to Greek *neuron* 'nerve'. Use of the word to mean 'audacity' (e.g. *have the nerve to*) dates from the late 19th century. The adjective **nervous**, also recorded in the late Middle English period meaning 'containing nerves' and 'relating to the nerves', is from Latin *nervosus* 'sinewy, vigorous', from Latin *nervus*. The sense 'easily agitated' dates from the mid 18th century. Of the phrases containing the word *nerve* are: *have the nerve* (late 19th century) and, from the Second World War, *war of nerves*.

nesh [Old English] The dialect word *nesh* 'feeble, over-sensitive to the cold' was *hnesce* in Old English. Germanic in origin, it is related to Dutch dialect *nes* 'soft or foolish'.

nest [Old English] Old English *nest* is from a Germanic source. It is related to Latin *nidus*, from the Indo-European bases of *nether* (meaning 'down') and *sit*, thus giving 'a place for sitting down'.

nestle [Old English] Old English *nestlian* is from *nest*; Dutch *nestelen* is a related form. Early use was in the context of birds building a nest. The transferred notion 'lie snugly' dates from the mid 16th century.
→ NEST

net¹ [Old English] Old English *net(t)* is Germanic in origin; it is related to Dutch *net* and German *Netz* and is probably from an Indo-European base meaning 'twist together'. The word **network** dates from the mid 16th century; its association with broadcasting began in the early 20th century leading to the phrase *network English* as the American English equivalent of BBC English. The abbreviation *Net* referring to the computing network known as the *Internet* became common towards the end of the 20th century, with words such as **Netizen** (= Network Citizen) being coined in the 1990s.

net² [Middle English] *Net* meaning 'free from deductions' was first recorded in late Middle English commercial documents. The word is from French *net* 'neat' and early senses included 'clean' and 'smart'.
→ NEAT

nether [Old English] *Nether* (Old English *nithera*, *neothera*) is from a Germanic source. It is related to Dutch *neder-* (found in compounds), *neer*, and German *nieder*, from an Indo-European root meaning 'down'.

nettle [Old English] Of Germanic origin, Old English *netle*, *netele* is related to Dutch *netel* and German *Nessel*. The verb dates from late Middle English when it meant both 'sting with nettles' and 'vex, irritate'.

neurosis [mid 18th century] This is modern Latin, from *neuro-* 'of nerves' and the suffix *-osis* (found as a Latin and Greek ending meaning 'action of', 'condition of').

neuter [late Middle English] *Neuter* came via Old French from Latin *neuter* 'neither', from *ne-* 'not' and *uter* 'either'. The verb meaning 'castrate' is found from the early 20th century. From the same period is **neutral**, first recorded as a noun: this is from Latin *neutralis* 'of neuter gender', from Latin *neuter*. The sense 'not taking sides' in a conflict situation dates from the mid 16th century.

never [Old English] Old English *næfre* is from *ne* 'not' and *æfre* 'ever'. The compound:
■ **never-never land** is often with allusion to the ideal country in J. M. Barrie's *Peter Pan* (1904).

new [Old English] Old English *nīwe*, *nēowe* is Germanic in origin, related to Dutch *nieuw* and German *neu*, from an Indo-European root shared by Sanskrit *nava*, Latin *novus*, and Greek *neos* 'new'. Late Middle English **news** is the plural of *new*, translating Old French *noveles* or medieval Latin *nova* 'new things'. Of the phrases: *no news is good news* is recorded from the late 16th century; *that's news to me* dates from the late 18th century; *in the news* is found from the 1930s, and *to be good news* (e.g. *this new employee is good news for the company*) is recorded from the 1980s. The compound:

■ **newfangle** (Middle English) is from *newfangle* (which is now restricted to dialect) meaning 'liking what is new', from the adverb *new* and a second element related to an Old English word meaning 'to take'.

newt [late Middle English] The word *newt* is from the phrase *an ewt* (*ewt* from Old English *efeta* which also gave the dialect word *eft* meaning 'newt'). It was interpreted, by wrong division, as *a newt*; *adder* underwent the same formation process.

next [Old English] Old English *nēhsta* 'nearest' is the superlative of *nēah* 'nigh'; Dutch *naast* and German *nächste* are cognates.

nib [late 16th century] A *nib* in early use was a 'beak, nose': it is probably from Middle Dutch *nib* or Middle Low German *nibbe*, a variant of *nebbe* 'beak'. Use of the word to refer to the point of a pen (originally a quill pen) dates from the early 17th century.
→ NEB

nibble [late 15th century] *Nibble* is probably of Low German or Dutch origin; Low German *nibbeln* 'gnaw' may be associated. The plural *nibbles* for light snacks before a meal dates from the early 20th century.

nibs [early 19th century] This word used in expressions such as *his nibs* is of unknown origin. The earlier word *nabs* was used similarly with a possessive adjective as in *his nabs*, influenced by references to the aristocracy such as *his lordship*.

nice [Middle English] 'Stupid' was the first sense recorded for *nice*. It comes from Old French, from Latin *nescius* 'ignorant', from *nescire* 'not know'. Other early senses (of which there were many including for example: 'wanton' and 'ostentatious') included 'coy, reserved'. This gave rise to 'fastidious, scrupulous', leading both to the sense 'fine, subtle' (regarded by some as the 'correct' sense) and to the main current senses. Middle English **nicety** had the meaning 'folly, foolish conduct'; it is from Old French *nicete*, based on Latin *nescius* 'ignorant'.

niche [early 17th century] This is an adoption of a French word whose literal meaning is 'recess', from *nicher* 'make a nest'. The Latin base is *nidus* 'nest'. Use of the word to mean 'place or position suited to somebody's capabilities and status' (e.g. *find one's niche*) is recorded from the early 18th century; in commercial contexts examples of the word as a 'position from which an entrepreneur can exploit a gap' (e.g. *new market niche*) are found from the 1960s.

nick [late Middle English] *Nick* meaning 'a small cut' is of unknown origin. The slang use 'prison' dates from the early 19th century, when the verb senses 'put in jail' and 'steal' were also first recorded.

nickname [late Middle English] This comes from the phrase *an eke-name*: here *eke* means 'addition'. The phrase was misinterpreted, by wrong division, as *a neke name*.

niece [Middle English] *Niece* is from Old French, based on Latin *neptis* 'granddaughter', the feminine of *nepos* 'nephew, grandson', from an Indo-European root shared by Dutch *nicht* and German *Nichte*. Down to about 1600, *niece* was commonly used to mean 'granddaughter'.
→ NEPHEW

niggle [early 17th century] *Niggle* had the sense 'do something in a fiddling or ineffectual way' in early examples. The word is apparently of Scandinavian origin; Norwegian *nigla* is a corresponding form. The sense 'cause annoyance' (as in *niggling pain*) dates from the late 18th century.

nigh [Old English] Old English *nē(a)h* is Germanic in origin, related to Dutch *na* and German *nah*.
→ NEAR

night [Old English] Old English *neaht*, *niht* is Germanic in origin, related to Dutch *nacht* and German *Nacht*, from an Indo-European root shared by Latin *nox* and Greek *nux*. The compound:

■ **nightmare** (Middle English) initially referred to a female evil spirit thought to lie upon and suffocate sleepers; it is based on *night* and Old English *mære* 'incubus'.

nil [mid 19th century] This is a use of a Latin word, a contraction of *nihil* 'nothing'.

nimble [Old English] Old English *næmel* meant 'quick to seize or comprehend'; it is related to *niman* 'take', of Germanic origin. Evidence of the early sense is scanty, the word becoming much more common once its use as 'quick and agile' became established. The -*b*- was added to facilitate pronunciation.

nincompoop [late 17th century] Various etymologies have been suggested for this word: it is perhaps from the given name *Nicholas*; or it may come from *Nicodemus* by association with the Pharisee of this name and his naive questioning of Christ (French *nicodème* means 'simpleton'). However it is probably only a fanciful formation. Another plausible origin is French *nic à poux* a term of derision in the late 16th century.

ninny [late 16th century] This word meaning 'simpleton' is perhaps from *Innocent* a given name for a man, shortened to *Ninny* as a pet-form.

nip¹ [late Middle English] This *nip* meaning 'pinch' is probably of Low German or Dutch origin. The transference of the sense to 'cause pain by a sharp chill' (e.g. *nipped by the cold*) dates from the mid 16th century. *Nip in the bud* is a phrase dating from the early 17th century. Slang use of *nip* in the sense 'move quickly' (e.g. *he nipped off to the bookie's*) is recorded in the early 19th century. Based on the verb *nip* are **nippy** (recorded from the end of the 16th century meaning 'inclined to nip') and **nipper** (early 16th century). The latter was a term in the mid 19th century for a boy working as an assistant for a costermonger or carter, and sometimes it referred to the most junior member of a group of workmen; it was also slang for any young boy.

nip² [late 18th century] This word (e.g. *a quick nip of brandy from a hip flask*) was originally a term for a half-pint of ale: it is probably an abbreviation of the rare term *nipperkin* 'small measure'. Low German and Dutch *nippen* 'to sip' may be related. In the US a *nip joint* was a name in the 1930s for a bar selling small quantities of liquor illegally.

nipple [mid 16th century] Early spellings included *neble* and *nible*: it may be a diminutive of *neb*.
→ NEB; NIB

nit [Old English] Old English *hnitu* 'the egg of a louse' is West Germanic in origin, related to Dutch *neet* and German *Nisse*. Use of the word to mean 'stupid person' is found from the late 16th century (Shakespeare *Love's Labour's Lost*: And his page,... Ah heavens, it is a most pathetical nit). The word **nitwit** (early 20th century) is apparently based on *nit*.

no [Old English] The Old English adverb *nō*, *nā* is from *ne* 'not' and *ō*, *ā* 'ever'. The determiner arose in Middle English (originally before words beginning with any consonant except *h-*): this was a reduced form of *non* from Old English *nān*. *No* is used in various colloquial phrases: *no strings* (early 20th century); *no bother* (1920s); *no kidding* (1940s); *no sweat* (1950s); and *no worries* and *no probs* (1980s). The compound:

■ **no-man's land** dates from Middle English and was originally the name of a plot of ground lying outside the north wall of the city of London, the site of a place of execution. During the First World War it defined the terrain between opposing entrenched armies.
→ NONE

nob [late 17th century] This slang word for a 'wealthy or socially distinguished person' is sometimes said to be from *noble* but the original form (Scots) was *knab* which makes the suggestion difficult to accept. The origin remains unknown.

nobble [mid 19th century] *Nobble* 'strike, beat up' is probably a variant of dialect *knobble*, *knubble* 'knock, strike with the knuckles'. Its use in the sense 'tamper with a horse by laming or drugging it' dates from the same period.

noble [Middle English] *Noble* is from Old French, from Latin (g)*nobilis* 'noted, high-born', from an Indo-European root shared by *know*. The word was once used as a term for an English gold coin first minted in the reign of Edward III and usually valued at 6s.8d. The noun **nobility** is late Middle English, from Old French *nobilite* or Latin *nobilitas*, from *nobilis*.
→ KNOW

nocturnal [late 15th century] *Nocturnal* is from late Latin *nocturnalis* 'of the night', based on Latin *nox*, *noct-* 'night'. The same Latin base is shared by Middle English **nocturn**, a word used in the Roman Catholic Church for part of matins originally said at night; the term **nocturne** (mid 19th century) is used in art for a picture of a night scene, and in musical contexts for a short composition, usually for piano, suggestive of night and meditation: this is an adoption of a French word, from Latin *nocturnus* 'of the night'

nocuous [mid 17th century] *Nocuous* 'harmful, poisonous' is based on Latin *nocuus* (from *nocere* 'to hurt').

nod [late Middle English] *Nod* was first used as a verb. It may be of Low German origin and related to Middle High German *notten* 'move about, shake'. The noun dates from the mid 16th century. The expression *nod off* 'fall asleep' is first recorded in Dickens's *The Chimes*: This cosy couple ... sat looking at the glowing sparks that dropped into the grate; now nodding off into a doze; now waking up again. The parliamentary phrase *nod through* (meaning record the vote of an MP who is within the precincts of Westminster but has not passed through the voting lobby because of illness or disability) dates from the 1970s.

node [late Middle English] A *node* was first recorded as 'a knotty swelling or a protuberance'; it is from Latin *nodus* 'knot'. The word **nodule**, also late Middle English, is from Latin *nodulus*, a diminutive of *nodus* 'knot'.

noise [Middle English] Early use of this word included the sense 'quarrelling': it is from Old French, from Latin *nausea* 'seasickness'. The sense development would appear to be from 'seasickness' to 'unease' to 'dispute' to 'din'. In technical applications, *noise* is a collective term for 'disturbances (interfering with the transfer of information)', e.g. *visual noise* in photography caused by graininess, *video noise* (= snow effect).
→ NAUSEA

noisome [late Middle English] This literary word meaning 'noxious, disagreeable, having an offensive smell' is based on obsolete *noy*, a shortened form of *annoy*.

nomad [late 16th century] *Nomad* is from French *nomade*, via Latin from Greek *nomas, nomad-* 'roaming in search of pasture', from the base of *nemein* 'to pasture'.

nomenclature [early 17th century] This comes from French, from Latin *nomenclatura*. The formative elements are *nomen* 'name' and *clatura* 'calling, summoning' (from *calare* 'to call').

nominate [late Middle English] Latin *nominat-* (the past participial stem of *nominare* 'to name') is the source of *nominate*, from *nomen, nomin-* 'a name'. It was originally used participially meaning 'called'; the verb senses are first found in English from the 16th century. **Nominee** (mid 17th century) is based on *nominate*. **Nomination**, a late Middle English word, is from Latin *nominatio(n-)*, from the verb *nominare*. The grammar term **nominative** (late Middle English) is from Latin *nominativus* 'relating to naming', a translation of Greek *onomastikē* (*ptōsis*) 'naming (case)'.

WORDBUILDING

The prefix **non-** [from Latin *non* 'not'] adds the sense

■ **not involved with** [non-aggression]

■ **not of the kind described** [non-believer]

■ **not of the importance implied** [non-issue]

■ **a lack of** [non-aggression]

■ **not in the way described** [non-uniformly]

■ **not causing** [non-skid]

■ **not requiring** [non-iron]

non- is also used when there is a need to make a differentiation with words prefixed by **un-** or **in-** [non-human / inhuman]

---

nonce [Middle English] *Nonce* (e.g. *nonce word, for the nonce*) is from *then anes* 'the one (purpose)', altered by misdivision; *newt* and *nickname* are similar formations. The word *nonce* used as a slang term from the 1970s for a person convicted of a sexual offence, is of unknown origin.

nonchalant [mid 18th century] This is an English use of a French word meaning literally 'not being concerned', from the verb *nonchaloir*; the *chaloir* element is from Latin *calere* 'be warm, be roused with zeal'.

nondescript [late 17th century] The sense in early scientific and medical examples of *nondescript* was 'not previously described or identified': it is formed from *non-* and obsolete *descript* 'described, engraved' (from Latin *descriptus*). The sense 'dull, drab, characterless' dates from the mid 19th century.

none [Old English] Old English *nān*, from *ne* 'not' and *ān* 'one' is Germanic in origin. German *nein!* 'no!' is a corresponding form.

nonentity [late 16th century] This word is from medieval Latin *nonentitas* 'non-existence'.

nonplus [late 16th century] This is from Latin *non plus* 'not more'. The noun originally meant 'a state in which no more can be said or done'. The verb (e.g. *competely nonplussed*) conveys the notion of being perplexed to the point of not being able to rationalize any further.

nook [Middle English] This word in early use referred to a corner or fragment. The origin is unknown. The word may be the base of **nooky**, an informal early 20th-century term for 'sexual activity'.

noon [Old English] Old English *nōn* meant 'the ninth hour from sunrise, i.e. approximately 3 p.m.', from Latin *nona* (*hora*) 'ninth hour'. The time change from 3 o'clock to midday appears to have occurred in English by the 14th century. There may be a connection with the time that *nones* were held: these were prayers said at the ninth hour of the day as part of the Divine Office, generally thought to be held at 3 in the afternoon but in recent research thought to have taken place closer to midday in Benedict's order in Italy, a practice which eventually spread to other orders.

noose [late Middle English] The word *noose* is probably via Old French *no(u)s* from Latin *nodus* 'knot'. It has only been in common use since 1600.

nor [Middle English] *Nor* is a contraction of Old English *nother* 'neither'.

normal [mid 17th century] This word comes from Latin *normalis*, from *norma* 'carpenter's square'. The early sense was 'right-angled'; current senses date from the early 19th century. **Norm**, also from Latin *norma* 'precept, rule, carpenter's square', dates from the early 19th century.

north [Old English] Of Germanic origin, *north* is related to Dutch *noord* and German *nord*. **Northern** was also found in Old English as *northerne*.

nose [Old English] Old English *nosu* is West Germanic in origin; and related to Dutch *neus*, and more remotely to German *Nase*, Latin *nasus*, and Sanskrit *nāsā*. Of the common expressions using the word *nose*: the phrase *follow one's nose* dates from the late 16th century; *poke one's nose into* dates from the early 17th century; *pay through the nose* is late 17th-century; *turn one's nose up at* is late 18th-century; *keep one's nose clean* is late 19th-century; *thumb one's nose at* is found from the early 20th century; *get up one's nose* originated in the 1950s. The compound:

■ **nosegay** (late Middle English) describing a small sweet-scented bunch of flowers is based on *nose*; the second element *gay* is in the obsolete sense 'ornament'.

■ **nosy parker** (early 20th century) is from the picture postcard caption: 'The adventures of Nosey Parker', referring to a peeping Tom in Hyde Park.

nosh [early 20th century] This Yiddish word was first found as a word for a snack bar. The sense 'food' dates from the 1960s.

nostalgia [late 18th century] The early sense of this word in English was 'acute homesickness'. It is modern Latin (translating German *Heimweh* 'homesickness'), from Greek *nostos* 'return home' and *algos* 'pain'.

nostril [Old English] Old English *nosterl*, *nosthyrl* is from *nosu* 'nose' and *thȳr(e)l* 'hole'.

not [Middle English] *Not* is a contraction of the adverb *nought*, a variant spelling of *naught* dating from Old English meaning literally 'no thing'.

notable [Middle English] This is from Old French, from Latin *notabilis* 'worthy of note', from the verb *notare* 'to note, mark'. **Notability** (late Middle English) is from Old French *notabilité* or late Latin *notabilitas*, from *notabilis*.

notary [Middle English] An early *notary* was a 'clerk or secretary'; it is from Latin *notarius* 'secretary', from *nota* 'mark'.

notch [mid 16th century] *Notch* is probably from Anglo-Norman French *noche*, a variant of Old French *osche*, of unknown origin.

note [Middle English] The early senses found were 'a single musical tone' and, as a verb, 'pay

particular attention to'. The word came via Old French from Latin *nota* 'a mark' and *notare* 'to mark': these forms are the base too of **notation** (late 16th century, from Latin *notatio(n-)*). **Notate** is recorded from the early 20th century as a back-formation (by removal of the suffix) from *notation*.

notice [late Middle English] The early sense recorded was 'warning of something'. The source is an Old French word, from Latin *notitia* 'being known', from *notus* 'known'.
→ NOTION

notify [late Middle English] This word is from Old French *notifier*, from Latin *notificare* 'make known', from *notus* 'known' and *facere* 'make'.
→ NOTION

notion [late Middle English] *Notion* is from Latin *notio(n-)* 'idea' (= the knowledge of something), from *notus*, the past participle of *noscere* 'know'. Late Middle English **notional** had the same sense as its source, medieval Latin *notionalis* 'relating to an idea', from *notio(n-)*.

notorious [late 15th century] The early sense recorded was 'generally known'. *Notorious* is based on medieval Latin *notorius*, from Latin *notus* 'known'.

noun [late Middle English] This grammatical term comes from Anglo-Norman French, from Latin *nomen* 'name'.

nourish [Middle English] *Nourish* is from Old French *noriss-*, the lengthened stem of *norir*, from Latin *nutrire* 'feed, cherish'.

nous [late 17th century] The informal word *nous* meaning 'common sense' was first recorded as a term in philosophy for 'the intellect'. It comes from a Greek word meaning 'mind, intelligence, intuitive apprehension'.

novel[1] [mid 16th century] The *novel* of literary contexts is from Italian *novella* (*storia*) 'new (story)', the feminine of *novello* 'new'; the base is Latin *novellus*, from *novus* 'new'. It described a 'short narrative' forming part of a series as in Boccaccio's *Decameron*; later (mid 17th century) it acquired the modern sense, 'a long fictitious prose narrative'. In non-literary contexts, the word *novel* was found earlier (from late Middle English until the 18th century) in the sense 'a novelty, a piece of news', from Old French *novelle*.
→ NOVEL[2]

novel[2] [late Middle English] Early use of the word was in the sense 'recent'; it comes via Old French from Latin *novellus*, from *novus* 'new'. The sense 'previously unknown, original' is found from the late 15th century. Late Middle

English **novelty** is from Old French *novelte*, from *novel* 'new, fresh'.

novice [Middle English] *Novice* is from Old French, from late Latin *novicius*, a base (from Latin *novus* 'new') shared by early 17th-century **novitiate** from ecclesiastical Latin *noviciatus*.

now [Old English] Old English *nū* is from a Germanic source; related forms are Dutch *nu*, German *nun*, from an Indo-European root shared by Latin *nunc* and Greek *nun*.

noxious [late 15th century] This word meaning 'harmful' is based on Latin *noxius*, from *noxa* 'harm'.

nozzle [early 17th century] *Nozzle* is based on *nose*. It was used as a slang term for 'nose' from the late 18th century.
→ NOSE

nuance [late 18th century] The French word *nuance* meaning 'shade, subtlety' has been adopted into English. It is from *nuer* 'to shade', based on Latin *nubes* 'cloud'.

nub [late 17th century] *Nub* is apparently a variant of dialect *knub* 'protuberance', from Middle Low German *knubbe*, *knobbe* 'knob'. The early sense led to the extension 'salient point, crux' (e.g. *nub of the matter*) in the mid 19th century.

nubile [mid 17th century] *Nubile* is from Latin *nubilis* 'marriageable', from *nubere* 'cover or veil oneself for a bridegroom'. The base is Latin *nubes* 'cloud'.
→ NUPTIAL

nucleus [early 18th century] This word comes from a Latin word with the literal meaning 'kernel, inner part': it is a diminutive of *nux*, *nuc-* 'nut'. It forms the base of the adjective **nuclear**, recorded from the mid 19th century. The colloquial abbreviation **nuke** dates from the 1950s, used to mean both 'nuclear bomb' and 'attack with a nuclear weapon'.

nude [late Middle English] 'Plain, explicit' was the early meaning of *nude* which comes from Latin *nudus*. The current sense 'naked' is first found in noun use in the early 18th century. **Nuddy** is a humorous alteration of *nude* dating from the 1950s.

nudge [late 17th century] In Norwegian dialect *nugga*, *nyggja* means 'to push, rub'. There may be a connection; it was in much earlier use than the English word *nudge*, the origin of which remains unknown.

nugget [mid 19th century] *Nugget* is apparently from dialect *nug* 'lump', the origin of which is unknown.

nuisance [late Middle English] 'Injury, hurt' was the early sense of *nuisance* from the Old French noun *nuisance* 'hurt'. The source is the verb *nuire*, from Latin *nocere* 'to harm' The use of *nuisance* to mean 'causing annoyance' was a mid 17th-century development.

null [late Middle English] French *nul, nulle* is the source of the English word, from Latin *nullus* 'none', from *ne* 'not' and *ullus* 'any'.

numb [late Middle English] The early spelling was *nome(n)*, the past participle of obsolete *nim* 'take', the notion being of power or sensation 'taken' away from a limb or faculty.

number [Middle English] The noun *number* is from Old French *nombre*; the verb is from Old French *nombrer*. The base, Latin *numerus* 'a number', is shared by late Middle English **numerous** (from Latin *numerosus*) and the contemporaneous **numeral** (from late Latin *numeralis*). It is also shared by **numerable** (mid 16th century from Latin *numerabilis*, from *numerare* 'to number'), and **numerical** (early 17th century from medieval Latin *numericus*). **Numerate** dates from the 1950s and is from Latin *numerus* on the pattern of *literate*.

nun [Old English] Old English *nonne* is from ecclesiastical Latin *nonna*, the feminine of *nonnus* 'monk', reinforced by Old French *nonne*.

nuptial [late 15th century] *Nuptial* is from Old French, or from Latin *nuptialis*, from *nuptiae* 'wedding', from *nubere* 'to wed'.
→ NUBILE

nurse [late Middle English] *Nurse* is a contraction of the earlier word *nourice*, from Old French, from late Latin *nutricia*: this is the feminine of Latin *nutricius* '(person) that nourishes', from *nutrix*, *nutric-* 'nurse' (from *nutrire* 'nourish'). The word was originally applied in English to a 'wet-nurse'. The verb was originally a contraction of *nourish*, altered under the influence of the noun. Late Middle English **nursery** is based on Old French *nourice* 'nurse'; its use in horticultural contexts for a 'place where young plants are reared' dates from the mid 16th century.

nurture [Middle English] *Nurture* is from Old French *noureture* 'nourishment', based on Latin *nutrire* 'feed, cherish'. It is often used in combination with the word *nature* as a determinant factor in the development of personality.

nut [Old English] Old English *hnutu* is Germanic in origin; Dutch *noot* and German *Nuss* are related. *Nut* came to be used as a slang term for 'head' in the mid 19th century, the time when the informal word **nuts** meaning 'crazy' is recorded; **nutty**, used in the same sense, is found towards the end of that century.

nutmeg [late Middle English] The early spelling was *notemuge*, a partial translation of Old French *nois muguede*, based on Latin *nux* 'nut' and late Latin *muscus* 'musk'.

nutrition [late Middle English] Latin *nutrire* 'feed, nourish' is the source of *nutrition* (from late Latin *nutritio(n-)*) and two other late Middle English words: **nutritive** (from medieval Latin *nutritivus*), and **nutriment** (from Latin *nutrimentum*). **Nutrient** and **nutritious** are both recorded from the mid 17th century: *nutrient* is from Latin *nutrient-*, the present participial stem of *nutrire*; *nutritious* is based on Latin *nutritius* 'that nourishes' (from *nutrex* 'a nurse').

nuzzle [late Middle English] The early sense recorded was 'grovel'; the word is a frequentative (= verb of repeated action) from *nose*, reinforced by Dutch *neuzelen* 'poke with the nose'.

nylon [1930s] This is an invented word, on the pattern of *cotton* and *rayon*. Its use in the plural for 'stockings' made of *nylon* dates from the 1940s.

nymph [late Middle English] *Nymph* is from Old French *nimphe* via Latin from Greek *numphē* 'nymph, bride'. Latin *nubere* 'be the wife of' is related. The word originally described a semi-divine spirit of classical mythology, thought to take the form of a maiden inhabiting places such as the sea, rivers, hills, and trees. Usage in the sense 'beautiful young woman' is recorded from the late 16th century; **nymphet**, based on *nymph* came to be used for an attractive young girl from the 1950s.

Oo

oaf [early 17th century] *Oaf* is a variant of obsolete *auf*, from Old Norse *álfr* 'elf'. The original meaning was 'elf's child, changeling', later developing to 'idiot child' and 'halfwit', notions which became generalized in the current sense (early 20th century) 'large clumsy man' (Rudyard Kipling *Islanders*: Then ye contented your souls With the flanelled fools at the wicket or the muddied oafs at the goals).

oak [Old English] Old English *āc* is from a Germanic source. It is related to Dutch *eik* and German *Eiche*, as well as to Latin *aesculus* 'species of oak sacred to Jupiter; mountain oak'. The horse race known as *the Oaks*, founded in 1779, owes its name to the estate of the 12th Earl of Derby who owned the first winner of this annual event for 3-year-old fillies run at Epsom on the Friday after the Derby.

oar [Old English] Danish and Norwegian *åre* are related to this Old English word of Germanic origin. The phrase *put one's oar in* meaning 'interfere' dates from the mid 16th century.

oasis [early 17th century] *Oasis* came via late Latin from Greek from an Egyptian word; it originally referred specifically to a fertile place in the Libyan desert. The figurative notion of 'a place of calm' dates from the early 19th century.

oast [Old English] Old English *āst* originally referred to any kiln before it was specifically applied to a kiln for drying malt and then for drying hops. Of Germanic origin, it is related to Dutch *eest*, from an Indo-European root meaning 'burn'.

oat [Old English] The origin of Old English *āte* (plural *ātan*) is unknown. Unlike other names of cereals (such as *wheat*, *barley*, etc.), *oat* is not a mass noun and may originally have denoted the individual grain: this may imply that oats were eaten in grains and not as meal. The slang use of the plural *oats* in the sense 'sexual gratification' (e.g. *have one's oats*, *sow one's wild oats*) is found from the 1920s.

oath [Old English] Old English *āth* 'solemn declaration', of Germanic origin, is related to Dutch *eed* and German *Eid*. The sense 'expletive, curse' dates from Middle English.

WORDBUILDING

The prefix **ob-** [from Latin *ob* 'towards, against, in the way of'] adds the sense

- **exposing** [obverse]
- **meeting** [occasion]
- **opposing** [opponent]
- **hindrance** [obviate]
- **completion** [obsolete]
- **inversely** [obconical]

---

obdurate [late Middle English] The original sense was 'hardened in sin, impenitent', the source being Latin *obduratus* 'hardened in heart', the past participle of *obdurare*. Here the elements are *ob-* 'in opposition' and *durare* 'harden' (from *durus* 'hard').

obelisk [mid 16th century] This word came via Latin from Greek *obeliskos*, a diminutive of *obelos* 'pointed pillar'. From the late 16th century it was also used as a term in printing (synonymous with *obelus*) for a dagger-shaped mark signifying obsolete use in some dictionaries.

obese [mid 17th century] *Obese* is from Latin *obesus* 'that has eaten itself fat', from *ob-* 'away, completely' and *esus* (the past participle of *edere* 'to eat').

obey [Middle English] *Obey* comes from Old French *obeir*, from Latin *oboedire* 'listen, pay attention to', from *ob-* 'in the direction of' and *audire* 'hear'. The same Latin verb gave rise, in the same period, to **obedience** (via Old French from Latin *oboedientia*) and **obedient** (also via Old French).

obfuscate [late Middle English] *Obfuscate* 'render obscure' is from late Latin *obfuscare* 'darken', based on Latin *fuscus* 'dark'.

obituary [early 18th century] This word for a 'notice of a death' (originally a 'register of deaths') is from medieval Latin *obituarius*, from Latin *obitus* 'death': this is from Latin *obire* 'to perish'. The word **obit** was already long in use from late Middle English; it is now regarded as an abbreviation of *obituary*, but originally it was also used in the senses 'death' and 'funeral service', from Latin *obitus* 'going down, death'.

object [late Middle English] *Object* is from medieval Latin *objectum* 'a thing presented to the mind', the neuter past participle (used as a noun) of Latin *obicere*, from *ob-* 'in the way of' and *jacere* 'to throw'. The phrase *no object* meaning 'not something aimed at or of significance', as in *money is no object*, dates from the late 18th century. The verb *to object* may also partly represent the Latin frequentative (= verb of repeated action) *objectare*, literally 'keep throwing against'. The related late Middle English noun **objection** is from Old French, or from late Latin *objectio(n-)* from *obicere*; **objective** is recorded from the early 17th century and is from medieval Latin *objectivus*, from *objectum*.

oblige [Middle English] 'Bind by oath' was the sense found for *oblige* in early examples. Old French *obliger* is the source, from Latin *obligare*, the elements of which are *ob-* 'towards' and *ligare* 'to bind'. The expression of gratitude *much obliged* dates from the early 19th century, first recorded in Jane Austen's *Letters*: Sackree is pretty well again, only weak;—much obliged to you for your message. The Latin verb *obligare* is also the base of **obligation** which, in Middle English, had the sense 'formal promise': it comes via Old French from Latin *obligatio(n-)*.

oblique [late Middle English] *Oblique* is from Latin *obliquus*. It is probably related to Latin *limus* 'transverse'. The figurative use 'not taking the direct course; indirect' is recorded in the same early period.

obliterate [mid 16th century] This is from Latin *obliterare* 'strike out, erase', based on *littera* 'letter, something written'. The figurative use 'get rid of from the mind' is found from the latter part of the 16th century.

oblivion [late Middle English] *Oblivion* came via Old French from Latin *oblivio(n-)*, from *oblivisci* 'forget'. In legal use the word has been used in the phrase *Act of (Indemnity and) Oblivion* referring to 'amnesty': in English historical contexts it was specifically applied to the Acts of 1660 and 1690, exempting those who had taken up arms against Charles II and William III respectively from the consequences of their actions. **Oblivious**, from the same period, is from Latin *obliviosus*, from *oblivio(n-)*. The first meaning recorded was 'forgetful, forgetting'; it was at the beginning of the 19th century that the sense 'unaware' occurred in examples.

oblong [late Middle English] *Oblong* is from Latin *oblongus* 'longish'. The noun dates from the early 17th century.

obnoxious [late 16th century] The early sense recorded was 'vulnerable' to harm of some sort (e.g. *obnoxious to criticism*); the origin is Latin *obnoxiosus*, from *obnoxius* 'exposed to

harm', from *ob-* 'towards' and *noxa* 'harm'. The current sense 'highly unpleasant and disagreeable', influenced by the sense conveyed by *noxious*, dates from the late 17th century.

obscene [late 16th century] *Obscene* is from French *obscène* or Latin *obscaenus* 'ill-omened or abominable' and, by transference, 'disgusting, indecent' (Shakespeare *Richard II*: That in a Christian climate souls refined, Should show so heinous black, obscene a deed). **Obscenity** from the same period is from French *obscénité* or Latin *obscaenitas*, from *obscaenus*.

obscure [late Middle English] This word conveying characteristics of both gloom and vagueness is from Old French *obscur*, from Latin *obscurus* 'dark', from an Indo-European root meaning 'cover'. The meaning 'insignificant, not illustrious' in describing a person dates from the mid 16th century. Late Middle English **obscurity** is from Old French *obscurite*, from Latin *obscuritas*, from *obscurus*.

obsequious [late 15th century] There is a notion of 'servility' in the modern word that did not exist in early use when it expressed 'prompt to serve and please' which was not depreciatory. The source is Latin *obsequiosus*, from *obsequium* 'compliance', from *obsequi* 'follow, comply with'.

observe [late Middle English] 'Comply with' was the sense in early examples (e.g. *all must observe the rules*). It is from Old French *observer*, from Latin *observare* 'to watch, pay attention to', from *ob-* 'towards' and *servare* 'attend to'. The sense 'make a comment' (as in '*Curious!*', *he observed*) dates from the early 17th century. **Observation**, late Middle English in the sense 'respectful adherence to the requirements of (rules, a ritual, etc.)', is from Latin *observatio(n-)*, from the verb *observare*. **Observance** is recorded slightly earlier and came via Old French from Latin *observantia*, from *observare*. Late Middle English **observant** is from the French *observant* meaning literally 'watching', the present participle of *observer*. The sense 'perceptive; attentive to detail' dates from the late 16th century. **Observatory** dates from the late 17th century and is from modern Latin *observatorium*, from Latin *observat-*, the past participial stem of *observare*.

obsess [late Middle English] *Obsess* had the early sense 'haunt, possess', referring to an evil spirit. It comes from Latin *obsess-*, the past participial stem of *obsidere* 'besiege': the formative elements are *ob-* 'opposite' and *sedere* 'sit'. The current sense 'fill the mind of' dates from the late 19th century. **Obsession** (early 16th century in the sense 'siege') is from Latin *obsessio(n-)*, from the verb *obsidere*. Use of the word for an 'idea which fills and troubles the mind' is found from the late 17th century, and as a term in psychology from the early 20th century.

obsolete [late 16th century] This word comes from Latin *obsoletus* meaning 'grown old, worn out': it is the past participle of *obsolescere* 'fall into disuse'. The noun **obsolescence** is recorded from the mid 18th century and means literally 'a (process of) falling into disuse', from the Latin verb *obsolescere*.

obstacle [Middle English] *Obstacle* came via Old French from Latin *obstaculum*, from *obstare* 'impede'. The elements here are *ob-* 'against' and *stare* 'stand'.

obstetric [mid 18th century] This is from modern Latin *obstetricus* from Latin *obstetricius* (based on *obstetrix* 'midwife'). The Latin verb *obstare* 'be present' is the base.

obstinate [Middle English] Latin *obstinatus*, the past participle of *obstinare* 'persist' is the source of *obstinate* in English. From the late 16th century, *obstinate* was applied in a specialized sense to disease meaning 'not responding readily to treatment'.

obstreperous [late 16th century] 'Clamorous, vociferous' was the meaning of *obstreperous* in early examples. The base is Latin *obstreperus* (from *obstrepere*), the base elements being *ob-* 'against' and *strepere* 'make a noise'.

obstruct [late 16th century] *Obstruct* is from Latin *obstruct-*, the past participial stem of *obstruere* 'block up', from *ob-* 'against' and *struere* 'pile up'. The noun **obstruction** is recorded slightly later, from Latin *obstructio(n-)*, from the verb *obstruere*.

obtain [late Middle English] The verb *obtain* is from Old French *obtenir*, from Latin *obtinere* 'obtain, gain'. Intransitive use of the verb in the sense 'hold good, be prevalent' dates from the early 17th century (e.g. *the price of silver fell to that obtaining elsewhere in the ancient world*).

obtrude [mid 16th century] Latin *obtrudere* (from *ob-* 'towards' and *trudere* 'to push') is the source of both *obtrude* meaning 'become noticeable' and mid 17th-century **obtrusive**.

obtuse [late Middle English] 'Blunt' was the first recorded meaning of *obtuse* from Latin *obtusus*, the past participle of *obtundere* 'beat against'. The sense 'stupid' dates from the early 16th century.

obvious [late 16th century] The sense 'frequently encountered' was recorded in early examples. Latin *obvius* is the base, from the phrase *ob viam* 'in the way'. Use of the word

meaning 'plain and evident to the mind' is first found in mid 17th-century examples.

occasion [late Middle English] *Occasion* 'occurrence, opportunity' is from Latin *occasio(n-)* 'juncture, reason', from *occidere* 'go down, set'. The formative elements here are Latin *ob-* 'towards' and *cadere* 'to fall', giving a notion of a set of circumstances converging and being conducive to an event.

occult [late 15th century] Early use was as a verb meaning 'to cut off from view'. It is from Latin *occultare* 'to secrete', a frequentative (= verb of repeated action) of *occulere* 'conceal', based on *celare* 'to hide'. The adjective and noun are from *occult-*, the past participial stem of *occulere* 'cover over'. *The occult* meaning 'the realm of the unknown' is a phrase dating from the 1900s

occupy [Middle English] This is formed irregularly from Old French *occuper*, from Latin *occupare* 'to seize'. A now obsolete vulgar sense 'have sexual relations with' seems to have led to the general avoidance of the word in the 17th and most of the 18th century. Middle English **occupation** came via Old French from Latin *occupatio(n-)*, from the verb *occupare*. The sense 'fill the mind' dates from the mid 16th century. **Occupant** dates from the late 16th century in legal contexts as a term for a 'person who establishes a title': this is from French, or from Latin *occupant-*, the present participial stem of *occupare* 'seize'.

occur [late 15th century] *Occur* is from Latin *occurrere* 'go to meet, present itself', from *ob-* 'against' and *currere* 'to run'. Use of the word to mean 'spring to mind as an idea' is found from the early 17th century. Mid 16th-century **occurrence** is probably from the plural of archaic *occurrent* used in the same sense: this comes via French from the present participial stem of Latin *occurrere* 'befall'.

ocean [Middle English] *Ocean* is from Old French *occean*, via Latin from Greek *ōkeanos* 'great stream encircling the earth's disc'. *The ocean* originally described the whole body of water ('the Great Outer Sea') regarded as encompassing the earth's single land mass: this was the Eastern hemisphere with its islands, the only land known.

ocular [late 16th century] *Ocular* is from late Latin *ocularis*, from Latin *oculus* 'eye', a base shared by **oculist** from French *oculiste*, recorded in the same period.

odd [Middle English] Early use was in contexts of number. The word is from Old Norse *odda-*, found in combinations such as *odda-mathr* 'third or odd man', from *oddi* 'angle'. The sense 'strange, peculiar' dates from the late 16th century (Shakespeare *Measure for Measure*: If she be mad … Her madness hath the oddest frame of sense). **Odds** is recorded from the early 16th century and is apparently the plural of the obsolete noun *odd* 'odd number or odd person'. It came to be used in betting contexts towards the end of the 16th century. The phrase *against all the odds* dates from the mid 18th century. **Oddment**, based on *odd*, is found from the late 18th century.

ode [late 16th century] *Ode* is from French, from late Latin *oda*, from Greek *ōidē*, an Attic form of *aoidē* 'song', from *ueidein* 'to sing'. In early use the word referred to ancient literature and poems intended to be sung (e.g. *Odes of Pindar*).

odious [late Middle English] The word *odious* is from Old French *odieus*, from Latin *odiosus*, from *odium* 'hatred'.

odour [Middle English] *Odour* is from Anglo-Norman French, from Latin *odor* 'smell, scent'. The spelling *odor* occurred occasionally in Middle English but became obsolete in the 14th century. Latin influence caused the spelling to reappear in the 16th century and become common in the 17th century. It has become usual in US English. Late Middle English **odorous** is based on Latin *odorus* 'fragrant' (from *odor* 'odour').

odyssey [late 19th century] This word for a long and eventful journey came via Latin from Greek *Odusseia*. This was the name of a Greek hexameter epic poem traditionally ascribed to Homer (8th century BC) , describing the travels of Odysseus during his ten years of wanderings after the sack of Troy.

of [Old English] Of Germanic origin, English *of* is related to Dutch *af* and German *ab*, from an Indo-European root shared by Latin *ab* and Greek *apo*. The primary sense was 'away from'. It came to mainly express the notions: removal, separation, privation, derivation, origin, and cause.
→ OFF

off [Old English] This was originally a variant of the preposition *of*, which combined the senses 'of' and 'off': these two forms were not differentiated till after 1600. Of the phrases: *they're off*, in horse racing, dates from the early 19th century; *it's a bit off* meaning 'it's unacceptable, or peculiar' is found from the early 20th century.

offal [late Middle English] In early use *offal* referred to 'refuse from a process' such as husks from milling grain, chips from carpentry. It was probably suggested by Middle Dutch *afval*, from *af* 'off' and *vallen* 'to fall'. The sense 'edible internal organs of a carcass' arose early but the word was usually plural.

offence [late Middle English] *Offence* is from Old French *offens* 'misdeed', from Latin *offensus* 'annoyance'. It was reinforced by French *offense*, from Latin *offensa* 'a striking against, a hurt, or displeasure'. The base is Latin *offendere* 'strike against' which (via Old French *offendre*) also gave **offend** in late Middle English; the latter's senses encompassed 'stumble', 'stumble morally' (= sin), 'transgress a law', 'attack', and 'harm'. The related form **offensive** is found from the mid 16th century; it comes from French *offensif*, *-ive* or medieval Latin *offensivus*, from Latin *offendere*. Use as a noun (as in *on the offensive*) dates from the early 18th century.

offer [Old English] Old English *offrian* meant 'sacrifice (something) to a god'. Of Germanic origin, it is from Latin *offerre* 'bestow, present', which in ecclesiastical Latin became 'offer to God'; it was reinforced by French *offrir* which continued to express the primary sense. The noun (late Middle English) is from French *offre*. The Christian Church term **offertory** describing an offering of bread and wine or a collection of money made at a religious service, dates from late Middle English and is from ecclesiastical Latin *offertorium* 'offering'. It is from late Latin *offert-* (which replaced Latin *oblat-*, the past participial stem of *offerre* 'to offer').

office [Middle English] *Office* came via Old French from Latin *officium* 'performance of a task', which in medieval Latin also meant 'divine service'. The formative elements are *opus* 'work' and *facere* 'do'. As well as being 'a duty', a 'kindness' (W. S. Maugham *Of Human Bondage*: He got her slippers and took off her boots. It delighted him to perform menial offices), the word is transferred in sense to the 'position to which duties are attached' (e.g. *office of parish priest*) and 'the place where duties are performed' (e.g. *an office on the third floor*). Middle English **officer** came via Anglo-Norman French from medieval Latin *officiarius*, from Latin *officium*, a base shared by Middle English **official** (via Old French from Latin *officialis*). The word **officiate** dates from the mid 17th century and is from medieval Latin *officiare* 'perform divine service', from *officium*.

officious [late 15th century] *Officious* is from Latin *officiosus* 'obliging', from *officium*. The original sense was 'performing its function, efficacious', which in the mid 16th century became 'ready to help or please'; later that century the word came to be used in a depreciatory way.
→ OFFICE

often [Middle English] *Often* is an extended form of *oft*, probably influenced by *selden* 'seldom'. Early examples appear to be northern English; the word became general in the 16th century. The phrase *as often as not* is found from the beginning of the 20th century; *more often than not* dates from the 1970s.

ogle [late 17th century] *Ogle* is probably from Low German or Dutch; Low German *oegeln*, a frequentative (= verb of repeated action) of *oegen* 'look at' may be associated. It first appeared in English as a cant word.

ogre [early 18th century] This is an adoption of a French word first used by the French writer Perrault in his narrative tales in 1697. The base is classical Latin *Orcus*, Hades, the god of the infernal regions.

oil [Middle English] *Oil* is from Old Northern French *olie*, Old French *oile*, from Latin *oleum* '(olive) oil'. The notion of *midnight oil* as a metaphor for late study in the light of an oil lamp (e.g. *burn the midnight oil*) dates from the mid 17th century; *oil the wheels* for 'cause to run more smoothly' is found from the late 19th century.

ointment [Middle English] This is an alteration of Old French *oignement*, from a popular Latin form of Latin *unguentum*. The change in form was influenced by obsolete *oint* 'anoint', from the past participle of Old French *oindre* 'anoint'.
➜ UNCTION

OK [mid 19th century] This was originally a US usage and is probably an abbreviation of *orl korrect*, a humorous form of *all correct*, popularized as a slogan during President Van Buren's re-election campaign of 1840 in the US. His nickname *Old Kinderhook*, derived from his birthplace, provided the initials.

old [Old English] Old English *ald* is West Germanic in origin, related to Dutch *oud* and German *alt*, from an Indo-European root meaning 'grown-up, adult', shared by Latin *alere* 'nourish'. The noun **oldster** arose in the early 19th century, based on *old* on the pattern of *youngster*.

olive [Middle English] This word came via Old French from Latin *oliva*, from Greek *elaia*, from *elaion* 'oil'. The cookery term in phrases such as *beef olive* dates from the late 16th century.

ombudsman [1950s] This term for an official appointed to investigate individuals' complaints against maladministration is the adoption of a Swedish word for 'legal representative'.

omen [late 16th century] This is an English use of a Latin word. **Ominous** dates from the same period and is from Latin *ominosus*, from *omen*.

omit [late Middle English] *Omit* is from Latin *omittere*, from *ob-* 'down' and *mittere* 'let go'. **Omission**, from the same period, is from late Latin *omissio(n-)*, from the same Latin source verb.

omnibus [early 19th century] *Omnibus* came via French from a Latin word meaning literally 'for all', the dative plural of *omnis* 'all'. It was originally a horse-drawn vehicle.

omnipotent [Middle English] Originally used as an attribute with the names of gods (e.g. *O God omnipotent!*), omnipotent came via Old French from Latin *omnipotent-* 'all-powerful'.

omniscient [early 17th century] This is from medieval Latin *omniscient-* 'all-knowing', based on Latin *scire* 'to know'.

omnivorous [mid 17th century] Literally 'all-eating', *omnivorous* is based on Latin *omnivorus* 'omnivorous'. Late 19th-century **omnivore** came via French from the same Latin adjective.

on [Old English] Old English *on*, *an* is Germanic in origin, related to Dutch *aan* and German *an*, from an Indo-European root shared by Greek *ana* 'upon'.

once [Middle English] The early spelling was *ones*, the genitive of *one*. The spelling change in the 16th century was in order to retain the unvoiced sound (= pronounced without vibration of the vocal cords) of the final consonant.
➜ ONE

one [Old English] Old English *ān* is Germanic in origin, related to Dutch *een* and German *ein*, from an Indo-European root shared by Latin *unus*. The initial *w* sound in the pronunciation developed before the 15th century and was occasionally represented in the spelling; it was not accepted into standard English until the late 17th century.

onerous [late Middle English] This word meaning 'burdensome' is from Old French *onereus*, from Latin *onerosus*, from *onus*, *oner-* 'burden'. In the mid 17th century the word **onus** started to be used in English as an adoption from Latin.

only [Old English] The Old English adjective *ānlic* is based on *one* suffixed with *-ly*.
➜ ONE

onslaught [early 17th century] Early use included the spelling *anslaight*: it comes from Middle Dutch *aenslag*, from *aen* 'on' and *slag* 'blow'. The change in the ending was due to association with the now obsolete word *slaught* meaning 'slaughter'.

ooze¹ [Old English] Old English *wōs* meant 'juice or sap'; the verb meaning 'trickle' dates from late Middle English.

ooze² [Old English] This *ooze* meaning 'mud at the bottom of a river or lake' was *wāse* in Old English; it is related to Old Norse *veisa* 'stagnant pool'. In Middle English and the 16th century, the spelling was *wose* (rhyming with *repose*), but from 1550 spellings imply a change in pronunciation and influence by *ooze* 'seeping'.
→ OOZE¹

opaque [late Middle English] The early spelling was *opake*, from Latin *opacus* 'darkened'. The current spelling (rare before the 19th century) has been influenced by the French form *opaque*. The noun **opacity** found from the mid 16th century is from French *opacité*, from Latin *opacitas*, from *opacus*.

open [Old English] The Old English adjective was *open*, the verb was *openian*. Of Germanic origin, the word is related to Dutch *open* and German *offen*, from the root of the adverb *up*.
→ UP

opera [mid 17th century] This is the adoption of Italian *opera* from a Latin word meaning literally 'labour, work'. The earliest examples in English consciously use the Italian word. **Operatic** is recorded from the mid 18th century, an irregular formation from *opera*, on the pattern of words such as *dramatic*. **Operetta** is a late 18th-century form from an Italian diminutive of *opera*.

operation [late Middle English] The noun *operation* came via Old French from Latin *operatio(n-)*, from the verb *operari* 'expend labour on'. The association with surgical procedures arose early. Latin *operari* also gave rise to the verb **operate** in the early 17th century. The base is Latin *opus*, *oper-* 'work'. Related words are mid 17th-century **operable** (from late Latin *operabilis*) and late Middle English **operative** (from Latin *operativus*). Use of the latter to mean 'skilled worker' (e.g. *factory operatives*) dates from the early 19th century.

ophthalmic [early 17th century] This word 'relating to the eye' came via Latin from Greek *ophthalmikos*, from *ophthalmos* 'eye'.

opiate [late Middle English] *Opiate* 'relating to opium' is from medieval Latin *opiatus*, based on Latin *opium*. **Opium** came via Latin from Greek *opion* 'poppy juice', from *opos* 'juice', from an Indo-European root meaning 'water'.

opinion [Middle English] *Opinion* came via Old French from Latin *opinio(n-)*, from the stem of *opinari* 'think, believe'. **Opinionated** dates from the early 17th century and is from the (rare) verb *opinionate* 'hold the opinion (that)'.

opportune [late Middle English] *Opportune* is from Old French *opportun(e)*, from Latin *opportunus*, from *ob-* 'in the direction of' and *portus* 'harbour': the Latin word originally described the wind driving towards the harbour, hence the English sense 'seasonable'. Late Middle English **opportunity** shares the same base and is from Old French *opportunite*, from Latin *opportunitas*. **Opportunist** (late 19th century) is based on *opportune*.

oppose [late Middle English] *Oppose* is from Old French *opposer*, from Latin *opponere* (from *ob-* 'against' and *ponere* 'to place'). It was influenced by Latin *oppositus* 'set or placed against' and Old French *poser* 'to place'. The chief use of the verb in Middle English was to mean 'confront (a person) with hard questions' (from late Latin *opponere*). Modern use with the notion of 'placing in opposition' mainly reflects classical Latin *opponere*. **Opponent** (late 16th century) originally referred to a person opening an academic debate by proposing objections to a philosophical or religious thesis. The source is Latin *opponent-*, the present participial stem of *opponere* 'set against'.

opposite [late Middle English] This came via Old French from Latin *oppositus*, the past participle of *opponere* 'set against'. **Opposition**, a word from the same period, is from Latin *oppositio(n-)*, from *opponere*. Its use in political contexts in the phrase *the Opposition* referring to the political party opposed to the one in office, dates from the early 18th century.
→ OPPOSE

oppress [late Middle English] *Oppress* is from Old French *oppresser*, from medieval Latin *oppressare*, from Latin *opprimere* 'press against, smother'. The classical Latin senses were reflected in early use of the English word. The same Latin verb gave rise to Middle English **oppression** (from Old French, from Latin *oppressio(n-)*) and **oppressive** (late 16th century from medieval Latin *oppressivus*).

opprobrious [late Middle English] This word meaning 'expressing scorn' is from late Latin *opprobriosus*, from Latin *opprobrium* 'infamy' (a word eventually adopted into English in the mid 17th century). The base elements are *ob-* 'against' and *probrum* 'disgraceful act'.

optic [late Middle English] *Optic* is from French *optique* or medieval Latin *opticus*, from Greek *optikos*, from *optos* 'seen'. An *Optic* fastened to the neck of a bottle for measuring out spirits is a proprietary name dating from the 1920s. **Optician** dates from the late 17th century, from French *opticien*, from medieval Latin *optica* 'optics; science of sight'.

optimism [mid 18th century] *Optimism* is from French *optimisme*, from Latin *optimum* 'best thing' (a word adopted into English in the late 19th century). *Optimism* was originally a term in philosophy; its use to mean 'tendency to hope for the best' dates from the early 19th century (Shelley *Essays*: Let us believe in a kind of optimism, in which we are our own gods). The verb **optimize** dates from the early 19th century and is based on Latin *optimus* 'best' (thus giving 'make the best').

option [mid 16th century] This is either from French, or from Latin *optio(n-)*, from the stem of *optare* 'choose'. The idiomatic expression *keep one's options open* was first recorded in the 1960s. **Opt** is a late 19th-century word from French *opter*, from Latin *optare* 'choose, wish'. The phrase *opt out of* is recorded in examples from the 1920s.

opulent [mid 16th century] The early meaning was 'wealthy, affluent'. The Latin present participial stem *opulent-* is the source meaning 'wealthy, splendid', from *opes* 'wealth'.

or [Middle English] This is a reduced form of the obsolete conjunction *other*, which superseded Old English *oththe* 'or'. The ultimate origin is unknown.

oracle [late Middle English] *Oracle* came via Old French from Latin *oraculum*, from *orare* 'speak'. In Greek and Roman history, this was 'the mouthpiece of the gods' with the power to prophesy (e.g. *Delphic oracle*); later it came to mean 'a person of great wisdom' (Shakespeare *Merchant of Venice*: I am sir Oracle, And when I ope my lips, let no dog bark).

oral [early 17th century] Late Latin *oralis* (from Latin *os*, *or-* 'mouth') is the source of *oral* in English. Use of the word in educational contexts to mean 'oral examination' was a late 19th-century development.

orange [late Middle English] This comes from Old French *orenge* (used in the phrase *pomme d'orenge*), based on Arabic *nāranj* from Persian. The native home of the *orange* may have been south-east Asia, the possible source of the name originally. In the Middle Ages the Seville orange was brought by the Arabs to Sicily from where it was introduced to the rest of Europe. The sweet orange was brought from China by the Portuguese in the 16th century and ousted the bitter orange while taking its name.

oration [late Middle English] An *oration*, now commonly 'a formal speech', was originally 'a prayer to God'. It comes from Latin *oratio(n-)* 'discourse, prayer', from *orare* 'speak, pray'. Late Middle English **orator** is from Anglo-Norman French *oratour*, from Latin *orator* 'speaker, pleader'.

orb [late Middle English] An *orb* once denoted 'a circle'; it now means 'a spherical body'. It comes from Latin *orbis* 'ring'. In poetical and rhetorical use, the word sometimes denotes a star or planet (Shakespeare *Merchant of Venice*: There's not the smallest orb which thou beholdest but in his motion like an Angel sings).

orbit [mid 16th century] Early use was as an anatomical term for 'eye socket'. It comes from Latin *orbita* which originally meant 'course or track', but which in medieval Latin came to mean 'eye socket'; it is the feminine form of *orbitus* 'circular', from *orbis* 'ring'. Use in astronomy contexts dates from the late 17th century. The phrase *go into orbit* arose in the 1970s.

orchard [Old English] The Old English spelling was *ortgeard*. The first element is from Latin *hortus* 'garden'; the second represents *yard*. The word once referred generally to a garden.
→YARD²

orchestra [early 17th century] *Orchestra* came via Latin from Greek *orkhēstra*, from *orkheisthai* 'to dance'. As part of the ancient Greek theatre it was a large circular or semi-circular space in front of the stage where the chorus danced and sang. Use of the word for a group of instrumentalists performing concert music began in the early 18th century. The word forms the base of the verb **orchestrate** found from the late 19th century; it was perhaps suggested by French *orchestrer*. First used literally meaning 'compose for an orchestra', it later (in the 1950s) gained the transferred sense 'bring together, organize' (e.g. *orchestrated pandemonium*).

ordain [Middle English] One of the early meanings of the word was 'put in order'. It comes from Anglo-Norman French *ordeiner*, from Latin *ordinare* 'put in order', from *ordo* 'order'. Another semantic branch is 'decree, appoint'; this is seen in a specialized use of the verb in the Christian Church meaning 'confer holy orders on' in appointing someone to the office of priest or other sacred office. The noun **ordination** in late Middle English had the general sense 'arrangement in order': it comes from Latin *ordinatio(n-)*, from Latin *ordinare*.
→ORDER

ordeal [Old English] Old English *ordāl*, *ordēl* is Germanic in origin and related to German *urteilen* 'give judgement', from a base meaning 'share out'. The word is not found in Middle English (except once in Chaucer's *Troylus*); the use of *ordeal* to refer to a kind of test of guilt or innocence by subjecting someone to pain to elicit a divine verdict gave rise to the prime current sense 'a painfully difficult experience' (mid 17th century).

order [Middle English] *Order* is from Old French *ordre*, from Latin *ordo*, *ordin-* 'row, series, rank'. The semantic strands include: 'rank, group' (e.g. *orders of society; Franciscan order*); 'regulation, command' (e.g. *give orders*), and 'sequence' (e.g. *the right order*). The phrase *out of order* (mid 16th century) at first meant 'out of proper sequence' gradually extending to 'not in a settled condition' (commonly 'indisposed, not in good health' in the 18th century), and 'not working'.

ordinal [Middle English] An *ordinal* first referred to a service book containing the forms of service used at ordinations. It comes from medieval Latin *ordinale* (neuter). The adjective (e.g. *ordinal number*) is from late Latin *ordinalis* 'relating to order in a series', from Latin *ordo*, *ordin-*.
→ ORDER

ordinary [late Middle English] The adjective *ordinary* is from Latin *ordinarius* 'orderly' (reinforced by French *ordinaire*), from *ordo*, *ordin-* 'order'. Early use of the word conveyed the sense 'orderly, regular' as well as 'customary'.

ore [Old English] Old English *ōra* meant 'unwrought metal'. Of West Germanic origin, it was influenced in form by Old English *ār* 'bronze' (related to Latin *aes* 'crude metal, bronze').

organ [late Old English] *Organ* came via Latin from Greek *organon* 'tool, instrument, sense organ', reinforced in Middle English by Old French *organe*. The word was first adopted in the 'musical instrument' sense. It came to mean 'an instrument, functioning part' generally (Shakespeare *Merchant of Venice*: Hath not a Jew hands, organs, dementions, senses, affections, passions), the figurative use of this led to 'means (of action or communication)': e.g. *a newspaper thought to be the organ of the government*. The adjective **organic** is late Middle English and is via Latin from Greek *organikos* 'relating to an organ or instrument'; in the context of agriculture (e.g. *organic food*) the word has been used meaning 'produced without the use of artificial chemicals' from the mid 19th century.

organize [late Middle English] *Organize* is from medieval Latin *organizare*, from Latin *organum* 'instrument, tool'. The word **organism** (early 18th century in the sense 'organization') is from *organize*: current senses ('living body', 'individual life form') derive from French *organisme*.
→ ORGAN

orgy [early 16th century] This word was originally used in the plural, the source being French *orgies*, via Latin from Greek *orgia* 'secret rites or revels'. The latter were practised in the worship of gods of Greek and Roman mythology such as during the festivals held in honour of Bacchus or Dionysus. The notion of 'excessive indulgence' in any activity dates from the late 19th century.

orient [late Middle English] *Orient* came via Old French from Latin *orient-*, the present participial stem of *oriri* 'to rise', with reference to the rising sun. **Oriental** is also a late Middle English word, from Old French, or from Latin *orientalis*, from *orient-*.
→ ORIGINAL

orientate [mid 19th century] This is probably a back-formation (by removal of the suffix) from the contemporaneous word **orientation** apparently based on *orient*. The term **orienteering**, a competitive sport in which participants have to find their way across rough terrain with a map and a compass, dates from the 1940s from Swedish *orientering*.
→ ORIENT

orifice [late Middle English] This word comes from French, from late Latin *orificium*, from *os, or-* 'mouth' and *facere* 'make'.

original [Middle English] The earliest use of this word was found in the phrase *original sin*: it comes from Old French, or from Latin *originalis*, from *origo, origin-* 'source'. The sense 'inventive, fresh, creative' was a mid 18th-century development. Latin *origo* also gave rise to early 16th-century **origin**, from French *origine*. The Latin base verb is *oriri* 'to rise'. **Originate** dates from the mid 17th century and is from medieval Latin *originare* 'cause to begin', from Latin *origo*.
→ ORIENT

ornament [Middle English] Early use included the sense 'accessory'. It comes from Old French *ournement*, from Latin *ornamentum* 'equipment, ornament', from *ornare* 'to adorn'. The verb dates from the early 18th century.

ornate [late Middle English] *Ornate* is from Latin *ornatus* 'adorned', the past participle of *ornare*.

ornithology [late 17th century] This word for the branch of zoology dealing with birds is from modern Latin *ornithologia*, from Greek *ornithologos* describing the 'treating of birds'.

orphan [late Middle English] *Orphan* came via late Latin from Greek *orphanos* 'bereaved'.

orthodontics [early 20th century] This word is composed of the prefix *ortho-* meaning 'straight' (from Greek *orthos* 'straight, right') and Greek *odous, odont-* 'tooth'.

orthodox [late Middle English] *Orthodox* (as in *Orthodox Church*) is from Greek *orthodoxos* (probably via ecclesiastical Latin), from *orthos* 'straight or right' and *doxa* 'opinion'.

orthography [late Middle English] This word came via Old French and Latin from Greek *orthographia*, from *orthos* 'correct' and *-graphia* writing.

oscillate [early 18th century] *Oscillate* is from Latin *oscillat-*, the past participial stem of *oscillare* 'to swing'. The base is Latin *oscillum* 'small face' which referred to a mask left swinging in the breeze.

osmosis [mid 19th century] This is a Latinized form of earlier *osmose*, from Greek *ōsmos* 'a push'. The 'pushing' refers in chemistry contexts to the tendency of molecules of a solvent to pass though a semi-permeable membrane from a less concentrated solution into a more concentrated one. By the end of the 19th century the word was being used figuratively for the gradual assimilation of ideas.

osseous [late Middle English] *Osseous* 'turned into bone' is based on Latin *osseus* 'bony'. The base is Latin *os* 'bone', shared by mid 17th-century **ossuary** 'place where the bones of dead people are placed' (from late Latin *ossuarium*, formed irregularly from Latin *os*) and early 18th-century **ossify** 'turn to bone' (from French *ossifier*).

ostentation [late Middle English] *Ostentation* came via Old French from Latin *ostentatio(n)-*, from the verb *ostentare*; this is a frequentative (= verb of repeated action) of *ostendere* 'stretch out to view'.

ostler [late Middle English] This word used formerly for a man employed to look after horses is from Old French *hostelier* 'innkeeper', from *hostel*.
→ HOTEL

ostracize [mid 17th century] *Ostracize* is from Greek *ostrakizein*, from *ostrakon* 'shell or potsherd': names were written on such fragments when voting to banish unpopular citizens.

other [Old English] Of Germanic origin, Old English *ōther* is related to Dutch and German *ander*, from an Indo-European root meaning 'different'. The original Old English sense was the Germanic 'one ... of two'. The phrase *the other day* originally meant 'the second day' (retained in Scots and Northern Irish use); the phrase *every other ...* as in *every other day* dates from the late 16th century. *One's other half* referring to one's spouse or partner dates from the late 17th century, originating in Milton's *Paradise Lost*: Return fair Eve ... Part of my soul I seek thee, and thee claim My other half).

otter [Old English] Old English *otr, ot(t)or* is of Germanic origin. Greek *hudros* 'water snake' is related.

ought¹ [Old English] Old English *āhte* in the context of duty, is the past tense of *āgan* 'owe'.
→ OWE

ought² [mid 19th century] This *ought* meaning 'nought' is perhaps from *an ought*, by wrong division of *a nought*. The word *adder* is an example of a word formed by misinterpreting word division in this way.

ounce [Middle English] This word for a unit of weight is from Old French *unce*, from Latin *uncia* 'twelfth part (of a pound or foot)'.
→ INCH

our [Old English] Old English *ūre* is of Germanic origin; German *unser* is related.
→ US

oust [late Middle English] Early use was as a legal term: it is from Anglo-Norman French *ouster* 'take away', from Latin *obstare* 'oppose, hinder'.

out [Old English] Old English *ūt* (adverb), *ūtian* (verb) are from a Germanic source, related to Dutch *uit* and German *aus*. Late Middle English **outer** is based on *out*; it replaced the earlier synonym *utter* which came to mean 'extreme'.
→ UTTER¹

outlaw [late Old English] The early forms were *ūtlaga* (as a noun) and *ūtlagian* (as a verb), from Old Norse *útlagi*, noun from *útlagr* 'outlawed or banished'.

outrage [Middle English] 'Lack of moderation' and 'violent behaviour' were the early senses of *outrage* from Old French *ou(l)trage* 'excess', based on Latin *ultra* 'beyond'. Sense development has been affected by the belief that the word is a compound of *out* and *rage*. Late Middle English **outrageous** is from Old French *outrageus*, from *outrage*.

oval [mid 16th century] *Oval* essentially means 'egg-shaped'; it is from French, or from modern Latin *ovalis*, from Latin *ovum* 'egg'.

ovary [mid 17th century] *Ovary* is from modern Latin *ovarium*, from Latin *ovum* 'egg'.

ovation [early 16th century] The first sense recorded for *ovation* is 'a processional entrance into Rome by a victorious commander'. The source is Latin *ovatio(n)-*, from *ovare* 'exult'. The word had the sense 'exultation' from the mid 17th to early 19th century. The sense 'enthusiastic reception, burst of applause' is found from the mid 19th century.

oven [Old English] Old English *ofen* has a Germanic origin; it is related to Dutch *oven*, German *Ofen*, from an Indo-European root shared by Greek *ipnos*.

over [Old English] Old English *ofer* is from a Germanic source. It is related to Dutch *over* and German *über*, from an Indo-European word (originally a comparative of the element represented by *-ove* in *above*) which is also the base of Latin *super* and Greek *huper*.

overhaul [early 17th century] The word *overhaul*, based on the verb *haul*, was originally in nautical use in the sense 'release (rope tackle) by slackening it'. The association with 'repair' dates from the early 18th century.

overt [Middle English] This is a use of the Old French past participle of *ovrir* 'to open', from Latin *aperire*.

overture [late Middle English] 'Aperture' was the early sense of *overture* which comes from Old French, from Latin *apertura* 'aperture'. The plural use in the sense 'initial negotiations' (e.g. *made overtures to them about the possibility of funding*) was also found in late Middle English. As a term in musical contexts for an orchestral piece introducing an opera or other extended composition, *overture* dates from the mid 17th century.

overwrought [late Middle English] This is the archaic past participle of *overwork*.

ovulate [late 19th century] *Ovulate* is a backformation (by removal of the suffix) from mid 19th-century **ovulation**, or it is based on medieval Latin *ovulum* 'little egg', a diminutive of *ovum* 'egg'.

owe [Old English] Old English *āgan* meant 'own, have as an obligation'. Of Germanic origin, it is from an Indo-European root shared by Sanskrit *īs* 'possess, own'.
→OUGHT[1]

own [Old English] Old English *āgen* (used as both an adjective and a pronoun) meant 'owned, possessed': it was the past participle of *āgan* 'owe'. The verb (Old English *āgnian* meaning both 'possess' and 'make own's own') was originally from the adjective, but later was probably reintroduced from *owner*.

oyez [late Middle English] This call asking for people's attention made by a public crier or by a court officer is from Old French *oiez!*, *oyez!* 'hear!': this is the imperative plural of *oir*, from Latin *audire* 'hear'.

ozone [mid 19th century] *Ozone* comes from German *Ozon*, from Greek *ozein* 'to smell'. One of the characteristics of *ozone* gas is that it has a pungent odour.

Pp

pace [Middle English] *Pace* is from Old French *pas*, from Latin *passus* 'stretch (of the leg)', from *pandere* 'to stretch'. As well as being associated with 'stepping', the word also meant 'journey, route' in early examples. The phrase *put through one's paces* arose in the mid 18th century in horse-riding contexts, extended to figurative use a century later. The notion of 'tempo' as in *change of pace* in a novel, narrative, or piece of music is reflected in use from the 1950s. The verb *pace oneself* meaning 'control one's actions to avoid undue tiredness' is found from the 1970s.

pachyderm [mid 19th century] This word for a large mammal such as an elephant, rhinoceros, or hippopotamus comes from French *pachyderme*, from Greek *pakhudermos* and relates the animals by skin type. The elements are *pakhus* 'thick' and *derma* 'skin'.

pacific [mid 16th century] In legal texts, the word *pacific* still retains an early meaning 'free from strife'. The source is French *pacifique* or Latin *pacificus* 'peacemaking', from *pax, pac-* 'peace'. Use of the word to refer to the *Pacific Ocean* was an early 17th-century development. The *Pacific Rim* was a phrase coined in the 1970s grouping together the Asiatic countries bordering the Pacific Ocean, regarded as sharing political, economic, and environmental interests.

pacify [late 15th century] This verb is from Old French *pacefier*, from Latin *pacificare*, based on *pax, pac-* 'peace'. The noun **pacifism** (from French *pacifisme*, from *pacifier* 'pacify') is recorded from the early 20th century.

pack [Middle English] This *pack* describing 'a container' (e.g. *pack of cigarettes*) or 'a collection, group' (e.g. *pack of reporters, wolf pack*) is from the Middle Dutch, Middle Low German noun *pak* and verb *pakken*. The verb appears early in Anglo-Latin and Anglo-Norman French in connection with the wool trade; trade in English wool was chiefly with the Low Countries. Early noun use was with reference to a 'bundle' specifically a pedlar's bundle of goods; the word became more generalized (*back pack*) during the 19th century with the widespread use of rucksacks. The connection with playing cards dates from the late 16th century. Associations from the early use of the word are 'putting belongings together ready for travel' (*pack one's bags, packed him off to work*), 'compacting' (*pack down*), and 'covering, protecting' (*packed with snow*).

package [mid 16th century] Early use was as a noun denoting the action or way of packing goods: it is based on the verb *pack*; Anglo-Latin *paccagium* is related. Use of the word to denote any 'grouping' (e.g. *package of philosophical and theological ideas* originated in the US in the 1930s; this then developed into the items being viewed as a single unit (usually by a purchaser): e.g. *with theatre tickets thrown in as part of the package*. The phrase *package holiday* dates from the 1960s.

packet [mid 16th century] This is a diminutive of *pack* (i.e. 'little pack'), perhaps from Anglo-Norman French; Anglo-Latin *paccettum* may be related. The colloquial sense 'large sum of money' (thus reversing the notion of small size) dates from the 1920s.
→ PACK

pact [late Middle English] *Pact* is from Old French, from Latin *pactum* 'something agreed', the neuter past participle form (used as a noun) of *paciscere* 'agree'.

pad¹ [mid 16th century] The first recorded sense for this *pad* was 'bundle of straw to lie on'. The various senses: 'thick wad of material' (*gauze pad*), 'underpart of an animal's foot' (*soft pad*), 'sheets fastened together for making notes' (*notepad*), 'area for take-off' (*helicopter pad*), 'person's home' (*a small pad in Peckham*) may not be of common origin. The meaning 'underpart of an animal's foot' for example is perhaps related to Low German *pad* 'sole of the foot', but the history remains obscure. The colloquial reference to 'a home' was originally a US slang usage (1930s) and referred to a room frequented by drug users or one used by a prostitute.

pad² [mid 16th century] This verb meaning 'walk with a soft dull tread' is from Low German *padden* 'to tread, go along a path'; it is partly imitative of the sound made.

paddle¹ [late Middle English] Early use of the word was to describe a small spade-like implement. The origin is unknown. The earliest of the current senses ('oar', 'part of a wheel', 'tool with a flat surface') dates from the 17th century.

paddle² [mid 16th century] This *paddle* describing the action of walking in shallow water is of obscure origin; Low German *paddeln* 'tramp about' may be related, but the association with water remains unexplained.

paddock [early 17th century] *Paddock* is apparently a variant of dialect *parrock*. The ultimate origin remains unknown.

paddy¹ [early 17th century] The *paddy* of *paddy field* is from Malay *pādī* meaning 'rice in the straw'.

paddy² [late 19th century] The *paddy* meaning 'fit of anger' is from the given name *Paddy*, associated with obsolete *paddywhack* meaning 'an Irishman (given to brawling)'. The name *Paddy* is an Irish pet-form of *Padraig* or *Patrick* and has been used colloquially as a form of address for an Irishman, considered offensive.

padlock [late 15th century] The first element (*pad-*) is of unknown origin. The obvious assumption would be that it is from *pad* (a late 16th-century variant of *ped*) meaning 'basket, hamper', but there is no early evidence that a padlock was used to fasten such a container.

pagan [late Middle English] *Pagan* is from Latin *paganus* 'villager, rustic', from *pagus* 'country district'. Latin *paganus* also meant 'civilian', becoming, in Christian Latin, 'heathen' (i.e. one not enrolled in the army of Christ).

page¹ [late 16th century] *Page* as in *page of a book* is from French, from Latin *pagina*, from *pangere* 'fasten'. The word *pagination* dates from the mid 19th century as a noun of action from **paginate**, from French *paginer*, based on Latin *pagina* 'a page'.

page² [Middle English] 'Youth, male of uncouth manners' was the early sense recorded for this *page* from Old French, perhaps from Italian *paggio*, from a Greek diminutive of *pais*, *paid-* 'boy'. Use of the word to denote a *page boy* at a wedding dates from the late 19th century. Early verb use (mid 16th century) was in the sense 'follow as or like a page'; its current sense 'summon over a public address system' dates from the early 20th century.

pageant [late Middle English] The early spelling was *pagyn*, the origin of which is unknown. Anglo-Latin *pagina* was contemporary with *pagyn*. The two main early senses were: 'scene dispayed on a stage' and 'stage on which a scene is exhibited'; examples suggest that the 'scene' sense was the earlier.

pagoda [late 16th century] *Pagoda* is from Portuguese *pagode*, perhaps based on Persian *butkada* 'temple of idols', influenced by Prakrit *bhagodī* 'divine'.

pail [Middle English] The origin of *pail* is uncertain; Old English *pægel* 'gill, small measure' and Old French *paelle* 'pan, liquid measure, brazier' may be related. It is a near-synonym of *bucket* but has come to be associated with the containment of liquids from the common combination *milk pail*.

pain [Middle English] 'Suffering inflicted as punishment for an offence' was the early meaning of *pain*. Old French *peine* is the source, from Latin *poena* which originally meant 'penalty' and later came to mean 'pain'. The phrase *pains and penalties* (mid 16th century) remains in legal contexts. The colloquial *pain in the neck* dates from the 1920s; from this, the reference of *a pain* to 'an annoying person' developed in the 1930s.

paint [Middle English] *Paint* is from *peint* 'painted', the past participle of Old French *peindre*, from Latin *pingere* 'to paint'. The expression *paint the town red* dates from the late 19th century; *paint oneself into a corner*, from the image of someone painting a floor and forgetting to start near a doorway to avoid crossing the wet paint, arose in the 1970s. The noun **painter** is Middle English from Anglo-Norman French *peintour*, based on Latin *pictor*, from the verb *pingere*.

pair [Middle English] *Pair* is from Old French *paire*, from Latin *paria* 'equal things', the neuter plural of *par* 'equal'. Formerly phrases such as *a pair of gloves* were expressed without *of*, as in *a pair gloves* (compare with German *ein Paar Handschuhe*). The colloquial phrase *the pair of us* dates from the late 19th century.

pal [late 17th century] *Pal* is an English Romany word originally meaning 'brother, mate', related to Turkish Romany *pral*, *plal* and based on Sanskrit *bhrātr* 'brother'. The informal phrase **palsy-walsy** arose in the 1930s as a noun in the sense 'friend'; this is a reduplication based on the noun *pal*.

palace [Middle English] This word is from Old French *paleis*, from Latin *Palatium*, the name of the Palatine Hill in Rome where the house of the emperor was situated. The adjective **palatial** is evidenced in use from the mid 18th century, based on Latin *palatium* 'palace'.

palate [late Middle English] *Palate* is from Latin *palatum*. Use of the word in the context of wine tasting dates from the 1970s.

palaver [mid 18th century] The first sense recorded was 'a talk between tribespeople and

traders': the word comes from Portuguese *palavra* 'word', from Latin *parabola* 'comparison'. The notion of 'fuss, rigmarole' (e.g. *what a palaver!*) dates from the late 19th century.
→ PARABLE

pale¹ [Middle English] *Pale* 'light in colour' is from Old French *pale*, from Latin *pallidus*; the verb is from Old French *palir*. The phrase *pale into insignificance* dates from the mid 19th century.

pale² [Middle English] This word for a 'stake' is from Old French *pal*, from Latin *palus* 'stake'. A figurative meaning is 'boundary' found in *beyond the pale* 'outside the bounds (of acceptable behaviour)', an idiom dating from the mid 19th century (C. Brontë *Jane Eyre*: *Without one overt act of hostility,... he contrived to impress me momently with the conviction that I was put beyond the pale of his favour*). **Palisade** (early 17th century) is from the same Latin base as *pale* via French from Provençal *palissada*, from *palissa* 'paling'.

palfrey [Middle English] *Palfrey* is from Old French *palefrei*, from medieval Latin *palefredus*: this is an alteration of late Latin *paraveredus*, from Greek *para* 'extra' and Latin *veredus* 'light horse'. It is a word used for an ordinary horse for riding as opposed to a warhorse.

pall¹ [Old English] Old English *pæll* meant 'rich (purple) cloth', 'cloth cover for a chalice', from Latin *pallium* 'covering, cloak'. The prime current sense (from Middle English) is a 'covering for a coffin'.

pall² [late Middle English] This *pall* as in *the initial enthusiasm began to pall* is a shortening of *appal*.
→ APPAL

pallet¹ [Middle English] This word for a 'straw mattress' is from Anglo-Norman French *paillete*, from *paille* 'straw', from Latin *palea*.

pallet² [late Middle English] The first sense recorded for this *pallet* was 'a flat wooden blade with a handle' used to shape clay or plaster: it comes from French *palette* 'little blade', from Latin *pala* 'spade' (related to *palus* 'stake'). In the early 20th century, the word came to be used for a small platform for moving or stacking goods by means of a forklift truck.
→ PALE²

palliasse [early 16th century] This word for a 'straw mattress' was first found in Scots: it comes from French *paillasse*, based on Latin *palea* 'straw'.

pall-mall [mid 16th century] This is from obsolete French *pallemaille*, from Italian *pallamaglio*, from *palla* 'ball' and *maglio* 'mallet'. It

was a 16th-century game in which a boxwood ball was driven through an iron ring suspended at the end of a long alley. The street *Pall Mall* in central London (running between St James's Street and Haymarket) developed from one of these alleys, later becoming famous as the centre of London club life.

pallor [late Middle English] This is an English use of a Latin word, from *pallere* 'be pale'; a related word is **pallid** (late 16th century) from Latin *pallidus* 'pale'.

palm¹ [Old English] This botanical term was *palm(a)* in Old English. Of Germanic origin, it is related to Dutch *palm* and German *Palme*, from Latin *palma*, literally 'palm (of a hand)', its leaf being likened to a spread hand.

palm² [Middle English] This word for the inner surface of the hand is from Old French *paume*, from Latin *palma*. The verb sense 'conceal (a card)' dates from the late 17th century. The noun **palmistry**, based on *palm* is late Middle English; the early suffix was *-estry* (of unknown origin), but it was later altered to *-istry*, perhaps on the pattern of *sophistry*.

palpable [late Middle English] This word is from late Latin *palpabilis*, from Latin *palpare* 'feel, touch gently', the source too of the medical term **palpate** 'examine by touch' dating from the mid 19th century.

palpitation [late Middle English] Latin *palpitatio(n-)* is the source of this word, from Latin *palpitare*, a frequentative (= verb of repeated action) of *palpare* 'touch gently'.

palsy [Middle English] This word is from Old French *paralisie*, from an alteration of Latin *paralysis*. Different forms of *palsy* are identified by a first element (e.g. *Bell's Palsy*, *cerebral palsy*). In early use, it was commonly referred to generally as *the palsy* as in the account of one of Jesus' miracles (Matthew 9:6: (*then saith he to the sick of the palsy*), *Arise, take up thy bed, and go into thine house*).
→ PARALYSIS

paltry [mid 16th century] *Paltry* is apparently based on the dialect word *pelt* meaning 'rubbish, rags'; Low German *paltrig* 'ragged' is probably related.

pamper [late Middle English] 'Cram with food' was the early sense of *pamper* which is probably of Low German or Dutch origin and associated with German dialect *pampfen* 'cram, gorge'. It is perhaps related to late Middle English *pap* (probably based on Latin *pappare* 'to eat') describing bland, soft, or semi-liquid food.

pamphlet [late Middle English] *Pamphlet* is from *Pamphilet*, the familiar name of the 12th-century Latin love poem *Pamphilus, seu de Amore*.

pan¹ [Old English] Old English *panne*, a utensil for heating food, is West Germanic in origin, related to Dutch *pan* and German *Pfanne*, perhaps based on Latin *patina* 'dish'.

pan² [1920s] This word used in filming contexts (e.g. *a slow pan over London*) is an abbreviation of *panorama* or *panoramic*.
→ PANORAMA

panacea [mid 16th century] This word for a 'remedy to heal all diseases' came via Latin from Greek *panakeia*, from *panakēs* 'all-healing'. The base elements are Greek *pan* 'all' and *akos* 'remedy'. The figurative meaning 'solution for all problems' dates from the early 17th century.

panache [mid 16th century] This is an adoption of a French word, from Italian *pennacchio*. The source is late Latin *pinnaculum*, a diminutive of *pinna* 'feather'. Historically a *panache* was a tuft or plume of feathers as a head-dress or on a helmet, which led to the generalized notion of flamboyant confidence.

pander [late Middle English] The early use of *pander* was as a noun: it comes from *Pandare*, the name of a character in Chaucer's *Troilus and Criseyde*. He acted as a lovers' go-between, a role which originated with the 14th-century Italian writer Boccaccio. The verb dates from the early 17th century (Shakespeare *Hamlet: Since Frost it self, as actively doth burn, As Reason panders Will*).

pane [late Middle English] A *pane* was originally a section or piece of something, such as a fence or strip of cloth. The word comes from Old French *pan*, from Latin *pannus* 'piece of cloth'. The sense 'division of a window' is found from the mid 15th century.

panel [Middle English] *Panel* is from Old French, literally 'piece of cloth', based on Latin *pannus* '(piece of) cloth'. The early sense 'piece of parchment' was extended to mean 'list'; this led to the notion 'advisory group' (e.g. *interview panel*). The sense 'rectangular section set into a door, wall, or ceiling' derives from the late Middle English use of the word to describe a 'distinct (usually framed) section of a surface'.

pang [late 15th century] *Pang* may be an alteration of *prong*. Early use was chiefly in the phrase *pangs of death*.
→ PRONG

panic [early 17th century] *Panic* is from French *panique*, from modern Latin *panicus*, from Greek *panikos*. This derives from the name *Pan*, the Greek god of flocks and herds. Strange or eerie woodland noises were attributed to him with an association of his causing terror.

pannier [Middle English] This word for a large basket (initially for carrying provisions) is from Old French *panier*, from Latin *panarium* 'bread basket'. The base is Latin *panis* 'bread'.

panoply [late 16th century] *Panoply* was first used to mean 'complete protection for spiritual warfare', often with biblical allusion to Ephesians 6:11, 13 (the whole armour of God). French *panoplie* or modern Latin *panoplia* 'full armour' gave the word in English. The base elements are Greek *pan* 'all' and *hopla* 'arms'.

panorama [late 18th century] The word *panorama* is composed of the prefix *pan-* 'all' (from Greek) and Greek *horama* 'view' (from *horan* 'see'). The word was invented in around 1789 by Robert Barker to describe a picture of a landscape arranged on the inside of a cylindrical surface round the spectator at the centre, or a picture gradually unrolled to show various sections in succession. The first one represented a view of Edinburgh.

pant [Middle English] *Pant* 'breathe spasmodically' is related to Old French *pantaisier* 'be agitated, gasp', based on Greek *phantasioun* 'cause to imagine', from *phantasia*.
→ FANTASY

pantaloon [late 16th century] The word was first used in reference to *Pantaloon*, a Venetian character in *commedia dell'arte*, represented as a foolish old man wearing *pantaloons*. It came via French from the the Italian name *Pantalone*. The word **pants** (mid 19th century) is an abbreviation of *pantaloons*; it became a slang expression for 'rubbish, no good' in the 1990s.

panther [Middle English] *Panther* is from Old French *pantere*, from Latin *panthera*, from Greek *panthēr*. In Latin, *pardus* 'leopard' existed alongside *panthera*. The two terms led to confusion: until the mid 19th century many taxonomists regarded the panther and the leopard as separate species.

pantomime [late 16th century] This word comes from French *pantomime* or Latin *pantomimus*, from Greek *pantomimos* 'imitator of all'. The Latin form was used in early examples, referring to an actor using mime. The English word now describes a dramatic performance associated with the Christmas festivities, but it originally consisted of action without speech; this developed later to a dramatized tale ending in a transformation scene followed by a comedy featuring clowns and Pantaloon and the dancing of Harlequin and Columbine. By the 20th century, the final Pantaloon and Harlequin features were lost.

→ MIMIC

pantry [Middle English] Latin *panis* 'bread' is the base of *pantry*. Originally a *pantry* was a room in a house where bread was kept. The direct source is Anglo-Norman French *panterie*, from *paneter* 'baker', based on late Latin *panarius* 'bread seller'.

papacy [late Middle English] This is from medieval Latin *papatia*, from *papa* 'pope, bishop (of Rome)', the base too of late Middle English **papal** (via Old French from medieval Latin *papalis*) and mid 16th-century **papist** (from French *papiste* or modern Latin *papista*).

→ POPE

paparazzi [1960s] This term for freelance photographers who pursue celebrities to obtain lucrative photos of them is from Italian; it comes from the name of a character in Fellini's film *La Dolce Vita* (1960).

paper [Middle English] *Paper* is from Anglo-Norman French *papir*, from Latin *papyrus* 'paper-reed', from Greek *papuros*. The Greek word originally referred to writing sheets made of thin strips of papyrus; the name was then transferred to paper made of cotton, and then to paper of linen and other fibres, all sense developments prior to the English word use. *Paper* meaning 'newspaper' dates from the mid 17th century; *papers* used to authenticate identity date from the late 17th century; *examination papers* are referred to from the mid 19th century.

par [late 16th century] *Par*, first recorded in the sense 'equality of value or standing', started to be used as a golfing term from the late 19th century. It is a use of a Latin word meaning both 'equal' and 'equality'. **Parity** is also a late 16th-century word, from late Latin *paritas*, from *par*.

WORDBUILDING

The prefix **para-¹** [from Greek *para* 'beside' in combinations often meaning 'amiss, irregular' and denoting alteration or modification] adds the sense

■ **beside; adjacent** [parataxis; parathyroid]

■ **beyond; distinct from but analogous to** [paramilitary; paramedic]

The prefix **para-²** [from French, from the Italian imperative singular of *parare* 'defend, shield'] adds the sense

■ **protecting from** [parachute; parasol]

---

parable [Middle English] *Parable* is from Old French *parabole*, from an ecclesiastical Latin sense 'discourse, allegory' of Latin *parabola* 'comparison'. The source is Greek *parabolē* 'placing side by side, application', from *para-* 'beside' and *bolē* 'a throw' (from the verb *ballein*). A *parable* places a simple story in juxtaposition with a moral principle to draw a comparison.

parachute [late 18th century] This is from French *para-* 'protection against' and *chute* 'fall'.

parade [mid 17th century] This word associated with 'ostentation' and 'display' was originally a French word meaning literally 'a showing', from Spanish *parada* and Italian *parata*, based on Latin *parare* 'prepare, furnish'.

paradise [Middle English] This comes from Old French *paradis*, via ecclesiastical Latin from Greek *paradeisos* 'royal (enclosed) park', from Avestan *pairidaēza* 'enclosure, park'. The earliest sense recorded in English was 'abode of the blessed'.

paradox [mid 16th century] Originally a *paradox* was a statement contrary to accepted opinion; it came via late Latin from Greek *paradoxon* 'contrary (opinion)' (a neuter adjective used as a noun). The formative elements are *para-* 'distinct from' and *doxa* 'opinion'.

paragon [mid 16th century] *Paragon* 'a person or thing regarded as a a perfect example' is from obsolete French, from Italian *paragone* which was a 'touchstone to try good (gold) from bad'. Medieval Greek *parakonē* 'whetstone' is the base.

parallel [mid 16th century] *Parallel* is from French *parallèle*, via Latin from Greek *parallēlos*, from *para-* 'alongside' and *allēlos* 'one another'.

paralysis [late Old English] This word came via Latin from Greek *paralusis*, from *paraluesthai* 'be disabled at the side'. Greek *para* 'beside' and *luein* 'loosen' are the formative elements. **Paralytic** is late Middle English, from Old French *paralytique*, via Latin from Greek *paralutikos* 'relating to paralysis'. The sense 'extremely drunk' dates from the late 19th century. **Paralyse** is recorded from the early 19th century, from French *paralyser*, from *paralysie* 'paralysis'.

paramount [mid 16th century] The early sense recorded was 'highest in jurisdiction' in the phrases *lord paramount* and *paramount chief*. The word is from Anglo-Norman French *paramont*, from Old French *par* 'by' and *amont* 'above'.

paranoia [early 19th century] This word is modern Latin, from Greek, from *paranoos* 'distracted', from *para* 'irregular' and *noos* 'mind'.

parapet [late 16th century] *Parapet* is from French, or from Italian *parapetto* 'breast-high wall', from *para-* 'protecting' and *petto* 'breast' (from Latin *pectus*). It was originally to screen and protect troops from the enemy.

paraplegia [mid 17th century] This is a modern Latin word, from Greek *paraplēgia*, from *paraplēssein* 'strike at the side', from *para* 'beside' and *plēssein* 'to strike'.

parasite [mid 16th century] *Parasite* came via Latin from Greek *parasitos* '(person) eating at another's table', from *para-* 'alongside' and *sitos* 'food'. Its use as a term in biology dates from the early 18th century. **Parasitic** (via Latin from Greek *parasitikos*) is from the same base and dates from the early 17th century.

parasol [early 17th century] *Parasol* is from French, from Italian *parasole*; the elements are *para-* 'protecting against' and *sole* 'sun' (from Latin *sol*).

parboil [late Middle English] This culinary term is from Old French *parbouillir*, from late Latin *perbullire* 'boil thoroughly'. Latin *per-* meaning 'through, thoroughly' (later confused with *part*) and *bullire* 'to boil' are the core elements.

parcel [late Middle English] The word was at first used chiefly in the sense 'small portion': it comes from Old French *parcelle*, from Latin *particula* 'small part'. The connection with postage dates from the mid 17th century.

parch [late Middle English] The origin of *parch* is unknown. The early sense was 'dry by exposure to great heat'; the association with thirst dates from the late 16th century.

parchment [Middle English] This comes from Old French *parchemin*, from a blend of late Latin *pergamina* 'writing material from Pergamum' and *Parthica pellis* 'Parthian skin' (a kind of scarlet leather)

pardon [Middle English] The noun is from Old French *pardun*, the verb from Old French *pardoner*. Medieval Latin *perdonare* 'concede, remit' is the source, from *per-* 'completely' and *donare* 'give'. Use of the word in I *beg your pardon* dates from the late 17th century; the shortened usage *pardon* meaning 'excuse me' is found from the late 19th century.

pare [Middle English] *Pare* is from Old French *parer* which meant both 'adorn, prepare' and 'peel, trim', from Latin *parare* 'prepare, make ready'.

parent [late Middle English] This is from an Old French word, from Latin *parent-*, the present participial stem of the verb *parere* 'bring forth'. It was common in the 16th century for the word simply to mean 'relative' reflecting French and other modern Romanic

usage. The noun **parenting** is recorded from the 1950s.

parenthesis [mid 16th century] This came via late Latin from Greek, from *parentithenai* 'put in beside'.

pariah [early 17th century] This word is from Tamil *paṟaiyar*, the plural of *paṟaiyan* of which the literal meaning is '(hereditary) drummer', (from *paṟai* 'large (festival) drum') but which serves as the name of the largest of the lower castes of southern India. Pariahs were not allowed to join in with a religious procession. Generalized use of the word for a 'social outcast' dates from the early 19th century.

parish [Middle English] *Parish* comes from Anglo-Norman French and Old French *paroche*, via late Latin from Greek *paroikia* 'sojourning'; this is based on *para-* 'beside, subsidiary' and *oikos* 'dwelling'. The modern parish became defined by geographical boundaries in an ecclesiastical hierarchy by the 13th century. The old minster system had started to break up by the 12th century; this system had been typified by a *minster parochia* (7th and 8th centuries) in which the secular clergy gave pastoral care to a large surrounding area; the following two centuries saw many local churches established, created and owned by major landowners; many had their permanence confirmed in the period around 1050–1150 when much rebuilding in stone was carried out. The word **parochial** dates from late Middle English: this is from Old French, from ecclesiastical Latin *parochialis* 'relating to an ecclesiastical district', from *parochia*.

park [Middle English] *Park* is from Old French *parc*, from medieval Latin *parricus*. Of Germanic origin, it is related to German *Pferch* 'pen, fold'. The word was originally a legal term for land held by royal grant for the keeping of game animals: the area was enclosed and therefore distinct from a *forest* or *chase*, and (also unlike a *forest*) had no special laws or officers. A military sense 'space occupied by artillery, wagons, stores, etc. in an encampment' (late 17th century) is the origin of the verb sense (mid 19th century).

→ PADDOCK

parley [late Middle English] A *parley* was originally a 'speech' or 'debate'. It is perhaps from Old French *parlee* '(something) spoken', the feminine past participle of the verb *parler*. This verb was also the source of late 16th-century **parlance** which was also initially a word for 'speech' or 'debate'. The base is Latin *parabola* 'comparison': in late Latin this came to mean 'speech'.

parliament [Middle English] This word is from Old French *parlement* 'speaking', from the verb *parler*. It was originally 'a formal conference or council', applied specifically to an assembly of magnates summoned by the monarch to discuss matters of general importance. The first *parliament* to include representations from the boroughs was established during the reign of Edward I (1272–1307).

parlour [Middle English] The source of the word *parlour* is Anglo-Norman French *parlur* 'place for speaking', from Latin *parlare* 'speak'.

parody [late 16th century] *Parody* came via late Latin from Greek *parōidia* 'burlesque poem', from *para-* 'mock-' and *ōidē* 'ode'. The sense 'feeble imitation' dates from the early 19th century.

parole [late 15th century] This word, common now in legal use, is from an Old French word meaning literally 'word' as well as 'formal promise'; it is from ecclesiastical Latin *parabola* 'speech'. Early use of the word was in military contexts.

paroxysm [late Middle English] French *paroxysme* is the source of this word which came via medieval Latin from Greek *paroxusmos*, from *paroxunein* 'exasperate'. Greek *para-* 'beyond' and *oxunein* 'sharpen' (from *oxus* 'sharp') are the formative elements.

parrot [early 16th century] *Parrot* is probably from dialect French *perrot*, a diminutive of the male given name *Pierre* 'Peter'. The word **parakeet** (mid 16th century) may essentially be a similar formation based on a diminutive of the Spanish given name *Pedro*. Another possiblity is that the word came via Italian based on a diminutive meaning 'little wig', referring to the bird's head plumage.

parry [late 17th century] This word probably represents French *parez!*, an imperative meaning 'ward off!', constantly heard as an instruction in fencing lessons. It is from *parer*, from Italian *parare* 'ward off'.

parse [mid 16th century] *Parse* is perhaps from Middle English *pars* 'parts of speech', from Old French *pars* 'parts' (influenced by Latin *pars* 'part'). The English meaning is 'split into component parts'.

parsimony [late Middle English] This is from Latin *parsimonia*, *parcimonia*, from *parcere* 'be sparing'.

parsnip [late Middle English] *Parsnip* is from Old French *pasnaie*, from Latin *pastinaca*, which is related to *pastinare* 'dig and trench the ground'. The change in the ending was due to association with *neep* a Scots and northern English word for 'turnip' (Old English, from Latin *napus*).

parson [Middle English] *Parson* is from Old French *persone*, from Latin *persona* 'person', which in medieval Latin had the sense 'rector'. → PERSON

part [Old English] A *part* in Old English referred to a part of speech. It is from Latin *pars*, *part-*. The verb (originally in Middle English in the sense 'divide into parts') is from Old French *partir*, from Latin *partire*, *partiri* 'divide, share'.

partake [mid 16th century] This is a back-formation (by removal of the suffix) from the earlier noun *partaker* 'person who takes a part'.

partial [late Middle English] 'Inclined to favour one party in a cause' was the early sense conveyed by *partial*. The notion 'biased' is from Old French *parcial* whereas that of 'incomplete' is from French *partiel*, from late Latin *partialis*, from *pars*, *part-* 'part'. The same Latin base gave rise to late Middle English **partiality** from Old French *parcialite*, from medieval Latin *partialitas*.

participant [late Middle English] This comes from Latin *participant-*, the present participial stem of *participare* 'share in'. **Participate** dates from the early 16th century from the same Latin verb, based on *pars*, *part-* 'part' and *capere* 'take'. The grammatical term **participle** (late Middle English) also shares the same base and is from an Old French by-form (= secondary form) of *participe*, from Latin *participium* 'that which shares' (i.e. a verbal form sharing the functions of a noun).

particle [late Middle English] *Particle* is from Latin *particula* 'little part', a diminutive of *pars*, *part-*.

particular [late Middle English] This word is from Old French *particuler*, from Latin *particularis* 'concerning a small part', from *particula* 'small part'. The sense 'attentive to detail' (e.g. *very particular about cleanliness*) dates from the early 17th century. In the mid 19th century the phrase *London particular* was used to refer to a dense fog associated with London (Dickens *Bleak House*: This is a London particular … A fog, miss). The noun **particularity** is found from the early 16th century when it was used in the plural as *particularities* for 'details': this is from Old French *particularite* or late Latin *particularitas*, from Latin *particularis*.

partisan [mid 16th century] *Partisan* is from French, via Italian dialect from Italian *partigiano*, from *parte* 'part' (from Latin *pars*, *part-*). The word is often used in an unfavourable sense when associated with unreasoning or prejudiced support or with fanatical adherence to a cause. In military contexts a *partisan* may be a member of a small group of irregular troops operating independently; a specific use of this was exemplified in the Second World War with reference to a resistance fighter in Italy or Eastern Europe, or specifically to a member of the Communist-led resistance forces in Yugoslavia.

partition [late Middle English] *Partition* is from Latin *partitio(n-)*, from *partiri* 'divide into parts'.

partner [Middle English] *Partner* is an alteration of *parcener* 'partner, joint heir', from Anglo-Norman French *parcener*, based on Latin *partitio(n-)* 'partition'. The change in the first syllable was due to association with *part*. Use of the word *partner* for a spouse dates from the early 17th century; the term came to be commonly applied to each person of an unmarried couple sharing a home towards the end of the 20th century. The phrase *partner in crime* dates from the early 19th century.

party [Middle English] The early use of *party* was to refer to a body of people united in opposition to others, as well as specifically to a political group. It comes from Old French *partie*, based on Latin *partiri* 'divide into parts'. The sense 'social gathering' dates from the early 18th century.

pass¹ [Middle English] *Pass* 'go by, go past' is from Old French *passer*, based on Latin *passus* 'pace'. **Passable** dates from late Middle English, from Old French, from *passer* 'to pass'; at first it meant 'able to be passed'; towards the end of the 15th century it came to mean 'adequate, tolerable'.

pass² [Middle English] This *pass* as in *mountain pass* was first used in the sense 'division of a text, passage through'. It is a variant of *pace* influenced by the verb *pass* and French *pas*. Use of the word to mean 'permission, a document giving permission' dates from the late 16th century. The expression *reach a pretty pass* arose in the mid 19th century; *make a pass at* is recorded from the 1920s.
→ PACE

passage [Middle English] *Passage* is from Old French, based on Latin *passus* 'pace'. The expression *of passage* meaning 'passing through, itinerant' is recorded from the late 17th century; *bird of passage* is found from the early 18th century.

passenger [Middle English] This is from the Old French adjective *passager* 'passing, transitory', used as a noun, from *passage*. The *-n-*

was added in late Middle English as in words such as *harbinger*, *messenger*, and *porringer*.
→ PASSAGE

passion [Middle English] *Passion* is from Old French, from late Latin *passio(n-)* (used chiefly as a term in Christian theology), from Latin *pati* 'suffer'. *The Passion* refers to the suffering of Jesus Christ. Use of the word in the sense 'great enthusiasm' (e.g. *passion for baroque music*) dates from the early 17th century. **Passionate** in late Middle English included the senses 'easily moved to passion' and 'enraged': this is from medieval Latin *passionatus* 'full of passion', from *passio*.

passive [late Middle English] Early use was as a grammatical term as well as expressing the sense '(exposed to) suffering, acted on by an external agency'. The source is Latin *passivus*, from *pass-* 'suffered', from the verb *pati*. The sense 'submissive' is found in examples (e.g. *passive obedience*) from the early 17th century.

passport [late 15th century] This word was first used to refer to authorization to depart from a port. It is from French *passeport*, from *passer* 'to pass' and *port* 'seaport'.

past [Middle English] This is a variant of *passed*, the past participle of *pass*.
→ PASS¹

paste [late Middle English] *Paste* is from Old French, from late Latin *pasta* 'medicinal preparation in the shape of a small square'; this is probably from Greek *pastē*, (plural) *pasta* 'barley porridge', from *pastos* 'sprinkled'. The adjective **pasty** dates from the mid 17th century in the sense 'resembling paste'; the meaning 'of the colour of dough, pale' (e.g. *pasty complexion*) is found from the mid 19th century.

pastel [mid 17th century] This word for a type of crayon made of powdered pigments bound with gum or resin came via French from Italian *pastello*, a diminutive of *pasta* 'paste'

pasteurize [late 19th century] This verb is based on the name of Louis *Pasteur*, the French chemist and bacteriologist (1822–95) who introduced pasteurization (partial sterilization usually involving heat treatment or irradiation) and made pioneering studies in vaccination techniques.

pastiche [late 19th century] This word for an artistic work in a style that imitates that of another work, artist, or period is from French, from Italian *pasticcio*, based on late Latin *pasta* 'paste'.

pastille [mid 17th century] This is an adoption of a French word, from Latin *pastillus* 'little loaf, lozenge', from *panis* 'loaf'.

pastime [late 15th century] *Pastime* is from the verb *pass* and the noun *time* translating French *passe-temps*.
→ PASS¹

pastor [late Middle English] *Pastor* is from Anglo-Norman French *pastour*, from Latin *pastor* 'shepherd, feeder', from *past-*, the past participial stem of *pascere* 'feed, graze'. Late Middle English **pastoral** is from Latin *pastoralis* 'relating to a shepherd', from *pastor* 'shepherd'. Its use in literary, art, and musical contexts dates from the late 16th century.

pastry [late Middle English] This was originally used as a collective term; it is based on *paste*, influenced by Old French *pastaierie*.

pasture [Middle English] *Pasture* is from Old French, from late Latin *pastura* 'grazing', from the verb *pascere* 'to graze'.
→ PASTOR

pasty [Middle English] This word for a type of pie is from Old French *paste(e)*, based on late Latin *pasta* 'paste'. Originally it was a pie of venison or other meat cooked in pastry without a dish, but later it came to be a turnover containing both meat and vegetables.

pat [late Middle English] *Pat* was first recorded in noun use for a blow with something flat; it is probably imitative of the noise. The verb dates from the mid 16th century. The related word *pat* used in phrases such as *he learnt his speech off pat* is a late 16th-century usage. It is apparently originally symbolic: a frequently found early use was *hit pat* (i.e. hit as if with flat blow).

patch [late Middle English] This is perhaps from a variant of Old French *pieche*, a dialect variant of *piece* 'piece'. Use of the word to mean 'small area' (e.g. *patch of blue sky*) dates from the mid 16th century.

pate [Middle English] The word *pate* is of unknown origin. Some believe the word to be a by-form (= secondary form) of *plate* comparing medieval Latin *platta* describing the clerical tonsure, and Dutch and German *platte* denoting 'a shaven head'. Evidence however is wanting.

patent [late Middle English] *Patent* is from Old French, from Latin *patent-*, the present participial stem of the verb *patere* 'lie open'. In early use it was found in the phrase *letters patent*, an open document issued by a monarch to record a contract or confer a privilege. It also meant more generally 'open to view'. Use of the word to denote a licence to manufacture, sell, or deal in a commodity, dates from the late 16th century.

paternal [late Middle English] Latin *paternus* 'fatherly, belonging to a father', from *pater* 'father' is the source of both *paternal* (from late Latin *paternalis*) and late Middle English **paternity** (from Old French *paternité*, from late Latin *paternitas*).

path [Old English] *Path* is of West Germanic origin, related to Dutch *pad* and German *Pfad*, of unknown ultimate origin. Originally it described a track formed by continual treading.

pathetic [late 16th century] 'Affecting the emotions' was the early sense of *pathetic* which came via late Latin from Greek *pathētikos* 'sensitive', based on *pathos* 'suffering'.

pathos [mid 17th century] This is an English use of Greek *pathos* 'suffering', related to *paskhein* 'suffer' and *penthos* 'grief'.
→ PATHETIC

patience [Middle English] *Patience* is from Old French, from Latin *patientia*, from the verb *pati* 'to suffer'. **Patient** from the same period is from Old French, from Latin *pati*; the noun *patient* for someone receiving medical treatment dates from late Middle English.

patio [early 19th century] This is an adoption of a Spanish word for an inner courtyard.

patriarch [Middle English] This word is from Old French *patriarche*, via ecclesiastical Latin from Greek *patriarkhēs*: the elements are *patria* 'family' and *arkhēs* 'ruling'.

patrimony [Middle English] This word referring to inherited property is from Old French *patrimoine*, from Latin *patrimonium*, from *pater*, *patr-* 'father'.

patriot [late 16th century] This is from French *patriote*, from late Latin *patriota* 'fellow countryman', which was the early sense in English. It is from Greek *patriōtēs*, from *patrios* 'of one's fathers', from *patris* 'fatherland'. **Patriotic** is found from the mid 17th century and came via late Latin from Greek *patriōtikos* 'relating to a fellow countryman'.

patrol [mid 17th century] English *patrol* came via German from French *patrouille*, from *patrouiller* 'paddle in mud'. The formative elements here are *patte* 'paw' and dialect (*gad*)*rouille* 'dirty water'.

patron [Middle English] *Patron* is from Old French, from Latin *patronus* 'protector of clients, defender', from *pater*, *patr-* 'father'. **Patronage** (from Old French, from *patron*) is a late Middle English word.

patter¹ [early 17th century] This word for a repeated light tapping sound is a frequentative (= verb of repeated action) of *pat*.
➔ PAT

patter² [late Middle English] This word for smooth-flowing continuous talk (e.g. *sales patter*) was first used in the sense 'recite (a prayer, charm, etc.) rapidly'. It comes from *paternoster*, literally 'Our Father', the Lord's prayer recited in Latin. The noun dates from the mid 18th century. Late Middle English **pitter-patter** is a reduplication (expressing rhythmic repetition) of the verb *patter*.

pattern [Middle English] *Pattern* comes from *patron* 'something serving as a model', from Old French. The change in sense is from the idea of a patron giving an example to others to be copied. Metathesis in the second syllable occurred in the 16th century, and by 1700 *patron* ceased to be used of things, the two forms becoming differentiated in sense.
➔ PATRON

patty [mid 17th century] This is an alteration of French *pâté*, by association with *pasty*.
➔ PASTY

paucity [late Middle English] This word indicating the 'presence of something in very small quantities' is from Old French *paucite* or Latin *paucitas*, from *paucus* 'few'.

paunch [late Middle English] *Paunch* is from Anglo-Norman French *pa(u)nche*, based on Latin *pantex, pantic-*, usually used in the plural in the sense 'intestines'.

pauper [late 15th century] *Pauper* is from a Latin word meaning literally 'poor'. The word's use in English originated partly in the Latin legal phrase *in forma pauperis* translating as 'in the form of a poor person' (which allowed non-payment of costs).

pause [late Middle English] *Pause* is from Old French, from Latin *pausa*, from Greek *pausis*, from *pausein* 'to stop'.

pave [Middle English] *Pave* is from Old French *paver* 'pave'. The phrase *pave the way* dates from the late 16th century. Middle English **pavement** is from Old French, from Latin *pavimentum* 'trodden down floor', from *pavire* 'beat, tread down'.

pavilion [Middle English] A *pavilion* originally denoted a large decorated tent. The word comes from Old French *pavillon*, from Latin *papilio(n-)* 'butterfly or tent'.

paw [Middle English] *Paw* is from Old French *poue*, probably of Germanic origin and related to Dutch *poot*. Humorous or contemptuous use of the word paw (e.g. *take your paws off me*) to

mean 'hand' dates from the early 17th century.

pawn¹ [late Middle English] The chess term *pawn* is from Anglo-Norman French *poun*, from medieval Latin *pedo, pedon-* 'foot soldier', from Latin *pes, ped-* 'foot'. Figurative use 'a person used by others for their own purposes' is recorded from the late 16th century.

pawn² [late 15th century] The *pawn* meaning 'deposit as security' is from Old French *pan* 'pledge, security'. Of West Germanic origin, it is related to Dutch *pand* and German *Pfand*.

pay [Middle English] The first sense recorded for *pay* was 'pacify'. The noun is from Old French *paie*, the verb from Old French *payer*, from Latin *pacare* 'appease'. The base is Latin *pax, pac-* 'peace'. The notion of 'payment' arose from the sense of 'pacifying' a creditor. Late Middle English **payment** is from Old French *paiement*, from *payer* 'to pay'.

pea [mid 17th century] This is a back-formation (by removal of the suffix) from *pease* which was interpreted as being a plural. This was *pise* 'pea', (plural) *pisan* in Old English and came via Latin from Greek *pison*. The phrase *as like as two peas (in a pod)* dates from the mid 18th century.

peace [Middle English] *Peace* is from Old French *pais*, from Latin *pax, pac-* 'peace'. The phrase *no peace for the wicked* comes from Isaiah 48:22 (There is no peace to the wicked, saith the Lord).

peaceable [Middle English] *Peaceable* is from Old French *peisible*, an alteration of *plaisible*, from late Latin *placibilis* 'pleasing', from Latin *placere* 'to please'.

peach [late Middle English] *Peach* is from Old French *pesche*, from medieval Latin *persica*, from Latin *persicum (malum)*, literally 'Persian apple'. The informal phrase:
■ **peachy-keen**, common since the mid 20th century in North American English meaning 'attractive, outstanding' is from *peachy* in the sense 'excellent' and *keen* meaning 'wonderful'.

peacock [Middle English] *Peacock* is from Old English *pēa* (from Latin *pavo*) 'peacock' and *cock*.

peak [mid 16th century] This is probably a back-formation (by removal of the suffix) from *peaked*, a variant of dialect *picked* meaning 'pointed'.

peal [late Middle English] This word is a shortening of *appeal*, perhaps from the call to prayers of a ringing bell.

pear [Old English] Old English *pere, peru* is West Germanic in origin, related to Dutch *peer*, from Latin *pirum*. The Middle English word

perry, an alcoholic drink made from the fermented juice of pears, is an alteration of Latin *pirum*.

pearl [late Middle English] *Pearl* is from Old French *perle* and may be based on Latin *perna* 'leg', extended in meaning to denote a leg-of-mutton-shaped bivalve (mentioned by Pliny). Matthew 7:6 has provided a common idiomatic expression: Neither cast ye your pearls before swine.

peasant [late Middle English] This word is from Old French *paisent* 'country dweller', from *pais* 'country', based on Latin *pagus* 'country district'.

peat [Middle English] *Peat* is from Anglo-Latin *peta*, perhaps of Celtic origin. It is found from about 1200 in Scoto-Latin documents.

pebble [late Old English] This was first recorded as the first element of the phrases *papel-stān* 'pebble-stone' and *pyppelrīpig* 'pebble-stream'. The origin is unknown, but the word is recorded in place names from the early 12th century onwards.

peck [late Middle English] This word meaning 'strike with the beak' is of unknown origin; Middle Low German *pekken* 'peck (with the beak)' may be related. It is apparently a by-form (= secondary form) of *pick* with which it was once commonly interchangeable. The compound:

■ **pecking order** translates the German word *Hackliste* (from animal psychology contexts) and describes a social hierarchy first observed in hens where those of higher rank are able to threaten those of lower rank without retaliation.

pectoral [late Middle English] *Pectoral* was once a word for 'breastplate'. It is from Latin *pectorale* 'breastplate', *pectoralis* 'of the breast', from *pectus, pector-* 'breast, chest'. Its use to mean *pectoral muscle* dates from the mid 18th century.

peculiar [late Middle English] 'Particular, special' was the early sense of *peculiar* from Latin *peculiaris* 'of private property'. The source is Latin *peculium* 'property', from *pecu* 'cattle': cattle constituted private property. The sense 'odd' dates from the early 17th century.

pecuniary [early 16th century] *Pecuniary* is from Latin *pecuniarius*, from *pecunia* 'money', from *pecu* 'cattle, money'.

pedagogue [late Middle English] *Pedagogue* came via Latin from Greek *paidagōgos*, the word for a slave who accompanied a child to school (from *pais, paid-* 'boy' and *agōgos* 'guide'). **Pedagogy** dates from the late 16th century and is

from French *pédagogie*, from Greek *paidagōgia* 'office of a pedagogue', from *paidagōgos*. The adjective **pedagogic** (from French *pédagogique*, from Greek *paidagōgikos*) arose in the late 18th century.

pedal [early 17th century] Early use of the word *pedal* was to denote a foot-operated lever of an organ. It came via French from Italian *pedale*, from Latin *pedalis* 'a foot in length'. Latin *pes, ped-* 'foot' is the base.

pedant [late 16th century] *Pedant* is from French *pédant*, from Italian *pedante* 'teacher', perhaps from the first element of Latin *paedogogus* 'teacher of boys'.
→PEDAGOGUE

pedestal [mid 16th century] *Pedestal* is from French *piédestal*, from Italian *piedestallo*. The elements are *piè* 'foot' (from Latin *pes, ped-*, which later influenced the spelling) and *di* 'of' and *stallo* 'stall'.

pedestrian [early 18th century] This word is from French *pédestre* or based on Latin *pedester* which meant both 'going on foot' and 'written in prose'. Early use in English was in the description of writing as 'prosaic'.

pedicure [mid 19th century] French *pédicure* is the source of this word, from Latin *pes, ped-* 'foot' and *curare* 'attend to'.

pedigree [late Middle English] This word is from Anglo-Norman French *pé de grue* 'crane's foot': this was a mark (consisting of three curved lines like the claws of a bird) used to denote succession in pedigrees. *Pedigree* was used in the context of animals from the early 17th century.

pediment [late 16th century] This word for the triangular upper part of the front of a building was formerly written as *periment*; it is perhaps an alteration of *pyramid*.

pedlar [Middle English] This is perhaps an alteration of the synonymous dialect word *pedder*, apparently from (chiefly eastern county) dialect *ped* 'pannier', which would have contained wares for sale. The verb **peddle** (early 16th century) is a back-formation (by removal of the suffix) from *pedlar*.

peek [late Middle English] Early spellings included *pike* (found in Chaucer and still heard in Yorkshire dialect) and *pyke*; the origin is unknown.

peel [Middle English] This verb (as in *peel fruit*) had the early sense 'to plunder'. It is a variant of dialect *pill*, from Latin *pilare* 'to strip hair from', from *pilus* 'hair'. The differentiation of *peel* and *pill* may have been by association with the French verbs *peler* 'to peel' and *piller* 'to pillage'. The phrase *peel off* meaning 'break away from a formation' (e.g. *the bombers peeled off one by one*) dates from the 1940s.

peep [late 15th century] The word *peep* (like *peek*) is symbolic of the action of looking quickly and furtively. The phrase:

■ **peeping Tom** is from the name of the person said to have watched the English noblewoman Lady Godiva (wife of Leofric Earl of Mercia) ride naked through Coventry. According to a 13th-century legend she agreed to her husband's proposition that he would reduce unpopular taxes, only if she rode naked on horseback through the marketplace. In later versions, it was said that only peeping Tom watched and he was struck blind as a punishment.

peer[1] [late 16th century] This word as in *she peered through the gloom* is perhaps a variant of dialect *pire* (Middle English); it is perhaps partly from a shortening of *appear*.

peer[2] [Middle English] *Peer* (as in *judged by his peers*) is from Old French *peer*, from Latin *par* 'equal'. The senses 'man of high rank' and 'member of one of the degrees of nobility' (e.g. *peers of the realm*) are found early in the word's history. The phrase *peer group* dates from the 1940s. In the British **peerage** (late Middle English), earldoms and baronetcies were the earliest to be conferred; dukes were created from 1337, marquesses from the end of the 14th century, and viscounts from 1440.

peevish [late Middle English] *Peevish* in early examples meant 'foolish, mad, spiteful'. The origin is unknown. The verb **peeve** is recorded from the early 20th century as a back-formation (by removal of the suffix) from *peevish*.

peg [late Middle English] *Peg* is probably of Low German origin; Dutch dialect *peg* 'plug, peg' may be related. Use of the word as a verb is found from the mid 16th century, extending from the notion of 'fixing with a peg' to one of figuratively 'pinning down, placing in a fixed category' (e.g. *I had him pegged as a chancer*). Early in the 19th century examples of the phrase *a round peg in a square hole* occur, and towards the end of that century *off the peg* is recorded.

pejorative [late 19th century] This word is from French *péjoratif*, *-ive*, from late Latin *pejorare* 'make worse', from Latin *pejor* 'worse'.

pelican [late Old English] The early spelling was *pellicane*; the word came via late Latin from Greek *pelekan*, probably based on *pelekus* 'axe',

referring to the shape of the bird's bill. The beak as a weapon is illustrated by the heraldic phrase *pelican in her piety* referring to the representation of a pelican wounding her breast in order to feed her young with her blood. The term:

■ **pelican crossing** dates from the 1960s: the first word is from the phrase *pe(destrian) li(ght) con(trolled)*, with alteration of the last syllable (*-con* to *-can*) to form an association with the bird's name.

pellet [late Middle English] *Pellet* is from Old French *pelote* 'metal ball', from a diminutive of Latin *pila* 'ball'. In shooting contexts it originally described a ball in English, usually one of stone used as a missile in the 13th and 14th centuries; later it came to be a term for smaller shot.

pell-mell [late 16th century] This comes from French *pêle-mêle*, from earlier *pesle mesle*, *mesle pesle*, a reduplication expressing confusion (from *mesler* 'to mix'). It has been suggested that the element *pesle* might be *pelle* 'shovel' (giving the sense 'mixed all together with a shovel') but Old French forms suggest this is a typical rhyming combination commonly found as in English *namby-pamby* and French *tirelire* 'piggy bank'.

pelmet [early 20th century] This is probably an alteration of French *palmette*, literally 'small palm', formerly a conventional ornament on window cornices.

pelt[1] [late 15th century] The origin of this *pelt* meaning 'attack by hurling things at somebody' is unknown. It is thought by some to be the same word as Middle English *pilt* 'to thrust' which was also sometimes spelt *pelt* but this remains doubtful. Use in phrases such as *pelt with rain* dates from the early 19th century.

pelt[2] [Middle English] This *pelt* as in *animal's pelt* is either from obsolete *pellet* 'skin' (from an Old French diminutive of *pel* 'skin', from Latin *pellis* 'skin') or a back-formation (by removal of the suffix) from *peltry*, a collective word for animal skins.

pelvis [early 17th century] This is a use of a Latin word meaning literally 'basin', describing the shape of the cavity.

pen[1] [Middle English] This was originally 'a feather with a sharpened quill'. Old French *penne* is the source of the word, from Latin *penna* 'feather' (which in late Latin came to mean 'pen').

pen[2] [Old English] Old English *penn*, a word for a small enclosure, is of unknown origin. The verb *pen* (e.g. *securely penned in*) was *pennen* in Middle English and is apparently formed from the Old English noun *penn*.

penal [late Middle English] This comes from Old French *penal*, from Latin *poenalis*, from *poena* 'pain, penalty'. Use of the word to mean 'appointed as a place of punishment' as in *penal colony* dates from the mid 19th century.

penalty [early 16th century] *Penalty* is probably via Anglo-Norman French: the reduction of the ending -*ity* to -*ty* suggests this. It is ultimately from medieval Latin *poenalitas*, based on *poena* 'pain'. Use of the word in sports such as football dates from the late 19th century.

penance [Middle English] The Latin verb *paenitere* 'be sorry' is the base of several words in English. *Penance* is from Old French, from Latin *paenitentia* 'repentance'; it was commonly found in the phrase *do penance* early in the word's history. Also Middle English is **penitent** which came via Old French; as a learned form in ecclesiastical use, it dominated and replaced the Middle English synonym *penant*. Late Middle English **penitentiary** was first used as a term in ecclesiastical law for a priest appointed to administer penance; this is from medieval Latin *paenitentiarius*, from Latin *paenitentia*. The North American usage meaning 'prison' dates from the early 19th century.

penchant [late 17th century] This is an adoption of a French word meaning 'leaning, inclining' (e.g. *penchant for fast cars*); it is from the present participle of the verb *pencher*.

pencil [Middle English] A *pencil* once denoted a fine paintbrush. It comes from Old French *pincel*, from a diminutive of Latin *peniculus* 'brush', itself a diminutive of *penis* 'tail'. The verb was originally used in the early 16th century in the sense 'paint with a fine brush'.

pendant [Middle English] This was originally a term for an architectural decoration projecting downwards. It comes from an Old French word meaning literally 'hanging', the present participle of the verb *pendre*, from Latin *pendere*. The word was used from late Middle English for a jewel attached to clothing but later it was applied to one attached to a necklace. Use of the word for a light fitting hanging from the ceiling dates from the mid 19th century.

pending [mid 17th century] This is an Anglicized spelling of French *pendant* 'hanging'. The sense 'awaiting decision' as in *pending tray* dates from the late 18th century.

pendulum [mid 17th century] This is a use of the Latin neuter form (functioning as a noun) of *pendulus* 'hanging down', a base shared by early 17th-century **pendulous**. The Latin source verb is *pendere* 'to hang'.

penetration [late Middle English] This is from Latin *penetratio(n-)*, from the verb *penetrare* 'place within or enter'. The verb **penetrate** from the same Latin root, dates from the mid 16th century; it is related to *penitus* 'inner'.

peninsular [mid 16th century] *Peninsular* is from Latin *paeninsula*, from *paene* 'almost' and *insula* 'island'.

pennant [early 17th century] This word for a flag is a blend of *pendant* and late Middle English **pennon**. The latter is a less common word for a 'flag', from Old French, from a derivative of Latin *penna* 'feather'.

penny [Old English] Old English *penig*, *penning* is Germanic in origin, related to Dutch *penning*, German *Pfennig*, and perhaps also to English *pawn* and *pan* (the latter from its round flat shape). For many centuries the *penny* was made of silver, then later of copper (hence the colloquial term *coppers*), and after 1860 of bronze. Before 15 February 1971 it was denoted by *d.* for *denarius* (the Latin word for an ancient Roman silver coin). The phrase:
■ **penny plain** meaning 'plain and simple' dates from the mid 19th century with reference to prints of characters sold for toy theatres, costing one penny for black-and-white ones, and two pennies for coloured ones.
→ PAN¹; PAWN²

pension [late Middle English] In early use a *pension* was a 'payment, tax, or regular sum paid to retain allegiance'. It comes from Old French, from Latin *pensio(n-)* 'payment', from *pendere* 'to pay'. Use of the word to describe an annuity paid to a retired employee has developed since the early 16th century. At first it was the Crown who paid *pensions* to retired civil servants or ex-servicemen; notable public figures also received such payments in recognition of their achievements. Gradually certain businesses granted *pensions* to former employees, this practice eventually spreading to include all people of retirement age. The current verb sense (e.g. *pension somebody off*) dates from the mid 19th century.

pensive [late Middle English] *Pensive* is from Old French *pensif*, -*ive*, from *penser* 'think': this is from Latin *pensare* 'to ponder', a frequentative (= verb of repeated action) of *pendere* 'to weigh'. The notion is of 'weighing up' the merits of various options.

pentathlon [early 17th century] This word, now a feature of the Olympic Games, once denoted the original five events of leaping, running, discus-throwing, spear-throwing, and wrestling of ancient Greek and Roman games. The origin is Greek, from *pente* 'five' and *athlon* 'contest'.

Pentecost [Old English] The Old English word was *pentecosten*, which came via ecclesiastical Latin from Greek *pentēkostē* (*hēmera*) 'fiftieth (day)'. The Jewish festival is held on the fiftieth day after the second day of Passover. The Christian festival is held on the seventh Sunday after Easter commemorating the descent of the Holy Spirit on the disciples as recorded in Acts 2.

penthouse [Middle English] In Middle English the word was *pentis* and meant 'an outhouse built on to the side of a building'. It was a shortening of Old French *apentis*, based on late Latin *appendicium* 'appendage', from Latin *appendere* 'hang on'. The change of form in the 16th century was by association with French *pente* 'slope' (first syllable) and English *house* (second syllable).

penultimate [late 17th century] Latin *paenultimus* is the source of this word, from *paene* 'almost' and *ultimus* 'last', following the pattern of *ultimate*.

penury [late Middle English] This word describing 'the condition of being destitute' is from Latin *penuria* 'need, scarcity'; it may be related to *paene* 'almost'.

people [Middle English] *People* is from Anglo-Norman French *poeple*, from Latin *populus* 'populace'. The phrase *of all people* expressing disbelief about somebody (e.g. *he of all people should know*) dates from the 1700s; the capitalized form in the phrase *the People* referring in US legal contexts to the State prosecution (e.g. *the People versus ...*), dates from the early 19th century.

pep [early 20th century] This word meaning 'energy and high spirits' is an abbreviation of *pepper*. It was originally a US usage.
→ PEPPER

pepper [Old English] Old English *piper*, *pipor* is from a West Germanic source and is related to Dutch *peper* and German *Pfeffer*; the word came via Latin from Greek *peperi*, from Sanskrit *pippalī* 'berry, peppercorn'. The phrase *peppercorn rent* is from the once common practice of stipulating the payment of a peppercorn as a nominal rent.

peptic [mid 17th century] *Peptic* is from Greek *peptikos* 'able to digest'.

WORDBUILDING

The prefix **per-** [from a Latin word meaning 'through, by means of'] adds the sense

■ **through; all over** [perforation; pervade]

■ **completely** [perfect; perturb]

In chemistry contexts, the prefix **per-** relates to the maximum proportion of some element in combination [peroxide]

---

perambulate [late Middle English] This is from Latin *perambulare* 'walk about', from *per-* 'all over' and *ambulare* 'to walk'. **Perambulator**, the full form of *pram* dates from the mid 19th century.

perceive [Middle English] *Perceive* is from a variant of Old French *perçoivre*, from Latin *percipere* 'seize, understand': the elements are Latin *per-* 'entirely' and *capere* 'take'. Related forms from the same base are: late Middle English **perception** (from Latin *perceptio(n-)*), late Middle English **perceptible** (from Latin *perceptibilis*), and mid 17th-century **perceptive** (from medieval Latin *perceptivus*).

perch [late Middle English] The noun (as in *perch for a bird's cage*) is from Middle English *perch* meaning 'pole, stick' (from Old French *perche*) which was also formerly used as a measure of length. The verb is from Old French *percher*.

percolate [early 17th century] *Percolate* is from Latin *percolare* 'strain through'; the formative elements are Latin *per-* 'through' and *colare* 'to strain' (from *colum* 'strainer'). The term **percolator** for a coffee-maker dates from the mid 19th century.

percussion [late Middle English] This is from Latin *percussio(n-)*, from the verb *percutere* 'to strike forcibly'. The elements here are Latin *per-* 'through' and *quatere* 'to shake, strike'. The word has been used in musical contexts since the late 18th century.

peremptory [late Middle English] This was first used as a legal term meaning 'admitting no refusal' when used of an order or decree; it came via Anglo-Norman French from Latin *peremptorius* 'deadly, decisive', from *perimere* 'destroy, cut off'. The base elements are Latin *per-* 'completely' and *emere* 'take'.

perennial [mid 17th century] The early sense recorded was 'remaining leafy throughout the year, evergreen'. It is based on Latin *perennis* 'lasting the year through'. Its use to mean 'perennial plant' dates from the mid 18th century.

perfect [Middle English] *Perfect* is from Old French *perfet*, from Latin *perfectus* 'completed', from the verb *perficere* 'to complete'. Latin *per-* 'through, completely' and *facere* 'do' are the formative elements and the base too of Middle English **perfection** (via Old French from Latin *perfectio(n-)*). The early sense of *perfection* was 'completeness'.

perfidy [late 16th century] This literary word for 'deceitfulness' came via Latin from Latin *perfidia* 'treachery', from *perfidus* 'treacherous', based on *per-* 'to ill effect' and *fides* 'faith'. The adjective **perfidious** (from Latin *perfidiosus*) dates from the same period.

perforation [late Middle English] This is from medieval Latin *perforatio(n-)*, from the verb *perforare* (from *per-* 'through' and *forare* 'pierce') which also gave rise to **perforate** in the same period.

perform [Middle English] *Perform* is from Anglo-Norman French *parfourmer*, an alteration (by association with *forme* 'form') of Old French *parfournir*, from *par* 'through, to completion' and *fournir* 'furnish, provide'. The connection with playing music, acting a play, etc. is recorded from the early 17th century.

perfume [mid 16th century] *Perfume* was originally pleasant-smelling smoke from a burning substance, especially in the process of fumigation. The noun comes from French *parfum*, the verb from *parfumer*, from obsolete Italian *parfumare* meaning literally 'to smoke through'.

perfunctory [late 16th century] This word meaning 'carried out with the minimum of effort' is from late Latin *perfunctorius* 'careless', from Latin *perfunct-*, the past participial stem of *perfungi* 'discharge'.

pergola [mid 17th century] This is an English use of an Italian word, from Latin *pergula* 'projecting roof', from *pergere* 'come or go forward'.

perhaps [late 15th century] This word is composed of Latin *per* 'by means of' and Middle English *hap* 'chance, fortune' (from Old Norse).

peril [Middle English] *Peril* is from Old French, from Latin *peric(u)lum* 'danger', from the base of *experiri* 'to try'. The phrase *at one's peril* is found from late Middle English. **Perilous** dating from the same period as *peril* is from Old French *perillous*, from Latin *periculosus*, from *periculum*.

perimeter [late Middle English] *Perimeter* came via Latin from Greek *perimetros*, from *peri-* 'around' and *metron* 'measure'. Attributive use in phrases such as *perimeter fence* dates from the 1970s.

period [late Middle English] When first used, *period* referred to the time during which something such as a disease, ran its course. It comes from Old French *periode*, via Latin from Greek *periodos* 'orbit, recurrence, course', from *peri-* 'around' and *hodos* 'way'. The sense 'portion of time' dates from the early 17th century, as does use of the word to mean 'full stop', now part of US English. **Periodic** is found from the mid 17th century, from French *périodique*, or via Latin from Greek *periodikos* 'coming round at intervals', from *periodos*.

peripatetic [late Middle English] A *peripatetic* was an early term for a philosopher holding the doctrines of Aristotle (384–322 BC), who would characteristically walk about while teaching. The word is from Old French *peripatetique*, via Latin from Greek *peripatētikos* 'walking up and down', from the verb *peripatein*.

periphery [late 16th century] Early use was to describe a line forming the boundary of something. The word came via late Latin from Greek *periphereia* 'circumference', from *peripherēs* 'revolving around'. Greek *peri-* 'around' and *pherein* 'to bear' are the base elements.

perish [Middle English] *Perish* is from Old French *periss-*, the lengthened stem of *perir*, from Latin *perire* 'pass away': the elements here are Latin *per-* 'through, completely' and *ire* 'go'. The word was once a common imprecation meaning 'May (something) perish!': this usage is retained in the phrase *perish the thought!* found from the late 19th century.

perjury [late Middle English] *Perjury* is from Anglo-Norman French *perjurie*, from Latin *perjurium* 'false oath', from the verb *perjurare*, literally 'to swear to ill effect'. This Latin verb also gave rise to late Middle English **perjure** originally used in the form *perjured* meaning 'guilty of perjury'.

perk¹ [late Middle English] This *perk* as in *perk up* was first recorded in the senses 'to perch, alight' and 'be lively'. It may be from an Old French dialect variant of *percher* 'to perch'.

perk² [early 19th century] The *perk* which refers to a benefit of money or goods (e.g. *perks of the job*) is an abbreviation of late Middle English **perquisite**, from Latin *perquisitum* 'acquisition'.

permanent [late Middle English] *Permanent* is from Latin *permanent-* 'remaining to the end' (perhaps via Old French), from *per-* 'through' and *manere* 'remain'. The abbreviation **perm** in hairdressing dates from the 1920s. The noun **permanence** is also a late Middle English word from medieval Latin *permanentia* (perhaps via French), from the verb *permanere*.

permeable [late Middle English] This word comes from Latin *permeabilis*, from *permeare* 'pass through'. The verb **permeate** is found in examples from the mid 17th century and also from the same Latin verb: the base elements are Latin *per-* 'through' and *meare* 'go'.

permit [late Middle English] This word was originally used in the sense 'commit, hand over': it is from Latin *permittere*, from *per-* 'through' and *mittere* 'send, let go'. The noun use for a 'written order giving permission' is recorded from the early 18th century. Late Middle English **permission** is (via Latin *permissio(n-)*) from the same Latin base verb, as is late 15th-century **permissive**. The latter was first found with the meaning 'tolerated, allowed' (Shakespeare *Measure for Measure*: When evil deeds have their permissive pass): it is from Old French, or from medieval Latin *permissivus*. The modern sense is 'allowing freedom' as in *permissive society* (1970s).

permutation [late Middle English] 'Exchange, barter' was the early meaning of *permutation* which came via Old French from Latin *permutatio(n-)*, from the verb *permutare* 'change completely'. The abbreviation **perm** dates from the 1950s in the context of the Football Pools where a combination of numbers from a larger group could be considered for a dividend.

pernicious [late Middle English] This word meaning 'having a harmful effect' is from Latin *perniciosus* 'destructive', from *pernicies* 'ruin', based on *nex, nec-* 'death'.

pernickety [early 19th century] This was originally Scots and perhaps northern English dialect. The origin is unknown; it is commonly found in US English and more recently has been introduced into literary English by writers of Scottish nationality. A shorter Scots form *pernicky* exists which may be a child's corruption of *particular*; *pernickety* could be an onomatopoeic extension.

perpendicular [late Middle English] Early use was as an adverb meaning 'at right angles'; it came via Old French from Latin *perpendicularis*, from *perpendiculum* 'plumb line'. The elements are Latin *per-* 'through' and *pendere* 'to hang'.

perpetrate [mid 16th century] *Perpetrate* is from Latin *perpetrare* 'perform', from *per-* 'to completion' and *patrare* 'bring about'. In Latin the act perpetrated might be good or bad; in English the verb was first used in the statutes referring to crime, which led to the negative association.

perpetual [Middle English] This came via Old French from Latin *perpetualis*, from *perpetuus* 'continuing throughout' (from *perpes, perpet-* 'continuous'). Latin *perpetuus* is also the base of late Middle English **perpetuity** (via Old French from Latin *perpetuitas*), and early 16th-century **perpetuate** (from Latin *perpetuare* 'make permanent').

perplexity [Middle English] *Perplexity* is from Old French *perplexite* or late Latin *perplexitas*, from Latin *perplexus* 'entangled, confused'. This is also the base of **perplex** formed under the influence of late 15th-century *perplexed*, a past participial adjective from obsolete *perplex* 'bewildered'. Latin *plexus* 'interwoven' is the source, from the verb *plectere* (Shakespeare *King John*: —I am perplext and know not what to say— What canst thou say, but will perplex thee more).

persecute [late Middle English] This word is from Old French *persecuter*, from Latin *persequi* 'follow with hostility', from *per-* 'through, utterly' *sequi* 'follow, pursue'.

perseverance [Middle English] Latin *perseverare* 'abide by strictly', from *perseverus* 'very strict' is the source of both **perseverance** (from Old French, from Latin *perseverantia*) and late Middle English **persevere** (from Old French *perseverer*).

persist [mid 16th century] *Persist* is from Latin *persistere*, from *per-* 'through, steadfastly' and *sistere* 'to stand'. The noun **persistence** dating from the same period is from French *persistance*, from the verb *persister*; it was influenced in spelling by Latin *persistent-* 'continuing steadfastly'.

person [Middle English] The word *person* is from Old French *persone*, from Latin *persona* 'actor's mask, character in a play', a sense later generalized to 'human being'. The word *parson* is a differentiated form of the same word. Of the phrases, *in person* is found from the mid 16th century and *in the person of* towards the end of that century. Also based on Latin *persona* is **personal**, a late Middle English word from Old French, from Latin *personalis* 'of a person'. **Personality** (late Middle English describing 'the fact or quality of being a person') is from Old French *personalite*, from medieval Latin *personalitas*, from Latin *personalis*. The prime current sense describing the qualities and characteristics in a person's make-up dates from the late 18th century.
→ PARSON

personage [late Middle English] This comes from Old French, reinforced by medieval Latin *personagium* 'effigy'. In early use the word was qualified by words such as *honourable* and *eminent*, but since the 19th century the notion 'significant, notable' has been implied in the word itself.

personnel [early 19th century] The word *personnel* is from a French adjective used as a noun, contrasted with *matériel* 'equipment or materials used in an organization or undertaking' and commonly in military contexts. Use of the word to designate a section of a company dealing with staff matters dates from the 1960s; this is now commonly referred to as *Human Resources*.

perspective [late Middle English] In early use this word was a name for the science of 'optics': it comes from medieval Latin *perspectiva (ars)* 'science of optics', from *perspicere* 'look at closely'. The base elements are *per-* 'thorough' and *specere* 'to look'. The notion of *perspective* in drawings dates from the end of the 16th century

perspicacious [early 17th century] This word meaning 'having a ready insight' is based on Latin *perspicax*, *perspicac-* 'seeing clearly'.

perspiration [early 17th century] A French word is the source of *perspiration* in English from the verb *perspirer*, which also gave mid 17th-century **perspire**. Latin *perspirare*, composed of *per-* 'through' and *spirare* 'breathe', is the base.

persuasion [late Middle English] *Persuasion* is from Latin *persuasio(n-)*, from the verb *persuadere*, the source also of **persuade** in the late 15th century. The base elements are Latin *per-* 'through, to completion' and *suadere* 'advise'. **Persuasive** (also late 15th century) is from French *persuasif*, *-ive* or medieval Latin *persuasivus*, from the same Latin base verb.

pert [Middle English] The early sense recorded was 'manifest', often used in contrast to *privy*. Another obsolete sense is 'quick to see and act; sharp'. The word is from Old French *apert*, from Latin *apertus* 'opened', the past participle of *aperire*, reinforced by Old French *aspert* (from Latin *expertus*). The common current sense 'attractive and jaunty' was also part of early usage of the word.
→ EXPERT

pertain [late Middle English] *Pertain* is from Old French *partenir*, from Latin *pertinere* 'extend to, have reference to', from *per-* 'through' and *tenere* 'to hold'. The same Latin verb is also the base of **pertinent** (from Old French) from the same period.

perturb [late Middle English] The word *perturb* is from Old French *pertourber*, from Latin *perturbare*, from *per-* 'completely' and *turbare* 'disturb'. **Perturbation** is also late Middle English, from Latin *perturbatio(n-)*, from the verb *perturbare*.

peruke [mid 16th century] This word is from French *perruque*, from Italian *perrucca*, of unknown origin. In early use a *peruke* referred to a natural head of hair; it was then used in phrases such as *false peruke*, *artificial peruke* which led to the meaning 'wig'.

peruse [late 15th century] *Peruse* in early examples meant 'use up, wear out'. This is perhaps from the prefix *per-* meaning 'thoroughly' added to the verb *use*. The later senses such as 'consider in detail' may involve a different formation of the verb; Anglo-Norman French *peruser* 'examine' may be related.

pervade [mid 17th century] Early examples included the sense 'traverse'. *Pervade* comes from Latin *pervadere*, from *per-* 'throughout' and *vadere* 'go'. The adjective **pervasive** dates from the mid 18th century based on the same Latin verb.

perverse [late Middle English] The early sense recorded was 'turned away from what is right or good'. The source is Old French *pervers(e)*, from Latin *perversus* 'turned about', from the verb *pervertere* 'turn to ill effect'. Based on the same Latin verb are: **perversion**, also late Middle English from Latin *perversio(n-)*, and **pervert**, late Middle English from Old French *pervertir*. The current noun sense 'person whose sexual behaviour is regarded as abnormal' dates from the late 19th century; the abbreviation **perv** is found from the 1940s.

pervious [early 17th century] *Pervious* is based on Latin *pervius* 'having a passage through' (based on *via* 'way').

pessimism [late 18th century] This comes from Latin *pessimus* 'worst', on the pattern of *optimism*. In the late 19th century it was the name given to the doctrine of Schopenhauer, Hartmann and other philosophers that this world is the worst possible or that evil will naturally prevail over good.

pest [late 15th century] The early use of the word was as a term for the bubonic plague. It comes from French *peste* or Latin *pestis* 'plague'. The informal word **pesky** (late 18th century) meaning 'annoying' may be related to *pest*.

pester [mid 16th century] Early use included the meanings 'overcrowd (a place)' and 'impede (a person)'. The source is French *empestrer* 'encumber', influenced by *pest*. The current sense 'annoy someone with frequent requests' is an extension of an earlier use, 'infest', referring to vermin.

pestilence [Middle English] This is from Old French, from Latin *pestilentia*, based on *pestis* 'a plague'. When first used, as well as referring to a disease, it denoted something morally corrupting.

pestle [Middle English] This comes from Old French *pestel*, from Latin *pistillum*, from the verb *pinsere* 'to pound'. The phrase *pestle and mortar* stems from the use of these by apothecaries in compounding drugs; they became symbolic of the profession.

pet [early 16th century] This word for a tame animal kept as part of a household was originally Scots and northern English. Its origin is unknown. It has been used as a term of endearment from the mid 19th century; *teacher's pet* is found as a phrase half a century later. The verb meaning 'stroke affectionately' is recorded from the early 17th century; sexual connotations have been associated with the word from the 1920s from US English.

petal [early 18th century] The word *petal* is from modern Latin *petalum*, from Greek *petalon* 'leaf', a neuter form (used as a noun) of *petalos* 'outspread'.

petard [mid 16th century] A *petard* historically was a small bomb made of a metal or wooden box filled with powder, for blowing down a door or for making a hole in a wall. It comes from French *pétard*, from *péter* 'break wind'. The phrase *hoist with one's own petard* meaning 'thwarted by having one's plan backfire' is from Shakespeare's *Hamlet*: *hoist* means 'lifted and removed' (from dialect *hoise*).

petition [Middle English] *Petition* is from Latin *petitio(n-)*, from *petit-*, the past participial stem of *petere* 'aim at, seek, lay claim to'. The verb dates from the early 17th century (Shakespeare *Coriolanus*: You have, I know, petition'd All the gods for my prosperity).

petrify [late Middle English] This word is from French *pétrifier*, from medieval Latin *petrificare*, from Latin *petra* 'rock', from Greek. The early English meaning was 'convert into stone'; the figurative use 'freeze through fear' dates from the late 18th century.

petticoat [late Middle English] This comes from the phrase *petty coat* which means literally 'small coat'. It was originally a small coat worn by men underneath a doublet; it was then applied more generally and may have been a kind of tunic worn by women before coming to denote an underskirt.

pettifogger [mid 16th century] This word for an inferior legal practitioner is from *petty* and obsolete *fogger* 'underhand dealer': the latter is probably from *Fugger*, the name of a family of merchants in Augsburg, Bavaria, in the 15th and 16th centuries. The verb **pettifog** (early 17th century) is a back-formation (by removal of the suffix) from *pettifogger*.

petty [late Middle English] The early sense recorded was 'small in size'; it is from a phonetic spelling of the pronunciation of French *petit* 'small'. The sense 'of small importance' dates from the late 16th century.

petulant [late 16th century] 'Immodest' was the early sense of *petulant* from French *pétulant*, from Latin *petulant-* 'impudent'; this is related to *petere* 'aim at, seek'. The current sense 'childishly sulky' (mid 18th century) is influenced by *pettish* meaning 'bad-tempered' (synonymous with the phrase *in a pet* 'in a sulk').

pew [late Middle English] This originally denoted a raised, enclosed place in a church, provided for particular worshippers. It comes from Old French *puye* 'balcony', from Latin *podia*, the plural of *podium* 'elevated place'. The use of *pew* for general seating for the congregation as opposed to the *pulpit* is found from the early 17th century.

pH [early 20th century] This abbreviation as in *pH factor* is from *p* representing German *Potenz* 'power' and *H*, the symbol for hydrogen.

phantom [Middle English] Early senses included 'illusion' and 'delusion'. It is from Old French *fantosme*, based on Greek *phantasma* 'mere appearance'.
→ FANTASTIC

pharaoh [Middle English] *Pharaoh* came via ecclesiastical Latin from Greek *Pharaō*, from Hebrew *par'ōh*, from Egyptian *pr-'o* 'great house'. Early English spellings included *Pharaon* and *Pharaoe*; the final *h* in later English spellings was influenced by the Hebrew.

pharmacy [late Middle English] *Pharmacy* was formerly the administration of drugs. It comes from Old French *farmacie*, via medieval Latin from Greek *pharmakeia* 'practice of the druggist', based on *pharmakon* 'drug'. This is also the base of **pharmaceutical** (mid 17th century) via late Latin from Greek *pharmakeutikos*, from *pharmakeutēs* 'druggist'.

phase [early 19th century] A *phase* first described an aspect of the moon. The word is from French *phase*, based on Greek *phasis* 'appearance', from the base of *phainein* 'to show'. The Latin form *phasis* was in use in English originally.

pheasant [Middle English] This is from Old French *fesan*, via Latin from Greek *phasianos* '(bird) of Phasis', the name of a river in the

Caucasus, from which the bird is said to have originated and spread westwards.

phenomenon [late 16th century] *Phenomenon* came via late Latin from Greek *phainomenon* 'thing appearing to view', based on *phainein* 'to show'. The word has also been used in the sense 'remarkable thing or person; prodigy' since the early 18th century (Dickens *Nicholas Nickleby*: 'This Sir', said Mr Vincent Crummles, bringing the maiden forward, 'this is the infant phenomenon—Miss Ninetta Crummles').

phial [Middle English] The word *phial* is from Old French *fiole*, via Latin from Greek *phialē* which described a broad flat container.

philander [mid 18th century] This comes from the earlier noun *philander* 'man, husband', often used in literature as the given name of a lover (and very often matched with the female character Phillis). It comes from Greek *philandros* 'fond of men', from *philein* 'to love' and *anēr* 'man'.

philanthropy [early 17th century] This word came via late Latin from Greek *philanthrōpia*, from *philanthrōpos* 'man-loving', from *philein* 'to love' and *anthrōpos* 'human being'. Related words from the same base are mid 18th-century **philanthrope**, and late 18th-century **philanthropic** (from French *philanthropique*).

philately [mid 19th century] This word for the collection of postage stamps is from French *philatélie*. The first element is from *philo-* 'loving', the second from Greek *ateleia* 'exemption from payment' (from *a-* 'not' and *telos* 'toll, tax'). The French word was proposed by M. Herpin, a postage-stamp collector, in *Le collectionneur de Timbres-poste* (15 November 1864); before postage stamps, letters were stamped with the word *franco* or *free* (i.e. 'without toll' because the carriage had been prepaid).

Philistine [late Middle English] This comes from French *Philistin*, via late Latin from Greek *Philistinos*, from Hebrew *pĕlištī*. In ancient history a *Philistine* was a member of a non-Semitic people (said to come from Crete) occupying the southern coast of Palestine in biblical times; they came into conflict with the Isralites during the 12th and 11th centuries BC. The figurative sense 'person hostile to culture' arose as a result of a confrontation between town and gown in Jena, Germany, in the late 17th century; a sermon on the conflict quoted: the Philistines are upon you (Judges 16), which associated the townspeople with hostility to culture.

philosopher [Middle English] The Latin words *philein* 'to love' and *sophos* 'wise' are the base of both *philosopher* (a variant of Old French *philosophe*, via Latin from Greek *philosophos* 'lover of wisdom') and Middle English **philosophy** (from Old French *philosophie*, via Latin from Greek *philosophia* 'love of wisdom').

phlegm [Middle English] Early spellings included *fleem* and *fleume*, from Old French *fleume*, from late Latin *phlegma* 'clammy moisture (of the body)'. The source is Greek *phlegma* 'inflammation', from *phlegein* 'to burn'. The spelling change in the 16th century was due to association with the Latin and Greek forms. Middle English **phlegmatic** first used in the sense 'relating to the humour phlegm', is from Old French *fleumatique*, via Latin from Greek *phlegmatikos*, from *phlegma*. The sense 'calm and self-possessed' dates from the late 16th century.

phobia [late 18th century] This is an independent usage of the suffix *-phobia* (via Latin from Greek) meaning 'fear'.

phonetic [early 19th century] *Phonetic* is from modern Latin *phoneticus*, from Greek *phōnētikos*, from *phōnein* 'speak'.

photography [early 19th century] This is from Greek *phōs*, *phōt-* 'light' and *-graphia* 'writing'. The word was apparently introduced (along with **photographic** and **photograph**) by Sir John Herschel in a paper presented to the Royal Society on 14 March 1839.

phrase [mid 16th century] 'Style, manner of expression' was the sense conveyed by *phrase* in early examples. It came via late Latin from Greek *phrasis*, from *phrazein* 'declare, tell'. The word **phraseology** (mid 17th century) is from modern Latin *phraseologia*, from Greek *phraseōn* (the genitive plural of *phrasis* 'a phrase') and *-logia* 'speaking'.

physical [late Middle English] *Physical* in early use meant 'medicinal, relating to medicine'. It comes from medieval Latin *physicalis*, from Latin *physica* 'things relating to nature'. The sense 'tangible' (e.g. *physical assets*) dates from the late 16th century; the sense 'relating to the body' (e.g. *physical exercise*) dates from the late 18th century.

physician [Middle English] This word is from Old French *fisicien*, based on Latin *physica* 'things relating to nature', from Greek.

physics [late 15th century] This was initially a term for natural science in general, especially the Aristotelian system. It is the plural of obsolete *physic* 'physical (thing)', suggested by Latin *physica*, Greek *phusika* 'natural things' from *phusis* 'nature'.

physiognomy [late Middle English] This word for a person's facial features is from Old French *phisonomie*, via medieval Latin from

Greek *phusiognōmonia* 'judging of a man's nature (by his features)'. The base is Greek *gnōmōn* 'a judge, interpreter'.

physiology [early 17th century] This biology term is from Latin *physiologia* (perhaps via French), from Greek *phusiologia* 'natural philosophy'.

physique [early 19th century] This is the adoption of a French adjective meaning literally 'physical', used as a noun.

pianoforte [mid 18th century] This formal word for a *piano* is from an Italian word, written earlier as *piano e forte* 'soft and loud', expressing gradation in tone. **Piano**, an abbreviation, is recorded from the early 19th century and, slightly later, examples of **pianist** (from French *pianiste*) are found.

pick[1] [Middle English] An earlier form of *pick* 'choose, take up' was *pike*, which continues in dialect use. The origin is unknown; Dutch *pikken* 'pick, peck', German *picken* 'peck, puncture', and French *piquer* 'to prick' may be related. The semantic strands include: 'pierce' (*pick a hole in*); 'remove pieces from, clear' (*pick a bone*); 'detach and take' (*pick a flower*); 'choose' (*pick a candidate*); 'plunder, steal' (*pick a pocket*); and 'separate by picking' (*pick cotton*).

pick[2] [Middle English] This *pick* describing a kind of long-handled tool for breaking up hard substances is a variant of *pike*.
→ PIKE

pickaxe [Middle English] The early spelling was *pikoys*, from Old French *picois*. It is related to *pike*; the change in the second syllable was due to association with *axe*.
→ PIKE

picket [late 17th century] A *picket* was initially a term for a 'pointed stake', on which a soldier was required to stand on one foot as a military punishment, common in the 17th and 18th centuries. It comes from French *piquet* 'pointed stake', from *piquer* 'to prick', from *pic* 'pike'. Use of the word in industrial disputes dates from the mid 19th century; this was an extension of a use of the word for a detachment of soldiers sent out to watch for the enemy (mid 18th century).

pickle [late Middle English] In early use *pickle* sometimes referred to a spicy sauce served with meat. It comes from Middle Dutch, Middle Low German *pekel*, but the ultimate origin remains unknown. The sense 'sorry predicament' (e.g. *in a right old pickle*) dates from the mid 16th century.

picnic [mid 18th century] This is from French *pique-nique*, of unknown origin. Originally it

was a fashionable social occasion for which each participant contributed provisions.

picture [late Middle English] *Picture* is from Latin *pictura*, from *pict-*, the past participial stem of *pingere* 'to paint'. The plural *pictures* referring to cinematographic films is found from the early 20th century. The phrase *every picture tells a story* was popularized by an advertising campaign for Doan's Backache Kidney pills in the early part of the 20th century. The Latin verb *pingere* is also the base of **pictorial** dating from the mid 17th century, based on late Latin *pictorius* (from Latin *pictor* 'painter').

picturesque [early 18th century] This is from French *pittoresque*, from Italian *pittoresco*, from *pittore* 'painter' (from Latin *pictor*). The change in spelling from *-tt-* to *-ct-* was due to association with *picture*.

pie [Middle English] This culinary term is probably the same word as the *pie* (from Old French, from Latin *pica* 'magpie') found in bird names such as *magpie*; the various combinations of ingredients are comparable to objects randomly collected by a magpie.

piebald [late 16th century] This word describing certain horse markings is from *pie* as in *magpie* (because of the magpie's black-and-white plumage) and *bald* in the obsolete sense 'streaked with white'.

piece [Middle English] *Piece* is from Old French *piece*; medieval Latin *pecia*, *petium* may be related but the ultimate origin is obscure. The Middle English word:

■ **piecemeal** owes the second element *-meal* to Old English *mælum* meaning 'measure, quantity taken at one time'.

pier [Middle English] *Pier* is from medieval Latin *pera*, of unknown origin. There is an Old French word *piro* meaning a 'breakwater' or 'barricade of piles' which might perhaps have given the English sense but the link between forms is unclear.

pierce [Middle English] Old French *percer* is the source of *pierce*, based on Latin *pertus-*, the past participial stem of *pertundere* 'bore through', from *per* 'through' and *tundere* 'to thrust'. The term **body piercing** dates from the 1970s.

pig [Middle English] *Pig* is probably represented in Old English by the first element of Old English *picbrēd* 'acorn', literally 'pig bread' (i.e. food for pigs). The further etymology is unknown.

pigeon [late Middle English] This comes from Old French *pijon*, a word for a young bird, especially a young dove; it is by alteration of late

Latin *pipio(n-)*, 'young cheeping bird', a word of imitative origin.

piggyback [mid 16th century] This was first used as an adverb; although analysed by folk etymology in various ways from an early date, the word's origin remains obscure. Early forms included *pickback* and *pick-a-pack*; this may have been a reference to a pack 'picked' (= pitched) on the shoulders or back.

pigment [Middle English] *Pigment* is from Latin *pigmentum*, from *pingere* 'to paint'. The verb dates from the early 20th century.

pike [early 16th century] This word for an infantry weapon in the form of a long wooden shaft is from French *pique*, a back-formation (by removal of the suffix) from *piquer* 'pierce'. French *pic* 'pick, pike' is the base. Old English *pīc* 'point, prick' (of unknown origin) may be an associated form; this gave rise to the Middle English term **pike** for a type of large freshwater fish, the association being its pointed jaw.

pile¹ [late Middle English] This *pile* meaning 'heap' is from Old French, from Latin *pila* 'pillar, pier'. The association with money (e.g. *make one's pile*) is from the phrase *pile of wealth* (Shakespeare *Henry VIII*: What piles of wealth hath he accumulated To his own portion?).

pile² [Old English] This word for a 'heavy post' driven into the ground to support a super-structure was *pil* 'dart, arrow' and 'pointed stake' in Old English. Of Germanic origin, it is related to Dutch *pijl* and German *Pfeil*, from Latin *pilum* '(heavy) javelin'.

pile³ [Middle English] The *pile* of *carpet pile* was first recorded in the sense 'downy feather'. It comes from Latin *pilus* 'hair'. The current sense dates from the mid 16th century.

pilfer [late Middle English] This is from Old French *pelfrer* 'to pillage', of unknown origin. Early use in English was as a noun meaning 'booty'; since the 1950s it has been found in the combination *pilfer-proof* with reference to packaging.

pilgrim [Middle English] *Pilgrim* is from Provençal *pelegrin*, from Latin *peregrinus* 'foreign'. The capitalized form *Pilgrim* in American history refers to one of the group of English Puritans who founded the colony of Plymouth, Massachusetts in 1620, regarded as the founding fathers of the United States. The Middle English noun **pilgrimage** is from Provençal *pelegrinatge*, from *pelegrin*.

pill [late Middle English] The *pill* referring to a small round mass, for example of a medicinal preparation, is ultimately from Latin *pilula* 'little ball', a diminutive of *pila*; Middle Dutch,

Middle Low German *pille* is related. *The Pill* as a name for a contraceptive dates from the 1950s.

pillage [late Middle English] *Pillage* was first used as a noun; it comes from Old French, from *piller* 'to plunder'.

pillar [Middle English] The word *pillar* is from Anglo-Norman French *piler*, based on Latin *pila* 'pillar'. Use of the word to mean 'a person as main supporter' arose early; examples of *pillar of society* date from the 1960s.

pillion [late 15th century] At first a *pillion* was a 'light saddle'; it comes from Scottish Gaelic *pillean*, Irish *pillín* 'small cushion', a diminutive of *pell*. Latin *pellis* 'skin' is the base.

pillory [Middle English] This is from Old French *pilori*, probably from Provençal *espilori*, associated by some with a Catalan word meaning 'peephole', of uncertain origin. A *pillory* was made up of two boards brought together leaving holes for the head and hands; in Great Britain this punishment was abolished except for the crime of perjury in 1815 and totally in 1837. Its use continued in the States until 1905.

pillow [Old English] Old English *pyle*, *pylu* is West Germanic in origin, related to Dutch *peluw* and German *Pfühl*, based on Latin *pulvinus* 'cushion'. The idiom *pillow talk* for 'intimate conversation' dates from the 1930s (James Joyce *Finnegans Wake*: Mid pillow talk and chithouse chat, on Marlborough Green as through Molesworth Fields).

pilot [early 16th century] This was initially used as a term for a person who steers a ship. It is from French *pilote*, from medieval Latin *pilotus*: this is an alteration of *pedota*, based on Greek *pēdon* 'oar', (plural) 'rudder'. Its use in aeronautics dates from the mid 19th century.

pimple [Middle English] *Pimple* is related to Old English *piplian* 'break out in pustules'.

pin [late Old English] Old English *pinn* is from a West Germanic source and is related to Dutch *pin* 'pin, peg', from Latin *pinna* 'point, tip, edge'. The primary sense in English is 'peg'. Use of the word to mean 'skittle' (as in *ninepins*) dates from the late 16th century. Based on *pin* are:
■ **pinafore** (late 18th century); the element *afore* is because the term originally denoted an apron with a bib pinned on the front of a dress.
■ **pin money**, a late 17th-century phrase for a small amount of money for spending on essentials is based on *pin* in the sense 'decorative clasp for the hair or a garment'.

pincers [Middle English] This is from Anglo-Norman French, from Old French *pincier* 'to pinch'. The military term *pincer movement* dates from the 1930s.

pinch [Middle English] *Pinch* is from an Old Northern French variant of Old French *pincier* 'to pinch'. Use of the word to mean 'hardship' dates from the early 17th century (Shakespeare *King Lear*: Necessity's sharp pinch); this sense is mainly reflected now in the phrase *feel the pinch*. The transferred slang sense 'steal' dates from the mid 17th century.

pine[1] [Old English] This *pine* used as the name for a type of evergreen coniferous tree is from Latin *pinus*, reinforced in Middle English by Old French *pin*. Based on *pine* is:
■ **pineapple** which in late Middle English meant 'a pine cone'. The word was applied to the fruit in the mid 17th century, because of its similarity in shape to a pine cone.

pine[2] [Old English] Old English *pīnian* meant 'suffer' and 'cause to suffer'. Of Germanic origin, it is related to Dutch *pijnen*, German *peinen* 'experience pain', and obsolete English *pine* 'punishment'. It is ultimately based on Latin *poena* 'punishment'.

ping [mid 19th century] This word is a formation imitative of the noise made. The game **ping-pong** derived its name in the early 20th century from the sound of a bat striking a ball.

pink[1] [mid 17th century] The colour *pink* is from early use of the adjective to describe the colour of the flowers of the plant known as *pink*: this term (dating from the late 16th century) was perhaps short for *pink eye*, literally 'small or half-shut eye'; the synonymous French plant name *oeillet* means literally 'little eye'. The informal word **pinkie** for 'the little finger' dates from the early 19th century and is partly from Dutch *pink* used in the same sense, reinforced by the English colour word *pink*.

pink[2] [early 20th century] The *pink* as in *the engine pinked* is a formation imitative of the sound made.

pinnacle [Middle English] *Pinnacle* is from Old French, from late Latin *pinnaculum*, a diminutive of *pinna* 'wing, point'. Figurative use meaning 'highest point' developed in late Middle English.

pint [late Middle English] This unit of measurement is from Old French *pinte*, of unknown origin. The word **pinta** is recorded from the 1950s, representing a pronunciation of *pint of*.

pioneer [early 16th century] *Pioneer* was first used as a military term for a member of the infantry. French *pionnier* 'foot soldier, pioneer'

is the source of the word, from Old French *paon*, from Latin *pedo*, *pedon-* 'footsoldier'.
➔ PAWN[1]

pious [late Middle English] This word is based on Latin *pius* 'dutiful, pious'; so too is early 16th-century **piety**, from Old French *piete*, from Latin *pietas* 'dutifulness'.

pip[1] [late 18th century] This *pip* as in *apple pip* is an abbreviation of Middle English **pippin** (from Old French *pepin*, of unknown ultimate origin). The late 19th-century verb **pip** used in phrases such as *he was pipped at the post* may be an extended sense.

pip[2] [early 20th century] This *pip* as in *telephone pips* is a formation imitative of the sound made.

pip[3] [late 16th century] The *pip* of a playing card or on a military uniform was originally spelt *peep*. The origin is unknown.

pipe [Old English] Old English *pīpe* 'musical tube' and *pīpian* 'play a pipe' are of Germanic origin. The word is related to Dutch *pijp* and German *Pfeife*, based on Latin *pipare* 'to peep, chirp', reinforced in Middle English by Old French *piper* 'to chirp, squeak'. The phrase:
■ **pipe dream** meaning 'fanciful hope' dates from the late 19th century referring to a dream experienced when smoking an opium pipe.
■ **piping hot** (late Middle English) was formed as a phrase because of the association with the whistling sound made by very hot liquid or food.

pique [mid 16th century] This was first used to denote animosity between two or more people: it is from French *piquer* 'prick, irritate'.

pirate [Middle English] *Pirate* is from Latin *pirata*, from Greek *peiratēs*, from *peirein* 'to attempt, attack' (from *peira* 'an attempt'). The noun **piracy** (mid 16th century) came via medieval Latin from Greek *pirateia*, from *peiratēs*.

pistol [mid 16th century] *Pistol* is from obsolete French *pistole*, from German *Pistole*. Czech *pišt'ala* is the source, of which the original meaning was 'whistle', which developed into 'firearm' by the resemblance in shape.

piston [early 18th century] This is an adoption of a French word from Italian *pistone*, a variant of *pestone* 'large pestle', an augmentative of *pestello* 'pestle'.

pit[1] [Old English] Old English *pytt* 'large hole' is West Germanic in origin. Related forms are Dutch *put* and German *Pfütze*, based on Latin *puteus* 'well, shaft'.

pit² [mid 19th century] This word for a stone of a fruit is apparently from Dutch and related to English *pith*.
→ PITH

pitch¹ [Middle English] The early senses of the verb *pitch* were 'thrust (something pointed) into the ground' and 'fall headlong'. The word may be related to Old English *picung* 'stigmata', of unknown ultimate origin. The sense development is obscure; semantic strands include: 'thrust in, place' (*pitch a tent*); 'set in order' (*pitched battle*); 'cast' (*pitch hay*); and 'incline forwards and downwards' (*pitched roof*). The compound:
■ **pitchfork** is late Middle English from the earlier word *pickfork*; it was influenced by the verb *pitch* because the tool is used for 'pitching' or throwing sheaves on to a stack.

pitch² [Old English] Old English *pic* denoting a 'sticky resinous substance' is Germanic in origin. Related forms are Dutch *pek* and German *Pech*, based on Latin *pix*, *pic-*.

pitcher [Middle English] This word for a large earthenware container is from Old French *pichier* 'pot', based on late Latin *picarium*.

piteous [Middle English] *Piteous* is from Old French *piteus*, from Latin *pietas* 'piety, pity'.
→ PIETY

pith [Old English] Old English *pitha* is from a West Germanic source.

pittance [Middle English] *Pittance* is from Old French *pitance*, from medieval Latin *pitantia*, from Latin *pietas* 'pity'.

pity [Middle English] Early use of the word included the sense 'clemency, mildness'. It comes from Old French *pite* 'compassion', from Latin *pietas* 'piety'. The adjective **pitiable** is also late Middle English, from Old French *piteable*, from *piteer* 'to pity'.
→ PIOUS

pivot [late Middle English] *Pivot* is from French, probably from the root of dialect *pue* 'tooth of a comb' and Spanish *pu(y)a* 'point'. The verb dates from the mid 19th century.

placard [late 15th century] A *placard* once referred to 'a warrant or licence'; these were under seal. The word comes from Old French *placquart*, from *plaquier* 'to plaster, lay flat', from Middle Dutch *placken*. The sense 'poster' dates from the mid 16th century.

placate [late 17th century] *Placate* is from Latin *placare* 'appease'.

place [Old English] *Place* is from Old French, from an alteration of Latin *platea* 'open space', from Greek *plateia* (*hodos*) 'broad (way)'. The word in English originally described an open space in a town such as a marketplace; this use came to specify a small square or form part of road names (e.g. *Marlborough Place*). The sense 'position' (e.g. *I know my place*) arose in Middle English.

placebo [late 18th century] This word for a medicine given for the psychological benefit it might bring rather than the physiological effect is from Latin. The word means literally 'I shall be acceptable or pleasing', from *placere* 'to please'.

placid [early 17th century] *Placid* is from French *placide*, from Latin *placidus*, from *placere* 'to please'.

plagiarism [early 17th century] This term for the practice of taking someone's ideas and passing them off as one's own is from Latin *plagiarius* 'kidnapper', from *plagium* 'a kidnapping' (from Greek *plagion*).

plague [late Middle English] Latin *plaga* 'stroke, wound' is the source of English *plague*. The origin is probably Greek (Doric dialect) *plaga*, from a base meaning 'strike'.

plaid [early 16th century] *Plaid* is from Scottish Gaelic *plaide* 'blanket', of which the ultimate origin is unknown. Describing a long piece of twilled woollen cloth with a tartan pattern, the *plaid* was formerly worn in all parts of Scotland and the north of England instead of a cloak. It is associated with Highland costume; the Lowland 'shepherd's plaid' (a black chequer pattern on white) is commonly called a *maud*.

plain [Middle English] The adjective *plain* once meant 'flat', a sense also reflected in the noun use (*Salisbury Plain*). It comes from Old French *plain*, from Latin *planus*, from a base meaning 'flat'. The meaning 'clear to the senses' was also recorded in Middle English. In this same period, the word was found meaning 'without armour' which developed later into 'without external marks' (*under plain cover*). Late Middle English saw the word used with the senses: 'open behaviour' (*to be plain with you*) and 'not outstanding' (*a plain face*). The phrase:
■ **plain sailing** (mid 18th century) was probably a popular use of *plane sailing*, denoting the practice of determining a ship's position on the theory that it is moving on a plane surface.

plaintiff [late Middle English] This is from Old French *plaintif* 'plaintive' (used as a noun). The masculine *-f* ending has come down through legal French; the word was originally the same as *plaintive* but diverged from it losing the sense of lamentation.
→ PLAINTIVE

plaintive [late Middle English] *Plaintive* is from Old French *plaintif, -ive*, from *plainte* 'lamentation', based on Latin *planctus* 'beating of the breast'. This particular word, in contrast with *plaintive*, shared the common history of adjectives ending in *-if, -ive*.
→ PLAINTIFF

plait [late Middle English] This is from Old French *pleit* 'a fold', based on Latin *plicare* 'to fold'. The word was formerly often pronounced like 'plate'; since late Middle English there has been an alternative spelling *plat*, to which the current pronunciation corresponds.

plan [late 17th century] *Plan* is from French, from earlier *plant* 'ground plan, plane surface', influenced in sense by Italian *pianta* 'plan of a building'. The notions of 'drawing on a flat surface', 'devising a scheme on paper', 'formulating a plan of action' all combine in the word.
→ PLANT

plane[1] [early 17th century] *Plane* 'flat surface' is from Latin *planum* 'flat surface', neuter of the adjective *planus* 'plain'. The adjective was suggested by French *plan(e)* 'flat'. The word was introduced to differentiate the geometrical senses, previously expressed by *plain*, from the latter's other meanings.

plane[2] [early 20th century] This *plane* as in *plane crash* is a shortened form of *aeroplane*.

plane[3] [Middle English] This word for a type of smoothing tool is from a variant of obsolete French *plaine* 'planing instrument'. This is from late Latin *plana* (used in the same sense), from Latin *planare* 'make level', from *planus* 'plain, level'.

plane[4] [late Middle English] This word for a type of tall spreading tree is from Old French, from Latin *platanus*, from Greek *platanos*, from *platus* 'broad'.

planet [Middle English] *Planet* is from Old French *planete*, from late Latin *planeta, planetes*, from Greek *planētēs* 'wanderer, planet'. The base verb is Greek *planan* 'wander'. The modern Latin word **planetarium** displaying images of stars, planets, and constellations dates from the mid 18th century, from Latin *planetarius* 'relating to the planets'.

plank [Middle English] *Plank* is from Old Northern French *planke*, from late Latin *planca* 'board', a feminine form (used as a noun) of *plancus* 'flat-footed'. The phrase *walk the plank*, a method of execution said to have been inflicted by pirates on their captives, dates from the early 19th century.

plankton [late 19th century] This word describing small and microscopic organisms floating in the sea is from German, from Greek *planktos* 'wandering', from the base of *plazein* 'wander'.

plant [Old English] Old English *plante* meant 'seedling'; it is from Latin *planta* 'sprout, cutting' (later influenced by French *plante*); the verb is from Latin *plantare* 'plant, fix in a place'. Use of the word in the phrase *plant oneself somewhere* meaning 'install oneself obstructively', dates from the early 18th century. Later that century *plant* came to be used for 'things installed', i.e. machinery, large pieces of apparatus (e.g. *plant hire*). The related late Middle English noun **plantation** described the action of planting seeds: this is from Latin *plantatio(n-)*, from the verb *plantare*. It has also been used to refer to an 'estate for the cultivation of crops such as coffee or tobacco' (early 18th century) and 'the settling of people in a conquered or dominated country': in the late 19th century it described the establishment of English landowners in Ireland.

plaque [mid 19th century] This word is an adoption from French, from Dutch *plak* 'tablet', from *plakken* 'to stick'. The notion of 'sticking' is often at the word's core, whether referring to an *ornamental plaque* attached to a wall (mid 19th century), *dental plaque* clinging to teeth (late 19th century), or in medicine a fatty deposit on an artery wall (late 19th century). The shape conveyed by the Dutch source word is reflected in the English use of the word for a gambling counter (early 20th century) and as a musical term for a thin metal plate inserted into the double reed of a wind instrument (mid 20th century).

plasma [early 18th century] The early sense recorded was 'mould, shape': it is from a late Latin word meaning 'mould', from Greek *plasma*, from *plassein* 'to shape'. Its use in medical contexts dates from the mid 19th century.

plaster [Old English] An early *plaster* was a bandage spread with a curative substance which usually became adhesive at body temperature. It comes from medieval Latin *plastrum*, a shortening of Latin *emplastrum*, from Greek *emplastron* 'daub, salve'; it was later reinforced by the Old French noun *plastre*. Use of the word to mean a soft mixture of lime mixed with sand or cement and water dates from late Middle English.

plastic [mid 17th century] The early sense of the word was 'characteristic of moulding'. French *plastique* or Latin *plasticus* gave the word in English; the base is Greek *plastikos*, from *plassein* 'to mould'. The noun **plasticine** (late 19th century) is based on *plastic*.

plate [Middle English] A *plate* first described a flat, thin sheet, usually made of metal. It is from Old French, from medieval Latin *plata* 'plate armour', based on Greek *platus* 'flat'. *Plate* as in *dinner plate* represents Old French *plat* which meant both 'platter, large dish', and 'dish of meat', a noun use of Old French *plat* 'flat'.

plateau [late 18th century] This is an English use of a French word, from Old French *platel*, a diminutive of *plat* 'level'. The verb (e.g. *the figures rose and then plateaued*) dates from the 1950s.

platform [mid 16th century] *Platform* is from French *plateforme* 'ground plan' (literally 'flat shape'). In early use in English the word was used both as a geometry term for a 'plane figure' and as a word for a 'raised level surface'.

platitude [early 19th century] This, used with reference to dull expression in speech or writing, is from French, from the adjective *plat* meaning 'flat'.

platonic [mid 16th century] This word (via Latin from Greek *Platōnikos*, from *Platōn* 'Plato') referred at first to the teachings of the Greek philosopher Plato (*c*.429–347 BC). From the mid 17th century the sense became applied to a type of relationship being 'intimate and affectionate but not sexual'.

platoon [mid 17th century] *Platoon* is from French *peloton* 'platoon', literally 'small ball', a diminutive of *pelote*. It captured the concept of a small body of footsoldiers acting as a closely-organized unit.

platter [Middle English] *Platter* is from Anglo-Norman French *plater*, from *plat* 'large dish'. In later use it came to denote a wooden plate commonly.
→ PLATE

plaudits [early 17th century] This plural word meaning 'praise' is from *plaudit* shortened from Latin *plaudite* 'applaud!': this imperative plural of *plaudere* 'to applaud' was said by Roman actors at the end of a play.

plausible [mid 16th century] Early use included the sense 'deserving applause or approval'; it comes from Latin *plausibilis* 'deserving applause', from *plaus-*, the past participial stem of *plaudere* 'applaud'.

play [Old English] Old English *pleg(i)an* meant 'to exercise'; the word is related to Middle Dutch *pleien* 'leap for joy, dance'. The Old English noun *plega* meant 'brisk movement';

its use to describe a dramatic performance on stage also dates from this early period.

plea [Middle English] A *plea* was originally a 'lawsuit'. It is from Old French *plait*, *plaid* 'agreement, discussion', from Latin *placitum* 'a decree' (the neuter past participle of *placere* 'to please'). The Middle English verb **plead** included the sense 'to wrangle' and was used in legal contexts; this is from Old French *plaidier* 'go to law', from *plaid*.

pleasant [Middle English] The early sense of *pleasant* was 'pleasing', from Old French *plaisant* 'pleasing', from the verb *plaisir*. **Pleasantry** dates from the late 16th century, from French *plaisanterie*, from Old French *plaisant*. In the plural it means 'light or humorous remarks', a usage from the early 18th century.
→ PLEASE

please [Middle English] *Please* is from Old French *plaisir* 'to please', from Latin *placere*. Use of the word in phrases such as *yes, please* and *please, sir* was apparently originally short for *may it please you, let it please you*; the use of *please* alone seems to have been unknown to Shakespeare who used *please you* (*As You Like It*: Will you hear the letter?—So please you, for I never heard it yet). Of the related words, the Old French noun *plaisir* gave **pleasure** in late Middle English; the second syllable was altered under the influence of English abstract nouns ending in *-ure*, such as *measure*. Late 16th-century **pleasurable** is based on *pleasure*, on the pattern of *comfortable*.

pleat [late Middle English] *Pleat* is a variant of *plait*. The written form of the word became obsolete between *c*.1700 and the end of the 19th century.
→ PLAIT

plebeian [mid 16th century] This word meaning 'of the lower social classes, lacking refinement' is based on Latin *plebeius*, from *plebs*, *pleb-* 'the common people'; the same base is shared by **plebiscite** dating from the same period. The latter came via French from Latin *plebiscitum*, from *plebs* and *scitum* 'decree' (from *sciscere* 'vote for'). The sense 'direct vote of the whole electorate' dates from the mid 19th century.

plectrum [late Middle English] This word came via Latin from Greek *plēktron* 'something with which to strike' (especially for striking the lyre), from *plēssein* 'to strike'.

pledge [Middle English] A *pledge* was originally a person acting as surety for another. It is from Old French *plege*, from medieval Latin *plebium*, perhaps related to the Germanic base of *plight*. An obsolete use was in the sense 'drink

to a health or toast which has been proposed' (Charles Kingsley *Heroes*: In his hand a sculptured goblet, as he pledged the merchant kings).
→ PLIGHT

plenary [late Middle English] *Plenary* as in *plenary session* is from late Latin *plenarius* 'complete', from *plenus* 'full'.

plenty [Middle English] 'Fullness' and 'perfection' were the early senses of *plenty* from Old French *plente*, from Latin *plenitas*. The base is Latin *plenus* 'full'.

plethora [mid 16th century] This was first used as a medical term in English for an excess of fluid. It came via late Latin from Greek *plēthōrē*, from *plēthein* 'be full'. The sense 'excess' dates from the early 18th century.

pliant [Middle English] This is from an Old French word meaning literally 'bending', the present participle of *plier*; this verb is also the source of late Middle English **pliable**, directly from French *pliable*.
→ PLY¹

pliers [mid 16th century] This word for a gripping tool is from dialect *ply* 'to bend', from French *plier* 'to bend', from Latin *plicare* 'to fold'.

plight [Middle English] *Plight* is from Anglo-Norman French *plit* 'fold' (conveying a notion of a complicated situation or predicament). The -*gh*- spelling is by association with Old English *plight* 'to promise' (as in *I plight thee my troth*).

plimsoll [late 19th century] A term for a light rubber-soled canvas shoe, *plimsoll* is probably from the resemblance of the side of the sole to a *Plimsoll line* on the side of the ship, marking the limit of legal submersion:
■ **Plimsoll line** derives its name from Samuel *Plimsoll* (1824–98), the English politician whose agitation in the 1870s resulted in the Merchant Shipping Act of 1876, ending the practice of sending to sea overloaded and heavily insured old ships, from which the owners profited if they sank.

plinth [late 16th century] *Plinth* is from Latin *plinthus*, from Greek *plinthos* 'tile, brick, squared stone'. The Latin form was in early use in English.

plod [mid 16th century] This is probably a symbolic formation conveying the notion of a heavy gait.

plonk¹ [late 19th century] This *plonk* meaning 'set down heavily' was originally dialect. It is imitative of the weight and sudden motion. Based on the verb *plonk* is mid 19th-century **plonker**, an informal word for 'idiot, oaf', first found in dialect meaning 'something large of its kind'.

plonk² [1930s] The *plonk* used informally in British English for 'cheap wine' was originally an Australian usage. It was probably an alteration of *blanc* in the French phrase *vin blanc* 'white wine'.

plot [late Old English] A *plot* was initially a 'piece of land'. The origin is unknown. The sense 'secret plan', dating from the late 16th century, is associated with Old French *complot* 'dense crowd, secret project'; the same term was used occasionally in English from the mid 16th century.

plough [late Old English] The early word, of Germanic origin, was spelt *plōh*; it is related to Dutch *ploeg* and German *Pflug*. The spelling *plough* became common in England in the 18th century; earlier, in the 16th–17th centuries, the noun was normally spelt *plough* but the verb was written as *plow*. The compound:
■ **ploughshare** (late Middle English) owes its second element to Old English *scær*, *scear* 'ploughshare' (related to *shear*).

ploy [late 17th century] The word *ploy* was originally Scots and northern English in the sense 'pastime'. Its origin is unknown; the notion of 'a calculated plan' dates from the 1950s.

pluck [late Old English] Early spellings included *ploccian* and *pluccian*. Of Germanic origin, it is related to Flemish *plokken*; probably from the base of Old French *(es)peluchier* 'to pluck'. The noun sense 'courage' (*such pluck in a difficult situation*) was originally boxers' slang.

plug [early 17th century] *Plug* is from Middle Dutch and Middle Low German *plugge*, of unknown ultimate origin. The informal phrase:
■ **plug-ugly**, found chiefly in US English where it originated in the mid 19th century, is probably by association with the verb *plug* in its informal sense 'hit with the fist'.

plum [Old English] Old English *plūme* is from medieval Latin *pruna*, from Latin *prunum*.
■ **plum pudding** dates from the early 18th century; it was originally made with plums and the word *plum* was retained later in the dish's name to denote 'raisin' which became a substituted ingredient.
→ PRUNE¹

plumb [Middle English] The first sense recorded for *plumb* (as in *plumb the depths*) was 'a sounding lead'; it came via Old French from Latin *plumbum* 'lead'. Sharing the same Latin base is late Middle English **plumber**, who was originally a person dealing in and working with lead: the direct source is Old French *plommier*, from Latin *plumbarius*. The verb *plumb* meaning 'work as a plumber' arose in the late 19th century as a back-formation (by removal of the suffix) from *plumber*.

plume [late Middle English] *Plume* is from Old French, from Latin *pluma* 'down, soft feather'. From the late 16th century the word was used to describe various objects resembling a feather (e.g. *plume of smoke*). Late Middle English **plumage** is from Old French, from *plume* 'feather'.

plummet [late Middle English] This word was first used as a noun describing a small ball of lead attached to a line for determining the vertical. It comes from Old French *plommet* 'small sounding lead', a diminutive of *plomb* 'lead'. The current verb sense 'drop straight down at high speed' dates from the 1930s.

plump¹ [late 15th century] 'Blunt, forthright' was the early sense of *plump*, a sense found until the early 17th century. It is related to Middle Dutch *plomp*, Middle Low German *plump*, *plomp* 'blunt, obtuse, blockish'. The sense has become appreciative, perhaps by association with *plum*.

plump² [late Middle English] The verb *plump* meaning 'set down heavily' is related to Middle Low German *plumpen*, Middle Dutch *plompen* 'fall into water'. The origin is probably imitative of the heavy sound of landing. The phrase *plump for* 'decide on' dates from the early 17th century; it was originally used in political contexts when voting for a single candidate.

plunder [mid 17th century] *Plunder* is from German *plündern* meaning literally 'rob of household goods', from Middle High German *plunder* 'household effects'. Early use of the verb was with reference to the Thirty Years War (reflecting German usage); on the outbreak of the Civil War in 1642, the word and the behaviour it expressed were associated with the forces led by Prince Rupert (of the Rhine).

plunge [late Middle English] *Plunge* is from Old French *plungier* 'thrust down', based on Latin *plumbum* 'lead, plummet'. The phrase *take the plunge* (also occasionally *make the plunge*) dates from the mid 19th century (Thackeray *Pendennis*: The poor boy had taken the plunge. Trembling with passionate emotion … poor Pen had said those words which he could withhold no more).

plural [late Middle English] The word *plural* is from Old French *plurel* or Latin *pluralis* 'relating to more than one', from *plus*, *plur-* 'more'. The noun **plurality** from the same period and is from Old French *pluralite*, from late Latin *pluralitas*, from Latin *pluralis*.

plus [mid 16th century] This is an English use is a Latin word meaning literally 'more'. The garment:
■ **plus fours** (1920s) associated with golf derive their name from the overhang at the knee requiring an extra four inches of material.

plush [late 16th century] *Plush* is from obsolete French *pluche*, a contraction of *peluche*, from Old French *peluchier* 'to pluck', based on Latin *pilus* 'hair'. The sense 'luxurious' dates from the 1920s.

ply¹ [late Middle English] This *ply* referring to 'thickness' (e.g. *two-ply wool*) was first recorded in the sense 'fold'. It comes from French *pli* 'a fold', from the verb *plier*, from Latin *plicare* 'to fold'.

ply² [late Middle English] The *ply* in phrases such as *plied them with drink* is a shortening of *apply*. The word conveys the notion of 'steady and busy occupation' and is used in various contexts. In the mid 16th century it had the sense 'work away at' which became 'to importune' (Shakespeare *Merchant of Venice*: He plies the Duke at morning and at night); it is also used of a ship travelling regularly between destinations (e.g. *ferries ply across the strait*).
→APPLY

pneumatic [mid 17th century] This word is from French *pneumatique* or Latin *pneumaticus*, from Greek *pneumatikos*, from *pneuma* 'wind'. Greek *pnein* 'breathe' is the base.

poach¹ [late Middle English] The culinary term *poach* is from Old French *pochier* which was in earlier use meaning 'enclose in a bag', from *poche* 'bag, pocket'.

poach² [early 16th century] The *poach* in contexts of illegally taking something was first recorded meaning 'push roughly together'; it is apparently related to *poke* (a sense present in English in early use). The sense 'catch and take (game) from somebody else's land' is perhaps partly from French *pocher* 'enclose in a bag'.
→POKE

pock [Old English] Old English *poc* 'pustule' is Germanic in origin, related to Dutch *pok* and German *Pocke*. Late Middle English **pox** is an alteration of *pocks*, the plural of *pock*.

pocket [Middle English] The first sense recorded for *pocket* was a 'bag, sack'; the word was also used as a measure of quantity. It comes from Anglo-Norman French *poket(e)*, a diminutive of *pouch* 'pouch' (which gave Scots *poke* 'small sack', as in *pig in a poke*). The verb dates from the late 16th century.

pod¹ [late 17th century] This word for a seed vessel (*peapod*) is a back-formation (by removal of the suffix) from dialect *podware, podder* 'field crops'. The origin is unknown.

pod² [mid 19th century] The *pod* as in *pod of whales* was originally US English; its origin is unknown.

podium [mid 18th century] *Podium* came via Latin from Greek *podion*, a diminutive of *pous*, *pod-* 'foot', giving the notion of a 'support'.

poet [Middle English] Greek *poiein* 'to create' is the base of a group of words: *poet* is from Old French *poete*, via Latin from Greek *poētēs*, a variant of *poiētēs* 'maker, poet'. Late Middle English **poetry**, in early use sometimes referring to creative literature in general, is from medieval Latin *poetria*, from Latin *poeta* 'poet'. Late 15th-century **poem** is from French *poème* or Latin *poema*, from Greek *poēma*, an early variant of *poiēma* 'fiction, poem'. Finally mid 16th-century **poetic** is via French from Latin *poeticus* 'poetic, relating to poets', from Greek *po(i)ētikos*, from *po(i)ētēs*.

po-faced [1930s] The first element is perhaps from *po* meaning 'chamber pot', influenced by *poker-faced*.

poignant [late Middle English] This is from an Old French word meaning literally 'pricking'; it is the present participle of *poindre*, from Latin *pungere* 'to prick'. In early use it described weapons in the sense 'pointed' and smells and food as 'sharp, pungent'. The sense 'distressing, moving' was also recorded early.

point [Middle English] This word expresses both precision and focused direction. The noun is partly from Old French *point*, from Latin *punctum* 'something that is pricked', giving rise to the meanings 'unit, mark, point in space or time'; it is also partly from Old French *pointe*, from Latin *puncta* 'pricking', giving rise to the senses 'tapering tip, promontory' (mid 16th century). The verb expressing the semantic strands 'give a point to' and 'indicate position or direction' is from Old French *pointer* or directly from the English noun. The compound:
■ **point-blank** (late 16th century) is probably from the verb *point* 'pierce' and *blank* meaning 'white spot (in the centre of a target)'.

poise [late Middle English] The early sense was '(measure of) weight'; the noun is from Old French *pois, peis*, the verb is from Old French *peser*, from an alteration of Latin *pensum* 'weight'. Latin *pendere* 'weigh' is the base. From the early senses arose the notion of 'equal weight, balance', leading to the extended senses 'composure' (mid 17th century) and 'elegant deportment' (late 18th century).

poison [Middle English] A *poison* originally referred to a harmful medicinal draught; it is

from Old French *poison* 'magic potion', from Latin *potio(n-)* 'potion', related to *potare* 'to drink'.

poke [Middle English] This word is of uncertain origin; Middle Dutch and Middle Low German *poken* may be related. The notion of 'searching and prying' (e.g. *poked around among the debris*) dates from the early 18th century. The noun dates from the late 18th century.

poker [mid 19th century] This is a word of US origin; it may be related to German *pochen* 'to brag' and *Pochspiel* 'bragging game'.

pokey [early 20th century] This informal word for 'prison' used mainly in North American English is an alteration of early 19th-century *pogey* (an early sense being 'hostel for the needy'). It may have been influenced by *poky* 'cramped and small'.
→ POKY

poky [mid 19th century] An early sense was 'concerned with petty matters'; it is based on *poke* in a contemporaneous sense 'confine'.

pole¹ [late Old English] Old English *pāl* 'stake', in early use was without reference to thickness or length. Of Germanic origin, it is related to Dutch *paal* and German *Pfahl*, based on Latin *palus* 'stake'. Of the idioms, *up the pole* dates from the late 19th century. The compound:
■ **pole position** (1950s) is from a 19th-century use of *pole* in horse racing, denoting the starting position next to the inside boundary fence.

pole² [late Middle English] The *pole* as in *North Pole, South Pole* is from Latin *polus* 'end of an axis', from Greek *polos* 'pivot, axis, sky'. The adjective **polar** dates from the mid 16th century and is from medieval Latin *polaris* 'heavenly', from Latin *polus*.

poleaxe [Middle English] This word for a type of battle axe is related to Middle Dutch *pol(l)aex*, Middle Low German *pol(l)exe*. The first syllable is Middle English *poll* 'head'; it may have referred to a special head of the axe or to the head of an enemy. The spelling change was due to association with *pole* meaning 'stake, handle'.
→ POLL

polecat [Middle English] The first part of *polecat* is perhaps from Old French *pole* 'chicken', referring to its prey.

polemic [mid 17th century] This came via medieval Latin from Greek *polemikos*, from *polemos* 'war'.

police [late 15th century] 'Public order' was the early sense of the word *police* which is from French. Medieval Latin *politia* 'citizenship, gov-

ernment' is the source. Current senses date from the early 19th century.
→ POLICY[1]

policy[1] [late Middle English] *Policy* 'course or principle of action' is from Old French *policie* 'civil administration', via Latin from Greek *politeia* 'citizenship', from *politēs* 'citizen'. Greek *polis* 'city' is the base.

policy[2] [mid 16th century] This word as in *insurance policy* is from French *police* 'bill of lading, contract of insurance', from Provençal *poliss(i)a*. This is probably from medieval Latin *apodissa*, *apodixa*, based on Greek *apodeixis* 'evidence, proof', from *apodeiknunai* 'demonstrate, show'.

polish [Middle English] The word *polish* is from Old French *poliss-*, the lengthened stem of *polir* 'to polish', from Latin *polire*. Use of the word to mean 'refinement' dates from the late 16th century.

polite [late Middle English] Latin *politus* 'polished, made smooth' (the past participle of *polire*) is the source of *polite* in English. The sense 'smoothed, burnished' was an early sense, reflecting Latin usage.

politic [late Middle English] *Politic* is from Old French *politique* 'political', via Latin from Greek *politikos*. This is from Greek *politēs* 'citizen', from *polis* 'city'. *Politics* as the science and art of government dates from the early 16th century.

poll [Middle English] The word may be of Low German origin. The original sense was 'head', which led to 'an individual person among a number'. This developed into the 'number of people ascertained by counting of heads' and then, in the 17th century, the 'counting of heads or of votes'. The compound:
■ **poll tax** as a tax levied on each person dates from the end of the 17th century.

pollen [mid 18th century] This is an English use of a Latin word meaning literally 'fine powder'. The verb **pollinate** is late 19th century based on Latin *pollen*.

pollute [late Middle English] *Pollute* is from Latin *polluere* 'to soil, defile', based on the root of *lutum* 'mud'. The noun **pollution** is late Middle English from Latin *pollutio(n-)*, from the verb *polluere*.

polo [late 19th century] This name for a game (originally played in the East) between two teams on horseback striking a ball with mallets into opposing goals, is from a Balti word meaning 'ball'.

poltergeist [mid 19th century] German *Poltergeist* is the source of the word in English,

from *poltern* 'create a disturbance' and *Geist* 'ghost'.

polygamy [late 16th century] Greek *polu-* 'much, often' and *-gamos* 'marrying' forming the adjective *polugamos* 'often marrying' are the base of both *polygamy* (from French *polygamie*, via late Latin from Greek *polugamia*) and **polygamous** dating from the early 17th century.

polyglot [mid 17th century] This is via French from Greek *poluglōttos*, from *polu-* 'many' and *glōtta* 'tongue'.

polytechnic [early 19th century] French *polytechnique* is the direct source of this word, from Greek *polutekhnos*, from *polu-* 'many' and *tekhnē* 'art'.

pomander [late 15th century] This word for a perforated container of sweet-smelling substances is from Old French *pome d'embre*, from medieval Latin *pomum de ambra* 'apple of amber-gris'.

pomegranate [Middle English] The name of this fruit is from Old French *pome grenate*, from *pome* 'apple' and *grenate* 'pomegranate'. Latin *(malum) granatum* meaning '(apple) having many seeds' is the source, based on Latin *granum* 'seed'.

pommel [Middle English] A *pommel* once described a ball or finial at the top point of a tower, corner of an altar, etc. It is from Old French *pomel*, from a diminutive of Latin *pomum* 'fruit, apple'.

pomp [Middle English] This is from Old French *pompe*, via Latin from Greek *pompē* 'procession, pomp', from *pempein* 'send'. Late Middle English **pompous** is from Old French *pompeux* 'full of grandeur', from late Latin *pomposus*, from *pompa* 'pomp'.

pond [Middle English] This is an alteration of *pound* now used to mean 'enclosure' but commonly used in dialect in the same sense as *pond*.
→ POUND[3]

ponder [Middle English] 'Appraise, judge the worth of' was the early sense of *ponder*, which is from Old French *ponderer* 'consider'. Latin *ponderare* 'weigh, reflect on' is the source, from *pondus, ponder-* 'weight'.

ponderous [late Middle English] This word meaning 'slow, clumsy, and weighty' came via French from Latin *ponderosus*, from *pondus, ponder-* 'weight'.

pontiff [late 17th century] Referring to the Pope, this word is from French *pontife*, from Latin *pontifex* meaning literally 'bridge-maker' but used as a term (in ancient Rome) for a member of the principal college of priests. This base is shared by **pontificate** already in late Middle English as a noun: the source is Latin *pontificatus*, from *pontifex*. The verb use 'express opinions in a pompous way' dates from the early 19th century.

pontoon [late 17th century] This word for any structure designed to provide buoyancy in the water is from French *ponton*, from Latin *ponto*, *ponton-*, from *pons*, *pont-* 'bridge'.

pony [mid 17th century] *Pony* is probably from French *poulenet* 'small foal', a diminutive of *poulain*, from late Latin *pullanus*. Latin *pullus* 'young animal' is the base. Slang use of *pony* as a term for twenty-five pounds sterling dates from the late 18th century.

poodle [early 19th century] The type of dog derives its name from German *Pudel(hund)*, from Low German *pud(d)eln* 'splash in water': the *poodle* is a water-dog. It sometimes has the figurative sense 'lackey'. The colloquial verb *poodle* meaning 'go around in leisurely manner' is found from the 1930s.

pool[1] [Old English] Old English *pōl* 'small area of standing water' is West Germanic in origin, related to Dutch *poel* and German *Pfuhl*. The word's use to mean 'swimming pool' dates from the 1920s.

pool[2] [late 17th century] The *pool* meaning 'grouping' originally referred to a game of cards with a kitty. It comes from French *poule* which means 'stake or kitty'. The game of *pool* owes its name to the notion of accumulating sums of money (agreed by each participant) by pocketing the balls of other players in a certain order, the overall winner taking the *pool*.

poop [late Middle English] This nautical term is from Old French *pupe*, from a variant of Latin *puppis* 'stern'.

poor [Middle English] *Poor* is from Old French *poure*, from Latin *pauper*. The word has been used to express 'unfortunate, hapless' (e.g. *poor thing*) since early times. Latin *pauper* is also the base of the contemporaneous noun **poverty** from Old French *poverte*, from Latin *paupertas*.

pop[1] [late Middle English] This word is an imitative formation of a sudden slapping sound; it was first used in the senses 'a blow, knock' and 'to strike'. The meaning 'abrupt explosive noise' dates from the late 16th century. The idiomatic phrase *pop the question* is recorded from the early 18th century.

pop[2] [late 19th century] This word used in phrases such as *pop music* is an abbreviation of *popular*.
→ POPULAR

pope [Old English] The word *pope* came via ecclesiastical Latin from ecclesiastical Greek *papas* 'bishop, patriarch', a variant of Greek *pappas* 'father'.

poppet [late Middle English] *Poppet* is based on Latin *pup(p)a* 'girl, doll'. In the mid 19th century, the word **popsy** 'attractive young woman' arose, an alteration of *poppet*.
→ PUPPET

poppycock [mid 19th century] This word meaning 'nonsense' is from Dutch dialect *pappekak*, from *pap* 'soft' and *kak* 'dung'.

populace [late 16th century] *Populace* is from French, from Italian *popolaccio* 'common people', based on *popolo* 'people'. The suffix *-accio* is pejorative.

popular [late Middle English] The early sense recorded was 'prevalent among the general public': it is from Latin *popularis*, from *populus* 'people'. The sense 'liked and admired' dates from the early 17th century.

populous [late Middle English] Latin *populus* 'people' is the base of *populous* (from late Latin *populosus*) and the following: **populate** (late 16th century) from medieval Latin *populare* 'supply with people'; **population** (also late 16th century) denoting initially an inhabited place, the source being late Latin *populatio(n-)*, from the verb *populare*; and **populist** (late 19th century).

porcelain [mid 16th century] *Porcelain* is from French *porcelaine*, from Italian *porcellana* 'cowrie shell': this led to 'chinaware', from a resemblance to the dense polished shells.

porch [Middle English] This is from Old French *porche*, from Latin *porticus* 'colonnade', from *porta* 'passage'. In North American English a *porch* has the meaning 'verandah': this is found from the early 19th century.

porcupine [Middle English] Forms in Middle English included *porke despyne*, a compound which may have arisen from a Latin type *porcus spinosus* meaning 'prickly pig'. Old French and Provencal *porc espin* provided the foreign word which was probably corrupted in English: the ending appears to have been identified with 'pen' and 'point' giving spellings such as *porkepyn* and *porkpen* amongst others. *Porpentine* was the word known to Shakespeare who uses it seven times in his work, four of these on inn signs. *Porcupine* was used figuratively towards the end of the 17th century in the sense 'prickly person or thing' and the quills of this animal have influenced use of the word in compounds such as *porcupine fish*, *porcupine grass*, *porcupine roller* (in a spinning machine), *porcupine wood* (with variegated markings from the coconut palm), etc.

pore¹ [late Middle English] This *pore* as in *pores of the skin* is from Old French, via Latin from Greek *poros* 'passage, pore'. Late Middle English **porous** is from Old French *poreux*, based on Latin *porus*.

pore² [Middle English] This *pore* as in *pored over the book* is perhaps related to *peer*.
→ PEER¹

pork [Middle English] *Pork* is from Old French *porc*, from Latin *porcus* 'pig'. In early use it was a term for a 'swine' or 'hog'.

porridge [mid 16th century] *Porridge* was originally a soup thickened with barley. It is an alteration of *pottage* (from Old French *potage* 'that which is put into a pot'). Use of the term informally to mean 'prison' dates from the 1950s.

port¹ [Old English] This is from Latin *portus* 'haven, harbour', reinforced in Middle English by Old French. The word *port* referring to the left side of a ship when moving forward (mid 16th century) probably referred originally to the side turned towards the port.

port² [Old English] The *port* meaning 'socket, opening' (as in *gun port, computer port*) was first used in the sense 'gateway'. It comes from Latin *porta* 'gate' and was reinforced in Middle English by Old French *porte*. The later sense 'opening in the side of a ship' led to the general sense 'aperture'.

port³ [Middle English] The *port* found in military contexts (*at the port*) and recently in computing contexts in connection with a transfer (literally 'a carrying') of software is from Old French *port* 'bearing', from the verb *porter*, from Latin *portare* 'carry'. The verb (from French *porter*) dates from the mid 16th century in military use: e.g. *port arms*.

portable [late Middle English] This is from Old French *portable*, from late Latin *portabilis*, from Latin *portare* 'carry'. The 1960s term **Portakabin** for a small temporary building is a blend of *portable* and an alteration of *cabin*.

portal [late Middle English] The word *portal* meaning 'a doorway or entrance' is from Old French, from medieval Latin *portale*, a neuter form (used as a noun) of *portalis* 'like a gate'. Latin *porta* 'door, gate' is the base. Use of the word in computing contexts (e.g. *Net portal*) arose in the 1990s.

portcullis [Middle English] *Portcullis* is from Old French *porte coleice* 'sliding door'. The elements are *porte* 'door' (from Latin *porta*) and *coleice*

'sliding' (the feminine of *couleis*, from Latin *colare* 'to filter').

portend [late Middle English] Latin *portendere* gave *portend* in English; the base elements are Latin *pro-* 'forth' and *tendere* 'to stretch'. These are the source too of late 16th-century **portent** from Latin *portentum* 'omen, token'.

porter¹ [Middle English] The word *porter* used to describe a person who carries objects (*station porter*) or patients (*hospital porter*) is from Old French *porteour*. This comes from medieval Latin *portator*, from Latin *portare* 'carry'. Use of *porter* as a term for a type of dark brown bitter beer derives from the fact that it was originally made as a drink for porters.

porter² [Middle English] The *porter* used as a term for a doorman (*hotel porter*) is from Old French *portier*, from late Latin *portarius*, from *porta* 'gate, door'.

portfolio [early 18th century] Italian *portafogli* is the source of this word, from *portare* 'carry' and *foglio* 'leaf, sheet of paper' (from Latin *folium*).

portico [early 17th century] This architectural term is from Italian, from Latin *porticus* 'porch'.

portion [Middle English] *Portion* is from Old French *porcion*, from Latin *portio(n-)*, from the phrase *pro portione* 'in proportion'. The word was once used for a 'dowry' (= marriage portion); examples of this are found from the early 16th century.

portly [late 15th century] This adjective meaning 'stout' is based on the noun *port* meaning 'bearing'. The early sense was 'stately, majestic'.
→ PORT³

portmanteau [mid 16th century] This word for a travelling bag is from French *portemanteau*, from *porter* 'carry' and *manteau* 'mantle'. The compound:
■ **portmanteau word** in the sense of a term blending both the sounds and meanings of other words (e.g. *motel*) was coined by Lewis Carroll in *Through the Looking Glass* (1872).

portray [Middle English] *Portray* is from Old French *portraire*, based on *traire* 'to draw', from an alteration of Latin *trahere*. The noun **portraiture** is recorded slightly later in the Middle English period from Old French, from *portrait*. Mid 16th-century **portrait** is from the French past participle (used as a noun) of Old French *portraire*.

pose [Middle English] The verb (as in *pose a problem, pose for a photograph*) is from Old French *poser*, from late Latin *pausare* 'to pause', which replaced Latin *ponere* 'to place'. The noun dates from the early 19th century. Towards the end of that century **poseur** was adopted from French describing a person affecting an attitude usually socially.

posh [early 20th century] This may be from the slang word *posh* meaning 'a dandy'. There is no evidence to support the folk etymology that *posh* is formed from the initials of *port out starboard home* explained by some as the practice of using the more comfortable accommodation out of the heat of the sun, on ships between England and India.

position [late Middle English] *Position* is from Old French, from Latin *positio(n-)*, from *ponere* 'to place'. The current sense of the verb dates from the early 19th century.

positive [late Middle English] *Positive* is from Old French *positif, -ive* or Latin *positivus*, from *posit-*, the past participial stem of *ponere* 'to place'. The original sense referred to laws as being formally 'laid down', which gave rise to the meaning 'explicitly laid down and admitting no question', and eventually 'very sure, convinced'.

posse [mid 17th century] Medieval Latin, from which this word came, had the literal meaning 'power', from Latin *posse* 'be able'. This is captured in English use in the power that such a group wields when summoned by a sheriff to enforce the law.

possess [late Middle English] *Possess* is from Old French *pussesser*, from Latin *possess-*, the past participial stem of *possidere* 'occupy, hold'. Latin *potis* 'able, capable' and *sedere* 'sit' are the formative elements. Use of the word in the contexts of demons *possessing* the body dates from the late 16th century. The related Middle English noun **possession** is from Old French, from Latin *possessio(n-)*.

possible [late Middle English] *Possible* is from Old French, or from Latin *possibilis* 'able to be done', from *posse* 'be able'. Dating from the same period and from the same base is **possibility**, from Old French *possibilite*, from late Latin *possibilitas*.

post¹ [Old English] This *post* (as in *gate post*) is from Latin *postis* which initially meant 'doorpost' but later came to mean 'rod, beam'. It was probably reinforced in Middle English by Old French *post* 'pillar, beam' and Middle Dutch, Middle Low German *post* 'doorpost'.

post² [early 16th century] The *post* (as in *delivered by post*) was first used to describe a 'courier on horseback travelling between stages'. It came via French from Italian *posta*, from a contraction of Latin *posita*, the feminine past participle of *ponere* 'to place'. Mid 19th-century **postal** is from French, from *poste* 'postal service'. The phrase:

■ **post-haste** arose in the mid 16th century from the use of the direction 'haste, post, haste', formerly written on letters.

post³ [mid 16th century] The *post* (as in *post as a software engineer*) is from French *poste*, from Italian *posto*: this is from a contraction of popular Latin *postum*, the neuter past participle of *ponere* 'to place'. Early use was with reference to the place where a soldier is stationed; the military phrase *the last post* is apparently linked to this, the bugle call being a summoning to or from one's station.

posterior [early 16th century] The plural *posteriors* once referred to descendants (= people following after). The source is the Latin comparative of *posterus* 'following', from *post* 'after'. Use of the word for the 'buttocks' dates from the early 17th century, when it was written in the plural.

posterity [late Middle English] This comes from Old French *posterite*, from Latin *posteritas*, from *posterus* 'following'. From the mid 16th to the mid 17th century the plural *posterities* was in use meaning 'later generations', but this is now obsolete.

posthumous [early 17th century] This is based on Latin *postumus* 'last' (a superlative from *post* 'after'); in late Latin it was spelt *posth-* by association with *humus* 'ground'.

postilion [mid 16th century] An early *postilion* was a 'forerunner acting as guide to the post-horse rider'. It comes from French *postillon*, from Italian *postiglione* 'post-boy', from *posta*. The term came to be used for a person riding the leading nearside horse of a team or pair drawing a coach, especially if no coachman was in charge.
→ POST²

postpone [late 15th century] *Postpone* is from Latin *postponere*, from *post* 'after' and *ponere* 'to place'.

postscript [mid 16th century] The source of this word is Latin *postscriptum*, the neuter past participle form (used as a noun) of *postscribere* 'write under, add'. The base elements are Latin *post* 'after, later' and *scribere* 'write'. The sense 'sequel' dates from the late 19th century (e.g. *as a postscript to this, Paul did finally marry*).

postulate [late Middle English] The verb *postulate* was first used in the sense 'nominate to an ecclesiastical office'. Latin *postulare* 'ask' is the source. The meaning 'suggest as a basis for reasoning' is found in examples from the mid 17th century. The term **postulant** for a 'candidate seeking admission to a religious order' dates from the mid 18th century; it comes from French *postulant* or Latin *postulant-*, the present participial stem of *postulare*.

posture [late 16th century] *Posture* once denoted the relative position of one thing to another. It comes from French, from Italian *postura*, from Latin *positura* 'position'. Latin *ponere* 'to place' is the base.

posy [late Middle English] A *posy* was first used to describe a short motto or line of verse inscribed inside a ring; it is a contraction of **poesy** (based on Greek *poēsis* 'creation, poetry'). The sense 'small bunch of flowers' dates from the late 15th century.

pot [late Old English] Old English *pott*, a word for a cylindrical container, was probably reinforced in Middle English by Old French *pot*. The ultimate origin is unknown; late Latin *potus* 'drinking cup' is probably related. Current senses of the verb date from the early 17th century. The colloquial usage 'shoot' (= take a potshot at) as in *potted a pigeon off the tree* is found from the mid 19th century: **potshot** is from the notion of shooting an animal 'for the pot', that is to say purely for food rather than for display (which would require skilled shooting). The noun **potter** (like *pot*) is a late Old English word and **pottery** (from Old French *poterie*, from *potier* 'a potter') is Middle English.

potash [early 17th century] This term for an alkaline compound is from the phrase *pot-ashes*, from obsolete Dutch *potasschen*: these were originally obtained by leaching vegetable ashes and evaporating the solution in iron pots.

potato [mid 16th century] *Potato* is from Spanish *patata*, a variant of Taino (an extinct Caribbean language) *batata* 'sweet potato'. The English word was originally used for the sweet potato and gained its current sense in the late 16th century.

potent [late Middle English] *Potent* meaning 'powerful' is from Latin *potent-*, the present participial stem of *posse* 'be powerful, be able'.

potentate [late Middle English] This word for a 'monarch, ruler' is from Latin *potentatus* 'dominion', from *potent-*, from *posse* 'be powerful'.
→ POTENT

potential [late Middle English] This is from late Latin *potentialis*, from *potentia* 'power', from *posse* 'be able'. The noun dates from the early 19th century.
→ POTENT

pothole [early 19th century] The first word of this compound is from Middle English *pot* 'pit', which may be of Scandinavian origin.

potion [Middle English] *Potion* is from Old French, from Latin *potio(n-)* 'drink, poisonous draught', related to *potare* 'to drink'.

potter [mid 16th century] The verb *potter* was first used in the sense 'poke repeatedly'; this use remains in dialect. It is a frequentative (= verb of repeated action) of dialect *pote* 'to push, kick, or poke', of which the origin is unknown. The sense 'occupy one's time in a desultory but pleasant manner' is found in examples from the mid 18th century.

pouch [Middle English] *Pouch* is from Old Northern French *pouche*, a variant of Old French *poche* 'bag'.

poultice [late Middle English] *Poultice* is from the Latin plural *pultes*, from *puls*, *pult-* 'pottage, pap'. It is a method of alleviating pain or of stimulating circulation by the local application of a soft moist heated substance to the skin.

poultry [Middle English] This word is from Old French *pouletrie*, from *poulet* 'pullet'.

pounce [late Middle English] This was first used as a noun for a stamping or punching tool. The origin is obscure; it may be from *puncheon* 'piercing instrument' (from Old French *poinson*). The noun sense 'claw, talon' arose in the late 15th century and gave rise to the verb 'spring or swoop upon' in the late 17th century.

pound[1] [Old English] Old English *pund* is Germanic in origin, related to Dutch *pond* and German *Pfund*. Latin (*libra*) *pondo*, denoting a Roman 'pound weight' of 12 ounces is the base. The word is used both as a unit of weight in English and as a unit of currency: the original money of account was a pound weight of silver equal to 20 shillings.

pound[2] [Old English] Old English *pūnian* meaning 'to strike heavily' is related to Dutch *puin* and Low German *pün* '(building) rubbish'. The colloquial phrase *pound the beat* in policing contexts was originally a US usage and is recorded from the early 20th century.

pound[3] [late Middle English] This word was found in compounds from late Old English and in early use referred to 'an enclosure' for the detention of stray or trespassing cattle. The origin is uncertain.

pour [Middle English] The origin of *pour* is unknown. Some have suggested a link with Old French *purer* (from Latin *purare* 'to purify with religious rites') but English shows no trace of an original sense 'purify' and no phonological link is clear.

pout [Middle English] This word was first used as a verb. It may be from the base of Swedish dialect *puta* 'be inflated'.

powder [Middle English] *Powder* is from Old French *poudre*, from Latin *pulvis*, *pulver-* 'dust'. Its use to describe a type of cosmetic is recorded early; it was formerly sprinkled on the hair or on a wig, later it was applied to the skin. The sense 'gunpowder' is late Middle English.

power [Middle English] *Power* is from Anglo-Norman French *poeir*, from an alteration of Latin *posse* 'be able'. The sense 'source of energy' such as electricity dates from the early 18th century.

pox [late Middle English]
→ POCK

practise [late Middle English] This verb is from Old French *practiser* or medieval Latin *practizare*, an alteration of *practicare* 'perform, carry out'; the source is Latin *practica* 'practice', from Greek *praktikē*, a feminine form (used as a noun), of *praktikos* 'concerned with action'. The late Middle English noun **practice** is from the verb *practise*, on the pattern of pairs such as *advise*, *advice*. Related words include: **practician** (late 15th century from Old French *practicien*, from *practique* 'practical') and **practitioner** (a mid-16th century extension of obsolete *practician*, a variant of *practician*). The word **practical** dates from the late 16th century and is based on the archaic word *practic* meaning 'practical', from Old French *practique*, via late Latin from Greek *praktikos* 'concerned with action'. The Greek verb *prattein* 'do, act' is the base.

pragmatic [late 16th century] This word was first recorded as meaning 'busy, interfering'. It comes via Latin from Greek *pragmatikos* 'relating to fact', from *pragma* 'deed' (from the stem of *prattein* 'do'). The current sense 'dealing with things sensibly in a way that is based on practical considerations', dates from the mid 19th century, the period when the noun **pragmatism** is first found, based on Greek *pragma*.

prairie [late 18th century] This is an adoption of a French word, from Old French *praerie*, from Latin *pratum* 'meadow'.

praise [Middle English] Early use included the sense 'set a price on, attach value to'. The source is Old French *preisier* 'to prize, praise', from late Latin *pretiare*, from Latin *pretium* 'price'.
→ PRIZE

pram [late 19th century]
→ PERAMBULATE

prance [late Middle English] Early use was as a verb in horse-riding contexts; it is of unknown origin. Early spellings (*praunse*, *pranse*) suggest a French origin but no corresponding word is recorded in French.

prank [early 16th century] Until the middle of the 18th century, a *prank* was a wicked or malicious deed; the origin is unknown.

prattle [mid 16th century] *Prattle* is from Middle Low German *pratelen*, from *praten*, a base shared by late Middle English **prate** 'talk foolishly'. The origin is probably imitative of the sound made.

pray [Middle English] 'Ask earnestly' was an early sense of *pray* from Old French *preier*, from late Latin *precare*, an alteration of Latin *precari* 'entreat'. The intransitive use (as in *pray to God*) was also recorded early. Middle English **prayer** is from Old French *preiere*, based on Latin *precarius* 'obtained by entreaty', from *prex*, *prec-* 'prayer'.

preach [Middle English] *Preach* is from Old French *prechier*, from Latin *praedicare* 'proclaim' (which in ecclesiastical Latin developed the sense 'preach'). The base elements are *prae* 'before' and *dicare* 'declare'. The same Latin base is shared by Middle English **preacher** from Old French *precheor*, from ecclesiastical Latin *praedicator*.

preamble [late Middle English] This is from Old French *preambule*, from medieval Latin *praeambulum*, from late Latin *praeambulus* 'going before'.

precarious [mid 17th century] *Precarious* is based on Latin *precarius* 'obtained by entreaty', from *prex*, *prec-* 'prayer'. The notion is one of something being dependent on the good grace of somebody else (needing entreaty) and therefore uncertain.

precaution [late 16th century] 'Prudent foresight' was the early sense from French *précaution*, from late Latin *praecautio(n-)*. Latin *praecavere* is the source, from *prae* 'before' and *cavere* 'take heed, beware of'.

precede [late Middle English] *Precede* is from Old French *preceder*, from Latin *praecedere*, from *prae* 'before' and *cedere* 'go'. Late Middle English **precedent** is from an Old French word meaning literally 'preceding'.

precept [late Middle English] This is from Latin *praeceptum*, the neuter past participle of *praecipere* 'warn, instruct', from *prae* 'before' and *capere* 'take'.

precinct [late Middle English] This word first described an administrative district; it is from medieval Latin *praecinctum*, the neuter past participle form (used as a noun) of *praecingere* 'encircle'. Latin *prae* 'before' and *cingere* 'gird' are the base elements. The early use is still reflected in US English where it is a term for an area under a particular police authority or a subdivision of a county for electoral purposes. The sense captured in *shopping precinct* dates from the middle of the 20th century.

precious [Middle English] *Precious* is from Old French *precios*, from Latin *pretiosus* 'of great value', from *pretium* 'price'. **Preciosity** 'over-refinement' in art, music, or language dates from the mid 19th century; it is a term suggested by French *préciosité*, derived from Molière's *Les Précieuses Ridicules* (1659), a comedy in which ladies frequenting the literary salons of Paris were satirized.

precipice [late 16th century] 'A headlong fall' was the first sense recorded for *precipice*. The origin is French *précipice* or Latin *praecipitium* 'abrupt descent', from *praeceps*, *praecip(it)-* 'steep, headlong'.

precipitation [late Middle English] Initially a *precipitation* was the action of falling or throwing down. It is from Latin *praecipitatio(n-)*, from *praecipitare* 'throw down or headlong'; Latin *praeceps*, *praecip(it)-* 'headlong' is the base (from *prae* 'before' and *caput* 'head'). Early 16th-century **precipitate** is also from Latin *praecipitare*. The original sense of the verb was 'hurl down, send violently'; hence 'cause to move rapidly', which gave rise in the early 17th century to 'cause to happen suddenly'. The word **precipitous** (mid 17th century) is from obsolete French *précipiteux*, from Latin *praeceps*.

precise [late Middle English] *Precise* is from Old French *prescis*, from Latin *praecis-*, the past participial stem of *praecidere* 'cut short', from *prae* 'in advance' and *caedere* 'to cut'. The noun **precision** dates from the mid 18th century, from French *précision* or Latin *praecisio(n-)*, from *praecidere*.

preclude [late 15th century] The early sense recorded was 'bar (a route or passage)'. The word is from Latin *praecludere*, from *prae* 'before' and *claudere* 'to shut'.

precocious [mid 17th century] This is based on Latin *praecox*, *praecoc-*, from *praecoquere* 'ripen fully', from *prae* 'before' and *coquere* 'to cook'. The sense in English is one of premature development.

precursor [late Middle English] This is from the Latin word *praecursor*, from *praecurrere* 'precede', from *prae* 'beforehand' and *currere* 'to run'.

predatory [late 16th century] Early use was in the sense 'relating to plundering'. The word

is from Latin *praedatorius*, from *praedator* 'plunderer', which also gave **predator** in the 1920s. Latin *praedari* 'seize as plunder' is the base verb, from *praeda* 'booty'.

predecessor [late Middle English] Late Latin *praedecessor* gave rise to this word in English, from Latin *prae* 'beforehand' and *decessor* 'retiring officer' (from *decedere* 'depart').

predestination [Middle English] This comes from ecclesiastical Latin *praedestinatio(n-)*, from *praedestinare* 'make firm beforehand'. Latin *prae* 'in advance' and *destinare* 'establish' are the formative elements. The verb **predestine** is late Middle English, from Old French *predestiner* or ecclesiastical Latin *praedestinare*.

predicament [late Middle English] This was first used as a term in Aristotelian logic for one of ten categories (substance or being, quantity, quality, relation, place, time, posture, possession, action, and passion). It comes from late Latin *praedicamentum* 'something predicated' (rendering Greek *katēgoria* 'category'), from Latin *praedicare*. From the sense 'category' arose the sense 'state of being, condition'; hence 'unpleasant situation'.
→ PREDICATE

predicate [late Middle English] Early use was as a noun. Latin *praedicatum* 'something declared' is the source, the neuter of *praedicatus* 'declared, proclaimed' (from the verb *praedicare*, from *prae* 'beforehand' and *dicare* 'make known'). The word **predicative** dates from the mid 19th century and is from Latin *praedicativus*, from *praedicare*.

prediction [mid 16th century] This comes from Latin *praedictio(n-)*, from *praedicere* 'make known beforehand', the source of **predict** recorded from the early 17th century. Latin *prae-* 'beforehand' and *dicere* 'say' are the base elements.

predilection [mid 18th century] French *predilection*, is the source of this word in English; from Latin *praedilect-*, the past participial stem of *praediligere* 'prefer'. The formative elements are *prae* 'in advance' and *diligere* 'to select'.

predominant [mid 16th century] This word comes from Old French, from medieval Latin *predominari* which also gave rise (late 16th century) to the verb **predominate**.

pre-eminent [late Middle English] Latin *praeeminent-*, the present participial stem of *praeeminere* 'tower above, excel' is the source of *pre-eminent* in English, from *prae* 'before' and *eminere* 'stand out'.

pre-empt [mid 19th century] This is a back-formation (by removal of the suffix) from early 17th-century **pre-emption** from medieval Latin *praeemptio(n-)*. The base verb is *praeemere*, from *prae* 'in advance' and *emere* 'buy'.

preen [late Middle English] This is apparently a variant of obsolete *prune* (based on Latin *ungere* 'anoint') used in the same sense, associated with Scots and northern English dialect *preen* 'to pierce, pin'. The association is the 'pricking' action of the bird's beak during grooming.

preface [late Middle English] *Preface* came via Old French from medieval Latin *praefatia*, an alteration of Latin *praefatio(n-)* 'words spoken beforehand'. Latin *praefari* is the source verb, from *prae* 'before' and *fari* 'speak'.

prefect [late Middle English] A *prefect* was initially an officer, governor, or magistrate. It comes from Old French, from Latin *praefectus*, the past participle of *praeficere* 'set in authority over'. Latin *prae* 'before' and *facere* 'make' are the base forms. Use of the word in educational contexts to mean 'a senior pupil with authority to discipline younger pupils' dates from the early 19th century.

prefer [late Middle English] *Prefer* is from Old French *preferer*, from Latin *praeferre*, from *prae* 'before' and *ferre* 'to carry'. The noun **preference** in late Middle English meant 'promotion' and is also from Old French, from medieval Latin *praeferentia*, from Latin *praeferre*. **Preferential**, based on *preference*, dates from the mid 19th century, formed on the pattern of *differential*.

prefix [mid 16th century] *Prefix* was first recorded in use as a verb. It is from Old French *prefixer*, from Latin *praefixus* 'fixed in front', from the verb *praefigere*. Latin *prae* 'before' and *figere* 'to fix' are the formative elements. The noun is from modern Latin *praefixum*, the neuter form (used as a noun) of *praefixus*, and dates from the mid 17th century.

pregnable [late Middle English] This is from Old French *prenable*, a word meaning literally 'takable', from Latin *prehendere* 'to seize'. The *g* of the English word was sometimes written in French, perhaps indicating palatal *n* (pronounced /ny/), but it has come to be pronounced as a separate sound in English.

pregnant [late Middle English] *Pregnant* is from Latin *praegnant-*, probably from *prae* 'before' and the base of *gnasci* 'be born'.

prejudice [Middle English] Early use of *prejudice* was as a legal term for 'harm or injury resulting from an action or judgement'. It is from Old French, from Latin *praejudicium*, from

prae 'in advance' and *judicium* 'judgement'. **Prejudicial** is late Middle English, from Old French *prejudiciel*, from *prejudice*.

prelate [Middle English] This formal term for a 'bishop' is from Old French *prelat*, from medieval Latin *praelatus* 'civil dignitary', the past participle form (used as a noun) of Latin *praeferre* meaning 'carry before' and 'place before in esteem'.

prelimininary [mid 17th century] This comes from modern Latin *praeliminaris* or French *préliminaire*, from Latin *prae* 'before' and *limen, limin-* 'threshold'. Use of *preliminaries* in publishing contexts for the front matter of a book is evidenced from the late 19th century.

prelude [mid 16th century] *Prelude* is from French *prélude*, from medieval Latin *praeludium*, from Latin *praeludere* 'play beforehand'. Latin *prae* 'before' and *ludere* 'to play' are the base forms. Use of *prelude* as a musical term is found from the mid 17th century.

premature [late Middle English] 'Ripe, mature' was the early meaning of *premature*, from Latin *praematurus* 'very early'. The formative elements are *prae* 'before' and *maturus* 'ripe'. As an obstetric term, *premature* is recorded from the mid 18th century.

premeditate [mid 16th century] The source of *premeditate* is Latin *praemeditat-*, the past participial stem of *praemeditari* 'think out before', from *prae* 'before' and *meditari* 'meditate'.

premier [late 15th century] This comes from an Old French word meaning 'first', from Latin *primarius* 'principal'. It has been used as a noun standing for *premier minister* since the early 18th century. **Premiere** (from French *première*, the feminine of *premier* 'first') as a name for the first performance of a musical or theatrical work, dates from the late 19th century.

premise [late Middle English] *Premise* is from Old French *premisse*, from medieval Latin *praemissa* (*propositio*) '(proposition) set in front'. Latin *praemittere* is the base, from *prae* 'before' and *mittere* 'send'.

premium [early 17th century] A *premium* in early use was a 'reward, prize'. It comes from Latin *praemium* 'booty, reward', from *prae* 'before' and *emere* 'buy, take'. Towards the middle of the 17th century, the word *premium* was taken up in insurance contexts. The phrase *at a premium* is seen in examples from the early 19th century onwards.

premonition [mid 16th century] 'Advance warning' was the early meaning of *premonition*. It comes from French *prémonition*, from late Latin *praemonitio(n-)*, from Latin *praemonere*.

Latin *prae* 'before' and *monere* 'warn' are the base forms.

preoccupy [mid 16th century] This English form was suggested by Latin *praeoccupare* 'seize beforehand', which is also the source (via Latin *praeoccupatio(n-)*), of late 16th-century **preoccupation**, first used in rhetoric in the sense 'anticipating and meeting objections beforehand'.

prepare [late Middle English] Latin *praeparare*, from *prae* 'before' and *parare* 'make ready', is the source of *prepare* (via French), **preparation** (via Old French from Latin *praeparatio(n-)*) and **preparatory** (from late Latin *praeparatorius*), all dating from the same period. The abbreviation **prep** dates from the mid 19th century, originally as school slang in the context of 'preparation' of lessons and exercises out of hours.

preponderate [early 17th century] The early senses recorded for *preponderate* are 'weigh more' and 'have greater intellectual weight'. The word comes from Latin *praeponderare*, from *prae* 'before' and *ponderare* 'weigh, consider'. **Preponderant** is recorded in the middle of the 17th century and comes from the same base; **preponderance** was formed slightly later from *preponderant*.

preposition [late Middle English] This grammar term, describing a part of speech such as *in*, *with*, *from*, is from Latin *praepositio(n-)*, from the verb *praeponere*, from *prae* 'before' and *ponere* 'to place'. The 'placing before' usually occurs before nouns and pronouns (e.g. *with a jolt*, *after her*).

preposterous [mid 16th century] *Preposterous* is based on Latin *praeposterus* 'reversed, absurd', from *prae* 'before' and *posterus* 'coming after'.

presage [late Middle English] This came via French from Latin *praesagium*, from *praesagire* 'forebode', from *prae* 'before' and *sagire* 'perceive keenly'.

presbytery [late Middle English] This was first used as an architectural term for the eastern part of a church chancel beyond the choir, reserved for the clergy and formerly consisting of three seats (*sedilia*). It is from Old French *presbiterie*, via ecclesiastical Latin from Greek *presbuterion*. The base is Greek *presbuteros* (the comparative of *presbus* 'old (man)') meaning 'elder', used in the New Testament to denote an elder of the early church. The term **Presbyterian** (from ecclesiastical Latin *presbyterium*) dates from the mid 17th century; **Presbyterianism** was first introduced in Geneva in 1541 under John Calvin, in the belief

that it best represented the pattern of the early church.

prescribe [late Middle English] Early use included the sense 'confine within bounds'; it was also a legal term meaning 'claim by prescription'. Latin *praescribere* 'direct in writing' is the source, from *prae* 'before' and *scribere* 'write'. **Prescription** was also a legal term in late Middle English: this is via Old French from Latin *praescriptio(n-)*, from the verb *praescribere*. Use of the word in medical contexts is found from the late 16th century. **Prescriptive** (from late Latin *praescriptivus* 'relating to a legal exception') dates from the mid 18th century.

present[1] [Middle English] This word referring to location (e.g. *persons here present*) and time (e.g. *the present and future*) is via Old French from Latin *praesent-*, the present participle of *praeesse* 'be at hand'. Latin *prae* 'before' and *esse* 'be' are the formative elements, shared by Middle English **presence** which came via Old French from Latin *praesentia* 'being at hand'.

present[2] [Middle English] This *present* as in *presented at court* is from Old French *presenter*. The source is Latin *praesentare* 'place before', which in medieval Latin came to mean 'present as a gift', from *praeesse* 'be at hand'. Use of the word in broadcasting contexts is found in examples from the 1930 onwards. The related noun **presentation** arose in late Middle English, via Old French from late Latin *praesentatio(n-)*, from Latin *praesentare*.
→ PRESENT[1]

present[3] [Middle English] This *present* as in *Christmas present* is from Old French, originally used in the phrase *mettre une chose en present à quelqu'un* 'put a thing into the presence of a person'. The phrase *a present from…* inscribed on holiday souvenirs is first found in the mid 19th century (Charles Dickens *Bleak House*: We found a mug with 'A Present from Tunbridge Wells' on it).

preserve [late Middle English] 'Keep safe from harm' was the early sense of *preserve* from Old French *preserver*, from late Latin *praeservare*. Latin *prae-* 'before, in advance' and *servare* 'to keep' are the base forms. Use of *preserve* as a term for 'jam' began in the early 17th century. Related late Middle English words are: **preservation** (via Old French from medieval Latin *praeservatio(n-)*, from late Latin *praeservare*) and **preservative** (via Old French from medieval Latin *praeservativus*) from the same base forms.

president [late Middle English] This word came via Old French from Latin *praesident-*, the present participial stem of *praesidere* 'sit before', from *prae* 'before' and *sedere* 'sit'. The term as a title for the elected head of the government was first used in the United States in the 1780s; this was apparently a continuation of the name of *president* or *presiding officer* of the congresses of the separate states. The related noun **presidency** dates from the late 16th century, from medieval Latin *praesidentia*, from *praesidere*, a source shared by **preside** (early 17th century), from French *présider*.

press[1] [Middle English] *Press* 'apply pressure to' is from Old French *presser*, from Latin *pressare* 'keep pressing', a frequentative (= verb of repeated action) of *premere*. The noun dates from the same period meaning 'throng, pressing'; use of the word to describe a printing press dates from the early 16th century and the phrase *the Press* 'newspapers' is found from the late 18th century. Late Middle English **pressure** is from Old French, from Latin *pressura*, from *press-*, the past participial stem of *premere* 'to press'. Its use to mean 'stress, strain' is found from the mid 17th century.

press[2] [late 16th century] This *press* as in *pressed into service* is an alteration (by association with the *press* meaning 'apply pressure to') of obsolete *prest* 'pay given on enlistment' or 'enlistment by such payment'. This is from Old French *prest* 'loan, advance pay', based on Latin *praestare* 'to provide'.

prestige [mid 17th century] *Prestige* was first recorded in the sense 'illusion, conjuring trick'. The source is a French word meaning literally 'illusion, glamour', from late Latin *praestigium* 'illusion' (from the Latin plural *praestigiae* 'conjuring tricks'). The transference of meaning occurred by way of the sense 'dazzling influence, glamour', at first depreciatory. The adjective **prestigious**, recorded a century before *prestige* initially had the sense 'practising legerdemain'. It is from late Latin *praestigiosus*, from *praestigiae*. The current sense 'inspiring admiration' dates from the early 20th century.

presumption [Middle English] Latin *praesumere* 'anticipate' (in late Latin 'take for granted'), from *prae* 'before' and *sumere* 'to take', is the source of several words in English: *presumption* is from Old French *presumpcion*, from Latin *praesumptio(n)* 'anticipation'. Middle English **presumptuous** is from Old French *presumptueux*, from late Latin *praesumptuosus* (a variant of *praesumptiosus* 'full of boldness', from *praesumptio*). The late Middle English verb **presume** is from Old French *presumer*.

pretend [late Middle English] *Pretend* is from Latin *praetendere* 'to claim', from *prae* 'before' and *tendere* 'stretch'. The same source is shared by late Middle English **pretence** via Anglo-Norman French and based on medieval Latin *pretensus* 'pretended' (an alteration of Latin

praetentus from *praetendere*); and, from the same period, **pretension**, from medieval Latin *praetensio(n-)*. The adjective **pretentious** (mid 19th century) is from French *prétentieux*, from *prétention*.

pretext [early 16th century] The word *pretext* is from Latin *praetextus* 'outward display'; the sense in English is 'a (diversionary) reason given in order to justify an action'. The Latin verb *praetexere* 'to disguise' is the source, from *prae* 'before' and *texere* 'weave'.

pretty [Old English] Old English *prættig* is related to Middle Dutch *pertich* 'brisk, clever' and obsolete Dutch *prettig* 'humorous, sporty', from a West Germanic base meaning 'trick'. The sense development 'deceitful, cunning, clever, skilful, admirable, pleasing, nice' has parallels in adjectives such as *canny*, *fine*, *nice*. Adverbial use in the sense 'considerably' (e.g. *pretty difficult*) is found from the mid 16th century.

prevail [late Middle English] *Prevail* is from Latin *praevalere* 'have greater power', from *prae* 'before' and *valere* 'have power'. **Prevalent**, from the same source verb, dates from the late 16th century.

prevaricate [mid 16th century] The early sense recorded for this word which now conveys 'evasion' is 'go astray, transgress'. It comes from Latin *praevaricari* 'walk crookedly, deviate', from *prae* 'before' and *varicari* 'straddle'. The base is Latin *varus* 'bent, knock-kneed'.

prevent [late Middle English] *Prevent* in early use meant 'act in anticipation of'. It comes from Latin *praevenire* 'precede, hinder', from *prae* 'before' and *venire* 'come'.

previous [early 17th century] This word is based on Latin *praevius* 'going before', from *prae* 'before' and *via* 'way'. The phrase *previous to* dates from the early 18th century.

prey [Middle English] Early noun use included the sense 'plunder taken in war' (= that which is 'seized'); it comes from Old French *preie*, from Latin *praeda* 'booty'. The verb is from Old French *preier*, based on Latin *praedari* 'seize as plunder', from *praeda*. The verbal phrase *prey (up)on* is found from early times.

price [Middle English] The noun is from Old French *pris*, from Latin *pretium* 'value, reward'. Middle English *pris* had all the senses of the Old French word: 'price, value, honour, prize, praise'. During the 15th century the noun *preise* (= praise) was formed and this sense was lost from *price*. During the last three hundred years, the sense 'prize' has also disappeared. The verb is a variant (by assimilation to the noun) of earlier *prise* 'estimate the value of'.

→ PRAISE; PRIZE

prick [Old English] In Old English the noun was *pricca* and the verb *prician*. The word is probably of West Germanic origin and related to Low German and Dutch *prik* (noun), *prikken* (verb). The semantic strands include: 'pierce' (*pricked herself with the needle*); 'urge, spur' (*pricked his horse on*); 'mark by pricking' (*each person is to prick only one of the nominees*); 'fix in position' (*prick the onions on sticks, prick out the seedlings*); 'insert' (*prick it with cloves*); and 'raise to a point' (*pricked up his ears*).

prickle [Old English] Old English *pricel* was an 'instrument for pricking', 'a sensation of being pricked'. Middle Dutch *prickel* is related, from the Germanic base of *prick*. The verb is partly a diminutive of the verb *prick*.

→ PRICK

pride [late Old English] The early spelling was *prȳde* 'excessive self-esteem', a variant of *prȳtu*, *prȳte*, from *prūd* 'proud'. The phrase *take a pride in* is first recorded in the form *take a pride to* (*do*) in Shakespeare's *Henry IV* part 2 (Men of all sorts take a pride to gird at me).

→ PROUD

priest [Old English] Old English *prēost* is Germanic in origin, related to Dutch *priester* and German *Priester*, based on ecclesiastical Latin *presbyter* 'elder'. In Old English the word *sacerd* was usually applied to a heathen or Jewish priest translating Latin *sacerdos*, whereas *prēost* was usually a Christian priest. *Sacerd* was no longer in use by the end of the Old English period.

→ PRESBYTERY

prig [mid 16th century] The origin of this word is uncertain. The earliest sense was 'tinker' or 'petty thief'; this may have developed into 'disliked person' giving, in the late 17th century 'someone affectedly and self-consciously precise'. However these later senses may represent a different word.

prim [late 17th century] Early use was as a verb; it is probably ultimately from Old French *prin*, Provençal *prim* 'excellent, delicate', from Latin *primus* 'first'. Late 19th-century **prissy** may be a blend of *prim* and *sissy*.

primate[1] [Middle English] This word used in the context of the Christian Church is from Old French *primat*, from Latin *primas*, *primat-* 'of the first rank', from *primus* 'first'. The reference is to the 'first' amongst the bishops of a province.

primate[2] [late 19th century] This zoology term is from Latin *primas*, *primat-* 'of the first rank', referring to mammals belonging to the order known as primates: this includes humans, apes, monkeys, lemurs, bushbabies, tarsiers, and marmosets.

→ PRIMATE[1]

prime[1] [Old English] Old English *prīm* was a service forming part of the Divine Office and said at the first hour of the day; it is from Latin *prima* (*hora*) 'first (hour)', reinforced in Middle English by Old French *prime*. English *prime* often conveys a notion of 'beginning' which sometimes extends to that of 'best stage' (e.g. *prime of life*). The adjective (as in *prime concern*) dates from late Middle English, via Old French from Latin *primus* 'first'. Late Middle English **primary** meaning 'original, not derivative' has as its source Latin *primarius*, from *primus*; noun uses date from the 18th century. **Primer**, describing an elementary textbook, (also late Middle English) is from medieval Latin *primarius* (*liber*) 'primary (book)' and *primarium* (*manuale*) 'primary (manual)'. Latin *primus* is also the base of **primal** meaning 'fundamental' (early 17th century) from medieval Latin *primalis*.

prime[2] [early 16th century] The early sense recorded for this *prime* (as in *primed his gun, primed him before the interview*) was 'fill, load'. The origin is uncertain; it is probably based on Latin *primus* 'first', since the sense expressed is a 'first' operation prior to something else.

primeval [mid 17th century] *Primeval* is based on Latin *primaevus*, from *primus* 'first' and *aevum* 'age'.

primitive [late Middle English] 'Original, not derivative' was the early sense of *primitive*. It comes from Old French *primitif, -ive*, from Latin *primitivus* 'first of its kind', from *primus* 'first'. The English word sometimes conveys 'earliest', sometimes 'fundamental', and occasionally 'naive, untrained'.

primordial [late Middle English] *Primordial* is from late Latin *primordialis* 'first of all', from *primordius* 'original'.

prince [Middle English] The word *prince* came via Old French from Latin *princeps, princip-* 'first, chief, sovereign', from *primus* 'first' and *capere* 'take'. An early use was to denote a ruler of a small state, a sense reflected in the title *Prince of Wales*: from the reign of Edward III, this came to be conferred customarily on the eldest surviving son of the King or Queen of England. The *Prince of Wales* was initially the only 'prince' in England but in the reign of James I it was extended to all the sons of the sovereign, and under Victoria to all the grandchildren together with the title **princess**. The latter is a late Middle English word from Old French *princesse*, from *prince*.

principal [Middle English] *Principal* came via Old French from Latin *principalis* 'first, original', from *princeps*, *princip-* 'first, chief'. **Principality** dates from the same period when it also denoted the rank of a prince; it is from Old French *principalite*, from late Latin *principalitas*, from Latin *principalis*.

principle [late Middle English] The word *principle* is from Old French, from Latin *principium* 'source', the plural of which (*principia*) meant 'foundations'. The base is Latin *princeps*, *princip-* 'first, chief'. The semantic strands are: 'origin, source', 'fundamental truth' and 'rudiment'.

print [Middle English] *Print*, initially, was the impression made by a stamp or seal. It comes from Old French *preinte* 'pressed', the feminine past participle of *preindre*, from Latin *premere* 'to press'. The phrase *the prints* has sometimes (since the mid 17th century) referred to the press; this is now chiefly a US usage. Use of the word *print* in photography dates from the mid 19th century.

prior¹ [early 18th century] This *prior* meaning 'going before' is an English use of a Latin word meaning literally 'former, elder', related to *prae* 'before'. The noun **priority** is recorded in use from late Middle English denoting precedence in time or rank: this is from Old French *priorite*, from medieval Latin *prioritas*, from Latin *prior*.

prior² [late Old English] This title for the male head of house of a religious order is from a medieval Latin noun use of Latin *prior* 'elder, former'. Middle English **priory** is from Anglo-Norman French *priorie*, medieval Latin *prioria*, from Latin *prior*.
→ PRIOR¹

prise [late 17th century] *Prise* as in *prise open* is from dialect *prise* 'lever', from Old French *prise* 'grasp, taking hold'.
→ PRY

prism [late 16th century] *Prism*, a term commonly used in geometry and optics, comes via late Latin from Greek *prisma* 'thing sawn', from *prizein* 'to saw'.

prison [late Old English] *Prison* is from Old French *prisun*, from Latin *prensio(n-)*, a variant of *prehensio(n-)* 'laying hold of' (from the verb *prehendere*). The word **prisoner** dates from late Middle English and is from Old French *prisonier*, from *prison*.

pristine [mid 16th century] Early senses included 'original', 'former', 'primitive', and 'undeveloped'. Latin *pristinus* 'former' is the source. The senses 'unspoilt' and 'spotless' date from the 1920s.

private [late Middle English] This originally denoted a person not acting in an official (i.e. public) capacity. It is from Latin *privatus* 'withdrawn from public life', a use of the past participle of *privare* 'bereave, deprive', from *privus* 'single, individual'.

privation [Middle English] *Privation* is from Latin *privatio(n-)*, from the verb *privare* 'deprive'.
→ PRIVATE

privilege [Middle English] This came via Old French from Latin *privilegium* which was a term in Roman Law for a 'bill or law affecting an individual', from *privus* 'private' and *lex*, *leg-* 'law'. The notion of 'individuality' led to one of 'special favour'.

privy [Middle English] This was originally used in the sense 'belonging to one's own private circle'. It comes from Old French *prive* 'private' (also used as a noun meaning 'private place' and 'familiar friend'), from Latin *privatus* 'withdrawn from public life'. The term *Privy Council* ilustrates the sense 'private', as a group of advisers to a ruler. Use of the word to denote a 'lavatory' (late Middle English) is from the notion of 'private place'. The phrase *privy to ...* was in early use conveying 'privately aware of'.
→ PRIVATE

prize [Middle English] The noun is a variant of *price*; the verb, originally in the sense 'estimate the value of', is from Old French *pris-*, the stem of *preisier* 'to praise, appraise'.
→ PRAISE; PRICE

WORDBUILDING

The prefix **pro-¹** [from Latin *pro* 'in front of, on behalf of, instead of, on account of'] adds the sense

■ favouring [pro-choice]

■ deputizing for [proconsul]

■ moving forwards, out, or away [proceed; propel; prostrate]

The prefix **pro-²** [from Greek *pro* 'before'] adds the sense

■ before [proactive]

---

probable [late Middle English] The early sense was 'worthy of belief'; the word is via Old French from Latin *probabilis* 'provable, credible', from *probare* 'to test, demonstrate'. The now common meaning 'likely' is found from the early 17th century (Shakespeare *Antony and Cleopatra*: Most probable That so she died). The related word **probability** is also late Middle English from Latin *probabilitas*, from *probabilis*.

probate [late Middle English] *Probate* is from Latin *probatum* 'something proved', the neuter past participle of *probare* 'to test, prove'. The word conveys the 'proving' of a will in law.

probation [late Middle English] *Probation* was first used for any 'testing', 'investigation', or 'examination'. It is from Old French *probacion*, from Latin *probatio(n-)*, from *probare* 'to test, prove'. The legal use dates from the late 19th century.
→ PROVE

probe [late Middle English] Early use was as a noun from late Latin *proba* 'proof', which in medieval Latin meant 'examination'; Latin *probare* 'to test' is the source. Use as a term for a small unmanned spacecraft used for transmitting information about the environment dates from the 1950s. The verb *probe* is found in examples from the mid 17th century.

probity [late Middle English] The source of this word is Latin *probitas*, from *probus* 'good'.

problem [late Middle English] A *problem* was originally a riddle or a question for academic discussion. It comes from Old French *probleme*, via Latin from Greek *problēma*. The base verb is Greek *proballein* 'put forth', from *pro* 'before' and *ballein* 'to throw'. The adjective **problematic** dates from the early 17th century, via French from late Latin *problematicus*, from Greek *problēmatikos*, from *problēma*.

proceed [late Middle English] *Proceed* is from Old French *proceder*, from Latin *procedere*, from *pro-* 'forward' and *cedere* 'go'. The word **proceeds** 'results, outcome' (= that which proceeds from something) is evidenced in use from the early 17th century, the plural of the obsolete noun *proceed* used in the same sense, but which earlier meant 'procedure'. **procedure** dates from the late 16th century and is from French *procédure*, from *procéder*.

process [Middle English] *Process* is via Old French *proces* from Latin *processus* 'progression, course', from the verb *procedere*. Current senses of the verb: 'perform a series of operations' (*processed the wool*) and 'deal with administratively' (*processed the application*) date from the late 19th century.
→ PROCEED

procession [late Old English] *Procession* came via Old French from Latin *processio(n-)*, from *procedere* 'move forward'. The verb **process** (as in *processed along the aisle*) dates from the early 19th century as a back-formation (by removal of the suffix) from *procession*.
→ PROCEED

proclaim [late Middle English] The early spelling was *proclame*, from Latin *proclamare* 'cry out', from *pro-* 'forth' and *clamare* 'to shout'. The change in the second syllable was due to association with the verb *claim*. The noun **proclamation** (via Old French from Latin *proclamatio(n-)*) dates from the same period and is from the same Latin source verb.

proclivity [late 16th century] This word meaning 'inclination towards' is from Latin *proclivitas*, from *proclivis* 'inclined'. The base forms are *pro-* 'forward, down' and *clivus* 'slope'.

procrastinate [late 16th century] This is from Latin *procrastinat-*, the past participial stem of *procrastinare* 'defer till the morning'. The formative elements are *pro-* 'forward' and *crastinus* 'belonging to tomorrow' (from *cras* 'tomorrow').

procreate [late Middle English] *Procreate* is from Latin *procreare* 'generate, bring forth', from *pro-* 'forth' and *creare* 'create'.

procurator [Middle English] This was originally a word for a 'steward'. It comes from Old French *procuratour* or Latin *procurator* 'administrator, finance agent', from *procurare* 'take care of, attend to'. Late Middle English **proctor** is a contraction of *procurator*. Latin *procurare* (from *pro-* 'on behalf of' and *curare* 'see to') is also the source of Middle English **procure**. **Procuration** is late Middle English via Old French from Latin *procuratio(n-)*.

prod [mid 16th century] This word was first recorded in verb use; it may be symbolic of a short poking movement, or a blend of *poke* and dialect *brod* 'to goad, prod'. The noun dates from the mid 18th century.

prodigal [late Middle English] *Prodigal* is from late Latin *prodigalis*, from Latin *prodigus* 'lavish'. The phrase *prodigal son* is with allusion to the parable in Luke 15:11–32, which tells of a son … who wasted his substance with riotous living but was welcomed back with open arms to his father's home.

prodigious [late 15th century] 'Portentous' was the early sense of *prodigious*, from Latin *prodigiosus*, from *prodigium* 'portent'. The sense 'extraordinarily large' (*prodigious sum*) dates from the beginning of the 17th century.
→ PRODIGY

prodigy [late 15th century] A *prodigy* initially was something extraordinary considered to be an omen. It comes from Latin *prodigium* 'portent'. It came to be applied to a person possessing an amazing quality or talent (*child prodigy*) in the mid 17th century.

produce [late Middle English] The first sense recorded was 'provide (something) for consideration' (as in *produced a contract*). It comes from Latin *producere*, from *pro-* 'forward' and *ducere* 'to lead'. Current noun senses (as in *farm* *produce, produce of their joint efforts*) date from the late 17th century. In the late Middle English period, the Latin verb *producere* also gave rise to: **product** (as a mathematical term) from the Latin neuter past participle *productum* '(something) produced'; **production** via Old French from Latin *productio(n-)*; and early 17th-century **productive** from French *productif, -ive* or late Latin *productivus*.

profane [late Middle English] The early sense was 'heathen'; it comes from Old French *prophane*, from Latin *profanus* 'outside the temple, not sacred'. Latin *pro-* (from Latin *pro* 'before') and *fanum* 'temple' are the base forms. The noun **profanity** (mid 16th century) is from late Latin *profanitas*, from Latin *profanus*.

profess [Middle English] Latin *profiteri* 'declare publicly' (from *pro-* 'before' and *fateri* 'confess') is the source of *profess* in English. This word was first recorded in *be professed* 'be received into a religious order'. Middle English **profession**, from the same source, referred to the vow made on entering a religious order; this is via Old French from Latin *professio(n-)*. The common current sense 'paid occupation' derives from the notion of an occupation that one 'professes' to be skilled in. **Professor**, from Latin *professor*, is late Middle English.

proffer [Middle English] *Proffer* is from Anglo-Norman French *proffrir*, from Latin *pro-* 'before' and *offerre* 'to offer'.

proficient [late 16th century] This word is from Latin *proficere* 'to advance, make progress', from *pro-* 'on behalf of' and *facere* 'do, make'. The main notion conveyed in English is 'skilful' (Marlowe *Faustus*: Who would not be proficient in this art?).

profile [mid 17th century] *Profile* is from obsolete Italian *profilo*, from the verb *profilare*. The base elements here are *pro-* 'forth' and *filare* meaning first 'draw a line' and later 'to spin' (from Latin *filare*, from *filum* 'thread').

profit [Middle English] This comes from Old French, from Latin *profectus* 'progress, profit', from *proficere* 'to advance', from *pro-* 'on behalf of' and *facere* 'do'. The verb is from Old French *profiter*.

profligate [mid 16th century] The early recorded sense was 'overthrown, routed'. It comes from Latin *profligatus* 'dissolute', the past participle of *profligare* 'overthrow, ruin'. The prefix *pro-* 'forward, down' and *fligere* 'strike down' are the base forms.

profound [Middle English] *Profound* is from Old French *profund*, from Latin *profundus* 'deep', from Latin *pro* 'before' and *fundus* 'bottom'. The

word was used earliest in the sense 'showing deep insight'.

profuse [late Middle English] 'Extravagant' was the early use of the word, from Latin *profusus* 'lavish, spread out', the past participle of *profundere* (from *pro-* 'forth' and *fundere* 'pour'). The noun **profusion** dates from the mid 16th century, coming via French from Latin *profusio(n-)*, from *profundere* 'pour out'. Early use expressed the senses 'extravagance', 'squandering', and 'waste'.

progeny [Middle English] This is from Old French *progenie*, from Latin *progenies*, from *progignere* 'beget'.

prognosticate [late Middle English] *Prognosticate* and **prognostication** (via Old French and medieval Latin *prognosticatio(n-)*) are from the verb *prognosticare* 'make a prediction'. Mid 17th-century **prognosis** came via late Latin from Greek *prognōsis*, from *pro-* 'before' and *gignōskein* 'know'.

programme [early 17th century] The early sense of *programme* was 'written notice'. It came via late Latin from Greek *programma*, from *prographein* 'write publicly', from *pro* 'before' and *graphein* 'write'. Use of the word in broadcasting contexts dates from the 1920s; it was adopted as a term in computing from the 1940s although the spelling *program* is now preferred.

progress [late Middle English] The noun (recorded first) is from Latin *progressus* 'an advance', from the verb *progredi*, from *pro-* 'forward' and *gradi* 'to walk'. The verb became obsolete in British English use at the end of the 17th century and was readopted from American English in the early 19th century. The noun **progression** is also late Middle English from Old French, from Latin *progressio(n-)*, from the same Latin source verb. **Progressive** is recorded from the early 17th century, from French *progressif, -ive* or medieval Latin *progressivus*.

prohibit [late Middle English] *Prohibit* is from Latin *prohibere* 'keep in check', from *pro-* 'in front' and *habere* 'to hold'. Late Middle English **prohibition** is from Old French, from Latin *prohibitio(n-)*, from *prohibere*. In the US of the mid 19th century, *Prohibition* referred to the forbidding of the manufacture and sale of intoxicating drinks, and became particularly famous as a term from 1920 to 1933 for restrictions under the Volstead Act.

project [late Middle English] A *project* initially was a 'preliminary design, tabulated statement'. It is from Latin *projectum* 'something prominent', the neuter past participle of *proicere* 'throw forth' (from *pro-* 'forth' and *jacere* 'to throw'). Early senses of the verb were 'plan, devise' and 'cause to move forward'. **Projection** dates from the mid 16th century when it was used to refer to the representation on a plane surface of any part of the surface of the earth: it is from Latin *projectio(n-)*, from *proicere* 'throw forth'. The word **projectile** is recorded from the mid 17th century and is modern Latin, based on the same Latin source verb.

proletarian [mid 17th century] This is based on Latin *proletarius* (from *proles* 'offspring') describing a person with no wealth in property and who only served the state by producing offspring. From the same base is **proletariat** (mid 19th century) via French *prolétariat*.

proliferation [mid 19th century] French *prolifération* is the source of English *proliferation*, from *prolifère* 'proliferous'. The verb **proliferate** dates from the late 19th century and is a back-formation (by removal of the suffix) from *proliferation*.

prolific [mid 17th century] *Prolific* is from medieval Latin *prolificus*, from Latin *proles* 'offspring'.

prologue [Middle English] This comes from Old French, via Latin from Greek *prologos*, from *pro-* 'before' and *logos* 'saying'.

prolong [late Middle English] *Prolong* is from Old French *prolonguer*, from late Latin *prolongare*, from *pro-* 'forward, onward' and *longus* 'long'.

promenade [mid 16th century] This word first described a leisurely walk in public. It is an adoption from French, from *se promener* 'to walk', the reflexive of *promener* 'take for a walk'.

prominent [late Middle English] The Latin verb *prominere* 'jut out' led to the first sense recorded in English for *prominent* which was 'projecting'. It comes from Latin *prominent-*, the present participial stem of *prominere* 'jut out'. The related word **prominence** is from obsolete French, from Latin *prominentia* 'jutting out'. The early sense in English was 'something that juts out'.
➔ EMINENCE

promiscuous [early 17th century] This word has as its base Latin *promiscuus* 'indiscriminate' (based on *miscere* 'to mix'). The early sense was 'consisting of elements mixed together', giving rise to 'indiscriminate' and 'undiscriminating', from which the notion of 'casual' arose.

promise [late Middle English] *Promise* is from Latin *promissum* 'something promised', the neuter past participle of *promittere* 'put forth, promise' (from *pro-* 'forward' and *mittere* 'to send'). Late Middle English **promissory** 'implying a promise' is from medieval Latin *promissorius*, from the same Latin source verb *promittere*.

promontory [mid 16th century] This word for a point of high land jutting out into the sea is from Latin *promontorium*, a variant (influenced by *mons*, *mont-* 'mountain') of *promunturium*.
➔ PROMINENT

promote [late Middle English] *Promote* is from Latin *promovere* 'move forward', from *pro-* 'forward, onward' and *movere* 'to move'. **Promotion** from the same period in sense is via Old French from Latin *promotio(n-)*, from *promovere*.

prompt [Middle English] Latin *promptus*, the past participle of *promere* 'to produce' (from *pro-* 'out, forth' and *emere* 'take') is the source of *prompt* in English. Early use was as a verb meaning 'incite to action'; its use in the context of assisting somebody at a loss to remember a recitation or part is recorded in late Middle English. The adjective is from Old French *prompt* or Latin *promptus* which meant both 'brought to light' and 'prepared, ready, at hand'. Early examples reflected the senses 'acting speedily' and 'ready and willing'.

promulgate [mid 16th century] This word meaning 'make widely known' is from Latin *promulgare* 'expose to public view', from *pro-* 'out, publicly' and *mulgere* 'cause to come forth' (literally 'to milk').

prone [late Middle English] *Prone* is from Latin *pronus* 'leaning forward', from *pro* 'forwards'. This notion of 'leaning forwards and downwards' is reflected at the core of the word's various meanings 'lying face downwards' (*prone and supine*); 'having a downwards direction' (C. Brontë *Villette*: The storm seemed to have burst at the zenith; it rushed down prone); 'liable to, tending to' (Shakespeare *Winter's Tale*: I am not prone to weeping (as our Sex Commonly are)): the latter was the earliest sense in English and remains the most common.

prong [late 15th century] A *prong* once denoted a forked implement. It is perhaps related to Middle Low German *prange* 'pinching instrument', or possibly to Middle English *prag* 'pin, nail' and its early 17th-century variant *prog* 'piercing instrument'. The verb *prong* dates from the mid 19th century.

pronoun [late Middle English] This is from *pro-* 'on behalf of', and *noun*, suggested by French *pronom*, Latin *pronomen* (from *pro-* 'for, in place of' and *nomen* 'name'). Pronouns stand in the stead of nouns to designate objects without naming them, when the reference is clear from the context or situation.

pronounce [late Middle English] *Pronounce* (from Old French *pronuncier*) and **pronunciation** (from Latin *pronuntiatio(n-)*) are both from the same period, from Latin *pronuntiare*. The base forms are *pro-* 'out, forth' and *nuntiare* 'announce' (from *nuntius* 'messenger'). The two main branches of the verb are: 'declare authoritatively' and 'articulate clearly'.

proof [Middle English] The early spelling was *preve*, from Old French *proeve*, from late Latin *proba*. Latin *probare* 'to test, prove' is the source verb. The change of vowel in late Middle English was due to the influence of *prove*. Current verb senses ('make waterproof', 'make a proof of (a printed work)', and in North American English 'knead (dough) until light') date from the late 19th century and all imply 'testing' in some respect.

prop[1] [late Middle English] Although its ulterior history is unknown, this *prop* meaning 'pole, support' is probably from Middle Dutch *proppe* 'support (for vines)'. Use of the word as a rugby term dates from the 1950s.

prop[2] [mid 19th century] This *prop* used in theatrical contexts is an abbreviation of *property*.
→ PROPERTY

propaganda This word came via Italian from modern Latin *congregatio de propaganda fide* 'congregation for propagation of the faith'. It referred to a committee of cardinals of the Roman Catholic Church responsible for foreign missions, founded in 1622 by Pope Gregory XV. Use of the word to mean 'biased information' dates from the early 20th century.

propagate [late Middle English] Latin *propagare* 'multiply from layers or shoots' is the source of this word in English, it is related to *propago* 'young shoot' (from a base meaning 'fix').

propel [late Middle English] The early sense was 'expel, drive out'. It is from Latin *propellere*, from *pro-* 'forward' and *pellere* 'to drive'. **Propeller**, from *propel*, is a late 18th-century word, sometimes abbreviated to **prop** from the early 20th century. The noun **propulsion** (via medieval Latin *propulsio(n-)*) meant 'expulsion, driving away' in the early 17th century and is also from Latin *propellere* 'drive before (oneself)'.

propensity [late 16th century] This word meaning 'leaning, tendency' is based on archaic *propense* which comes from Latin *propensus* 'inclined'. This is the past participle of

propendere, from *pro-* 'forward, down' and *pendere* 'hang'.

proper [Middle English] *Proper* is from Old French *propre*, from Latin *proprius* 'one's own, special'. The word had already undergone much sense development in Latin, Romanic, and French before being taken into English. The semantic branches include: 'individually applicable, own' (Shakespeare *Tempest*: Even with such like valour, men hang, and drown their proper selves); 'conforming with rule, accurate, strictly applicable' (*that is not, in a proper sense, true*); and 'fitting, appropriate' (*only right and proper*).

property [Middle English] An Anglo-Norman French variant of Old French *propriete* gave *property* in English. The source is Latin *proprietas*, from *proprius* 'one's own, particular'. *Property* may belong to a person (*personal property*) or to a thing as an attribute (*properties of a triangle*).
→ PROPER

prophet [Middle English] *Prophet* is from Old French *prophete*, via Latin from Greek *prophētēs* 'spokesman', from *pro* 'before' and *phētēs* 'speaker' (from *phēnai* 'speak'). The Greek base also gave Middle English **prophecy** from Old French *profecie*, via late Latin from Greek *prophēteia*, and Middle English **prophesy** from Old French *profecier*, from *profecie*. The differentiation of the spellings *prophesy* and *prophecy* as verb and noun was not established until after 1700. **Prophetic** dates from the late 15th century and is from French *prophétique* or late Latin *propheticus*, from Greek *prophētikos* 'predicting'.

propitious [late Middle English] This is from Old French *propicieus* or based on Latin *propitius* 'favourable, gracious'.

proportion [late Middle English] The Latin phrase *pro portione* 'in respect of (its or a person's) share' is the source of *proportion* which came via Old French from Latin *proportio(n-)*. The phrase *out of proportion* arose in the early 18th century. The related word **proportional** is late Middle English from late Latin *proportionalis*, from *proportio(n-)*).

propose [Middle English] *Propose* is from Old French *proposer*, from Latin *proponere* 'put forth', but influenced by Latin *propositus* 'put or set forth' and Old French *poser* 'to place'. Latin *proponere* also gave rise to: Middle English **proposition** (from Old French, from Latin *propositio(n-)*), the verb dating from the 1920s. **Propound** (mid 16th century) is an alteration of archaic *propone*, from Latin *proponere* 'set forth'. The addition of the final -*d* may be compared with that in *expound* and *compound*. **Proponent**

(late 16th century) is from Latin *proponent-*, the present participial stem of *proponere*.

proprietary [late Middle English] A *proprietary* was originally a member of a religious order who held property. It is from late Latin *proprietarius* 'proprietor', from *proprietas*. The adjective, recorded from the late 16th century, conveys 'belonging to a proprietor' and is commonly applied in modern use to manufactured items which are patented (*proprietary brand*).
→ PROPERTY

propriety [late Middle English] The early sense recorded for *propriety* is 'peculiarity, essential quality'. It is from Old French *propriete*, from Latin *proprietas*. An obsolete sense of the word is 'piece of land, private possession' found in North American historical records. Current uses of the word relate to the various senses of *proper*.
→ PROPER; PROPERTY

proscribe [late Middle English] 'To outlaw' was the early sense of *proscribe* from Latin *proscribere*, from *pro-* 'in front of' and *scribere* 'write'. The notion is one of 'writing out publicly' for all to see.

prose [Middle English] This came via Old French from Latin *prosa* (*oratio*) 'straightforward (discourse)', the feminine of *prosus*, earlier *prorsus* 'direct'. Late 16th-century **prosaic** was first used as a noun for a prose writer. It is from late Latin *prosaicus*, from Latin *prosa* 'straightforward (discourse)'. Current senses of the adjective 'lacking poetic beauty', 'commonplace', date from the mid 18th century.

prosecute [late Middle English] The early sense was 'continue with (a course of action)'. The word is from Latin *prosequi* 'pursue, accompany', from *pro-* 'onward' and *sequi* 'follow'. **Prosecution** dates from the mid 16th century when it meant 'the continuation of a course of action'. This is from Old French, or from late Latin *prosecutio(n-)*, from *prosequi*.

proselyte [late Middle English] *Proselyte* came via late Latin from Greek *prosēluthos* 'stranger, convert', from *proseluth-*, the past stem of *proserkhesthai* 'to approach'.

prospect [late Middle English] *Prospect* was first used as a noun describing the action of looking towards a distant object. It derives from Latin *prospectus* 'view', from *prospicere* 'look forward' (from *pro-* 'forward' and *specere* 'to look'). Early use, referring to a view of landscape, gave rise in the mid 16th century to the meaning 'mental picture', which developed into 'anticipated event' (e.g. *the prospect is daunting*). The word **prospective** is late 16th-

century in origin in the sense 'looking forward, having foresight': it is from obsolete French *prospectif*, *-ive* or late Latin *prospectivus*, from Latin *prospectus*.

prospectus [mid 18th century] This is an English use of a Latin word meaning literally 'view, prospect', from the verb *prospicere*, from *pro-* 'forward' and *specere* 'to look'.
→ PROSPECT

prosperity [Middle English] Old French *prosperite* is the source, from Latin *prosperitas*, from *prosperus* 'doing well': this is a base shared by late Middle English **prosper** from Old French *prosperer*, from Latin *prosperare*. **Prosperous** is also late Middle English from Old French *prospereus*, from Latin *prosperus*.

prostitute [mid 16th century] This word was first used as a verb. It comes from Latin *prostituere* 'expose publicly, offer for sale', from *pro-* 'before' and *statuere* 'set up, place'.

prostrate [Middle English] *Prostrate* is from Latin *prostratus*, the past participle of *prosternere* 'throw down', from *pro-* 'before' and *sternere* 'lay flat'.

protagonist [late 17th century] This word for a 'major character' in a drama is from Greek *prōtagōnistēs*, from *prōtos* 'first in importance' and *agōnistēs* 'actor'.

protection [Middle English] An Old French word gave *protection* in English, from late Latin *protectio(n-)*. The source is Latin *protegere* 'cover in front', which also gave rise to late Middle English **protect**, the base forms being *pro-* 'in front' and *tegere* 'to cover'. Late Middle English **protector** is from Old French *protectour*, from late Latin *protector*.

protein [mid 19th century] This is from French *protéine*, German *Protein*, from Greek *prōteios* 'primary', from *prōtos* 'first'. *Proteins* are an essential, therefore 'primary', part of all living organisms.

protest [late Middle English] *Protest* was first used as a verb in the sense 'make a solemn declaration'. The word derives from Old French *protester*, from Latin *protestari*, from *pro-* 'forth, publicly' and *testari* 'assert'. Latin *testis* 'witness' is the base, shared by Middle English **protestation** via Old French from late Latin *protestatio(n-)* (from *protestari*). The religious term **Protestant** came into English via German or French; this was from the declaration (*protestatio*) of Martin Luther and his supporters dissenting from the Diet of Spires (1529) which reaffirmed the Diet of Worms against the Reformation. The Protestant rejection was of the authority of the papacy, finding authority instead in the text of the Bible made available to all in vernacular translation. The compound:

■ **Protestant ethic**, the view that a person's responsibility is to achieve success through hard work, translates the German *die protestantische Ethik*, coined in 1904 by the economist Max Weber in his thesis on the relationship between the teachings of Calvin and the rise of capitalism.

WORDBUILDING

The prefix **proto-** [from Greek *prōtos* 'first'] adds the sense

■ original; primitive [prototype]

■ first; anterior [protozoon]

---

protocol [late Middle English] This originally denoted the original minute of an agreement, forming the legal authority for future dealings relating to it. It is from Old French *prothocole*, via medieval Latin from Greek *prōtokollon* 'first page, flyleaf', from *prōtos* 'first' and *kolla* 'glue'. The sense 'official procedure' governing such things as affairs of state derives from French *protocole*, summarizing the collection of set forms of etiquette to be observed by the French head of state, and used as a name for the government department responsible for this (in the 19th century).

protract [mid 16th century] *Protract* is from Latin *protrahere* 'prolong', from *pro-* 'out' and *trahere* 'to draw'. *Protract time* was an early phrase, now obsolete. From the same period, **protraction** is from French, or from late Latin *protractio(n-)*, from *protrahere*.

protrude [early 17th century] 'Thrust (something) forward or onward' was the early sense of *protrude* from Latin *protrudere*, from *pro-* 'forward, out' and *trudere* 'to thrust'.

protuberant [mid 17th century] This is from late Latin *protuberant-*, the present participial stem of *protuberare* 'swell out', from *pro-* 'forward, out' and *tuber* 'bump'. *Protuberant* is the base of **protuberance** dating from the same period.

proud [late Old English] Late Old English *prūt*, *prūd* meant 'having a high opinion of one's own worth', from Old French *prud* 'valiant', based on Latin *prodesse* 'be of value'. The notion 'slightly projecting' (*stood proud of the surrounding surface*) is first recorded as a distinct sense in English dialect of the 19th century, but it was seen in the phrase *proud flesh* (referring to raised flesh along the edges of a healing wound) in late Middle English.

prove [Middle English] *Prove* is from Old French *prover*, from Latin *probare* 'test, approve, demonstrate', from *probus* 'good'. Use of the term in the context of bread baking is found from the mid 19th century.

provenance [late 18th century] This word is from French, from the verb *provenir* 'come or stem from'. Latin *provenire* is the source, from *pro-* 'forth' and *venire* 'come'.

proverb [Middle English] *Proverb* is from Old French *proverbe*, from Latin *proverbium*, from *pro-* '(put) forth' and *verbum* 'word'. It is a saying 'put forth' as a truth familiar to all. Late Middle English **proverbial** is from Latin *proverbialis*, from *proverbium*.

provide [late Middle English] Early use included the sense 'prepare to do, get ready'. It is from Latin *providere* 'foresee, attend to', from *pro-* 'before' and *videre* 'to see'. Late Middle English **provision** also had the sense 'foresight' and came via Old French from Latin *provisio(n-)*, from *providere*. Use of the plural *provisions* for 'food supplies' is recorded from the early 17th century. The verb dates from the early 19th century.

providence [late Middle English] *Providence* is from Old French, from Latin *providentia*, from *providere* 'foresee, attend to'. Late Middle English **provident** is from the same source verb; mid 17th-century **providential** is from *providence*, on the pattern of *evidential*.
→ PROVIDE

province [late Middle English] *Province* is from Old French, from Latin *provincia* 'charge, province', which is of uncertain ultimate origin. **Provincial** is late Middle English from Old French, from Latin *provincialis* 'belonging to a province'. The notion of 'narrowness, limited view' began to be associated sometimes with the word from the mid 18th century.

proviso [late Middle English] *Proviso* is from the medieval Latin phrase *proviso (quod)* 'it being provided (that)', from Latin *providere* 'foresee, provide, attend to'. **Provisory** (early 17th century) is from the same Latin verb via French *provisoire* or medieval Latin *provisorius*.

provoke [late Middle English] Early use included the sense 'invoke, summon'. It comes from Old French *provoquer*, from Latin *provocare* 'call forth, challenge' (from *pro-* 'forth' and *vocare* 'to call'). The Latin base is shared by **provocation** (also late Middle English) from Old French, from Latin *provocatio(n-)*, and, from the same period, **provocative** from Old French *provocatif*, *-ive*, from late Latin *provocativus*.

provost [late Old English] The early spelling was *profost* 'head of a chapter, prior'. This was reinforced in Middle English by Anglo-Norman French *provost*, from medieval Latin *propositus*, a synonym of Latin *praepositus* 'head, chief'.

prow [mid 16th century] *Prow* is from Old French *proue*, from Provençal *proa*, probably via Latin from Greek *prōira*, from a base represented by Latin *pro* 'in front'.

prowess [Middle English] 'Bravery in battle' was the early sense of *prowess*. Old French *proesce* is the source, from *prou* 'valiant'. The sense 'skill in a particular activity' dates from the early 20th century.

prowl [late Middle English] This word is of unknown origin; there is apparently no related word outside English. Early use was in the sense 'move about in search of something'.

proximity [late 15th century] *Proximity* is from French *proximité*, from Latin *proximitas*, from *proximus* 'nearest', a base shared by late 16th-century **proximate** (from Latin *proximatus*, the past participle of *proximare* 'draw near').

proxy [late Middle English] *Proxy* is a contraction of *procuracy*, denoting the office of a procurator.
→ PROCURATOR

prude [early 18th century] This comes from French as a back-formation (by removal of the suffix) from *prudefemme*: this is the feminine of *prud'homme* 'good man and true', from *prou* 'worthy'. Old French *prude* was laudatory but the word in English was usually applied adversely from early use.

prudent [late Middle English] *Prudent* is from Old French, or from Latin *prudent-*, a contraction of *provident-* 'foreseeing, attending to'. Late Middle English **prudential** is from *prudent*, on the pattern of words such as *evidential*.
→ PROVIDENCE

prune[1] [Middle English] This word for a plum preserved by drying comes from Old French, via Latin from Greek *prou(m)non* 'plum'.

prune[2] [late 15th century] This verb in early use had the sense 'abbreviate, reduce by rejecting superfluities'. The source is Old French *pro(o)ignier*, possibly based on Latin *rotundus* 'round'. The word features in gardening contexts from the late 16th century.

prurient [late 16th century] The early sense recorded was 'having a mental itching'. Latin *prurient-* is the source, the present participial stem of the verb *prurire* 'to itch, long' and 'be wanton'.

pry [Middle English] 'Peer inquisitively' was the sense found in early examples. The origin

remains unknown. The verb *peer* is near in form but appears later.

psalm [Old English] Old English *(p)sealm* came via ecclesiastical Latin from Greek *psalmos* 'song sung to harp music', from *psallein* 'to pluck'. The noun **psalmist** is late 15th century, from late Latin *psalmista*, based on Greek *psalmos*.

pseud [1960s] *Pseud* is an abbreviation of late Middle English **pseudo**, an independent use of the prefix *pseudo-*, from Greek *pseudēs* 'false', *pseudos* 'falsehood'.

pseudonym [mid 19th century] This is from French *pseudonyme*, from Greek *pseudōnymos*, from *pseudēs* 'false' and *onoma* 'name'.

psyche [mid 17th century] *Psyche* came via Latin from Greek *psukhē* 'breath, life, soul'. Early 19th-century **psychic** is from Greek *psukhikos*, from *psukhē*. This base is involved in the first element of the science terms **psychology** (late 17th century from modern Latin *psychologia*) and **psychiatry** (mid 19th century from Greek *psukhē* and *iatreia* 'healing', from *iatros* 'healer').

psychedelic [1950s] This word used in drug contexts where there is an association of increased awareness of the senses was formed irregularly from *psyche* and Greek *dēlos* 'clear, manifest', suffixed by *-ic*. The noun **psychedelia** dates from the 1960s and is a back-formation (by removal of the suffix) from *psychedelic*.

pub [mid 19th century] This term is an abbreviation of *public house*.

puberty [late Middle English] *Puberty* is from Latin *pubertas*, from *puber* 'adult', related to *pubes* 'genitals'. Greek *pubes* 'groin' is the base of mid 17th-century **pubescent** from French, or from Latin *pubescent-*, the present participial stem of *pubescere* 'reach puberty'.

public [late Middle English] *Public* is from Old French, from Latin *publicus*, a blend of *poplicus* 'of the people' (from *populus* 'people') and *pubes* 'adult'. The compound:
■ **public school** (late 16th century) is from Latin *publica schola*, a school maintained at the public expense; in England *public school* (a term recorded from 1580) originally denoted a grammar school under public management, founded for the benefit of the public (contrasting with *private school*, run for the profit of the proprietor); since the 19th century the term has been applied to the old endowed English grammar schools, and newer schools modelled on them, which have developed into fee-paying boarding schools.
→ PUBLISH

publican [Middle English] This was first used in the sense 'collector of taxes' (as in the *publicans and sinners* of biblical reference). It comes from Old French *publicain*, from Latin *publicanus*, from *publicum* 'public revenue' a neuter form (used as a noun) of *publicus* 'of the people'. The sense 'person who manages a pub' dates from the early 18th century.

publish [Middle English] The early sense recorded was 'make generally known'. It is from the stem of Old French *puplier*, from Latin *publicare* 'make public', from *publicus*. The noun **publication** referred in late Middle English to a 'public announcement or declaration': this is via Old French from Latin *publicatio(n-)*, from *publicare*. **Publicity**, from French *publicité*, from *public* 'public', is recorded from the late 18th century.
➔ PUBLIC

puce [late 18th century] This colour term is from a French word for 'flea', giving 'flea(-colour)', from Latin *pulex, pulic-*.

pucker [late 16th century] This is probably a frequentative (= verb of repeated action), from the base of *pocket*, suggesting the formation of small purse-like gatherings.

pudding [Middle English] A *pudding* originally referred to a sausage such as *black pudding*. It is apparently from Old French *boudin* 'black pudding', from Latin *botellus* 'sausage, small intestine'. In early times ingredients were apparently boiled in a bag (*pudding cloth*) but the method of cooking gradually changed included boiling, steaming, and later baking.

puddle [Middle English] *Puddle* is a diminutive of Old English *pudd* 'ditch, furrow'; German dialect *Pfudel* 'pool' is related.

puerile [late 16th century] 'Like a boy' was the early meaning. It comes from French *puéril* or Latin *puerilis*, from *puer* 'boy'. The depreciative sense arose in the late 17th century.

puff [Middle English] This is imitative of the sound of a breath, perhaps from Old English *pyf* (noun), *pyffan* (verb). The word includes the senses 'a burst of breath' as well as 'inflated shape' (*puff sleeves*), 'boaster' (a now archaic sense) and 'effeminacy'.

pugnacious [mid 17th century] *Pugnacious* is based on Latin *pugnax, pugnac-*, from *pugnare* 'to fight', from *pugnus* 'fist'.

puke [late 16th century] This is probably imitative and was first recorded as a verb in: At first the infant, mewling, and puking in the nurse's arms, in Shakespeare's *As You Like It*.

pull [Old English] Old English *pullian* 'pluck, snatch' is of uncertain origin; the sense has developed from expressing a short sharp action to one of sustained force. If *pull* and *pluck* went back to early Germanic, a primitive connection between them would be conceivable but historical evidence is lacking.

pullet [late Middle English] The word *pullet* is from Old French *poulet*, a diminutive of *poule*, from the feminine of Latin *pullus* 'chicken, young animal'.

pulley [Middle English] *Pulley* is from Old French *polie*, probably from a medieval Greek diminutive of *polos* 'pivot, axis'.

pulp [late Middle English] At first *pulp* referred to the soft fleshy part of fruit. The origin is Latin *pulpa*. The verb dates from the mid 17th century. The phrase *pulp fiction* is from an originally US usage of *pulp* meaning 'ephemeral literature of poor quality' (1930s).

pulpit [Middle English] *Pulpit* is from Latin *pulpitum* 'scaffold, platform'. This was an early sense recorded in English but now obsolete; such platforms were for public representations or discussions. In medieval Latin *pulpitum* came to mean 'pulpit'. It was in the early 17th century that the connection with sermons arose in English.

pulse¹ [late Middle English] The *pulse* referring to the rhythmic throbbing of the arteries is from Latin *pulsus* 'beating', from *pellere* 'to drive, beat'. The verb **pulsate** is found in examples from the late 18th century and is from Latin *pulsare* 'throb', a frequentative (= verb of repeated action) of *pellere* 'to drive, beat'.

pulse² [Middle English] This word for an edible seed is from Old French *pols*, from Latin *puls* 'porridge of meal or pulse'.
➔ POLLEN

pulverize [late Middle English] *Pulverize* is from late Latin *pulverizare*, from *pulvis, pulver-* 'dust'.

pummel [mid 16th century] This is a variant of *pommel*.
➔ POMMEL

pump¹ [late Middle English] *Pump* is related to Dutch *pomp* 'ship's pump', recorded earlier in the sense 'wooden or metal conduit'. The word is probably partly of imitative origin. Machines for raising water were in ancient and medieval use but no evidence of the term *pump* is found in English before the 15th century; early use was as a nautical term referring to the pumping out of bilge water.

pump² [mid 16th century] This *pump* as in *tennis pumps* is of unknown origin. No word similar in form and sense has been found in other languages.

pun [mid 17th century] This is perhaps an abbreviation of obsolete *pundigrion*, as a fanciful alteration of *punctilio* 'petty point' (from Italian *puntiglio* 'little point').

punch¹ [late Middle English] This *punch* meaning 'strike' was first used as a verb in the sense 'puncture, prod'. It is a variant of *pounce*.
→ POUNCE

punch² [early 16th century] The *punch* as a term for a device for making holes is perhaps an abbreviation of Middle English *puncheon* (via Old French from Latin *pungere* 'to puncture'), or from the verb *punch*.
→ PUNCH¹

punch³ [mid 17th century] This *punch* as a name for a drink made from wine or spirits is apparently from Sanskrit *pañca* 'five, five kinds of': this is because the drink originally had five ingredients.

punch⁴ [mid 17th century] This *punch* as in *as pleased as Punch* is connected with the grotesque hook-nosed male character of the Punch and Judy Show, the English variant of a stock character derived from Italian *commedia dell'arte*. The word was first used as a dialect term for a short, fat person (whence the extended use in *Suffolk punch* a horse of a short-legged thickset breed). In origin it is an abbreviation of *Punchinello*, an alteration of Neapolitan dialect *Polecenella* (which may be a diminutive of *pollecena* 'young turkey cock with a hooked beak').

punctilious [mid 17th century] This comes from French *pointilleux*, from *pointille*, from Italian *puntiglio* 'little point'. The notion is one of being attentive to minute detail.

punctual [late Middle English] This comes from medieval Latin *punctualis*, from Latin *punctum* 'a point'. The word has four main semantic branches: obsolete 'sharp-pointed' (*punctual instrument*); 'made by a point' (*punctual mark*); 'to the point' (*a punctual story*); 'accurate, precise, timely' (*punctual time, punctual revolt*); and 'exactly observant of an appointed time' (*always punctual for his appointment*).

punctuate [mid 17th century] The early sense was 'point out': it comes from medieval Latin *punctuare* 'bring to a point', from *punctum* 'a point'. Use in examples such as *she punctuated her speech with giggles* dates from the early 19th century. **Punctuation** comes, via medieval Latin *punctuatio(n-)*, from the same source verb.

puncture [late Middle English] This word, originally having the general sense 'perforation with a sharp instrument, pricking' is from Latin *punctura*, from *pungere* 'to prick'. The verb dates from the late 17th century. Use in combinations such as *puncture wound*, *puncture proof* is recorded from the late 19th century.

pundit [late 17th century] Sanskrit *paṇḍita* 'learned' is the source of this word in English. The transferred use 'learned expert' dates from the early 19th century.

pungent [late 16th century] The early sense was 'very painful or distressing'. Latin *pungere* 'to prick' is the source. A now obsolete sense 'keenly affecting the mind' was found from the early 17th century (Pepys *Diary*: A very good and pungent sermon … discoursing the necessity of restitution).

punish [Middle English] *Punish* is from Old French *puniss-*, the lengthened stem of *punir* 'punish', from Latin *punire*. Latin *poena* 'penalty' is the base. The transferred use meaning 'cause difficulty and hardship to' (as in *punishing work schedule*) dates from the early 19th century. From the same Latin source are: late Middle English **punishment** (from Old French *punissement*, from the verb *punir*) and early 17th-century **punitive**, from French *punitif, -ive* or medieval Latin *punitivus*, from *punire*.

punk [late 17th century] This was originally a North American term for soft crumbly wood that has been attacked by fungus, used as tinder. It may, in some senses, be related to archaic *punk* 'prostitute' and to *spunk* 'touchwood, tinder'. Since the beginning of the 20th century, it has been used disparagingly in US English (e.g. *stop right there, punk!*); it has been used to mean 'punk-rocker' (interested in a style of rock music characterized by aggressive lyrics) since the 1970s.

punnet [early 19th century] This is perhaps a diminutive of the dialect word *pun* for the unit of weight 'a pound'.

punt [Old English] The sailing term *punt* is from Latin *ponto*, denoting a flat-bottomed ferry boat; it was readopted in the early 16th century from Middle Low German *punte* or Middle Dutch *ponte* 'ferry boat', of the same origin.

punter [early 18th century] This was originally a term for a player playing against the bank in certain card games. In the late 19th century it came to be a term in horse racing for a small professional backer of horses. Colloquial generalized use in the sense 'client' or merely 'person' dates from the 1960s (e.g. *the bootsale went well, with most punters satisfied with their bargains*). The word is from the early 18th-century verb **punt** meaning 'lay a stake against the bank', from French *ponter* in the same sense.

puny [mid 16th century] This was first used as a noun denoting a younger or more junior person; it is a phonetic spelling of *puisne* (a legal term for a junior judge) from an Old French word meaning literally 'born after'.

pupil[1] [late Middle English] Early use of this *pupil* (as in *school pupil*) was in the sense 'orphan, ward (under the care of a guardian)'. It is from Old French *pupille*, from Latin *pupillus* (a diminutive of *pupus* 'boy') and *pupilla* (a diminutive of *pupa* 'girl').

pupil[2] [late Middle English] This *pupil* (as in *pupil of the eye*) is from Old French *pupille* or Latin *pupilla* 'female child', a diminutive of *pupa* 'doll': this is from the tiny reflected images visible in the eye.

puppet [mid 16th century] An early *puppet* meant simply 'doll'; it is a later form of *poppet* but generally having a more unfavourable connotation. Its use in political contexts to mean 'a person or state controlled by another' dates from the late 16th century.
→ POPPET

puppy [late 15th century] A *puppy* was initially a 'lapdog' kept as a lady's pet. It is perhaps from Old French *poupee* 'doll, plaything'; it may have an association with *puppet*, synonymous with dialect *puppy* (as in *puppy-show* 'puppet show'). Use as a contemptuous term (e.g. *young, shallow-brained puppy*) meaning 'impertinent young man' dates from the late 16th century. At this same time **pup** was recorded meaning 'arrogant young man'; it is a back-formation (by removal of the suffix) from *puppy*, misinterpreted as a diminutive.
→ PUPPET

purchase [Middle English] *Purchase* is from Old French *pourchacier* 'seek to obtain or bring about', which was also the earliest sense in English. This soon gave rise to the senses 'gain', seen in nautical use where the notion of 'gaining' is one portion of rope after another (hand over hand) as the anchor is hauled up. From 'gain' came the sense 'buy'.

pure [Middle English] *Pure* is from Old French *pur* 'pure', from Latin *purus*. The word branches semantically into 'not mixed (physically) with anything else' (e.g. *pure gold*); 'not mixed (generally)' (e.g. *pure lineage*); and 'free from corruption or defilement' (e.g. *pure French, a maiden pure*). Latin *purus* is a base shared by: Middle English **purify** (from Old French *purifier*, from Latin *purificare*); Middle English **purity** (from Old French *purete*, later assimilated to late Latin *puritas*); and early 18th-century **purist**

(from French *puriste*, from *pur* 'pure'). The term **Puritan** for a member of a group of English Protestants of the late 16th and 17th centuries who sought simplification in forms of worship, is based on late Latin *puritas* 'purity'.

purgatory [Middle English] This word for a place of spiritual purging and purification is from Anglo-Norman French *purgatorie* or medieval Latin *purgatorium*, a neuter form (used as a noun) of late Latin *purgatorius* 'purifying'. The source verb, as in the case of *purge*, is Latin *purgare* 'purify'.
→ PURGE

purge [Middle English] This is from Old French *purgier*, from Latin *purgare* 'purify', from *purus* 'pure'. The same Latin verb gave rise to late Middle English **purgative** in medical contexts, from Old French *purgatif*, *-ive*, from late Latin *purgativus*.

purloin [Middle English] This formal word was first used in the sense 'put at a distance'. It comes from Anglo-Norman French *purloigner* 'put away', from *pur-* 'forth' and *loign* 'far'.

purple [Old English] When first used this word described the distinctive colour associated with an emperor's clothing, originally 'crimson'. It is an alteration of *purpre*, from Latin *purpura* 'purple', from Greek *porphura*: this denoted molluscs that yielded a crimson dye as well as the cloth dyed with this. Use of the word to mean 'splendid, brilliant' is seen in phrases such as *purple patch, purple prose* in literary composition, from the late 16th century.

purport [late Middle English] The early sense recorded was 'express, signify'. It comes from Old French *purporter*, from medieval Latin *proportare* composed of Latin *pro-* 'forth' and *portare* 'carry, bear'. The sense 'appear, seem' (*it purported to have been written by the same author*) dates from the late 18th century.

purpose [Middle English] *Purpose* is from Old French *porpos*, from the verb *porposer*, a variant of *proposer*. As well as meaning an 'object in view' (e.g. *served my purpose well*) it may be used to mean 'determination, intention' (Shakespeare *Macbeth*: Infirm of purpose: Give me the Daggers). The phrase *on purpose* meaning 'by design' is found from the late 16th century (Shakespeare *Comedy of Errors*: Belike his wife … On purpose shut the doors against his way).
→ PROPOSE

purse [late Old English] This is an alteration of late Latin *bursa* 'purse', from Greek *bursa* 'hide, leather'. The current verb sense derived from the notion of drawing purse strings dates from the early 17th century (Shakespeare

Othello: Thou … did'st contract, and purse thy brow together).

pursue [Middle English] This was originally used in the sense 'follow with enmity'. It comes from Anglo-Norman French *pursuer*, from an alteration of Latin *prosequi* 'prosecute'. It is used to mean 'prosecute' in a court of law, in Scottish legal contexts. The same Latin source is shared by late Middle English **pursuit**, from Anglo-Norman French *pursuete* 'following after', from *pursuer*; early senses included 'persecution, annoyance' and in the legal domain 'petition, prosecution'.

purulent [late Middle English] This is from Latin *purulentus* 'festering', from *pus, pur-* 'pus' (a word adopted into English in this same period).

purvey [Middle English] *Purvey* is from Anglo-Norman French *purveier*, from Latin *providere* 'foresee, attend to'. Early senses included 'foresee', 'attend to in advance', and 'equip'. The notion 'provide' has come to dominate; the noun **purveyor** (also Middle English) is commonly found in phrases such as *purveyors of fine food* in commercial or military supply contexts.
→ PROVIDE

push [Middle English] This is from Old French *pousser*, from Latin *pulsare* 'to push, beat, pulse'. The early sense was 'exert force on', giving rise later to 'make a strenuous effort, endeavour'. The colloquial phrase *push off* (early 18th century) is from the image of a person pushing a boat away from the shore and leaving; the idiomatic phrase *when push comes to shove* dates from the 1950s.
→ PULSE[1]

pusillanimous [late Middle English] This word meaning 'timid, showing lack of courage' is from ecclesiastical Latin *pusillanimis*, translating Greek *olugopsukhos*. The base forms are *pusillus* 'very small' and *animus* 'mind', giving a notion of 'having a feeble spirit'.

puss [early 16th century] Informal *puss* is probably from Middle Low German *pūs* (also *pūskatte*) or Dutch *poes*, of unknown origin. It is a word common to several Germanic languages as a calling name for a cat; it is rarely found as a synonym for cat as it is in English. The compound:
■ **pussy willow** dates from the mid 19th century and was originally a child's word, because of the resemblance of the soft fluffy catkins to a cat's fur.

put [Old English] In Old English this was recorded only in the verbal noun *putung*. The origin is unknown; dialect *pote* 'to push, thrust'

(an early sense of the verb *put*) may be related. The main semantic strands include: 'thrust' (Shakespeare *Othello*: Wear thy good Rapier bare, and put it home), 'move to another position' (*put on the table*); and 'bring into some condition or state' (*put to bed, put in prison*).

putrefy [late Middle English] Latin *puter, putr-* 'rotten' is the base of several words dating from the same period: *putrefy* (via French from Latin *putrefacere* 'make rotten'); **putrefaction** (from Old French, or from late Latin *putrefactio(n-)*, from *putrefacere*) and **putrid** (from Latin *putridus*, from *putrere* 'to rot').

putt [mid 17th century] This golfing term was originally Scots; the doubling of the *t* is a differentiation from the verb *put*.

putty [mid 17th century] *Putty* is from French *potée* which means literally 'potful', from *pot* 'pot'. The phrase *to be like putty in someone's hands* dates from the 1920s.

puzzle [late 16th century] *Puzzle* was first found in examples as a verb. The origin is obscure and the noun did not appear until somewhat later (*c.*1612). A connection has been suggested between *puzzle* and *pose* (as in *pose a problem*) but it is likely that these were two originally distinct words which subsequently attracted each other by certain similarities.

pygmy [late Middle English] Originally this was used in the plural, denoting a mythological race of small people. The word is via Latin from Greek *pugmaios* 'dwarf', from *pugmē* 'the length measured from elbow to knuckles'. Use of the word descriptively to mean 'very small' in combinations such as *pygmy goat* date from the late 16th century.

pyjamas [early 19th century] This word comes from Urdu and Persian, from *pāy* 'leg' and *jāma* 'clothing'. These were loose trousers usually of silk or cotton worn by both sexes in Turkey, Iran, and India, etc: the garment was adopted for night wear by Europeans living in those countries and gradually the term came to be applied outside Asia.

pylon [mid 19th century] *Pylon* is from Greek *pulōn*, from *pulē* 'gate'.

pyramid [late Middle English] *Pyramid* was first used in the geometrical sense of the term. It came via Latin from Greek *puramis, puramid-*, which also denoted a type of cake. This is taken by some to be the earlier sense, the geometrical sense arising from a resemblance in shape. An Egyptian origin is now generally rejected.

pyre [mid 17th century] This word came via Latin from Greek *pura* 'hearth', from *pur* 'fire'.

Qq

quack¹ [mid 16th century] This *quack* describing the sound made by a duck is imitative of the harsh noise; the first use recorded was as a verb.

quack² [mid 17th century] This *quack* used informally to refer to a 'doctor' is an abbreviation of an earlier word *quacksalver* which comes from Dutch; it probably derives from obsolete *quacken* 'to prattle' and *salf*, *zalf* (the equivalent of English *salve*). Thus *quacksalver* paints an image of someone prattling about his remedies to potential customers.
→ SALVE

quadrangle [late Middle English] Latin *quattuor* 'four' and *angulus* 'corner, angle' are the base elements of *quadrangle* from Old French, or from late Latin *quadrangulum* 'square (thing)'. The prefix *quadr-* is also found in the forms *quadri-* and *quadru-* (from *quattuor*) and is exemplified in many English words. Late Middle English **quadrant** (from Latin *quadrans*, *quadrant-* 'quarter') is now a technical term for 'each of four quarters of a circle' but was first recorded as a term for an astronomical instrument. In the mid 17th century other words arose sharing this common prefix: **quadratic** (via French or from modern Latin *quadraticus*, from *quadrare* 'make square'); **quadrilateral** (based on late Latin *quadrilaterus* 'four-sided'); **quadruped** (from French *quadrupède* or Latin *quadrupes*, *quadruped-* 'four-footed'). In the late 18th century **quadruplet** became another member of this prefix-related group; it is from the late Middle English verb *quadruple* (via French from Latin *quadruplus*) influenced by the pattern of *triplet*.

quaff [early 16th century] This word is probably imitative of the sound of drinking.

quagmire [late 16th century] The first syllable *quag* is an archaic word meaning 'marshy place', probably related to the dialect verb *quag* 'shake, shiver'. The initial *qu-* is probably symbolic of the trembling movement as in *quake*.
→ MIRE

quail [late Middle English] The verb *quail* as in *she quailed at his heartless words* was first found meaning 'waste away, come to nothing'. The origin is unknown. The bird name *quail* is not associated; a Middle English word, it is from Old French *quaille* (from medieval Latin *coacula*, a word probably imitating the call).

quaint [Middle English] The original senses of *quaint* were 'wise, clever' and 'ingenious, cunningly devised'. 'Showing skill' was the core notion. Later development led to 'out of the ordinary'. Old French *cointe* is the source, from Latin *cognitus*, the past participle of *cognoscere* 'ascertain'. Current use reflects the meaning 'interestingly unusual or old-fashioned' found in examples from the late 18th century; the appreciative connotation of the word has weakened.

quake [Old English] In Old English the verb was *cwacian*. The term **Quaker** (member of the Society of Friends) is derived from this. It may allude to the direction given by the movement's founder, preacher George Fox (1624–91), to his followers to 'tremble at the name of the Lord', or it may be associated with the fits supposedly experienced by worshippers when moved by the Spirit.

qualify [late Middle English] To *qualify* (from French *qualifier*, from medieval Latin *qualificare*) was originally to 'describe (something) in a particular way'. The base is Latin *qualis* 'of what kind, of such a kind', shared by the noun **qualification** found from the mid 16th century from medieval Latin *qualificatio(n-)*, from the verb *qualificare*.

quality [Middle English] The early senses recorded were 'character, disposition' and 'particular property or feature'. It comes from Old French *qualite*, from Latin *qualitas* (translating Greek *poiotēs*), from *qualis* 'of what kind, of such a kind'.

qualm [early 16th century] A *qualm* was originally a 'momentary sick feeling'. It may be related to Old English *cw(e)alm* 'pain', of Germanic origin.

quandary [late 16th century] This word is perhaps partly from Latin *quando* 'when', capturing the notion of 'indecision'.

quango [1970s] Originally a US term *quango* is an acronym from *quasi* (or *quasi-autonomous*) *non-government(al) organization*.

quantity [Middle English] This comes from Old French *quantite*, from Latin *quantitas* (translating Greek *posotēs*). The base is Latin *quantus* 'how great, how much'. The verb **quantify** dates from the mid 16th century and is from medieval Latin *quantificare*, from Latin *quantus*.

quarantine [mid 17th century] *Quarantine* is from Italian *quarantina* 'forty days', from *quaranta* 'forty'. The word represented the number of days of isolation imposed to test for disease but the length of time is no longer fixed at forty.

quarrel [Middle English] A *quarrel* was originally a 'reason for disagreement with somebody'. Old French *querele* is the source, from Latin *querel(l)a* 'complaint', from *queri* 'complain'.
→ QUERULOUS

quarry[1] [Middle English] This *quarry* as a place from which stone, for example, is extracted is from a variant of medieval Latin *quareria*, from Old French *quarriere*. Latin *quadrum* 'a square' is the base. The verb dates from the late 18th century.

quarry[2] [Middle English] This *quarry* meaning 'pursued animal' is from Old French *cuiree*, an alteration (influenced by *cuir* 'leather' and *curer* 'clean, disembowel') of *couree*. The Latin source is *cor* 'heart'. Originally the term referred to the parts of a deer that were placed on the hide and given as a reward to the hounds.

quarry[3] [mid 16th century] This *quarry* is a term for a diamond-shaped pane of glass or an unglazed floor tile. The latter was the early sense. It is an alteration of Middle English *quarrel* (via Old French based on late Latin *quadrus* 'square') which in late Middle English denoted a latticed windowpane.

quart [Middle English] *Quart* as a unit of capacity measuring a quarter of a gallon is from Old French *quarte*, from Latin *quarta* (*pars*) 'fourth (part)'. The source is Latin *quartus* 'fourth', from *quattuor* 'four'. The same base is shared by Middle English **quarter** (via Old French *quartier* from Latin *quartarius* 'fourth part of a measure') and early 17th century **quartet** 'set of four' (from French *quartette*, from Italian *quartetto* from *quarto* 'fourth').

quartz [mid 18th century] *Quartz*, a hard mineral consisting of silica, is from German *Quarz*, from Polish dialect *kwardy*, corresponding to Czech *tvrdý* 'hard'.

quash [Middle English] The word *quash* is from Old French *quasser* 'annul', from late Latin *cassare* (in medieval Latin the alternative spelling *quassare* existed), from *cassus* 'null, void'. *Quash* was found early in legal use. The verb *squash* is a mid 16th-century alteration of *quash*.

quasi [late 15th century] This is a use of a Latin word meaning literally 'as if, almost'.

quaver [late Middle English] This was first used as a verb in the general sense 'tremble'. It is from dialect *quave* 'quake, tremble', probably from an Old English word related to *quake*. The noun is first recorded in the mid 16th century as a musical term.
→ QUAKE

quay [late Middle English] The early spelling was *key*, from Old French *kay*, of Celtic origin. The change of spelling occurred in the late 17th century, influenced by the modern French spelling *quai*.

queasy [late Middle English] Early spellings included *queisy* and *coisy* 'causing nausea', of uncertain origin. The word may be related to Old French *coisier* 'to hurt'. Early English examples reflected the sense 'unsettled, troubled' referring to a state of affairs as well as to the stomach.

queen [Old English] Old English *cwēn* is Germanic in origin, related to Old English *cwene* 'woman' (now archaic **quean** 'badly behaved girl'). Dutch *kween* 'barren cow' is related, from an Indo-European root shared by Greek *gunē* 'woman'. The English word from earliest times denoted a woman of distinction, a female sovereign.

queer [early 16th century] This word is considered to be from German *quer* 'oblique, perverse', but the origin is doubtful. Early senses included 'eccentric' and 'strange' but there was also the notion 'of questionable character'. The word was associated with illness from the late 18th century (*feel queer*); the offensive association with homosexuality is recorded from the late 19th century in slang.
→ THWART

quell [Old English] Old English *cwellan* meant 'kill'. Of Germanic origin, it is related to Dutch *kwellen* and German *quälen*. The attenuated sense 'subdue' is found from the early 16th century.

quench [Old English] Old English -*cwencan* was recorded in *acwencan* 'to put out, extinguish'. The sense 'satisfy (thirst or desire)' arose in Middle English. The origin is Germanic.

querulous [late 15th century] *Querulous* is from late Latin *querulosus*, from Latin *querulus*, from *queri* 'complain'.
→ QUARREL

query [mid 17th century] This is an Anglicized form of the Latin imperative *quaere!*, used in the 16th century in English as a verb in the sense 'inquire' and as a noun meaning 'query'. The source is Latin *quaerere* 'to ask, seek'.

quest [late Middle English] *Quest* as a noun is from Old French *queste*, and in early use meant both 'inquest' and 'a search'. As a verb it is from Old French *quester*; early use often described the activity of a hound searching for game. The base is Latin *quaerere* 'ask, seek'.
→ QUERY; QUESTION; INQUEST

question [late Middle English] The noun is from Old French *question*, the verb from Old French *questionner*, from Latin *quaestio(n-)*. Latin *quaerere* 'ask, seek' is the base. The sense 'call into question' (*questioned his ethics*) dates from the mid 17th century. The noun **questionnaire** (late 19th century) is an adoption of a French word, from *questionner* 'to question'.

queue [late 16th century] This was initially used as a heraldic term for the tail of an animal. It comes from French, based on Latin *cauda* 'tail'. The word also described a 'pigtail' in the mid 18th century. The notion of forming an orderly line is associated with the word from the mid 19th century.

quibble [early 17th century] The early sense recorded was 'play on words, pun'; it is a diminutive of obsolete *quib* 'a petty objection'. Latin *quibus* is the likely source, a dative and ablative form of *qui, quae, quod* 'who, what, which', frequently used in legal documents and thereby associated with subtle distinctions or verbal niceties.

quick [Old English] Old English *cwic, cwicu* meant 'alive, animated, alert' (e.g. *the quick and the dead*). Of Germanic origin, it is related to Dutch *kwiek* 'sprightly' and German *keck* 'saucy', from an Indo-European root shared by Latin *vivus* 'alive' and Greek *bios*, *zōē* 'life'. The sense 'mentally agile' (e.g. *quick at maths*) was already in Old English.

quid [late 17th century] This informal word for one pound sterling originally denoted a sovereign. The origin remains obscure.

quiet [Middle English] Originally a noun denoting peace as opposed to war, *quiet* came via Old French, based on Latin *quies, quiet-* 'repose, quiet'. the same base is shared by mid 17th-century **quiescent** 'inactive' from Latin *quiescere* 'be still'.
→ QUIT; QUITE

quiff [late 19th century] This was originally a lock of hair plastered down on the forehead, a hairstyle adopted particularly by soldiers. The origin is unknown. The word now refers to a tuft of hair brushed upwards from the forehead.

quill [late Middle English] 'Hollow stem' (of a reed) and 'shaft of a feather' were the early meanings of *quill* which is probably from Middle Low German *quiele*.

quilt [Middle English] This comes from Old French *cuilte*, from Latin *culcita* 'mattress, cushion'. The Latin word described a soft item for lying upon but in its adoption into other languages, the purpose became one of covering. Until the late 17th century a quilted bed cover was also known as a *counterpoint* (later *counterpane*), a word altered from medieval Latin *culcita puncta* 'pricked (= by sewing) mattress').
→ COUNTERPANE

quintessence [late Middle English] This was first used as a term in philosophy. It came via French from medieval Latin *quinta essentia* 'fifth essence'. In classical and medieval philosophy it was thought that there was a fifth substance in addition to the four elements (air, earth, fire, and water), latent in all things and composing the celestial bodies. Extension of the word to mean 'most typical or perfect example' is found from the late 16th century.

quintet [late 18th century] *Quintet* is from French *quintette* or Italian *quintetto*, from *quinto* 'fifth', from Latin *quintus*.

quip [mid 16th century] This is perhaps from Latin *quippe* 'indeed, forsooth'. *Quip* was originally a sharp or sarcastic remark; the notion of 'cleverness' was a later association.

quire [Middle English] This word for 'four sheets of paper' is from Old French *quaier*, from Latin *quaterni* 'set of four'. The Latin base is *quattuor* 'four'.
→ QUART

quirk [early 16th century] The origin of *quirk*, first used as a verb meaning 'move jerkily', is unknown. The early sense of the noun (mid 16th century) was 'subtle verbal twist, quibble', which later became 'unexpected twist'.

quisling [Second World War] This word for a traitor cooperating with an enemy comes from the name of Major Vidkun *Quisling* (1887–1945). He was the Norwegian army officer and diplomat who ruled Norway on behalf of the German occupying forces during the Second World War, encouraging non-resistance by the population. He was executed for treason at the end of the war.

quit [Middle English] The early sense recorded was 'set free, redeem'. It is from Old French *quiter* (verb), *quite* (adjective), from Latin *quietus*, the past participle of *quiescere* 'be still'. Latin *quies* 'calm, quiet' is the base. The use of *quit* to

mean 'discontinue' an activity such as a job, dates from the mid 17th century.
→ QUIET; QUITE; QUITS

quite [Middle English] *Quite* is from the obsolete adjective *quite*, a variant of *quit* and conveying 'completely, fully'. The notion of moderation in the sense 'fairly' (e.g. *quite nice*) was not reflected until the middle of the 19th century.
→ QUIT

quits [late 15th century] The first sense recorded for *quits* (as in *call it quits*) was 'freed from a liability or debt'. It may be a colloquial abbreviation of medieval Latin *quittus* used as a receipt (from Latin *quietus* 'quiet').

quiver[1] [Middle English] This *quiver* meaning 'tremble' is from the Old English adjective *cwifer* 'nimble, quick', a word now obsolete but still found occasionally in dialect. The initial *qu-* is probably symbolic of quick movement (as in *quaver* and *quick*).

quiver[2] [Middle English] This *quiver* describing an archer's portable case for arrows is from Anglo-Norman French *quiveir*. Of West Germanic origin, it is related to Dutch *koker* and German *Köcher*, forms reflected during the Old English and Middle English period by *cocker*, a synonym for *quiver*.

quixotic [late 18th century] This is based on the name *Don Quixote*, the hero of a romance (1605–15) by Cervantes, a satirical account of chivalric conduct. Don Quixote, in his exploits, shows naive unworldly idealism, captured in the idiom *tilting at windmills* inspired by the episode where Quixote sees windmills as giants and attacks them on his charger.

quiz[1] [mid 19th century] This *quiz* was first used as a verb meaning 'ask questions' in US English. It is possibly from *quiz* 'look curiously at', influenced by *inquisitive*.
→ QUIZ[2]

quiz[2] [late 18th century] This *quiz* meaning 'practical joke' and 'look curiously at (someone)' (e.g. *deep-set eyes quizzed her in the moonlight*) is sometimes said to have been invented by a Dublin theatre proprietor. Having made a bet that a nonsense word could

be made known within 48 hours throughout the city, and that the public would give it a meaning, he purportedly had the word written up on walls all over the city. There is no evidence to support this theory.

quorum [late Middle English] This originally referred to justices of the peace whose presence was needed to constitute a deciding body. It was used in commissions for committee members to attend, in the Latin phrase *quorum vos ... unum* (*duos*, etc.) *esse volumus* meaning 'of whom we wish that you ... be one (two, etc.)'.

quota [early 17th century] The source of this word is medieval Latin *quota* (*pars*) 'how great (a part)', the feminine of *quotus*, from *quot* 'how many'. *Quota* is a limited number or amount to be contributed, paid, supplied, etc.
→ QUOTE

quote [late Middle English] This comes from medieval Latin *quotare*, from *quot* 'how many', or from medieval Latin *quota* The original sense was 'mark a book with numbers, or with marginal references'; later it came to mean 'give a reference by page or chapter' which led in the late 16th century to 'cite a text or person'. The phrase *quote ... unquote* has been used informally since the 1930s by a speaker referring to somebody else's words, sometimes to show the speaker's dissociation from the opinion. **Quotation** (apart from a rare appearance in Middle English meaning 'a numbering') dates from the mid 16th century when it was 'a marginal reference to a passage of text': it derives from medieval Latin *quotatio(n-)*, from the verb *quotare*.
→ QUOTA

quoth [Middle English] *Quoth* is the past tense of the obsolete verb *quethe* 'say, declare' which was recorded in use until the mid 16th century. The origin is Germanic. *Quoth* iself is now archaic or part of dialect use.

quotient [late Middle English] This mathematical term for the result of dividing one quantity by another comes from Latin *quotiens* 'how many times' (from *quot* 'how many'). The final *-ent* spelling is because of a confused association with participial forms ending in *-ens*, *-ent-*.

Rr

rabbit [late Middle English] The now archaic English synonym *cony* was in earlier use than *rabbit*, which is apparently from Old French, related to French dialect *rabotte* meaning 'young rabbit'. It may be of Dutch origin and have a link with Flemish *robbe*. The verb sense 'talk incessantly' dates from the middle of the 20th century.

rabble [late Middle English] A *rabble* initially was a 'string of meaningless words' as well as describing 'pack of animals'. The early notion was 'string, series'. It may be related to dialect *rabble* 'to gabble' (expressive of hurry and confusion); this is probably from a Low German source imitative of the gabbling sound.

rabies [late 16th century] This is from Latin, from *rabere* 'to rave', the source too (via Latin *rabidus*) of early 17th-century **rabid** of which the early sense was 'furious, madly violent' (Dickens *Dombey and Son*: He was made so rabid by the gout). The sense 'affected with rabies' arose in the early 19th century.

race¹ [late Old English] This *race* involves propulsion and progression. The equivalent Old Norse *rás* was a '(water) current'. *Race* was originally a northern English word coming into general use around the middle of the 16th century. The early sense was 'rapid forward movement', which became specified as 'contest of speed' in the early 16th century, and 'channel, path' (as in *mill race*) in the mid 16th century. The latter sense may be connected with Old French *rase* 'watercourse'. Verb use dates from the late 15th century.

race² [early 16th century] This *race* (as in *of every race and creed*) is basically a 'group' or 'set' and was first used to denote a group with common features. The phrase *the human race* dates from the late 16th century. *Race* came via French from Italian *razza*, of unknown ultimate origin. The notion of 'set' led to one of 'characteristic peculiarity' in figurative use (e.g. *race and flavour of the conversation*), extended to a notion of 'liveliness, piquancy' illustrated by the adjective **racy** (e.g. *racy stories*).

rack¹ [Middle English] The *rack* meaning 'framework for storing' is from Middle Dutch *rec*, Middle Low German *rek* 'horizontal bar or shelf', probably from *recken* 'to stretch, reach'. This verb is possibly the source of the English sense 'cause extreme pain or stress to', associated with *the rack* (recorded in the 15th century) as a former instrument of torture.

rack² [late 15th century] This wine term meaning 'draw off from the sediment in the barrel' is from Provençal *arracar*, from *raca* 'stems and husks of grapes, dregs'.

racket¹ [early 16th century] *Racket* as a sports term for a 'bat' is from French *raquette*. The plural **rackets** recorded in late Middle English referred to a ball game played with rackets in a plain four-walled court but with a solid, harder ball than the type used in the modern game of squash; the word's development was via French and Italian from Arabic *rāḥa*, *rāḥat-* 'palm of the hand'.

racket² [mid 16th century] This word for a 'din' is an imitative formation reflecting the sound of clattering. Some cite Gaelic *racaid* as the source but this Gaelic word is undoubtedly itself from English.

radiant [late Middle English] Latin *radiare* 'emit rays' (from *radius* 'ray, spoke') is the source of several words. *Radiant* initially meant 'emitting rays' reflecting the Latin sense but in the early 17th century this was extended to a person's appearance reflecting a state of joy or beauty; **radiation** (via Latin *radiatio(n-)*) arose in the same period as *radiant* and referred at first to the action of projecting rays of light. **Radiate** dates from the early 17th century; its extension to contexts of giving out an aura such as confidence or happiness, began in the early 19th century.

radical [late Middle English] Early senses of *radical* included 'forming the root' and 'inherent'. Late Latin *radicalis* is the source of the word, from Latin *radix*, *radic-* 'root'. The notion of 'fundamental' became associated with *radical* from the mid 17th century when used in the context of action, and came to be applied more specifically as a political term meaning 'extreme' towards the beginning of the 19th century. The phrase:
■ **radical chic** capturing the fashionable affectation of radical left-wing views, was coined by the American writer, Tom Wolfe, in the 1970s.

radio [early 20th century] This is an abbreviation of *radio-telephony* used as an independent word (from Latin *radius* 'ray'). It started to be used to name particular radio stations from the 1920s (e.g. *Radio Holland*); the four national radio networks of the BBC (*Radio 1, 2, 3, and 4*) were inaugurated on 30 September 1967. *Radio* is one of the elements in the composition of the 1940s term **radar** from the phrase *ra(dio) d(etection) a(nd) r(anging)*.

radish [Old English] Old English *rædic* is from Latin *radix, radic-* 'root'. A related word is **radicle** (late 17th century) from Latin *radicula* 'little root', a diminutive of *radix*; this term identifies the part of a plant embryo that develops into the primary root.

radius [late 16th century] This was first used as an English term in anatomy for a bone in the forearm and is a use of a Latin word meaning literally 'staff, spoke, ray'. Its use in mathematics dates from the mid 17th century. *Radius* is also the base of late 16th-century **radial** (from medieval Latin *radialis*), and both **radium** and **radian** from the late 19th century.

raffish [early 19th century] The word *raffish* meaning 'unconventional and slightly disreputable' is based on *riff-raff*.
→ RIFF-RAFF

raffle [late Middle English] A *raffle* was originally a kind of dice game played with three dice in which a triplet was the winning throw, then the highest doublet etc. The word is from Old French, but earlier details are unknown. The current sense relating to the sale of tickets to take part in a draw for prizes, dates from the mid 18th century.

raft¹ [late Middle English] This type of *raft* made of logs bound together to form a floating platform was first exemplified in the sense 'beam, rafter'. Old Norse *raptr* 'rafter' is the source. The verb (e.g. *rafted ashore*) dates from the late 17th century. **Rafter** (in Old English *ræfter*, of Germanic origin) is related to *raft*.

raft² [mid 19th century] This *raft* meaning 'large amount' (e.g. *raft of government initiatives*) is an alteration of dialect *raff* 'abundance', by association with *raft* 'floating mass'. The word may have a Scandinavian origin.

rag [Middle English] *Rag* is probably a backformation (by removal of the suffix) from late Old English **raggy** or Middle English **ragged**, both of Scandinavian origin. Old Norse *rǫgvathr* 'tufted' and Norwegian *ragget* 'shaggy' are comparable forms. The jazz term **rag**, a late 19th-century word may also be from *ragged* reflecting the syncopation. However the *rag* associated with student stunts and fancy-dress parades and, as a verb, meaning 'make fun of' (*ragged him mercilessly*) is of unknown origin; it is first found in examples from the mid 18th century. Of the compounds:

■ **raggle-taggle** meaning 'untidy and scruffy' is apparently a fanciful early 20th-century variant of early 19th-century **ragtag**: this superseded the earlier *tag-rag* and *tag and rag*.

■ **ragamuffin** (Middle English) is probably based on *rag*, with a fanciful suffix. The 1990s term **ragga** for a style of dance music is taken from *ragamuffin*, because of the style of clothing worn by its devotees.

rage [Middle English] In early use this word was also used in the sense 'madness'. The noun comes from Old French *rage*, the verb from Old French *rager*, from a variant of Latin *rabies*. The phrase *all the rage* associated with temporary enthusiasm, first recorded as *the rage*, is found from the late 18th century.
→ RABIES

raid [late Middle English] This is a Scots variant of *road* in the early senses 'military journey on horseback' and 'foray', which referred to incursions across the border into England. The noun became rare from the end of the 16th century but was revived by Sir Walter Scott; the meaning was extended to include any sudden attack to seize or suppress (*police raid*) in the late 19th century; the verb dates from the mid 19th century.

rail¹ [Middle English] *Rail* as a steel bar or series of bars is from Old French *reille* 'iron rod', from Latin *regula* 'straight stick, rule'. The late Middle English verb *rail* gave the verbal noun **railing**, both words associated with the provision of rails for vines to be trained in early examples. The word **railway** dates from the late 18th century and was used alongside **railroad** with equal frequency; the construction of these ways (originally laid with wooden rails) was for heavy goods wagons first used in Newcastle at the beginning of the 17th century. Cast-iron rails were introduced around the middle of the 18th century and wrought-iron ones from about 1820. The extension to a wider use of the railways for passenger travel began with the opening of the line between Stockton and Darlington in 1825 and Liverpool and Manchester in 1830.

rail² [late Middle English] This *rail* meaning 'complain strongly' (*he railed at human fickleness*) is from French *railler*, from Provençal *ralhar* 'to jest'. This is based on an alteration of Latin *rugire* 'to bellow'.

rain [Old English] *Rain* (in Old English *regn* as a noun, and *regnian* as a verb) is of Germanic origin. Related forms are Dutch *regen* and

German *Regen*. The phrase *it never rains but it pours* is found from the early 18th century. The compounds **rainbow** and **raindrop** were also recorded in Old English (as *regnboga* and *regndropa* respectively).

raise [Middle English] *Raise* is from Old Norse *reisa*; the verb *rear* is related. Use of the word to mean 'an increase in salary' was originally a US usage of the late 19th century. *Raise* was often reinforced by the word *up* in early examples, but this is not very common now.
→ REAR²

rake¹ [Old English] Old English *raca, racu* 'implement for levelling the ground, gathering leaves, etc.' is Germanic in origin, related to Dutch *raak* and German *Rechen*, from a base meaning 'heap up'. The verb is partly from Old Norse *raka* 'to scrape, shave'.

rake² [mid 17th century] This *rake* referring to a fashionable or wealthy man of dissolute habits is an abbreviation of archaic *rakehell* used in the same sense (Spenser *Faerie Queene*: Amid their rakehell bands, They spied a Lady).

rally [early 17th century] The early sense recorded was 'bring together again'. The source is French *rallier*, from *re-* 'again' and *allier* 'to ally'. Use of the word in health contexts to mean 'start to recover' is found from the mid 19th century. At this same time the noun is recorded in US English describing a gathering of supporters of a cause. Since the mid 20th century it has also described a competition for motor vehicles held over a long distance or over rough terrain.

ram [Old English] Old English *ram(m)* 'male sheep' and 'battering ram' is Germanic in origin, related to Dutch *ram*. It may be related to Old Norse *ramm-r* meaning 'strong'. The verb may come from the noun but the early uses in English ('beat down earth with a heavy implement') do not confirm this clearly.

ramble [late Middle English] *Ramble* was first recorded as a verb in the sense 'talk in a confused way'; it is probably related to Middle Dutch *rammelen*, used of animals in the sense 'wander about on heat', as well as to the English noun *ram*. The word's use in the context of a walk for recreation dates from the mid 17th century.
→ RAM

ramekin [mid 17th century] This term for a small baking dish is from French *ramequin*, of Low German or Dutch origin; obsolete Flemish *rameken* is an associated form meaning 'toasted bread'.

ramify [late Middle English] This verb is from Old French *ramifier*, from medieval Latin *ram-*

ificare, from Latin *ramus* 'branch'. The noun **ramification** (mid 17th century) is from French, from *ramifier* 'form branches'.

ramp [Middle English] Early use was as a verb in the sense 'rear up', also used as a heraldic term: from Old French *ramper* 'creep, crawl', the origin of which is unknown. The noun sense 'inclined plane connecting two different levels' dates from the late 18th century.

rampage [late 17th century] *Rampage* is perhaps based on the Middle English verb *ramp* 'assume a threatening posture, rush in a wild manner' (from Old French *ramper* 'to creep, climb') and the noun *rage*. It was originally a Scots verb and the noun is based on this (Dickens *Great Expectations*: She's been on the Ram-page this last spell, about five minutes).

rampant [Middle English] This was first used as a heraldic term meaning 'rearing on its hind legs', from an Old French word with the literal sense 'crawling', the present participle of *ramper*. The original use described a wild animal, which then gave rise to the sense 'fierce', leading to the current notion of 'unrestrained'.
→ RAMPAGE

rampart [late 16th century] *Rampart* is from French *rempart*, from *remparer* 'fortify, take possession of again'. The Latin base forms are *ante* 'before' and *parare* 'prepare'.

ramshackle [early 19th century] This was originally dialect in the sense 'irregular, disorderly'. It is an alteration of the earlier word *ramshackled*, which is an altered form of obsolete *ransackled* meaning 'ransacked'.

ranch [early 19th century] This is an Anglicized form of Spanish *rancho* 'group of persons eating together'. The phrase *Meanwhile, back at the ranch* was originally used in cowboy stories and westerns, introducing a subsidiary plot.

rancid [early 17th century] Latin *rancidus* which means 'stinking' is the source of *rancid* in English.
→ RANCOUR

rancour [Middle English] *Rancour* came via Old French from late Latin *rancor* 'rankness', used in the Vulgate in the sense 'bitter grudge'. The word is related to Latin *rancidus* 'stinking'.

random [Middle English] In early use *random* referred to an 'impetuous headlong rush'. It comes from Old French *randon* 'great speed', from *randir* 'gallop', from a Germanic root. Initially it was mainly found in the phrase *with great randon* or *in great randon*, reflecting the Old French spelling. The expression *at random* was first most commonly exemplified in *run at random* (mid 16th century).

range [Middle English] Originally this word was a 'line of people or animals'. The origin is Old French *range* 'row, rank', from *rangier* 'put in order', from *rang* 'rank'. Early usage also included the notion of 'movement over an area'. The US use of the word to mean 'an extensive stretch of grazing ground' dates from the beginning of the 20th century.

rank¹ [Middle English] This word relating to position in a hierarchy (e.g. *rank of captain*) is from Old French *ranc*, of Germanic origin and related to *ring*. The early sense 'row of things' remains in modern usage in *taxi rank*. The phrase **rank and file** is found from the late 16th century referring to the 'ranks' and 'files' into which privates and non-commissioned officers form on parade; it was later extended to ordinary members of any group.
➔ RING¹

rank² [Old English] Old English *ranc* meant 'proud, rebellious, sturdy' and 'fully grown'. The origin is Germanic. An early sense 'luxuriant' gave rise to 'too luxuriant', whence the negative connotation of offensive abundance of modern usage (e.g. *rank with cigar smoke*).

rankle [Middle English] This word meaning 'cause annoyance' is from Old French *rancler*, from *rancle*, *draoncle* 'festering sore'. An early English sense was 'fester'. The source is an alteration of medieval Latin *dracunculus*, a diminutive of *draco* 'serpent, dragon'.

ransack [Middle English] *Ransack* is from Old Norse *rannsaka*, from *rann* 'house' and a second element related to *sækja* 'seek'. The Old Norse term relates to legal use and the searching of property for stolen goods. An early sense in English was 'search (a person) for a stolen or missing item'.

ransom [Middle English] The noun is from Old French *ransoun*, the verb from *ransouner*. Latin *redemptio(n-)* 'ransoming, releasing' is the source of the form. Early use also occurred in theological contexts expressing 'deliverance' and 'atonement'.
➔ REDEEM

rant [late 16th century] 'Behave in a boisterous way' was an early meaning of *rant* from Dutch *ranten* 'talk nonsense, rave'. It also expressed 'declaim in a high-flown manner' (Shakespeare *Hamlet*: Nay, and thou'lt mouth, I'll rant as well as thou).

rap [Middle English] *Rap* was originally in the noun sense 'severe blow with a weapon' and verb sense 'deliver a heavy blow'. It is probably imitative and of Scandinavian origin; asso-

ciated forms are Swedish *rappa* 'beat, drub' and English *clap* and *flap*.
➔ CLAP; FLAP

rapacious [mid 17th century] Latin *rapax*, *rapac-* (from *rapere* 'to snatch') is the base of this word meaning 'aggressively greedy' in English.

rape¹ [late Middle English] This originally referred to the violent seizure of property, and later to the carrying off of a woman by force. It comes via Anglo-Norman French from Latin *rapere* 'seize'.

rape² [late Middle English] This plant name originally referred to the turnip. It is from Latin *rapum*, *rapa* 'turnip'.

rapid [mid 17th century] *Rapid* is from Latin *rapidus*, from *rapere* 'take by force, seize'. The noun use is usually plural as *rapids* (mid 18th century) referring to a part of the river where the bed forms a steep descent; it was first recorded in US English.
➔ RAPE¹

rapier [early 16th century] *Rapier* is from French *rapière*, from *râpe* 'rasp, grater': the perforated hilt resembles a rasp.

rapport [mid 17th century] This is an English use of a French word, from *rapporter* 'bring back'. This notion of 'return' is reflected in the sense 'harmonious communication and understanding between people'.

rapscallion [late 17th century] This is an alteration of earlier *rascallion*, perhaps from *rascal*.
➔ RASCAL

rapt [late Middle English] This was first used in the sense 'transported by religious feeling'. It is from Latin *raptus* 'seized', the past participle of *rapere*. The sense 'deeply engaged in (a feeling)' as in *rapt in thought* dates from the early 16th century.
➔ RAPE¹

rapture [late 16th century] The early sense was 'seizing and carrying off'. It is from obsolete French, or from medieval Latin *raptura* 'seizing', partly influenced by *rapt*.
➔ RAPT

rare¹ [late Middle English] This *rare* meaning 'not occurring very often' was first used in the sense 'widely spaced, infrequent'. Latin *rarus* is the source of this and late Middle English **rarity** (from Latin *raritas*); it is also the base of the first element of late Middle English verb **rarefy** from Old French *rarefier*, or medieval Latin *rareficare*. **Rarefaction** is an early 17th-century word from medieval Latin *rarefactio(n-)*, from *rarefacere* 'grow thin, become rare'.

rare² [late 18th century] This *rare* meaning 'lightly cooked' is a variant of obsolete *rear* 'half-cooked', used to refer to soft-boiled eggs from the mid 17th to mid 19th centuries.

raring [1920s] This word as in *raring to go* is the present participle of *rare*, a dialect variant of *roar* or *rear*.
→ REAR²; ROAR

rascal [Middle English] In early examples a *rascal* was 'a mob' and 'a member of the rabble'. It comes from Old French *rascaille* 'rabble', which is of uncertain origin. The meaning 'rogue, scamp' dates from the late 16th century.

rash¹ [late Middle English] This *rash* referring to decisions taken unwisely and without enough forethought was also found in Scots and northern English in the sense 'nimble, eager'. It is of Germanic origin; related to German *rasch*.

rash² [early 18th century] This word used in medical contexts is probably related to Old French *rasche* 'eruptive sores, scurf'; Italian *raschia* 'itch' is an associated form. The figurative use 'sudden outbreak and proliferation' (e.g. *rash of burglaries*) is found from the early 19th century.

rasher [late 16th century] *Rasher* may be from the obsolete verb *rash*, an alteration of *rase* 'tear with something sharp' (from Latin *radere* 'scrape') but it may also have a notion of a food prepared for hasty cooking. Many other suggestions as to the derivation have also been explored but the origin remains unknown.

rasp [Middle English] Early use was as a verb in the sense 'scrape, abrade'. Old French *rasper* is the source and the origin is perhaps Germanic. The notion of 'rough sound' dates from the mid 19th century.

raspberry [early 17th century] The first element is from dialect *rasp*, an abbreviation of obsolete *raspis* 'raspberry' which was also used as a collective. The origin is unknown. Use of the word for a derisive sound (late 19th century) is a shortening of *raspberry tart*, rhyming slang for 'fart'.

rat [Old English] Old English *ræt* was reinforced in Middle English by Old French *rat*. The word was probably first adopted in the Germanic languages when the animal came to be known in western Europe, and it also occurs in the Romance languages. The ultimate origin is unknown. The verb dates from the early 19th century.

ratchet [mid 17th century] This word for a bar or wheel with a set of angled teeth is from French *rochet*, originally a term for a blunt lance head and later used to describe a 'bobbin or ratchet'. It is related to the base of archaic *rock* 'a quantity of wool on a distaff for spinning'.

rate [late Middle English] The word originally expressed a notion of 'estimated value'. It comes from Old French, from medieval Latin *rata*; this was part of the Latin phrase *pro rata parte* (or *portione*) 'according to the proportional share'. Latin *ratus* is the base, the past participle of *reri* 'reckon'. The phrase *at any rate* is found in examples from the early 17th century; the notion of 'degree of speed' (e.g. *at a cracking rate*; *at the rate of knots*) dates from the mid 17th century.

rather [Old English] Old English *hrathor* 'earlier, sooner' was the comparative of *hræthe* 'without delay', from *hræth* 'prompt'.

ratify [late Middle English] *Ratify* 'make valid' is from Old French *ratifier*, from medieval Latin *ratificare*. Latin *ratus* 'fixed' is the base.
→ RATE

ratio [mid 17th century] This is an adoption of a Latin word meaning literally 'reckoning', from *rat-*, the past participial stem of *reri* 'reckon'. The word's use in mathematics is also found in the mid 17th century.

ration [early 18th century] This comes from French, from Latin *ratio(n-)* 'reckoning, ratio'. In English the word has the sense 'fixed allowance'; the verbal noun **rationing** associated with the control of food supplies during periods of scarcity dates from the First World War.

rational [late Middle English] The early sense was 'having the ability to reason'. It is from Latin *rationalis*, from *ratio(n-)* 'reckoning, reason'. Use of the word to mean 'based on reason' dates from the early 16th century.
→ RATIO

rationale [mid 17th century] This is a modern Latin word, the neuter form (used as a noun) of Latin *rationalis* 'endowed with reason'. Its use in English refers to 'a reasoned exposition of principles'.
→ RATIONAL

rattle [Middle English] This word was first recorded in use as a verb. It is related to Middle Dutch and Low German *ratelen*, a form imitative of the sound. It has reflected the meaning 'talk rapidly' since the late 16th century, and 'annoy, irritate' (e.g. *rattled by the insult*) since the mid 19th century. Noun use included 'short sharp sound' in early examples and was soon extended to instruments making this type of noise, such as a *baby's rattle*.

raucous [mid 18th century] *Raucous* is based on Latin *raucus* 'hoarse'.

ravage [early 17th century] *Ravage* is from French *ravager*, from earlier *ravage*, an alteration of *ravine* 'rush of water'. Plural use in the sense 'destructive actions' (e.g. *ravages of time*) dates from the late 17th century.
→ RAVINE

rave [Middle English] 'Show signs of madness' was the sense reflected in early examples. Its source is probably Old Northern French *raver*, related obscurely to (Middle) Low German *reven* 'be senseless, rave'. The sense 'highly enthusiastic' (as in *rave reviews*) dates from the 1920s, first found as a US usage. Use of the word to mean 'lively party' dates from the 1960s.

ravel [late Middle English] The early sense recorded was 'entangle, confuse'; it is probably from Dutch *ravelen* 'fray out, tangle'. In ordinary use the word *ravel* is a synonym of *unravel*, sometimes reinforced by *out* (Shakespeare *Richard II*: Must I ravel out My weav'd up folies?). The opposite notion of 'tangling' found originally remains in Scots and dialect use.

raven [Old English] Old English *hræfn* is Germanic in origin, related to Dutch *raaf* and German *Rabe*. The word is common in compounds relating to the colour black, for example *raven-haired*; this particular compound is first recorded in the mid 19th century.

ravenous [late Middle English] Old French *ravineus*, from *raviner* 'to ravage', gave rise to English *ravenous*. Original use included 'addicted to plundering' (Daniel Defoe *Voyage round the World*: Nations who were ravenous and mischievous, treacherous and fierce), but association with hunger was also early.
→ RAVAGE; RAVINE

ravine [late 18th century] This word for a deep gorge is from a French word meaning 'violent rush (of water)'. In Old French *ravine* meant 'pillage, violent seizure'.
→ RAVENOUS

ravish [Middle English] *Ravish* is from Old French *raviss-*, the lengthened stem of *ravir*, from an alteration of Latin *rapere* 'seize'. **Ravishing** dates from late Middle English; its notion of 'carrying away' soon came to have an association with delight and ecstasy.

raw [Old English] Old English *hrēaw* 'uncooked' has a Germanic origin; it is related to Dutch *rauw* and German *roh*, from an Indo-European root shared by Greek *kreas* 'raw flesh'. The word has also conveyed the sense 'unprotected' from Middle English (e.g. *raw wounds*) and has been associated with the weather (e.g. *raw evening air*) from the middle of the 16th century. The word came to be applied to facts such as *raw data* in the sense 'not yet subjected to a process; unadjusted' at the beginning of the 20th century.

ray [Middle English] *Ray* is from Old French *rai*, based on Latin *radius* 'spoke, ray'. The word is usually distinguished from *beam* in that it describes a smaller quantity of light; *beam* in scientific use is a collection of parallel rays. *Ray* also tends to be associated with the heat of the sun rather than its light.
→ RADIUS

raze [Middle English] *Raze* meaning 'efface' as in *razed to the ground* had the early sense 'scratch, incise'. The source is Old French *raser* 'shave closely', from the verb *radere* 'to scrape'. The verb once (mid 16th century) meant 'remove by scraping, cut off' in English (Sir Walter Scott *Lord of the Isles*: An axe has razed his crest). Middle English **razor** is from Old French *rasor*, from *raser*.

razzle [early 20th century] This word forming part of the phrase *on the razzle* is an abbreviation of late 19th-century **razzle-dazzle** which is itself a reduplication of *dazzle*. An alteration probably of the compund *razzle-dazzle* is the informal word **razzmatazz** (late 19th century) referring to showy and noisy activity.
→ DAZZLE

WORDBUILDING

The prefix **re-** [from Latin *re-* or *red-* 'again, back'] adds the sense

- **once more; afresh** [reaccustom; reactivate]
- **with return to a previous state** [restore; revert]
- **in return; mutually** [react; resemble]
- **in opposition** [resistance]
- **behind; after** [relic; remain]
- **in a withdrawn state** [recluse; reticent]

The prefix **re-** adds intensity to a word [refine; resound] or negates a word's force [recant]

---

reach [Old English] The Old English verb *ræcan* is from a West Germanic origin, related to Dutch *reiken* and German *reichen*. The notion is one of extending and stretching; the noun, in late Middle English, referred to an enclosed stretch of water, a sense now long obsolete except in Canadian dialect.

react [mid 17th century] *React* is from the prefix *re-* (expressing intensive force or reversal) and *act*, originally suggested by medieval Latin *react-*, the past participial form of *reagere* 'do again'. The noun **reaction**, also mid 17th century based on *react* was originally suggested by medieval Latin *reactio(n-)*, from *reagere*. Its use in chemistry dates from the early 19th century.

read [Old English] Old English *rædan* is of Germanic origin, related to Dutch *raden* and German *raten* 'advise, guess'. Early senses included 'believe, think, suppose', 'advise', and 'interpret (a riddle or dream)'. Use of the word to mean 'study' as in *she read French at Manchester* is found from the late 19th century. The related Old English *rædere* (= **reader**) meant 'interpreter of dreams, reader'.

ready [Middle English] *Ready* is based on Old English *ræde* from a Germanic base meaning 'arrange, prepare'; related to Dutch *gereed*, the word captures the notion 'in a state of preparation'.

real [late Middle English] First used as a legal term meaning 'relating to things, especially real property', English *real* comes from Anglo-Norman French, from late Latin *realis* 'relating to things' (from Latin *res* 'thing'). The noun **reality** is found from the late 15th century, via French from medieval Latin *realitas*, from late Latin *realis*. **Realize** (early 17th century) was formed from *real* on the pattern of French *réaliser*. The sense 'become aware' started in American English in the late 18th century; it was often condemned as such by English writers in the middle of the 19th century.

realm [Middle English] The earliest English spelling was *reaume*, an adoption of the Old French form, from Latin *regimen* 'government'. The spelling with -*l*- (standard from about 1600) was influenced by Old French *reiel* 'royal'.

ream [late Middle English] The *ream*, formerly for 480 sheets of paper and now a term for 500 sheets (allowing for wastage), is from Old French *raime*, based on Arabic *rizma* 'bundle'. The phrase *reams of* meaning 'a large quantity' arose at the beginning of the 20th century.

reap [Old English] Old English *ripan*, *reopan*, is of unknown origin. It is not represented in the cognate languages; early use related to the action of cutting grain or any similar crop with a sickle. Figurative use 'get in return, obtain (some profit)' began in Middle English.

rear¹ [Middle English] The *rear* which means 'back part' was first used as a military term and probably originated in the phrase *th'arrear*. It is from Old French *rere*, based on Latin *retro* 'back'. It was used colloquially to mean 'buttocks' from the late 18th century. The compound:

■ **rearguard** in late Middle English referred to the rear part of an army; this is from Old French *rereguarde*.

rear² [Old English] Old English *ræran* 'set upright, construct, elevate' is Germanic in origin, related to *raise* (which has supplanted *rear* in many applications) and also to *rise*. The word was used to express the notion of *rearing cattle* and other animals from Middle English and was applied in the context of educating children from the late 16th century (Shakespeare *A Midsummer Night's Dream*: For her sake I do rear up her boy).
→ RAISE; RISE

reason [Middle English] The noun is from Old French *reisun*, the verb from Old French *raisoner*, from a variant of Latin *ratio(n-)*, from the verb *reri* 'consider'. Of the phrases: (*with*)*in reason* arose early; *it stands to reason* is found from the early 16th century; *to see reason* from the late 16th century; *for reasons best known to oneself* dates from the early 17th century. The *age of reason* captures the period in the late 17th and 18th centuries in western Europe when cultural life was characterized by faith in human reason. Late Middle English **reasonable** is from Old French *raisonable*, suggested by Latin *rationabilis* 'rational', from *ratio*.
→ RATIO

rebate¹ [late Middle English] This *rebate* found in financial or commercial contexts was first used as a verb in the sense 'diminish (a sum or amount)'. It is from Anglo-Norman French *rebatre* which meant both 'beat back' and 'deduct'. The noun dates from the mid 17th century.

rebate² [late 17th century] The *rebate* found in joinery contexts is an alteration of late Middle English **rabbet** from Old French *rabbat* 'abatement, recess'.

rebel [Middle English] The noun is from Old French *rebelle*, the verb from Old French *rebeller*. Latin *rebellis* is the source, a word used originally with reference to an enemy making a fresh declaration of war after being defeated, based on Latin *bellum* 'war'. The phrase *rebel without a cause* is from the title of a film released in the US in 1955, which defined a young person with a sense of frustration linked to aggressive behaviour, rather than one motivated by loyalty to a cause. The noun **rebellion** is also Middle English, from Old French, from Latin *rebellio(n-)*, from *rebellis*.

rebound [late Middle English] *Rebound* is from Old French *rebondir*, from *re* 'back' and *bondir* 'bounce up'. The phrase *on the rebound* referring to emotional attachments was first recorded with the wording *in the rebound* in the middle of the 19th century.

rebuff [late 16th century] *Rebuff* is from the obsolete French verb *rebuffer* and the noun *rebuffe*. The source elements are Italian *ri-* (expressing opposition) and *buffo* 'a gust, puff' (of imitative origin), giving a notion of being repelled by a sudden gust.

rebuke [Middle English] The original sense recorded was 'force back, repress'. It is from Anglo-Norman French and Old Northern French *rebuker*, from *re-* 'back, down' and *bukier* 'to beat': this verb originally meant 'cut down wood' (from Old French *busche* 'log').

rebut [Middle English] The early senses of *rebut* were 'rebuke' and 'repulse'. The word comes from Anglo-Norman French *rebuter*, from Old French *re-* (a prefix expressing opposition) and *boter* 'to butt'. The sense 'claim that (an accusation) is false' was originally a legal use of the early 19th century.

recalcitrant [mid 19th century] This word descriptive of uncooperative behaviour is from Latin *recalcitrare* 'kick out with the heels', based on *calx, calc-* 'heel'.

recall [late 16th century] This was first used as a verb, composed of the prefix *re-* 'again' and the verb *call*, suggested by Latin *revocare* or French *rappeler* 'call back'. Association with memory dates from the mid 17th century in psychology contexts.

recant [mid 16th century] This verb meaning 'withdraw and renounce (a statement)' is from Latin *recantare* 'revoke', based on *cantare* 'sing, chant'. The prefix *re-* here expressing negation and reversal.

recapitulation [late Middle English] This comes from Old French *recapitulation* or late Latin *recapitulatio(n-)*, from the verb *recapitulare* 'go through heading by heading', a source shared by late 16th-century **recapitulate**. The base is late Latin *capitulum* 'chapter' (a diminutive of *caput* 'head'). The abbreviation **recap** dates from the 1950s.

recede [late 15th century] This word had the early sense 'depart from (a usual state or standard)', a use that was common in the second half of the 17th century but which is now obsolete. From Latin *recedere*, the formative elements are *re-* 'back' and *cedere* 'go'. **Recess** dates from the mid 16th century in the sense 'withdrawal, departure' and is from Latin *recessus* from *recedere* 'go back'; the sense 'niche' dates from the late 18th century. **Recession** is mid 17th-century, from Latin *recessio(n-)*, from the same source verb; its use as a term in economics for a 'temporary decline' began in the 1920s.

receive [Middle English] *Receive* is from Anglo-Norman French *receivre*, based on Latin *recipere*, from *re-* 'back' and *capere* 'take'. Latin

recipere, in the medieval Latin feminine past participle form of *recepta* meaning 'received', is the source of late Middle English **receipt** (via Anglo-Norman French *receite*). The *-p-* was inserted in imitation of the Latin spelling. Early use included the meaning 'recipe' and 'statement of ingredients' in a medical compound. Also late Middle English and from Latin *recipere* are: **receptive** (from medieval Latin *receptivus*) and **reception** (from Old French, or from Latin *receptio(n-)*); this word's use to mean 'party, formal receiving of guests' is found from the mid 19th century. Finally **receptor** joined this family in the early 20th century, coined in German from Latin *receptor*, from the verb *recipere*.
→ RECIPE

recent [late Middle English] *Recent* is from Latin *recens, recent-* or French *récent*. The word was used from the beginning of the 17th century to mean 'fresh' and in poetry this occasionally extended to 'freshly arrived' (Pope *Iliad*: All heaven beholds me recent from thy arms).

receptacle [late Middle English] This is from Latin *receptaculum*, from *receptare* 'receive back', a frequentative (= verb of repeated action) of *recipere*. Its use as a scientific term dates from the mid 16th century.
→ RECEIVE

recipe [late Middle English] This is a use of a Latin word meaning literally 'receive!', first used as an instruction in medical prescriptions. It is the imperative form of *recipere*. Culinary contexts contain examples from the early 18th century.
→ RECEIVE

recipient [mid 16th century] This word means literally 'person receiving' coming from the Latin present participial stem *recipient-* from *recipere* 'receive'.
→ RECEIVE

reciprocal [late 16th century] Latin *reciprocus* (based on the prefixes *re-* 'back' and *pro-* 'forward') forms the basis of *reciprocal* in English. An early use was in phrases such as *reciprocal tides*. **Reciprocate** dating from the same period is from Latin *reciprocare* 'move backwards and forwards', from *reciprocus*.

recite [late Middle English] This was first used as a legal term in the sense 'state (a fact) in a document', but the sense 'repeat aloud something learned by heart' soon followed. It comes from Old French *reciter* or Latin *recitare* 'read out', from *re-* (a sense intensifier here) and *citare* 'cite'.

reckless [Old English] Old English *recceléas* is from the Germanic base (meaning 'care') of

Old English **reck** 'care, heed, regard', a commonly found word in rhetorical and poetic language in the 19th century.

reckon [Old English] Old English (ge)recenian 'recount, relate', of West Germanic origin, is related to Dutch rekenen and German rechnen 'to count (up)'. Early senses included 'give an account of items received' and 'mention things in order', which led to the notion of 'calculation' and consequently 'coming to a conclusion'. The phrase *I reckon* used parenthetically (R. L. Stevenson *Treasure Island*: You would just as soon save your lives, I reckon) dates from the early 17th century. It was formerly very common in literary English and remains in dialect; in the southern states of America it is a common equivalent of the northern *I guess*.

reclaim [Middle English] This was first used as a falconry term in the sense 'recall'. Old French reclamer is the source, from Latin reclamare 'cry out against', from re- 'back' and clamare 'to shout'. The sense 'make (waste land or water-covered land) suitable for cultivation' is recorded from the mid 18th century.

recline [late Middle English] 'Cause to lean back' was the first meaning recorded for recline, from Old French recliner or Latin reclinare 'bend back, recline'. The elements here are re- 'back' and clinare 'to bend'.

recluse [Middle English] Recluse is from Old French reclus, the past participle of reclure, from Latin recludere 'enclose'. The prefix re- means 'again' and Latin claudere 'to shut' is the base verb. As well as referring to a person shut away from the world, the word was used from early times as an adjective in English, especially in the phrase to be recluse 'to be secluded from society'.

recognizance [Middle English] This legal term for a 'bond' comes from Old French reconnissance, from reconnaistre 'recognize'. The related word **recognition** is found from the late 15th century as 'the acknowledgement of a service'. This is from Latin recognitio(n-), from the verb recognoscere 'know again, recall to mind', the source too of the slightly earlier word **recognize** first attested as a term in Scots law. Old French reconniss- is the source here, the stem of reconnaistre, from Latin recognoscere. Its use to mean 'know by some distinctive feature' dates from the early 18th century.

recoil [Middle English] This word first denoted the act of retreating. It is from Old French reculer 'move back', based on Latin culus 'buttocks'. The sense 'spring back in horror' dates from the early 16th century.

recollect [early 16th century] 'Gather' was the early sense found for recollect which comes from Latin recolligere, composed of re- 'back' and colligere 'collect'. The association with memory dates from the mid 16th century. Late 16th-century **recollection** denoted gathering things together again: it is from French or medieval Latin recollectio(n-), from the verb recolligere.

recommend [late Middle English] This is from medieval Latin recommendare, from Latin re- (an intensifier here) and commendare 'commit to the care of'. Early use was in the context of committing one's soul or spirit to God. Examples in the sense 'mention with approbation' (e.g. highly recommended) date from the late 16th century.

recompense [late Middle English] Recompense is from Old French, from the verb recompenser 'do a favour to requite a loss'. This is from late Latin recompensare, from Latin re- 'again' and compensare 'weigh one thing against another'.

reconcile [late Middle English] This word is from Old French reconcilier or Latin reconciliare, from Latin re- (a prefix meaning 'back' which also adds intensive force to the sense) and conciliare 'bring together'.

reconnaissance [early 19th century] This is an English use (in military contexts) of a French word, from reconnaître 'recognize'.
→ RECONNOITRE

reconnoitre [early 18th century] The word reconnoitre common in military and naval contexts, is from obsolete French reconnoître, from Latin recognoscere 'know again'. The abbreviation **recce** dates from the 1940s.
→ RECOGNIZANCE

record [Middle English] English record is from Old French record 'remembrance', from recorder 'bring to remembrance'. Latin recordari 'remember' is the source, based on cor, cord- 'heart'. The noun was earliest used in law as 'the fact of something having been written down as evidence'. It was at the end of the 19th century that the word came to be used in connection with recorded sound, first on a cylinder and later on a disc. The phrase off the record (originally a US usage) dates from the 1930s. Verb use originally included both 'narrate orally or in writing' and 'repeat so as to commit to memory'. The related word **recorder** is late Middle English when it referred to a kind of judge: it comes from Anglo-Norman French recordour, from Old French recorder. It was partly reinforced by the verb record in the now obsolete sense 'practise a tune', which influenced the term *recorder* for a musical instrument.

recount [late Middle English] *Recount* is from Old Northern French *reconter* 'tell again', based on Old French *counter*.
→COUNT¹

recoup [early 17th century] *Recoup* was first used as a legal term meaning 'keep back, make a deduction'. It is from French *recouper* 'retrench, cut back', from *re-* 'back' and *couper* 'to cut'.

recourse [late Middle English] Early use included the sense 'running or flowing back'. Old French *recours* gave rise to this, from Latin *recursus*, whose elements are *re-* 'back, again' and *cursus* 'course, running'. The phrase *have recourse to* reflecting the sense 'resort to' arose early.

recover [Middle English] This was originally with reference to health. The source is Anglo-Norman French *recoverer*, from Latin *recuperare* 'get again'. The noun **recovery** is a late Middle English word for 'a means of restoration': it comes from Anglo-Norman French *recoverie*, from *recovrer* 'get back'.

recreation [late Middle English] This word referring to 'activity done for enjoyment' also had the sense 'mental or spiritual consolation' in early examples. It came via Old French from Latin *recreatio(n)*, from *recreare* 'create again, renew', which gives the word the notion of 'refreshment'.

recriminate [early 17th century] Medieval Latin *recriminari* 'accuse mutually' (from *re-* expressing opposition and *criminare* 'accuse') is based on Latin *crimen* 'crime' and gave rise to both the verb *recriminate* and the noun **recrimination** in the same period. The latter came into English via French *récrimination* or medieval Latin *recriminatio(n-)*.

recruit [mid 17th century] The early noun sense was 'fresh body of troops'; it comes from obsolete French dialect *recrute*, based on Latin *recrescere* 'grow again'. The early verb sense was 'supplement the numbers in (a group)', from French *recruter*, which made its first appearance in literary use in gazettes published in Holland and was disapproved of by French critics in the later stages of the 17th century. The context of *recruiting* staff stems from a US use of the early 20th century when athletes were *recruited*, that is induced to sign on as students in a college or university to improve the institution's prestige. The word **rookie** for a 'new recruit' dating from the late 19th century may be an alteration of *recruit*.

rectify [late Middle English] Latin *rectus* 'right, straight' is the base of several words: *rectify* is from Old French *rectifier*, from medieval Latin *rectificare*; late Middle English **rectitude** originally recorded in the sense 'straightness' came from Old French, from late Latin *rectitudo*. Late 16th-century **rectangle** is from medieval Latin *rectangulum*, from late Latin *rectiangulum* (the other base element here being *angulus* 'an angle').

rector [late Middle English] This word is from Latin *rector* 'ruler', from *rect-*, the past participial stem of *regere* 'to rule'. The Latin sense was also reflected in English use originally. **Rectory** dates from the mid 16th century, from Old French *rectorie* or medieval Latin *rectoria*, from the same base.

recumbent [mid 17th century] This comes from Latin *recumbent-*, the present participial stem of *recumbere* 'recline', from *re-* 'back' and a verb related to *cubare* 'to lie'.

recuperate [mid 16th century] Latin *recuperare* 'regain', from *re-* 'back' and *capere* 'take', is the source of *recuperate* in English. The noun **recuperation**, from the same Latin base, is recorded slightly earlier (late 15th century): Latin *recuperatio(n-)* is the direct source.

recur [Middle English] *Recur* in early examples had the sense 'return to'. It is from Latin *recurrere*, from *re-* 'again, back' and *currere* 'run'. The same Latin verb gave rise to **recurrent** in the late 16th century in anatomy contexts; it referred to a nerve or blood vessel 'turning back' so as to reverse direction. **Recursive**, again from the same base, is found from the late 18th century used generally to mean 'characterized by repetition'; its specialized uses in contexts such as computing, mathematics, and linguistics arose in the 20th century. **Recursion** is not recorded before the 1930s and is from late Latin *recursio(n-)*, from *recurrere*.

red [Old English] Old English *rēad* is Germanic in origin, related to Dutch *rood* and German *rot*, from an Indo-European root shared by Latin *rufus, ruber*, Greek *eruthros*, and Sanskrit *rudhira* 'red'. The original long vowel sound of the English word is retained in the surname *Reid, Reed*, etc. Use of the word in political contexts to mean 'Communist' dates from the mid 19th century, inspired by the colour of a party badge. Of the compounds:

■ **red book** for a book of economic or political significance owes its derivation to the fact that *red* was the conventional colour of the binding of official books.

■ **red cent** (early 19th century) meaning a one-cent coin derives its name from the fact that it was formerly made of copper.

■ **red-letter day** (early 18th century) for a memorable day is associated with the practice of highlighting church festivals or saints' days in red letters on a calendar.

■ **red tape** (early 18th century) is with reference to the red or pink tape used to bind and secure official documents.

redeem [late Middle English] 'Buy back' was the early sense recorded for *redeem* which is from Old French *redimer* or Latin *redimere*. The formative elements are *re-* 'back' and *emere* 'buy'. Use of the word to mean 'make up for' (as in *his bravery that day redeemed his former reputation*) is found from the late 16th century. **Redemption** is also late Middle English from Old French, from Latin *redemptio(n-)*, from *redimere* 'buy back'.

redoubtable [late Middle English] This word meaning 'formidable' is from Old French *redoutable*, from *redouter* 'to fear'; the elements here are *re-* used to intensify the meaning and *douter* 'to doubt'.

redress [Middle English] This word meaning 'set right' is from Old French *redresser*; the noun came via Anglo-Norman French *redresse*. The word was formerly used in phrases such as *beyond redress*, *past redress*, *without redress*, now obsolete (Shakespeare *Richard II*: Things past redress, are now with me past care).

reduce [late Middle English] *Reduce* is from Latin *reducere*, from *re-* 'back, again' and *ducere* 'bring, lead'. The original sense was 'bring back' which led to 'restore' surviving in the medical sense 'restore (a dislocated part) to its proper position by manipulation or surgery'. Sense development led to 'bring to a different state', then 'bring to a simpler or lower state' (hence change '(a substance) to a more basic form)'; and finally 'diminish in size or amount' (the prime current sense) dating from the late 18th century. Late Middle English **reduction** denoted 'the action of bringing back', coming via Old French, or from Latin *reductio(n-)*, it is also derived from *reducere*.

redundant [late 16th century] 'Abundant' was the early sense of *redundant* from Latin *redundare* 'surge up'. In the mid 16th century, the sense developed into 'having some superfluous element' which in the 1920s was extended to employment contexts.

reed [Old English] Old English *hrēod* has a West Germanic origin; it is related to Dutch *riet* and German *Ried*. Its use in musical contexts for part of a mouthpiece dates from the early 16th century.

reef [late 16th century] An earlier spelling of the *reef* found in *coral reef* was *riff*. It comes from Middle Low German and Middle Dutch *rif*, *ref*, from Old Norse *rif* which means literally 'rib' but was used in the same sense.

reek [Old English] Old English *rēocan* 'give out smoke or vapour' and *rēc* 'smoke' are Germanic in origin, related to Dutch *rieken* 'to smell', *rook* 'smoke' and German *riechen* 'to smell', *Rauch* 'smoke'. *Auld Reekie* meaning 'Old Smoky' once was a nickname for Edinburgh.

reel [Old English] Old English *hrēol* was a rotatory device on which spun thread was wound. The origin of the word is unknown; it is not represented in the cognate languages. It may have given the term *reel* for a lively Scottish or Irish folk dance; another source commonly cited is Gaelic *righil*, probably from Lowland Scots. The Middle English verb *reel* 'sway, whirl' may be related to the noun, but the origin remains uncertain.

refectory [late Middle English] This word for a room used for communal meals comes from late Latin *refectorium*, from Latin *reficere* 'refresh, renew'. The base elements are *re-* 'back' and *facere* 'make'.

refer [late Middle English] *Refer* is from Old French *referer* or Latin *referre* 'carry back', from *re-* 'back' and *ferre* 'bring'. **Referee**, formed from *refer*, dates from the early 17th century, but did not appear in sports contexts until the mid 19th century. The Latin verb *referre* is also the source of mid 19th-century **referendum** from its gerund (meaning 'referring'), or the neuter gerundive (meaning 'something to be brought back or referred').

refine [late 16th century] This word is made up of the prefix *re-* 'again' and the verb *fine* 'clarify' (from Old French *fin*, based on Latin *finire* 'to finish'), influenced by French *raffiner*. Early contexts involved the purification or separation of metals from extraneous matter. The noun **refinement** (early 17th century) is based on *refine*, influenced by French *raffinement*.

reflect [late Middle English] *Reflect* is from Old French *reflecter* or Latin *reflectere*, from *re-* 'back' and *flectere* 'to bend'. The sense 'turn one's thoughts back' is exemplified from the early 17th century. Late Middle English **reflection** is from Old French *reflexion* or late Latin *reflexio(n-)*, from Latin *reflectere*. Its connection with casting back light rays is found early. **Reflex** (early 16th-century) was first used as a noun denoting reflection; it is from Latin *reflexus* 'a bending back', from *reflectere*.

reform [Middle English] *Reform* was first used as a verb in the senses 'restore (peace)' and 'bring back to the original condition'. Its source is Old French *reformer* or Latin *reformare*, from re- 'back' and *formare* 'to form, shape'. The noun dates from the mid 17th century. Late Middle English **reformation** is from Latin *reformatio(n-)*, from *reformare*. It was in the 16th century that the *Reformation* movement worked for the reform of what were perceived as abuses in the Roman Church resulting in the establishment of the Reformed and Protestant Churches. The *Counter-Reformation* followed on and ran counter to the Protestant Reformation.

refrain[1] [Middle English] This verb was first recorded in the sense 'restrain (a thought or feeling)'. It is from Old French *refrener*, from Latin *refrenare*. The notion of control (here self-control) comes from the Latin base *frenum* 'bridle'.

refrain[2] [late Middle English] This *refrain* of music or poetry contexts is from Old French, from *refraindre* 'to break'. It is based on Latin *refringere* 'break up', because the refrain 'broke' the sequence.

refresh [late Middle English] *Refresh* is from Old French *refreschier*, from re- 'back' and *fres(che)* 'fresh'. The notion of *refresh the memory* dates from the mid 16th century. The noun **refreshment** dates from the same period as *refresh*; the plural *refreshments* for 'food' and more commonly now for 'drinks' dates from the mid 17th century.

refrigerate [late Middle English] This comes from the Latin verb *refrigerare*, from re- 'back' and *frigus, frigor-* 'cold'. **Refrigerant** is a late 16th-century word for a substance for cooling or allaying fever: it is from French *réfrigérant* or Latin *refrigerant-*, the present participial stem of *refrigerare*. The word **refrigerator** in the context of preserving food dates from the mid 19th century.

refuge [late Middle English] *Refuge* is from Old French, from Latin *refugium*, from Latin re- 'back' and *fugere* 'to flee'. The phrase *take refuge* is recorded in examples from the mid 18th century. The word **refugee** dates from the late 17th century, from French *réfugié* 'gone in search of refuge'.

refund [late Middle English] Early senses included 'pour back' and 'restore'. It is from Old French *refonder* or Latin *refundere*, from the prefix re- meaning 'back' and *fundere* 'to pour'. Later it became associated with the verb *fund*. The sense 'repay' dates from the mid 16th century. The noun ('repayment') dates from the mid 19th century.

refuse[1] [Middle English] This verb is from Old French *refuser*, which is probably an alteration of Latin *recusare* 'to refuse', influenced by *refutare* 'refute'. Early use included the senses

'keep clear of' (e.g. *refused evil to do good*) and 'renounce' (e.g. *refused the world to become a monk*), both now obsolete.

refuse[2] [late Middle English] This word meaning 'waste matter' is perhaps from Old French *refusé* meaning 'refused', the past participle of *refuser*. Early use in English was adjectival.
→ REFUSE[1]

refute [mid 16th century] *Refute* is from Latin *refutare* 'repel, rebut'. The core meaning of *refute* is 'prove (a theory) to be wrong'; a more general sense developed from this expressing 'deny' (as in *refute the allegations*), felt by some to be a degradation of the language; it has become widely accepted however in standard English.

regal [late Middle English] *Regal* is from Old French, or from Latin *regalis*, from *rex, reg-* 'king'. The word **regalia** for 'royal emblems' meant, in mid 16th-century examples, 'royal powers'. It is a medieval Latin form meaning literally 'royal privileges', from the Latin neuter plural of *regalis* 'regal'.

regale [mid 17th century] The word *regale* is from French *régaler*, from re-, here serving the purpose of an intensifier, and Old French *gale* 'pleasure'. Early use included the contexts of both delighting people with the provision of food and pleasing the minds of people with entertainment.

regard [Middle English] *Regard* is from Old French *regarder* 'to watch', from re- 'back' (here also serving as an intensifier) and *garder* 'to guard'. The noun once meant 'appearance' (Milton *Paradise Lost*: To whom with stern regard thus Gabriel spake) and 'importance, value, estimation' (Shakespeare *Troilus and Cressida*: What things there are Most abject in regard, and dear in use).

regatta [early 17th century] This is an English use of an Italian (Venetian dialect) word meaning literally 'a fight, contest'. It was used as a name for certain boat races held on the Grand Canal; the first English *regatta* was held on the Thames on 23 June 1775.

regeneration [Middle English] This comes from Latin *regeneratio(n-)*, from *regenerare* 'create again', a source shared by late Middle English **regenerate**, from the Latin past participle *regeneratus*. It was first found in adjectival use; the verb dates from the mid 16th century.

regent [late Middle English] *Regent* is from Old French, or from Latin *regere* 'to rule'. The general sense 'ruler' existed originally alongside that of 'person invested with royal authority'. **Regency** is also late Middle English, from medieval Latin *regentia*, from the same Latin source verb. One of its uses is to designate a style of architecture and furniture characteristic of the *Regency* of 1811–20 when George, Prince of Wales was *regent*.

reggae [1960s] This word for a popular style of music with a strongly accented subsidiary beat may be related to Jamaican English *rege-rege* 'quarrel, row'.

regime [late 15th century] The word *regime* was first used in medical contexts to describe a 'regimen', i.e. 'a prescribed course of medical treatment'. It is from French *régime*, from Latin *regimen* 'rule'. The prime current sense relating to a form of government dates from the late 18th century, with original reference to the Ancien Régime (the political and social system in France before the Revolution of 1789).

regiment [late Middle English] This was first used in the sense 'rule or government over a person, people, or country', very common between 1550 and 1680. It came via Old French from late Latin *regimentum* 'rule', from *regere* 'to rule'. Military use of the word dates from the late 16th century; the application of the word in the British Army was considerably altered by changes made in 1881 when the old numbered infantry regiments were converted into battalions of the new Territorial Regiments. The verb *regiment* was an early 17th-century development.

region [Middle English] The word *region* is from Old French, from Latin *regio(n-)* 'direction, district', from *regere* 'to rule, direct'. The sense of the Latin verb influenced early use in English ('realm', 'kingdom'). The phrase *in the region of* meaning 'approximately' dates from the 1960s.

register [late Middle English] This comes from Old French *regestre* or medieval Latin *regestrum, registrum*, an alteration of *regestum* (the singular form of late Latin *regesta* 'things recorded'). The source is Latin *regerere* 'enter, record'. **Registration** dates from the mid 16th century from medieval Latin *registratio(n-)*, based on Latin *regerere*; **registrar** is late 17th-century from medieval Latin *registrarius*, from *registrum*.

regress [late Middle English] This word comes from Latin *regressus*, from *regredi* 'go back, return', from *re-* 'back' and *gradi* 'walk'. **Regression** dates from the same period and is from Latin *regressio(n-)*, from *regredi*; its use as a term in psychology is found from the beginning of the 20th century.

regret [late Middle English] *Regret* is from Old French *regreter* 'bewail (the dead)', perhaps

from the Germanic base of the Scots *greet* 'weep, cry' (recorded in Old English). The noun dates from the early 16th century.

regular [late Middle English] This comes from Old French *reguler*, from Latin *regularis*, from *regula* 'rule'. The colloquial use meaning 'absolute' (e.g. *a regular goody-two-shoes*) dates from the early 19th century. The word's use in relation to size or quality as 'medium, standard' (e.g. *regular fries*) was originally a US usage of the 1950s.

regulate [late Middle English] The sense in early examples was 'control by rules'. Late Latin *regulare* 'direct, regulate' (from Latin *regula* 'rule') is the source.

regurgitate [late 16th century] This is from medieval Latin *regurgitare*, from *re-* 'again, back' and *gurges, gurgit-* 'whirlpool'. It was a word first applied to fluids or gases in the sense 'gush, pour back again'; it was in the mid 18th century that the meaning was transferred to contexts of rejection by the stomach.

rehabilitate [late 16th century] Early use was in the sense 'restore (by a formal act or declaration) to former privileges' (e.g. *he was rehabilitated on payment of the fine*). Medieval Latin *rehabilitare* is the source. The common current use of the word meaning 'restore (someone) to a degree of normal life by training' started in the 1940s; the abbreviation **rohab** also dates from that time.

rehearse [Middle English] 'Repeat aloud' is the first meaning recorded for *rehearse* from Old French *rehercier*. This word may be from *re-* 'again' and *hercer* 'to harrow', from *herse* 'harrow'. The word is found in theatrical contexts from the late 16th century.
→ HEARSE

reign [Middle English] The verb is from Old French *reignier* 'to reign', the noun from Old French *reigne* 'kingdom'. Latin *regnum* is the base, related to *rex, reg-* 'king'.

reimburse [early 17th century] This word is made up of *re-* 'back, again' and the obsolete verb *imburse* 'put in a purse', from medieval Latin *imbursare*. The elements are *in-* 'into' and late Latin *bursa* 'purse'.

rein [Middle English] *Rein* is from Old French *rene*, based on Latin *retinere* 'retain'. The phrase *give rein to* 'allow full scope to' dates from the late 16th century.

reindeer [late Middle English] Old Norse *hrein-indýri* gave rise to English *reindeer*, from *hreinn* 'reindeer' and *dýr* 'animal'.

reinforce [late Middle English] This is from French *renforcer*, influenced by *inforce*, an obsolete spelling of *enforce*; the sense of providing military support is probably from Italian *rinforzare*. The word's use as a psychology term is found from the beginning of the 20th century.

reiterate [late Middle English] This was first recorded as meaning 'do (an action) repeatedly'. It derives from Latin *reiterare* 'go over again', from *re-* 'again' and *iterare* 'do a second time'.

reject [late Middle English] *Reject* is from Latin *reject-*, the past participial stem of *reicere* 'throw back', based on *jacere* 'to throw'. As a noun the word was applied to people considered to be unsuitable for some activity from the 1920s, originally in the context of military service.

rejoice [Middle English] 'Cause joy to' was an early sense of this word, from Old French *rejoiss-*, the lengthened stem of *rejoir*. The prefix *re-* is here used as an intensifier of the sense; *joir* means 'experience joy'.

rejoinder [late Middle English] This word for a 'reply' comes from the Anglo-Norman French infinitive *rejoindre* (literally 'a joining again') used as a noun.

rejuvenate [early 19th century] This is based on the Latin adjective *juvenis* 'young', suggested by French *rajeunir*.

relapse [late Middle English] Latin *relaps-*, the past participial stem of *relabi* 'slip back', is the source of English *relapse*. Early senses referred to a return to heresy or wrongdoing; the word's use in contexts of illness dates from the late 16th century.

relation [Middle English] This is from Old French, or from Latin *relatio(n-)*, from *referre* 'bring back'. The phrase *no relation* used to deny any association by blood despite having the same surname, dates from the 1930s. Related words from the same base are late Middle English **relative** (from Old French *relatif, -ive*, from late Latin *relativus* 'having reference or relation') and **relate** dating from the mid 16th century.
➔ REFER

relax [late Middle English] *Relax* is from Latin *relaxare*, based on *laxus* 'lax, loose'. The prefix *re-* here intensifies the meaning. The sense 'become less tense, cease to worry' is a usage from the 1930s. The noun **relaxation** from late Middle English started out in contexts referring to the 'partial remission of a penalty'. It is from Latin *relaxatio(n-)*, from the verb *relaxare*.

relay [late Middle English] This once referred to the provision of fresh hounds on the track of a deer. The Old French noun *relai* and the verb *relayer* led to the English form, based on

Latin *laxare* 'slacken'. The sense 'pass on (broadcast signals)' dates from the late 19th century.

release [Middle English] The noun is from Old French *reles*, the verb from Old French *relesser*, from Latin *relaxare* 'stretch out again, slacken'. An early sense was 'grant discharge of', still retained in legal use (e.g. *released the debt*). Use of the word to mean 'make available for publication' started at the beginning of the 20th century.
➔ RELAX

relegate [late Middle English] An early sense of *relegate* was 'send into exile'. The word comes from Latin *relegare* 'send away, refer', from *re-* 'again' and *legare* 'send'. The use of *relegate* in sporting contexts dates from the early 20th century.

relent [late Middle English] 'Dissolve, melt' was the early meaning of *relent* (Pope *Spring*: All nature mourns, the Skies relent in show'rs). The word is based on Latin *re-* 'back' and *lentare* 'to bend' (from *lentus* 'flexible').

relevant [early 16th century] *Relevant* was first used as a Scots legal term meaning 'legally pertinent'. It is from medieval Latin *relevare* 'raise up'.

relic [Middle English] *Relic* is from Old French *relique*, which was originally plural from Latin *reliquiae* 'remains'. Early use was in religious contexts for an 'object remaining as a memorial of a departed holy person, held in veneration' but it was also used early as *relics* referring to the 'remains of a dead person'. Colloquial use as 'old person' dates from the mid 19th century.

relieve [Middle English] *Relieve* is from Old French *relever*, from Latin *relevare* 'raise again, alleviate', based on *levare* 'to raise' (from *levis* 'light'). The prefix *re-* here intensifies the meaning. Late Middle English **relief** is from Old French, from *relever* 'raise up, relieve'; the word was associated from early times with money and the assistance it provided. Its use to mean 'replacement of a sentinel by a fresh man or body of men' dates from the early 16th century.

religion [Middle English] This was originally used in the sense 'life under monastic vows'. The source is Old French, or Latin *religio(n-)* 'obligation, bond, reverence', perhaps based on Latin *religare* 'to bind'. Middle English **religious** is from Old French, from Latin *religiosus*, from *religio*.

relinquish [late Middle English] *Relinquish* is from Old French *relinquiss-*, the lengthened stem of *relinquir*, from Latin *relinquere*, from *re-*

(here used as an intensifier) and *linquere* 'to leave'.

relish [Middle English] *Relish* is an alteration of obsolete *reles* which comes from Old French *reles* 'remainder' (from *relaisser* 'to release'). The early noun sense was 'odour, taste' giving rise in the mid 17th century to 'appetizing flavour, piquant taste': this led to its use as a term for a 'condiment' in the late 18th century. Verb use meaning 'have a liking for' (e.g. *relished the prospect*) is found from the late 16th century.

reluctant [mid 17th century] The early sense was 'writhing, offering opposition' (Milton *Paradise Lost*: Down he fell A Monstrous Serpent on his Belly prone, Reluctant, but in vain). It is from Latin *reluctari* 'struggle against', from *re-* (expressing intensive force) and *luctari* 'to struggle'.

rely [Middle English] *Rely* is from Old French *relier* 'bind together', from Latin *religare*. The original sense was 'gather together', later 'turn to, associate with', which then led to 'depend upon with confidence'.

remain [late Middle English] *Remain* is from Old French *remain-*, the stressed stem of *remanoir*, from Latin *remanere* (from *re-* used as an intensifier and *manere* 'to stay'). **Remains** also late Middle English was occasionally treated as singular in early examples: it is from Old French *remain*, from *remaindre*, from an informal form of Latin *remanere*. From the same period, **remainder** (first a legal term) is from Anglo-Norman French, from Latin *remanere*.

remand [late Middle English] This was first used as a verb in the sense 'send back again'. It derives from late Latin *remandare*, from *re-* 'back' and *mandare* 'commit'. Its use as a legal term dates from the early 16th century; noun use, arising in legal contexts, dates from the late 18th century.

remark [late 16th century] This was first used in the sense 'notice'. French *remarquer* 'note again' is the source, from *re-* which here intensifies the sense and *marquer* 'to mark, note'. The noun sense 'observation, comment' arose in the late 17th century. **Remarkable** dates from the early 17th century and is from French *remarquable*, from *remarquer*.

remedy [Middle English] *Remedy* is from Anglo-Norman French *remedie*, from Latin *remedium*, from *re-* 'back' (also here giving intensive force) and *mederi* 'heal'. The related word **remedial** (mid 17th century) is from late Latin *remedialis*, from Latin *remedium* 'cure, medicine'. The association with education dates from the 1920s.

remember [Middle English] This is from Old French *remembrer*, from late Latin *rememorari* 'call to mind'. The formative elements here are *re-* expressing intensive force and Latin *memor* 'mindful'. **Remembrance**, also Middle English, is from Old French, from *remembrer*; a well-known use is in the phrase *Remembrance Day* for the day on which the dead of the First and Second World Wars are commemorated by the wearing of an artificial poppy.

remind [mid 17th century] This word is made up of the prefix *re-* 'again' and the verb *mind*, probably suggested by obsolete *rememorate* which had the same sense.

reminisce [early 19th century] This is a back-formation (by removal of the suffix) from late 16th-century **reminiscence** which referred to 'the action of remembering'. The source is late Latin *reminiscentia*, from Latin *reminisci* 'remember'. **Reminiscent** made its appearance in the mid 18th century from Latin *reminisci*.

remit [late Middle English] *Remit* is from Latin *remittere* 'send back, restore', from *re-* 'back' and *mittere* 'send'. The noun dates from the early 20th century. **Remiss** is a late Middle English word from Latin *remissus* 'slackened', the past participle of *remittere*. The early senses were 'weakened in colour or consistency' and (in describing sound) 'faint, soft'. **Remission** is recorded as a Middle English word coming from either Old French or from Latin *remissio(n-)*, from *remittere*; its use in medical contexts is found from the late 17th century.

remnant [Middle English] This is a contraction of obsolete *remenant* from Old French *remenant*, from *remenoir*, *remanoir* 'remain'. The use in drapery contexts arose early.

remonstrate [late 16th century] This was first recorded in the sense 'make plain'; it is from medieval Latin *remonstrare* 'demonstrate, show', from *re-* serving as an intensifier and *monstrare* to show'. The noun **remonstrance** dating from the same period in the sense 'evidence' is from Old French, or from medieval Latin *remonstrantia*, from *remonstrare*. The *Grand Remonstrance* refers to a formal statement of grievances presented by the House of Commons to the Crown in 1641.

remorse [late Middle English] *Remorse* is from Old French *remors*, from medieval Latin *remorsus*, from Latin *remordere* 'vex'. The elements here are *re-* expressing intensive force and *mordere* 'to bite'.

remote [late Middle English] 'Far apart' was the sense found in early examples. It is from Latin *remotus*, the past participle of *removere* 'remove'. The sense 'performed at a distance' as in *remote control* dates from the beginning of the 20th century.

remove [Middle English] This is from the Old French stem *remov-*, from Latin *removere*, from *re-* 'back' and *movere* 'to move'. The sense 'change residence' was found in late Middle English.

remunerate [early 16th century] Latin *remunerari* 'reward, recompense' is the source of *remunerate* in English, based on *munus, muner-* 'gift'. The prefix *re-* here intensifies the meaning.

renal [mid 17th century] *Renal* is from French *rénal*, from late Latin *renalis*, from Latin *renes* 'kidneys'.

rend [Old English] Old English *rendan* is related to Middle Low German *rende*; the word is not represented in the other Germanic languages. The word expresses 'split, tear'; its association with sounds dates from the early 17th century (Shakespeare *Hamlet*: Anon the dreadful Thunder Doth rend the region).

render [late Middle English] *Render* is from Old French *rendre*, from an alteration of Latin *reddere* 'give back', from *re-* 'back' and *dare* 'give'. The earliest senses were 'recite', 'translate', and 'give back' (which led to 'represent' and 'perform'); 'hand over' (hence 'give (help)' and 'submit for consideration'); 'cause to be'; and 'melt down' (e.g. *rendered fat*). The related word **rendition** (early 17th century) is from obsolete French, from *rendre* 'give back, render'.

rendezvous [late 16th century] This is from the French imperative *rendez-vous!* 'present yourselves!', from *se rendre*.

renegade [late 15th century] *Renegade* is from Spanish *renegado*, from medieval Latin *renegatus*, the past participle (used as a noun) of *renegare* 'renounce'. The base here is Latin *negare* 'deny'. The core notions in the English word are desertion and betrayal.

renege [mid 16th century] The early sense recorded was 'desert (especially a faith or a person)'. It is from medieval Latin *renegare*, from Latin *re-* (an intensifier here) and *negare* 'deny'.

rennet [late 15th century] This word for curdled milk from an unweaned calf's stomach, used in curdling milk for cheese, is probably related to *run*.
➔ RUN

renounce [late Middle English] *Renounce* is from Old French *renoncer*, from Latin *renuntiare* 'protest against', from *re-* (expressing reversal) and *nuntiare* 'announce'. The noun **renun-**

ciation is also late Middle English from late Latin *renuntiatio(n-)*, from Latin *renuntiare*.

renovate [early 16th century] This word comes from Latin *renovare* 'make new again', from *re-* 'back, again' and *novus* 'new'.

renown [Middle English] *Renown* is from Anglo-Norman French *renoun*, from Old French *renomer* 'make famous'. The elements are the intensifying prefix *re-* and *nomer* 'to name' (from Latin *nominare*).

rent[1] [Middle English] The word *rent* meaning 'regular payment' for the use of property or land is from Old French *rente*, from a root shared by *render*. **Rental** dates from late Middle English and is from Anglo-Norman French, or from Anglo-Latin *rentale*, from Old French *rente*.
➔ RENDER

rent[2] [mid 16th century] This *rent* meaning 'large tear' is from obsolete *rent* 'pull to pieces, lacerate', a variant of *rend*.
➔ REND

repair[1] [late Middle English] *Repair* 'mend, make good' is from Old French *reparer*, from Latin *reparare*. The formative elements are *re-* 'back' and *parare* 'make ready'. Late Middle English **reparation** is from Old French, from late Latin *reparatio(n-)*, from *reparare*.

repair[2] [Middle English] This *repair* (as in *we repaired to the nearest café*) is from Old French *repairer*, from late Latin *repatriare* 'return to one's country'.
➔ REPATRIATE

repartee [mid 17th century] *Repartee* derives from French *repartie* 'replied promptly', the feminine past participle of *repartir* 'set off again'.

repast [late Middle English] This comes from Old French, based on late Latin *repascere*, based on *pascere* 'to feed'. The prefix *re-* is an intensifier.

repatriate [early 17th century] Late Latin *repatriare* 'return to one's country', from *re-* 'back' and Latin *patria* 'native land' is the source of the English word *repatriate*. The abbreviation **repat** came into use in the 1940s.

repeal [late Middle English] *Repeal* is from Anglo-Norman French *repeler*, from Old French *re-* expressing reversal and *apeler* 'to call, appeal'. Early verb use was in the sense 'call back (from banishment)'.

repeat [late Middle English] This word is from Old French *repeter*, from Latin *repetere* 'attack again, do or say again', from *re-* 'back' and *petere* 'seek'. Use of the word in the context of food (e.g. *onions tend to repeat*) dates from the late

19th century. Late Middle English **repetition** is from Old French *repeticion* or Latin *repetitio(n-)*, from *repetere*.

repel [late Middle English] *Repel* is from Latin *repellere*, from *re-* 'back' and *pellere* 'to drive'. Mid 17th-century **repellent** is from the same source, usually meaning 'warding off' but also, from the late 18th century, 'causing aversion'.

repent [Middle English] The word *repent* is from Old French *repentir*, composed of the intensifying prefix *re-* and *pentir* based on Latin *paenitere* 'cause to repent'.

repercussion [late Middle English] This was first used as a medical term meaning 'repressing of infection'. It comes from Old French, or from Latin *repercussio(n-)*, from *repercutere* 'cause to rebound, push back' (from *re-* 'back, again' and *percutere* 'to strike'). An early sense of the mid 16th century ('driving back, rebounding') gave rise later to 'blow given in return', hence the word's use to describe an unintended consequence occurring some time after an event (early 20th century).

repertoire [mid 19th century] French *répertoire* gave rise to this English word, from late Latin *repertorium*.
➔ REPERTORY

repertory [mid 16th century] A *repertory* was once an index or catalogue. It comes from late Latin *repertorium*, from Latin *reperire* 'find, discover'. The sense 'performance of plays at regular intervals' (arising from the fact that a company has a 'repertory' of pieces for performance) dates from the late 19th century.

replenish [late Middle English] The early sense recorded was 'supply abundantly'. It is from Old French *repleniss-*, the lengthened stem of *replenir*. The elements here are *re-* 'again' (also expressing intensive force) and *plenir* 'fill' from Latin *plenus* 'full'.

replete [late Middle English] *Replete* is from Old French *replet(e)* or Latin *repletus*, the past participle of *replere* 'fill up', from *re-* 'back, again' and *plere* 'fill'.

replicate [late Middle English] The early sense was 'repeat'. It comes from Latin *replicare*, from *re-* 'back, again' and *plicare* 'to fold'. The current senses 'make an exact copy' and 'reproduce' date from the late 19th century. The word **replica** (adopted from Italian in the mid 18th century) is also from *replicare* and was first used as a musical term in the sense 'a repeat'.

reply [late Middle English] This is from Old French *replier*, from Latin *replicare* 'repeat', later 'make a reply'. The noun dates from the mid 16th century.
➔ REPLICATE

report [late Middle English] *Report* is from Old French *reporter* (verb), *report* (noun), from Latin *reportare* 'bring back'. The elements are *re-* 'back' and *portare* 'carry'. The sense 'give an account' gave rise to 'submit a formal report', hence 'inform an authority of one's presence' (mid 19th century) and 'be accountable (to a superior)' (late 19th century). The noun sense 'resounding noise' (e.g. *report of a distant gun*) is found from the late 16th century.

repose [late Middle English] The noun is from Old French *repos*, the verb from Old French *reposer*, from late Latin *repausare*. Latin *pausare* 'to pause' is the base, intensified by the prefix *re-*.

repository [late 15th century] *Repository* is from Old French *repositoire* or Latin *repositorium*, from *reposit-*, the past participial stem of *reponere* 'place back'.

reprehensible [late Middle English] This is from late Latin *reprehensibilis*, from *reprehendere* 'rebuke'.

represent [late Middle English] *Represent* is from Old French *representer* or Latin *repraesentare* 'exhibit', from *re-* (here expressing intensive force) and *praesentare* 'to present'. **Representation** is also a late Middle English word meaning originally 'image, likeness'; it is from Old French *representation* or Latin *repraesentatio(n-)*, from *repraesentare*. The same Latin source verb gave rise to **representative** in the same period from Old French *representatif*, *-ive* or medieval Latin *repraesentativus*, from the verb *repraesentare*.

repress [Middle English] Originally, *repress* had the sense 'keep back (something objectionable)'. It comes from Latin *repress-*, the past participial stem of the verb *reprimere* 'press back, check', from *re-* 'back' and *premere* 'to press'.

reprieve [late 15th century] This was first recorded as the past participle *repryed*. The source is Anglo-Norman French *repris*, the past participle of *reprendre*, from Latin *re-* 'back' and *prehendere* 'seize'. The insertion of *-v-* in the 16th century remains unexplained. Sense development has undergone a reversal, from the early meaning 'send back to prison', via 'postpone (a legal process)', to the current sense 'rescue from impending punishment'.

reprimand [mid 17th century] *Reprimand* is from French *réprimande*, via Spanish from Latin *reprimenda* meaning 'things to be held in check', the neuter plural gerundive of *repri-mere*.

→ REPRESS

reprisal [late Middle English] The word *reprisal* is from Anglo-Norman French *reprisaille*, from the medieval Latin neuter plural *reprisalia*: the base here is Latin *repraehens-*, the past participial stem of *repraehendere* 'seize'. The early sense was 'seizing (property) by force'; the current sense 'act of retaliation' dates from the early 18th century.

→ REPREHENSIBLE

reproach [Middle English] This word is from the Old French verb *reprochier*, from a base meaning 'bring back close', either based on Latin *prope* 'near' or on Latin *reprobare* 'disapprove of'. The latter is probably more plausible as the senses are similar to those of French *reprouver* 'to reprove'.

reprobate [late Middle English] This word was initially used as a verb meaning 'disapprove of'. It is from Latin *reprobare* 'disapprove', from *re-* (expressing reversal) and *probare* 'approve'.

reproof [Middle English] The word *reproof* is from Old French *reprove*, from *reprover* 'reprove'. Early senses included 'ignominy, personal shame' and 'scorn'. The Middle English verb **reprove** included, in early use, the senses 'reject' and 'censure'. It is from Old French *reprover*, from late Latin *reprobare* 'disapprove'.

→ REPROACH; REPROBATE

reptile [late Middle English] The word *reptile* is an English use of the late Latin neuter form of *reptilis*, from Latin *repere* 'to crawl'. It was used generally at first for any creeping or crawling animal.

republic [late 16th century] *Republic* is from French *république*, from Latin *respublica*, from *res* 'concern' and *publicus* 'of the people, public'. The phrase *republic of letters* referring to the 'collective body of people engaged in literary pursuits; field of literature' dates from the early 18th century.

repudiate [late Middle English] This was originally an adjective in the sense 'divorced'. It comes from Latin *repudiatus* 'divorced, cast off', from *repudium* 'divorce'.

repugnance [late Middle English] 'Opposition' was the early meaning of *repugnance* from Old French *repugnance* or Latin *repugnantia*. Latin *repugnare* 'oppose' is the source of these forms, from *re-* (giving a sense of opposition) and *pugnare* 'to fight'. Late Middle English **repugnant** had the sense 'offering resistance', from Old French *repugnant* or Latin *repugnant-*, the present participial stem of *repugnare*.

repulse [late Middle English] *Repulse* is from Latin *repuls-*, the past participial stem of verb *repellere* 'drive back'. The same Latin verb is the base of the contemporaneous words **repulsion** (from late Latin *repulsio(n-)*) and **repulsive** (from French *répulsif, -ive*).

reputation [Middle English] The word *reputation* (first recorded in the sense 'opinion') is from Latin *reputatio(n-)*, from *reputare* 'think over'; the same source is shared by late Middle English **repute** from Old French *reputer* or Latin *reputare*. **Reputable** was first recorded in the early 17th century, from obsolete French, or from medieval Latin *reputabilis*, from Latin *reputare*.

request [Middle English] The Old French noun *requeste* gave rise to English *request*, based on Latin *requirere* 'require'. Use of the word to refer to a wish to hear a particular record or song to be played on a radio programme, dates from the 1920s.

→ REQUIRE

requiem [Middle English] This is the accusative form of Latin *requies* 'rest', the first word of the Mass for the Dead, said or sung for the repose of their souls. The Introit reads: Requiem aeternam dona eis, Domine.

require [late Middle English] *Require* is from Old French *requere*, from Latin *requirere* 'search for, deem necessary', from *re-*, here intensifying the sense, and *quaerere* 'seek'. Early use included the senses 'ask', 'ask for', and 'enquire'. Also from the same base is late Middle English **requisition** (from Old French, or from Latin *requisitio(n-)*) first used as a noun in the sense 'request, demand'. The verb dates from the mid 19th century when it was used in military contexts for 'require (something) to be provided'. Latin *requirere* also gave rise to late Middle English **requisite** (from Latin *requisitus*, the past participle of *requirere*) first recorded as an adjective meaning 'necessary, indispensable'; noun use is found in examples from the beginning of the early 17th century.

rescind [mid 16th century] *Rescind* is from Latin *rescindere*, from *re-*, here serving as an intensifier of the sense, and *scindere* 'to divide, split'.

rescue [Middle English] *Rescue* is from Old French *rescoure* based on Latin *excutere* 'shake out, discard'. The prefix *re-* intensifies the sense. The notion here is of 'shaking out' a captive from the hands of an enemy.

research [late 16th century] The noun is from the obsolete French form *recerche*, the verb from *recercher*, based on *cerchier* 'to search'.

The prefix re- here is an intensifier of the meaning.

resemble [Middle English] *Resemble* is from Old French *resembler*, based on Latin *similare* (from *similis* 'like'). Middle English **resemblance** is from Anglo-Norman French, from the verb *resembler*.

resent [late 16th century] The word *resent* is from obsolete French *resentir*, from *re-* serving as an intensifier and *sentir* 'to feel' (from Latin *sentire*). The early sense was 'experience (an emotion or sensation)' which later developed into 'feel deeply', giving rise to 'feel aggrieved by'. The noun **resentment** dates from the early 17th century, from Italian *risentimento* or French *ressentiment*, from obsolete French *resentir*.

reserve [Middle English] *Reserve* is from Old French *reserver*, from Latin *reservare* 'keep back', based on *servare* 'to keep'. The word **reservation** made its appearance in late Middle English when it referred to the Pope's right of nomination to a benefice; its source is either Old French, or late Latin *reservatio(n-)*, from *reservare* 'keep back'. The word's use in the context of booking rooms or places started out in US English at the beginning of the 20th century.

reservoir [mid 17th century] This comes from French *réservoir*, from *réserver* 'to reserve, keep'.

resident [Middle English] *Resident* is from Latin *residere* 'remain' (from *re-* 'back' and *sedere* 'sit'), the source too of late Middle English **reside** first recorded in the sense 'be in residence as an official'. This is probably a back-formation (by removal of the suffix) from *resident*, influenced either by French *résider* or by Latin *residere* 'remain'. Late Middle English **residence** 'the fact of living in a place' is from Old French, or from medieval Latin *residentia*, from Latin *residere*.

residue [late Middle English] *Residue* is from Old French *residu*, from Latin *residuum* 'something remaining'.

resign [late Middle English] *Resign* is from Old French *resigner*, from Latin *resignare* 'unseal, cancel', from *re-* 'back' and *signare* 'sign, seal'. The noun **resignation** is also late Middle English and came via Old French from medieval Latin *resignatio(n-)*, from *resignare*.

resilient [mid 17th century] This is from Latin *resilire* 'leap back'. The first senses recorded were 'returning to the original position' and 'looking back'; the prime current sense 'cheerful, buoyant' dates from the early 19th century.

resist [late Middle English] *Resist* is from Old French *resister* or Latin *resistere*. The formative elements are *re-* expressing opposition and *sistere* 'to stop' (a reduplication of *stare* 'to stand'). Latin *resistere* is also the base of late Middle English **resistance**, from French *résistance*, from late Latin *resistentia*. This was used as a name (*the Resistance*) in the Second World War for the underground movement in France formed in June 1940 with the aim of resisting the authority of the German occupying forces.

resolve [late Middle English] The early senses recorded were 'dissolve, disintegrate' and 'solve (a problem)'. The source is Latin *resolvere* 'loosen, release', from *re-* (expressing intensive force) and *solvere* 'loosen'. **Resolution** (from Latin *resolutio(n-)*) dates from the same period and comes from the same source verb as does **resolute**: this was first used in the sense 'paid' referring to a rent. It is from Latin *resolutus*, the past participle of *resolvere*. The sense 'determined, intent' dates from the early 16th century.

resonance [late Middle English] This word comes from Old French, from Latin *resonantia* 'echo', from *resonare* 'resound'; the prefix *re-* is an intensifier and *sonare* 'to sound' is the base verb. Late 16th-century **resonant** is from French *résonnant* or Latin *resonant-*, the present participial stem of *resonare*. **Resonate** dates from the late 19th century, from Latin *resonare*.

resort [late Middle English] A *resort* was initially 'something to turn to for assistance'. Old French *resortir* is the source, from *re-* 'again' and *sortir* 'come or go out'. The sense 'place frequently visited' (as in *holiday resort*) dates from the mid 18th century.

resound [late Middle English] This is formed from the prefix *re-* 'again' and the verb *sound*, suggested by Old French *resoner* or Latin *resonare* 'sound again'.

resource [early 17th century] This word comes from obsolete French *ressource*, the feminine past participle (used as a noun) of Old French dialect *resourdre* 'rise again, recover' (based on Latin *surgere* 'to rise').

respect [late Middle English] The word *respect* is from Latin *respectus*, from *respicere* 'look back at, regard', from *re-* 'back' and *specere* 'look at'. Use of the word to mean 'detail' (as in *in all respects, in some respects, in this respect*) dates from the late 16th century. Late Middle English **respective** had the sense 'relative, comparative': it comes from medieval Latin *respectivus*, from *respicere*, reinforced by French *respectif, -ive*.

respire [late Middle English] *Respire* is from Old French *respirer* or Latin *respirare* 'breathe out', from *re-* 'again' and *spirare* 'breathe'. **Respiration** dates from the same period from Latin *respiratio(n-)*, from *respirare*. **Respirate** arose in the mid 17th century, a back-formation (by removal of the suffix) from *respiration*.

respite [Middle English] This word for a 'short period of rest' or 'delay' comes from Old French *respit*, from Latin *respectus* 'refuge, consideration'.

resplendent [late Middle English] This is from Latin *resplendere* 'shine out', from *re-* (adding intensive force) and *splendere* 'to glitter'.

response [Middle English] *Response* is from Old French *respons* or Latin *responsum* 'something offered in return', the neuter past participle of *respondere* 'to answer, offer in return', the source of late Middle English **respond** (via Old French). The base elements are *re-* 'again' and *spondere* 'to pledge'. The verb dates from the mid 16th century. **Respondent** dates from the early 16th century meaning 'a person who replies to something' from Latin *respondere*. **Responsive** is also late Middle English from French *responsif*, *-ive* or late Latin *responsivus*, from the verb *respondere*. **Responsible** dates from the late 16th century (in the sense 'answering to, corresponding'): from obsolete French *responsible*, from the same Latin source verb.

rest¹ [Old English] Of Germanic origin, the Old English forms *ræst*, *rest* (noun), *ræstan*, *restan* (verb) are from a root meaning 'league' or 'mile' referring to a distance after which a rest is taken. Briefly in the Old English period only, the word *rest* meant 'bed'; the association was 'repose' obtained through sleep. From the late 16th century the word also came to denote a 'support', that is 'a thing upon which something else rests'. The colloquial phrase *give it a rest* is found from the 1920s.

rest² [late Middle English] The *rest* meaning as a noun 'a remaining part' and as a verb 'remain' is from Old French *reste* (noun), *rester* (verb). Latin *restare* 'remain' is the source, from *re-* 'back' and *stare* 'to stand'.

restaurateur [late 18th century] The word *restaurateur* describing 'a person who owns and manages a restaurant' is an adoption of a French word, from the verb *restaurer* 'provide food for' (literally 'restore to a former state'). Early 19th-century **restaurant** is also from French, from *restaurer*.

restitution [Middle English] This comes from Old French, or from Latin *restitutio(n-)*, from *restituere* 'restore', from *re-* 'again' and *statuere* 'establish'.

restive [late 16th century] *Restive* is from Old French *restif*, *-ive*, from Latin *restare* 'remain'. The original sense, 'inclined to remain still, inert', has undergone a reversal; the association with the refractory movements of a horse led to the current sense which is 'fidgety, restless'.

restore [Middle English] The word *restore* is from Old French *restorer*, from Latin *restaurare* 'rebuild, restore'. The noun **restoration** is late 15th-century denoting the action of restoring to a former state. This is partly from Old French, partly an alteration of obsolete *restauration* (from late Latin *restauratio(n-)*, from the verb *restaurare*), suggested by *restore*.

restrain [Middle English] A group of Middle English words derive from Latin *restringere*, from *re-* 'back' and *stringere* 'to tie, pull tight'. *Restrain* is from Old French *restreign-*, the stem of *restreindre* 'hold back'; **restraint** is from Old French *restreinte*, a noun use of the feminine past participle of *restreindre*; **restriction** is from Old French, or from Latin *restrictio(n-)*; **restrictive** is from Old French *restrictif*, *-ive*, from medieval Latin *restrictivus*. The verb **restrict** arose later (mid 16th century) but it comes from the same Latin source verb.

result [late Middle English] *Result* is from medieval Latin *resultare* 'to result'; earlier this verb had the sense 'spring back', based on *saltare*, a frequentative (= verb of repeated action) of *salire* 'to jump'. The noun dates from the early 17th century. **Resultant** dates from the mid 17th century as an adjective: it comes from Latin *resultant-*, the present participial stem of *resultare*.

resume [late Middle English] *Resume* is from Old French *resumer* or Latin *resumere*, from *re-* 'back' and *sumere* 'take'. It commonly means 'take on again' (Dickens *Pickwick Papers*: Mr Pickwick's countenance resumed its customary benign expression). The sense 'begin to speak again' dates from the early 19th century (Dickens *Pickwick Papers*: Mr Weller smoked for some minutes in silence, and then resumed).

resurrection [Middle English] This is from Old French, from late Latin *resurrectio(n-)*, from the verb *resurgere* 'rise again'. As *Resurrection* it refers in Christian contexts to the rising of Christ from the dead. The verb **resurrect** made its appearance in the late 18th century as a back-formation (by removal of the suffix) from *resurrection*. In the early 19th century, **resurgent** came into use, also from Latin *resurgere*.

resuscitate [early 16th century] Latin *resuscitare* 'raise again' is the source of this word, from *re-* 'back' and *suscitare* 'raise'.

retail [late Middle English] *Retail* is from an Anglo-Norman French use of Old French *retaille* 'a piece cut off', from *retaillier*, from *re-* (an intensifier here) and *tailler* 'to cut'. The association with 'cutting' is related to the sale of commodities in small quantities.

retain [late Middle English] *Retain* came via Anglo-Norman French from Old French *retenir*, from Latin *retinere*, from *re-* 'back' and *tenere* 'hold'. The contemporaneous word **retention** initially denoted the power to retain something: it is from Old French, from Latin *retentio(n-)*, from *retinere*. Late Middle English **retentive** is from Old French *retentif*, *-ive* or medieval Latin *retentivus*, from the same source verb.

retaliate [early 17th century] The word *retaliate* is from Latin *retaliare* 'return in kind', from *re-* 'back' and *talis* 'such'. Early contexts referred to repaying kindness as well as ill-treatment.

retch [mid 19th century] *Retch* is a variant of dialect *reach*, from a Germanic base meaning 'spittle'.

reticent [mid 19th century] This is from Latin *reticent-*, the present participial stem of *reticere* 'remain silent', from *re-* (expressing intensive force) and *tacere* 'be silent'.

retinue [late Middle English] The word *retinue* is from Old French *retenue*, the feminine past participle form (used as a noun) of *retenir* 'keep back, retain'. The notion is one of advisers 'kept back' for personal support.
→ RETAIN

retire [mid 16th century] This was first used in the sense 'withdraw (to a place of safety or seclusion)'. French *retirer* is the source, from *re-* 'back' and *tirer* 'draw'. The phrase *retire oneself* 'withdraw' was very common in the sixteenth and seventeenth centuries. The sense 'withdraw from a post' (e.g. *retired after thirty years' service*) dates from the late 17th century.

retort [late 15th century] The early sense recorded was 'hurl back (an accusation or insult)'. The word derives from Latin *retort-*, the past participial stem of the verb *retorquere* 'twist back, cast back', from *re-* 'in return' and *torquere* 'to twist'. The scientific term **retort** for a 'container' or 'furnace' is found from the early 17th century. This is from French *retorte*, from medieval Latin *retorta*, the feminine past participle of *retorquere* 'twist back', referring to the long recurved neck of the laboratory container.

retract [late Middle English] *Retract* is from Latin *retract-*, the past participial stem of *retrahere* 'draw back'; the senses 'withdraw (a statement)' and 'go back on' came via Old French from *retractare* 'reconsider' (based on *trahere* 'drag').

retreat [late Middle English] The noun is from Old French *retret*, the verb from Old French *retraiter*, from Latin *retrahere* 'pull back'. Use of the word in religious contexts for a withdrawal from everyday life to devote oneself to reflection and prayer in seclusion, dates from the mid 18th century.
→ RETRACT

retrench [late 16th century] *Retrench* is from obsolete French *retrencher*, a variant of *retrancher*, from *re-* (here a prefix expressing reversal) and *trancher* 'to cut, slice'. The early meaning, now obsolete, was 'cut short, repress'. The sense 'economize' dates from the mid 17th century (Pepys *Diary*: For his family expenses and others, he would labour, however, to retrench in many things convenient).

retribution [late Middle English] Early use included the sense 'recompense for merit or a service'. It comes from Latin *retributio(n-)*, from the verb *retribuere* 'assign again', from *re-* 'back' and *tribuere* 'assign'. The notion of 'recompense for evil' is reflected in the word's use from the late 16th century.

retrieve [late Middle English] The early sense was 'find lost game' when talking about a hunting dog. It is from Old French *retroeve-*, the stressed stem of *retrover* 'find again'.

retrograde [late Middle English] This was originally a term in astronomy referring to planets appearing to move in a direction from east to west. It comes from Latin *retrogradus*, from *retro* 'backwards' and *gradus* 'step' (from *gradi* 'to walk'). The 1960s term **retro** is from French *rétro*, an abbreviation of *rétrograde* 'retrograde'.

retrospect [early 17th century] This is from Latin *retrospicere* 'look back', formed on the pattern of *prospect*. The adjective **retrospective** appeared slightly later, around the middle of the 17th century; it is probably from *retrospect* used as a verb.

return [Middle English] The verb is from Old French *returner*, from Latin *re-* 'back' and *tornare* 'to turn'; the noun came via Anglo-Norman French. The use of the noun in *many happy returns* is first suggested in a letter from Johnson to a Mrs Aston on 2 January 1779: Now the new year is come, of which I wish you and dear Mrs Gastrel many and many returns.

reunion [early 17th century] *Reunion* is from French *réunion* or Anglo-Latin *reunio(n-)*, from Latin *reunire* 'unite'.

reveal [late Middle English] *Reveal* is from Old French *reveler* or Latin *revelare* 'lay bare', based on *velum* 'veil'. The prefix *re-* here expresses reversal, that is a 'lifting of a veil'. The noun **revelation** appeared slightly before the verb in the theological sense (Joseph Butler to John Wesley 16 August 1739: Sir, the pretending to extraordinary revelations and gifts of the Holy Ghost is a horrid thing—a very horrid thing); it derives from Old French, or from late Latin *revelatio(n-)*, from *revelare*.

reveille [mid 17th century] This military term is from French *réveillez!* 'wake up!', the imperative plural of *réveiller*, based on Latin *vigilare* 'keep watch'.

revel [late Middle English] The word *revel* is from Old French *reveler* 'rise up in rebellion, make noise', from Latin *rebellare* 'to rebel'.

revenge [late Middle English] *Revenge* is from Old French *revencher*, from late Latin *revindicare*, from *re-* (here serving as an intensifier) and *vindicare* 'claim, avenge'.

revenue [late Middle English] The word *revenue* is from Old French *revenu(e)* meaning 'returned', the past participle form (used as a noun) of *revenir*. The source is late Latin *revenire* 'return', from *re-* 'back' and *venire* 'come'. An obsolete and rare use was 'return to a place'; it was more commonly 'yield from lands and property'.

reverberate [late 15th century] The early sense was 'drive or beat back'. Latin *reverberare* 'strike again' is the source, from *re-* 'back' and *verberare* 'to lash'. The noun base is the Latin plural *verbera* 'scourge'.

reverence [Middle English] *Reverence* is from Old French, from Latin *reverentia*, from *revereri* 'stand in awe of': the prefix *re-* here intensifies the sense of Latin *vereri* 'to fear'. Related late Middle English words from the same base are **reverend** (from Old French, or from Latin *reverendus* 'person to be revered') and **reverent** (from Latin *reverent-*, the present participial stem of *revereri*). The verb **revere** dates from the mid 17th century, from French *révérer* or Latin *revereri*.

reverie [early 17th century] This comes from obsolete French *resverie*, from Old French *reverie* meaning 'rejoicing, revelry'. The source verb is *rever* 'be delirious'; the ultimate origin is unknown.

reverse [Middle English] Middle English words which come from Latin *revertere* 'turn back' include *reverse* (via Old French from Latin *reversus*, the past participle of *revertere*), and **revert** (via Old French *revertir*). Early senses of *revert* were 'recover consciousness', 'return to a position', and 'return to a person (after estrangement)'. The word **reversion** is late Middle English when it referred to the 'action of returning to or from a place': this is either from Old French, or from Latin *reversio(n-)*, from *revertere*. **Reversal** (based on the verb *reverse*) is recorded from the late 15th century as a legal term.

review [late Middle English] *Review* was first recorded as a noun denoting a formal inspection of military or naval forces. It comes from obsolete French *reveue*, from *revoir* 'see again'. The words use in journalism for a 'periodical publication' began in the early 18th century.

revile [Middle English] *Revile* is from Old French *reviler*, based on *vil* 'vile'. An early sense but one which was rarely found was 'degrade, abase'.

revise [mid 16th century] The early sense recorded for *revise* was 'look again or repeatedly (at)'. The form is from French *réviser* 'look at', or Latin *revisere* 'look at again': the latter is based on *visere*, an intensive form of *videre* 'to see'. The noun **revision** came into use in the early 17th century, from French *révision* or late Latin *revisio(n-)*, from the verb *revisere*. The sense of looking over something again to make improvements is found from the early 17th century (Johnson *Boswell* 29 August 1771: I am engaging in a very great work, the revision of my Dictionary); it came to be associated with preparation for examinations in the early 20th century. The verb *revise* did not reflect this sense before the 1940s.

revive [late Middle English] *Revive* is from Old French *revivre* or late Latin *revivere*, from Latin *re-* 'back' and *vivere* 'live'.

revoke [late Middle English] This is from Old French *revoquer* or Latin *revocare*, from *re-* 'back' and *vocare* 'to call'. 'Recall, bring back' was an early sense in English, now obsolete; the sense 'annul, repeal' was also early.

revolve [late Middle English] *Revolve* had the senses 'turn (the eyes) back', 'restore', and 'consider' in early use. It comes from Latin *revolvere*, from *re-* 'back' (also intensifying the sense here) and *volvere* 'to roll'. The word **revolution** is also late Middle English from Old French, or from late Latin *revolutio(n-)*, from *revolvere*. The semantic strands are: 'moving round' (e.g. *revolution of the heavens*), 'turning round (in the mind)' (now obsolete), and 'alteration, change' (e.g. *the green revolution*). The early 20th-century

rev is an abbreviation of *revolution* in motoring contexts.

revolt [mid 16th century] The noun is from French *révolte*, the verb from French *révolter*, from Italian *rivoltare*, based on Latin *revolvere* 'roll back'. Early use was in the context of casting off allegiance (e.g. *revolt against the king*); it was in the mid 18th century that the meaning 'affect with disgust' was reflected.
→ REVOLVE

revulsion [mid 16th century] This word was first used as a medical term meaning 'drawing of disease or blood congestion from one part of the body to another'. It comes from French, or from Latin *revulsio(n-)*, from *revuls-*, the past participial stem of the verb *revellere*. The formative elements are *re-* 'back' and *vellere* 'pull'. The prime current meaning 'sense of disgust and loathing' dates from the early 19th century.

reward [Middle English] This comes from an Anglo-Norman French variant of Old French *reguard* 'regard, heed', also an early sense of the English word. The notion of recompense was also early, reflected as 'a payment' offered for the capture of a criminal or missing person or for the return of lost property from the late 16th century (Shakespeare *Henry VI* part iii: Is Proclamation made, That who finds Edward, Shall have a high reward, and he his Life).

rhapsody [mid 16th century] An early *rhapsody* referred to 'an epic poem' suitable for recitation at one time. It came via Latin from Greek *rhapsōidia*, from *rhaptein* 'to stitch' and *ōidē* 'song, ode'. The word was used to mean 'collection, miscellany' from the late 16th century but this use became obsolete. It is recorded as a musical term from the late 19th century (*Liszt's Hungarian Rhapsodies*).

rhetoric [Middle English] *Rhetoric* is from Old French *rethorique*, via Latin from Greek *rhētorikē* (*tekhne*) '(art) of rhetoric', from *rhetor* 'rhetor'. **Rhetorical** dates from late Middle English when it was first used in the sense 'eloquently expressed'; this came via Latin from Greek *rhetorikos* (from *rhētor* 'rhetor').

rheumatic [late Middle English] This word originally referred to infection characterized by rheum, a watery fluid collecting in the eyes or nose. The source of the form is either Old French *reumatique* or (via Latin) Greek *rheumatikos*, from *rheuma* 'bodily humour, flow'. **Rheumatism** dates from the late 17th century, from French *rhumatisme*, or via Latin from Greek *rheumatismos*. The source is Greek *rheumatizein* 'to snuffle', from *rheuma* 'stream', the disease was originally supposed to be caused by the internal flow of 'watery' humours.

rhyme [Middle English] In Middle English the spelling was *rime*, from Old French, from medieval Latin *rithmus*, via Latin from Greek *rhuthmos*. The current spelling was introduced in the early 17th century under the influence of **rhythm** (also from Greek *rhuthmos* and originally in the sense 'rhyme'). *Rhime* was a common spelling until the end of the 18th century and was affected by some writers in the 19th century.

rib [Old English] The Old English noun *rib(b)* is of Germanic origin; it is related to Dutch *rib(be)* and German *Rippe*. The verb meaning 'mark with ridges' dates from the mid 16th century; the sense 'tease' was originally a US slang usage meaning 'to fool, dupe', which arose in the 1930s.

ribald [Middle English] This was first used as a noun for a 'lowly retainer' or a 'licentious or irreverent person'. It comes from Old French *ribauld*, from *riber* 'indulge in licentious pleasures', from a Germanic base meaning 'prostitute'.

ribbon [early 16th century] *Ribbon* is a variant of Middle English *riband* (from Old French *riban*, probably from a Germanic compound of the noun *band*). The French spelling *ruban* was also frequent in the 16th to 18th centuries.
→ BAND¹

rich [Old English] Old English *rīce* meant both 'powerful' and 'wealthy'. Of Germanic origin, it is related to Dutch *rijk* and German *reich*; ultimately from Celtic; it was reinforced in Middle English by Old French *riche* 'rich, powerful'. The sense 'highly amusing, outrageous' (e.g. *that's rich coming from him*) dates from the mid 18th century (coming from a notion of 'unstinted'). Middle English **riches** is a variant (later interpreted as a plural form) of archaic *richesse*, from Old French *richeise* (from *riche* 'rich').

rick¹ [Old English] Old English *hrēac* 'stack of hay, corn, peas, etc.' is Germanic in origin, related to Dutch *rook*.

rick² [late 18th century] The verb *rick* as in *ricked his neck* is from southern dialect. It is probably a variant spelling of *wrick*.

rickety [late 17th century] *Rickety* is based on mid 17th-century *rickets* (a disease in children due to vitamin D deficiency, causing bow legs) which is perhaps an alteration of Greek *rhakhitis*, from *rhakhis* 'spine'.

rid [Middle English] *Rid* is from Old Norse *rythja*. The original sense 'to clear' described clearing land of trees and undergrowth; this gave rise to 'free from rubbish or encumbrances', later becoming used in more general contexts.

riddle[1] [Old English] Old English *rædels*, *rædelse* meant 'opinion, conjecture, riddle'; it is related to Dutch *raadsel*, German *Rätsel* and English *read*.

→ READ

riddle[2] [late Old English] An early spelling of this word for a type of sieve was *hriddel*. Of Germanic origin, the word is from an Indo-European root shared by Latin *cribrum* 'sieve', *cernere* 'separate', and Greek *krinein* 'decide'.

ride [Old English] Old English *rīdan* is Germanic origin, related to Dutch *rijden* and German *reiten*. The main sense of sitting on or being carried along on horseback has transferred to other forms of transport (e.g. *ride a bike*) and has generalized as simply 'move' (e.g. *riding high*). Of the idioms, *to have a rough ride* dates from the early 19th century; *take for a ride* 'mislead' was originally US English from the 1920s; *for the ride* 'for fun' arose in the 1960s. The related **rider** was *rīdere* in Old English meaning 'mounted warrior, knight'; this was generalized to any person riding a horse in Middle English.

ridge [Old English] Old English *hrycg* meant 'spine, crest'. Of Germanic origin, it is related to Dutch *rug* and German *Rücken* 'back'. The senses 'top of a roof', 'elevated narrow ground' were also early.

ridiculous [mid 16th century] This comes from Latin *ridiculosus*, from *ridiculus* 'laughable', from *ridere* 'to laugh'. The word **ridicule** dates from the late 17th century; this is from French, or from Latin *ridiculum*, a neuter form (used as a noun) of *ridiculus*.

riding [Old English] Old English *trithing* describing an administrative district is from Old Norse *thrithjungr* 'third part', from *thrithi* 'third'. The initial *th-* was lost due to assimilation with the preceding *-t* of *East*, *West*, or with the *-th* of *North* (*East Riding, West Riding, North Riding of Yorkshire*).

rife [late Old English] Late Old English *rȳfe* may be from Old Norse *rīfr* 'acceptable'; however it was common in early southern texts which favours its being native in English rather than an adoption from Scandinavian.

riff-raff [late 15th century] This was formerly written as *riff and raff*; it is from Old French *rif et raf* 'one and all, every bit', which is of Germanic origin.

rifle[1] [mid 17th century] The word *rifle* is from French *rifler* 'graze, scratch', of Germanic origin. The earliest noun usage was in *rifle gun*, which had 'rifles' or spiral grooves cut into the inside of the barrel.

rifle[2] [Middle English] This *rifle* meaning 'search through' is from Old French *rifler* 'graze, plunder'. The origin is Germanic. An early sense in English was 'plunder'.

rift [Middle English] The word *rift* is of Scandinavian origin; Norwegian and Danish *rift* 'cleft, chink' are related.

rig[1] [late 15th century] *Rig* was first in nautical use in the sense 'make ready for sea'. It may be of Scandinavian origin, associated with Norwegian *rigga* 'bind or wrap up'. The noun ('arrangement of masts and sails') dates from the early 19th century.

rig[2] [late 18th century] This was originally recorded in the noun sense 'trick, way of swindling'. The origin is unknown; the verb ('set up (something) fraudulently') is related to the noun.

right [Old English] The Old English forms *riht* (adjective and noun), *rihtan* (verb), *rihte* (adverb) are Germanic in origin, related to Latin *rectus* 'ruled', from an Indo-European root denoting movement in a straight line. The adjectival semantic strands include: 'straight', 'upright, righteous', 'legitimate', as well as indicating the opposite of left. **Rightful** (in Old English *rihtful* 'upright, righteous') is based on *right*; the notion of 'legitimacy' dates from Middle English. The word **righteous** also dates from Old English (as *rihtwīs*, from *riht* 'right' and *wīs* 'manner, state, condition'). The change in the ending in the 16th century was due to association with words such as *bounteous*.

rigid [late Middle English] *Rigid* is from Latin *rigidus*, from *rigere* 'be stiff'. The notion is one of inflexibility and lack of pliancy.

rigmarole [mid 18th century] This is apparently an alteration of *ragman roll*, originally a legal document recording a list of offences. The phrase appears to have gone out of literary use in about 1600.

rigour [late Middle English] *Rigour* is from Old French *rigour* from Latin *rigor* 'stiffness'. The same base is shared by late Middle English **rigorous** from Old French *rigorous* or late Latin *rigorosus*.

rile [early 19th century] *Rile* is a variant of late 16th-century *roil* 'make turbid' which may be from Old French *ruiler* 'mix mortar', from late Latin *regulare* 'regulate'.

rim [Old English] Old English *rima* meant 'a border, coast'; Old Norse *rimi* 'ridge, strip of land' is the only known cognate. It is recorded as the edge of a circular object from the early

17th century and in the plural *rims* for spectacles from the mid 19th century.

rind [Old English] Old English *rind(e)* 'bark of a tree' is related to Dutch *run* and German *Rinde*, of which the origin is unknown. The word refers to the outer peel of fruit and vegetables from Middle English.

ring[1] [Old English] Old English *hring* 'small circular band' is Germanic in origin, related to Dutch *ring*, German *Ring*, aand English *rank*. The semantic strands also include: 'border, rim' (Middle English), 'circle of people' (Old English), and 'enclosed circular space' (Middle English). Verb use dates from late Middle English; its use in the context of drawing a circle around something such as a date to draw attention to it is found from the 1970s.
→ RANK[1]

ring[2] [Old English] Old English *hringan* 'give out a clear sound' is Germanic in origin and may be an imitative formation.

rink [late Middle English] This was originally a Scots term for a jousting-ground. It is perhaps originally from Old French *renc* 'rank'. It was used to describe a stretch of ice marked off for the sport of curling from the late 18th century. The word remained limited to Scots use until the later part of the 19th century.

rinse [Middle English] The source of this word is Old French *rincer*, but the ultimate origin is unknown. An early sense was 'to clear or clean by removal'.

riot [Middle English] This word was originally used in the sense 'dissolute living'. It comes from Old French *riote* 'debate', from *rioter* 'to quarrel' of unknown ultimate origin. The idiomatic phrase *read the riot act* is an extension from the *Riot Act* of 1715, when a specified portion of this was read out by a legal authority, any assembly of more than twelve people was required to disperse or be declared guilty of a felony; this Act was repealed in 1973. The adjective **riotous** (via Old French from *riote*) is also Middle English when it meant 'troublesome'.

rip [late Middle English] This *rip* meaning 'tear' is of unknown origin; there may be a link with *reap*. Phrases such as *let it rip* were originally US recorded from the middle of the 19th century. The slang use *rip off* meaning 'steal' was also originally a US usage of the 1960s; *rip* alone had this sense at the start of the 20th century. The noun dates from the early 18th century. The *rip* of *rip tide* (late 18th century) may be a related word.
→ REAP

ripe [Old English] Old English *rīpe* is West Germanic in origin, related to Dutch *rijp* and German *reif*. The stem may be related to that of the verb *reap*.

riposte [early 18th century] This word came via French from French from Italian *risposta* 'response'.

rise [Old English] Old English *rīsan* meant 'make an attack' and 'wake, get out of bed'. Of Germanic origin, it is related to Dutch *rijzen* and German *reisen*. The semantic strands include: 'get up from lying or sitting', 'ascend', 'reach a higher degree', and 'spring up, come into existence'. The phrase *rise and shine!* was originally used in the armed forces in the early 20th century as a summons to get out of bed.

risk [mid 17th century] The noun is from French *risque*, the verb from French *risquer*, from Italian *risco* 'danger' and *rischiare* 'run into danger'. The phrase *run the risk* dates from the mid 17th century; *at risk* is recorded from the early 20th century.

rite [Middle English] *Rite* is from Latin *ritus* '(religious) usage'. Late 16th-century **ritual** was first used as an adjective and is from Latin *ritualis*, from *ritus*. *Rituals* meaning 'ritual observances' dates from the mid 17th century; the sense became more trivialized (Laurie Lee *I Can't Stay Long*: The ritual of bargaining was long and elaborate).

rival [late 16th century] *Rival* is from Latin *rivalis*, originally in the sense 'person living on the opposite bank and using the same stream as another', from *rivus* 'stream'.

river [Middle English] *River* is from Anglo-Norman French, based on Latin *riparius*, from *ripa* 'bank of a river'. The phrase *sell down the river* was originally a US usage (mid 19th century) in the context of selling a troublesome slave to the owner of a sugar-cane plantation on the lower Mississippi, where the conditions were harsher.

rivet [Middle English] *Rivet* is from Old French, from *river* 'fix, clinch'. The ultimate origin is unknown.

rivulet [late 16th century] This is an alteration of obsolete *riveret* (from a French word meaning literally 'small river'). It was perhaps suggested by Italian *rivoletto*, a diminutive of *rivolo*, based on Latin *rivus* 'stream'.

road [Old English] Old English *rād* meant 'journey on horseback', 'foray'. Of Germanic origin, it is related to the verb *ride*. The now common sense of *road* as the equivalent of *street* did not appear before the end of the 16th century. The phrase *one for the road* dates from the 1950s. The compound:

■ **roadstead** (mid 16th century) is based on *road* and obsolete *stead* meaning 'a place'.
→ RIDE

roar [Old English] Old English *rārian* is imitative of a deep prolonged cry. Of West Germanic origin, it is related to German *röhren*. The noun dates from late Middle English.

roast [Middle English] The word *roast* is from Old French *rostir*, of West Germanic origin. Frequently in modern use the word means 'cook in an oven'; this was originally a use of *bake* whereas *roast* was 'cook before a fire'. The colloquial sense 'ridicule, criticize' (e.g. *roasted in the press*) dates from the early 18th century.

rob [Middle English] *Rob* is from Old French *rober*. Of Germanic origin, it is related to the archaic verb *reave* 'carry out raids'. The noun **robber** is Middle English, from Anglo-Norman French and Old French *robere*, from the same Old French verb, as is Middle English **robbery** (from Anglo-Norman French and Old French *roberie*).

robe [Middle English] *Robe* is from Old French, from the Germanic base (in the sense 'booty') of *rob*: clothing was an important component of booty.
→ ROB

robot [1920s] This is from Czech *robota* 'forced labour'. The term was coined in Karel Čapek's play *R.U.R.* 'Rossum's Universal Robots' (1920), when it described a mechanical man or woman.

robust [mid 16th century] *Robust* is from Latin *robustus* 'firm and hard', from *robus*, an earlier form of *robur* 'oak, strength'.

rock[1] [Middle English] This *rock* as a large mass of stone is from Old French *rocque*, from medieval Latin *rocca*, of unknown ultimate origin. The phrase *between a rock and a hard place* dates from the 1920s; so too does the slang use of the word for a precious stone, particularly a diamond. *On the rocks* referring to ice in a drink, is an expression recorded from the 1940s.

rock[2] [late Old English] This *rock* 'move to and fro' (originally *roccian*) is probably from a Germanic base meaning 'remove, move'; it is related to Dutch *rukken* 'jerk, tug' and German *rücken* 'move'. The noun dates from the early 19th century.

rocket [early 17th century] *Rocket* is from French *roquette*, from Italian *rocchetto*, a diminutive of *rocca* 'distaff (for spinning)': the reference is to the cylindrical shape. The sense 'severe reprimand' (e.g. *gave him a rocket for being late*) was originally military slang of the 1940s.

rod [late Old English] Old English *rodd* referred to both a 'slender shoot growing on or cut from a tree' and a 'straight stick or bundle of twigs used to inflict punishment'. It is probably related to Old Norse *rudda* 'club'.

rodent [mid 19th century] *Rodent* is from Latin *rodere* 'to gnaw'.

rogue [mid 16th century] A *rogue* was once an 'idle vagrant'; it is probably from Latin *rogare* 'beg, ask', and related to obsolete slang *roger* 'vagrant beggar'. Many similar cant terms were introduced towards the middle of the 16th century.

role [early 17th century] This word is from obsolete French *roule* 'roll', referring originally to the roll of paper on which the actor's part was written.

roll [Middle English] The noun is from Old French *rolle*, the verb from Old French *roller*, from Latin *rotulus* 'a roll': this is a variant of *rotula* 'little wheel', a diminutive of *rota*. The adjective **roly-poly** (early 17th century) is a fanciful formation from the verb *roll*.

rollick [early 19th century] This is probably dialect, perhaps a blend of *romp* and *frolic*.

Romance [Middle English] This word was originally a term for the vernacular language of France as opposed to Latin. It comes from Old French *romanz*, based on Latin *Romanicus* 'Roman'. The lower case spelling **romance** is of the same origin, originally referring to 'a composition in the vernacular' as opposed to works in Latin. Early use was related to vernacular verse on the theme of chivalry; the sense 'genre centred on romantic love' dates from the mid 17th century. Mid 17th-century **romantic** referred to the characteristics of romance in a narrative: it is from archaic *romaunt* 'tale of chivalry', from an Old French variant of *romanz*. The context of 'appealing to the feelings' dates from the early 18th century.

romp [early 18th century] This may be an alteration of *ramp*. The sense 'cover the ground quickly' is chiefly found as racing slang from the late 19th century (e.g. *romped home*).
→ RAMP

roof [Old English] Old English *hrōf* is Germanic in origin, related to Old Norse *hróf* 'boat shed' and Dutch *roef* 'deckhouse'. English alone has the general sense 'covering of a house'; other Germanic languages use forms related to *thatch*.

room [Old English] Old English *rūm* has a Germanic origin; it is related to Dutch *ruim* and German *Raum*. The word branches semantically into: 'space' (e.g. early 20th century *room at the* top), 'portion of space' (e.g. *rooms in the cottage*), and the now obsolete 'assigned place; place in which one is seated' (e.g. *the best room of the playhouse*).

roost [Old English] Old English *hrōst* is related to Dutch *roest*; the ultimate origin is unknown. The phrase *rule the roost* (sometimes *rule the roast*) dates from the late 18th century. The verb dates from the early 16th century. **Rooster** dates from the late 18th century and is mainly part of US English and dialect.

root[1] [late Old English] Old English *rōt* (as in *tree root*) is from Old Norse *rót*, related to Latin *radix*, and English *wort*. *Take root* dates from the early 16th century.

root[2] [Old English] Old English *wrōtan* 'turn up the soil' is Germanic in origin, related to Old English *wrōt* 'snout', German *Rüssel* 'snout', and perhaps ultimately to Latin *rodere* 'gnaw'. The phrase *root for* 'support' dates from the late 19th century as a US usage.

rope [Old English] Old English *rāp* is from a Germanic source; related forms are Dutch *reep* and German *Reif*. Use of the word in its plural as a demarcation of a ring for fighting dates from the early 19th century; *on the ropes* is found from the 1950s.

rosary [late Middle English] In early use a *rosary* referred to a 'rose garden': it is from Latin *rosarium* 'rose garden', based on *rosa* 'rose'. The religious term is found from the mid 16th century.

rose [Old English] Old English *rōse* is from a Germanic source, from Latin *rosa*; it was reinforced in Middle English by Old French *rose*. The children's game *ring-a-roses* is said to refer to the inflamed ('rose-coloured') ring of buboes, symptomatic of the plague. The word **rosette** (mid 18th century) is from a French diminutive of *rose*.

roster [early 18th century] A *roster* was originally a list of duties and leave for military personnel. It comes from Dutch *rooster* 'list', earlier 'gridiron', from *roosten* 'to roast', with reference to its parallel lines.

rostrum [mid 16th century] This is an English use of a Latin word meaning literally 'beak' (from *rodere* 'gnaw'). The word was originally used (initially in the plural *rostra*) to refer to part of the Forum in Rome, decorated with the beaks of captured galleys, used as a platform for public speakers.

rot [Old English] The Old English verb *rotian* is Germanic in origin, related to Dutch *rotten*; the noun (Middle English) may have come via Scandinavian. The slang use meaning 'non-

sensical rubbish' (e.g. *he was speaking complete rot*) dates from the mid 19th century.

rotation [mid 16th century] This comes from Latin *rotatio(n-)*, from the verb *rotare*, the source too of late 17th-century **rotate** based on Latin *rota* 'wheel'. The related word **rotary** dates from the mid 18th century, from medieval Latin *rotarius*, from *rota*. The worldwide charitable society of businessmen and women formed in 1905 known as *Rotary International* owes its name to the fact that its members hosted events in rotation. It has been suggested that the Middle English word **rote** (as in *learn by rote*) may be based on Latin *rota* 'wheel' but there is no evidence to support this; the origin remains unknown.

rotor [early 20th century] This is an irregular formation from late 17th-century *rotator* (from Latin *rotare*, based on *rota* 'wheel'). It was chosen as a mathematical term for a quantity, the first example cited being a velocity of rotation about an axis.

rotten [Middle English] *Rotten* is from Old Norse *rotinn*. The compound:
■ **rotten borough** is a historical reference to a borough that was able to elect an MP despite having very few voters, the choice usually being in the hands of one person or family. It owes its name to the fact that the borough was found to have 'decayed' to the point of no longer having a constituency.

rotund [late 15th century] *Rotund* is from Latin *rotundus*, from *rotare* 'rotate'. The word **rotunda** describing a round building or room dates from the early 17th century; it is an alteration of Italian *rotonda (camera)* 'round (chamber)', the feminine of *rotondo* 'round'.

rough [Old English] Old English *rūh* is West Germanic in origin, related to Dutch *ruw* and German *rauh*. The word refers to surfaces, to water and weather, to temperament, to sounds, to undressed materials (*rough timber*), and to lack of finish generally (e.g. *rough copy*). The phrase *rough and ready* dates from the early 19th century and was originally boxing slang.

round [Middle English] *Round* is from the Old French stem *round-*, from a variant of Latin *rotundus* 'rotund'. The historical reference:
■ **Roundhead** comes from the short-cropped hairstyle of the Puritans, who formed an important element in this Parliamentary party of the English Civil War.

rouse [late Middle English] *Rouse* was originally a hawking and hunting term: it is probably from Anglo-Norman French, but the origin remains obscure. General use became common from around 1585, often in combination with the word *up*.

rout [Middle English] This word for a 'decisive defeat' is ultimately based on Latin *ruptus* 'broken', from the verb *rumpere*; the meaning 'disorderly retreat' and the verb (late 16th century) are from obsolete French *route*, probably from Italian *rotta* 'break-up of an army'. The sense 'disorderly crowd' came via Anglo-Norman French *rute*.

route [Middle English] *Route* is from Old French *rute* 'road', from Latin *rupta (via)* 'broken (way)', the feminine past participle of *rumpere*. The word was found in Middle English and towards the end of the 16th century but not finally adopted before the start of the 18th century, when the spelling was usualy *rout* until the beginning of the 19th century.

routine [late 17th century] *Routine* is from French, from *route* 'road'. Use in theatrical contexts dates from the 1920s (e.g. *learned the same routine*); the word has been used in computing since the 1940s.
→ ROUTE

rover [Middle English] *Rover* is from Middle Low German, Middle Dutch *rōver*, from *rōven* 'rob'; it is, like *rob*, related to the archaic verb *reave* 'carry out raids'. The verb *rove* is late 15th-century; it was originally a term in archery meaning 'shoot at a casual mark of undetermined range'. This may be from dialect *rave* 'to stray', probably of Scandinavian origin.

row[1] [Old English] Old English *rāw* 'orderly line' is of Germanic origin; related to Dutch *rij* and German *Reihe*. The phrase *in rows* dates from late Middle English; it was in this period too that the word came to denote a narrow street edged by houses. In Scots and northern English it became common in street names.

row[2] [Old English] Old English *rōwan* 'propel with oars' is Germanic in origin; related to *rudder*; from an Indo-European root shared by Latin *remus* 'oar' and Greek *eretmon* 'oar'.
→ RUDDER

row[3] [mid 18th century] This word for a noisy 'quarrel' is of unknown origin. It became common from around 1800 and was considered low speech.

rowdy [early 19th century] This was originally a US noun usage in the sense 'lawless backwoodsman'. The origin is unknown.

royal [late Middle English] The word *royal* is from Old French *roial*, from Latin *regalis* 'regal'. The French origin is reflected in early use by the common placing of the word after the noun (e.g. *blood royal*). Late Middle English **royalty** is

from Old French *roialte*, from *roial*. The sense 'royal right (especially over the ownership of minerals)', recorded in the late 15th century, developed in the mid 19th century into the sense 'payment made by a mineral producer to the site owner'; this was then transferred to payments for the use of patents and published materials.

rub [Middle English] *Rub* was first used as a verb: it is perhaps from Low German *rubben*, but the ultimate origin is unknown. The noun dates from the late 16th century. The word **rubber**, recorded from the mid 16th century, is based on the verb *rub*. The original sense was 'an implement (such as a hard brush) used for rubbing and cleaning'. Because an early use of the elastic substance once known as *caoutchouc* was to rub out pencil marks, *rubber* acquired the sense 'eraser' in the late 18th century. The meaning was subsequently generalized in the mid 19th century to refer to the substance in any form or use, at first often differentiated as *India rubber*. The sports term *rubber* found from the late 16th century is of unknown origin; early use was as a term in bowls.

rubbish [late Middle English] This is from Anglo-Norman French *rubbous*; it may be related to Old French *robe* 'spoils'. The change in the ending was due to assocation with words ending in -*ish*. The verb meaning 'denigrate', found from the 1950s, was originally Australian and New Zealand slang.
→ RUBBLE

rubble [late Middle English] *Rubble* may be from an Anglo-Norman French alteration of Old French *robe* 'spoils'.
→ RUBBISH

rubric [late Middle English] The early spelling *rubrish* originally referred to a heading, or section of text written in red to stand out. It is from Old French *rubriche*, from Latin *rubrica (terra)* 'red (earth or ochre as writing material)', from the base of *rubeus* 'red'; the later spelling is influenced by the Latin form.

ruby [Middle English] *Ruby* is from Old French *rubi*, from medieval Latin *rubinus*, from the base of Latin *rubeus* 'red'.

ruck[1] [Middle English] This rugby term for a loose scrum was first found in the sense 'stack of fuel, heap'. It is apparently of Scandinavian origin; Norwegian *ruke* 'heap of hay' is associated.

ruck[2] [late 18th century] This *ruck* meaning 'an untidy fold, crease' is from Old Norse *hrukka*.

ruck[3] [1950s] The informal *ruck* meaning 'quarrel, fight' is perhaps a shortened form of early 19th-century **ruction** (whose origin is unknown) or of late 19th-century *ruckus* meaning 'commmotion' (which may be related to *rumpus*).

rucksack [mid 19th century] This is an adoption of a German word, from *rucken* (a dialect variant of *Rücken* 'back') and *Sack* 'bag, sack'.

rudder [Old English] Old English *rōther* was a 'paddle, oar'. Of West Germanic origin, it is related to Dutch *roer*, German *Ruder*, and to English *row*.
→ ROW²

ruddy [late Old English] Late Old English *rudig* is from the base of archaic *rud* 'red colour'; it is related to *red*. The word's use as a euphemism for *bloody* dates from the early 20th century.
→ RED

rude [Middle English] Early senses included 'roughly made' and 'uncultured'. The source of the word is Old French, from Latin *rudis* 'unwrought', an adjective referring to handicraft, but used figuratively to mean 'uncultivated'. Latin *rudus* 'broken stone' is related. The phrase *rude awakening* appeared towards the end of the 19th century.

rudiment [mid 16th century] *Rudiment* is from French, or from Latin *rudimentum* 'beginning, first principle', from *rudis* 'unwrought', on the pattern of *elementum* 'element'.

rue [Old English] The Old English noun *hrēow* meant 'repentance'; the verb *hrēowan* meant 'affect with contrition'. The origin is Germanic and related forms include Dutch *rouw* 'mourning' and German *Reue* 'remorse'. The phrase *rue the day* stems from late 16th-century use (Shakespeare *King John*: France, thou shalt rue this hour within this hour).

ruff [early 16th century] This *ruff*, now commonly referring to a type of frill worn round the neck, was first used for a frill around a sleeve: it is probably from a variant of *rough*.
→ ROUGH

ruffian [late 15th century] This is from Old French *ruffian*, from Italian *ruffiano*, perhaps from dialect *rofia* 'scab, scurf', of Germanic origin.

ruffle [Middle English] Early use was as a verb. The origin is unknown. Current noun senses ('ornamental frill' and 'vibrating drum beat') date from the late 17th century.

rug [mid 16th century] *Rug* was once a name for a type of coarse woollen cloth. The origin is probably Scandinavian; Norwegian dialect *rugga* 'coverlet' and Swedish *rugg* 'ruffled hair'

are associated; The sense 'small carpet' dates from the early 19th century.
→ RAG; RUGGED

rugby [mid 19th century] The sport term *rugby* is named after *Rugby* School in Warwickshire, a public school where the game was first played.

rugged [Middle English] 'Shaggy' was an early sense of *rugged* as was 'rough-coated' (in descriptions of horses). It is probably of Scandinavian origin; Swedish *rugga* 'roughen' is associated.
→ RUG

ruin [Middle English] The early word meant 'collapse of a building'. It comes via Old French from Latin *ruina*, from *ruere* 'to fall'. **Ruinous**, a late Middle English word which included the sense 'falling down' is from Latin *ruinosus*, from *ruina*. The noun **ruination** is first recorded in the mid 17th century, based on the obsolete verb *ruinate*, which was common between 1550 and 1700 meaning 'reduce to ruins'.

rule [Middle English] The noun is from Old French *reule*, the verb from Old French *reuler*, from late Latin *regulare*, from Latin *regula* 'straight stick'. Semantic strands include: 'principle governing conduct' (*rules of action*), 'principle governing procedure' (*rules of art*), 'criterion' (*hard and fast rule*), 'good order, discipline' (now obsolete), and 'graduated strip for measuring'.

rumble [late Middle English] *Rumble* is probably from Middle Dutch *rommelen*, *rummelen*, imitative of a low continuous noise. The sense 'discover (an illicit activity)' found from the late 19th century (e.g. *you've been rumbled*) may be a different word.

rumbustious [late 18th century] This word is probably an alteration of archaic *robustious* common during the 17th century meaning 'boisterous, robust'.

ruminate [mid 16th century] This word is from Latin *ruminari* 'chew over'; the figurative use 'meditate' soon developed. The related **ruminant** (mid 17th century) is from the same Latin verb, from *rumen* 'throat'.

rummage [late 15th century] *Rummage* is from Old French *arrumage*, from *arrumer* 'stow (in a hold)', from Middle Dutch *ruim* 'room'. In early use the word referred to the arranging of items such as casks in the hold of a ship, giving rise in the early 17th century to the verb meaning 'make a search of (a vessel)'.

rumour [late Middle English] *Rumour* is from Old French *rumur*, from Latin *rumor* 'noise'. An early now obsolete use was to mean 'widespread report in praise of someone'.

rump [late Middle English] *Rump* is probably of Scandinavian origin; Danish and Norwegian *rumpe* 'backside' are associated forms. The origin of the phrase:

■ **Rump Parliament** is uncertain. It is said to derive from *The Bloody Rump*, the name of a paper written before the trial resulting in the execution of Charles I (the Rump here was the part of the Long Parliament which continued to sit after Pride's Purge in 1648 and voted for the trial). The word was popularized after a speech by Major General Brown, given at a public assembly. It is also said to have been coined by Clem Walker in his *History of Independency* (1648), as a term for those strenuously opposing the king.

rumple [early 16th century] This word was first as a noun in the sense 'wrinkle'. It is from Middle Dutch *rompel*.

rumpus [mid 18th century] The word *rumpus* is probably fanciful.

run [Old English] The Old English verb *rinnan*, *irnan* is Germanic in origin, probably reinforced in Middle English by Old Norse *rinna*, *renna*. The current form with *-u-* in the present tense is first recorded in the 16th century. The word *rennet* may be from *renne*, an obsolete form of *run*.
→ RENNET

rune [Old English] Old English *rūn* meant 'a secret, mystery'; it was not recorded between Middle English and the late 17th century, when it was reintroduced under the influence of Old Norse *rúnir*, *rúnar* 'magic signs, hidden lore'.

rung [Old English] Old English *hrung* meant 'stout stick, spoke, cross-bar' related to Dutch *rong* and German *Runge*.

runt [early 16th century] The first sense recorded for *runt* was 'old or decayed tree stump'. The origin is unknown. Its use in phrases such as *runt of the litter* is found from the mid 19th century.

rupture [late Middle English] Early use was as a noun; the word derives from Old French *rupture* or Latin *ruptura*, from *rumpere* 'to break'. Its use to mean 'hernia' dates from the early 16th century. The verb made its appearance in examples around the middle of the 18th century.

rural [late Middle English] *Rural* is from Old French, or from late Latin *ruralis*, from *rus*, *rur-* 'country'. In early use little difference exists between *rural* and *rustic*, but later usage shows *rural* in connection with locality and country scenes, with *rustic* being reserved for the primitive qualities of country life.

ruse [late Middle English] *Ruse* was first used as a hunting term for a 'detour' or a 'turning' of a hunted animal to escape the dogs. It comes from Old French, from *ruser* 'use trickery', used prior to that in the sense 'drive back', perhaps based on Latin *rursus* 'backwards'.

rush[1] [late Middle English] The verb *rush* is from an Anglo-Norman French variant of Old French *ruser* 'drive back'. This was an early sense in English and the word was sometimes combined with intensifiers such as *down*, *up*, or *aside* (Shakespeare *Romeo and Juliet*: The kind Prince Taking thy part, hath rushed aside the Law).
→ RUSE

rush[2] [Old English] Old English *risc*, *rysc*, the name for a plant of the order *Juncaceae* is Germanic in origin. The sense 'made of rushes' (as in *rush-matting*) dates from the end of the 19th century.

russet [Middle English] *Russet* is from an Anglo-Norman French variant of Old French *rousset*; this is a diminutive of *rous* 'red', from Provençal *ros*, from Latin *russus* 'red'. It was originally a name for a coarse homespun woollen cloth that was reddish-brown, grey, or neutral in colour, used formerly for making clothing for landworkers. When adjectival use started in the 15th century it was usually applied to cloth; this continued throughout the 16th century (Cromwell *Letters*: A russet-coated Captain who knows what he fights for).

rust [Old English] Old English *rūst* is Germanic in origin, related to Dutch *roest*, German *Rost* and English *red*. The adjective **rusty** is also Old English (as *rūstig*).
→ RED

rustic [late Middle English] The early sense recorded was 'rural'. It comes from Latin *rusticus*, from *rus* 'the country'. The sense 'unsophisticated; plain and simple' dates from the beginnning of the 17th century (Shakespeare *As You Like It*: Meantime, forget this new falne dignity, And fall into our Rustic Revelry). The noun *rustic* meaning 'peasant' dates from the mid 16th century.

rustle [late Middle English] The word *rustle* is imitative and was first found in verb use; Flemish *rijsselen* and Dutch *ritselen* are comparable forms. The noun dates from the mid 18th century. The phrase *rustle up* in connection with the notion of 'getting together quickly' is also mid 19th-century; the verb *rustle* in the context of stealing animals such as cattle, is found from the early 20th century.

rut[1] [late 16th century] This *rut* meaning 'deep furrow' may be from Old French *rute*. It is often regarded as a variant of *route* but this word was rare in the 16th century and the vowel difference makes the link improbable.

rut² [late Middle English] This *rut* in the context of male deer in mating periods is from Old French, from Latin *rugitus*, from *rugire* 'to roar'.

ruthless [Middle English] This is based on the now archaic Middle English word *ruth* 'compassion' from the verb *rue* probably influenced by Old Norse *hrygth*.
➔ RUE

Ss

sabbath [Old English] The word *sabbath* is from Latin *sabbatum*, via Greek from Hebrew *šabbāṯ*, from *šābaṯ* 'to rest'. Originally it referred to the seventh day of the week, Saturday, which was considered a day of religious rest. In English *Sabbath* as a synonym for Sunday was not common before the 17th century.

sable [late Middle English] This word for a marten with dark brown fur native to Japan and Siberia, is from an Old French word meaning 'sable fur': this in turn is from medieval Latin *sabelum*, of Slavic origin. The *sable* meaning 'black' is from an Old French heraldic term, generally taken to be identical with the term for sable fur despite its characteristic dark brown colour.

sabotage [early 20th century] This is an English use of a French word, from *saboter* 'kick with sabots, wilfully destroy'. The word **sabot** has been in English use since the early 17th century, a blend of *savate* 'shoe' and *botte* 'boot'. **Saboteur** is found from the early 20th century, from French, from the verb *saboter*.

sabre [late 17th century] This word for a type of cavalry sword is from a French alteration of obsolete *sable*, from German *Sabel*: the latter is a local variant of *Säbel*, from Hungarian *szablya*.

sack¹ [Old English] Old English *sacc* is from Latin *saccus* 'sack, sackcloth, bag', from Greek *sakkos*, of Semitic origin. The verb sense 'dismiss from employment' dates from the mid 19th century. Latin *saccus* is also the source of mid 18th-century **sac** first used as a term in biology, and the source of mid 19th-century **sachet** (from a French word meaning literally 'little bag', a diminutive of *sac*): this initially denoted any small perfumed bag used to scent clothes.

sack² [mid 16th century] This *sack* referring to the 'pillaging' of a town is from French *sac*, in the phrase *mettre à sac* 'put to sack'. The French phrase was on the model of Italian *fare il sacco*, *mettere a sacco*, which perhaps originally referred to filling a sack with plunder.

sacrament [Middle English] This comes via Old French from Latin *sacramentum* 'solemn oath' (from *sacrare* 'to hallow', from *sacer* 'sacred'), used in Christian Latin as a translation of Greek *mustērion* 'mystery'.

sacred [late Middle English] This is the past participle of the now archaic verb *sacre* 'consecrate'. The source is Old French *sacrer*, from Latin *sacrare*, from *sacer*, *sacr-* 'holy'. Early English use reflected the sense 'consecrated', but the word is now closer to the meaning of Latin *sacer*.

sacrifice [Middle English] *Sacrifice* is from Old French, from Latin *sacrificium*; it is related to *sacrificus* 'sacrificial', from *sacer* 'holy'.

sacrilege [Middle English] This word for 'violation of what is considered holy' came via Old French from Latin *sacrilegium*, from *sacrilegus* 'stealer of sacred things'. The elements here are *sacer*, *sacr-* 'sacred' and *legere* 'take possession of'.

sacristy [late Middle English] Latin *sacer*, *sacr-* 'sacred' is the base of *sacristy* (from French *sacristie*, from medieval Latin *sacristia*) and provides the first element (in the ablative case) of late 15th-century **sacrosanct**. The latter is from Latin *sacrosanctus*, literally 'holy by sacred rite'; *sanctus* 'holy' is the second element.

sad [Old English] Old English *sæd* meant both 'sated, weary' and 'weighty, dense'. Of Germanic origin, it is related to Dutch *zat* and German *satt*, from an Indo-European root shared by Latin *satis* 'enough'. The original meaning was replaced in Middle English by the senses 'steadfast, firm' (Milton *Paradise Lost*: Settl'd in his face, I see Sad resolution and secure), 'serious, sober' (*Romance of the Rose*: She, demurely sad of chere), and later 'sorrowful'. The colloquial use meaning 'pitiably dull, uncool' became popularized in the 1980s (*what a sad dress she's wearing!*).

saddle [Old English] Old English *sadol*, *sadul* is Germanic in origin, related to Dutch *zadel* and German *Sattel*, perhaps from an Indo-European root shared by Latin *sella* 'seat' and *sit*. The figurative phrase *be in the saddle* referring to a position of control and management dates from the mid 16th century. The word's use in cookery, for a joint of mutton (originally consisting of the two loins) is found from the mid 18th century.
→ SIT

sadism [late 19th century] This comes from French *sadisme*, from the name of the Marquis de Sade (1740–1814), a French writer and soldier. His career as a cavalry officer was interrupted by periods of imprisonment for cruelty and debauchery. While in prison he wrote a number of sexually explicit works: the cruel sexual practices that he described led to the coining of *sadism*.

safe [Middle English] Early use was as an adjective. It comes from Old French *sauf*, from Latin *salvus* 'uninjured'. The noun is from the verb *save*, later assimilated to the adjectival form; it was first used to describe a chest for protecting food from insects, later (early 19th century) coming to describe a burglar-proof container for valuables. Also based on Latin *salvus* 'safe' is Middle English **safety** from Old French *sauvete*, from medieval Latin *salvitas*. The late Middle English compound **safeguard** was first found meaning 'protection' or 'a safe conduct': this is from Old French *sauve garde*, from *sauve* 'safe' and *garde* 'guard'.
→ SAVE¹

sag [late Middle English] This is apparently related to Middle Low German *sacken* and Dutch *zakken* 'subside'. Further details of the history are unknown.

saga [early 18th century] *Saga* is from an Old Norse word with the literal meaning 'narrative'; it is related to English *saw* meaning 'proverb' (in Old English *sagu* 'a saying'). The more general use of the word for any 'long drawn-out story' arose in the mid 19th century. In the 1990s the phrase *Aga-saga* came to be applied to a type of popular novel about the domestic and emotional lives of middle-class characters: this is from the association of Aga stoves with the middle classes.

sail [Old English] The word *sail* (in Old English *segel* as a noun and *seglian* as a verb) is Germanic in origin, related to Dutch *zeil* and German *Segel* (both nouns). The notion of 'gliding, moving smoothly' became transferred to other contexts (*she sailed along, singing happily*; *clouds sailed over*). Mid 17th-century **sailor** is a variant of obsolete *sailer*.

saint [Middle English] *Saint* is from Old French *seint*, from Latin *sanctus* 'holy', the past participle of *sancire* 'consecrate'. The word has been used in the names of many diseases (e.g. *St Vitus' dance*) with the supposition that the associated saint would ward off the illness. Also based on Latin *sanctus* and where the form *sanct* has prevailed are: late Middle English **sanctify** (via Old French from ecclesiastical Latin *sanctificare*); late Middle English **sanctity** first used in the sense 'saintliness' (from Old French

sainctite, reinforced by Latin *sanctitas*); and early 17th-century **sanctimonious** originally meaning 'holy in character' (based on Latin *sanctimonia* 'sanctity'). The word **sanctum** (late 16th century) for a sacred place within a church is a use of the neuter form of Latin *sanctus*, giving 'consecrated place'.

sake [Old English] Old English *sacu* 'contention, crime' is from a Germanic source; related forms are Dutch *zaak* and German *Sache*, from a base meaning 'affair, legal action, thing'. The phrase *for the sake of*, the only surviving modern use, was not in Old English and may be from Old Norse. Down to the middle of the 19th century, the apostrophe used to express possession of abstract and common nouns (e.g. *for conscience's sake*) was often omitted probably because of the final *s* sound: the phrases *for goodness sake*, *for conscience sake* continue to be written without the apostrophe.

salacious [mid 17th century] The word *salacious* which conveys 'undue interest in sexual matters' is based on Latin *salax*, *salac-* (from *salire* 'to leap').

salad [late Middle English] *Salad* is from Old French *salade*, from Provençal *salada*, based on Latin *sal* 'salt'. The word is based on the 'seasoning' of the mixed vegetables. The phrase *salad days* referring to a time of inexperience is from Shakespeare's *Antony and Cleopatra*: (My salad days when I was green in judgement, cold in blood).

salary [Middle English] This is from Anglo-Norman French *salarie*, from Latin *salarium*, originally a Roman soldier's allowance to buy salt, from *sal* 'salt'. From around 1390 to 1520 the word was commonly applied to the stipend of a priest. A *salary* is now often restricted to payment for non-manual work, contrasting with *wage*.

sale [late Old English] Late Old English *sala* is from Old Norse *sala*, of Germanic origin; it is related to *sell*. Use of the word for the selling of goods at a lower price for quick disposal dates from the mid 19th century (e.g. *end-of-season sale*).
→ SELL

salient [mid 16th century] This was first used as a heraldic term meaning 'leaping'. It comes from Latin *salient-*, the present participial stem of the verb *salire* 'to leap'. The sense 'outstanding, significant' as in *salient point* is found from the mid 19th century.

saliva [late Middle English] This is a use of a Latin word. Mid 17th-century **salivate** is from Latin *salivare* 'produce saliva', from *saliva*. Extension of the use in the phrase *salivate at* meaning 'relish the prospect of (doing something)' arose in the 1970s.

sallow [Old English] This word meaning 'of an unhealthy yellow colour' is from *salo* 'dusky'. It is from a Germanic source related to Old Norse *sǫlr* 'yellow', from a base meaning 'dirty'.

sally [late Middle English] This word for a 'sortie, sudden rush' is from French *saillie*, the feminine past participle form (used as a noun) of *saillir* 'come or jut out'. This is from Old French *salir* 'to leap', from Latin *salire*.

saloon [early 18th century] Early examples of the word reflected the sense 'drawing room'. It is from French *salon*, from Italian *salone* 'large hall', an augmentative of *sala* 'hall'. It started to be used for a large area in a passenger boat from the early 19th century, and in the contexts of rail travel (*dining saloon*) and the sale of alcohol (*saloon bar*) from the middle of that century. At the start of the 20th century, examples are found of *saloon* as a type of car.

salt [Old English] *Salt* (in Old English *sealt* as a noun, and *sealtan* as a verb) has a Germanic origin; related noun forms are Dutch *zout* and German *Salz*, from an Indo-European root shared by Latin *sal* and Greek *hals* 'salt'. Late Middle English **souse** (from Old French *sous* 'pickle') is related to *salt*; it was first used as a name for pickled meat. The late Middle English compound:

■ **salt cellar** has, as its second element, the obsolete *saler*, from Old French *salier* 'salt-box', from Latin *salarium*. The change in the spelling was due to sense association with *cellar*.
→ SALARY

salutary [late Middle English] Early use of this word was as a noun meaning 'remedy'. It comes from French *salutaire* or Latin *salutaris*, from *salus*, *salut-* 'health'. The sense in English is 'conducive to health', comparable to mid 16th-century **salubrious** (based on Latin *salubris*) which also shares the base *salus* 'health'.

salute [late Middle English] *Salute* is from Latin *salutare* 'greet, pay one's respects to', from *salus*, *salut-* 'health, welfare, greeting'; the noun is partly from Old French *salut*.
→ SALUTARY

salvage [mid 17th century] Originally *salvage* was 'payment for saving a ship or its cargo'. The word comes from French, from medieval Latin *salvagium*, from Latin *salvare* 'to save'. The verb dates from the late 19th century.

salvation [Middle English] This comes from Old French *salvacion*, from ecclesiastical Latin *salvation-* (from *salvare* 'to save'), translating Greek *sōtēria*. It is generally 'saving and deliverance' but most commonly it is in the religious context of 'saving the soul'.

salve [Old English] The Old English noun *sealfe* and verb *sealfian* have a Germanic origin, related to Dutch *zalf* and German *Salbe*, from a base meaning 'clarified butter, grease'.

salver [mid 17th century] This is from French *salve* 'tray for presenting food to the king', from Spanish *salva* 'sampling of food', from *salvar* 'make safe'. The tray therefore openly displayed the cup from which the tasting had been done, thereby proving the safety of the contents.

salvo [late 16th century] This word for a 'volley of shots' was written formerly as *salve*. The source is French *salve*, Italian *salva* 'salutation'.

same [Middle English] *Same* is from Old Norse *sami*, from an Indo-European root shared by Sanskrit *sama*, Greek *homos*. The slang **samey** is recorded from the 1920s.

sample [Middle English] This comes from an Anglo-Norman French variant of Old French *essample* 'example'. An early but now obsolete use of the word was 'suppositious case, fact serving as an illustration'. Scientific application in the sense 'specimen' started in the late 19th century. Current verb meanings date from the mid 18th century. Middle English **sampler** described 'an example to be imitated': this comes from Old French *essamplaire* 'exemplar'; from the early 16th century it referred to a beginner's exercise in embroidery.

sanction [late Middle English] A *sanction* was once 'an ecclesiastical decree'. It comes from French, from Latin *sanctio(n-)*, from *sancire* 'ratify'. The word's use a legal term for a type of 'penalty' dates from the early 17th century. The verb dates from the late 18th century.

sanctuary [Middle English] The source of English *sanctuary* is Old French *sanctuaire*, from Latin *sanctuarium*, from *sanctus* 'holy'. The early sense was 'a church or other sacred place where a fugitive was immune, by the law of the medieval church, from arrest'.

sand [Old English] Of Germanic origin, *sand* is related to Dutch *zand* and German *Sand*. The idiomatic phrase *happy as a sandboy* (early 19th century) is probably with original reference to a boy hawking sand for sale; *bury one's head in the sand* came into use from the mid 19th century.

sandal [late Middle English] This came via Latin from Greek *sandalion*, a diminutive of *san-*

dalon 'wooden shoe', probably of Asiatic origin and related to Persian *sandal*.

sandwich [mid 18th century] This word derives its name from the 4th Earl of *Sandwich* (1718–92), an English nobleman said to have eaten food in this form so that he would not have to leave the gaming table thereby losing precious time.

sanguine [Middle English] This comes from Old French *sanguin(e)* 'blood red', from Latin *sanguineus* 'of blood', from *sanguis*, *sanguin-* 'blood'. In medieval physiology *sanguine* was one of the four complexions, characterized by the predominance of the blood over the other three humours. A ruddy countenance, with a positive, amorous, and hopeful character, were signs of this complexion or temperament.

sanitary [mid 19th century] *Sanitary* is from French *sanitaire*, from Latin *sanitas* 'health', from *sanus* 'healthy'. From the same period, **sanitation** was formed irregularly from *sanitary*.

sanity [late Middle English] The early sense recorded was 'health', the source being Latin *sanitas* in this sense, from *sanus* 'healthy'. Current meanings relating to mental health date from the early 17th century when **sane** was first recorded. This is from Latin *sanus* 'healthy'; its use to mean 'mentally sound' is due to the antithesis with *insane*, exclusively used in the context of mental ill health.

sap [Old English] Old English *sæp* 'vital fluid' is probably of Germanic origin. The verb (as in *sapped his energy*) dating from the mid 18th century is often interpreted as a figurative use of the notion 'drain the sap from'; it derives however originally from the late 16th-century verb *sap* 'dig a tunnel or covered trench' thus meaning 'undermine'. The latter is from French *super*, from Italian *zappare*, from *zappa* 'spade, spadework', probably from Arabic *sarab* 'underground passage', or *sabora* 'probe a wound, explore'.

sarcasm [mid 16th century] *Sarcasm* is from French *sarcasme*, or via late Latin from late Greek *sarkasmos*, from *sarkazein* 'gnash the teeth, speak bitterly' (earlier found meaning 'tear flesh', from *sarx*, *sark-* 'flesh'). Late 17th-century **sarcastic** is from French *sarcastique*, from *sarcasme*, on the pattern of pairs such as *enthousiasme*, *enthousiastique*.

sarcophagus [late Middle English] This word for a 'stone coffin' came via Latin from Greek *sarkophagos* 'flesh-consuming', from *sarx*, *sark-* 'flesh' and *-phagos* '-eating'. The word was first used for a type of stone reputed amongst the Greeks to have the property of consuming the flesh of dead bodies in contact with it.

sash[1] [late 16th century] This word for a loop of cloth worn round the body was written earlier as *shash*, a term for fine fabric twisted round the head as a turban. The source is Arabic *šāš* 'muslin, turban'.

sash[2] [late 17th century] This *sash* as in *sash window* is an alteration of *chassis* which was apparently interpreted as a plural and shortened.

Satan [Old English] This came via late Latin and Greek from Hebrew *śāṭān*, literally 'adversary', from *śāṭan* 'plot against'.

satchel [Middle English] *Satchel* is from Old French *sachel*, from Latin *saccellus* 'small bag'.

sate [early 17th century] This word meaning 'satisfy' is probably an alteration of dialect *sade* 'make weary of', from Old English *sadian* 'become sated or weary' (related to *sad*). The change in the final consonant was due to association with *satiate*.
→ SAD; SATIATE

satellite [mid 16th century] The early word had the sense 'follower, obsequious underling'. It comes from French *satellite* or Latin *satelles*, *satellit-* 'attendant'. The association of the word with an orbit around an astronomical body dates from the end of the 19th century.

satiate [late Middle English] This comes from Latin *satiatus*, the past participle of *satiare* 'satiate', from *satis* 'enough'.

satin [late Middle English] The word *satin* came via Old French. Arabic *zaytūnī* 'of Tsinkiang' is apparently synonymous and refers to a town in China the locality of which is disputed. Late 19th-century **sateen** is an alteration of *satin*, on the pattern of *velveteen*.

satire [early 16th century] This is from French, or from Latin *satira*, a later form of *satura* 'poetic medley' in which follies or vices were held up to ridicule. The adjective **satirical** (based on late Latin *satiricus* from *satira*) dates from the same period.

satisfaction [Middle English] This is either from Old French, or from Latin *satisfactio(n-)*, from *satisfacere* 'satisfy, content', from *satis* 'enough' and *facere* 'make'. The earliest recorded use referred to the last part of religious penance after 'contrition' and 'confession': this involved fulfilment of the observance that the confessor asked and expected, in contrast with the current meaning 'fulfilment of one's own expectations'. The related word **satisfactory** is late Middle English when it meant 'leading to the atonement of sin'; this is from Old French *satisfactoire* or medieval Latin *satisfactorius*, from Latin *sat-*

isfacere; current senses date from the mid 17th century. Late Middle English **satisfy** is from Old French *satisfier*, formed irregularly from Latin *satisfacere*.

saturate [late Middle English] This was first recorded as an adjective in the sense 'satisfied'. It is from Latin *saturare* 'fill, glut', from *satur* 'full'. The early sense of the verb in the mid 16th century was 'satisfy'; the noun dates from the 1950s. The noun **saturation** (mid 16th century) is from late Latin *saturatio(n-)*, from the same Latin source verb.

sauce [Middle English] *Sauce* is from Old French, based on Latin *salsus*, the past participle of *salere* 'to salt', from *sal* 'salt'. Early 16th-century **saucy**, based on *sauce*, was first recorded with the sense 'savoury, flavoured with sauce'; it started to reflect the sense 'insolent' in the early 16th century, but later mellowed into 'cheeky'. **Sassy** is a mid 19th-century variant of *saucy*.
→ SALAD

saucer [Middle English] This was initially a term for a condiment dish. It is from Old French *saussier(e)* 'sauce boat', probably suggested by late Latin *salsarium*. It started to describe a small shallow dish to support a cup from the early 18th century.

saunter [late Middle English] The early sense recorded was 'to muse, wonder' but the word's origin is unknown. The current sense dates from the mid 17th century.

sausage [late Middle English] This is from Old Northern French *saussiche*, from medieval Latin *salsicia*, from Latin *salsus* 'salted'. The colloquial phrase *silly old sausage* arose at the beginning of the 20th century; *not a sausage* meaning 'nothing at all' dates from the 1930s.
→ SAUCE

savage [Middle English] *Savage* is from Old French *sauvage* 'wild', from Latin *silvaticus* 'of the woods', from *silva* 'a wood'. The noun sense 'uncivilized person, living a primitive life' dates from the late 16th century (Shakespeare *Love's Labour's Lost*: Vouchsafe to show the sunshine of your face, That we (like savages) may worship it). *Noble savage* came to be used as a phrase appreciating the virtues of a simple state of development (Dryden *Conquest of Granada*: I am as free as Nature first made man 'Ere the base Laws of Servitude began When wild in woods the noble savage ran); the French writer Rousseau (1712-78) conceived of the *noble savage* as morally superior to civilized man.

save¹ [Middle English] *Save* 'rescue, protect' (*save someone's life*), 'reserve, lay aside' (*save money*), and 'avoid' (*it will save wear and tear*) is from Old French *sauver*, from late Latin *salvare* (from Latin *salvus* 'safe'). The noun dates from the late 19th century as a sports term. **Savings** referring to money put by for use later is found from the early 18th century. The word **saviour** is a Middle English word from Old French *sauveour*, from ecclesiastical Latin *salvator* (translating Greek *sōtēr*), from late Latin *salvare* 'to save'.

save² [Middle English] This *save* meaning 'except' (as in *the room was empty save for a single chair*) is from Old French *sauf, sauve*, from Latin *salvo, salva*: this is the ablative singular of *salvus* 'safe', used in phrases such as *salvo jure, salva innocentia* 'with no violation of right or innocence'.

savour [Middle English] *Savour* is from Old French, from Latin *sapor*, from *sapere* 'to taste', a base shared by Middle English **savoury** first recorded in the sense 'pleasing to the sense of taste or smell': this comes from Old French *savoure* 'tasty, fragrant'.

saw [Old English] Old English *saga* describing a cutting tool is Germanic in origin, related to Dutch *zaag*. Middle English **sawyer** was written earlier as *sawer*. The compound **see-saw** dates from the mid-17th century and was originally used by sawyers as a rhythmical refrain in the to-and-fro motion of their work: it is a reduplication of the verb *saw*.

say [Old English] Old English *secgan* is of Germanic origin, related to Dutch *zeggen* and German *sagen*. *Say, speak*, and *tell* are near-synonyms but *say* is usually followed by the words or statement actually said, giving the verb the sense 'utter, declare'. Of the idiomatic phrases, *when all is said and done* dates from the mid 16th century; *to say it with flowers* arose in the early 20th century as an advertising slogan of the Society of American Florists. *You can say that again* was originally a US usage from the 1940s. The phrase *I say, I say, I say* to introduce a joke started in the 1960s.

scab [Middle English] This comes from Old Norse *skabb*; related forms are dialect *shab*. The sense 'contemptible person' dating from the late 16th century was probably influenced by Middle Dutch *schabbe* 'slut'. It was used to refer to a blackleg in a strike from the mid 18th century; the usage was originally US.
→ SHABBY

scabbard [Middle English] *Scabbard*, a sheath for the blade of a dagger, is from Anglo-Norman French *escalberc*, from a Germanic compound of words meaning 'cut' (related to *shear*) and 'protect' (related to the second element of *hauberk*).

scaffold [Middle English] A *scaffold* first denoted a temporary platform from which to repair or erect a building. It comes from Anglo-Norman French, from Old French (e)*schaffaut*, from the base of *catafalque*. It was around the middle of the 16th century that the word came to be used for a platform for the execution of criminals.

scald [Middle English] This was first recorded in verb use and comes from Anglo-Norman French *escalder*, from late Latin *excaldare* 'wash in hot water': the elements here are Latin *ex-* 'thoroughly' and *calidus* 'hot'. The noun dates from the early 17th century.

scale¹ [Middle English] This *scale* found commonly in the plural meaning an instrument for weighing had the early sense 'drinking cup', a meaning which survives in South African English. It comes from Old Norse *skál* 'bowl' from a Germanic source; related forms are Dutch *schaal*, German *Schale* 'bowl', and English dialect *shale* 'dish' (which is related to mid 18th-century **shale** describing a type of rock). The Germanic base is shared by the *scale* of *fish scales*; this is a shortening of Old French *escale* in Middle English.

scale² [late Middle English] This *scale* for a graduated range of values is from Latin *scala* 'ladder'. The verb (as in *scaled the cliff face*) came via Old French *escaler* or medieval Latin *scalare* 'climb', from the base of Latin *scandere* 'to climb'.

scalp [Middle English] This word was originally a term for the skull or cranium and is probably of Scandinavian origin. The modern sense arose at the beginning of the 17th century.

scamp [mid 18th century] A *scamp* was once a highwayman: it comes from obsolete *scamp* 'rob on the highway', probably from Middle Dutch *schampen* 'slip away', from Old French *eschamper*. Early usage (still reflected in West Indian English) was derogatory, whereas the tone is now more playful.

scamper [late 17th century] The first recorded sense was 'run away'; it was very common between 1687 and 1700; it may have been military slang either from obsolete Dutch *schampen* 'escape, be gone' or from Italian *scampare* 'decamp'.

scan [late Middle English] This was first used as a verb in the sense 'analyse the metre (of a line of verse)'. The source is Latin *scandere* 'climb' (in late Latin 'scan (verses)'), by analogy with the raising and lowering of one's foot when marking rhythm. From this 'analyse (metre)', the sense developed into 'estimate the

correctness of' and 'examine minutely', which in turn led to 'look at searchingly' in the late 18th century. The related noun **scansion** is found in examples from the mid 17th century, from Latin *scansio(n-)*, from *scandere*.

scandal [Middle English] *Scandal* originally had the sense 'a discredit to religion (by the reprehensible behaviour of a cleric)'. It comes from Old French *scandale*, from ecclesiastical Latin *scandalum* 'cause of offence', from Greek *skandalon* 'snare, stumbling block'. The sense 'damage to reputation' is first found recorded in Shakespeare's *Comedy of Errors*: I wonder much That you would put me to this shame and trouble, And not without some scandal to your self, With circumstance and oaths, so to deny this chain, which now you wear so openly. The late 15th-century verb **scandalize** meant 'make a public scandal of': this is from French *scandaliser* or ecclesiastical Latin *scandalizare*, from Greek *skandalizein*.

scant [Middle English] *Scant* is from Old Norse *skamt*, the neuter form of *skammr* 'short'. The adjective **scanty** dating from the late 16th century is based on *scant*.

scapegoat [mid 16th century] This is from the archaic word *scape* meaning 'escape' and *goat*. The reference was to the ritual of the Day of Atonement (Leviticus 16) where one goat was selected for sacrifice and a second was chosen to be sent alive into the wilderness symbolically bearing the sins of the people ('escaping' death). The sense was generalized in the early 19th century.

scar [late Middle English] *Scar* is probably a truncation of Old French *escharre*, via late Latin from Greek *eskhara* 'scab from a burn' (literally 'hearth').

scarce [Middle English] *Scarce* once had the sense 'restricted in quantity or size' and 'parsimonious'. It is from a shortening of Anglo-Norman French, from a Romance word meaning 'plucked out, selected'.

scare [Middle English] *Scare* is from Old Norse *skirra* 'to frighten', from *skjarr* 'timid'.

scarf [mid 16th century] A *scarf* once described a 'sash (around the waist or over the shoulder)'. Worn chiefly by officials or soldiers it served for carrying things. It is likely that it is based on Old Northern French *escarpe*, probably identical with Old French *escharpe* 'pilgrim's bag or pouch'.

scarlet [Middle English] This word originally denoting any brightly coloured cloth, but often bright red. It is shortening of Old French *escarlate*, from medieval Latin *scarlata*: this came via Arabic and medieval Greek from late Latin *sigillatus* 'decorated with small images', from *sigillum* 'small image'. The sense 'red with shame or indignation' dates from the mid 19th century. The phrase *scarlet woman* arose in the early 19th century, originally applied (as *scarlet lady*) as a derogatory reference with allusion to Revelation 17 to the Roman Catholic Church, by those who perceived it as devoted to showy ritual.

scarper [mid 19th century] This is probably from Italian *scappare* 'to escape', influenced by the rhyming slang *Scapa Flow* 'go'.

scathe [Middle English] *Scathe* is from Old Norse *skathi* (noun), *skatha* (verb), related to the Dutch and German verb *schaden*. The early meaning, now archaic or Scots, was 'injure, hurt'; the modern sense 'wither with satire' started in the mid 19th century, reflected too in the adjective **scathing**.

scatter [Middle English] First found as a verb, *scatter* is probably a variant of *shatter*. The word **scat** in use from the mid 19th century may be an abbreviation of *scatter*, or may be from the sound of a hiss (used to drive an animal away) combined with -*cat*.

scatty [early 20th century] This is an abbreviation of late 18th-century **scatterbrained**.
→ SCATTER

scavenge [mid 16th century] This is an alteration of the earlier word *scavager* which comes from Anglo-Norman French *scawager*, from Old Northern French *escauwer* 'inspect'; Flemish *scauwen* 'to show' is the base. The term originally referred to an officer who collected *scavage*, a toll on foreign merchants' goods offered for sale in a town; later it was a word for a person who kept the streets clean. The mid 17th-century verb **scavenge** had the early sense 'clean out (dirt)': this is a back-formation (by removal of the suffix) from *scavenger*.

scenario [late 19th century] This is an adoption of an Italian word from Latin *scena* 'scene'.

scene [mid 16th century] In early use a *scene* was a subdivision of a play, or (a piece of) stage scenery. It comes from Latin *scena*, from Greek *skēnē* 'tent, stage'. **Scenic** in the early 17th century when it was first recorded, had the sense 'theatrical': this came via Latin from Greek *skēnikos* 'of the stage', from *skēnē*. Mid 18th-century **scenery** had the early spelling *scenary* and is from Italian *scenario*; the change in the ending was due to association with English words ending in -*ery*.
→ SCENARIO

scent [late Middle English] This was first used as a term in hunting to refer to the sense of smell. It comes from Old French *sentir* 'perceive, smell', from Latin *sentire*. The addition of -*c*- in the 17th century is unexplained. Use of the word to mean 'perfume' dates from the mid 18th century.

sceptic [late 16th century] This word was first used to refer to a philosopher denying the possibility of knowledge in a certain sphere; the leading ancient *sceptic* was Pyrrho whose followers at the Academy vigorously opposed Stoicism. The origin is either French *sceptique* or (via Latin) Greek *skeptikos*, from *skepsis* 'inquiry, doubt'.

sceptre [Middle English] *Sceptre* is from Old French *ceptre*, via Latin from Greek *skēptron*, from *skēptein* an alteration of *skēptesthai* 'lean on'.

schedule [late Middle English] An early *schedule* was a 'scroll, explanatory note, appendix'. It comes via Old French from late Latin *schedula* 'slip of paper', a diminutive of *scheda*, from Greek *skhedē* 'papyrus leaf'. The sense 'timetable' is found from the mid 19th century in US usage; it was during this period that the verb came into use.

scheme [mid 16th century] This was a term in rhetoric originally for 'a figure of speech'; it comes from Latin *schema*, from Greek. An early sense was 'diagram of the position of celestial objects', giving rise to 'diagram, outline', which led to the current senses. The unfavourable notion of 'plot' arose in the mid 18th century. Late 18th-century **schema** (from Greek *skhēma* 'form, figure') was first used as a term in philosophy; **schematic** pre-dated this (early 17th century) and comes from modern Latin *schematismus*, from Greek *skhēmatismos* 'assumption of a certain form', from *skhēma*.

schism [late Middle English] This comes from Old French *scisme*, via ecclesiastical Latin from Greek *skhisma* 'cleft', from *skhizein* 'to split'.

school[1] [Old English] Old English *scōl*, *scolu* 'place for instruction' came via Latin from Greek *skholē* 'leisure, philosophy, lecture-place', reinforced in Middle English by Old French *escole*. **Scholar** was written in Old English as *scol(i)ere* 'schoolchild, student', from late Latin *scholaris*, from Latin *schola*.

school[2] [late Middle English] This *school* as in *school of whales* is from Middle Low German, Middle Dutch *schōle*, from a West Germanic source. Old English *scolu* 'troop' is related.
→ SHOAL[1]

science [Middle English] The early word *science* simply meant 'knowledge'. It comes from Old French, from Latin *scientia*, from *scire* 'know'. The more specific use of the term for a branch of study such as biology and physics arose in the early 18th century. Prior to that in the Middle Ages, the phrase *the seven liberal sciences* was synonymous with *the seven liberal arts* for the Trivium (Grammar, Logic, and Rhetoric) and the Quadrivium (Arithmetic, Music, Geometry, and Astronomy). The adjective **scientific** dates from the late 16th century, from French *scientifique* or late Latin *scientificus* 'producing knowledge', from *scientia*. Early use described the liberal arts (or sciences) as opposed to the 'mechanic' arts (i.e. those requiring manual skill).

scintillate [early 17th century] This comes from Latin *scintillare* 'sparkle', from *scintilla* 'spark'.

scissors [late Middle English] *Scissors* is from Old French *cisoires*, from late Latin *cisoria*, the plural of *cisorium* 'cutting instrument'. The prefix *cis-* here is a variant of *caes-*, the stem of *caedere* 'to cut'. The spelling with *sc-* occurred in the 16th century by association with the Latin stem *sciss-* 'cut'.

scoff[1] [Middle English] This *scoff* was first used as a noun in the sense 'mockery, scorn' and was often found in the phrase *make scoff*. It may be of Scandinavian origin.

scoff[2] [late 18th century] This informal word for 'eat ravenously' was originally a variant of Scots and dialect *scaff*. The noun meaning 'food' is from Afrikaans *schoff*, representing Dutch *schoft* meaning 'quarter of a day', and by extension each of the four meals of the day.

scold [Middle English] This is probably from Old Norse *skáld* 'poet'; there may have been an intermediate sense 'lampooner'. In early use in English the word often referred to a woman using ribald language; the verb started out with the meaning 'behave as a scold' and gained the sense 'chide' in the early 18th century.

scoop [Middle English] This was originally a word for a utensil for pouring liquids. It comes from Middle Dutch, Middle Low German *schōpe* 'waterwheel bucket'; from a West Germanic base meaning 'draw water'. The use of the word in journalism for an 'exclusive story' dates from the late 19th century in US English.
→ SHAPE

scope [mid 16th century] This was originally a 'target for shooting at'. It comes from Italian *scopo* 'aim', from Greek *skopos* 'target', from *skeptesthai* 'look out'. The sense 'reach, range' (e.g. *limited in scope*) developed in the early 17th century.

scorch [Middle English] This word, first used as a verb, is perhaps related to Old Norse *skorpna* 'be shrivelled'. *Scorched earth policy* (translating a Chinese phrase) came into use in

the 1930s describing the policy of destroying all means of sustenance in a country which could be of use to an invading army.

score [late Old English] Late Old English *scoru* meant 'set of twenty'; it comes from Old Norse *skor* 'notch, tally, twenty' from a Germanic source; English *shear* is related. The verb (late Middle English) is from Old Norse *skora* 'make an incision'.
→ SHEAR

scorn [Middle English] *Scorn* is a shortening of Old French *escarn* (noun), *escharnir* (verb), of Germanic origin. The phrase *hell hath no fury like a woman scorned* is found in the following form initially in 1697: Heav'n has no Rage, like Love to Hatred turn'd, Nor Hell a Fury, like a Woman scorn'd (William Congreve *Mourning Bride*).

scotch [early 17th century] *Scotch* as in *scotched the rumours* was first recorded in noun use for 'a block placed under a wheel'. This sense 'put an end to' dates from the early 19th century and is from the notion of wedging or blocking something so as to render it inoperative. The word's origin is unknown but it may be related to *skate*. The sense 'injure and temporarily render harmless' (e.g. *feudal power was scotched, though far from killed*) is based on an emendation of Shakespeare's We have scotch'd the snake, not kill'd it (*Macbeth*), originally understood as a use of late Middle English *scotch* 'score, cut the surface of'.

scour[1] [Middle English] *Scour* 'cleanse by hard rubbing' is from Middle Dutch, Middle Low German *schüren*, from Old French *escurer*. Late Latin *excurare* 'clean (off)' is the source, from *ex-* 'away' and *curare* 'to clean'.

scour[2] [late Middle English] This *scour* meaning 'range about in search of something' (as in *scoured the country*) is related to obsolete *scour* 'moving hastily', of unknown origin.

scourge [Middle English] *Scourge* is a shortening of Old French *escorge* (noun), *escorgier* (verb), from Latin *ex-* 'thoroughly' and *corrigia* 'thong, whip'. It is a word used most often figuratively as in the *Scourge of God* (= instrument of divine chastisement), the title given by historians to Attila the Hun in the 5th century.

scout [late Middle English] The verb was the first recorded, from Old French *escouter* 'listen'; the earlier form was *ascolter*, from Latin *auscultare*. The noun is from Old French *escoute* 'act of listening'. Early phrases in English were *on the scout* and *in scout* meaning 'on the lookout'. Military use arose in the mid 16th century; the word *Scout* (originally *Boy Scout*) has also been used for a member of the organization established General Baden-Powell in 1908.

scowl [late Middle English] Scowl is probably of Scandinavian origin related to Danish *skule* 'scowl'. The noun dates from the early 16th century.

scrabble [mid 16th century] 'Make marks at random, scrawl' was the early sense of *scrabble* from Middle Dutch *schrabbelen*: this is a frequentative (= verb of repeated action) of *schrabben* 'to scrape'. The noun sense 'a scramble to obtain something' (e.g. *the scrabble for the dropped coins*) is originally a North American usage dating from the late 18th century.

scramble [late 16th century] This is an imitative word comparable to the dialect words *scamble* meaning 'stumble' and *cramble* meaning 'crawl'. The word **scram** which appeared in the early 20th century is probably from the verb *scramble*.

scrap¹ [late Middle English] This was first found as a plural noun referring to fragments of uneaten food. It comes from Old Norse *skrap* 'scraps', related to *skrapa* 'to scrape'. The verb 'make refuse of' dates from the late 19th century.

scrap² [late 17th century] This *scrap* meaning 'fight' was first used in the sense 'sinister plot, scheme'. It may be from the noun *scrape*.

scrape [Old English] Old English *scrapian* meant 'scratch with the fingernails'. Of Germanic origin, it was reinforced in Middle English by Old Norse *skrapa* or Middle Dutch *schrapen* 'to scratch'. The sense 'awkward predicament' (e.g. *got himself into a scrape*) dates from the early 18th century and is probably from the notion of being 'scraped' making one's way along a narrow passage.

scratch [late Middle English] Scratch is probably a blend of the synonymous dialect words *scrat* and *cratch*, both of uncertain origin; Middle Low German *kratsen* and Old High German *krazzōn* may be related. The idiomatic phrase *scratch the surface of* dates from the early 20th century. Use of the word in sport in the phrase *scratch from* (*a race or competition*) is from the notion of scratching out one's name from the list of competitors; it was originally with reference to Oxford undergraduates taking part of an examination but withdrawing before the viva voce.

scrawl [early 17th century] This is apparently an alteration of the verb *crawl*, perhaps influenced by the obsolete *scrawl* 'sprawl'.

scrawny [mid 19th century] Scrawny is a variant of dialect *scranny*; archaic *scrannel* 'weak, feeble' referring to sound, is related (Milton *Lycidas*: Their lean and flashy songs Grate on their scrannel Pipes of wretched straw).

scream [Middle English] The origin of *scream* is uncertain; it may be from Middle Dutch. The sense 'express oneself angrily' (e.g. *screamed at her for breaking the glass*) dates from the late 19th century.

screech [mid 16th century] This is an alteration of archaic *scritch* 'utter a loud cry', which is imitative of the sound.

screed [Middle English] Screed is probably a variant of the noun *shred*. The early sense was 'fragment cut from a main piece', then 'torn strip, tatter', which gave in the late 18th century (via the notion of a long roll or list) the meaning 'long, tedious speech'. Use of the word in the context of plastering a wall or ceiling dates from the early 19th century.

screen [Middle English] Screen is a shortening of Old Northern French *escren* which has a Germanic origin. Use of the verb to mean 'examine to determine suitability' (e.g. *screened applicants before shortlisting them*) dates from the 1940s.

screw [late Middle English] This is from Old French *escroue* 'female screw, nut', from Latin *scrofa* which is literally 'sow', but which later gained the sense 'screw'. The slang term 'prison warder' dates from the early 19th century. The early sense of the verb was 'contort (the features), twist around' (late 16th century); the slang use 'deceive, defraud', originally North American English, dates from the early 20th century.

scribble [late Middle English] Scribble is from medieval Latin *scribillare*, a diminutive of Latin *scribere* 'write'.

scribe [Middle English] Scribe is from Latin *scriba*, from *scribere* 'write'. The verb was first used in the sense 'write down'; the sense 'mark with a pointed instrument' in technical contexts is perhaps partly a shortening of *describe*.

scrimp [mid 18th century] This was first recorded in the sense 'keep short of (food)'. It comes from Scots *scrimp* 'meagre' and may be related to Middle English *shrimp* (perhaps linked with Middle Low German *schrempen* 'to wrinkle' and Middle High German *schrimpfen* 'to contract'). The sense 'economize' as in *scrimp and save* dates from the mid 19th century.

script [late Middle English] The early sense was 'something written'. It is a shortening of Old French *escript*, from Latin *scriptum*, the neuter past participle form (used as a noun) of *scribere* 'write'. Use of the word in contexts such as *film script* dates from the 1930s.

scripture [Middle English] Scripture is from Latin *scriptura* 'writings', from *script-*, the past participial stem of the verb *scribere* 'write'. Use of the word *Scripture* as the name of a school subject devoted to the study of the Bible and the Christian religion began in the 1920s.

scroll [late Middle English] This is an alteration of obsolete *scrow* 'roll', itself a shortening of *escrow* 'bond, deed' (related to *shred*).
➔ SHRED

scrounge [early 20th century] *Scrounge* is a variant of dialect *scrunge* 'steal'.

scrub[1] [late 16th century] This *scrub* meaning 'clean by brushing vigorously' is probably from Middle Low German, Middle Dutch *schrobben*, *schrubben*.

scrub[2] [late Middle English] The early sense of this *scrub* for brushwood undergrowth was 'stunted tree'; it is a variant of *shrub*.
➔ SHRUB

scruff[1] [late 18th century] This *scruff* as in *scruff of the neck* is an alteration of dialect *scuff* used in this same sense, of which the origin is obscure.

scruff[2] [early 16th century] This *scruff* meaning 'dirty untidy person' had the early sense 'scurf'; it is a variant of *scurf*. The word came to mean 'worthless thing', which led to the current sense in the mid 19th century.

scrunch [late 18th century] 'Eat or bite noisily' was the early sense of *scrunch* which is probably imitative like *crunch*.

scruple [late Middle English] This is from French *scrupule* or Latin *scrupulus*, from *scrupus* which has the literal meaning 'rough pebble' and the figurative meaning (used by Cicero) 'cause of unease or anxiety'. Late Middle English **scrupulous** is originally recorded in the sense 'troubled with doubts': it comes from French *scrupuleux* or Latin *scrupulosus*, from *scrupulus*.

scrutiny [late Middle English] *Scrutiny* is from Latin *scrutinium*, from *scrutari* 'to search' but with the earlier meaning 'sort rubbish', from *scruta* 'rubbish'. Early use referred to the taking of individual votes in an election procedure.

scuffle [late 16th century] This may have a Scandinavian origin and be related to Swedish *skuffa* 'to push'. English *shove* and *shuffle* may also be associated.

scullery [late Middle English] This was first used to refer to the part of a household devoted to kitchen utensils. It comes from Old French *escuelerie*, from *escuele* 'dish', from Latin *scutella* 'salver' (a diminutive of *scutra* 'wooden platter').

sculpture [late Middle English] This comes from Latin *sculptura*, from *sculpere* 'to carve, hollow out'. Mid 17th-century **sculptor** is an English use of a Latin word, also from *sculpere*. The verb **sculpt** is mid 19th-century from French *sculpter*, from *sculpteur* 'sculptor' but regarded as a back-formation (by removal of the suffix) from *sculptor* or *sculpture*.

scum [Middle English] *Scum* is from Middle Low German, Middle Dutch *schūm*, of Germanic origin. Use of the word as a derogatory reference to people (e.g. *scum of the earth*) dates from the late 16th century.

scupper [late 19th century] This was first used as military slang in the sense 'kill, especially in an ambush'. The origin is unknown; the sense 'sink' dates from the 1970s.

scurf [late Old English] Late Old English *sceorf* is from the base of *sceorfan* 'gnaw', *sceorfian* 'cut to shreds'.

scurrilous [late 16th century] This word meaning 'spreading scandalous claims about (someone)' is based on French *scurrile* or Latin *scurrilus* (from *scurra* 'buffoon').

scurry [early 19th century] This is an abbreviation of *hurry-scurry*, a reduplication of *hurry*.

scuttle[1] [late Old English] This *scuttle* as in *coal scuttle* was *scutel* in late Old English meaning 'dish, platter'. It comes from Old Norse *skutill*, from Latin *scutella* 'dish'.

scuttle[2] [late 15th century] This *scuttle* as in *scuttled along the corridor* is perhaps an altered form of dialect *scuddle*, a frequentative (= verb of repeated action) of *scud* 'move quickly'. The latter may be an alteration of the noun *scut* 'hare' giving 'run like a hare'.

scuttle [late 15th century] This *scuttle* in nautical contexts is perhaps from Old French *escoutille*, from the Spanish diminutive *escotilla* 'hatchway'. The verb dates from the mid 17th century.

scythe [Old English] Old English *sīthe* is of Germanic origin, related to Dutch *zeis* and German *Sense*. The etymologically correct spelling *sithe* was preferred by Johnson but did not prevail against the spelling with *sc-* which was probably influenced by Latin *scindere* 'to cut' (as was the spelling of the word *scissors*).

sea [Old English] Old English *sǣ* is Germanic in origin, related to Dutch *zee* and German *See*. Of the phrases: *high sea*, later *high seas*, was found early; *sea change* referring to a profound transformation is from Shakespeare's *Tempest* 1610 (Nothing of him that doth fade, But doth suffer a Sea-change Into something rich and strange) literally referring to someone thought to have drowned; *all at sea* in the context of uncertainty and perplexity dates from the mid 18th century; *worse things happen at sea* is found from the early 19th century.

seal [Middle English] A *seal* originally indicated a piece of wax impressed with a mark and attached to a document as evidence of authenticity. It comes from Old French *seel* (as a noun) and *seeler* (as a verb), from Latin *sigillum* 'small picture': this is a diminutive of *signum* 'a sign'.
→ SCARLET

seam [Old English] Old English *sēam* is of Germanic origin, related to Dutch *zoom* and German *Saum*. Use of the word in geology (*coal seam*) dates from the late 16th century. The word **seamstress** (also late 16th century) is based on archaic *seamster*, *sempster* 'tailor, seamstress', which originally referred to a woman but which in Old English was already starting to be applied to a male tailor.

sear [Old English] Old English *sēarian* is Germanic in origin. The base means 'dry' and the early sense was 'dry up'. In the early 16th century the word is recorded in medical contexts with the meaning 'burn (tissue) by the application of a hot iron'. It became more generalized as 'burn' towards the end of that century.

search [Middle English] This is from the Old French verb *cerchier* from late Latin *circare* 'go round', from Latin *circus* 'circle'. The main semantic strands are 'explore thoroughly' (*search the premises*) and 'try to find' (*search out the truth*).

season [Middle English] *Season* is from Old French *seson*, from Latin *satio(n-)* which initially meant 'sowing' but which later came to mean 'time of sowing', from the root of *serere* 'to sow'. The verb sense 'add savoury flavouring to (a dish)' was in early use; it comes from the primary sense in Old French which was 'to ripen, make (fruit) palatable by the influence of the seasons'.

seat [Middle English] Early use was as a noun. It comes from Old Norse *sæti*, from the Germanic base of *sit*. The verb dates from the late 16th century. Use of the word to mean 'place of abode' as in *country seat* dates from the early 17th century.
→ SIT

seclude [late Middle English] The early sense recorded was 'obstruct access to' and the word was often used loosely as a synonym of *exclude*. It comes from Latin *secludere*, from *se-* 'apart' and *claudere* 'to shut'. Early 17th-century **seclusion** is from medieval Latin *seclusio(n-)*, from *secludere* 'shut off'.

second[1] [Middle English] The *second* referring to two in a series came via Old French from Latin *secundus* 'following, second', from the base of *sequi* 'follow'. The verb dates from the late 16th century. **Secondary** is late Middle English from Latin *secundarius* 'of the second quality or class', from *secundus*.

second[2] [late Middle English] The time word *second* is from medieval Latin *secunda (minuta)* 'second (minute)', the feminine form (used as a noun) of *secundus*, referring to the 'second' operation of dividing an hour by sixty.

second[3] [early 19th century] The verb *second* as in *seconded to another department for six months* is from French *en second* 'in the second rank (of officers)'. The use was originally military involving the removal of an officer temporarily from his regiment to an extra-regimental appointment.

secret [late Middle English] *Secret* is from Old French, from the Latin adjective *secretus* meaning 'separate, set apart', from *secernere* (from *se-* 'apart' and *cernere* 'to sift'). Late Middle English **secrecy** is from *secret*, probably formed on the pattern of *privacy*. Mid 19th-century **secretive** is a back-formation (by removal of the suffix) from *secretiveness*, suggested by French *secrètivité*, from *secret*.

secretary [late Middle English] This originally referred to a 'person entrusted with a secret'. It comes from late Latin *secretarius* 'confidential officer', from Latin *secretum* 'secret', the neuter of *secretus*. The early 19th-century word **secretariat** is via French from medieval Latin *secretariatus*, from *secretarius*.
→ SECRET

secrete [mid 18th century] This verb meaning 'keep hidden' is an alteration of the obsolete verb *secret* 'keep secret'.

secretion [mid 17th century] *Secretion* comes from French *sécrétion* or Latin *secretio(n-)* 'separation', from *secernere* 'move apart'. The verb **secrete** 'produce and discharge' (*secreting insulin*) dates from the early 18th century as a back-formation (by removal of the suffix) from *secretion*.

sect [Middle English] *Sect* is from Old French *secte* or Latin *secta* with the literal meaning 'following', thus giving 'faction, party', from the stem of *sequi* 'follow'. Mid 17th-century **sectarian** is based on *sectary* 'a member of a sect', reinforced by the word *sect*.

section [late Middle English] This comes from French *section* or Latin *sectio(n-)*, from *secare* 'to cut (off)'. The verb dates from the early 19th century; the transferred use 'cause (someone) to be compulsorily detained in a mental hospital' dates from the 1980s. The related word **sector** (late 16th century in mathematical contexts) is from late Latin, a technical use of Latin *sector* 'cutter', from *secare*.

secular [Middle English] Use of the word in contexts where there is a contrast between religious life and civil or lay life is from Old French *seculer*, from Latin *saecularis*. Latin *saeculum* 'generation, age' is the base, used in Christian Latin to mean 'the world' as opposed to the Church. Use of *secular* in astronomy or economics (*secular acceleration*, *secular trend*) dating from the early 19th century, is from Latin *saecularis* 'relating to an age or period'.

security [late Middle English] *Security* is from Old French *securite* or Latin *securitas*, from *securus* 'free from care', the source of mid 16th-century **secure**: this meant 'feeling no apprehension' in early examples. The Latin base elements are *se-* 'without' and *cura* 'care'. Also from Latin *securitas* is Middle English **surety** (via Old French) which referred in early use to 'something given to support an undertaking that someone will fulfil an obligation'.

sedate [late Middle English] This word meaning 'calm and dignified' was originally a medical term meaning 'not sore or painful' and 'tranquil'. It comes from Latin *sedatus*, the past participle of *sedare* 'settle', from *sedere* 'sit'.

sedative [late Middle English] *Sedative* is from Old French *sedatif* or medieval Latin *sedativus*, from Latin *sedare* 'settle'. **Sedation** dates from the mid 16th century, from French *sédation* or Latin *sedatio(n-)*, from *sedare*. From this as a back-formation (by removal of the suffix), came **sedate** found from the 1960s.
→ SEDATE

sedentary [late 16th century] 'Not migratory' was the early sense of *sedentary* from French *sédentaire* or Latin *sedentarius*, from *sedere* 'sit'.

sediment [mid 16th century] This word is from French *sédiment* or Latin *sedimentum* 'settling', from *sedere* 'sit'.

seduce [late 15th century] This was originally used in the sense 'persuade (someone) to abandon their duty'. Latin *seducere* is the source, from *se-* 'away, apart' and *ducere* 'to lead'. The same Latin base is shared (from the early 16th century) by **seduction**, from French *séduction* or Latin *seductio(n-)*; and (from the mid 18th century) **seductive** from *seduction* influenced by pairs such as *induction*, *inductive*. **Seductress** appeared in the early 19th century from obsolete *seductor* 'male seducer', also from *seducere*.

see[1] [Old English] Old English *sēon* 'perceive by sight' is Germanic in origin, related to Dutch *zien* and German *sehen*, perhaps from an Indo-European root shared by Latin *sequi* 'follow'. The imperative *see!* as in *see! I told you he would come* and *now see here!* was common from early times; it was often accompanied by a personal pronoun which is still seen in the dialect *sithee*, the equivalent of *look you*. The sense 'deem' (e.g. *see fit*) dates from Middle English; 'escort' (as in *see them to the door, please*) dates from the early 17th century (Shakespeare *Coriolanus*: Go see him out at Gates … Give him deserv'd vexation).

see[2] [Middle English] This *see* as in *bishop's see* is from Anglo-Norman French *sed*, from Latin *sedes* 'seat', from *sedere* 'sit'.

seed [Old English] Old English *sǣd* is Germanic in origin, related to Dutch *zaad*, German *Saat* and English *sow*. The phrase *go to seed* dates from the 1920s.
→ SOW[1]

seek [Old English] Old English *sēcan* is Germanic in origin, related to Dutch *zieken* and German *suchen*, from an Indo-European root shared by Latin *sagire* 'perceive by scent'.

seem [Middle English] Early senses included 'suit, befit, be appropriate' in phrases such as *ill it seemed me them to censure*. Old Norse *sœma* 'to honour' is the source, from *sœmr* 'fitting'. Middle English **seemly** is from Old Norse *sœmiligr*, from *soemr* 'fitting'.

seep [late 18th century] This is perhaps a dialect form of Old English *sīpian* 'to soak'.

seethe [Old English] Old English *sēothan* meant 'make or keep boiling'. Of Germanic origin it is related to Dutch *zieden*. The sense 'be in a state of inner turmoil' (e.g. *seething with anger*) dates from the early 17th century (Shakespeare *Troilus and Cressida*: I will make a complemental assuault upon him, for my business *soothes*).

segment [late 16th century] This was first used as a term in geometry. It is from Latin *segmentum*, from *secare* 'to cut'. The verb dates from the mid 19th century.

segregate [mid 16th century] This comes from Latin *segregare* 'separate from the flock', from *se-* 'apart' and *grex*, *greg-* 'flock'. **Segregation** comes from the same base and dates from the same period via late Latin *segregatio(n-)*.

seize [Middle English] *Seize* is from Old French *seizir* 'give seisin', from medieval Latin *sacire*, in the phrase *ad proprium sacire* 'claim as one's own', from a Germanic base meaning 'procedure'. The sense 'jam, cease to function' in mechanical contexts dates from the late 19th century.

seldom [Old English] Old English *seldan* is Germanic in origin; related forms are Dutch *zelden* and German *selten*, from a base meaning 'strange, wonderful'.

select [mid 16th century] *Select* is from Latin *select-*, the past participial stem of *seligere* 'select by separating off', from *se-* 'apart' and *legere* 'choose'. The adjective *select* as in *a select group, carefully chosen* meaning 'of special excellence' dates from the late 16th century. **Selection**, an early 17th-century word, is from Latin *selectio(n-)*, from *seligere*.

self [Old English] This is a word of Germanic origin, related to Dutch *zelf* and German *selbe*. Early use was emphatic, expressing the sense '(I) myself', '(he) himself', etc. The verb (e.g. *pollination is usually by selfing*) dates from the early 20th century.

sell [Old English] The Old English verb *sellan* is from a Germanic source, related to Old Norse *selja* 'give up, sell'. Early use included the sense 'give, hand (something) over voluntarily in response to a request', but the chief current sense 'hand over something in return for money' was also recorded early, as was 'betray (someone)'. *Sell oneself* arose in the late 18th century. The word is not common in compounds but *sell-by-date* has been popularized since the 1970s.

semblance [Middle English] This is from Old French, from *sembler* 'seem', from Latin *similare*, *simulare* 'simulate'.

senate [Middle English] *Senate* is from Old French *senat*, from Latin *senatus*, from *senex* 'old man'. Middle English **senator** was first used to refer to a member of the ancient Roman senate: it is from Old French *senateur*, from Latin *senator*.

send [Old English] Old English *sendan* is from a Germanic source, related to Dutch *zenden* and German *senden*. The word branches semantically into: 'order to go' (*sent a messenger*) and 'cause to go' (*sent him flying*); of the idiomatic verbal phrases, *send down* meaning 'send to prison' dates from the mid 19th century and was originally US English; *send up* in the sense 'make fun of' dates from the 1930s.

senior [late Middle English] This is an English use of a Latin word meaning literally 'older, older man', the comparative of *senex*, *sen-* 'old man, old'. The same base is shared by the adjective **senile** (from French *sénile* or Latin *senilis*) which has been in use since the mid 17th century.

sense [late Middle English] Latin *sensus* 'faculty of feeling, thought, meaning' (from *sentire* 'feel') is the source of many English words including, in the late Middle English period: *sense* (a direct derivation), **sensible** (from Old French, or from Latin *sensibilis* 'that can be perceived by the senses'), **sensibility** (from late Latin *sensibilitas*, from *sensibilis*), **sensitive** (via Old French or from medieval Latin *sensitivus*, formed irregularly from Latin *sentire*), **sensual** (from late Latin *sensualis*), and, recorded slightly earlier than these, **sensuality** (from Old French *sensualite*, from late Latin *sensualitas*). Later words in this group are: **sensation** (recorded from the early 17th century from medieval Latin *sensatio(n-)*), **sensuous** (mid 17th century based on Latin *sensus* 'sense'), and **sensory** (mid 18th century either coming from Latin *sens-*, the past participial stem of *sentire* or based on the noun *sense*). **Sensor** dates from the 1950s from *sensory*, on the pattern of *motor*.

sentence [Middle English] 'Way of thinking, opinion', 'court's declaration of punishment', and 'gist (of a piece of writing)' were early senses reflected by *sentence*. This came via Old French from Latin *sententia* 'opinion', from *sentire* 'feel, be of the opinion'. **Sententious** dates from late Middle English, from Latin *sententiosus*, from *sententia* 'opinion'. The original sense 'full of meaning or wisdom' became depreciatory.

sentiment [late Middle English] Early use included the meanings 'personal experience' and 'physical feeling, sensation'. Old French *sentement* is the source, from medieval Latin *sentimentum*, from Latin *sentire* 'feel'.

sentinel [late 16th century] *Sentinel* is from French *sentinelle*, from Italian *sentinella*, of which the origin is unknown. Obsolete *centrinel*, a variant of *sentinel* may have given the word **sentry** dating from the early 17th century.

separate [late Middle English] Latin *separare* 'disjoin, divide' (from *se-* 'apart' and *parare* 'prepare') is the source of both *separate* and late Middle English **separation**(via Old French from Latin *separatio(n-)*).

septic [early 17th century] *Septic* came via Latin from Greek *sēptikos*, from *sēpein* 'make rotten'.

sepulchre [Middle English] This word came via Old French from Latin *sepulcrum* 'burial place', from *sepelire* 'bury'.

sequel [late Middle English] Early senses included 'body of followers', 'descendants' and 'consequence'. It comes from Old French *sequelle* or Latin *sequella*, from *sequi* 'follow'. This Latin verb is also the source of late Middle English **sequence** from late Latin *sequentia*. **Sequential** did not appear before the early

19th century when it was used as a medical term meaning 'following as a secondary condition': this is from *sequence*, on the pattern of *consequential*.

sequester [late Middle English] This comes from Old French *sequestrer* or late Latin *sequestrare* 'commit for safe keeping', from Latin *sequester* 'trustee'. The contemporaneous word **sequestrate** started out with the sense 'separate from general access'; this is also from late Latin *sequestrare*.

serenade [mid 17th century] Serenade is from French *sérénade*, from Italian *serenata*, from *sereno* 'serene'.

serene [late Middle English] This adjective was first used to describe the weather or sky as 'clear, fine, and calm'. It derives from Latin *serenus*. The noun **serenity** (from Old French *serenite*, from Latin *serenitas*, from *serenus*) is recorded from the same period.

sergeant [Middle English] Sergeant is from Old French *sergent*, from Latin *servient-*, the present participial stem of *servire* 'serve'. Early use was as a general term meaning 'attendant, servant' and 'common soldier'; the term was later applied to specific official roles. The Middle English word **serjeant** is a variant commonly used in legal contexts.

series [early 17th century] This is an English use of a Latin word meaning literally 'row, chain', from *serere* 'join, connect'. **Serial** dates from the mid 19th century, based on *series*, perhaps suggested by French *sérial*. It was applied to a film broadcast, radio or television play in a series of episodes from the early 20th century.

serious [late Middle English] Serious is from Old French *serieux* or late Latin *seriosus*, from Latin *serius* 'earnest, serious'. The sense 'significant, important' (e.g. *making serious progress*) dates from the late 16th century.

sermon [Middle English] Early use included the general sense 'speech, discourse, something that is said'. It comes from Old French, from Latin *sermo(n-)* 'discourse, talk'. The word's application to an instructive religious talk given from a pulpit stems from the discourses of Jesus in Christian contexts: an example is *The Sermon on the Mount* recorded in the book of Matthew, introduced by the words: he went up into a mountain … and taught them, saying ….

serpent [Middle English] Serpent came via Old French from Latin *serpent-*, the present participial stem of the verb *serpere* 'to creep'. It is sometimes used to refer to the Devil from the biblical story of the temptation of Eve and is occasionally found in the phrase (from the Book of Revelation) *The Old Serpent* (Tennyson *Geraint and Enid*: Some, whose souls the old serpent long had drawn Down).

serrated [early 18th century] This is based on late Latin *serratus*, from Latin *serra* 'saw'.

serried [mid 17th century] Thought to have been popularized by Sir Walter Scott's use of it in his novels, *serried* is apparently the past participle of *serry* 'press close': this is probably from French *serré* 'close together', based on Latin *sera* 'lock'. It could also be a form of *serred* (pronounced as a disyllable) from obsolete *serr* 'press close together', from the same Latin base.

service [Old English] Early use was to refer to religious devotion or a form of liturgy. The word comes from Old French *servise* or Latin *servitium* 'slavery', from *servus* 'slave'. The semantic branches of the noun *service* include: 'the condition of being a servant' (*in service*); 'the duty of a servant' (*my share of the service was the pantry-work*); 'worship' (*church service*); 'help' (*services rendered*); 'waiting at table', 'supply' (*silver service*); and 'action of serving' in technical contexts (*service in tennis*). The plural *Services* has been used to refer to motorway stations providing food and petrol since the 1960s. The early sense of the verb *service*, found from the mid 19th century, was 'be of service to, provide with a service'. Related words also based on Latin *servus* 'slave' are Middle English **serve** (from Old French *servir*), Middle English **servant** (an adoption of an Old French form meaning literally '(person) serving', a noun use of the present participle of *servir* 'to serve'), and late Middle English **servile** (from Latin *servilis*), originally meaning 'suitable for a slave or for the working class'.

session [late Middle English] Session is from Old French, or from Latin *sessio(n-)*, from *sess-*, the past participial stem of *sedere* 'sit'. Some of the transferred senses do not depend on the notion of sitting but rather reflect a period of time set aside for an activity, such as in *recording session*.

set¹ [Old English] Old English *settan* is from a Germanic source and is related to Dutch *zetten*, German *setzen*, and English *sit*. Confusion between *set* and *sit* began as early as the 14th century from similarity of certain past forms and certain senses. Meanings branch into: 'cause to sit' (*set them upon the camel's back*); 'sink' (*the sun has set*); 'put in a definite place' (*sleeves set into the shirt*); 'appoint, establish' (*set a boundary*); 'arrange, adjust' (*set a snare*); 'place mentally' (*set at naught*); 'come into a settled condition' (*her face set in a sulky stare*); and 'cause to take a

certain direction' (*set our course at north north-east*). The late Old English adjective *set* (e.g. *at set times*) is the past participle of the verb *set*.
→ SIT

set² [late Middle English] This *set* meaning a 'group or collection' is partly from Old French *sette*, from Latin *secta* 'sect', and partly from *set* 'fix, place, etc.'.
→ SET¹

sett [Middle English] This word for the earth or burrow of a badger is a variant of *set*. The spelling with -*tt* prevailed in technical senses of *set*.
→ SET²

settle¹ [Old English] Old English *setlan* meant 'to seat, place', from *setl* 'a place to sit'. In some uses the verb became synonymous with Middle English *saytle* which was similar in sound and meant 'appease, reconcile'; this may have influenced some of the senses (e.g. *settle an argument*).
→ SETTLE²

settle² [Old English] Old English *setl* meant 'a place to sit'. In the middle of the 16th century it came to describe a wooden bench with a high back and arms with a box under the seat. Of Germanic origin, it is related to German *Sessel* and Latin *sella* 'seat', as well as to English *sit*. Early 18th-century **settee** may be a fanciful variant of *settle*.
→ SIT

sever [Middle English] *Sever* is from Anglo-Norman French *severer*, from Latin *separare* 'disjoin, divide'; this is a base shared with late Middle English **severance** also from Anglo-Norman French. This noun started to be used in the context of discharge from contractual employment in the 1940s.

several [late Middle English] *Several* is from Anglo-Norman French, from medieval Latin *separalis*, from Latin *separ* 'separate, different'. Early use in English included the sense 'existing apart, separate' (Dryden *Fables* (Preface): The Reeve, the Miller, and the Cook, are several men).

severe [mid 16th century] The early sense recorded was 'strict, harsh' (e.g. *severe reprimand*); it comes from French *sévère* or Latin *severus*. The sense 'sober, austerely plain' (e.g. *severe dress*) dates from the mid 17th century; the first example of *severe* in the context of weather dates from the late 17th century.

sew [Old English] Old English *siwan* is Germanic origin, from an Indo-European root shared by Latin *suere* and Greek *suein*. The colloquial sense 'bring to a conclusion' of *sew up* arose at the beginning of the 20th century (e.g. *the deal was sewn up within seconds*).

sewer [Middle English] This initially referred to a watercourse to drain marshy land. The source is Old Northern French *seuwiere* 'channel to drain the overflow from a fish pond', based on Latin *ex-* 'out of' and *aqua* 'water'. The noun **sewage**, based on *sewer* by substitution of the suffix -*age* dates from the mid 19th century.

sex [late Middle English] This word which originally denoted either of the two categories, male and female, is from Old French *sexe* or Latin *sexus*. *Sex* denoting *sexual intercourse* dates from the 1920s; the adjective in this phrase (mid 17th-century **sexual**) is from late Latin *sexualis*, from Latin *sexus*.

shabby [mid 17th century] The first syllable of *shabby* is from dialect *shab* 'scab' from a Germanic base meaning 'itch'. Johnson wrote: A word that has crept into conversation and low writing, but ought not to be admitted into the language.

shack [late 19th century] *Shack* is perhaps from Mexican *jacal*, Nahuatl *xacatli* 'wooden hut'. The early sense of the verb, originally a US usage, was 'live in a shack'.

shackle [Old English] Old English *sc(e)acul* 'fetter' is Germanic in origin, related to Dutch *schakel* 'link, coupling'. The root appears to be 'something to fasten or attach' rather than 'shake'.

shade [Old English] Old English *sc(e)adu* is Germanic origin. The association with 'depth of colour' (*shades of blue*) dates from the late 17th century. The word's use for a 'protective globe to diffuse light' (*light shade*) is found from the late 18th century. Late 16th-century **shady** is based on *shade*; colloquial use meaning 'questionable, disreputable' arose in the mid 19th century perhaps from university slang. The related noun **shadow** was *scead(u)we* in Old English, the oblique case of *sceadu*; the verb form *sceadwian* meant 'screen or shield from attack'. Of Germanic origin, *shadow* is related to Dutch *schaduw* and German *Schatten* (nouns), from an Indo-European root shared by Greek *skotos* 'darkness'. The idiomatic phrase *be afraid of one's own shadow* dates from the mid 16th century. Use of the word in political contexts in combinations such as *shadow cabinet* dates from the early 20th century.

shaft [Old English] Old English *scæft*, *sceaft* meant 'handle, pole'; early senses of the verb (late Middle English) were 'fit with a handle' and 'send out shafts of light'. The word is Germanic in origin, related to Dutch *schaft*, German *Schaft*, and perhaps also to *sceptre*. The word *shaft* describing an excavation (*mine shaft*) appears in the 15th century and is thought to be an application of *shaft* 'slender staff, columnar part'.

shag [late Old English] *Shag* as in *shagpile carpet* was *sceacga* 'rough matted hair' in Old English. Of Germanic origin, it is related to Old Norse *skegg* 'beard'. The mid 16th-century bird name *shag* is perhaps a specific use of the word, with reference to the bird's 'shaggy' crest.

shake [Old English] Old English *sc(e)acan* (verb) is Germanic in origin. Early examples include the poetical sense 'depart, flee' as well as the senses 'tremble' and 'cause to vibrate'. The phrase *shake hands* dates from the early 16th century. Use of *shake* with the meaning 'disturb, upset the composure of' (*shaken by the news*) dates from the mid 16th century.

shallow [late Middle English] This is obscurely related to *shoal*. Use of the word in connection with feelings, reasoning, or lack of depth of character dates from the late 16th century (Shakespeare *The Rape of Lucrece*: Out, idle words, servants to shallow fools).
→ SHOAL²

sham [late 17th century] *Sham* may be a northern English dialect variant of the noun *shame*. It appeared as slang around 1677 and became common immediately.
→ SHAME

shamble [late 16th century] *Shamble* as in *shamble along* is probably from dialect *shamble* 'ungainly'; it may be from the phrase *shamble legs* referring to the legs of trestle tables such as those used in a meat market.
→ SHAMBLES

shambles [late Middle English] This word was initially a term for a 'meat market'. It is the plural of earlier *shamble* 'stool, stall', of West Germanic origin, from Latin *scamellum*: this is a diminutive of *scamnum* 'bench'. From the late 16th century, the sense was transferred in some contexts to 'a place of carnage' and from the 1920s was generalized to a 'scene of disorder'. **Shambolic** which arose in the 1970s, is from *shambles* and is probably on the pattern of *symbolic*.

shame [Old English] Old English *sc(e)amu* (noun), *sc(e)amian* 'feel shame' are of Germanic origin; related forms are the Dutch verb *schamen*, the German noun *Scham*, and the German verb *schämen*. Old English compounds include **shameful** (as *sc(e)amful* 'modest, shamefaced') and **shameless** (as *sc(e)amlēas*). **Shamefaced** in the mid 16th century meant 'modest, shy' and is an alteration of archaic *shamefast*; the spelling change was by association with *face*. The sense 'ashamed' appeared in the late 19th century.

shampoo [mid 18th century] This was first recorded in the sense 'massage' as part of a Turkish bath process. It comes from Hindi *cāmpo!* 'press!', the imperative of *cāmpnā*.

shank [Old English] Old English *sceanca* is West Germanic in origin, related to Dutch *schenk* 'leg bone' and High German *Schenkel* 'thigh'. The use of the verb as a golfing term dates from the 1920s. *Shanks's Pony* 'on foot' is first recorded in 1785 as *shanks-nag* in R. Fergusson's *Poems* (And auld shanks-naig wad tire, I dread, To pace to Berwick).

shanty¹ [early 19th century] This *shanty* as in *shanty town* was originally a North American usage; it may be from Canadian French *chantier* 'lumberjack's cabin, logging camp'.

shanty² [mid 19th century] This *shanty* as in *sea shanty* is probably from French *chantez!* 'sing!', the imperative plural of *chanter*.

shape [Old English] Of Germanic origin, Old English *gesceap* meant 'external form' and 'creation'; the verb *sceppan* expressed 'create'. The phrase *in the shape of* (*femininity, in the shape of the token woman, was represented*) dates from the mid 18th century. A century later the word began to refer to 'state of health or fitness' (*in pretty good shape*) originally in US English. The phrase *in all shapes and sizes* arose in the 1950s.

shard [Old English] Old English *sceard* meant 'gap, notch, potsherd'. Of Germanic origin, it is related to Dutch *schaarde* 'notch' and to *shear*.
→ SHEAR

share [Old English] Old English *scearu* was a 'division, part into which something may be divided'. From a Germanic source, it is related to Dutch *schure* and German *Schar* 'troop, multitude', and to English *shear*. The phrase *share and share alike* dates from the mid 16th century in the context of splitting up spoils. The commercial use as in *stocks and shares* is found from the early 17th century. Verb use dates from the late 16th century.
→ SHEAR

shark [late 16th century] *Shark* as in *loan shark* is perhaps from German *Schurke* 'worthless rogue', influenced by the zoological term *shark* (a late Middle English word of unknown origin).

sharp [Old English] Old English *sc(e)arp* is of Germanic origin, related to Dutch *scherp* and German *scharf*. English *scrape* may also be related. The meaning 'of quick intellect' appeared early; the phrase *you're so sharp you'll cut yourself* appeared in the early 20th century. Use of *sharp* to mean 'stylish' (*sharp dresser*) dates from the 1940s.
→ SCRAPE

shatter [Middle English] 'Scatter, disperse' was the early sense of *shatter* which may be an imitative formation or may have a connection with *scatter*.

shave [Old English] Old English *sc(e)afan* 'scrape away the surface of (something) by paring' is of Germanic origin, related to Dutch *schaven* and German *schaben*. The phrase *a close shave* (sometimes *a near shave*) appeared in texts from the early 19th century.

shawl [mid 17th century] *Shawl* is from Urdu and Persian *šāl*, probably from *Shāliāt*, the name of a town in India. The material referred to in the original manufacture was made in Kashmir from the hair of the *shawl-goat* (*capra lanigera* from Tibet).

she [Middle English] *She* is probably a phonetic development of the Old English feminine personal pronoun *hēo*, *hīe*.

sheaf [Old English] Old English *scēaf*, of Germanic origin, is related to Dutch *schoof* 'sheaf' and German *Schaub* 'wisp of straw', and also to the English verb *shove*. **Sheave**, another term for *sheaf* is found from the late 16th century from the plural *sheaves*.
→ SHOVE

shear [Old English] Old English *sceran* originally had the meaning 'cut through with a weapon'. Of Germanic origin, it is related to Dutch and German *scheren*, from a base meaning 'divide, shear, shave'. **Shears** (in Old English *scēara* 'scissors, cutting instrument') is related to Dutch *schaar*, German *Schere*, as well as to *shear*.

sheath [Old English] Old English *scæth*, *scēath* 'scabbard', from Germanic, is related to Dutch *schede*, German *Scheide*, and the English verb *shed*. The notion of shape and that of covering are reflected in the variation of senses: its use to mean 'contraceptive' started in the mid 19th century; its use in fashion contexts (*sheath dress*) dates from the early 20th century. Late Middle English **sheathe** is from *sheath*.
→ SHED²

shed¹ [late 15th century] This *shed* as in *garden shed* is apparently a variant of the noun *shade*. The sense 'send forth' illustrated in *shed tears*, *shed light*, arose in Middle English; 'cast off' in contexts such as *shed bark* is found from the late 16th century.
→ SHADE

shed² [Old English] The Old English verb *sc(e)ādan* meant both 'separate out (one selected group), divide' (still found in sheep farming contexts) and 'scatter'. Of Germanic origin, it is related to Dutch and German *scheiden*.
→ SHEATH

sheen [early 17th century] *Sheen* is from obsolete *sheen* 'beautiful, resplendent' and is apparently related to the verb *shine*.
→ SHINE

sheep [Old English] Old English *scēp*, *scæp*, *scēap* is West Germanic in origin, related to Dutch *schaap* and German *Schaf*. Many of the associations with the word (such as 'timidity', 'meek defencelessness') arose from biblical stories. The phrase *black sheep* (late 18th century) became known from the proverb *there is a black sheep in every flock* which focused on 'singularity' and therefore 'dubious character'. The Old English noun **shepherd** (spelt in early times *scēaphierde*) has as its second element the obsolete word *herd* meaning 'herdsman'.

sheer [Middle English] 'Exempt, cleared' was the early sense recorded for this *sheer* commonly found since the early 19th century in the sense 'steep, perpendicular' (*sheer cliff*). It is probably an alteration of dialect *shire* 'pure, clear', from the Germanic base of the verb *shine*. In the mid 16th century the word was used to describe clear, pure water, and also in the description of textiles as 'very thin, diaphanous'.
→ SHINE

sheet¹ [Old English] Old English *scēte*, *scīete* 'piece of linen for swathing or protecting' is from a Germanic source and is related to the verb *shoot* in its primary sense 'to project'. Use of the word as in *sheet of paper* dates from the early 16th century. The sense 'broad expanse of' (*sheet of water*) is recorded from the late 16th century.
→ SHOOT

sheet² [Old English] This word for a rope attached to a sail was, in Old English, *scēata* meaning 'lower corner of a sail'. Of Germanic origin, it is related to Old Norse *skauti* 'kerchief'. The phrase *three sheets to the wind* meaning 'very drunk' dates from the early 19th century. This nautical *sheet* influenced late 15th-century **sheet anchor** initially a term for an additional anchor for emergency use: the first word of this compound may in fact be related to obsolete *shot* which denoted two cables spliced together.
→ SHEET¹

shelf [Middle English] *Shelf* is from Middle Low German *schelf*; related forms are Old English *scylfe* 'partition', *scylf* 'crag'. The late 16th-century verb **shelve** had the sense 'project like a shelf', a Shakespearean usage (*Two Gentlemen of Verona*: Her chamber is aloft. And built so shelving, that one cannot climb it). The form is from *shelves*, the plural of *shelf*. The late Middle English verb *shelve* meaning 'slope' (*the land* *shelved gently downwards*) is of uncertain origin but may be associated with *shelf*.

shell [Old English] The Old English noun *scell* is Germanic in origin, related to Dutch *schel* 'scale, shell' and English *scale*. The verb dates from the mid 16th century when it meant 'remove the pod from'. Use of the word as a term for an explosive projectile (*mortar shell*) dates from the mid 17th century, sugggested by the metal protective casing for the powder. The First World War phrase *shell shock* is associated with this type of *shell* in reference to psychological disturbance from exposure to shellfire. The notion of a *shell* as a place to which to withdraw (*go into one's shell*) dates from figurative use of the early 19th century.
→ SCALE¹

shelter [late 16th century] This may be, according to the common view, an alteration of obsolete *sheltron* 'phalanx', from Old English *scieldtruma* meaning literally 'shield troop'. The main objection to the theory is that *sheltron* became obsolete in the 15th century and *shelter* has not been found earlier than 1585.

shield [Old English] Of Germanic origin, the Old English noun *scild* and verb *scildan* are related to Dutch *schild* and German *Schild*, from a base meaning 'divide, separate'. The notion of protection is at the core of the verb also dating from Old English.

shift [Old English] Old English *sciftan*, of Germanic origin, meant 'arrange, divide, apportion'; a related form is German *schichten* 'to layer, stratify'. A common Middle English sense 'change, replace' gave rise to the noun sense 'period of work' as in *night shift* (via the concept of replacement relays of workers) and 'straight unwaisted dress' (via the notion of changing one's clothes). This latter use started in the 17th century when *shift* replaced *smock* as being a more 'delicate' expression; in the 19th century, *shift* gave way to *chemise* for the same reasons.

shilly-shally [mid 18th century] This was originally written *shill I, shall I*, a reduplication of *shall I?*, expressing doubt and hesitation.

shimmer [late Old English] Old English *scymrian*, from a Germanic source, is related to German *schimmern* and to *shine*. The noun dates from the early 19th century.
→ SHINE

shin [Old English] Old English *scinu* is probably from a Germanic base meaning 'narrow or thin piece', related to German *Schiene* 'thin plate' and Dutch *scheen*. Use of the word in butchery contexts (*shin of beef*) dates from the early 18th century. The verb was originally in nautical use in the early 19th century.

shine [Old English] Old English *scinan* is of Germanic origin; related forms are Dutch *schijnen* and German *scheinen*. The phrase *shine through* meaning 'be clearly evident' arose in the late 16th century (Shakespeare: *Two Gentlemen of Verona*: These follies are within you, and shine through you like the water in an Urinall).

shingle¹ [late Middle English] This *shingle* referring to small stones is of unknown origin but the formation may be echoic (as in the case of *chink*). There may be a connection with Norwegian *singl* 'coarse sand'.

shingle² [Middle English] This *shingle* as in *shingle roof* is apparently from Latin *scindula*, earlier spelt *scandula* meaning 'a split piece of wood'.

ship [Old English] The Old English noun *scip* and late Old English verb *scipian* are related to Dutch *schip* and German *Schiff*. The phrase *ships that pass in the night* is from a phrase by Longfellow (1873 Ships that pass in the night, and speak each other in passing ... So on the ocean of life we pass and speak one another, Only a look and a voice, then darkness again). The related noun **shipper** has reflected its current senses from the mid 18th century but it existed in late Old English (*scipere*) meaning 'sailor'.

shire [Old English] Old English *scir* meant 'care, official charge, county', a word of Germanic origin. *The Shires* is a term used in reference to parts of England regarded as strongholds of traditional rural culture, especially the rural Midlands. *Shire* forms the first element of Old English **sheriff** (*scirgerefa*); the second element is *reeve*, which historically was a local official and in particular the chief magistrate of a district in Anglo-Saxon England.

shirk [mid 17th century] 'Practise fraud or trickery' was the early sense recorded for *shirk* from obsolete *shirk* 'sponger', perhaps from German *Schurke* 'scoundrel'. The sense 'avoid work' dates from the late 18th century.

shirt [Old English] Old English *scyrte*, of Germanic origin, is related to Old Norse *skyrta*, Dutch *schort*, German *Schürze* 'apron', and English *short*. It is probably from a base meaning 'short garment'. In Chaucer's *Wife of Bath's Tale* there is an early example of an association between the possession of a *shirt* and money (I holde him rich al hadde he nat a sherte); this continued in phrases such as *the shirt off one's back* (mid 17th century) and *lose one's shirt* in betting contexts (also worded in various similar phrases from the mid 19th century).
→ SHORT; SKIRT

shiver¹ [Middle English] The Middle English spelling was *chivere*, which is perhaps an alteration of dialect *chavele* 'to chatter', from Old English *ceafl* 'jaw', giving an association of teeth chattering due to the cold.

shiver² [Middle English] This *shiver* as in *shiver of glass* is from a Germanic base meaning 'to split'; German *Schiefer* 'slate' is related.

shoal¹ [late 16th century] This *shoal* as in *shoal of fish* is probably from Middle Dutch *schōle* 'troop'.
→ SCHOOL²

shoal² [Old English] This *shoal*, a term for a sandbank or place where the water is shallow, is from the Old English adjective *sceald* of Germanic origin; *shallow* is related.
→ SHALLOW

shock¹ [mid 16th century] The noun is from French *choc*, the verb from French *choquer*, words of unknown origin. The original senses sprang from military contexts: 'throw (troops) into confusion by charging at them' and, as a noun, 'an encounter between charging forces'. The latter gave rise to the notion of 'sudden violent blow or impact'. Medical use of the term dates from the early 19th century; the phrase *culture shock* is found from the 1940s.

shock² [Middle English] This *shock* referring to a group of sheaves of grain may be from Middle Dutch and Middle Low German *schok* 'number of sheaves, group of sixty units'. The origin is unknown.

shock³ [mid 17th century] The origin of this *shock* as in *shock of hair* is uncertain; obsolete *shough*, a term for a breed of lapdog, may be associated. The word was originally a name for a dog with long shaggy hair, and was then used as an adjective meaning 'unkempt, shaggy'. The current sense dates from the early 19th century.

shoddy [mid 19th century] *Shoddy* is of unknown origin. One sense of the word is 'smaller stones of a quarry', a dialect use, which may suggest a connection with *shoad* denoting loose fragments of tin, lead, or copper ore, lying near the surface mixed with earth.

shoe [Old English] The Old English noun *scōh* and the verb *scōg(e)an* are Germanic in origin, related to Dutch *schoen* and German *Schuh*. Scholars have referred the word to two semantic roots: 'take a walk' and 'covering'. The phrase *shoe a horse* dates from Middle English.

shoot [Old English] Old English *scēotan* is related to Dutch *scieten* and German *schiessen*, as well as to English *sheet*, *shut*, and *shot*. The senses branch into: 'go swiftly and suddenly' (*shot off to call his mother*); 'send forth' (*shot flames out*); and 'send missiles' (*shot an arrow*). Use in

film contexts (*shoot a film*) dates from the late 19th century.
→ SHEET¹; SHOT; SHUT

shop [Middle English] This is a shortening of Old French *eschoppe* 'lean-to booth', of West Germanic origin, related to German *Schopf* 'porch' and English dialect *shippon* 'cattle shed'. The verb is first recorded in the mid 16th century in the sense 'imprison' from an obsolete slang use of the noun for 'prison': this led to 'inform on (someone)' (*shopped him to the police*).

shore¹ [Middle English] This *shore* as in *sea shore* is from Middle Dutch, Middle Low German *schōre*; it may be from the root of the verb *shear* but the core notion remains unclear. It could be 'division' between water and land.
→ SHEAR

shore² [Middle English] The *shore* of the phrase *shore up* is from Middle Dutch, Middle Low German *schōre* 'prop'. The ultimate origin is unknown.

short [Old English] Of Germanic origin, Old English *sceort* is related to *shirt* and *skirt*. The main semantic branches are: 'small in length'; 'of little duration in time'; 'not reaching a standard' (*short change*) and, from the 15th century, 'easily crumbled' (*short pastry*). The latter may owe its sense to 'having little length of fibre'. The phrase *short and sweet* dates from the early 16th century; the sense 'having insufficient money' (*short of cash*) is found from the mid 18th century. The application of the verb *short* in electrical contexts is from *short-circuit*.
→ SHIRT; SKIRT

shot [Old English] Old English *sc(e)ot*, *gesc(e)ot* 'rush, dash' and later 'act of shooting' is of Germanic origin, related to German *Geschoss*, from the base of the verb *shoot*.
→ SHOOT

shoulder [Old English] Old English *sculdor*, of West Germanic origin, is related to Dutch *schouder* and German *Schulter*. The verb dates from Middle English, the sense 'bear' (*shoulder a responsibility*) being reflected in examples from the late 16th century.

shout [late Middle English] *Shout* may be related to the root of *shoot*; Old Norse *skúta* 'a taunt' may be related, so too the rare English verb *scout* meaning 'reject a proposal with scorn'.
→ SHOOT

shove [Old English] Old English *scūfan*, of Germanic origin, is related to Dutch *schuiven*, German *schieben*, and English *shuffle*.
→ SHOVEL; SHUFFLE

shovel [Old English] Old English *scofl* is from a Germanic source; related words are Dutch *schoffel*, German *Schaufel*, and English *shove*.
➔ SHOVE

show [Old English] Old English *scēawian* meant 'look at, inspect' from a West Germanic base meaning 'look'; it is related to Dutch *schouwen* and German *schauen*. The change in sense around 1200 from 'look at' to 'cause to be looked at' is difficult to account for. The noun is from the verb; its sense 'spectacle for entertainment' dates from the mid 16th century; the use 'large-scale display of objects for public viewing' (*flower show*) appeared at the beginning of the 19th century.

shower [Old English] Old English *scūr* meant 'light fall of rain, hail, etc.'. Of Germanic origin, it is related to Dutch *schoer* and German *Schauer*. Derogatory use with reference to people (*such a shower of idiots*) dates from the 1940s.

shred [late Old English] Late Old English *scrēad* meant 'piece cut off'; the verb *scrēadian* meant 'trim, prune'. Its origin is West Germanic, English *shroud* being a related form.
➔ SHROUD

shrew [Old English] Old English *scrēawa*, *scrǣwa* is from a Germanic source related to words with senses such as 'dwarf', 'devil', or 'fox'. It was frequently used from Middle English for a scolding or troublesome wife.

shrewd [Middle English] 'Evil in nature or character' was an early sense recorded for *shrew*, either from *shrew* in the sense 'evil person or thing' or as the past participle of obsolete *shrew* 'to curse'. The word developed the sense 'cunning', and gradually gained a favourable connotation during the 17th century.
➔ SHREW

shriek [late 15th century] *Shriek* is imitative of the noise; dialect *scruak*, Old Norse *skrækja* and *screech* are similar.
➔ SCREECH

shrill [late Middle English] Of Germanic origin, *shrill* is related to Low German *schrell* 'sharp in tone or taste'.

shrine [Old English] Old English *scrīn* was a 'cabinet, chest, reliquary'. Its source is Germanic and it is related to Dutch *schrijn* and German *Schrein*, from Latin *scrinium* 'chest for books'.

shrink [Old English] Old English *scrincan*, of Germanic origin, is related to Swedish *skrynka* 'to wrinkle'. The sense 'draw back' in an action of recoiling in abhorrence or timidity dates from the early 16th century. The slang use meaning 'psychiatrist' comes from *head-shrinker* and started out as a US usage in the 1960s.

shrivel [mid 16th century] *Shrivel* may be Scandinavian in origin; Swedish dialect *skryvla* 'to wrinkle' is perhaps associated.

shroud [late Old English] Late Old English *scrūd* meant 'garment, clothing' and is from a Germanic source from a base meaning 'cut'; English *shred* is related. An early sense of the verb in Middle English was 'cover so as to protect'. Use of the noun to specifically denote the sheet in which a corpse is laid out, dates from the late 16th century.
➔ SHRED

shrub [Old English] Old English *scrubb*, *scrybb* meant 'shrubbery'; West Flemish *schrobbe* 'vetch', Norwegian *skrubba* 'dwarf cornel', and English *scrub* are related.
➔ SCRUB²

shrug [late Middle English] An early sense recorded was 'fidget, shudder from cold'. The origin is unknown. The phrase *shrug off* meaning 'reject in an offhand manner' first appeared in the early years of the 20th century.

shudder [Middle English] *Shudder* comes from Middle Dutch *schūderen*, from a Germanic base meaning 'shake'. The phrase *I shudder to think* was first recorded in 1872 in the *Letters* of George Eliot: I shudder a little to think what a long book it will be.

shuffle [mid 16th century] This is perhaps from Low German *schuffeln* which meant 'walk clumsily' as well as 'deal dishonestly, shuffle (cards)'. Of Germanic origin, it is related to *shove* and *scuffle*.
➔ SCUFFLE; SHOVE

shun [Old English] Old English *scunian* had the sense 'abhor, shrink back with fear, seek safety from an enemy'; its origin remains unknown. If the primary sense were 'hide oneself (from) the verb might be a derivative of a Germanic root (*sku-*) meaning 'cover, hide'. Middle English **shunt**, originally meaning 'move suddenly aside' may be from *shun*.

shut [Old English] Old English *scyttan* 'put (a bolt) in position to hold fast' is West Germanic in origin, related to Dutch *schutten* 'shut up, obstruct' and English *shoot*. The phrase *get shut of* is found from around 1500. The colloquial *shut up!* 'stop talking!' is recorded from the mid 19th century.
➔ SHOOT

shuttle [Old English] Old English *scytel* 'dart, missile' is from a Germanic source; Old Norse *skutill* 'harpoon' is associated. The verb and the

noun use for a form of transport going back-wards and forwards between two fixed places stem from association with the movement of the bobbin (in weaving) from one side of the loom to the other and back. The word's use in space travel is from the 1960s.
→ SHOOT

shy [Old English] Old English *scēoh* was applied to horses meaning 'easily frightened'. Coming from a Germanic source, it is related to German *scheuen* 'shun' and *scheuchen* 'scare'. The word's application to people is seen from the start of the 17th century; the verb dates from the mid 17th century. The *shy* meaning 'fling, throw' of *coconut shy* is a late 18th-century word of unknown origin.

shyster [mid 19th century] This word for a person using deceptive methods in business is said to be from *Scheuster*, the name of a lawyer whose behaviour provoked accusations of 'scheuster' practices; it was perhaps reinforced by the German word *Scheisser* 'worthless person'.

sibling [Old English] A *sibling* was originally a 'relative'. The current sense referring to children of common parentage dates from the early 20th century.

sick [Old English] Old English *sēoc* 'affected by illness' is of Germanic origin, related to Dutch *ziek* and German *siech*. The association with vomiting dates from the early 17th century, the phrase *sick as a dog* appearing in the early 18th century; this has been transformed humorously occasionally to *sick as a parrot* since the 1970s. The word's application in the sense 'macabre' (*sick joke*) dates from the 1950s. The adjective **sickly** (late Middle English) is based on *sick*, probably suggested by Old Norse *sjúkligr*.

sickle [Old English] Old English *sicol, sicel* is Germanic in origin and related to Dutch *sikkel* and German *Sichel*, based on Latin *secula*, from *secare* 'to cut'.

side [Old English] Old English *sīde* referred to the 'left or right part of the body'. Germanic in origin, it is related to Dutch *zijde* and German *Seite*, probably from a base meaning 'extending lengthways'. The word describes lateral surfaces but also alternative aspects (*the bright side*) and opposing views (*on his side in the argument*). The notion of dishonesty in the expression *on the side* dates from the late 19th century in US English. The compound
■ **sideburn** appeared in the late 19th century, inverted from the original *burnside*: this came from the name of General *Burnside* (1824–81), who affected this style.

sidle [late 17th century] This is probably a back-formation (by removal of the suffix) from *sideling* which meant 'with a sideward movement': the latter developed the parallel altered form **sidelong** in late Middle English.

siege [Middle English] *Siege* is from Old French *sege*, from *asegier* 'besiege'.

sieve [Old English] The Old English noun *sife* is from West Germanic and is related to Dutch *zeef* and German *Sieb*. The word has been used occasionally since the early 17th century to refer to someone who cannot keep a secret (Shakespeare *All's Well That Ends Well*: Yet in this captious, and intenable Sieve I still pour in the waters of my love). The verb **sift** (in Old English *siftan*), also of West Germanic origin, is related to Dutch *ziften*.

sigh [Middle English] This was first used as a verb and is probably a back-formation (by removal of the suffix) from *sighte*, the past tense of obsolete *siche* which also meant 'sigh' (Old English *sīcan*).

sight [Old English] Old English (*ge*)*sihth* meant 'something seen'. Of West Germanic origin, it is related to Dutch *zicht* and German *Gesicht* 'sight, face, appearance'. The sense 'eyesight' is Middle English; *sights* as in *all the sights of Brussels* is late 16th-century, the period when the word was also used as a technical term for a device to assist aim (*sights of a gun*). The sense (mid 16th century) was first recorded as 'take aim by looking through the sights of a gun'. Of the phrases, *a sight for sore eyes* originated in the early 18th century; (*not*) *by a long sight* was a US English colloquial phrase found from the early 19th century.

sign [Middle English] *Sign* is via Old French from Latin *signum* 'mark, token'. The noun expresses both 'gesture, symbol' and 'indication, suggestion'; the verb splits broadly into 'make a sign' and 'give an indication'. **Signet** (late Middle English) meaning 'small seal' is from Old French, or from medieval Latin *signetum*, a diminutive of *signum*; the word is found in the title *Writer to the Signet*, a Scots term originally for a clerk in the Secretary of State's office who prepared writs to pass the royal signet. Mid 16th-century **signature** is related, first used as a Scots legal term for a document presented by a writer for royal approval and seal; it comes from medieval Latin *signatura* 'sign manual', from Latin *signare* 'to sign, mark'.

signal [late Middle English] *Signal* is from Old French, from medieval Latin *signale*, the neuter of late Latin *signalis*, from Latin *signum* 'mark, token'. The verb dates from the early 19th century.

→ SIGN

signify [Middle English] *Signify* is from Old French *signifier*, from Latin *significare* 'indicate, portend', from *signum* 'token'. From the same Latin source come late Middle English **significance** (from Old French, or from Latin *significantia*) and late 16th-century **significant** (from the Latin present participial stem *significant-*).

→ SIGNAL

silence [Middle English] *Silence* is from Old French, from Latin *silentium*, from *silere* 'be silent'. The phrase *silence is golden* dates from the early 19th century. **Silent**, from the same Latin source verb as *silence*, appeared in the late 15th century in the sense 'not speaking'.

silhouette [late 18th century] This word derives from the name (although the reason remains obscure) of Étienne de *Silhouette* (1709-67), a French author and politician. Explanations include: his short tenure of the office of Controller-General in 1759; or a possible allusion to the outline portraits with which de Silhouette is said to have decorated the walls of his chateau at Bry-sur-Marne.

silk [Old English] Old English *sioloc, seolec* is from late Latin *sericum*, the neuter form of Latin *sericus*, based on Greek *Sēres*: this was the name given to the inhabitants of the Far Eastern countries from which silk first came overland to Europe. The word **silken** is also Old English (*seolcen*); the sense 'soft, glossy' dates from the early 16th century.

sill [Old English] Old English *syll, sylle* was a 'horizontal beam forming a foundation of a wall'. Of Germanic origin, it is related to German *Schwelle* 'threshold'. Its use to mean 'window sill' started in late Middle English.

silly [late Middle English] 'Deserving of pity or sympathy' was the early sense recorded for *silly*, an alteration of dialect *seely* which originally meant 'happy' and later 'innocent, feeble': this is from a West Germanic base meaning 'luck, happiness'. The sense 'foolish' developed via the stages 'feeble' and 'unsophisticated, ignorant'.

silt [late Middle English] Originally, this probably referred to a salty deposit and may be from a Scandinavian source related to Danish and Norwegian *sylt* 'salt marsh'.

→ SALT

silver [Old English] Old English *seolfor*, of Germanic origin, is related to Dutch *zilver* and German *Silber*. The word's application to articles made of silver (*silverware*) arose early; its

use to mean 'money' in general is chiefly Scots.

similar [late 16th century] This was also originally a term in anatomy meaning 'homogeneous'. It comes from French *similaire* or medieval Latin *similaris*, from Latin *similis* 'like'. The literary device **simile** for drawing comparisons (late Middle English) is a use of the neuter of *similis*. This Latin adjective is also the base of **simulate** in the mid 17th century, from Latin *simulare* 'copy, represent'.

simmer [mid 17th century] *Simmer* is an alteration of dialect *simper* (which expressed the same sense) and may be imitative of the noise of the light bubbling.

simper [mid 16th century] The origin of *simper* is unknown; there may be a connection with German *zimpfer* 'elegant, delicate'.

simple [Middle English] *Simple* is from Old French, from Latin *simplus*. The main semantic branches are: 'free from duplicity, straightforward'; 'poor, humble'; 'deficient in knowledge'; and 'with nothing added'. The phrase *pure and simple* dates from the late 19th century. **Simplicity** (late Middle English) is from Old French *simplicite* or Latin *simplicitas*, from *simplex* 'single'. **Simpleton** and **simplify** both date from the mid 17th century: *simpleton* is a fanciful formation based on *simple*; *simplify* is from French *simplifier*, from medieval Latin *simplificare*, from Latin *simplus*.

simultaneous [mid 17th century] This word is based on Latin *simul* 'at the same time', probably influenced by late Latin *momentaneus*.

sin [Old English] Old English *synn* (noun), *syngian* (verb) are probably related to Latin *sons, sont-* 'guilty'. **Sinful** also dates from Old English (*synfull*). The weakening to 'reprehensible' is found from the mid 19th century (*sinful waste of money*).

since [late Middle English] *Since* is a contraction of obsolete *sithence*, or from dialect *sin* (both from dialect *sithen* 'thereupon, afterwards, ever since').

sincere [mid 16th century] Early senses included 'not falsified' and 'unadulterated'. The source is Latin *sincerus* 'clean, pure'. The notion 'containing no deception' was also early.

sing [Old English] Germanic in origin, the Old English verb *singan* is related to Dutch *zingen* and German *singen*. The criminals' slang use meaning 'admit to a crime' dates from the early 17th century.

singe [Old English] Old English *sencgan*, of West Germanic origin, is related to Dutch *zengen*. There may be a connection between the stem of *singe* and the verb *sing*, from an association with the hissing sound of intense singeing.

single [Middle English] *Single* came via Old French from Latin *singulus*, related to *simplus* 'simple'. The word **singlet** in the mid 18th century was originally a term for a man's short jacket; it is based on *single* because the garment was unlined, on the pattern of *doublet*.

singular [Middle English] Early use reflected the senses 'solitary, single, living alone' and 'beyond the average'. The word derives from Old French *singuler*, from Latin *singularis* 'alone (of its kind)', from *singulus* 'single'. Use as a grammatical term was also early. **Singularity** (via Old French from late Latin *singularitas*, from *singularis*) dates from the same Middle English period.
➔ SINGLE

sinister [late Middle English] 'Malicious, underhand' was the early sense of *sinister* in English, from Old French *sinistre* or Latin *sinister* 'left' (Ben Jonson *Poetaster*: The sinister application Of the malicious, ignorant, and base Interpreter). The Latin sense 'left' was also reflected early and is seen in heraldic phrases such as *bend sinister*. The sense 'indicating misfortune' (*sinister token*, *sinister presage*) dates from the late 16th century and originally referred to omens seen on the left hand, thought to be the unlucky side.

sink [Old English] Old English *sincan*, of Germanic origin, is related to Dutch *zinken* and German *sinken*. The word expresses movement downwards as well as submersion and dropping to a lower level, expressed both literally and figuratively. The notion *sink or swim* contrasting success and failure dates from Middle English. The noun **sink** dating from Middle English and originally a word for a pool or pit, is based on the verb; its use as in *kitchen sink* dates from the mid 16th century.

sinuous [late 16th century] *Sinuous* is from French *sinueux* or Latin *sinuosus*, from *sinus* 'a bend'.

sip [late Middle English] *Sip* may be a modification of Old English **sup** (now dated or part of northern English), as symbolic of a less vigorous action.

siphon [late Middle English] *Siphon* is from French, or via Latin from Greek *siphōn* 'pipe'. The verb dates from the mid 19th century.

sir [Middle English] *Sir* is a reduced form of Middle English **sire** first used as a respectful form of address to a king: the latter is from Old French, from an alteration of Latin *senior*.
➔ SENIOR

siren [Middle English] In early use the word *siren* denoted both an imaginary type of snake and a monster part woman part bird (of classical mythology) said to lure sailors to their death. The source is Old French *sirene*, from late Latin *Sirena*, the feminine form of Latin *Siren*, from Greek *Seirēn*. In the early 19th century *siren* was applied to an accoustical instrument invented by Cagniard de la Tour in 1819 for producing musical tones; in the later part of the century the same word was applied to a similar but larger instrument for giving fog and other warnings from steam ships. The phrase *siren suit* from the 1930s was from its use as a one-piece garment for women in air-raid shelters.

sister [Old English] Of Germanic origin, *sister* is related to Dutch *zuster* and German *Schwester*, from an Indo-European root shared by Latin *soror*. The word **sissy** (mid 19th century) was first used meaning 'sister' and is based on the first element; it soon came to be used in the sense 'effeminate person, coward'.

sit [Old English] Old English *sittan*, from Germanic, is related to Dutch *zitten* and German *sitzen*, from an Indo-European root shared by Latin *sedere* and Greek *hezesthai*. The main semantic branches are 'be seated', 'be situated', and 'take a seat'; it is also used in many verb phrases (*sit back*, *sit around*, etc.).

site [late Middle English] This was first used as a noun. It comes from Anglo-Norman French, or from Latin *situs* 'local position'. The verb 'locate, place' dates from the late 16th century.

situate [late Middle English] *Situate* is from medieval Latin *situare* 'to place', from Latin *situs* 'site'. **Situation** is also late Middle English, from French, or from medieval Latin *situatio(n-)*, from *situare*. Use of the word to mean 'position in life' (*my situation as a soldier*) dates from the early 18th century; 'post of employment' is a meaning expressed by the word from the early 19th century.

size [Middle English] Early use of the word was as a synonym for *assize* (of which it is a shortening) or as a word for an 'ordinance fixing a rate of payment'. This is from Old French *sise*, from *assise* 'ordinance'. The notion of fixing an amount led to the word's use to express magnitude and bulk. The verb phrase *size up* ('try to form an opinion of (somebody)') appeared in the late 19th century. The Middle English term **size** in decorating contexts for a glutinous wash to form a background for painting may be the same word, but the history is not clear.
➔ ASSIZE

skate [mid 17th century] This *skate* as in *ice skates* was originally written as the plural *scates*; it comes from Dutch *schaats* (a singular form but interpreted as plural), from Old French *eschasse* 'stilt'. The phrase *get one's skates on* 'hurry up' was originally military slang in the late 19th century.

skeleton [late 16th century] This is modern Latin, from the Greek neuter of *skeletos* 'dried up', from *skellein* 'dry up'. The general sense 'supporting framework' is found from the mid 17th century.

sketch [mid 17th century] *Sketch* is from Dutch *schets* or German *Skizze*, from Italian *schizzo*; this is from *schizzare* 'make a sketch', based on Greek *skhedios* 'done extempore'. It was in the late 18th century that the word was applied to a short comic drama.

skew [late Middle English] *Skew* was first used as a verb in the sense 'move obliquely'; it is a shortening of Old Northern French *eskiuwer*, a variant of Old French *eschiver* 'eschew'. The adjective (*skew mouth*) and noun (*the skew of the trajectory*) dating from the early 17th century are from the verb. The first element of the word **skewbald** in the description of ponies (mid 17th century) is unconnected: it is from obsolete *skewed* 'skewbald' (which is of uncertain origin), on the pattern of *piebald*.

skewer [late Middle English] This word is of unknown origin but is probably a variant of dialect *skiver* in the same sense.

skid [late 17th century] This was first used as a noun in the sense 'supporting beam'; it may be related to Old Norse *skíth* 'billet, snowshoe' (which also gave English **ski** in the mid 18th century via Norwegian). The verb was first used meaning 'fasten a skid to (a wheel) to slow its motion', later coming to mean 'slip'. The compound:
■ **skid row** (1930s) as a term for a rundown area is an alteration of *skid road*, a North American term originally applied to a downtown area occupied by loggers.

skill [late Old English] Old English *scele* meant 'knowledge, discrimination', from Old Norse *skil* 'discernment, knowledge'.

skim [Middle English] 'Remove scum from (a liquid)' was the early sense recorded. It is a back-formation (by removal of the suffix) from *skimmer*, a utensil used for skimming, or it derives from Old French *escumer*, from *escume* 'scum, foam'. The sense 'read rapidly' dates from the late 18th century, as does the sense 'move rapidly over the surface of (something)'.

skin [late Old English] Late Old English *scinn* is from Old Norse *skinn*, related to Dutch *schinden* 'flay, peel' and German *schinden*. The slang expression *gimme some skin* said before slapping hands in solidarity dates from the 1940s. The colloquial word **skint** first found in the 1920s is a variant of colloquial *skinned* used in the same sense (the past participle of *skin*).

skip¹ [Middle English] This *skip* meaning 'move along lightly' is probably of Scandinavian origin. The sense 'abscond' was also early. Use of the word to mean 'pass over in reading' dates from the early 16th century.

skip² [early 19th century] This *skip* as a term for a container for rubbish or quarry materials is a variant of *skep* from Old Norse *skeppa* 'basket'.

skipper [late Middle English] This is from Middle Dutch, Middle Low German *schipper*, from *schip* 'ship'.

skirmish [Middle English] *Skirmish* first used as a verb is from Old French *eskirmiss-*, the lengthened stem of *eskirmir*, from a Germanic verb meaning 'defend'. The noun came to be generalized to any 'contest, encounter' from the late 16th century.

skirt [Middle English] *Skirt* is from Old Norse *skyrta* 'shirt' associated with the synonymous Old English *scyrte* and *short*. Verb use is found in texts from the early 17th century.
→ SHORT

skit [early 18th century] This was first used as a word for a 'satirical comment or attack'. It is related to the rare verb *skit* 'move lightly and rapidly', perhaps from Old Norse and related to *skjóta* 'shoot'. Late Middle English **skittish** may also be from this same rare English verb *skit*.

skulk [Middle English] *Skulk* is apparently of Scandinavian origin; Norwegian *skulka* 'lurk', and Danish *skulke*, Swedish *skolka* 'shirk' are probably related.

skull [Middle English] This was originally written *scolle*. The origin is unknown but there may be a link with Old Norse *skoltr*. Use in the phrase *skull and crossbones* as an emblem on a pirate's flag dates from the early 19th century. The expression *out of one's skull* meaning 'crazy' dates from the 1960s.

sky [Middle English] This was commonly used in the plural denoting clouds in early use; it is from Old Norse *ský* 'cloud'. The word was applied to a shade of blue in the mid 17th century; the phrase *out of a clear (blue) sky* made its appearance towards the end of the 19th century; *the sky's the limit* dates from the 1920s.

slack [Old English] Old English *slæc* meant 'inclined to be lazy, unhurried'. From a Germanic source, it is related to Latin *laxus* 'loose'. The senses branch broadly into: 'remiss, negligent' (*slack parenting*); 'lacking energy; dull, slow' (*slack digestion*); and 'not drawn tightly' (*slack rope*).

slag [mid 16th century] *Slag* is from Middle Low German *slagge*, perhaps from *slagen* 'strike', with reference to fragments formed by hammering. Slang use meaning 'worthless person' dates from the late 18th century. The verb sense 'criticize' dates from the 1970s (*slagged them off mercilessly*).

slake [Old English] Old English *slacian* meant 'become less eager' and 'slacken', from the adjective *slæc* 'slack'; Dutch *slaken* 'diminish, relax' is associated. The sense 'allay' in association with thirst is recorded from Middle English.

slam [late 17th century] The *slam* as in *slammed the door* was originally a dialect word meaning 'slap vigorously'; it is probably of Scandinavian origin and Old Norse *slam(b)ra* may be related. The sense 'be severely critical of' was originally a US usage from the early 20th century. The phrase *slam on the brakes* is found from the 1950s.

slander [Middle English] *Slander* is from Old French *esclandre*, an alteration of *escandle*, from late Latin *scandalum* 'scandal'.
→ SCANDAL

slant [late Middle English] *Slant* is a variant of dialect *slent* which is Scandinavian in origin, probably influenced by *aslant* 'in a sloping direction'. The sense 'interpretation' (*new slant on the issue*) is found from the early 20th century in US English originally.

slap [late Middle English] *Slap* is probably an imitative formation. The noun dates from the mid 17th century. The phrase *slap in the face* was originally *slap on the face* (mid 19th century); *slap and tickle* for 'amorous play' is recorded from the 1920s.

slash [late Middle English] *Slash* may be imitative, or it may be from Old French *esclachier* 'break in pieces'. Use of the word to mean 'reduce severely' as in *slash prices* dates from the beginning of the 20th century.

slat [late Middle English] A *slat* when first recorded in use was a 'roofing slate'. The word is a shortening of Old French *esclat* 'splinter', from *esclater* 'to split'. The current sense dates from the mid 18th century.

slate [Middle English] Middle English *sclate*, *sklate*, is a shortening of Old French *esclate*, a feminine form synonymous with *esclat* 'piece broken off'. The phrase *clean slate* dates from the late 19th century. The verb sense 'find fault

with, scold' appeared around the middle of the 19th century.
→ SLAT

slaughter [Middle English] *Slaughter* is from Old Norse *slátr* 'butcher's meat'; it is related to *slay*. The verb dates from the mid 16th century.
→ SLAY

slave [Middle English] *Slave* is a shortening of Old French *esclave*, the equivalent of medieval Latin *sclava* (feminine) 'Slavonic (captive)': the Slavonic peoples had been reduced to a servile state by conquest in the 9th century. The verb dates from the late 16th century, the sense 'toil away like a slave' appearing in the early 18th century.

slay [Old English] Old English *slēan* 'strike, kill' is Germanic in origin, related to Dutch *slaan* and German *schlagen*. The sense 'overwhelm with delight, convulse with laughter' (*he slays me with his comments*) was already in Middle English.
→ SLAUGHTER

sled [Middle English] This term is from Middle Low German *sledde* and is related to the English verb *slide*. Related to *sled* is late 16th-century **sledge** (from Middle Dutch *sleedse*) and early 17th-century **sleigh** (originally a North American usage from Dutch *slee*).
→ SLIDE

sledge [Old English] Old English *slecg* 'hammer' is from a Germanic base meaning 'to strike'; it is related to *slay*. The compound **sledge-hammer** is found from the late 15th century describing a large heavy hammer used by blacksmiths; the idiom (*take*) *a sledgehammer to crack a nut* in the context of taking drastic measures to solve a small problem dates from the 1970s.
→ SLAY

sleek [late Middle English] *Sleek* is a later variant of *slick* (adjective and verb). It sometimes means 'fawning, plausible' (Shelley *Hellas*: After the war is fought, yield the slick Russian That which thou canst not keep).
→ SLICK

sleep [Old English] Old English *slēp*, *slæp* (noun forms), and *slēpan*, *slæpan* (verb forms) are of Germanic origin, related to Dutch *slapen* and German *schlafen*. The phrase *sleep like a top* arose in the late 17th century.

sleet [Middle English] From a Germanic source, *sleet* is probably related to Middle Low German *slōten* (plural) 'hail' and German *Schlosse* 'hailstone'.

sleeve [Old English] Old English *slēfe*, *slīefe*), *slȳf* are forms related to Middle Dutch *sloove* 'covering'. The idiom *have something up one's sleeve* originated from the notion of a card being secreted up there, from the early 16th century.

sleight [Middle English] Old English *sleghth* meant 'cunning, skill', from Old Norse *slœgth*, from *slœgr* 'sly'.

slender [late Middle English] *Slender* is of unknown origin; an Anglo-Norman French source is the most probable.

sleuth [Middle English] *Sleuth* originally meant 'track' and was part of the compound *sleuth-hound*, a species of bloodhound formerly used in Scotland for tracking fugitives or for searching out game. Old Norse *slóth* is the source. Current senses date from the late 19th century.

slice [Middle English] *Slice* in early use included the sense 'fragment or splinter'. It is a shortening of Old French *esclice* 'splinter', from the verb *esclicier*, related to German *schleissen* 'to slice' and English *slit*.
→ SLIT

slick [Middle English] 'Glossy' and 'make smooth or glossy' were the early senses. It is probably from Old English and related to Old Norse *slíkr* 'smooth'. The sense 'plausible' dates from the late 16th century; 'skilful, adroit' dates from the early 19th century.
→ SLEEK

slide [Old English] The Old English verb *slídan* is related to *sled* and *sledge*. The noun, first used in the sense 'act of sliding', is recorded from the late 16th century. Its use to describe a piece of playground equipment dates from the late 19th century.
→ SLED

slight [Middle English] The adjective is from Old Norse *sléttr* 'smooth' (an early sense in English and remaining in dialect); this is Germanic in origin and related to Dutch *slechts* 'merely' and German *schlicht* 'simple', *schlecht* 'bad'. The verb, originally reflecting the sense 'make smooth or level', is from Old Norse *slétta*. The sense 'treat with disrespect' is found from the late 16th century.

slim [mid 17th century] *Slim* is from Low German or Dutch (from a base meaning 'slant-ing, cross, bad'), of Germanic origin. The pejorative sense found in Dutch and German existed originally in the English noun *slim* 'lazy or worthless person'; South African usage still reflects the meaning 'crafty, sly'. It has reflected the sense 'poor, slight' (*slim chance*) from the late 17th century.

slime [Old English] Old English *slím*, of Germanic origin, is related to Dutch *slijm* and German *Schleim* 'mucus, slime', Latin *limus* 'mud', and Greek *limnē* 'marsh'.

sling [Middle English] This is probably from Low German, of symbolic origin; compare with German *Schlinge* 'noose, snare'. Use of the word to express a cloth support for an injured arm dates from the early 18th century. The verb sense 'throw' (*sling a few things into your bag*) is from Old Norse *slyngva*.

slink [Old English] Old English *slincan* meant 'crawl, creep'; Middle Dutch and Middle Low German *slinken* 'subside, sink' may be related.

slip¹ [Middle English] 'Move quickly and softly' was the early sense, probably from the Middle Low German verb *slippen*. The phrase *slip someone's memory* arose in the mid 17th century; *slip through the net* dates from the early 20th century. The noun *slip* is from or related to the verb; its use to denote a female's under-skirt is a 20th-century usage; earlier (from the mid 18th century) it was an outer garment. **Slippery** (late 15th century) is from dialect *slipper* meaning 'slippery', probably suggested by German dialect *schlipfferig*. The noun **slipper** (based on *slip*) dates from the late 15th century and the first element of **slipshod** (late 16th century) is associated: this was originally in the sense 'wearing slippers or loose shoes'.

slip² [late Middle English] This *slip* as in *slip of paper* is probably from Middle Dutch, Middle Low German *slippe* 'cut, strip'. An early sense in English was 'twig, sprig', which led to 'young person' and the phrase *slip of a girl* (mid 17th century).

slit [late Old English] The Old English noun *slite* is related to Old English *slītan* 'split, rend' (of Germanic origin).

slither [Middle English] *Slither* is an alteration of the dialect verb *slidder*, a frequentative (= verb of repeated action) from the base of *slide*. The change from the -dd- spelling to -th- is normal as in *gather* and *hither*.
→ SLIDE

sliver [late Middle English] This word for a long thin piece is from dialect *slive* 'cleave'.

slobber [late Middle English] This is probably from Middle Dutch *slobberen* meaning both 'walk through mud' and 'feed noisily', imi-tative of the noise.

slogan [early 16th century] *Slogan* is from Scottish Gaelic *sluagh-ghairm*, from *sluagh* 'army' and *gairm* 'shout'. It was originally used in the sense 'battle cry'.

slop [mid 16th century] The early sense was 'to spill, splash'; it is from the obsolete noun *slop* meaning 'muddy place', related to Old

English *slip* 'semi-liquid mass'. Early use of the noun was as a word for 'slushy mud', the first of the current senses ('unappetizing food') dating from the mid 17th century.

slope [late 16th century] First used as a verb, *slope* is from the obsolete adverb *slope*, a shortening of *aslope* 'in a sloping manner'. The use of the verb with reference to aimless or unobtrusive movement (*sloped off unheard*) may be related to *lope*.
→ LOPE

slot [late Middle English] A *slot* was originally a 'slight depression running down the middle of the chest', a use which survives in Scots. It comes from Old French *esclot*, of obscure origin.

slouch [early 16th century] *Slouch*, first used meaning a 'lazy, slovenly person' is of unknown origin. *Slouching* was used to mean 'hanging down, drooping' (specifically when describing a hat with a brim hanging over the face), and 'having an awkward posture' from the 17th century.

slough[1] [Old English] Old English *slōh*, *slō(g)* meaning 'swamp' is of unknown origin. The sense 'state into which someone sinks' developed in Middle English; *Slough of Despond* is from Bunyan's use of the phrase in his *Pilgrim's Progress*: They drew near to a very Miry Slough … The name of the Slough was Despond.

slough[2] [Middle English] This *slough* pronounced 'sluff' was first used as a noun denoting a skin, especially the outer skin shed by a snake. It is perhaps related to Low German *slu(we)* 'husk, peel'. The verb dates from the early 18th century.

sloven [late 15th century] The original sense of *sloven* was 'person with base manners'; the word is perhaps from Flemish *sloef* 'dirty' or Dutch *slof* 'careless, negligent'. The adjective **slovenly** based on *sloven* dates from the late 16th century; its early sense was 'lewd, base'.

slow [Old English] Old English *slāw* meant 'slow-witted, sluggish'; it comes from a Germanic source. Other semantic branches include 'taking a comparatively long time' and 'moving in a sluggish manner'; it also combines with other words (*slow-witted*, *slow-motion*) which reinforce these senses.

sludge [early 17th century] This word is a variant of dialect *slutch* used in the same sense but of uncertain origin; it may, like *slush*, be imitative of the sound made by the soft semi-liquid substance when walking through it.
→ SLUSH

slug [late Middle English] This meant 'sluggard' in early examples. It is probably of Scan-

dinavian origin and associated with Norwegian dialect *slugg* 'large heavy body'. Use of the word to describe a type of land snail dates from the early 18th century.

sluggard [Middle English] *Sluggard* is based on the rare verb *slug* 'be lazy or slow' which may be Scandinavian in origin. Late Middle English **sluggish** is probably based on the same verb.

sluice [Middle English] *Sluice* is from Old French *escluse* 'sluice gate', based on Latin *excludere* 'exclude'. The verb dates from the late 16th century, the sense 'swill with water' dating from the mid 18th century.

slum [early 19th century] This word was originally slang in the sense 'room'. Its origin is unknown. The verb phrase *slum it* made its appearance in the late 19th century.

slumber [Middle English] *Slumber* is an alteration of Scots and northern English *sloom* which had the same sense. The *-b-* was added to facilitate pronunciation.

slump [late 17th century] This verb was first recorded in the context 'fall into a bog'. It is probably imitative of the dull splashing sound and related to Norwegian *slumpe* 'to fall'. Use of the noun in connection with prices arose in the late 19th century.

slur [early 17th century] The origin of *slur* is unknown. The Middle English noun *slur* meaning 'thin, fluid mud' gave rise to the early verb senses 'smear, smirch' and 'disparage (a person)': later sense development led to 'gloss over (a fault)', which influenced current usage 'speak indistinctly' (late 19th century).

slurry [late Middle English] This is related to dialect *slur* 'thin mud', of which the origin is unknown.
→ SLUR

slush [mid 17th century] *Slush* is probably imitative. The compound:
■ **slush fund** (mid 19th century) was originally nautical slang for money collected to buy luxuries from the sale of watery food referred to as *slush*.

sly [Middle English] Early use of *sly* included the sense 'dexterous, skilful'. It derives from Old Norse *slœgr* 'cunning', which was originally 'able to strike' from the verb *slá*. The phrase *on the sly* is recorded in use from the early 19th century.
→ SLEIGHT

smack[1] [mid 16th century] The early sense reflected by *smack* was 'part (one's lips) noisily'. It comes from Middle Dutch *smacken* which is an imitative formation similar to German *sch-*

matzen 'eat or kiss noisily'. Use of the word to mean 'strike (a person)' dates from the early 19th century (Dickens *Seven Dials*: Mrs. A. smacks Mrs. B.'s child for 'making faces').

smack² [Old English] This *smack* as in *it smacks of fish* in contexts of flavour (*smæc* 'flavour, smell' in Old English) is of Germanic origin; it is related to Dutch *smaak* and German *Geschmack*.

small [Old English] Old English *smæl* is Germanic in origin, related to Dutch *smal* and German *schmal*. The senses branch into: 'of relatively little girth' (*small waist*); 'of limited size' (*small piece*); and 'weak' (*small beer*).

smart [Old English] The Old English verb *smeortan* is West Germanic in origin; German *schmerzen* is related. The adjective is related to the verb, the original sense in late Old English being 'causing sharp pain'; from this arose 'keen, brisk', which in turn gave rise to the current senses of 'mentally sharp' (*smart at maths*) and 'neat in a brisk, sharp style' (*smart dresser*).

smash [early 18th century] First recorded in noun use, *smash* is probably imitative, representing a blend of words such as *smack* and *smite* with *bash* and *mash*.

smattering [mid 16th century] This word is from *smatter* meaning 'talk ignorantly, prate', which survives in Scots. Its origin is unknown.

smear [Old English] Old English *smeoru* 'ointment, grease' and the verb *smierwan* come from a Germanic source; the German verb *schmieren* and the noun *Schmer* are related. Figurative use in contexts of attempting to discredit someone's reputation, dates from the mid 16th century.

smell [Middle English] This is not a word represented in any of the cognate languages and its origin is unknown. The sense 'give out an unpleasant odour' is found early; the notion of 'raise suspicion' (*this extortion case smells*) is found from the 1930s.

smile [Middle English] *Smile* may be of Scandinavian origin and related to **smirk** (*sme(a)rcian* in Old English), from a base shared by *smile*. The early sense of *smirk* was 'to smile' but it later gained a notion of smugness or silliness.

smock [Old English] Old English *smoc* referred to a 'woman's loose-fitting undergarment' and is probably related to both Old English *smūgan* 'to creep' and Old Norse *smjúga* 'put on a garment, creep into'. The use of the verb as a needlework term dates from the late 19th century.

smoke [Old English] Old English *smoca* (noun) and *smocian* (verb) are from the Germanic base of *smēocan* 'emit smoke'; Dutch *smook* and German *Schmauch* are related forms. Early 20th-century **smog** is a blend of *smoke* and *fog*.

smooth [Old English] Old English *smōth* is probably from a Germanic source though no cognates are known. Use of the word to mean 'speaking in a plausible way' (often implying insincerity) dates from late Middle English; its application in the sense 'stylish, suave' is found from the 1920s. The verb dates from Middle English.

smother [Middle English] *Smother* was first recorded in use as a noun in the sense 'stifling smoke'. It comes from the base of Old English *smorian* 'suffocate'. The senses 'prevent from flourishing' (*smothered his ambition*) and 'extinguish (a fire)' date from the late 16th century.

smoulder [late Middle English] *Smoulder* is related to Dutch *smeulen*. During the 17th and 18th centuries, both noun and verb fell into disuse apart from poetical use of *smouldering*; in 1755 Johnson said (of *smouldering*): This word seems a participle, but I know not whether the verb *smoulder* be in use. Sir Walter Scott's novels apparently revived the word's use in the 19th century.

smug [mid 16th century] *Smug* is from Low German *smuk* 'pretty' and originally had the sense 'neat, spruce' in descriptions of men; it was used commonly between about 1590 and 1650 to describe women and girls in this original sense. The notion of complacency developed later but it is difficult to date because of the extremely common use of the word.

smuggle [late 17th century] This is apparently from Low German *smuggelen*, of which the ultimate origin is unknown.

snack [Middle English] The early sense recorded was 'snap, bite'; it is from Middle Dutch *snac(k)*, from *snacken* 'to bite', a variant of *snappen*. Senses relating to food date from the late 17th century; use of the word to mean 'light incidental meal' dates from the mid 18th century.

snag [late 16th century] *Snag* is probably of Scandinavian origin. The early sense 'stump sticking out from a tree trunk' gave rise to a US sense 'submerged piece of timber obstructing navigation': this led to the current main sense 'hitch' as a figurative use (e.g. *the snag is I've no money*). Current verb senses arose in the 19th century.

snap [late 15th century] Early use included the senses 'make a sudden audible bite' and 'quick sharp biting sound'. It probably derives from Middle Dutch or Middle Low German *snappen* 'seize' and is partly imitative. The sense 'utter sharp words' (*snapped at him angrily*) dates from the late 16th century; 'break suddenly' (*the rubber band snapped*) is recorded from the early 17th century; the word's use in photography (*snapped him as he played*) from the notion of a quick movement, is found from the late 19th century.

snare [late Old English] Old English *sneare* is from Old Norse *snara*; the Middle English verb is from the noun.

snarl¹ [late 16th century] This *snarl* (as in *the dog snarled*) is an extension of obsolete *snar* of Germanic origin; it is related to German *schnarren* 'rattle, snarl' which is probably imitative of the sound.

snarl² [late Middle English] This *snarl* (as in *snarled up in the netting*) had the early senses 'snare, noose' and 'catch in a snare'; it comes from *snare*.
→ SNARE

snatch [Middle English] The early spelling was *sna(c)che* expressing the senses 'suddenly snap at' and 'a snare'; the word may be related to *snack*.
→ SNACK

sneak [late 16th century] *Sneak* is probably dialect and is perhaps related to obsolete *snike* 'to creep'. The sense 'inform' is school slang of the late 19th century; in this same period the verb also meant 'steal in a stealthy manner' (*they would sneak a smoke behind the sheds*).

sneer [late Middle English] This is probably a word of imitative origin; it was used from the middle of the 16th century in the sense 'snort' when referring to a horse. The sense 'smile scornfully' is found from the late 17th century.

sneeze [Middle English] *Sneeze* is apparently an alteration (due to misreading or misprinting) of Middle English *fnese* because this initial *fn-* had become an unfamiliar combination. The *sn-* was later adopted because it sounded appropriate to the sound and action.

snip [mid 16th century] The early noun sense was 'a shred'. *Snip* is from Low German *snip* meaning 'small piece' and is imitative in origin. Use of the word to mean 'bargain' dates from the 1920s. The verb started out meaning 'take something suddenly', now obsolete; 'cut by scissors' is late 16th- century.

snivel [late Old English] This was first recorded only in the verbal noun *snyflung* 'mucus', from *snofl* used in the same sense. The verb sense 'be or appear to be upset and in tears' (*stop snivelling boy*) dates from the late 17th

century. There may be an association with late 16th-century **snuffle** (which is probably from Low German and Dutch *snuffelen*).

snob [late 18th century] This was originally dialect in the sense 'cobbler'; its origin is unknown. Early senses conveyed a notion of 'lower status or rank'; later the word described a person seeking to imitate people they perceived as superior in social standing or wealth. Folk etymology connects the word with Latin *sine nobilitate* 'without nobility' but the first recorded sense has no connection with this.

snoop [mid 19th century] This word meaning 'pry' (*snooping around hoping to find proof*) is from Dutch *snœpen* 'eat on the sly', an early sense in US English.

snooty [early 20th century] This is based on mid 19th-century **snoot**, a variant of *snout*. Late Middle English **snot** and late 16th century **snotty** are also related to Middle English **snout** (from Middle Dutch, Middle Low German *snūt*).

snore [Middle English] The early sense recorded was 'a snort, snorting'; it is probably imitative of the noise in the same way as late Middle English **snort** which was first used as a verb also in the sense 'snore'.

snow [Old English] Old English *snāw* is of Germanic origin, related to Dutch *sneeuw* and German *Schnee*, from an Indo-European root shared by Latin *nix*, *niv-* and Greek *nipha*.

snub [Middle English] Early use was as a verb originally in the sense 'rebuke with sharp words'. Old Norse *snubba* 'chide, check the growth of' is the source. The adjective, first recorded in the early 18th century, was chiefly used in the phrase *snub nose*.

snuff¹ [late Middle English] This *snuff* meaning 'suppress, extinguish' is of obscure origin. The noun originally described the portion of a wick partly consumed during burning as it gave off light. The slang phrase *snuff it* meaning 'to die' dates from the late 19th century.

snuff² [late Middle English] This *snuff* was first in verb use meaning 'inhale throught the nostrils'; it comes from Middle Dutch *snuffen* 'to snuffle'. The noun as a term for a preparation of tobacco inhaled through the nostrils dates from the late 17th century and is probably an abbreviation of Dutch *snuftabak*.

snug [late 16th century] This was originally in nautical use in the sense 'shipshape, compact, prepared for bad weather' and is probably of Low German or Dutch origin. The dialect and slang use of the word as a noun meaning 'bar of a public house' dates from the early 19th century. Late 17th-century **snuggle** is a frequentative (– verb of repeated action) of the verb *snug* meaning 'nestle closely'.

soak [Old English] Old English *socian* meant 'become saturated with a liquid by immersion'; it is related to *sūcan* 'to suck'. Use of the noun in the sense 'heavy drinker' (*old soak*) dates from the early 19th century.

soap [Old English] Old English *sape* is West Germanic in origin, related to Dutch *zeep* and German *Seife*. The verb dates from the mid 16th century. The application of the noun *soap* to a radio or television serial (*soap opera*) dates from the 1930s as a result of early sponsorship of such programmes by soap manufacturers.

soar [late Middle English] *Soar* is a shortening of Old French *essorer*, based on the Latin elements *ex-* 'out of' and *aura* 'breeze'.

sob [Middle English] *Sob* is perhaps of Dutch or Low German origin; Dutch dialect *sabben* 'to suck' may be related. The compound *sob story* appeared in the early 20th century.

sober [Middle English] Latin *sobrius* is the base of *sober* (via Old French) and late Middle English **sobriety** (from Old French *sobriete* or Latin *sobrietas*). *Sober* expresses 'temperate, avoiding excess' and 'grave, serious'. In Scots the word once meant 'insignificant, small, paltry'.

social [late Middle English] Latin *socius* 'companion' is the base of several English words: *social* is from Old French, or from Latin *socialis* 'allied'; mid 16th-century **sociable** is from French, or from Latin *sociabilis*, from *sociare* 'unite'; **society** (also mid 16th century in the sense 'companionship, friendly association with others') is from French *société*, from Latin *societas*; early 19th-century **socialism** is apparently from French *socialisme*, from *social*. The early history of the word *socialism* is obscure. The French word made its appearance in 1832 contrasted with *personnalité*, three or four years later the modern political sense was attributed to a use by either Leroux or Reybaud in their writings. However the source has also been attributed to an English use in 1835 during the discussions of a society founded by Robert Owen.

sock [Old English] Old English *socc* was a 'light shoe'. Of Germanic origin, it is from Latin *soccus* 'comic actor's shoe, light low-heeled slipper', from Greek *sukkhos*. The phrase *knock the socks off* was originally US English from the early 19th century; *pull one's socks up* arose in the late 19th century; *put a sock in it* is early 20th-century.

socket [Middle English] The early use was as a term for the 'head of a spear, resembling a ploughshare'. It comes from an Anglo-Norman French diminutive of Old French *soc* 'ploughshare', probably of Celtic origin. The notion of a hollow part in a cylindrical shape for fitting together with another part dates from the 15th century.

soft [Old English] Old English *sōfte* meant 'agreeable, calm, gentle'. Of West Germanic origin, it is related to Dutch *zacht* and German *sanft*. Its meanings branch broadly into 'calm, pleasing' (Shakespeare *Antony and Cleopatra*: Till that the conquering Wine hath steep't our sense, In soft and delicate Lethe), 'gentle, mild' (*a softer approach*), and 'yielding' (*soft heart*). The idiomatic phrase *have a soft spot for* dating from the late 17th century expresses tenderness.

soggy [early 18th century] *Soggy* once meant 'boggy, soaked with water'; it is based on dialect *sog* 'a swamp'.

soil¹ [late Middle English] This *soil* describing the upper layer of earth is from Anglo-Norman French, perhaps representing Latin *solium* 'seat', by association with *solum* 'ground'. It once referred to a land or country and still reflects the sense 'native land'.

soil² [Middle English] This *soil* meaning 'make dirty' is from Old French *soiller*, based on Latin *sucula*, a diminutive of *sus* 'pig'. The earliest use of the noun (late Middle English) was as a term for a 'muddy wallow for wild boar'; current noun use referring to 'waste matter' dates from the early 16th century.

solace [Middle English] *Solace* is from the Old French noun *solas* and verb *solacier*, based on Latin *solari* 'to console'.

solar [late Middle English] This is from Latin *solaris*, from *sol* 'sun', a base shared by mid 19th-century **solarium**, a use of a Latin word meaning literally 'sundial, place for sunning oneself'.

solder [Middle English] *Solder* is from Old French *soudure*, from the verb *souder*, from Latin *solidare* 'fasten together'. The base is Latin *solidus* 'solid'.

soldier [Middle English] This word derives from Old French *soldier*, from *soulde* '(soldier's) pay', from Latin *solidus* (a gold coin of the later Roman Empire). Early use also reflected its figurative use referring to spiritual service (*soldiers of Christ*). The verb dates from the early 17th century meaning 'serve as a soldier'; the figurative *soldier on* arose in the 1950s.

sole¹ [Middle English] This *sole* referring to the underpart of the foot is from Old French, from Latin *solea* 'sandal, sill', from *solum* 'bottom, pavement, sole'; Dutch *zool* and German *Sohle* are associated. Use of the word *sole* for a type of marine flatfish (Middle English via Old French, from Provençal *sola*) is by shape association.

sole² [late Middle English] This *sole* meaning 'only' also meant 'secluded' and 'unrivalled' in early examples. It is from Old French *soule*, from Latin *sola*, the feminine of *solus* 'alone'.

solemn [Middle English] *Solemn* initially was a word meaning 'associated with religious rites' (*solemn Mass*; *Solemn Requiem*). It comes from Old French *solemne*, from Latin *sollemnis* 'customary, celebrated at a fixed date', from *sollus* 'entire'. **Solemnity** in Middle English meant 'observance of formality and ceremony' and was frequently found in the phrases *in solemnity* and *with solemnity*; this is from Old French *solemnite*, from Latin *sollemnitas*, from *sollemnis*.

solicit [late Middle English] *Solicit* is from Old French *solliciter*, from Latin *sollicitare* 'agitate', from *sollicitus* 'anxious': the base forms are *sollus* 'entire' and *citus* (the past participle of *ciere* 'set in motion'). The word expresses the notions 'entreat' and 'sue for, seek by petition'. **Solicitor** in this same Middle English period referred to an agent or deputy or generally to 'a person instigating (something)'; its source is Old French *solliciteur*, from *solliciter*. The rise of *solicitors* as a class of legal practitioners dates from the late 16th century. A later (mid 16th-century) word in this group, **solicitous**, is also based on Latin *sollicitus* 'anxious'.

solid [late Middle English] *Solid* is from Latin *solidus*, related to *salvus* 'safe' and *sollus* 'entire'. The word's application to reasoned judgement based on sound principles (*solid argument*) is found from the early 17th century. **Solidarity** dates from the mid 19th century and is from French *solidarité*, from *solidaire* 'solidary'. Its use in English became very common in the late 20th century in reference to the independent Polish trade union movement registered in September 1980 and officially banned in October 1982.

soliloquy [Middle English] *Soliloquy* is from late Latin *soliloquium* (a word introduced by Saint Augustine), from Latin *solus* 'alone' and *loqui* 'speak'.

solitary [Middle English] Latin *solus* 'alone' is the base of several words: *solitary* (from Latin *solitarius*), Middle English **solitude** (from Old French, or from Latin *solitudo*) and late 17th-century **solo** first used as a musical term adopted from Italian.

solstice [Middle English] *Solstice* is from Old French, from Latin *solstitium*, from *sol* 'sun' and *stit-* (the past participial stem of *sistere* 'stop').

solve [late Middle English] The early senses of *solve* were 'loosen, dissolve, untie'; the source

is Latin *solvere* 'loosen, unfasten'. Other words sharing this base are late Middle English **soluble** (from late Latin *solubilis*) and, in the same period, **solution** (from Old French, from Latin *solutio(n-)*). **Solvent** dates from the mid 17th century, from Latin *solvent-*, the present participial stem of *solvere*.

sombre [mid 18th century] *Sombre* is from French, based on Latin *sub* 'under' and *umbra* 'shade'. It expresses the notions dark and gloomy referring to both objects and people.

some [Old English] Old English *sum*, of Germanic origin, is from an Indo-European root shared by Greek *hamōs* 'somehow' and Sanskrit *sama* 'any, every'.

somersault [mid 16th century] This word, first used as a noun, is from Old French *sombresault*, from Provençal *sobresaut*, from *sobre* 'above' and *saut* 'leap'.

somnolent [late Middle English] 'Causing sleepiness' was the early meaning recorded for *somnolent* from Old French *sompnolent* or Latin *somnolentus*. Latin *somnus* 'sleep' is the base, which also provides the first element of **somnambulist** (late 18th century, from French *somnambulisme*): Latin *ambulare* 'to walk' is the source of the second element.

son [Old English] Old English *sunu*, of Germanic origin, is related to Dutch *zoon* and German *Sohn*, from an Indo-European root shared by Greek *huios*. The word's use as an affectionate form of address occurred early; the phrase *son and heir* appeared in Middle English.

song [Old English] Old English *sang* is of Germanic origin, related to Dutch *zang* and German *Sang*, as well as to *sing*. The phrase *song and dance* was originally US (early 17th century) and referred to a form of entertainment; it was later applied to a vaudeville act; the sense 'rigmarole' developed in the late 19th century (*made a song and dance about it*).
→ SING

sonorous [early 17th century] This is based on Latin *sonorus* from *sonor* 'sound'.

soon [Old English] Old English *sōna*, of West Germanic origin, had the early sense 'immediately'. The idiomatic phrase *sooner you than me* is recorded from the 15th century; *as soon* meaning 'rather' (W. B. Yeats *Hour-Glass*: I'd as soon listen to dried peas in a bladder as listen to your thoughts) dates from the late 16th century as a Shakespearean usage.

soot [Old English] Old English *sōt*, of Germanic origin, is related to German dialect *Sott*, from an Indo-European root shared by the verb *sit*.

→ SIT

soothe [Old English] Old English *sōthian* 'verify, show to be true' is from Old English *sōth* 'true, genuine' (Middle English **soothsayer**, using this same word as its first element, originally referred to a 'person who speaks the truth'). In the 16th century the verb *soothe* passed through the senses 'corroborate (a statement)', 'humour (a person) by expressing assent' and 'flatter by giving assent', from which arose 'mollify, appease' in the later part of the 17th century.

sop [Old English] Old English *soppian* meant 'dip (bread) in liquid'; it is probably from the base of Old English *sūpan* 'sup'. The sense 'thing done or offered as a concession to appease someone' (mid 17th century) alludes to the sop used by Aeneas on his visit to Hades to appease Cerberus, the monstrous watchdog guarding the entrance (an account from Virgil's *Aeneid*). The word **sopping** (the present participle of *sop*) dates from the mid 19th century. **Soppy** which first made its appearance in the early 19th century in the sense 'soaked with water' is based on *sop*.

sorcerer [late Middle English] The early spelling was *sorser*, from Old French *sorcier*, based on Latin *sors, sort-* 'lot'.

sordid [late Middle English] This was first used as a medical term in the sense 'purulent'; it is from French *sordide* or Latin *sordidus*, from *sordere* 'be dirty'. The current senses date from the early 17th century, for example in the description of actions or habits as being 'despicable, stemming from ignoble motives'.

sore [Old English] Old English *sār* (noun and adjective), *sāre* (adverb), are forms of Germanic origin, related to Dutch *zeer* 'sore' and German *sehr* 'very'. The original sense was 'causing intense pain, grievous', which led to the adverbial use (*sore troubled*). **Sorely** is also Old English (as *sārlice*); it has tended to be used as an intensifier of meaning (*sorely missed*).

sorrow [Old English] Old English *sorh, sorg* (noun), *sorgian* (verb), are Germanic in origin, related to Dutch *zorg* and German *Sorge*. Its relationship to forms outside Germanic is not clear.

sorry [Old English] Old English *sārig* meant 'pained, distressed'; this sense weakened later in the commonly used *I'm sorry*. Of West Germanic origin, it is from the base of the noun *sore*. The shortening of the root vowel has given

the word an apparent connection with *sorrow* but this is unrelated.

→ SORE

sort [late Middle English] *Sort* is from Old French *sorte*, from an alteration of Latin *sors, sort-* 'lot, condition'. The phrase *of sorts* arose in the late 16th century and meant 'of various kinds'; in the early 20th century it gained a colloquial disparaging usage (*he's an artist of sorts*). Of the other phrases, *out of sorts* is recorded from the early 17th century; the contrasting pair *something of the sort* and *nothing of the sort* date from the early 19th century.

soul [Old English] Old English *sāwol, sāw(e)l*, is of Germanic origin, related to Dutch *ziel* and German *Seele*. It expresses the spiritual or emotional part of man (*his soul isn't in it*), the disembodied spirit of someone deceased (*his departed soul*), and figuratively the essential part of something (*the very soul of history*). It has also, from Middle English been used to mean 'person' (*not a soul stirred*).

sound[1] [Middle English] The early spelling of this *sound* (as in *made a loud sound*) was *soun*, from Anglo-Norman French *soun* as a noun and *suner* as a verb, from Latin *sonus*. The form with *-d* was established in the 16th century. The phrase *I like the sound of* was first recorded in Mrs Gaskell's *Letters*: I like the 'sound' of him extremely, and I hope he will like me when we come to know each other.

sound[2] [Middle English] This *sound* meaning 'in good condition, not damaged or diseased' is from Old English *gesund*, of West Germanic origin, related to Dutch *gezond* and German *gesund* 'healthy'. In Middle English the prominent sense was 'uninjured, unwounded'. Use of *sound* to mean 'having well-grounded opinions' dates from the early 16th century; the phrase *as sound as a bell* appeared in the late 16th century.

sound[3] [late Middle English] *Sound* 'ascertain the depth of water' is from Old French *sonder*, based on Latin *sub-* 'below' and *unda* 'wave'.

sound[4] [Middle English] This *sound* as a term for a narrow stretch of water is from Old Norse *sund* 'swimming, strait', related to *swim*.

→ SWIM

sour [Old English] Old English *sūr* is Germanic in origin, related to Dutch *zuur* and German *sauer*. The word branches semantically into: 'having a tart taste' and 'unpleasant, embittered, peevish'. These leading senses are also prominent in the cognate languages.

source [late Middle English] *Source* is from Old French *sours(e)*, the past participle of *sourdre* 'to rise', from Latin *surgere*. The word has been used to refer to a work supplying evidence of a primary nature (*authentic source*) from the late 18th century.

south [Old English] Old English *sūth* is Germanic in origin, related to Low German *sud*. The adjective **southern** was *sūtherne* in Old English.

souvenir [late 18th century] This is an adoption of a French word from *souvenir* 'remember', from Latin *subvenire* 'occur to the mind'.

sovereign [Middle English] *Sovereign* (based on Latin *super* 'above') is from Old French *soverain*; the change in the ending was due to association with *reign*. The word was used as a term for a gold coin minted in England from the time of Henry VII to Charles I; it was originally worth 22s. 6d. **Sovereignty** is also late Middle English from Old French *sovereinete*, from the same base.

sow[1] [Old English] Old English *sāwan* 'to plant' is Germanic in origin; related forms are Dutch *zaaien* and German *säen*. It was also used figuratively meaning 'disseminate' from early times.

sow[2] [Old English] Old English *sugu* 'female pig' is related to Dutch *zeug*, German *Sau*, from an Indo-European root shared by Latin *sus* and Greek *hus* 'pig'.

sozzled [late 19th century] This is the past participle of dialect *sozzle* 'mix sloppily', which is probably imitative in origin.

space [Middle English] *Space* is a shortening of Old French *espace*, from Latin *spatium*. It refers to 'time and duration' (*in the space of seven days*) and 'area or extension' (*a large enough space*). Use of the word in reference to the immeasurable expanse containing the solar and star systems dates from the late 17th century, as do current verb senses. Also based on Latin *spatium* are late Middle English **spacious** (from Old French *spacios* or Latin *spatiosus*) and mid 19th-century **spatial**.

spade [Old English] Old English *spadu, spada* is from a Germanic source, related to Dutch *spade*, German *Spaten*, and to Greek *spathē* 'blade, paddle'. The phrase *to call a spade a spade* dates from the mid 16th century in a reference to an early source in Plutarch's *Apophthegmata* (178 BC).

span [Old English] This *span* as in *a span of three feet* was originally a 'distance between the tips of the thumb and little finger'. Of Germanic origin, it is rare in Old English but was reinforced from 1300 by Old French *espan*. The meaning 'a short space of time' (*mortal span*) dates from the late 16th century. The word was applied to the 'arch of a bridge' from the early 19th century.

spanner [late 18th century] The word *spanner* is based on German *spannen* 'draw tight'.

spar[1] [Middle English] This *spar* as a word for a 'pole, rafter' is a shortening of Old French *esparre*, or from Old Norse *sperra*; it is related to Dutch *spar* and German *Sparren*.

spar[2] [Old English] The *spar* of sparring partner was, in Old English, *sperran, spyrran* 'strike out rapidly'. The origin is unknown; Old Norse *sperrask* 'kick out' may be related.

spare [Old English] Old English *spær* meant 'not plentiful, meagre'; the verb *sparian* meant 'refrain from injuring', 'refrain from using'. From a Germanic source, *spare* is related to Dutch and German *sparen* 'to spare'. The compound:
■ **spare rib** (late 16th century) is probably from Middle Low German *ribbesper* (by transposition of the syllables), associated with the adjective *spare*.

spark [Old English] Old English *spærca, spearca* is of unknown origin; it is not represented in the other Germanic languages. The Middle English verb **sparkle** is a frequentative (= verb of repeated action) or diminutive noun of *spark*.

sparse [early 18th century] This was first used to describe writing in the sense 'widely spaced': it is from Latin *sparsus*, the past participle of *spargere* 'scatter'. Its use in connection with population or groups of people was originally US.

spasm [late Middle English] *Spasm* is from Old French *spasme*, or via Latin from Greek *spasmos, spasma*, from *span* 'pull'. Late 17th-century **spasmodic** is from modern Latin *spasmodicus*, from Greek *spasmōdēs*, from *spasma*.

spate [late Middle English] This was originally Scots and northern English in the sense 'flood, inundation'; the origin is unknown. Figurative use is recorded from the early 17th century.

spatter [mid 16th century] A person could *spatter* when the word was first in use: it had the sense 'splutter while speaking'. As a form, it is a frequentative (= verb of repeated action) from a base shared by Dutch and Low German *spatten* 'burst, spout'.

spawn [late Middle English] This is a shortening of Anglo-Norman French *espaundre* 'to shed roe', a variant of Old French *espandre* 'pour out', from Latin *expandere* 'expand'. The contemptuous use 'give birth' was first recorded in Shakespeare's *Measure for Measure*: Some

report, a Seamaid spawn'd him. Some, that he was
begot betweene two Stock-fishes.

spay [late Middle English] *Spay* is a shortening
of Old French *espeer* 'cut with a sword', from
espee 'sword', from Latin *spatha*.

speak [Old English] Old English *sprecan*, later
specan, from a West Germanic source, is related
to Dutch *spreken* and German *sprechen*. The
phrase *speak for yourself* is recorded from Middle
English; *speak for itself* appeared in the late 18th
century. Related to *speak* is **speech** (*sprǣc, sprēc*
in Old English); Dutch *spraak*, and German
Sprache are cognates.

special [Middle English] This is a shortening
of Old French *especial* 'especial' or Latin *specialis*,
from *species* 'appearance'. This base form (from
Latin *specere* 'to look') was adopted as an English
word in its own right (e.g. *various species*) in
late Middle English. **Speciality** in late Middle
English referred to the quality of being special
or distinctive; this comes from Old French *espe-
cialite* or late Latin *specialitas*, from Latin *specialis*.
The verb **specialize** is early 17th-century from
French *spécialiser*, from *spécial* 'special'.

specify [Middle English] *Specify* is from Old
French *specifier* or late Latin *specificare*, the base
too of late 16th-century **specification** (from
medieval Latin *specificatio(n-)*) and mid 17th-
century **specific** (from late Latin *specificus*,
from Latin *species*) used originally to mean
'having a special determining quality'.

specimen [early 17th century] This was initially a 'pattern, model'; it is an adoption of a
Latin word, from *specere* 'to look'. The Latin
plural *specimina* was fairly common in the later
half of the 17th century.

speck [Old English] Old English *specca* was a
small spot or discoloration; it is not found in
the cognate languages. Late Middle English
speckle had the same sense and is from Middle
Dutch *spekkel*; the verb (late 16th century)
derives from the noun or it is a back-formation
(by removal of the suffix) from *speckled*.

spectacle [Middle English] *Spectacle* came
via Old French from Latin *spectaculum* 'public
show', from *spectare*; this is a frequentative
(= verb of repeated action) of *specere* 'to look'.
The phrase *make a spectacle of* meaning 'exhibit'
(usually as an object of contempt) was also
early. The word's use (at first in the singular)
for a device to assist eyesight was late Middle
English. **Spectacular** (from *spectacle* on the
pattern of words such as *oracular*) dates from
the late 17th century.

spectator [late 16th century] *Spectator* is
from French *spectateur* or Latin *spectator*, from
spectare 'gaze at, observe'. The verb **spectate**

is recorded from the early 18th century as a
back-formation (by removal of the suffix) from
spectator.
→ SPECTACLE

spectre [early 17th century] *Spectre* is from
French *spectre* or Latin *spectrum* literally 'image,
apparition', from *specere* 'to look'; **spectrum**
was adopted into English in the early 17th
century, when it too originally meant 'spectre'
(its use in physics dates from the late 17th
century).

speculation [late Middle English] Latin
speculari 'spy out, watch' from *specula* 'watchtower' is the source of *speculation* (via Old
French, or from late Latin *speculatio(n-)*), the
contemporaneous **speculative** (from Old
French *speculatif*, *-ive* or late Latin *speculativus*),
and **speculate** in the late 16th century. The
latter has been used in the context of buying
and selling commodities from the late 18th
century.

speed [Old English] Old English *spēd* as a
noun, and *spēdan* as a verb, are from the Germanic base of Old English *spōwan* 'prosper, succeed', a sense reflected in early usage (and
found in the expression *God speed!*). The noun
splits semantically into 'abundance' (now
obsolete), 'success, prosperity' (*more haste less
speed*) and 'rapidity'.

spell¹ [Middle English] This *spell* as in (*spell
correctly*) is a shortening of Old French *espeller*,
from the Germanic base of Old English **spell**
meaning 'narration' and later 'incantation'
(*magic spell*).

spell² [late 16th century] *Spell* as in a *spell of
activity* is a variant of dialect *spele* 'take the place
of', of unknown origin. The early sense of the
noun was 'shift of relief workers'

spend [Old English] Old English *spendan* is
partly from Latin *expendere* 'pay out' and partly
also a shortening of obsolete *dispend*, from Latin
dispendere 'pay out'. English senses broadly split
into 'disburse' and 'allow time to pass'.

sphere [Middle English] *Sphere* is from Old
French *espere*, from late Latin *sphera*, earlier
sphaera, from Greek *sphaira* 'ball'. **Spherical**
(via late Latin from Greek *sphairikos*, from
sphaira) is recorded from the late 15th century.

spick and span [late 16th century] The
early sense was 'brand new' from the phrase
spick and span new, an emphatic extension of
dialect *span new*. Old Norse *spán-nýr* is the
source, from *spánn* 'chip' and *nýr* 'new'. The
addition of the element *spick* was influenced by
Dutch *spiksplinternieuw*, literally 'splinter new'.

spike [Middle English] *Spike* 'thin pointed piece of metal' is perhaps from Middle Low German, Middle Dutch *spiker*, related to *spoke*. The verb dates from the early 17th century; its use in *spike someone's drink* from the late 18th century is from the notion of making it sharper.
→ SPOKE

spill [Old English] Old English *spillan* meant 'kill, destroy' (common from about 1300 till 1600) and 'shed (blood)'. The origin is unknown. The sense 'allow liquid to pour out or over' arose in late Middle English.

spin [Old English] Old English *spinnan* meant 'draw out and twist (fibre)'; it is related to German *spinnen*. The noun dates from the mid 19th century. In the late 20th century in US political contexts the word *spin* acquired the meaning 'bias, slant' (*put a spin on something*) and in the 1980s is seen in **spin doctor** for a political press agent employed to promote a favourable interpretation of events to journalists. Of related words, **spider** (in late Old English *spīthra*) is from *spinnan*; Old English **spindle** (first as *spinel*) is from the base of the verb *spin*.

spine [late Middle English] *Spine* is a shortening of Old French *espine*, or from Latin *spina* 'thorn, prickle, backbone'. The word has been used to denote the back of a book from the 1920s.

spinney [late 16th century] *Spinney* is a shortening of Old French *espinei*, from an alteration of Latin *spinetum* 'thicket', from *spina* 'thorn'.
→ SPINE

spinster [late Middle English] This was once a word for a 'woman who spins' based on the verb *spin*; in early use the term was appended to names of women to denote their occupation. The current sense in the context of marriage dates from the early 18th century.

spire [Old English] Old English *spīr* was a 'tall slender stem of a plant', related to German *Spier* 'tip of a blade of grass'. The shape association led to the word being used in the late 16th century as a name for a slender structure such as a *spire of rock* or a *church spire* (Matthew Arnold *Thyrsis*: And that sweet city with her dreaming spires ... Lovely all times she lies, lovely to-night).

spiral [mid 16th century] This was first used as an adjective; it is from medieval Latin *spiralis*, from Latin *spira* 'coil', the source too of mid 16th-century **spire**, now a zoology term for the upper part of a spiral shell, but first used in the general sense 'a spiral'.

spirit [Middle English] This is from Anglo-Norman French, from Latin *spiritus* 'breath, spirit', from *spirare* 'breathe'. The use of the word to refer to alcoholic liquor dates from the late 17th century in the plural (Bunyan *Pilgrim's Progress*: He gave me also a piece of an Honeycomb, and a little Bottle of Spirits). The sense 'liveliness, vivacity' dates from the early 18th century; so too phrases such as *low spirits*, *high spirits*. The related word **spiritual** is also Middle English from Old French *spirituel*, from Latin *spiritualis*, from *spiritus*.

spit[1] [Old English] Old English *spittan* 'eject saliva' is imitative of the action and sound. Association with this word led to **spittle** (late 15th century), an alteration of dialect *spattle* used in the same sense.

spit[2] [Old English] Old English *spitu* 'thin pointed rod' (*roasted on the spit*) is West Germanic in origin and related to Dutch *spit* and German *Spiess*.

spite [Middle English] This is a shortening of Old French *despit* 'contempt', *despiter* 'show contempt for'. The spelling *spight* influenced by other English words with this *-ght* ending was common from about 1575 to 1700. The phrase *in spite of* dates from the early 16th century.

splay [Middle English] 'Unfold to view, display' in the context of opening a banner was the early sense of *splay*, a shortening of the verb *display*.
→ DISPLAY

splendid [early 17th century] *Splendid* is from French *splendide* or Latin *splendidus*, from *splendere* 'shine, be bright'. The notion of 'grandeur' is at the core of the word; its use to mean 'excellent' started in the mid 17th century. The phrase *in splendid isolation* illustrates the word in expressions where a contrast is given with a noun of a very different connotation; this specific phrase was in use at the end of the 19th century to refer to the political and commercial uniqueness of Great Britain in Europe.

splice [early 16th century] This is probably from Middle Dutch *splissen*. The origin is doubtful but there may be a connection with *split*. Early use was chiefly nautical; it was applied in the context of film and magnetic or paper tapes from the early 20th century.

splint [Middle English] This once denoted a section of armour; it comes from Middle Dutch, Middle Low German *splinte* 'metal plate or pin' and is related to *splinter*. Use of the word in medical contexts arose in Middle English. The Middle English word **splinter** is related to *splint* (from Middle Dutch *splinter*, *splenter*).

split [late 16th century] This was originally in the sense 'break up (a ship)', describing the force of a storm or rock; it comes from Middle

Dutch *splitten*, of which the ultimate origin is unknown. The idiom *split hairs* dates from the late 17th century; *split the difference* arose in the early 18th century; *split the atom* is recorded from the early 20th century.

spoil [Middle English] 'Plunder' was the early sense of *spoil*, a shortening of Old French *espoille* (as a noun), and *espoillier* (as a verb). Latin *spoliare* is the source of some senses, from *spolium* 'plunder, skin stripped from an animal'; others reflect a shortening of *despoil*. Use of *spoil* to mean 'impair, mar' dates from the mid 16th century.

spoke [Old English] Old English *spāca* is West Germanic in origin, related to Dutch *speek* and German *Speiche*, from the base of *spike*. The idiomatic phrase *put a spoke in one's wheels* (early 17th century) in the context of obstruction is probably a mistranslation of Dutch *een spaak in 'twiel steeken* 'put a stave in the wheel'. The phrase had variants such as *set a spoke in one's cog* and *set a spoke in one's cart*.
→ SPIKE

sponge [Old English] This word came via Latin from Greek *spongia*, a later form of *spongos*, reinforced in Middle English by Old French *esponge*. The verb sense 'live from others in a parasitic way' (from the notion of 'soaking up' benefits) dates from the late 17th century.

sponsor [mid 17th century] This was first used as a noun. An adoption from Latin, it is from *spondere* 'promise solemnly'. The verb dates from the late 19th century in the general sense 'favour strongly'; the notion of 'contribute towards the expenses of' was expressed by *sponsor* from the 1930s.

spontaneous [mid 17th century] This is based on late Latin *spontaneus*, from the phrase (*sua*) *sponte* 'of (one's) own accord'.

spool [Middle English] This once denoted a cylinder on which to wind spun thread in weaving; it is a shortening of Old French *espole* or comes from Middle Low German *spōle*; related forms are Dutch *spoel* and German *Spule*. The verb dates from the early 17th century.

spoon [Old English] Old English *spōn* meant 'chip of wood, splinter'. Of Germanic origin, it is related to German *Span* 'shaving'. The word's use as a term for a utensil (late Middle English) is of Scandinavian origin. The verb dates from the early 18th century; a century later it started to be used colloquially to mean 'be amorous together'. This is perhaps from the notion of being close together (fitting closely like spoons); the word was used in the sense 'lie close together' in the 19th century.

sporadic [late 17th century] This came via medieval Latin from Greek *sporadikos*, from *sporas*, *sporad-* 'scattered'. It is related to *speirein* 'to sow', the source too of mid 19th-century **spore** (from modern Latin *spora*, from Greek *spora* 'sowing, seed').

sport [late Middle English] *Sport* in its early use meant 'pastime, entertainment'; it is a shortening of the noun *disport*. The phrase *in sport* 'in jest' arose in the 15th century; *the sport of kings* (mid 17th century) once referred to war-making but was later applied to hunting and horse-racing. Use of the word in the common current specialized sense of 'game undertaken for physical exercise' began in the early 16th century. The verb sense 'display' (*sporting a dapper tie*) arose in the early 18th century and was particularly common from about 1770 to 1830.

spot [Middle English] This is perhaps from Middle Dutch *spotte*. In early use it had the sense 'moral stain' as well as 'small stain' more generally; it was also applied to a location. The phrase *put on the spot* was originally a US usage of the 1920s. The verb sense 'notice, recognize' (*spotted him at once*) arose from the early 19th-century slang use 'note as a suspect or criminal'.

spouse [Middle English] *Spouse* is from Old French *spous(e)*, a variant of *espous(e)* 'betrothed person', from Latin *sponsus* (masculine), *sponsa* (feminine), past participles of *spondere* 'betroth'.

spout [Middle English] This is from Middle Dutch *spouten*, from an imitative base shared by Old Norse *spýta* 'to spit'. The verb expressed 'discharge a liquid in a copious stream'. Early noun association was with the draining of water from a roof, which then became generalized. The extended sense 'utter volubly' (*constantly spouting about his achievements*) dates from the early 17th century.

sprawl [Old English] Old English *spreawlian* meant 'move the limbs convulsively'; it is related to Danish *sprælle* 'kick or splash about'. The noun dates from the early 18th century.

spray[1] [early 17th century] An earlier spelling of this *spray* meaning 'scatter in minute drops' was *spry*; it is related to Middle Dutch *spra(e)yen* 'to sprinkle'.

spray[2] [Middle English] This *spray* as in *spray of flowers* represents late Old English (*e*)*sprei*, recorded in personal and place names. Its origin is unknown.

spread [Old English] Old English -*sprædan* is first recorded in combinations. Of West Germanic origin, it is related to Dutch *spreiden* and

German *spreiten*. The senses split broadly into 'open out to display or cover' and 'grow larger, extend'.

sprig [Middle English] This word for a small shoot or twig may be related to Low German *sprick* 'dry twig'.

sprightly [late 16th century] This word is based on *spright*, a rare variant of Middle English **sprite** which is an alteration of *sprit* (a contraction of *spirit*).
→ SPIRIT

spring [Old English] Old English *spring* (noun), *springan* (verb) are of Germanic origin, related to Dutch and German *springen*. Early use in the senses 'head of a well' and 'rush out in a stream' gave rise to the figurative use 'originate'.

sprint [late 18th century] This was first used as a dialect term meaning 'a bound or spring'; it is related to Swedish *spritta*. Its use to express 'move at full speed' dates from the late 19th century.

sprout [Middle English] *Sprout* 'shoot forth' is West Germanic in origin and related to Dutch *spruiten* and German *spriessen*. Its elliptical use for *Brussels sprouts* is recorded from the mid 19th century.

spruce [late 16th century] This *spruce* meaning 'neat, smart' is perhaps from an early use of another *spruce* meaning 'Prussian' (now obsolete) used in the phrase *spruce (leather) jerkin*. This early *spruce* (eventually, from the early 17th century, used as a tree name) is an alteration of obsolete *Pruce* 'Prussia'.

spur [Old English] Old English *spora, spura* 'spike for pricking the side of a horse' is Germanic in origin, related to Dutch *spoor*, German *Sporn*, and English *spurn*. The notion of 'projection' led to the word's use in phrases such as *spur of land, spurs from a branch*. The notion of 'sharpness' led to such phrases as *on the spur of the moment* (early 19th century).
→ SPURN

spurious [late 16th century] 'Born out of wedlock' was the early sense of *spurious* based on Latin *spurius* 'false'. The sense became generalized to 'of doubtful origin'.

spurn [Old English] Old English *spurnan, spornan* 'trip, stumble, strike against something with the foot' and 'reject with contempt' is related to Latin *spernere* 'to scorn'.
→ SPUR

spy [Middle English] This is a shortening of Old French *espie* 'espying', *espier* 'espy'. Germanic in origin, it is from an Indo-European root shared by Latin *specere* 'behold, look'.

squad [mid 17th century] *Squad* is a shortening of French *escouade*, a variant of *escadre*, from Italian *squadra* 'square'. The latter is a base shared by the word **squadron** (from Italian *squadrone*) which originally in the mid 16th century denoted a group of soldiers in square formation.

squalid [late 16th century] Latin *squalere* meaning 'be rough or dirty' is the source of both *squalid* (from Latin *squalidus*) and early 17th-century **squalor** (adopted from Latin).

squall [mid 17th century] This is probably an alteration of *squeal*, influenced by *bawl*.

square [Middle English] *Square* in its various parts of speech is a shortening of the Old French noun *esquare*, of *esquarre* (a past participle, used as an adjective), and of the verb *esquarrer*. The base is Latin *quadra* 'square'. The compound:
■ **square meal** is said to derive from nautical use referring to the square platters on which meals were served on board ship.

squat [Middle English] The early sense recorded was 'thrust down with force'; it is from Old French *esquatir* 'flatten', based on Latin *coactus*, the past participle of *cogere* 'compel'. The current sense of the adjective 'short and thick-set' dates from the mid 17th century. Use of the verb to mean 'occupy a building illegally' dates from the late 19th century.
→ COGENT

squeak [late Middle English] This imitative word was first used as a verb; Swedish *skväka* 'croak', Middle English **squeal** and late 15th-century *shriek* are comparable forms.

squeamish [late Middle English] This is an alteration of dialect *squeamous*, from Anglo-Norman French *escoymos*, of unknown origin.

squeeze [mid 16th century] *Squeeze* is from earlier *squise*, from obsolete *queise*, of unknown origin. It has been used in the sense 'pressure from a crowd' (*a bit of a squeeze in the passage*) since the early 19th century; the colloquial use 'strong financial pressure' is late 19th-century.

squire [Middle English] This word, originally a term for a young nobleman acting as an attendant to a knight before becoming a knight himself, is a shortening of Old French *esquier* 'esquire'.
→ ESQUIRE

squirm [late 17th century] This is symbolic of writhing movement and is probably associated with *worm*.

stab [late Middle English] The origin of *stab* is unknown. It is related to the synonymous dialect verb *stob* which is probably from the Scots and dialect noun *stob* meaning 'stump'.

stability [Middle English] This is from Old French *stablete*, from Latin *stabilitas*, from *stabilis* 'stable', from the base of *stare* 'to stand'. Middle English **stable** is from Anglo-Norman French, from Latin *stabilis*, and **stabile** dates from the 1940s, also from Latin *stabilis* and influenced by *mobile*.

stable [Middle English] This *stable* (*riding stables*) is a shortening of Old French *estable* 'stable, pigsty', from Latin *stabulum*, from the base of *stare* 'to stand'.

stack [Middle English] *Stack* is from Old Norse *stakkr* 'haystack', of Germanic origin. It has been used to express a large quantity from the late 19th century (*stacks of money*).

stadium [late Middle English] A *stadium* (via Latin from Greek *stadion*) was a term for an ancient Greek and Roman measure of length (rendered in the Authorized Version of the Bible by 'furlong'). Use of the word as in *sports stadium* dates from the mid 19th century.

staff [Old English] Old English *stæf* first referred to a stick to assist walking; of Germanic origin, it is related to Dutch *staf* and German *Stab*. Use of the word in musical contexts for a set of horizontal lines for notes to be placed indicating pitch dates from the mid 17th century. The sense 'body of officers' in the Army (*General Staff, Chief of Staff*) is found from the early 18th century; the generalized application 'body of employees' dates from the mid 19th century.

stage [Middle English] This word was first applied in early examples to a floor of a building, a platform, or a stopping-place. A shortening of Old French *estage* 'dwelling', it is based on Latin *stare* 'to stand'. The sense 'division of a journey or process' (*stage coach, stage in her life*) arose in the early 17th century; the period when current senses of the verb came into use.

stagger [late Middle English] This is an alteration of dialect *stacker*, from Old Norse *stakra*, a frequentative (= verb of repeated action) of *staka* 'push, stagger'. The noun dates from the late 16th century. The verb sense 'arrange in a stepped way' (*staggered banks of lighting*) is found from the mid 19th century.

stagnate [mid 17th century] Latin *stagnare* 'settle as a still pool', from *stagnum* 'pool', is the source shared by *stagnate* and the contemporaneous **stagnant**.

staid [mid 16th century] This is the archaic past participle of *stay*, from the notion of one's character staying fixed and free from capricious changes.
→ STAY[1]

stain [late Middle English] *Stain* is a shortening of archaic *distain*, from Old French *desteindre* 'tinge with a colour different from the natural one'. Early use meant 'deprive of colour'. The noun was first recorded in the mid 16th century in the sense 'defilement, disgrace'.

stair [Old English] Old English *stæger* is Germanic origin and related to Dutch *steiger* 'scaffolding', from a base meaning 'climb'.

stake [Old English] Old English *staca* 'stout stick' is West Germanic in origin, related to Dutch *staak* and English *stick*. The *stake* meaning 'sum of money placed at risk' is perhaps a specialized usage from the notion of an object being placed as a wager on a post or stake. The phrase *have a stake in* dates from the late 18th century.

stale [Middle English] This word first described beer in the sense 'clear from long standing, strong'; it is probably from Anglo-Norman French and Old French, from *estaler* 'to halt, be placed'. The word was applied to food from the early 16th century. The first element of the compound **stalemate** (a chess term from the mid 18th century) is from obsolete *stale*, from Anglo-Norman French *estale* 'position', from *estaler*.
→ STALL

stalk[1] [Middle English] This *stalk* as in *flower stalk* is probably a diminutive of dialect *stale* 'rung of a ladder, long handle'.

stalk[2] [late Old English] Late Old English *stealcian* was first found in *bistealcian* 'walk cautiously or stealthily'. Of Germanic origin, it is related to *steal*. In late Middle English the word was used in contexts of pursuing game. In the late 20th century, this notion of stealth and attempting to corner a prey was transferred to the context of persistently following another person causing harrassment.
→ STEAL

stall [Old English] Old English *steall* 'stable or cattle shed' is from a Germanic source, related to Dutch *stal* and to *stand*. Many of the noun senses include a notion of 'separate place' or 'division'; its use to mean a fixed seat in a church dates from late Middle English; its application to seats in a theatre dates from the early 19th century. Early senses of the verb included 'reside, dwell' and 'bring to a halt'.
→ STAND

stallion [Middle English] This is from an Anglo-Norman French variant of Old French

estalon, from a derivative of a Germanic base shared by *stall*. Early use reflected the notions 'strong' and 'sturdy'.
→ STALL

stalwart [late Middle English] This is a Scots variant of obsolete *stalworth*, from Old English *stæl* 'place' and *weorth* 'worth'.

stamina [late 17th century] The early sense was 'rudiments, essential elements of something'; it is a use of the plural of Latin *stamen* in the sense 'threads spun by the Fates'. The notion of threads was extended in the early 18th century to the 'vital capacities' or 'vigour' that sustain a person.

stammer [late Old English] Old English *stamerian* is West Germanic in origin and related to Middle English **stumble** (from Old Norse) with which it shares a base. The noun dates from the late 18th century.

stamp [Middle English] 'Crush to a powder' was the sense reflected in early examples. Of Germanic origin, it is related to German *stampfen* 'stamp with the foot', reinforced by Old French *estamper* 'to stamp'. An early 19th-century variant of the verb *stamp* is **stomp** (originally US dialect). Use of the noun to denote an embossed or impressed mark by a government office, and later an adhesive label, dates from the late 17th century; as a shortened form of *postage stamp*, examples are found from the early 19th century.

stampede [early 19th century] This is a Mexican Spanish use of Spanish *estampida* 'crash, uproar', of Germanic origin; it is related to the verb *stamp*.
→ STAMP

stance [Middle English] When first recorded this word denoted a standing place; it is from French, from Italian *stanza*.

stand [Old English] The Old English verb *standan* and noun *stand* are Germanic in origin, from an Indo-European root shared by Latin *stare* and Greek *histanai*, and the English noun *stead*. The verb branches semantically into: 'maintain an erect attitude on the feet' (*stand to attention*), 'be upright supported from below' (*the statue stood on a plinth*), 'remain in a certain condition without deterioration' (*stood the test of time*), 'remain motionless' (*the water stood in pools*), and 'cause to stand' (*stood it on the shelf*).
→ STEAD

standard [Middle English] This once denoted 'a flag raised on a pole as a rallying point'; the word appeared first (*standard-general*) with reference to the 'Battle of the Standard' in 1138. Richard of Hexham, a contemporary writer told the story of the battle and mentioned a mast of a ship being used there with flags at the top as a *standard* mounted from a machine brought on to the battle field. In early use the word was also a term for 'the authorized exemplar of a unit of measurement' and an 'an upright timber'. It is a shortening of Old French *estendart*, from *estendre* 'extend'. *Stand* has influenced many of the senses.

staple¹ [Old English] Old English *stapol* is of Germanic origin, related to Dutch *stapel* 'pillar', a sense reflected in English in early use. The semantic base seems to be 'something supporting'. Use of the word in the context of stationery dates from the late 19th century.

staple² [Middle English] *Staple* seen attributively in *staple diet* is from Old French *estaple* 'market', from Middle Low German, Middle Dutch *stapel* 'pillar, emporium'. It was once used to describe a place appointed by royal authority where a body of merchants had the exclusive right of purchase of certain classes of goods destined for export. Adjectival use was originally in *staple commodities*.
→ STAPLE¹

star [Old English] Old English *steorra*, from a Germanic source, is related to Dutch *ster* and German *Stern*, from an Indo-European root shared by Latin *stella* and Greek *astēr*. The reference to *stars* in astrology dates from Middle English; variants of *thank one's lucky stars* are found from the late 16th century. The word's application to a celebrity dates from the late 18th century.

starboard [Old English] Old English *stēorbord* meant 'rudder side' because early Teutonic sailing vessels were steered with a paddle over the right side.
→ STEER; BOARD

starch [Old English] In Old English, this was recorded only in the past participle *sterced* 'stiffened'. Of Germanic origin, it is related to Dutch *sterken*, German *stärken* 'strengthen', and English *stark*. Figurative use of the noun began in the early 18th century in the phrase *take the starch out of* meaning 'remove the formality or stiffness from' something.
→ STARK

stare [Old English] Old English *starian*, of Germanic origin, is from a base meaning 'be rigid'. The phrase *stare (somebody) out* was first found in *stare out of countenance* recorded in the late 17th century.

starling [late Old English] The first element of *starling* is the archaic or dialect word *stare* (*stær* in Old English) which alone means 'starling'.

stark [Old English] Of Germanic origin, Old English *stearc* meant 'unyielding, severe'; it is related to Dutch *sterk* and German *stark* 'strong', a sense prevailing in other Germanic languages. The sense 'stiff, rigid' may be the original. The bird name **stork** (in Old English *storc*), of Germanic origin, is probably related to *stark* because of its rigid stance.

start [Old English] Old English *styrtan* meant 'to caper, leap'. Of Germanic origin, it is related to Dutch *storten* 'push' and German *stürzen* 'fall headlong, fling'. The noun is from the verb. From the sense 'sudden movement' arose the meaning 'initiation of movement, setting out on a journey' which then gave 'beginning (of a process, etc.)'.

startle [Old English] From the base of *start*, Old English *steartlian* meant 'kick, struggle'. The early sense gave rise to 'move quickly, caper' (typically in the context of cattle) which gave '(cause to) react with fear' in the late 16th century.
→ START

starve [Old English] Old English *steorfan* meant 'to die'. From a Germanic source, it is probably from a base meaning 'be rigid'; related forms are Dutch *sterven* and German *sterben*.
→ STARE

state [Middle English] *State* is partly a shortening of *estate*, partly from Latin *status* 'manner of standing, condition'. The current verb senses date from the mid 17th century.
→ STATUS

static [late 16th century] *Static* was formerly a term for the science of weight and its effects. It came via modern Latin from Greek *statikē* (*tekhne*) 'science of weighing'. The adjective is from modern Latin *staticus*, from Greek *statikos* 'causing to stand', from the verb *histanai*.

station [Middle English] *Station* came via Old French from Latin *statio(n-)*, from *stare* 'to stand'. Early use referred generally to 'position', especially 'position in life, status', and specifically, in ecclesiastical use, to 'a holy place of pilgrimage (visited one after another)'. The phrase *Stations of the Cross* has referred from the mid 16th century to a series of images (usually 14 in number) depicting successive incidents of the Passion, visited one after the other in church for meditation and prayer. Verb use of *station* dates from the late 16th century.

stationary [late Middle English] This is from Latin *stationarius* (originally in the sense 'belonging to a military station'), from *statio(n-)* 'standing'. In English the word was first used

in astronomy referring to planets as 'having no apparent motion'.
→ STATION

stationery [early 18th century] This is based on Middle English *stationer*, originally a term for a 'bookseller' from medieval Latin *stationarius* 'a tradesman (at a fixed location, i.e. not itinerant)'. This is a later Latin word from the one which gave rise to *stationary*.

statistic [late 18th century] This is from the German adjective *statistisch*, and the noun *Statistik*. This German noun was used by a German writer called Aschenwall in 1748 as a name for the area of knowledge dealing with the constitutions and resources of the various States of the world. French writers of the 18th century refer to Aschenwall as having introduced the word which then gave rise to French *statistique*. In English the word was first found in the phrase *statistic science* (a collection of numerical facts to do with economic conditions).

statue [Middle English] *Statue* is from Old French, from Latin *statua*, from *stare* 'to stand'. The same base is shared by mid 16th-century **statuary** (from Latin *statuarius*) and late 18th-century **statuesque** from *statue*, on the pattern of *picturesque*. Mid 19th-century **statuette** is a diminutive of French *statue*.

stature [Middle English] *Stature* came via Old French from Latin *statura*, from *stare* 'to stand'. The early sense referred to 'height when standing'. The sense 'importance' dates from the mid 19th century.

status [late 18th century] This was first used as a legal term meaning 'legal standing'; it is a use of a Latin word with the literal meaning 'standing', from *stare* 'to stand'.

statute [Middle English] *Statute* is from Old French *statut*, from late Latin *statutum*, the neuter past participle of Latin *statuere* 'set up' from *status* 'standing'.
→ STATUS

staunch [late Middle English] 'Watertight' was the meaning of the adjective *staunch* in early examples. The source is Old French *estanche*, the feminine of *estanc*, from a Romance base meaning 'dried up, weary'. Use of the word to mean 'loyal' (*staunch supporter*) dates from the early 17th century. The same base is shared by the Middle English verb **staunch** 'stop (the flow of)', from Old French *estanchier*.

stave [Middle English] This is a back-formation (by removal of the suffix) from *staves* the plural of *staff*. Use as a musical term for a set of lines for musical notation dates from the early 19th century. Current senses of the verb date from the early 17th century, with *stave off* found from the middle of that same century.

stay[1] [late Middle English] The *stay* meaning 'remain' is from Anglo-Norman French *estai-*, the stem of Old French *ester*, from Latin *stare* 'to stand'. The sense 'support' (*stayed with bolts*) is partly from the Old French noun *estaye*, partly from the verb *estayer*, of Germanic origin. The noun *stays* (early 17th century) for a supportive corset for women is plural from the make-up of the garment, formed of two pieces laced together.

stay[2] [Old English] Old English *stæg*, a nautical term for a large rope used to support a mast and later any supporting guy, wire, or cable, is related to Dutch *stag*, from a base meaning 'be firm'.

stead [Old English] Old English *stede* meant 'place'. From a Germanic source, it is related to Dutch *stad* 'town', German *Statt* 'place' and *Stadt* 'town', from an Indo-European root shared by the verb *stand*. The idiom *stand somebody in good stead* 'be of benefit to somebody' was originally worded (late Middle English) *stand someone in stead*. The adjective **steadfast** (*stedefæst* in Old English) is literally 'standing firm'.
→ STAND

steady [Middle English] 'Unwavering, without deviation' was the early meaning of *steady*, based on *stead*. The verb dates from the mid 16th century.
→ STEAD

steal [Old English] The Old English verb *stelan* is Germanic in origin, related to Dutch *stelen* and German *stehlen*. The main sense strands include: 'take dishonestly' (*stole his watch*) and 'go secretly' (*stole into her room*). The word has a central notion of clandestine activity (*stole a kiss, stole a look*). The colloquial noun sense meaning 'bargain' (*it's a steal at that price*) arose in the 1940s in US usage.

stealth [Middle English] 'Theft' was the early sense recorded, probably representing an Old English word related to *steal*. The phrase *by stealth* originally meant 'by theft' in late Middle English.
→ STEAL

steam [Old English] Of Germanic origin, the Old English noun *stēam* meant 'vapour', the verb *stēman* meant 'emit a scent, be exhaled'. Dutch *stoom* 'steam' is related. The idiomatic phrase *let off steam* was originally in the context of steam engines in the early 19th century.

steed [Old English] Old English *stēda* 'stallion' is related to *stud*. From the 16th century the word became common in poetry combined with an appreciatory adjective as in *trusty steed*.
→ STUD[2]

steel [Old English] Old English *stȳle*, *stēli* is Germanic in origin, related to Dutch *staal*, German *Stahl*. The word was associated early with robust trustworthy qualities of character. The verb dates from the late 16th century in its figurative sense 'strengthen' (*steeled himself to face the ordeal*).
→ STAY[2]

steep[1] [Old English] Old English *stēap* meant 'extending to a great height'. Of West Germanic origin, it is related to *steeple* and *stoop*. The word was connected colloquially with prices from the mid 19th century (*a bit steep at that price*).
→ STEEPLE; STOOP

steep[2] [Middle English] This *steep* meaning 'soak in water' is Germanic in origin; Scots **stoup** 'pail' is related.

steeple [Old English] Old English *stēpel* is from Germanic; the adjective *steep* is related. The racing term **steeplechase** dating from the late 18th century has *steeple* as its first element because originally a steeple marked the finishing point across country.

steer [Old English] The Old English verb *stīeran* meaning 'guide the course of' has a Germanic origin; related forms are Dutch *sturen* and German *steuern*. The idiom *steer clear of* arose in the early 18th century.

stem[1] [Old English] Old English *stemn*, *stefn* is Germanic in origin; related forms are Dutch *stam* and German *Stamm* meaning 'trunk of a tree'. The verb (late 16th century) meant originally 'rise erect'; the common modern use meaning 'originate from, spring from' (*it stems from his childhood*) started out in the US in the 1930s.

stem[2] [Middle English] 'To stop, delay' was the early meaning recorded for this *stem* (*stemmed the flow*). It comes from Old Norse *stemma*, of Germanic origin. The skiing term (early 20th century) meaning 'decelarate before a turn' is from the German verb *stemmen*.

stench [Old English] Old English *stenc* 'smell' is Germanic in origin; related forms are Dutch *stank*, German *Gestank*, and the verb *stink*.
→ STINK

step [Old English] Of Germanic origin, Old English *stæpe*, *stepe* (as a noun) and *stæppan*, *steppan* (as a verb) are related to Dutch *steppen* and German *stapfen*. The phrase *to take a step* or *take steps* in the context of taking an action originated in the early 17th century. Use of the plural to mean 'step-ladder' began in the late

17th century. The idiom *watch* or *mind one's step* is found from the 1930s.

stereotype [late 18th century] This is from the French adjective *stéréotype*.

sterile [late Middle English] This is from Old French, or from Latin *sterilis*; Greek *steira* 'barren cow' is related. The sense 'free from bacteria' dates from the late 19th century.

sterling [Middle English] This word as in *pound sterling* is probably based on *steorra* 'star' because some early Norman pennies bore a small star. Its use to define character or qualities as 'thoroughly excellent' started in the mid 17th century.

stern[1] [Old English] Old English *styrne* 'severe, inflexible' is probably from the West Germanic base of the verb *stare*.
→ STARE

stern[2] [Middle English] The nautical word *stern* is probably from Old Norse *stjörn* 'steering', from *stýra* 'to steer'.

stethoscope [early 19th century] This is from French *stéthoscope*, from Greek *stēthos* 'breast' and *skopein* 'look at'.

stew [Middle English] A *stew* originally was a 'cauldron'; it is from Old French *estuve* (related to *estuver* 'heat in steam'), probably based on Greek *tuphos* 'smoke, steam'. Use of the word to describe a dish of meat and vegetables cooked slowly in broth (mid 18th century) is directly from the verb dating from late Middle English.

steward [Old English] Old English *stīweard* is composed of *stig* (probably in the sense 'house, hall') and *weard* 'ward'. Early use in English was as a term for an official controlling the domestic affairs of a household, or as a term for an officer of a royal household. The verb dates from the early 17th century.

stick[1] [Old English] Old English *sticca* 'peg, stick, spoon' is West Germanic in origin; related forms are Dutch *stek* 'cutting from a plant' and German *Stecken* 'staff, stick'. The idiom *get hold of the wrong end of the stick* originated in the mid 19th century; so too did *give somebody some stick* from the notion of a thrashing. Use of the phrase *the sticks* to refer to a remote rural area (the backwoods) arose in the early years of the 20th century in US English.

stick[2] [Old English] The Old English verb *stician* 'to spear' is from a Germanic source; German *sticken* 'embroider' is related, from an Indo-European root shared by Greek *stizein* 'to prick', *stigma* 'a mark' and Latin *instigare* 'spur on'. Early senses included 'pierce' and 'remain fixed (by its embedded pointed end)', which

gave rise in late Middle English to 'cause to adhere'. The general notion in Middle English of 'fix in position' led to looser usage meaning 'put' (*stick the kettle on*).

stickler [mid 16th century] The sense 'umpire' was the first recorded for *stickler*; this is from obsolete *stickle* 'act as umpire', an alteration of obsolete *stightle* 'to control', a frequentative (= verb of repeated action) of Old English *stiht(i)an* 'set in order'.

stiff [Old English] Old English *stif* is Germanic in origin, related to Dutch *stijf*. The main semantic strands are: 'rigid' (*stiff muscles*), 'strong' (*stiff drink*), and 'difficult' (*stiff competition*). The slang noun use for 'a corpse' dates from the mid 19th century.

stifle [late Middle English] This is perhaps from a frequentative (= verb of repeated action) of Old French *estouffer* 'smother, stifle'. Figurative use (*stifled ambition*) is illustrated from the early 17th century.

stigma [late 16th century] A *stigma* was once a mark made by pricking or branding; it came via Latin from Greek *stigma* 'a mark made by a pointed instrument, a dot'; *stick* is related. The *stigmata* refer in Christian contexts (early 17th century) to marks resembling the wounds on Christ's crucified body, said to have been supernaturally reproduced on the bodies of certain saints or other devout followers. The verb **stigmatize** dates from the same period when it meant 'mark with a brand'; via French or medieval Latin, it is from Greek *stigmatizein* from the base *stigma*.
→ STICK[1]

stile [Old English] Old English *stigel* is from a Germanic root meaning 'to climb'.

stiletto [early 17th century] This is an English use of an Italian diminutive of *stilo* 'dagger'.

still[1] [Old English] Old English *stille* 'motionless' and *stillan* 'quieten' are West Germanic in origin, from a base meaning 'be fixed, stand'.

still[2] [mid 16th century] This *still* as in *whisky still* is from the rare verb *still* 'extract by distillation', a shortening of *distil*.
→ DISTIL

stilt [Middle English] *Stilt* is of Germanic origin perhaps from a base meaning 'walk stiffly'; related forms are Dutch *stelt* and German *Stelze*. The word *stilted* describing language is found from the early 20th century (Byron *To Murray*: You are taken in by that false, stilted, trashy style); the reference is to the use of an artificially elevated style.

stimulate [mid 16th century] The early sense recorded was 'sting, afflict'; it is from Latin *stimulare* 'urge', 'goad'. **Stimulus** is a late 17th-century use of a Latin word meaning 'goad, spur, incentive'. The related **stimulant** is early 18th-century from *stimulare*.

sting [Old English] Old English *sting* (as a noun) and *stingan* (as a verb) are of Germanic origin. The slang use *sting somebody for money* where exploitation is used to extort cash dates from the early 20th century. The word **stingy** meaning 'mean' (mid 17th century) may be a dialect variant of the noun *sting*.

stink [Old English] Old English *stincan* is West Germanic origin; related forms are Dutch and German *stinken*, and *stench*.
→ STENCH

stint [Old English] Old English *styntan* meaning 'make blunt' is from a Germanic source; *stunt* is related. The word commonly conveyed the notion 'cease, come to a halt' in Middle English. The most frequent use currently 'limit the supply of (something) unduly' (*don't stint on the wine*) started in the early 18th century.
→ STUNT¹

stipulate [early 17th century] This is from Latin *stipulari* 'demand as a formal promise'.

stir [Old English] Old English *styrian* has a Germanic origin; German *stören* 'to disturb' is related. The sense 'arouse feelings in' (*his poetry stirred my soul*) arose in Middle English. In colloquial use since the early 19th century, the phrase *Stir-up Sunday* refers to the Sunday next before Advent, suggested by the opening words (*Stir up ...*) of the Collect for the day; it is also humorously associated with the stirring of the Christmas mincemeat, the preparation of which was traditionally started during that week. The informal noun *stir* meaning 'time in prison' is unconnected with the *stir* meaning 'agitate, disturb'; in use from the mid 19th century, it may be from Romany *sturbin* 'jail'.

stirrup [Old English] Old English *stigrāp* is made up of two elements: the first is from the Germanic base of obsolete *sty* 'climb' and the second is *rope*. The original *stirrup* must have been a looped rope.

stitch [Old English] Old English *stice* meant 'a puncture, stabbing pain'. It is Germanic in origin, related to German *Stich* 'a sting, prick' and English *stick*. The sense 'loop' (in sewing etc.) arose in Middle English. Use of the phrase *stitch someone up* in the context of a criminal informing on someone to cause a conviction dates from the 1970s.
→ STICK²

stock [Old English] Old English *stoc(c)* 'trunk, block of wood, post' is Germanic in origin; related forms are Dutch *stok* and German *Stock* 'stick'. The notion 'store, fund' (*stock of food*; *company's stock*) arose in late Middle English and is of obscure origin, perhaps expressing 'growth from a central stem' or 'firm foundation'.

stockade [early 17th century] *Stockade* 'a defensive barrier made from stakes' is a shortening of obsolete French *estocade*, an alteration of *estacade*, from Spanish *estacada*. This is from the Germanic base of the noun *stake*.
→ STAKE

stocking [late 16th century] This is from *stock* in the dialect sense 'stocking'.
→ STOCK

stodge [late 17th century] This was first used as a verb in the sense 'stuff to stretching point'; it is symbolic, suggested by *stuff* and *podge*.

stoical [late Middle English] *Stoical* comes via Latin from Greek *stōïkos*, from *stoa*: this is with reference to Zeno's teaching in the *Stoa Poikilē* or Painted Porch, at Athens. Zeno of Citium was the founder of Stoicism in around 300 BC, a philosophy which taught that virtue, the highest good, is based on knowledge.

stoke [mid 17th century] This is a back-formation (by removal of the suffix) from **stoker**: the latter is from Dutch, from *stoken* 'stoke (a furnace)', from Middle Dutch *stoken* 'push, poke'.
→ STICK¹

stole [Old English] The early term *stole* described either a 'long robe' or a 'priest's vestment'. It came via Latin from Greek *stolē* 'clothing', from *stellein* 'array'.

stolid [late 16th century] This is from obsolete French *stolide* or Latin *stolidus* (perhaps related to *stultus* 'foolish').

stomach [Middle English] This is from Old French *estomac*, *stomaque*, via Latin from Greek *stomakhos* 'gullet', from *stoma* 'mouth'. The early sense of the verb was 'be offended at, resent' in the early 16th century.

stone [Old English] The Old English noun *stān* is Germanic in origin; related forms are Dutch *steen* and German *Stein*. The verb dating from Middle English is first recorded with the meaning 'throw stones at'; the use of *stoned* in the context of intoxication by alcohol or drugs is found from the 1950s.

stool [Old English] Of Germanic origin, *stool* is related to Dutch *stoel*, German *Stuhl*, and English *stand*. The word used in reference to faeces began as a name for the place where evacuation of the bowels took place, i.e. the seat enclosing a chamber pot. The term:

■ **stool pigeon** for a police informer (late 19th-century) is from the original use of a pigeon fixed to a stool as a decoy for wildfowl.
→ STAND

stoop [Old English] The Old English verb *stūpian*, of Germanic origin, is related to the adjective *steep*.
→ STEEP[1]

stop [Old English] Old English (*for*)*stoppian*, of West Germanic origin, meant 'block up (an aperture)'; German *stopfen* is related, from late Latin *stuppare* 'to stuff'. The strands of meaning branch broadly into: 'plug, close up' (*stopped the gap*), 'bring to a stand' (*stopped the taxi*), and 'come to a stand' (*stopped dead*). The phrases *stop at nothing* and *stop short* are found from the late 17th century.

store [Middle English] *Store* is a shortening of Old French *estore* (as a noun) and *estorer* (as a verb), from Latin *instaurare* 'renew'. Use of the noun to mean 'shop' was, in early use, a large establishment selling a great variety of articles. The word is more common outside the UK; within the UK it is chiefly in the combinations *chain store*, *department store*, and *store detective*.

storey [late Middle English] This is a shortening of Latin *historia* 'history, story' which had a specialized use in Anglo-Latin, perhaps with original reference to a tier of painted windows or sculptures on the front of a building, representing a historical subject.

storm [Old English] *Storm* is Germanic in origin; related forms are Dutch *storm* and German *Sturm*, and probably also the English verb *stir*. The verb dates from late Middle English in phrases referring to the weather; its use to mean 'rush at in an assault' (*stormed the building*) dates from the early 17th century; the meaning 'rush with violence' (*stormed off in anger*) is early 19th-century.
→ STIR

story [Middle English] A *story* initially was a historical account or representation; this usually involved passages of bible history and legends of the saints. It is a shortening of Anglo-Norman French *estorie*, from Latin *historia*. The word became associated with fictitious events for the entertainment of the listener or reader from the 1500s.
→ HISTORY

stout [Middle English] This is from Anglo-Norman French and Old French dialect, of West Germanic origin and may be related to *stilt*. From the late 17th century the noun was a term for any strong beer and is probably elliptical for *stout ale*.
→ STILT

stove [Middle English] A *stove* was originally a 'sweating-room'; it is from Middle Dutch or Middle Low German *stove* and may be related to the noun *stew*. Use of the word in phrases such as *cooking stove*, *oil stove* dates from the late 16th century.
→ STEW

stow [late Middle English] *Stow* is a shortening of *bestow*. Its early sense was 'put in a certain place'.
→ BESTOW

straddle [mid 16th century] *Straddle* is an alteration of dialect *striddle*, a back-formation (by removal of the suffix) from dialect *striddling* 'astride', from *stride*.
→ STRIDE

strafe [early 20th century] This is a humorous adaptation of the German First World War catchphrase *Gott strafe England* 'may God punish England'.

straight [Middle English] This is the archaic past participle of *stretch*. The phrase *the straight and narrow* (mid 19th century) indicating the conventional and moral path is a mis-interpretation of a biblical reference in Matthew 7:14: Because strait is the gate, and narrow is the way which leadeth unto life, and few there be that find it. The colloquial phrase *think straight* is recorded from the beginning of the 20th century.
→ STRETCH

strain[1] [Middle English] The *strain* 'subject to tension', 'stretch' is from Old French *estreindre*, from Latin *stringere* 'draw tight' (the earliest sense in English). Now obsolete senses of the word in English include 'bind fast', 'compress, contract', 'stretch (limbs) and hold extended'.

strain[2] [Old English] Old English *strīon* meaning 'acquisition, gain' is from a Germanic source; Latin *struere* 'to build up' is related. Another sense strand of this *strain* is 'ancestry, race; variety developed by breeding' (*a new strain or breed*)

strait [Middle English] *Strait* is a shortening of Old French *estreit* 'tight, narrow', from Latin *strictus* 'drawn tight'.
→ STRICT

strand[1] [Old English] This *strand* meaning 'leave aground' was first recorded as a noun meaning 'land bordering water'. Verb use dates from the early 17th century. Dutch *strand* and German *Strand* may be related.

strand[2] [late 15th century] This *strand* meaning 'thread' is of unknown origin. A connection has been suggested with obsolete *strain* 'thread, line, streak' or with Old French *estran* 'rope' but these theories are not proven.

strange [Middle English] *Strange* is a shortening of Old French *estrange*, from Latin *extraneus* 'external, strange'. Late Middle English **stranger** is a shortening of Old French *estrangier*, from the same Latin base.

strangle [Middle English] *Strangle* is a shortening of Old French *estrangler*, from Latin *strangulare*. The Greek verb *strangalan* is the source, from *strangalē* 'halter', related to *strangos* 'twisted'. The word **strangulation** dates from the mid 16th century, from Latin *strangulatio(n-)*, from *strangulare* 'choke'.

strap [late 16th century] Initially this was a term for a trap for birds as well as for a piece of timber fastening two objects together. It is a dialect form of late Middle English *strop* 'a strip of leather' for sharpening razors

stratagem [late 15th century] This was, in early times, a word for a 'military ploy'; it came into English via French and Latin from Greek *stratēgēma*, from *stratēgein* 'be a general', based on *stratos* 'army'. **Strategy** dates from the early 19th century, from French *stratégie*, from Greek *stratēgia* 'generalship', from *stratēgos*. The Greek base is shared by **strategic** from the same period (from French *stratégique*, from Greek *stratēgikos*).

stratum [late 16th century] The early sense recorded was 'layer or coat of a substance'. It is modern Latin, from a Latin word meaning literally 'something spread or laid down', the neuter past participle of *sternere* 'strew'.

straw [Old English] Old English *strēaw*, of Germanic origin, is related to Dutch *stroo*, German *Stroh*, and English **strew** (in Old English *stre(o)wian*, from an Indo-European root shared by Latin *sternere* 'lay flat').

stray [Middle English] *Stray* as a noun is from the Anglo-Norman French noun *strey*; as a verb it is a shortening of the Anglo-Norman French and Old French verb *estrayer*; the adjectival form (*stray animals*) is from *astray*.

streak [Old English] Old English *strica* is Germanic in origin; related forms are Dutch *streek* and German *Strich*, and English *strike*. The sense 'run naked' was originally US slang. Use of the word *streaks* in hairdressing started in the 1940s.
→ STRIKE

stream [Old English] The Old English noun *strēam* is originally Germanic; related forms are Dutch *stroom* and German *Strom*, from an Indo-European root shared by Greek *rhein* 'to flow'. The word was used figuratively from early times. The phrase *stream of consciousness* is recorded from the mid 19th century; it became generalized from 'an individual's thoughts experienced as a continuous flow' (in psychology) to an 'uncontrolled train of thought'.

street [Old English] Old English *strǣt*, of West Germanic origin, is from late Latin *strāta (via)* 'paved (way)', the feminine past participle of *sternere* 'lay down'. The phrase *the man on the street* referring to an ordinary person as opposed to an expert is recorded from the early 19th century. The compound *streetwise* dates from the 1960s in American English usage.

strenuous [early 17th century] This is based on Latin *strenuus* 'brisk'.

stress [Middle English] *Stress* first denoted hardship or force exerted on a person to compel a certain response or for extortion. It is a shortening of *distress*, or comes partly from Old French *estresse* 'narrowness, oppression', based on Latin *strictus* 'drawn tight'.
→ STRICT

stretch [Old English] Old English *streccan*, of West Germanic origin, is a verb related to Dutch *strekken* and German *strecken*. The noun dates from the late 16th century. The phrase *at full stretch* was originally (late 17th century) *on the full stretch* referring to mental strain. The slang use of the word for 'a period in jail' was initially a term of hard labour (early 19th century); the word had been associated, in verb use, with suffering first in connection with the rack (Middle English) and hanging in the late 16th century.
→ STRAIGHT

strict [late Middle English] This first meant 'restricted in space or extent' in early examples (*strict passage*). It comes from Latin *strictus*, the past participle of *stringere* 'tighten, draw tight'. **Stricture** dating from the same period is from Latin *strictura*, from *stringere* 'draw tight'. An early meaning of *stricture* was 'incidental remark'; this came from another sense of *stringere* ('touch lightly'); the sense developed into 'censorious remark'.

stride [Old English] Old English *stride* was a 'single long step'; the verb *strīdan* was 'stand or walk with the legs wide apart'. It is probably from a Germanic base meaning 'strive, quarrel'; related forms are Dutch *strijden* 'fight' and German *streiten* 'quarrel'. The idiom *take something in one's stride* appeared in the early 19th century.

strident [mid 17th century] This is from Latin *strident-*, the present participial stem of *stridere* 'to creak'.

strife [Middle English] *Strife* is a shortening of Old French *estrif*, related to Old French *estriver* 'strive'. As well as expressing conflict, the word in early examples meant 'striving together'. The verb **strive** is also Middle English, a shortening of Old French *estriver* (related to *estrif*).

strike [Old English] Old English *strīcan* meant 'go, flow' and 'rub lightly'. West Germanic in origin, it is related to German *streichen* 'to stroke' and English *stroke*. The sense 'deliver a blow' dates from Middle English. The word's application in the context of industrial disputes dates from the early 19th century.
➔ STROKE

string [Old English] The Old English noun *streng* is Germanic in origin; German *Strang* and English *strong* are related. The verb dating from late Middle English is first recorded in the senses 'arrange in a row' and 'fit with a string'. Of the idioms: *have on a string* came into use in the late 16th century; *pull the strings* meaning 'control' (as of a puppet) is mid 19th-century; *no strings attached* appeared in the 1950s from an earlier (late 19th-century) US use of *string* meaning 'limitation, condition'.
➔ STRONG

stringent [mid 17th century] 'Compelling, convincing' was the early meaning of *stringent* from Latin *stringere* 'draw tight'.

strip[1] [Middle English] This *strip* meaning 'unclothe' and 'peel away' is Germanic in origin; Dutch *stropen* is related. The figurative use in the context of stripping someone of honours, titles, or rights, arose early. The sense 'dismantle' (*stripped down the engine*) arose in the late 17th century.

strip[2] [late Middle English] This word for a 'long narrow piece' of something such as cloth is either from or related to Middle Low German *strippe* 'strap, thong' and probably also to English *stripe*. The word **stripling** (Middle English) is probably from this *strip* from the notion of 'narrowness, slimness'.
➔ STRIPE

stripe [late Middle English] *Stripe* may be a back-formation (by removal of the suffix) from *striped* adopted from Dutch or Low German; Middle Dutch and Middle Low German *stripe* may be related. The noun was not found until the 17th century in connection with textiles. In the early 19th century, the word *stripes* entered military contexts referring to a narrow strip of braid worn on a coat sleeve indicating rank.

stroke [Old English] Old English *strācian* meant 'caress lightly'. Germanic in origin, it is related to Dutch *streek* 'a stroke', German *streichen* 'to stroke', and English *strike*. The earli-est noun sense 'blow' (George Eliot *Romola*: [He] remained obstinately silent under all the strokes from the knotted cord) is first recorded in Middle English. The idiom *stroke of luck* is mid 19th-century in origin; *pull a stroke* 'play a dirty trick' appeared in the 1970s, perhaps from a sport association.
➔ STRIKE

stroll [early 17th century] 'Roam as a vagrant' was the early sense expressed by *stroll*, with the notion of leisure appearing towards the end of the century. It is probably from German *strollen*, *strolchen*, from *Strolch* 'vagabond', but the ultimate origin is unknown.

strong [Old English] *Strong* is of Germanic origin; related to Dutch and German *streng*, and English *string*. It has been used to mean 'not moderate' in the context of language since the late 17th century. From the early 19th century *strong* has been used colloquially as an adverb in phrases such as *come on strong* and *going strong*. **Strength** (in Old English *strengthu*) is from the Germanic base of *strong*.
➔ STRING

structure [late Middle English] Early use of *structure* was to refer to the process of building. It comes from Old French, or from Latin *structura*, from *struere* 'to build'. The verb is rarely found before the 20th century.

struggle [late Middle English] This is a frequentative (= verb of repeated action) and may be imitative in origin. The noun dates from the late 17th century. The initial letters of the word (str-) may symbolize effort as in *strive* and *strong*.

strut [Old English] Old English *strūtian*, a Germanic word in origin, meant 'protrude stiffly'. Chaucer uses the word in his *Miller's Tale* to refer to hair sticking up. Current senses such as 'swagger' date from the late 16th century.

stub [Old English] Germanic in origin, Old English *stub(b)* was a 'stump of a tree'; the notion of a portion being left behind when something has been removed led to the word's use in the sense 'counterfoil' (late 19th century). The verb is first recorded in late Middle English in the meaning 'grub up (a plant) by the roots'; the meaning 'accidentally strike' (*stubbed his toe*) was originally a US usage of the mid 19th century.

stubble [Middle English] *Stubble* first referred to stalks left in the ground after reaping. It comes from Anglo-Norman French *stuble*, from Latin *stupla*, *stupula*, variants of *stipula* 'straw'; the word was applied to bristly growth of hair on a man's face, from the late 16th century.

stubborn [Middle English] *Stubborn* was originally in the sense 'untameable, implacable'. The word's origin is unknown; it is commonly assumed that the word is from *stub*, a theory which holds up with regard to sense (a stub being difficult to move) but not to form.

stud[1] [Old English] Old English *studu*, *stuthu* was a 'post, upright prop'; German *stützen* 'to prop' is related. The sense 'ornamental metal knob' arose in late Middle English.

stud[2] [Old English] Old English *stōd* as in *stud farm*, *at stud* is Germanic in origin; related words are German *Stute* 'mare' and English *stand*.
→ STAND

study [Middle English] The noun is a shortening of Old French *estudie*, the verb is a shortening of *estudier*, both based on Latin *studium* 'zeal, painstaking application'. The same base is shared by Middle English **studious** (from Latin *studiosus*), late Middle English **student** (from the verb *studere* 'apply oneself to') and early 19th-century **studio** (via Italian).

stuff [Middle English] *Stuff* was first used to refer to material for making clothes. It is a shortening of Old French *estoffe* 'material, furniture' and *estoffer* 'equip, furnish (a garrison)', from Greek *stuphein* 'draw together'. The noun splits broadly into 'equipment, stores', 'material from which something is made', and 'matter of an unspecified kind'. Of the phrases, *do one's stuff* is found from the mid 17th century and *that's the stuff* from the 1920s, from the notion *that's the stuff to give the troops*.

stump [Middle English] A *stump* in early use referred to a part of a limb remaining after an amputation. It comes from Middle Low German *stump(e)* or Middle Dutch *stomp*. The early sense of the verb was 'stumble', coming to mean 'cause to be at a loss' (*the problem has completely stumped me*) in US English in the early 19th century, probably from the notion of coming across stumps in ploughing which halt progress.

stun [Middle English] This is a shortening of Old French *estoner* 'astonish'.

stunt[1] [late 16th century] *Stunt* first meant 'bring to an abrupt halt'. It is from dialect *stunt* 'foolish, stubborn', of Germanic origin and perhaps related to *stump*.
→ STUMP

stunt[2] [late 19th century] The *stunt* of *stunt man*, *film stunt* was originally US college slang but it is not clear how this arose. It was an event in college athletics in response to a challenge. The word's meaning was extended in the early 20th century, in British English regarded initially as a soldiers' word. A connection with US colloquial *stump* 'dare' is not borne out in the etymology.

stupefy [late Middle English] This is from French *stupéfier*, from Latin *stupefacere*, from *stupere* 'be struck senseless', the base too of mid 17th-century **stupefaction**.

stupendous [mid 16th century] Latin *stupendus* 'to be wondered at' (the gerundive of *stupere*) is the base of English *stupendous*.

stupid [mid 16th century] This word is from French *stupide* or Latin *stupidus*, from *stupere* 'be amazed or stunned' (the source too of **stupor** in late Middle English). The notion is of being dulled through shock. Dryden used the word often in the sense 'stunned' (*Aeneis*: Men, Boys, and Women stupid with Surprise, Where ere she passes, fix their wond'ring Eyes). The sense 'slow-witted' arose in the early 16th century.

sturdy [Middle English] Early use included the senses 'reckless, violent' and 'intractable, obstinate'. The word is a shortening of Old French *esturdi* 'stunned, dazed'. It is thought by some to be based on Latin *turdus* 'a thrush'; further association with this particular bird and being dazed is illustrated by the French phrase *soûl comme une grive* 'drunk as a thrush'; the derivation of the English word however remains obscure. The sense 'solidly built' and 'robust' arose early.

stutter [late 16th century] This is a frequentative (= verb of repeated action) of dialect *stut*, of Germanic origin; German *stossen* 'strike against' is a related form.

sty[1] [Old English] Old English *stī-* (found in *stīfearh* 'sty pig'), is probably identical with *stig* 'hall', the first element of *steward*.
→ STEWARD

sty[2] [early 17th century] This *sty* as an inflammation of the eyelid is from dialect *styany*, composed of *styan* (from Old English *stīgend* 'riser') and *eye*.

style [Middle English] A *style* in early use could be a stylus, a literary composition (*a mournful style*), an official title (*under the style of Denby and Co*), or a characteristic manner of literary expression (*in point of style*). It comes from Old French *stile*, from Latin *stilus*. The verb dates from the early 16th century.

suave [late Middle English] The early sense recorded was 'gracious, agreeable'. It is from

Old French, or from Latin *suavis* 'agreeable'. The current sense dates from the mid 19th century.

WORDBUILDING

The prefix **sub-** [from Latin *sub* 'under, close to'] adds the sense

■ **at, to,** or **from a lower level** [subalpine]

■ **lower in rank** [subaltern]

■ **of a smaller size** [subculture]

■ **somewhat, nearly** [subantarctic]

■ **indicative of secondary action** [sublet]

■ **indicative of support** [subvention]

---

subdue [late Middle English] This is from Anglo-Norman French *suduire*, from Latin *sub-ducere*, literally 'draw from below'.

subject [Middle English] *Subject* when first in use as a noun referred to a '(person) owing obedience'. Old French *suget* is the source, from Latin *subjectus* meaning 'brought under', the past participle of *subicere*, (from *sub-* 'under' and *jacere* 'throw'). The sense 'theme of a literary composition' is found from the late 16th century; its use in art contexts to denote a person being drawn dates from the early 17th century; the sense 'subject matter' in an educational context dates from the mid 19th century. The verb sense 'cause to undergo' (*subjected him to hours of questioning*) is a mid 16th-century usage originally.

subjugate [late Middle English] This is from late Latin *subjugare* 'bring under a yoke', based on *jugum* 'yoke'.

sublimate [late Middle English] This word first expressed the meaning 'raise to a higher status'. It comes from Latin *sublimare* 'raise up'.

sublime [late 16th century] A word meaning originally 'dignified, aloof', *aloof* is from Latin *sublimis*, from *sub-* 'up to' and a second element perhaps related to *limen* 'threshold' and *limus* 'oblique'. The word's use in phrases such as *sublime view, sublime beauty* expressing a mental reaction of feeling overwhelmed dates from the early 18th century.

submerse [late Middle English] Latin *submergere* (from *sub-* 'under' and *mergere* 'to dip') is the source of the synonyms *submerse* and early 17th-century **submerge**.

submit [late Middle English] This is from Latin *submittere*, from *sub-* 'under' and *mittere* 'send, put'. The sense 'present for judgement' dates from the mid 16th century. Late Middle English **submission** is from the same source verb via Old French, or from Latin *submissio(n-)*.

Submissive appeared in the late 16th century, from *submission*, on the pattern of pairs such as *remission* and *remissive*.

subordinate [late Middle English] This word is from medieval Latin *subordinatus* 'placed in an inferior rank', from Latin *sub-* 'below' and *ordinare* 'ordain'.

subscribe [late Middle English] First recorded in the sense 'sign at the bottom of a document', *subscribe* is from Latin *subscribere*, from *sub-* 'under' and *scribere* 'write'. The related noun **subscription** (also late Middle English) is from Latin *subscriptio(n-)*, from *subscribere*. The word as a term for a payment for the regular purchase of a periodical or as a recurrent payment to a charitable fund is found in use from the late 17th century.

subsequent [late Middle English] This is from Old French, or from Latin *subsequent-*, the present participial stem of *subsequi* 'follow after'.

subservient [mid 17th century] This word with a notion of servility is from Latin *subservient-*, the present participial stem of the verb *subservire* 'subject to, comply with'.

subside [late 17th century] The word *subside* is from Latin *subsidere*, from *sub-* 'below' and *sidere* 'settle' (a verb related to *sedere* 'to sit'). The noun **subsidence** recorded slightly earlier is from Latin *subsidentia* 'sediment', from the same source verb.

subsidy [late Middle English] This is from Anglo-Norman French *subsidie*, from Latin *subsidium* 'assistance, support'. When **subsidiary** was first recorded in the mid 16th century, it had the sense 'serving to help or supplement' (from Latin *subsidiarius*, from *subsidium*). Use of the word to mean 'subsidiary company' is recorded from the late 19th century.

subsist [mid 16th century] The sense in early examples was 'continue to exist': it is from Latin *subsistere* 'stand firm', from *sub-* 'from below' and *sistere* 'set, stand'.

substance [Middle English] This word was first used to refer to the essential nature of something. It comes from Old French, from Latin *substantia* 'being, essence', from the verb *substare* 'stand firm'. The word was used to refer to a 'solid thing' (Shakespeare *Titus Andronicus*: So He takes false shadows, for true substances) from the late 16th century. Middle English **substantial** is from Old French *substantiel* or Christian Latin *substantialis*, from *substantia*. Mid 17th-century **substantiate** is from medieval Latin *substantiare* 'give substance'.

substitute [late Middle English] A *substitute* formerly referred to a deputy or delegate. It comes from Latin *substitutus*, the past participle of *substituere* 'put in place of', based on *statuere* 'set up'.

subterfuge [late 16th century] This word derives from French, or comes from late Latin *subterfugium*, from Latin *subterfugere* 'escape secretly', from *subter-* 'beneath' and *fugere* 'flee'.

subterranean [early 17th century] Latin *subterraneus* (from *sub-* 'below' and *terra* 'earth') is the base of *subterranean* in English.

subtle [Middle English] 'Not easily understood' was an early sense of *subtle*, from Old French *sotil*, from Latin *subtilis* meaning 'fine, delicate'. Middle English **subtlety** (from Old French *soutilte*, from Latin *subtilitas*) is also based on Latin *subtilis*.

subtract [mid 16th century] *Subtract* is from Latin *subtract-*, the past participial stem of *subtrahere* 'draw away (from below)'.

suburb [Middle English] The word *suburb* is from Old French *suburbe* or Latin *suburbium*, from *sub-* 'near to' and *urbs*, *urb-* 'city'. **Suburban** is also Middle English from Latin *suburbanus*, from *suburbium*.

subvert [late Middle English] This is from Old French *subvertir* or Latin *subvertere*, from *sub-* 'from below' and *vertere* 'to turn'. The word **subversive** is mid 17th-century from medieval Latin *subversivus*, from the verb *subvertere*.

successor [Middle English] The word *successor* is from Old French *successour*, from Latin *successor*. This is from the Latin verb *succedere* 'come close after', a source shared by: Middle English **succession** (from Old French, or from Latin *successio(n-)*) which first denoted the legal transmission of an estate or the throne to another, as well as 'heirs'; late Middle English **succeed** (via Old French *succeder*); late Middle English **successive** (from medieval Latin *successivus*); and mid 16th-century **success** (from Latin *successus*). The latter originally referred to the outcome of something whether good or bad.

succinct [late Middle English] 'Encircled' was the early meaning of *succinct* from Latin *succinctus* 'tucked up': this is the past participle of *succingere*, from *sub-* 'from below' and *cingere* 'gird'.

succulent [early 17th century] This is from Latin *succulentus*, from *succus* 'juice'.

succumb [late 15th century] 'Bring low, overwhelm' was the meaning conveyed by *succumb* when it was first exemplified. It comes from Old French *succomber* or Latin *succumbere*, from *sub-* 'under' and a verb related to *cubare* 'to lie'.

such [Old English] Old English *swilc*, *swylc* is related to Dutch *zulk* and German *solch*, from the Germanic bases of *so* and *alike*. The phrase *such and such* appeared in the mid 16th century.

suck [Old English] The Old English verb *sūcan* is from an Indo-European imitative root; English *soak* is related. The phrase *suck up to* was originally schoolboys' slang of the mid 19th century. Late Middle English **suckle** is probably a back-formation (by removal of the suffix) from the slightly earlier **suckling** from the verb *suck*. The word **suction** made its appearance in the early 17th century, from late Latin *suctio(n-)*, from Latin *sugere* 'suck'.
→ SOAK

sudden [Middle English] This is from Anglo-Norman French *sudein*, from an alteration of Latin *subitaneus*, from *subitus* 'sudden'.

suds [mid 19th century] This word is of uncertain sense development but may have originally denoted the flood water of the fens; Middle Low German *sudde*, Middle Dutch *sudse* 'marsh, bog', and English *seethe* are probably related.
→ SEETHE

sue [Middle English] This is from Anglo-Norman French *suer*, based on Latin *sequi* 'follow'. Early senses were very similar to those of the verb *follow*.

suffer [Middle English] *Suffer* is from Anglo-Norman French *suffrir*, from Latin *sufferre*, from *sub-* 'from below' and *ferre* 'to bear'. The senses broadly include 'undergo, endure' (*suffered hours of interrogation*) and 'tolerate' (*suffer fools gladly*). The word **sufferance** is also Middle English from Anglo-Norman French *suffraunce*, from late Latin *sufferentia*, from *sufferre*.

suffice [Middle English] This is from Old French *suffis-*, the stem of *suffire*, from Latin *sufficere* 'put under, meet the need of'. Latin *sub-* 'under' and *facere* 'make' are the formative elements.

sufficient [Middle English] This was first recorded in the sense 'legally satisfactory'. The source is either Old French, or Latin *sufficient-*, the present participial stem of *sufficere* 'meet the need of'. This same base is shared by late 15th-century **sufficiency** (from late Latin *sufficientia*) first used referring to 'sufficient means or wealth'.

suffocate [late 15th century] This is from Latin *suffocare* 'stifle', from *sub-* 'below' and *fauces* 'throat'.

suffrage [late Middle English] *Suffrage* was initially a word for 'intercessory prayers' and 'assistance'. Latin *suffragium* gave the word in English, reinforced by French *suffrage*. The modern sense of 'right to vote' was originally US from the late 18th century.

suffuse [late 16th century] This is from Latin *suffus-*, from *sub-* 'below, from below' and *fundere* 'pour'.

sugar [Middle English] The word *sugar* is from Old French *sukere*, from Italian *zucchero*, probably via medieval Latin from Arabic *sukkar*. The figurative sense 'make palatable' arose in late Middle English; the phrase *sugar the pill* originated in the late 18th century. *Sugar* became a term of endearment in the 1930s.

suggestion [Middle English] A *suggestion* was initially 'an incitement to evil', but the use soon became generalized to 'proposal, thought put forward'. The word came via Old French from Latin *suggestio(n-)*, from the verb *suggerere* 'suggest, prompt', the source too of early 16th-century **suggest**.

suicide [mid 17th century] This is from modern Latin *suicida* 'act of suicide', *suicidium* 'person who commits suicide'. Latin *sui* 'of oneself' and *caedere* 'kill' are the elements here.

suit [Middle English] This is from Anglo-Norman French *siwte* from a feminine past participle of a Romance verb based on Latin *sequi* 'follow'. Early senses included 'attendance at a court' and 'legal process'. Use of the word as in *suit of clothes* and *suit of cards* derives from an earlier meaning 'set of things to be used together'. A relatively recent addition (1970s) to the word's sense development has been *a suit* meaning 'a business executive', a slang use which started in US English. The verb sense 'accommodate, make appropriate' is recorded from the late 16th century (Shakespeare *As You Like It*: He ... That ... therein suits His folly to the mettle of my speech). The adjective **suitable** is late 16th-century from the verb *suit*, on the pattern of *agreeable*.

suitor [late Middle English] An early sense was 'member of a retinue'; the origin is Anglo-Norman French *seutor*, from Latin *secutor*, from *sequi* 'to follow'. It started to be used to refer to a man seeking a woman in marriage in the late 16th century.

sulk [late 18th century] *Sulk* may be a back-formation (by removal of the suffix) from mid 18th-century **sulky** which is perhaps from obsolete *sulke* 'hard to dispose of'. Earlier details are unknown.

sullen [Middle English] 'Solitary, averse to company', and 'unusual' were early meanings of *sullen* from Anglo-Norman French *sulein*, from *sol* 'sole'.

sully [late 16th century] *Sully* is perhaps from French *souiller* 'to soil'.

sultry [late 16th century] The word *sultry* is from obsolete *sulter* 'swelter'.

sum [Middle English] Latin *summa* 'main part, sum total' (the feminine of *summus* 'highest') is the source of *sum* which came into English via Old French, and late Middle English **summary** from Latin *summarius*.

summer [Old English] Old English *sumor* is Germanic in origin; related forms are Dutch *zomer*, German *Sommer*, as well as Sanskrit *samā* 'year'.

summit [late Middle English] This was first used in the general sense 'top part'. It derives from Old French *somete*, from *som* 'top': this in turn comes from Latin *summum*, the neuter form of *summus* 'highest'. A *summit* in political contexts (*summit meeting*) is a use dating from the 1950s.

summon [Middle English] This is from Old French *somondre*, from Latin *summonere* originally meaning 'give a hint' but later used in the sense 'call, summon'. Latin *sub-* 'secretly' and *monere* 'warn' are the base elements. Middle English **summons** as an 'authoritative call to attend' is from Old French *sumunse*, from an alteration of Latin *summonita*, the feminine past participle of *summonere*.

sump [Middle English] A *sump* was once a word for a 'marsh'. It comes from Middle Dutch or Low German *sump*, or (in the mining sense) from German *Sumpf*; *swamp* is related.
→ SWAMP

sumptuous [late Middle English] The early sense referred was 'made or produced at great cost'. It comes from Old French *somptueux*, from Latin *sumptuosus*, from *sumptus* 'expenditure'.

sun [Old English] Old English *sunne* is Germanic in origin; related forms are Dutch *zon* and German *Sonne*, from an Indo-European root shared by Greek *hēlios* and Latin *sol*.

sundae [late 19th century] This word for an ice-cream dessert was originally US and may be an alteration of **Sunday**, either because the dish was made with ice cream left over from Sunday and sold cheaply on the Monday, or because it was sold only on Sundays, a practice devised (according to some accounts) to circumvent Sunday legislation. The word *Sunday* was, in Old English, *Sunnandæg* 'day of the sun', a translation of Latin *dies solis*.

sundry [Old English] Old English *syndrig* meant 'distinct, separate, special'. The current use 'various' arose in late Middle English.

WORDBUILDING

The prefix **super-** [from Latin *super-*, from *super* 'above, beyond'] adds the sense

- **above, over, beyond** [superstructure]
- **to an extreme degree** [superabundant]
- **extra large** [supercontinent]
- **having greater influence** or **capacity** [superbike; superpower]
- **of a higher kind** [superfamily]

---

superb [mid 16th century] *Superb* was first used in the description of buildings and monuments, from Latin *superbus* 'proud, magnificent'.

supercilious [early 16th century] This is from Latin *superciliosus* 'haughty', from *supercilium* 'eyebrow' and is inpired by the air of contempt achieved from a disdainful look with raised eyebrows.

superficial [late Middle English] This is from late Latin *superficialis*, from Latin *superficies* 'surface'. The word came to be applied to people meaning 'shallow' in the early 17th century (Shakespeare *Measure for Measure*: A very superficial, ignorant, unweighing fellow).

superfluous [late Middle English] This word is from Latin *superfluus*, from *super-* 'over' and *fluere* 'to flow'.

superintendent [mid 16th century] *Superintendent* is from ecclesiastical Latin *superintendere* 'oversee', the same verb which gave early 17th-century **superintend** (translating Greek *episkopein*).

superior [late Middle English] This is from Old French *superiour*, from Latin *superior*, the comparative of *superus* 'that is above', from *super* 'above'. The noun use meaning 'person of higher rank' is recorded from the late 15th century.

supersede [late 15th century] The early sense recorded for *supersede* is 'postpone, defer'. It comes from Old French *superseder*, from Latin *supersedere* 'be superior to', from *super-* 'above' and *sedere* 'sit'. The current sense 'take the place of' dates from the mid 17th century.

superstitious [Middle English] This is from Old French, or from Latin *superstitio(n-)*, from *super-* 'over' and *stare* 'to stand': this may be

from the notion of 'standing over' something in awe.

supervise [late 15th century] The early sense was 'survey, peruse'; it comes from medieval Latin *supervis-*, the past participial stem of *supervidere* 'survey, supervise'. Latin *super-* 'over' and *videre* 'to see' are the formative elements.

supper [Middle English] *Supper* is from Old French *super* 'to sup' (a verb form used as a noun). Formerly this was the last of the three main meals of the day, the others being breakfast and dinner. The word is now usually applied to a less formal meal than dinner.

supplant [Middle English] This is from Old French *supplanter* or Latin *supplantare* 'trip up', from *sub-* 'from below' and *planta* 'sole of the foot'.

supple [Middle English] This word which originally meant 'of yielding consistency' is from Old French *souple*, from Latin *supplex*, *supplic-* 'submissive', from *sub-* 'under' and the root of *plicare* 'to fold'.

supplement [late Middle English] *Supplement* is from Latin *supplementum*, from *supplere* 'fill up, complete'. Use of the word in the context of publications dates from the late 16th century.
→ SUPPLY

supply [late Middle English] This is from Old French *soupleer*, from Latin *supplere* 'fill up', from *sub-* 'from below' and *plere* 'fill'. The early sense of the noun was 'assistance, relief', chiefly a Scots use. The plural *supplies* meaning 'provisions' dates from the early 17th century. In the context of education the phrase *supply teacher* is recorded from the early 20th century.

support [Middle English] *Support* in early examples had the sense 'tolerate, put up with'. It comes from Old French *supporter*, from Latin *supportare*, from *sub-* 'from below' and *portare* 'carry'. The notion of standing by somebody and offering encouragement (*supported him openly*) started out in the military context of giving assistance in battle by a second line of troops; this same sense was transferred in the 1950s to the action of giving encouragement to a sports team (*supporting Sheffield Wednesday*).

suppose [Middle English] *Suppose* is from Old French *supposer*, from Latin *supponere* (from *sub-* 'from below' and *ponere* 'to place'); it was influenced by Latin *suppositus* 'set under' and Old French *poser* 'to place'. Late Middle English **supposition** was first used as a term in scholastic logic; it derives from Old French, or from late Latin *suppositio(n-)* (translating Greek *hupothesis* 'hypothesis').

suppress [late Middle English] This is from Latin *suppress-*, the past participial stem of *supprimere* 'press down', from *sub-* 'down' and *premere* 'to press'.

supreme [late 15th century] 'Highest' was the early meaning of *supreme*; it was used literally but was gradually restricted to poetry. The source is Latin *supremus*, the superlative of *superus* 'that is above', from *super* 'above'. The notions 'paramount' and 'exalted' are seen in its application to rulers and to God (Shakespeare *Richard III*: Take heed you dally not before your King, Lest he that is the supreme King of Kings Confound your hidden falsehood).

sure [Middle English] This is from Old French *sur*, from Latin *securus* 'free from care'. The main sense strands are: 'safe, secure' (Shakespeare *Two Gentlemen of Verona*: The Forest is not three leagues off, If we recover that, we are sure enough); 'steadfast, unfaltering' (*sure of foot*); subjectively certain (*I'm absolutely sure*); and 'objectively certain' (*a sure thing*).

surf [late 17th century] *Surf* is apparently from obsolete *suff*, the origin of which is unknown; it may have been influenced by *surge*.

surface [early 17th century] *Surface* is an adoption of a French word, suggested by Latin *superficies*. One of the main modern developments in the sense of *surface* has been to refer to the 'earth' in phrases such as *surface to air missiles* and *surface mail*.

surge [late 15th century] A *surge* in early examples (from Old French *sourgeon*) referred to a 'fountain' or 'stream'. The verb is partly from the Old French stem *sourge-*, based on Latin *surgere* 'to rise'; early senses included 'rise and fall on the waves' and 'swell with great force'.

surgery [Middle English] This is from Old French *surgerie*, a contraction of *serurgerie*, from *serurgien*, a contraction of which gave Middle English **surgeon**. The Latin base is *chirurgia*, from Greek *kheirourgia* 'handiwork, surgery', from *kheir* 'hand' and *ergon* 'work'. The Latin spelling was reflected in the late 18th century in *chirurgical*, the early spelling of **surgical** (from French *cirurgical*, from Old French *sirurgie*).

surly [mid 16th century] *Surly* once expressed 'lordly, haughty, arrogant'. It is an alteration of obsolete *sirly* 'in the manner of a lord'. The notion 'churlish and ill-humoured' arose in the mid 17th century.

surmise [late Middle English] 'Formal allegation' was the early noun sense; 'allege formally' the early verb sense (both of which are now obsolete). The word is from Anglo-Norman French and Old French *surmise*, the feminine past participle of *surmettre* 'accuse', from late Latin *supermittere* 'put in afterwards'. Latin *super-* 'over' and *mittere* 'send' are the base elements. The current verb sense 'form a notion that something is the case' (*I surmised that he was to be her successor*) dates from the early 18th century.

surmount [late Middle English] Early senses of *surmount* included 'surpass' and 'be superior to'. It derives from Old French *surmonter*.

surname [Middle English] This is a partial translation of Anglo-Norman French *surnoun*, suggested by medieval Latin *supernomen*. An early use was as a term for a name title or epithet added to a person's name derived from his birthplace (*Jesus of Nazareth*) or from some achievement or association (*Edward the Confessor*).

surpass [mid 16th century] *Surpass* is from French *surpasser*, from *sur-* 'above' and *passer* 'to pass'.

surplice [Middle English] This word for a clerical garment worn over a cassock is from Old French *sourpelis*, from medieval Latin *superpellicium*. The Latin formative elements, *super-* 'above' and *pellicia* 'fur garment', point to the early tradition of wearing a surplice over the fur garments needed to keep the wearer warm in a very cold church.

surplus [late Middle English] This is from Old French *sourplus*, from medieval Latin *superplus*, from *super-* 'in addition' and *plus* 'more'.

surprise [late Middle English] A *surprise* was originally an 'unexpected seizure of a place, or attack on troops'. It comes from the Old French feminine past participle of *surprendre*, from medieval Latin *superprehendere* 'seize'. The idiom *take by surprise* is late 17th-century; *surprise, surprise!* said in fun or irony dates from the 1950s.

surrender [late Middle English] This word was first found mainly in legal use. It is from Anglo-Norman French partly based on *render*.
→ RENDER

surreptitious [late Middle English] Early use reflected the sense 'obtained by suppression of the truth'. The word is based on Latin *surreptitius*, from the verb *surripere*, from *sub-* 'secretly' and *rapere* 'seize'. The meaning 'done stealthily or secretly' dates from the mid 17th century.

surrogate [early 17th century] This is from Latin *surrogatus*, the past participle of *surrogare* 'elect as a substitute', from *super-* 'over' and *rogare* 'ask'.

surround [late Middle English] 'Overflow' was the early meaning of *surround*. This is from Old French *souronder*, from late Latin *superundare*; the Latin base elements are *super-* 'over' and *undare* 'to flow' (from *unda* 'a wave'). The word *surround* was later associated with *round*. Military use ('enclose on all sides so as to cut off') arose in the mid 17th century.

surveillance [early 19th century] This is an adoption of a French word, from *sur-* 'over' and *veiller* 'watch' (from Latin *vigilare* 'keep watch').

survey [late Middle English] The early sense recorded was 'examine and ascertain the condition of'. Anglo-Norman French *surveier* is the source of the form, from medieval Latin *supervidere*, from *super-* 'over' and *videre* 'to see'. The early (late 15th-century) sense of the noun was 'supervision'. In late Middle English a **surveyor** (from Anglo-Norman French *surveiour*, from the verb *surveier*) was a supervisor.

survive [late Middle English] *Survive* is from Old French *sourvivre*, from Latin *supervivere*, from *super-* 'in addition' and *vivere* 'live'.

susceptive [late Middle English] This is from late Latin *susceptivus*, from *suscept-*, the past participial stem of *suscipere* 'take up', a source shared by early 17th-century **susceptible** (from late Latin *susceptibilis*). The base elements are *sub-* 'from below' and *capere* 'take'.

suspect [Middle English] Three Middle English words come from the Latin source *suspicere* 'mistrust', from *sub-* 'from below' and *specere* 'to look'. *Suspect* was originally used as an adjective from Latin *suspectus* 'mistrusted' (the past participle of *suspicere*). **Suspicion** is from Anglo-Norman French *suspeciun*, from medieval Latin *suspectio(n-)*; the change in the second syllable was due to association with Old French *suspicion* (from Latin *suspicio(n-)* 'suspicion'). **Suspicious** is from Old French *suspicious*, from Latin *suspiciosus*, from *suspicio(n-)*.

suspend [Middle English] This is from Old French *suspendre* or Latin *suspendere*, from *sub-* 'from below' and *pendere* 'hang'. Several senses reflect *suspend* as a synonym of 'hang'; others develop the literal notion of attachment by a cord (*a light shade suspended from the ceiling*) or the figurative notion of being held at bay but not completely cut off (*suspended from his post pending enquiries*). Latin *suspendere* also gave late Middle English **suspension** (from French, or from Latin *suspensio(n-)*); its past participle (*suspensus* meaning 'suspended, hovering, doubtful') is the base of **suspense**. The latter is also late Middle English and came via Old French *suspens* 'abeyance'.

sustain [Middle English] This is from Old French *soustenir*, from Latin *sustinere*, the elements of which are *sub-* 'from below' and *tenere* 'hold'. Middle English **sustenance** is from Old French *soustenance*, from the verb *soustenir*. The core notions are 'a means of living' and 'means of support'.

swab [mid 17th century] A *swab* was initially a 'mop for cleaning the decks'. It is a back-formation (by removal of the suffix) from *swabber* 'a sailor detailed to swab decks': this derives from early modern Dutch *zwabber*, from a Germanic base meaning 'splash' or 'sway'.

swagger [early 16th century] This is apparently a frequentative (= verb of repeated action) of the contemporaneous verb **swag** meaning 'cause to sway or sag', from the Middle English noun *swag* which meant 'bulging bag' (probably of Scandinavian origin): this eventually in the late 18th century denoted a thief's booty (*escaped with the swag*).

swallow [Old English] Old English *swelgan*, of Germanic origin; related forms are Dutch *zwelgen* and German *schwelgen*. This has no connection with the bird name *swallow* (in Old English *swealwe*); this is Germanic in origin, related to Dutch *zwaluw* and German *Schwalbe*.

swamp [early 17th century] This is probably ultimately from a Germanic base meaning 'sponge' or 'fungus'.

swan [Old English] Of Germanic origin, *swan* is related to Dutch *zwaan* and German *Schwan*. The current sense of the verb (*swanned around while others slaved away*) originated as military slang, referring to the free movement of armoured vehicles. The word **swansong** (early 19th century) for any final performance was suggested by German *Schwanengesang* referring to a song like that reputedly sung by a dying swan.

swap [Middle English] This word was originally used in the sense 'throw forcibly'. It is probably imitative of a resounding blow. Current senses have arisen from an early use meaning 'strike hands as a token of agreement'.

swarm [Old English] The Old English noun *swearm* is Germanic in origin; German *Schwarm* is related and so too, probably, is the base of Sanskrit *svarati* 'it sounds, resounds'. The semantic base may however be 'agitated', 'deflected' as is the case with *swerve*.

swarthy [late 16th century] *Swarthy* is an alteration of obsolete *swarty* from *swart* 'black, dusky' (in Old English *sweart*), of Germanic origin. Dutch *zwart* and German *schwarz* are related.

sway [Middle English] This corresponds in sense to Low German *swājen* 'be blown to and fro' and Dutch *zwaaien* 'swing, walk totteringly'. The word *sway* in the context of putting pressure on someone to change their opinion is a late 16th-century usage.

swear [Old English] Old English *swerian* 'make a solemn declaration' is Germanic in origin; related forms are Dutch *zweren*, German *schwören*, and English *answer*. The word's use in the context of expressing anger by expletives arose in late Middle English.
➔ ANSWER

sweat [Old English] The Old English noun *swāt* and verb *swǣtan* are of Germanic origin; related forms are Dutch *zweet* and German *Schweiss*, from an Indo-European root shared by Latin *sudor*. The word **swot** in the context of academic study is a mid 19th-century dialect variant of *sweat*.

sweep [Old English] Old English *swāpan* is Germanic in origin; German *schweifen* 'sweep in a curve' is related. The word branches semantically into 'clear with a broom' (*swept the leaves*), 'clean with a broom' (*swept the carpet*), and 'pass over swiftly' (*she swept down the staircase*). Mid 18th-century **swipe** may be a variant of *sweep*.

sweet [Old English] Old English *swēte* is Germanic in origin, related to Dutch *zoet* and German *süss*, from an Indo-European root shared by Latin *suavis* and Greek *hēdus*. Adjectival use to express the speaker's attraction to and fondness for something (*isn't it sweet!*) dates from the late 18th century. The noun *sweet* meaning 'pudding, dessert' is early 19th-century; its use to refer to confectionery (*bags of sweets*) is mid 19th-century.

swell [Old English] The Old English verb *swellan* is Germanic in origin and related to German *schwellen*. Current senses of the noun date from the early 16th century; the informal adjectival use 'great, wonderful' (*a swell time they had*) derives from the late 18th century use to refer to a 'fashionable or distinguished man'.

swelter [Middle English] *Swelter* is from the base of dialect *swelt* 'perish', of Germanic origin.

swerve [Old English] Of Germanic origin, Old English *sweorfan* meant 'depart, leave, turn aside'. Middle Dutch *swerven* 'to stray' is related. The semantic base may have been 'agitated, irregular' or 'deflected'.

swift [Old English] This word expressing the notions of rapidity and lack of delay is from the Germanic base of Old English *swīfan* 'move

in a course, sweep'. The bird name dates from the mid 17th century.

swill [Old English] Old English *swillan*, *swilian* 'wash out a container', 'bathe, drench' is of unknown origin; there are no certain cognates. The noun meaning 'kitchen refuse in liquid form' dates from the mid 16th century.

swim [Old English] The Old English verb *swimman* is Germanic in origin; related forms are Dutch *zwemmen* and German *schwimmen*. Of the idiomatic phrases, *sink or swim* dates from late Middle English often in the context of the ducking of a woman in the ordeal testing witchcraft; *in the swim* meaning 'in tune with the fashion' is late 19th-century.

swindle [late 18th century] This is a back-formation (by removal of the suffix) from *swindler*, from German *Schwindler* 'extravagant maker of schemes, swindler': this comes from German *schwindeln* meaning both 'be giddy' and 'tell lies'. The early 20th-century word **swizzle** is probably an alteration of *swindle*.

swing [Old English] Of Germanic origin, Old English *swingan* meant both 'to beat, whip' and 'rush, fling oneself'; the noun *geswing* meant 'a stroke with a weapon'. German *schwingen* 'brandish' is related. The specialized use meaning 'suffer death by hanging' is found in examples from the mid 16th century. The noun *swing* as in *playground swings* dates from the late 17th century.

swirl [late Middle English] *Swirl* was originally Scots in the sense 'whirlpool'. The word may be Low German or Dutch in origin related to Dutch *zwirrelen* 'to whirl'.

swish [mid 18th century] The word *swish* is imitative. The sense 'elegant, fashionable' is a colloquial use from the late 19th century.

switch [late 16th century] A *switch* was initially a thin tapering riding whip; the source is probably Low German. From the early 17th century the word came to be applied to various mechanical devices for altering the direction of something (*railway switch*) or for making or breaking contact (*light switch*). The verb sense 'exchange' sometimes with intent to deceive (*switched briefcases*) dates from the late 19th century.

swivel [Middle English] This word is from the base of Old English *swīfan* 'to move (along a course), sweep'.

swoon [Middle English] The verb is from obsolete *swown* 'fainting', the noun from *aswoon* 'in a faint', both from Old English *geswōgen* 'overcome'.

swoop [mid 16th century] 'Sweep along in a stately manner' was the early sense recorded for *swoop* which may be a dialect variant of Old English *swāpan* 'sweep'. The sense 'come down upon sudddenly' is found from the late 18th century. The early sense of the noun was 'a blow or stroke'.

→ SWEEP

sword [Old English] Old English *sw(e)ord* is Germanic in origin and related to Dutch *zwaard* and German *Schwert*. The expression *put to the sword* dates from late Middle English.

sycophant [mid 16th century] This was initially 'an informer'. It is from French *sycophante*, or via Latin from Greek *sukophantēs* 'informer', from *sukon* 'fig' and *phainein* 'to show'. The explanation that there was an association with informing against the illegal exportation of figs from ancient Athens (recorded by Plutarch) is not substantiated. The term may have referred to an obscene gesture.

syllable [late Middle English] *Syllable* is from an Anglo-Norman French alteration of Old French *sillabe*, via Latin from Greek *sullabē*, from *sun-* 'together' and *lambanein* 'take'. A syllable is basically a group of sounds 'taken together' and uttered with a single effort.

syllabus [mid 17th century] An early *syllabus* was a 'concise table of headings of a discourse'. Modern Latin, it was originally a misreading of Latin *sittybas*, the accusative plural of *sittyba*, from Greek *sittuba* 'title slip, label'. Use of the word in educational contexts for a programme of study is recorded from the late 19th century.

symbol [late Middle English] This comes from Latin *symbolum* 'symbol, Creed (as the mark of a Christian)'; it was first used in English to refer to the Apostles' Creed; the source is Greek *sumbolon* 'mark, token', from *sun-* 'with' and *ballein* 'to throw'. From the mid 17th-century **symbolic** is recorded, from French *symbolique* or late Latin *symbolicus*, from Greek *sumbolikos*. The adjective *symbolical* dates from the early 17th century.

symmetry [mid 16th century] *Symmetry* in early examples referred to 'proportion'. It is from French *symétrie* or Latin *symmetria*, from Greek; the elements are *sun-* 'with' and *metron* 'measure'.

sympathy [late 16th century] This was first used to express 'understanding between people'; it came via Latin from Greek *sumpatheia*, from *sumpathēs* (from *sun-* 'with' and *pathos* 'feeling'). The word **sympathise** from the same period in the sense 'suffer with another person', is from French *sympathiser*, from *sympathie* 'sympathy, friendly under-

standing'. In the mid 17th century the adjective **sympathetic** (on the pattern of *pathetic*) joined this group of related words and meant 'relating to a paranormal influence'; the phrase *sympathetic magic* illustrates its use in the context of magical ritual involving objects associated with an event.

symphony [Middle English] This once denoted any of various instruments such as the dulcimer or the virginal; it comes from Old French *symphonie*, via Latin from Greek *sumphōnia*, from *sumphōnos* 'harmonious'. The base elements are *sun-* 'together' and *phōnē* 'sound'.

symptom [late Middle English] An early spelling was *synthoma*, from medieval Latin, based on Greek *sumptōma* 'chance, symptom'; this comes from *sumpiptein* 'happen'. The word was later influenced in spelling by French *symptome*.

synagogue [Middle English] This came via Old French and late Latin from Greek *sunagōgē* 'meeting', from *sun-* 'together' and *agein* 'bring'.

synchronous [mid 17th century] This is based on late Latin *synchronus*, from Greek *sunkhronos*, from *sun-* 'together' and *khronos* 'time'.

syncopate [early 17th century] This comes from late Latin *syncopat-*, the past participial stem of *syncopare* 'to swoon'. The notion of temporary loss of consciousness led to associations of weakening and strengthening of musical beats (*syncopated rhythm*) or omission of sounds.

syndicate [early 17th century] A *syndicate* was initially a committee of syndics (= government officials); it comes from French *syndicat*, from medieval Latin *syndicatus*, from late Latin *syndicus* 'delegate of a corporation'. Current verb senses such as 'control by a syndicate' date from the late 19th century.

syndrome [mid 16th century] This is a modern Latin word, from Greek *sundromē*, from *sun-* 'together' and *dramein* 'to run'.

synergy [mid 19th century] This is from Greek *sunergos* 'working together', from *sun-* 'together' and *ergon* 'work'.

synod [late Middle English] A word for an assembly of the clergy and occasionally the laity of a diocese came via late Latin from Greek *sunodos* 'meeting', from *sun-* 'together' and *hodos* 'way'.

synopsis [early 17th century] This word for a brief summary came via late Latin from Greek, from *sun-* 'together' and *opsis* 'seeing'.

synthesis [early 17th century] This came via Latin from Greek *sunthesis*, from *suntithenai* 'place together'. In the latter part of the 17th century, the word **synthetic** came into English from French *synthétique* or modern Latin *syntheticus*, from Greek *sunthetikos* (based on *suntithenai* 'place together').

system [early 17th century] This word is from French *système* or late Latin *systema*, from Greek *sustēma*, of which the base elements are *sun-* 'with' and *histanai* 'set up'. The related form **systematic** is found from the early 18th century, from French *systématique*, via late Latin from late Greek *sustēmatikos*, from *sustēma*. Early 19th-century **systemic** was formed irregularly from *system*.

Tt

tab [late Middle English] This *tab* describing a small flap or strip to be gripped or held is perhaps related to *tag*. It was apparently first used in dialect. In American English in the late 19th century, *tab* meant 'an account', commonly reflected in the idiom *keep tabs on* meaning 'keep a regular check on' someone. This is the same word used to mean 'bill' in a restaurant (*pick up the tab*).
➔ TAG

tabby [late 16th century] The word *tabby* used to describe a type of cat is said to be from its stripes, reflecting an earlier use of the word for a kind of silk taffeta, that was originally striped; later it referred to silk with a watered finish. The origin is French *tabis*, based on Arabic *al-'Attābiyya*, the name of the quarter of Baghdad where *tabby* was manufactured. *Tabby*, from the mid 18th century, has also been used as a term for an elderly maiden lady often with humorous overtones alluding to certain cat-like characteristics.

table [Old English] Old English *tabule* referred to 'a flat slab' or 'an inscribed tablet'. Latin *tabula* 'plank, tablet, list' is the source, reinforced in Middle English by Old French *table*. The idiom *turn the tables on someone* is a metaphor of the early 17th century from the notion of swivelling a games board to reverse the positions and fortunes of the players. The phrase:
■ **table d'hôte** adopted from French in the early 17th century is literally 'host's table'. The term originally described a table in a hotel or restaurant where all guests ate together, which led to its use for a meal served there at a stated time and for a fixed price.

tablet [Middle English] This Middle English word is from Old French *tablete*, from a diminutive of Latin *tabula*. In early use it referred to a small slab of stone or metal for an inscription, later to a stiff sheet of something such as card (Shakespeare *Cymbelene*: This Tablet lay upon his Brest, wherein Our pleasure, his full Fortune, doth confine). The notion of a compressed drug or confection in the shape of a lozenge dates from the late 16th century. The word **tabloid** (late 19th century and based on *tablet*) was originally the proprietary name of a medicine sold in tablets; the term then came to denote any small medicinal tablet of any brand. The application

of *tabloid* to a newspaper (early 20th century) is from the notion of the stories being concentrated into an easily assimilable form.
➔ TABLE

taboo [late 18th century] This word comes from Tongan *tabu* 'set apart'; it was introduced into English by the explorer Captain Cook in 1777 in the narrative of his voyages (Not one of them would sit down, or eat a bit of any thing … On expressing my surprize at this, they were all *taboo*, as they said; which word has a very comprehensive meaning; but in general signifies that a thing is forbidden). The stress on the second syllable in pronunciation is an English feature; in the native languages which feature this word, the stress is on the first syllable and it is only used adjectivally. English use of *taboo* in linguistic contexts meaning 'considered offensive, prohibited by social custom' (*taboo terms*) dates from the 1930s.

tacit [early 17th century] An early meaning of *tacit* was 'wordless, noiseless'. It is from Latin *tacitus*, the past participle of *tacere* 'be silent'. **Taciturn** appeared in the late 18th century, from Latin *taciturnus*, from *tacitus*.

tack[1] [Middle English] The word *tack* (in *tin tack, tacks along the hem*) was used very generally at first for 'something that fastens one thing to another' such as a buckle or clasp. It is probably related to Old French *tache* 'clasp, large nail'. It is also used in nautical contexts, originally as a term for a rope, wire, or hook for holding the corners of the lower square sails of a sailing ship; the notion of changing direction is from the changing of the tacks to brace the yards and turn the ship's head to the wind.

tack[2] [late 18th century] The *tack* associated with horse-riding was originally dialect in the general sense 'apparatus, equipment' and is a contraction of *tackle*. The current sense (as in *tack room*) dates from the 1920s.

tack[3] [1980s] The *tack* referring to cheap and shoddy things is a back-formation (by removal of the suffix) from early 19th century **tacky**. The origin of the latter is unknown but early use was as a noun for a horse of little value; it was later applied to a poor white in some southern states of the US, which led to the extended meaning 'shabby, in bad taste' in the mid 19th century.

tackle [Middle English] *Tackle* in early use referred to equipment or utensils for a specific task; it is probably from Middle Low German *takel*, from *taken* 'lay hold of'. Early senses of the verb found in late Middle English were in the context of providing and handling a ship's equipment; later it was used in connection with harnessing a horse. Use of the word to mean 'lay hold of, grip' (*tackled his opponent*) arose colloquially in the early 19th century, and was adopted as a rugby term later that century.

tact [mid 17th century] *Tact* in early examples referred to the sense of touch. It comes via French from Latin *tactus* 'touch, sense of touch', from *tangere* 'to touch'. The word developed a notion of 'sensitivity' and in the late 18th century gained its modern sense 'delicacy in dealing with others'. The Latin source verb, *tangere*, also gave (via Latin *tactilis*) the English word **tactile** which in the early 17th century meant 'perceptible by touch, tangible'.

tactical [late 16th century] The word *tactical* was first used meaning 'relating to military or naval tactics'; it comes from Greek *taktikos* from *tuktos* 'ordered, arranged', from the base of *tassein* 'arrange'. **Tactic** dates from the mid 18th century, from modern Latin *tactica*, from Greek *taktikē* (*tekhnē*) '(art) of tactics', the feminine of *taktikos*.

tag [late Middle English] When first recorded, this word referred to a narrow hanging section of a skirt slashed as a decorative feature. It is of unknown origin but may be related to late Middle English *dag* similarly describing a pointed part of ornamental edging on a piece of clothing. Use of *tag* for a label indicating ownership began in US English in the mid 19th century; the notion of *electronic tagging* for surveillance of for example a convicted person allowed beyond the confines of prison dates from the late 20th century.

tail [Old English] Old English *tæg(e)l* is apparently from a Germanic base meaning 'hair, hairy tail'; it is related to Middle Low German *tagel* 'twisted whip, rope's end'. The early sense of the verb in use from the early 16th century was 'fasten to the back of something'; the meaning 'follow closely' appeared at the beginning of the 20th century (*tailed by a detective she'd hired*).

tailor [Middle English] This comes from Anglo-Norman French *taillour* meaning literally 'cutter', based on late Latin *taliare* 'to cut'. The verb dates from the mid 17th century.

taint [Middle English] First evidence of use is as a verb in the sense 'convict, prove guilty': in this sense *taint* is a shortening of *attaint* (from Old French) 'affect with disease'. In late Middle English *taint* also meant 'tinge, dye', from Old French *teint* 'tinged', based on Latin *tingere* 'to dye'. The word was sometimes applied to the damage of honour and reputation (Shakespeare *Henry VIII*: We come not by the way of Accusation, To taint that honour every good Tongue blesses).

take [late Old English] Late Old English *tacan* meant 'get (especially by force), capture', from Old Norse *taka* 'grasp, lay hold of', apparently from a primary notion of 'touch, put the hand on'. Essentially the verb has a sense of 'transfer' involving 'seizing' and 'receiving'. The main semantic strands include 'touch' (long obsolete), 'grip' (*took me in his arms*), 'choose' (*took the opportunity*), 'receive' (*took the call*), 'comprehend' (*couldn't take in the news*), 'undertake, perform' (*I'll take a look*), 'convey, deliver' (*take it by courier*), and many idiomatic uses.

tale [Old English] Old English *talu* was 'telling, something told'. Germanic in origin, it is related to Dutch *taal* 'speech' and German *Zahl* 'number', and to English *tell*. The plural *tales* meaning 'confidences', 'malicious gossip' as in *tell tales* has been in use since late Middle English.
→ TELL

talent [Old English] Old English *talente, talentan* referred to a unit of weight used by ancient nations such as the Babylonians, Assyrians, Romans, and Greeks, and comes from Latin *talenta*, the plural of *talentum* 'weight, sum of money' (from Greek *talanton*). The word's use to mean 'natural aptitude or skill' is a figurative use with biblical allusion to the parable of the talents (Matthew 25:14–30) in which a master gives one, two, and ten talents of silver to each of three servants: two of them use their talents well and double the number whereas the third with one talent buries his coin and fails to benefit from it.

talisman [mid 17th century] *Talisman* is based on Arabic *ṭilsam*, apparently from an alteration of late Greek *telesma* 'completion, religious rite'. This is from *telein* 'complete, perform a rite', from *telos* 'result, end'.

talk [Middle English] *Talk* is a frequentative (= verb of repeated action) from the Germanic base of *tale* or *tell*. Colloquial phrases such as *you can talk!*, *hark who's talking*, pointing out to the speaker that he may not be in a position to criticize, appeared in the mid 19th century (Thackeray *Vanity Fair*: A person can't help their birth … I am sure Aunt Bute need not talk: she wants to marry Kate to young Hooper, the wine-merchant). Another colloquial use, based on *talk* arose in the early 20th century in US English: the phrase

the talkies (influenced by *movie*) came to refer to films with a soundtrack.
→ TALE; TELL

tall [late Middle English] This is a word of remarkable sense development as is often the case with adjectives which subjectively 'estimate' such as *pretty, clean, handsome, elegant*. Its source is probably Old English *getæl* 'swift, prompt'; early senses also included 'fine, handsome' and 'bold, strong, good at fighting'. The notion 'high in stature' is expressed in examples from the early 16th century; this was soon applied to anything lofty such as trees, mountains, and ships, especially square-riggers (1902 John Masefield *Salt-water Ballads*: All I ask is a tall ship and a star to steer her by). The phrase *tall, dark, and handsome* is recorded from the early years of the 20th century.

tallow [Middle English] This may have come from Middle Low German and corresponds to forms such as Dutch *talk* and German *Talg*. Despite the indication from many comparable Germanic forms that there is a common origin, examples of the word before the 13th century have not been found.

tally [late Middle English] A *tally* in early examples was a notched tally stick. The notches indicated the amount of a debt and the stick was cleft lengthwise so that both parties had a record of the agreement. The word comes from Anglo-Norman French *tallie*, from Latin *talea* 'twig, cutting'.

tame [Old English] The Old English adjective *tam* and the verb *temmian* are Germanic in origin, related to Dutch *tam* and German *zahm*, from an Indo-European root shared by Latin *domare* and Greek *daman* 'tame, subdue'. The word developed a depreciatory aspect as 'lacking animation or effect' in the early 17th century (Shakespeare *Hamlet*: Be not too tame neyther: but let your owne Discretion be your Tutor: suit the action to the word).

tamper [mid 16th century] *Tamper* was initially 'busy oneself to a particular end', 'machinate' (1823 Sir Walter Scott *Peveril*: You shall … [not] tamper … amongst my servants, with impunity). It is an alteration of the verb *temper*. The notion of 'meddling' became associated with the word from the mid 16th century.
→ TEMPER

tan [late Old English] Late Old English *tannian* 'convert into leather' is probably from medieval Latin *tannare* and may be of Celtic origin; it was reinforced in Middle English by Old French *tanner*. The crushed bark of the oak was made into an infusion for converting hide into leather. A word which is related to *tan* is Middle

English **tawny** from Old French *tane*, from *tan* 'tanbark'.

tandem [late 18th century] The word *tandem* for a type of bicycle ridden by two people is a humorous use of a Latin word meaning literally 'at length'.

tang [Middle English] There are two main semantic branches to this word: it is both 'a projecting pointed part' (and originally referred to both a snake's tongue, once believed to be a stinging organ, and to the sting of an insect) and 'a penetrating flavour' (*fruity tang*). Old Norse *tangi* 'point, tang of a knife' is the source.

tangent [late 16th century] This was first used in geometry and meant 'touching', the meaning of the Latin present participle *tangent-* from the verb *tangere*. The same Latin verb gave the contemporaneous word **tangible** which came via French, or from late Latin *tangibilis*. Figurative use of the phrase *off at a tangent* dates from the late 18th century.

tangle [Middle English] The early sense reflected in examples of this word's use is 'entangle, catch in a tangle'. It is probably Scandinavian in origin and related to Swedish dialect *taggla* 'disarrange'.

tank [early 17th century] The word *tank* may be from Gujarati *tānkū* or Marathi *tānkē* 'underground cistern', from Sanskrit *tadāga* 'pond'. It was probably influenced by Portuguese *tangue* 'pond', from Latin *stagnum*. *Tank* came to be applied to an armoured vehicle from its use as a secret code word during their manufacture in 1915.

tankard [Middle English] A *tankard* initially referred to a large tub for carrying liquid. It then, in the late 15th century, came to describe a drinking cup made of wooden staves secured by hoops. It is perhaps related to Dutch *tanckaert*.

tannoy [1920s] The word *tannoy* is a contraction of *tantalum alloy*, which is used as a rectifier in this sound reproduction and amplification system. *Tannoy* was originally a proprietary name.

tantalize [late 16th century] *Tantalize* is based on *Tantalus*, the name of a Lydian King in Greek Mythology whose punishment for killing his son Pelops was to be provided for eternity with fruit and water which he could never reach.

tantamount [mid 17th century] This comes from the earlier verb *tantamount* 'amount to as much', from Italian *tanto montare*.

tap¹ [Old English] Old English *tæppa* was a 'peg for the vent-hole of a cask', the verb *tæppian* was 'provide (a cask) with a stopper'. The phrase *on tap* is recorded from the late 15th century. From a Germanic source, *tap* is related to Dutch *tap* and German *Zapfen* (both nouns). Use of the word to describe a listening device attached to a telephone dates from the 1920s, from the notion of 'siphoning off' information; verb use in this sense appeared in the late 19th century when current was diverted to intercept a telegraphic communication.

tap² [Middle English] This *tap* meaning 'strike lightly' is from Old French *taper*, of imitative origin; *clap* and *rap* are similar formations.

tape [Old English] Old English *tæppa, tæppe* is perhaps related to Middle Low German *teppen* 'pluck, tear'. The word first described a narrow woven strip of stout linen used for tying garments or as a measuring line. The word came to be applied in recording contexts (*magnetic tape*) from the 1940s.

taper [Old English] An early *taper* was a wax candle. It is a dissimilated form (by alteration of *p-* to *t-*) of Latin *papyrus*, the pith of which was used for candle wicks. The verb was first used in the late 16th century to describe the action of rising like a flame; the notion of coming to a point influenced its sense development (*tapered away from one metre wide to barely an inch*).

tapestry [late Middle English] This is from Old French *tapisserie*, from *tapissier* 'tapestry worker' or the verb *tapisser* 'to carpet', from *tapis* 'carpet'.

tar [Old English] Old English *teru, teoru* is Germanic in origin and related to Dutch *teer*, German *Teer*, and ultimately perhaps to *tree*. The phrase *tar with the same brush* is associated with the practice by shepherds of protecting all their sheep uniformly with a curative coating of tar. *Tar* forms the first element of **tarpaulin** (a word originating in the early 17th century; the second element is probably the *pall* of *funeral pall* reminiscent of the blackness of the tarred canvas. The suffix *-in* here represents *-ing*.
→ TREE

tardy [mid 16th century] *Tardy* is from French *tardif, -ive*, from Latin *tardus* 'slow'.

target [late Middle English] *Target* is a diminutive of the archaic synonym *targe* and was originally a term for a light round shield. The noun came later to denote various round objects and to refer generally to anything at which aim was directed (Tennyson *Locksley Hall*: They to whom my foolish passion were a target for their scorn). The verb dates from the early 17th century.

tariff [late 16th century] A *tariff* once referred to an arithmetical table. It came via French from Italian *tariffa*, based on Arabic *ṭarrafa* 'notify'. The word became less specific in the context of customs duties; it was not until around 1890 that the sense 'classified list of charges' in a hotel or other business came into common English use (although more frequent earlier in Europe and the US). Since the 1950s *tariff* has also entered legal contexts to denote a series of scales suggesting standard minimum penalties for certain categories of crimes and injuries reflecting their severity, used as a point of reference for calculating sentences.

tarnish [late Middle English] *Tarnish* is from French *terniss-*, the lengthened stem of *ternir*, from *terne* 'dark, dull'. Figurative use (*tarnished her reputation*) is recorded from the late 17th century.

tart¹ [late Middle English] The *tart* of culinary contexts was originally a savoury pie. It is from Old French *tarte* or medieval Latin *tarta*, of unknown origin. Slang use of the word to refer to a female was originally in a tone of endearment in the mid 19th century and is probably an abbreviation of *sweetheart*; later that century it was applied disparagingly.

tart² [Old English] Old English *teart* meant 'harsh, severe' and was used in connection with punishment; its origin is unknown but some suggest a shared base with *tear*. 'Sharp to the taste' was a late Middle English sense development and its connection with speech and words (*tart comments*) is early 17th-century.

task [Middle English] *Task* is from an Old Northern French variant of Old French *tasche*, from medieval Latin *tasca*: this is an alteration of *taxa*, from Latin *taxare* 'censure, charge'. An early use of the noun was to refer to a fixed payment to a lord or feudal superior; an early verb sense was 'impose a tax on'. Its general use as 'something that has to be done' is found from the late 16th century (Shakespeare *Richard II*: Alas poore Duke, the taske he undertakes is numbring sands, and Drinking Oceans drie).
→ TAX

tassel [Middle English] This once referred to a clasp for a cloak. It comes from Old French *tassel* 'clasp' but earlier details of the origin are unknown.

taste [Middle English] When first found, the word *taste* also had the sense 'touch'. The noun comes from Old French *tast*, the verb from Old French *taster* 'touch, try, taste'; this is perhaps based on a blend of Latin *tangere* 'to touch' and *gustare* 'to taste'. The notion of 'discernment in knowing what is beautiful' (*such taste in his use of colours*) dates from the late 17th century, but the sense 'judgement, discriminative faculty' was already in Middle English.

tat [mid 19th century] This word referring to worthless articles was first exemplified in the senses 'rag' and 'person in rags'. It is probably a back-formation (by removal of the suffix) from early 16th-century **tatty**, originally Scots for 'tangled, matted, shaggy'; this is apparently ultimately related to Old English *tættec* 'rag', of Germanic origin.
➔ TATTERED

tattered [Middle English] *Tattered* expressed the sense 'dressed in decoratively slashed or jagged clothing' originally and is apparently from the noun *tatter* 'scrap of cloth'; it was later treated as a past participle. Late Middle English **tatters** also had the singular meaning 'scrap of cloth'; it comes from Old Norse *totrar* 'rags'.

tattoo¹ [mid 17th century] The *tattoo* of *military tattoo* was originally written *tap-too* and comes from Dutch *taptoe!* This meant literally 'close the tap (of the cask)!' said to soldiers who were then expected to return to their quarters. The *tattoo* in practical terms was originally a signal given by the beat of a drum or by a bugle call.

tattoo² [mid 18th century] This *tattoo* as a word for an indelible design of pigment inserted into the skin is from Tahitian, Tongan, and Samoan *ta-tau* or Marquesan (aboriginal Polynesian) *ta-tu*.

taunt [early 16th century] *Taunt* is apparently from French *tant pour tant* 'like for like, tit for tat', from *tant* 'so much'. The base is Latin *tantum*, the neuter of *tantus* 'so much', giving a notion of 'exchange' and 'rejoinder'. An early use of the verb was 'exchange banter, retort with banter'.

taut [Middle English] The early spelling was *tought* and the meaning 'distended'; the word is perhaps originally a variant of *tough*.
➔ TOUGH

tavern [Middle English] *Tavern* is from Old French *taverne*, from Latin *taberna* 'hut constructed of boards, tavern'.

tawdry [early 17th century] *Tawdry* is short for *tawdry lace*, a fine silk lace or ribbon worn as a necklace in the 16th and 17th centuries, a contraction of *St Audrey's lace. Audrey* was a later form of the name *Etheldrida*, the patron saint (died 679) of Ely where *tawdry laces*, along with cheap imitations and other cheap finery, were traditionally sold at the fair of St Etheldrida. St Audrey is said to have died of a throat tumour which she considered just retribution for the many showy necklaces she had worn in her youth.

tax [Middle English] The word *tax* was also used originally to mean 'estimate or determine the amount of a penalty or damages'. This survives in legal use in the sense 'examine and assess the costs of a case'. The origin is Old French *taxer*, from Latin *taxare* 'to censure, charge, compute', perhaps from Greek *tassein* 'fix'. Use of the verb to mean 'burden, make serious demands on' (*taxed his brain*) dates from the late 17th century. Middle English **taxation** formerly referred to 'the assessment of a penalty or of damages': this is via Old French from Latin *taxatio(n-)*, from *taxare*.

tea [mid 17th century] The word *tea* probably came via Malay from Chinese (Min dialect) *te*; it is related to Mandarin *chá*. The idiom *not for all the tea in China* originated in Australian English in the 1890s; *tea and sympathy* became popularized from a film title of 1956.

teach [Old English] Old English *tæcan* meant 'offer to view, present, point out'. Of Germanic origin, it is related to *token*, from an Indo-European root shared by Greek *deiknunai* 'show', *deigma* 'sample'. The sense 'dissuade' (*that will teach you!*) arose in Middle English.
➔ TOKEN

team [Old English] Old English *tēam* was a 'team of draught animals'. Related forms are German *Zaum* 'bridle', English *teem* and *tow*, from an Indo-European root shared by Latin *ducere* 'to lead'. The word was transferred to a group of people in a joint endeavour from the early 16th century.
➔ TEEM¹; TOW

tear¹ [Old English] Old English *teran* 'pull apart, rend' is of Germanic origin, related to Dutch *teren* and German *zehren*, from an Indo-European root shared by Greek *derein* 'flay'. The noun dates from the early 17th century. The verb has been associated with rushing and speed since the late 16th century (*tore off down the street*) as if tearing through obstacles. *Tear apart* meaning 'destroy by criticism' dates from the 1950s.

tear² [Old English] Old English *tēar* as in *tears of joy* is Germanic in origin. It is related to German *Zähre*, from an Indo-European root shared by Old Latin *dacruma* (Latin *lacrima*) and Greek *dakru*. The phrase *without tears* meaning 'without difficulty' first appeared in titles, the first recorded being *Reading without Tears* in 1857 by F. L. Mortimer.

tease [Old English] Old English *tæsan*, of West Germanic origin, is first recorded meaning 'comb or card wool in preparation for spinning'; it is related to Dutch *teezen*, German dialect *zeisen*, and **teasel** (in Old English *tæsl*, *tæsel*). The sense 'make fun of' is a development of the earlier and more serious 'irritate by annoying actions' (early 17th century), a figurative use of the word's original sense.

technical [early 17th century] This is based on **technic** dating from the same period first used as an adjective meaning 'to do with art or an art'; it comes from Latin *technicus*, from Greek *tekhnikos*, from *tekhnē* 'art'. **Technology** from the same period is from Greek *tekhnologia* 'systematic treatment', from *tekhnē* 'art, craft' and *-logia* 'speaking, discourse'. Early 19th-century **technique**, like *technical*, is from Latin *technicus* (via French).

teddy [early 20th century] This word for a toy bear is from *Teddy*, the pet form of the given name *Theodore*, alluding to *Theodore Roosevelt*, the 26th President of the United States who was an enthusiastic bear-hunter.

tedious [late Middle English] *Tedious* is from Old French *tedieus* or late Latin *taediosus*, from Latin *taedium*: the latter is the source of English **tedium**, a word recorded from the mid 17th century. Latin *taedere* 'be weary of' is the base.

teem[1] [Old English] Old English *tēman*, *tīcman* 'bring forth' is from a Germanic source, related to *team*. The original senses included 'give birth to' and 'be or become pregnant' giving rise to 'be full of' in the late 16th century (*teeming with insects*).
→TEAM

teem[2] [Middle English] This *teem* as in *teeming with rain* is from Old Norse *tœma* 'to empty', from *tómr* 'empty'. The original sense was specifically 'to drain liquid from, pour liquid out'; the current sense 'flow in a stream' was originally dialect and dates from the early 19th century.

teeter [mid 19th century] This is a variant of dialect *titter*, from Old Norse *titra* 'shake, shiver'.

teetotal [mid 19th century] The first element of this word is sometimes thought to be *tea* but it is in fact an emphatic extension (by reproducing the first letter) of *total*. It was apparently first used by Richard Turner, a worker from Preston, in a speech made in 1833 urging total abstinence from all alcohol rather than mere abstinence from spirits, advocated by some early temperance reformers.

telescope [mid 17th century] This is from Italian *telescopio* or modern Latin *telescopium*, from *tele-* 'at a distance' and *-scopium* 'looking'.

television [early 20th century] This is made up of the prefix *tele-* meaning 'at a distance' (from Greek *tēle-*) and the noun *vision*. **Televise** dates from the 1920s as a back-formation (by removal of the suffix) from *television*.

tell [Old English] Old English *tellan* meant 'relate, count, estimate'. The notion of counting is seen in the noun *teller*, a term for a bank official. Of Germanic origin, *tell* is related to German *zählen* 'reckon, count', *erzählen* 'recount, relate', and to English *tale*. The sense 'disclose, reveal' (*you mustn't tell!*) dates from Middle English.
→TALE

temerity [late Middle English] *Temerity* is from Latin *temeritas*, from *temere* 'rashly'.

temper [Old English] Old English *temprian* meant 'bring something into the required condition by mixing it with something else'. Latin *temperare* 'mingle, restrain oneself' is the source. Sense development was probably influenced by Old French *temprer* 'to temper, moderate'. The noun originally referred to a proportionate mixture of elements or qualities, as well as to the combination of the four bodily humours believed in medieval times to be the basis of **temperament**. This led to the common meaning of *temper* as a 'state of mind' (*in a good temper*). Late Middle English **temperament** comes from Latin *temperamentum* 'correct mixture', from *temperare*; in early use it was synonymous with the noun *temper*.

temperature [late Middle English] This is from French *température* or Latin *temperatura*, from *temperare* 'restrain'. The word originally described 'the state of being tempered or mixed', later becoming synonymous with *temperament* as a combination of bodily humours or a state of mind. The modern sense in the context of heat intensity dates from the late 17th century.
→TEMPER

tempest [Middle English] Latin *tempus* 'time, season' is the base of *tempest* (from Old French *tempeste*, from Latin *tempestas* 'season, weather, storm') and late Middle English **tempestuous** (from late Latin *tempestuosus*, from Latin *tempestas*).

template [late 17th century] The early spelling was *templet*; it is probably based on late Middle English *temple*, a term (from Old French) for a device for keeping cloth stretched. The change in the ending in the 19th century was due to association with *plate*.

temple[1] [Old English] Old English *templ*, *tempel* describing a building devoted to worship was reinforced in Middle English by Old French *temple*, both from Latin *templum* 'open or consecrated space'.

temple[2] [Middle English] This *temple* as part of the forehead is from Old French, from an alteration of Latin *tempora*, the plural of *tempus* 'temple of the head'.

tempo [mid 17th century] *Tempo* was first used as a fencing term for the timing of an attack. It is the adoption of an Italian word, from Latin *tempus* 'time'.

temporal [Middle English] *Temporal* 'relating to worldly matters' is from Old French *temporel* or Latin *temporalis*, from *tempus*, *tempor-* 'time'. When first used it meant 'lasting only for a time', synonymous with mid 16th-century **temporary** (from Latin *temporarius*, from *tempus*).

tempt [Middle English] *Tempt* is from Old French *tempter* 'to test', from Latin *temptare* 'handle, test, try', a base shared by Middle English **temptation** (from Old French *temptacion*, from Latin *temptatio(n-)*). Early use of *temptation* was with biblical reference (Matthew 4) to the temptation of Jesus by the Devil in the wilderness and then to the temptation of medieval saints by evil spirits.

tenant [Middle English] *Tenant* is from an Old French word meaning literally 'holding', the present participle of *tenir*, from Latin *tenere*. This Latin verb also gave rise to late 16th-century **tenable** (from French, from *tenir* 'to hold') and early 17th-century **tenacious** (from Latin *tenax*, *tenac-*).

tend[1] [Middle English] The early sense recorded for this *tend* as in *he tends to make mistakes* was 'move or be inclined to move in a certain direction'. It comes from Old French *tendre* 'stretch, tend', from Latin *tendere*. The noun **tendency** did not appear in use until the early 17th century, from medieval Latin *tendentia*, from *tendere*.

tend[2] [Middle English] This *tend* as in *tending his flock* is a shortening of *attend*.
→ ATTEND

tender[1] [Middle English] The *tender* of *tender thoughts*, *tender area* is from Old French *tendre*, from Latin *tener* 'tender, delicate'. Its use in connection with feelings arose early. Of the phrases: *tender mercies* is a biblical phrase from the Psalms: Call to remembrance, O Lorde, thy tender mercies and thy loving kindnesses; the phrase *tender loving care* and its abbreviation *TLC* date from the 1960s in allusion to care given by nurses.

tender[2] [mid 16th century] The *tender* of *invitation to tender* was initially a legal term meaning 'formally offer a plea, evidence, or money to discharge a debt'. It comes from Old French *tendre*, from Latin *tendere* 'to stretch, hold forth'.
→ TEND[1]

tender[3] [late Middle English] The *tender* of *fire tender* was first found expressing the meaning 'attendant, nurse'; it is from *tend* 'take care of' or it is a shortening of *attender*.
→ TEND[2]

tenet [late 16th century] The earlier spelling was *tenent*; *tenet* is from Latin meaning literally 'he holds', from the verb *tenere*.

tennis [late Middle English] Early spellings were *tenetz* and *tenes*, terms for 'real tennis', apparently from Old French *tenez!* 'take, receive!', the imperative of *tenir*: this was a command called out by the server to an opponent.

tenor [Middle English] The *tenor* meaning 'content, import' in *the general tenor of the debate* is from Old French *tenour*, from Latin *tenor* 'course, substance, import of a law'. Latin *tenere* 'to hold' is the source of both this word and the musical term *tenor* dating from late Middle English (via Old French from medieval Latin); the tenor part was allotted the melody and therefore 'held' it.

tension [mid 16th century] *Tension* was first used as a medical term for the condition or feeling of being physically strained; it comes from French, or from Latin *tensio(n-)*, from *tendere* 'to stretch'. The adjective **tense** as in *tense atmosphere* appeared in the late 17th century, from Latin *tensus*, the past participle of the verb *tendere*, expressing the literal sense 'stretched'.

tense [Middle English] This *tense* in grammar contexts such as *present tense*, *past tense* was first used in the general sense 'time'. It from Old French *tens*, from Latin *tempus* 'time'.

tent [Middle English] This is from Old French *tente*, based on Latin *tent-*, the past participial stem of *tendere* 'stretch'. Early tents were made of skins or cloth stretched on poles. The verb dates from the mid 16th century.

tentacle [mid 18th century] This word has been Anglicized from modern Latin *tentaculum*, from Latin *tentare*, *temptare* 'to feel, try'.

tentative [late 16th century] *Tentative* is from medieval Latin *tentativus*, from *tentare*, a variant of *temptare* 'handle, try'.

tenuous [late 16th century] This is an irregular formation from Latin *tenuis* 'thin'. Figurative use in the sense 'flimsy, unsubstantial, of slight importance' (*tenuous link between his presence there and the crime*) is found from the early 19th century.

tenure [late Middle English] *Tenure* is from Old French, from *tenir* 'to hold', from Latin *tenere*. This same verb gave rise to **tenement** in Middle English in the sense 'tenure, property held by tenure'. This came via Old French from medieval Latin *tenementum*.

tepid [late Middle English] *Tepid* is from Latin *tepidus*, from *tepere* 'be warm'.

term [Middle English] In early examples, a *term* referred to a limit in space or time (Gibbon *Decline and Fall*: He had now reached the term of his prosperity); as the plural *terms*, the early meaning was 'limiting conditions'. The source is Old French *terme*, from Latin *terminus* 'end, boundary, limit'. The notions of 'limit' and 'specification' have passed into legal contexts, e.g. *term of years* (= right to land for a specified, limited period), linguistic contexts, e.g. *scientific term* (= a word specific to scientific use), the field of logic, e.g. *terms of the proposition* (= the two extremes of the proposition), and maths contexts, e.g. *reduced to its lowest terms* (= with both numerator and denominator at their lowest limit, i.e. with no common factor). The Latin base of *term*, **terminus**, was adopted as an English word in the mid 16th century in the sense 'final point in space or time'; it has been used as a 'stopping point' for a vehicle from the early 19th century, initially for trains and then for trams and buses. The same base is shared by **terminal**, which dates from the early 19th century, from Latin *terminalis*.

termination [late Middle English] The early sense of *termination* was 'determination, decision'. It comes from Old French, or from Latin *terminatio(n-)*, from *terminare* 'to limit, end'. Late 16th-century **terminate** had the sense 'direct an action towards a specified end': this too is from Latin *terminare*, from *terminus* 'end, boundary'.
→ TERM

terrace [early 16th century] An early *terrace* was an open gallery; later it came to denote a platform or balcony in a theatre. An Old French word meaning literally 'rubble, platform' is the source, based on Latin *terra* 'earth'. The word often describes a raised level place for walking; this may be on the bank of a river as for example The Terrace at the Palace of Westminster. A *terrace of houses* initially described a row of houses raised above the level of the roadway. The Terraces have referred to raised tiers for standing spectators at sports stadia since the 1950s.

terrain [early 18th century] This once referred to part of the training ground where horses were exercised in a riding school. It comes from French, from a popular Latin variant of Latin *terrenum*, the neuter of *terrenus* 'of the earth'. The word soon became generalized to refer to any 'tract of country'.

terrestrial [late Middle English] 'Temporal, worldly, mundane' were the senses reflected by early use of *terrestrial*, which is based on Latin *terrestris* from *terra* 'earth'.
→ TERRITORY

terrible [late Middle English] *Terrible* once meant 'causing terror' (reflected in the name *Ivan the Terrible* (1533–84), a Tsar of Russia). Coming via French from Latin *terribilis*, from *terrere* 'frighten', the word developed a notion of 'dread' and the negative connotation led to its use colloquially as an intensive (*it's a terrible shame*). It also has the sense 'outrageous' (*a terrible man to tease me like that!*) illustrated in the phrase *the terrible twins* (*Evening Advertiser*, Swindon, 31 December 1976: The 'Terrible Twins' of yesteryear, Mr Jack Jones, general secretary of the Transport and General Workers, and Mr Hugh Scanlon, president of the Engineering Workers, have mellowed).

territory [late Middle English] This word is from Latin *territorium*, from *terra* 'land'. The word originally designated the district surrounding a town or city and under its jurisdiction, in particular a Roman or provincial city. Early 17th-century **territorial** is from late Latin *territorialis*, from Latin *territorium*; the notion of 'defending one's territory' arose in the early 20th century.

terror [late Middle English] Latin *terrere* 'to frighten' has given rise to several English words. *Terror* is from Old French *terrour*, from Latin *terror*, a base shared by **terrorist** dating from the late 18th century from French *terroriste*. The word was originally applied to supporters of the Jacobins in the French Revolution, who advocated repression and violence in pursuit of democracy and equality. The related verb **terrify** (late 16th century) is from Latin *terrificare*, from *terrificus* 'frightening', a base shared by mid 17th-century **terrific** which initially reflected this Latin sense (Milton *Paradise Lost*: The Serpent … with brazen eyes And hairie Main terrific). *Terrific* came to be an enthusiastic term meaning 'marvellous' from the 1930s.

terse [early 17th century] *Terse* is from Latin *tersus* 'wiped, polished', from the verb *tergere*. The original sense was 'polished, trim, spruce' (Ben Jonson *Poetaster*: I am enamour'd of this street … 'tis so polite and terse); in the context of language it meant 'polished, polite' (Warton *History of English Poetry*: a terse and polite Latin poet of this period). The sense developed into 'concise and to the point' (*terse explanation of the facts*) in the late 18th century.

test [late Middle English] A *test* once denoted a cupel used to treat gold or silver alloys or ore. This is the source of the expressions *put to the test* and *stand the test*. The English word comes via Old French from Latin *testu, testum* 'earthen pot', a variant of *testa* 'jug, shell'. Verb use appeared in the early 17th century. The notion of academic *testing* dates from the early 20th century.

testament [Middle English] This word is from Latin *testamentum* 'a will' (from *testari* 'testify') which as a Christian Latin word also translated Greek *diathēkē* 'covenant'. The late Middle English word **testate** 'having left a will at death' is from Latin *testatus* 'witnessed', the past participle of *testari* from *testis* 'a witness'. The latter is the base too of late Middle English **testify** from Latin *testificari*.

testimony [Middle English] *Testimony* (from Latin *testimonium*) and late Middle English **testimonial** (from Old French *testimonial* 'testifying, serving as evidence', from late Latin *testimonialis*) are based on Latin *testis* 'a witness'. *Testimonial* has been used as a word for 'a public gift as a mark of esteem' (*testimonial football match*) from the mid 19th century.
→ TESTAMENT

tetchy [late 16th century] The word *tetchy* is probably from a variant of Scots *tache* 'blotch, fault', from Old French *teche*.

tether [late Middle English] *Tether* is from Old Norse *tjóthr*, from a Germanic base

meaning 'fasten'. The figurative notion of being *at the end of one's tether* dates from the early 16th century.

text [late Middle English] A *text* is essentially 'something woven'; it comes from Old Northern French *texte*, from Latin *textus* meaning 'tissue, literary style' and later in medieval Latin coming to mean 'Gospel'. The source of the form is *text-*, the past participial stem of the verb *texere* 'to weave'.

texture [late Middle English] A *texture* once referred to a woven fabric or something resembling this. It comes from Latin *textura* 'weaving', from *texere* 'to weave', the source too of the related word **textile** (early 17th century from Latin *textilis*).

thanks [Old English] Old English *thancas*, the plural of *thanc* '(kindly) thought, gratitude', is Germanic in origin and related to Dutch *dank*, German *Dank*, and English *think*. **Thank** (in Old English *thancian*) is related to Dutch and German *danken*. Also dating from this same early period are **thankful** (in Old English *thancful*) and **thankfully** (in Old English *thancfullīce*).
→ THINK

that [Old English] Old English *thæt* is the nominative and accusative singular neuter of *se* 'the'. Of Germanic origin, it is related to Dutch *dat* and German *das*. Old English **this** is a related word, the neuter of *thes*. Of West Germanic origin, it is also related to *the*.
→ THE

thatch [Old English] Old English *theccan* meant 'to cover'. From a Germanic source, it is related to Dutch *dekken* and German *decken*. The word has been used in slang since the mid 17th century for 'a covering of hair'.

thaw [Old English] The Old English verb *thawian* is West Germanic in origin and related to Dutch *dooien*. The noun, first recorded in Middle English, developed its figurative use in the mid 19th century.

the [Old English] Old English *se, sēo, thæt* was ultimately superseded by forms from Northumbrian and North Mercian *thē*, Germanic in origin. Dutch *de, dat*, and German *der, die, das* are related.
→ THAT

theatre [late Middle English] *Theatre* is from Old French, or from Latin *theatrum*, from Greek *theatron*, from *theasthai* 'behold'. The American English spelling *theater* was prevalent in England from about 1550 to 1700 but was dropped between 1720 and 1750. The adjective **theatrical** dates from the mid 16th century, based on Greek *theatrikos* (from *theatron* 'theatre'); its use to mean 'irrelevantly histrionic' (*such a theatrical reaction to something so trivial*) is found from the early 18th century.

theme [Middle English] *Theme* comes via Old French from Latin *thema*, from the Greek word meaning literally 'proposition'; it is related to *tithenai* 'to set or place'. Relatively recent combinations with *theme* are *theme music* (1950s), *theme park* (1960s), and *theme pub*, *theme restaurant* (1980s); these all refer to some recurring or unifying idea. The word **thematic** dates from the late 17th century, from Greek *thematikos*, from *thema*.

then [Old English] This Old English word is Germanic in origin; related forms are Dutch *dan*, German *dann*, and English *that* and *the*. Old English **than** was originally the same word as *then*.
→ THAT; THE

theology [late Middle English] This word originally applied only to Christianity. It comes from French *théologie*, from Latin *theologia*, from Greek. Greek *theos* 'god' is the base, the suffix *-logia* meaning 'discourse'. **Theological** dating from the same period and expressing the sense 'relating to the word of God or the Bible', is from medieval Latin *theologicalis* via late Latin from Greek *theologikos* (from *theologia*). **Theologian** is recorded from the late 15th century, from French *théologien*, from *théologie* or Latin *theologia*.

theory [late 16th century] When first recorded this word meant 'a mental scheme of something to be done'. It comes via late Latin from Greek *theōria* 'contemplation, speculation', from *theōros* 'spectator'. Early 17th century **theoretical** reflected the sense 'conjectural' originally; it is via late Latin from Greek *theōrētikos*, from *theōrētos* 'that may be seen', from *theōrein*. The maths term **theorem** via late Latin from Greek (mid 16th century) is from the same base verb.

therapeutic [mid 17th century] This comes via modern Latin from Greek *therapeutikos*, from *therapeuein* 'minister to, treat medically', a base shared by the noun **therapy** which made its appearance in the mid 19th century (from modern Latin *therapia*, from Greek *therapeia* 'healing').

there [Old English] Old English *thær*, *thēr* is Germanic in origin, related to Dutch *daar* and German *da*, English *that*, and *the*. Amongst the many idioms, the phrase *there*, *there* said to comfort someone, dates from the early 16th century; *not all there* meaning 'not have all one's faculties' is found from the mid 19th century.
→ THAT; THE

thermal [mid 18th century] The original sense recorded for *thermal* was 'relating to hot springs'. It comes from French, from Greek *thermē* 'heat'.

thesaurus [late 16th century] This word comes via Latin from Greek *thēsauros* 'storehouse, treasure'. The original sense 'dictionary or encyclopedia' was narrowed to the current meaning by the publication of Roget's *Thesaurus of English Words and Phrases* in 1852.

thesis [late Middle English] This term originally referred to the setting down of the foot or the lowering of the hand in beating time. It comes via late Latin from Greek, literally 'placing, a proposition', from the root of *tithenai* 'to place'. *Thesis* was used from the late 16th century to mean a 'proposition' laid down to be proved; its use in academic contexts for a dissertation presented by a candidate for a University degree, began in the mid 17th century.

thespian [late 17th century] The word *thespian* is based on *Thespis*, the name of a Greek dramatic poet (6th century BC), regarded as the founder of Greek tragedy.

they [Middle English] The personal pronoun *they* is from Old Norse *their*, the nominative plural masculine of *sá*; it is related to Middle English **them** (from Old Norse *theim* 'to those, to them', the dative plural of *sá*); and **their** (from Old Norse *their(r)a* 'of them', the genitive plural of the demonstrative *sá*); also to *that* and *the*.
→ THAT; THE

thick [Old English] Old English *thicce* is Germanic in origin, related to Dutch *dik* and German *dick*. The transferred sense 'stupid, slow-witted' dates from the late 16th century (compare Shakespeare *Henry IV* part ii: Hang him Baboone, his Wit is as thicke as Tewksburie Mustard). The idiom *thick and fast* dates from the early 18th century; *lay it on thick* appeared around the mid 18th century. Old English nouns related to *thick* are **thickness** (*thicnes*) and **thicket** (*thiccet*).

thief [Old English] Old English *thīof*, *thēof* is from a Germanic source, related to Dutch *dief* and German *Dieb*. The verb **thieve** (in Old English *thēofian*) is from *thēof*. Transitive uses began in the late 17th century. Also related to *thief* is **theft** (in Old English *thīefth*, *thēofth*).

thigh [Old English] Of Germanic origin, Old English *thēh*, *thēoh* is related to Dutch *dij*; the form *thee* still remains in Scots and northern dialect.

thin [Old English] Old English *thynne* has a Germanic origin and is related to Dutch *dun* and German *dünn*, from an Indo-European root shared by Latin *tenuis*. The main senses include: 'of little thickness' and 'not dense or bushy'. The phrase *a thin time* meaning 'a wretched period' dates from the 1920s; *thin on the ground* dates from the 1950s (Winston Churchill *2nd World War*: the Australians were thin on the ground and enemy parties go ashore at many points).

thing [Old English] Of Germanic origin, *thing* included the early senses 'meeting' (a sense which did not extend beyond the Old English period) and 'matter, concern', as well as 'inanimate object'. It is related to German *Ding*. The idiom *do one's (own) thing* is recorded from the mid 19th century, but it did not become widespread until the 1960s during the hippie culture; *have a thing with (somebody)* dates from this same decade.

think [Old English] Old English *thencan*, of Germanic origin, is related to Dutch and German *denken*. Of the idioms, *think twice* and *think nothing of* date from the late 19th century; *think again* and *I should think not* appeared in the early 20th century. The compound:

■ **think-tank** referring to a research organization providing advice on national problems dates from the 1950s.

thirst [Old English] The Old English noun *thurst* and the verb *thyrstan* are from a Germanic source, related to Dutch *dorst* (noun), *dorsten* (verb) and German *Durst* (noun), *dürsten* (verb).

thong [Old English] The spellings in Old English included *thwang* and *thwong*. Of Germanic origin, the word is related to German *Zwang* 'compulsion' and English *twinge*. A *thong* in early use was a 'shoelace'; it then referred to any narrrow strip of leather, and eventually to any thin strip. This led to the word's application in clothing contexts, referring to a type of sandal (1960s) and to a style of ladies' knickers (1990s).

thorn [Old English] From a Germanic source, this word is related to Dutch *doorn* and German *Dorn*. The phrase *a thorn in one's side* comes from a biblical reference (Numbers 33:55: Those which ye let remain of them, shall be … thorns in your sides). It is an example of the figurative use of *thorn* as something that is a source of continual trouble or grief (Shakespeare: *Hamlet*: Those Thornes that in her bosome lodge).

thorough [Old English] Old English *thuruh* was an alteration of *thurh* 'through'. Original use was as an adverb and preposition in the same senses as those reflected by *through*. The adjective 'carried out in every detail' dates from the late 15th century, a period when it also meant 'going or extending through something' surviving in late Middle English *thoroughfare* (literally 'a track going through').

though [Old English] Old English *thēah*, of Germanic origin, is related to Dutch and German *doch*; superseded in Middle English by forms from Old Norse *thó, thau*.

thought [Old English] Germanic in origin, Old English *thōht* is related to Dutch *gedachte* as well as to English *think*. The phrase *(on) second thoughts* dates from the mid 17th century; *lost in thought* is early 19th-century; *it's the thought that counts* is recorded from the 1930s.
→ THINK

thrall [Old English] Old English *thrǽl* meant 'slave', from Old Norse *thrǽll*, perhaps from a base meaning 'to run'.

thrash [Old English] *Thrash* is a variant of *thresh* which was an early sense reflected in examples of *thrash*. The Germanic root was probably 'to tramp with the feet' and the word came to be applied in English to treading out corn by men or oxen; however the method of threshing gradually changed to involve, in the main, beating with a flail, which led to the extended more generalized notions of knocking, beating and striking (leaving *thresh* in contexts of producing grain).
→ THRESH

thread [Old English] The Old English noun *thrǽd* is from a Germanic source, related to Dutch *draad* and German *Draht*, and to the English verb *throw*. The verb dates from late Middle English. The idiom *hang by a thread* arose in the early 16th century suggested by the story of the sword of Damocles: this flatterer had enthused about the happiness of Dionysius, the tyrant of Syracuse, who then, at a banquet, suspended a sword precariously over Damocles' head by a hair to impress upon him how precarious happiness can be. Of the other idioms, *pick up the thread* originated in the mid 17th century, with *lose the thread* appearing in the 1980s.
→ THROW

threat [Old English] Old English *thrēat* meant 'oppression'. Of Germanic origin, it is related to Dutch *verdrieten* 'grieve' and German *verdriessen* 'irritate'. Based on *thrēat* is the verb **threaten** (in Old English, *thrēatnian*) which originally expressed 'urge or induce' especially by the use of threats.

thresh [Old English] Old English *therscan* changed later to *threscan*. A Germanic word in origin, it is related to Dutch *dorsen* and German *dreschen*. The compound:

■ **threshold** (in Old English *therscold*, *threscold*) is related to German dialect *Drischaufel*; the first element is related to *thresh* in the Germanic sense 'tread', but the origin of the second element remains unknown.
→ THRASH

thrift [Middle English] The early sense recorded was 'prosperity, acquired wealth, success'. *Thrift* comes from Old Norse, from *thrífa* 'grasp, get hold of'. The word eventually, in the mid 16th century, became associated more with the parsimony of saving and sparing use rather than with the results and benefits of making savings. The related verb *thrive* has maintained a positive connotation.
→ THRIVE

thrill [Middle English] This was first used as a verb in the sense 'pierce or penetrate'; it is an alteration of dialect *thirl* 'pierce, bore'. The sense 'affect with a sudden wave of emotion' dates from the early 17th century (Shakespeare *King Lear*: A servant that he bred, thrill'd with remorse, Oppos'd against the act). The colloquial use of *thrilled* meaning 'delighted' arose in the early 20th century.

thrive [Middle English] This was originally in the sense 'grow, increase'; it comes from Old Norse *thrífask*, the reflexive of *thrífa* 'grasp, get hold of'. The sense 'flourish, prosper' developed early without the association of parsimony found in *thrift*.
→ THRIFT

throat [Old English] Old English *throte*, *throtu* comes from a Germanic source and is related to German *Drossel*. Late Middle English **throttle** is perhaps a frequentative (= verb of repeated action) from *throat*; the noun dating from the mid 16th century is perhaps a diminutive of *throat* (this was its early meaning), but the history of the word is not clear. Use of the word to refer to a valve controlling the flow of fuel dates from the early 19th century.

throb [late Middle English] This word is probably imitative of pulsating movement.

throes [Middle English] The early word was the singular *throwe* 'violent spasm'; it is perhaps related to Old English *thréa*, *thrawu* 'calamity', influenced by *thrówian* 'suffer'.

throne [Middle English] This comes from Old French *trone*, via Latin from Greek *thronos* 'elevated seat'.

throng [Old English] Old English *(ge)thrang* 'crowd, tumult' comes from a Germanic source. The early sense of the verb in Middle English was 'press violently, force one's way'.

through [Old English] Old English *thurh* functioned as a preposition and an adverb. Of Germanic origin, it is related to Dutch *door* and German *durch*. The spelling change to *thr-* appears in around 1300, becoming standard from Caxton onwards.

throw [Old English] Old English *thráwan* meant 'to twist, turn'. Of West Germanic origin, it is related to Dutch *draaien* and German *drehen*, from an Indo-European root shared by Latin *terere* 'to rub' and Greek *teirein* 'wear out'. The main current sense expressing propulsion and sudden action, dates from Middle English. Use of the noun as a word for a piece of decorative fabric thrown over a piece of furniture dates from the late 19th century originally in North American English.

thrust [Middle English] Early use was as a verb; it comes from Old Norse *thrýsta* and is perhaps related to Latin *trudere* 'to thrust'. The noun is first recorded (early 16th century) in the sense 'act of pressing'. It came to be used in US English in the mid 20th century to mean 'gist, theme' (*the main thrust of his argument*).

thud [late Middle English] This was originally Scots; it is probably from Old English *thyddan* 'to thrust, push', related to *thoden* 'violent wind'. The noun is recorded first as a word for a sudden blast or gust of wind, and later for the sound of a thunderclap: this led to a generalization for a dull, heavy sound. The verb dates from the early 16th century.

thug [early 19th century] *Thug* was first used as a term for a member of an organization of professional robbers and assassins in India who strangled their victims. It comes from Hindi *thag* 'swindler, thief', based on Sanskrit *sthagati* 'he covers or conceals'. The word was soon generalized to any violent bully.

thumb [Old English] Old English *thuma*, from West Germanic, is related to Dutch *duim* and German *Daumen*, from an Indo-European root shared by Latin *tumere* 'to swell'. The verb dates from the late 16th century when it had the sense 'play (a musical instrument) with the thumbs'. **Thimble** (in Old English *thýmel*) started out as a word for a 'finger-stall' and is based on *thumb*.

thump [mid 16th century] This is imitative of a heavy striking sound.

thunder [Old English] Old English *thunor* (as a noun) and *thunrian* (as a verb) are of Germanic origin; Dutch *donder* and German *Donner*, both nouns, are related, from an Indo-European root shared by Latin *tonare* 'to thunder'. The verb became associated with angry words from Middle English. The noun **thunderer** was applied in late Middle English to God or to a deity such as Jupiter or Thor; from the late 16th century it was a word for a 'powerful orator' and *The Thunderer*, from the early 19th century, was a sobriquet for the London *Times* newspaper.

thwart [Middle English] The early spelling was *thwerte*, from the adjective *thwert* 'perverse, obstinate, adverse'. Old Norse *thvert* is the source, the neuter of *thverr* 'transverse', from an Indo-European root shared by Latin *torquere* 'to twist'.

tiara [mid 16th century] This was originally used to refer to a Persian royal headdress, in particular a kind of turban worn by kings in ancient Persia. It comes via Latin from Greek, partly via Italian. Use of the word for a jewelled coronet or headband dates from the early 18th century.

tick [Middle English] This *tick* as in *ticked every box of the questionnaire* was first used as a verb meaning 'pat, touch'. It is probably of Germanic origin and related to the Dutch noun *tik* and the verb *tikken* 'to pat, touch'. The noun is recorded from late Middle English as 'a light tap'; current senses date from the late 17th century.

ticket [early 16th century] *Ticket* (a shortening of obsolete French *étiquet*, from Old French *estiquet(te)*) was first used in the general senses 'short written note' and 'a licence or permit'. The source is Old French *estiquier* 'to fix', from Middle Dutch *steken*. The phrase *on tick* (mid 17th century) in the context of delaying payment is apparently from the phrase *on the ticket*, referring to a written IOU or promise to pay.
→ ETIQUETTE

tickle [Middle English] The early sense recorded was 'be delighted or thrilled'. It is perhaps a frequentative (= verb of repeated action) of *tick* or an alteration of Scots and dialect *kittle* 'to tickle'. The sense 'amuse' dates from late Middle English.
→ TICK,

tiddly [mid 19th century] This, in early examples, was a noun for an alcoholic drink, particularly spirits. The source may be slang *tiddlywink*, a term for an unlicensed public house. The current sense 'slightly drunk' dates from the early 20th century.

tide [Old English] Old English *tīd* was a 'time, period, era' (e.g. *Eastertide*). From Germanic, it is related to Dutch *tijd* and German *Zeit*, and to English *time*. Use of the word in connection with the sea dates from late Middle English.
→ TIME

tidings [late Old English] Late Old English *tīdung* meant 'announcement, piece of news'. It is probably from Old Norse *títhindi* 'news of events', from *títhr* 'occurring'.

tidy [Middle English] *Tidy* is based on the noun *tide*. The original meaning was 'timely, opportune'; it later had various senses associated with approval, usually in connection with a person, including 'attractive', 'healthy', and 'skilful'; the sense 'orderly, neat' dates from the early 18th century. Perhaps based on *tidy* is the verb **titivate** which in the early 19th century was also spelt *tidivate*.

tie [Old English] The Old English verb was *tīgan*, the noun *tēah*, words of Germanic origin. Use of the noun to mean 'necktie' dates from the mid 18th century.

tier [late 15th century] *Tier* is from French *tire* 'sequence, order', from *tirer* 'elongate, draw'.

tight [Middle English] *Tight* started out with the meaning 'healthy, vigorous'; later it came to mean 'firm, solid'. It is probably an alteration of *thight* which meant 'firm, solid' and later 'close-packed, dense'. This word is from a Germanic source and is related to German *dicht* 'dense, close'. The colloquial sense 'stingy' (*tight with his money*) dates from the early 19th century.

tile [Old English] Old English *tigele* is from Latin *tegula*, from an Indo-European root meaning 'cover'. The word was used as a slang term for 'hat' from the early 19th century.

till¹ [Old English] Old English *til* 'until' is Germanic in origin, related to Old Norse *til* 'to', and also ultimately to the *till* of farming contexts.
→ TILL³

till² [late Middle English] The *till* associated with registering cash taken in transactions was first used in the general sense 'drawer or compartment for valuables'. The word's origin is unknown.

till³ [Old English] Old English *tilian* meant 'strive for, obtain by effort' and is Germanic in origin, related to Dutch *telen* 'produce, cultivate' and German *zielen* 'aim, strive', as well as ultimately to the *till* meaning 'until'. The current sense in agricultural contexts dates from Middle English.
→ TILL¹

tiller [late Middle English] This nautical word is from Anglo-Norman French *telier* 'weaver's beam, stock of a crossbow', from medieval Latin *telarium*, from Latin *tela* 'web'.

tilt [late Middle English] In early use the word *tilt* had the sense 'fall or cause to fall, topple'. It may be related to Old English *tealt* 'unsteady', or it may be Scandinavian in origin and related to Norwegian *tylten* 'unsteady' and Swedish *tulta* 'totter'.

timber [Old English] *Timber* originally referred to 'a building' as well as to 'building material'. Of Germanic origin, it is related to German *Zimmer* 'room', from an Indo-European root meaning 'build'.

time [Old English] Old English *tīma*, of Germanic origin, is related to *tide*, which it superseded in temporal senses, leaving *tide* to refer to the movements of the sea. The earliest of the current verb senses (dating from late Middle English) is 'do (something) at a particular moment'.
→ TIDE

timid [mid 16th century] *Timid* is from Latin *timidus*, from *timere* 'to fear', the source too of the late Middle English word **timorous** which expressed 'feeling fear' (from Old French *temoreus*, from medieval Latin *timorosus*, from Latin *timor* 'fear').

tin [Old English] Of Germanic origin, *tin* is related to Dutch *tin* and German *Zinn*. Use of the word for a container for food or drink hermetically sealed to preserve freshness, dates from the late 18th century.

tincture [late Middle English] A *tincture* once referred to a dye or pigment. It comes from Latin *tinctura* 'dyeing', from *tingere* 'to dye or colour'. The sense 'slight trace of' as in *tincture of irony in her voice* (early 17th century) comes from the obsolete sense 'imparted quality', likened to a tint imparted by a dye. Pharmaceutical use of the word began in the late 17th century.

tinder [Old English] Old English *tynder*, *tyndre* is Germanic in origin, related to Dutch *tonder* and German *Zunder*.

tinge [late 15th century] *Tinge* is from Latin *tingere* 'to dip or colour'. The noun dates from the mid 18th century and soon developed the figurative sense 'trace (of some quality)' (*tinge of sadness*).

tingle [late Middle English] *Tingle* may be a variant of *tinkle*. The original notion was perhaps 'ring in response to a loud noise', but the term was very early applied to the result of hearing something shocking resulting in a prickling sensation.

tinker [Middle English] This word was first recorded in Anglo-Latin as a surname; its origin is unknown.

tinkle [late Middle English] The sense 'tingle' was included in early examples of this word's use. It is a frequentative (= verb of repeated action) of obsolete *tink* 'to chink or clink', of imitative origin.

tinsel [late Middle English] *Tinsel* was originally fabric interwoven with metallic thread or spangled. It comes from Old French *estincele* 'spark', or *estinceler* 'to sparkle', based on Latin *scintilla* 'a spark'. Use of the word to describe 'metallic threads' such as those for decorating a Christmas tree, dates from the late 16th century. The figurative notion of glitter was picked up in the term *Tinseltown* (1970s) as a nickname for Hollywood, and by extension the Hollywood cinema and its perceived glamour.

tint [early 18th century] This is an alteration (perhaps influenced by Italian *tinta*) of obsolete *tinct* 'to colour, tint', from Latin *tinctus* 'dyeing'. The base verb is Latin *tingere* 'to dye or colour'.
→ TINGE

tiny [late 16th century] *Tiny* is an extension of obsolete *tine*, 'small, diminutive', of unknown origin. Early 19th-century **teeny** is a variant of *tiny* and **teensy** (late 19th century and originally US dialect) is probably an extension of *teeny*.

tip¹ [late Middle English] The *tip* which means 'extremity' is from the Old Norse noun *typpi*, the verb *typpa*, and *typptr* 'tipped'. It is related to *top*.
→ TOP

tip² [late Middle English] The *tip* meaning 'tilt over' is perhaps of Scandinavian origin, influenced later by the verb *tip* in the sense 'touch with a tip or point'. Current senses of the noun date from the mid 19th century. The notion of 'falling over' was transferred to the word **tipsy** in the late 16th century.

tip³ [early 17th century] This *tip* in the context of rewarding service for example in a restaurant or hotel, originally meant 'give, hand, pass'; it is probably from the *tip* meaning 'culmination'.
→ TIP¹

tipple [late 15th century] To *tipple* was originally 'sell (alcoholic drink) by retail'. It is a back-formation (by removal of the suffix) from late Middle English *tippler* 'a retailer of alcoholic liquor', a word of unknown origin. Norwegian dialect *tipla* 'drip slowly' may be related.

tire [Old English] Old English *tēorian* meant 'fail, come to an end' as well as 'become physically exhausted'. The origin is unknown.

tissue [late Middle English] *Tissue* is from Old French *tissu* 'woven', the past participle of *tistre*, from Latin *texere* 'to weave'. The word originally denoted a rich material, often interwoven with gold or silver threads; later in the mid 16th century, it came to describe any woven fabric, which led to the notion of 'intricacy' (*tissue of lies*).

titbit [mid 17th century] Early spellings included *tyd bit*, *tid-bit*. It is based on dialect *tid* 'tender' of which the origin is unknown.

titillate [early 17th century] *Titillate* is from Latin *titillare* 'to tickle'.

title [Old English] Old English *titul* was reinforced by Old French *title*, both from Latin *titulus* 'inscription, title'. The word originally referred to a placard or inscription placed on an object giving information about it, which led to *title* as a descriptive heading in a book or other composition. The late 16th-century word **titular** had the sense 'existing only in name': this is from French *titulaire* or modern Latin *titularis*, from *titulus*.

to [Old English] Old English *tō* functioned as both an adverb and preposition. Of West Germanic origin, it is related to Dutch *toe* and German *zu*. Compounds of *to* include **toward** (in Old English *tōweard*) and **towards** (in Old English *tōweardes*).

toad [Old English] Old English *tādde*, *tāda* is an abbreviation of *tādige*, of unknown origin. **Toady**, dating from the early 19th century, is said to be a contraction of *toad-eater*, a charlatan's assistant who ate toads; toads were regarded as poisonous, and the assistant's miraculous survival was thought to be due to the efficacy of the charlatan's remedy. The compound:
■ **toadstool** (late Middle English) is a fanciful name from the image of a toad sitting on the rounded stool-like cap.

toast [late Middle English] *Toast* was first used as a verb in the sense 'burn as the sun does, parch'. It is from Old French *toster* 'roast', from Latin *torrere* 'parch'. The practice of drinking a toast goes back to the late 17th century, originating in the practice of naming a lady at a banquet, whose health the company was requested to drink: the idea was that the lady's name flavoured the drink like the pieces of spiced toast formerly placed in drinks such as wine.

tobacco [mid 16th century] This is from Spanish *tabaco*; said to be from a Carib word for a tobacco pipe or from a Taino word for a primitive cigar. An alternative is an Arabic source.

toboggan [early 19th century] The origin of this word is Canadian French *tabaganne*, from Micmac *topaǧan* 'sled'.

today [Old English] Old English *tō dæg* meant 'on (this) day'. **Tonight** (*tō niht* 'on (this) night') dates from the same period and **tomorrow** is Middle English when it was written as two words.

toddle [late 16th century] The early spelling was *todle* a Scots and northern English word, of which the origin is obscure.

toddy [early 17th century] The word *toddy* is from Marathi *tāḍī*, Hindi *tārī*, from Sanskrit *tāḍī* 'palmyra'. The word originally referred to the sap obtained from the palmyra and other species of palm, used as a drink (sometimes in a fermented and alcoholic form) in tropical countries. It came to describe a liquor such as whisky mixed with hot water and sugar from the late 18th century.

toe [Old English] Old English *tā*, from a Germanic source, is related to Dutch *tee* and German *Zeh*, *Zehe*. Current senses of the verb date from the mid 19th century. The idiom *toe the line* from an athletics analogy originated in the early 19th century. The derogatory word:
■ **toerag** (mid 19th century) originally referred to a rag wrapped round the foot as a sock or, by extension, to the wearer, a vagrant for example.

toff [mid 19th century] *Toff* is perhaps an alteration of *tuft*, a word used for a gold tassel worn on the cap by titled undergraduates at Oxford and Cambridge.
→ TUFT

toffee [early 19th century] This was apparently originally a dialect word, an alteration of early 19th-century *taffy* retained in North American English usage. Early spellings also included *tuffy* and *toughie* inspired apparently by the sweet's toughness.

tog [early 18th century] The *tog* of *togs* 'clothing' was first used as a slang term for a coat or outer garment. It is apparently an abbreviation of the obsolete criminals' slang *togeman(s)* 'a light cloak', from French *toge* or Latin *toga*. As a term for a unit of thermal resistance (e.g. 12 tog duvet rating), *tog* dates from the 1940s, suggested by an earlier unit called the *clo* (the first element of *clothes*).

together [Old English] Old English *tōgædere* is based on the preposition *to* and a West Germanic word related to *gather*. The adjective dates from the 1960s.
→ GATHER

toggle [mid 18th century] *Toggle* was originally in nautical use, a term for a short pin passed through a loop of a rope to keep it in place. The origin is obscure but there is probably a relationship with *tangle*. The word's generalization to a 'fastener' on a strap or garment dates from the late 19th century. It has been used as a term in computing since the 1980s for a command that has the opposite effect on successive occasions: the notion is one of turning through 90 degrees.

toil [Middle English] The early senses recorded were 'contend verbally' and, as a noun, 'strife'. The word is from Anglo-Norman French *toiler* 'strive, dispute' and *toil* 'confusion', from Latin *tudiculare* 'stir about'. The base is Latin *tudicula* 'machine for crushing olives', related to *tundere* 'crush'.

toilet [mid 16th century] *Toilet* is from French *toilette* 'cloth, wrapper', a diminutive of *toile*. It was originally a word for a cloth wrapper for clothes; later (in the 17th century) it came to describe a cloth cover for a dressing table, articles used in dressing, the process of dressing, and later also the process of washing oneself. In the 19th century a *toilet* was also a dressing room, and, in the US, one with washing facilities; this resulted in use of the word for 'a lavatory' in the early 20th century.

token [Old English] Old English *tāc(e)n* is Germanic in origin, related to Dutch *teken*, German *Zeichen*, and to English *teach*. Early use was in the sense 'symbol, sign'; it came to denote a coin-shaped piece of metal from the late 16th century when there was a scarcity of small coin from the reign of Queen Elizabeth I to 1813 and tradesmen issued *tokens* to exchange for goods or cash. Use of the word to mean 'voucher' (*book token*) dates from the early 20th century.
➔ TEACH

tolerance [late Middle English] Latin *tolerare* 'bear, endure' is the source of a group of words: *tolerance* (via Old French from Latin *tolerantia*) was originally the action of bearing hardship, or the ability to bear pain and hardship. **Tolerable** dates from the same period as *tolerance* and comes via Old French from Latin *tolerabilis*; **toleration** (from French *tolération*, from Latin *toleratio(n-)*) initially referred to the granting of permission by authority; the verb **tolerate** (early 16th century in the sense 'endure (pain)') is from the past participial stem of *tolerare*; late 18th-century **tolerant** is from French *tolérant*, the present participle of *tolérer*, from Latin *tolerare*.

toll¹ [Old English] This *toll* as in *toll gate* was originally a charge, tax, or duty; it is from medieval Latin *toloneum*, an alteration of late Latin *teloneum*, from Greek *telōnion* 'toll house', from *telos* 'tax'. Use of the word to mean 'number' (*death toll*) arose in the late 19th century from the notion of paying a toll or tribute in human lives (to an adversary or to death).

toll² [late Middle English] This *toll* associated with the ringing of a bell is probably a special use of dialect *toll* 'to drag, pull'.

tomb [Middle English] *Tomb* is from Old French *tombe*, from late Latin *tumba*, from Greek *tumbos*.

tome [early 16th century] This was originally a word for one volume of a larger work. It comes from French, via Latin from Greek *tomos* 'section, roll of papyrus, volume'; related to *temnein* 'to cut'.

ton [Middle English] *Ton* is a variant of *tun*, both spellings being used for the container and the weight. The senses were differentiated in the late 17th century, with *tun* specifying a 'cask'.

tone [Middle English] *Tone* is from Old French *ton* via Latin from Greek *tonos* 'tension, tone'. Greek *teinein* 'to stretch' is the source. The main semantic branches are: 'sound considered in terms of its quality' (*sweet tone of the instrument*), 'degree of firmness in body tissue' (*improved muscle tone*), and 'degree of light and shade' (*darker tone*). The Greek base of *tone* is shared by mid 17th-century **tonic** (from French *tonique*, from Greek *tonikos* 'of or for stretching'). Its literal sense 'producing tension' is extended to noun use in contexts such as *a nerve tonic* (a medicine to strengthen) and *gin and tonic* (where *tonic* is a stimulant).

tongs [Old English] In Old English the spelling was *tang(e)*, a singular form. Of Germanic origin from a base meaning 'bite', it is related to Dutch *tang* and German *Zange*.

tongue [Old English] Old English *tunge* is from a Germanic source; related to Dutch *tong*, German *Zunge*, and Latin *lingua*. The word has referred to a part of the body and the speech associated with that organ from early times; the idiom *hold one's tongue* is also found in early examples. The verb *tongue* in musical contexts dates from the 1930s.

too [Old English] This is a stressed form of *to*; it began to be spelt as *too* from the 16th century.

tool [Old English] Old English *tōl* is from a Germanic base meaning 'prepare'. The verb dates from the early 19th century meaning 'shape with a tool'; its use in bookbinding where an ornamental design is impressed on the binding of a book dates from the late 19th century.

tooth [Old English] Old English forms were *tōth* (singular) and *tēth* (plural). Of Germanic origin, the word is related to Dutch *tand* and German *Zahn*, from an Indo-European root shared by Latin *dent-*, Greek *odont-*. The verb **teethe** is late Middle English, based on *teeth*.

top [late Old English] The word *top* as a term for a child's spherical spinning toy dates from late Old English but its origin is unknown. *Top* as in *top shelf*, *top executive* however is from a Germanic source (spelt *topp* in late Old English) and is related to Dutch *top* 'summit, crest'. Its main semantic branches include: 'crest, tuft' (now obsolete or dialect), 'highest part' (*top of the hill*), 'covering' (*gold top milk*), and 'first place in time' (*top of the morning*). The compound:
■ **topsy-turvy** (early 16th century) is a jingle apparently based on *top* and obsolete *terve* meaning 'overturn'.

topiary [late 16th century] *Topiary* is from French *topiaire*, from Latin *topiarius* 'ornamental gardener', from *topia opera* 'fancy gardening'. A diminutive of Greek *topos* 'place' is the source.

topic [late 15th century] A *topic* was originally a word for a set or book of general rules or ideas. It comes from Latin *topica*, from Greek *ta topika*, meaning literally 'matters concerning commonplaces' (the title of a treatise by Aristotle), from *topos* 'a place'. Late 16th-century **topical** is based on Greek *topikos*. Early use was as a term in logic and rhetoric describing a rule or argument as 'applicable in most but not all cases'.

topple [mid 16th century] 'Tumble about' was the early meaning of *topple*, a frequentative (= verb of repeated action) of *top*.
→ TOP

torch [Middle English] *Torch* is via Old French from Latin *torqua*, a variant of *torques* 'necklace, wreath', from *torquere* 'to twist'. The current verb sense 'set alight' was originally US slang dating from the 1930s.

torment [Middle English] In early use, this was found as both noun (from Old French *torment*) and verb (from Old French *tormenter*) referring to the infliction or suffering of torture. Latin *tormentum* 'instrument of torture' is the base, from *torquere* 'to twist'.

tornado [mid 16th century] *Tornado* was first used to refer to a violent thunderstorm of the tropical Atlantic Ocean; it may be an alteration of Spanish *tronada* 'thunderstorm' (from *tronar* 'to thunder') by association with Spanish *tornar* 'to turn'.

torpedo [early 16th century] This is a use of a Latin word which had the literal meaning 'stiffness, numbness' and by extension 'electric ray (fish)' (which gives a shock causing numbness), from *torpere* 'be numb or sluggish'. The *torpedo* of military contexts dates from the late 18th century and first described a timed explosive device for detonation under water.

torrent [late 16th century] Latin *torrere* 'parch, scorch, bubble' is the base of *torrent* (which comes via French from Italian *torrente*) and, from the same period, *torrid* (from French *torride* or Latin *torridus*). Whereas *torrent* captures the notion of 'bubbling' associated with boiling, *torrid* focuses on the intense heat, both aspects of the original Latin source.

torso [late 18th century] *Torso* is from an Italian word meaning literally 'stalk, stump', from Latin *thyrsus* 'stalk of a plant'.

torture [late Middle English] *Torture* had the early sense 'distortion, twisting', or it referred to a physical disorder characterized by twisting; it comes via French from late Latin *tortura* 'twisting, torment', from Latin *torquere* 'to twist', a source shared by the contemporaneous word **tortuous** (via Old French from Latin *tortuosus*, from *tortus* 'twisting, a twist').

Tory [mid 17th century] The word *Tory* is probably from Irish *toraidhe* 'outlaw, highwayman', from *tóir* 'pursue'. The word was used of Irish peasants dispossessed by English settlers and making their living as robbers; it was extended to other marauders in particular to Scottish Highlanders. It was then adopted in around 1679 as an abusive nickname for those who opposed the exclusion of the Catholic James, Duke of York, from accession to the throne: he later became James II. *Tory* remained the name for the members of the English, later British, parliamentary party supporting the established religious and political order until the emergence of the Conservative Party in the 1830s.

toss [early 16th century] *Toss* came into use soon after 1500 and was found in nearly all its senses by 1550. Of unknown origin, the only cognate appears to be Norwegian and Swedish dialect *tossa* 'to strew, spread'. The compound *toss-up* in the context of throwing up a coin to decide something dates from the early 18th century, figurative use expressing doubt as to an outcome (*it's a toss-up whether he'll come*) occurring about a century later.

tot[1] [early 18th century] This word for a very young child was originally dialect and is of unknown origin. It was first recorded in 1725. *Tommel-tot* has been recorded in Danish for Tom Thumb and *Tottr* is an Icelandic nickname of a dwarfish person, but no connection with the English word has been traced.

tot[2] [mid 18th century] This *tot* as in *totted up all the winnings* is from archaic *tot* 'a set of figures to be added up'; it is an abbreviation of *total* or of Latin *totum* 'the whole'.

tot³ [late 19th century] The *tot* which means 'salvage saleable items from refuse' is from slang *tot* 'bone', of unknown origin. There may be an association with *tat*.

total [late Middle English] *Total* comes via Old French from medieval Latin *totalis*, from *totum* 'the whole' (the neuter form of Latin *totus* 'whole, entire'). The verb, first used in the sense 'add up', dates from the late 16th century; it gained the sense 'damage beyond repair' (*totalled his car in the collision*) in the late 19th century.

tote¹ [late 19th century] The *tote* of betting contexts is an abbreviation of *totalizator*, a device showing how many bets have been staked on a race, to facilitate the eventual division of the total amongst the backers of the winner.

tote² [late 17th century] This word in phrases such as *tote bag* and *hoodlums toting revolvers* is probably a dialect word originally. It is first recorded in US English.

totter [Middle English] *Totter* is from Middle Dutch *touteren* 'to swing to and fro' (the original sense in English). The sense 'reel and stagger' dates from the early 17th century.

touch [Middle English] The verb is from Old French *tochier*, probably from a Romance word of imitative origin; the noun is originally from Old French *touche*, and later (in certain senses) directly from the verb. Use of the word in connection with feelings was found early alongside the physical senses. Of the idioms: *touched in the head* originated from early 18th-century usage in the sense 'slightly deranged'; *in touch with* dates from the mid 19th century; *lose one's touch* is recorded from the 1920s; *soft touch* dates from the 1940s.

touchy [early 17th century] *Touchy* is perhaps an alteration of *tetchy*, influenced by *touch*.
→ TETCHY

tough [Old English] Old English *tōh* is related to Dutch *taai* and German *zäh*. The sense 'difficult to do' is recorded from the early 17th century. The idiom *tough it out* is recorded in the early 19th century, with *tough as old boots* found slightly later.

toupee [early 18th century] A *toupee* was initially a curl or a lock of artificial hair; it is an alteration of French *toupet* 'hair-tuft', a diminutive of Old French *toup* 'tuft', ultimately of Germanic origin and related to *top*.
→ TOP

tour [Middle English] This was a word for a 'turn' or 'spell of work' in early examples (*tour of duty*) from an Old French word meaning 'turn', via Latin from Greek *tornos* 'lathe'. The notion of visiting a number of places was associated with *tour* from the mid 17th century.

tournament [Middle English] *Tournament* is from Anglo-Norman French variants of Old French *torneiement*, from *torneier* 'take part in a tourney', the source of Middle English **tourney**, based on Latin *tornus* 'a turn'.
→ TOUR

tousle [late Middle English] *Tousle* had the sense 'handle roughly or rudely'; it is a frequentative (= verb of repeated action) of dialect *touse* 'handle roughly', of Germanic origin and related to German *zausen*.
→ TUSSLE

tout [Middle English] The early spelling was *tute* and the meaning 'look out'. From a Germanic source, *tout* is related to Dutch *tuit* 'spout, nozzle' (from the notion of 'protruding, poking one's head out'). Later senses were 'watch, spy on' (late 17th century) and 'solicit custom' (mid 18th century). The noun is first recorded in examples from the early 18th century in the slang use 'thieves' lookout'.

tow [Old English] Old English *togian*, of Germanic origin, meant 'draw, drag'; *tug* is related. The noun dates from the early 17th century; *in tow* is a phrase from the early 18th century.
→ TUG

towel [Middle English] *Towel* is from Old French *toaille*, of Germanic origin. It was once used as a word for a table napkin. The idiom *to throw in the towel* dates from the early 20th century from a boxing analogy.

tower [Old English] Old English *torr* was reinforced in Middle English by Old French *tour*, from Latin *turris*, from Greek. The phrase *tower of strength* is from a use in the Book of Common Prayer: O Lord … be unto them a tower of strength; the alliterative *tower and town* dates from Middle English referring to the inhabited places of a region generally.

town [Old English] Old English *tūn* was an 'enclosed piece of land, homestead, village'. Germanic in origin, the word is related to Dutch *tuin* 'garden' and German *Zaun* 'fence'. The phrase *town and gown* is associated with Oxford and Cambridge, contrasting the civic community with the student body. *Go to town* as an idiom dates from the 1930s. **Township** was, in Old English, *tūnscipe* referring to 'the inhabitants of a village'.

toxic [mid 17th century] *Toxic* is from medieval Latin *toxicus* 'poisoned', from Latin *toxicum* 'poison': this comes from the Greek phrase *toxikon* (*pharmakon*) '(poison for) arrows', from *toxon* 'bow'.

toy [late Middle English] The word *toy* is of unknown origin. It originally denoted a funny story or remark, and later an antic, trick, or a frivolous entertainment. The verb dates from the early 16th century (*toyed with the idea*). The compound:
■ **toyboy** (1980s) is a colloquial term for the young male lover of an older woman.

trace[1] [Middle English] *Trace* is first recorded as a noun in the sense 'path that someone or something takes'. The noun comes from Old French *trace*, the verb from Old French *tracier*, based on Latin *tractus*. The main semantic branches include: 'follow step by step' (*trace back*), 'mark, imprint' (Tennyson *Palace of Art*: The deep-set windows, stain'd and traced, Would seem slow-flaming crimson fires From shadow'd grots of arches interlaced), and 'reproduce a shape' (*traced the outline*).
➔ TRACT[1]

trace[2] [Middle English] This was originally (as *trays*) a collective term for a pair of ropes, chains, and eventually leather straps for connecting draught animals to the swingle-tree. It comes from Old French *trais*, the plural of *trait*.
➔ TRAIT

track [late 15th century] 'Trail, marks left behind' was the early sense of *track*; the noun is from Old French *trac*, perhaps from Low German or Dutch *trek* 'draught, drawing'. The early sense seems to have been the line or mark made on the ground by dragging something over it, then apparently following the sense development of *trace*. The verb is from French *traquer* or directly from the noun.
➔ TRACE[1]

tract[1] [late Middle English] This *tract* as in *tract of forest* had the early sense 'duration or course (of time)' before it came to be applied to area or territory (mid 16th century). It is from Latin *tractus* 'drawing, draught', from *trahere* 'draw, pull'. Use was often interchangeable with *trace* and *track*.
➔ TRACE[1]; TRACK

tract[2] [late Middle English] This *tract* first denoted a written work discussing a particular topic; it is apparently an abbreviation of Latin *tractatus* 'a handling, treatise, discussion'. The current sense 'short treatise in pamphlet form' dates from the early 19th century.

traction [late Middle English] *Traction* in early examples was 'contraction', such as that of a muscle. It comes from French, or from medieval Latin *tractio(n-)*, from Latin *trahere*

'draw, pull'. Current senses date from the early 19th century. The word **tractor** (late 18th century) is from the same Latin source verb and was first used to mean 'someone or something that pulls'.

trade [late Middle English] First used as a noun, *trade* is from a Middle Low German word meaning literally 'track'. Of West Germanic origin, the word is related to *tread*. Early senses included 'course, way of life', which gave rise in the 16th century to 'habitual practice of an occupation' or 'skilled handicraft'. Current verb senses date from the late 16th century. The compound:
■ **trade wind** (mid 17th century) is from the phrase *blow trade* 'blow steadily in the same direction'. Because of the importance of these winds to navigation, 18th-century etymologists were led erroneously to connect the word *trade* with 'commerce'.
➔ TREAD

tradition [late Middle English] *Tradition* is from Old French *tradicion*, or from Latin *traditio(n-)*, from *tradere* 'deliver, betray'. The base elements are *trans-* 'across' and *dare* 'give'. The abbreviation **trad** dates from the 1950s, usually in the context of jazz.

traffic [early 16th century] This once referred to the commercial transportation of merchandise or passengers. It is from French *trafique*, Spanish *tráfico*, or Italian *traffico*, but earlier details of the origin are unknown. Use of *traffic* to mean 'vehicles moving on a highway' dates from the early 19th century. The phrase *traffic calming*, a translation of German *Verkehrsberuhigung*, arose in the 1980s describing the deliberate slowing of traffic by measures such as road humps.

tragedy [late Middle English] *Tragedy* is from Old French *tragedie*, via Latin from Greek *tragōidia*, apparently from *tragos* 'goat' (the reason remains unexplained) and *ōidē* 'song, ode'. The adjective **tragic** appeared in use in the mid 16th century, from French *tragique*, via Latin from Greek *tragikos*, from *tragos*; it was associated with *tragōidia*.

trail [Middle English] First recorded in use as a verb, *trail* is from Old French *traillier* 'to tow', or Middle Low German *treilen* 'haul (a boat)'. The Latin base is *tragula* 'dragnet', from *trahere* 'to pull'. The noun was originally a word for the train of a robe, later becoming generalized to denote anything trailing.
➔ TRAWL

train [Middle English] This is from Old French *train* (masculine), *traine* (feminine), from the verb *trahiner*, from Latin *trahere* 'pull, draw'. Early use was as a noun in the sense 'delay' (from the notion of 'dragging'). Other early senses included 'trailing part of a robe' and 'retinue'; the latter gave rise to 'line of travelling people or vehicles' and later 'a connected series of things' (*train of events*). The phrase *train of thought* from the idea of a 'series' dates from the late 18th century. The early verb sense 'cause (a plant) to grow in a desired shape' was the basis of the use 'educate, instruct, teach'.

traipse [late 16th century] The origin of *traipse* is unknown. The noun is first recorded in the sense 'slovenly woman' in the late 17th century.

trait [mid 16th century] This is from French, from Latin *tractus* 'drawing, draught'. An early sense was 'stroke of the pen or pencil in a picture' giving rise to 'a particular feature' of mind or character in the mid 18th century.
→ TRACT[1]

traitor [Middle English] *Traitor* is from Old French *traitour*, from Latin *traditor*, from *tradere* 'hand over'.

trajectory [late 17th century] This comes from modern Latin *trajectoria*, from Latin *traject-*, the past participial stem of *traicere* 'throw across', from *trans-* 'across' and *jacere* 'to throw'.

tram [early 16th century] Early use of the word *tram* was as a term of a shaft of a barrow. It comes from Middle Low German and Middle Dutch *trame* 'beam, barrow shaft'. In the early 19th century the word was used for the parallel wheel tracks used in a mine, on which the public tramway was modelled; hence the word's use for the passenger vehicle itself.

trammel [late Middle English] The first use recorded for *trammel* was 'dragnet'. It comes from Old French *tramail*, from a medieval Latin variant of *trimaculum*, perhaps from Latin *tri-* 'three' and *macula* 'mesh'. Figurative use of the word (usually in the plural) meaning 'something that hinders' is found in the mid 17th century.

tramp [late Middle English] *Tramp* was first used as a verb; it is probably of Low German origin. The noun dates from the mid 17th century meaning 'a stamp, heavy tread'; its use to describe a vagrant is recorded a century later. The verb **trample** dating from late Middle English in the sense 'tread heavily' is a frequentative (= verb of repeated action) of *tramp*.

trampoline [late 18th century] This is from Italian *trampolino*, from *trampoli* 'stilts'.

trance [Middle English] *Trance* was originally used as a verb in the sense 'be in a trance'. It comes from Old French *transir* 'depart, fall into trance', from Latin *transire* 'go across'.

tranquil [late Middle English] *Tranquil* is from French *tranquille* or Latin *tranquillus*.

transaction [late Middle English] This was first used as a term in Roman Law. It comes from late Latin *transactio(n-)*, from *transigere* 'drive', the source too of **transact** in the late 16th century; the base elements are *trans-* 'through' and *agere* 'do, lead'

transcend [Middle English] *Transcend* is from Old French *transcendre* or Latin *transcendere*, from *trans-* 'across' and *scandere* 'climb'. **Transcendent** is late Middle English from the present participial stem of the same verb; the related word **transcendental** is recorded from the early 17th century from medieval Latin *transcendentalis*.

transcript [Middle English] *Transcript* is from Old French *transcrit*, from Latin *transcriptum*, the neuter past participle of *transcribere*. The spelling change in the 15th century was due to association with the Latin. **Transcribe** (from Latin *transcribere*) is found in examples from the mid 16th century. The early sense was 'make a copy in writing'. **Transcription** from French, or from Latin *transcriptio(n-)*, from the verb *transcribere* dates from the late 16th century.

transfer [late Middle English] This word was first in use as a verb. It comes from French *transférer* or Latin *transferre*, from *trans-* 'across' and *ferre* 'to bear'. The earliest use of the noun (late 17th century) was as a legal term in the sense 'conveyance of property'.

transfigure [Middle English] This word meaning 'transform into something more beautiful or elevated' is from Old French *transfigurer* or Latin *transfigurare*, from *trans-* 'across' and *figura* 'figure'. The late Middle English **transfiguration** was first used with biblical reference to Christ's appearance in radiant form in a more spiritual state; this is from Old French, or from Latin *transfiguratio(n-)*, from the verb *transfigurare*.

transfix [late 16th century] *Transfix* was first used in the sense 'pierce with a sharp implement'; it comes from Latin *transfigere* 'pierce through', from *trans-* 'across' and *figere* 'fix, fasten'. The figurative use 'make motionless with astonishment or fear' dates from the mid 17th century.

transform [Middle English] This word is from Old French *transformer* or Latin *transformare*. The noun **transformation** dates from late Middle English and is from Old French, or from late Latin *transformatio(n-)*, from the verb *transformare*.

transfuse [late Middle English] *Transfuse* had the sense 'cause to pass from one person to another' in early examples. It comes from Latin *transfus-*, the past participial stem of *transfundere* 'pour from one container into another', from *trans-* 'across' and *fundere* 'pour'. Late 16th-century **transfusion** is from Latin *transfusio(n-)*, from *transfundere*.

transgress [late 15th century] *Transgress* is from Old French *transgresser* or Latin *transgress-*, the past participial stem of *transgredi* 'step across', from *trans-* 'across' and *gradi* 'go'.

transient [late 16th century] This is from Latin *transient-*, the present participial stem of *transire* 'go across', from *trans-* 'across' and *ire* 'go'.

transistor [1940s] *Transistor* is a blend of *transfer* and *resistor*, influenced by the pattern of words such as *varistor* (= varying resistor) a semiconductor diode with resistance dependent on the applied voltage.

transit [late Middle English] *Transit* initially meant 'passage from one place to another'. It is from Latin *transitus*, from *transire* 'go across', the base of the contemporaneous **transitory** (from Old French *transitoire*, from Christian Latin *transitorius*). In the mid 16th-century, examples started to be found of **transition** (from French, or from Latin *transitio(n-)*) and **transitive** in the sense 'transitory' (from late Latin *transitivus*) from the same Latin source verb.

translate [Middle English] *Translate* is from Latin *translatus*, the past participle of *transferre* 'carry across', a sense also reflected by the English word from early times. Middle English **translation** is from Old French, or from Latin *translatio(n-)*, from the same base verb.
→ TRANSFER

translucent [late 16th century] 'Shining through' was the early sense recorded, reflecting that of the Latin source *translucent-*, the present participial stem of *translucere*. The base elements are *trans-* 'through' and *lucere* 'to shine'. The sense 'allowing the passage of light' dates from the late 18th century.

transmit [late Middle English] *Transmit* is from Latin *transmittere*, from *trans-* 'across' and *mittere* 'send'.

transparent [late Middle English] *Transparent* is from Old French, from medieval Latin *transparent-*, the present participial stem of *transparere* 'shine through'. The same base is shared by **transparency** dating from the late 16th century, first used as a general term for a transparent object. Its use to denote a photograph on a transparent substance (intended to be seen by transmitted light) dates from the mid 19th century. It comes from medieval Latin *transparentia*.

transpire [late Middle English] *Transpire* had the early sense 'emit as vapour through the surface'. It comes from French *transpirer* or medieval Latin *transpirare*, from Latin *trans-* 'through' and *spirare* 'breathe'. The sense 'happen, occur' (Dickens *Dombey and Son*: Few changes—hardly any—have transpired among his ship's company) is a figurative use from a notion of 'leak out, become known, come to the surface'.

transplant [late Middle English] This was first used as a verb describing the repositioning of a plant. The source is late Latin *transplantare*, from Latin *trans-* 'across' and *plantare* 'to plant'. The noun, first in the sense 'something or someone moved to a new place', dates from the mid 18th century; use of the word in surgical contexts where an organ is taken from one person or animal and replaced in another, arose in the 1950s with advances in technology.

transport [late Middle English] *Transport* is from Old French *transporter* or Latin *transportare*, from *trans-* 'across' and *portare* 'carry'. The word's use to denote 'a means of transportation' arose in the use of *transport ships* to transport soldiers or convicts and later army supplies.

transpose [late Middle English] Early use included the meaning 'transform, convert'. It is from Old French *transposer*, from *trans-* 'across' and *poser* 'to place'. The word **transposition** dating from the mid 16th century is from late Latin *transpositio(n-)*.

transvestite [1920s] This is from German *Transvestit*, from Latin *trans-* 'across' and *vestire* 'clothe'.

trap [Old English] Old English *træppe* 'snare' is attested earliest in the compound *coltetræppe* 'Christ's thorn'. It is related to Middle Dutch *trappe* and medieval Latin *trappa*, of uncertain origin. The idioms *shut one's trap* and *keep one's trap shut* originated in the late 18th century. Verb use dates from late Middle English.

trapeze [mid 19th century] *Trapeze* is from French *trapèze*, from late Latin *trapezium*, a word adopted into English as a term in geometry in the late 16th century (from late Latin from Greek *trapezion*, from *trapeza* 'table'). The term has been used in anatomy (describing a bone of the wrist) since the mid 19th century.

trappings [late Middle English] This word is a derivative of the late Middle English verb *trap* 'adorn (a horse) with trappings' from the obsolete noun *trap* 'trappings', from Old French *drap* 'drape'. The extended meaning 'superficial embellishments' dates from the late 16th century (Shakespeare *Hamlet*: These, but the Trappings, and the Suites of woe).

trash [early 16th century] This word is of unknown origin. Early use was in the sense 'refuse' whether 'cuttings from a hedge', 'sugar canes stripped of their juice' or other leftovers. It was used of people from the early 17th century (Shakespeare *Othello*: I do suspect this Trash To be a party in this Injurie); more recent examples (late 19th century) include *white trash*. The verb is first recorded in the mid 18th century in the sense 'strip (sugar canes) of their outer leaves to encourage faster ripening'; the other senses ('vandalize', 'impair the quality of something') have arisen in the 20th century.

trauma [late 17th century] This is an English use of a Greek word meaning literally 'wound'. It was transferred to the notion of a 'mental wound' in the late 19th century. **Traumatic** in psychiatry (via late Latin from Greek *traumatikos*, from *trauma*) dates from the same period; its much looser generalized use is evidenced from the 1960s.

travel [Middle English] *Travel* is a variant of Middle English **travail** which comes via Old French from medieval Latin *trepalium* (from *tres* 'three' and *palus* 'stake'). It was originally used in the same sense 'engage in painful effort'; the sense 'make a journey' arose early. The compound **travelator** dating from the 1950s is based on *travel*, suggested by *escalator*.

traverse [Middle English] *Traverse* was first used as a legal term in the verb sense 'deny (an allegation) in pleading', from a notion of 'throwing an argument across' in contradiction. The source is Old French *traverser* 'to cross, thwart', from late Latin *traversare*. The noun is from Old French *travers* (masculine), *traverse* (feminine), partly based on *traverser*.

travesty [mid 17th century] This was first used as an adjective in the sense 'dressed to appear ridiculous'. It comes from French *travesti* 'disguised', the past participle of *travestir*, from Italian *travestire*. The base elements are Latin *trans-* 'across' and *vestire* 'to clothe'.

trawl [mid 16th century] *Trawl* was first used as a verb. It is probably from Middle Dutch *traghelen* 'to drag' (related to *traghel* 'dragnet'), perhaps from Latin *tragula* 'dragnet'.

tray [late Old English] Late Old English *trīg* is from the Germanic base of *tree*. The primary sense may have been 'wooden container'.
→ TREE

treachery [Middle English] Old French *trechier* 'to cheat' is a source shared by *treachery* (from Old French *trecherie*) and Middle English **treacherous** (from Old French *trecherous*, from *trecheor* 'a cheat').

treacle [Middle English] *Treacle* was originally a word for an antidote against venom made of many ingredients in the form of a salve originally. It is from Old French *triacle*, via Latin from Greek *thēriakē* 'antidote against venom' (the feminine of the adjective *thēriakos*, from *thērion* 'wild beast'). Current senses relating to uncrystallized syrup date from the late 17th century. The compound
■ **Treacle Bible** started to be used by bible collectors from the late 19th century for any of the English versions or editions of the Bible having the word 'treacle' in contrast to those having the word 'balm' in their translation.

tread [Old English] The Old English verb *tredan* is West Germanic in origin, related to Dutch *treden* and German *treten*. The idiom *tread on air* dates from the late 18th century. **Treadle** (in Old English *tredel* 'stair, step') is from the verb *tread*.

treason [Middle English] *Treason* is from Anglo-Norman French *treisoun*, from Latin *traditio(n-)* 'handing over', from the verb *tradere*. In Old English law, *treason* was either *high treason* (an offence against the king's majesty or the safety of the commonwealth) or *petty treason* (an offence committed against a subject). The latter is now punished as 'murder' and *high treason* is now simply *treason*.

treasure [Middle English] The word *treasure* is from Old French *tresor*, based on Greek *thesauros*. Also Middle English are: **treasurer** (from Old French *tresorier*, from *tresor*, influenced by late Latin *thesaurarius*) and **treasury**.
■ **Treasure trove** (late Middle English) is from Anglo-Norman French *tresor trové* meaning literally 'found treasure'.
→ THESAURUS

treat [Middle English] *Treat* is first recorded with the meanings 'negotiate' and 'discuss (a subject)'. It is from Old French *traitier*, from Latin *tractare* 'handle', a frequentative (= verb of repeated action) of *trahere* 'draw, pull'. The current noun sense 'event that gives great pleasure' dates from the mid 17th century. Late Middle English **treatise** from Anglo-Norman French *tretis*, is also from Old French *traitier*.

treaty [late Middle English] *Treaty* is from Old French *traite*, from Latin *tractatus* 'treatise'.

treble [Middle English] *Treble* comes via Old French from Latin *triplus*. The musical term *treble* (late Middle English) arose from the fact that it was the highest part in a three-part contrapuntal composition.
➔ TRIPLE

tree [Old English] Old English *trēow, trēo* is from a Germanic variant of an Indo-European root shared by Greek *doru* 'wood, spear', *drus* 'oak'.

trek [mid 19th century] The noun is from South African Dutch *trek*, the verb from *trekken* 'pull, travel'. The informal word **Trekkie** has become popularized from the 1970s to describe a devotee of the US science fiction television programme *Star Trek*.

trellis [late Middle English] This once referrred to any latticed screen. It is from Old French *trelis*, from Latin *trilix* 'three-ply', from *tri-* 'three' and *licium* 'warp thread'. Current senses in gardening contexts date from the early 16th century.

tremble [Middle English] *Tremble* is from Old French *trembler*, from medieval Latin *tremulare*, from Latin *tremulus* (from *tremere* 'to tremble'), the base too of early 17th-century **tremulous**. Latin *tremere* is also the source of **tremor** an adoption of a Latin form.

tremendous [mid 17th century] *Tremendous* is based on Latin *tremendus*, the gerundive of *tremere* 'to tremble'.

trench [late Middle English] *Trench* had the early senses 'track cut through a wood' and 'sever by cutting'. The noun comes from Old French *trenche*, the verb from Old French *trenchier*, based on Latin *truncare*. Use of the word in military contexts is commonly exemplified by the phrase *the trenches* referring to battle positions in northern France and Belgium in the First World War. Middle English **trenchant** (first used meaning 'having a sharp edge') is from an Old French word meaning literally 'cutting', the present participle of *trenchier*.

trend [Old English] Old English *trendan* had the meaning 'revolve, rotate'. Of Germanic origin, it is related to *trundle*. The verb sense 'turn in a specified direction' dates from the late 16th century, and gave rise to the figurative use 'assume a general tendency' in the mid

19th century, a development paralleled in the noun.
➔ TRUNDLE

trepidation [late 15th century] This comes from Latin *trepidatio(n-)*, from *trepidare* 'be agitated, tremble', from *trepidus* 'alarmed'.

trespass [Middle English] The verb *trespass*, initially meaning 'commit an offence against, sin', is from Old French *trespasser* 'pass over, trespass'. The noun is from Old French *trespas* 'passing across', from medieval Latin *transpassare*.

tress [Middle English] *Tress* is from Old French *tresse*, perhaps based on Greek *trikha* 'threefold'.

trestle [Middle English] The word *trestle* is from Old French *trestel*, based on Latin *transtrum* 'beam'.

triad [mid 16th century] *Triad* meaning 'set of three' is from French *triade*, or via late Latin from Greek *trias, triad-*, from *treis* 'three'.

triage [early 18th century] This is an English use of a French word, from *trier* 'separate out'. The medical sense dates from the 1930s, from the military system of assessing the wounded on the battle field.

trial [late Middle English] *Trial* is from Anglo-Norman French, or from medieval Latin *triallum*. Legal use of the word was early. Phrases such as *trial by combat, trial by the sword* when guilt or innocence was determined, date from the late 16th century; the notion of testing ability or achievement is found associated with the word from the late 17th century. *Trial and error* was originally a mathematical phrase of the early 19th century. Verb use dates from the 1980s.

triangle [late Middle English] This comes from Old French *triangle* or Latin *triangulum*, the neuter form of *triangulus* 'three-cornered'. **Triangular** dates from the mid 16th century from late Latin *triangularis*, from Latin *triangulum*. The word's use in connection with a group of three people involving adultery (*eternal triangle*) dates from the early 20th century.

tribe [Middle English] *Tribe* is from Old French *tribu* or Latin *tribus* (singular and plural); perhaps related to *tri-* 'three' and referring to the three divisions of the early people of Rome.

tribulation [Middle English] The base of *tribulation* is Latin *tribulum* 'threshing board (constructed of sharp points)', from *terere* 'to rub'. It comes via Old French from ecclesiastical Latin *tribulatio(n-)*, from Latin *tribulare* 'press, oppress'.

tribunal [late Middle English] A *tribunal* was originally a word for a seat for judges. It is from Old French, or from Latin *tribunal* 'a raised platform provided for magistrates' seats'. The base is Latin *tribunus*, a name for 'an official of ancient Rome' and literally 'head of a tribe', from *tribus* 'tribe'. This gave the English word **tribune**, first to refer to an officer of the ancient Roman administration, and in the 20th century, in connection with radical left-wing policies. It was the title of a British weekly journal founded in 1937 and formed part of the name of a group of Labour MPs holding radical left-wing views (*Tribune group*).

tribute [late Middle English] *Tribute*, when first used, referred to a payment made periodically by one state or ruler to another. It comes from Latin *tributum*, the neuter past participle (used as a noun) of *tribuere* meaning initially 'divide between tribes' and later 'assign', from *tribus* 'tribe'. Late Middle English **tributary** (from Latin *tributarius*, from *tributum*) is first recorded in use meaning 'paying a tribute, subject to payment to another state'; the word's use in geography to mean 'a stream flowing or feeding into a larger river' dates from the early 19th century.

trice [late Middle English] A *trice* is literally 'a tug', and figuratively 'an instant' (*in a trice*), coming from Middle Dutch *trīsen* 'pull sharply', related to *trīse* 'pulley'.

trick [late Middle English] This is from an Old French dialect variant of *triche*, from *trichier* 'deceive', of unknown origin. The idiom *up to one's old tricks* dates from the early 19th century, from a late 16th-century use of the word meaning 'habit'. Current senses of the verb date from the mid 16th century. The phrase *trick or treat* (originally US) is recorded from the 1940s at Hallowe'en when children call at houses threatening to play a trick on the householder unless a treat is produced in the form of sweets or money.

trickle [Middle English] The history of *trickle* is uncertain. It may be imitative of the sound and movement and was first applied to describe tears falling in successive drops.

trident [late Middle English] This word for a three-pronged spear is from Latin *trident-*, from *tri-* 'three' and *dens, dent-* 'tooth'.

trifle [Middle English] Early use included the sense 'an idle story told to deceive or amuse'. It is from Old French *trufle*, a by-form of *trufe* 'deceit', of unknown origin. The word soon came to be generalized to any 'trivial or paltry thing or matter'. Its use as a name for a dessert (now of sponge cake, jelly, cream, and custard but originally principally of cream boiled with various ingredients) dates from the late 16th century. The verb *trifle* derives from Old French *truffler* 'mock, deceive'.

trigger [early 17th century] *Trigger* is from dialect *tricker*, from Dutch *trekker*, from *trekken* 'to pull'.

trill [mid 17th century] The noun is from Italian *trillo*, the verb from *trillare*.

trim [Old English] Old English *trymman*, *trymian* meant 'make firm, arrange', of which the adjective appears to be a derivative. The word's history is obscure; current verb senses date from the early 16th century when usage became frequent and served many purposes: this is possibly explained by spoken or dialect use in the Middle English period not recorded in extant literature.

trinity [Middle English] *Trinity* is from Old French *trinite*, from Latin *trinitas* 'triad', from *trinus* 'threefold'.

trinket [mid 16th century] The *-et* ending suggests this is a diminutive but the origin of the word remains unknown. Some have suggested a link with *trenket* 'small (shoemaker's) knife' (from Old French, from *trencher* 'to cut') but evidence is lacking.

trio [early 18th century] *Trio* is from Italian, from Latin *tres* 'three', on the pattern of *duo*.

trip [Middle English] *Trip* is from Old French *triper*, from Middle Dutch *trippen* 'to skip, hop'.

tripe [Middle English] This is from an Old French word for the 'entrails of an animal', but earlier details of the origin are unknown. The transferred meaning 'rubbish' dates from the late 17th century.

triple [Middle English] *Triple* is from Old French, or from Latin *triplus*, from Greek *triplous*. The adjective **triplicate** (late Middle English) is from Latin *triplicare* 'to triple, make three'; the verb dates from the early 17th century. **Triplet** (mid 17th century) is based on *triple*, on the pattern of *doublet*.

tripod [early 17th century] *Tripod* comes via Latin from Greek *tripous, tripod-*, from *tri-* 'three' and *pous, pod-* 'foot'.

trite [mid 16th century] The word *trite* is from Latin *tritus*, the past participle of *terere* 'to rub' giving a notion of irritation through repetition.

triumph [late Middle English] *Triumph* is from the Old French *triumphe*, from Latin *triump(h)us*, probably from Greek *thriambos* 'hymn to Bacchus'. Current senses of the verb date from the early 16th century. **Triumphal** (from Old French *triumphal* or Latin *triumphalis*, from *triump(h)us*) and **triumphant** (from Old French, or from Latin *triumphare* 'celebrate a victory') date from the same period.

trivet [late Middle English] *Trivet* is apparently from Latin *tripes*, *triped-* 'three-legged', from *tri-* 'three' and *pes*, *ped-* 'foot'.

trivia [early 20th century] This is modern Latin, the plural of *trivium* 'place where three roads meet', influenced in sense by *trivial*.
→TRIVIAL

trivial [late Middle English] Early use reflected the sense 'belonging to the trivium', that is to the lower division of the liberal arts comprising rhetoric, grammar, and logic in medieval university studies. It comes from medieval Latin *trivialis*, from Latin *trivium* 'place where three roads meet'. The other main semantic branch of the word reflected the sense 'commonplace' in the late 16th century as well as 'of little account' (Shakespeare *Henry VI* part ii: We have but trivial argument, More then mistrust, that shewes him worthy death).

troll¹ [early 17th century] This *troll* describing a gigantic or dwarfish mythical cave-dwelling being of ugly appearance is from Old Norse and Swedish *troll*, Danish *trold*.

troll² [late Middle English] The verb *troll* had the early sense 'stroll, roll'. Its origin is uncertain; Old French *troller* 'wander here and there (in search of game)' and Middle High German *trollen* 'stroll' may be related. The word has become part of computing slang from the 1990s, referring to a message posted to a newsgroup with the intention of inciting flame mail (= an abusive response); the notion is one of 'random search of a prey'. The word **trolley** recorded from the early 19th century, of dialect origin, may be from *troll*.

troop [mid 16th century] *Troop* is from French *troupe*, a back-formation (by removal of the suffix) from *troupeau*, a diminutive of medieval Latin *troppus* 'flock', probably of Germanic origin. Use of the verb in general phrases such as *troop off* dates from the mid 16th century.

trophy [late 15th century] A *trophy* once referred to a display of weapons taken from a defeated army. From French *trophée*, the word comes via Latin from Greek *tropaion*, from *tropē* 'a rout', from *trepein* 'to turn'.

tropic [late Middle English] The word *tropic* was originally used as a term for the 'turning' point on the ecliptic reached by the sun at the solstice. It comes via Latin from Greek *tropikos*, from *tropē* 'turning', from *trepein* 'to turn'. Its application in geographical contexts to the two parallels of latitude (*tropic of Cancer* and *tropic of Capricorn*) as boundaries of the torrid zone, dates from the early 16th century: the terms

were used to correspond to the same names given to two circles of the celestial sphere parallel to the equator and touching the ecliptic at the solstitial points.

trot [Middle English] The noun is from Old French *trot*, the verb from Old French *troter*, from medieval Latin *trottare*, of Germanic origin. The idiom *trot out* meaning 'declare' (Thackeray *Book of Snobs*: She began to trot out scraps of French) arose in the early 19th century; it stems from the notion of leading out a horse to show off its paces.

trouble [Middle English] *Trouble* is, as a noun, from Old French *truble*; the verb is form Old French *trubler*, based on Latin *turbidus* 'turbid'. Expressions such as *get into trouble* and *be in trouble* are found from the mid 16th century; *look for trouble* appeared in the 1920s. The phrase *the Troubles* has been applied to various rebellions, civil wars, and periods of unrest in Ireland for example in 1919–23, and in Northern Ireland from the 1970s.

trough [Old English] Old English *trog* is Germanic in origin, related to Dutch *trog* and German *Trog*, also to *tree*. The primary meaning is 'wooden vessel'. The notion of a downturn on a graph or similar representation dates from the late 19th century in meteorology, the early 20th century in economics, and generally (*peaks and troughs*) from the 1930s.
→TREE

trousers [early 17th century] This is from archaic *trouse*, a singular word from Irish *triús* and Scottish Gaelic *triubhas* (which also gave rise to mid 16th-century **trews**). The spelling of *trousers* was influenced by the pattern of *drawers*.

trout [late Old English] Late Old English *truht* is from late Latin *tructa*, based on Greek *trōgein* 'gnaw'. Use of the derogatory phrase *old trout* referring to an elderly woman is found from the late 19th century.

trove [late 19th century] This word for a store of valuable things is from *treasure trove*.
→TREASURE

trowel [Middle English] *Trowel* is from Old French *truele*, from medieval Latin *truella*: this is an alteration of Latin *trulla* 'scoop', a diminutive of *trua* 'skimmer'.

truant [Middle English] A *truant* once referred to a person begging through choice rather than necessity. It comes from Old French and is probably ultimately of Celtic origin; Welsh *truan* and Scottish Gaelic *truaghan* 'wretched' may be related. During the 15th century, the word came to be applied to a lazy person, especially a child absenting himself from school. The idiom *play truant* dates from the mid 16th century.

truce [Middle English] Early use of this Germanic word was usually in the plural as *trewes* or *trues*. The word comes from Old English *trēowa*, the plural of *trēow* 'belief, trust'; related forms are Dutch *trouw*, German *Treue*, and English *true*.
→ TRUE

truck[1] [Middle English] A *truck* was initially 'a solid wooden wheel'; it is perhaps short for *truckle* in the sense 'wheel, pulley'. The sense 'wheeled vehicle' dates from the late 18th century.

truck[2] [Middle English] The *truck* of the idiom *have no truck with* is probably from Old French *troquer* 'to barter, exchange'; medieval Latin *trocare* 'to barter' may be associated. *Truck* in early use referred to trading by exchange of commodities.

truculent [mid 16th century] This word meaning 'quick to argue' is from Latin *truculentus*, from *trux, truc-* 'fierce'.

trudge [mid 16th century] First used as a verb, *trudge* is of unknown origin. One suggestion is that it comes from French *trucher* 'beg from laziness' but the semantic link is not evidenced.

true [Old English] Old English *trēowe*, *trȳwe* meant 'steadfast, loyal'; it is related to Dutch *getrouw*, German *treu*, and English *truce*. **Truth** was, in Old English *trīewth*, *trēowth* meaning 'faithfulness, constancy'; the variant **troth** is found from Middle English including phrases such as *plight one's troth*. **Truly** also dates from Old English (as *trēowlīce* 'faithfully') with the phrase *well and truly* arising in the 15th century. The word's use in letter writing as *Yours truly* dates from the late 18th century, later developing the humorous sense 'myself' (*You did it?— Yes, yours truly!*).
→ TRUCE

truffle [late 16th century] This word for a type of fungus is probably via Dutch from obsolete French *truffle*, perhaps based on Latin *tubera*, the plural of *tuber* 'hump, swelling'. Use of the word in confectionery dates from the 1920s.

trump [early 16th century] The *trump* of games such as bridge and whist is an alteration of *triumph*, once used in card games in the same sense. The idiom *come up trumps* originated as *turn up trumps* in the late 16th century.

trumpet [Middle English] *Trumpet* is from Old French *trompette*, a diminutive of *trompe* meaning 'trumpet'. The idiomatic expression *blow one's own trumpet* arose in the mid 15th century from a notion of declaring public

triumph for oneself. The verb dates from the mid 16th century, with figurative use from the early 17th century (Shakespeare *Othello*: That I love the Moor,... My ... storm of Fortunes, May trumpet to the world).

truncate [late 15th century] This is from Latin *truncare* 'maim'.

truncheon [Middle English] In early use this referred to a piece broken off from, for example, a spear; it was also a word for a cudgel. It comes from Old French *tronchon* 'stump', based on Latin *truncus* 'trunk'. The word came to refer to a staff carried as a symbol of office from the late 16th century and eventually (late 19th century) to a short club carried by a police officer.

trundle [mid 16th century] A *trundle* was initially 'a small wheel or roller'. It is a parallel formation to the obsolete or dialect verb *trendle*, *trindle* '(cause to) revolve'; related to *trend*. The general use of *trundle* to mean 'go' (*trundled off happily*) arose in the late 17th century.
→ TREND

trunk[1] [late Middle English] This *trunk* as in *trunk of a tree*, *trunk full of old clothes* is from Old French *tronc*, from Latin *truncus* 'main stem of a tree'. The word has been used to refer to the main part of the human body since the late 15th century. It often carries a notion of 'central connection' as for example in telephony. The sense 'chest, box' arose because early *trunks* were made out of tree-trunks. Another semantic branch of the word is 'hollow tube' (*elephant's trunk*), from a shape association with the mid 16th-century use of the word to describe cylindrical objects such as a case for explosives, a pea-shooter, etc. In the late 19th century in US usage, the plural *trunks* came to be used for 'men's shorts' from an earlier theatrical term (*trunk-hose*) for short breeches of thin material worn over tights. It has been suggested that the *trunk* refers either to the body or to the tube-like shape of the legs of the garment.

truss [Middle English] 'Bundle' was the early sense of *truss*. The noun is from Old French *trusse*, the verb from *trusser* 'pack up, bind in', based on late Latin *tors-*, the past participial stem of *torquere* 'to twist'. Use of the word as a medical term dates from the mid 16th century; the sense 'framework' in building contexts is found a century later.

trust [Middle English] This is from Old Norse *traust*, from *traustr* 'strong'; the verb is from Old Norse *treysta*, assimilated to the noun spelling. The phrase *in trust* is found from the mid 16th century; *on trust* was expressed originally as *of trust* and *upon trust* in the late 16th century.

Colloquial use in ironic phrases such as *trust Sarah to pipe up!* dates from the early 19th century. The noun **trustee** dates from the mid 17th century.

try [Middle English] *Try* is from Old French *trier* 'sift', of unknown origin. Early use was in the sense 'separate (one thing) from another' or as *try out* meaning 'ascertain by examination'. Legal use of the word was also early. The common current meaning 'make an effort' is found from the early 17th century, the period when the noun sense 'attempt' was found. The cliché *try anything once* is recorded from the 1920s.

tryst [late Middle English] This was in Scots use originally, a variant of obsolete *trist* 'an appointed place in hunting', from French *triste* or medieval Latin *trista*.

tub [Middle English] *Tub* is probably of Low German or Dutch origin; Middle Low German and Middle Dutch *tubbe* may be related. The word was applied to a bath from the late 16th century, a slow clumsy ship from the early 17th century, and to a fat person from the late 19th century, from associations of shape.

tube [mid 17th century] This is from French *tube* or Latin *tubus*. It is a more recent word than *pipe* and more generic. The phrase *the tube* started to be used in reference to the television set from the 1960s from the use of *tube* as a term in electronics; some associate the phrase *couch potato* with *tube* (from *tuber* = 'potato'). Other phrases include: *down the tube* meaning 'lost, finished' (= down the drain) which also arose in the 1960s; *have one's tubes tied* in medical contexts referring to sterilization by tubal ligation, is recorded from the 1970s. Of related words, the adjective **tubular** dates from the late 17th century based on Latin *tubulus* 'small tube'.

tuber [mid 17th century] This is an adoption of a Latin word meaning literally 'hump, swelling'.

tuck [Old English] Old English *tūcian* meant 'to punish, ill-treat'; it was influenced in Middle English by Middle Dutch *tucken* 'pull sharply' and was used in English in the sense 'pull at and pluck (herbs or fruit)'. Of West Germanic origin, it is related to *tug*. Use of the word to mean 'pleat, gather in folds' dates from the mid 15th century.
→TUG

tuft [late Middle English] This is probably from Old French *tofe*, of unknown origin. The final -*t* is typical of phonetic confusion between -*f* and -*ft* at the end of words; *graft* illustrates the same

process. The word **tuffet** dating from the mid 16th century is an alteration of *tuft*.

tug [Middle English] *Tug* is from the base of *tow*. The noun is first recorded in late Middle English as a term for a 'loop from a horse's saddle' for supporting a shaft or trace. The phrase *tug of war* is found from the late 17th century; *tug of love* arose in the 1970s in the context of custody battles over minors. The word's use for a small powerful steamer for towing other boats dates from the early 19th century.
→TOW

tuition [late Middle English] 'Custody, care' was the early meaning of *tuition* which comes via Old French from Latin *tuitio(n-)*, from *tueri* 'to watch, guard'. Current senses to do with instruction date from the late 16th century.

tumble [Middle English] An early sense was 'dance with contortions'. This is from Middle Low German *tummelen*; Old English *tumbian* 'to dance' may be related. The sense was probably influenced by Old French *tomber* 'to fall'. The noun, first used in the sense 'tangled mass', dates from the mid 17th century.

tumult [late Middle English] This is from Old French *tumulte* or Latin *tumultus*, from Latin *tumere* 'to swell'. The adjective **tumultuous** dating from the mid 16th century is from Old French *tumultuous* or Latin *tumultuosus*, from *tumultus*.

tune [late Middle English] The word *tune* is an unexplained alteration of *tone*. The figurative phrases *in tune* and *out of tune* are found from the middle of the 15th century; of the other idioms, *change one's tune* is early 16th-century; *to the tune of* dates from the early 17th century. The verb is first recorded in the late 15th century in the sense 'celebrate in music, sing'.
→TONE

tunic [Old English] *Tunic* is from Old French *tunique* or Latin *tunica*.

tunnel [late Middle English] *Tunnel* had the early senses 'tunnel-net (for catching water fowl)' and 'flue of a chimney'. It comes from Old French *tonel*, a diminutive of *tonne* 'cask'. The noun sense 'artificial underground passage' in engineering contexts dates from around the middle of the 18th century.

turban [mid 16th century] The word *turban* comes via French from Turkish *tülbent*, from Persian *dulband*.

turbine [mid 19th century] *Turbine* comes from French, from Latin *turbo, turbin-* 'spinning top, whirl'.

turbulence [late Middle English] *Turbulence* is from Old French, or from late Latin *turbulentia*, from *turbulentus* 'full of commotion', which also gave **turbulent** in the same period. The base is Latin *turba* 'crowd'.

tureen [mid 18th century] *Tureen* is an alteration of earlier *terrine*, from French *terrine*: this is a feminine form of Old French *terrin* 'earthen' (hence 'earthern container'), based on Latin *terra* 'earth'.

turf [Old English] Of Germanic origin, *turf* is related to Dutch *turf* and German *Torf*, from an Indo-European root shared by Sanskrit *darbha* 'tuft of grass'. The word has referred colloquially to horse-racing from the mid 18th century. The phrase:
■ **turf war** dates from the 1970s from the notion of a *war* over *turf* expressing the informal sense 'area regarded as personal territory', originally the area controlled by, for example, a street gang or criminal.

turgid [early 17th century] The word *turgid* as in *turgid river* is from Latin *turgidus*, from *turgere* 'to swell'.

turkey [mid 16th century] *Turkey* is short for *turkeycock* or *turkeyhen*, originally applied to the guineafowl (which was imported through Turkey), and then erroneously to the American bird.

turmoil [early 16th century] The origin of *turmoil* is unknown; there is no corresponding word in French but some have suggested a connection with Old French *tremouille*, modern French *trémie (de moulin)* 'mill-hopper'.

turn [Old English] The Old English verb *tyrnan, turnian* is from Latin *tornare*, based on Greek *tornos* 'lathe, circular movement', probably reinforced in Middle English by Old French *turner*. The noun recorded in Middle English is partly from Anglo-Norman French *tourn*, and partly from the verb. Its use as a theatrical term for a public appearance on stage is found from the early 18th century. Of the phrases: *in turn(s)*, *in one's turn*, and *at every turn* are late 16th-century (Shakespeare *A Midsummer Night's Dream*: Ile lead you about a Round, Through bogge, through bush, through brake, … And neigh, and barke, and grunt, … Like horse, hound, hog … at every turn); *turn and turn about* is mid 17th-century; *on the turn* is mid 19th-century; *speak out of turn* is late 19th-century.

turret [Middle English] *Turret* is from Old French *tourete*, a diminutive of *tour* 'tower'.

tusk [Old English] Old English *tux* is a variant of Old English *tusc* used in the same sense; the spelling of the latter became *tush*, a now archaic word or one restricted to dialect.

tussle [late Middle English] This was originally Scots and northern English; it is perhaps a diminutive of dialect *touse* 'handle roughly'.
→ TOUSLE

tutor [late Middle English] *Tutor* is from Old French *tutour* or Latin *tutor*, from *tueri* 'to watch, guard'. The word **tutorial** (based on Latin *tutorius*) dates from the early 18th century when it was used in connection with legal guardianship. Noun use in the sense 'period of individual instruction' is found from the 1920s.

twaddle [late 18th century] This word for 'nonsense' is an alteration of the earlier *twattle* known as a verb from 1573 and as a noun from 1639 but of unknown origin.

tweak [early 17th century] *Tweak* is probably an alteration of dialect *twick* 'pull sharply'.
→ TWITCH

twee [early 20th century] *Twee* represents a child's pronunciation of *sweet*.

tweezers [mid 17th century] *Tweezers* is an extended form of obsolete *tweeze* 'a case of surgical instruments': this is a shortening of *etweese*, the plural of *etui* 'case' (from French). The verb **tweeze** dates from the 1930s as a back-formation (by removal of the suffix) from *tweezer*.

twiddle [mid 16th century] Early use of the word was in the sense 'concern oneself with trifles'. It is apparently imitative, combining the notion *twirl* or *twist* with that of trifling action expressed by *fiddle*. The idiom *twiddle one's thumbs* dates from the mid 19th century.

twig [Old English] Old English *twigge* is Germanic in origin, related to Dutch *twijg* and German *Zweig*, also to *twain* (Old English *twegen*) and *two* (Old English *twā*). The origin of the slang verb *twig* 'understand' (mid 18th century) remains unascertained.

twilight [late Middle English] The first element of *twilight* is from Old English *twi-* 'two' used in an obscure sense in this compound: Middle High German *zwischenliecht* literally 'between-light' was used in the same sense.

twill [Middle English] This is from a Scots and northern English variant of obsolete *twilly*, from Old English *twi-* 'two', suggested by Latin *bilix* 'two-threaded'. Mid 19th-century **tweed** was originally a misreading of *tweel*, a Scots form of *twill*, influenced by association with the river Tweed.

twin [late Old English] Late Old English *twinn* meant 'double', from *twi-* 'two'; it is related to Old Norse *tvinnr*. Current verb senses date from late Middle English.

twine [Old English] Old English *twīn* was 'thread, linen'. From the Germanic base of *twi-* 'two', the word is related to Dutch *twijn*.

twinge [Old English] Of Germanic origin, Old English *twengan* meant 'pinch, wring'. The noun dates from the mid 16th century.

twinkle [Old English] The Old English verb *twinclian* is Germanic in origin. *In a twinkle* and *in the twinkle of an eye* date from the late 16th century (Marlowe *Jew of Malta*: Vanish, and return in a twinkle).

twirl [late 16th century] *Twirl* is probably an alteration (by association with *whirl*) of *tirl*, a variant of archaic *trill* 'twiddle, spin'.

twist [Old English] *Twist* is Germanic in origin, probably from the base of *twin* and *twine*. Current verb senses date from late Middle English. The word **twizzle** dating from the late 18th century is probably imitative, influenced by *twist*.
➔ TWIN; TWINE

twitch [Middle English] *Twitch* is Germanic in origin, related to Old English *twiccian* 'to pluck, pull sharply'. The word has been used as a slang term in the sense 'watch out obsessively for rare birds' from the late 20th century.

tycoon [mid 19th century] This is from Japanese *taikun* 'great lord'.

type [late 15th century] 'Symbol, emblem' was the early meaning recorded for *type*; it is from French, or from Latin *typus*, from Greek *tupos* 'impression, figure, type', from *tuptein* 'to strike'. Use of the word in printing dates from the early 18th century; the general sense 'category with common characteristics' arose in the mid 19th century. The related word **typical** (early 17th century) comes from medieval Latin *typicalis*, via Latin from Greek *tupikos*, from *tupos*. Mid 17th-century **typify** is based on Latin *typus*.

typhoon [late 16th century] This is partly via Portuguese from Arabic *ṭūfān* (perhaps from Greek *tuphōn* 'whirlwind'); it was reinforced by Chinese dialect *tai fung* 'big wind'.

tyrant [Middle English] *Tyrant* is from Old French, via Latin from Greek *turannos*, a base shared by late Middle English **tyranny** from Old French *tyrannie*, from late Latin *tyrannia*, from Latin *turannus*.

tyre [late 15th century] A *tyre* was initially a term for a curved piece of iron plate with which carriage wheels were formerly shod. The word may be a variant of archaic *tire*, a shortening of *attire* expressing the notion that the tyre was the 'clothing' of the wheel.

Uu

ubiquitous [mid 19th century] The base of *ubiquitous* 'present or appearing in every place' is modern Latin *ubiquitas*, from Latin *ubique* meaning 'everywhere', based on *ubi* 'where'.

udder [Old English] Old English *ūder* is West Germanic in origin, related to Dutch *uier* and German *Euter*.

ugly [Middle English] *Ugly* is from Old Norse *uggligr* 'to be dreaded', from *ugga* 'to dread', therefore the primary sense reflects the effect on the observer rather than the appearance itself of the person or object observed. The phrase *ugly duckling* in contexts where someone's hidden beauty is suddenly revealed is from the title of one of Hans Christian Andersen's fairy tales, in which the plain duckling becomes a beautiful swan. This story was first translated into English in 1846.

ukulele [late 19th century] This is an English adoption of an Hawaiian word meaning literally 'jumping flea'. The *ukulele* was developed from a Portuguese instrument introduced into Hawaii around 1879.

ulcer [late Middle English] The word *ulcer* is from Latin *ulcus, ulcer-*. Figurative use expressing the sense 'corrupting influence' is recorded from the late 16th century. The verb **ulcerate** (late Middle English) is from Latin *ulcerare* 'make ulcerous'.

ulterior [mid 17th century] This is an adoption into English of a Latin word meaning literally 'further, more distant'. The sense 'beyond what is openly stated' (*ulterior motive*) dates from the early 18th century.

ultimate [mid 17th century] *Ultimate* is from late Latin *ultimatus*, the past participle of *ultimare* 'come to an end'. Phrasal use as *the ultimate* meaning 'the last word' (*the ultimate in fashion*) dates from the late 17th century. The noun **ultimatum** is mid 18th-century and is an English use of the neuter form of late Latin *ultimatus* in the medieval Latin senses 'final' and 'completed'.

umbilical [mid 16th century] This comes from French *ombilical*, or is based on Latin *umbilicus*. Use of the word to mean 'maintaining an essential supply' in astronautical contexts (*umbilical pipe; umbilical connection*) dates from the 1940s.

umbrage [late Middle English] *Umbrage* is from Old French, from Latin *umbra* 'shadow' (the base too of early 17th-century **umbrella** from Italian). An early sense was 'shadowy outline', which then gave rise to 'ground for suspicion': this led to the current notion of 'offence' as in *she took umbrage at the comment*.

umpire [late Middle English] The early spelling was *noumpere* 'an arbitrator' from Old French *nonper* 'not equal' (Milton *Paradise Lost*: Chaos umpire sits And by decision more embroils the fray By which he reigns; next him high arbiter Chance governs all). The *n* of the early form was lost by wrong division of the phrase *a noumpere*; the word *adder* underwent the same process. *Umpire* became a term in sports such as tennis in the early 18th century.

umpteen [early 20th century] *Umpteen* is a humorous formation based on the numbers ending in *-teen*. In the late 19th century the word *umpty* expressed an indefinite number following the pattern of *twenty, thirty*, etc.

WORDBUILDING

1. The prefix **un-** [Old English, of Germanic origin; from an Indo-European root shared by Latin *in-* and Greek *a*] adds the sense

- **not** [unacademic; unrepeatable]
- **the reverse of** (with a notion of approval or disapproval) [unselfish; unprepossessing]
- **a lack of** [unrest]

2. The prefix **un-** [Old English *un-, on-*, of Germanic origin; related to Dutch *ont-* and German *ent-*] adds the sense

- **cancellation of, reversal** [untie]
- **separation, reduction** [unmask, unman]
- **release** [unburden]

---

unanimous [early 17th century] This is based on Latin *unanimus*, from *unus* 'one' and *animus* 'mind', giving 'of one opinion'.

unbeknown [mid 17th century] This word is based on the archaic word *beknown* meaning 'known', prefixed by *un-* 'not'.

uncanny [late 16th century] *Uncanny* was originally Scots in the sense 'relating to the occult, malicious'. It is made up of the prefix *un-* 'not' and the late 16th-century (originally Scots) adjective *canny* 'knowing'.

➜CAN¹

uncle [Middle English] *Uncle* is from Old French *oncle*, from late Latin *auunculus*, an alteration of Latin *auunculus* 'maternal uncle'. The regional form *nuncle* is a late 16th-century variant of the English word (Dryden *Wild Gallant*: Alas, alas poor Nuncle!). In the 1920s the word *uncle* was used in BBC Radio for a male announcer or story-teller for children's programmes.

uncouth [Old English] Old English *uncūth* meant 'unknown', from the prefix *un-* 'not' and *cūth* (the past participle of *cunnan* 'know, be able'). The sense 'lacking sophistication' in the context of language dates from the late 17th century; the sense 'ill-mannered, rough' in the description of people and their behaviour dates from the mid 18th century.

unction [late Middle English] *Unction* is from Latin *unctio(n-)*, from *unguere* 'anoint'. The phrase *extreme unction* in the Roman Catholic Church refers to a final anointing of a sick person in danger of death. The word *unction* is sometimes used to express the 'manifestation of deep religious feeling' (*clerical unction*) from a link between religious fervour and an 'anointing' with the Holy Spirit; this usage became associated with self-satisfaction and developed a derogatory connotation. The Latin verb *unguere* is also the base of late Middle English **unctuous** (via medieval Latin *unctuosus* from Latin *unctus* 'anointing'): this had the early sense 'greasy; like an ointment'. Another word from the same period and the same Latin source verb (*unguere*) is **unguent** via Latin *unguentum*.

under [Old English] Of Germanic origin, *under* is related to Dutch *onder* and German *unter*. It has provided the first element of many words: dating from Old English are *undergān* (= **undergo**) meaning in early examples 'undermine'; **underhand** first recorded in the sense 'in subjection, under control'; *underlecgan* (= **underlay**); *underlicgan* (= **underlie**) meaning originally 'be subject or subordinate to'; *underneothan* (= **underneath**); and *understandan* (= **understand**).

undermine [Middle English] This word was probably suggested by Middle Dutch *ondermineren*. Figurative use from late Middle English expressed 'work stealthily against' (*undermined him with their carefully-worded arguments*); from the mid 16th century, the sense was extended to 'weaken, ruin' (*undermined their faith*).

underwhelm [1950s] The humorous formation *underwhelm* was suggested by *overwhelm*.

undulate [mid 17th century] Based on Latin *unda* 'a wave', *undulate* is from late Latin *undulatus*.

ungainly [mid 17th century] The word *ungainly* is composed of the prefix *un-* 'not' and obsolete *gainly* 'graceful', based on Old Norse *gegn* 'straight'.

uniformity [late Middle English] This is from Old French *uniformite* or late Latin *uniformitas*, from Latin *uniformis* 'of one form'. **Uniform** (mid 16th century) is from French *uniforme* or Latin *uniformis*. The noun sense describing clothing of a fixed style and colour designed to be worn by each member of a group such as schoolchildren, flight stewards, etc., dates from the mid 18th century.

unique [early 17th century] *Unique* is an adoption of a French word, from Latin *unicus*, from *unus* 'one'. The word's absolute sense 'being only one of its kind' means that strictly it cannot be modified by adverbs such as *really*, *quite*, or *very*. However if *unique* is used in the gradable sense 'remarkable, unusual', it may be argued that a submodifying adverb is possible (*a really unique opportunity*).

unison [late Middle English] This is from Old French, or from late Latin *unisonus*, from Latin *uni-* 'one' and *sonus* 'sound'; *unison* was initially a term in music (= a note of the same pitch as another) and acoustics. The phrase *in unison* is recorded from the early 17th century.

unity [Middle English] Latin *unus* 'one' is the base of several words: *unity* is from Old French *unite*, from Latin *unitas*; the late Middle English verb **unite** is from Latin *unit-*, the past participial stem of *unire* 'join together'. The *three unities* refer since the late 17th century to the three principles of the Aristotelian canon of dramatic composition, expanded by French classical dramatists (expressed in a play by one action, occurring in one place, in one limited period of time). Late Middle English **union** is from Old French, or from ecclesiastical Latin *unio(n-)* 'unity'; the word's use for a group of people associated together for a common purpose (e.g. *trade union*) dates from the mid 17th century. **Unify** (early 16th century) is from French *unifier* or late Latin *unificare* 'make into a whole'. Finally **unit**, first used as a mathematical term in the late 16th century, is also from Latin *unus*, the ending probably suggested by *digit*.

university [Middle English] The word *university* is from Old French *universite*, from Latin *universitas* which meant 'the whole' and in late Latin 'society, guild'. In English the term was first applied to a corporation of teachers and students formed for the purpose of giving and receiving instruction in a fixed range of subjects to a level higher than that achieved in school. The base is Latin *universus* 'combined into one', from *uni-* 'one' and *versus* 'turned' (the past participle of *vertere*). The same base is shared by late Middle English **universe** (from Latin *universum*, the neuter of *universus*) and the contemporaneous **universal** (from Old French, or from Latin *universalis*). The phrase *the universe* referring to 'all existing matter' is recorded from the late 16th century.

unkempt [late Middle English] This word is based on *kempt* 'combed', the past participle of archaic *kemb*, related to *comb*. The prefix *un-* means 'not'.
→ COMB

unless [late Middle English] This is a later form of *in less* or *on less*, assimilated, through lack of stress on the initial word, to *unless*.

unlike [Middle English] This is perhaps originally an alteration of Old Norse *úlíkr*; Old English *ungelīc* 'not of the same kind, not comparable' may be related.

unruly [late Middle English] This is made up of the prefix *un-* 'not' and archaic *ruly* meaning 'amenable to discipline or order' (from *rule*).
→ RULE

until [Middle English] *Until* is from Old Norse *und* 'as far as' and *till* 'until'; the sense in the English word is thus duplicated. Middle English **unto** is from *until*, with *to* replacing *till* (being synonymous with 'to' in northern dialect).

untold [Old English] Old English *unteald* meant 'not counted, unspecified'. In late Middle English this became 'not able to be counted' (*untold suffering*).

untrue [Old English] Old English *untrēowe* meant 'unfaithful'. The sense 'contrary to fact' appeared in examples in Middle English. The noun **untruth** (in Old English *untreowth*) had the early meaning 'unfaithfulness'.

unwieldy [late Middle English] The early meaning recorded was 'lacking strength, infirm'. The word is composed of the prefix *un-* 'not' and *wieldy* in the obsolete sense 'active'. The word came to mean 'huge and awkward in shape' from the late 16th century.

up [Old English] Old English *up(p)*, *uppe*, of Germanic origin, is related to Dutch *op* and German *auf*. Based on *up* are: **upward** (in Old English *upweard(es)*), Middle English **upon** suggested by Old Norse *upp á*, Middle English **upper**, and late 19th-century **uppity**, a fanciful formation. The compound

■ **upper case** referred originally to two type cases positioned on an angled stand, the case containing the capital letters being higher and further away from the compositor, the *lower case* being closer.

upbraid [late Old English] Late Old English *upbrēdan* meant 'allege (something) as a basis for censure', based on *braid* in the obsolete sense 'brandish' thus giving a notion of holding something aloft for public disapproval. The current sense *find fault with* dates from Middle English.

upbringing [late 15th century] This is from the obsolete Middle English verb *upbring* 'to rear'.

upholsterer [early 17th century] This is from the obsolete noun *upholster* based on *uphold* in the obsolete sense 'keep in repair'. The verb **upholster** dates from the mid 19th century as a back-formation (by removal of the suffix) from *upholsterer*.

upright [Old English] Old English *upriht* is related to Dutch *oprecht* and German *aufrecht*. The sense 'having integrity' (*upright citizen*) dates from the mid 16th century.

uproar [early 16th century] *Uproar* is from Middle Dutch *uproer*, from *op* 'up' and *roer* 'confusion' which was associated with English *roar*. Its early use expressed the sense 'insurrection, rising' which soon developed into 'loud confused noise'.

upside down [Middle English] This was originally *up so down*, perhaps in the sense 'up as if down'.

urbane [mid 16th century] This word was first used in the sense 'urban'; it comes from French *urbain* or Latin *urbanus* 'belonging to the city', the source too of early 17th-century **urban**. Latin *urbs*, *urb-* 'city' is the base.

urchin [Middle English] The early spelling was *hirchon*, *urchon* 'hedgehog', from Old Northern French *herichon*, based on Latin *hericius* 'hedgehog'. The word meant 'hedgehog' in Middle English but the use is now archaic. It came to be applied to a poor raggedly dressed child in the mid 16th century. The compound *sea urchin* is of the genus *Echinus* from Greek *ekhinos* 'hedgehog' with reference to the spines on the shell.

urgent [late 15th century] This word comes from Old French, from Latin *urgent-*, the present participial stem of *urgere* 'press, drive', a verb which also gave **urge** in the mid 16th century.

urn [late Middle English] *Urn* is from Latin *urna*, related to *urceus* 'pitcher'. Early use was as a term for a *funeral urn*; it was applied to other containers later such as one for dispensing tea or storing hot water (late 18th century).

us [Old English] Old English *ūs* was the accusative and dative of *we*, related to Dutch *ons* and German *uns*. The notion of *us and them* contrasting ordinary people with authority dates from the 1940s.

usage [Middle English] Latin *usus* 'a use' (from *uti* 'to use') is the base of *usage*, **use**, and **usual**. *Usage* had the early sense 'customary practice' and comes from Old French, from *us* 'a use'; Middle English **use** is also, as a noun, from Old French *us*, the verb from Old French *user*, based on Latin *uti*. The positive sense 'make use of, employ' soon developed (in late Middle English) the negative sense 'take advantage of, manipulate' in parallel with the positive one. Late Middle English **usual** is from Old French, or from late Latin *usualis*.

usher [late Middle English] An *usher* was originally a term for a doorkeeper, from Anglo-Norman French *usser*, from medieval Latin *ustiarius*, from Latin *ostiarius*. The base is Latin *ostium* 'door'. The function often involved showing people to their seats, for example in a court of law. The word was applied to a schoolmaster's assistant from the early 16th century and in US English to a person assisting people at a wedding, in the late 19th century. The verb dates from the late 16th century.

usurp [Middle English] 'Appropriate (a right) wrongfully' is the sense of *usurp* in early examples. It comes from Old French *usurper*, from Latin *usurpare* 'seize for use'.

usury [Middle English] This word describing the practice of lending money at interest is from Anglo-Norman French *usurie*, or from medieval Latin *usuria*, from Latin *usura*. Latin *usus* 'a use' is the base. Middle English **usurer** referring to a 'moneylender' is from Anglo-Norman French, from Old French *usure*, from Latin *usura*.
→ USEAGE

utensil [late Middle English] *Utensil* was once a collective term for domestic implements or containers. It comes from Old French *utensile*, from the medieval Latin neuter form of *utensilis* 'usable', from *uti* 'to use'.
→ USAGE

utility [late Middle English] Old French *utilite* gave *utility* in English, from Latin *utilitas*, from *utilis* 'useful'. The word was commonly used to mean 'usefulness' from around 1540–1650 and from around 1755. Early 19th-century **utilize** is from French *utiliser*, from Italian *utilizzare*, from *utile* 'useful'.

utmost [Old English] Old English *ūt(e)mest* meant 'outermost' (Spenser *Faerie Queene*: Corineus had that Province utmost west To him assigned). The phrase *one's utmost* meaning 'one's very best' dates from the early 17th century.

Utopia [mid 16th century] This is from the name of an imaginary island depicted by Sir Thomas More in his book entitled *Utopia* written in 1516: it was described as enjoying a perfect social, legal, and political system, based on Greek *ou* 'not' and *topos* 'place'.

utter[1] [Old English] Old English *ūtera*, *ūttra* meaning 'outer', is the comparative of *ūt* 'out'; it was in very frequent use in this sense from around 1400 to 1620 (Milton *Paradise Lost*: Drive them out From all Heav'ns bounds into the utter Deep). The sense 'extreme, complete' became very common from around 1515 (Shakespeare *Henry VI Part 1*: The utter losse of all the Realme).
→ OUT

utter[2] [late Middle English] This *utter* as in *uttered a whispered sound* is from Middle Dutch *ūteren* 'speak, make known, give currency to (coins)'. An early, now obsolete use, was 'put (goods) on to the market, sell'; later the verb meant 'circulate (money) as legal tender' and 'publish'. The basic notion is one of 'put forth' which is carried over into the meaning 'declare, speak'.

Vv

vacant [Middle English] *Vacant* is from Old French, or from Latin *vacant-*, the present participial stem of *vacare* 'remain empty, be unoccupied, leave empty'. Examples of the word in connection with lack of intelligence are found from the early 18th century. Latin *vacare* is also the source of late Middle English **vacation** 'freedom from an occupation' (from Old French, or from Latin *vacatio(n-)*) and mid 17th-century **vacate**: this was first used as a legal term meaning 'make void, annul' (*vacating all grants of property*) and also in the sense 'make ineffective', now obsolete.

vaccine [late 18th century] *Vaccine* is from Latin *vaccinus*, from *vacca* 'cow', a derivation linked to the early use of the cowpox virus against smallpox.

vacillate [late 16th century] The notion of wavering between different opinions or choices became associated with the word *vacillate* in the early 17th century but the early sense recorded was 'sway unsteadily'; it comes from Latin *vacillare* 'sway'.

vacuum [mid 16th century] This modern Latin word is the neuter of Latin *vacuus* 'empty', a base shared by mid 17th-century **vacuous** meaning, in early examples, 'empty of matter'. 'Unintelligent' became one of the word's meanings in the mid 19th century (Thackeray *Book of Snobs*: A vacuous, solemn … Snob.).

vagabond [Middle English] A *vagabond* was originally 'a vagrant, someone of no fixed abode'. The source of the word is Old French, or from Latin *vagabundus*, from *vagari* 'wander'. An additional notion of 'rogue, rascal' was evidenced in the use of the word from the late 17th century (Dickens *Dombey and Son*: No young vagabond could be brought to bear its contemplation for one moment).

vagary [late 16th century] Early use of *vagary* included the now obsolete verb use 'roam'. It comes from Latin *vagari* 'wander'. The noun meant 'roaming, a ramble', later applied to speech or written expression (*wordy vagary*) and subsequently (early 17th century) to 'capricious action' (*vagaries of the weather*).

vagrant [late Middle English] This word is from Anglo-Norman French *vagarant* 'wandering about', from the verb *vagrer*, associated with Latin *vagari* 'wander'.
→ VAGABOND

vague [mid 16th century] *Vague* is from French, or from Latin *vagus* 'wandering, uncertain'. The sense 'unable to think or communicate with clarity' (*he's so vague in his responses*) dates from the early 19th century.

vain [Middle English] 'Devoid of real worth' was the early meaning conveyed by examples of *vain*. The word is via Old French from Latin *vanus* 'empty, without substance'. The phrase *in vain* reflecting the Latin *in vanum* and Old French *en vein* (later *en vain*) is found early. The word's appliction to people describing them as 'having a high opinion of [their] own appearance' is recorded from the late 17th century. This has its associations with late 15th-century **vainglorious** 'showing unwarranted pride in one's qualities', suggested by Old French *vaine gloire*, Latin *vana gloria*. The Middle English noun **vanity** is from Old French *vanite*, from Latin *vanitas*, from *vanus*.

valance [late Middle English] This word for a length of decorative drapery (*curtain valance*) is perhaps Anglo-Norman French, from a shortened form of Old French *avaler* 'descend'.

valediction [mid 17th century] This formal word for 'leave-taking' is based on Latin *vale* 'goodbye' and *dicere* 'to say', on the pattern of *benediction*.

valency [early 17th century] The source of this word originally quoted solely in dictionaries, meaning 'power, strength', and since the mid 19th century used in chemistry contexts, is late Latin *valentia* 'vigour, capacity', from *valere* 'be well or strong'.

valentine [late Middle English] A *valentine* formerly referred to a person chosen, sometimes by lot, as a sweetheart or special friend. It is from Old French *Valentin*, from Latin *Valentinus*, the name of two early Italian saints with feast days on 14 February.

valet [late 15th century] An early *valet* was a footman acting as an attendant to a horseman. It comes from French and is related to late Middle English **vassal** (via Old French from medieval Latin *vassallus* 'retainer', of Celtic origin). The verb **valet** dates from the mid 19th century, with its use in the context of cleaning clothes arising in the 1930s (from the mid 19th-century use of the verbal noun *valeting*) and, in the context of car cleaning, from the 1970s. A related word is late Middle English **varlet** from Old French, a variant of *valet*; the sense 'rogue' dates from the mid 16th century.

valiant [Middle English] Early senses included 'robust' and well-built'. The source is Old French *vaillant*, based on Latin *valere* 'be strong'. The notion of 'courage' became associated with the word in late Middle English. The same Latin verb is the source of Middle English **valour** (via Old French from late Latin *valor*) which at first referred to 'worth derived from personal qualities or rank' and later (towards the end of the 16th century) to 'courage'.

valid [late 16th century] *Valid* is from French *valide* or Latin *validus* 'strong', from *valere* 'be strong'. The word was used early in contexts of legal authority; its application to arguments or assertions as being 'well-founded' was a mid 17th-century development. The verb **validate** is from medieval Latin verb *validare* 'make legally valid', from the same source and is recorded from the mid 17th century in the Latin sense.

valley [Middle English] The word *valley* is from Old French *valee*, based on Latin *vallis, valles*, the base too of Middle English **vale** (via Old French *val*).

value [Middle English] *Value* is from the Old French feminine past participle of *valoir* 'be worth', from Latin *valere* 'be strong'. Use of the word in mathematical contexts (*values of x and y*) dates from the mid 16th century, and in musical contexts (*value or length of the breve*) from the mid 17th century.

valve [late Middle English] A *valve* (from Latin *valva* 'leaf of a door') was once a term for a leaf of a folding or double door; later (towards the end of the 18th century) it described a door or flap controlling the flow of water. Use of the word in anatomy (*heart valve*) is found from the early 17th century.

vamoose [mid 19th century] The word *vamoose* used as an informal word for 'depart' is from Spanish *vamos* 'let us go'.

vamp [Middle English] A *vamp* was once a term for 'the foot of a stocking' and currently refers to the upper front part of a boot or shoe; it is a shortening of Old French *avantpie*, from *avant* 'before' and *pie* 'foot'. In jazz and popular music the word is a term for 'a short introductory passage'; the current musical sense of the verb, 'repeat a short simple passage' devel-

oped from the general meaning 'improvise' (late 18th century), which itself developed from a notion of 'patching'.

vampire [mid 18th century] This comes from French, from Hungarian *vampir*, perhaps from Turkish *uber* 'witch'. The word **vamp** found from the early 20th century in reference to a 'woman using sexual attraction to exploit men' is an abbreviation of *vampire*.

van [early 19th century] This *van* as a term for a type of delivery or service vehicle is a shortening of *caravan*, to which the word also sometimes refers.

vandal [mid 16th century] *Vandal* is from Latin *Vandalus*, a word of Germanic origin. The current meaning 'person who deliberately damages private property' dates from the mid 17th century. The word originally (as *Vandal*) described a member of a Germanic people that completely sacked Rome in 455 BC and ravaged Gaul, Spain, and North Africa in the 4th and 5th centuries.

vane [late Middle English] This word for a 'broad blade (driven by the wind)' is a dialect variant of obsolete *fane* 'banner', of Germanic origin.

vanguard [late Middle English] A *vanguard*, a term originally for the front section of an army, is a shortening of Old French *avan(t)garde*, from *avant* 'before' and *garde* 'guard'. The early 17th-century word **van** found as part of the phrase *in the van of* is an abbreviation of *vanguard*.

vanilla [mid 17th century] This word for a flavouring is from Spanish *vainilla* 'pod', a diminutive of *vaina* 'sheath, pod', from Latin *vagina* 'sheath'. The spelling change was due to association with French *vanille*. Since the 1970s the word has been used to mean 'plain, basic, conventional' from the popular perception of *vanilla* as the basic or usual flavour of ice-cream.

vanish [Middle English] *Vanish* is a shortening of Old French *e(s)vaniss-*, the lengthened stem of *e(s)vanir*, from Latin *evanescere* 'die away'.

vanquish [Middle English] The source of *vanquish* is Old French *vencus, venquis* (the past participle and past tense of *veintre*), later influenced by *vainquiss-* the lengthened stem of *vainquir*, from Latin *vincere* 'conquer'.

vantage [Middle English] *Vantage* is from Anglo-Norman French, a shortening of Old French *avantage* 'advantage'.

vapid [mid 17th century] The word *vapid* was used originally in descriptions of drinks as 'lacking in flavour'; it comes from Latin *vapidus* 'savourless'. The sense 'devoid of animation' dates from the mid 18th century.

vapour [late Middle English] *Vapour* is from Old French, or from Latin *vapor* 'steam, heat'. The current verb sense 'talk in a vacuous way' (*vapoured on about his youth*) dates from the early 17th century. In the mid 17th century and remaining common until 1750, *vapours* referred to a morbid condition caused by a nervous disorder; it was commonly called *the vapours* during the 18th century, describing depression and a state of being generally out of sorts.

variegated [mid 17th century] This is based on Latin *variegare* 'make varied', from *varius* 'diverse'.

various [late Middle English] Latin *varius* 'changing, diverse' is the base of *various* as well as of late 15th-century **variety** (from French *variété* or Latin *varietas*). The sense 'sort, type' (*many varieties of confectionery*) dates from the early 17th century. Examples of *variety* in the context of entertainment (*variety show*) are found from the early 20th century.

varnish [Middle English] *Varnish* is from Old French *vernis*, from medieval Latin *veronix* 'fragrant resin, sandarac' or medieval Greek *berenikē* (probably from *Berenice*, the name of a town in Cyrenaica, a region of NE Libya).

varsity [mid 17th century] *Varsity* is a shortening of *university*, reflecting an archaic pronunciation.

vary [Middle English] A group of words in English sprang from Latin *variare*: those in Middle English include *vary*, and **variance** (via Old French from Latin *variantia* 'difference'); then in late Middle English came **variable** (via Old French from Latin *variabilis*), **variant** (from an Old French present participle meaning literally 'varying') first used as an adjective in the sense 'tending to vary', and **variation** (from Old French, or from Latin *variatio(n-)*) first used in the sense 'variance or conflict'.

vase [late Middle English] This is an adoption of a French word, from Latin *vas* 'vessel'. The earlier pronunciations (rhyming with *mace* and *maize*) are still current in the US.
➔ VESSEL

vast [late Middle English] *Vast* is from Latin *vastus* 'void, immense'.

vat [Middle English] A southern and western dialect variant of obsolete *fat* 'container', *vat* is Germanic in origin and related to Dutch *vat* and German *Fass*.

vaudeville [mid 18th century] This term for a type of entertainment is from French, spelt earlier as *vau de ville* or *vau de vire*, reputedly a

name originally given to songs composed by Olivier Basselin, a 15th-century fuller born in *Vau de Vire* in Normandy.

vault¹ [Middle English] This *vault* meaning 'arched roof' is from Old French *voute*, based on Latin *volvere* 'to roll'. It has been used as a term for a 'burial chamber' since the mid 16th century, originally describing one with an arched roof.

vault² [mid 16th century] This *vault* meaning 'leap, spring (pushing with the hands)' is from Old French *volter* 'to turn (a horse), gambol', based on Latin *volvere* 'to roll'.

vaunt [late Middle English] The noun is a shortening of obsolete *avaunt* 'boasting, a boast'; the verb (originally in the sense 'use boastful language') is from Old French *vanter*, from late Latin *vantare*, based on Latin *vanus* 'vain, empty'.

veal [Middle English] *Veal* is from Anglo-Norman French *ve(e)l*, from Latin *vitellus*, a diminutive of *vitulus* 'calf'.

veer [late 16th century] The verb *veer* is from French *virer*, perhaps from an alteration of Latin *gyrare*. The original use in English was nautical in reference to the wind, meaning 'change gradually'; it came to mean 'change course' from the early 17th century.
➔ GYRATE

vegetable [late Middle English] The early use was adjectival in the sense 'growing as a plant', from Old French, or from late Latin *vegetabilis* 'animating': this is from Latin *vegetare* 'enliven', from *vegetus* 'active', from *vegere* 'be active'. The noun dates from the late 16th century. Related words include: late Middle English **vegetative** (from Old French *vegetatif*, *-ive* or medieval Latin *vegetativus*) which had the early meaning 'capable of growth'; mid 16th-century **vegetation** (from medieval Latin *vegetatio(n-)* 'power of growth', from the verb *vegetare*), and early 17th-century **vegetate** (from Latin *vegetare*). The slang use *veg out* meaning 'pass the time in mindless activity' arose in the 1980s. **Vegetarian** is an irregular formation of the mid 19th century based on *vegetable*; the abbreviation **veggie** dates from the 1970s.

vehement [late Middle English] This word once described pain or temperature in the sense 'intense, high in degree'. French *véhément* or Latin *vehement-* 'impetuous, violent' gave rise to the word in English; the Latin word is perhaps from an unrecorded adjective meaning 'deprived of mind', influenced by Latin *vehere* 'carry'.

vehicle [early 17th century] *Vehicle* is from French *véhicule* or Latin *vehiculum*, from *vehere* 'carry'.

veil [Middle English] *Veil* is from Anglo-Norman French *veil(e)*, from Latin *vela*, the plural of *velum*. The idiom *take the veil* for 'become a nun' dates from early times; *draw a veil over (something)* arose in the early 18th century.

vein [Middle English] *Vein* is from Old French *veine*, from Latin *vena*. The earliest senses were 'blood vessel' and 'small natural underground channel of water'. Another early use was as a term in mining for a crack or fissure filled with, for example, metallic ore. This led in the mid 16th century to figurative associations of 'inter-mixture' of qualities (*vein of sarcasm, vein of humour*) sometimes extended to 'mood, temporary state of mind' (*carried on in the same vein*).

vellum [late Middle English] This word for fine parchment is from Old French *velin*, from *veel*.
→VEAL

velocity [late Middle English] *Velocity* is from French *vélocité* or Latin *velocitas*, from *velox, veloc-* 'swift'.

velvet [Middle English] The word *velvet* is from Old French *veluotte*, from *velu* 'velvety', from medieval Latin *villutus*. The *velvet revolution* is a term applied to a non-violent political revolution, especially the relatively smooth change from Communism to a Western-style democracy in Czechoslovakia at the end of 1989. Latin *villus* 'tuft, down' is the base shared by both *velvet* and **velour** (early 18th century) from French *velours* 'velvet', from Old French *velour*, from Latin *villosus* 'hairy'.

venal [mid 17th century] This adjective meaning 'motivated by susceptibility to bribery' was initially used in the sense 'available for purchase', referring to merchandise or a favour. Latin *venalis* is the source, from *venum* 'thing for sale'.

vendor [late 16th century] This comes from Anglo-Norman French *vendour* from a base shared by early 17th-century **vend** which first reflected the sense 'be sold'. The source is French *vendre* or Latin *vendere* 'sell' (composed from Latin *venum* 'something for sale' and a variant of *dare* 'give').

vendetta [mid 19th century] An Italian word in origin, *vendetta* is from Latin *vindicta* 'vengeance'.

veneer [early 18th century] An early spelling was *fineer* and the origin of the word is German *furni(e)ren*, from Old French *fournir* 'furnish', giving the notion of 'furnishing' a piece of furniture with a thin surface. Figurative use (*veneer of courtesy*) is mid 19th-century.

venerable [late Middle English] The word *venerable* is from Old French, or from Latin *venerabilis*, from the verb *venerari*, a source shared by the early 17th-century verb **venerate** 'adore, revere'.

vengeance [Middle English] *Vengeance* is from Old French, from *venger* 'avenge'. The word **vengeful** (late 16th century) is from obsolete *venge* 'avenge', on the pattern of *revengeful*.

venison [Middle English] *Venison* is from Old French *veneso(u)n*, from Latin *venatio(n-)* 'hunting', from *venari* 'to hunt'.

venom [Middle English] The source of *venom* in English is Old French *venim*, a variant of *venin*, from an alteration of Latin *venenum* 'poison'. *Venom* is the base of Middle English **venomous** from Old French *venimeux*.

vent¹ [late Middle English] This *vent* meaning 'opening' or 'provide with an opening' is partly from French *vent* 'wind', from Latin *ventus*; it was reinforced by French *évent*, from *éventer* 'expose to air', based on Latin *ventus* 'wind'. The verb sense 'give free expression to' (*vented his anger*) is found from the late 16th century.

vent² [late Middle English] The *vent* which means 'slit' is an alteration of dialect *fent*, from Old French *fente* 'slit', based on Latin *findere* 'cleave'.

ventilate [late Middle English] When first used, *ventilate* had the sense 'winnow, scatter'. Latin *ventilare* 'blow, winnow' is the source, from *ventus* 'wind'. The sense 'cause air to circulate in' dates from the mid 18th century. The noun **ventilation** dates from late Middle English when it meant 'current of air'; it comes from Old French, or from Latin *ventilatio(n-)*, from the verb *ventilare*.

ventriloquist [mid 17th century] This is based on modern Latin *ventriloquium* (from Latin *venter* 'belly' and *loqui* 'speak').

venture [late Middle English] This word, a shortening of *adventure*, was first used in the noun sense 'adventure' and in the verb sense 'risk the loss of'. The sense 'dare to go' (*ventured out*) dates from the mid 16th century; 'dare to put forward' (*ventured his opinion*) dates from the mid 17th century.

venue [late 16th century] From Old French, *venue* is literally 'a coming'; the form is the feminine past participle of *venir* 'to come' from Latin *venire*. It was first used as a term for 'a thrust or bout' in fencing and as a legal term meaning 'the county or district within which a criminal or civil case must be heard'.

veracity [early 17th century] *Veracity* is from French *véracité* or medieval Latin *veracitas*, from *verax* 'speaking truly'.

veranda [early 18th century] This is from Hindi *varaṇḍā*, from Portuguese *varanda* 'railing, balustrade'.

verb [late Middle English] The English word *verb* is from Old French *verbe* or Latin *verbum* 'word, verb'. Latin *verbum* is also the source of: (in the late 15th century) **verbal** from French, or from late Latin *verbalis*, and **verbatim** from medieval Latin; (in the late 17th century) **verbose** from Latin *verbosus*.

verdant [late 16th century] *Verdant* is perhaps from Old French *verdeant*, the present participle of *verdoier* 'be green', based on Latin *viridis* 'green'. The same base is shared by late Middle English **verdure** which comes via French from Old French *verd* 'green'.

verdict [Middle English] *Verdict* is from Anglo-Norman French *verdit*, from Old French *veir* 'true' (from Latin *verus*) and *dit* (from Latin *dictum* 'saying').

verge[1] [late Middle English] *Verge* comes via Old French from Latin *virga* 'rod'. The word branches semantically into: 'rod' (*verge carried in procession before the bishop*), the now obsolete 'measure of length' (*verge of land*), 'area of jurisdiction' (*the verge of the court*), and 'edge, rim, border' (*grass verge*). The current verb sense 'border on' (*verges on rudeness*) was a late 18th century development. The ecclesiastical term **verger** ('a person carrying a rod of office' in Middle English) is related and is from Anglo-Norman French.

verge[2] [early 17th century] This *verge* meaning 'incline towards' as in *his style verged into the art nouveau school* had the early sense 'descend (to the horizon)' (*Sir Walter Scott Talisman: The light was now verging low, yet served the knight still to discern that they two were no longer alone in the forest*). The source is Latin *vergere* 'to bend, incline'.

verify [Middle English] *Verify*, first found as a legal term, is from Old French *verifier*, from medieval Latin *verificare*, from *verus* 'true'. Early 16th-century **verification** is from Old French or from medieval Latin *verificatio(n-)*, from *verificare*.

verisimilitude [early 17th century] This word meaning 'appearance of being real or true' is from Latin *verisimilitudo*, from *verisimilis* 'probable': the elements here are *veri* (the genitive of *verus* 'true') and *similis* 'like'.

veritable [late Middle English] Old French *verite* 'truth' gave rise to *veritable* (whose early senses included 'true' and 'speaking the truth', later coming to mean 'genuine, actual') and the contemporaneous **verity** (from Latin *veritas*, from *verus* 'true').

vermin [Middle English] This was originally a collective term for animals such as reptiles and snakes regarded as objectionable. It comes from Old French, based on Latin *vermis* 'worm'. The word **varmint** (a synonym for 'vermin' in the mid 16th century) is an alteration of *vermin*.

vernacular [early 17th century] Latin *vernaculus* 'domestic, native' (from *verna* 'home-born slave') is the base of *vernacular*, a word referring to 'language or dialect' spoken by the ordinary people of a particular district.

versatile [early 17th century] 'Inconstant, fluctuating' was the sense conveyed by *versatile* in early examples. The source is either the French form, or Latin *versatilis*, from *versare* 'turn about, revolve': this is a frequentative (= verb of repeated action) of *vertere* 'to turn'.

verse [Old English] Old English *fers* is from Latin *versus* 'a turn of the plough, a furrow, a line of writing', from *vertere* 'to turn'; it was reinforced in Middle English by Old French *vers*, from Latin *versus*.

version [late Middle English] A *version* was originally a 'translation': the word is from French, or from medieval Latin *versio(n-)*, from Latin *vertere* 'to turn'. It was in the late 18th century that the word came to be used to refer to a 'variant form' or 'an account embodying a particular point of view' (*his version of events*).

verso [mid 19th century] This word used to refer to the left-hand page of an open book (i.e. the back of the turned page) or to the reverse of something such as a coin or medal, is from Latin *verso (folio)* 'on the turned (leaf)'.

versus [late Middle English] This is from a medieval Latin use of Latin *versus* 'towards'.

vertical [mid 16th century] The early word is recorded as meaning 'directly overhead'. It comes from French, or from late Latin *verticalis*, from Latin *vertex* 'whirlpool, crown of a head, vertex' (from *vertere* 'to turn').
→ VORTEX

vertigo [late Middle English] This is an English use of a Latin word meaning 'whirling', from *vertere* 'to turn'. The adjective **vertiginous** dates from the early 17th century from Latin *vertiginosus*, from *vertigo*.

verve [late 17th century] *Verve* started out in reference to 'special talent in writing'. It is from a French word meaning 'vigour', and before that 'form of expression', from Latin *verba* 'words'. The word came to be used in the generalized sense 'energy, vigour' in the middle of the 19th century.

very [Middle English] This was first used as an adjective in the sense 'real, genuine'; it is from Old French *verai*, based on Latin *verus* 'true'. The Middle English word **verily** is based on *very* and suggested by Old French *verrai(e)ment*.

vespers [late 15th century] This word for a service of evening prayer is from Old French *vespres* 'evensong', from Latin *vesperas* (accusative plural), on the pattern of *matutinas* 'matins'.

vessel [Middle English] Anglo-Norman French *vessel(e)* is the source of *vessel* in English, from late Latin *vascellum*, a diminutive of *vas* 'vessel'. From 1300 to 1600, the word was commonly used as a collective for table utensils. Later the main notion was one of 'containment', whether for liquids (*glass vessel of water*), for people (*sea-going vessel*), or for spirituality (*vessel of the soul*). *Vessel* has been used as a term in anatomy from late Middle English.
→ VASE

vest [late Middle English] The verb *vest* (as in *the power vested in me*) is from Old French *vestu* 'clothed', the past participle of *vestir*, from Latin *vestire*. The noun (from French *veste*, via Italian from Latin *vestis* 'garment') dates from the early 17th century when it referred to a loose outer garment; it came to describe an undergarment for the upper body in the early 19th century, and, towards the end of the 20th century, was used in the specific context of athletics wear.

vestibule [early 17th century] Formerly a *vestibule* was the space in front of the main entrance of a Roman or Greek building. It comes from French, or from Latin *vestibulum* 'entrance court'.

vestige [late Middle English] This word meaning 'trace' comes from French, from Latin *vestigium* 'footprint'.

vestry [late Middle English] This is probably from an Anglo-Norman French alteration of Old French *vestiarie*, from Latin *vestiarium*, a source shared by its Middle English synonym **vestiary**.

veteran [early 16th century] The word *veteran* is from French *vétéran* or Latin *veteranus*, from *vetus* 'old'. **Vet**, the abbreviation, is recorded in use from the mid 19th century.

veterinary [late 18th century] The source of this word is Latin *veterinarius*, from *veterinae* 'cattle'. Noun use as a term for a veterinary

surgeon is recorded from the mid 19th century, as is the abbreviation **vet**.

veto [early 17th century] This is a use of a Latin word meaning literally 'I forbid', used by Roman tribunes of the people when opposing measures of the Senate. Verb use is found from the beginning of the 18th century.

vex [late Middle English] *Vex* is from Old French *vexer*, from Latin *vexare* 'shake, disturb'. The contemporaneous noun **vexation** is from the same source via Old French, or from Latin *vexatio(n-)*.

via [late 18th century] This is an English use of the Latin ablative of *via* 'way, road'. The literal meaning is 'by way of'. The first contexts involved routes and places; later (from the 1930s) the word acquired the sense 'by means of' (*communication via satellite*).

viable [early 19th century] A French word is the source of *viable* based on *vie* 'life', from Latin *vita*. The literal sense is 'able to live'; figurative use expressing 'workable, practicable' arose in the mid 19th century.

viaduct [early 19th century] This word for an arched structure for carrying a railway or road over a valley or low-lying ground is based on Latin *via* 'way', on the pattern of *aqueduct*. The literal meaning is 'way carrier'.

vial [Middle English] This word is an alteration of *phial*.
→ PHIAL

vibrate [late Middle English] The early sense recorded was 'give out (light or sound) as if by vibration' (Tennyson *Aylmer's Field*: Star to star vibrates light). Latin *vibrat-* is the source, the past participial stem of *vibrare* 'move to and fro'. The related word **vibrant** is recorded from the early 17th century when it meant 'move rapidly, vibrate': the form is from the present participial stem of Latin *vibrare*. The noun **vibration** dates from the mid 17th century, from Latin *vibratio(n-)*, from the same Latin verb source.

vicar [Middle English] *Vicar* comes via Anglo-Norman French from Old French *vicaire*, from Latin *vicarius* 'substitute', from *vic-* 'change, turn, place'. The phrase *the Vicar of Christ* is sometimes applied to the Pope in reference to his being an earthly representative of God.

vicarious [mid 17th century] This is based on Latin *vicarius* 'substitute'.
→ VICAR

vice[1] [Middle English] This *vice* in the context of immorality or depravity is via Old French from Latin *vitium* 'vice'. The general sense 'defect, failing' dates from late Middle English

(Chaucer *Squire's Tale*: He with a manly voys sith this message ... Withouten vice of silable or of lettre). Middle English **vicious** had the early sense 'characterized by immorality': it comes from Old French *vicious* or Latin *vitiosus*, from *vitium*. The extension of meaning to 'savage' was first found in descriptions of bad-tempered horses (early 18th century); later (early 19th century) it came to mean 'spiteful' (*vicious tongue*).

vice² [Middle English] This term for a type of tool was originally a word for a 'screw' or 'winch'. It comes from Old French *vis*, from Latin *vitis* 'vine' (the association being the spiral growth of the vine's tendrils).

viceroy [early 16th century] This word for a ruler exercising authority in a colony on behalf of a sovereign is from archaic French, from *vice-* '(standing) in place of' and *roi* 'king'.

vice versa [early 17th century] This is an English use of a Latin phrase meaning literally 'the position being reversed'.

vicinity [mid 16th century] 'Proximity' was the early meaning of *vicinity* from Latin *vicinitas*, from *vicinus* 'neighbour'.

vicissitude [early 17th century] The early word meant 'alternation'; it is from French, or from Latin *vicissitudo*, from *vicissim* 'by turns', from *vic-* 'turn, change'. Current use is in the sense 'change of circumstances' usually with an implication of unpleasantness.

victim [late 15th century] A *victim* (from Latin *victima*) originally referred to a 'creature killed as a religious sacrifice'. The phrase *fall a victim to* arose in the mid 18th century.

victor [Middle English] This word comes from either Anglo-Norman French *victo(u)r* or Latin *victor*, from *vincere* 'conquer', Middle English **victory** is from Anglo-Norman French *victorie*, from Latin *victoria*, a base shared by the late Middle English adjective **victorious**, from Anglo-Norman French *victorious*, from Latin *victoriosus*.

video [1930s] The word *video* is from Latin *videre* 'to see', on the pattern of *audio*.

vie [mid 16th century] This verb meaning 'compete eagerly' is probably a shortening of obsolete *envy* which came via Old French from Latin *invitare* 'to challenge'.

view [Middle English] *View* is from Anglo-Norman French *vieue*, the feminine past participle of *veoir* 'see', from Latin *videre*. The word has been used to describe a 'pictorial representation of a scene' from the late 17th century. The verb dates from the early 16th century.

vigil [Middle English] The early use of *vigil* was to refer to the 'eve' of a festival or holy day. It comes via Old French from Latin *vigilia* 'wakefulness', from *vigil* 'awake'. The phrase *keep vigil* in the context of holding a nocturnal service on the eve of a church festival dates from the mid 16th century; the same phrase in the more general context of keeping watch during a period of sleep dates from the late 17th century. Related words include: late 15th-century **vigilant** (from Latin *vigilant-*, the present participial stem of *vigilare* 'keep awake'), late 16th-century **vigilance** (from French, or from Latin *vigilantia*, from *vigilare*), and mid 19th-century **vigilante** adopted from a Spanish word with the literal meaning 'vigilant'.

vignette [Middle English] Originally as *vyn(n)ett*, this was once used as an architectural term for a carved representation of a vine: it is a use of a French diminutive of *vigne* 'vine'. In later use (mid 18th century), the word came to describe any decorative design in the midst of printed matter or a photographic portrait (mid 19th century), or even a brief verbal description painting a portrait of a person or scene (late 19th century).

vigour [Middle English] *Vigour* is from Old French, from Latin *vigor*, from *vigere* 'be lively'. The adjective **vigorous** (also Middle English) comes via Old French from medieval Latin *vigorosus*, from Latin *vigor*.

vile [Middle English] This comes via Old French from Latin *vilis* 'cheap, base, of low value'. The late Middle English verb **vilify** had the early sense 'lower in value': this is from late Latin *vilificare*, from Latin *vilis*.

village [late Middle English] *Village* is from Old French, from Latin *villa* 'country house', a base which gave (via Italian) the English word **villa** in the early 17th century.

villain [Middle English] *Villain* comes from Old French *vilein*, based on Latin *villa*. The early sense recorded was 'a rustic, boor'; the Middle English word **villein** is a variant spelling which now refers back to a feudal tenant of medieval England, working the land to pay dues to a lord of a manor. Middle English **villainy** is from Old French *vilenie*, from *vilein*.
→ VILLAGE

vim [mid 19th century] Originally a US word, *vim* is commonly thought to be from the Latin accusative of *vis* 'energy'. Some early citations however suggest a purely imitative origin.

vindicate [mid 16th century] 'Deliver, rescue' was the early sense expressed by *vindicate*, from Latin *vindicare* 'claim, avenge', from *vindex, vindic-* 'claimant, avenger'.

vindictive [early 17th century] This word is based on Latin *vindicta* 'vengeance'.

vine [Middle English] Latin *vinum* 'wine' is the base of several words in English: *vine* is from Old French, from Latin *vinea* 'vineyard, vine'; late Middle English **vintage** is an alteration (influenced by *vintner*) of the earlier word *vendage*, from Old French *vendange*, from Latin *vindemia* (literally 'wine removal'); late Middle English **vintner** comes via Anglo-Latin from Old French *vinetier*, from medieval Latin *vinetarius*, from Latin *vinetum* 'vineyard'; late 19th-century **viniculture** is composed of Latin *vinum* and *culture*, on the pattern of words such as *agriculture*.

vinegar [Middle English] The word *vinegar* is from Old French *vyn egre*, based on Latin *vinum* 'wine' and *acer* 'sour'.

violent [Middle English] In early use, *violent* meant 'having a marked or powerful effect'. The source of the word is Old French from Latin *violent-* 'vehement, violent', a base shared by Middle English **violence** (via Old French from Latin *violentia*). The late Middle English verb **violate** is from Latin *violare* 'treat violently'.

violin [late 16th century] This term is from Italian *violino*, a diminutive of *viola* (which also gave early 18th-century **viola** from Italian and Spanish); late 15th-century **viol** is related and originally denoted a violin-like instrument; this is from Old French *viele*, from Provençal *viola* and is probably related to *fiddle*.
→ FIDDLE

viper [early 16th century] *Viper* is from French *vipère* or Latin *vipera*, from *vivus* 'alive' and *parere* 'bring forth' (because the snake gives birth to live young).

virgin [Middle English] *Virgin* is from Old French *virgine*, from Latin *virgo, virgin-*, the base too of Middle English **virginity** from Old French *virginite*, from Latin *virginitas*.

virile [late 15th century] The early sense of the word *virile* was 'characteristic of a man'; it comes from French *viril* or Latin *virilis*, from *vir* 'man'.

virtue [Middle English] *Virtue* is from French *vertu*, from Latin *virtus* 'valour, merit, moral perfection' (from *vir* 'man'). References were made from early times to the *seven virtues* as opposed to the *seven deadly sins*. Latin *virtus* is a source shared by Middle English **virtuous** from Old French *vertuous*, from late Latin *virtuosus*. The early 17th-century word **virtuoso** (from an Italian word meaning literally 'learned, skilful', from late Latin *virtuosus*) is related. The adjective **virtual** dating from late Middle English (and also from Latin *virtus* 'virtue') included the early sense 'possessing certain virtues': this is from medieval Latin *virtualis*, suggested by late Latin *virtuosus*. The meaning 'in effect, in essence (but not actual)' dates from the mid 17th century; this was extended to computing contexts from the 1950s in the sense 'not existing physically' (*virtual memory*).

virus [late Middle English] This was originally a term for the 'venom of a snake'; it is a use of a Latin word meaning literally 'slimy liquid, poison'. The early medical sense (superseded by the current use as a result of improved scientific understanding) was 'a substance produced in the body as the result of disease, especially one that is capable of infecting others with the same disease'. Late Middle English **virulent** originally described a poisoned wound: this is from Latin *virulentus*, from *virus* 'poison'.

visa [mid 19th century] *Visa* comes via French from Latin *visa*, the feminine past participial form of *videre* 'to see'.

viscount [late Middle English] *Viscount* is from Old French *visconte*, from medieval Latin *vicecomes, vicecomit-*. Historically a *viscount* was a person acting as the deputy of a count or earl in the administration of a district. Later use of the term was as a title for a member of the fourth order of the British peerage ranking between an earl and a baron, a use which dates from the reign of Henry VI, when John, Baron Beaumont, was created Viscount Beaumont by letters patent of 12 February 1440.

viscous [late Middle English] *Viscous* is from Anglo-Norman French *viscous* or late Latin *viscosus*, from Latin *viscum* 'birdlime'.

vision [Middle English] A *vision* initially referred to a 'supernatural apparition'; it comes via Old French from Latin *visio(n-)*. The source verb is Latin *videre* 'to see', the base too of Middle English **visible** (from Old French, or from Latin *visibilis*) and late Middle English **visibility** (from French *visibilite* or late Latin *visibilitas*, from Latin *visibilis*).

visit [Middle English] *Visit* is from Old French *visiter* or Latin *visitare* 'go to see, go to inspect', a frequentative (= verb of repeated action) of *visare* 'to view', from *videre* 'to see'. Early use included a notion of inflicting hurt or punishment (*visited with the Plague*) as well as of going to be with someone socially. Late Middle English **visitor** is from Anglo-Norman French *visitour*, from Old French *visiter*.

visor [Middle English] The word *visor* is from Anglo-Norman French *viser*, from Old French *vis* 'face', from Latin *visus* 'face'.

vista [mid 17th century] An English adoption of an Italian word, *vista* means literally 'view', from *visto* 'seen', the past participle of *vedere* 'see', from Latin *videre*.

visual [late Middle English] This word originally described a beam imagined to project from the eye making vision possible; it comes from late Latin *visualis*, from Latin *visus* 'sight', from *videre* 'to see'. The current noun sense referring to a 'picture' serving as an illustration dates from the 1950s.

vital [late Middle English] *Vital* comes via Old French from Latin *vitalis*, from *vita* 'life'. The sense 'essential' dates from the early 17th century; the plural *vitals* meaning 'essential organs of the body' dates from the same period. **Vitality** is late 16th-century from Latin *vitalitas*, from *vitalis*.

vitamin [early 20th century] *Vitamin* is a combination of Latin *vita* 'life' and the word *amine*, because *vitamins* were originally thought to contain an amino acid.

vitreous [late Middle English] This word is based on Latin *vitreus* (from *vitrum* 'glass').

vitriol [late Middle English] The cruel and bitter criticism referred to as *vitriol* is by association with its use to mean 'sulphuric acid'. It comes from Old French, or from medieval Latin *vitriolum*, from Latin *vitrum* 'glass'.

vivacious [mid 17th century] The word *vivacious* is based on Latin *vivax*, *vivac-* 'lively, vigorous' (from *vivere* 'to live').

vivid [mid 17th century] Latin *vividus* (from *vivere* 'to live') is the source of *vivid* in English. The early sense was 'full of life, vigorous'; later the word was applied to colours in the sense 'bright, intense' and, in the mid 19th century to feelings (Charlotte Brontë *Villette*: His passions were strong, his aversions and attachments alike vivid).

vivisect [mid 19th century] The verb is a back-formation (by removal of the suffix) from early 18th-century **vivisection**, from Latin *vivus* 'living', on the pattern of *dissection*.

vixen [late Middle English] The early spelling was *fixen*, perhaps from the Old English adjective *fyxen* 'of a fox'. The *v-* is from the form of the word in southern English dialect. The word was applied to an ill-tempered quarrelsome woman from the late 16th century.

vocabulary [mid 16th century] This was first used to denote a list of words with definitions or translations; it is from medieval Latin *vocabularius*, from Latin *vocabulum*, from *vocare* 'to name, call'.

vocation [late Middle English] A *vocation* as a 'calling' is from Old French, or from Latin *vocatio(n-)*, from *vocare* 'to call'. The word was first used in reference to God calling someone to fulfil a particular role; it was generalized to mean 'one's ordinary occupation' from the mid 16th century.

vogue [late 16th century] The *vogue* was the early phrasal use, referring to 'the prime place in popular opinion'. It is from French, from Italian *voga* 'rowing, fashion', from *vogare* 'row, go well'. The sense 'the prevailing fashion' is found from the mid 17th century.

voice [Middle English] *Voice* is from Old French *vois*, from Latin *vox, voc-*, the source too of late Middle English **vocal** (via Latin *vocalis*). Current senses of the noun *vocal* date from the 1920s. The late 16th-century verb **vociferate** (also based on Latin *vox*) is from the Latin verb *vociferari* 'exclaim'; Latin *ferre* 'to carry' is the other formative element.

void [Middle English] *Void* formerly meant 'unoccupied' either in relation to a see, benefice, or secular office having no incumbent, or of a place having no inhabitants. It is from a dialect variant of Old French *vuide*, related to Latin *vacare* 'vacate'. The verb is partly a shortening of *avoid*, reinforced by Old French *voider*. Figurative noun use indicating 'an empty feeling, a feeling of unsatisfied desire' (Tennyson *In Memoriam*: [Tears] Which weep a loss for ever new, A void where heart on heart reposed) is first recorded in the late 17th century.

volatile [Middle English] This was first used as a noun meaning a 'creature that flies', and it was also a collective word for 'birds'. It derives from Old French *volatil* or Latin *volatilis*, from *volare* 'to fly'. The association of the word with temperament is found from the mid 17th century (*volatile temper*).

volcano [early 17th century] This is an adoption of an Italian word from Latin *Volcanus* 'Vulcan', the god of fire and of metal-working in Roman mythology. The adjective **volcanic** is late 18th-century from French *volcanique*, from *volcan*.

volition [early 17th century] This word often found in the phrase *of one's own volition* was first used in reference to a 'decision or choice made after deliberation'. The source is either French, or medieval Latin *volitio(n-)*, from *volo* 'I wish'.

volley [late 16th century] *Volley* is from French *volée*, based on Latin *volare* 'to fly'. Early use included the context of firearms discharging a salvo or of missiles flying (Milton *Paradise Lost*: Over head the dismal hiss Of fiery Darts in flaming volies flew); this was also extended early figuratively to words and oaths (*volley of abuse*). The sports term *volley* in tennis is also late 16th-century.

voluble [late 16th century] *Voluble* is from French, or from Latin *volubilis*, from *volvere* 'to roll'. Earlier use in late Middle English included the senses 'rotating about an axis' (Milton *Paradise Lost*: Or this less volubil Earth By shorter flight to th' East had left him there) and 'having a tendency to change', which were also meanings of the Latin word.

volume [late Middle English] *Volume* was originally a roll of parchment containing written matter; it is from Old French *volum(e)*, from Latin *volumen* 'a roll', from *volvere* 'to roll'. Another semantic branch of the word involves 'quantity, amount': this springs from the obsolete meaning 'size or extent (of a book)' (dating from the early 16th century). Early 17th-century **voluminous** is partly from late Latin *voluminosus* 'having many coils', partly from Latin *volumen*, *volumin-*.

voluntary [late Middle English] *Voluntary* is from Old French *volontaire* or Latin *voluntarius*, from *voluntas* 'will'. The word **volunteer** dates from the late 16th century as a noun, mid 18th century as a verb, with military reference; it comes from French *volontaire* 'voluntary'.

voluptuous [late Middle English] *Voluptuous* is from Old French *voluptueux* or Latin *voluptuosus*, from *voluptas* 'pleasure'. The word became associated with fullness of form suggesting sensuous pleasure from the early 19th century.

vomit [late Middle English] *Vomit* is from the Old French noun *vomite* or Latin *vomitus*, from *vomere* 'to vomit'.

voracious [mid 17th century] *Voracious* is based on Latin *vorax*, *vorac-* (from *vorare* 'devour').

vortex [mid 17th century] This is an English use of the Latin word *vortex*, *vortic-* meaning literally 'eddy', a variant of *vertex*.
→ VERTICAL

vote [late Middle English] *Vote* is from Latin *votum* 'a vow, wish', from *vovere* 'to vow'. The verb dates from the mid 16th century. The word **votive** (late 16th century) meaning 'offered in fulfilment of a vow' is from Latin *votivus*, from *votum*. The original sense 'expressing a desire' is preserved in *votive Mass*, a Mass celebrated in the Roman Catholic Church for a special occasion.

vouch [Middle English] First used as a legal term in the sense 'summon (a person) to court to prove title to property', *vouch* is from Old French *voucher* 'summon', based on Latin *vocare* 'to call'. The noun **voucher** (early 16th century) is from *vouch*; this was also found earliest as a legal term as a 'summoning to court'. In the early 17th century, the word came to mean 'a piece of evidence' and in the late 17th century 'a written document as proof of delivery or attesting the correctness of accounts'. It was in the 1940s that the word started to be used as a term for a document exchangeable for goods or services. Middle English **vouchsafe** was originally expressed by the phrase *vouch* something *safe* on someone, i.e. 'warrant the secure conferment of (something on someone)'.

vow [Middle English] *Vow* is from Old French *vou*, from Latin *votum*; *vows* in the ecclesiastical context 'engagement to follow a religious life of devotion to God' dates from late Middle English. It was applied in the sense 'solemn promise of fidelity' from the late 16th century (Shakespeare *Midsummer Night's Dream*: By all the vowes that ever men have broke, (In number more than ever women spoke)). The verb *vow* is from Old French *vouer*.
→ VOTE

vowel [Middle English] This is from Old French *vouel*, from Latin *vocalis* (*littera*) 'vocal (letter)'.

voyage [Middle English] *Voyage* was first used as a noun denoting a 'journey' by sea or by land; it is from Old French *voiage*, from Latin *viaticum* initially meaning 'provisions for a journey' and, in late Latin, 'journey'. From the late 15th century the phrase *boon voyage* became common meaning 'prosperous journey'; after 1600 *boon* was consciously recognized as French and dropped: *bon voyage* is recorded from the late 17th century.

vulgar [late Middle English] *Vulgar* is from Latin *vulgaris*, from *vulgus* 'common people'. The original senses were 'used in ordinary calculations' (surviving in *vulgar fraction*) and 'in ordinary use, used by the people' (surviving in *vulgar tongue*). The sense 'coarse and common, uncultured' dates from the mid 17th century.

vulnerable [early 17th century] This comes from late Latin *vulnerabilis*, from Latin *vulnerare* 'to wound', from *vulnus* 'wound'.

vulture [late Middle English] The word *vulture* is from Anglo-Norman French *vultur*, from Latin *vulturius*. Figurative use in application to people as rapacious arose in the early 17th century.

wacky [mid 19th century] This was originally a dialect word based on the noun *whack*.
→ WHACK

wad [mid 16th century] *Wad* originally referred to 'wadding'; it is perhaps related to Dutch *watten*, French *ouate* 'padding, cotton wool'. In the late 16th century, *wad* was used as a term for 'a bundle of hay or straw' or a 'small bundle' of a flexible material used as a plug. In US usage it came to refer to a 'roll of banknotes' from the late 18th century.

waddle [late 16th century] The word *waddle* is perhaps a frequentative (= verb of repeated action) of *wade*. In Stock Exchange slang the phrase *waddle out* has been used in connection with someone becoming a 'lame duck' or defaulter since the late 18th century.
→ WADE

wade [Old English] Old English *wadan* included the senses 'move onward' and 'penetrate'; it is from a Germanic word meaning 'go (through)', from an Indo-European root shared by Latin *vadere* 'go'. The sense 'walk through (water or a soft substance such as mud)' was also found early.

wafer [late Middle English] *Wafer* (originally *wafre*) is from an Anglo-Norman French variant of Old French *gaufre* from Middle Low German *wâfel* 'waffle'. The word was originally used for a 'light thin crisp cake' but from the early 18th century it was also applied to a small disc of flour mixed with gum which could then be moistened and used for sealing letters.

waffle¹ [late 17th century] This word meaning 'idle chatter' (a usage in printers' slang) was originally dialect used in the sense 'yap, yelp (of a small dog)'. Imitative in origin, it is a frequentative (= verb of repeated action) of dialect *waff* 'yelp'.

waffle² [mid 18th century] This *waffle* referring to a type of cake made from batter is from Dutch *wafel*.
→ WAFER

waft [early 16th century] 'Escort (a ship)' was the early sense recorded for *waft*, a back-formation (by removal of the suffix) from obsolete *wafter* 'armed convoy vessel'. Low German and Dutch *wachter* is the source, from *wachten* 'to guard'. A sense 'convey by water, carry over' gave rise to the current use of the verb 'carry through the air'.

wag¹ [Middle English] *Wag* was first used as a verb. It is from the Germanic base of Old English *wagian* 'to sway'. The general early sense was 'be in motion': this was sometimes applied to boats expressing the sense 'rock'; sometimes to tongues (*set tongues wagging*) with a notion of idle gossip, sometimes simply in the sense 'make one's way' (Bunyan *Pilgrim's Progress*: They made a pretty good shift to wagg along). The word **waggle** (late 16th century) is a frequentative (= verb of repeated action) of *wag*.

wag² [mid 16th century] This *wag* is a dated term for someone making facetious jokes; it originally denoted a young man or mischievous boy, as well as being used as a term of endearment to an infant. The word is probably from obsolete *waghalter* (*halter* here meaning 'rope, noose'), used as a term for a 'person likely to be hanged'.

wage [Middle English] *Wage* is from Anglo-Norman French and Old Northern French, of Germanic origin. Early use was in the sense 'pledge, security' synonymous with Middle English *gage* to which it is related along with Scots *wed* meaning 'a pledge'. *Wage* was also in use early as a term for 'a payment for services rendered' (often in the plural *wages*). The phrase *wage war* (late Middle English) developed from the sense 'offer promises that something would be fulfilled'.
→ WED

wager [Middle English] *Wager* in early use included the sense 'solemn pledge'. It source is Anglo-Norman French *wageure*, from *wager* 'to wage'. Its use in reference to a 'sum of money laid down as a stake' is also exemplified early.

wagon [late 15th century] *wagon* is from Dutch *wagen*; it is related to the archaic synonym **wain** (in Old English *wæg(e)n*) of Germanic origin and related to Dutch *wagen* and German *Wagen*, as well as to *way* and *weigh*.
→ WAY; WEIGH

waif [late Middle English] *Waif* is from an Anglo-Norman French variant of Old Northern French *gaif*, probably of Scandinavian origin.

Early use was often in *waif and stray*, as a legal term for a piece of property found and (if unclaimed) falling to the lord of the manor. The sense 'abandoned and neglected child' dates from the late 18th century; the notion of 'thinness' through hunger led to the word being used in fashion contexts referring to a very thin model, in the 1990s.

wail [Middle English] *Wail* is from Old Norse; it is related to *woe*. The word has positive connotations as US slang in jazz contexts when *wailing* refers to exceptional playing with feeling (1950s).
→ WOE

wainscot [Middle English] This is from Middle Low German *wagenschot*, apparently from *wagen* 'wagon' and *schot*, probably meaning 'partition'.

waist [late Middle English] *Waist* apparently represents the development of an Old English word from the Germanic root of *wax* 'increase'.
→ WAX²

wait [Middle English] *Wait* is from Old Northern French *waitier*, of Germanic origin; related to *wake*. Early senses included 'lie in wait (for)', 'observe carefully', and 'be watchful'. Noun use has included, from early times, use as a term for a 'watchman'. The plural *waits* from late Middle English described a small group of wind instrumentalists employed by a city at the public expense to entertain councillors or citizens as a municipal band; this was applied more particularly from the late 18th century to a band of musicians and singers playing seasonal music for gratuities in the lead up to Christmas.
→ WAKE¹

waive [Middle English] *Waive* was originally a legal term relating to removal of the protection of the law. It is from an Anglo-Norman French variant of Old French *gaiver* 'allow to become a waif, abandon'. The sense 'refrain from applying or enforcing' dates from the mid 17th century.

wake¹ [Old English] In Old English the verb *wake* is only recorded in the strong past tense *wōc*. The strong verb probably had the sense 'become awake' but in Middle English the weak verb *wacian* 'remain awake, hold a vigil' had its influence causing indiscriminate use of the two verbs. Dutch *waken* and German *wachen* are related. Also of Germanic origin and related to *wake* is Old English **waken** (as *wæcnan*) meaning 'be aroused'.
→ WATCH

wake² [late 15th century] This *wake* now meaning 'trail of disturbed water' originally denoted a track made by a person or thing. It is probably via Middle Low German from Old Norse *vǫk*, *vaka* 'hole or opening in ice'.

walk [Old English] Old English *wealcan*, of Germanic origin, meant 'roll, toss' and 'wander'. The sense 'move about', and specifically 'go about on foot', arose in Middle English. The specific noun use 'branch of activity' (*various walks of science*) dates from the mid 18th century, the period from which the phrase *walk of life* is recorded.

wall [Old English] Old English *wall* is from Latin *vallum* 'rampart', from *vallus* 'stake'. Of the idioms: *go to the wall* 'succumb' is found from the late 16th century; *go over the wall* 'escape from prison' is 1930s; *up the wall* meaning 'angry' dates from the 1950s; *off the wall* 'zany' is 1960s.

wallet [late Middle English] A *wallet* was initially 'a bag for provisions'. It comes probably via Anglo-Norman French from a Germanic word related to *well*. Current use as a term for a flat holder for bank notes (originally US) dates from the mid 19th century.
→ WELL²

wallop [Middle English] *Wallop* was first used as a noun denoting 'a horse's gallop'. It is from Old Northern French *walop* (as a noun) and *waloper* (as a verb), perhaps from a Germanic phrase meaning 'run well', from the bases of *well* and *leap*. Sense extension from 'gallop' led to the senses 'bubbling noise of a boiling liquid' and then 'sound of a clumsy movement', which gave the current sense 'strike'.
→ GALLOP; WELL¹

wallow [Old English] Old English *walwian* meant 'to roll about' It is Germanic in origin, from an Indo-European root shared by Latin *volvere* 'to roll'. Figurative use was early (*wallow in self-pity*).

wally [1960s] This informal word is perhaps a shortened form of the given name *Walter*. There are many theories of the origin: one story tells of a *Wally* who became separated from companions at a 1960s pop festival; the name, announced at frequent intervals over a loudspeaker, was taken up as a chant by the crowd.

waltz [late 18th century] This word is from German *Walzer*, from *walzen* 'revolve'. The transferred verb use 'move nimbly' (*turned and waltzed off down the corridor*) arose in the mid 19th century.

wan [Old English] The origin of Old English *wann* is unknown; it was mainly used in poetry in the sense 'dark, black'; it also referred to the face as 'discoloured by disease'. The meaning 'pallid' is Middle English with the phrase *pale and wan* recorded from late Middle English.

wand [Middle English] *Wand* is from Old Norse *vǫndr*, probably of Germanic origin and related to *wend* and the verb *wind*; the semantic base is 'suppleness, flexibility'. The word became connected with magic in late Middle English; the notion of transformation was taken up again in the 1970s when a *wand* was adopted as a term for a hand-held electronic device passed over a bar code to read the data and convert it into computer-compatible form.
→ WEND; WIND²

wander [Old English] Old English *wandrian*, of West Germanic origin, is related to *wend* and *wind*. The word has been used of the mind losing concentration since late Middle English and of the eyes straying to other objects of interest from the late 16th century.
→ WEND; WIND²

wane [Old English] Old English *wanian* 'lessen' (*wax and wane*) is Germanic in origin and related to Latin *vanus* 'vain'.

wangle [late 19th century] *Wangle* is first recorded as printers' slang. The origin is unknown but is perhaps based on the verb *waggle*.
→ WAG¹

want [Middle English] The noun is from Old Norse *vant*, the neuter of *vanr* 'lacking'; the verb is from Old Norse *vanta* 'be lacking'. The original notion of 'lack' was early extended to 'need' and from this developed the sense 'desire'. The 1980s term **wannabe** represents a pronunciation of *want to be*.

wanton [Middle English] The spelling in Middle English was *wantowen* 'rebellious, lacking discipline', from *wan-* 'badly' and Old English *togen* 'trained' (related to *team* and *tow*).
→ TEAM; TOW

war [late Old English] Late Old English *werre* is from an Anglo-Norman French variant of Old French *guerre*, from a Germanic base shared by *worse*. Curiously, no Germanic nation in early historic times had any word properly meaning 'war', although there were poetical words, ones used in proverbs and in personal names expressing that sense. The Romanic-speaking peoples took Germanic *werra* 'confusion, discord' as the closest term; the continental Germanic languages later developed separate words (e.g. German *Krieg*). The Middle English word **warrior** is from Old Northern French *werreior*, a variant of Old French *guerreior*, from *guerreier* 'make war', from *guerre* 'war'.
→ WORSE

warble [late Middle English] From Old French *werble*, English *warble* was in early use 'a tune or melody' with a basic notion of 'trilling'; later, influenced by the verb, it came to denote an act of warbling such as gentle bird-song.

ward [Old English] One meaning of the Old English noun *weard* was 'keeping a look-out'; the verb *weardian* meant 'keep safe, guard'. Of Germanic origin, the word was reinforced in Middle English by the Old Northern French noun *warde*, and the verb *warder* meaning 'to guard'. In this period, 'guardianship' was specifically applied to a child or minor legally incapable of governing his own affairs; it was also (during the 15th century) applied to the minor himself. Other semantic branches of *ward* include 'administrative area' (*wards in this borough*): this developed from an Old English sense 'body of guards' which led to 'place for guarding', 'garrison', 'appointed station'.

warden [Middle English] A *warden* was originally 'a guardian or protector'. The word comes from Anglo-Norman French and Old Northern French *wardein*, a variant of Old French *guarden* 'guardian'. In current use *warden* refers to various offices involving the overseeing of work, the custodianship of property, authority over an area or a group.

warder [late Middle English] A *warder* once denoted a watchman or sentinel; it is from Anglo-Norman French *wardere*, from Old Northern French *warder* 'to guard'. The current sense 'prison guard' dates from the mid 19th century.

wardrobe [Middle English] The early sense was 'private chamber', often one adjoining the 'chamber' (= bedroom) where clothing and sometimes armour were kept. In the 16th to 18th centuries it referred commonly to a room for keeping costly objects. It is from Old Northern French *warderobe*, a variant of Old French *garderobe* (from *garder* 'to keep' and *robe* 'dress').

ware [Old English] Old English *waru*, of Germanic origin, meant 'commodities' and may be the same word as Scots *ware* 'cautiousness', having the primary sense 'object of care'.

warlock [Old English] Old English *wærloga* was a word for a 'traitor, scoundrel, monster' as well as for 'the Devil'; it comes from *wær* 'covenant' and an element related to *leogan* 'belie, deny'. From its application to the Devil, the word was transferred in Middle English to a person in league with the Devil, and hence a sorcerer. It was chiefly Scots until given wider currency by the popularity of Sir Walter Scott's novels.

warm [Old English] Old English *wearm* (as an adjective) and *werman*, *wearmian* (verb forms) are Germanic in origin; Dutch and German *warm* are related, from an Indo-European root shared by Latin *formus* 'warm' and Greek *thermos* 'hot'.

warn [Old English] A West Germanic base meaning 'be cautious' gave rise to Old English *war(e)nian, wearnian* 'to warn'; the noun **warning** is also Old English (as *war(e)nung*).

warp [Old English] The Old English forms were *weorpan* (as a verb) and *wearp* (as a noun); the word is from a Germanic source and related to Dutch *werpen* and German *werfen* 'to throw'. Early verb senses included 'throw', 'fling open', and 'hit (with a missile)'; the sense 'bend' dates from late Middle English. The noun was originally a term in weaving.

warrant [Middle English] The early noun senses were 'protector' and 'safeguard'; as a verb, it meant 'keep safe from danger'. The form comes from variants of Old French *guarant* (noun), *guarantir* (verb), of Germanic origin. Middle English **warranty** is from Anglo-Norman French *warantie*, a variant of *garantie*. Early use was as a legal term for a covenant annexed to a conveyance of property, in which the vendor affirmed the security of the title.
→ GUARANTEE

warren [late Middle English] The word *warren* is from an Anglo-Norman French and Old Northern French variant of Old French *garenne* 'game park', of Gaulish origin. In English the word was first applied to a piece of enclosed land for breeding game; it was subsequently applied to a piece of land for breeding rabbits and hares.

wart [Old English] Old English *wearte*, of Germanic origin, is related to Dutch *wrat* and German *Warze*. The idiom *warts and all* dates from the 1930s (W. S. Maugham *Cakes and Ale*: *Don't you think it would be more interesting if you went the whole hog and drew him warts and all?*). The reference is a popular summary of Cromwell's instructions to the court painter Lely in 1763: *I desire you would use all your skill to paint my picture truly like me and not flatter me at all; but remark all these roughnesses, pimples, warts, and everything as you see me.*

wary [late 15th century] The word *wary* is based on Old English (now archaic) *ware* 'aware'.

wash [Old English] The Old English verb *wæscan* is Germanic in origin, related to Dutch *wassen*, German *waschen*, and to English *water*. The main noun senses branch into: 'act of cleansing' (*a quick wash and brush-up*), 'washing movement of water' (*the wash of the waves*), 'liquid refuse' (*hogwash*), 'alluvial deposit' (*left

its wash on the plateau*), and 'watery infusion' in the context of beer brewing.
→ WATER

wasp [Old English] Old English *wæfs, wæps, wæsp* is West Germanic in origin, from an Indo-European root shared by Latin *vespa*; it may be related to *weave* (from the web-like form of the insect's nest).
→ WEAVE¹

waste [Middle English] The noun *waste* is from Old Northern French *wast(e)*, the verb from Old Northern French *waster*, based on Latin *vastus* 'unoccupied, uncultivated'. The idiomatic phrase *lay waste* dates from the early 16th century; *waste* in the sense 'refuse' is found from the late 17th century.

watch [Old English] Old English *wæcce* meant 'watchfulness'; *wæccende* meant 'remaining awake'; the word is related to *wake*. The sense 'small timepiece' probably developed by way of a sense 'alarm device attached to a clock'.
→ WAKE¹

water [Old English] The Old English noun *wæter* and verb *wæterian* are Germanic in origin and related to Dutch *water* and German *Wasser*, from an Indo-European root shared by Russian *voda*, also by Latin *unda* 'wave' and Greek *hudōr* 'water'. Of the compounds:

■ **waterlogged** (mid 18th century) is the past participle of the verb *waterlog* 'make (a ship) unmanageable by flooding'. The meaning of the *log* element is obscure but may convey 'reduce (a ship) to the condition of a log'.

■ **watershed** (early 19th century) had the early meaning 'ridge of high ground', suggested by German *Wasserscheide*.

wave [Old English] The Old English verb *wafian* is from the Germanic base of *waver*; the noun is by alteration of Middle English *wawe* '(sea) wave', influenced by the verb. Use of the word in the context of hairdressing dates from the mid 19th century (Dickens *Our Mutual Friend*: Bella ... employed both her hands in giving her hair an additional wave). In the same period the word was also starting to be used for any swell of feeling or opinion (Dickens *Haunted House*: What flood of thought came, wave upon wave, across my mind!). The idiom *make waves* dates from the 1960s. Combinations such as *Mexican wave* describing a wavelike effect when spectators stand, raise their arms, and sit again in successive crowd sections, originated at the World Cup football competition held in Mexico City in 1986.
→ WAVER

waver [Middle English] *Waver* is from Old Norse *vafra* 'flicker, move unsteadily', of Germanic origin. Early use included both 'show signs of indecision' and 'wander, rove without a fixed destination'.

→ WAVE

wax¹ [Old English] Old English *wæx, weax* 'beeswax' is Germanic in origin, related to Dutch *was* and German *Wachs*. The verb dates from late Middle English. It is possible that the root is identical with that of *wax* meaning 'grow' with the etymological sense 'that which grows in the honeycomb'.

wax² [Old English] Old English *weaxan* 'grow, increase' is Germanic in origin, related to Dutch *wassen* and German *wachsen*, from an Indo-European root shared by Greek *auxanein* and Latin *augere* 'to increase'. The word was used early in connection with the moon *waxing and waning*; it also expressed 'become' without the notion of increase (*waxed lyrical*). The compound *waxwork* describing an object modelled in wax dates from the late 17th century.

way [Old English] Old English *weg*, of Germanic origin, is related to Dutch *weg* and German *Weg*, from a base meaning 'move, carry'. It has the main senses: 'track, path' (*parting of the ways*), 'course of travel' (*knew his way around*; *the food went down the wrong way*), and 'course of action' (Gray *Elegy*: They kept the noiseless tenor of their way). Of the idiomatic phrases: *by way of* is late Middle English; *out of the way* is recorded from the late 15th century; *way of thinking, have a way with one,* and *have everything one's own way* date from the early 18th century; *in a small way* is found from the mid 18th century; *in a big way* dates from the 1920s.

wayward [late Middle English] *Wayward* is a shortening of obsolete *awayward* 'turned away'.

we [Old English] Of Germanic origin, *we* is related to Dutch *wij* and German *wir*. Use of *we* by a sovereign (*royal 'we'*) to mean 'I' dates from early times.

weak [Old English] Old English *wāc* meant 'pliant', 'of little worth', and 'not steadfast'; it was reinforced in Middle English by Old Norse *veikr*, from a Germanic base meaning 'yield, give way'. The sense 'over-diluted' (*weak tea*) is found from the late 16th century; so too 'ineffective' (Shakespeare *Henry VI part 1*: My ancient Incantations are too weak). The phrase *weakest link* dates from the mid 19th century.

weal [early 19th century] This *weal* describing a red swollen mark is a variant of *wale* (describing a ridge on a textured woven fabric), influenced by the obsolete verb *wheal* meaning 'to suppurate'.

wealth [Middle English] The early spelling was *welthe*: this is from *well* or Old English *wela* meaning 'wealth, well-being' (of West Ger-

manic origin; related to *well*) on the pattern of *health*.

→ WELL¹

wean [Old English] Old English *wenian* 'accustom (a child) to the loss of its mother's milk', of Germanic origin, is related to Dutch *wennen* and German *entwöhnen*.

weapon [Old English] Old English *wǣp(e)n* comes from a Germanic source; it is related to Dutch *wapen* and German *Waffe*.

wear [Old English] Old English *werian*, of Germanic origin, is from an Indo-European root shared by Latin *vestis* 'clothing'. The main sense strands are: 'be clothed in', 'waste or destroy by use' (*worn shoes*) used primarily in connection with clothing initially, 'deteriorate, suffer gradual destruction' (*his patience wore out*), 'last' (*he's wearing well*), 'pass away' in time contexts in poetical use (Tennyson *Love and Duty*: Till now the dark was worn, and overhead The lights of sunset and of sunrise mix'd in that brief night), and the Scots use 'proceed' (*wore westward out of sight*). The phrase *the worse for wear* dates from the late 18th century.

weary [Old English] Old English *wērig, wǣrig* is from a West Germanic source. The primary sense was perhaps 'bewildered, stupefied'.

weasel [Old English] Old English *wesle, wesule*, of West Germanic origin, is related to Dutch *wezel* and German *Wiesel*. Certain characteristics of the animal have been transferred to its derogatory use in the description of people from the late 16th century (Shakespeare *Henry V*: For once the Eagle (England) being In prey, To her unguarded Nest, the Weazell (Scot) Comes sneaking, and so sucks her Princely Eggs). The US phrase *weasel word* (early 20th century) refers to an ambiguous word used to reduce the force of a concept being expressed (from the analogy of a weasel sucking out the contents of an egg); the more general verb sense 'extricate' (*weaseled his way out of doing the chores*) arose in the 1950s.

weather [Old English] Old English *weder*, of Germanic origin, is related to Dutch *weer* and German *Wetter*, and probably also to the English noun *wind* from a root meaning 'to blow'. The phrase *weather permitting* dates from the early 18th century; *under the weather* meaning 'indisposed' is recorded from the early 19th century. Verb use in the sense 'come safely through' dates from the mid 17th century, with *weather the storm* recorded in the later years of that century.

→ WIND¹

weave¹ [Old English] Old English *wefan*, of Germanic origin, is from an Indo-European root shared by Greek *huphē* 'web' and Sanskrit *ūrṇavābhi* 'spider', literally 'wool-weaver'. Figurative use dates from the mid 16th century (Shakespeare *Henry VI part 2*: My Brayne, more busie than the laboring spider, Weaves tedious Snares to trap mine Enemies). Related to *weave* is Old English **weft** (*weft(a)*).

weave² [late 16th century] This verb meaning 'thread one's way' (*weaving in and out of the traffic*) is probably from Old Norse *veifa* 'to wave, brandish'.

web [Old English] Old English *web(b)* was a term for 'woven fabric'. Of Germanic origin, it is related to Dutch *web* and to English *weave*. Early use of the verb was in the sense 'weave (fabric) on a loom'. The past participial adjective *webbed* as in *webbed feet* dates from the mid 17th century.
→WEAVE¹

wed [Old English] Old English *weddian* is from the Germanic base of Scots *wed* 'a pledge'; it is related to Latin *vas* 'surety'. The noun **wedding** is also Old English (*weddung*). **Wedlock** dates from late Old English as *wedlāc* meaning 'marriage vow', from *wed* 'pledge' and the suffix *-lāc* expressing action.

wedge [Old English] The Old English noun *wecg* is from a Germanic source, related to Dutch *wig*. The shape and use of the object have led to various applications of the word: *wedge of cheese* (late 16th century), *a wedge of troops* (early 17th century), *wedge of high pressure* (late 19th century), *wedge heel* (1950s), *wedge hairstyle* (1970s). The idiom *the thin end of the wedge* dates from the mid 19th century.

wee [Middle English] This word meaning 'extremely small' was originally a noun in Scots, usually as *a little wee* 'a little bit'. It comes from Old English *wēg(e)* and was rare as an adjective in Scottish writers before 1721 despite being recorded as early as the 15th century and despite evidence in Shakespeare that it was known in English use early in the 17th century. The phrase *the wee small hours* appears to have been inspired by an alteration (by Charlotte Brontë in *Shirley*) of a line in Burns's poem *Death and Dr. Hornbook* in his *Poems and Songs* 1787: the auld kirk-hammer strak the bell Some wee, short hour ayont the twal. **Weeny**, based on *wee* dates from the late 18th century, on the pattern of *tiny*.

weed [Old English] The Old English noun *wēod* and verb *wēodian* are of unknown origin; the Dutch verb *wieden* is related. The plural *weeds* was used to mean 'mourning clothes' from the late 16th century, surviving in the phrase *widow's weeds*. Use of the noun as a term of contempt for a thin person with no muscle

or stamina dates from the mid 19th century. Figurative verb use (*weeded out the less qualified applicants*) is found in examples from the early 16th century.

week [Old English] Old English *wice*, of Germanic origin, is related to Dutch *week* and German *Woche*, from a base probably meaning 'sequence, series'. There is no reason to suppose that the word referred to a specific period of seven days, before the Germanic peoples came into contact with the Romans.

weep [Old English] A Germanic word in origin, Old English *wēpan* is probably imitative of the sound of moaning and sobbing, although in modern use the verb indicates the more or less silent shedding of tears. *Weep* is now normally restricted to literary use, because the later commonly used word *cry* conveys sound as well as tears.

weigh [Old English] Old English *wegan*, of Germanic origin, is related to Dutch *wegen* 'weigh' and German *bewegen* 'move', from an Indo-European root shared by Latin *vehere* 'convey'. Early senses included 'transport from one place to another' and 'raise up'.

weight [Old English] Old English *(ge)wiht*, of Germanic origin, is related to Dutch *wicht* and German *Gewicht*. The form of the word has been influenced by *weigh*.
→WEIGH

weir [Old English] Old English *wer* is from *werian* 'dam up'.

weird [Old English] Old English *wyrd*, of Germanic origin, meant 'destiny'. The adjective originally meant (late Middle English) 'having the power to control destiny', and was used especially in *the Weird Sisters*, originally referring to the Fates, later the witches in Shakespeare's *Macbeth*; the latter use gave rise to the sense 'unearthly' (early 19th century).

welcome [Old English] The Old English word *wilcuma* meant 'a person whose coming is pleasing'; the verb form was *wilcumian*, from *wil-* 'desire, pleasure' and *cuman* 'come'. The first element was later changed to *wel-* 'well', influenced by Old French *bien venu* or Old Norse *velkominn*.

weld [late 16th century] 'Become united' was the early meaning of *weld*, an alteration (probably influenced by the past participle) of *well* in the obsolete sense 'melt or weld (heated metal)'.
→WELL²

well¹ [Old English] Old English *wel(l)* 'happy, in a state of good fortune', of Germanic origin, is related to Dutch *wel* and German *wohl*, and

probably also to the verb *will*. Vowel lengthening in Middle English gave rise to the current Scots form *weel*. Middle English **welfare** is from the adverb *well* and the verb *fare* 'perform'.
→ WILL¹

well² [Old English] Old English *wella* 'spring of water', of Germanic origin from a base meaning 'boil, bubble up', is related to Dutch *wel* and German *Welle* 'a wave'.

Welsh [Old English] The Old English noun *Welisc*, *Wælisc* is from a Germanic word meaning 'foreigner', from Latin *Volcae*, the name of a Celtic people.

wench [Middle English] *Wench* is an abbreviation of obsolete *wenchel* 'child, servant, prostitute'; it is perhaps related to Old English *wancol* 'unsteady, inconstant'.

wend [Old English] Old English *wendan* meant 'to turn, depart'. Of Germanic origin, it is related to Dutch and German *wenden* and to the verb *wind*.
→ WIND²

werewolf [late Old English] The first element of *werewulf* has usually been identified with Old English *wer* 'man'. In modern use the word has been revived through folklore studies.

west [Old English] Of Germanic origin, *west* is related to Dutch and German *west*, from an Indo-European root shared by Greek *hesperos* and Latin *vesper* 'evening'. **Western** is also Old English (as *westerne*) and **westerly** is late 15th-century based on obsolete *wester* 'western'.

wet [Old English] The Old English adjective and noun form *wæt* and verb *wætan* are related to *water*. The sense 'inept, ineffectual' dates from the early 20th century. The word has been used as a term for a politician with liberal or middle of the road views on controversial issues since the 1930s; it was often applied to members of the Conservative party opposed to the monetarist policies of Margaret Thatcher.
→ WATER

whack [early 18th century] This word is probably imitative, or it may be an alteration of *thwack*.

whale [Old English] *hwæl* is Germanic in origin.

wham [1920s] This is a word imitative of a heavy blow. The term **whammy** (based on *wham*) has been applied since the 1940s to an 'evil influence'; in the 1950s it was often with reference to its use in a comic strip called *Li'l Abner* and was sometimes part of the phrase *double whammy* indicating the full force of the 'hex'.

wharf [late Old English] Old English *hwearf* is from a Germanic source. An early combination was *merehwearf* meaning 'seashore'. It was used to refer to the bank of a river from the early 17th century but this meaning is now obsolete (Shakespeare *Hamlet*: The fat weede That rots it selfe in ease, on Lethe Wharfe).

what [Old English] Old English *hwæt*, Germanic in origin, is related to Dutch *wat* and German *was*, from an Indo-European root shared by Latin *quod*. **Why** was *hwī*, *hwȳ* in Old English meaning 'by what cause': this is the instrumental case of *hwæt* 'what', of Germanic origin.

wheat [Old English] The Old English form of the word was *hwǣte* from a Germanic source related to Dutch *weit*, German *Weizen*, and English *white*. In figurative contexts, *wheat* is sometimes opposed to *chaff* alluding to separating the good from the bad.
→ WHITE

wheedle [mid 17th century] The origin of *wheedle* is obscure but it may be from German *wedeln* 'cringe, fawn', from *Wedel* 'tail, fan'.

wheel [Old English] The Old English noun *hwēol* is Germanic in origin, from an Indo-European root shared by Sanskrit *cakra* 'wheel, circle' and Greek *kuklos* 'circle'.

wheeze [late Middle English] *Wheeze* is probably from Old Norse *hvæsa* 'to hiss'.

whelp [Old English] The Old English noun *hwelp*, of Germanic origin, is related to Dutch *welp* and German *Welf*.

when [Old English] Old English *hwanne*, *hwenne*, of Germanic origin, is related to German *wenn* 'if', *wann* 'when'. Middle English **whence** (as *whennes*) is from the earlier *whenne* from Old English *hwanon*; it was later respelt with the ending *-ce* to denote the unvoiced sound.

where [Old English] Old English *hwǣr*, of Germanic origin, is related to Dutch *waar* and German *wo*.

whet [Old English] Old English *hwettan*, of Germanic origin, is related to German *wetzen*, based on an adjective meaning 'sharp'.

whether [Old English] Old English *hwæther*, *hwether*, of Germanic origin, is related to German *weder* 'neither'.

which [Old English] Old English *hwilc* is from the Germanic bases of *who* and *alike*.

whicker [mid 17th century] This imitative word started out in the sense 'to snigger, titter'.

whiff [late 16th century] *Whiff* was originally a noun for a 'gust of wind' and 'an inhalation of tobacco smoke' as well as a verb meaning 'blow with a slight gust': it is imitative of the sound.

while [Old English] Old English *hwīl* was a 'period of time'. A Germanic word in origin, it is related to Dutch *wijl* and German *Weile*; the conjunction is an abbreviation of Old English *thā hwīle the* 'the while that'.

whim [late 17th century] The origin of *whim* is unknown but it is related to early 16th-century *whim-wham* 'fanciful object, trifle' which, like *flim-flam* and *jim-jam*, is a fanciful reduplication probably symbolic of something frivolous. Early 17th-century *whimsy* had the sense 'caprice' and is probably based on *whim-wham* (as *flimsy* is to *flim-flam*).

whimper [early 16th century] *Whimper* is from dialect *whimp* 'to whimper', of imitative origin.

whine [Old English] Old English *hwīnan* meant 'whistle through the air'; it is related to late Old English **whinge** (*hwinsian*) and German *winseln*.

whinny [late Middle English] This word was first recorded as a verb and is imitative of the sound made. The noun dates from the early 19th century.

whip [Middle English] *Whip* is probably from Middle Low German and Middle Dutch *wippen* 'swing, leap, dance', from a Germanic base meaning 'move quickly'. The noun is partly from the verb, reinforced by Middle Low German *wippe* 'quick movement'. The compound:
■ **whipping boy** is an extended use of the original mid 17th-century term for a boy educated with a young prince or other royal person and punished instead of him.

whirl [Middle English] The verb *whirl* is probably from Old Norse *hvirfla* 'turn about'; the noun is partly from Middle Low German, Middle Dutch *wervel* 'spindle', or from Old Norse *hvirfill* 'circle', from a Germanic base meaning 'rotate'. Late Middle English **whirligig** is composed of *whirl* and the obsolete noun *gig* meaning 'whipping-top'.

whirr [late Middle English] The early sense was 'move with a whirring sound'; it is probably Scandinavian in origin like *whirl*.
➔ WHIRL

whisk [late Middle English] *Whisk* is of Scandinavian origin. The card game **whist** was spelt *whisk* in the mid 17th century, and is perhaps from the verb *whisk* (with reference to whisking away the tricks).

whisker [late Middle English] *Whisker* was originally a bundle of material such as feathers or twigs, used for whisking; it is based on the verb *whisk*. Use of the word to refer to male facial hair dates from the early 17th century.

whisper [Old English] Old English *hwisprian* is Germanic in origin, related to German *wispeln*, from the imitative base of *whistle*.
➔ WHISTLE

whistle [Old English] This imitative word (in Old English *(h)wistlian* as a verb, and *(h)wistle* as a noun) is related to Swedish *vissla* 'to whistle'.

whit [late Middle English] This is apparently an alteration of obsolete *wight* 'small amount'.

white [late Old English] Late Old English *hwīt*, of Germanic origin, is related to Dutch *wit* and German *weiss*, also to *wheat*. In late Old English **Whit Sunday** was *Hwīta Sunnandæg*, literally 'white Sunday', probably with reference to the white robes of those newly baptized at Pentecost. Of the many compounds of *white*:
■ **white feather** (late 18th century) in the context of cowardice is with reference to a white feather in the tail of a game bird, being a mark of bad breeding.
■ **white-knuckle ride** (1970s) is with reference to the effect caused by gripping tightly to side rails of a fairground ride to steady oneself.
➔ WHEAT

whittle [mid 16th century] The verb *whittle* is from the dialect noun *whittle* meaning a 'knife'.

who [Old English] Old English *hwā*, of Germanic origin, is related to Dutch *wie* and German *wer*. **Whose** was *hwæs* in Old English, the genitive of *hwā* 'who' and *hwæt* 'what'.

whole [Old English] Old English *hāl*, of Germanic origin, is related to Dutch *heel* and German *heil*, also to *hail*. The spelling with *wh*- (reflecting a dialect pronunciation with *w*-) first appeared in the 15th century. The words **wholesome** and **wholly** although not recorded until Middle English were probably already in Old English. The late Middle English word **wholesale** was originally in the phrase *by whole sale* meaning 'in large quantities'.
➔ HAIL²

whoops [1920s] This is probably an alteration of *upsy-daisy*.

whore [late Old English] Late Old English *hōre*, of Germanic origin, is related to Dutch *hoer* and German *Hure*, from an Indo-European root shared by Latin *carus* 'dear'.

whorl [late Middle English] When first used, this word referred to a a small flywheel; it is apparently a variant of *whirl*, influenced by Old English *wharve* 'whorl of a spindle'.
→ WHIRL

wick [Old English] Old English *wēoce* (*wick of a candle*) is West Germanic origin and related to Dutch *wiek* and German *Wieche* 'wick yarn'. The *wick* of the phrase *get on someone's wick* dating from the 1940s and meaning 'annoy someone' is sometimes said to derive from *Hampton Wick*, rhyming slang for *prick*.

wicked [Middle English] *Wicked* is probably based on Old English *wicca* 'witch'.

wicker [Middle English] Of Scandinavian origin, *wicker* is associated with Swedish *viker* 'willow' and related to *vika* 'to bend'.

wicket [Middle English] A *wicket* was originally a 'small door or grille'; it is from Anglo-Norman French and Old Northern French *wiket*; it is usually referred to the Germanic root of Old Norse *víkja* 'to turn, move'. Cricket senses date from the late 17th century.

wide [Old English] Of Germanic origin, Old English *wīd* meant 'spacious, extensive', *wīde* meant 'over a large area'. The early 17th-century noun **width** is from *wide*, on the pattern of *breadth* (replacing *wideness*).

widget [1930s] This word was originally US and is perhaps an alteration of *gadget*.
→ GADGET

widow [Old English] Old English *widewe* is from an Indo-European root meaning 'be empty'; Sanskrit *vidh* 'be destitute', Latin *viduus* 'bereft, widowed', and Greek *ēitheos* 'unmarried man' are related. Of the compounds:

■ **widow's cruse** refers to a small supply which apparently has no end, with biblical allusion to 1 Kings 17:10–16 which tells the story of a widow's cruse of oil which does not run out because of her kindness in sharing her tiny supply of food despite drought and famine.

■ **widow's mite** refers to a small monetary contribution from someone who is poor, with biblical allusion to Mark 12:43 in which a widow contributes two mites to a treasury, her total wealth.

■ **widow's walk** (a North American usage of the 1930s) is a term for a railed platform built on a roof originally in early New England houses and typically providing an unimpeded view of the sea; this is with reference to its use as a viewpoint for the hoped-for return of a seafaring husband.

■ **widow's weeds** dating form the early 18th century was expressed earlier as *mourning weeds*: here *weeds* is in the obsolete general

sense 'garments' from Old English *wæd(e)*, of Germanic origin.

wield [Old English] Old English *wealdan*, *wieldan* 'govern, subdue, direct', of Germanic origin; related to German *walten*.

wife [Old English] Old English *wīf* was a word for 'woman'. Of Germanic origin, it is related to Dutch *wijf* and German *Weib*.

wig [late 17th century] This is a shortening of *periwig*. The verb *wig* meaning 'rebuke' dates from the early 19th century apparently comes from the notion of a person of importance such as a judge (*bigwig*) issuing a reprimand.

wiggle [Middle English] This word is from the Middle Low German and Middle Dutch frequentative (= verb of repeated action) *wiggelen*.

wigwam [early 17th century] This is from Ojibwa *wigwaum*, Algonquian *wikiwam* meaning 'their house'.

wild [Old English] Old English *wilde*, of Germanic origin, is related to Dutch and German *wild*.

wilderness [Old English] Old English *wildēornes* was a 'land inhabited only by wild animals', based on *wild dēor* 'wild deer' and the noun suffix -*ness*.

wile [Middle English] *Wile* is perhaps from an Old Norse word related to *vél* 'craft'.

will[1] [Old English] Old English *wyllan* (the *will* of future tense formation) is Germanic in origin and related to Dutch *willen* and German *wollen*, from an Indo-European root shared by Latin *velle* 'will, wish'. **Would** was in Old English *wolde*, the past of *wyllan*.

will[2] [Old English] This *will* as in *free will* was *willa* (as a noun) and *willian* (as a verb) in Old English from a Germanic origin. The word is related to Dutch *wil* and German *Wille*, and the English adverb *well*. Middle English **wilful** is based on *will*.
→ WILL[1]

will-o'-the-wisp [early 17th century] This was originally *Will with the wisp*, a *wisp* being a 'handful of (lighted) hay'.

willy-nilly [early 17th century] This is a later spelling of *will I, nill I* 'I am willing, I am unwilling'.

wilt [late 17th century] *Wilt* was originally dialect and may be an alteration of dialect *welk* meaning 'lose freshness', of Low German origin.

wimp [1920s] The origin of *wimp* is uncertain but it may be from *whimper*.
→ WHIMPER

win [Old English] Old English *winnan* meant 'strive, contend' as well as 'subdue and take possession of, acquire'. The source of the word is Germanic.

wince [Middle English] *Wince* was originally used in the sense 'kick restlessly from pain or impatience'. It comes from an Anglo-Norman French variant of Old French *guenchir* 'turn aside'.

winch [late Old English] Late Old English *wince* was a term for a 'reel, pulley'. Of Germanic origin, it is related to the verb *wink*. The verb dates from the early 16th century.
→WINK

wind[1] [Old English] Of Germanic origin this *wind* (as in *wind and rain*) is related to Dutch *wind* and German *Wind*, from an Indo-European root shared by Latin *ventus*.

wind[2] [Old English] Old English *windan* meant 'go rapidly', 'twine'. It comes from a Germanic source and is related to *wander* and *wend*.
→WANDER; WEND

window [Middle English] The word *window* is from Old Norse *vindauga*, from *vindr* 'wind' and *auga* 'eye'. The idiomatic phrase *window of opportunity* dates from the 1970s.

wine [Old English] Old English *wīn*, of Germanic origin, is related to Dutch *wijn* and German *Wein*, based on Latin *vinum*.

wing [Middle English] This was originally recorded in the plural coming from Old Norse *vængir*, the plural of *vængr*.

wink [Old English] Old English *wincian* meaning 'close the eyes' is Germanic in origin, related to German *winken* 'to wave' and to *wince*. The idiom *not to sleep a wink* dates from Middle English. The proverb *a nod's as good as a wink to a blind horse* illustrates *wink* in the sense 'glance' (dating from the early 16th century).
→WINCE

winnow [Old English] Old English *windwian* is from *wind*.
→WIND[1]

winsome [Old English] Old English *wynsum* is based on *wyn* 'joy'.

winter [Old English] Of Germanic origin, *winter* is related to Dutch *winter* and German *Winter*, and probably also to *wet*. **Wintry** is also Old English (*wintrig*).
→WET

wipe [Old English] Related to *whip*, Old English *wīpian* is from a Germanic source. It has been used to mean both 'rub gently' and 'erase'. The idiom *wipe the floor with* dates from the late 19th century. The noun is recorded from the mid 16th century meaning 'a slashing blow, swipe' (*a wipe over the shins*); it has been used as a noun referring to a soft piece of absorbent cloth from the 1970s.
→WHIP

wire [Old English] Old English *wīr* is Germanic in origin, probably from the base of Latin *viere* 'plait, weave'. The phrase *by wire* dates from the mid 19th century in reference to communication by telegraphic messaging; in the early 20th century *over the wire(s)* referred to communication via the telephone system. The word *wire* as a conductor of electric current is recorded from this same period (end of the 19th/beginning of the 20th century) with *live wire* extended early to its figurative sense 'vivacious person'.

wise [Old English] Old English *wīs*, from a Germanic source, is related to Dutch *wijs* and German *weise*, and to English *wit*. **Wisdom** (in Old English *wīsdōm*) is based on *wise*.
→WIT[2]

wish [Old English] Old English *wȳscan*, of Germanic origin, is related to German *wünschen* and to English *wont*.
→WONT

wishy-washy [early 18th century] This is a reduplication of *washy* from *wash*.
→WASH

wisp [Middle English] The origin of *wisp* is uncertain; it is perhaps related to *whisk*.
→WHISK

wistful [early 17th century] *Wistful* is apparently from obsolete *wistly* 'intently', influenced by *wishful*.

wit[1] [Old English] Old English *wit(t)*, *gewit(t)* referred to the mind as the seat of consciousness. From a Germanic source, it is related to Dutch *weet* and German *Witz*, and to English *wit*. **Witty** (in Old English *wit(t)ig*) originally meant 'having wisdom'. **Witless** (in Old English *witlēas*) is first recorded as meaning 'crazy, dazed'. Finally, the noun **witticism** was coined in 1677 by Dryden from *witty*, on the pattern of *criticism*.
→WIT[2]

wit[2] [Old English] Old English *witan* 'have knowledge of' is the *wit* of *to wit*. Of Germanic origin, it is related to Dutch *weten* and German *wissen*, from an Indo-European root shared by Sanskrit *veda* 'knowledge' and Latin *videre* 'see'.

witch [Old English] Old English *wicca* (masculine), *wicce* (feminine), *wiccian* (verb); current senses of the verb are probably a shortening of Middle English *bewitch*, the prefix *be-* here meaning 'thoroughly'.

with [Old English] *With* is probably a shortening of a Germanic preposition related to obsolete English *wither* meaning 'adverse, opposite'.

withdraw [Middle English] This is based on the verb *draw* prefixed by Old English *with-* meaning 'away'.

wither [late Middle English] This is apparently a variant of *weather* ultimately differentiated for certain senses. Originally applied to plants, it was later (early 16th century) extended figuratively in the sense 'lose freshness, languish'. The phrase *wither away* originated in tracts about Marxist philosophy describing the decline of the state after a dictatorship has effected changes in society such that the state's domination is no longer necessary.
→ WEATHER

withers [early 16th century] This term for the highest part of a horse's back is apparently a reduced form of *widersome*, the first element of which is from obsolete *wither-* 'against, contrary' (as the part that resists the strain of the collar); the second element *-some* is of obscure origin.

withhold [Middle English] This is based on the verb *hold* prefixed by *with-* meaning 'away'.
→ HOLD¹

without [Old English] Old English *withūtan* meant 'on the outside'. **Within** had the form *withinnan* in late Old English and meant 'on the inside'.

withstand [Old English] Old English *withstandan* is based on the verb *stand* prefixed by *with-* 'against' (the preposition *with* commonly expressed 'opposition' in early use).
→ STAND

witness [Old English] Old English *witnes* is based on Old English *wit* 'understanding'. Early use included the sense 'understanding, knowledge, evidence' (Shakespeare *Merchant of Venice*: An evil soule producing holy witnesse, Is like a villaine with a smiling cheeke). The phrase *bear witness* arose in Middle English; later in that period the word *witness* came to be applied to a 'person testifying for Christ' as a martyr.
→ WIT¹

witter [early 19th century] This originally Scots and dialect word is probably imitative of chattering.

wizard [late Middle English] A *wizard* was once a word for a 'philosopher or sage'; it is based on *wise*. It became a term for someone practising witchcraft in the mid 16th century, later (early 17th century) coming to be applied to any person 'performing wonders' in a particular area (*financial wizard*).
→ WISE

wizened [early 16th century] This is the past participle of archaic *wizen* 'shrivel', of Germanic origin.

wobble [mid 17th century] An earlier spelling was *wabble*. Of Germanic origin, the word is connected with Old Norse *vafla* 'waver' and related to the verb *wave*.
→ WAVE

wodge [mid 19th century] The word *wodge* is an alteration of *wedge*.
→ WEDGE

woe [Old English] *Woe* is a natural exclamation of lament, recorded as *wā* in Old English and found in several Germanic languages. Middle English **woebegone** had the sense 'afflicted with grief'; the second element *begone* conveys 'surrounded' (the past participle of obsolete *bego* 'go around, beset'). *See box over.*

wold [Old English] Old English *wald* meant 'wooded upland'. **Weald**, a formerly wooded district including parts of Kent, Surrey, and East Sussex, is an Old English variant of *wald*. Of Germanic origin, *wold* is perhaps related to *wild*.
→ WILD

wolf [Old English] Old English *wulf*, from a Germanic source, is related to Dutch *wolf* and German *Wolf*, from an Indo-European root shared by Latin *lupus* and Greek *lukos*. The verb dates from the mid 19th century.

woman [Old English] Old English *wīfmon*, *-man* (from *wif* 'woman' and *man* or *mon* 'human being'), a formation peculiar to English, the ancient word being *wife*. The word has also been used without an article from early times to refer to the female sex (Dryden *Aeneis*: Woman's a various and a changeful Thing). The phrase *one's own woman* meaning 'independent' dates from the early 17th century.
→ WIFE

womb [Old English] Old English *wamb*, *womb* is Germanic in origin. Early use was also as a term for the 'abdomen' or 'stomach'. Figurative use indicating 'conception and development' dates from the late 16th century (Shakespeare *Richard II*: This England, This Nurse, this teeming wombe of Royall Kings).

wonder [Old English] The Old English noun *wundor* and verb *wundrian* are in origin Germanic words related to Dutch *wonder* and German *Wunder*; their ultimate origin is unknown. Based on *wonder* is late Old English **wonderful** and late 15th-century **wondrous**, an alteration, on the pattern of *marvellous*, of obsolete *wonders* (adjective and adverb), the genitive form of *wonder*.

Natural exclamations

woe is one of many natural exclamations in English. The dates below indicate when these were first recorded.

■ **aw** [mid 19th century in American English] expressing mild protest.

■ **faugh** [mid 16th century] expressing disgust.

■ **hey** [Middle English] said in attracting attention.

■ **hi** [late Middle English] said in greeting.

■ **ho** [Middle English] expressing surprise or derision.

■ **hoots** [early 19th century, but mid 16th century as *hoot*] expressing impatience.

■ **hoy** [late Middle English] said to attract attention.

■ **lo** [Old English as *lā*] said to indicate an amazing event.

■ **oh** [Middle English] expressing entreaty or mild surprise.

■ **oof** [mid 19th century] expressing alarm or annoyance.

■ **ooh** [early 20th century] expressing delight or pain.

■ **oops** [1930s] said on making an error.

■ **ouch** [mid 17th century] expressing pain.

■ **ow** [mid 19th century] expressing pain.

■ **pooh** [late 16th century] expressing disgust.

■ **pshaw** [late 17th century] expressing impatience or contempt.

■ **shoo** [late Middle English] said to frighten off the hearer.

■ **whee** [1920s] expressing delight.

■ **whisht** [mid 16th century] said to hush the hearer.

■ **whoo** [early 17th century] expressing surprise or delight.

■ **wow** [early 16th century] expressing admiration.

■ **yah** [early 17th century] expressing derision.

■ **yahoo** [1970s] expressing excitement.

■ **yeehaw** [1970s in American English] expressing exuberance.

■ **yeow** [1920s in American English] expressing shock.

■ **yippee** [1920s in American English] expressing wild excitement.

■ **yo** [late Middle English] said in greeting.

■ **yoo-hoo** [1920s] said to attract attention.

■ **zowie** [early 20th century in American English] expressing astonishment.

---

wont [Old English] This word used in the phrase *as is his wont* was *gewunod* in Old English,

the past participle of *wunian*, 'dwell, be accustomed', of Germanic origin. Late Middle English **wonted** is formed from *wont*.

woo [late Old English] Late Old English *wōgian* 'make love' was the intransitive verb, *āwōgian* 'court' was used transitively; the word's origin is unknown. In later use the word has become restricted to literary contexts.

wood [Old English] Old English *wudu* is from a Germanic word related to Welsh *gwŷdd* 'trees'. Early examples reflect the sense 'tree' as well as the substance and a 'collection of trees'. The idiom *not to see the wood for the trees* dates from the mid 16th century; *be out of the wood* meaning 'be out of trouble' dates from the late 18th century.

wool [Old English] Old English *wull*, of Germanic origin, is related to Dutch *wol* and German *Wolle*, from an Indo-European root shared by Latin *lana* 'wool', *vellus* 'fleece'. The idiomatic phrase *pull the wool over someone's eyes* (originally *spread the wool over someone's eyes*) is recorded from the early 19th century. The word **woollen** dates from late Old English (as *wullen*).

word [Old English] Germanic in origin, *word* is related to Dutch *woord* and German *Wort*, from an Indo-European root shared by Latin *verbum* 'word'. Of the phrases: *word for word* is late Middle English; *of few words* is mid 15th-century; *by word of mouth* is mid 16th century; *in a word* and *upon one's word* are late 16th-century.

work [Old English] The Old English noun *weorc* and verb *wyrcan* are Germanic in origin and related to Dutch *werk* and German *Werk*, from an Indo-European root shared by Greek *ergon*. The word **wright** (in Old English *wryhta*, *wyrhta*) found in compounds such as *wheelwright* meaning 'wheel-maker' is of West Germanic origin and related to *work*.

world [Old English] Old English *w(e)oruld* is from a Germanic compound meaning 'age of man'; it is related to Dutch *wereld* and German *Welt*. **Worldly** was *woruldlic* in Old English.

worm [Old English] The Old English word *wyrm* is of Germanic origin, related to Latin *vermis* 'worm' and Greek *rhomox* 'woodworm'. The word has been applied contemptuously to a person regarded as an object of scorn since earliest times. The idiom *can of worms* dates from the 1960s. Verb use has included a notion of 'prying' from the late 16th century; this gave rise in the early 17th century to the sense 'make one's way insidiously (into someone's confidence'), which led to the phrase *worm one's way* from the early 19th century.

worry [Old English] Old English *wyrgan*, of West Germanic origin, meant 'strangle'. In

Middle English the original sense of the verb gave rise to 'seize by the throat and tear' and later figuratively 'harass', which led to 'cause anxiety to': this was in the early 19th century, the date also of the noun.

worse [Old English] In Old English the adjectival form was *wyrsa* or *wiersa* and the adverbial form was *wiers* from a Germanic source; *war* is a related word; so too is **worst** (in Old English, *wierresta*, *wyrresta* as an adjective and *wierst*, *wyrst* as an adverb, also of Germanic origin).
➔WAR

worship [Old English] Old English *weorthscipe* (based on *worth*) had the sense 'worthiness, acknowledgement of worth'. The word started to be used as a title of honour (*your worship*) from the mid 16th century, later coming to be applied specifically to magistrates.
➔WORTH

worth [Old English] Old English *w(e)orth* is Germanic in origin, related to Dutch *waard* and German *wert*. The phrases *of worth* meaning 'of high merit', *of little worth*, and *of great worth* date from the late 16th century. **Worthy**, from *worth*, is Middle English.

wotcha [late 19th century] This informal greeting is a corruption of *what cheer?*

wound [Old English] Old English *wund* (noun) and *wundian* (verb), from a Germanic source, are related to Dutch *wond* and German *Wunde*; earlier details of the origin are unknown.

wrangle [late Middle English] English *wrangle* may be related to Low German *wrangeln*, a frequentative (= verb of repeated action) of *wrangen* 'to struggle'.
➔WRING

wrap [Middle English] The origin of *wrap* is obscure; its dialect variant *wrop* formerly had greater currency. The phrase *wrap up* meaning 'bring to an end' dates from the 1920s with the phrase *it's a wrap* meaning 'the recording is complete' in filming contexts recorded from the 1970s.

wrath [Old English] Old English *wrǣththu* is from Old English *wrāth* 'angry'.

wreak [Old English] Old English *wrecan* meant 'drive (out)' (now obsolete), 'give vent to' (Shelley *Cenci*: 'Tis my hate and the deferred desire To wreak it, which extinguishes their blood), and 'avenge' (Tennyson *Gareth and Lynette*: Grant me some knight to … Kill the foul thief, and wreak me for my son). Of Germanic origin,

it is related to Dutch *wreken* and German *rächen*
➔WRECK; WRETCH

wreath [Old English] Old English *writha* is related to *writhe*.
➔WRITHE

wreck [Middle English] A legal term initially, *wreck* was a term for 'wreckage washed ashore'. It comes from Anglo-Norman French *wrec*, from the base of Old Norse *reka* 'to drive'; related to *wreak*.
➔WREAK

wrench [late Old English] Late Old English *wrencan* meant 'to twist' and is of unknown origin. It came to mean 'sprain, rick' in the early 16th century. The word was applied as the name of a tool from the late 18th century.

wrestle [Old English] This is a frequentative (= verb of repeated action) of Old English *wrǣstan* 'wrest, twist, tighten', of Germanic origin; it is related to Danish *vriste*, and to English *wrist*.
➔WRIST

wretch [Old English] Old English *wrecca* also referred to a 'banished person'. Of West Germanic origin, it is related to German *Recke* 'warrior, hero' and the English verb *wreak*. Middle English **wretched** is formed irregularly from *wretch*.
➔WREAK

wriggle [late 15th century] *Wriggle* is from Middle Low German *wriggelen*, a frequentative (= verb of repeated action) of *wriggen* 'twist, turn'. The figurative phrase *wriggle out of* 'evade, shirk' dates from the mid 17th century.

wring [Old English] The Old English verb *wringan*, of West Germanic origin, is related to Dutch *wringen* and English *wrong*. The phrases *wring out* and *wring one's hands* are late Middle English.
➔WRONG

wrinkle [late Middle English] The origin of *wrinkle* is obscure; it may be a back-formation (by removal of the suffix) from the Old English past participle *gewrinclod* 'sinuous', of which no infinitive is recorded.

wrist [Old English] *Wrist*, of Germanic origin, is probably from the base of *writhe*.
➔WRITHE

write [Old English] The Old English verb *wrītan* had the meaning 'score, form (letters) by carving, write'. Germanic in origin, it is related to German *reissen* 'sketch, drag'. Old English **writ** first used as a general term for written matter is from the Germanic base of *write*.

writhe [Old English] Related to *wreathe*, Old English *wriþan* 'make into coils, plait, fasten with a cord' is Germanic in origin.

wrong [late Old English] Late Old English *wrang* is from Old Norse *rangr* 'awry, unjust'; it is related to *wring*. Adjectival use branches broadly into the following semantic strands: 'twisted, bent' (now archaic), 'unjust, perverse' (*morally wrong*), and 'unlawful' (*wrong title*).
➔WRING

wrought [Middle English] *Wrought* is the archaic past and past participle of *work*.
➔WORK

wry [early 16th century] The early sense recorded is 'contorted'. The origin is Old English *wrigian* 'tend, incline' which came in Middle English to mean 'deviate, swerve, contort'.

Xerox [1950s] *Xerox* is an invented name, based on *xerography*, a term for a dry-copying process, from Greek *xero-* 'dry' and *-graphia* 'writing'.

Xmas [mid 18th century] The initial letter *X* represents the initial letter chi of Greek *Khristos* 'Christ'.

X-ray [late 19th century] This is a translation of German *X-Strahlen* (a plural form), from the letter *X-* (chosen because, when discovered in 1895, the nature of the rays was unknown) and *Strahl* 'ray'.

Yy

yacht [mid 16th century] *Yacht* is from early modern Dutch *jaghte*, from *jaghtschip* 'fast pirate ship', from *jag(h)t* 'hunting' and *schip* 'ship'.

yahoo [mid 18th century] This informal word for a loud brash person is from the name of an imaginary race of brutish creatures in Swift's *Gulliver's Travels* published in 1726.

yammer [late Middle English] This was originally used as a verb meaning 'lament, cry out'; it is an alteration of earlier *yomer*, from Old English *geōmrian* 'to lament', suggested by Middle Dutch *jammeren*.

yank [late 18th century] This is first recorded as a Scots word in the sense 'sudden sharp blow'; its origin is unknown.

Yankee [mid 18th century] The origin of *Yankee* is uncertain; it is recorded from the late 17th century as a nickname and may be from Dutch *Janke*, a diminutive of *Jan* 'John'.

yap [early 17th century] This word was first used as a term for a barking dog; it is imitative of a short sharp sound. The verb sense 'chatter' dates from the late 19th century.

yard¹ [Old English] Old English *gerd* 'twig, stick, rod' is West Germanic in origin and related to Dutch *gard* 'twig, rod' and German *Gerte*. The word was used as a measure of length from early times and as the standard unit of English long measure equal to three feet from late Middle English. The earlier standard was the *ell* (= 45 inches), succeeded by the *verge* during the reign of Edward III, the equivalent of the *yard*.

yard² [Old English] Old English *geard* meant 'building, home, enclosure within the precincts of a house', from a Germanic base related to Russian *gorod* 'town'. *Garden* and *orchard* are related.
→ GARDEN; ORCHARD

yarn [Old English] Old English *gearn* is Germanic in origin, related to Dutch *garen* apparently from a base meaning 'guts' and related outside Germanic to Latin *hariolus* 'soothsayer' and *haruspex* 'person who predicts the future from inspecting entrails'. The idiom *spin a yarn* is originally nautical slang for 'tell a story' recorded as a usage from the early 19th century.

yawn [Old English] Of Germanic origin, Old English *geonian* is from an Indo-European root shared by Latin *hiare* and Greek *khainein*. Early use included the sense 'have the mouth wide open, gape'. Current noun senses date from the early 18th century.

you [Old English] Old English *ēow*, is the accusative and dative form of *gē* (= ye) of West Germanic origin; it is related to Dutch *u* and German *euch*. During the 14th century *you* began to replace Old English *ye* (related to Dutch *gij* and German *ihr*), *thou*, and *thee*; by the 17th century it had become the ordinary second person pronoun for any number and case. **Your** (in Old English *ēower*, the genitive of *gē*) is related to German *euer*.

year [Old English] Old English *gē(a)r*, of Germanic origin, is related to Dutch *jaar* and German *Jahr*, from an Indo-European root shared by Greek *hōra* 'season'.

yearn [Old English] Old English *giernan* is from a Germanic base meaning 'eager'. The verb was also used transitively ('have a strong desire for') in early use.

yeast [Old English] Of Germanic origin, *yeast* is related to Dutch *gist* and German *Gischt* 'froth, yeast', from an Indo-European root shared by Greek *zein* 'to boil'.

yell [Old English] The Old English verb *g(i)ellan*, of Germanic origin, is related to Dutch *gillen* and German *gellen*.

yellow [Old English] Old English *geolu, geolo* is West Germanic in origin, related to Dutch *geel* and German *gelb*, as well as to English *gold*. The figurative sense 'cowardly' is recorded in US English from the mid 19th century.
→ GOLD

yelp [Old English] The Old English verb *g(i)elpan* meant 'to boast' and is from a Germanic imitative base. From late Middle English the sense was 'cry or sing with a loud voice'; the current sense 'utter a squealing bark' arose in the 16th century.

yen [late 19th century] This was originally used in the sense 'craving (of a drug addict) for a drug'; it comes from Chinese *yǎn*.

yeoman [Middle English] The *yeo* of *Yeoman* is probably from *young*; *youngman* itself was once used as a term for a 'servant' or 'attendant'.

yes [Old English] Old English *gēse*, *gīse* is probably from an unrecorded phrase meaning 'may it be so'. The compound *yes-man* describing someone who always agrees with the views of a superior to please, dates from the early 20th century in US English.

yesterday [Old English] The first element of Old English *giestran dæg* is from *geostran* 'yester-' of Germanic origin; it is related to Dutch *gisteren* and German *gestern* 'yesterday', from an Indo-European root shared by Latin *heri* and Greek *khthes*.

yet [Old English] Old English *gīet(a)* is of unknown origin.

yield [Old English] Old English *g(i)eldan*, of Germanic origin, meant 'pay, repay'. The senses 'produce, bear' (*yielding honey*) and 'surrender' (*yield to the enemy*) arose in Middle English.

yob [mid 19th century] This is back slang for *boy*.

yoke [Old English] The Old English noun *geoc* and verb *geocian* are from a Germanic source related to Dutch *juk* and German *Joch*, from an Indo-European root shared by Latin *jugum* and Greek *zugon*, also by Latin *jungere* 'to join'.

yokel [early 19th century] The word *yokel* may be a figurative use of dialect *yokel* 'green woodpecker'.

yolk [Old English] Old English *geol(o)ca* is from *geolu* 'yellow'.

yon [Old English] Old English *geon*, of Germanic origin, is related to German *jener* 'that one' and also to Middle English **yonder** and Dutch *ginder* 'over there'.

yonks [1960s] The origin of *yonks* is unknown but there may be a connection with *donkey's years*.

young [Old English] Of Germanic origin, Old English *g(e)ong* is related to Dutch *jong*, German *jung*, and **youth** (in Old English *geoguth*), from an Indo-European root shared by Latin *juvenis*. The word *youth* has been used to refer to a young man between boyhood and maturity from Middle English.

Yule [Old English] Old English *geol(a)* was a word for 'Christmas Day'; it is related to Old Norse *jól* originally applied to a heathen festival lasting twelve days, and later applied to Christmas.

yummy [late 19th century] This is based on the imitative phrase *yum-yum*.

yuppie [1980s] This is an elaboration of the acronym *yup* from *young urban professional*.

Zz

zany [late 16th century] *Zany* is from French *zani* or Italian *zan(n)i*, a Venetian form of *Gianni*, *Giovanni* 'John': this was the stock name of servants acting as clowns in the *commedia dell'arte*.

zap [1920s] This was originally a US usage imitative of the sound of a ray gun. The verb meaning 'kill' dates from the 1940s; its use in connection with moving rapidly through video or television channels is found from the 1980s.

zeal [late Middle English] *Zeal* comes via ecclesiastical Latin from Greek *zēlos*. Early 16th-century **zealous** is from a medieval Latin derivative of Latin *zelus* 'zeal, jealousy'. The word **zealot** is recorded from the mid 16th century when it was a term for a member of a Jewish sect which fiercely resisted the Romans until the fall of Jerusalem in AD 70: it comes via ecclesiastical Latin from Greek *zēlōtēs*, from *zēloun* 'be jealous', from *zēlos*. Its association with 'someone full of zeal' is found from the early 17th century.

zebra [early 17th century] This comes from Italian, Spanish, or Portuguese, originally in the sense 'wild ass', perhaps ultimately from Latin *equiferus*, from *equus* 'horse' and *ferus* 'wild'. The phrase *zebra crossing* for a type of pedestrian crossing distinguished by black-and-white stripes dates from the 1950s.

zenith [late Middle English] This is from Old French or medieval Latin *cenit*, based on Arabic *samt (ar-ra's)* 'path (over the head)'.

zero [early 17th century] *Zero* is from French *zéro* or Italian *zero*, via Old Spanish from Arabic *ṣifr* 'cipher'.

zest [late 15th century] *Zest* is from French *zeste* 'orange or lemon peel', of unknown origin. The figurative use 'keen enjoyment' (*zest for life*) dates from the late 18th century.

zigzag [early 18th century] The word *zigzag* is from French, from German *Zickzack*, symbolic of alternation of direction, first applied to the line taken by trenches in fortifications.

zillion [1940s] This is made up of the letter *z* (perhaps as a symbol of an unknown quantity) and *million*.

zip [mid 19th century] This word is imitative of a light sharp sound; early use included a notion of quick movement. It has been used colloquially to mean 'nothing, zero' in US English from the beginning of the 20th century; its use as a term for a fastener for clothes dates from the 1920s.

zip code [1960s] This compound used in postal addresses in the US is based on *Zip*, an acronym from *zoning improvement plan*.

zodiac [late Middle English] *Zodiac* is from Old French *zodiaque*, via Latin from Greek *zōidiakos*, from *zōidion* 'sculptured animal figure': this is a diminutive of *zōion* 'animal'.

zombie [early 19th century] This is of West African origin; Kikongo *zumbi* 'fetish' is a related form. Figurative use meaning 'dull, slow-witted person' is found from the 1930s.

zone [late Middle English] *Zone* is from French, or from Latin *zona* 'girdle', from Greek *zōnē*. It was first used to refer to each of the five belts or encircling regions (differentiated by climate) into which the surface of the earth is divided by the tropics. From this early use, the word came to be applied to various areas defined by certain boundaries or subject to certain restrictions (*building zone, Soviet Zone*).

zoology [mid 17th century] *Zoology* is from modern Latin *zoologia*, from Greek *zōion* 'animal' and *-logia* 'discourse, treatise'. The word was originally used to refer to the part of medical science dealing with the medicines or remedies obtainable from animals. Mid 19th-century **zoo** is an abbreviation of *zoological garden*, originally applied specifically to that of Regent's Park, London.

zoom [late 19th century] The imitative word *zoom* described, in early use, a low-pitched continuous humming sound. It soon became associated with movement and was used as aircraft slang from the early 20th century describing the action of climbing at a dangerously sharp angle. From the 1970s it is found in contexts of prices soaring (*costs started to zoom*). The word's use in cinematography and photography is evidenced from the 1940s.

Oxford Paperback Reference

The Concise Oxford Dictionary of Art & Artists
Ian Chilvers

Based on the highly praised *Oxford Dictionary of Art*, over 2,500 up-to-date entries on painting, sculpture, and the graphic arts.

'the best and most inclusive single volume available, immensely useful and very well written'

Marina Vaizey, *Sunday Times*

The Concise Oxford Dictionary of Art Terms
Michael Clarke

Written by the Director of the National Gallery of Scotland, over 1,800 entries cover periods, styles, materials, techniques, and foreign terms.

A Dictionary of Architecture
James Stevens Curl

Over 5,000 entries and 250 illustrations cover all periods of Western architectural history.

'splendid ... you can't have a more concise, entertaining, and informative guide to the words of architecture'

Architectural Review

'excellent, and amazing value for money ... by far the best thing of its kind'

Professor David Walker

AskOxford**.**COM

Oxford Dictionaries Passionate about language

For more information about the background to Oxford Quotations and Language Reference Dictionaries, and much more about Oxford's commitment to language exploration, why not visit the world's largest language learning site, www.AskOxford.com

Passionate about English?

What were the original 'brass monkeys'?   **Ask**Oxford**.**COM

How do new words enter the dictionary?   **Ask**Oxford**.**COM

How is 'whom' used?   **Ask**Oxford**.**COM

Who said, 'For also knowledge itself is power?'   **Ask**Oxford**.**COM

How can I improve my writing?   **Ask**Oxford**.**COM

If you have a query about the English language, want to look up a word, need some help with your writing skills, are curious about how dictionaries are made, or simply have some time to learn about the language, bypass the rest and ask the experts at www.AskOxford.com.

Passionate about language?

If you want to find out about writing in French, German, Spanish, or Italian, improve your listening and speaking skills, learn about other cultures, access resources for language students, or gain insider travel tips from those   **Ask**Oxford**.**COM
in the know, ask the experts at

Oxford Companions

'Opening such books is like sitting down with a knowledgeable friend. Not a bore or a know-all, but a genuinely well-informed chum ... So far so splendid.'

Sunday Times [of *The Oxford Companion to Shakespeare*]

For well over 60 years Oxford University Press has been publishing Companions that are of lasting value and interest, each one not only a comprehensive source of reference, but also a stimulating guide, mentor, and friend. There are between 40 and 60 Oxford Companions available at any one time, ranging from music, art, and literature to history, warfare, religion, and wine.

Titles include:

The Oxford Companion to English Literature
Edited by Margaret Drabble
'No guide could come more classic.'

Malcolm Bradbury, *The Times*

The Oxford Companion to Music
Edited by Alison Latham
'probably the best one-volume music reference book going'

Times Educational Supplement

The Oxford Companion to Western Art
Edited by Hugh Brigstocke
'more than meets the high standard set by the growing number of Oxford Companions'

Contemporary Review

The Oxford Companion to Food
Alan Davidson
'the best food reference work ever to appear in the English language'

New Statesman

The Oxford Companion to Wine
Edited by Jancis Robinson
'the greatest wine book ever published'

Washington Post

OXFORD

Great value ebooks from Oxford!

An ever-increasing number of Oxford subject reference dictionaries, English and bilingual dictionaries, and English language reference titles are available as ebooks.

All Oxford ebooks are available in the award-winning Mobipocket Reader format, compatible with most current handheld systems, including Palm, Pocket PC/Windows CE, Psion, Nokia, SymbianOS, Franklin eBookMan, and Windows. Some are also available in MS Reader and Palm Reader formats.

Priced on a par with the print editions, Oxford ebooks offer dictionary-specific search options making information retrieval quick and easy.

For further information and a full list of Oxford ebooks please visit: www.askoxford.com/shoponline/ebooks/

Oxford Paperback Reference

The Kings of Queens of Britain
John Cannon and Anne Hargreaves

A detailed, fully-illustrated history ranging from mythical and pre-conquest rulers to the present House of Windsor, featuring regional maps and genealogies.

A Dictionary of Dates
Cyril Leslie Beeching

Births and deaths of the famous, significant and unusual dates in history – this is an entertaining guide to each day of the year.

'a dipper's blissful paradise ... Every single day of the year, plus an index of birthdays and chronologies of scientific developments and world events.'

Observer

A Dictionary of British History
Edited by John Cannon

An invaluable source of information covering the history of Britain over the past two millennia. Over 3,600 entries written by more than 100 specialist contributors.

Review of the parent volume
'the range is impressive ... truly (almost) all of human life is here'
Kenneth Morgan, *Observer*

Oxford Paperback Reference

The Concise Oxford Dictionary of English Etymology
T. F. Hoad

A wealth of information about our language and its history, this
reference source provides over 17,000 entries on word origins.

'A model of its kind'

Daily Telegraph

A Dictionary of Euphemisms
R. W. Holder

This hugely entertaining collection draws together euphemisms from all
aspects of life: work, sexuality, age, money, and politics.

Review of the previous edition
'This ingenious collection is not only very funny but extremely
instructive too'

Iris Murdoch

The Oxford Dictionary of Slang
John Ayto

Containing over 10,000 words and phrases, this is the ideal reference for
those interested in the more quirky and unofficial words used in the
English language.

'hours of happy browsing for language lovers'

Observer

Oxford Paperback Reference

The Concise Oxford Companion to English Literature
Margaret Drabble and Jenny Stringer

Based on the best-selling *Oxford Companion to English Literature*, this is an indispensable guide to all aspects of English literature.

Review of the parent volume
'a magisterial and monumental achievement'

Literary Review

The Concise Oxford Companion to Irish Literature
Robert Welch

From the ogam alphabet developed in the 4th century to Roddy Doyle, this is a comprehensive guide to writers, works, topics, folklore, and historical and cultural events.

Review of the parent volume
'Heroic volume ... It surpasses previous exercises of similar nature in the richness of its detail and the ecumenism of its approach.'

Times Literary Supplement

A Dictionary of Shakespeare
Stanley Wells

Compiled by one of the best-known international authorities on the playwright's works, this dictionary offers up-to-date information on all aspects of Shakespeare, both in his own time and in later ages.

Oxford Paperback Reference

The Concise Oxford Dictionary of Quotations
Edited by Elizabeth Knowles

Based on the highly acclaimed *Oxford Dictionary of Quotations*, this paperback edition maintains its extensive coverage of literary and historical quotations, and contains completely up-to-date material. A fascinating read and an essential reference tool.

The Oxford Dictionary of Humorous Quotations
Edited by Ned Sherrin

From the sharply witty to the downright hilarious, this sparkling collection will appeal to all senses of humour.

Quotations by Subject
Edited by Susan Ratcliffe

A collection of over 7,000 quotations, arranged thematically for easy look-up. Covers an enormous range of nearly 600 themes from 'The Internet' to 'Parliament'.

The Concise Oxford Dictionary of Phrase and Fable
Edited by Elizabeth Knowles

Provides a wealth of fascinating and informative detail for over 10,000 phrases and allusions used in English today. Find out about anything from the 'Trojan house' to 'ground zero'.